SAXON® MATH

Course 3

Teacher's Manual
Volume 1

Stephen Hake

SAXON®

An imprint of HMH Supplemental Publishers, Inc.

www.SaxonPublishers.com

1-800-531-5015

Acknowledgements

This book was made possible by the significant contributions of many individuals and the dedicated efforts of a talented team at Harcourt Achieve.

Special thanks to:

- Melody Simmons and Chris Braun for suggestions and explanations for problem solving in Courses 1-3,

- Elizabeth Rivas and Bryon Hake for their extensive contributions to lessons and practice in Course 3,

- Sue Ellen Fealko for suggested application problems in Course 3.

The long hours and technical assistance of John and James Hake on Courses 1-3, Robert Hake on Course 3, Tom Curtis on Course 3, and Roger Phan on Course 3 were invaluable in meeting publishing deadlines. The saintly patience and unwavering support of Mary is most appreciated.

– Stephen Hake

Staff Credits

Editorial: Jean Armstrong, Shelley Farrar-Coleman, Marc Connolly, Hirva Raj, Brooke Butner, Robin Adams, Roxanne Picou, Cecilia Colome, Michael Ota

Design: Alison Klassen, Joan Cunningham, Deborah Diver, Alan Klemp, Andy Hendrix, Rhonda Holcomb

Production: Mychael Ferris-Pacheco, Heather Jernt, Greg Gaspard, Donna Brawley, John-Paxton Gremillion

Manufacturing: Cathy Voltaggio

Marketing: Marilyn Trow, Kimberly Sadler

E-Learning: Layne Hedrick, Karen Stitt

ISBN 13: 978-1-5914-1886-3
ISBN 10: 1-5914-1886-0

© 2007 Saxon, an imprint of HMH Supplemental Publishers, Inc. and Stephen Hake

7 8 9 10 0868 14 13 12 11 10
4500229183

SAXON MATH™

Course 3
Content Overview

ABOUT THE AUTHOR

Stephen Hake has authored five books in the Saxon Math series. He writes from 17 years of classroom experience as a teacher in grades 5 through 12 and as a math specialist in El Monte, California. As a math coach, his students won honors and recognition in local, regional, and statewide competitions.

Stephen has been writing math curriculum since 1975 and for Saxon since 1985. He has also authored several math contests including Los Angeles County's first Math Field Day contest. Stephen contributed to the 1999 National Academy of Science publication on the Nature and Teaching of Algebra in the Middle Grades.

Stephen is a member of the National Council of Teachers of Mathematics and the California Mathematics Council. He earned his BA from United States International University and his MA from Chapman College.

EDUCATIONAL CONSULTANTS

Nicole Hamilton
Consultant Manager
Richardson, TX

Joquita McKibben
Consultant Manager
Pensacola, FL

John Anderson
Lowell, IN

Beckie Fulcher
Gulf Breeze, FL

Heidi Graviette
Stockton, CA

Brenda Halulka
Atlanta, GA

Marilyn Lance
East Greenbush, NY

Ann Norris
Wichita Falls, TX

Melody Simmons
Nogales, AZ

Benjamin Swagerty
Moore, OK

Kristyn Warren
Macedonia, OH

Mary Warrington
East Wenatchee, WA

Integrated Strands

Connections are the foundation for long-term retention of learning.

Rather than separating decimals from fractions from geometry, as in a typical chapter approach, Saxon Math integrates and connects strands on a daily basis. Students see the relationships within mathematics as they develop their understanding of a concept.

In addition to its integrated instructional approach, the textbook also provides integrated review, practice and assessment throughout.

- Skills and concepts are kept alive through daily practice.
- Math connections are strengthened and made meaningful.
- Written practice sets are rich and varied – just like the state test.

Traditional Unit Structure

Saxon Integrated and Distributed Structure

Saxon Math's INTEGRATED LEARNING results in students developing and retaining a deep understanding of mathematics.

Incremental Learning

Content is mastered through small increments followed by integrated practice and strategically-placed assessments.

Rather than learning all of a strand in a single chapter, Saxon Math instructs in smaller, more easily assimilated increments that are spread across the year. Students practice, review, and build connections to other strands every step of the way.

Before the next increment of a strand is introduced, students are assessed to check their progress. A level of mastery is reached for each increment of a strand through this consistent and integrated practice and assessment, which is distributed throughout the year.

Saxon Math's INCREMENTAL LEARNING provides a built-in system for tracking and benchmarking student mastery of every part of the standards.

Do you want students to be successful problem solvers?

Saxon Math: The New Look of Results

Saxon Math believes that *all* of mathematics is about **PROBLEM SOLVING.**

The organizing principle for the Saxon Math approach is mathematical thinking.
Skills, concepts and problem solving are bridged by consistent mathematic language.

Mathematical Thinking Balances

Math Background	Word Problems
Relationship of Standards	Problem Solving Skills
Meanings of Operation	Problem Solving Strategies

Problem solving is more than word problems. Word problems cannot be successfully solved without an understanding of the meanings of operations and the relationship between the numbers in a problem. Teaching through mathematical thinking is the foundation for helping students become successful problem solvers.

Saxon Math's daily Problem Solving opportunities are:

- *Guided*

- *Embedded*

- *Applied*

Guided Problem Solving

In addition to specific lessons on solving word problems, every lesson begins and ends with Problem Solving.

Guided problem solving instruction occurs every day and builds students' confidence as they are encouraged to use a variety of strategies to solve problems.

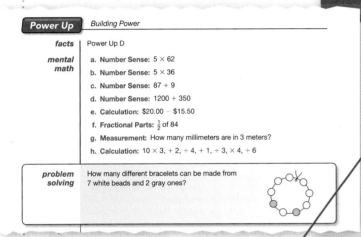

Power Up	Building Power
facts	Power Up D
mental math	a. Number Sense: 5×62
	b. Number Sense: 5×36
	c. Number Sense: $87 + 9$
	d. Number Sense: $1200 + 350$
	e. Calculation: $\$20.00 - \$15.50$
	f. Fractional Parts: $\frac{1}{2}$ of 84
	g. Measurement: How many millimeters are in 3 meters?
	h. Calculation: $10 \times 3, + 2, \div 4, + 1, \div 3, \times 4, \div 6$
problem solving	How many different bracelets can be made from 7 white beads and 2 gray ones?

A suggested discussion guide following the four-step plan is provided in the **Teacher's Manual** to allow for a rich discussion of how and why a problem can be solved.

Power Up Discussion For use with Power Up, p. 123

Problem-Solving Strategy: Use Logical Reasoning/ Draw a Diagram

Problem: How many different bracelets can be made from 7 white beads and 2 gray ones?

[Understand] Understand the Problem

"What information are we given?"
A bracelet is made of 9 beads: 7 white beads and 2 gray beads.

"What are we asked to do?"
Determine how many different bracelets can be made from 7 white beads and 2 gray beads.

"Is this a combination or permutation problem?"
It is a combination problem. Order is not important to our answer.

"What do we already know?"
We know that bracelets form a continuous circuit when clasped, which means we need to be careful not to mistakenly repeat any of our combinations.

[Plan] Make a Plan

"What problem-solving strategy will we use?"
We will *use logical reasoning* to *draw a diagram*.

"How can we modify the bracelet?"
It can be unclasped to form a string of beads, but keep in mind the bracelet will be clasped again to form a continuous circuit.

[Solve] Carry out the Plan

"What are the possible positionings for the two gray beads?"
The two gray beads can be right next to each other, or they can be separated by one, two or three beads.

"Are there bracelets with the gray beads separated by more than three beads?"
Yes, but they are the same as the bracelets above. Gray beads separated by 1 white bead are also separated by 6 white beads; by 2 white beads are also separated by 5 white beads; by 3 white beads are also separated by 4 white beads.

"So how many different bracelets can be made?"
Five.

[Check] Look Back
Verify your solutions by drawing the four combinations as clasped bracelets instead of unclasped.

123B   *Saxon Math Course 1*

---

problem solving	What is the sum of the first ten even numbers?

[Understand] We are asked to find the sum of the first ten even numbers.

[Plan] We will begin by *making the problem simpler*. If the assignment had been to add the first *four* even numbers, we could simply add $2 + 4 + 6 + 8$. However, adding columns of numbers can be time-consuming. We will try to *find a pattern* that will help add the even numbers 2–20 more quickly.

[Solve] We can find pairs of addends in the sequence that have the same sum and multiply by the number of pairs. We try this pairing technique on the sequence given in the problem:

$$2 + 4 + 6 + 8 + 10 + 12 + 14 + 16 + 18 + 20 = 22 \times 5 = 110$$

[Check] We found the sum of the first ten even numbers by pairing the addends and multiplying. We can verify our solution by adding the numbers one-by-one with pencil and paper or a calculator.

Extended problems in the **student text** provide students with more in-depth support for each problem solving strategy.

SAXON MATH™

Embedded Problem Solving

Saxon Math develops higher-order thinking skills through the meaningful Math Conversations that occur every day in the cumulative Written Practice.

Students learn to express their understanding through these rich mathematical discussions. This is important in today's high-stakes testing, where it is not enough to compute and solve. Students have to explain their reasoning and thinking.

---

c. The distance from the center to the circle.

d. **Explain** If the diameter of a circle is 10 in., what is its radius? Describe how you know.

Written Practice | Strengthening Concepts

1. **Analyze** What is the product of the sum of 55 and 45 and the difference of 55 and 45?
(12)

* 2. **Model** Potatoes are three-fourths water. If a sack of potatoes weighs 20 pounds, how many pounds of water are in the potatoes? Draw a diagram to illustrate the problem.
(22)

3. **Formulate** There were 306 students in the cafeteria. After some went outside, there were 249 students left in the cafeteria. How many students went outside? Write an equation and solve the problem.
(11)

* 4. **Explain** a. If the diameter of a circle is 5 in., what is the radius of the circle?
(27)

b. What is the relationship of the diameter of a circle to its radius?

5. **Classify** Which of these numbers is divisible by both 2 and 3?
(21)
A 122   B 123   C 132

6. Round 1,234,567 to the nearest ten thousand.
(16)

7. **Formulate** If ten pounds of apples costs $12.90, what is the price per pound? Write an equation and solve the problem.
(15)

8. What is the denominator of $\frac{23}{24}$?
(6)

* 9. **Model** What number is $\frac{3}{5}$ of 65? Draw a diagram to illustrate the problem.
(22)

* 10. **Model** How much money is $\frac{2}{3}$ of $15? Draw a diagram to illustrate the problem.
(22)

Model Use your fraction manipulatives to help answer problems 11–18.

11. $\frac{1}{6} + \frac{2}{6} + \frac{3}{6}$ **12.** $\frac{7}{8} - \frac{3}{8}$
(Inv. 2)   (Inv. 2)

13. $\frac{6}{6} - \frac{5}{6}$ **14.** $\frac{2}{8} + \frac{5}{8}$
(Inv. 2)   (Inv. 2)

15. a. How many $\frac{1}{8}$s are in 1?
(Inv. 2)
b. How many $\frac{1}{8}$s are in $\frac{1}{2}$?

* 16. Reduce: $\frac{4}{6}$
(26)

17. What fraction is half of $\frac{1}{4}$?
(Inv. 2)

18. What fraction of a circle is 50% of a circle?
(Inv. 2)

---

3 Written Practice

Math Conversations
Discussion opportunities are provided below.

Problem 2 Model
Extend the Problem
"How can you find $\frac{3}{4}$ of 20 using mental math?" Sample: The denominator 4 means that the whole or 20 is divided into 4 equal parts, and each equal part is $20 \div 4$ or 5. The numerator represents 3 of those equal parts, so $5 + 5 + 5 = 15$.

Problem 4 Explain
Extend the Problem
"What is the relationship of the radius of a circle to its diameter?" In any circle, a radius is one-half the length of a diameter.

Problem 16 Explain
"Name the operation that is used to reduce a fraction, and explain how that operation is used." Division; divide the numerator and the denominator by a common factor of the numerator and the denominator. If the factor is the greatest common factor, the division will produce a fraction in simplest form.

Errors and Misconceptions
Problems 17
When students find one-half of a whole number, they simply divide the whole number by 2. However, when they are asked to find one-half of a unit fraction, simply dividing the denominator by 2 is a mistake. For example, $\frac{1}{2}$ of $\frac{1}{4} = \frac{1}{4 \div 2}$ is a common error.

Encourage students to use fraction manipulatives when finding a fractional part of a fraction. The manipulatives can help students see, for example, that $\frac{1}{2}$ of $\frac{1}{4}$ of a circle represents a part of the circle that is smaller than $\frac{1}{4}$.

(continued)

Teacher's Manual

| **Early Finishers** *Real-World Application* | Mrs. Akiba bought 3 large bags of veggie sticks for her students. Each bag contains 125 veggie sticks. If $\frac{5}{6}$ of Mrs. Akiba's 30 students eat the same amount of veggie sticks, how many sticks will each student eat? |

Students put it all together to solve multi-step problems in the Written Practice.

Applied Problem Solving

Saxon Math provides students with opportunities to dive more deeply into mathematics and its connections – within mathematical strands, to other subject areas, and as real-world applications.

Investigations
Every 10 Lessons

Students explore math in more depth through the Investigations. Using mathematical thinking, activities, and extensions, these Investigations allow students to develop a broader and deeper understanding of math concepts and connections.

---

13. **Connect** Form a whole circle using six of the $\frac{1}{6}$ pieces. Then remove (subtract) $\frac{1}{6}$. What fraction of the circle is left? What equation represents your model?

14. Demonstrate subtracting $\frac{1}{3}$ from 1 by forming a circle of $\frac{3}{3}$ and then removing $\frac{1}{3}$. What fraction is left?

Reading
< means
than
= means
equal to
> means
greater tha

Thinking Skill
Connect
What percent is one whole circle?

INVESTIGATION 2

Focus on
• Investigating Fractions with Manipulatives

In this investigation you will make a set of fraction manipulatives to help you answer questions in this investigation and in future problem sets.

Activity
Using Fraction Manipulatives

Materials needed:
- Investigation Activities 2A–2F
- scissors
- envelope or zip-top bag to store fraction pieces

Preparation:
To make your own fraction manipulatives, cut out the fraction circles on the Investigation Activities. Then cut each fraction circle into its parts.

Model Use your fraction manipulatives to help you with these exercises:

1. What percent of a circle is $\frac{1}{2}$ of a circle?
2. What fraction is half of $\frac{1}{2}$?
3. What fraction is half of $\frac{1}{4}$?
4. Fit three $\frac{1}{4}$ pieces together to form $\frac{3}{4}$ of a circle. Three fourths of a circle is what percent of a circle?
5. Fit four $\frac{1}{8}$ pieces together to form $\frac{4}{8}$ of a circle. Four eighths of a circle is what percent of a circle?
6. Fit three $\frac{1}{6}$ pieces together to form $\frac{3}{6}$ of a circle. Three sixths of a circle is what percent of a circle?
7. Show that $\frac{4}{8}$, $\frac{3}{6}$, and $\frac{2}{4}$ each make one half of a circle. (We say that $\frac{4}{8}$, $\frac{3}{6}$, and $\frac{2}{4}$ all *reduce* to $\frac{1}{2}$.)
8. The fraction $\frac{2}{8}$ equals which single fraction piece?
9. The fraction $\frac{6}{8}$ equals how many $\frac{1}{4}$s?
10. The fraction $\frac{2}{6}$ equals which single fraction piece?
11. The fraction $\frac{4}{8}$ equals how many $\frac{1}{3}$s?
12. The sum $\frac{1}{8} + \frac{1}{8} + \frac{1}{8}$ is $\frac{3}{8}$. If you add $\frac{3}{8}$ and $\frac{2}{8}$, what is the sum?

112   Sa

Investigation 2 **111**

Teacher Rubric

Criteria Performance	Knowledge and Skills Understanding	Communication and Representation	Process and Strategies
	The student got it! The	The student clearly	The student had an

Performance Task 3

The Four Corners States
Assign after Lesson 20 and Cumulative Test 3

Objectives
- Make a bar graph and a circle graph to display the same data.
- Formulate a question that can be answered by data.
- Communicate ideas through writing.

Materials

Name _____

Performance Task **3A**
For use with Performance Task 3

Did you know that you could stand in four states at the same time? The boundaries of Utah, Colorado, New Mexico and Arizona—*The Four Corners States*—form a common geographic point. It is the only place in the United States where this occurs.

We can use data and graphs to gain understanding about the size and geographic characteristics of this unique area. Use the *The Four Corners States Data Charts* to complete all tasks.

1. Make a bar graph and sketch a circle graph to display the land areas of the four states.

Land Areas of *The Four Corner States*

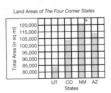

Land Areas of *The Four Corner States*

Performance Tasks and Activities
Every 5 Lessons

Students apply math to real-world situations within a performance environment. Integrating problem solving with math concepts, these Tasks and Activities allow students to explore topics in the real world and to explain their thinking with open ended questions. Both teacher and student rubrics are included.

Do you want students to develop strong proportional thinking?

Saxon Math: The New Look of Results

Saxon Math focuses on how to SET UP THE PROPORTION and give meaning to the numbers in the problem.

The hardest part that students have with solving problems involving proportions is to ask themselves the right questions to set up the proportion. Students' natural inclination is to go directly to the computing!

Proportional Thinking

Proportional thinking development begins in Saxon Math with the meaning of ratio and how to solve a proportion. Then students solve simple ratio problems and build to the more complex applications of proportion.

Proportional thinking is very important to understanding mathematics because proportions are used in a variety of real-world situations and across math strands. Students use proportions to solve problems involving ratios, percents, measurement, scale drawings, and similar triangles in geometry.

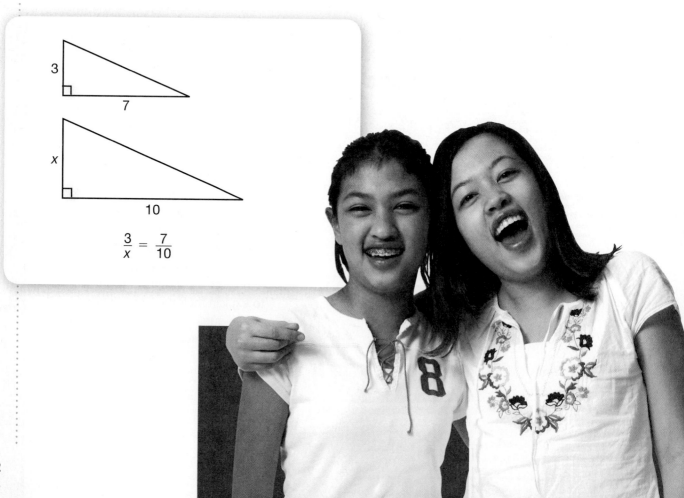

$$\frac{3}{x} = \frac{7}{10}$$

The Ratio Box

The ratio box is a graphic organizer that helps students to translate the words of a problem into a proportional form.

The ratio box helps students to:

- translate the words to establish the relationship of the information,
- set up an equation or proportion to solve, and
- eliminate the chance they will make an error.

> The ratio of parrots to macaws was 5 to 7 at a bird sanctuary. If there were 75 parrots, how many macaws were there?
>
> In this problem there are two kinds of numbers: ratio numbers and actual count numbers. The ratio numbers are 5 and 7. The number 75 is an actual count of parrots. We will arrange these numbers in two columns and two rows to form the ratio box.
>
> | | Ratio | Actual Count |
> |---|---|---|
> | Parrots | 5 | 75 |
> | Macaws | 7 | m |
>
> We were not given the actual count for macaws so we used m to stand for the number of macaws. The numbers in this ratio box can be used to write a proportion.
>
> | | Ratio | Actual Count |
> |---|---|---|
> | Parrots | 5 | 75 |
> | Macaws | 7 | m |
>
> $$\frac{5}{7} = \frac{75}{m}$$
> $$5m = 525$$
> $$m = 105$$
>
> There were 105 macaws.

The ratio box provides a consistent way to help students translate problems, especially application problems and more complex problems. Using the same graphic organizer for ratio, rate, proportion, and percent helps students understand, connect, and solve problems that involve proportional thinking.

> ### Skills and Concept Trace
>
> See the complete trace for ratios and proportional thinking in the Scope and Sequence starting on p. T879.

Do you want students to develop strong algebraic thinking?

Saxon Math: The New Look of Results

Saxon Math embeds ALGEBRAIC THINKING throughout the curriculum – not as a separate math topic.

Embedded Algebraic Thinking

There is no new math in algebra—only new language and symbolism. Without connections to arithmetic thinking, algebra has little meaning to students. Saxon Math provides that link from arithmetic to algebra.

Algebraic thinking in Saxon Math is embedded and distributed across the course in small increments, as part of every strand, not as a separate unit of instruction or topic. The distributed approach in the textbook lends itself better to providing this kind of natural integration.

Preparing for Algebra 1 Success

Although Saxon Math uses a distributed approach, all the expected algebraic topics are covered in the textbook. Patterns, relations, and functions are presented early in the student text and are reviewed and practiced throughout the year. Order of operations are applied to whole numbers, integers, rational numbers, and exponents. Students build on their understanding of variables and expressions and extend them to equations and inequalities. Students also analyze patterns and functions leading to graphing on the coordinate plane.

The development of algebraic thinking progresses from Course 1 to Course 3, building a solid foundation for students to have confidence and success in Algebra 1.

Algebraic Patterns in Problem Solving

Saxon Math provides support for helping students move from the WORDS in a problem to a non-numeric representation to writing an equation.

The Saxon Math approach to writing an equation to solve word problems:

Read ⟩ Translate ⟩ Write a word equation ⟩ Draw a diagram ⟩ Write an equation ⟩ Solve

The most intimidating part of algebra is word problems — translating a situation into an equation, a mathematical model.

Rather than categorize word problems, Saxon Math focuses students on the "plot." What is this story about? Are we combining or separating? Are we comparing? Are we making equal groups?

If students can identify the plot, then they can define the relationship in an equation: $a + b = c$, or $a - b = c$, or $ab = c$. When they know the plot and its corresponding relationship or formula, then students substitute, use a variable for the unknown, and solve for the unknown.

Saxon Math uses word problems to teach students how to model algebraically the commonly encountered mathematical relationships of everyday life.

Read the problem and identify the plot or pattern:

The trip odometer in Odell's car read 47 miles when he started. At the end of his trip, the odometer read 114 miles. How many miles did he travel?

Translate:

   SOME + SOME MORE = TOTAL

Write a word equation and draw a diagram:

   $S + M = T$

114	
SOME	SOME MORE
47	?

Write an equation:

   $47 + M = 114$

Solve:

   $114 - 47 = 67$

Odell travelled 67 miles.

Saxon Math teaches a variety of patterns or relationships that can be found in word problems.

• Addition pattern
• How many more/fewer pattern
• Larger-smaller-difference pattern
• Later-earlier-difference pattern
• Some and some more
• Subtraction pattern: Some went away

Do you want higher student achievement and increased test scores?

Saxon Math: The New Look of Results

Saxon Math has a long history of MEASURABLE STUDENT IMPROVEMENT – backed by years of research.

Immediate, Measurable, and Long-Lasting Results

The demands of today's state testing environment make clear the importance of selecting a math program that can deliver results. Saxon Math's look and approach have a proven track record of higher standardized test scores and subject mastery.

The evidence found on these pages is *just a selection* from the extensive body of

- independent research studies,
- case histories and
- efficacy studies

that all point to Saxon Math's power to achieve better results for students and their schools.

See how Saxon Math has built long-lasting achievement in classrooms across the nation. Saxon's results are immediate and schools show growth in one year's time. Their results are measurable quantitatively and qualitatively through test scores and customer testimonials. Saxon Math's results speak for themselves.

SEE THE RESULTS FOR YOURSELF!

For a complete report on Saxon Math Results, go to www.SaxonPublishers.com.

"Our students' test scores, math abilities and confidence have sky-rocketed."

Scott Neuman, Seventh and Eighth Grade Teacher, Humboldt Park Elementary, Milwaukee, Wisconsin

Discover What Schools Think

"The continual review and practice of concepts is very effective with my students. I also believe the mental math has developed the students to be better mathematical thinkers and has taught them how to use strategies to solve problems."

Jan Stevenson, Math Teacher, Davis County Middle School, Bloomfield, Iowa

"At a school where over 80 percent of our kids qualify for free lunch and their average grade-level equivalency upon entering fifth grade is 2.5, I have been phenomenally impressed with how well Saxon works for our kids... Saxon has helped our kids see the connections between mathematical concepts. None of the skills are taught in isolation and each new skill is woven into subsequent lessons. Our kids experience such a dramatic shift in the way they see numbers and operations that I know they are getting the foundation they need for higher-level mathematics."

Sarah Hayes, Vice Principal KIPP D.C., KEY Academy, Washington, D.C.

"We have been using Saxon Math for the past 13 years and have no desire to change to another series. Saxon works. Students and parents consistently express positive attitudes about Saxon and math in general. Students feel confident they can do math. Our students excel in all areas, including problem solving and computation. We have consistently scored among the top schools in the state since we started using Saxon. Teachers are confident that students understand how to use math concepts even when confronted with new problems."

David W. Schweltzer, Math Chairman, Michael Grimmer Middle School, Schererville, Indiana

"We have found that Saxon Math eliminates the gaps in our students' achievement. Students are excited to learn. They can see a real-world connection to their learning. The fact practice ensures future success of recalling facts and ensures immediate recall... "

Dianne Tetreault, Principal, Cambridge Educational Academy, Boca Raton, Florida

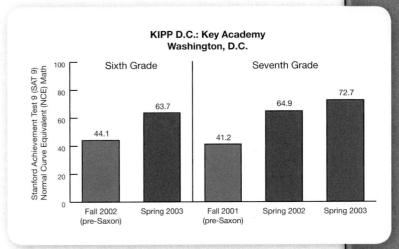

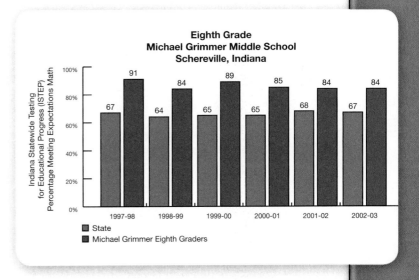

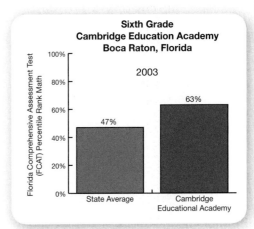

SAXON MATH™

Saxon Math Works . . .
with a Consistent Lesson Structure that Enhances Success

Every lesson in Saxon Math follows the same three-part lesson plan.

This regular format allows students to become comfortable with the lessons and to know what to expect each day. By not including loud colorful photographs, Saxon Math with its predictable format lets students focus solely on the mathematics. The color and vibrancy of mathematics comes from the students' learning.

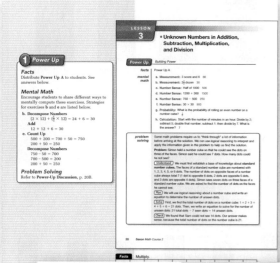

1 Power Up
Prevention Through Built-In Intervention

The **Power Up** at the beginning of every lesson provides daily reinforcement and building of:

- basic skills and concepts
- mental math
- problem solving strategies

Daily work on these problems results in automaticity of basic skills and mastery of mental math and problem solving strategies. For those students who need extra time, the Saxon approach allows for mastery gradually over time.

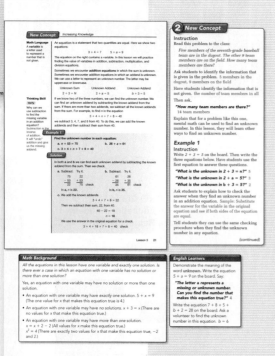

2 New Concepts
Increase Student Knowledge

Using clear explanations and a set of examples that build in depth, the **New Concepts** expand students' knowledge. Thinking skill questions, reading math hints, and math language tips help students understand how and why the math works.

Through the in-lesson **Activities**, students explore math concepts using manipulatives and other materials.

Have students work the **Practice Set** in class to see how well each student understands today's new skills and concepts.

③ *Written Practice* — Distributed and Integrated

Students attain a depth of understanding on a particular concept by practicing it over time and in a variety of ways. The **Written Practice** provides that depth with its integrated and distributed practice—allowing students to review, maintain, and build on concepts and skills previously taught.

To help students build their mathematical language, Saxon Math provides continual exposure to and review of **math vocabulary.**

Once a skill has been taught, students move to **higher order thinking skills** and applications of that concept. Students become confident and successful with both basic concepts and the richer, deeper mathematics that is the foundation of later math courses.

The distributed mixed practice is unpredictable and therefore challenging. It mirrors the format of state tests, giving students a **test prep** experience every day!

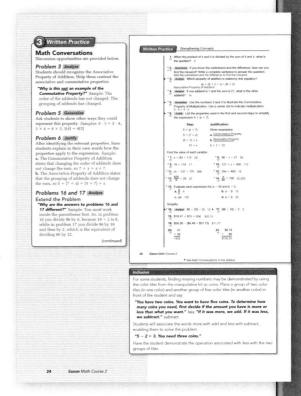

Recommended Daily Pacing

The Saxon distributed approach is unique in that the focus of the day is mainly on the rich depth of content in the distributed Written Practice.

In a typical 60-min class period, the author suggests you spend about half of the class period having the students complete the Written Practice problems. This allows you to have meaningful math conversations with students as they work out the problems.

SAXON MATH™

Saxon Math Works...
for All Students

Saxon Math has built-in support to help you customize and differentiate instruction.

The consistent lesson format of Saxon Math provides a predictable routine that enables all learners to be successful. By focusing on the mathematics and not the "fluff" seen in other math texts, Saxon Math makes higher-level mathematical thinking accessible for every student.

English Language Learners

Throughout the student text, ESL/ELL students will find structures to help them acquire mathematical understanding and mathematical language. Visual models, hands-on activities, mathematical conversations, and math language prompts all help students in their daily learning.

The **English Learners** teacher notes focus on language acquisition, not on reteaching or simplifying the math.

Proven Approach
- Define/Hear
- Model/Connect
- Discuss/Explain
- Apply/Use

For Spanish speakers, the **Glossary** in the student text provides a Spanish translation of each math term. The complete program is also available in Spanish.

Advanced Learners

The **Early Finishers** in the Written Practice offers the opportunity to deepen mathematical learning with problem solving, cross-curricular, and enrichment activities.

The **Extensions** in the Investigations allow students to expand their knowledge of the Investigation concepts, sharpen their higher-order thinking skills, and explore more connections.

The **Extend the Problem** suggestions in the Teacher's Manual provide even more ways to engage the advanced learner.

English Learners

For example 4, explain the meaning of the word **occupied**. Say:

"The word occupied means taken up by or filled by."

Write 4.63271 on the board. Point to the seven and say:

"The number 7 fills up this space."

Have students find the place occupied by 2, 3 and 4, answering with the phrase: "The place occupied by 3 is...", and so on.

Special Education Students

Adaptations for Saxon Math: A Complete and Parallel Program

The flexible curriculum design of *Adaptations for Saxon Math* can be integrated into inclusion classrooms, pullout programs, or self-contained resource classrooms —**ensuring that Special Education students keep pace with the core curriculum.**

The unique design organizes exercises in ways that open the doors to success for students with a variety of learning disabilities, such as:

- Visual-motor integration
- Distractibility or lack of focus
- Receptive language
- Fine motor coordination
- Number reversal in reading and copy work
- Math anxiety
- Verbal explanation
- Spatial organization

Each adapted lesson begins with a **lesson summary**— an important reference tool for special education students and valuable for parents.

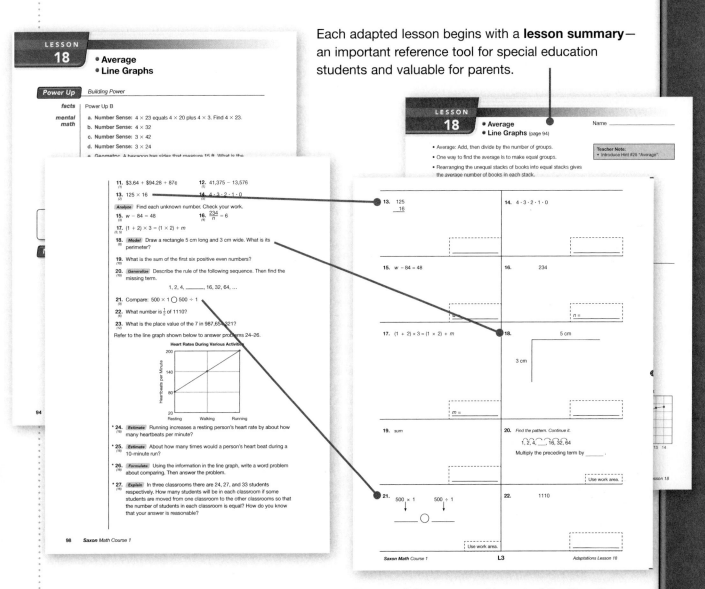

The carefully-structured layout of the **Practice exercises** helps special education students focus on mastering the concept, rather than figuring out the directions.

SAXON **MATH**

Saxon Math Works...

in Assessing for Learning and for Accountability

Assessments can be categorized in two ways, both of which are valuable and necessary in helping students succeed in mathematics.

Saxon Math provides opportunities for "Assessment for Learning" and for "Assessment of Learning."

Assessment *FOR* Learning	Assessment *OF* Learning
Purpose: Improvement	*Purpose:* Accountability
Assess continuously **during** teaching to influence learning.	Assess periodically **after** teaching to gather evidence of learning.
Use for immediate **feedback** to intervene, if necessary, on a particular concept.	Use **to judge** learning, usually in the form of a grade or score.

Assessment *FOR* Learning

The instructional design of Saxon Math effectively helps you to identify immediately any learning gaps and to provide intervention to keep students on track. Assessments to gauge student progress are throughout every lesson. You can use these classroom assessments and their continuous flow of information about student achievement to advance, not merely check on, student progress.

Daily Checks on New Content

Highlighted questions in the student text provide point-of-use prompts that students can use to clarify their thinking. Use the **Practice Set** each day to assess student understanding of the New Concepts.

Daily Checks on Previously-Taught Content

Because Saxon Math's **Written Practice** is distributed and integrated, you can daily assess students' retention and understanding of previously-taught content. Each problem references the lesson where the concept was first taught. By checking student homework, you can easily keep track of which concepts need reinforcement. You can remediate by reviewing the lesson again or by assigning the Reteaching Master.

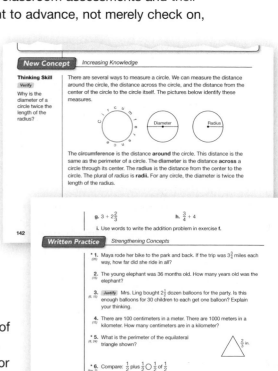

Assessment *OF* Learning

The assessments in Saxon Math are frequent and consistently placed to offer a regular method of ongoing testing and tracking of student mastery.

Every Five Lessons

After every five lessons there is a **Power-Up Test** and a **Cumulative Test**. Use the Power-Up Test to assess basic facts and skills, as well as problem solving strategies. The Cumulative Test checks mastery of concepts from previous lessons.

Every Section (10 lessons)

Every Section also ends with a Power-Up Test and a Cumulative Test. In addition, the Teacher's Manual contains a guide for creating individualized tests.

Every Quarter

Use the **Benchmark Tests** to check student progress after lessons 30, 60 and 90. Benchmark Tests assess student knowledge of all concepts and skills up to that point in the course.

Final Test

Use the **End-of-Course Exam** to measure student progress against your beginning-of-year benchmarks.

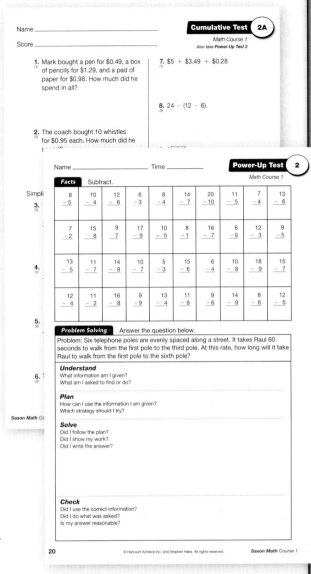

Tracking and Benchmarking the Standards

A **Standards Benchmark Checkpoint** occurs every ten lessons, at the end of each Section. Create **customized Benchmark Assessments** by using the Test and Practice Generator CD and the convenient guide in the Teacher's Manual.

If you need to create benchmark tests for a specific time frame (say, for a six-week period), you can easily use the Teacher's Manual guide for which test items on the CD to choose.

Print out **Standards Reports** to quickly track student progress against your benchmarks.

SAXON **MATH**™

Course 1

Course 2

Course 3

Components

Core Program

Student Edition

Student Edition eBook
complete student text on CD

Teacher's Manual
two-volume hardbound

Teacher's Manual eBook
complete teacher edition on CD

Resources and Planner CD
an electronic pacing calendar
with standards, plus assessment,
reteaching, and instructional masters

Meeting the Needs of All Students

Written Practice Workbook
no need to carry the textbook home

Power Up Workbook
consumable worksheets for every lesson

Reteaching Masters
one for every lesson

Manipulatives Kit
use with lesson Activities and
Investigations

Adaptations for Saxon Math
A complete, parallel program for Special
Education students

Classroom package,
with Teacher's Guide and CD

Title 1 Resource package
for pullout programs

Special Education Resource package
for special education or self-contained
resource classrooms

Building the Depth of the Standards

Instructional Masters
performance tasks and activities,
activity masters, Power-Up worksheets,
recording forms, and more

Instructional Transparencies
overheads of all Instructional Masters

Graphing Calculators Activities
correlated to lessons

Instructional Posters
in English and Spanish

Answer Key CD
student answers for displaying to
check homework

Online Activities – real world, graphing
calculator, and exploration activities

Tracking and Benchmarking the Standards

Course Assessments
numerous assessments to check student
progress, plus recording forms for easy
tracking and analysis of scores

Test and Practice Generator CD
test items, correlated to standards, in
multiple formats and in both English and
Spanish; customize by editing questions
or writing new ones

eGradebook
electronic gradebook to track progress
on benchmark tests; generate a variety of
reports, including standards reports

Saxon Math Works . . .
by providing a comprehensive program that is easy to plan, easy to manage, and easy to teach!

Available in Spanish

Student Edition, Teacher's Manual,
plus worksheets, blackline
masters, posters, test generator
questions, and online activities

Table of Contents
Integrated and Distributed Units of Instruction

Standards Benchmark Check Point

Math Focus:
Number & Operations • Geometry

Distributed Strands:
Number & Operations • Algebra • Measurement • Geometry • Problem Solving

Maintaining & Extending

Power Up
Facts pp. 72, 78, 85, 92, 97, 103, 108, 114, 120, 126

Mental Math Strategies
pp. 72, 78, 85, 92, 97, 103, 108, 114, 120, 126

Problem Solving Strategies
pp. 72, 78, 85, 92, 97, 103, 108, 114, 120, 126

Enrichment
Early Finishers pp. 107, 119, 125

Standards Benchmark Check Point

Section 3 — Lessons 21–30, Investigation 3

Math Focus:
Number & Operations

Distributed Strands:
Number & Operations • Algebra • Geometry • Problem Solving

Maintaining & Extending

Power Up
Facts pp. 139, 146, 153, 159, 163, 169, 176, 181, 186, 192

Mental Math Strategies
pp. 139, 146, 153, 159, 163, 169, 176, 181, 186, 192

Problem Solving Strategies
pp. 139, 146, 153, 159, 163, 169, 176, 181, 186, 192

Enrichment
Early Finishers pp. 158, 180, 185, 191

Standards Benchmark Check Point

Math Focus:
Algebra • Measurement

Distributed Strands:
Number & Operations • Algebra • Geometry • Measurement • Data Analysis & Probability
• Problem Solving

    Activity 1   **Sketching Prisms and Cylinders**
Using Parallel Projection
    Activity 2   **Sketching Pyramids and Cones**
    Activity 3   **Create a Multiview Drawing**
    Activity 4   **One-Point Perspective Drawing**

Maintaining & Extending

Power Up
Facts pp. 202, 210, 218, 223, 229, 237, 245, 250, 257, 264

Mental Math Strategies
pp. 202, 210, 218, 223, 229, 237, 245, 250, 257, 264

Problem Solving Strategies
pp. 202, 210, 218, 223, 229, 237, 245, 250, 257, 264

Enrichment
Early Finishers pp. 217, 222, 244, 263, 270

Extensions p. 275

Standards Benchmark Check Point

Section 5 | *Lessons 41–50, Investigation 5*

Math Focus:
Number & Operations • Algebra

Distributed Strands:
Number & Operations • Algebra • Geometry • Measurement • Problem Solving

---

Maintaining & Extending

Power Up
Facts pp. 277, 287, 294, 300, 308, 313, 319, 326, 330, 336

Mental Math Strategies
pp. 277, 287, 294, 300, 308, 313, 319, 326, 330, 336

Problem Solving Strategies
pp. 277, 287, 294, 300, 308, 313, 319, 326, 330, 336

Enrichment
Early Finishers pp. 307, 341

Standards Benchmark
Check Point

Section 6 — *Lessons 51–60, Investigation 6*

Math Focus:
Number & Operations • Data Analysis & Probability

Distributed Strands: Number & Operations • Algebra • Geometry • Measurement • Data Analysis & Probability • Problem Solving

---

Maintaining & Extending

Power Up
Facts pp. 346, 354, 360, 367, 375, 382, 389, 394, 400, 406

Mental Math Strategies
pp. 346, 354, 360, 367, 375, 382, 389, 394, 400, 406

Problem Solving Strategies
pp. 346, 354, 360, 367, 375, 382, 389, 394, 400, 406

Enrichment
Early Finishers pp. 353, 366, 374, 381, 399

Standards Benchmark Check Point

Section 7 — Lessons 61–70, Investigation 7

Math Focus:
Algebra

Distributed Strands:
Number & Operations • Algebra • Geometry • Measurement • Data Analysis & Probability
• Problem Solving

Maintaining & Extending

Power Up
Facts pp. 415, 422, 429, 435, 440, 446, 452, 457, 463, 470

Mental Math Strategies
pp. 415, 422, 429, 435, 440, 446, 452, 457, 463, 470

Problem Solving Strategies
pp. 415, 422, 429, 435, 440, 446, 452, 457, 463, 470

Enrichment
Early Finishers pp. 462, 475

Standards Benchmark Check Point

Starting with Lesson 61, you can include additional instruction and practice on Algebra topics by using the Appendix that begins on page 785.

Math Focus:
Algebra • Measurement

Distributed Strands:
Number & Operations • Algebra • Measurement • Data Analysis & Probability

Activity **Make a Scatterplot and Graph a Best-fit Line**

Maintaining & Extending

Power Up
Facts pp. 479, 486, 491, 496, 502, 507, 514, 519, 525, 531

Mental Math Strategies
pp. 479, 486, 491, 496, 502, 507, 514, 519, 525, 531

Problem Solving Strategies
pp. 479, 486, 491, 496, 502, 507, 514, 519, 525, 531

Enrichment
Early Finishers pp. 485, 530

Standards Benchmark Check Point

Section 9 — Lessons 81–90, Investigation 9

Math Focus:
Algebra • Measurement

Distributed Strands:
Number & Operations • Algebra • Geometry • Measurement • Data Analysis & Probability
• Problem Solving

Maintaining & Extending

Power Up
Facts pp. 545, 550, 557, 563, 568, 574, 580, 585, 593, 599

Mental Math Strategies
pp. 545, 550, 557, 563, 568, 574, 580, 585, 593, 599

Problem Solving Strategies
pp. 545, 550, 557, 563, 568, 574, 580, 585, 593, 599

Enrichment
Early Finishers pp. 567, 573, 584, 592, 598, 605

Standards Benchmark
Check Point

Math Focus:
Algebra • Measurement

Distributed Strands:
Algebra • Measurement • Geometry • Data Analysis & Probability

Maintaining & Extending

Power Up
Facts pp. 610, 617, 624, 629, 634, 640, 646, 651, 658, 664

Mental Math Strategies
pp. 610, 617, 624, 629, 634, 640, 646, 651, 658, 664

Problem Solving Strategies
pp. 610, 617, 624, 629, 634, 640, 646, 651, 658, 664

Enrichment
Early Finishers pp. 623, 645, 657, 669

Standards Benchmark Check Point

Section 11 | *Lessons 101–110, Investigation 11*

Math Focus:
Algebra • Data Analysis & Probability

Distributed Strands:
Algebra • Data Analysis & Probability • Measurement • Geometry • Number & Operations • Problem Solving

Activity 1 **Modeling Freefall**

Activity 2 **Using the Graph of a Quadratic Function**

Activity 3 **Maximization**

Maintaining & Extending

Power Up
Facts pp. 675, 681, 686, 691, 697, 702, 707, 712, 717, 722

Mental Math Strategies
pp. 675, 681, 686, 691, 697, 702, 707, 712, 717, 722

Problem Solving Strategies
pp. 675, 681, 686, 691, 697, 702, 707, 712, 717, 722

Enrichment
Early Finishers p. 690

Standards Benchmark Check Point

Math Focus:
Geometry • Algebra

Distributed Strands:
Geometry • Algebra • Measurement • Number & Operations • Data Analysis & Probability

Maintaining & Extending

Power Up
Facts pp. 731, 737, 742, 748, 754, 758, 763, 768, 773, 778

Mental Math Strategies
pp. 731, 737, 742, 748, 754, 758, 763, 768, 773, 778

Problem Solving Strategies
pp. 731, 737, 742, 748, 754, 758, 763, 768, 773, 778

Enrichment
Early Finishers pp. 736, 741, 747, 781

Standards Benchmark Check Point

Contents by Strand

This chart gives you an overview of the instructions of math concepts by strand in *Saxon Math* Course 3. The chart shows where in the textbook each topic is taught and references the New Concepts section of a lesson or the instructional part of an Investigation.

	LESSONS
NUMBER AND OPERATIONS	
Numeration	
read and write whole numbers and decimals	12
place value to trillions	12
place value to hundred trillions	12
number line (integers, fractions)	1, 10
number line (rational and irrational numbers)	15, 31, 36
comparison symbols ($=, <, >$)	1, 77, 94
comparison symbols ($=, <, >, \leq, \geq$)	62, 77, 94
compare and order rational numbers	1, 5, 10, 30, 63
compare and order real numbers	16
scientific notation	28, 51, 57
Basic operations	
add, subtract, multiply, and divide integers	2, 31, 33, 36
add, subtract, multiply, and divide decimal numbers	24, 25, 46
add, subtract, multiply, and divide fractions and mixed numbers	2, 13, 22, 23
add, subtract, multiply, and divide algebraic terms	15, 21, 27, 31, 36
add and subtract polynomials	80
add, subtract, multiply, and divide radical expressions	96, 120
multiply binomials	92
mental math strategies	1-120
regrouping in addition, subtraction, and multiplication	2, 31, 33, 46
multiplication notations: $a \times b, a \cdot b, a(b)$	2, 36
division notations: division box, division sign, and division bar	2, 36
division with remainders	4
Properties of numbers and operations	
even and odd integers	1
factors, multiples, and divisibility	9
prime and composite numbers	9
greatest common factor (GCF)	9, 10
least common multiple (LCM)	13
divisibility tests (2, 3, 5, 9, 10)	9
divisibility tests (4, 6, 8)	9
prime factorization of whole numbers	9, 10, 15
positive exponents of whole numbers, decimals, fractions	15, 27, 46
positive exponents of integers	27, 36, 46
negative exponents of whole numbers	51, 57
negative exponents of rational numbers	51, 57, 68
square roots	15, 36, 74
cube roots	15
order of operations	31, 33
inverse operations	38

	LESSONS
Estimation	
round whole numbers, decimals, mixed numbers	17, 117
estimate sums, differences, products, quotients	17
estimate squares and square roots	16, 118
determine reasonableness of solution	17
approximate irrational numbers	16; Investigation 2
ALGEBRA	
Ratio and proportional reasoning	
fractional part of a whole, group, set, or number	5, 22, 30, 45
equivalent fractions	10, 34
convert between fractions, terminating decimals, and percents	11, 12, 71, 119
convert between fractions, repeating decimals, and percents	30, 63, 71, 110
reciprocals of numbers	22
complex fractions involving one term in numerator/denominator	119
complex fractions involving two terms in numerator/denominator	119
identify/find percent of a whole, group, set, or number	11, 12, 45, 48, 58, 63, 84, 109
percents greater than 100%	67, 71
percent of change	67, 71
solve proportions with unknown in one term	34, 35, 37, 45, 48, 87
find unit rates and ratios in proportional relationships	7, 25, 29, 34, 38, 44, 49, 102, 105
apply proportional relationships such as similarity, scaling, and rates	26, 38, 37, 49, 70, 89; Investigation 12
estimate and solve application problems involving percent	48, 58, 63, 67, 71; Investigation 10
estimate and solve application problems involving proportional relationships such as similarity and rate	7, 35, 37, 45, 49, 64, 70, 89; Investigation 10
compare and contrast proportional and non-proportional linear relationships (direct and inverse variation)	34, 41, 47, 69, 84, 98
Patterns, relations, and functions	
generate a different representation of data given another representation of data	69
use, describe, extend arithmetic sequence (with a constant rate of change)	61, 73
input-output tables	41, 47, 97, 99
analyze a pattern to verbalize a rule	61, 73
analyze a pattern to write an algebraic expression	61, 97
evaluate an algebraic expression to extend a pattern	61, 73, 97
compare and contrast linear and nonlinear functions	41, 88, 98, 99; Investigations 10, 11
Variables, expressions, equations, and inequalities	
formulate a problem situation for a given equation with one unknown variable	3
formulate an equation with one unknown variable given a problem situation	3, 4
formulate an inequality with one unknown variable given a problem situation	62, 77
solve one-step equations with whole numbers	2, 3, 14, 38
solve one-step equations with fractions and decimals	3, 4, 14, 38
solve two-step equations with whole numbers	19, 50, 79

	LESSONS
solve two-step equations with fractions and decimals	**50, 79**
solve equations with exponents	**93**
solve systems of equations with two unknowns by graphing	**56, 82, 89**
graph an inequality on a number line	**62, 77**
graph pairs of inequalities on a number line	**94**
solve inequalities with one unknown	**62, 77**
validate an equation solution using mathematical properties	**19, 90; Investigation 8**

GEOMETRY

Describe basic terms

point	**18**
segment	**18**
ray	**18**
line	**18, 44, 54**
angle	**18, 54**
plane	**18; Investigation 1**

Describe properties and relationships of lines

parallel, perpendicular, and intersecting	**18, 54; Investigation 1**
horizontal, vertical, and oblique	**44; Investigation 1**
slope	**44**

Describe properties and relationships of angles

acute, obtuse, right	**18, 54; Investigation 3**
straight	**18, 54**
complementary and supplementary	**54**
angles formed by transversals	**54**
vertical angles	**54**
adjacent angles	**54**
calculate to find unknown angle measures	**20, 54, 81, 115; Investigation 3**

Describe properties and relationships of polygons

regular	**19**
sum of angle measures	**20, 115**
diagonals	**66, 74**
effects of scaling on area	**8, 26, 71, 88, 108; Investigation 5**
effects of scaling on volume	**35, 60, 71, 76, 91, 106, 108**
similarity and congruence	**19**
classify triangles	**20, 35**
classify quadrilaterals	**Investigation 3**

Use Pythagorean theorem to solve problems

Pythagorean theorem involving whole numbers	**74; Investigation 2**
Pythagorean theorem involving radicals	**66, 74, 78, 96; Investigation 2**
trigonometric ratios	**112, 118**

3-Dimensional figures

represent in 2-dimensional world using nets	**55, 95, 100**
draw 3-dimensional figures	**Investigation 4**

	LESSONS
Coordinate geometry	
name and graph ordered pairs	**41, 60, 89;** **Investigations 1, 5, 11**
intercepts of a line	**56, 82**
determine slope from the graph of line	**44, 56, 113; Investigation 8**
identify reflections, translations, rotations, and symmetry	**26; Investigation 3**
graph reflections across the horizontal or vertical axes	**26; Investigation 5**
graph translations	**Investigation 5**
graph rotations	**Investigation 5**
graph dilations	**60, 71; Investigation 5**
graph linear equations	**41, 47, 56, 82**
MEASUREMENT	
Measuring physical attributes	
use customary units of length, area, volume, weight, capacity	**6, 31, 42**
use metric units of length, area, volume, weight, capacity	**6, 8, 42, 104**
use temperature scales Fahrenheit, Celsius	**31**
use units of time	**80**
Systems of measurement	
convert units of measure	**6, 23, 52, 72, 80, 104**
convert between systems	**9, 52**
unit multipliers	**52, 64, 72**
Solving measurement problems	
perimeter of polygons, circles, complex figures	**8, 31, 39, 60**
area of triangles, rectangles, and parallelograms	**8, 17, 20, 37, 60, 66, 92, 96**
area of trapezoids	**75**
area of circles	**40, 101, 114**
area of semicircles and sectors	**40**
area of complex figures	**37**
surface area of right prisms and cylinders	**43, 44, 85**
surface area of spheres	**111**
surface area of cones and pyramids	**100, 114**
estimate area	**37, 40, 43; Investigation 1**
volume of right prisms, cylinders, pyramids, and cones	**42, 76, 104, 117**
volume of spheres	**111**
estimate volume	**42, 76, 104, 117**
Solving problems of similarity	
scale factor	**26, 35, 60, 66, 87, 91**
similar triangles	**35, 115; Investigation 12**
indirect measurement	**65, 118**
scale drawings two-dimensional	**35, 60**
scale drawings three-dimensional	**91**
Use appropriate measurement instruments	
compass	**39**
protractor	**18**
DATA ANALYSIS AND PROBABILITY	
Data collection and representation	
collect and display data	**53; Investigation 6**
tables and charts	**Investigations 8, 11**
frequency tables	**Investigation 6**

	LESSONS
histograms	**53; Investigation 6**
bar graphs	**53; Investigation 6**
circle graphs	**Investigation 6**
Venn diagrams	**90; Investigation 3**
scatter plots	**113; Investigation 8**
line plots	**53, 109**
box-and whisker plots	**103**
choose an appropriate graph	**103; Investigations 6, 9**
identify bias in data collection	**Investigation 6**
analyze bias in data collection	**Investigations 6, 9**
draw and compare different representations	**Investigation 6**
Data set characteristics	
mean, median, mode, and range	**7, 53, 103, 105**
select the best measure of central tendency for a given situation	**7, 53**
determine trends from data	**53, 98, 113**
predict from graphs	**98, 113**
recognize misuses of graphical or numerical information	**53**
evaluate predictions and conclusions based on data analysis	**53**
Probability	
experimental probability	**32, 59**
make predictions based on experiments	**32, 59**
accuracy of predictions in experiments	**59**
theoretical probability	**32, 59, 110**
sample spaces	**32, 68, 83**
simple probability	**32, 59**
probability of compound events	**32, 68**
probability of the complement of an event	**32**
probability of independent events	**32, 83**
probability of dependent events	**83**
select and use different models to simulate an event	**59**
PROBLEM SOLVING	
Four-step problem-solving process	**1-120**
Problem-solving strategies	**1-120**
ALGEBRA APPENDIX TOPICS	
graph sequences	**A73**
formulate the equation of a line with given characteristics	**A66, A68, A71, A119, A120**
formulate the equation of a line parallel/perpendicular to a given line	**A119, A120**
solve proportions with an unknown in two terms	**A83**
graph linear inequalities	**A106, A108**
factor quadratics	**A101, A105, A110**
solve quadratic equations	**A105, A110, A116, A117**
solve systems of linear equations using substitution	**A97, A102**
solve systems of linear equations using elimination	**A87 A99, A104**
formulate an equation with two unknown variables given a problem situation	**A87**
solve systems of linear inequalities with two unknowns	**A114**
graph systems of linear inequalities	**A112**

• Problem Solving

Objectives

- Use the four-step problem-solving process to solve real-world problems.
- Select or develop a problem-solving strategy for different types of problems.

Lesson Preparation

Materials

- **Problem-Solving Model poster**
- **Problem-Solving Strategies poster**

Problem-Solving Model

Understand
- ✔ What information am I given?
- ✔ What am I asked to find or do?

Plan
- ✔ How can I use the information I am given to solve the problem?
- ✔ Which strategy should I try?

Solve
- ✔ Did I follow the plan?
- ✔ Did I show my work?
- ✔ Did I write the answer?

Check
- ✔ Did I look back at the problem to see if I used the correct information?
- ✔ Did I answer the question or do what I was asked to do?
- ✔ Is my answer reasonable, does it make sense?

Problem-Solving Model

Problem-Solving Strategies

- ● **Act It Out or Make a Model**
- ● **Use Logical Reasoning**
- ● **Draw a Picture or Diagram**
- ● **Write an Equation**
- ● **Make It Simpler**
- ● **Find a Pattern**
- ● **Make an Organized List**
- ● **Guess and Check**
- ● **Make or Use a Table, Chart, or Graph**
- ● **Work Backwards**

Problem-Solving Strategies

Meeting Standards

• Problem Solving

As we study mathematics we learn how to use tools that help us solve problems. We face mathematical problems in our daily lives, in our careers, and in our efforts to advance our technological society. We can become powerful problem solvers by improving our ability to use the tools we store in our minds. In this book we will practice solving problems every day.

four-step problem-solving process

Solving a problem is like arriving at a destination, so the process of solving a problem is similar to the process of taking a trip. Suppose we are on the mainland and want to reach a nearby island

Problem-Solving Process	Taking a Trip
Step 1: (Understand) Know where you are and where you want to go.	We are on the mainland and want to go to the island.
Step 2: (Plan) Plan your route.	We might use the bridge, the boat, or swim.
Step 3: (Solve) Follow the plan.	Take the journey to the island
Step 4: (Check) Check that you have reached the right place.	Verify that you have reached your desired destination.

Problem-Solving Overview   **1**

In this lesson students are reminded how to use the four-step problem-solving process, problem-solving strategies, and when they need to do some writing while problem solving.

Four-Step Problem-Solving Process
Instruction

Give students the opportunity to describe different types of problems they have encountered. Suggestions may include:
- word problems
- real-world problems
- finding a sum, difference, product, or quotient
- any math problems

To help students understand that reasoning is a part of problem solving, ask,

> *"If you know exactly what to do so you can accomplish a goal, are you solving a problem?"*

Help students understand that uncertainty is a part of problem solving. Uncertainty gives us the opportunity to apply reasoning skills. Also explain that making errors and correcting errors is a part of the problem-solving process.

Before reading through the student page with the class, display the *Problem-Solving Model* concept poster. Point out that this problem-solving model is flexible and can be adapted to any problem.

(continued)

Math Background

What is problem solving?

Many mathematicians would say that problem solving occurs whenever we do not know exactly how to proceed. Problem-solving abilities vary from student to student. Some students engage in problem solving while working on routine one-step problems. Other students need to be presented with more complex problems to engage in problem solving.

The goal of problem solving is to give students the tools they need to solve a wide range of problems. One tool is a process that helps them interpret and represent a problem. Another tool is a set of problem solving strategies that can be used to solve a variety of problems. In this program, problem solving is a daily experience as students encounter both routine word problems and non-routine strategy problems in every lesson.

Four-Step Problem-Solving Process (continued)

Instruction

As you discuss the chart at the top of the student page, emphasize the importance of asking questions during the problem-solving process.

Example

Instruction

"How do you know that the problem requires more than one step?" If the problem asked how much more money Josh needs to buy a specific television it would be one step. Since it asks us to decide which television he can buy after working five weekends, it is a multi-step problem.

Have a volunteer describe the steps of the solution.

- Determine how much money Josh earns in five weekends.
- Add that amount to the money he has saved.
- Compare the total to the prices of the television to see which one Josh can buy.

(continued)

When we solve a problem, it helps to ask ourselves some questions along the way.

Follow the Process	Ask Yourself Questions
Step 1: Understand	What information am I given? What am I asked to find or do?
Step 2: Plan	How can I use the given information to solve the problem? What strategy can I use to solve the problem?
Step 3: Solve	Am I following the plan? Is my math correct?
Step 4: Check (Look Back)	Does my solution answer the question that was asked? Is my answer reasonable?

Below we show how we follow these steps to solve a word problem.

Example

Josh wants to buy a television. He has already saved $68.25. He earns $35 each Saturday stocking groceries in his father's store. The sizes and prices of the televisions available are shown at right. If Josh works and saves for 5 more weekends, what is the largest television he could buy?

Televisions
15" $149.99
17" $199.99
20" $248.99

Solution

Step 1: Understand the problem. We know that Josh has $68.25 saved. We know that he earns $35.00 every weekend. We are asked to decide which television he could buy if he works for 5 more weekends.

Step 2: Make a plan. We cannot find the answer in one step. We make a plan that will lead us toward the solution. One way to solve the problem is to find out how much Josh will earn in 5 weekends, then add that amount to the money he has already saved, then determine the largest television he could buy with the total amount of money.

Step 3: Solve the problem. (Follow the Plan.) First we multiply $35 by 5 to determine how much Josh will earn in 5 weekends. We could also find 5 multiples of $35 by making a table.

Weekend	1	2	3	4	5
Amount	$35	$70	$105	$140	$175

English Learners

Students will encounter unfamiliar words when they read word problems. Sometimes these words will be math vocabulary and other times they will be non-math words.

Demonstrate a difficult word by drawing or showing a picture or touching an item that represents the word. The ideas provided in this program follow a similar approach.

- Identify the word.
- Demonstrate the word and how to use it.
- Ask the students to use the word in a sentence or identify the word in a similar situation.

Creating a *word wall* of unfamiliar words will provide a visual reference throughout the year.

$$\begin{array}{r} \$35 \\ \times\ 5 \\ \hline \$175 \end{array}$$

Josh will earn $175 in 5 weekends.

Now we add $175 to $68.25 to find the total amount he will have.

$$\begin{array}{r} \$175 \\ +\quad 68.25 \\ \hline \$243.25 \end{array}$$

We find that Josh will have $243.25 after working 5 more weekends. When we compare the total to the prices, we can see that **Josh can buy the 17″ television.**

Step 4: Check your answer. (Look Back.) We read the problem again. The problem asked which television Josh could buy after working five weekends. We found that in five weekends Josh will earn $175.00, which combined with his $68.25 savings gives Josh $243.25. This is enough money to buy the 17″ television.

1. List in order the four steps in the problem-solving process.
   understand, plan, solve, check

2. What two questions do we answer to help us understand a problem?   What information am I given? What am I asked to find or do to solve the problem?

Refer to the text below to answer problems **3–8.**

> *Mary wants to put square tiles on the kitchen floor. The tile she has selected is 12 inches on each side and comes in boxes of 20 tiles for $54 per box. Her kitchen is 15 feet 8 inches long and 5 feet 9 inches wide. How many boxes of tile will she need and what will be the price of the tile, not including tax?*

▶ 3. What information are we given?   Mary's kitchen is 15 ft 8 in. by 5 ft 9 in. The tiles are 12 in. by 12 in. (1 ft by 1 ft). A box of 20 tiles costs $54.

▶ 4. What are we asked to find?   The number of boxes of tile needed and the total price.

5. Which step of the four-step problem-solving process have you completed when you have answered problems **3** and **4**?   Understand

6. Describe your plan for solving the problem. Besides the arithmetic, is there anything else you can draw or do that will help you solve the problem?

7. Solve the problem by following your plan. Show your work and any diagrams you used. Write your solution to the problem in a way someone else will understand.

8. Check your work and your answer. Look back to the problem. Be sure you used the information correctly. Be sure you found what you were asked to find. Is your answer reasonable?   I estimated the room is 6 ft by 16 ft. That means the room will need 6 tiles across and 16 tiles down. 6 × 16 = 96. There are 20 tiles in each box. 20 × 5 = 100. There are enough tiles in 5 boxes, so my answer is reasonable.

Sample: Sketch [a] rectangle to [vi]sualize the problem. [C]alculate the number of tiles [n]eeded. Find the number of [b]oxes to buy. Find the cost [of] the boxes.

5 ft 9 in.
(6 tiles)

15 ft 8 in.
(16 tiles)

7. Sample: Tiles needed: 16 × 6 = 96. Whole boxes needed: 96 ÷ 20 = 4 r 16. Whole boxes + 16 tiles = 5 boxes. Cost: 5 × $54 = $270.

Problem-Solving Overview   **3**

▶ See Math Conversations in the sidebar.

Four-Step Problem-Solving Process (continued)

Example (continued)
Instruction
Extend the Problem
You may wish to extend the problem by asking students how many weekends Josh would need to work to buy a 20″ television. 6 weekends

Math Conversations
Discussion opportunities are provided below.

Problem 3   Represent
As students list the given information in the problem, ask a volunteer to list the information on the board. Ask the class to check that all the necessary information is included.

Problem 4   Verify
Ask another volunteer to write the goal of the problem on the board using his or her own words. Have the class verify that they agree with the goal.

Problem-Solving Strategies

Instruction

Ten strategies are presented and practiced in this program. You can use the following problems to give examples of each type. Use the strategy indicated to solve each given problem.

Make a Model

Give the dimensions of a rectangular prism that is made from 36 cubes with a length that measures twice its height. **6 units long, 3 units high, 2 units wide**

Use Logical Reasoning

Five candidates ran for class president. Tanya received 8 more votes than Bruce who received 6 fewer votes than Emily. Juanita received more votes than Tanya but fewer votes than Jason. Who was elected class president? **Jason**

Draw a Diagram

Mr. Ortega has red, yellow, and green apples in a basket. One half of the apples are red. One fourth of the apples are green. Sixteen apples are yellow. How many apples are in the basket? **64**

Write an Equation

Bethany collects coins. She paid $28 for a coin. This new coin cost $8 less than twice the price of the last coin she bought. How much was the last coin she bought?
$2p - 8 = \$28$; **$18**

Make It Simpler

A radio station is offering prizes to its callers. Every 10th caller receives a hat. Every 25th caller receives a T-shirt. Every 50th caller receives a music CD. The prizes will be offered to the first 1000 callers. How many prizes of each kind is the radio station planning to give away? **100 hats; 40 T-shirts; 20 CDs**

Find a Pattern

One school is sponsoring a recycling program for tin cans. The first week they received 100 cans. Each week after the first week, the number of cans increased by 50. Predict the number of cans they will collect after 4 months. (Use 4 weeks = 1 month) **850 cans**

Make An Organized List

How many different three-digit numbers can be made from the numbers 0, 6, and 9? **4**

Guess and Check

Thirteen pigs and chickens are on a farm. Altogether the animals have 42 legs. How many are pigs and how many are chickens? **8 pigs, 5 chickens**

(continued)

problem-solving strategies

As we consider how to solve a problem we choose one or more strategies that seem to be helpful. Referring to the picture at the beginning of this lesson, we might choose to swim, to take the boat, or to cross the bridge to travel from the mainland to the island. Other strategies might not be as effective for the illustrated problem. For example, choosing to walk or bike across the water are strategies that are not reasonable for this situation.

Problem-solving **strategies** are types of plans we can use to solve problems. Listed below are ten strategies we will practice in this book. You may refer to these descriptions as you solve problems throughout the year.

Act it out or make a model. Moving objects or people can help us visualize the problem and lead us to the solution.

Use logical reasoning. All problems require reasoning, but for some problems we use given information to eliminate choices so that we can close in on the solution. Usually a chart, diagram, or picture can be used to organize the given information and to make the solution more apparent.

Draw a picture or diagram. Sketching a picture or a diagram can help us understand and solve problems, especially problems about graphs or maps or shapes.

Write a number sentence or equation. We can solve many word problems by fitting the given numbers into equations or number sentences and then finding the unknown numbers.

Make it simpler. We can make some complicated problem easier by using smaller numbers or fewer items. Solving the simpler problem might help us see a pattern or method that can help us solve the complex problem.

Find a pattern. Identifying a pattern that helps you to predict what will come next as the pattern continues might lead to the solution.

Make an organized list. Making a list can help us organize our thinking about a problem.

Guess and check. Guessing a possible answer and trying the guess in the problem might start a process that leads to the answer. If the guess is not correct, use the information from the guess to make a better guess. Continue to improve your guesses until you find the answer.

Make or use a table, chart, or graph. Arranging information in a table, chart, or graph can help us organize and keep track of data. This might reveal patterns or relationships that can help us solve the problem.

Work backwards. Finding a route through a maze is often easier by beginning at the end and tracing a path back to the start. Likewise, some problems are easier to solve by working back from information that is given toward the end of the problem to information that is unknown near the beginning of the problem.

Inclusion

Some students may need help focusing when they read. It may be beneficial for them to use an index card while reading new concepts and word problems. They should slide the card to uncover one line at a time to help them keep their place as they read.

Teacher Tip

Instruction

You may wish to display the *Problem-Solving Strategies* poster throughout the year as a reference for students.

9. Name some strategies used in this lesson.   Answers will vary.

The chart below shows where each strategy is first introduced in this textbook.

Strategy	Lesson
Act It Out or Make a Model	Lesson 1
Use Logical Reasoning	Lesson 15
Draw a Picture or Diagram	Lesson 1
Write a Number Sentence or Equation	Lesson 31
Make It Simpler	Lesson 4
Find a Pattern	Lesson 19
Make an Organized List	Lesson 38
Guess and Check	Lesson 8
Make or Use a Table, Chart, or Graph	Lesson 21
Work Backwards	Lesson 2

writing and problem solving

Sometimes a problem will ask us to explain our thinking. Writing about a problem solving can help us measure our understanding of math.

For these types of problems, we use words to describe the steps we used to follow our plan.

This is a description of the way we solved the problem about tiling a kitchen.

First, we round the measurements of the floor to 6 ft by 16 ft. We multiply to find the approximate area: 6 × 16 = 96 sq. ft. Then we count by 20s to find a number close to but greater than 96: 20, 40, 60, 80, **100.** *There are 20 tiles in each box, so Mary needs to buy 5 boxes of tiles. We multiply to find the total cost: $54 × 5 = $270.*

10. Write a description of how we solved the problem in the example.
Answers will vary.
Other times, we will be asked to write a problem for a given equation.
Be sure to include the correct numbers and operations to represent the equation.

11. Write a word problem for the equation $b = (12 \times 10) \div 4$.
Answers will vary.

Problem-Solving Overview   **5**

Problem-Solving Strategies
Make a Table
Mrs. Whong can average 55 mph on a highway. She plans to stop every 2 hours for 15 minutes. About how long it will take her to drive 300 miles?

Hours	1	2	3	4	5	6
Miles	55	110	165	220	275	330
Stops	15 min		15 min		15 min	

Sample: about 6 hr; about $5\frac{1}{2}$ hours driving and 30 min in stops.

Work Backwards
On Monday Angela's mother gave her some money. On Tuesday she spent half of it. On Wednesday she earned $10. On Thursday she went shopping and came home with one third of the amount she had yesterday. On Friday, she spent half of the amount and had $4 left. How much money did her mother give her? $28

Writing and Problem Solving
Instruction
Point out that sometimes students will be asked to describe their thinking in words. These directions will be presented in different ways.
• Explain how you found your answer.
• Explain how you know your answer is correct.
• Explain why your answer is reasonable.

Students should write brief, accurate descriptions of their methods. Encourage them to use appropriate mathematical language.

Periodically, students will be asked to write a problem for a given situation or equation. Give students the opportunity to share the word problems they write for problem 11.

Looking Forward
Students will use the problem-solving process and strategies in each lesson of this text. Routine and non-routine strategy problems are presented every day in the Power Up section of each lesson. One-step, two-step, and multi-step problems are presented in the Written Practice section of each lesson.

Section 1 Overview

Lesson Planner

LESSON	NEW CONCEPTS	MATERIALS	RESOURCES
1	• Number Line: Comparing and Ordering Integers	none	Power Up A
2	• Operations of Arithmetic	none	Power Up A
3	• Addition and Subtraction Word Problems	none	Power Up A
4	• Multiplication and Division Word Problems	none	Power Up A
5	• Fractional Parts	Manipulative Kit: color tiles, fraction circles	Power Up A
6	• Converting Measures	Manipulative Kit: inch and metric rulers Yardsticks and/or metersticks	Power Up B
7	• Rates and Average • Measures of Central Tendency	Manipulative Kit: color cubes index cards	Power Up B
8	• Perimeter and Area	Manipulative Kit: color tiles Tape measure, metersticks, or yardsticks	Power Up B
9	• Prime Numbers	Manipulative Kit: color tiles Calculators, grid paper	Power Up B Lesson Activity 1
10	• Rational Numbers • Equivalent Fractions	Manipulative Kit: fraction circles	Power Up B
Inv. 1	• The Coordinate Plane	Manipulative Kit: inch rulers Graph paper	Investigation Activity 2

Problem Solving

Strategies

- **Act It Out or Make a Model**   Lessons 1, 6
- **Find a Pattern**   Lessons 5, 10
- **Make It Simpler**   Lessons 4, 7
- **Make an Organized List**   Lesson 10
- **Draw a Diagram**   Lessons 1, 9
- **Work Backwards**   Lesson 2
- **Write an Equation**   Lesson 3
- **Guess and Check**   Lesson 8

Real-World Applications

pp. 11, 19–23, 25, 27–29, 32–34, 37–40, 42–45, 51–53, 57, 58, 66

4-Step Process

Student Edition   Lessons 1, 2, 4, 8, 9

Teacher Edition   Lessons 1–10 (Power-Up Discussions)

Communication

Explain

pp. 16, 58, 61, 67, 70

Formulate a Problem

pp. 22, 29, 34, 46, 52

Connections

Math and Other Subjects

- **Math and Geography**   p. 39
- **Math and History**   pp. 22, 45
- **Math and Sports**   pp. 20, 29, 38, 45, 53

Math to Math

- **Problem Solving and Measurement**   Lessons 1, 3–10
- **Algebra and Problem Solving**   Lessons 2–9, Inv. 1
- **Fractions, Percents, Decimals, and Problem Solving**   Lessons 1, 3–5, 7–9
- **Fractions and Measurement**   Lessons 5, 6, 8, 10
- **Measurement and Geometry**   Lessons 8–10
- **Algebra, Measurement, and Geometry**   Inv. 1

Representation

Model

pp. 9, 39, 57, 65, 66

Represent

pp. 14, 15, 29, 34, 57, 65, 66

Technology

Student Resources

- **eBook**   Anytime
- **Online Resources** at
  www.SaxonPublishers.com/ActivitiesC3
  Graphing Calculator Activities   Lesson 7 and Inv. 1

Teacher Resources

- **Resources and Planner CD**
- **Adaptations CD**   Lessons 1–10
- **Test & Practice Generator CD**
- **eGradebook**
- **Answer Key CD**

The course begins with a review of number and operations. Introductory measurement lessons in these lessons include units of measure and converting measures in Lesson 6, measuring perimeter and area in Lesson 8, and relating measures with rates in Lesson 7. The initial statistics lesson appears in Lesson 7 as students identify and find various measures of central tendency.

Algebra is a major emphasis in this textbook. As early as Lessons 3 and 4 students are taught to recognize the underlying plot in word problems and to use equations to model the plot. Students then solve the equations they have written to represent the word problems. A necessary vehicle for conveying algebraic ideas is the coordinate plane. The first investigation in this course introduces the coordinate plane and related terminology.

Beginning the Year

Establish productive routines early in the school year.

Saxon Math is uniquely organized to develop and practice the various strands of mathematics concurrently. Consequently the early lessons in the book are foundational and usually seem easy to students. **If a student seems unusually challenged by early lessons, take steps to assure that the student is properly placed in the series.**

Power-Up

Each day, work through the Power-Up Section with students.

Fact practice fosters quick recall of essential knowledge and skills that allow students to focus their mental energies on problem solving. Mental Math develops facility with numbers and familiarity with commonly encountered applications of mathematics. Daily Problem Solving employs strategies that are useful for solving a wide range of real-world problems.

New Concepts

Involve students in working through each example.

Draw students' attention to new terminology. Involve students in working through each example as part of the assignment. Guide student work on the Practice Set questions at the end of the New Concept section. These lesson practice problems should be considered part of the daily assignment. This dose of massed practice is an essential component of instruction.

Written Practice

Suggestions for Math Conversations provide support for guiding and extending problems.

Try to allow half of the class period for students to work on the Written Practice. Asterisks indicate potentially challenging problems that students should work on first, during class, where help is available. Exercises not finished in class become homework. Help students through difficult problems on the day's assignment to reduce the chance of misconceptions and to minimize the number of incorrectly answered homework problems.

Assessment

A variety of weekly assessment tools are provided.

After Lesson 10:
- Power-Up Test 1
- Cumulative Test 1
- Customized Benchmark Test
- Performance Task 1

LESSON	NEW CONCEPTS	PRACTICED	ASSESSED
1	• Number Line: Comparing and Ordering Integers	Lessons 1, 2, 3, 4, 5, 6, 7, 8, 9, 10, 11, 12, 13, 14, 15, 16, 18, 19, 21, 22, 23, 24, 25, 26, 29, 30, 32, 34, 35, 36, 38, 39, 49, 54, 92, 93	Tests 1, 2
2	• Operations of Arithmetic	Lessons 2, 3, 4, 5, 6, 7, 8, 9, 10, 11, 12, 13, 14, 15, 16, 17, 18, 20, 21, 23, 25, 26, 28, 31, 32,	Tests 1, 2, 3
3	• Addition and Subtraction Word Problems	Lessons 3, 4, 5, 6, 7, 8, 9, 10, 12, 13, 14, 16, 17, 18, 19, 20, 21, 22, 23, 25, 26, 28, 32, 34, 35, 36, 38, 39, 40, 41, 42, 47, 51, 55, 56, 58, 61, 63, 64, 65, 66, 67, 68, 105, 112, 114, 115, 117	Tests 1, 2, 3
4	• Multiplication and Division Word Problems	Lessons 4, 5, 6, 7, 8, 10, 11, 12, 14, 15, 17, 18, 19, 20, 21, 28, 29, 32, 35, 36, 37, 38, 39, 41, 42, 47, 50, 51, 52, 55, 56, 58, 61, 63, 64, 65, 66, 67, 95, 96, 102, 105, 112, 114, 115, 117	Tests 1, 3, 4, 6, 10
5	• Fractional Parts	Lessons 5, 6, 7, 8, 9, 10, 11, 12, 13, 14, 15, 16, 17, 18, 22, 23, 24, 26, 27, 30, 39, 48, 49, 50	Tests 1, 2, 6, 8
6	• Converting Measures	Lessons 6, 7, 8, 9, 10, 11, 13, 14, 17, 18, 21, 24, 28, 38, 41, 46, 83	Tests 2
7	• Rates and Average	Lessons 7, 8, 9, 10, 11, 12, 13, 14, 16, 18, 19, 20, 21, 22, 24, 25, 26, 27, 29, 30, 36, 37, 38, 43, 44, 45, 58, 59, 65, 67, 100, 103, 109, 111, 117	Tests 3, 4, 5, 12
7	• Measures of Central Tendency	Lessons 8, 9, 10, 14, 15, 17, 20, 29, 40, 61, 62, 65, 67, 117	Tests 2, 4, 5, 8
8	• Perimeter and Area	Lessons 8, 9, 10, 11, 12, 13, 14, 15, 16, 17, 18, 19, 21, 22, 23, 24, 25, 26, 27, 28, 30, 32, 33, 37, 38, 39, 41, 44, 46, 47, 50, 81, 83, 94, 96	Tests 2–4, 6
9	• Prime Numbers	Lessons 9, 10, 11, 12, 13, 14, 15, 16, 17, 18, 19, 20, 24, 26, 27, 30, 32, 35, 37, 43, 44, 94	Tests 2–4, 7
10	• Rational Numbers	Lessons 10, 11, 12, 13, 14, 15, 17, 18, 19, 20, 21, 25, 27, 28, 29, 30, 31, 33, 37	Tests 2, 5
10	• Equivalent Fractions	Lessons 10, 11, 12, 13, 20, 31	Tests 2, 4, 5
Inv. 1	• The Coordinate Plane	Lessons 17, 19, 20, 21, 23, 25, 26, 28, 29, 30, 32, 33, 34, 36, 37, 38, 39, 40, 51, 52, 53, 54, 60, 86, 91, 92, 93	Tests 3, 4

• Number Line: Comparing and Ordering Integers

Objectives
- Graph points on a number line.
- Compare and order integers.
- Recognize the sets of counting numbers, whole numbers, integers, even numbers, and odd numbers.
- Find the absolute value of a number.

Lesson Preparation

Materials
- **Power Up A** (in *Instructional Masters*)

Optional
- **Teacher-provided material:** index cards

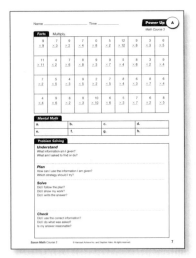

Power Up A

Math Language

New	Maintain	English Learners (ESL)
absolute value	counting numbers	composed
elements	negative numbers	
even numbers	number line	
integers	origin	
odd numbers	positive numbers	
sequence		
sets		
whole numbers		

Technology Resources

Student eBook Complete student textbook in electronic format.

Resources and Planner CD Assessment, reteaching, and instructional masters, plus a pacing calendar with standards.

Test and Practice Generator CD Create additional practice sheets and custom-made tests.

www.SaxonPublishers.com Visit for more student activities and planning materials.

Inclusion

Adaptations CD Adapted lessons, investigations, practice and assessments.

Meeting Standards

Communication

Problem-Solving Strategy: Draw a Diagram/ Act It Out

Some problems describe physical movement. To solve such problems, we might act out the situation to understand what is happening. We can also draw a diagram to represent the movement in the problem. We try to keep diagrams simple so they are easy to understand.

Problem: A robot is programmed to take two steps forward, then one step back. The robot will repeat this until it reaches its charger unit, which is ten steps in front of the robot. How many steps back will the robot take before it reaches the charger unit?

Understand We are told a robot takes two steps forward and then one step back. We are asked to find how many steps back the robot will take before it reaches the charger unit, which is ten steps away.

Plan We will draw a diagram to help us count the steps. Your teacher might also select a student to act out the robot's movements for the class.

Solve We use a number line for our diagram. We count two spaces forward from zero and then one space back and write "1" above the tick mark for 1. From that point, we count two spaces forward and one space back and write "2" above the tick mark for 2. We continue until we reach the tick mark for 10. The numbers we write represent the total number of backward steps by the robot. We reach 10 after having taken eight steps back. The robot reaches the charger unit after taking eight steps back.

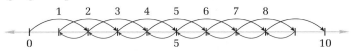

Check To check for reasonableness, we rethink the problem situation with our answer in mind. It makes sense that the robot takes eight steps back before reaching the charger unit. Two steps forward and one step back is the same as one step forward. After completing this pattern 8 times, we expect the robot to be able to take 2 steps forward and reach its destination.

1 **Power Up**

Facts
Distribute **Power Up A** to students. See answers below.

Mental Math
Encourage students to share different ways to mentally compute these exercises. Strategies for exercises **e** and **f** are listed below.

e. Add 2, Subtract 2
$$98 + 37 =$$
$$(98 + 2) + (37 - 2) =$$
$$100 + 35 = 135$$
Add the Tens, Add the Ones
$$98 + 37$$
$$90 + 30 = 120$$
$$7 + 8 = 15$$
$$120 + 15 = 135$$

f. Find a Fraction
$$50\% = \frac{1}{2}$$
$$\frac{1}{2} \times 50 = 25$$
Double and Halve
$$50\% \text{ of } 50 = 100\% \text{ of } 25 = 25$$

Problem Solving
Refer to **Power-Up Discussion**, p. 6B.

• Number Line: Comparing and Ordering Integers

Power Up *Building Power*

facts Power Up A

mental math

a. Calculation: Danielle drives 60 miles per hour for 2 hours. How far does she drive in total?   120 miles

b. Number Sense: 100×100 10,000

c. Estimation: 4.034×8.1301 $4 \times 8 = 32$

d. Measurement: How long is the key? $2\frac{1}{4}$ inches

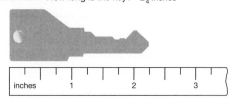

e. Number Sense: $98 + 37$ 135

f. Percent: 50% of 50   25

g. Geometry: This figure represents a   **B**   •————————•
    A line   **B** line segment   **C** ray

h[1]. Calculation: $7 + 5, + 3, + 1, \div 8, \times 2, \times 4$ 16

problem solving

Some problems describe physical movement. To solve such problems, we might act out the situation to understand what is happening. We can also draw a diagram to represent the movement in the problem. We try to keep diagrams simple so they are easy to understand.

Problem: A robot is programmed to take two steps forward, then one step back. The robot will repeat this until it reaches its charger unit, which is ten steps in front of the robot. How many steps back will the robot take before it reaches the charger unit?

（Understand） We are told a robot takes two steps forward and then one step back. We are asked to find how many steps back the robot will take before it reaches its charger unit, which is ten steps away.

（Plan） We will draw a diagram to help us count the steps. Your teacher might also select a student to act out the robot's movements for the class.

---

[1] As a shorthand, we will use commas to separate operations to be performed sequentially from left to right. This is not a standard mathematical notation.

Facts Multiply.

9 ×9 **81**	7 ×3 **21**	9 ×2 **18**	7 ×4 **28**	0 ×8 **0**	5 ×2 **10**	12 ×12 **144**	9 ×8 **72**	3 ×3 **9**	6 ×5 **30**
11 ×11 **121**	4 ×2 **8**	7 ×6 **42**	8 ×8 **64**	9 ×3 **27**	9 ×7 **63**	5 ×4 **20**	8 ×6 **48**	3 ×2 **6**	9 ×4 **36**
7 ×2 **14**	5 ×5 **25**	4 ×3 **12**	9 ×5 **45**	2 ×2 **4**	7 ×5 **35**	8 ×4 **32**	6 ×3 **18**	8 ×7 **56**	6 ×4 **24**
4 ×4 **16**	9 ×6 **54**	8 ×2 **16**	8 ×3 **24**	10 ×10 **100**	6 ×6 **36**	5 ×3 **15**	7 ×7 **49**	6 ×2 **12**	8 ×5 **40**

Solve We use a number line for our diagram. We count two spaces forward from zero and then one space back and write "1" above the tick mark for 1. From that point, we count two spaces forward and one space back and write "2" above the 2. We continue until we reach the tick mark for 10. The numbers we write represent the total number of backward steps by the robot. We reach 10 after having taken eight steps back. The robot reaches the charger unit after taking eight steps back.

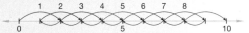

Check To check for reasonableness, we rethink the problem situation with our answer in mind. It makes sense that the robot takes eight steps back before reaching the charger unit. Two steps forward and one step back is the same as one step forward. After completing this pattern 8 times, we expect the robot to be able to take two steps forward and reach its destination.

New Concept   *Increasing Knowledge*
___

The numbers we use in this book can be represented by points on a number line.

Number line

Points to the right of zero (the *origin*) represent positive numbers. Points to the left of zero represent negative numbers. Zero is neither positive nor negative.

The tick marks on the number line above indicate the locations of **integers,** which include **counting numbers** (1, 2, 3, …) and their opposites (… −3, −2, −1) as well as zero. Thus all **whole numbers** (0, 1, 2, …) are integers, but not all integers are whole numbers. We will study numbers represented by points between the tick marks later in the book.

Classify Give an example of an integer that is not a whole number.   any negative number, such as −2

Counting numbers, whole numbers, and integers are examples of different **sets** of numbers. A set is a collection of items, like numbers or polygons. We use braces to indicate a set of numbers, and we write the **elements** (members) of the set within the braces.

The set of integers

{…, −3, −2, −1, 0, 1, 2, 3, …}

The set of whole numbers

{0, 1, 2, 3, …}

Analyze How are the sets of whole numbers and integers different?
The set of whole numbers does not include negative numbers.

2 **New Concepts**

Instruction
This lesson reviews important concepts learned in previous years. After going through this instructional material, you can assess students' understanding by discussing questions such as:

"Is zero a whole number?" yes

"Is zero a counting number?" no

"Why does the number line have arrowheads on both ends?" Sample: The numbers go on in both directions.

"Why do you think zero is called the origin?" Sample: The positive numbers start to its right and the negative numbers start to its left.

Tell students that the terms *counting numbers* and *natural numbers* can be used interchangeably.

(continued)

Math Background

The opposite of a number is also called the additive inverse of that number. The Inverse Property of Addition states that the sum of a number and its opposite is zero. In symbolic form:

For every number a, $a + (-a) = 0$.

In future lessons, students will frequently use additive inverses when solving equations for unknowns.

Instruction

After introducing absolute value, ask:

"Why does absolute value have to be positive?" Sample: It is a distance, and distances can't be negative.

Example 1

Instruction

If students can't order these numbers by inspection, have them use the number line.

Example 2

Instruction

Be sure that students understand how to choose the correct inequality symbol.

You can extend the discussion of the *Connect* question by asking whether the way numbers change as you move on the number line is the same on both sides of zero. Sample: Yes, no matter where you are, if you move to the right, the numbers increase.

Instruction

You may want to sketch a number line on the board or overhead to demonstrate graphing a point on a number line. As you plot the points for the given even numbers, ask students to follow along with you. Discuss the notation used for the set of even numbers.

(continued)

The **absolute value** of a number is the distance between the number and the origin on a number line. Absolute value is always a positive number because it represents a distance. Thus, the absolute value of −5 (negative five) is 5, because −5 is 5 units from zero. Two vertical bars indicate absolute value.

"The absolute value of negative five is five."

$$|-5| = 5$$

We can order and compare numbers by noting their position on the number line. We use the equal sign and the greater than/less than symbols (> and <, respectively) to indicate a comparison. When properly placed between two numbers, the small end of the symbol points to the lesser number.

Example 1

Arrange these integers in order from least to greatest.

−3, 3, 0, 1

Solution

We write the integers in the same order as they appear on the number line.

−3, 0, 1, 3

Example 2

Compare:

a. −3 ◯ −1   b. |−3| ◯ |−1|

Solution

Thinking Skill

Connect

When you move from left to right on a number line, do the numbers increase or decrease? What happens to the numbers when you move from right to left? *increase; the numbers decrease*

a. We replace the circle with the correct comparison symbol. Negative three is less than negative one.

$$-3 < -1$$

b. The absolute value of −3 is 3 and the absolute value of −1 is 1, and 3 is greater than 1.

$$|-3| > |-1|$$

We graph a point on a number line by drawing a dot at its location. Below we graph the numbers −4, −2, 0, 2, and 4.

These numbers are members of the set of **even numbers.** The set of even numbers can be expressed as a **sequence,** an ordered list of numbers that follows a rule.

The set of even numbers

$$\{\ldots -4, -2, 0, 2, 4, \ldots\}$$

Inclusion

Some students need a physical demonstration of the number line. Write ten different integers on pieces of paper. Hand them to ten different students. Then call one student at a time to stand in number order at the front of the classroom. Have each student distance him/herself from the others according to the values of their numbers. Discuss with the class what happens to the order and distance of the students when each one is called up to the board.

Teacher Tip

The early lessons in this book review foundational concepts and skills that will be built on in later lessons. Use these lessons to establish the following important practices:

• Present a complete lesson or test each day.

• Ensure students complete all the problems in the practice set and the written practice.

• Emphasize that students should develop neat work habits and show all the steps in algorithms and problem-solving procedures.

• Leave enough time for the written practice so that students can complete most of it during class.

Example 3

Graph the numbers in this sequence on a number line.

$$\{\dots, -3, -1, 1, 3, \dots\}$$

Solution

This is the sequence of **odd numbers**. We sketch a number line and draw dots at −3, −1, 1, and 3. The ellipses show that the sequence continues, so we darken the arrowheads to show that the pattern continues.

Example 4

Graph two numbers that are four units from zero.

Solution

Both **4** and **−4** are four units from zero.

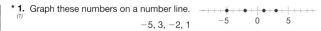

Practice Set

a. Arrange these integers in order from least to greatest.

$$-4, 3, 2, -1, 0 \quad -4, -1, 0, 2, 3$$

▶ b. Which number in problem **a** is an even number but not a whole number? −4

▶ c. Compare: $-2 \, \ominus \, -4$

d. **Model** Graph the numbers in this sequence on a number line.
$$\dots, -4, -2, 0, 2, 4, \dots$$

Simplify.

e. $|-3|$ 3   f. $|3|$ 3

▶ g. **Analyze** Write two numbers that are ten units from zero.   10, −10

▶ h. Write an example of a whole number that is not a counting number.   0

Written Practice   *Strengthening Concepts*

* **1.** Graph these numbers on a number line.
  (1)
$$-5, 3, -2, 1$$

▶ * **2.** **Analyze** Arrange these numbers from least to greatest.   −5, −2, 1, 3
  (1)
$$-5, 3, -2, 1$$

---

* Asterisks indicate exercises that should be completed in class with teacher support as needed.

▶ See Math Conversations in the sidebar.

Example 3
Instruction
Sketch the graph of this sequence and use the terms *origin*, *tick marks*, and *integers* to describe the graph. Also explain that the arrowheads are darkened to show that the sequence goes on without end in both directions.

Example 4
Instruction
Relate example 4 to absolute value. Point out that the absolute value of both 4 and −4 is 4 because both numbers are 4 units from the origin.

Practice Set
Problems b and h
To help students compare and contrast counting numbers, whole numbers, and integers, they may benefit from writing and labeling each set of numbers in their math notebooks or on a index card that can be used as a bookmark. Students can then refer to each set of numbers as needed.

Problem c
Write the greater than symbol (>) and the less than symbol (<) on the board or overhead, then invite students to share different ways to remember what each symbol represents.

Problem g   Analyze
Students should conclude that the numbers are opposites because they are the same distance from zero, but opposite in direction.

3 Written Practice

Math Conversations
Discussion opportunities are provided below.

Problem 2   Analyze
When ordering numbers using a number line, make sure students generalize that the number farthest to the left is least and the number farthest to the right is greatest.

(continued)

3 Written Practice *(Continued)*

Math Conversations

Discussion opportunities are provided below.

Problem 11 [Analyze]

Ask a volunteer to write the set of counting numbers and the set of counting-number opposites using braces and digits on the board or overhead. Sample:
{1, 2, 3, 4, 5, ...}; {..., −5, −4, −3, −2, −1}

Ask another volunteer to write the set of integers using braces and digits on the board or overhead. Sample:
{..., −3, −2, −1, 0, 1, 2, 3, ...}

Have students name a number that is common to each set to prove that the given statement in problem 11 is true.

Problem 17 [Evaluate]

"If we would plot these integers on a number line, what would be the location of each integer with respect to zero?" Sample: Both integers would be to the left of zero.

"Which integer would be closest to zero?" −2

"Which integer is greatest? Why?" −2; Sample: On a number line, −2 is to the right of −3.

Errors and Misconceptions

Problem 6

A common misconception is that the set of counting numbers begins with 0 because 0 can be an answer for some counting questions. For example, "How many months of the year have 32 days?"

Remind students that 0 is the first whole number and 1 is the first counting number.

Problem 19

Students who believe that the absolute value of a number can be negative misunderstand the concept.

Emphasize that absolute value is a measure of distance, not direction, from zero on a number line. To help students understand this concept, point out that it is not sensible to consider distance as a negative measure. For example, the distance from school to each student's home is a positive number of feet or miles. In the same way, the distance between any two numbers on a number line is a positive distance.

(continued)

---

* **3.** Use braces and digits to indicate the set of whole numbers.
  (1) {0, 1, 2, 3, ...}

* **4.** Use braces and digits to indicate the set of even numbers.   {..., −4,
  (1) −2, 0, 2, 4, ...}

5. Which number in problem **1** is an even number?   −2
(1)

▶ **6.** Which whole number is *not* a counting number?   0
(1)

7. Write the graphed numbers as a sequence of numbers. (Assume the
(1) pattern continues.)   ..., −4, −2, 0, 2, 4, ...

* **8.** The sequence of numbers in problem 7 is part of what set of
  (1) numbers?   the set of even integers

[Analyze]   Decide if the statements in **9–11** are true or false, and explain why.

9. All whole numbers are counting numbers.   False. Zero is a whole
(1) number, but not a counting number.

10. All counting numbers are whole numbers.   True; The whole numbers
(1) include all the counting numbers.

▶* **11.** If a number is a counting number or the opposite of a counting number,
  (1) then it is an integer.   True; Integers include counting numbers, their
  opposites, and zero.

12. What is the absolute value of 21?   21
(1)

13. What is the absolute value of −13?   13
(1)

14. What is the absolute value of 0?   0
(1)

15. Compare: $5 \, \textcircled{>} \, -7$
(1)

16. Compare: $-3 \, \textcircled{<} \, -2$
(1)

▶* **17.** [Evaluate]   Compare: $|-3| \, \textcircled{>} \, |-2|$
  (1)

18. Graph these numbers on a number line: −5, 0, 5
(1)

▶* **19.** If $|n| = 5$, then n can be which two numbers?   5, −5
  (1)

20. Write two numbers that are five units from zero.   −5, 5
(1)

21. Graph these numbers on a number line.
(1)   −3, 0, 3

22. Write two numbers that are 3 units from 0.   3, −3
(1)

23. Graph the numbers in this sequence on a number line.
(1)   ..., −15, −10, −5, 0, 5, 10, 15, ...

24. What number is the opposite of 10?   −10
(1)

23.
−15 −10 −5   0   5   10 15

▶ See Math Conversations in the sidebar.

English Learners

For problem **8**, explain the meaning of the word **composed.** Say:

"When you compose something, you put things together to make a group. A class is composed of the teacher and all the students in the classroom."

Write the number 23,471 on the board. Ask students what digits the number is composed of. The number is composed of the digits 2, 3, 4, 7, and 1.

25. What is the sum when you add 10 and its opposite?   0
(1)

* 26. What number is the opposite of −2?   2
(1)

▶* 27. `Conclude` What is the sum when you add −2 and its opposite?   0
(1)

For multiple choice problems **28–30,** choose *all* correct answers from
the list.

    A counting numbers (natural numbers)

    B whole numbers

    C integers

    D none of these

* 28. Negative seven is a member of which set of numbers?   **C**
(1)

29. Thirty is a member of which set of numbers?   **A, B, C**
(1)

30. One third is a member of which set of numbers?   **D**
(1)

Early Finishers
*Real-World
Application*

A group of eight students wants to ride a roller coaster at the local fair. Each passenger must be at least 48 inches tall to ride. The list below represents the number of inches each student's height differs from 48 inches. (A negative sign indicates a height less than 48 inches.)

    −4   −3   −1   5   0   −2   1   4

  a. Write each student's height in inches, then arrange the heights from least to greatest.   44, 45, 46, 47, 48, 49, 52, 53

  b. How many of the students represented by the list may ride the roller coaster?   four students

Lesson 1   **11**

▶ See Math Conversations in the sidebar.

3 **Written Practice** (Continued)

Math Conversations
Discussion opportunities are provided below.

Problem 27 `Conclude`
When working with opposite numbers, students should understand and apply the following generalizations.

- The opposite of a positive number is a negative number.
- The opposite of a negative number is a positive number.
- The sum of a number and its opposite is zero.

The Math Background feature in this lesson contains additional information about the sum of a number and its opposite.

Looking Forward

Comparing and ordering integers on a number line prepares students for:

- **Lesson 2,** working with operations of arithmetic.
- **Lesson 31,** adding integers.
- **Lesson 33,** subtracting integers.
- **Lesson 36,** multiplying and dividing integers.
- **Lesson 62,** graphing solutions to inequalities on a number line.
- **Lesson 90,** identifying and manipulating sets.
- **Lesson 94,** graphing pairs of inequalities on a number line.

• Operations of Arithmetic

Objectives

- Understand and use the four operations of arithmetic and the relationships between them.
- Use variables to represent missing or unknown values.
- Learn and apply some properties of addition and multiplication.
- Find unknown numbers in equations by using inverse operations.

Lesson Preparation

Materials

- **Power Up A** (in *Instructional Masters*)

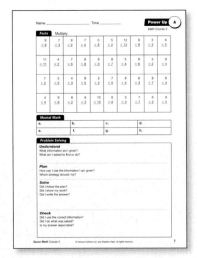

Power Up A

Math Language

New	Maintain	English Learners (ESL)
variables	addend	rearrange
	difference	
	dividend	
	divisor	
	factor	
	minuend	
	product	
	quotient	
	subtrahend	
	sum	

Technology Resources

Student eBook Complete student textbook in electronic format.

Resources and Planner CD Assessment, reteaching, and instructional masters, plus a pacing calendar with standards.

Test and Practice Generator CD Create additional practice sheets and custom-made tests.

www.SaxonPublishers.com Visit for more student activities and planning materials.

Inclusion

Adaptations CD Adapted lessons, investigations, practice and assessments.

Meeting Standards

National Council of Teachers of Mathematics (NCTM)

Numbers and Operations

NO.2a Understand the meaning and effects of arithmetic operations with fractions, decimals, and integers

NO.2b Use the associative and commutative properties of addition and multiplication and the distributive property of multiplication over addition to simplify computations with integers, fractions, and decimals

Connections

CN.4a Recognize and use connections among mathematical ideas

Problem-Solving Strategy: Work Backwards

A number of problems in this book will ask us to "fill in the missing digits" in an addition, subtraction, multiplication, or division problem. We can work backwards to solve such problems.

Problem: Copy this problem and fill in the missing digits:

$$\begin{array}{r} \$\_0\_8 \\ -\ \$432\_ \\ \hline \$4\_07 \end{array}$$

(Understand) We are shown a subtraction problem with missing digits. We are asked to fill in the missing digits.

(Plan) We will work backwards and use number sense to find the missing digits one-by-one. This is a subtraction problem, so we can look at each column and think of "adding up" to find missing digits.

(Solve) We look at the first column and think, "7 plus what number equals 8?" (1). We write a 1 in the blank. We move to the tens column and think, "0 plus 2 is what number?" We write a 2 in the tens place of the minuend (the top number). Then we move to the hundreds column and think, "What number plus 3 equals a number that ends in 0?" We write a 7 in the difference and remember to regroup the 1 in the thousands column. We move to the thousands column and think, "4 plus 4 plus 1 (from regrouping) equals what number?" We write a 9 in the remaining blank.

(Check) We filled in all the missing digits. Using estimation our answer seems reasonable, since $4700 + $4300 = $9000. We can check our answer by performing the subtraction or by adding.

$$\begin{array}{r} \$9028 \\ -\ \$4321 \\ \hline \$4707 \end{array} \qquad \begin{array}{r} \$4707 \\ +\ \$4321 \\ \hline \$9028 \end{array}$$

• Operations of Arithmetic

Power Up   *Building Power*

facts   Power Up A

mental math

a. Calculation: Kyle rides his bicycle 15 miles per hour for 2 hours. How far does he travel?   30 miles

b. Number Sense: 203 + 87   290

c. Measurement: How long would a row of 12 push pins be?
12 inches, or 1 foot

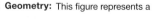

d. Percent: 10% of 100   10

e. Estimation: 25.032 + 49.994   75

f. Geometry: This figure represents a

     A line   **B** line segment   **C** ray

g. Number Sense: 2 × 16   32

h. Calculation: 4 + 3, + 2, + 1, + 0   10

problem solving

A number of problems in this book will ask us to "fill in the missing digits" in an addition, subtraction, multiplication, or division problem. We can work backwards to solve such problems.

Problem: Copy this problem and fill in the missing digits:

$$
\begin{array}{r}
\$\_0\_8 \\
- \ \$432\_ \\
\hline
\$4\_07
\end{array}
$$

(**Understand**) We are shown a subtraction problem with missing digits. We are asked to fill in the missing digits.

(**Plan**) We will work backwards and use number sense to find the missing digits one-by-one. This is a subtraction problem, so we can look at each column and think of "adding up" to find missing digits.

(**Solve**) We look at the first column and think, "7 plus what number equals 8?" (1). We write a 1 in the blank. We move to the tens column and think, "0 plus 2 is what number?" We write a 2 in the tens place of the minuend (the top number). Then we move to the hundreds column and think, "What number plus 3 equals a number that ends in 0? We write a 7 in the difference and remember to regroup the 1 in the thousands column. We move to the thousands column and think, "4 plus 4 plus 1 (from regrouping) equals what number?" We write a 9 in the remaining blank.

Facts   Multiply.

9 × 9 81	7 × 3 21	9 × 2 18	7 × 4 28	0 × 8 0	5 × 2 10	12 × 12 144	9 × 8 72	3 × 3 9	6 × 5 30
11 × 11 121	4 × 2 8	7 × 6 42	8 × 8 64	9 × 3 27	9 × 7 63	5 × 4 20	8 × 6 48	3 × 2 6	9 × 4 36
7 × 2 14	5 × 5 25	4 × 3 12	9 × 5 45	2 × 2 4	7 × 5 35	8 × 4 32	6 × 3 18	8 × 7 56	6 × 4 24
4 × 4 16	9 × 6 54	8 × 2 16	8 × 3 24	10 × 10 100	6 × 6 36	5 × 3 15	7 × 7 49	6 × 2 12	8 × 5 40

We filled in all the missing digits. Using estimation our answer seems reasonable, since $4700 + $4300 = $9000. We can check our answer by performing the subtraction or by adding.

$$\begin{array}{r} \$9028 \\ -\ \$4321 \\ \hline \$4707 \end{array} \qquad \begin{array}{r} \$4707 \\ +\ \$4321 \\ \hline \$9028 \end{array}$$

New Concept   *Increasing Knowledge*

The fundamental operations of arithmetic are addition, subtraction, multiplication, and division. Below we review some terms and symbols for these operations.

Terminology

addend + addend = sum
minuend − subtrahend = difference
factor × factor = product
dividend ÷ divisor = quotient

Example 1

What is the quotient when the product of 3 and 6 is divided by the sum of 3 and 6?

Solution

First we find the product and sum of 3 and 6.

product of 3 and 6 = 18

sum of 3 and 6 = 9

Then we divide the product by the sum.

$18 \div 9 = \mathbf{2}$

Three numbers that form an addition fact also form a subtraction fact.

$5 + 3 = 8$

$8 - 3 = 5$

Likewise, three numbers that form a multiplication fact also form a division fact.

$4 \times 6 = 24$

$24 \div 6 = 4$

We may use these relationships to help us check arithmetic answers.

Lesson 2   13

---

2 New Concepts

Example 1
Instruction
You might extend this example by asking students whether other pairs of one-digit numbers will give a one-digit answer when their product is divided by their sum. The only pairs besides 3 and 6 are 2 and 2, 4 and 4, 6 and 6, and 8 and 8.

Instruction
Point out that students learned fact families of four related facts for addition and subtraction and for multiplication and division in earlier grades. These inverse relationships are useful in simplifying expressions, solving equations, and for checking answers.

(continued)

Math Background

Although students are often encouraged to use an inverse operation to check their work, the same operation can often be used.

For example, students are likely to use subtraction to solve $x + 61 = 95$ for x.

$$x + 61 = 95$$
$$x + 61 - 61 = 95 - 61$$
$$x = 34$$

Subtraction can also be used to check the answer.

$$\begin{array}{r} 95 \\ -\ 34 \\ \hline 61 \end{array} \checkmark$$

Encourage students to check their work using a variety of methods.

Inclusion

Students may need a more direct connection between numbers and their terminology. Ask a student to write an addition, subtraction, multiplication, or division equation on the board. Then ask another student to label the parts of the problem using the correct terminology. Examples:

5 + 6 = 11
addend + addend = sum

25 ÷ 5 = 5
dividend ÷ divisor = quotient

2 New Concepts (Continued)

Example 2

Instruction

If there is time, discuss how rounding and making estimates could also be used to check these answers.

Instruction

When presenting the table of symbols, point out that the operations of addition and subtraction have only one symbol each while there are several ways to show the operations of multiplication and division.

Be sure that students understand the properties and can give examples of each. If students do not have immediate recall of the properties, refer them to the *Student Reference Guide*.

(continued)

Example 2

Simplify and check:

a. $706 - 327$ b. $450 \div 25$

Solution

Thinking Skill

Represent

Form another addition fact and another subtraction fact using the numbers 706, 327, and 379.
$706 - 379 = 327$;
$327 + 379 = 706$

We simplify by performing the indicated operation.

a.
$$\begin{array}{r} 706 \\ -\ 327 \\ \hline 379 \end{array}$$

b.
$$\begin{array}{r} 18 \\ 25\overline{)450} \end{array}$$

We can check subtraction by adding, and we can check division by multiplying.

a.
$$\begin{array}{r} 379 \\ +\ 327 \\ \hline 706\ \checkmark \end{array}$$

b.
$$\begin{array}{r} 25 \\ \times\ 18 \\ \hline 200 \\ 250 \\ \hline 450\ \checkmark \end{array}$$

Symbols for Multiplication and Division

"three times five"	3×5, $3 \cdot 5$, $3(5)$, $(3)(5)$
"six divided by two"	$6 \div 2$, $2\overline{)6}$, $\frac{6}{2}$

Math Language

The term **real numbers** refers to the set of all numbers that can be represented by points on a number line.

The table below lists important properties of addition and multiplication. In the second column we use letters, called **variables** to show that these properties apply to all real numbers. A variable can take on different values.

Some Properties of Addition and Multiplication

Name of Property	Representation	Example
Commutative Property of Addition	$a + b = b + a$	$3 + 4 = 4 + 3$
Commutative Property of Multiplication	$a \cdot b = b \cdot a$	$3 \cdot 4 = 4 \cdot 3$
Associative Property of Addition	$(a + b) + c = a + (b + c)$	$(3 + 4) + 5 = 3 + (4 + 5)$
Associative Property of Multiplication	$(a \cdot b) \cdot c = a \cdot (b \cdot c)$	$(3 \cdot 4) \cdot 5 = 3 \cdot (4 \cdot 5)$
Identity Property of Addition	$a + 0 = a$	$3 + 0 = 3$
Identity Property of Multiplication	$a \cdot 1 = a$	$3 \cdot 1 = 3$
Zero Property of Multiplication	$a \cdot 0 = 0$	$3 \cdot 0 = 0$

We will use these properties throughout the book to simplify expressions and solve equations.

14   *Saxon* Math Course 3

---

14   **Saxon** Math Course 3

Demonstrate the Associative Property of Addition using the numbers 3, 5, and 8.   Sample: $(3 + 5) + 8 = 3 + (5 + 8)$; $8 + 8 = 3 + 13$; $16 = 16$

Example 3

Show two ways to simplify this expression, justifying each step.

$$(25 \cdot 15) \cdot 4$$

Solution

There are three factors, but we multiply only two numbers at a time. We multiply 25 and 15 first.

Step:	Justification:
$(25 \cdot 15) \cdot 4$	Given
$375 \cdot 4$	Multiplied 25 and 15
1500	Multiplied 375 and 4

Instead of first multiplying 25 and 15, we can use properties of multiplication to rearrange and regroup the factors so that we first multiply 25 and 4. Changing the arrangement of factors can make the multiplication easier to perform.

Step:	Justification:
$(25 \cdot 15) \cdot 4$	Given
$(15 \cdot 25) \cdot 4$	Commutative Property of Multiplication
$15 \cdot (25 \cdot 4)$	Associative Property of Multiplication
$15 \cdot 100$	Multiplied 25 and 4
1500	Multiplied 15 and 100

Notice that the properties of addition and multiplication do not apply to subtraction and division. Order matters when we subtract or divide.

$$5 - 3 = 2 \quad \text{but} \quad 3 - 5 = -2$$
$$8 \div 4 = 2 \quad \text{but} \quad 4 \div 8 = \frac{1}{2}$$

Example 4

Simplify $100 - 365$.

Solution

Reversing the order of the minuend and the subtrahend reverses the sign of the difference.

$$365 - 100 = 265$$
$$\text{so } 100 - 365 = -265$$

Example 5

Find the value of x and y in the equations below.

   a. $6 + x = 30$ b. $6y = 30$

Lesson 2   15

---

2 New Concepts (Continued)

Example 3
Instruction
Ask students to explain each step of the two ways shown in the book. Although using the properties may seem to add a step or two, emphasize that the multiplication is much easier and can be done using mental math.

Instruction
Have students give other examples showing that order matters when subtracting or dividing, but not when adding or multiplying.
Sample: $9 + 7 = 16$ and $7 + 9 = 16$, but $9 - 7 = 2$ and $7 - 9 = -2$.

Example 4
Instruction
Refer students who need help with this concept to the section on "Subtracting Signed Numbers" in the *Student Reference Guide*.

(continued)

English Learners

For the solution to example 3, explain the meaning of the word **rearrange.** Say:

"When you rearrange numbers, you place them in a different order."

Write an addition fact on the board and say:

"I will rearrange these numbers to make a subtraction fact."

Rearrange the numbers. Write another addition fact and ask a volunteer to rearrange them.

Teacher Tip

The first few lessons in this program cover much of the arithmetic learned in earlier grades. You may help students who are having difficulty remembering particular topics by referring them to the appropriate parts of the *Student Reference Guide*.

2 New Concepts (Continued)

Example 5
Instruction
You might point out that the procedures used for **a** and **b** are similar to work students did in earlier grades, finding an unknown number in a number sentence. The procedures are equivalent to performing the same operation on both sides of the equation.

Practice Set

Problem f [Error Alert]
Students should immediately recognize that the difference will be negative because the subtrahend (87) is greater than the minuend (36).

Problems h and i [Explain]
Students should conclude that the following statements are also true: an addition answer can be checked using subtraction, and a multiplication answer can be checked using division.

3 Written Practice

Math Conversations
Discussion opportunities are provided below.

Problem 1 [Analyze]
"**What operation is often used to compare two numbers?**" subtraction

Problem 2 [Analyze]
"**What operation does the product of two numbers represent?**" multiplication

"**What operation does the sum of two numbers represent?**" addition

"**What operation produces a quotient?**" division

(continued)

Solution

The letters x and y represent numbers and are unknowns in the equations.

   a. We can find an unknown addend by subtracting the known addend(s) from the sum.

$$30 - 6 = 24$$

Thus, **$x = 24$.**

   b. We can find an unknown factor by dividing the product by the known factor(s).

$$30 \div 6 = 5$$

Thus, **$y = 5$.**

Practice Set   Name each property illustrated in **a–d.**

   a. $4 \cdot 1 = 4$ **b.** $4 + 5 = 5 + 4$
     Identity Property of Multiplication   Commutative Property of Addition

   c. $(8 + 6) + 4 = 8 + (6 + 4)$ Associative Property of Addition

   d. $0 \cdot 5 = 0$ Zero Property of Multiplication

   e. What is the difference when the sum of 5 and 7 is subtracted from the product of 5 and 7?   23

   f. Simplify: $36 - 87$ -51

   g. [Justify] Lee simplified the expression $5 \cdot (7 \cdot 8)$. His work is shown below. What properties of arithmetic did Lee use for steps 1 and 2 of his calculations?

$5 \cdot (7 \cdot 8)$	Given
$5 \cdot (8 \cdot 7)$	Commutative Property of Multiplication
$(5 \cdot 8) \cdot 7$	Associative Property of Multiplication
$40 \cdot 7$	$5 \cdot 8 = 40$
280	$40 \cdot 7 = 280$

   h. [Explain] Explain how to check a subtraction answer.   Add the difference to the subtrahend. The result should be the minuend.

   i. [Explain] Explain how to check a division answer.   Multiply the divisor and quotient, then add the remainder if any. The result should be the dividend.

For **j** and **k,** find the unknown.

   j. $12 + m = 48$ $m = 36$ **k.** $12n = 48$ $n = 4$

Written Practice   *Strengthening Concepts*

   * 1. [Analyze] The product of 20 and 5 is how much greater than the sum of
    (2)   20 and 5?   75

   * 2. [Analyze] What is the quotient when the product of 20 and 5 is divided
    (2)   by the sum of 20 and 5?   4

          ▶ See Math Conversations in the sidebar.

3. The sum of 10 and 20 is 30.
(2)
$$10 + 20 = 30$$

Write two subtraction facts using these three numbers.
30 − 20 = 10; 30 − 10 = 20

4. The product of 10 and 20 is 200.
(2)
$$10 \cdot 20 = 200$$

Write two division facts using the same three numbers.
200 ÷ 20 = 10; 200 ÷ 10 = 20

* **5.** **a.** Using the properties of multiplication, how can we rearrange the
(2)   factors in this expression so that the multiplication is easier?
       one answer (4 · 25) · 17
                        (25 · 17) · 4

   b. What is the product?   1700

   c. Which properties did you use?   one answer: Commutative Property
       4 · (25 · 17), Associative Property (4 · 25) · 17

6. Use braces and digits to indicate the set of counting numbers.
(1) {1, 2, 3, …}

7. Use braces and digits to indicate the set of whole numbers.
(1) {0, 1, 2, 3, …}

8. Use braces and digits to indicate the set of integers.
(1) {…, −2, −1, 0, 1, 2, …}

Justify   Decide if the statements in **9–10** are true or false, and explain why.

9. All whole numbers are counting numbers.   False. Zero is a whole
(1) number, but not a counting number.

10. All counting numbers are integers.
(1) True. Integers include all the counting numbers.

11. Arrange these integers from least to greatest: 0, 1, −2, −3, 4
(1) −3, −2, 0, 1, 4

12. **a.** What is the absolute value of −12?   12
(1)

   b. What is the absolute value of 11?   11

Analyze   In **13–17**, name the property illustrated.

►* **13.** 100 · 1 = 100   Identity Property of Multiplication
(2)

* **14.** a + 0 = a   Identity Property of Addition
(2)

* **15.** (5)(0) = 0   Zero Property of Multiplication
(2)

►* **16.** 5 + (10 + 15) = (5 + 10) + 15   Associative Property of Addition
(2)

* **17.** 10 · 5 = 5 · 10   Commutative Property of Multiplication
(2)

18. **a.** Name the four operations of arithmetic identified in Lesson 2.
(2)   addition, subtraction, multiplication, division
   b. For which of the four operations of arithmetic do the Commutative
       and Associative Properties not apply?   subtraction and division

* **19.** If |n| = 10, then n can be which two numbers?   10, −10
(1)

►* **20.** **Analyze**   Compare:
(1)
   a. 0 ⊖ −1   **b.** −2 ⊖ −3   **c.** |−2| ⊘ |−3|

► See Math Conversations in the sidebar.

Math Conversations
Discussion opportunities are provided below.

Problem 13   Summarize
Extend the Problem
"What does the Identity Property of Multiplication state?" Sample: The product of any number and 1 is that number.

Problem 16   Analyze
"Why isn't this equation an example of the Commutative Property of Addition?" Sample: The order of the addends on the left side of the equation is the same as the order of addends on the right side of the equation.

Problem 20   Analyze
"How can a number line be used to compare two numbers?" Sample: Plot each number. The number farther to the right is greater.

(continued)

Math Conversations
Discussion opportunities are provided below.

Problem 28 Generalize
"Will the difference of these numbers be positive or negative? Explain why."
Negative; the subtrahend (5010) is greater than the minuend (846).

"One way to check our work is to make an estimate of the difference before we subtract. What is a reasonable estimate of this difference? Explain your answer." Sample: −4000 is a reasonable estimate because when rounding to the nearest thousand, 846 rounds to 1000 and 5010 rounds to 5000; 1000 − 5000 = −4000.

Errors and Misconceptions
Problem 27
Students may regroup across the zero in the hundreds place incorrectly. Perform the computation at the board or overhead, and discuss each regrouping with students.

For additional practice regrouping across zeros, ask students to complete the following subtractions.

2070 − 385 1685   6004 − 957 5047

Problem 30
Use the given division, or a division such as 4575 ÷ 15 or 7038 ÷ 34, to demonstrate that if two numbers are brought down from the divisor, a zero must be written in the quotient.

* 21. Graph the numbers in this sequence on a number line:
   (1)
   ..., −4, −2, 0, 2, 4, ...

22. What number is the opposite of 20?   −20
   (1)

23. Which integer is neither positive nor negative?   0
   (1)

For multiple choice problems **24–26,** choose *all* correct answers.

* 24. One hundred is a member of which set of numbers?   **A, B, C**
   (1)
   A counting numbers (natural numbers)

   B whole numbers

   C integers

   D none of these

* 25. Negative five is a member of which set of numbers?   **C**
   (1)
   A counting numbers (natural numbers)

   B whole numbers

   C integers

   D none of these

* 26. One half is a member of which of these set of numbers?   **D**
   (1)
   A counting numbers (natural numbers)

   B whole numbers

   C integers

   D none of these

Generalize Simplify

▶ 27. 5010 − 846   4164   ✒ 28. 846 − 5010   −4164
   (2)   (2)

29. 780(49)   38,220   ▶ 30. $\frac{5075}{25}$ 203
   (2)   (2)

▶ See Math Conversations in the sidebar.

Looking Forward
Working with operations of arithmetic prepares students for:

• **Lesson 3,** solving addition and subtraction word problems.

• **Lesson 4,** solving multiplication and division word problems.

• **Lesson 21,** working with the order of operations.

• **Lesson 31,** adding integers.

• **Lesson 33,** subtracting integers.

• **Lesson 36,** multiplying and dividing integers.

• Addition and Subtraction Word Problems

Objectives

- Find missing numbers in problems about combining, separating, comparing, and elapsed time.
- Write and solve equations from word problems.

Materials

- **Power Up A** (in *Instructional Masters*)

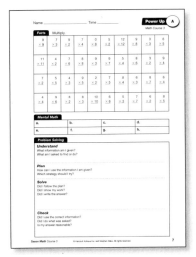

Power Up A

Math Language

Maintain	English Learners (ESL)
combining	elapsed
comparing	
elapsed time	
equation	
formula	
minuend	
separating	

Technology Resources

Student eBook Complete student textbook in electronic format.

Resources and Planner CD Assessment, reteaching, and instructional masters, plus a pacing calendar with standards.

Test and Practice Generator CD Create additional practice sheets and custom-made tests.

www.SaxonPublishers.com Visit for more student activities and planning materials.

Inclusion

Adaptations CD Adapted lessons, investigations, practice and assessments.

Meeting Standards

National Council of Teachers of Mathematics (NCTM)

Numbers and Operations

NO.2a Understand the meaning and effects of arithmetic operations with fractions, decimals, and integers

Algebra

AL.2c Use symbolic algebra to represent situations and to solve problems, especially those that involve linear relationships

AL.2d Recognize and generate equivalent forms for simple algebraic expressions and solve linear equations

Connections

CN.4b Understand how mathematical ideas interconnect and build on one another to produce a coherent whole

Problem-Solving Strategy: Write an Equation

Thirty-eight cars are waiting to take a ferry across a lake. The ferry can carry six cars. If the ferry starts on the same side of the lake as the cars, how many times will the ferry cross the lake to deliver all 38 cars to the other side of the lake?

(Understand) **Understand the problem.**

"What information are we given?"

A ferry can carry 6 cars at a time. Thirty-eight cars are waiting to take the ferry. The ferry is currently on the same side of the lake as the cars.

"What are we asked to do?"

We are asked to determine the number of times the ferry will cross the lake to carry all the cars across.

(Plan) **Make a plan.**

"What problem-solving strategy will we use?"

We can *write an equation* to find the number of times the ferry will cross the lake.

(Solve) **Carry out the plan.**

"How many groups of 6 cars need to be ferried?

We divide to find the answer: $38 \div 6 = 6$ r2. The ferry will need to carry across six groups of six cars and one group of two cars.

"How many times will the ferry need to cross the lake to carry across all the cars?"

The ferry will cross the lake twice (across and back) for each of the first six groups of cars. The ferry will only need to cross the lake once to carry over the last group of cars. Altogether, the ferry will need to cross the lake $(2 \cdot 6) + 1$, or 13 times, to deliver all 38 cars to the other side.

(Check) **Look back.**

"Did we find the answer to the question that was asked?"

Yes. The ferry will need to cross the lake 13 times.

• Addition and Subtraction Word Problems

facts | Power Up A

mental math |
a. **Calculation:** Sophie drives 35 miles per hour for 3 hours. How far does she drive?   105 miles

b. **Estimation:** 21 + 79 + 28   20 + 80 + 30 = 130

c. **Number Sense:** 1108 + 42   1150

d. **Measurement:** If object A weighs 7 pounds, how much does object B weigh?   4 pounds

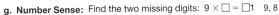

e. **Percent:** 50% of 100   50

f. **Geometry:** This figure represents a   **C**
   A line   **B** line segment   **C** ray

g. **Number Sense:** Find the two missing digits: 9 × □ = □1   9, 8

h. **Calculation:** 3 dozen roses, minus 5 roses, plus a rose, minus a dozen roses, ÷ 2   10 roses

problem solving | Thirty-eight cars are waiting to take a ferry across a lake. The ferry can carry six cars. If the ferry starts on the same side of the lake as the cars, how many times will the ferry cross the lake to deliver all 38 cars to the other side of the lake?   13 crossings

New Concept   Increasing Knowledge

When we read a novel or watch a movie we are aware of the characters, the setting, and the plot. The plot is the storyline. Although there are many different stories, plots are often similar.

Many word problems we solve with mathematics also have plots. Recognizing the plot helps us solve the problem. In this lesson we will consider word problems that are solved using addition and subtraction. The problems are like stories that have plots about combining, separating, and comparing.

Problems about **combining** have an addition thought pattern. We can express a combining plot with a **formula,** which is an **equation** used to calculate a desired result.

$$some + more = total$$
$$s + m = t$$

Lesson 3   19

Facts   Multiply.

9 ×9 = 81	7 ×3 = 21	9 ×2 = 18	7 ×4 = 28	0 ×8 = 0	5 ×2 = 10	12 ×12 = 144	9 ×8 = 72	3 ×3 = 9	6 ×5 = 30
11 ×11 = 121	4 ×2 = 8	7 ×6 = 42	8 ×8 = 64	9 ×3 = 27	9 ×7 = 63	5 ×4 = 20	8 ×6 = 48	3 ×2 = 6	9 ×4 = 36
7 ×2 = 14	5 ×5 = 25	4 ×3 = 12	9 ×5 = 45	2 ×2 = 4	7 ×5 = 35	8 ×4 = 32	6 ×3 = 18	8 ×7 = 56	6 ×4 = 24
4 ×4 = 16	9 ×6 = 54	8 ×2 = 16	8 ×3 = 24	10 ×10 = 100	6 ×6 = 36	5 ×3 = 15	7 ×7 = 49	6 ×2 = 12	8 ×5 = 40

1 Power Up

Facts
Distribute **Power Up A** to students. See answers below.

Mental Math
Encourage students to share different ways to mentally compute these exercises. Strategies for exercises **a** and **c** are listed below.

a. **Add to Solve**
   35 mi + 35 mi = 70 mi
   70 mi + 35 mi = 105 mi
   Regroup and Multiply
   35 mi × 3 = (30 + 5) × 3 =
   (30 × 3) + (5 × 3) =
   90 + 15 = 105 mi

c. **Add 2, Subtract 2**
   1108 + 42 =
   (1108 + 2) + (42 − 2) =
   1110 + 40 = 1150
   Add the Ones, Then the Tens
   1108 + 2 = 1110
   1110 + 40 = 1150

Problem Solving
Refer to **Power-Up Discussion,** p. 19B.

2 New Concepts

Instruction
Point out that problem solving is a goal of mathematics. Explain that the word problems in this lesson involve very simple arithmetic because the goal is to understand the different problem types, not to practice arithmetic.

Explain that problems about combining may involve more than two addends. If you have time, ask students to make up some combining problems for the class to solve.

(continued)

Example 1
Instruction
Have students work along with you as you demonstrate the problem on the board or overhead.

As you discuss the information that follows the solution, have students make up and share other problems based on this story. Have them explain how to decide which operation to use for each problem.

Instruction
After you discuss word problems about *separating,* ask students how the parts of the combining formula could be made into a separating formula. Sample: $t - m = s$

Have students explain how separating problems are different from combining problems.

(continued)

See how the numbers in this story fit the formula.

> *In the first half of the game, Heidi scored 12 points. In the second half, she scored 15 points. In the whole game, Heidi scored 27 points.*

In this story, two numbers are combined to make a total. (In some stories, more than two numbers are combined.)

$$s + m = t$$
$$12 + 15 = 27$$

A story becomes a word problem if one of the numbers is missing, as we see in the following example.

Example 1

In the first half of the game, Heidi scored 12 points. In the whole game, she scored 27 points. How many points did Heidi score in the second half?

Solution

Heidi scored some in the first half and some more in the second half. We are given the total.

$$s + m = t$$
$$12 + m = 27$$

The "more" number is missing in the equation. Recall that we can find an unknown addend by subtracting the known addend from the sum. Since $27 - 12 = 15$, we find that Heidi scored **15 points** in the second half. The answer is reasonable because 12 points in the first half of the game plus 15 points in the second half totals 27 points.

Example 1 shows one problem that we can make from the story about Heidi's game. We can use the same formula no matter which number is missing because the missing number does not change the plot. However, the number that is missing does determine whether we add or subtract to find the missing number.

- If the sum is missing, we add the addends.
- If an addend is missing, we subtract the known addend(s) from the sum.

$$s + m = t$$

Find by subtracting. —————↑ ↑ ↑————— Find by adding.

Now we will consider word problems about **separating.** These problems have a subtraction thought pattern. We can express a separating plot with a formula.

$$\text{starting amount} - \text{some went away} = \text{what is left}$$
$$s - a = l$$

Here is a story about separating.

> *Alberto went to the store with a twenty dollar bill. He bought a loaf of bread and a half-gallon of milk for a total of $4.83. The clerk gave him $15.17 in change.*

Math Background

Students can be distracted from the meaning of a problem if they try to focus on key words. Even the words sum, difference, product, and quotient do not assure that a problem is solved by addition, subtraction, multiplication, and division, respectively.

Instead of searching for key words students should seek to understand the actions or relationships described in a problem and to express the actions or relationships with equations. The equation then determines the operation required to find the unknown.

In this story some of Alberto's money went away when he bought the bread and milk. The numbers fit the formula.

$$s - a = l$$
$$\$20.00 - \$4.83 = \$15.17$$

We can make a problem from the story by omitting one of the numbers, as we show in example 2. If a number in a subtraction formula is missing, we add to find the minuend. Otherwise we subtract from the minuend.

$$s - a = l$$

Find by adding. ———————— Find by subtracting.

Math Language
Recall that the **minuend** is the number in a subtraction problem from which another number is subtracted.

Example 2

Alberto went to the store with a twenty dollar bill. He bought a loaf of bread and a half-gallon of milk. The clerk gave him $15.17 in change. How much money did Alberto spend on bread and milk? Explain why your answer is reasonable.

Solution

This story has a separating plot. We want to find how much of Alberto's money went away. We write the numbers in the formula and find the missing number.

$$s - a = l$$
$$\$20.00 - a = \$15.17$$

We find the amount Alberto spent by subtracting $15.17 from $20.00. We find that Alberto spent **$4.83** on bread and milk. Since Alberto paid $20 and got back about $15, we know that he spent about $5. Therefore $4.83 is a reasonable answer. We can check the answer to the penny by subtracting $4.83 from $20. The result is $15.17, which is the amount Alberto received in change.

Example 3

The hike to the summit of Mt. Whitney began from the upper trailhead at 8365 ft. The elevation of Mt. Whitney's summit is 14,496 ft. Which equation shows how to find the elevation gain from the trailhead to the summit?

A $8365 + g = 14{,}496$ **B** $8365 + 14{,}496 = g$

C $g - 14{,}496 = 8365$ **D** $8365 - g = 14{,}496$

Solution

A $8365 + g = 14{,}496$

One way of **comparing** numbers is by subtraction. The difference shows us how much greater or how much less one number is compared to another number. We can express a comparing plot with this formula.

$$\text{greater} - \text{lesser} = \text{difference}$$
$$g - l = d$$

Example 2

Instruction

After working through the example, ask how the answer could be checked. Lead students to see that the subtrahend and difference can be added and compared to the minuend or that an estimate could be used.

Example 3

Instruction

Ask students to identify which parts of equation A represent "some", "more", and "total". The starting point at 8365 ft represents "some." The elevation gain, g, represents "more." The height of the summit (14,496 ft) represents "total."

Instruction

When presenting comparing problems, ask for examples of comparing situations that students have experienced. Samples: Who is taller? How much more does a cheeseburger cost than a veggie burger? Which book is shorter?

(continued)

Example 4

Instruction

You may want to explain that when the comparing relationship is used with ages, the difference is correct only after the birthday has taken place that year. Since John F. Kennedy was born on May 29, 1917, he was 43 when he was elected in November 1960. If the election had been before May 29, the equation would produce the year 1918, a year later than the year he was born.

Practice Set

Problems d and e `Evaluate`

A number of different equations can be used to represent each problem. For example, the equations $215,768 - 180,635 = d$ and $d + 180,635 = 215,768$ can be used to represent problem **d,** and the equations $\$20.00 - a = \$10.50$ and $\$20.00 - \$10.50 = a$ can be used to represent problem **e.**

You might choose to challenge students to write two different equations to represent each problem.

We can use a similar formula for **elapsed time.**

$$\text{later} - \text{earlier} = \text{difference}$$
$$l - e = d$$

Here is a comparing story. See how the numbers fit the formula.

From 1990 to 2000, the population of Fort Worth increased from 447,619 to 534,694, a population increase of 87,075.

$$\text{greater} - \text{lesser} = \text{difference}$$
$$534,694 - 447,619 = 87,075$$

In word problems a number is missing. We find the larger number (or later time) by adding. Otherwise we subtract.

$$l - s = d$$
$$l - e = d$$

Find by adding. ⟶   ⟵ Find by subtracting.

Example 4

President John F. Kennedy was elected in 1960 at the age of 43. In what year was he born?

Solution

A person's age is the difference between the given date and their birth. We are missing the year of birth, which is the earlier date.

$$l - e = d$$
$$1960 - e = 43$$

We subtract and find that John F. Kennedy was born in **1917.**

Practice Set

a. Which three words identify the three types of plots described in this lesson? combining, separating, comparing

b. In example 2 we solved a word problem to find how much money Alberto spent on milk and bread. Using the same information, write a word problem that asks how much money Alberto gave to the clerk. Sample: Alberto spent $4.83 on milk and bread. The clerk gave him $15.17 in change. How much money did Alberto give to the clerk?

c. `Formulate` Write a story problem for this equation. See student work. Answers vary.
$$\$20.00 - a = \$8.45$$

`Evaluate` For problems **d–f,** identify the plot, write an equation, and solve the problem.

e. separating, $20.00 - a = $10.50, $9.50; Twenty dollars is $10 + $10. Since Binh left the theater with a little more than $10, he must have spent a little less than $10.

▶ **d.** From 1990 to 2000 the population of Garland increased from 180,635 to 215,768. How many more people lived in Garland in 2000 than in 1990? comparison, $215,768 - 180,635 = d$, 35,133 people

▶ **e.** Binh went to the theater with $20.00 and left the theater with $10.50. How much money did Binh spend at the theater? Explain why your answer is reasonable.

▶ See Math Conversations in the sidebar.

Teacher Tip

To connect writing and math, ask students to write and solve a story problem for each type of problem situation: combining, separating, and comparing. You may have students exchange problems for solving, post some of the problems on a bulletin board, or use them as "Problems of the Week."

English Learners

For the solution to example 3, explain the meaning of the word **elapsed.** Say:

"When you are sitting in class, time passes by, or elapses. How much time has elapsed since class began?"

Ask students how much time has elapsed since they were born. Emphasize the use of the word "elapsed."

    f. In the three 8th-grade classrooms at Washington school, there are 29 students, 28 students, and 31 students. What is the total number of students in the three classrooms? combining, $29 + 28 + 31 = t$, 88 students

    g. Which equation shows how to find how much change a customer should receive from \$10.00 for a \$6.29 purchase? **B**

        A $\$10.00 + \$6.29 = c$ **B** $\$10.00 - \$6.29 = c$

        C $\$6.29 + \$10.00 = c$ **D** $\$10.00 + c = \$6.29$

Written Practice   *Strengthening Concepts*

    Evaluate For problems **1–6,** identify the plot, write an equation, and solve the problem.

▶ *** 1.** The seventh-grade winner ran the mile in 5 minutes and 8 seconds.
  (3) The eighth-grade winner ran the mile in 4 minutes and 55 seconds. How many more seconds did it take for the seventh-grade winner to run a mile? comparing; 5 min 8 sec − 4 min 55 sec = d; 13 seconds

▶ *** 2.** Laurie, Moesha, and Carrie went to the mall. Laurie spent \$20,
  (3) Moesha spent \$25, and Carrie spent \$30. How much did they spend in all? combining; $\$20 + \$25 + \$30 = t$; \$75

* 3. Karl bought a foot-long sandwich. After he cut off a piece for his friend,
  (3) his sandwich was 8 inches long. How much did he cut off for his friend? separating; 12 in. − a = 8 in.; 4 inches

* 4. Irina and her sister put their money together to buy a gift. Irina
  (3) contributed \$15. Together, they spent \$32. How much did Irina's sister contribute? combining; $\$15 + m = \$32$; \$17

* 5. Last week, Benji read 123 pages. This week Benji read 132 pages. How
  (3) many more pages did Benji read this week than last week? comparing; 132 − 123 = d; 9 pages

* 6. Ahnly's mother bought a dozen eggs. Ahnly ate two eggs on her salad.
  (3) How many eggs are left? separating; 12 − 2 = d; 10 eggs

7. Write a story for this equation: $\$10 - \$4.05 = c$. See student work.
(3)

8. Which two values of n make this equation true?
(1)
$$|n| = 3 \quad 3, -3$$

9. Arrange these numbers from least to greatest: −6, 5, −4, 3, −2.
(1) −6, −4, −2, 3, 5

10. Compare:
(1)
  a. −5 ⊘ 1   **b.** −1 ⊖ −2

11. Compare:
(1)
  a. −10 ⊘ 10   **b.** |−10| ⊜ |10|

12. Compare: |−5| ⊜ (the distance from zero to −5 on a number line)
(1)

▶ See Math Conversations in the sidebar.

---

③ Written Practice

Math Conversations
Discussion opportunities are provided below.

Problem 1 Evaluate
"One way to solve this problem is to change both times to seconds. How many seconds is the same as 5 minutes and 8 seconds?" 308

"How many seconds is the same as 4 minutes and 55 seconds?" 295

"What is 295 subtracted from 308?" 13

"Describe a way you could solve this problem using only mental math." Sample: Count up from 4 minutes 55 seconds to 5 minutes 8 seconds.

Problem 2 Evaluate
Extend the Problem
"The values \$20, \$25, and \$30 are addends. When finding the sum of three addends, in how many different ways can the addends be arranged?" six different ways

"What is true about the sum of each arrangement?" Sample: Each sum is the same.

(continued)

Math Conversations

Discussion opportunities are provided below.

Problem 15 [Evaluate]

Extend the Problem

"Suppose that a student named 4000 as a reasonable estimate of this product. Describe the arithmetic that the student completed to make the estimate." Sample: Round 37 to 40. The product of 40 and 25 is 1000, and the product of 1000 and 4 is 4000.

Problem 25 [Analyze]

"What operation does the expression 5t represent?" multiplication

Errors and Misconceptions
Problem 22

When working with fact families, students may assume that every fact family must consist of four related facts. To address this misconception, ask students to form an addition and subtraction fact family using the numbers 4, 4, and 8.

Students will discover that the numbers can be arranged to form only one addition fact $(4 + 4 = 8)$ and only one subtraction fact $(8 - 4 = 4)$.

Lead students to conclude from the example that it is possible for a fact family to consist of fewer than four related facts.

(continued)

---

13. Refer to these expressions to answer the questions that follow:
    (2)
    $$6 + 4 = 10 \qquad 12 - 7 = 5$$

    a. Which number is the minuend? 12

    b. Which numbers are the addends? 6 and 4

14. Refer to these expressions to answer the questions that follow:
    (2)
    $$2 \cdot 3 = 6 \qquad \frac{20}{5} = 4$$

    a. Which number is a divisor? 5

    b. Which numbers are factors? 2 and 3

▶* 15. Consider the following expression:
     (2)
     $$4 \cdot (37 \cdot 25)$$

     a. How can the numbers in this expression be arranged to make the multiplication easier? $(4 \cdot 25) \cdot 37$

     b. Which properties did you use to rearrange the factors? Commutative: $4 \cdot (25 \cdot 37)$, and Associative: $(4 \cdot 25) \cdot 37$

     c. What is the product? 3700

16. Simplify, then compare: $19 > -19$
    (1, 2)
    $$36 - 17 \bigcirc 17 - 36$$

17. Use the numbers 5 and 12 to provide an example of the Commutative Property of Addition. $5 + 12 = 12 + 5$
    (2)

18. Use the numbers 2, 3, and 5 to provide an example of the Associative Property of Addition. One possible answer: $(2 + 3) + 5 = 2 + (3 + 5)$
    (2)

19.
    $-3 \ -2 \ -1 \ 0 \ 1 \ 2 \ 3$

19. Graph the numbers in this sequence on a number line:
    (1)
    $$\dots, -3, -1, 1, 3, \dots$$

20. When 15 is subtracted from 10, what is the difference? -5
    (2)

21. If $6 + 3 = 9$, then what other addition fact and two subtraction facts are true for 6, 3, and 9? $3 + 6 = 9; 9 - 6 = 3; 9 - 3 = 6$
    (2)

▶ 22. If $2 \cdot 4 = 8$, then what other multiplication fact and two division facts are true for 2, 4, and 8? $4 \cdot 2 = 8; \frac{8}{4} = 2; \frac{8}{2} = 4$
    (2)

23. Which whole number is not a counting number? 0
    (1)

24. What number is the opposite of -5? 5
    (1)

Analyze For problems **25–27,** find the value of the variable and name the property illustrated.

▶* 25. If $5t = 5$, then t is what number? 1; Identity Property of Multiplication
     (1)

* 26. If $5 + u = 5$, then u is what number? 0; Identity Property of Addition
    (1)

* 27. If $4x = 0$, then x is what number? 0; Zero Property of Multiplication
    (1)

▶ See Math Conversations in the sidebar.

Generalize Simplify.

28. $100 − $90.90 $9.10
(1)

29. 89 · $0.67 $59.63
(1)

▶ **30.** $\dfrac{\$72.18}{18}$ $4.01
(1)

Early Finishers
Real-World Application

On Monday, Robert's bank account balance was $140.00. On Tuesday, Robert withdrew $56.00. On Thursday, Robert deposited money into his account. On Friday, Robert's account balance was $180.00. How much money did Robert deposit in his bank account on Thursday? $96

▶ See Math Conversations in the sidebar.

Looking Forward

Solving addition and subtraction word problems prepares students for:

• **Lesson 4,** solving multiplication and division word problems.

• **Lesson 49,** solving rate problems with proportions and equations.

• **Lesson 50,** solving multi-step equations.

Math Conversations
Discussion opportunities are provided below.

Errors and Misconceptions
Problem 30 *Generalize*
Use the given division or a division such as $48.32 ÷ 16$ or $50.75 ÷ 25$ to demonstrate that if two digits are brought down from the divisor, a zero must be written in the quotient.

• Multiplication and Division Word Problems

Objectives

- Find missing numbers in equal groups problems.
- Write and solve equations from word problems.
- Match a problem situation to an equation representing the situation.

Lesson Preparation

Materials

- **Power Up A** (in *Instructional Masters*)

Power Up A

Math Language

English Learners (ESL)

sorted

Technology Resources

Student eBook Complete student textbook in electronic format.

Resources and Planner CD Assessment, reteaching, and instructional masters, plus a pacing calendar with standards.

Test and Practice Generator CD Create additional practice sheets and custom-made tests.

www.SaxonPublishers.com Visit for more student activities and planning materials.

Inclusion

Adaptations CD Adapted lessons, investigations, practice and assessments.

Meeting Standards

National Council of Teachers of Mathematics (NCTM)

Numbers and Operations

NO.2a Understand the meaning and effects of arithmetic operations with fractions, decimals, and integers

NO.2c Understand and use the inverse relationships of addition and subtraction, multiplication and division, and squaring and finding square roots to simplify computations and solve problems

Algebra

AL.2c Use symbolic algebra to represent situations and to solve problems, especially those that involve linear relationships

AL.2d Recognize and generate equivalent forms for simple algebraic expressions and solve linear equations

Connections

CN.4b Understand how mathematical ideas interconnect and build on one another to produce a coherent whole

Problem-Solving Strategy: Make It Simpler

There are often multiple ways to solve a problem. We might find that certain solution methods are easier than others. Sometimes we can find a way to make it simpler. For example, to find the sum of 7, 8, 9, and 10, we can add 7 and 8 to get 15, then add 9 to get 24, and then add 10 to get 34. But notice how we can find the sum more simply:

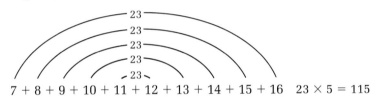

$$7 + 8 + 9 + 10 \qquad 17 \times 2 = 34$$

We paired addends that have equal sums. Then we multiplied the sums by the number of pairs.

Problem: What is the sum when we add 7, 8, 9, 10, 11, 12, 13, 14, 15, and 16?

(**Understand**) We are asked to find the sum of a set of numbers.

(**Plan**) We can pair the addends at the ends of the list to get a sum of 23. We can work inward to form other pairs that each have a sum of 23. Then we can count the pairs and multiply that number by 23.

(**Solve**) We count five pairs (7 and 16; 8 and 15; 9 and 14; 10 and 13; 11 and 12). Those five pairs account for all the addends in the problem. We multiply 23 by 5 and get 115.

$$7 + 8 + 9 + 10 + 11 + 12 + 13 + 14 + 15 + 16 \qquad 23 \times 5 = 115$$

(**Check**) Multiplication is a short way of adding equal groups, so it is reasonable that we can simplify an addition problem by multiplying. By making the problem simpler, we found a quick and easy solution method.

Facts
Distribute **Power Up A** to students. See answers below.

Mental Math
Encourage students to share different ways to mentally compute these exercises. Strategies for exercises **c** and **g** are listed below.

c. Double and Halve
50% of 30 =
100% of 15 = 15

Find a Fraction
50% = $\frac{1}{2}$
$\frac{1}{2} \times 30 = 15$

g. Add 2, Subtract 2
98 + 102 =
(98 + 2) + (102 − 2) =
100 + 100 = 200

Add Each Place Separately
Ones: 8 + 2 = 10
Tens: 90 + 0 = 90
Hundreds: 100 + 0 = 100
Total: 10 + 90 + 100 = 200

Problem Solving
Refer to **Power-Up Discussion**, p. 26B.

• Multiplication and Division Word Problems

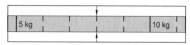

Power Up *Building Power*

facts | Power Up A

mental math

a. Calculation: Ivan exercises about 40 minutes a day. About how many minutes does he exercise during the month of September?
40 × 30 = 1200 minutes

b. Number Sense: 1000 × 1000   1,000,000

c. Percent: 50% of 30   15

d. Measurement: What mass is indicated on this scale?   8 kg

5 kg			10 kg

e. Estimation: 99 × 102   10,000

f. Geometry: A polygon with 6 sides is called a   B
  A pentagon.   **B** hexagon.   **C** heptagon.

g. Number Sense: 98 + 102   200

h. Calculation: One score is 20. Two score is 40. Three score and 5 is 65. How many is four score and 7?   87

problem solving

There are often multiple ways to solve a problem. We might find that certain solution methods are easier than others. Sometimes we can find a way to make it simpler. For example, to find the sum of 7, 8, 9, and 10, we can add 7 and 8 to get 15, then add 9 to get 24, and then add 10 to get 34. But notice how we can find the sum more simply:

$$\overset{\displaystyle \overset{17}{\overset{17}{7 + 8 + 9 + 10}}}{} \qquad 17 \times 2 = 34$$

We paired addends that have equal sums. Then we multiplied the sums by the number of pairs.

Problem: What is the sum when we add 7, 8, 9, 10, 11, 12, 13, 14, 15, and 16?

[Understand] We are asked to find the sum of a set of numbers.

[Plan] We can pair the addends at the ends of the list to get a sum 23. We can work inward to form other pairs that each have a sum of 23. Then we can count the pairs and multiply that number by 23.

Facts | Multiply.

9 × 9 81	7 × 3 21	9 × 2 18	7 × 4 28	0 × 8 0	5 × 2 10	12 × 12 144	9 × 8 72	3 × 3 9	6 × 5 30
11 × 11 121	4 × 2 8	7 × 6 42	8 × 8 64	9 × 3 27	9 × 7 63	5 × 4 20	8 × 6 48	3 × 2 6	9 × 4 36
7 × 2 14	5 × 5 25	4 × 3 12	9 × 5 45	2 × 2 4	7 × 5 35	8 × 4 32	6 × 3 18	8 × 7 56	6 × 4 24
4 × 4 16	9 × 6 54	8 × 2 16	8 × 3 24	10 × 10 100	6 × 6 36	5 × 3 15	7 × 7 49	6 × 2 12	8 × 5 40

Solve We count five pairs (7 and 16; 8 and 15; 9 and 14; 10 and 13; 11 and 12). Those five pairs account for all the addends in the problem. We multiply 23 by 5 and get 115.

$$7 + 8 + 9 + 10 + 11 + 12 + 13 + 14 + 15 + 16$$

Check Multiplication is a short way of adding equal groups, so it is reasonable that we can simplify an addition problem by multiplying. By making the problem simpler, we found a quick and easy solution method.

New Concept   *Increasing Knowledge*

In Lesson 3 we considered word problems that involve addition and subtraction. In this lesson we will look at problems that involve multiplication and division. Many word problems have an equal groups plot that can be expressed with this formula.

number of groups × number in group = total

$$n \times g = t$$

See how the numbers in the following story fit the formula.

In the auditorium there were 24 rows of chairs with 15 chairs in each row. There were 360 chairs in all.

The words "in each" are often used when describing the size of a group (*g*). We write the numbers in the formula.

$$n \times g = t$$
$$24 \times 15 = 360$$

An equal groups story becomes a problem if one of the numbers is missing. If the missing number is the product, we multiply. If the missing number is a factor, we divide the product by the known factor.

$$n \times g = t$$

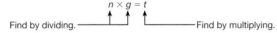

Find by dividing. ————————— Find by multiplying.

Example 1

Analyze

What information are we given? What are we asked to find?
given: 15 chairs in each row, 360 chairs total;
find: The number of rows

In the auditorium the chairs were arranged in rows with 15 chairs in each row. If there were 360 chairs, how many rows of chairs were there?

Solution

We use the formula to write an equation:

$$n \times g = t \qquad n \times 15 = 360$$

To find the missing factor in the equation, we divide 360 by 15. We find that there were **24 rows.**

---

2 New Concepts

Instruction

When you finish reading the introduction, discuss the steps for solving word problems. Lead students to see that these four steps represent the problem-solving process and can be used to solve any word problem.

1. **Understand** Read the problem and decide what type of problem the situation describes.
2. **Plan** Use the given information to write an equation.
3. **Solve** Solve the equation.
4. **Check** Check the arithmetic and look back at the problem to see that the answer fits the situation. Write the answer, using a complete sentence when needed.

You may need to explain that checking the answer to the equation is not the same as checking that the answer makes sense in the problem situation.

Example 1

Instruction

Guide students to see that the *Analyze* questions are part of the first step in solving this problem. This is the information needed to understand the problem.

Have students write all the steps needed to solve this problem. Stress the importance of writing each step on a separate line. You may need to demonstrate this on the board or overhead.

(continued)

Math Background

Although addition, subtraction, multiplication, and division represent the fundamental operations of arithmetic, there are additional operations of arithmetic that enable us to manipulate numbers. Two of those additional operations are raising to powers (for example, 2^3), and taking roots (for example, $\sqrt{36}$).

Students will work with powers and roots in future lessons.

Example 2

Instruction

If students have difficulty deciding which equation can be used to find the price of each ticket, suggest that they read each equation using the words "the cost of each ticket" for t and decide whether it makes sense. Sample: Equation C says that the cost of each ticket divided by 5 equals $28.75, but this doesn't make sense because the total is $28.75.

Example 3

Instruction

Discuss how students can explain why an answer is reasonable. Point out that a good explanation references the original problem, and not just the computation. The explanation should show that the answer makes sense in the context of the problem situation, that an estimate of the answer is close to the answer, or that the answer has the correct units.

Practice Set

Problem b Analyze

One way for students to check their answer is to make an estimate of the cost of each ticket, then decide if the value of the unknown in the equation they chose approximates the estimate.

For example, $100 \div 4$, or $25, is a reasonable estimate of the cost of each ticket, and answer choice D is the only equation that has a value of about $25 for t.

Example 2

The total cost for five student tickets to the county fair was $28.75. The cost of each ticket can be found using which of these equations?

  A $5t = \$28.75$ B $\$28.75t = 5$
  C $\dfrac{t}{5} = \$28.75$ D $\dfrac{t}{\$28.75} = 5$

Solution

  A $5t = \$28.75$

Example 3

Cory sorted 375 quarters into groups of 40 so that he could put them in rolls. How many rolls can Cory fill with the quarters? Explain why your answer is reasonable.

Solution

We are given the total number of quarters (375) and the number in each group (40). We are asked to find the number of groups.

$$n \times 40 = 375$$

We find the unknown factor by dividing 375 by 40.

$$375 \div 40 = 9 \text{ r } 15$$

The quotient means that Cory can make 9 groups of 40 quarters, and there will be 15 quarters remaining. Therefore, **Cory can fill 9 rolls.**

The answer is reasonable because 375 quarters is nearly 400 quarters, and 400 is ten groups of 40. So 375 quarters is not quite enough to fill ten rolls.

Practice Set

  a. Carver gazed at the ceiling tiles. He saw 30 rows of tiles with 32 tiles in each row. How many ceiling tiles did Carver see?   960 ceiling tiles

  ▸ b. Analyze   Four student tickets to the amusement park cost $95.00. The cost of each ticket can be found by solving which of these equations? **D**

   A $\dfrac{4}{\$95.00} = t$ B $\dfrac{t}{4} = \$95.00$
   C $4 \cdot \$95.00 = t$ D $4t = \$95.00$

  c. Amanda has 632 dimes. How many rolls of 50 dimes can she fill? Explain why your answer is reasonable.   12 rolls; Since 600 is 12×50, it is reasonable that Amanda can fill 12 rolls.

Written Practice   *Strengthening Concepts*

  1. The band marched in 14 rows with an equal number of members in
  (4) each row. If there were 98 members in the band, how many members were in each row?   7

  2. Olga bought five cartons of one dozen eggs. How many eggs did she
  (4) buy?   60

  ▸ See Math Conversations in the sidebar.

Teacher Tip

Since you have now taught several lessons, it may be helpful to read or reread the material in the front matter of this guide about the program, its philosophy, and the approach to teaching with it. The information about pacing instructional time within lessons may be more useful now that you know more about the instructional needs of your students.

English Learners

For example 3, explain the meaning of the word **sorted.** Say:

  "When you sort a group of objects or numbers, you separate them using some rule."

Write the following numbers on the board: 23, $\frac{1}{2}$, 0.9, 2, $\frac{3}{4}$, $\frac{9}{5}$, 0.13. Then say:

  "We will sort these numbers into whole numbers, fractions, and decimal numbers."

23, 2; $\frac{1}{2}$, $\frac{3}{4}$, $\frac{9}{5}$; 0.9, 0.13

3. The 5 km (5000 meters) hiking trail will have markers placed every
(4) 800 m. How many markers will be used? Explain why your answer
is reasonable.   Sample: 6 markers. Since 6 × 800 m is 4800 m, it is
reasonable that 6 markers will be used.

▶ * **4.** (Represent) Fadi bought 3 pounds of apples at $1.98 per pound. The
(4) total cost of the apples can be found using which equation?   **B**

A $C = \dfrac{\$1.98}{3}$ B $C = 3 \times \$1.98$

C $\$1.98 = C \cdot 3$ D $\dfrac{3}{C} = \$1.98$

5. 4 buses. Since
60 × 3 is 180,
three buses will
not be enough to
fit the students
and chaperones.
Another bus is
necessary.

▶ * **5.** There are a total of two hundred students and chaperones going on a
(4) field trip. Each bus can hold 60 passengers. How many buses will be
used for the field trip? Explain why your answer is reasonable.

6. On Lee's first attempt at the long jump, she jumped 297 cm. On her
(3) second attempt she jumped 306 cm. How much farther was her second
mark than her first mark?   9 cm

7. Zoe, Ella, and Mae ate lunch at the deli. The cost of Zoe's meal was $8,
(3) Ella's was $9, and Mae's was $7. What was the total of their bill (before
tax)? $24

8. Aaron was awake for 14 hours. He spent six of these hours at school.
(3) For how many of Aaron's wakeful hours was he not at school?   8

9. Write a word problem for this equation:
(3)
$$\$5 - p = \$1.50 \quad \text{See student work.}$$

10. Write a word problem for this equation:
(4)
$$n \,(\$25) = \$125 \quad \text{See student work.}$$

▶ **11.** (Analyze) Arrange these numbers from least to greatest.
(1)
$$-1, 2, -3, -4, 5 \quad -4, -3, -1, 2, 5$$

12. Compare:
(1)
a. $-7 \, \text{>} \, -8$ b. $5 \, \text{>} \, -6$

13. Compare:
(1)
a. $|-7| \, \text{<} \, |-8|$ b. $|11| \, \text{=} \, |-11|$

14. Name two numbers that are 7 units from zero on a number line.   7, −7
(1)

15. Which two integer values for n make this equation true?
(1)
$$|n| = 1 \quad 1, -1$$

16. Use braces and digits to indicate the set of odd numbers.
(1) $\{\ldots, -3, -1, 1, 3, \ldots\}$

17. Graph the set of odd numbers on a number line.
(1)
$-3 \; -2 \; -1 \;\; 0 \;\; 1 \;\; 2 \;\; 3$

▶ See Math Conversations in the sidebar.

Math Conversations
Discussion opportunities are provided below.

Problem 4 Represent

If students have difficulty choosing the
equation, ask them to first estimate the cost of
three pounds of apples. Sample: 3 × $2 or $6

Ask students to then compare the equations
and, using mental math, choose the equation
that has a value of about $6 for C.

Make sure students recognize that the problem
can be solved using multiplication ($3 \times \$1.98$)
or repeated addition ($\$1.98 + \$1.98 + \$1.98$).

Problem 11 Analyze

*"How can a number line can be used to
compare and order these integers?"*
Sample: Plot each integer on a number
line. Since we must write the integers in order
from least to greatest, write the integers as
they appear from left to right on the number
line.

Errors and Misconceptions
Problem 5
For some division problems, students must
interpret the remainder to successfully
solve the problem. The exact quotient for
problem 5 is $3\frac{1}{3}$. However, the context of the
problem requires students to interpret the $\frac{1}{3}$
and decide that $3\frac{1}{3}$ buses is not a sensible
number of buses. It is sensible, however, to
name 4 buses as the correct number because
3 buses will only provide transportation for
60×3 or 180 passengers.

(continued)

Math Conversations

Discussion opportunities are provided below.

Problem 20
Extend the Problem
"Using only mental math, what is the sum of the addends?" 48

Problem 21 [Analyze]
"Does subtracting 5 from 12 produce a positive number or a negative number?" a positive number

"Does subtracting 12 from 5 produce a positive number or a negative number?" a negative number

"Is a positive number greater than or less than a negative number?" greater than

Problem 26 [Evaluate]
Challenge students to explain how this problem can be solved using only mental math. Sample: Compare each change to 10: a change from 54 to 63 is less than 10 and a change from 48 to 59 is greater than 10, so the change from 48 to 59 is the greater change.

Problem 27 [Analyze]
"Why isn't division used to solve this problem?" Sample: Division would be used if the total cost was given and we were asked to find the cost of one ticket. In this problem, we are given the cost of one ticket and asked to find the total cost of a greater number of tickets.

Problem 29 [Classify]
"How is the set of integers different from the set of counting (natural) numbers?" Positive whole numbers and their opposites, and zero, represent the set of integers. Another name for the set of counting numbers is the set of natural numbers, which include only the positive whole numbers.

---

18. Refer to these expressions to answer the questions that follow:
(2)

$$6 \times 5 = 30 \qquad \frac{12}{3} = 4$$

   a. Which numbers are factors? 6, 5

   b. Which number is the quotient? 4

19. Refer to these expressions to answer the questions that follow:
(2)

$$3 + 5 = 8 \qquad 17 - 7 = 10$$

   a. Which number is the sum? 8

   b. Which number is the difference? 10

▶* **20.** [Justify] Consider the following expression:
(2)

$$3 + (28 + 17)$$

   a. How can the numbers in the expression be arranged to make the addition easier? $(3 + 17) + 28$

   b. Which properties did you use? Commutative Property of Addition, $3 + (17 + 28)$; Associative Property of Addition, $(3 + 17) + 28$

▶* **21.** [Analyze] Simplify and compare: $12 - 5 \, \ominus \, 5 - 12$
(1, 2)

22. If $3 \cdot 7 = 21$, what other multiplication fact and what two division facts
(2) are true for 3, 7, and 21? $7 \cdot 3 = 21, \frac{21}{3} = 7, \frac{21}{7} = 3$

23. If $2 + 4 = 6$, then what other addition fact and what two subtraction
(2) facts are true for 2, 4, and 6? $4 + 2 = 6, 6 - 4 = 2, 6 - 2 = 4$

24. What number is the opposite of 10? -10
(1)

* **25.** Which is the greater total: 4 groups of 20 or 5 groups of 15?
(4) 4 groups of 20

▶* **26.** [Evaluate] Which change in height is greater: 54 in. to 63 in. or 48 in. to
(3) 59 in.? 48 in. to 59 in.

▶* **27.** [Analyze] Which total cost is less: 25 tickets for $5 each or 20 tickets for
(4) $6 each? 20 tickets for $6 each

* **28.** Use braces and digits to indicate the set of whole numbers.
(1) {0, 1, 2, 3, ...}

▶* **29.** [Classify] Consider the sets of integers and counting numbers. Which set
(1) includes the whole numbers? integers

* **30.** Which two numbers satisfy this equation? $\frac{1}{2}, -\frac{1}{2}$
(1)

$$|n| = \frac{1}{2}$$

▶ See Math Conversations in the sidebar.

Looking Forward

Solving multiplication and division word problems prepares students for:

- **Lesson 5,** working with fractional parts and solving fractional-parts problems.
- **Lesson 7,** calculating with and solving problems involving rates and average.
- **Lesson 49,** solving rate problems with proportions and equations.
- **Lesson 50,** solving multi-step equations.
- **Lesson 58,** solving percent problems with equations.
- **Lesson 70,** solving direct variation problems.

• Fractional Parts

Objectives

- Find fractional parts of numbers.
- Compare and order fractions by comparing them to $\frac{1}{2}$.

Lesson Preparation

Materials

- **Power Up A** (in *Instructional Masters*)

Optional

- **Manipulative Kit:** color tiles or overhead fraction circles

Power Up A

Math Language

New	English Learners (ESL)
denominator	budgeted
numerator	

Technology Resources

Student eBook Complete student textbook in electronic format.

Resources and Planner CD Assessment, reteaching, and instructional masters, plus a pacing calendar with standards.

Test and Practice Generator CD Create additional practice sheets and custom-made tests.

www.SaxonPublishers.com Visit for more student activities and planning materials.

Inclusion

Adaptations CD Adapted lessons, investigations, practice and assessments.

Meeting Standards

National Council of Teachers of Mathematics (NCTM)

Numbers and Operations

NO.1a Work flexibly with fractions, decimals, and percents to solve problems

NO.1b Compare and order fractions, decimals, and percents efficiently and find their approximate locations on a number line

Representation

RE.5b Select, apply, and translate among mathematical representations to solve problems

Problem-Solving Strategy: Find a Pattern

What are the next three numbers in this sequence?

5, 3, 8, 6, 11, …

(Understand) **Understand the problem.**

"What information are we given?"

We are shown the first five numbers in a sequence.

"What are we asked to do?"

We are asked to determine the next three numbers in the sequence.

(Plan) **Make a plan.**

"What problem-solving strategy will we use?"

We will *find the pattern* in order to extend the sequence.

(Solve) **Carry out the plan.**

"What rule has been followed to generate the sequence?"

The second term equals the first term minus 2. The third term equals the second term plus 5. This sequence of operations (subtract 2, add 5) continues through the remaining given terms.

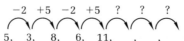

"What are the next three terms of the sequence?"

9, 14, and 12

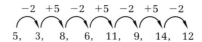

(Check) **Look back.**

"Did we complete the task?"

Yes. We found that the next three numbers in the sequence are 9, 14, and 12.

LESSON
5
• Fractional Parts

facts | Power Up A

mental math

a. Calculation: Pedro completes six multiplication facts every ten seconds. How many does he complete in one minute?   36

b. Estimation: $1.49 + $2.49 + $5.99 $1.50 + $2.50 + $6.00 = $10.00

c. Number Sense: Find the two missing digits: $11 \times \square = \square 7$ 7, 7

d. Geometry: In this triangle, x must be greater than how many cm?   8 cm

e. Percent: 10% of 90   9

f. Measurement: Sam measured from the wrong end of the ruler. How long is his pencil? $4\frac{1}{2}$ inches

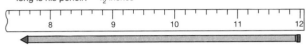

g. Number Sense: 230 + 230   460

h. Calculation: $3 + 5, - 2, \times 7, - 2, \div 5, \times 2, - 1, \div 3$ 5

problem solving | What are the next three numbers in this sequence?

5, 3, 8, 6, 11, ...   9, 14, 12

New Concept *Increasing Knowledge*

We often use fractions to describe part of a group. A fraction is composed of a **numerator** and a **denominator**.

$$\begin{array}{l} \text{numerator} \\ \text{denominator} \end{array} \quad \frac{1}{3} \quad \begin{array}{l} \text{number of parts described} \\ \text{number of equal parts} \end{array}$$

We can find a fractional part of a group by dividing by the denominator and multiplying by the numerator.

A quart is 32 ounces. To find the number of ounces in $\frac{3}{4}$ of a quart we can divide 32 ounces by 4 ($32 \div 4 = 8$) to find the number of ounces in $\frac{1}{4}$. Then we can multiply by 3 ($3 \times 8 = 24$) to find the number of ounces in $\frac{3}{4}$.

$$\frac{3}{4} \times 32 \text{ oz} = 24 \text{ oz}$$

Lesson 5   **31**

---

1 Power Up

Facts
Distribute **Power Up A** to students. See answers below.

Mental Math
Encourage students to share different ways to mentally compute these exercises. Strategies for exercises **e** and **f** are listed below.

e. Multiply by 10, Divide by 10
   10% of 90 = 100% of 9 = 9
   Use a Fraction
   $10\% = \frac{1}{10}$
   $\frac{1}{10} \times 90 = 9$

f. Count Back
   Start at 12 in., count 1 for 11 in., count 2 for 10 in., count 3 for 9 in., count 4 for 8 in., then add the remaining $\frac{1}{2}$ in. to get $4\frac{1}{2}$ in.
   Subtract
   $12 - 7\frac{1}{2} = 12 - 8 + \frac{1}{2} = 4\frac{1}{2}$ inches

Problem Solving
Refer to **Power-Up Discussion**, p. 31B.

2 New Concepts

Instruction
Discuss situations for which students have used fractions to name part of a group. Samples: a half dozen eggs, seven-eighths of a pizza, three-fourths of a cup

You might point out that we can also think of $\frac{3}{4}$ of a quart as $\frac{1}{4}$ of 3 quarts, so we could multiply 32 ounces by 3, and divide that result, 96, by 4 to get 24 ounces. We get the same answer either way.

(continued)

Facts | Multiply.

9 × 9 81	7 × 3 21	9 × 2 18	7 × 4 28	0 × 8 0	5 × 2 10	12 × 12 144	9 × 8 72	3 × 3 9	6 × 5 30
11 × 11 121	4 × 2 8	7 × 6 42	8 × 8 64	9 × 3 27	9 × 7 63	5 × 4 20	8 × 6 48	3 × 2 6	9 × 4 36
7 × 2 14	5 × 5 25	4 × 3 12	9 × 5 45	2 × 2 4	7 × 5 35	8 × 4 32	6 × 3 18	8 × 7 56	6 × 4 24
4 × 4 16	9 × 6 54	8 × 2 16	8 × 3 24	10 × 10 100	6 × 6 36	5 × 3 15	7 × 7 49	6 × 2 12	8 × 5 40

Example 1

Instruction

Before demonstrating the solutions, ask students to close their books. Have volunteers explain how to solve the two problems and let the class discuss the explanations. Then have students open their books and review the solutions.

Instruction

Present the instruction on comparing fractions by comparing them to $\frac{1}{2}$. This strategy is known as using a benchmark. Help students master this technique by naming fractions, having the class respond with "less than $\frac{1}{2}$," "equal to $\frac{1}{2}$," or "greater than $\frac{1}{2}$" for each fraction, and asking a volunteer to explain the reasoning for the answer. Some fractions to use: $\frac{5}{8}$, $\frac{7}{16}$, $\frac{6}{12}$, $\frac{3}{8}$, $\frac{9}{16}$, and $\frac{5}{10}$.

Example 2

Instruction

Ask students what they notice about the denominators and the answers. Sample: Fractions with greater denominators are less than fractions with lesser denominators when the numerators are the same. You may want to mention that a strategy for comparing fractions with the same numerator is that the fraction with the lesser denominator will be the greater fraction. Likewise, a strategy for comparing fractions with the same denominators is that the fraction with the greater numerator is the greater fraction. Use the Thinking Skill *Connect* question to discuss this concept further.

(continued)

Example 1

There were 30 questions on the test. One third of the questions were true-false, and two fifths were multiple choice.

    a. How many questions were true-false?

    b. How many questions were multiple choice?

Solution

    a. To find $\frac{1}{3}$ of 30 we can divide 30 by the denominator 3. There were **10 true-false questions.**

    b. To find $\frac{2}{5}$ of 30 we can divide 30 by the denominator 5 and find there are 6 questions in each fifth. Then we multiply 6 by the numerator 2 to find the number of questions in $\frac{2}{5}$ of 30. There were **12 multiple choice questions.**

We will learn many strategies to compare fractions. One strategy we can use is to determine if the fraction is greater than or less than $\frac{1}{2}$. To estimate the size of a fraction, we compare the numerator to the denominator. For example, if Tyler has read $\frac{3}{10}$ of a book, then he has read less than half the book because 3 is less than half of 10. If Taylor has read $\frac{3}{4}$ of a book, then she has read more than half of the book because 3 is greater than half of 4.

Example 2

Arrange these fractions from least to greatest.
$$\frac{3}{6}, \frac{3}{5}, \frac{3}{8}$$

Solution

Thinking Skill

Connect

What do you notice about the denominators of the fractions when listed from least to greatest? The numerators? Use your observations to quickly arrange these fractions from least to greatest:
$$\frac{1}{10}, \frac{1}{4}, \frac{1}{8}, \frac{1}{12}$$
The denominators are listed from greatest to least. The numerators are the same.
$$\frac{1}{12}, \frac{1}{10}, \frac{1}{8}, \frac{1}{4}$$

For each fraction we can ask, "Is the fraction less than $\frac{1}{2}$, equal to $\frac{1}{2}$, or greater than $\frac{1}{2}$?" To answer the question we compare the numerator and the denominator of each fraction.

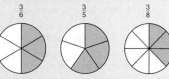

We find that $\frac{3}{8}$ is less than $\frac{1}{2}$, that $\frac{3}{6}$ is equal to $\frac{1}{2}$, and that $\frac{3}{5}$ is greater than $\frac{1}{2}$. Therefore, from least to greatest, the fractions are
$$\frac{3}{8}, \frac{3}{6}, \frac{3}{5}$$

Math Background

A fraction whose numerator is 1 is called a unit fraction. Examples of unit fractions include $\frac{1}{2}$, $\frac{1}{3}$, $\frac{1}{4}$, and $\frac{1}{5}$. To find a unit fraction of a whole or group, students need only to divide the whole or group by the denominator of the unit fraction.

However, this method of simply dividing by the denominator is used only with unit fractions. Two computations are needed to find other fractional parts of a whole or group (such as $\frac{2}{3}$ or $\frac{5}{8}$).

Manipulative Use

To give students hands-on experience with **fractional parts,** you may use the **color tiles** or the **fraction circles** in the manipulative kit. Students can make groups of tiles and show how many tiles would be in different fractions of the group. The fraction circles can help students compare fractions, especially those with either the same numerator or the same denominator.

Example 3

Compare $\frac{2}{3}$ of an hour and $\frac{2}{5}$ of an hour. Explain why your answer is reasonable.

Solution

$$\frac{2}{3} \text{ of an hour} > \frac{2}{5} \text{ of an hour}$$

The answer is reasonable because $\frac{2}{3}$ of an hour is greater than half an hour and $\frac{2}{5}$ of an hour is less than half an hour.

Practice Set

b. 18; Since $\frac{3}{5}$ is slightly greater than $\frac{1}{2}$, 18 is reasonable because 18 is slightly greater than $\frac{1}{2}$ of 30.

  a. How many minutes is $\frac{1}{6}$ of an hour?   10 minutes

▶ b. **Justify** Three fifths of the 30 questions on the test were multiple-choice. How many multiple-choice questions were there? Explain why your answer is reasonable.

  c. Greta drove 288 miles and used 8 gallons of fuel. Greta's car traveled an average of how many miles per gallon of fuel?   36 miles

▶ d. Arrange these fractions from least to greatest.

$$\frac{5}{10}, \frac{5}{6}, \frac{5}{12} \qquad \frac{5}{12}, \frac{5}{10}, \frac{5}{6}$$

Written Practice   *Strengthening Concepts*

▶ * 1. **Connect** How many yards is $\frac{1}{4}$ of a mile? (A mile is 1760 yards.)   440 yards
   (5)

* 2. Arrange these fractions from least to greatest. $\frac{2}{5}, \frac{2}{4}, \frac{2}{3}$
   (5)
$$\frac{2}{4}, \frac{2}{5}, \frac{2}{3}$$

* 3. Two thirds of the game attendees were fans of the home team. If
   (5) 600 people attended the game, how many were fans of the home team?   400

* 4. Risa typed 192 words in 6 minutes. She typed on average how many
   (5) words per minute?   32 words

▶ * 5. To prepare for the banquet, Ted bought eleven packages of rolls with
   (4) 24 rolls in each package. How many rolls did he buy?   264

* 6. Patricia has a cell phone plan that includes 500 minutes of use per
   (3, 5) month. During the first week of a month, Patricia spoke on her phone for two and a half hours. How many minutes of her plan for the month remain?   350 minutes

* 7. Volunteers collected non-perishable food items and packaged 14 items
   (4) per box. If the volunteers collected a total of 200 items, how many boxes could they fill?   14 boxes

8. Jenna budgeted $300 to redecorate a room. If she spent $54 on paint,
   (3) how much money remains? $246

Lesson 5   33

▶ See Math Conversations in the sidebar.

Practice Set
Problem b [Error Alert]

If students have difficulty solving the problem, encourage them to first solve a simpler problem. For example, students can suppose that $\frac{1}{5}$ of the questions were multiple choice, then decide how to find $\frac{1}{5}$ of 30. divide 30 by 5

Problem d [Error Alert]

Watch for students who assume that a fraction with a greater denominator is greater than a fraction with a lesser denominator. For this problem suggest students compare each fraction to $\frac{1}{2}$ to determine their relative sizes.

3 Written Practice

Math Conversations

Discussion opportunities are provided below.

Problem 1 [Connect]

"Finding $\frac{1}{4}$ of an amount is the same as dividing that amount by what number?" 4

Problem 5 [Explain]

Extend the Problem

"How many dozens of rolls did Ted buy? Explain how to use only mental math to find the answer." 22 dozen; Sample: Because each package contains 24 rolls, and $24 \div 12 = 2$, each package contains 2 dozen rolls. Since Ted bought 11 packages, he bought 11×2 or 22 dozen rolls.

(continued)

English Learners

For problem 8, explain the meaning of the word **budgeted**. Say:

"When you budget, you plan how you will spend your money. Each week you might have a budget of how much you can spend on lunch. For example, your weekly lunch budget might be $15.00."

Ask students how much money is "budgeted" in this situation: Anna can spend $35 for a new T-shirt and shorts. Anna has budgeted $35.

Math Conversations

Discussion opportunities are provided below.

Problem 10 | Represent

One way for students to check their answer is to make an estimate of the total cost of the sketchbooks, then decide if the value of the unknown in the equation they chose approximates the estimate.

For example, $20 \times \$3$ or $\$60$ is a reasonable estimate of the total cost of the sketchbooks, and answer choice A is the only equation that has a value of about $\$60$ for c.

Problem 17 | Analyze

"Describe a way you could complete this comparison using only mental math."

Sample: Compare 7 and 15. Since 7 is less than half of 15, the fraction $\frac{7}{15}$ is less than $\frac{1}{2}$, and the greater than symbol completes the comparison.

(continued)

---

* 9. Three-fourths of the voters supported the bond measure. If there were 8000 voters, how many supported the bond measure?   6000
(5)

▶* 10. **Represent**   The art teacher bought 19 sketchbooks for $2.98 per book. What equation can be used to find the total cost of the sketchbooks?   **A**
(4)

   A $c = 19 \cdot \$2.98$ **B** $\dfrac{19}{\$2.98} = c$

   C $\$2.98 \cdot c = 19$ **D** $\dfrac{\$2.98}{19} = c$

11. The children sold lemonade for 25¢ per cup. If they sold forty cups of lemonade, how much money did they collect? $10
(4)

12. If the children collected $10 at their lemonade stand but had spent $2 on supplies, what was their profit? $8
(3)

13. Write a word problem for this equation.   *See student work.*
(4)
$$3 \times 20 \text{ sec} = t$$

14. Write a word problem for this equation.   *See student work.*
(3)
$$10 \text{ lb} - w = 3 \text{ lb}$$

15. The water level in the beaker was 10 mL before the small toy was placed into it. After the toy was submerged in the water, the level was 23 mL. The toy has as much volume as how many mL of water?   13 mL
(3)

16. Arrange these numbers from least to greatest. $-5, -3, 0, 4, 7$
(1)
$$-5, 7, 4, -3, 0$$

▶* 17. **Analyze**   Compare: $\dfrac{1}{2} \bigcirc\!\!> \dfrac{7}{15}$
(5)

18. What two numbers have an absolute value of 6?   6, −6
(1)

19. Name a pair of addends with a sum of 6.   *See student work. Sample:*
(2)   1 & 5, 2 & 4

20. Name a pair of factors with a product of 6.   *See student work. Sample:*
(2)   2 & 3, or 1 & 6

* 21. Use the numbers 2, 3, and 4 to provide an example of the Associative Property of Multiplication. $(2 \cdot 3) \cdot 4 = 2 \cdot (3 \cdot 4)$
(2)

22. Graph the numbers in this sequence on a number line:
(1)
$$\dots, -6, -3, 0, 3, 6, \dots$$

23. Identify two numbers that are 50 units from zero on a number line.
(1)   50, −50

24. If $10 - 6 = 4$, what other subtraction fact and what two addition facts are true for 10, 6, and 4? $10 - 4 = 6$; $6 + 4 = 10$; $4 + 6 = 10$
(2)

25. If $6 \times 5 = 30$, what other multiplication fact and what two division facts are true for 6, 5, and 30? $5 \cdot 6 = 30$; $30 \div 6 = 5$; $30 \div 5 = 6$
(2)

26. What is the sum of 5 and its opposite?   0
(1)

▶ See Math Conversations in the sidebar.

▶ **27.** Compare: $-8 \bigcirc -6$
   (1)

   Explain Decide if the statements in **28–29** are true or false and explain why.
   If the answer is false, provide a counterexample (an example that disproves
   the statement).

* **28.** Some integers are counting numbers.   True; Integers include all counting
   (1) numbers.

* **29.** All fractions are integers.   False; The fraction $\frac{1}{2}$ is not an integer.
   (1, 5)

   30. Use the Associative and Commutative Properties to make this
   (1) calculation easier. Justify the steps.

$$6 \cdot (17 \cdot 50)$$

Step:	Justification:
$6 \cdot (50 \cdot 17)$	Commutative Property
$(6 \cdot 50) \cdot 17$	Associative Property
$300 \cdot 17$	Multiplied 6 and 50
5100	Multiplied 300 and 17

▶ See Math Conversations in the sidebar.

Math Conversations
Discussion opportunities are provided below.

Errors and Misconceptions
Problem 27
Watch for students who write a greater
than symbol to complete the comparison.
A common error when comparing negative
numbers is to compare them as if they were
positive numbers. For example, because
$8 > 6$, students might mistakenly assume that
$-8 > -6$.

Ask these students to plot the integers on
a number line, then remind them of the
generalization that on a number line, the
number farthest to the left is least and the
number farthest to the right is greatest.

Looking Forward

Working with fractional parts and solving fractional-parts problems prepares
students for:

• **Lesson 10,** finding equivalent fractions.

• **Lesson 13,** adding and subtracting fractions and mixed numbers.

• **Lesson 22,** multiplying and dividing fractions.

• **Lesson 23,** multiplying and dividing mixed numbers.

• **Lesson 29,** writing and solving problems involving ratios.

• **Lesson 63,** simplifying fractions with negative exponents.

• **Lesson 119,** simplifying complex fractions.

• Converting Measures

Objectives

- Use a constant to convert between units of measure.
- Learn conversions between several units of measure in the U.S. Customary and metric systems.

Lesson Preparation

Materials

- **Power Up B** (in *Instructional Masters*)

Optional
- **Manipulative Kit:** metric and inch rulers
- **Teacher-provided material:** yardsticks, metersticks

Power Up B

Math Language

Maintain	
capacity	U.S. Customary
mass	system
metric system	

Technology Resources

Student eBook Complete student textbook in electronic format.

Resources and Planner CD Assessment, reteaching, and instructional masters, plus a pacing calendar with standards.

Test and Practice Generator CD Create additional practice sheets and custom-made tests.

www.SaxonPublishers.com Visit for more student activities and planning materials.

Inclusion

Adaptations CD Adapted lessons, investigations, practice and assessments.

Meeting Standards

National Council of Teachers of Mathematics (NCTM)

Measurement

ME.1a Understand both metric and customary systems of measurement

ME.1b Understand relationships among units and convert from one unit to another within the same system

Connections

CN.4c Recognize and apply mathematics in contexts outside of mathematics

Problem-Solving Strategy: Act It Out

Alberto, Bonnie, and Carl are sitting around a small table. They share a pencil. Alberto writes the number 1 with the pencil and passes it to Bonnie. Bonnie writes the number 2 and passes the pencil to Carl. Carl writes the number 3 and passes the pencil to Alberto. If the pattern continues, who will write the number 11?

(Understand) **Understand the problem.**

"What information are we given?"

Three students take turns writing counting numbers.

"What are we asked to do?"

We are asked to determine which student will write the number 11.

(Plan) **Make a plan.**

"What problem-solving strategy will we use?"

We will *act out* the problem.

(Solve) **Carry out the plan.**

"How do we begin?"

We will select students to role-play as Alberto, Bonnie, and Carl.

Teacher's Note: Choose three volunteers to play the roles of Alberto, Bonnie, and Carl.

"How do we proceed?"

The selected students can call out the numbers or write them on the board in order. Following the pattern, we find that Bonnie writes the number 11.

(Check) **Look back.**

"Did we find the answers to the questions that were asked?"

Yes. Bonnie will write the number 11.

Facts

Distribute **Power Up B** to students. See answers below.

Mental Math

Encourage students to share different ways to mentally compute these exercises. Strategies for exercises **a**, **d**, and **g** are listed below.

a. Use Logical Reasoning
   1 min = 60 sec
   In 1 sec: 10 ft
   In 6 sec: 60 ft
   In 60 sec: 600 ft
   Multiply
   10 ft per sec × 60 sec = 600 ft

d. Regroup
   25 × 200 = 25 × 2 × 100 =
   50 × 100 = 5000
   Double and Halve
   25 × 200 = 50 × 100 = 5000

g. Find a Fraction
   50% = $\frac{1}{2}$
   $\frac{1}{2}$ × 10 = 5
   Double and Halve
   50% of 10 = 100% of 5 = 5

Problem Solving

Refer to **Power-Up Discussion**, p. 36B.

• Converting Measures

Power Up | *Building Power*

facts | Power Up B

mental math

a. Calculation: The trolley rolled at a rate of 10 feet per second. How far does it go in a minute?   600 feet

b. Estimation: 29 × 98   30 × 100 = 3000

c. Geometry: In this triangle, *x* must be more than how many cm?   2 cm

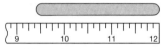

d. Number Sense: 25 × 200   5000

e. Measurement: How long is this object? $2\frac{5}{8}$

f. Power/Roots: $\sqrt{100} \times \sqrt{1}$ 10 × 1 = 10

g. Percent: 50% of 10   5

h. Calculation: 63 ÷ 9, × 3, + 1, ÷ 2, × 3, − 1, ÷ 4, + 1, ÷ 3, − 4   −1

problem solving

Alberto, Bonnie, and Carl are sitting around a small table. They share a pencil. Alberto writes the number 1 with the pencil, and passes it to Bonnie. Bonnie writes the number 2 and passes the pencil to Carl. Carl writes the number 3 and passes the pencil to Alberto. If the pattern continues, who will write the number 11?   Bonnie

New Concept | *Increasing Knowledge*

Most math problems are about counts or measures. In the following tables, we show some common units from the two systems of measure used in the United States. The tables also show equivalent measures and abbreviations.

Abbreviations

Customary				Metric			
inches	in.	ounces	oz	millimeters	mm	milliliters	mL
feet	ft	pints	pt	centimeters	cm	liters	L
		quarts	qt	meters	m	grams	g
yards	yd	gallons	gal	kilometers	km	kilograms	kg
miles	mi	pounds	lb				

Facts | Multiply.

10 ×10 = 100	6 ×9 = 54	2 ×4 = 8	5 ×0 = 0	4 ×6 = 24	3 ×3 = 9	5 ×8 = 40	4 ×9 = 36	2 ×7 = 14	3 ×8 = 24
2 ×9 = 18	5 ×5 = 25	7 ×9 = 63	3 ×7 = 21	6 ×6 = 36	8 ×9 = 72	2 ×3 = 6	5 ×9 = 45	4 ×8 = 32	8 ×8 = 64
4 ×7 = 28	2 ×6 = 12	3 ×9 = 27	7 ×7 = 49	2 ×8 = 16	11 ×11 = 121	5 ×6 = 30	4 ×4 = 16	6 ×7 = 42	3 ×5 = 15
3 ×4 = 12	7 ×8 = 56	4 ×5 = 20	2 ×2 = 4	6 ×8 = 48	5 ×7 = 35	3 ×6 = 18	12 ×12 = 144	2 ×5 = 10	9 ×9 = 81

Equivalent Measures

Measure	U.S. Customary	Metric
Length	12 in. = 1 ft 3 ft = 1 yd 5280 ft = 1 mi	1000 mm = 1 m 100 cm = 1 m 1000 m = 1 km
	1 in. = 1 mi ≈	2.54 cm 1.6 km
Capacity	16 oz = 1 pt 2 pt = 1 qt 4 qt = 1 gal	1000 mL = 1 L
	1 qt ≈	0.95 Liters
Weight/ Mass	16 oz = 1 lb 2000 lb = 1 ton	1000 mg = 1 g 1000 g = 1 kg 1000 kg = 1 tonne
	2.2 lb ≈ 1.1 ton ≈	1 kg 1 metric tonne

Reading Math

The symbol ≈ means "approximately equal to."

Converting from one unit to another unit involves multiplication or division by a constant that defines the relationship between units.

number of first unit × constant = number of second unit

Example 1

Reggie took 36 big steps to walk the length of the hallway. If each big step was about a yard, then the hallway was about how many feet long?

Solution

The units are yards and feet. The constant is 3 ft per yd.

36 yd × 3 ft per yd = **108 ft**

The hallway is about 108 feet long. The answer is reasonable because it takes more feet than yards to measure a distance.

Example 2

A full 2-liter beverage bottle contains how many milliliters of liquid?

2-liter bottle

Solution

The units are liters (L) and milliliters (mL). The constant is 1000 mL per L.

2 L × 1000 mL per L = **2000 mL**

Lesson 6   37

---

2 New Concepts

Instruction

The equivalents and abbreviations in the two tables should be familiar to students. Tell any students who have not learned them that they should try to commit them to memory, as they will be used throughout this program. They will find similar information in the *Student Reference Guide*.

Point out that the symbol ≈ is read "is approximately equal to".

The equivalents in the table as well others that can be found in various tables of measures in dictionaries and handbooks are used as the constants for converting from one unit to another using the formula given in the text: number of first unit × constant = number of second unit.

To review units of capacity in the U.S. Customary system, draw the diagram shown below on the board or overhead.

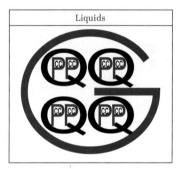

Liquids

The diagram shows that a gallon (G) contains 4 quarts (Q), that each quart contains two pints (P), and that each pint contains two cups (C).

Point out that a quart is equal to 32 fluid ounces, then ask students to use the diagram to name the number of fluid ounces in one pint, one cup, and one gallon. 16; 8; 128

Example 1
Instruction

Point out that checking whether the answer is reasonable is always an important part of solving a problem. Discuss how knowing the relationship between feet and yards shows that the answer is reasonable.

Example 2
Instruction

Emphasize that the constant for conversion must show the relationship between the units mentioned in the problem.

(continued)

2 New Concepts (Continued)

Example 3
Instruction
Caution students to be careful when converting measures because, as with this problem, the operation to use is not always multiplication. Ask a volunteer to explain why this answer is reasonable. Sample: A kilometer is much longer than a meter, so there would be fewer kilometers than meters in the same distance.

Example 4
Instruction
Have students work along with you as you model solving this two-step problem on the board or overhead. When the first part of the problem is completed, ask why 128 ounces is not the answer. Sample: James weighed 8 pounds 10 ounces, and 128 ounces represents only the 8 pounds. Once again, stress the importance of writing each step clearly on its own line.

3 Written Practice

Math Conversations
Discussion opportunities are provided below.

Problem 1 Analyze
"How can you use a division fact to help solve this problem using only mental math?" Sample: Because there are 60 minutes in one hour, divide 180 by 60 to find the answer: $18 \div 6 = 3$, so $180 \div 60 = 3$.

Problem 3
A helpful strategy to help students recognize how to solve the problem is for them to apply the measurement generalizations described below.

- To change from a larger unit to a smaller unit, multiply.
- To change from a smaller unit to a larger unit, divide.

Students should conclude that multiplying by 1000 will change kilograms to an equivalent number of grams, and that multiplying a number by 1000 is the same as moving the decimal point in that number three places to the right.

(continued)

Example 3
The 5000 meter run is an Olympic event. How many kilometers is 5000 meters?

Solution
The units are meters (m) and kilometers (km). The constant is 1000 m per km.

$$k \cdot 1000 \text{ m per km} = 5000 \text{ m}$$

By dividing we find that 5000 m is **5 km.**

Example 4
James weighed 8 pounds 10 ounces at birth. How many ounces did James weigh?

Solution
This is a two-step problem. The first step is an equal groups problem. There are 8 groups (pounds) and 16 oz in each group.

$$n \times g = t$$

$$8 \text{ lbs} \times 16 \text{ oz per lb} = t$$

We multiply 8 pounds times 16 ounces, which is 128 ounces.

The second step of the problem is a combining problem. The expression "8 pounds 10 ounces" means 8 pounds plus 10 ounces, so we add 10 ounces to 128 ounces.

$$s + m = t$$

$$128 \text{ oz} + 10 \text{ oz} = t$$

We find that James weighed **138 ounces** at birth.

Practice Set

a. A room is 15 feet long and 12 feet wide. What are the length and width of the room in yards?   5 yards long and 4 yards wide

b. Nathan is 6 ft 2 in. tall. How many inches tall is Nathan?   74 in.

c. Seven kilometers is how many meters?   7000 meters

Written Practice *Strengthening Concepts*

▶ * 1. (6) *Analyze* A movie is 180 minutes long. How long is the movie in hours?   3 hr

* 2. (6) A recipe calls for a half pint of cream. How many ounces of cream are required?   8 oz

▶ * 3. (6) The bottle of water weighed 2 kg. What is its weight in grams?   2000 g

* 4. (5) Three quarters of the students wore the school colors. If there are 300 students, how many wore school colors?   225 students

38   *Saxon* Math Course 3

▶ See Math Conversations in the sidebar.

Manipulative Use
Give students hands-on experience with **measuring and converting measures** by having them measure various classroom objects. Unless you have balances available, it makes most sense to have them measure distances. Let some students use **metric rulers** or **metersticks,** while others use **inch rulers** or **yardsticks.**

Have them measure something in one unit, convert it to another measure in the same system (for example, feet to inches), and then measure again using the converted unit to check the conversion.

38   *Saxon* Math Course 3

5. Each book that Violet carried weighed 2 pounds. If she carried
(4) 12 books, how heavy was her load?   24 lbs

6. Jorge read 23 pages before dinner and 18 pages after dinner. How
(3) many pages did he read in all?   41 pages

▶ * **7.** *Analyze*   The students were divided evenly into five groups to work
(5) on a project. Two of the groups completed the project before class
ended. What fraction of the students completed the project before class
ended? $\frac{2}{5}$

8. After the demolition, there were 20 tons of rubble to remove. Each truck
(4) could carry 7 tons of rubble. How many trucks were required to carry
the rubble away?   3 trucks

9. The driving distance from San Antonio to Dallas is 272 miles. Along the
(3) route is Austin, which is 79 miles from San Antonio. What is the driving
distance from Austin to Dallas?   193 mi

10. A serving of three cookies of a certain kind contains 150 calories. There
(4) are how many calories in one cookie of this kind?   50 calories

11. How many hours are in a week?   168 hr
(4, 6)

12. Valerie rode her bicycle from home to the market in 12 minutes, spent
(3) 20 minutes at the market, then rode her bicycle home in 15 minutes.
When she arrived home, how much time had passed since Valerie left
home?   47 min

* **13.** The glass is three-quarters full. If the glass can hold 12 ounces, how
(5) many ounces are in it now?   9 oz

14. Arrange these numbers from least to greatest: $-2, \frac{5}{7}, 1, 0, \frac{1}{2}$ $-2, 0, \frac{1}{2}, \frac{5}{7}, 1$
(1, 5)

15. Compare: $-5 \; \textcircled{<} \; 4$ **16.** Compare: $|-2| \; \textcircled{<} \; |-3|$
(1)   (1)

17. Compare: $5 \; \textcircled{=} \; |-5|$
(1)

18. Use the numbers 5 and 3 to provide an example of the Commutative
(2) Property of Addition. $5 + 3 = 3 + 5$

19. Use braces and digits to indicate the set of even counting numbers.
(1) $\{2, 4, 6, \ldots\}$

20. What is the absolute value of zero?   0
(1)

▶* **21.** *Model*   Graph 1 on a number line and two numbers that are 3 units
(1) from 1.   ◄–+–+–┼–+–●–┼–┼–●–┼–+–+►
　　　　　　　 -5　　0　　5

22. If $12 + 3 = 15$, what other addition fact and what two subtraction facts
(2) are true for 12, 3, and 15? $3 + 12 = 15$; $15 - 3 = 12$; $15 - 12 = 3$

23. If $40 \div 8 = 5$, what other division fact and what two multiplication facts
(2) are true for 40, 8, and 5? $40 \div 5 = 8$; $5 \times 8 = 40$; $8 \times 5 = 40$

▶ See Math Conversations in the sidebar.

Math Conversations
Discussion opportunities are provided below.

Problem 7   Analyze
Make sure students infer that because the five
groups are each equal in number, each group
represents a unit fraction ($\frac{1}{5}$) of the whole.

Problem 21
Extend the Problem
*"Why aren't the two numbers that
are each three units from 1 opposite
numbers?"*   Sample: On a number line,
opposite numbers are the same distance
from zero. In this problem, the numbers -2
and 4 are not the same distance from zero.

(continued)

Math Conversations

Discussion opportunities are provided below.

Problem 30 `Connect`

"What do the symbols on each side of the unknown represent?" absolute value

"In a general way, what is the absolute value of a number?" its distance from zero on a number line

Errors and Misconceptions
Problem 30

Because the left side of the equation represents absolute value, students may not recognize that the right side of the equation represents distance from zero on the number line.

If students have difficulty naming the values of *x*, ask them:

"What numbers are 7 units from zero?"
7, −7

---

24. What number is the opposite of 100?   −100
    (1)

* 25. Give an example of an integer that is not a whole number.
    (1)   Sample: −1, −2

* 26. Give an example of an integer that is a whole number.   See student
    (1)   work for any whole number.

`Explain`   Decide if the statements in problems **27–29** are true or false, and explain why. If the statement is false, give a counterexample (an example that disproves the statement).

* 27. Every counting number is greater than every integer.
    (1)

* 28. Every positive number is greater than every negative number.
    (1)

* 29. Every fraction is less than 1.   false; counter example: $\frac{3}{2}$ is a fraction and it
    (1)   is greater than 1

▶* 30. `Connect`   Find two solutions for this equation.
    (1)
$$|x| = 7 \quad x = 7, -7$$

27. false; counter example: 4 is a counting number and 5 is an integer, but 4 is not greater than 5.

28. true; Every positive number is greater than zero and every negative number is less than zero.

Early Finishers
Real-World Application

Recycling helps to preserve landfill space and save natural resources for the future. Suppose Americans recycle approximately $\frac{3}{5}$ of the 62 million newspapers bought daily. At that rate, how many newspapers are recycled in one week?
260,400,000 newspapers

▶ See Math Conversations in the sidebar.

Looking Forward

Converting measures prepares students for:

• **Lesson 7,** calculating with and solving problems involving rates.

• **Lesson 52,** using unit multipliers to convert measures and converting mixed-unit to single-unit measures.

• **Lesson 64,** using a unit multiplier to convert a rate.

• **Lesson 72,** using multiple unit multipliers.

• **Lesson 80,** adding and subtracting mixed measures.

• **Lesson 104,** converting between volume, capacity, and mass in the metric system.

• Rates and Average
• Measures of Central Tendency

Objectives

- Form rates and unit rates given two measures.
- Solve rate problems by multiplying by a unit rate.
- Find the average of a set of numbers.
- Determine the best measure of central tendency to use to represent a set of data.

Lesson Preparation

Materials

- **Power Up B** (in *Instructional Masters*)

Optional

- **Manipulative Kit: color cubes**
- **Teacher-provided material: index cards**

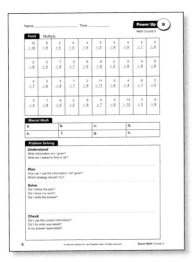

Power Up B

Math Language

New		English Learners (ESL)
average	range	misleading
mean	rate	
median	unit rate	
mode		

Technology Resources

Student eBook Complete student textbook in electronic format.

Resources and Planner CD Assessment, reteaching, and instructional masters, plus a pacing calendar with standards.

Test and Practice Generator CD Create additional practice sheets and custom-made tests.

www.SaxonPublishers.com Visit for more student activities and planning materials.

Inclusion

Adaptations CD Adapted lessons, investigations, practice and assessments.

Meeting Standards

National Council of Teachers of Mathematics (NCTM)

Numbers and Operations

NO.1d Understand and use ratios and proportions to represent quantitative relationships

Measurement

ME.1b Understand relationships among units and convert from one unit to another within the same system

ME.2f Solve simple problems involving rates and derived measurements for such attributes as velocity and density

Data Analysis and Probability

DP.1b Select, create, and use appropriate graphical representations of data, including histograms, box plots, and scatterplots

DP.2a Find, use, and interpret measures of center and spread, including mean and interquartile range

Problem-Solving Strategy: Make It Simpler

The sum of the odd numbers from one to seven is 16.

$$1 + 3 + 5 + 7$$

Find the sum of the odd numbers from one to fifteen.

(Understand) **Understand the problem.**

"What information are we given?"

The sum of the odd numbers from 1 to 7 is 16.

"What are we asked to do?"

We are asked to find the sum of 1, 3, 5, 7, 9, 11, 13, and 15.

(Plan) **Make a plan.**

"What problem-solving strategy will we use?"

We will *make it simpler* by using the pairing technique we learned in problem solving 4.

(Solve) **Carry out the plan.**

"What is the sum of the greatest and least addends?"

$1 + 15 = 16$

"Where are other pairs of addends that sum to 16?"

By working inward from both ends of the list we find other pairs (3 and 13; 5 and 11; 7 and 9) that each have a sum of 16.

"How many pairs of addends exist?"

There are 4 pairs of addends that sum to 16.

"What is the sum of the odd numbers from one to fifteen?"

We multiply 16 by 4 to get 64.

(Check) **Look back.**

"Did we do what we were asked to do?"

Yes. We found that the sum of the odd numbers from 1 to 15 is 64.

• Rates and Average
• Measures of Central Tendency

Power Up *Building Power*

facts | Power Up B

mental math

a. **Calculation:** How many miles per minute is 300 miles per hour?
   5 miles per minute
b. **Estimation:** $2.99 + $9.99 + $6.99 $3 + $10 + $7 = $20

c. **Number Sense:** 45 × 200   9000

d. **Percent:** 10% of 50   5

e. **Measurement:** Two of these sewing needles laid end-to-end would be how long? $4\frac{1}{2}$ in.

f. **Geometry:** In this triangle, *x* must be more than how many inches?   7

g. **Number Sense:** 1527 + 23   1550

h. **Calculation:** 16 ÷ 2, ÷ 2, ÷ 2, ÷ 2, ÷ 2 $\frac{1}{2}$

problem solving | The sum of the odd numbers from one to seven is 16.

$$1 + 3 + 5 + 7 \qquad 8 \times 2 = 16$$

Find the sum of the odd numbers from one to fifteen.   64

New Concepts *Increasing Knowledge*

rates and average

A **rate** is a division relationship between two measures. We usually express a rate as a **unit rate,** which means that the number of the second measure is 1. Here are some unit rates:

65 miles per hour (65 mph)

24 miles per gallon (24 mpg)

32 feet per second (32 ft/sec)

15 cents per ounce ($0.15/oz)

Rate problems involve the two units that form the rate.

number of **hours** × 65 **miles per hour** = number of **miles**

number of **gallons** × 24 **miles per gallon** = number of **miles**

Lesson 7   41

---

1 Power Up

Facts
Distribute **Power Up B** to students. See answers below.

Mental Math
Encourage students to share different ways to mentally compute these exercises. Strategies for exercises **c** and **g** are listed below.

c. **Double and Halve**
   45 × 200 = 90 × 100 = 9000
   Regroup, then Multiply
   45 × (200) = 45 × (2 × 100) =
   (45 × 2) × 100 = 90 × 100 = 9000
g. **Add 3, Subtract 3**
   1527 + 23 =
   (1527 + 3) + (23 − 3) =
   1530 + 20 = 1550
   Subtract 7, Add 7
   1527 + 23 =
   (1527 − 7) + (23 + 7) =
   1520 + 30 = 1550

Problem Solving
Refer to **Power-Up Discussion**, p. 41B.

Facts | Multiply.

10 ×10 = 100	6 ×9 = 54	2 ×4 = 8	5 ×0 = 0	4 ×6 = 24	3 ×3 = 9	5 ×8 = 40	4 ×9 = 36	2 ×7 = 14	3 ×8 = 24
2 ×9 = 18	5 ×5 = 25	7 ×9 = 63	3 ×7 = 21	6 ×6 = 36	8 ×9 = 72	2 ×3 = 6	5 ×9 = 45	4 ×8 = 32	8 ×8 = 64
4 ×7 = 28	2 ×6 = 12	3 ×9 = 27	7 ×7 = 49	2 ×8 = 16	11 ×11 = 121	5 ×6 = 30	4 ×4 = 16	6 ×7 = 42	3 ×5 = 15
3 ×4 = 12	7 ×8 = 56	4 ×5 = 20	2 ×2 = 4	6 ×8 = 48	5 ×7 = 35	3 ×6 = 18	12 ×12 = 144	2 ×5 = 10	9 ×9 = 81

2 New Concepts

Instruction

Explain that the relationship in a *rate* is a comparison of two different units. Rates are used in many real-world situations, as can be seen from the list of rates given here. Have students give examples of other rates they are familiar with.

Example 1
Instruction

You might point out the hour units are not included in the answer because they are canceled during the computation.

Example 2
Instruction

Help students see that a unit rate is like a division problem with a divisor of 1. When writing a rate, it should be simplified so that its divisor is 1. The label for a rate is made up of the two units of the rate.

Example 3
Instruction

Point out that in this example the rate and distance are given, and we are asked to find the time. Students can think of a rate problem as a multiplication or a division problem and write an equation to find any unknown.

Instruction

The term average can mean any one of several measures of central tendency, though it usually refers to the mean, which is the average described here.

(continued)

---

number of **seconds** × 32 **feet per second** = number of **feet**

number of **ounces** × 15 **cents per ounce** = number of **cents**

Example 1

Driving at an average speed of 55 mph, about how far will the driver travel in 6 hours?

Solution

We are given the rate and the number of hours. We will find the number of miles.

$$6 \text{ hours} \times 55 \text{ miles per hour} = n \text{ miles}$$

The driver will travel about 55 miles each hour, so in 6 hours the trucker will drive 6 × 55, or **330 miles.**

Example 2

Heather finished the 100 km bike race in four hours. What was her average speed in kilometers per hour?

Solution

We are given the two units and asked for the rate. The desired rate is kilometers per hour. This means we divide the number of kilometers by the number of hours.

$$\frac{100 \text{ km}}{4 \text{ hr}} = 25 \frac{\text{km}}{\text{hr}}$$

We divide the numbers. We can use a division bar to indicate the division of units as shown or we can use the word "per." Heather's average speed was **25 kilometers per hour.**

Example 3

Traveling at an average rate of 58 miles per hour, about how long would it take a car to travel 20 miles?

Solution

At 60 mph a car travels one mile each minute. Since 58 mph is nearly 60 mph, the trip would take **a little more than 20 minutes.**

In the examples above, we used the term *average speed*. The speed of the truck in example 1 probably fluctuated above and below its average speed. However, the total distance traveled was the same as if the truck had traveled at a steady speed—the average speed.

In common usage, the **average** of a set of numbers is a central number that is found by dividing the sum of the elements of a set by the number of elements. This number is more specifically called the **mean.**

Math Background

Measures of central tendency that students typically work with include mean, median, and mode. For the same set of data, it is possible for two or more of these measures to be equal.

For example, 4 represents the mean, the median, and the mode of the data set {2, 4, 4, 6}.

Calculating an average often involves two steps. First we find the total by *combining*, then we make *equal groups.* As an example, consider these five stacks of coins:

There are 15 coins in all (1 + 5 + 3 + 4 + 2 = 15). Finding the average number of coins in each stack is like leveling the stacks (15 ÷ 5 = 3).

Referring to the original stacks, we say the average number of coins in each stack is three.

Example 4

In the four 8th grade classrooms at Keeler School there are 28, 29, 31, and 32 students. What is the average number of students in an 8th grade classroom at Keeler School?

Solution

Thinking Skill

Predict

Without calculating, could we predict whether 35 is a reasonable answer for this problem? Explain.

measures of central tendency

We could predict that 35 is an unreasonable average since it is greater than the greatest number of students in any 8th grade classroom at Keeler School.

The average is a central number in a range of numbers. The average is more than the least number and less than the greatest number. We add the four numbers and then divide the sum by four.

$$\text{Average} = \frac{28 + 29 + 31 + 32}{4} = \frac{120}{4} = 30$$

The average number of students in an 8th grade classroom at Keeler School is **30 students.**

The average, or mean, is one measure of central tendency. Other measures include the **median**, which is the central number in a set of data, and the **mode**, which is the most frequently occurring number.

To find the median we arrange the numbers in order from least to greatest and select the middle number or the average of the two middle numbers. To find the mode we select the number that appears most often.

Example 5

Below we show the prices of new homes sold in a certain neighborhood. Find the mean, median, and mode of the data. Which measure should a researcher use to best represent the data?

Home Prices (in thousand $)	
170	191
208	175
185	175
209	187
181	195
183	219

Prices of New Homes Sold (in thousand $)

Instruction

You might demonstrate the concept of equal groups using color cubes in place of the coins. Make five stacks of 1, 2, 3, 4, and 5 cubes and then level them to five stacks of 3 cubes each. You can show that the total (15) divided by the number of groups (5) is the average or mean (3).

Example 4

Instruction

As you work through this example, you may want to write the general formula for average on the board or overhead before writing the equation given in the text.

$$\text{Average} = \frac{\text{sum of the addends}}{\text{number of addends}}$$

Explain that the formula can be used to find any part that is unknown.

You can extend the *Predict* question by asking why predicting an average of 25 would also be unreasonable for this problem. Sample: 25 is less than the least number of students in any of the classrooms.

Instruction

The three measures of central tendency described in this lesson are useful ways to describe a set of data, but it is interesting to note that each one can be used to present a set of data in a way that supports a particular position or point of view.

(continued)

Teacher Tip

To provide students with real-world experience with data, assign them independently or in pairs to collect a set of data. Possible topics include:

- Heights of classmates in centimeters.
- Prices for various kinds of products at a grocery store or at different stores.
- Selling prices for local real estate as listed in the newspaper.

After they gather the data, have them analyze the data by finding the mean, median, mode, and range. Students can then use those measures to write a description of the data.

Example 5

Instruction

Encourage discussion of the differences among the three measures of central tendency and what the *mean, median,* and *mode* might convey to different audiences. Ask why the mode might be misleading to a buyer. Sample: It would indicate that there are many homes at that value, when there are only two and they are at the low end of the prices.

Instruction

The *range* can be helpful in showing how close or far apart the numbers in the set are. A small range indicates that the numbers are all close in value, while a large range shows that the data may be quite scattered.

Practice Set

Problem c Estimate

Students should conclude that the problem describes the movement of the train between stops, and the length of time the train is at each stop is unimportant.

Accept reasonable estimates that may be different than the given estimate of 18 minutes. For example, a reasonable estimate is 20 minutes if 62 is rounded to 60 and 18 is rounded to 20.

Visit www. SaxonPublishers. com/ActivitiesC3 for a graphing calculator activity.

Solution

Mean:

$$\text{mean} = \frac{170 + 191 + 208 + 175 + 185 + 175 + 209 + 187 + 181 + 195 + 183 + 219}{12}$$

$$\text{mean} \approx 190$$

Median: Order the numbers to find the central value.

170 175 175 181 183 185 187 191 195 208 209 219

$$\text{median} = \frac{185 + 187}{2} = 186$$

Mode: The most frequently occurring number is **175.**

If the researcher is reporting to someone interested in property tax revenue, the **mean** is a good statistic to report. It may be useful in predicting revenue from property taxes.

However, if the researcher is reporting to prospective buyers, the **median** is a good statistic to report. It tells the buyer that half of the new homes cost less than $186,000.

The mean may be misleading to a buyer—its value is greater than the median because of a few expensive homes. Only $\frac{1}{3}$ of the homes were sold for more than $190,000.

We may also refer to the **range** of a set of data, which is the difference between the greatest and least numbers in the set. The range of home prices in example 4 is

$$\$219,000 - \$170,000 = \$49,000$$

Practice Set

a. Alba ran 21 miles in three hours. What was her average speed in miles per hour? 7 mph

b. How far can Freddy drive in 8 hours at an average speed of 50 miles per hour? 400 miles

▶ c. Estimate If a commuter train averages 62 miles per hour between stops that are 18 miles apart, about how many minutes does it take the train to travel the distance between the two stops? about 18 minutes

d. Analyze If the average number of students in three classrooms is 26, and one of the classrooms has 23 students, then which of the following must be true? **D**

A At least one classroom has fewer than 23 students.

B At least one classroom has more than 23 students and less than 26 students.

C At least one classroom has exactly 26 students.

D At least one classroom has more than 26 students.

e. What is the mean of 84, 92, 92, and 96? 91

▶ See Math Conversations in the sidebar.

English Learners

To help students understand the meaning of the word **misleading** in the solution to example 5, say:

"When information is misleading, it makes you think something that is not true. If I tell you that there are five items on a math test, what do you think?" the test is not long

"When you take the test, every question has five parts. Was my statement misleading? Why?" Discuss the question using the word "misleading."

f. The heights of five basketball players are 184 cm, 190 cm, 196 cm, 198 cm, and 202 cm. What is the average height of the five players?   194 cm

The price per pound of apples sold at different grocery stores is reported below. Use this information to answer problems **g–i.**

| $0.99 | $1.99 | $1.49 | $1.99 |
| $1.49 | $0.99 | $2.49 | $1.49 |

g. Display the data in a line plot.

h. Compute the mean, median, mode, and range of the data.
mean = $1.62; median = $1.49; mode = $1.49; range = $1.50

i. *Verify* Rudy computed the average price and predicted that he would usually have to pay $1.62 per pound for apples. Evaluate Rudy's prediction based on your analysis of the data.

. Sample:

```
          x
   x    x    x
x  x    x    x
$1 $1.50 $2 $2.50
```

Written Practice   *Strengthening Concepts*

i. Rudy's statement is inaccurate. Although the mean price per pound is $1.62, the median is only $1.49. This tells us that he would pay $1.49 or less at half the grocery stores. In fact, the mode is $1.49, signifying that it is the most common price charged among the stores.

1. In the act there were 12 clowns in each little car. If there were
(4)   132 clowns, how many little cars were there?   11 cars

▶ * **2.** There were 35 trees on the property. Four fifths are deciduous (they lose
(5)   their leaves in the fall and winter). How many trees on the property are deciduous?   28 trees

* **3.** Melody weighed 7 pounds, 7 ounces at birth. How many ounces did
(6)   Melody weigh?   119 ounces

▶ * **4.** The bird flew 80 km in four hours. What was the bird's average speed in
(7)   km/hr?   20 km/hr

* **5.** If the plane travels at 400 miles per hour, how far will it fly in 5 hours?
(7)   2000 miles

▶ * **6.** How many pints are in a gallon of milk?   8 pints
(6)

* **7.** The number of points scored by the starting players on the basketball
(7)   team were 8, 12, 16, 19, and 20. What was the average number of points scored per starting player?   15 points per player

In problems **8–11,** identify the plot, write an equation, and solve the problem.

* **8.** In the package were three rows of 8 colored pencils. How many colored
(4)   pencils were there in all?   equal groups; $3 \cdot 8 = t$; 24 pencils

* **9.** Felicia scored 15 points in the first half and 33 points in all. How many
(3)   points did she score in the second half?
combining; $15 + m = 33$; 18 points

* **10.** There were 20 ounces of birdseed in the feeder before the birds came.
(3)   When the birds left, there were 11 ounces of birdseed in the feeder. How many ounces of birdseed did the birds remove from the feeder?
separating; $20 - l = 11$; 9 ounces

* **11.** President Ronald Reagan ended his second term in office in 1989. He
(3)   had served two terms of 4 years each. What year did he begin his first term?   elapsed time; $1989 - e = 8$; 1981

▶ See Math Conversations in the sidebar.

3 Written Practice

Math Conversations
Discussion opportunities are provided below.

Problem 2 Connect
Extend the Problem
Challenge students to describe a way to find $\frac{4}{5}$ of 35 using mental math. Sample: The denominator 5 represents the whole divided into 5 equal parts, and each equal part is $35 \div 5$ or 7. The numerator represents four of those equal parts, and $4 \times 7 = 28$.

Problem 4
"Explain how a division fact can be used to help solve this problem." $8 \div 4 = 2$, so $80 \div 4 = 20$

Errors and Misconceptions
Problem 6
If students have difficulty converting from one unit to another, encourage them to make a list of the various Customary and metric relationships in their math notebooks or on an index card. The index card can be used as a bookmark, and students can refer to the bookmark or to their notebook as needed.

(continued)

Math Conversations

Discussion opportunities are provided below.

Problem 16 [Analyze]

Extend the Problem

"One of these equations can be written in a simpler way. Which equation can be written in a simpler way? Describe the simplified equation." $d \cdot e = f$; The dot that is used to represent multiplication is unnecessary, and $de = f$ is a simpler way to write the equation.

Problem 27 [Generalize]

Remind students that one way to check a computation is to make an estimate before completing any arithmetic.

"Explain how we could estimate the answer to this subtraction problem." Sample: Round 2020 to 2000 and round 10,101 to 10,000, then subtract; $2000 - 10,000 = -8000$.

"How can an estimate such as −8000 be used to decide if our exact answer is reasonable?" Sample: If the exact answer is close to the estimate, it is reasonable to assume that the exact answer is correct.

Errors and Misconceptions
Problem 27

Watch for students who do not immediately recognize that the difference will be a negative number. Ask these students to solve a simpler problem, such as $2 - 10$, to help recognize that the difference will be negative when the subtrahend is greater than the minuend.

---

12. Write a word problem for this equation: 5 lbs $\times$ 9 = w See
(4)   student work.

13. Write a word problem for this equation: $14 - x = \$3$ See
(3)   student work.

14. Arrange these numbers from least to greatest: $0, -1, \frac{2}{3}, 1, \frac{2}{5}$.
(1, 5) $-1, 0, \frac{2}{5}, \frac{2}{3}, 1$

* 15. Compare: $-11 \, \bigcirc \, -10$
(1)   <

▶*** 16.** [Analyze]   For each letter, write a word to describe its role: Sample:
(2) a: addend; b: addend; c: sum; d: factor; e: factor; f: product
$$a + b = c \qquad d \cdot e = f$$

17. Use the numbers 3 and 8 to provide an example of the Commutative
(2)   Property of Multiplication.   Sample: $3 \cdot 8 = 8 \cdot 3$

18. Use the numbers 1, 2, and 3 to provide an example of the Associative
(2)   Property of Addition.   Sample: $(1 + 2) + 3 = 1 + (2 + 3)$

19. Graph the numbers in this sequence on a number line:
(1)
$$\ldots, -5, -2, 1, 4, 7, \ldots$$

20. When 20 is subtracted from zero, what is the result? -20
(2)

21. If $7 - 5 = 2$, what other subtraction fact and what two addition facts are
(2)   true for 7, 5, and 2? $7 - 2 = 5; 5 + 2 = 7; 2 + 5 = 7$

22. If $12 \div 4 = 3$, what other division fact and what two multiplication facts
(1)   are true for 3, 4 and 12? $12 \div 3 = 4; 3 \cdot 4 = 12; 4 \cdot 3 = 12$

23. True or false: Every whole number is a counting number. Explain your
(1)   answer.   False; The number 0 is not a counting number.

24. What number is the absolute value of -90?   90
(1)

25. What number is the opposite of 6? -6
(1)

* 26. Find the value of the variable that makes the equation true and name
(2)   the property illustrated.

   a. If $6x = 6$, then x is what number?   1; Identity Property of Multiplication

   b. If $7 + y = 7$, then y is what number?   0; Identity Property of Addition

[Generalize]   Simplify.

▶*** 27.** $2020 - 10,101$ -8081
(2)

28. $48 \cdot \$0.79$ $\$37.92$
(2)

29. $\dfrac{\$60.60}{12}$ $\$5.05$
(2)

30. Use the Associative and Commutative Properties to make the
(2)   calculations easier. Justify the steps.

$$4 \cdot (12 \cdot 75)$$

$4 \cdot (75 \cdot 12)$	Commutative Property
$(4 \cdot 75) \cdot 12$	Associative Property
$300 \cdot 12$	Multiplied 4 and 75
3600	Multiplied 300 and 12

▶ See Math Conversations in the sidebar.

Looking Forward

Calculating with and solving problems involving rates and averages prepares students for:

- **Lesson 49,** solving rate problems with proportions and equations.
- **Lesson 64,** using a unit multiplier to convert a rate.
- **Lesson 105,** solving compound average and rate problems.

Finding measures of central tendency prepares students for:

- **Lesson 53,** solving problems using measures of central tendency.
- **Investigation 6,** collecting, displaying, and interpreting data.
- **Lesson 103,** using line plots and box-and-whisker plots.

• Perimeter and Area

Objectives

- Find the perimeters and areas of rectangles.
- Understand floor tiles as a model of area and baseboards as a model of perimeter.
- Determine how changing the dimensions of a shape by a factor changes its perimeter and area.
- Find the perimeters and areas of complex shapes formed from multiple rectangles.

Lesson Preparation

Materials

- **Power Up B** (in *Instructional Masters*)

Optional
- **Manipulative Kit: color tiles**
- **Teacher-provided material: tape measures, metersticks, or yardsticks**

Power Up B

Math Language

New	Maintain
area	formula
perimeter	

Technology Resources

Student eBook Complete student textbook in electronic format.

Resources and Planner CD Assessment, reteaching, and instructional masters, plus a pacing calendar with standards.

Test and Practice Generator CD Create additional practice sheets and custom-made tests.

www.SaxonPublishers.com Visit for more student activities and planning materials.

Inclusion

Adaptations CD Adapted lessons, investigations, practice and assessments.

Meeting Standards

National Council of Teachers of Mathematics (NCTM)

Algebra

AL.3a Model and solve contextualized problems using various representations, such as graphs, tables, and equations

Geometry

GM.4d Use geometric models to represent and explain numerical and algebraic relationships

GM.4e Recognize and apply geometric ideas and relationships in areas outside the mathematics classroom, such as art, science, and everyday life

Measurement

ME.1c Understand, select, and use units of appropriate size and type to measure angles, perimeter, area, surface area, and volume

ME.2c Develop and use formulas to determine the circumference of circles and the area of triangles, parallelograms, trapezoids, and circles and develop strategies to find the area of more-complex shapes

Representation

RE.5c Use representations to model and interpret physical, social, and mathematical phenomena

Problem-Solving Strategy: Guess and Check

Guess and check is a strategy in which we try a possible answer and then check the result. If our guess is incorrect, we use the result to improve our next guess. To solve some problems, we might find it useful to simply try all the possible answers and then compare the results.

Problem: ◯ · ▢ + △

The numbers 3, 4, and 5 are placed in the shapes above and the numbers are multiplied and added as shown. In order to make the result the least, which number should go in the triangle?

Understand Two of the three numbers are multiplied, and then the third number is added to the product.

Plan We will try each possible arrangement and find the one with the least result, then record which number goes in the triangle.

Solve There are six possible arrangements:

$3 \cdot 4 + 5 = 17$ $3 \cdot 5 + 4 = 19$ $4 \cdot 5 + 3 = 23$
$4 \cdot 3 + 5 = 17$ $5 \cdot 3 + 4 = 19$ $5 \cdot 4 + 3 = 23$

We might notice that the order of the first two numbers does not affect the result, since reversing factors does not change their product. In both arrangements with a result of 17 (the least result), we see that 5 is in the third location, which corresponds to the triangle.

Check We tried each possible arrangement and then found the answer. It makes sense that 5 must be in the triangle to produce the least result. When we multiply numbers greater than 2, we get greater results than when we add the same numbers. So multiplying the lesser two of the three numbers will produce the least result.

• Perimeter and Area

facts | Power Up B

mental math |

a. **Calculation:** Dante rode his bike a mile in 5 minutes. At that rate, how many miles can he ride in an hour?   12 miles

b. **Number Sense:** Find the two missing digits: $7 \times \square = \square 1$
$7 \times \boxed{3} = \boxed{2}1$

c. **Measurement:** What is the mass of 3 pumpkins this size?   24 kg

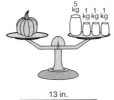

d. **Powers/Roots:** $\sqrt{16} + \sqrt{4}$ 6

e. **Number Sense:** 651 + 49   700

f. **Percent:** 10% of 40   4

g. **Geometry:** In this triangle, x must be more than how many inches?   4 in.

13 in.

9 in.   x

h. **Calculation:** 3 dozen, ÷ 4, + 1, ÷ 2, + 1, ÷ 2, + 1, ÷ 2   2

problem solving | Guess and check is a strategy in which we try a possible answer and then check the result. If our guess is incorrect, we use the result to improve our next guess. To solve some problems, we might find it useful to simply try all the possible answers and then compare the results.

Problem:

$\bigcirc \cdot \square + \triangle$

The numbers 3, 4, and 5 are placed in the shapes above and the numbers are multiplied and added as shown. In order to make the result the least, which number should go in the triangle?

[**Understand**] Two of the three numbers are multiplied, and then the third number is added to the product.

[**Plan**] We will try each possible arrangement and find the one with the least result, then record which number goes in the triangle.

[**Solve**] There are six possible arrangements:

$3 \cdot 4 + 5 = 17$	$3 \cdot 5 + 4 = 19$	$4 \cdot 5 + 3 = 23$
$4 \cdot 3 + 5 = 17$	$5 \cdot 3 + 4 = 19$	$5 \cdot 4 + 3 = 23$

We might notice that the order of the first two numbers does not affect the result, since reversing factors does not change their product. In both arrangements with a result of 17 (the least result), we see that 5 is in the third location, which corresponds to the triangle.

---

1 Power Up

Facts
Distribute **Power Up B** to students. See answers below.

Mental Math
Encourage students to share different ways to mentally compute these exercises. Strategies for exercises **a**, **b**, and **e** are listed below.

a. **Use a Pattern**
  5 minutes → 1 mile
  10 minutes → 2 miles
  60 minutes or 1 hour → 12 miles
  Use Logical Reasoning
  One hour has 12 parts of 5 minutes. In each part, Dante rides 1 mile. In 12 parts, he rides 12 miles.

b. **Think of a Fact**
  What multiple of 7 ends in 1? Only 21, so $7 \times 3 = 21$.
  Guess and Check
  It has to be an odd number.
  Try 5: $7 \times 5 = 35$ → no
  Try 7: $7 \times 7 = 49$ → no
  Try 3: $7 \times 3 = 21$ → yes

e. **Subtract 1, Add 1**
  $651 + 49 =$
  $(651 - 1) + (49 + 1) =$
  $650 + 50 = 700$
  Add 9, Subtract 9
  $651 + 49 =$
  $(651 + 9) + (49 - 9) =$
  $660 + 40 = 700$

Problem Solving
Refer to **Power-Up Discussion**, p. 47B.

Facts | Multiply.

10 × 10 —— 100	6 × 9 —— 54	2 × 4 —— 8	5 × 0 —— 0	4 × 6 —— 24	3 × 3 —— 9	5 × 8 —— 40	4 × 9 —— 36	2 × 7 —— 14	3 × 8 —— 24
2 × 9 —— 18	5 × 5 —— 25	7 × 9 —— 63	3 × 7 —— 21	6 × 6 —— 36	8 × 9 —— 72	2 × 3 —— 6	5 × 9 —— 45	4 × 8 —— 32	8 × 8 —— 64
4 × 7 —— 28	2 × 6 —— 12	3 × 9 —— 27	7 × 7 —— 49	2 × 8 —— 16	11 × 11 —— 121	5 × 6 —— 30	4 × 4 —— 16	6 × 7 —— 42	3 × 5 —— 15
3 × 4 —— 12	7 × 8 —— 56	4 × 5 —— 20	2 × 2 —— 4	6 × 8 —— 48	5 × 7 —— 35	3 × 6 —— 18	12 × 12 —— 144	2 × 5 —— 10	9 × 9 —— 81

Instruction

Have students relate *perimeter* and *area* to projects they and their families may have done. Ask how many have helped paint or wallpaper a wall, put new grass seed on a lawn, tie a package or stack of old newspapers with string, or build a fence. Point out that all of these involve finding or using the perimeter or area of something. Have students describe other projects they have done that may have involved perimeter or area in some way.

Example 1

Instruction

Ask volunteers to explain how they remember that *perimeter* is the distance around something and *area* is the measure of a surface or region. Some students, for example, associate *perimeter* with *meter*, a measure of length.

For part a, ask whether the answer would be the same if the dimensions were changed to feet before finding the perimeter and have students justify their answer. **Yes; Multiplying first is using the Distributive Property and does not change the answer.**

(continued)

> **Check** We tried each possible arrangement and then found the answer. It makes sense that 5 must be in the triangle to produce the least result. When we multiply numbers greater than 2, we get greater results than when add the same numbers. So multiplying the lesser two of the three numbers will produce the least result.

New Concept — *Increasing Knowledge*

The floor of a room can help us understand perimeter and area. Many rooms have a baseboard trim around the edge of the floor. The baseboard represents the **perimeter** of the room, which is the distance around the room. The total length of the baseboards in a room is a measure of the perimeter of the room. (The actual perimeter of a room includes the opening for each doorway as well.)

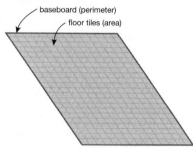

baseboard (perimeter)
floor tiles (area)

Some rooms are covered with floor tiles. The tiles cover the **area** of the floor, which is a measure of its surface. The number of floor tiles used to cover the floor is a measure of the area of the room.

Example 1

A rectangular room is five yards long and four yards wide.

a. How many feet of baseboard are needed to reach around the room?

b. How many square yards of carpet are needed to cover the floor?

c. Describe whether the tasks in a and b are similar to finding the perimeter or the area.

5 yd

4 yd

Solution

a. To find the distance around the room we add the lengths of the four sides.

$$5 \text{ yd} + 4 \text{ yd} + 5 \text{ yd} + 4 \text{ yd} = 18 \text{ yd}$$

Math Background

Is it possible for the same number to represent both the perimeter and the area of a rectangle?

Yes. A 4-by-4 rectangle has a perimeter of 16 units and an area of 16 square units, and a 3-by-6 rectangle has a perimeter of 18 units and an area of 18 square units.

Although the numbers may be the same, the measures are not equal because units and square units are different kinds of units.

We are asked for the number of *feet* of baseboard needed. Each yard is 3 feet so we multiply:

18 yd × 3 ft per yd = 54 ft

We find that **54 feet** of baseboard are needed. (In actual construction we would subtract from the total length the opening for each doorway.)

b. A one yard-by-one yard square is a square yard. We can find the number of square yards needed by multiplying the length in yards by the width in yards.

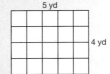

5 yd · 4 yd = 20 sq. yd

We find that **20 square yards** of carpet are needed to cover the floor.

c. In part a we found the distance around the room, which is its **perimeter.** In part b we found the **area** of the room.

We often refer to the length and width of a rectangle.

To find the perimeter of a rectangle, we add two lengths and two widths. To find the area of a rectangle, we multiply the length and width.

Formulas for the Perimeter and Area of a Rectangle

$$P = 2l + 2w$$
$$A = lw$$

In example 2 we compare the effects of doubling the length and width of a rectangle on the perimeter and area.

Example 2

The figures below show the dimensions of room A and room B.

a. Find the perimeter of each room in yards.

b. Find the area of each room in square yards.

c. How does doubling the length and width affect the perimeter of the rectangle?

d. How does doubling the length and width affect the area of the rectangle?

---

2 New Concepts (Continued)

Instruction

As you review the formulas for a rectangle, you may want to show how the formulas for a square are related to the formulas for a rectangle. The *length* and *width* of a rectangle are the values needed to find both the area and perimeter of the rectangle. In the formulas, s can replace both l and w since the length of a square is equal to the width of a square.

- Perimeter of a rectangle: $P = 2l + 2w$
- Perimeter of a square: $P = 2s + 2s = 4s$
- Area of a rectangle: $A = lw$
- Area of a square: $A = s \cdot s = s^2$

(continued)

Example 2

Instruction

Read through the questions for the four parts before working on the solutions. As you read the questions for parts c and d, ask students to predict what the effect of doubling the dimensions will be on both perimeter and area. Make a class tally of the predictions. Go back to check them after the solutions have been found.

You may extend this problem by having students find the answers to the four parts of this example after converting the dimensions in the drawings to feet. Figure A: perimeter = 54 ft, area = 180 ft²; Figure B: perimeter = 108 ft, area = 720 ft² Point that the answers to parts c and d do not change with a change in units.

Instruction

The floor plan of this room with a closet is a complex figure made up of two shapes. Its perimeter is found just as all perimeters are found—by adding the lengths of its sides. Caution students not to add the lengths of all sides of both rectangles, as not all sides are included in the perimeter of the combined figure. The areas of the parts of the figure can be added to find the area of the entire figure.

Example 3

Instruction

After working the example, ask whether the figure could have been divided into parts differently. You might take time to show that the figure could have been divided into 2 different rectangles or into 3 rectangular parts.

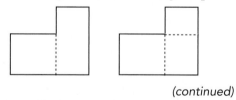

(continued)

---

a. The perimeter of room A is **18 yd,** and the perimeter of room B is **36 yd.**

b. The area of room A is **20 sq. yd,** and the area of room B is **80 sq. yd.**

c. Doubling the length and width also doubles the perimeter.

d. Doubling the length and width results in an area four times as large.

The floor plan of a room with a closet might look like two joined rectangles. To find the perimeter we add the lengths of each side. To find the area we add the areas of the two rectangles. In the following example we first find the lengths of the sides that are not labeled.

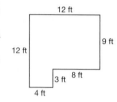

Example 3

Find the perimeter and area of this figure. All angles are right angles (square corners).

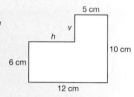

Sample: We could find the area of a 10-by-12 cm rectangle and subtract the area of a 4-by-7 cm rectangle.

Thinking Skill

Analyze

Describe another way we could find the area of the figure in example 3 by first finding the area of two different rectangles.

Solution

The horizontal segments labeled h and 5 cm must total 12 cm, so h must be 7 cm. The vertical segments labeled 6 cm and v must total 10 cm, so v must be 4 cm. We add the six sides to find the perimeter.

$$\text{Perimeter} = 5 \text{ cm} + 10 \text{ cm} + 12 \text{ cm} + 6 \text{ cm} + 7 \text{ cm} + 4 \text{ cm}$$
$$= \textbf{44 cm}$$

The area is the sum of the areas of the two rectangles.

$$\text{Area} = 4 \text{ cm} \cdot 5 \text{ cm} + 6 \text{ cm} \cdot 12 \text{ cm}$$
$$= 20 \text{ sq. cm} + 72 \text{ sq. cm}$$
$$= \textbf{92 sq. cm}$$

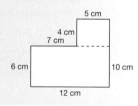

Teacher Tip

To give students hands-on experience with perimeter and area, have them measure the classroom and determine its perimeter and area. They might choose another room in the building, measure it, calculate its perimeter and area, and compare the results with those for the classroom.

Manipulative Use

Have students use **color tiles** from the manipulative kit to find the **perimeters and areas** of a variety of figures. Let them create figures, find the lengths of sides in "tile units," calculate the perimeter and area, and then count the "tile units" along the sides to check the perimeter, and count the tiles to check the area.

Practice Set ▶ **a.** *Evaluate* Jarrod is placing baseboards and one-foot-square floor tiles in a 12 ft-by-8 ft room. Ignoring doorways, how many feet of baseboard does he need? How many tiles does he need?   **40 ft of baseboard, 96 tiles**

Find the perimeter and area of each rectangle.

b. *P* = 14 cm, *A* = 12 sq. cm

c. *P* = 42 cm, *A* = 108 sq. cm

b.

c.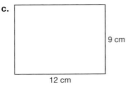

d. The perimeter of the rectangle in **c** is 3 times the perimeter in **b**. The area of the rectangle in **c** is 9 times the area in **b**.

d. *Analyze* The length and width of the rectangle in **c** are three times the length and width of the rectangle in **b**. The perimeter and area of the rectangle in **c** are how many times those measures in **b**?

▶ **e.** Placing 12 tiles side by side, Pete can make a 12-by-1 rectangle. Name two other rectangles Pete can make with the 12 tiles.   **6 by 2, 4 by 3**

f. Find the perimeter and area of a room with these dimensions.   *P* = 54 ft, *A* = 152 ft²

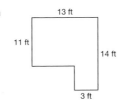

Written Practice   *Strengthening Concepts*

▶ ***1.*** *(8)* *Connect* Joel will fence a rectangular yard measuring 20 yards by 15 yards. How many yards of fencing will he need? What will be the area of the fenced yard?   **70 yards of fencing; 300 yd²**

▶ ***2.*** *(8)* *Evaluate* Joel fences a larger yard with dimensions that are four times the dimensions in problem 1. Find the dimensions of the larger yard and then find its perimeter and area.   **80 yards by 60 yards; perimeter = 280 yards; area = 4800 yd²**

3. The perimeter in problem 2 is 4 times the perimeter in problem 1. The area in problem 2 is 16 times the area in problem 1.

3. *(8)* The perimeter and area of the yard in problem 2 are how many times those measured in problem 1?

4. *(8)* Placing 30 tiles side by side, Patricia can make a 30-by-1 rectangle. Name three other rectangles Patricia can make with the 30 tiles.   **2 by 15; 3 by 10; 6 by 5.**

5. *(4)* Each volume contains 12 chapters. If there are 5 volumes, how many chapters are there in all?   **60 chapters**

▶ ***6.*** *(6)* The net weight of the bag of almonds is 2 lb 8 oz. How many ounces of almonds are there?   **40 oz**

Lesson 8   51

▶ See Math Conversations in the sidebar.

---

② New Concepts *(Continued)*

Practice Set
Problem a [Error Alert]
Students will name fewer than 96 tiles if they assume a fixed amount of space exists between adjacent tiles.

Problem e [Error Alert]
Point out that a 12-by-1 arrangement and a 1-by-12 arrangement count as one arrangement, not two.

③ Written Practice

Math Conversations
Discussion opportunities are provided below.

Problem 1 Connect
"Why are only two measures—a length and a width—needed to find the perimeter of a rectangle?" Sample: The opposite sides of a rectangle are congruent.

Problem 2 Evaluate
Prior to completing the problem, ask students to predict how the area of the rectangle will change after the length and width of the rectangle become four times greater. Encourage students to record their predictions, and refer to them after completing Problem 3.

Problem 6
"Will the exact answer be greater than, or less than, 32 ounces? Explain why." greater than; Sample: 1 pound is equivalent to 16 ounces, and 2 pounds is equivalent to 16 × 2 or 32 ounces. So 2 pounds 8 ounces is a greater weight than 32 ounces.

(continued)

Math Conversations

Discussion opportunities are provided below.

Problem 8 Evaluate

Before completing the problem, have students note that the data range from 7 to 12, and then using only mental math, ask them to predict how the mean, median, and mode of the data will compare to that range. Sample: The mean and the median will be greater than 7 and less than 12. The least possible mode (assuming there is at least one mode) is 7, and the greatest possible mode is 12.

After completing the problem, ask students to compare their answers to their predictions. Then challenge them to choose one number from the data set and describe how that number should be changed to increase the average of all of the numbers from 9.7 to 10. Increase the chosen number by 3.

Errors and Misconceptions
Problem 12

A misconception some students may have about the average rate is that Tina must have driven exactly 56 miles per hour for each of the 3 hours. Explain that although Tina may have driven at that rate for that amount of time, it is more likely that Tina's speed was not constant throughout the trip, and it is possible, for example, that Tina stopped for a relatively short length of time.

Help students recognize that elapsed time and distance represent the only data that are needed to compute an average rate of speed, and generalize that a computed average is likely to not represent an event exactly as it occurred.

(continued)

---

* 7. A video game was discounted and now costs two thirds of its original
(5) price. If it originally cost $45, how much does it cost now? $30

▶ *** 8.** **Evaluate** Mahesh rides a bus to work. The number of minutes his daily
(7) bus ride took over a two-week period are recorded below:

	M	T	W	Th	F
Week 1	12	8	10	9	12
Week 2	8	7	12	9	10

   a. Find the mean, median, mode, and range of the data.   mean: 9.7 minutes, median: 9.5 minutes, mode: 12 minutes, range: 5 minutes
   b. Which measure would Mahesh use to describe how many minutes the duration of his bus ride may differ from day to day?   range

9. The auditorium has twelve rows of 24 seats. How many seats are there
(4) in all?   288 seats

10. What is the quotient when the sum of 15 and 12 is divided by the
(2) difference of 15 and 12?   9

* 11. A mile-high city is how many feet above sea level?   5280 ft
(6)

▶*** 12.** Tina drove 168 miles in 3 hours. What was her average rate in miles per
(7) hour?   56 mph

13. Write a word problem for this equation: See student work.
(4)
$$5 \text{ mi} \times 4 = d$$

14. Write a word problem for this equation: See student work.
(3)
$$12 \text{ in.} - x = 7 \text{ in.}$$

15. Arrange these numbers from least to greatest.
(1, 5)
$$\frac{1}{2}, -1, \frac{5}{7}, -2, \frac{2}{6}, 1 \quad -2, -1, \frac{2}{6}, \frac{1}{2}, \frac{5}{7}, 1$$

16. Compare: $-100 \,\text{\textcircled{<}}\, 10$
(1)

17. Compare: $-3 \,\text{\textcircled{>}}\, -4$
(1)

18. Compare: $|-3| \,\text{\textcircled{<}}\, |-4|$
(1)

* 19. Use the numbers 5 and 7 to provide an example of the Commutative
(2) Property of Addition.   Sample: $5 + 7 = 7 + 5$

20. Graph the numbers in this sequence on a number line.
(1)
$$\ldots, -7, -3, 1, 5, 9, \ldots$$

21. What is the absolute value of 15?   15
(1)

22. If $3 + 4 = 7$, what other addition fact and what two subtraction facts are
(2) true for 3, 4, and 7? $4 + 3 = 7; 7 - 4 = 3;$ and $7 - 3 = 4$

20.

▶ See Math Conversations in the sidebar.

23. What is the opposite of 3? −3
(1)

24. What two numbers are 5 units from 0? 5, −5
(1)

Explain For problems **25–27**, state whether the sentence is true or false, and explain why. If the answer is false, provide a counterexample.

* **25.** Every negative number is an integer. false; counterexample: $-\frac{1}{2}$ is not an
(1) integer.

26. Every natural number is an integer. true; Integers include natural
(1) numbers.

27. The sum of two whole numbers is a whole number. true; Adding two
(1) positive integers results in another positive integer.

28. Find two solutions to this equation: $|x| = 15$. $x = 15, −15$
(1)

29. Find the product of 37 and 68. 2516
(2)

▶ **30.** *Analyze* Three out of every four restaurant patrons did not order the
(5) special. What fraction did order the special? $\frac{1}{4}$

Early Finishers
Real-World Application

The Tour de France is a well-known cycling competition in which cyclists from around the world are chosen to participate. The Tour's length varies from year to year but is usually between 3000 and 4000 km in length. If one mile is approximately 1.6 km, approximately how long is the Tour de France in miles? between 1875 and 2500 miles

▶ See Math Conversations in the sidebar.

---

3 Written Practice (Continued)

Math Conversations

Discussion opportunities are provided below.

Problem 30 Analyze

Students should conclude that when working with one (or more than one) fractional parts of a whole, 1 is typically used to represent the whole.

When one of two fractional parts of a whole is given, students should generalize that subtraction is used (subtract the known fractional part from the whole) to find the unknown fractional part.

Looking Forward

Finding the perimeters and areas of polygons prepares students for:

• **Investigation 2,** understanding and applying the Pythagorean Theorem.

• **Lesson 37,** calculating areas of combined polygons.

• **Lesson 39,** calculating circumferences of circles.

• **Lesson 40,** calculating areas of circles.

• **Lesson 42,** calculating volumes.

• **Lesson 43,** calculating surface areas.

• **Lesson 60,** calculating areas of parallelograms.

• **Lesson 75,** calculating areas of trapezoids.

• Prime Numbers

Objectives

- Identify counting numbers as prime or composite.
- Use an area model to demonstrate prime and composite numbers.
- Use factor trees and division by prime numbers to find the prime factorization of counting numbers.
- Understand and apply tests of divisibility.

Lesson Preparation

Materials

- **Power Up B** (in *Instructional Masters*)

Optional

- **Manipulative Kit: color tiles**
- **Lesson Activity 1** (in *Instructional Masters*) **or grid paper**
- **Teacher-provided material: calculators**

Power Up B

Math Language

New	Maintain
composite numbers	factor
divisible	
prime factorization	
prime numbers	

Technology Resources

Student eBook Complete student textbook in electronic format.

Resources and Planner CD Assessment, reteaching, and instructional masters, plus a pacing calendar with standards.

Test and Practice Generator CD Create additional practice sheets and custom-made tests.

www.SaxonPublishers.com Visit for more student activities and planning materials.

Inclusion

Adaptations CD Adapted lessons, investigations, practice and assessments.

Meeting Standards

National Council of Teachers of Mathematics (NCTM)

Numbers and Operations

NO.1f Use factors, multiples, prime factorization, and relatively prime numbers to solve problems

Geometry

GM.4d Use geometric models to represent and explain numerical and algebraic relationships

Reasoning and Proof

RP.2b Make and investigate mathematical conjectures

Communication

CM.3d Use the language of mathematics to express mathematical ideas precisely

Connections

CN.4b Understand how mathematical ideas interconnect and build on one another to produce a coherent whole

Problem-Solving Strategy: Draw a Diagram

Fraction problems can be difficult to visualize but are often easy to draw. Drawing a fraction problem can help us sort through what is actually being asked.

Problem: Given that $\frac{1}{7}$ of a number is $\frac{1}{5}$, what is $\frac{5}{7}$ of that number?

Understand We have been told that $\frac{1}{7}$ of a number is $\frac{1}{5}$ and have been asked to determine what $\frac{5}{7}$ of that number is.

Plan We know that $\frac{1}{7}$ of a number is one piece of seven pieces the number can be divided into. We will draw a diagram of the number divided into its seven parts.

Solve We draw a whole divided into seven equal parts. Each seventh represents one-seventh of the value of the whole, unknown number. We then label one of the sevenths as $\frac{1}{5}$, because we are told that each seventh has the value $\frac{1}{5}$:

We want to know the value of $\frac{5}{7}$ of the number, so we label five of the sevenths as $\frac{1}{5}$:

We see that $\frac{5}{7}$ of the number is $\frac{1}{5} + \frac{1}{5} + \frac{1}{5} + \frac{1}{5} + \frac{1}{5}$, which is 1.

Check It may seem unusual to consider that $\frac{1}{7}$ of a whole can have the value $\frac{1}{5}$, or that $\frac{5}{7}$ of a whole can have the value 1, but drawing a diagram showed us that it is possible.

Facts

Distribute **Power Up B** to students. See answers below.

Mental Math

Encourage students to share different ways to mentally compute these exercises. Strategies for exercises **c** and **f** are listed below.

c. Double and Halve Twice
$2 \times 32 = 4 \times 16 = 8 \times 8 = 64$
Regroup
$2 \times 32 = 2 \times (30 + 2) = 60 + 4 = 64$

f. Add 3, Subtract 3
$1307 + 13 =$
$(1307 + 3) + (13 - 3) =$
$1310 + 10 = 1320$
Add the Ones, then the Tens
$1307 + 13 \longrightarrow$
$1307 + 3 = 1310$
$1310 + 10 = 1320$

Problem Solving

Refer to **Power-Up Discussion**, p. 54B.

Power Up   *Building Power*

facts   Power Up B

mental math
a. Calculation: Eight cups per day is how many cups per week?   56 cups per week
b. Estimation: $\$99.50 \times 4$ $\$100 \times 4 = \$400$
c. Number Sense: 2×32 64
d. Measurement: Find the mass of 10 of these cups.   170 g

e. Geometry: In this triangle, x must be greater than what number?   3
f. Number Sense: $1307 + 13$ 1320
g. Percent: 50% of 40   20
h. Calculation: $49 \div 7, \times 2, + 1, \div 3, \times 9, + 5, \div 5, - 11$ $= -1$

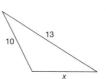

problem solving
Fraction problems can be difficult to visualize but are often easy to draw. Drawing a fraction problem can help us sort through what is actually being asked.

Problem: Given that $\frac{1}{7}$ of a number is $\frac{1}{5}$, what is $\frac{5}{7}$ of that number?

(**Understand**) We have been told that $\frac{1}{7}$ of a number is $\frac{1}{5}$ and have been asked to determine what $\frac{5}{7}$ of that number is.

(**Plan**) We know that $\frac{1}{7}$ of a number is one of seven pieces the number can be divided into. We will draw a picture of the "number" divided into its seven fractional parts.

(**Solve**) We draw a whole divided into seven equal parts. Each seventh represents one-seventh of the value of the whole, unknown number. We then label one of the sevenths as $\frac{1}{5}$, because we are told that each seventh has the value $\frac{1}{5}$:

Facts   Multiply.

10 × 10 100	6 × 9 54	2 × 4 8	5 × 0 0	4 × 6 24	3 × 3 9	5 × 8 40	4 × 9 36	2 × 7 14	3 × 8 24
2 × 9 18	5 × 5 25	7 × 9 63	3 × 7 21	6 × 6 36	8 × 9 72	2 × 3 6	5 × 9 45	4 × 8 32	8 × 8 64
4 × 7 28	2 × 6 12	3 × 9 27	7 × 7 49	2 × 8 16	11 × 11 121	5 × 6 30	4 × 4 16	6 × 7 42	3 × 5 15
3 × 4 12	7 × 8 56	4 × 5 20	2 × 2 4	6 × 8 48	5 × 7 35	3 × 6 18	12 × 12 144	2 × 5 10	9 × 9 81

We want to know the value of $\frac{5}{7}$ of the number, so we label five of the sevenths as $\frac{1}{5}$:

We see that $\frac{5}{7}$ of the number is $\frac{1}{5} + \frac{1}{5} + \frac{1}{5} + \frac{1}{5} + \frac{1}{5}$, which is **1.**

(Check) It may seem unusual to consider that $\frac{1}{7}$ of a whole can have the value $\frac{1}{5}$, or that $\frac{5}{7}$ of a whole can have the value 1, but drawing a diagram showed us that it is possible.

New Concept   *Increasing Knowledge*

Prime numbers are counting numbers greater than 1 that have exactly two different counting number factors: the number itself and 1. For example, the numbers 2, 3, 5, 7, 11, and 13 are prime. We may use an area model to illustrate numbers that are prime and numbers that are not prime.

Suppose we have six square tiles. Fitting the tiles side by side we can form two different rectangles, a 6-by-1 rectangle and a 3-by-2 rectangle.

These two rectangles illustrate the two counting number factor pairs of 6, which are 6×1 and 3×2. If we have 7 square tiles, we can form only one rectangle, a 7-by-1 rectangle. This is because there is only one factor pair for 7, which is 7×1.

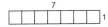

A prime number has only one factor pair, so a prime number of tiles can only form a "by 1" rectangle. The rectangles above illustrate that 7 is prime and that 6 is not prime.

Counting numbers with more than two factors are **composite numbers.** Six is a composite number. The numbers 4, 8, 9, 10, and 12 are other examples of composite numbers. Counting numbers greater than 1 are either prime or composite.

Composite numbers are so named because they are *composed* of two or more prime factors. For example, 6 is composed of the prime factors 2 and 3. We write the **prime factorization** of a composite number by writing the number as a product of prime numbers. The prime factorization of 6 is $2 \cdot 3$.

Example 1

Write the prime factorization of

a. **36.**

b. **45.**

2 New Concepts

Instruction

Students may use square tiles, **Lesson Activity 1** Square Centimeter Grid, or grid paper to explore the concept of *prime* and *composite* numbers. Have them create or draw arrays and determine whether another array can be formed using the same number of tiles.

They should discover that different arrays can be formed from the same number of tiles by making a "by 1" array, unless the only possible array is a "by 1" array. Those arrays for which no other array can be made represent prime numbers; the others represent composite numbers.

Point out that writing the *prime factorization* of a number is different from listing all the different factors of a number.

• In listing all the factors of a number, the number itself and 1 are included, as well as any composite numbers that are factors.

• In a prime factorization, a number is factored until all the factors are prime numbers.

(continued)

Math Background

If the greatest common factor (GCF) of two numbers (or more than two numbers) is 1, the numbers are said to be *relatively prime.*

For example, 8 and 13 are relatively prime numbers. The factors of 8 are 1, 2, 4, and 8. The factors of 13 are 1 and 13. The only factor that is common to both numbers is 1.

The concept of relatively prime numbers is applied each time a fraction is reduced to lowest terms. The only common factor of the numerator and the denominator of a fraction in lowest terms is 1.

2 New Concepts (Continued)

Example 1
Instruction

Guide students to see that several different *factor trees* can be made for 36. Tell students to choose any factor pair of 36 to begin the factor tree and to factor those factors any way they choose. Let volunteers draw factor trees on the board or overhead so that the class can see a variety of factor trees and how they all produce the same prime factorization. Stress that the factors are rewritten in ascending order for the prime factorization, using dots to indicate multiplication.

One way to apply the successive divisions method is to start with the smallest possible prime factor used as often as possible, then the next greater factor, and so on. One advantage of this method is that (unless a factor was not noticed at the correct time) the factors are ordered in ascending order, and need only be copied.

Suggest that students now make a factor tree for 45 and use successive divisions to find the prime factorization of 36. Have them check whether both methods yield the same prime factorization.

Instruction

Testing for divisibility with the tests described here is a quick way to see whether a number is composite. Have students analyze what tests and combinations are given on the student page to see what numbers they have divisibility tests for. 2, 3, 4, 5, 6, 9, 10

You may want to tell them that the test for divisibility by 8 is whether the last three digits are divisible by 8, and that if a number is divisible by 3 and by 4, it is also divisible by 12.

If students need more help, the *Student Reference Guide* has a concise list of these tests.

(continued)

Solution

a. A factor tree can help us find the prime factorization of a number. Here we show one possible factor tree for 36. We split 36 into the factors 6 and 6. Then we split each 6 into the factors 2 and 3. We stop when the factors are prime; we do not use the number 1 in a factor tree. We order the prime numbers at the end of the "branches" to write the prime factorization.

$$36 = 2 \cdot 2 \cdot 3 \cdot 3$$

b. Another method for finding the prime factorization of a number is by dividing the number by a prime number and then dividing the quotient by a prime number. We continue dividing in this way until the quotient is prime.

$$\begin{array}{r} 3 \\ 3\overline{)9} \\ 5\overline{)45} \end{array}$$

We use the divisors, 5 and 3, and the final quotient, 3, to write the prime factorization.

$$45 = 3 \cdot 3 \cdot 5$$

One way to test if a counting number is prime or composite is to determine if it is **divisible** (can be divided) by a counting number other than 1 and itself. For example, 2 is prime, but other multiples of 2 are composite because they are divisible by 2. Thus, even numbers greater than 2 are composite. In the table below we list some tests for divisibility.

Divisibility Tests

Condition	Number is Divisible by	Example Using 3420
the number is even (ends with 0, 2, 4, 6, or 8)	2	342<u>0</u>
the sum of the digits is divisible by 3	3	3 + 4 + 2 + 0 = <u>9</u> and 9 is divisible by 3
the number ends in 0 or 5	5	342<u>0</u>

We can combine these tests to build divisibility tests for other numbers. Here are some examples:

- A number divisible by 2 and 5 is divisible by 10 (2 × 5). Thus, 3420 is divisible by 10.
- A number divisible by 2 and 3 is divisible by 6 (2 × 3). Thus, 3420 is divisible by 6.
- A number is divisible by 9 if the sum of its digits is divisible by 9 (3 × 3). Thus, 3420 is divisible by 9 because the sum of its digits (3 + 4 + 2 + 0 = 9) is divisible by 9.

Inclusion

Students may have difficulty connecting prime numbers to rectangles. Provide 6 color tiles from the manipulative kit and have students stack the tiles in groups of two or more.

"Can you stack 6 into equal groups? Explain." Sample: Yes, into 2 groups of 3.

Have the student rearrange the groups into a rectangle. The result should be a 3-by-2 rectangle. Provide 7 tiles and have the student stack them into groups.

"Can you stack 7 into equal groups? Explain." Sample: No, because stacking them into groups of 2 or 3 each results in one leftover tile.

Have the student rearrange the 7 tiles into a rectangle. 1 by 7 rectangle

"What kind of number is 7, prime or composite? Explain." Sample: prime; Seven cannot be stacked evenly into groups or arranged into a rectangle other than a "by 1" rectangle.

- A number is divisible by 4 if its last two digits are divisible by 4. Thus, 3420 is divisible by 4 since its last two digits (20) are divisible by 4.

Example 2

Determine whether the following numbers are prime or composite and state how you know.

a. 1,237,526   b. 520,611

Solution

a. The number is **composite** because it is even and thus divisible by 2.

b. The number is **composite** because the sum of its digits is divisible by 3 ($5 + 2 + 0 + 6 + 1 + 1 = \underline{15}$).

Practice Set

a. **Model** Is 9 a prime or composite number? Draw rectangles using 9 squares to support your answer. composite; Student drawings should include a 9 × 1 rectangle and a 3 × 3 rectangle.

b. Write the first 10 prime numbers. 2, 3, 5, 7, 11, 13, 17, 19, 23, 29

c. **Represent** Draw a factor tree for 36. Make the first two branches 4 and 9.

d. Find the prime factors of 60 by dividing by prime numbers.

c.
```
        36
       /  \
      4    9
     / \  / \
    ②  ② ③  ③
```

d.
```
        5
    2)‾10‾
    3)‾30‾
    2)‾60‾;
60 = 2 · 2 · 3 · 5
```

h. **D** 7, Multi-digit numbers ending in 4, 5, or 6 cannot be prime because a last digit of 4 or 6 means the number has 2 as a factor, and a last digit of 5 means it has 5 as a factor.

Write the prime factorization of each number in **e–g**.

e. 25 $25 = 5 \cdot 5$ f. 100 $100 = 2 \cdot 2 \cdot 5 \cdot 5$

g. 16 $16 = 2 \cdot 2 \cdot 2 \cdot 2$

h. Choose a number to complete the statement. Justify your choice.

A multi-digit number might be prime if its last digit is _____.

A 4   B 5   C 6   D 7

i. Six squares can be arranged to form two different rectangles.

The models illustrate that 6 is composite and not prime. Illustrate that 12 is composite by sketching three different rectangles with 12 squares each.

Written Practice   *Strengthening Concepts*

* 1. Three thousand, six hundred ninety people finished the half-marathon.
(5) If $\frac{2}{3}$ of the finishers walked a portion of the course, how many finishers walked during the race? 2460 people

2. A doorway that is 2 meters high is how many centimeters high? 200 cm
(6)

3. Driving at 80 km per hour, how far will Curtis drive in 2 hours, in 3 hours,
(7) and in 4 hours? 160 km, 240 km, 320 km

Lesson 9   57

▶ See Math Conversations in the sidebar.

Math Conversations

Discussion opportunities are provided below.

Problem 4a [Evaluate]

At least two different equations can be used to represent the problem. For example, $150 + m = 320$ and $320 - 150 = m$ can both be used to find the length of track that was installed during the second month.

You might encourage students to write two different equations to represent the problem. Students can then solve one equation to find the answer and use the second equation to check their work.

Problem 4b [Evaluate]

"Describe how to find the average of a group of numbers." Sample: Divide the sum of the numbers by the number of addends.

Problem 5 [Explain]

Extend the Problem

You might choose to ask students to work in pairs or in small groups to solve the following problem.

"Suppose that two of the seven numbers in the group are deleted and the median of the remaining five numbers is 182. Which two numbers were deleted? (Hint: There is more than one answer.)" There are six possible answers: 190 and 205; 190 and 208; 190 and 214; 205 and 208; 205 and 214; 208 and 214.

Problem 15a [Connect]

"Is the question asking us to find the perimeter or the area of the room? Explain how you know." perimeter; Sample: Perimeter is a measure of the distance around.

"Explain how multiplication and addition can be used to find the perimeter of a rectangle." Multiply the length by 2 and multiply the width by 2. Then find the sum of the products.

Errors and Misconceptions

Problem 7

Watch for students who list 1 as the first prime number. Use other prime numbers (such as 2, 5, and 13) to demonstrate that a prime number has exactly two different factors.

(continued)

▶ * **4.** [Evaluate] Identify the plot, write an equation, and solve the problem:
(3, 7) The railroad workers laid 150 miles of track in the first month. At the end of the two months, the total was up to 320 miles.

    a. How many miles did they lay in the second month?
    Combining; $150 + m = 320$; 170 miles

    b. The workers laid an average of how many miles of track each month? 160 miles

▶ **5.** [Explain] A traffic counter recorded the number of vehicles heading
(7) north through an intersection for a seven-day period. The following counts were recorded for the seven days.

$$86, 182, 205, 214, 208, 190, 126$$

    a. What was the median number of vehicles counted? 190

    b. What was the mean number of vehicles counted? 173

    c. Are most of the counts closer to the median or mean? Why?

5. c. median; one low count (86) lowers the mean below most of the counts, while the median is near most of the counts.

6. A mile is 5280 ft. How many yards is a mile? 1760 yd
(6)

▶ **7.** List the first eight prime numbers. 2, 3, 5, 7, 11, 13, 17, 19
(9)

Simplify.

8. 100 cm − 68 cm   32 cm
(2)

9. $2970.98 − $1429.59 $1541.39
(2)

10. 5280 ÷ 30   176
(2)

11. $123.45 ÷ 3 $41.15
(2)

* **12.** Find the perimeter and area.
(8)

* **13.** Find the perimeter.
(8)

32 in.

44 in.

$P = 152$ in.; $A = 1408$ in.^{2}

12 m   15 m

19 m

$P = 46$ m

14. Find the perimeter and area of this figure.   Perimeter 30 in.; Area 39 sq. in.
(8)

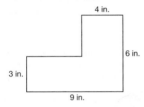
4 in.

6 in.

3 in.

9 in.

* **15.** [Connect] A rectangular room is 15 feet long and 12 feet wide.
(8)

▶   **a.** How many feet of baseboard are needed to reach around the room? (Ignore door openings.) 54 ft

    b. How many one-foot-square tiles are needed to cover the floor? 180 tiles

▶ See Math Conversations in the sidebar.

16. $a = 5$;
Commutative
Property of
Addition

17. $b = 18$;
Commutative
Property of
Multiplication

18. $c = 1$; Identity
Property of
Multiplication

19. 0; Zero
Property of
Multiplication

For problems **16–19,** find the value of the variable that makes the equation true and state the property illustrated.

16. $5 + 4 = 4 + a$
(2)

17. $17 \cdot 18 = b \cdot 17$
(2)

18. $20 \cdot c = 20$
(2)

19. $21d = 0$
(2)

20. a. What is the absolute value of 9?   9
(1)

   b. Simplify and compare: $|-12|$ ⊘ $|11|$

21. If 13 and 5 are the factors, what is the product?   65
(2)

22. If 225 is the dividend and 15 is the divisor, then what is the
(2) quotient?   15

For problems **23–26,** choose *all* the correct answers.

23. Twenty-seven is a member of which set(s) of numbers?   **A, B, C**
(1)
   A whole numbers   **B** counting numbers   **C** integers

24. Zero is a member of which set(s) of numbers?   **A, C**
(1)
   A whole numbers   **B** counting numbers   **C** integers

25. Negative two is a member of which set(s) of numbers?   **C**
(1)
   A whole numbers   **B** counting numbers   **C** integers

▶* **26.** *Analyze*   The number 5280 is divisible by which of these numbers?
(9)
   A 2   **B** 3   **C** 4   **D** 5
   A, B, C, D

▶* **27.** *List*   List all the prime numbers between 30 and 50.   31, 37, 41, 43, 47
(9)

* **28.** Use a factor tree to find the prime factors of 490. Then write the prime
(9) factorization of 490. $2 \cdot 5 \cdot 7 \cdot 7$

* **29.** Use division by primes to find the prime factors of 48. Then write the
(9) prime factorization of 48. $2 \cdot 2 \cdot 2 \cdot 2 \cdot 3$

30. Rearrange factors to make the calculation easier. Then simplify. Justify
(2) your steps.

$$40 \cdot (23 \cdot 50)$$

Step:	Justification:
$40 \cdot (50 \cdot 23)$	Commutative Property of Multiplication
$(40 \cdot 50) \cdot 23$	Associative Property of Multiplication
$2000 \cdot 23$	Multiplied 40 and 50
46,000	Multiplied 2000 and 23

Lesson 9   **59**

▶ See Math Conversations in the sidebar.

Math Conversations
Discussion opportunities are provided below.

Problem 26   Analyze
"Explain how you know if one number is divisible by another." Sample: The division of the numbers does not produce a remainder (or the remainder is zero).

Problem 27   List
Before solving the problem, invite a volunteer to name a whole number between 30 and 50, then discuss with students how to decide if that number is prime or composite.

• Rational Numbers
• Equivalent Fractions

Objectives

- Understand how the sets of numbers (whole numbers, integers, rational numbers) are closed or open under the operations of arithmetic.
- Identify numbers as rational numbers.
- Find equivalent fractions for a given fraction.
- Use prime factorization to reduce fractions.
- Compare fractions by rewriting them with common denominators.
- Write improper fractions as whole numbers or mixed numbers.

Lesson Preparation

Materials

- **Power Up B** (in *Instructional Masters*)

Optional

- **Manipulative Kit: overhead fraction circles**

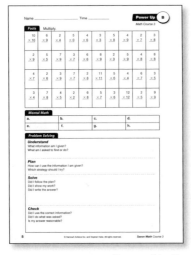

Power Up B

Math Language

New	Maintain	English Learners (ESL)
equivalent fractions	denominator	further
greatest common factor	integers	
improper fraction	numerator	
mixed number	whole numbers	
rational numbers		
reduce		

Technology Resources

Student eBook Complete student textbook in electronic format.

Resources and Planner CD Assessment, reteaching, and instructional masters, plus a pacing calendar with standards.

Test and Practice Generator CD Create additional practice sheets and custom-made tests.

www.SaxonPublishers.com Visit for more student activities and planning materials.

Inclusion

Adaptations CD Adapted lessons, investigations, practice and assessments.

Meeting Standards

National Council of Teachers of Mathematics (NCTM)

Numbers and Operations

NO.1a Work flexibly with fractions, decimals, and percents to solve problems

NO.1b Compare and order fractions, decimals, and percents efficiently and find their approximate locations on a number line

NO.1g Develop meaning for integers and represent and compare quantities with them

NO.2a Understand the meaning and effects of arithmetic operations with fractions, decimals, and integers

Problem-Solving Strategy: Find a Pattern/Make an Organized List

Alan, Bianca, and Charles are counting in turn. Alan says "one," Bianca says "two," and Charles says "three." Then it's Alan's turn again and he says "four." If the pattern continues, who will say "fifty-nine"?

(Understand) **Understand the problem.**

"What information are we given?"

Three students take turns counting aloud.

"What are we asked to do?"

We are asked to determine which student will say "fifty-nine."

(Plan) **Make a plan.**

"What problem-solving strategy will we use?"

Instead of acting it out, as we did with the easier problem in Lesson 6, we will *make an organized list* and use our list to *find a pattern*.

(Solve) **Carry out the plan.**

"How should we begin our list?"

We will record the first dozen numbers and the speaker's initial to see if a pattern emerges:

A	B	**C**	A	B	**C**	A	B	**C**	A	B	**C**
1	2	**3**	4	5	**6**	7	8	**9**	10	11	**12**

"How could we describe the numbers that Charles says?"

They are the multiples of 3.

"How could we describe the numbers that Alan says?"

They are one more than the multiples of 3.

"How could we describe the numbers that Bianca says?"

They are two more than the multiples of 3.

"What relation is 59 to the nearest multiple of 3?"

Since $59 \div 3 = 19 \text{ r2}$, it is two more than the nearest multiple of 3.

"Who will say fifty-nine?"

Because 59 is 2 more than a multiple of 3, Bianca will say it.

(Check) **Look back.**

"Did we find the answer to the question that was asked?"

Yes. Bianca will say fifty-nine.

• Rational Numbers
• Equivalent Fractions

facts   Power Up B

mental math

a. **Calculation:** The windmill rotated once every 15 seconds. How many rotations per minute is this?   4

b. **Number Sense:** 324 + 16   340

c. **Algebra:** Solve for *x*: 5 + *x* = 14.   9

d. **Measurement:** Francisco measured the florist box with a yardstick. How long is the florist box?   25 in.

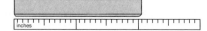

e. **Geometry:** In this triangle, *x* must be less than what number?   15

f. **Number Sense:** 2 × 64   128

g. **Power/Roots:** $\sqrt{81} - \sqrt{1}$ 8

h. **Calculation:** $|-10| - 1, \sqrt{\ }, \times 5, + 1, \sqrt{\ }, \sqrt{\ }, - 2$ 0

problem solving   Alan, Bianca, and Charles are counting in turn. Alan says "one," Bianca says "two," and Charles says "three." Then it's Alan's turn again and he says "four." If the pattern continues, who will say "fifty-nine"?   Bianca

New Concepts   Increasing Knowledge

rational numbers   In the loop is the set of whole numbers.

Whole numbers
0, 1, 2, 3, 4, …

• If we add any two whole numbers, is the sum a whole number?   yes

• If we multiply any two whole numbers, is the product a whole number?   yes

---

Power Up 1

Facts
Distribute **Power Up B** to students. See answers below.

Mental Math
Encourage students to share different ways to mentally compute these exercises. Strategies for exercises **a** and **b** are listed below.

a. **Use a Pattern**

   15 s ➝ 1 rotation
   30 s ➝ 2 rotations
   45 s ➝ 3 rotations
   60 s or 1 min ➝ 4 rotations

  Divide
   1 min = 60 s
   60 ÷ 15 = 4

b. **Add the Ones, Then the Tens**

   324 + 16 ➝
   324 + 6 = 330
   330 + 10 = 340

  Subtract 4, Add 4
   324 + 16 =
   (324 − 4) + (16 + 4) =
   320 + 20 = 340

Problem Solving
Refer to **Power-Up Discussion**, p. 60B.

Facts   Multiply.

10 × 10 100	6 × 9 54	2 × 4 8	5 × 0 0	4 × 6 24	3 × 3 9	5 × 8 40	4 × 9 36	2 × 7 14	3 × 8 24
2 × 9 18	5 × 5 25	7 × 9 63	3 × 7 21	6 × 6 36	8 × 9 72	2 × 3 6	5 × 9 45	4 × 8 32	8 × 8 64
4 × 7 28	2 × 6 12	3 × 9 27	7 × 7 49	2 × 8 16	11 × 11 121	5 × 6 30	4 × 4 16	6 × 7 42	3 × 5 15
3 × 4 12	7 × 8 56	4 × 5 20	2 × 2 4	6 × 8 48	5 × 7 35	3 × 6 18	12 × 12 144	2 × 5 10	9 × 9 81

Math Language
Remember that the set of whole numbers includes the counting numbers and zero.

We say that the set of whole numbers is **closed** under addition and multiplication because every sum or product is a whole number. Referring to our illustration we might say that we can find any sum or product of whole numbers within the whole numbers loop.

Let us consider subtraction.

• If we subtract any two whole numbers, is the result a whole number?   no

Certainly 3 − 1 is a whole number, but 1 − 3 is −2, which is not a whole number. The result is outside the loop.

More inclusive than the set of whole numbers is the set of integers, which includes the whole numbers as well as the negatives of whole numbers. The set of integers is closed under addition, subtraction and multiplication. Every sum, difference, and product can be found inside the integers loop.

Now we will consider division.

• If we divide any two integers, is the result an integer?   no

The divisions 1 ÷ 2, 3 ÷ 2, 3 ÷ 4, 4 ÷ 3, and many others all have quotients that are fractions and not integers. These quotients are examples of rational numbers.

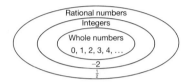

Thinking Skill

Explain

Explain why every integer is a rational number but not every rational number is an integer.

Rational numbers are numbers that can be expressed as a ratio of two integers. Any integer can be written as a fraction with a denominator of 1, so integers are rational numbers. The set of rational numbers is closed under addition, subtraction, multiplication, and division. That means any sum, difference, product, or quotient of two rational numbers is a rational number, with one exception: we guard against division by zero. That is, we do not use zero as a divisor or denominator. Reasons for this provision appear later in the book.

On the number line, rational numbers include the integers as well as many points between the integers.

Examples of Rational Numbers

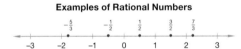

Every integer can be expressed as a ratio of two integers. Therefore, every integer is a rational number. Only some rational numbers can be expressed as a whole number or a negative of a whole number. Therefore, only some rational numbers are integers.

Lesson 10   61

---

2 New Concepts

Instruction

Use the *Math Language* callout to remind students that the *whole numbers* include 0. Ask why the ellipsis is only at the right of this sequence of numbers. Sample: The numbers to the left of zero are not whole numbers, so the sequence does not extend in that direction.

Point out that it makes sense that the set of whole numbers is closed to both addition and multiplication because multiplication is a way to show repeated addition.

Discuss how the set of *integers* is different from the set of whole numbers. Sample: The set of integers includes negative numbers. Be sure that students notice that this set is closed to another operation—subtraction.

As you read the description of *rational numbers,* point out that the rational numbers with the exception of zero are closed to yet another operation—division. Have students notice that as each set of numbers becomes more inclusive, the set is closed to more operations.

With the Thinking Skill *Explain* question, you might also discuss how each set of numbers contains another set. Ask if students can think of a set of numbers that is included in the set of whole numbers. Samples: counting (natural) numbers, odd numbers, even numbers, prime numbers, composite numbers

(continued)

Math Background

A rational number is any number that can be expressed as $\frac{a}{b}$, where a and b are integers and $b \neq 0$. In a more general way, a rational number is any number that can be written as a ratio of two integers.

A number line represents real numbers, which consist of all the rational numbers and irrational numbers. Any real number that is not a rational number is an irrational number.

Between any two consecutive integers on an integer number line, there are infinitely many rational numbers and infinitely many irrational numbers.

Example 1

Instruction

After students graph the numbers, point out that all numbers that can be classified as rational numbers can be graphed on a number line.

Instruction

As you discuss *equivalent fractions* and the different ways shown to name one half, ask whether it would be possible to list all the ways to name one half. Sample: No, because there is always another greater even number that could be used as the denominator.

(continued)

Example 1

Describe each number in a–c as a whole number, an integer, or a rational number. Write every term that applies. Then sketch a number line and graph each number.

a. −3 b. 2 c. $\frac{3}{4}$

Solution

a. The number −3 is an **integer** and a **rational number**.

b. The number 2 is a **whole number**, an **integer**, and a **rational number**.

c. The number $\frac{3}{4}$ is a **rational number**.

We draw dots on the number line to graph the numbers. To graph $\frac{3}{4}$, we divide the distance between 0 and 1 into four equal parts and graph the point that is three fourths of the way to 1.

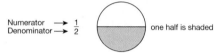

equivalent fractions

One way to express a rational number is as a fraction. Recall that a fraction has two terms, a numerator and a denominator.

Numerator → $\frac{1}{2}$ ← Denominator   one half is shaded

Many different fractions can name the same number. Here we show four different ways to name the same shaded portion of a circle.

$\frac{4}{8}$ $\frac{3}{6}$ $\frac{2}{4}$ $\frac{1}{2}$

The fractions $\frac{4}{8}$, $\frac{3}{6}$, $\frac{2}{4}$, and $\frac{1}{2}$ are **equivalent fractions.** We can find equivalent fractions on an inch ruler.

Math Language

When we *reduce* a fraction we write it in its simplest form. We can also say that we *simplify* the fraction.

The segment is $\frac{1}{2}$ in., $\frac{2}{4}$ in., $\frac{4}{8}$ in., and $\frac{8}{16}$ in. long. The last three fractions **reduce** to $\frac{1}{2}$. We reduce a fraction by removing pairs of factors that the numerator and denominator have in common. For example, we can reduce $\frac{12}{18}$ by dividing the terms of the fraction by a number that is a factor of both 12 and 18, such as 2 or 3 or 6.

$$\frac{12 \div 2}{18 \div 2} = \frac{6}{9} \qquad \frac{12 \div 3}{18 \div 3} = \frac{4}{6} \qquad \frac{12 \div 6}{18 \div 6} = \frac{2}{3}$$

Inclusion

Expand on the number line demonstration from Lesson 1 with rational numbers. Write ten numbers (whole, integer, rational) on pieces of paper. Hand them to ten students and call them one at a time to stand in order. Have the students stand at the correct distance from each other according to number value. Discuss with the class what happens to the order and distance of the students when each one is called up. Also discuss how this demonstration is different from that in Lesson 1.

The last result, $\frac{2}{3}$, cannot be reduced further, so we say that it is in its "simplest form." If we begin by dividing the terms by 2 or 3, then we need to reduce twice to write the fraction in its simplest form. We only reduce once if we divide the terms by 6 because 6 is the greatest common factor of 12 and 18. The **greatest common factor** of a set of numbers is the largest whole number that is a factor of every number in the set.

In this lesson we will practice reducing fractions by first writing the prime factorization of the terms of the fraction. Then we remove pairs of like terms from the numerator and denominator and simplify.

$$\frac{4}{8} = \frac{\overset{1}{\cancel{2}} \cdot \overset{1}{\cancel{2}}}{\underset{1}{\cancel{2}} \cdot \underset{1}{\cancel{2}} \cdot 2} = \frac{1}{2} \qquad \frac{3}{6} = \frac{\overset{1}{\cancel{3}}}{2 \cdot \underset{1}{\cancel{3}}} = \frac{1}{2} \qquad \frac{2}{4} = \frac{\overset{1}{\cancel{2}}}{\underset{1}{\cancel{2}} \cdot 2} = \frac{1}{2}$$

Example 2

Using prime factorization, reduce $\frac{72}{108}$.

Solution

We write the prime factorization of the numerator and denominator.

$$\frac{72}{108} = \frac{2 \cdot 2 \cdot 2 \cdot 3 \cdot 3}{2 \cdot 2 \cdot 3 \cdot 3 \cdot 3}$$

Each identical pair of factors from the numerator and denominator reduces to 1 over 1.

$$\frac{\overset{1}{\cancel{2}} \cdot \overset{1}{\cancel{2}} \cdot 2 \cdot \overset{1}{\cancel{3}} \cdot \overset{1}{\cancel{3}}}{\underset{1}{\cancel{2}} \cdot \underset{1}{\cancel{2}} \cdot 3 \cdot \underset{1}{\cancel{3}} \cdot \underset{1}{\cancel{3}}} = \frac{2}{3}$$

We can form equivalent fractions by multiplying a fraction by a fraction equal to 1. Here we illustrate some fractions equal to 1.

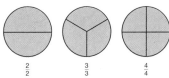

$$\frac{2}{2} \qquad \frac{3}{3} \qquad \frac{4}{4}$$

Notice that a fraction equals 1 if the numerator and denominator are equal. Multiplying by a fraction equal to 1 does not change the size of the fraction, but it changes the name of the fraction.

$$\frac{1}{2} \cdot \frac{2}{2} = \frac{2}{4} \qquad \frac{1}{2} \cdot \frac{3}{3} = \frac{3}{6} \qquad \frac{1}{2} \cdot \frac{4}{4} = \frac{4}{8}$$

Connect What property of multiplication are we using when we multiply by a fraction equal to 1? Identity Property of Multiplication

(continued)

2 New Concepts (Continued)

Instruction
Help students see that there can be several ways to reduce a fraction such as $\frac{12}{18}$. The term "simplest form" is sometimes called "lowest terms," meaning that the terms of the numerator and the denominator are the lowest (or the least) whole numbers they can be.

You may want to explain that some people call the process of removing pairs of common factors from the numerator and the denominator "canceling."

Example 2
Instruction
Tell students that a good method to use when reducing fractions is to remove one factor pair at a time by striking out both factors and writing small 1s above the factor in the numerator and below the factor in the denominator.

Instruction
To form *equivalent fractions,* we follow a process opposite to the process of reducing fractions—instead of removing factors, we put in factors. Help students observe that in both cases we use a fraction equivalent to 1 to change the way we name the fraction. Use the *Connect* question to show it is the Identity Property of Multiplication that allows us to form equivalent fractions.

English Learners

For the example 1 solution, explain the meaning of the word **further**. Say:

"When we say that a number cannot be reduced further, it means it cannot be reduced any more. It is in its simplest form."

Write these fractions and mixed numbers on the board and ask which can be reduced further.

$$3\frac{1}{2}, \frac{15}{2}, \frac{7}{8}, \frac{16}{24}, 4\frac{3}{6} \qquad \frac{15}{2} = 7\frac{1}{2}, \frac{16}{24} = \frac{2}{3}, 4\frac{3}{6} = 4\frac{1}{2}$$

Example 3
Instruction
Ask students to explain how to find the fraction equal to 1 that is needed when forming an equivalent fraction. Sample: You look at the denominator you are starting with to determine what you have to multiply by to get the denominator you want.

Example 4
Instruction
If necessary, review the inequality symbols ($<$ and $>$) as you start this example. Ask whether this is the only common denominator that could be used. no Guide students to see that the answer would be the same even if 30 or 45 had been used as the common denominator.

Instruction
You can extend the instruction for *improper fractions* and *mixed numbers* by asking students to tell how they are alike and different. Samples: They both name a fraction that is equal to or greater than 1. Only a mixed number has an integer part.

(continued)

 Example 3

Write a fraction equivalent to $\frac{1}{2}$ that has a denominator of 100.

Solution

We multiply $\frac{1}{2}$ by a fraction equal to 1 that changes the denominator from 2 to 100.

$$\frac{1}{2} \cdot \frac{50}{50} = \frac{50}{100}$$

Writing fractions with common denominators is one way to compare fractions.

Example 4

Compare: $\frac{2}{3} \bigcirc \frac{3}{5}$

Solution

A common denominator for the two fractions is 15.

$$\frac{2}{3} \cdot \frac{5}{5} = \frac{10}{15} \qquad \frac{3}{5} \cdot \frac{3}{3} = \frac{9}{15}$$

We see that $\frac{2}{3}$ equals $\frac{10}{15}$ and $\frac{3}{5}$ equals $\frac{9}{15}$. It is clear that $\frac{10}{15}$ is greater than $\frac{9}{15}$, therefore,

$$\frac{2}{3} > \frac{3}{5}$$

An **improper fraction** is a fraction equal to or greater than 1. These fractions are improper fractions:

$$\frac{5}{2}, \frac{4}{4}, \frac{10}{3}, \frac{12}{6}$$

The following fractions are not improper fractions.

$$\frac{2}{5}, \frac{1}{4}, \frac{3}{10}, \frac{6}{12}$$

Conclude How can we tell from observation that a fraction is improper?   The numerator is equal to or greater than the denominator.

A **mixed number** is a whole number plus a fraction, such as $2\frac{3}{4}$. Since an improper fraction is equal to or greater than 1, an improper fraction can be expressed as an integer or mixed number. The shaded circles illustrate that $\frac{5}{2}$ equals $2\frac{1}{2}$.

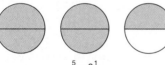

$$\frac{5}{2} = 2\frac{1}{2}$$

We see that $\frac{5}{2} = \frac{2}{2} + \frac{2}{2} + \frac{1}{2} = 2\frac{1}{2}$.

Manipulative Use

Students who may need a more concrete introduction to **equivalent fractions** may benefit from using **fraction circles** to show different ways to represent the same fraction. For example: Students can place 2 fourths, 3 sixths, and 4 eighths over 1 half or 2 sixths over 1 third to see the equivalence of the fractions.

Example 5

Express each improper fraction as a whole or mixed number.

a. $\frac{10}{3}$　　　　　　　　　b. $\frac{12}{6}$

Solution

a. The thirds form three groups of $\frac{3}{3}$ leaving $\frac{1}{3}$.

$$\frac{10}{3} = \frac{3}{3} + \frac{3}{3} + \frac{3}{3} + \frac{1}{3} = 3\frac{1}{3}$$

b. Twelve sixths form two groups of $\frac{6}{6}$.

$$\frac{12}{6} = \frac{6}{6} + \frac{6}{6} = 2$$

We can quickly convert an improper fraction to a whole or mixed number by performing the division indicated by the fraction bar and writing any remainder as a fraction.

$$\frac{10}{3} = 3\overline{)10} \begin{array}{c} 3\frac{1}{3} \\ \underline{-9} \\ 1 \end{array} \qquad \frac{12}{6} = 6\overline{)12} \begin{array}{c} 2 \end{array}$$

Practice Set ▶ **Classify** Describe each number in **a–c** as a whole number, an integer, or a rational number. Use every term that applies.

a. 5　　　　　　**b.** -2　integer, rational **c.** $-\frac{2}{5}$　rational
whole, integer, rational

▶ **Generalize** Use prime factorization to reduce each fraction in **d–f**.

d. $\frac{20}{36}$ $\frac{2 \cdot 2 \cdot 5}{2 \cdot 2 \cdot 3 \cdot 3} = \frac{5}{9}$　　　**e.** $\frac{36}{108}$ $\frac{2 \cdot 2 \cdot 3 \cdot 3}{2 \cdot 2 \cdot 3 \cdot 3 \cdot 3} = \frac{1}{3}$

f. $\frac{75}{100}$ $\frac{3 \cdot 5 \cdot 5}{2 \cdot 2 \cdot 5 \cdot 5} = \frac{3}{4}$

Complete each equivalent fraction in **g–i**. Show the multiplication.

g. $\frac{3}{5} = \frac{}{20}$ $\frac{3}{5} \cdot \frac{4}{4} = \frac{12}{20}$　　　**h.** $\frac{3}{4} = \frac{}{20}$ $\frac{3}{4} \cdot \frac{5}{5} = \frac{15}{20}$

i. $\frac{1}{4} = \frac{}{100}$ $\frac{1}{4} \cdot \frac{25}{25} = \frac{25}{100}$

j. Compare: $\frac{3}{5} \enspace \bigcirc \enspace \frac{3}{4}$

k. Sketch a number line and graph the points representing $-1, \frac{3}{4}, 0, \frac{3}{2}$, and $-\frac{1}{2}$.

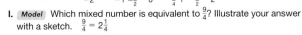

l. **Model** Which mixed number is equivalent to $\frac{9}{4}$? Illustrate your answer with a sketch. $\frac{9}{4} = 2\frac{1}{4}$

m. What property of multiplication did you use to form the equivalent fractions in **g–i**? Identity Property of Multiplication

▶ **n.** **Represent** Write an example to show that the set of whole numbers is not closed under subtraction. Sample: $3 - 5 = -2$, because 3 and 5 are whole numbers, but -2 is not a whole number.

▶ See Math Conversations in the sidebar.

Example 5
Instruction
Have students explain why $\frac{10}{3}$ and $3\frac{1}{3}$ name the same number. Sample: They are both at the same place on a number line. Then ask if anyone notices a relationship between the numerator and denominator of an improper fraction that names a whole number. Samples: The numerator is a multiple of the denominator. The denominator is a factor of the numerator.

Practice Set
Problems a–c [Error Alert]
To preclude students from simply making guesses, you might choose to ask them to explain why each number is or is not a whole number, an integer, and/or a rational number.

Problems d–f [Error Alert]
Watch for students who cancel two factors in the numerator or in the denominator of the fractions.

Remind these students that in order to cancel terms, one factor must be in the numerator and one factor must be in the denominator. At the board or overhead, write an example such as $\frac{2}{2} = 2 \div 2 = 1$ to help reinforce this concept.

Problem l [Model]
Before making a sketch, ask students to name the operation that a fraction bar represents. division

Regardless of the type of figure that is used to represent $\frac{9}{4}$ (such as a square divided into four equal parts, for example), students should infer that two or more congruent figures will be needed because the numerator of the fraction is greater than its denominator. In other words, the fraction is greater than 1.

Problem n [Represent]
To share their answers with their classmates and to promote discussion, invite volunteers to write their answers on the board or overhead.

Math Conversations

Discussion opportunities are provided below.

Problem 1 | Model

Students should infer that more than one rectangle is possible when rectangles are used to represent the factors of a composite number.

Point out that a 1-by-15 rectangle and a 15-by-1 rectangle do not count as two different rectangles because each rectangle represents the same factor pair.

Problem 2 | Represent

You might choose to invite one or more volunteers to list the answers to the following question on the board or overhead.

"Name the different factor pairs we could use as the first pair of factors in our tree."
2×45; 3×30; 5×18; 6×15; 9×10

Lead students to generalize that although any of the factor pairs can be used to start the tree, a factor pair such as 9×10 is more likely to produce a tree that has branches of nearly the same length. Such "balanced" trees are sometimes easier for students to complete. Tell students that we do not choose the factor pair 1 and 90 to begin with, because we do not use the factor 1 when creating factor trees.

Errors and Misconceptions
Problem 19

Watch for students who assume that to compare the given fractions, they must choose a common denominator and use that denominator to write two equivalent fractions.

Ask students if they can mentally compare the fractions in this exercise. Yes, because the signs of the fractions are different.

Make sure students recognize that on a number line, the fraction $-\frac{4}{3}$ is to the left of zero and the fraction $\frac{3}{4}$ is to the right of zero.

(continued)

1.

2.

4.
$$11$$
$$3\overline{)33}$$
$$5\overline{)165}$$
$$165 = 5 \cdot 3 \cdot 11$$

9.

▶ **1.** (9) **Model** Illustrate that 15 is composite by drawing two different rectangles that can be formed by 15 squares.

▶ **2.** (9) **Represent** Draw a factor tree for 90, then list the prime factors of 90. $2 \cdot 3 \cdot 3 \cdot 5$

* **3.** (9) Which of these numbers has 5 and 3 as factors?   **D**

A 621   B 425   C 333   D 165

* **4.** (9) Find the prime factors of 165 by dividing by prime numbers.

For **5–6**, use prime factorization to reduce each fraction.

* **5.** (10) $\frac{22}{165}$ $\frac{2 \cdot 11}{3 \cdot 5 \cdot 11} = \frac{2}{15}$

* **6.** (10) $\frac{35}{210}$ $\frac{5 \cdot 7}{2 \cdot 3 \cdot 5 \cdot 7} = \frac{1}{6}$

For **7–8**, complete each equivalent fraction.

* **7.** (10) $\frac{2}{3} = \frac{}{45}$ $\frac{2 \cdot 15}{3 \cdot 15} = \frac{30}{45}$

* **8.** (10) $\frac{2}{5} = \frac{}{100}$ $\frac{2 \cdot 20}{5 \cdot 20} = \frac{40}{100}$

* **9.** (10) Sketch a number line and graph the points representing $\frac{2}{3}, \frac{3}{2}$, 0, and 1.

10. (8) What are the perimeter and area of a room that is 13 feet by 10 feet? Perimeter 46 ft; Area 130 ft²

* **11.** (7) The daily high temperatures (in degrees Fahrenheit) for a week are shown below. Find the mean, median, mode, and range of the data.

84   85   88   89   82   78   82
mean 84, median 84, mode 82, range 11

* **12.** (7) Which of the four measures from problem 11 would you report as the temperature which an equal number of data points are greater or less than?   median: 84

13. (6) A two and a half hour performance is how many minutes?   150 min

14. (5) Three quarters of the 84 crayons are broken. How many crayons are broken?   63

15. (4) A total of 100 coins are arranged in 25 equal stacks. How many coins are in each stack?   4 coins

16. (3) Phil planned to send 178 invitations. If he has already sent 69, how many are left to be sent?   109

17. (3) Write a word problem for this equation: See student work.
$$5 \text{ lb} - w = 3\frac{1}{2} \text{ lb}$$

18. (4) Write a word problem for this equation: See student work.
$$\$2 \times n = \$18$$

▶ **19.** (10) Arrange the numbers from least to greatest: $0, \frac{3}{4}, -\frac{4}{3}, 1, -1$.
$-\frac{4}{3}, -1, 0, \frac{3}{4}, 1$

20. (1) Compare: $-7 \lessdot -6$

21. (1) Compare: $|-7| \gtrdot |-6|$

▶ See Math Conversations in the sidebar.

22. Compare: $-\frac{3}{4}$ $\bigcirc$ $-\frac{1}{4}$
(1, 10)

23. What is the absolute value of $-\frac{3}{4}$? $\quad \frac{3}{4}$
(1)

24. What two numbers are 7 units from 0? $\quad$ 7, -7
(1)

Explain For problems **25–27,** state whether the sentence is true sometimes, always, or never. Explain your answer.

▶* **25.** A whole number is an integer. $\quad$ always true; Integers include whole
(2) numbers.

▶* **26.** A mixed number is a whole number. $\quad$ never true; A mixed number
(2) contains a fraction less than 1, so it can never be an integer.

▶* **27.** A rational number is an integer. $\quad$ sometimes true; The rational number $\frac{4}{2}$ is
(2) an integer (equal to 2) but $\frac{1}{2}$ is not.

28. $30.00 \div 8 \quad$ $3.75 $\qquad$ **29.** $8.57 \times 63 \quad$ $539.91
(2) $\qquad\qquad\qquad\qquad\qquad$ (2)

30. The product of 17 and 6 is how much greater than the sum of 17 and 6?
(2) 79

▶ See Math Conversations in the sidebar.

Lesson 10 $\quad$ 67

Math Conversations

Discussion opportunities are provided below.

Problems 25–27 Explain

Encourage volunteers to share with their classmates an example to support or a non-example to disprove each statement.

Looking Forward

Working with rational numbers prepares students for:

• **Lesson 16,** working with irrational numbers.

• **Lesson 30,** working with repeating decimals.

• **Lesson 84,** selecting an appropriate rational number.

• **Lesson 110,** converting repeating decimals to fractions.

Finding equivalent fractions prepares students for:

• **Lesson 13,** adding and subtracting fractions and mixed numbers.

• **Lesson 17,** rounding and estimating.

• **Lesson 34,** working with proportions.

Assessment   30–40 minutes   For use after Lesson 10

Distribute **Cumulative Test 1** to each student. Two versions of the test are available in *Saxon Math Course 3 Course Assessments Book*. Have students complete the **Power-Up Test** first. Allow 10 minutes. Then have students work the 20 numbered items on the **Cumulative Test.** Students may use copies of the answer sheet to record their work. Track individual and class progress with the **Test Analysis** forms.

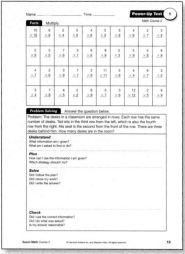

Power-Up Test 1

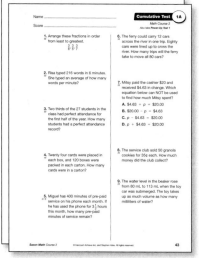

Cumulative Test 1A

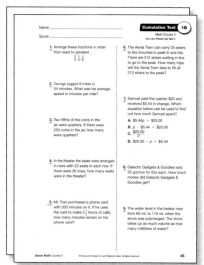

Alternative Cumulative Test 1B

Optional Answer Forms

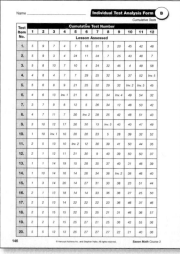

Individual Test Analysis Form

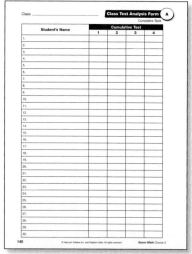

Class Test Analysis Form

Reteaching

Students who score below 80% on the assessment may be in need of reteaching. Look for the causes of student mistakes. If errors are conceptual, refer to the *Reteaching Masters* for reteaching.

Customized Benchmark Assessment

You can develop customized benchmark tests using the Test Generator located on the *Test & Practice Generator CD*.

This chart shows the lesson, the standard, and the test item question that can be found on the *Test & Practice Generator CD*.

LESSON	NEW CONCEPTS	LOCAL STANDARD	TEST ITEM ON CD
1	• Number Line: Comparing and Ordering Integers		1.1.1
2	• Operations of Arithmetic		1.2.1
3	• Addition and Subtraction Word Problems		1.3.1
4	• Multiplication and Division Word Problems		1.4.1
5	• Fractional Parts		1.5.1
6	• Converting Measures		1.6.1
7	• Rates and Average		1.7.1
7	• Measures of Central Tendency		1.7.2
8	• Perimeter and Area		1.8.1
9	• Prime Numbers		1.9.1
10	• Rational Numbers		1.10.1
10	• Equivalent Fractions		1.10.2

Using the Test Generator CD

• Develop tests in both English and Spanish.
• Choose from multiple-choice and free-response test items.
• Clone test items to create multiple versions of the same test.
• View and edit test items to make and save your own questions.
• Administer assessments through paper tests or over a school LAN.
• Monitor student progress through a variety of individual and class reports —for both diagnosing and assessing standards mastery.

Predicting Shoe Sales

Assign after Lesson 10 and Test 1

Objectives
- Interpret data from a table.
- Calculate measures of central tendency.
- Choose a measure of central tendency that best describes the data.
- Communicate their ideas through writing.

Materials
Performance Task 1A and **1B**

Preparation
Make copies of **Performance Task 1A** and **1B**. (One each per student.)

Time Requirement
25 minutes; Begin in class and complete at home.

Task
Explain to students that for this task they will be examining sales data for a shoe store. Students will be asked to make important decisions for the store owner based on past sales. They will need to calculate the mean, median, and mode of the given data and then select an appropriate measure of central tendency to predict future sales. Students must then justify why a particular measure best describes the data for each given situation. Point out that all necessary information is provided on **Performance Task 1A** and **1B**.

Criteria for Evidence of Learning
- Calculates the correct mean, median, and mode.
- Draws valid conclusions based on calculations and the given data sets.
- Chooses the best measure of central tendency to describe a data set.
- Communicates ideas clearly through writing.

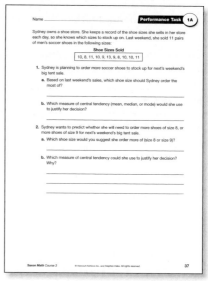

Performance Task 1A

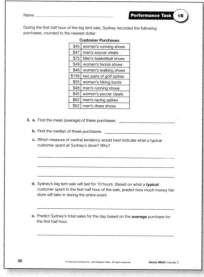

Performance Task 1B

National Council of Teachers of Mathematics (NCTM)

Algebra

AL.3a Model and solve contextualized problems using various representations, such as graphs, tables, and equations

Data Analysis and Probability

DP.2a Find, use, and interpret measures of center and spread, including mean and interquartile range

Communication

CM.3a Organize and consolidate their mathematical thinking through communication

Connections

CN.4c Recognize and apply mathematics in contexts outside of mathematics

Focus on
• The Coordinate Plane

Objectives
- Graph points a coordinate plane.
- Identify the axes, origin, and quadrants of a coordinate plane.

Lesson Preparation

Materials
- **Investigation Activity 2**
  (in *Instructional Masters*) or
  graph paper
- **Manipulative Kit: inch rulers**

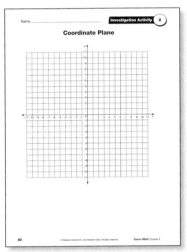

Investigation Activity 2

Math Language

New

coordinate plane	quadrant
coordinates	*x*-axis
intersect	*y*-axis

Technology Resources

Student eBook Complete student textbook in electronic format.

Resources and Planner CD Assessment, reteaching, and instructional masters, plus a pacing calendar with standards.

Test and Practice Generator CD Create additional practice sheets and custom-made tests.

www.SaxonPublishers.com Visit for more student activities and planning materials.

Inclusion

Adaptations CD Adapted lessons, investigations, practice and assessments.

Meeting Standards

National Council of Teachers of Mathematics (NCTM)

Geometry

GM.2a Use coordinate geometry to represent and examine the properties of geometric shapes

GM.2b Use coordinate geometry to examine special geometric shapes, such as regular polygons or those with pairs of parallel or perpendicular sides

GM.4c Use visual tools such as networks to represent and solve problems

Problem Solving

PS.1c Apply and adapt a variety of appropriate strategies to solve problems

The coordinate plane is also called the *Cartesian plane* after René Descartes. Explain to students that in the 1600s, Descartes showed how the solution to an algebraic equation could be found by graphing the equation on a coordinate plane. His work laid the foundation for analytic geometry, a combination of algebra and geometry.

Instruction

Explain to students that using the *x*- and *y*-coordinates to name locations on a coordinate plane is similar to the way we use longitude and latitude to name locations on a map.

You may need to remind students that *clockwise* means moving in the direction of the hands of a clock. The word *counterclockwise* means moving in the opposite direction of the hands of a clock.

Point out that each coordinate supplies us with two different pieces of information: distance and direction. The value of the number tells us the horizontal or vertical distance the point is from the origin. The sign of the number tells us the direction.

(continued)

Focus on
● The Coordinate Plane

Two perpendicular number lines form a **coordinate plane.** The horizontal number line is called the *x*-**axis.** The vertical number line is called the *y*-**axis.** The point at which the *x*-axis and the *y*-axis **intersect** (cross) is called the **origin.**

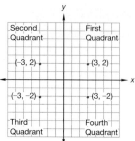

Thinking Skill

Infer

What are the signs of the *x*- and *y*-coordinates of points in each quadrant?
first quadrant: positive, positive;
second quadrant: negative, positive;
third quadrant: negative, negative;
fourth quadrant: positive, negative

We can identify any point on the coordinate plane with two numbers called **coordinates** of the point. The coordinates are written as a pair of numbers in parentheses, such as (3, 2). The first number shows the horizontal (↔) direction and distance from the origin. The second number shows the vertical (↕) direction and distance from the origin. The sign of the number indicates the direction. Positive coordinates are to the right or up. Negative coordinates are to the left or down. The origin is at point (0, 0).

The two axes divide the plane into four regions called **quadrants,** which are numbered counterclockwise beginning with the upper right as first, second, third, and fourth.

Example 1

Math Language

A **vertex** (plural: vertices) of a polygon is a point where two sides meet.

Find the coordinates of the vertices of △ABC on this coordinate plane. Then count squares and half squares on the grid to find the area of the triangle in square units.

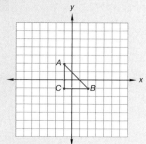

Math Background

Why is a pair of coordinates representing one point called an ordered pair?

A set of coordinate points must be written in the correct order, (*x, y*). They give us the information we need to plot a particular point on a coordinate plane. The first number in the ordered pair identifies the position as it relates to the *x*-axis, while the second number identifies the position as it relates to the *y*-axis.

We first find the point on the x-axis that is directly above, below, or on the designated point. That number is the first coordinate. Then we determine how many units above or below the x-axis the point is. That number is the second coordinate.

Point A (−1, 2)

Point B (2, −1)

Point C (−1, −1)

There are 3 full squares and 3 half squares within the triangle, so the area of the triangle is $4\frac{1}{2}$ **square units.**

We can visually represent or graph pairs of related numbers on a coordinate plane. Suppose Kim is a year older than Ivan. We can let x represent Ivan's age and y represent Kim's age. Then we can record pairs of ages for Kim and Ivan in a table and graph the pairs on a coordinate plane.

x	y
1	2
2	3
3	4
4	5

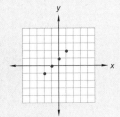

Each point represents two numbers, Kim's age and Ivan's age.

Visit www. SaxonPublishers. com/ActivitiesC3 *for a graphing calculator activity.*

Graph the pairs of numbers from this table on a coordinate plane.

x	y
−2	−1
−1	0
0	1
1	2

Example 1
Instruction
Some students may remember the formula for the area of a triangle.

"How could you compute the area of the triangle?"
Sample: Use the formula $A = \frac{1}{2}bh$; $b = 3$; $h = 3$; $A = \frac{1}{2}(3 \cdot 3) = 4.5$ units^2

Instruction
Point out that each point represents both Kim's age and Ivan's age. We can see that there is a constant relationship between their ages. Each time Kim's age increases by one, Ivan's age increases by one.

Example 2
Instruction
Discuss the relationship between x and y. Each time x increases by 1, y increases by 1. Some students may be able to generalize this to $y = x + 1$.

(continued)

Activity

Math Conversations

Discussion opportunities are provided below.

Problem 1 [Explain]

"If you connected the points on this graph, would you form a parallelogram? Why or why not?" no; both pairs of opposite sides are not parallel

Math Conversations

Discussion opportunities are provided below.

Problem 5 [Model]

Ask a volunteer to draw a table of value pairs on the board to represent the line in the problem. First, have the student write the points on the x-axis in a column in consecutive order. Then have the student complete the table.

x	y
4	2
3	1
2	0
1	−1
0	−2
−1	−3
−2	−4

Some students may be able to generalize the equation $y = x - 2$.

Problem 7 [Connect]

Extend the Problem

"How can you use subtraction to find the perimeter of the rectangle?"
subtract the x-coordinates $3 - (-2) = 5$;
subtract the y-coordinates $4 - (-2) = 6$;
$5 + 5 + 6 + 6 = 22$

(continued)

1.

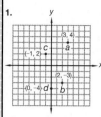

2. See student work. Sample:
a. I counted three units to the right of the origin, and then four units up from the x-axis
b. I counted two units to the right of the origin, and then three units down from the x-axis.
c. I counted left of the origin one unit, and up two units from the x-axis.
d. I counted four units down from the origin along the y-axis (x = 0).

3.

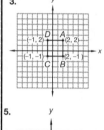

5.

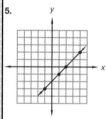

Activity

Coordinate Plane

Materials needed:

- Graph paper or copies of Lesson Activity 1
- Ruler

We suggest students work in pairs or in small groups. If using graph paper, begin by darkening two perpendicular lines on the graph paper to represent the x-axis and y-axis. For this activity we will let the distance between adjacent lines on the graph paper represent one unit. Label the tick marks on each axis from −5 to 5.

1. Graph and label the following points on a coordinate plane:

   a. (3, 4)   **b.** (2, −3)   **c.** (−1, 2)   **d.** (0, −4)

▶ **2.** [Explain] Explain how you located each point in problem 1.

3. The vertices of rectangle *ABCD* are located at *A*(2, 2), *B*(2, −1), *C*(−1, −1), and *D*(−1, 2). Draw the square and find its perimeter and area.   The perimeter is 12 units, and the area is 9 square units.

4. Which vertex of rectangle *ABCD* in problem 3 is located in the third quadrant?   *C*

▶ **5.** [Model] Graph these three points: (4, 2), (2, 0), and (−1, −3). Then draw a line that passes through these points. Name a point in the fourth quadrant that is also on the line.   Sample: (1, −1); See student work.

6. One vertex of a square is the origin. Two other vertices are located at (−3, 0) and (0, −3). What are the coordinates of the fourth vertex? (−3, −3)

▶ **7.** [Connect] Find the perimeter and area of a rectangle whose vertices are located at (3, −2), (−2, −2), (−2, 4), and (3, 4).   22 units, 30 sq. units

8. Points (4, 4), (4, 0), and (0, 0) are the vertices of a triangle. Find the area of the triangle by counting the whole squares and the half squares. 8 sq. units

9. The point (−3, 2) lies in which quadrant?   second

70   *Saxon Math Course 3*

▶ See Math Conversations in the sidebar.

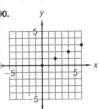

0.

10. A pint is half of a quart. Letting x represent the number of pints and y the number of quarts, we can make a table of x, y pairs. Graph the pairs from this table on a coordinate plane.

x	y
0	0
2	1
4	2
6	3

▶ **11.** *Represent* On a coordinate plane, graph these points and draw segments from point to point in the order given.

1. $(0, 4)$ **2.** $(-3, -4)$

3. $(5, 1)$ **4.** $(-5, 1)$

5. $(3, -4)$ **6.** $(0, 4)$

12. *Model* Plan and create a straight-segment drawing on graph paper. Determine the coordinates of the vertices. Then write directions for completing the dot-to-dot drawing for other classmates to follow. Include the directions "lift pencil" between consecutive coordinates of points not to be connected.   See student work.

11.

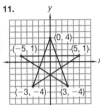

▶ See Math Conversations in the sidebar.

Looking Forward

Investigating the coordinate plane prepares students for:

- **Lesson 47,** graphing functions.
- **Investigation 5,** graphing transformations.
- **Lesson 56,** understanding the slope-intercept equation of a line.
- **Lesson 82,** graphing equations using intercepts.
- **Lesson 89,** solving problems with two unknowns by graphing.

Lesson Planner

LESSON	NEW CONCEPTS	MATERIALS	RESOURCES
11	• Percents	none	Power Up C
12	• Decimal Numbers	Newspapers and magazines, grid paper	Power Up C
13	• Adding and Subtracting Fractions and Mixed Numbers	Manipulative Kit: fraction circles	Power Up C
14	• Evaluation • Solving Equations by Inspection	none	Power Up C
15	• Powers and Roots	none	Power Up C
16	• Irrational Numbers	Calculators, 10 pieces of paper	Power Up D
17	• Rounding and Estimating	Newspapers or news magazines, tape measure, calculators	Power Up D Investigation Activity 2
18	• Lines and Angles	Manipulative Kit: protractors, calculators	Power Up D
19	• Polygons	Newspapers or magazines	Power Up D
20	• Triangles	White index cards, 3 other color index cards, grid paper	Power Up D
Inv. 2	• Pythagorean Theorem	Scissors, envelopes or locking plastic bags	Investigation Activity 3

Problem Solving

Strategies

- **Act It Out**   Lesson 11
- **Find a Pattern**   Lessons 16, 18, 19, 20
- **Make a Table**   Lessons 17, 18
- **Make It Simpler**   Lessons 13, 19
- **Use Logical Reasoning**   Lessons 12, 15, 17
- **Work Backwards**   Lesson 14
- **Write an Equation**   Lesson 19

Real-World Applications

pp. 75, 76, 82–84, 89–92, 94–97, 100,
101, 105–108, 110–113, 117, 118,
124, 125, 127, 129–130, 138

4-Step Process

Student Edition   Lessons 11, 14, 15, 19

Teacher Edition   Lessons 11–20
(Power-Up Discussions)

Communication

Discuss

pp. 78, 87, 94, 110, 122

Explain

pp. 76, 93, 98, 104, 105, 112

Connections

Math and Other Subjects

- **Math and Geography**   p. 111
- **Math and History**   pp. 95, 106
- **Math and Science**   pp. 107, 119
- **Math and Sports**   pp. 106, 124

Math to Math

- **Problem Solving and Measurement**
Lessons 11–19
- **Algebra and Problem Solving**   Lessons 11, 12, 14–17, 19, Inv. 2
- **Fractions, Percents, Decimals, and Problem Solving**   Lessons 11–20
- **Fractions and Measurement**   Lessons 13–15, 17, 20
- **Measurement and Geometry**   Lessons 11–20, Inv. 2
- **Algebra, Measurement, and Geometry**   Inv. 2

Representation

Manipulatives/Hands On

pp. 80, 84, 88, 103, 104

Represent

pp. 84, 91, 106, 112, 123

Technology

Student Resources

- **eBook**   Anytime
- **Calculator**   Lessons 16, 17, 18
- **Online Resources** at
www.SaxonPublishers.com/ActivitiesC3
Graphing Calculator Activities   Lessons 13, 15
Real-Word Investigation 1   after Lesson 19

Teacher Resources

- **Resources and Planner CD**
- **Adaptations CD**   Lessons 11–20
- **Test & Practice Generator CD**
- **eGradebook**
- **Answer Key CD**

In this section, students are working with fractions, decimals, and percents. They solve equations and evaluate expressions. The section closes with two-dimensional figures and the Pythagorean Theorem.

Equivalence

Students learn to represent numbers in a variety of forms.

Rational numbers can be expressed in various ways. In Lesson 11 students express fractional parts as percents, and in Lesson 12 students begin work with the decimal form of rational numbers. Students add and subtract fractions and mixed number in Lesson 13.

Estimation

The ability to estimate is applicable across a broad spectrum of mathematics.

Rounding numbers and estimation is a valuable consumer skill. Lesson 17 begins instruction on rounding and estimating.

Algebraic Thinking

Solving equations and evaluating expressions are fundamental skills in algebra.

In Lesson 14 students learn to evaluate expressions and to solve equations by inspection. Students must be comfortable with the exponential expressions to succeed in algebra. In Lesson 15 student begin work with powers and roots, which leads to an introduction to irrational numbers in Lesson 16.

Spatial Thinking

Analyzing two-dimensional figures is the focus of these lessons.

Geometric terminology relating to lines and angles is taught in Lesson 18 where students also measure angles. Students classify polygons in Lesson 19 and they classify triangles in Lesson 20. Students also calculate the perimeters and areas of triangles. Investigation 2 provides students with a full class period of experience with the widely applicable Pythagorean Theorem.

Assessment

A variety of weekly assessment tools are provided.

After Lesson 15:
- Power-Up Test 2
- Cumulative Test 2
- Performance Activity 2

After Lesson 20:
- Power-Up Test 3
- Cumulative Test 3
- Customized Benchmark Test
- Performance Task 3

LESSON	NEW CONCEPTS	PRACTICED	ASSESSED
11	• Percents	Lessons 12, 15, 16, 17, 18, 19, 28, 29, 30, 32, 33, 34, 38, 41, 43, 44, 45, 48, 50, 56, 72, 77, 92	Tests 3, 4, 6
12	• Decimal Numbers	Lessons 12, 14, 18, 19, 22, 24, 25, 26, 28, 29, 30, 32, 33, 35, 36, 37, 38, 39, 41, 43, 45, 46, 47, 48, 49, 50, 51, 52, 53, 54, 56, 58, 59, 61, 62, 92, 93, 96	Tests 3, 5, 6, 9
13	• Adding and Subtracting Fractions and Mixed Numbers	Lessons 13, 14, 15, 16, 17, 18, 19, 20, 21, 23, 24, 25, 26, 27, 28, 29, 30, 31, 32, 34, 35, 36, 37, 38, 39, 40, 41, 42, 43, 44, 46, 47, 48, 49, 50, 51, 52, 56, 58, 59, 62, 63, 71, 72, 106	Tests 3, 4, 7
14	• Evaluation	Lessons 14, 15, 16, 17, 18, 19, 20, 21, 22, 23, 25, 26, 28, 29, 30, 31, 32, 34, 35, 36, 37, 38, 39, 40, 41, 42, 43, 44, 45, 46, 47, 49, 50, 51, 52, 53, 59, 63, 77, 89, 106	Tests 3, 5
14	• Solving Equations by Inspection	Lessons 14, 15, 16, 17, 18, 20, 21, 22, 23, 24, 25, 26, 27, 28, 29, 30, 33, 44, 57, 77	Tests 3–6
15	• Powers and Roots	Lessons 15, 16, 17, 18, 19, 20, 21, 22, 23, 24, 25, 26, 27, 28, 29, 30, 31, 32, 33, 34, 35, 37, 38, 39, 40, 41, 42, 43, 45, 47, 48, 49, 50, 57, 64, 65, 66, 67, 74, 105	Tests 3–5, 13, 15
16	• Irrational Numbers	Lessons 16, 17, 18, 20, 21, 32, 49, 73, 78, 92, 93, 97, 110	Test 4
17	• Rounding and Estimating	Lessons 17, 18, 19, 21, 22, 24, 26, 27, 28, 29, 30, 32, 35, 36, 39, 73, 87	Test 4
18	• Lines and Angles	Lessons 18, 20, 22, 24, 25, 27, 28, 29, 32, 36, 37, 38, 39, 40, 41, 42, 43, 49, 56	Tests 4, 6
19	• Polygons	Lessons 22, 24, 27, 33, 34, 36, 38, 40, 116	Test 4
20	• Triangles	Lessons 20, 21, 22, 23, 24, 25, 26, 27, 28, 29, 30, 31, 32, 33, 35, 36, 37, 38, 39, 40, 45, 48, 49, 53, 56, 60, 67, 82, 84, 88, 91, 92, 94, 95, 97, 98, 99, 101, 110, 112, 115	Tests 4–6, 9, 13
Inv. 2	• Pythagorean Theorem	Lessons 21, 23, 25, 26, 27, 28, 29, 30, 32, 33, 35, 39, 40, 41, 46, 47, 48, 51, 52, 54, 60, 61, 62, 63, 65, 67, 68, 72, 75, 76, 80, 81, 82, 83, 84, 85, 86, 87, 88, 89, 90, 91, 92, 94, 95, 97, 99, 100, 103, 104, 107, 108, 110, 111, 112, 115	Tests 5, 6, 9, 10, 13, 15–17

• Percents

Objectives

- Understand that a percent sign is a way to indicate a fraction with a denominator of 100.
- Write percents as reduced fractions and write fractions as percents.
- Find a percent of a group by finding an equivalent fractional part of the group.

Lesson Preparation

Materials

- **Power Up C** (in *Instructional Masters*)

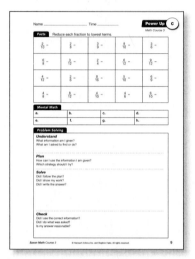

Power Up C

Math Language

Maintain	English Learners (ESL)
denominator	converted
percent	
reduce	

Technology Resources

Student eBook Complete student textbook in electronic format.

Resources and Planner CD Assessment, reteaching, and instructional masters, plus a pacing calendar with standards.

Test and Practice Generator CD Create additional practice sheets and custom-made tests.

www.SaxonPublishers.com Visit for more student activities and planning materials.

Inclusion

Adaptations CD Adapted lessons, investigations, practice and assessments.

Meeting Standards

National Council of Teachers of Mathematics (NCTM)

Numbers and Operations

NO.1a Work flexibly with fractions, decimals, and percents to solve problems

NO.1b Compare and order fractions, decimals, and percents efficiently and find their approximate locations on a number line

NO.3a Select appropriate methods and tools for computing with fractions and decimals from among mental computation, estimation, calculators or computers, and paper and pencil, depending on the situation, and apply the selected methods

Problem Solving

PS.1b Solve problems that arise in mathematics and in other contexts

Connections

CN.4a Recognize and use connections among mathematical ideas

Problem-Solving Strategy: Act it Out

Six friends have organized themselves by age. Molly is older than Jenna, but younger than Brett. Brett is younger than Cynthia, but older than Jenna. Jenna is older than Tina and Marcus. Marcus is younger than Cynthia and Tina. Who is the oldest and who is the youngest?

(Understand) Six friends are organized by age, and we are asked to determine which friend is the oldest and which is the youngest.
1. Molly is older than Jenna, but younger than Brett.
2. Brett is younger than Cynthia, but older than Jenna.
3. Jenna is older than Tina and Marcus.
4. Marcus is younger than Cynthia and Tina.

(Plan) We will act it out, arranging the actors from oldest to youngest, from left to right.

Teacher's Note: It may help to write "oldest" on the left side of the chalkboard and "youngest" on the right, then position the students between the labels in the proper order.

(Solve) *Step 1:* We position Molly between Brett and Jenna. Brett is the oldest, so we position him on the left. Jenna is the youngest, so we position her on the right.

Step 2: Brett is in position as older than Jenna. We position Cynthia to his left.

Step 3: Marcus and Tina are younger than Jenna, so we will position them both to her right until step 4 clarifies which one of them is the youngest.

Step 4: Cynthia is already in the postion of oldest. Marcus is younger than Tina, so he is the youngest, and will be in the right-most position.

(Check) Cynthia is the oldest, and Marcus is the youngest. We can verify the solution by rereading the given statements while our actors remain in position.

1 Power Up

Facts
Distribute **Power Up C** to students. See answers below.

Mental Math
Encourage students to share different ways to mentally compute these exercises. Strategies for exercises **d** and **f** are listed below.

d. Use Number Sense
The digits of multiples of 9 sum to 9, so the missing digit in the product is 5. Then the other missing digit has to be 6, because $9 \times 6 = 54$.

Guess and Check
The multiplier has to be an even number.
Try 8: $9 \times 8 = 72$ → no
Try 4: $9 \times 4 = 36$ → no
Try 6: $9 \times 6 = 54$ → yes

f. Change Feet to Inches
$6 \text{ ft} \times \frac{12 \text{ in.}}{\text{ft}} = 72$ in.
$72 \text{ in.} + 7\frac{1}{2} \text{ in.} = 79\frac{1}{2}$ in.

Change Feet to Yards First
6 ft = 2 yd
$2 \text{ yd} \times \frac{36 \text{ in.}}{\text{yd}} = 72$ in.
$72 \text{ in.} + 7\frac{1}{2} \text{ in.} = 79\frac{1}{2}$ in.

Problem Solving
Refer to **Power-Up Discussion,** p. 72F.

• Percents

Power Up *Building Power*

facts Power Up C

mental math

a. Calculation: The rocket traveled 2000 feet per second. How many feet per minute did the rocket travel? 120,000

b. Estimation: 11×29 $11 \times 30 = 330$

c. Geometry: What is the measure of $\angle QSR$? 100°

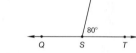

d. Number Sense: $123 + 77$ 200

e. Algebra: What are the missing digits?
$9 \times \square = \square 4$ $9 \times \boxed{6} = \boxed{5}4$

f. Measurement: The door was 6 ft $7\frac{1}{2}$ inches high. How many inches is that? $79\frac{1}{2}$ inches

g. Percent: 100% of 351   351

h. Calculation: 7×8, $+ 4$, $\div 2$, $+ 6$, $\sqrt{\ }$, $+ 4$, square that number   100

problem solving

Six friends have organized themselves by age. Molly is older than Jenna, but younger than Brett. Brett is younger than Cynthia, but older than Jenna. Jenna is older than Tina and Marcus. Marcus is younger than Cynthia and Tina. Who is the oldest and who is the youngest?

Understand Six friends are organized by age, and we are asked to determine which friend is the oldest and which is the youngest.

1. Molly is older than Jenna, but younger than Brett.

2. Brett is younger than Cynthia, but older than Jenna.

3. Jenna is older than Tina and Marcus.

4. Marcus is younger than Cynthia and Tina.

Plan We will act it out, arranging the actors from oldest to youngest, from left to right.

Solve

Step 1: We position Molly between Brett and Jenna. Brett is the oldest, so we position him on the left. Jenna is the youngest, so we position her on the right.

Step 2: Brett is in position as older than Jenna. We position Cynthia to his left.

Step 3: Marcus and Tina are younger than Jenna, so we will position them both to her right until step 4 clarifies which one of them is the youngest.

Step 4: Cynthia is already in the postion of oldest. Marcus is younger than Tina, so he is the youngest, and will be in the right-most position.

Facts Reduce each fraction to lowest terms.

$\frac{2}{10} = \frac{1}{5}$	$\frac{2}{8} = \frac{1}{4}$	$\frac{3}{9} = \frac{1}{3}$	$\frac{8}{10} = \frac{4}{5}$	$\frac{3}{6} = \frac{1}{2}$
$\frac{6}{8} = \frac{3}{4}$	$\frac{3}{12} = \frac{1}{4}$	$\frac{2}{4} = \frac{1}{2}$	$\frac{6}{12} = \frac{1}{2}$	$\frac{9}{12} = \frac{3}{4}$
$\frac{4}{12} = \frac{1}{3}$	$\frac{2}{6} = \frac{1}{3}$	$\frac{8}{16} = \frac{1}{2}$	$\frac{5}{10} = \frac{1}{2}$	$\frac{6}{9} = \frac{2}{3}$
$\frac{4}{8} = \frac{1}{2}$	$\frac{8}{12} = \frac{2}{3}$	$\frac{4}{10} = \frac{2}{5}$	$\frac{4}{6} = \frac{2}{3}$	$\frac{6}{10} = \frac{3}{5}$

New Concept — *Increasing Knowledge*

In Lesson 10 we compared fractions with common denominators by rewriting them. One way to express rational numbers with common denominators is as percents. The word percent means *per hundred*. The denominator 100 is indicated by the word *percent* or by the symbol %. One hundred percent equals one whole.

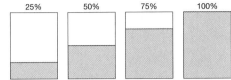

Thus, 50% means $\frac{50}{100}$, which reduces to $\frac{1}{2}$, and 5% means $\frac{5}{100}$, which equals $\frac{1}{20}$.

Example 1

Write each percent as a reduced fraction.

a. 1%   b. 10%   c. 100%

Solution

We write each percent as a fraction with a denominator of 100. Then we reduce if possible.

a. $1\% = \frac{1}{100}$ b. $10\% = \frac{10}{100} = \frac{1}{10}$ c. $100\% = \frac{100}{100} = 1$

One way to write a fraction as a percent is to find an equivalent fraction with a denominator of 100.

$$\frac{1}{4} = \frac{25}{100} = 25\%$$

Example 2

Write each fraction as a percent.

a. $\frac{3}{4}$ b. $\frac{3}{5}$ c. $\frac{3}{10}$

Solution

We write each fraction with a denominator of 100.

a. $\frac{3}{4} \cdot \frac{25}{25} = \frac{75}{100} = 75\%$

b. $\frac{3}{5} \cdot \frac{20}{20} = \frac{60}{100} = 60\%$

c. $\frac{3}{10} \cdot \frac{10}{10} = \frac{30}{100} = 30\%$

Lesson 11   73

---

② New Concepts

Instruction

Write the word "percent" and the % symbol on the board or overhead. Ask students where they have seen the word or symbol. Responses may include:

- advertisements for sales telling what amount will be saved.
- labels for juice drinks telling how much real juice is in the product.
- clothing tags telling how much of each kind of fiber is in the fabric.

Example 1
Instruction

Discuss why each percent is rewritten as a fraction with 100 as the denominator. Emphasize that a percent symbol is one way of indicating a fraction that has 100 as its denominator.

Example 2
Instruction

Point out that knowing all the factor pairs of 100 is helpful when writing fractions as percents. Ask a volunteer to describe how to find an appropriate fraction equal to 1 if you do not remember the factor pairs of 100. Sample: Divide 100 by the denominator of the fraction you are rewriting. The quotient will be the numerator and denominator of the fraction equal to 1.

(continued)

Math Background

Some fraction-percent equivalents are quite common. These include the following, which students should be able to recall instantly.

$\frac{1}{2} = 50\%$ $\frac{1}{3} = 33\frac{1}{3}\%$ $\frac{1}{4} = 25\%$ $\frac{3}{4} = 75\%$

$\frac{1}{5} = 20\%$ $\frac{2}{5} = 40\%$ $\frac{3}{5} = 60\%$ $\frac{4}{5} = 80\%$

$\frac{1}{10} = 10\%$ $\frac{3}{10} = 30\%$ $\frac{7}{10} = 70\%$ $\frac{9}{10} = 90\%$

Example 3

Instruction

Call attention to the percents that include a fraction, such as $33\frac{1}{3}\%$. You may want to tell students that any fraction, even an improper fraction, can be written as a percent.

Example 4

Instruction

Caution students that it can be easy to make mistakes when rewriting fractions and percents if each step is not carefully written, especially when there are several zeros involved in the computation.

Call attention to part c and guide students through the process of changing the mixed number to a fraction before removing the percent symbol.

(continued)

Another way to convert a fraction to a percent is to multiply the fraction by 100%. This method applies the Identity Property of Multiplication since 100% is equal to 1. For example, to convert $\frac{2}{3}$ to a percent we can multiply $\frac{2}{3}$ by 100% (or $\frac{100\%}{1}$).

$$\frac{2}{3} \cdot \frac{100\%}{1} = \frac{200\%}{3}$$

We complete the process by dividing 200% by 3 and writing any remainder as a fraction.

$$\frac{200\%}{3} = 66\frac{2}{3}\%$$

Example 3

Write each fraction as a percent.

a. $\frac{1}{3}$ b. $\frac{5}{6}$ c. $\frac{3}{8}$

Solution

Since the denominators 3, 6, and 8 are not factors of 100, we cannot easily find an equivalent fraction with a denominator of 100. Instead we multiply each fraction by 100%. We express remainders as reduced fractions.

a. $\frac{1}{3} \cdot \frac{100\%}{1} = \frac{100\%}{3} = 33\frac{1}{3}\%$

b. $\frac{5}{6} \cdot \frac{100\%}{1} = \frac{500\%}{6} = 83\frac{1}{3}\%$

c. $\frac{3}{8} \cdot \frac{100\%}{1} = \frac{300\%}{8} = 37\frac{1}{2}\%$

To write a percent as a fraction we replace the percent sign with a denominator of 100 and reduce if possible. If the percent is a mixed number, we rewrite it as an improper fraction before multiplying the denominator by 100 to remove the percent symbol.

Example 4

Write each percent as a reduced fraction.

a. 4%   b. 40%   c. $33\frac{1}{3}\%$

Solution

a. $4\% = \frac{4}{100} = \frac{1}{25}$

b. $40\% = \frac{40}{100} = \frac{2}{5}$

c. $33\frac{1}{3}\% = \frac{100}{3}\% = \frac{100}{300} = \frac{1}{3}$

Notice in **c** that we converted the mixed number $33\frac{1}{3}$ to $\frac{100}{3}$. The denominator is 3. To remove the percent sign, we multiplied the denominator by 100, making the denominator 300.

English Learners

For the solution to example 1 explain the meaning of the word **converted**. Say:

"If the 4 feet is converted to inches, we write the measure in inches."

Write on the board 4 ft × 12 in. per ft = 48 in. and say:

"I converted 4 feet to 48 inches."

Ask volunteers to convert these measures: 5 ft to in., 12 m to cm. 60 in., 1200 cm Stress the use of the word "converted."

Fractional part problems are often expressed as percents.

Forty percent of the 30 students rode the bus.

To perform calculations with percents we first convert the percent to a fraction or decimal. In this lesson we will convert percents to fractions. In the next lesson we will convert percents to decimals.

Example 5

Forty percent of the 30 students rode the bus. How many of the students rode the bus?

Solution

Thinking Skill

Connect

If 100% represents all of the students, what percent of the students did *not* ride the bus?   60%

We convert 40% to a fraction and find the equivalent fractional part of 30.

$$40\% = \frac{40}{100} = \frac{2}{5}$$

$$\frac{2}{5} \text{ of } 30 = 12$$

Twelve of the students rode the bus.

Example 6

A quart is what percent of a gallon?

Solution

Since four quarts equal a gallon, a quart is $\frac{1}{4}$ of a gallon. We convert $\frac{1}{4}$ to a percent to answer the question.

$$\frac{1}{4} = \frac{25}{100} = 25\%$$

A quart is 25% of a gallon.

Practice Set

Write each fraction as a percent.

a. $\frac{4}{5}$ 80%   **b.** $\frac{7}{10}$ 70%   **c.** $\frac{1}{6}$ $16\frac{2}{3}\%$

Write each percent as a reduced fraction.

d. 5% $\frac{1}{20}$ **e.** 50% $\frac{1}{2}$ **f.** $12\frac{1}{2}\%$ $\frac{1}{8}$

Arrange these numbers in order from least to greatest.

g. 75%, 35%, 3%, 100%   ▶ **h.** $\frac{1}{2}$, $33\frac{1}{3}\%$, $\frac{1}{10}$, 65% $\frac{1}{10}$, $33\frac{1}{3}\%$, $\frac{1}{2}$, 65%
3%, 35%, 75%, 100%

Solve.

i. Three of the five basketball players scored more than 10 points. What percent of the players scored more than 10 points?   60%

▶ **j.** Janice scored 30% of the team's 50 points. How many points did Janice score?   15 points

▶ See Math Conversations in the sidebar.

Example 5
Instruction
You may want to discuss or demonstrate that the answer will be the same even if the fraction for the percent is not completely reduced at first. Point out that completely reducing the fraction first makes calculating the fractional part easier.

Example 6
Instruction
Ask why $\frac{1}{4}$ is first changed to an equivalent fraction with a denominator of 100 to find the percent. Sample: Because percent means per hundred.

Practice Set
Problem h
Students may assume that the fractions and the percents cannot be compared until the fractions are changed to percents or the percents are changed to fractions.

Students should continue to use mental math strategies to determine relative sizes of rational numbers. Most of the ordering of these numbers can be done by comparing the numbers to $\frac{1}{2}$ (50%).

Problem j
Asking students to write an equation to represent the problem can help them decide that multiplication is used to find 30% of 50.

A way for students to check their work is to decide that since 30% is less than $\frac{1}{2}$, the correct answer is less than $\frac{1}{2}$ of 50.

Teacher Tip

Some teachers who have used this program present the instruction and examples to the class with all student books closed. Then students open their books and quickly review the material before beginning the practice set and written practice. You may want to use this approach for some of your lessons.

Math Conversations

Discussion opportunities are provided below.

Problem 2 Analyze

Extend the Problem

"How many cubic feet of sand were delivered? Explain your answer." 108 ft^3; Sample: One cubic yard measures 3 ft by 3 ft by 3 ft, or 27 cubic feet, and 27 × 4 = 108.

Problem 3 Explain

Extend the Problem

"Suppose a gardener decreased the height of one bush by 20 cm. Using only mental math, name the new average height of the five bushes, and explain how you found the answer." 97 cm; Sample: Since the sum of the five heights is 20 fewer cm, the average height will decrease by 20 cm ÷ 5, or 4 cm: 101 cm − 4 cm = 97 cm

Problem 5 Generalize

Help students recall the divisibility rules that are typically used to help name prime factors.

- A number is divisible by 2 if the digit in the ones place of the number is even.
- A number is divisible by 3 if the sum of the digits in the number is divisible by 3.
- A number is divisible by 5 if the digit in the ones place of the number is 0 or 5.

Problem 10 Conclude

"One operation can be used to find both the perimeter and the area of the classroom. Name the operation and explain how it is used." multiplication; Sample: We find the product of 25 × 4 and the product of 25 × 25.

Errors and Misconceptions

Problem 5

Students should recognize that $\frac{2}{2}$, $\frac{2}{2}$, and $\frac{3}{3}$ represent the factor pairs that can be canceled. The factor pairs can be canceled because each pair is equivalent to 1, and the product of 1 and any number is that number.

Use the prime factorization of the numerator and the denominator to demonstrate that if only some of the factor pairs (in this case, one or two) are canceled, the product of the remaining factors will not be in lowest terms.

(continued)

---

1. There are 1000 envelopes in unopened boxes in the office closet. If
(4) one box holds 250 envelopes, how many boxes of envelopes are in the office closet?   4 boxes

▶ *** 2.** **Analyze**   A dump truck delivered four cubic yards of sand for the
(4, 6) playground. The sand weighed five tons and 800 pounds. How many pounds of sand were delivered?   10,800 pounds

▶ **3.** The heights of the rose bushes in the garden are 98 cm, 97 cm, 100 cm,
(7) 109 cm, and 101 cm. What is the average height of the rose bushes in the garden?   101 cm

4. Identify the plot, write an equation, and solve the problem: Tucker
(3) purchased comic books. He paid with a $10 bill and received $3.25 in change. What was the cost of the comic books?   separating; $10.00 − a = $3.25; $6.75

▶ *** 5.** **Generalize**   Using prime factorization, reduce $\frac{60}{72}$. Show your work.
(10) $\frac{2 \cdot 2 \cdot 3 \cdot 5}{2 \cdot 2 \cdot 2 \cdot 3 \cdot 3} = \frac{5}{6}$

* 6. Complete the equivalent fraction. Show the multiplication: $\frac{2}{3} = \frac{\square}{18}$
(10) $\frac{2}{3} \times \frac{6}{6} = \frac{12}{18}$

* 7. What property of multiplication is used to find equivalent
(10) fractions?   Identity Property of Multiplication

For problems **8** and **9** refer to this figure.

* 8. Find the perimeter of the figure.   44 cm
(8)

9. What is the area of the figure?   96 cm^2
(8)

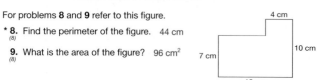

▶ *** 10.** **Conclude**   If each side of a square classroom is 25 feet, then what is the
(8) perimeter of the room? What is the area of the floor of the room? P = 100 ft; A = 625 ft^2

11. Jim rode his bike for four hours at 16 miles per hour. How far did Jim
(7) ride in two hours, in three hours, and in four hours?   32 mi, 48 mi, 64 mi

12. Steph was paid $50 for 4 hours of work. What was her rate of pay in
(7) dollars per hour? $12.50 per hour

13. Of the 150 people surveyed, $\frac{7}{10}$ said they owned at least one pet. How
(5) many of the people surveyed owned pets?   105 people

14. Find the perimeter of a triangle if each side measures 9 cm.   27 cm
(8)

▶ See Math Conversations in the sidebar.

* **15.** (1, 10) *Analyze* Compare:

a. $|-4| \bigcirc\!\!\!\!> -3$ **b.** $\frac{4}{5} \bigcirc\!\!\!\!> \frac{7}{10}$

For problems **16–18,** find the missing number and name the property illustrated.

16. (2) $7 + 2 = 2 + \square$ 7; Commutative Property of Addition

17. (2) $13 \cdot 200 = 200 \cdot \square$ 13; Commutative Property of Multiplication

18. (2) $5 + (4 + 7) = (5 + 4) + \square$ 7; Associative Property of Addition

19. (10) What two equivalent fractions are illustrated by the shaded circles? $\frac{3}{4} = \frac{9}{12}$

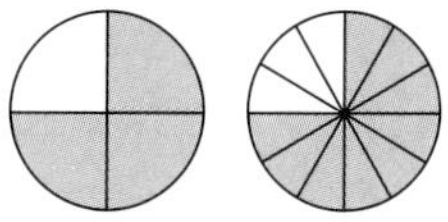

20. (2) What is the difference between the product of 20 and 2 and the difference of 20 and 2? 22

21. (2) If 3 is a factor, and 21 is the product, then what is the other factor? 7

▶* **22.** (2) *Justify* Rearrange factors to make the calculations easier. Then simplify. Justify your steps.

$$8 \cdot (7 \cdot 5)$$

): Justification:
· 7) Commutative Property
·7 Associative Property
7 Multiplied 8 and 5
Multiplied 40 and 7

Classify For problems **23–25,** choose *all* the correct answers from the list below.

A whole numbers **B** counting numbers

C integers **D** rational numbers

* **23.** (10) The number $\frac{22}{23}$ is a member of which sets of numbers? **D**

* **24.** (1) The number -5 is a member of which sets of numbers? **C, D**

* **25.** (1) Zero is a member of which sets of numbers? **A, C, D**

* **26.** (9) List all the prime numbers between 50 and 70. 53, 59, 61, 67

▶* **27.** (9) **a.** Use a factor tree to find the prime factors of 81. Then write the prime factorization of 81. $3 \cdot 3 \cdot 3 \cdot 3$

b. Use division by primes to find the factors of 80. Then write the prime factorization of 80. $2 \cdot 2 \cdot 2 \cdot 2 \cdot 5$

Simplify.

28. (2) $\frac{9450}{30}$ 315 **29.** (2) \$100.00 − \$69.86 \$30.14 **30.** (5) $\frac{3}{4}$ of 48 36

▶ See Math Conversations in the sidebar.

3 Written Practice (Continued)

Math Conversations

Discussion opportunities are provided below.

Problem 22 *Justify*

"Why is the product of 40 and 7 easier to find than the product of 56 and 5?" Sample: The multiplication fact 4×7 can be used to find the product of 40×7.

Errors and Misconceptions

Problem 27

Arranging like factors together and all factors in ascending order prepares students for writing prime factorization with exponents, which is presented in Lesson 15.

Looking Forward

Working with percents prepares students for:

- **Lesson 48,** finding percents of a whole.
- **Lesson 58,** solving percent problems with equations.
- **Lesson 63,** working with rational numbers, non-terminating decimals, and percents.
- **Lesson 67,** working with percents of change.
- **Lesson 71,** working with percent changes of dimensions.

• Decimal Numbers

Objectives

- Understand the relationship between place values and the function of the decimal point in our number system.
- Write decimal numbers using words.
- Compare and order decimal numbers.
- Convert between fractions, decimal numbers, and percents.
- Compare and order different forms of rational numbers.
- Convert between forms of rational numbers to solve problems.

Lesson Preparation

Materials

- **Power Up C** (in *Instructional Masters*)

Optional

- **Teacher-provided material:** grid paper, newspapers, magazines

Power Up C

Math Language

Maintain	English Learners (ESL)
decimal number	non-terminating
percent	
rational number	

Technology Resources

Student eBook Complete student textbook in electronic format.

Resources and Planner CD Assessment, reteaching, and instructional masters, plus a pacing calendar with standards.

Test and Practice Generator CD Create additional practice sheets and custom-made tests.

www.SaxonPublishers.com Visit for more student activities and planning materials.

Inclusion

Adaptations CD Adapted lessons, investigations, practice and assessments.

Meeting Standards

National Council of Teachers of Mathematics (NCTM)

Numbers and Operations

NO.1a Work flexibly with fractions, decimals, and percents to solve problems

NO.1b Compare and order fractions, decimals, and percents efficiently and find their approximate locations on a number line

NO.2a Understand the meaning and effects of arithmetic operations with fractions, decimals, and integers

NO.3a Select appropriate methods and tools for computing with fractions and decimals from among mental computation, estimation, calculators or computers, and paper and pencil, depending on the situation, and apply the selected methods

NO.3b Develop and analyze algorithms for computing with fractions, decimals, and integers and develop fluency in their use

Problem-Solving Strategy: Use Logical Reasoning

The numbers 2, 4, and 6 are placed in the shapes. The same number is put into both triangles. What is the least possible result? What is the greatest possible result?

$$\frac{\triangle + \bigcirc}{\square} \cdot \triangle$$

Understand **Understand the problem.**

"What information are we given?"

The numbers 2, 4, and 6 will be placed in the provided expression. The same number will be placed in both triangles.

"What are we asked to do?"

We are asked to determine both the *least* and the *greatest* possible values for the expression.

Plan **Make a plan.**

"What problem-solving strategy will we use?"

We will use *logical reasoning* and *number sense* to find the desired results.

Solve **Carry out the plan.**

"How does the value of the divisor affect the value of a quotient?"

The greater the divisor, the lesser the quotient. The lesser the divisor, the greater the quotient.

"How does the value of a factor affect the value of a product?"

The greater the factor, the greater the product. The lesser the factor, the lesser the product.

To find the *least* value of the expression:

"What will the triangle/multiplier be?" 2.

"What will the square/divisor be?" 6.

"What will the value be?" $\left[\frac{(2 + 4)}{6}\right] \times 2 = 2.$

To find the *greatest* value of the expression:

"What will the triangle/multiplier be?" 6.

"What will the square/divisor be?" 2.

"What will the value be?" $\left[\frac{(6 + 4)}{2}\right] \times 6 = 30.$

Check **Look back.**

"Did we do what we were asked to do?"

Yes. We found that 2 is the least value, and 30 is the greatest value.

1 Power Up

Facts

Distribute **Power Up C** to students. See answers below.

Mental Math

Encourage students to share different ways to mentally compute these exercises. Strategies for exercises **a** and **c** are listed below.

a. Multiply Rate by Time
$$\frac{1}{2} \text{ hr} \times 8\frac{\text{mi}}{\text{hr}} = 4 \text{ mi}$$
Use Logical Reasoning
1 hr ➝ 8 mi
$\frac{1}{2}$ hr ➝ 4 mi

c. Complementary Angles
$$m\angle A + m\angle B = 90°$$
$$m\angle B = 90° - m\angle A$$
$$m\angle B = 90° - 70° = 20°$$
Sum of Angles of a Triangle
$$m\angle A + m\angle B + m\angle C = 180°$$
$$70° + m\angle B + 90° = 180°$$
$$m\angle B = 180° - (90° + 70°)$$
$$m\angle B = 180° - (160°) = 20°$$

Problem Solving

Refer to **Power-Up Discussion**, p. 78B.

2 New Concepts

Instruction

Ask whether students have heard about number systems with other bases. Some may mention that computers use a base two or binary system.

Have several volunteers answer the *Discuss* question. This will help you see whether students have a good grasp of the decimal system and how the place values relate to one another on both sides of the decimal point.

(continued)

---

facts | Power Up C

mental math |
a. Calculation: Samantha skates 8 miles per hour for $\frac{1}{2}$ an hour. How far does she skate?   4 miles

b. Number Sense: What is the average (mean) of 30 and 40?   35

c. Geometry: What is the measure of $\angle B$?   20°

d. Algebra: $\frac{20}{x} = 5$ 4

e. Measurement: Ten yards is how many feet?   30 feet

f. Power/Roots: $\sqrt{36} + \sqrt{9}$ 9

g. Percent: 50% of 90   45

h. Calculation: Half a dozen $\times 4, + 1, \sqrt{}, \times 10, - 1, \sqrt{}, + 1, \div 4$ 2

problem solving | The numbers 2, 4, and 6 are placed in the shapes. The same number is put into both triangles. What is the least possible result? What is the greatest possible result?   Least: 2; Greatest: 30

New Concept | *Increasing Knowledge*

Our number system is a base ten system. There are ten different digits, and the value of a digit depends on its place in the number. In the United States we use a decimal point to separate whole-number places from fraction places.

Decimal Place Values

millions	hundred thousands	ten thousands	thousands	hundreds	tens	ones	decimal point	tenths	hundredths	thousandths	ten-thousandths	hundred-thousandths	millionths
1,000,000	100,000	10,000	1,000	100	10	1	.	$\frac{1}{10}$	$\frac{1}{100}$	$\frac{1}{1,000}$	$\frac{1}{10,000}$	$\frac{1}{100,000}$	$\frac{1}{1,000,000}$

Discuss How do the place values in our number system relate to one another?   Sample: The value of each place is 10 times the value of the place to its right.

Facts | Reduce each fraction to lowest terms.

$\frac{2}{10} = \frac{1}{5}$	$\frac{2}{8} = \frac{1}{4}$	$\frac{3}{9} = \frac{1}{3}$	$\frac{8}{10} = \frac{4}{5}$	$\frac{3}{6} = \frac{1}{2}$
$\frac{6}{8} = \frac{3}{4}$	$\frac{3}{12} = \frac{1}{4}$	$\frac{2}{4} = \frac{1}{2}$	$\frac{6}{12} = \frac{1}{2}$	$\frac{9}{12} = \frac{3}{4}$
$\frac{4}{12} = \frac{1}{3}$	$\frac{2}{6} = \frac{1}{3}$	$\frac{8}{16} = \frac{1}{2}$	$\frac{5}{10} = \frac{1}{2}$	$\frac{6}{9} = \frac{2}{3}$
$\frac{4}{8} = \frac{1}{2}$	$\frac{8}{12} = \frac{2}{3}$	$\frac{4}{10} = \frac{2}{5}$	$\frac{4}{6} = \frac{2}{3}$	$\frac{6}{10} = \frac{3}{5}$

To read a decimal number, we read the whole number part (to the left of the decimal point), say "and" at the decimal point, and then read the fraction part (to the right of the decimal point). To read the fraction part of a decimal number we read the digits as though the digits formed a whole number, and then we name the place value of the final digit.

Example 1

Use words to write each number.

a. 12.05   b. 0.125

Solution

a. twelve and five hundredths

b. one hundred twenty-five thousandths

Example 2

Order these numbers from least to greatest.

0.5   0.41   0.05   0.405

Solution

Writing the numbers with decimal points aligned helps us compare the digits in each place.

$$0.5$$
$$0.41$$
$$0.05$$
$$0.405$$

All four numbers have a zero in the ones place. In the tenths place 0.05 has a zero, so it is least, and 0.5 has a 5 so it is greatest. Two numbers have 4 in the tenths place so we look at the hundredths place to compare. We see that 0.405 is less than 0.41. In order, the numbers are:

0.05, 0.405, 0.41, 0.5

Naming a decimal number also names a fraction. To write a decimal number as a fraction or mixed number, we write the digits to the right of the decimal point as the numerator and write the denominator indicated by the place value of the last digit. We reduce the fraction if possible.

$$12.25 = 12\frac{25}{100} = 12\frac{1}{4}$$

$$0.125 = \frac{125}{1000} = \frac{1}{8}$$

Example 3

Name each decimal number. Then write the decimal number as a reduced fraction.

a. 2.8   b. 0.75

Instruction

Caution students that they may hear people say "two point five" when they mean "two and five tenths." Explain that such usage is a short way of reading a number but in this course we will write the proper names of decimal numbers.

Example 1
Instruction

Explain that when we write numbers in words, we write what we say when we say numbers. The word *and* is used for the decimal point. Point out that when the number is a decimal fraction with no whole number part we do not say or write the zero so there is no need to use the word *and*.

Example 2
Instruction

You may extend this example by asking students to explain how comparing decimals less than 1 is like comparing whole numbers. Sample: For both, you line up the places and you compare from left to right.

(continued)

Math Background

The following generalizations can be used by students when changing the word form of a decimal number to standard form.

Place Value	Number of Digits to the Right of the Decimal Point
tenths	one
hundredths	two
thousandths	three
ten-thousandths	four
hundred-thousandths	five

2 New Concepts (Continued)

Example 3

Instruction

You may want to point out that when 2.8 is written as a reduced fraction, the whole number part (2) remains the same, but that when 0.75 is written as a reduced fraction, the whole number part (0) is not included.

Instruction

When presenting the content on converting fractions to decimals, you may wish to reinforce the concept that a fraction represents a division. Remind students that the fraction bar tells us to divide.

Example 4

Instruction

Have students explain the differences among the decimal numbers found in parts **a** and **b**. Students must be alert not to include the whole number part when converting the fractional part of a mixed number to a decimal as in part **b**.

(continued)

Solution

a. two and eight tenths; $2.8 = 2\frac{8}{10} = 2\frac{4}{5}$

b. seventy-five hundredths; $0.75 = \frac{75}{100} = \frac{3}{4}$

To express a fraction as a decimal number, we perform the division indicated. For example, to convert $\frac{3}{4}$ to a decimal number, we divide 3 by 4. We divide as though we are dividing money. We write 3 as 3.00 and place the decimal point in the quotient directly above the decimal point in the dividend.

$$
\begin{array}{r}
0.75 \\
4\overline{)3.00} \\
\underline{2\,8} \\
20 \\
\underline{20} \\
0
\end{array}
$$

Notice that we used a decimal point and zeros to write 3 as 3.00 so that we could perform the division. Some fractions convert to decimal numbers that have repeating digits in the quotient (they never divide evenly). We will address decimal numbers with repeating digits in Lesson 30.

Example 4

Express each fraction or mixed number as a decimal number.

  a. $\frac{3}{8}$ b. $2\frac{1}{2}$

Solution

a. We divide 3 by 8. We place the decimal point on the 3 and write as many zeros as necessary to complete the division. We divide until the remainder is zero or until the digits in the quotient begin to repeat.

$$
\begin{array}{r}
0.375 \\
8\overline{)3.000} \\
\underline{2\,4} \\
60 \\
\underline{56} \\
40 \\
\underline{40} \\
0
\end{array}
$$

b. The mixed number $2\frac{1}{2}$ is a whole number plus a fraction. The whole number, 2, is written to the left of the decimal point. The fraction $\frac{1}{2}$ converts to 0.5.

$$2\frac{1}{2} = \mathbf{2.5}$$

Note that converting a rational number to decimal form has three possible outcomes.

1. The rational number is an integer.

2. The rational number is a terminating decimal number.

Teacher Tip

To help students **relate the topic** of this lesson **to everyday life,** ask them to look in newspapers or magazines to find ads or articles that mention decimals, fractions, or percents. You might post them on the bulletin board for a few days.

3. The rational number is a non-terminating decimal number with repeating digits. We will learn more about this type of rational number in Lesson 30.

We can use the Identity Property of Multiplication to convert a number to a percent. Since 100% is equivalent to 1, we can multiply a decimal by 100% to find an equivalent percent.

$$0.4 \times 100\% = 40\%$$

Converting decimals to percents shifts the decimal point two places to the right.

Example 5

Convert each number to a percent by multiplying each number by 100%

   a. 0.2   **b.** 0.125   **c.** 1.5

Solution

   a. $0.2 \times 100\% = 20\%$

   b. $0.125 \times 100\% = 12.5\%$

   c. $1.5 \times 100\% = 150\%$

Fractions and decimals greater than 1 convert to percents greater than 100%.

Converting from a percent to a decimal shifts the decimal point two places to the left.

Example 6

Convert the following percents to decimals.

   a. 5%   **b.** 225%

Solution

   a. $5\% = \dfrac{5}{100} = 0.05$

   b. $225\% = \dfrac{225}{100} = 2.25$

Example 7

Arrange in order from least to greatest: $\frac{1}{2}$, 12%, 1.2, −1.2.

Solution

Converting fractions and percents to decimals can help us compare different forms of rational numbers.

$$\frac{1}{2} = 0.5$$

$$12\% = 0.12$$

The negative number is least. Then 0.12 is less than 0.5, which is less than 1.2. The correct order is **−1.2, 12%, $\frac{1}{2}$, 1.2.**

---

2 New Concepts (Continued)

Example 5
Instruction

You may need to demonstrate that shifting the decimal point two places to the right is the same as multiplying by 100.

Example 6
Instruction

If needed, demonstrate that shifting the decimal point two places to the left is the same as dividing by 100.

Example 7
Instruction

Discuss other ways that these three numbers could have been ordered. Samples: Locate them all on a number line. Change them all to percents.

(continued)

English Learners

Explain the meaning of the term **non-terminating.** Say:

"If something terminates, it stops or ends. If something is non-terminating, it never stops."

Have students use calculators to simplify the fractions $\frac{5}{4}$ and $\frac{5}{3}$. Ask which fraction is non-terminating. $\frac{5}{4} = 1.25$ while $\frac{5}{3} = 1.6...$, so $\frac{5}{3}$ is non-terminating.

Example 8
Instruction

Point out that this lesson has covered different ways to express numbers and how to convert among the ways. Explain that this example will help demonstrate why it is important to be able to use various forms to express a number. Before looking at the solution, ask volunteers to explain how they would decide which form of the percent would be easiest to use for each part of the example. Sample: For part a, I would change 80% to $\frac{8}{10}$ so I could reduce the 40 and the 10.

Practice Set
Problems j–m

To convert a decimal number to a percent, some students may multiply the decimal number by 100% and write a percent symbol. Encourage these students to check their work by applying the generalization that multiplying a decimal number by 100% is the same as moving the decimal point in that number two places to the right and writing a percent symbol.

Example 8

a. **How much money is 80% of $40?**

b. **How much money is 75% of $40?**

c. **Estimate 8.25% sales tax on a $19.95 purchase.**

Solution

To find a percent of a number we change the percent to a decimal or fraction and then multiply. Usually one form or the other is easier to multiply.

a. We choose to change 80% to a decimal.

$$80\% \text{ of } \$40$$
$$0.8 \times \$40 = \mathbf{\$32}$$

b. We choose to change 75% to a fraction.

$$75\% \text{ of } \$40$$
$$\frac{3}{\cancel{4}} \times \$\cancel{40}^{\,10} = \mathbf{\$30}$$

c. We round 8.25% to 8% and 19.95 to $20.

Step:	Justification:
8% of $20	Rounded
0.08 × $20	8% = 0.08
$1.60	Multiplied

Practice Set Use words to write the decimal numbers in problems **a** and **b**.

a. 11.12 b. 0.375
a. eleven and twelve hundredths b. three hundred seventy-five thousandths

Write each fraction in problems **c–e** as a decimal number.

c. $\frac{3}{5}$ 0.6   d. $2\frac{1}{4}$ 2.25   e. $\frac{1}{200}$ 0.005

Write each decimal in problems **f–i** as a fraction.

f. 0.05 $\frac{1}{20}$ g. 0.025 $\frac{1}{40}$ h. 1.2 $1\frac{1}{5}$ i. 0.001 $\frac{1}{1000}$

▶ Write each decimal in problems **j–m** as a percent.

j. 0.8 80%   k. 1.3 130%   l. 0.875 87.5% m. 0.002 0.2%

Write each percent in problems **n–q** as a decimal.

n. 2% 0.02   o. 20% 0.2   p. 24% 0.24   q. 0.3% 0.003

r. Order from least to greatest: $-0.4, 2.3, 0.6, \frac{1}{2}$. $-0.4, \frac{1}{2}, 0.6, 2.3$

s. What length is 75% of 12 inches?   9 inches

t. If the sales-tax rate is 7.5%, what is the sales tax on a $48.00 purchase? $3.60

u. Estimate 8.25% sales tax on a $39.79 purchase. $3.20

▶ See Math Conversations in the sidebar.

1. Lashonna passed back 140 papers. If these papers were in stacks of 28, how many stacks of papers did Lashonna pass back?   5 stacks
   (4)

▸ 2. The players on the junior high basketball team had heights of 71″, 69″, 69″, 67″, and 64″. What was the average height of the players on the team?   68″
   (7)

▸ 3. *Evaluate* Identify the plot, write an equation, and solve: This week, Kay ran a mile in 8 minutes 6 seconds. Last week, her time was 8 minutes 25 seconds. How much did her time improve?   compare. 8 min 25 sec − 8 min 6 sec = d; 19 sec
   (3)

▸ * 4. Using prime factorization, reduce $\frac{50}{75}$. $\frac{2 \cdot 5 \cdot 5}{3 \cdot 5 \cdot 5} = \frac{2}{3}$
   (10)

* 5. Use words to write 4.02.   four and two hundredths
   (12)

* 6. Write $\frac{5}{8}$ as a decimal number.   0.625
   (12)

* 7. Convert 0.17 to a fraction. $\frac{17}{100}$
   (12)

* 8. How much money is 15% of $60? $9
   (12)

▸ * 9. Complete the equivalent fraction:
   (10)

$$\frac{1}{7} = \frac{\square}{35}   \quad 5$$

▸* 10. Compare: $\frac{5}{5} \bigcirc \frac{7}{7}$ =
   (10)

For problems **11** and **12**, refer to the figure at right.

11. Find the perimeter.   28 m
   (8)

12. Find the area.   34 m²
   (8)

7 m
2 m
3 m
5 m
4 m

13. Brad mowed the field for 4 hours and mowed 2 acres per hour. How many acres did Brad mow?   8 acres
   (7)

▸ 14. Mr. Osono was paid $168 for 8 hours of work. What was his hourly rate of pay? $21 per hour
   (7)

15. Find the perimeter of a square with side length 9 m.   36 m
   (8)

Analyze For problems **16–18,** find the missing number and state the property illustrated.

16. $6 \cdot 4 = 4 \cdot \square$ 6; Commutative Property of Multiplication
   (2)

17. $4 + (5 + 1) = (4 + 5) + \square$ 1; Associative Property of Addition
   (2)

18. $6\frac{1}{2} + 1\frac{1}{8} = 1\frac{1}{8} + \square$ $6\frac{1}{2}$; Commutative Property of Addition
   (2)

Lesson 12   83

▸ See Math Conversations in the sidebar.

3 Written Practice

Math Conversations

Discussion opportunities are provided below.

Problem 2 Formulate

You may need to remind students that the symbol ′ stands for feet and the symbol ″ stands for inches.

Extend the Problem

Ask students to write the answer in feet and inches. 5 feet 8 inches

Problem 3 Evaluate

After completing the problem, encourage students to write and solve a different equation to check their work.

Problem 4 Explain

Extend the Problem

"Explain how you can reduce $\frac{50}{75}$ to lowest terms using only mental math." Sample: The greatest common factor (GCF) of 50 and 75 is 25; 50 ÷ 25 = 2 and 75 ÷ 25 = 3, so $\frac{50}{75}$ in lowest terms is $\frac{2}{3}$.

Problem 9 Analyze

Extend the Problem

"What is the equivalent fraction for 1 that is used to change $\frac{1}{7}$ to $\frac{5}{35}$?" $\frac{5}{5}$

"Why is $\frac{5}{5}$ equivalent to 1?" Sample: A fraction bar represents division, and 5 ÷ 5 = 1.

Problem 14 Explain

Extend the Problem

"Suppose Mr. Osono saves 20% of his hourly salary. Explain how you can use mental math to find the amount of his hourly salary he saves." Sample: 10% of a number is the same as moving the decimal point in that number one place to the left. Since 10% of $21.00 is $2.10, 20% of $21.00 is $2.10 + $2.10, or $4.20.

Errors and Misconceptions
Problem 10

Watch for students who do not quickly recognize that the fractions can be compared without renaming. Remind these students that a fraction bar represents division, and that the quotient of a non-zero number divided by itself is 1. Students should conclude that the fractions are equivalent because each fraction is another name for 1.

(continued)

3 Written Practice (Continued)

Math Conversations
Discussion opportunities are provided below.

Problem 26 Represent
Invite two volunteers to work at the board or overhead. Ask one volunteer to demonstrate how to use a factor tree to find the prime factorization. Ask the other volunteer to demonstrate how to use the division-by-primes method.

Errors and Misconceptions
Problem 30
Students sometimes have alignment difficulties when adding and subtracting decimal numbers. To help maintain correct alignment of the place values, encourage these students to complete the computation on grid paper or on lined paper turned sideways.

---

19. Compare:
(1, 10)
   a. $|-2| \ominus 2$ **b.** $\frac{3}{4} \ominus \frac{3}{8}$

20. What equivalent fractions are illustrated?
(10) $\frac{1}{2} = \frac{3}{6}$

21. The product of two numbers is 10. Their sum is 7. Name the
(12) numbers.   5 and 2

22. The product of two numbers is 6. Their difference is 1. Name the
(2) numbers.   2 and 3

23. Arrange from least to greatest: $-0.12, -1.2, -\frac{1}{2}$. $-1.2, -\frac{1}{2}, -0.12$
(12)

* 24. The number -4 is a member of which sets of numbers?   rational
(1, 10) numbers, integers

* 25. List all the prime numbers between zero and twenty.
(9)   2, 3, 5, 7, 11, 13, 17, 19

▶*** 26.** **Represent** Write the prime factorization of 60. $2 \cdot 2 \cdot 3 \cdot 5$
(9)

27. What is $\frac{2}{3}$ of 18?   12
(5)

28. Suzanne is collecting money for T-shirts from the 12 members of
(4) her band section. Each shirt costs $11.40. What is the total amount Suzanne should collect? $136.80

29. Darren ran three miles in 27 minutes. At that rate, how long will it take
(7) him to run 5 miles?   45 minutes

▶*** 30.** Simplify: $18.7 + 9.04 - 1.809$ 25.931
(10)

▶ See Math Conversations in the sidebar.

Looking Forward

Working with decimal numbers prepares students for:

- **Lesson 17,** rounding and estimating.
- **Lesson 24,** adding and subtracting decimal numbers.
- **Lesson 25,** multiplying and dividing decimal numbers.
- **Lesson 30,** converting fractions to repeating decimals.
- **Lesson 63,** working with rational numbers, non-terminating decimals, and percents.
- **Lesson 110,** converting repeating decimals to fractions.

• Adding and Subtracting Fractions and Mixed Numbers

Objectives

- Add and subtract fractions and mixed numbers with and without common denominators.
- Represent fraction addition and subtraction on a number line.
- Add and subtract fractions and mixed numbers to solve word problems.

Lesson Preparation

Materials

- **Power Up C** (in *Instructional Masters*)

Optional

- **Manipulative Kit: overhead fraction circles**

Power Up C

Math Language

Maintain	English Learners (ESL)
common denominators	rename
improper fraction	
reduce	

Technology Resources

Student eBook Complete student textbook in electronic format.

Resources and Planner CD Assessment, reteaching, and instructional masters, plus a pacing calendar with standards.

Test and Practice Generator CD Create additional practice sheets and custom-made tests.

www.SaxonPublishers.com Visit for more student activities and planning materials.

Inclusion

Adaptations CD Adapted lessons, investigations, practice and assessments.

Meeting Standards

National Council of Teachers of Mathematics (NCTM)

Numbers and Operations

NO.1a Work flexibly with fractions, decimals, and percents to solve problems

NO.2a Understand the meaning and effects of arithmetic operations with fractions, decimals, and integers

NO.3a Select appropriate methods and tools for computing with fractions and decimals from among mental computation, estimation, calculators or computers, and paper and pencil, depending on the situation, and apply the selected methods

Problem-Solving Strategy: Make It Simpler

Find the sum of the even numbers from 2 to 20.

(Understand) **Understand the problem.**

"What are we asked to do?"

We are asked to find the sum of 2, 4, 6, 8, 10, 12, 14, 16, 18, and 20.

(Plan) **Make a plan.**

"What problem-solving strategy will we use?"

We will *make it simpler* by using the pairing technique we've developed.

(Solve) **Carry out the plan.**

"What is the sum of the greatest and least addends?"

$2 + 20 = 22$.

"Where are other pairs of addends that sum to 22?"

By working inward from both ends of the list we find other pairs (4 and 18; 6 and 16; 8 and 14; 10 and 12) that each have a sum of 22.

"How many pairs of addends totaling 22 exist?"

There are 5 pairs of addends that sum to 22.

"What is the sum of the even numbers from 2 to 20?"

We multiply 22 by 5 to get 110.

(Check) **Look back.**

"Did we find the answer to the question that was asked?"

Yes. We found that the sum of the even numbers from 2 to 20 is 110.

• Adding and Subtracting Fractions and Mixed Numbers

facts | Power Up C

mental math | a. **Calculation:** Miguel rode his bike at a rate of 18 miles per hour for $1\frac{1}{2}$ hours. How far did Miguel ride? $18 + 9 = 27$ miles

b. **Estimation:** The tires cost $78.99 each. About how much would four new tires cost? $320

c. **Measurement:** Two inches is about how many centimeters?   ≈5 cm

one inch

d. **Algebra:** $3x = 33$ 11

e. **Geometry:** In this triangle, x must be between what two lengths?   5 m and 13 m

f. **Fractional Parts:** $\frac{3}{4}$ of 8 muffins   6 muffins

g. **Number Sense:** 33×3000 99,000

h. **Calculation:** $\sqrt{81} + 1, \times 5, - 1, \sqrt{}, \times 5, + 1, \sqrt{}, - 7$ −1

problem solving | Find the sum of the even numbers from 2 to 20.   110

Leftover from the pizza party were $\frac{3}{8}$ of a ham and pineapple pizza and $\frac{2}{8}$ of a vegetarian pizza. What fraction of a whole pizza was left? If Mario eats two of the slices of ham and pineapple pizza, what fraction of the ham and pineapple pizza will be left?

We can add $\frac{3}{8}$ and $\frac{2}{8}$ to find the fraction of a whole pizza remaining. We can subtract $\frac{2}{8}$ from $\frac{3}{8}$ to find how much ham and pineapple pizza will be left if Mario eats two slices.

$$\frac{3}{8} + \frac{2}{8} = \frac{5}{8} \qquad\qquad \frac{3}{8} - \frac{2}{8} = \frac{1}{8}$$

Together the remaining pieces are $\frac{5}{8}$ of a whole pizza. If Mario eats two slices of the ham and pineapple pizza, $\frac{1}{8}$ of that pizza will be left.

Equal parts of a circle, like slices of pizza, is one model for fractions. Another model for fractions is a number line.

Lesson 13   85

$\frac{2}{10} = \frac{1}{5}$	$\frac{2}{8} = \frac{1}{4}$	$\frac{3}{9} = \frac{1}{3}$	$\frac{8}{10} = \frac{4}{5}$	$\frac{3}{6} = \frac{1}{2}$
$\frac{6}{8} = \frac{3}{4}$	$\frac{3}{12} = \frac{1}{4}$	$\frac{2}{4} = \frac{1}{2}$	$\frac{6}{12} = \frac{1}{2}$	$\frac{9}{12} = \frac{3}{4}$
$\frac{4}{12} = \frac{1}{3}$	$\frac{2}{6} = \frac{1}{3}$	$\frac{8}{16} = \frac{1}{2}$	$\frac{5}{10} = \frac{1}{2}$	$\frac{6}{9} = \frac{2}{3}$
$\frac{4}{8} = \frac{1}{2}$	$\frac{8}{12} = \frac{2}{3}$	$\frac{4}{10} = \frac{2}{5}$	$\frac{4}{6} = \frac{2}{3}$	$\frac{6}{10} = \frac{3}{5}$

---

1 Power Up

Facts
Distribute **Power Up C** to students. See answers below.

Mental Math
Encourage students to share different ways to mentally compute these exercises. Strategies for exercises **c** and **g** are listed below.

c. Regroup
$33 \times 3000 = 33 \times 3 \times 1000 = 99 \times 1000 = 99,000$
Multiply by 3, Divide by 3
$33 \times 3000 = (33 \times 3) \times (3000 \div 3) = 99 \times 1000 = 99,000$

g. Multiply by Numerator First
$\frac{3}{4} \times 8 = \frac{24}{4} = 6$
Divide by Denominator First
$\frac{3}{4} \times 8 = 3 \times 2 = 6$

Problem Solving
Refer to **Power-Up Discussion**, p. 85B.

---

2 New Concepts

Instruction
Ask students to tell about any times they or their families needed to add or subtract fractions or mixed numbers. Responses may include:
- measuring wood or fabric for a carpentry or sewing project.
- helping a younger sibling with homework.
- making calculations with time in hours and parts of hours.

Help students see that because the pizzas were cut into 8 equal parts (eighths), we can add or subtract them just by operating on the number of pieces, or the numerators.

Point out that we can add or subtract fractions using a number line just as we do whole numbers.

(continued)

Instruction

Mention that another phrase sometimes used to describe denominators that are the same is "like denominators."

Example 1

Instruction

Point out the word *simplify* in the direction line. Explain that the exercises in parts **a** and **b** are expressions and that the task is to make them as simple as possible. This means more than just adding or subtracting; the number that is the answer should also be completely reduced, or simplified.

Be sure that students notice that the operations can be done either by using arithmetic or by using a number line. Guide them through both methods for both parts.

(continued)

On the number lines below, we represent fraction addition and subtraction.

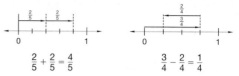

$$\frac{2}{5} + \frac{2}{5} = \frac{4}{5} \qquad\qquad \frac{3}{4} - \frac{2}{4} = \frac{1}{4}$$

Math Language

Recall that when two fractions have the same denominator, we say that they have **"common denominators."**

Notice that the fractions in each example have common denominators. To add or subtract fractions that have common denominators, we add or subtract the numerators and leave the denominators unchanged.

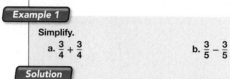

Simplify.

a. $\dfrac{3}{4} + \dfrac{3}{4}$
b. $\dfrac{3}{5} - \dfrac{3}{5}$

Solution

a. The fractions have common denominators. We add the numerators.

$$\frac{3}{4} + \frac{3}{4} = \frac{6}{4}$$

Math Language

Recall that an **improper fraction** is a fraction equal to or greater than 1. A mixed number is a whole number plus a fraction.

Fraction answers that can be reduced should be reduced. Improper fractions should be converted to whole or mixed numbers.

$$\frac{6}{4} = \frac{\overset{1}{\cancel{2}} \cdot 3}{\underset{1}{\cancel{2}} \cdot 2} = \frac{3}{2}$$

$$\frac{3}{2} = \frac{2}{2} + \frac{1}{2} = 1\frac{1}{2}$$

We illustrate this addition on a number line.

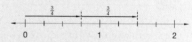

b. The fractions have common denominators. We subtract the numerators.

$$\frac{3}{5} - \frac{3}{5} = \frac{0}{5} = 0$$

We illustrate the subtraction.

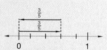

We often need to add or subtract fractions that do not have common denominators. We can do this by first renaming one or more of the fractions so that they have common denominators. Recall from Lesson 11 that we use the Identity Property of Multiplication to rename a fraction by multiplying the fraction by a fraction equal to 1.

Math Background

The least common denominator (LCD) of two or more fractions is the least common multiple (LCM) of the denominators.

To find the LCD of two or more fractions, students often use a list. An alternative method to making a lengthy list involves prime factors.

For example, to find the LCD of 27 and 60, first write the prime factorization of each number.

$$27 = 3^3$$
$$60 = 2^2 \cdot 3 \cdot 5$$

Then identify all of the primes factors that are present. In the factorizations 3^3 and $2^2 \cdot 3 \cdot 5$, the prime factors 2, 3, and 5 are present. Then find the product of the greatest powers of each factor that is present to find the LCD.

$$2^2 \cdot 3^3 \cdot 5 = 540 \qquad \text{The LCD of 27 and 60 is 540.}$$

$$\frac{1}{2} \cdot \frac{2}{2} = \frac{2}{4} \qquad \frac{1}{2} \cdot \frac{3}{3} = \frac{3}{6} \qquad \frac{1}{2} \cdot \frac{4}{4} = \frac{4}{8}$$

Forming equivalent factions enables us to add or subtract fractions that have different denominators.

Example 2

Simplify.

a. $\frac{2}{3} + \frac{3}{4}$

b. $\frac{3}{4} - \frac{1}{6}$

Solution

a. One way to find a common denominator is to multiply the denominators of the fractions that are being added or subtracted. The denominators are 3 and 4. Since $3 \times 4 = 12$, we rename the fractions so that both denominators are 12.

Find the common denominator:

$$\frac{2}{3} \quad = \frac{}{12}$$
$$+\frac{3}{4} \quad = \frac{}{12}$$

Rename the fractions:

$$\frac{2}{3} \cdot \frac{4}{4} = \frac{8}{12}$$
$$+\frac{3}{4} \cdot \frac{3}{3} = \frac{9}{12}$$
$$\frac{17}{12} \text{ or } 1\frac{5}{12}$$

b. The denominators are 4 and 6, and $4 \times 6 = 24$, so a common denominator is 24. However, 24 is not the least common denominator. Since 12 is the least common multiple of 4 and 6, the least common denominator of the two fractions is 12. We perform this subtraction twice using 24 and then 12 as the common denominator.

$$\frac{3}{4} \cdot \frac{6}{6} = \frac{18}{24}$$
$$-\frac{1}{6} \cdot \frac{4}{4} = \frac{4}{24}$$
$$\frac{14}{24} = \frac{7}{12}$$

$$\frac{3}{4} \cdot \frac{3}{3} = \frac{9}{12}$$
$$-\frac{1}{6} \cdot \frac{2}{2} = \frac{2}{12}$$
$$\frac{7}{12}$$

Using the least common denominator often makes the arithmetic easier and often avoids the need to reduce the answer.

Discuss Why did we arrange the fractions vertically in example 2 but not in example 1? We did not need to write equivalent fractions with a common denominator in example 1.

When adding and subtracting mixed numbers it is sometimes necessary to regroup.

Example 3

Simplify:

a. $3\frac{1}{2} + 1\frac{3}{4}$

b. $3\frac{1}{2} - 1\frac{3}{4}$

Instruction

Emphasize the need for using common denominators when adding and subtracting fractions with unlike denominators.

Example 2

Instruction

Model the procedures explained in both parts of this example on the board or overhead. Have students follow along, doing each step as you do. This is a good time to emphasize neatness and the need to write each step next to or below the one before it. Point out that if work is done carelessly, it is easy to make errors and difficult to find them when checking the work.

Instruction

When you finish example 2, ask whether it is necessary to use the least common denominator. no Point out that the answer will be the same no matter what common denominator is used. Tell students that they can always find a common denominator by multiplying the denominators of the fractions being added or subtracted.

Use the *Discuss* question to give students practical pointers for working with fractions.

(continued)

Example 3

Instruction

Work through both parts of this example on the board or overhead as students follow along on their papers.

Be sure that students know how to carry out the process for renaming or regrouping so that the subtraction can take place. This is similar to regrouping when subtracting with whole numbers, except that the number that is regrouped is a 1 and it is regrouped in fractional parts.

Instruction

You may use the summary to check student understanding of addition and subtraction of fractions. Ask students to explain how to carry out each step.

(continued)

Solution

It is helpful to arrange the numbers vertically. We rewrite the fractions with common denominators.

a. We add the fractions, and we add the whole numbers.

$$3\frac{1}{2} = \quad 3\frac{2}{4}$$
$$+ 1\frac{3}{4} = + 1\frac{3}{4}$$
$$\overline{\quad = \quad 4\frac{5}{4}}$$

In this case the sum includes an improper fraction. We convert the improper fraction to a mixed number and combine it with the whole number to simplify the answer.

$$4\frac{5}{4} = 4 + \frac{5}{4} = 4 + 1\frac{1}{4} = 5\frac{1}{4}$$

b. We rewrite the fractions with common denominators.

$$3\frac{1}{2} = \quad 3\frac{2}{4}$$
$$- 1\frac{3}{4} = - 1\frac{3}{4}$$
$$\overline{\qquad\qquad}$$

In this case we must rename a whole number as a fraction so that we can subtract, because $\frac{2}{4}$ is less than $\frac{3}{4}$. We sometimes call this process regrouping.

We rename $3\frac{2}{4}$ as $2\frac{6}{4}$.

$$3\frac{2}{4} = 2 + \frac{4}{4} + \frac{2}{4} = 2\frac{6}{4}$$

Now we can subtract.

$$2\frac{6}{4}$$
$$- 1\frac{3}{4}$$
$$\overline{\quad 1\frac{3}{4}}$$

In this table we summarize the steps for adding and subtracting fractions and mixed numbers.

Adding and Subtracting Fractions and Mixed Numbers
1. Write fractions with common denominators.
2. Add or subtract numerators as indicated, regrouping if necessary.
3. Simplify the answer if possible by reducing.

Manipulative Use

You may want to use the **fraction circles** in the Manipulative Kit to demonstrate addition and subtraction of fractions, either for the whole class or for any students who may need the extra support of a more **concrete representation of the fraction operations.**

English Learners

For the solution to b, explain the meaning of **rename.** Say:

"If you rename something, you give it a different name. Watch while I rename this number."

Write the following on the board: twenty-nine and three fourths $= 29\frac{3}{4} = 29.75$. Then say:

"I renamed the number in two different ways."

Ask who can rename these numbers as decimals: $10\frac{1}{2}$ and $45\frac{1}{4}$. 10.5, 45.25

Example 4

The end of a 2″ by 4″ piece of lumber is actually about $1\frac{1}{2}$-by-$3\frac{1}{2}$ in. If one 2-by-4 is nailed on top of another 2-by-4, what will be the dimensions of the combined ends?

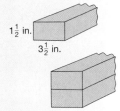

$1\frac{1}{2}$ in.

$3\frac{1}{2}$ in.

Solution

The width of the ends is not changed. We add $1\frac{1}{2}$ in. and $1\frac{1}{2}$ in. to find the boards' combined thickness.

$$1\frac{1}{2} + 1\frac{1}{2} = 2\frac{2}{2} = 3$$

The combined boards will be about **3 inches thick and $3\frac{1}{2}$ inches wide.**

Example 5

Visit www.SaxonPublishers.com/ActivitiesC3 *for a graphing calculator activity.*

The carpenter cut $15\frac{1}{2}$ inches from a 2-by-4 that was $92\frac{5}{8}$ inches long. How long was the resulting 2-by-4?

Solution

We subtract $15\frac{1}{2}$ inches from $92\frac{5}{8}$ after writing the fractions with common denominators.

$$\begin{aligned} 92\frac{5}{8} &= 92\frac{5}{8} \\ - 15\frac{1}{2} &= 15\frac{4}{8} \\ \hline & 77\frac{1}{8} \end{aligned}$$

The resulting 2-by-4 is **$77\frac{1}{8}$ inches long.**

Practice Set

Simplify:

a. $\frac{4}{9} + \frac{5}{9}$ 1

b. $\frac{2}{3} - \frac{2}{3}$ 0

c. $\frac{1}{8} + \frac{1}{4}$ $\frac{3}{8}$

d. $\frac{5}{6} - \frac{1}{2}$ $\frac{1}{3}$

e. $\frac{4}{5} + \frac{1}{2}$ $\frac{13}{10}$ or $1\frac{3}{10}$

f. $\frac{1}{3} - \frac{1}{4}$ $\frac{1}{12}$

▶ g. $3\frac{1}{3} + 2\frac{1}{2}$ $5\frac{5}{6}$

▶ h. $6\frac{5}{6} - 2\frac{1}{3}$ $4\frac{1}{2}$

▶ i. $3\frac{1}{2} + 1\frac{2}{3}$ $5\frac{1}{6}$

▶ j. $7\frac{1}{3} - 1\frac{1}{2}$ $5\frac{5}{6}$

Lesson 13   89

▶ See Math Conversations in the sidebar.

Example 4
Instruction

Ask a volunteer to use the diagram to explain why the width of the ends is not changed.

You might explain why a 2″ by 4″ piece of lumber is not exactly 2″ by 4″. The wood is rough cut to those dimensions but then some wood is removed when the lumber is planed to make it smooth, and later the wood shrinks a little more as it dries.

Example 5
Instruction

Ask what numbers in the problem are not used to find the answer. 2-by-4 Point out that examples 4 and 5 show a practical use for addition and subtraction of fractions.

Practice Set
Problems g–j

A way for students to check their work is to perform the computations by first changing each mixed number to an improper fraction. The sum or difference of the fractions is then found using the standard algorithm for adding and subtracting fractions with unlike denominators. For example, the solution for problem **g** is shown below.

$$3\frac{1}{3} + 2\frac{1}{2} = \frac{10}{3} + \frac{5}{2} = \frac{20}{6} + \frac{15}{6} = \frac{35}{6} = 5\frac{5}{6}$$

(continued)

Practice Set
Problem l [Error Alert]
Make sure students look carefully at the diagram and recognize that the solution is the sum of $32\frac{1}{4}$, $1\frac{5}{8}$, and $1\frac{5}{8}$.

Remind students who name $35\frac{4}{8}$ inches or $35\frac{2}{4}$ inches to always express their answers in simplest form.

3 Written Practice

Math Conversations
Discussion opportunities are provided below.

Problem 1 [Analyze]
One way for students to solve the problem is to find $\frac{4}{5}$ of 65,000. Using equivalent forms of rational numbers sometimes makes the calculations easier. In this case students could find $\frac{8}{10}$ or 0.8 of 65,000.

Encourage students to choose one method and use it to solve the problem.

Then ask students to compare the answers produced by each method to check their work.

Problems 8 and 9 [Generalize]
"For problems 8 and 9, how must we change one or both fractions before we can find the sum or the difference of the fractions?" Sample: A common denominator must be used to rewrite one or both fractions as equivalent fractions.

"When choosing a common denominator, why is it helpful to choose the least common denominator, or LCD?" Sample: Choosing the LCD simplifies the arithmetic that needs to be completed and often produces an answer that is already in simplest form.

Problems 12 and 13 [Generalize]
A way for students to check their work, or an alternative algorithm for completing the computations, is to change each mixed number to an improper fraction, find the sum or difference of those fractions, and then reduce the sum or difference to lowest terms.

Problem 14 [Justify]
"Why is it easier to find the sum of $3\frac{1}{2}$ and $2\frac{1}{2}$ than to find the sum of $4\frac{9}{10}$ and $2\frac{1}{2}$?" Sample: The mixed numbers $3\frac{1}{2}$ and $2\frac{1}{2}$ have common denominators.

(continued)

---

k. [Justify] In problem **h**, did you need to rename a whole number to subtract? Why or why not? No, because $\frac{1}{3}$ is less than $\frac{5}{6}$ we can subtract without renaming a whole number.

▶ **l.** Nelson wants to replace a piece of molding across the top of a door. The door frame is $32\frac{1}{4}$ inches wide and is trimmed with molding on each side that is $1\frac{5}{8}$ inches wide. How long does the molding across the top need to be? $35\frac{1}{2}$ in.

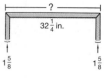

m. If the top of a bulletin board is $74\frac{3}{4}$ inches above the floor and the bottom is $38\frac{1}{2}$ inches above the floor, then what is the vertical measurement of the bulletin board? $36\frac{1}{4}$ in.

Written Practice   *Strengthening Concepts*

▶ ***1.** [Analyze] There were 65,000 people at the stadium. Eighty percent of the people had been to the stadium previously. How many of the people at the stadium had been there previously? 52,000 people
(12)

2. A dime is about 1 mm thick. How many dimes are in a stack 1 cm high? 10 dimes
(6)

3. Flying at an average speed of 525 miles per hour, how far can a passenger fly in two hours, in three hours, and in four hours? 1050 mi, 1575 mi, 2100 mi
(7)

For problems **4** and **5**, identify the plot, write an equation, and solve the problem.

4. Separating;
$\frac{8}{8} - \left(\frac{3}{8} + \frac{1}{4}\right) = p$; $\frac{3}{8}$

4. A whole pizza was cut into eighths. If Hector eats $\frac{3}{8}$ of the pizza and Rita eats $\frac{1}{4}$ of the pizza, then what fraction of the pizza remains?
(3, 13)

5. The ceiling fan company sold 7400 fans this year and 6900 fans last year. How many more fans did they sell this year compared to last year? comparing; $7400 - 6900 = d$; $d = 500$ fans
(3)

[Generalize] Simplify.

6. $\frac{5}{8} + \frac{2}{8}$ $\frac{7}{8}$
(13)

7. $\frac{5}{8} - \frac{2}{8}$ $\frac{3}{8}$
(13)

▶ ***8.** $\frac{2}{3} + \frac{1}{6}$ $\frac{5}{6}$
(13)

▶ ***9.** $\frac{2}{3} - \frac{1}{6}$ $\frac{1}{2}$
(13)

10. $1\frac{1}{4} + 2\frac{1}{4}$ $3\frac{1}{2}$
(13)

11. $2\frac{1}{4} - 1\frac{1}{4}$ 1
(13)

▶ ***12.** $3\frac{4}{5} - 2\frac{1}{10}$ $1\frac{7}{10}$
(13)

▶ ***13.** $3\frac{4}{5} + 2\frac{1}{10}$ $5\frac{9}{10}$
(13)

▶ ***14.** [Justify] Rearrange the addends to make the calculations easier. Then simplify. Justify your steps.
(2, 13)

$$3\frac{1}{2} + \left(4\frac{9}{10} + 2\frac{1}{2}\right)$$

14.

Step:	Justification:
$3\frac{1}{2} + \left(2\frac{1}{2} + 4\frac{9}{10}\right)$	Commutative Property
$\left(3\frac{1}{2} + 2\frac{1}{2}\right) + 4\frac{9}{10}$	Associative Property
$6 + 4\frac{9}{10}$	Added $3\frac{1}{2}$ and $2\frac{1}{2}$
$10\frac{9}{10}$	Added 6 and $4\frac{9}{10}$

▶ See Math Conversations in the sidebar.

* 15. Write each fraction as a decimal.
(12)
 a. $\frac{3}{25}$ 0.12   **b.** $3\frac{2}{5}$ 3.4

* 16. Write each decimal as a reduced fraction.
(12)
 a. 0.15 $\frac{3}{20}$ **b.** 0.015 $\frac{3}{200}$

* 17. Choose every correct answer. The set of whole numbers is closed
(1, 10) under   **A, C**

 A addition.   **B** subtraction.

 C multiplication.   **D** division.

▶*** 18.** [Generalize] Use prime factorization to reduce $\frac{75}{125}$. Show your work.
(9, 10) $\frac{5 \cdot 5 \cdot 3}{5 \cdot 5 \cdot 5} = \frac{3}{5}$

▶*** 19.** [Connect] Write a fraction equivalent to $\frac{3}{5}$ with a denominator of 100.
(10) $\frac{60}{100}$

20. Find the perimeter of a triangle with side lengths $1\frac{1}{2}$ in., 2 in., and
(8, 13) $2\frac{1}{2}$ in.   6 in.

21. Find the area of the ceiling of a room that is 14 feet wide and
(8) 16 feet long.   224 ft^2

22. List all the prime numbers between 70 and 90.   71, 73, 79, 83, 89
(9)

23. Write the prime factorization of 120. $2 \cdot 2 \cdot 2 \cdot 3 \cdot 5$
(9)

24. Find the average (mean) of 1, 3, 5, and 7.   4
(7)

25. The lengths of the tennis rackets on the shelf were 22 inches, 24 inches,
(7) 26 inches, 28 inches, and 20 inches. What was the average length of
 the racquets?   24 inches

26. Kimberly and Kerry delivered 280 papers in 4 weeks. What was the
(7) average number of papers delivered per week?   70 papers per week

▶ **27.** [Represent] Graph the numbers $\frac{1}{2}$, $\frac{1}{3}$, and $\frac{5}{6}$ on a number line. (*Hint:* First
(1, 10) find the common denominator of the fractions to determine the proper
 spacing on the number line.)

Simplify. Then choose one of the problems **28–30** to write a word problem
involving the given numbers and operation.   See student work.

28. $64.32 ÷ 16   **29.** 2007 − 1918   **30.** $\frac{\$52.70}{17}$ $3.10
(2) $4.02   (2) 89   (2)

27.
 ┬──●──●────●──┬
 0   $\frac{1}{3}$ $\frac{1}{2}$ $\frac{5}{6}$ 1

▶ See Math Conversations in the sidebar.

Looking Forward

Adding and subtracting fractions
and mixed numbers prepares
students for:

• **Lesson 22,** multiplying and
  dividing fractions.

• **Lesson 23,** multiplying and
  dividing mixed numbers.

• **Lesson 32,** finding probabilities.

• **Lesson 83,** finding probabilities
  of dependent events.

Math Conversations
Discussion opportunities are provided below.

Problem 18 [Generalize]
Extend the Problem
*"Explain how you can reduce $\frac{75}{125}$
to lowest terms using only mental math."*
Sample: The greatest common factor (GCF)
of 75 and 125 is 25; 75 ÷ 25 = 3 and 125 ÷
25 = 5, so $\frac{75}{125}$ in lowest terms is $\frac{3}{5}$.

Problem 19 [Connect]
After completing the problem, ask,

*"How many other fractions are equivalent
to $\frac{3}{5}$?"* Samples: an infinite number; too
many to count

Errors and Misconceptions
Problem 27
Students may not recognize that the least
common denominator of the fractions
represents the least number of equal divisions
that the number line must have between any
two consecutive integers.

To help students understand this concept,
draw a number line from 0 to 1 with a tick
mark at $\frac{1}{2}$ on the board or overhead. Ask
students where they would place a point for
$\frac{1}{3}$ and for $\frac{5}{6}$ if the locations of the points must
be exact. Students should conclude that a
number line divided into sixths is needed to
plot the given fractions because the LCD of the
denominators is 6.

You might choose to point out that a number
line would not be needed (although it could
be used) to *compare* the fractions.

• Evaluation
• Solving Equations by Inspection

Objectives
- Evaluate expressions by substituting numbers in place of variables.
- Solve simple equations by inspection.

Lesson Preparation

Materials
- **Power Up C** (in *Instructional Masters*)

Power Up C

Math Language

New	Maintain
constant	equation
evaluate	expression
solution	variable

Technology Resources

Student eBook Complete student textbook in electronic format.

Resources and Planner CD Assessment, reteaching, and instructional masters, plus a pacing calendar with standards.

Test and Practice Generator CD Create additional practice sheets and custom-made tests.

www.SaxonPublishers.com Visit for more student activities and planning materials.

Inclusion

Adaptations CD Adapted lessons, investigations, practice and assessments.

Meeting Standards

National Council of Teachers of Mathematics (NCTM)

Numbers and Operations

NO.3c Develop and use strategies to estimate the results of rational-number computations and judge the reasonableness of the results

Algebra

AL.2a Develop an initial conceptual understanding of different uses of variables

AL.3a Model and solve contextualized problems using various representations, such as graphs, tables, and equations

AL.2c Use symbolic algebra to represent situations and to solve problems, especially those that involve linear relationships

AL.2d Recognize and generate equivalent forms for simple algebraic expressions and solve linear equations

Problem Solving

PS.1b Solve problems that arise in mathematics and in other contexts

Problem-Solving Strategy: Work Backwards

Sometimes the given information in a problem requires us to work backwards to find an answer.

Problem: Samantha's age is half of Juan's age. Paul's age is half of Samantha's age. If Paul is eight years old, how old is Juan?

(Understand) We are given Paul's age. We are told how Paul's age relates to Samantha's age and how Samantha's age relates to Juan's age. We are asked to find Juan's age.

(Plan) We will work backwards from Paul's age to first find Samantha's age and then Juan's age.

(Solve) Paul is eight years old, and we know that his age is half of Samantha's. So we multiply 8 by 2 and find that Samantha is 16 years old.

We are told that Samantha's age is half of Juan's age, so we multiply 16 by 2 to find that Juan is 32 years old.

(Check) We worked backwards from Paul's age to find Juan's age. To find Juan's age, we first had to find Samantha's age. We check our math and find that 8 years (Paul's age) is half of 16 years (Samantha's age), which in turn is half of 32 years (Juan's age).

- **Evaluation**
- **Solving Equations by Inspection**

1 Power Up

Facts
Distribute **Power Up C** to students. See answers below.

Mental Math
Encourage students to share different ways to mentally compute these exercises. Strategies for exercises **a**, **e**, and **g** are listed below.

a. Use Logical Reasoning
1 hr has 30 2-min parts.
1 part → 1 page
30 parts → 30 pages

e. Use Math Sense
Only one multiple of 9 has a 3 in the ones place.
$9 \times 7 = 63$, so the missing ones digit is 7.
Then we find $17 \times 9 = 153$.

g. Double and Halve
50% of 44 = 100% of 22 = 22
Find a Fraction
$50\% = \frac{1}{2}$
$\frac{1}{2} \times 44 = 22$

Problem Solving
Refer to **Power-Up Discussion**, p. 92B.

Power Up *Building Power*

facts | Power Up C

mental math

a. Calculation: Kerry reads a page every two minutes. How many pages does she read per hour?   30

b. Measurement: How long is the segment? $1\frac{5}{8}$ inches

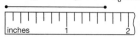

c. Power/Roots: $\sqrt{25} \times \sqrt{25}$ $5 \times 5 = 25$

d. Fractional Parts: What number is $\frac{5}{8}$ of 48?   30

e. Number Sense: What are the missing digits? $1\square \times 9 = 1\square 3$
$1\boxed{7} \times 9 = 1\boxed{5}3$

f. Geometry: What is the measure of $\angle S$?   50°

g. Percent: 50% of 44   22

h. Calculation: $5^2 - 4, \div 3, + 2, \sqrt{}, \times 5, + 1, \sqrt{}, \times 12, + 1, \sqrt{}$ 7

problem solving

Sometimes the given information in a problem requires us to work backwards to find an answer.

Problem: Samantha's age is half of Juan's age. Paul's age is half of Samantha's age. If Paul is eight years old, how old is Juan?

(**Understand**) We are given Paul's age. We are told how Paul's age relates to Samantha's age and how Samantha's age relates to Juan's age. We are asked to find Juan's age.

(**Plan**) We will work backwards from Paul's age to first find Samantha's age and then Juan's age.

(**Solve**) Paul is eight years old, and we know that his age is half of Samantha's. So we multiply 8 by 2 and find that Samantha is 16 years old.

We are told that Samantha's age is half of Juan's age, so we multiply 16 by 2 to find that Juan is 32 years old.

(**Check**) We worked backwards from Paul's age to find Juan's age. To find Juan's age, we first had to find Samantha's age. We check our math and find that 8 years (Paul's age) is half of 16 years (Samantha's age), which in turn is half of 32 years (Juan's age).

Facts   Reduce each fraction to lowest terms.

$\frac{2}{10} = \frac{1}{5}$	$\frac{2}{8} = \frac{1}{4}$	$\frac{3}{9} = \frac{1}{3}$	$\frac{8}{10} = \frac{4}{5}$	$\frac{3}{6} = \frac{1}{2}$
$\frac{6}{8} = \frac{3}{4}$	$\frac{3}{12} = \frac{1}{4}$	$\frac{2}{4} = \frac{1}{2}$	$\frac{6}{12} = \frac{1}{2}$	$\frac{9}{12} = \frac{3}{4}$
$\frac{4}{12} = \frac{1}{3}$	$\frac{2}{6} = \frac{1}{3}$	$\frac{8}{16} = \frac{1}{2}$	$\frac{5}{10} = \frac{1}{2}$	$\frac{6}{9} = \frac{2}{3}$
$\frac{4}{8} = \frac{1}{2}$	$\frac{8}{12} = \frac{2}{3}$	$\frac{4}{10} = \frac{2}{5}$	$\frac{4}{6} = \frac{2}{3}$	$\frac{6}{10} = \frac{3}{5}$

evaluation

Math Language
Recall that an **expression** is a mathematical phrase made up of variables, numbers, and/or symbols. To **evaluate** an expression means "to find the value of" the expression.

Sometimes we use a letter to represent an unidentified number. For example, "Four times a number *s*" can be expressed as $4 \cdot s$, or $4s$.

In the expression $4s$, the number 4 is a **constant,** because its value does not change, and the letter *s* is a **variable,** because its value can change. (If an algebraic term is composed of both constant and variable factors, we customarily write the constant factor first.)

Recall that a formula is an expression or equation used to calculate a desired result. For example, the formula for the perimeter (*P*) of a square guides us to multiply the length of a side (*s*) by 4.

$$P = 4s$$

We **evaluate** an expression by substituting numbers in place of variables and calculating the result.

For example, in the expression $4s$, if we substitute 6 for *s* we get 4(6), which equals 24.

Example 1

A formula for the perimeter of a rectangle is $P = 2l + 2w$. Find *P* when *l* is 15 cm and *w* is 12 cm.

Solution

We substitute 15 cm for *l* and 12 cm for *w* in the formula. Then we perform the calculations.

$$P = 2l + 2w$$
$$P = 2(15 \text{ cm}) + 2(12 \text{ cm})$$
$$P = 30 \text{ cm} + 24 \text{ cm}$$
$$P = \textbf{54 cm}$$

Explain How can we use the formula $A = lw$ to find the area of the same rectangle? Substitute 15 cm for *l* and 12 cm for *w* in the formula. Multiply: $15 \cdot 12 = 180$. A = 180 cm^2

solving equations by inspection

Sample:
$\frac{n}{7} = 4$; $n = 28$

An **equation** is a mathematical sentence stating that two quantities are equal. An equation can have one or more variables. A **solution** to an equation with one variable is a number that satisfies the equation (makes the equation true). In the equation $4x = 20$, the solution is 5 because $4(5) = 20$.

Formulate Write and solve an equation that has one operation and one variable. Use any operation and variable you wish.

In this book we will learn and practice many strategies for solving equations, but first we will practice solving equations by inspection. That is, we will study equations and mentally determine the solutions.

2 New Concepts

Instruction
Point out that we evaluate the expression $4s$ to find the value for *P* in this formula. Guide students to see that $P = 4s$ is a formula and $4s$ is an expression. Explain that an expression will not have an equals sign.

Example 1
Instruction
Have students notice that this formula, like most geometric formulas, uses units. The units are carried through the computation and used to label the answer.

As you discuss the *Explain* question, point out that the units are multiplied in the computation and therefore the answer is expressed in square units.

Instruction
As you introduce solving equations by inspection, point out that the quantities on both sides of the equals sign in an *equation* are expressions. Have students use the definition of an expression in the sidebar to explain why $4x$ and 20 are both expressions.

Ask volunteers to share the equations they wrote and solved. Let others solve the equations and explain what they did to solve them.

Explain that solving an equation by inspection means just that—you look at ("inspect") the equation and use mental math to solve it.

(continued)

Math Background

It is customary to write algebraic expressions in a way that creates the greatest likelihood that the terms of the expression will be interpreted correctly.

For example, when an expression includes a constant and a variable (such as $2c$), the constant is given first to minimize the likelihood that it will be interpreted as an exponent.

Example 2
Instruction
After you work through the problem, use the *Discuss* question to explore how we know that $3m$ equals 18. Lead students to describe the mental math they do to arrive at that conclusion.

Practice Set
Problem a [Error Alert]
Remind students that the height of a parallelogram is a measure that is perpendicular to its base.

Problem c [Error Alert]
Make sure students recognize that the expression $4ac$ represents the product of three factors.

Example 2

If a taxi company charges a \$2 flat fee plus \$3 per mile (*m*), then the cost (*c*) in dollars of a taxi ride is shown by this formula:

$$3m + 2 = c$$

Suppose that the cost of a taxi ride is \$20. Find the length of the taxi ride by solving the equation $3m + 2 = 20$.

Solution

This equation means that the number of miles is multiplied by 3, then 2 is added making the total 20.

$$3m + 2 = 20$$

That means that $3m$ equals 18. Since $3m$ equals 18, m must equal 6.

$$m = 6$$

So the taxi ride was **6 miles.**

Discuss Why does $3m + 2 = 20$ mean that $3m = 18$? $3m$ is 18 because 18 plus 2 is 20.

Practice Set ▶

a. A formula for the area (*A*) of a parallelogram is $A = bh$. Find the area of a parallelogram with a base (*b*) of 12 in. and a height (*h*) of 4 in.   48 in.²

4 in.
12 in.

b. In the expression $4ac$, what is the constant?   4

▶ c. Evaluate $4ac$ for $a = 1$ and $c = 12$.   48

Analyze Solve each equation by inspection.

d. $w + 5 = 16$ $w = 11$ e. $m - 6 = 18$ $m = 24$

f. $25 - n = 11$ $n = 14$ g. $5x = 30$ $x = 6$

h. $\dfrac{d}{4} = 8$ $d = 32$ i. $\dfrac{12}{z} = 6$ $z = 2$

j. $2a - 1 = 9$ $a = 5$ k. $20 = 3f - 1$ $f = 7$

l. Admission to the county fair is \$3. Each ride costs \$2. Nate has \$15. Solve the following equation to find how many rides he can take.

$$2r + 3 = 15 \quad r = 6;\ 6\ \text{rides}$$

Written Practice   *Strengthening Concepts*

1. There were 256 farmers in the county 30 years ago. Five eighths of
(5) those farmers have changed occupations. How many of the 256 farmers changed occupations?   160 farmers

2. Averaging 35 pages per hour, how many pages can Karina read in
(7) 2 hours, in 3 hours, and in 4 hours?   70 pgs, 105 pgs, 140 pgs

▶ See Math Conversations in the sidebar.

Teacher Tip

As you move through this program, your students are **building their knowledge of mathematical concepts and skills** and increasing their ability to use them. It is important that they get sufficient practice to reinforce and maintain understanding and proficiency.

You can accomplish this easily by teaching all the lessons in the sequence of the program and making sure that students do all the exercises in the practice set and written practice. The practice plan has been carefully developed to ensure that all students get the practice they need to be successful.

3. Each package of light bulbs contains 4 bulbs. If an employee at a construction office needs to order 480 bulbs, how many packages should she order?   120 packages
(4)

For problem **4**, identify the plot, write an equation, and solve the problem.

4. When Betsy Ross made the American flag, it had 13 stars. On July 4, 1960, the 50th star was added to the flag for Hawaii. How many more stars were on the flag by July 4, 1960, than were on the Betsy Ross flag?   comparing; $50 - 13 = d$; 37 stars
(3)

Analyze   Solve by inspection.

5. $15 = m - 4$ $m = 19$ **6.** $15 - m = 4$ $m = 11$
(14)   (14)

7. $3w = 36$ $w = 12$ * **8.** $5x + 5 = 20$ $x = 3$
(14)   (14)

▶ * **9.** $\frac{x}{3} = 4$ $x = 12$ ▶ * **10.** $\frac{x}{2} + 3 = 12$ $x = 18$
(14)   (14)

▶ *Generalize*   Simplify.

* **11.** $\frac{3}{8} + \frac{1}{3}$ $\frac{17}{24}$ * **12.** $1\frac{1}{4} - \frac{3}{16}$ $1\frac{1}{16}$
(13)   (13)

* **13.** *Justify*   Rearrange the addends to make the calculations easier. Then
(2, 13)   simplify. Justify your steps.

$$\frac{3}{8} + \left(1\frac{1}{2} + 2\frac{5}{8}\right)$$

14. Arrange in order from least to greatest. $-1, -0.5, 0, \frac{3}{8}, \frac{1}{2}, 0.8, 1$
(1, 12)

$$\frac{1}{2}, -1, 0, \frac{3}{8}, 0.8, 1, -0.5$$

Evaluate   For problems **15–18**, use the given information to find the value of each expression.

▶ * **15.** Find ac when $a = 2$ and $c = 9$.   18
(14)

* **16.** The formula for the perimeter of a square is $P = 4s$. Find P when $s = 12$. $P = 48$
(14)

* **17.** For $y = x - 9$, find y when $x = 22$. $y = 13$
(14)

▶ * **18.** For $d = rt$, find d when $r = 60$ and $t = 4$. $d = 240$
(14)

19. Arrange these fractions in order from least to greatest.
(10)

$$\frac{2}{3}, \frac{3}{4}, \frac{5}{12} \quad \frac{5}{12}, \frac{2}{3}, \frac{3}{4}$$

20. Write the prime factorization of 990. $2 \cdot 3 \cdot 3 \cdot 5 \cdot 11$
(9)

21. What is the difference between the product of 6 and 8 and the sum of 8 and 12?   28
(2)

22. If 4 is the divisor, and 8 is the quotient, what is the dividend?   32
(2)

▶ See Math Conversations in the sidebar.

(left margin partial)

ep:	Justification:
$\frac{5}{8} + 1\frac{1}{2})$	Commutative Property of Addition
$\frac{5}{8}) + 1\frac{1}{2}$	Associative Property of Addition
$1\frac{1}{2}$	Added $\frac{3}{8}$ and $2\frac{5}{8}$
$\frac{1}{2}$	Added 3 and $1\frac{1}{2}$

③ Written Practice

Math Conversations
Discussion opportunities are provided below.

Problems 9 and 10   *Analyze*
Invite a volunteer to translate the equation in problem 9 to words. Sample: x divided by three is equal to four.

"What number divided by three is equal to four?" 12

Invite a volunteer to translate the equation in problem 10 to words. Sample: The quotient of a number and two, increased by three, is twelve.

"For the moment, let's ignore the increase of three. What number divided by two is equal to twelve?" 24

"Explain how we can use 24 to help learn the value of x." Sample: Since $\frac{x}{2}$ is increased by 3 to equal 12, the value of x must be less than 24.

"What is the value of x, and how can we check our work?" 18; check by substitution

Problem 11   *Generalize*
Before completing the arithmetic, ask students to make an estimate of the sum. Sample: A reasonable estimate is less than 1 because both fractions are less than $\frac{1}{2}$.

After completing the arithmetic, remind students to compare the exact answer and the estimate to decide the reasonableness of the exact answer.

Problem 12   *Generalize*
Before completing the arithmetic, ask students to make an estimate of the sum and use it to check the exact answer for reasonableness after the arithmetic has been completed. Sample: An estimate is 1 because $\frac{3}{16}$ is about the same as $\frac{4}{16}$ or $\frac{1}{4}$, and $1\frac{1}{4} - \frac{1}{4}$ is 1.

Problem 15   *Evaluate*
"What operation does the expression ac represent?" multiplication

Problem 18   *Evaluate*
Challenge a volunteer to explain how to learn the value of d using only mental math. Sample: rt represents the product of 60 and 4. Since the product of 6 and 4 is 24, the product of 60 and 4 is 240.

(continued)

Math Conversations

Discussion opportunities are provided below.

Problem 30 *Generalize*

It is important for students to note that the dimensions of the room are given in feet and the flooring is sold in units of square yards.

---

* **23.** If each side of a square is $2\frac{1}{2}$ in., then what is the perimeter of the
(8, 13) square?   10 in.

24. Compare:
(1)
   a. $|-5| \lessgtr |-6|$ **b.** $-5 \gtrless -6$

25. The data below show the number of students in seven classrooms.
(7) What is the median number of students?   30

27, 30, 29, 31, 30, 32, 29

26. Estimate 8.25% sales tax on a $39.89 purchase. $3.20
(12)

27. Express each percent as a decimal.
(12)
   a. 125%   1.25   **b.** 8.25%   0.0825

Find each perimeter.

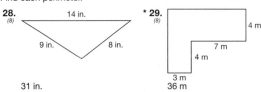

28. 14 in.   *** 29.**
(8)   9 in.   8 in.   *(8)*   4 m   7 m   4 m   3 m

31 in.   36 m

▶* **30.** *Generalize* Leah wants to carpet a room that is 12 feet wide and 15 feet
(6, 8) long. Carpeting is sold by the square yard. Find the length and width of the room in yards. Then find the number of square yards needed to carpet the room.   5 yards long, 4 yards wide, 20 square yards

▶ See Math Conversations in the sidebar.

Looking Forward

Solving equations by inspection prepares students for:

• **Lesson 38,** using properties of equality to solve equations.

• **Lesson 50,** solving multi-step equations.

•Powers and Roots

Objectives

- Use exponents to show repeated multiplication.
- Simplify exponential expressions.
- Write prime factorizations using exponents.
- Find the nth root of a number.

Materials

- **Power Up C** (in *Instructional Masters*)

Power Up C

Math Language

New	Maintain
index	base
perfect square	exponent
radicand	power
	radical

Technology Resources

Student eBook Complete student textbook in electronic format.

Resources and Planner CD Assessment, reteaching, and instructional masters, plus a pacing calendar with standards.

Test and Practice Generator CD Create additional practice sheets and custom-made tests.

www.SaxonPublishers.com Visit for more student activities and planning materials.

Inclusion

Adaptations CD Adapted lessons, investigations, practice and assessments.

National Council of Teachers of Mathematics (NCTM)

Numbers and Operations

NO.1f Use factors, multiples, prime factorization, and relatively prime numbers to solve problems

NO.2c Understand and use the inverse relationships of addition and subtraction, multiplication and division, and squaring and finding square roots to simplify computations and solve problems

Algebra

AL.3a Model and solve contextualized problems using various representations, such as graphs, tables, and equations

Problem-Solving Strategy: Use Logical Reasoning

In some problem situations, we are given enough information to use logical reasoning to find other information.

Problem: Dora, Eric, and Francis went to the restaurant and each ordered a different sandwich. Dora ordered a tuna sandwich, and Eric did not order a ham sandwich. If their order was for tuna, grilled cheese, and ham sandwiches, what did each person order?

Understand In the problem, three people order three sandwiches. We know what one person ordered, and we know what one other person did not order. We are asked to find each person's sandwich order.

Plan We will make a table to keep track of the information. We will place checkmarks to represent sandwich orders that we know are true and X's to represent orders that we know are false.

Solve We draw a table with a row for each person and a column for each sandwich. We use abbreviations for the names. We start by placing a checkmark in the box that corresponds to "Dora orders the tuna sandwich." Then we place an X in the box that corresponds to "Eric orders the ham sandwich."

	T	H	GC
D	✓		
E		X	
F			

	T	H	GC
D	✓	X	X
E	X	X	
F	X		

	T	H	GC
D	✓	X	X
E	X	X	✓
F	X	✓	X

Now we use logical reasoning to fill the table. Dora ordered the tuna sandwich, so it is implied that neither Eric nor Francis ordered tuna. We write X's in the boxes below Dora's checkmark. By ordering tuna, it is also implied that Dora did not order the ham or grilled cheese. So we write X's in the boxes to the right of Dora's checkmark.

Each person's order was different, so only one checkmark should appear in each row and column. Since there are two X's in the column for "ham sandwich," we conclude that Francis ordered the ham sandwich. Now we know Francis did not order the grilled cheese, so we place an X in the lower-right box. The only possible order for Eric is grilled cheese.

Check We created a table and filled in the information we knew. Then we used logical reasoning to find each person's order (Dora: tuna; Eric: grilled cheese; Francis: ham).

• Powers and Roots

Power Up *Building Power*

facts	Power Up C
mental math	**a. Calculation:** Wendy walked 8 miles in 2 hours. What was her average rate in miles per hour? 4 mph
	b. Estimation: $19.95 × 4 $80
	c. Fractional Parts: $\frac{1}{4}$ of $84 $21
	d. Measurement: Jeremiah's forearm (elbow to wrist) is 11 inches long. His hand is 6 inches long. He measures a cabinet by placing his hand and forearm against it. He has to do this twice to reach the end. About how long is the cabinet? about 34 inches
	e. Powers/Roots: $\sqrt{100} - \sqrt{25}$ 5
	f. Geometry: In this triangle, x must be between what two numbers? 3 and 7
	g. Percent: 10% of $6.50 $0.65
	h. Calculation: 200 − 50, ÷ 3, − 1, $\sqrt{}$, − 5, × 50, $\sqrt{}$, + 3, minus a dozen 1

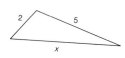

	problem solving	In some problem situations, we are given enough information to use logical reasoning to find other information.

Problem: Dora, Eric, and Francis went to the restaurant and each ordered a different sandwich. Dora ordered a tuna sandwich, and Eric did not order a ham sandwich. If their order was for tuna, grilled cheese, and ham sandwiches, what did each person order?

[**Understand**] In the problem, three people order three sandwiches. We know what one person ordered, and we know what one other person did **not** order. We are asked to find each person's sandwich order.

[**Plan**] We will make a table to keep track of the information. We will place checkmarks to represent sandwich orders that we know are true and X's to represent orders that we know are false.

[**Solve**] We draw a table with a row for each person and a column for each sandwich. We use abbreviations for the names. We start by placing a checkmark in the box that corresponds to "Dora orders tuna sandwich." Then we place an X in the box that corresponds to "Eric orders ham sandwich."

	T	H	GC
D	✓		
E		X	
F			

---

1 Power Up

Facts
Distribute **Power Up C** to students. See answers below.

Mental Math
Encourage students to share different ways to mentally compute these exercises. Strategies for exercises **a**, **f**, and **g** are listed below.

a. Use Math Sense
Average rate = miles per hour
Wendy's rate = 8 miles in 2 hours
Wendy's average rate = 4 miles per hour

f. Use Math Sense
side x < sum of the other two sides
side x > difference of the other two sides
side x > 3 and x < 7

g. Multiply by 10, Divide by 10
10% of $6.50 = 100% of $0.65 = $0.65
Find a Fraction
10% = $\frac{1}{10}$
$\frac{1}{10} × $6.50 = $0.65

Problem Solving
Refer to **Power-Up Discussion**, p. 97B.

Facts	Reduce each fraction to lowest terms.

$\frac{2}{10} = \frac{1}{5}$	$\frac{2}{8} = \frac{1}{4}$	$\frac{3}{9} = \frac{1}{3}$	$\frac{8}{10} = \frac{4}{5}$	$\frac{3}{6} = \frac{1}{2}$
$\frac{6}{8} = \frac{3}{4}$	$\frac{3}{12} = \frac{1}{4}$	$\frac{2}{4} = \frac{1}{2}$	$\frac{6}{12} = \frac{1}{2}$	$\frac{9}{12} = \frac{3}{4}$
$\frac{4}{12} = \frac{1}{3}$	$\frac{2}{6} = \frac{1}{3}$	$\frac{8}{16} = \frac{1}{2}$	$\frac{5}{10} = \frac{1}{2}$	$\frac{6}{9} = \frac{2}{3}$
$\frac{4}{8} = \frac{1}{2}$	$\frac{8}{12} = \frac{2}{3}$	$\frac{4}{10} = \frac{2}{5}$	$\frac{4}{6} = \frac{2}{3}$	$\frac{6}{10} = \frac{3}{5}$

Instruction

Review the vocabulary (*base* and *exponent*) associated with powers of numbers and be sure that students can read these numbers.

Example 1

Instruction

Move quickly through this example if students are familiar with the topic. Students who need some review may use the *Student Reference Guide*. Discuss the differences mentioned in the Thinking Skill *Explain* feature.

Have students note that when a base is a power of 10, the exponents represents the number of zeros in the standard form of the number.

(continued)

Now we use logical reasoning to fill the table. Dora ordered the tuna sandwich, so it is implied that neither Eric nor Francis ordered tuna. We write X's in the boxes below Dora's checkmark. By ordering tuna, it is also implied that Dora did not order the ham or grilled cheese. So we write X's in the boxes to the right of Dora's checkmark.

	T	H	GC
D	✓	X	X
E	X	X	
F	X		

Each person's order was different, so only one checkmark should appear in each row and column. Since there are two X's in the column for "ham sandwich," we conclude that Francis ordered the ham sandwich. Now we know Francis did not order the grilled cheese, so we place an X in the lower-right box. The only possible order for Eric is grilled cheese.

	T	H	GC
D	✓	X	X
E	X	X	✓
F	X	✓	X

(Check) We created a table and filled in the information we knew. Then we used logical reasoning to find each person's order (Dora: tuna; Eric: grilled cheese; Francis: ham).

New Concept   *Increasing Knowledge*

To show repeated multiplication we can use an exponent.

$$\text{base} \rightarrow 5^2 \leftarrow \text{exponent}$$

If the exponent is a counting number, it indicates how many times the base is used as a factor.

$$5^3 = 5 \cdot 5 \cdot 5 = 125$$

We read 5^2 as "five squared." We read 5^3 as "five cubed." We say "to the *n*th power" if the exponent *n* is greater than 3. For example, 5^4 is read as "five to the fourth power" or just "five to the fourth."

Example 1

Simplify:

a. 5^4 b. 10^4

Solution

Thinking Skill

Explain

Explain the difference between 5^4 and $5 \cdot 4$.

The exponent, 4, indicates that the base is a factor four times.

a. $5 \cdot 5 \cdot 5 \cdot 5 = \textbf{625}$

b. $10 \cdot 10 \cdot 10 \cdot 10 = \textbf{10,000}$

Notice that the number of zeros in 10,000 matches the exponent of 10. 5^4 means four 5s are multiplied. $5 \cdot 4$ means four 5s are added.

Math Background

The perfect squares from 1 to 400 are shown in bold below.

$1 \times 1 = \textbf{1}$	$2 \times 2 = \textbf{4}$	$3 \times 3 = \textbf{9}$	$4 \times 4 = \textbf{16}$
$5 \times 5 = \textbf{25}$	$6 \times 6 = \textbf{36}$	$7 \times 7 = \textbf{49}$	$8 \times 8 = \textbf{64}$
$9 \times 9 = \textbf{81}$	$10 \times 10 = \textbf{100}$	$11 \times 11 = \textbf{121}$	$12 \times 12 = \textbf{144}$
$13 \times 13 = \textbf{169}$	$14 \times 14 = \textbf{196}$	$15 \times 15 = \textbf{225}$	$16 \times 16 = \textbf{256}$
$17 \times 17 = \textbf{289}$	$18 \times 18 = \textbf{324}$	$19 \times 19 = \textbf{361}$	$20 \times 20 = \textbf{400}$

Each perfect square is the product of its square root raised to the second power.

Example 2

Write the prime factorization of 72 using exponents.

Solution

The prime factorization of 72 is $2 \cdot 2 \cdot 2 \cdot 3 \cdot 3$. We can group like factors with an exponent.

$$72 = 2^3 \cdot 3^2$$

We can use exponents with units of length to indicate units of area. We show this in example 3 with the area of a square. The formula for the area of a square is $A = s^2$. In this formula, A represents area and s represents the length of the side.

Example 3

The figure shows a square floor tile that is one foot on each side. Find the area covered by the tile in square inches using the formula $A = s^2$.

12 in. ☐

Solution

Reading Math
We read in.^{2} as "square inch."

Squaring a length results in square units.

Step:	Justification:
$A = s^2$	Formula for area of a square
$= (12 \text{ in.})^2$	Substituted 12 in. for s and squared
$= 144 \text{ in.}^2$	Notice that one square foot equals 144 square inches.

12 in.

144 square inches

12 in.

Exponents can be applied to variables. If the same variable is a factor in an expression a number of times, we can simplify the expression by writing the variable with an exponent.

Example 4

Express with exponents.

$$2xxyyyz$$

Solution

Since x is a factor twice, we use the exponent 2, and since y is a factor 3 times, we use the exponent 3.

$$2x^2y^3z$$

The inverse of raising a number to a power is taking a root of a number. We may use a **radical** sign, $\sqrt{}$, to indicate a root of a number.

$$\sqrt{25} = 5 \qquad \text{"The } \textbf{square root} \text{ of 25 is 5."}$$
$$\sqrt[3]{125} = 5 \qquad \text{"The } \textbf{cube root} \text{ of 125 is 5."}$$

The number under the radical sign is the **radicand**.

Lesson 15   99

Example 2
Instruction
Call attention to the form used for the answer. The bases are ordered from least to greatest. You may want to have students practice carrying out two or three more prime factorizations. Some examples to use are 144 $(2^4 \cdot 3^2)$, 600 $(2^3 \cdot 3 \cdot 5^2)$, and 44,100 $(2^2 \cdot 3^2 \cdot 5^2 \cdot 7^2)$.

Example 3
Instruction
Point out that the label for the answer is square inches. Although area is always expressed in square units, you may want to point out that inches were multiplied by inches in the computation, which produces inches^2, or square inches.

Instruction
When introducing roots, relate the inverse relationship of powers and roots to the other inverse relationships students are familiar with (addition and subtraction; multiplication and division). Spend some time making sure that students understand the new vocabulary and can read roots correctly.

(continued)

Example 5

Instruction

Work through the example and then discuss the *Analyze* question. Point out that 64 could also be called a perfect sixth power, because the sixth root of 64 is a whole number. Have students use the pattern of the square and cube roots of 64 and what they have learned in this lesson to predict which is greater, the square root or the sixth root of 64? $\sqrt{64}$ is 8, $\sqrt[6]{64}$ is 2.

Examples 6 and 7

Instruction

Tell students that knowing the squares of the first 10 or so counting numbers is helpful when working on word problems involving squares or square roots.

(continued)

The small 3 in $\sqrt[3]{125}$ is the **index** of the root. If the index is 4 or more, we say **"the *n*th root."**

$$\sqrt[5]{32} \text{ is read "the fifth root of 32"}$$
$$\sqrt[5]{32} = 2 \text{ because } 2 \cdot 2 \cdot 2 \cdot 2 \cdot 2 = 32$$

Example 5

Visit www.SaxonPublishers.com/ActivitiesC3 for a graphing calculator activity.

Simplify:

a. $\sqrt{144}$ b. $\sqrt[3]{27}$

Solution

a. We find the number which, when multiplied by itself, equals 144. Since $12 \cdot 12 = 144$, $\sqrt{144}$ equals **12**.

b. We find the number which, when used as a factor three times, equals 27. Since $3 \cdot 3 \cdot 3 = 27$, $\sqrt[3]{27}$ equals **3**.

A number that is a square of a counting number is a **perfect square**. For example, 25 is a perfect square because $5^2 = 25$.

Analyze The number 64 is both a perfect square and a perfect cube. Is $\sqrt{64}$ less than or greater than $\sqrt[3]{64}$? Since $8 \cdot 8 = 64$ and $4 \cdot 4 \cdot 4 = 64$, we find that $\sqrt{64} = 8$ and $\sqrt[3]{64} = 4$. Thus $\sqrt{64}$ is greater than $\sqrt[3]{64}$.

Example 6

The floor of a square room is covered with square-foot floor tiles. If 100 tiles cover the floor, how long is each side of the room?

100 ft²

Solution

The side length of a square is the square root of the area of the square. Therefore, the length of each side is $\sqrt{100 \text{ ft}^2}$, which is **10 ft**.

Example 7

Name the first three counting numbers that are perfect squares. Then find their positive square roots.

Solution

Here we show several counting numbers in order.

$$1, 2, 3, 4, 5, 6, 7, 8, 9, 10, 11, 12, \ldots$$

The numbers 1 (1×1) and 4 (2×2) and 9 (3×3) are perfect squares. We find the square roots.

$$\sqrt{1} = 1 \qquad \sqrt{4} = 2 \qquad \sqrt{9} = 3$$

Teacher Tip

Some students may find it interesting (and helpful for learning some of the squares and square roots) to **make a chart of the squares and look for patterns.**

1	4	9	16
25	36	49	64
81	100	121	144
169	196	225	256
289	324	361	400

For example: When the first 20 squares are arranged in rows of 4, notice that all the squares in the last column are multiples of 16. You may wish to ask students how that pattern changes if the first 20 squares are arranged in rows of 5.

Practice Set

Simplify:

a. 10^5 100,000   b. 3^4 81   c. $(15 \text{ cm})^2$ 225 cm²

d. $\sqrt{121}$ 11   e. $\sqrt[3]{8}$ 2   f. $\sqrt{5^2}$ 5

Express with exponents.

g. $5xyyyzz$ $5xy^3z^2$ h. $aaab$ a^3b i. $3xyxyx$ $3x^3y^2$

j. Mr. Chin wants to cover the floor of his garage with a non-slip coating. His garage measures 20 feet on each side. Use the formula $A = s^2$ to find the number of square feet of floor that need to be coated. 400 ft²

20 ft

Written Practice   *Strengthening Concepts*

1. At the baseball game, 40% of the fans joined in singing the national anthem, while the rest listened quietly. If there were 25,000 fans in the stadium, how many joined in singing? 10,000 fans
(12)

2. A gallon of milk contains 128 oz. How many 8-oz cups can be filled with a gallon of milk? 16 cups
(4)

3. Jackie played the drums in the band. If he beat the drum at a rate of 110 beats per minute, how many beats would he play in $4\frac{1}{2}$ minutes? 495 beats
(7)

Generalize Simplify.

▶ * **4.** $(4 \text{ in.})^3$ 64 in.³   ▶ * **5.** $\sqrt[3]{1}$ 1   * **6.** $\sqrt{8^2}$ 8
(15)   (15)   (15)

7. Express with exponents: $2xxxmrr$ $2x^3mr^2$
(15)

Analyze Solve by inspection.

▶ * **8.** $\frac{x}{4} = 12$ $x = 48$ * **9.** $2x + 5 = 5$ $x = 0$ * **10.** $9 - m = 7$ $m = 2$
(14)   (14)   (14)

Simplify.

▶ * **11.** $\frac{4}{5} - \frac{1}{2}$ $\frac{3}{10}$ ▶ * **12.** $1\frac{1}{4} + 1\frac{1}{3}$ $2\frac{7}{12}$
(13)   (13)

▶ * **13.** *Justify* Compare and justify your answer with a property of addition.
(2, 13)
$$\left(\frac{1}{3} + \frac{1}{2} + \frac{2}{3}\right) \ominus \left(\frac{1}{3} + \frac{2}{3} + \frac{1}{2}\right)$$
Commutative Property of Addition

14. Arrange in order from least to greatest: $0, -2, \frac{1}{3}, 0.3, 3, -1.5$.
(1, 12) $-2, -1.5, 0, 0.3, \frac{1}{3}, 3$

* **15.** Find $4ac$ when $a = 1$ and $c = 9$. 36
(14)

* **16.** What is the difference between the sum of $\frac{1}{2}$ and 10 and the product of $\frac{1}{2}$ and 10? $5\frac{1}{2}$
(2)

* **17.** For $y = \frac{1}{3}x + 2$, find y when $x = 6$. $y = 4$
(14)

Lesson 15   101

▶ See Math Conversations in the sidebar.

Math Conversations

Discussion opportunities are provided below.

Problem 5 *Generalize*

Students should generalize that to simplify the expression, they must find a factor that when used three times has a product of 1.

Problem 8 *Analyze*

To solve for x by inspection, explain that it makes sense to look for a multiple of 4 because the denominator of the fraction is 4. In other words, students should consider values such as 4, 8, 12, 16, and so on, for the initial values of x.

Problem 11

"Are the denominators of the fractions the same or different?" different

"How must we change the fractions in order to subtract $\frac{1}{2}$ from $\frac{4}{5}$?" Sample: Rewrite one or both fractions as equivalent fractions that share a common denominator.

"What is the least common denominator, or LCD, of 5 and 2?" 10

Problem 12

Before completing the arithmetic, ask students to make an estimate of the sum. Sample: Both addends are less than $1\frac{1}{2}$. So the sum of the addends will be less than $1\frac{1}{2} + 1\frac{1}{2}$, or 3.

Problem 13 *Justify*

"How do the addends on the left side of the equation compare to the addends on the right side of the equation?" Sample: The same three addends are on both sides of the equation.

"How are the addends on the left side of the equation different from the addends on the right side of the equation?" Sample: The order of the addends is different.

Errors and Misconceptions
Problem 4

A common error is to label the product as 64 inches. To help students recognize that the label *inches* is not correct, demonstrate the arithmetic shown below on the board or overhead.

$(4 \text{ in.})^3 = 4 \cdot 4 \cdot 4 \cdot \text{in.} \cdot \text{in.} \cdot \text{in.}$

$4 \cdot 4 \cdot 4 \cdot \text{in.} \cdot \text{in.} \cdot \text{in.} = (4)^3 \cdot (\text{in.})^3 = 64 \text{ in.}^3$

Students should recognize that the parentheses represent a grouping symbol, and the exponent 3 represents raising *everything* inside the grouping symbol to the third power.

(continued)

3 Written Practice (Continued)

Math Conversations

Discussion opportunities are provided below.

Problem 19 [Analyze]

If students use a common denominator to compare the fractions, remind them they can find and compare the decimal equivalents of the fractions to check their work.

Errors and Misconceptions
Problem 21

Watch for students who do not include two decimal places in the answer, and remind them that that one way to check a product of decimal factors is to count decimal places in those factors. The total number of decimal places in the factors should be the same as the number of decimal places in the product.

---

* 18. How much money is 20% of $65? $13
(11, 12)

▶* 19. [Analyze] Arrange these fractions in order from least to greatest.
(10)
$$\frac{3}{8}, \frac{2}{5}, \frac{1}{4} \quad \frac{1}{4}, \frac{3}{8}, \frac{2}{5}$$

* 20. Write the prime factorization of 630 using exponents. $2 \cdot 3^2 \cdot 5 \cdot 7$
(9, 15)

▶ 21. A formula for the area of a square is $A = s^2$. Find A when $s = 15$ cm.
(14) $A = 225$ cm^2

22. If the subtrahend is 12 and the difference is 12, what is the
(2)   minuend?   24

23. If each side of a square is $7\frac{1}{2}$ in., what is the perimeter of the
(8, 13)   square?   30 in.

24. Compare: $0.625 \bigotimes \frac{3}{5}$
(12)

25. What is the median number of bears in the zoos in the state if the zoos
(7)   contain 11 bears, 3 bears, 18 bears, 2 bears, and 5 bears?   5 bears

26. Write 0.07 as a fraction. Then name both numbers.
(12) $\frac{7}{100}$; seven hundredths

27. Explain why the following statement is false: "Every whole number is
(1)   positive."   Zero is a whole number but is not positive.

Find the perimeters.

28.
(8)

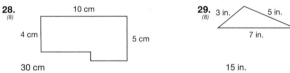

30 cm

29.   3 in.   5 in.
(8)
         7 in.
         15 in.

* 30. A 15-foot square room is going to be carpeted. Use $A = s^2$ to find the
(15)   number of square feet of carpet that is needed.   225 ft^2

▶ See Math Conversations in the sidebar.

Looking Forward

Working with powers and roots prepares students for:

- **Lesson 16,** working with irrational numbers.
- **Lesson 21,** learning the order of operations.
- **Lesson 27,** understanding the Laws of Exponents.
- **Lesson 51,** working with negative exponents.
- **Lesson 63,** simplifying fractions with negative exponents.
- **Lesson 74,** simplifying square roots.
- **Lesson 78,** finding products of square roots.
- **Lesson 93,** solving equations with exponents.

Assessment   *30–40 minutes*   *For use after Lesson 15*

Distribute **Cumulative Test 2** to each student. Two versions of the test are available in *Saxon Math Course 3 Course Assessments Book*. Have students complete the **Power-Up Test** first. Allow 10 minutes. Then have students work the 20 numbered items on the **Cumulative Test.** Students may use copies of the answer sheet to record their work. Track individual and class progress with the **Test Analysis** forms.

Power-Up Test 2

Cumulative Test 2A

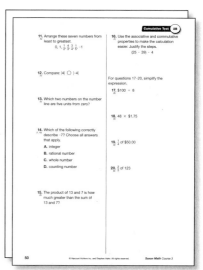

Alternative Cumulative Test 2B

Optional Answer Forms

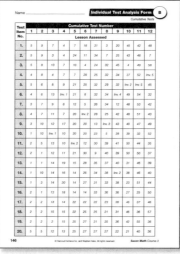

Individual Test Analysis Form

Class Test Analysis Form

Reteaching

Students who score below 80% on the assessment may be in need of reteaching. Look for the causes of student mistakes. If errors are conceptual, refer to the *Reteaching Masters* for reteaching.

Orders of Magnitude and Power Prefixes
Assign after Lesson 15 and Test 2

Objectives
- Identify differences in order of magnitude.
- Relate orders of magnitude to metric prefixes.
- Relate orders of magnitude to powers of 10.
- Relate power prefixes to extremely small or great measures.

Materials
Performance Activity 2A and **2B**

Preparation
Make copies of **Performance Activities 2A** and **2B.** (One each per student.)

Time Requirement
15–30 minutes; Begin in class and complete at home.

Activity
Explain to students that an order of magnitude means a tenfold difference in size. For example, a penny, a dime, a dollar, a $10 bill, and a $100 bill differ in value from one denomination to the next larger or next smaller denomination by one order of magnitude. Students will refer to a table comparing the masses of animals to a man in order to identify differences in magnitude. Students then relate metric prefixes separated by one order of magnitude. Students conclude the activity by referring to a table listing prefixes separated by three orders of magnitude—prefixes that have entered into common usage through advances in computer technology. Point out that all necessary information is provided on **Performance Activities 2A** and **2B.**

Criteria for Evidence of Learning
- Correctly identifies differences in size by orders of magnitude.
- Identifies relationship between metric prefixes by order of magnitude.
- Selects proper prefix and base unit to name a measure.

Performance Activity 2A and 2B

National Council of Teachers of Mathematics (NCTM)

Numbers and Operations

NO.1e Develop an understanding of large numbers and recognize and appropriately use exponential, scientific, and calculator notation

NO.1f Use factors, multiples, prime factorization, and relatively prime numbers to solve problems

NO.1g Develop meaning for integers and represent and compare quantities with them

Measurement

ME.1a Understand both metric and customary systems of measurement

Communication

CM.3a Organize and consolidate their mathematical thinking through communication

• Irrational Numbers

Objectives

- Approximate the value of square roots with and without a calculator.
- Identify numbers as members of the sets of irrational numbers and real numbers.
- Compare and order rational and irrational numbers.
- Find the length of a side of a square given its area.

Lesson Preparation

Materials

- **Power Up D** (in *Instructional Masters*)
- **Teacher-provided material:** calculators

Optional

- **Teacher-provided material:** 10 pieces of paper

Power Up D

Math Language

New

irrational numbers

real numbers

Technology Resources

Student eBook Complete student textbook in electronic format.

Resources and Planner CD Assessment, reteaching, and instructional masters, plus a pacing calendar with standards.

Test and Practice Generator CD Create additional practice sheets and custom-made tests.

www.SaxonPublishers.com Visit for more student activities and planning materials.

Inclusion

Adaptations CD Adapted lessons, investigations, practice and assessments.

Meeting Standards

National Council of Teachers of Mathematics (NCTM)

Problem Solving

PS.1b Solve problems that arise in mathematics and in other contexts

PS.1c Apply and adapt a variety of appropriate strategies to solve problems

Connections

CN.4b Understand how mathematical ideas interconnect and build on one another to produce a coherent whole

Problem-Solving Strategy: Find a Pattern

Problem: Find the next four numbers in this sequence:

$$\frac{1}{24}, \frac{1}{12}, \frac{1}{8}, \frac{1}{6}, \frac{5}{24}, —, —, —, —$$

Understand Understand the problem.

"What information are we given?"

The first five terms of a sequence are $\frac{1}{24}, \frac{1}{12}, \frac{1}{8}, \frac{1}{6}$ and $\frac{5}{24}$.

"What are we asked to do?"

We are asked to extend the sequence for three more terms.

Plan Make a plan.

"What problem-solving strategies could we use?"

We will to *find a pattern* to extend the sequence.

"Do we need to adapt any of the information?"

Because the fractions have different denominators, it is difficult to see the pattern. It would be easier to find a pattern if the fractions have the same denominator.

Solve Carry out the plan.

"How do we begin?"

The lowest common denominator of 24, 12, 8, and 6 is 24. We will convert the fractions to twenty-fourths:

$$\frac{1}{24} \quad \frac{1}{12} \quad \frac{1}{8} \quad \frac{1}{6} \quad \frac{5}{24}$$

$$\frac{1}{24} \quad \frac{2}{24} \quad \frac{3}{24} \quad \frac{4}{24} \quad \frac{5}{24}$$

"How do we proceed?"

We can see that the sequence increases by $\frac{1}{24}$ with each term. We will extend the sequence, and then simplify (reduce) the fractions when possible:

$$\frac{1}{24} \quad \frac{1}{12} \quad \frac{1}{8} \quad \frac{1}{6} \quad \frac{5}{24} \quad \frac{1}{4} \quad \frac{7}{24} \quad \frac{1}{3} \quad \frac{3}{8}$$

$$\frac{1}{24} \quad \frac{2}{24} \quad \frac{3}{24} \quad \frac{4}{24} \quad \frac{5}{24} \quad \frac{6}{24} \quad \frac{7}{24} \quad \frac{8}{24} \quad \frac{9}{24}$$

Check Look back.

"Did we complete the task that was assigned?"

Yes. We found that the next four terms of the sequence are $\frac{1}{4}, \frac{7}{24}, \frac{1}{3}$, and $\frac{3}{8}$.

• **Irrational Numbers**

facts | Power Up D

mental math

a. **Calculation:** Chrissy drove 100 miles in 2 hours. What was her average speed in miles per hour?   50 mph

b. **Geometry:** What is the measure of ∠PMR?
110°

c. **Fractional Parts:** $\frac{1}{5}$ of 35   7

d. **Measurement:** Half of a kilogram is how many grams?   500 g

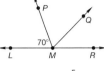

e. **Algebra:** What is the mass of 8 of the objects in the left tray?   56 kg

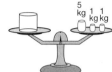

f. **Calculation:** 18, ÷ 3, ÷ 3, × 3, × 3, + 2, + 1, ÷ 3, × 2, + 1, ÷ 3, square it, √   5

problem solving

Find the next four numbers in the sequence:

$$\frac{1}{24}, \frac{1}{12}, \frac{1}{8}, \frac{1}{6}, \frac{5}{24}, \underline{\quad}, \underline{\quad}, \underline{\quad}, \underline{\quad} \quad \frac{1}{4}, \frac{7}{24}, \frac{1}{3}, \frac{3}{8}$$

Recall that the set of rational numbers is closed under addition, subtraction, multiplication, and division. However, the square roots of many rational numbers, such as $\sqrt{2}$ and $\sqrt{3}$, are not rational numbers. Since $\sqrt{2}$ and $\sqrt{3}$ are greater than $\sqrt{1}$ and less than $\sqrt{4}$, their values are more than 1 and less than 2.

To find the approximate value of $\sqrt{2}$ and $\sqrt{3}$, we can use a calculator.

Most calculators have a square root key, ▣. If we enter a number and then press ▣, the display shows the square root of the entered number.

• Use a calculator to find $\sqrt{1}$ and $\sqrt{4}$.

• Use a calculator to find $\sqrt{2}$ and $\sqrt{3}$.

How do the displays for $\sqrt{2}$ and $\sqrt{3}$ differ from the displays for $\sqrt{1}$ and $\sqrt{4}$?

Lesson 16   103

---

1 Power Up

Facts
Distribute **Power Up D** to students. See answers below.

Mental Math
Encourage students to share different ways to mentally compute these exercises. Strategies for exercises **b** and **d** are listed below.

b. **Divide by 5**
$35 \div 5 = 7$
Multiply by One Fifth
$\frac{1}{5} \times 35 = 7$

d. **Supplementary Angles**
$m\angle LMP + m\angle PMR = 180°$
$70° + m\angle PMR = 180°$
$m\angle PMR = 180° - 70° = 110°$

Problem Solving
Refer to **Power-Up Discussion**, p. 103B.

2 New Concepts

Instruction
Students will need to use calculators for the following activity. Be sure that they know how to use the square root key.

(continued)

Facts   Simplify each power.

$10^2 = 100$	$20^2 = 400$	$2^2 = 4$	$2^3 = 8$	$5^2 = 25$
$3^2 = 9$	$6^2 = 36$	$9^2 = 81$	$4^2 = 16$	$8^2 = 64$
$7^2 = 49$	$1^2 = 1$	$11^2 = 121$	$30^2 = 900$	$10^3 = 1000$
$12^2 = 144$	$13^2 = 169$	$25^2 = 625$	$15^2 = 225$	$\left(\frac{1}{2}\right)^2 = \frac{1}{4}$

Instruction

Call attention to the differences in the calculator displays. Explain that even if the display could continue, no pattern would be found for $\sqrt{2}$ or $\sqrt{3}$.

Example 1

Instruction

Help students understand how to find the two whole numbers between which a square root is located. Use a few more examples, if needed, to solidify this skill: $\sqrt{13}$ (between $\sqrt{9}$ and $\sqrt{16}$, or between 3 and 4), $\sqrt{75}$ (between $\sqrt{64}$ and $\sqrt{81}$, or between 8 and 9), and $\sqrt{136}$ (between $\sqrt{121}$ and $\sqrt{144}$, or between 11 and 12). Point out that knowing the perfect squares makes the estimates easier to complete.

Example 2

Instruction

If students have trouble getting started on this example, show them how to use a number line to plot the numbers they know first. Remind them that they need to think about what two perfect squares 5 is between. 4 and 9, so $\sqrt{5}$ is between 2 and 3

(continued)

No matter how many digits a calculator displays, the displays for $\sqrt{2}$ and $\sqrt{3}$ will be filled with digits without a repeating pattern. The display fills because there is no rational number—no fraction or repeating decimal—that equals $\sqrt{2}$ or $\sqrt{3}$.

The numbers $\sqrt{2}$ and $\sqrt{3}$ are examples of **irrational numbers.** The prefix *ir-* means *not,* so "irrational numbers" means "non-rational numbers." The square root of any counting number that is not a perfect square is an irrational number. Later we will consider other examples of irrational numbers.

Example 1

Which number is irrational?

   A $\sqrt{0}$ **B** $\sqrt{4}$ **C** $\sqrt{8}$ **D** $\sqrt{16}$

Solution

The numbers 0, 4, and 16 are perfect squares.

$$\sqrt{0} = 0 \qquad \sqrt{4} = 2 \qquad \sqrt{16} = 4$$

Since 0 is not a perfect square, $\sqrt{8}$ is an irrational number. (Since $\sqrt{8}$ is between $\sqrt{4}$ and $\sqrt{9}$, its value is greater than 2 and less than 3.)

Thinking Skill

Explain

How can you determine which two counting numbers the square root of 108 falls between? Find the two perfect squares closest in value: $10^2 = 100$ and $11^2 = 121$, so the square root of 108 is between 10 and 11.

Rational numbers and irrational numbers together form the set of **real numbers.**

Real Numbers

Rational Numbers	Irrational Numbers

All of the real numbers can be represented by points on a number line, and all of the points on a number line represent real numbers.

Examples of Real Numbers

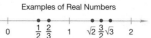

Example 2

Arrange these real numbers in order from least to greatest.

$$2, \sqrt{5}, \frac{5}{9}, 0, 3, 1.2, 1$$

Solution

The irrational number $\sqrt{5}$ is greater than $\sqrt{4}$, which equals 2, and less than $\sqrt{9}$, which equals 3.

$$0, \frac{5}{9}, 1, 1.2, 2, \sqrt{5}, 3$$

Inclusion

Expand on the number line demonstration from Lesson 10. Write ten numbers (whole, integer, rational, irrational) on pieces of paper. Hand them to ten students and call one at a time to stand in order. Have the students stand at the correct distance from each other according to number value. Discuss with the class what happens to the order and distance of the students when each one is called up. Also discuss how this demonstration is different from that in Lesson 10.

Math Background

Since there is exactly one point on a number line that corresponds to every real number, a number line can be used to compare real numbers.

For example, to order $\sqrt{8}$, $\frac{3}{8}$, and $-\frac{5}{2}$ from least to greatest, first use a number line to compare the numbers.

- The point corresponding to $\sqrt{8}$ is between 2 and 3, and it is located to the right of the points corresponding to $\frac{3}{8}$ and $-\frac{5}{2}$. So the greatest number is $\sqrt{8}$.

- The point corresponding to $-\frac{5}{2}$ is located to the left of zero, and it is to the left of the points corresponding to $\frac{3}{8}$ and $\sqrt{8}$. So the least number is $-\frac{5}{2}$.

The order of the numbers, from least to greatest, is $-\frac{5}{2}, \frac{3}{8}, \sqrt{8}$.

Example 3

The area of this square is 2 cm². What is the length of each side?

2 cm²

Solution

The side length of a square is the square root of its area. Therefore, the length of each side is $\sqrt{2cm^2}$, which is $\sqrt{2}$ **cm.**

Notice that $\sqrt{2}$ cm is an actual length that is approximately equal to 1.4 cm.

Practice Set

a. If a real number is not rational, then it is what type of number?   irrational

▶ **b.** Which of the following numbers is irrational?   **D**

   A -3 **B** $\sqrt{9}$ **C** $\dfrac{9}{2}$ **D** $\sqrt{7}$

c. D $\sqrt{5}$. The square root of 5 is between $\sqrt{4}$ and $\sqrt{9}$. The square root of 4 is 2, and $\sqrt{9}$ is 3. So $\sqrt{5}$ is between 2 and 3 on the number line.

▶ **c.** [Explain] Which of these numbers is between 2 and 3 on the number line? How do you know?

   A $\sqrt{2}$ **B** $\sqrt{3}$ **C** $\sqrt{4}$ **D** $\sqrt{5}$

d. Arrange these real numbers in order from least to greatest.

   0, 1, $\sqrt{2}$, $\frac{3}{4}$, 0.5, -0.6 -0.6, 0, 0.5, $\frac{3}{4}$, 1, $\sqrt{2}$

Find the length of each side of these squares.

e.   20 mm   **f.** $\sqrt{3}$ cm

400 mm²   3 cm²

Use a calculator to find the square roots of these numbers. Round to the nearest hundredth.

▶ **g.** $\sqrt{10}$ 3.16   ▶ **h.** $\sqrt{20}$ 4.47   ▶ **i.** $\sqrt{40}$ 6.32

j. Refer to your answers to problems **g, h,** and **i** to answer this question: Which number is twice as much as the square root of ten, $\sqrt{20}$ or $\sqrt{40}$? $\sqrt{40}$

Written Practice   *Strengthening Concepts*

1. Bonnie drove 108 miles in 2 hours. What was her average speed?
(7) 54 miles per hour

2. Before the gift was revealed, only $\frac{2}{7}$ of the crowd guessed correctly. If
(5) there were 294 people in the crowd, how many guessed correctly before it was revealed?   84 people

For problems **3** and **4,** identify the plot, write an equation, and solve the problem.

3. Roger completed 28 of 41 math exercises during school. How many
(3) exercises are left to complete after school?   separating, $41 - 28 = l$, $l = 13$

Lesson 16   105

▶ See Math Conversations in the sidebar.

Example 3
Instruction

Help students understand that we "undo" what we know about the area of a square—that it is the square of the side length—by taking its square root to find the length of a side.

Practice Set
Problem b [Error Alert]

If students look for more than one correct answer, they can generalize that the words *which* and *is* imply there is only one correct answer.

Problem c [Explain]

When solving problems of this nature, explain that it makes sense to first look for perfect squares (such as 1, 4, 9, 16, 25, and so on) because the square roots of perfect squares are easily recognized. For example, 4 is a perfect square, and its square root is 2. Students can then infer that because they are looking in problem c for a number that is greater than 2, they must look for a number that is greater than $\sqrt{4}$.

Problems g, h, and i [Error Alert]

When rounding a number to the hundredths place, students must remember to consider the digit in the thousandths place of the number.

Teacher Tip

Continue to **require that written work be done neatly,** with each step on its own line. As the work with mathematical concepts and skills grows more complex, it is even more important that the students are able to go back easily over their work in order to locate an error when one has been made.

Math Conversations

Discussion opportunities are provided below.

Problem 5 Generalize

Students should generalize that simplifying the expression involves naming a factor that when used three times has a product of 64.

Problem 7 Generalize

"The LCD or least common denominator of 7 and 14 is 14. Explain how you can find an equivalent fraction in fourteenths for $\frac{6}{7}$ using only mental math." Sample: Since 7 times 2 is 14, multiply the numerator by 2; $\frac{6}{7} \times \frac{2}{2} = \frac{12}{14}$.

Problem 14

Ask students to describe their thought processes for finding the value of m. Steps should include "$5m$ is 40 because 40 plus 10 is 50" and "m is 8 because 5 times 8 is 40."

Errors and Misconceptions
Problem 6

Some students may think that 10^3 is simpler in form than 1000 because 10^3 contains fewer digits. To address this misconception, explain that a number in standard form (such as 1000) is considered to be a simpler form of 10^3 because 10^3 represents operations ($10 \times 10 \times 10$) that have not yet been completed.

(continued)

4. In Major League Baseball in 1960 there were two leagues of eight teams each. By 1998 the total number of teams had expanded to 30. How many teams were added from 1960 to 1998? comparing, $30 - 16 = d$, $d = 14$
   (3)

Generalize Simplify.

▸ * 5. $\sqrt[3]{64}$ 4
   (15)

▸ * 6. 10^3 1000
   (15)

▸ * 7. $\frac{6}{7} + \frac{1}{14}$ $\frac{13}{14}$
   (13)

* 8. $2\frac{5}{8} - 1\frac{1}{4}$ $1\frac{3}{8}$
   (13)

9. Find the perimeter and area of this figure. 26 m, 30 m²
   (8)

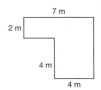

10. *Represent* Express with exponents:
    (15)
    a. $4xyzxy$ $4x^2y^2z$

    b. $3aabbbc$ $3a^2b^3c$

11. *Analyze* Compare:
    (15)
    a. $\sqrt{16}$ $\bigcirc$ 7 ($<$)

    b. $\sqrt{81}$ $\bigcirc$ 3^2 ($=$)

Analyze Solve problems **12–15** by inspection.

* 12. $4z - 2 = 30$ $z = 8$
   (14)

* 13. $200 - a = 140$ $a = 60$
   (14)

▸* 14. $50 = 5m + 10$ $m = 8$
   (14)

* 15. $7 = \frac{x}{3}$ $x = 21$
   (14)

16. Compute 75% of $800. $600
    (11)

17. Find $4ac$ when $a = 3$ and $c = 39$. 468
    (14)

18. Rearrange the factors to make the calculation easier. Then simplify, justifying your steps.
    (2)

$$8 \cdot (49 \cdot 25)$$

* 19. *Conclude* Momentum is the product of mass and velocity, $p = mv$. Find p when $m = 40$ and $v = 11$. $p = 440$
    (14)

20. What is the mean and the median of 2, 4, 6, and 8? 5, 5
    (7)

21. Write the prime factorization of 400. Use exponents for repeated factors. $2^4 \cdot 5^2$
    (9, 15)

22. What is the product of the sum of 10 and 5 and the difference of 10 and 5? 75
    (2)

18.

Step:	Justification:
$8 \cdot (25 \cdot 49)$	Commutative Property
$(8 \cdot 25) \cdot 49$	Associative Property
$200 \cdot 49$	Multiplied 8 and 25
9800	Multiplied 200 and 49

▸ See Math Conversations in the sidebar.

23. Express $\frac{1}{8}$ as a decimal and as a percent.   0.125; $12\frac{1}{2}$ or 12.5%
(12)

▶ **24.** (Conclude) The relationship between rate (r), time (t), and distance (d) is
(14)   expressed in the formula $d = rt$. Find d when $r = 55$ miles per hour and
    $t = 2$ hours. $d = 110$ miles

25. List the even prime numbers.   2
(1, 9)

Simplify.

26. $123 - 321$ -198 **27.** $\frac{2001 \text{ hours}}{3}$ 667 hours
(2)   (2)

(Classify)   For problems **28–30,** choose from this list *all* correct answers.

    A integers   **B** whole numbers   **C** natural numbers

    D rational numbers   **E** irrational numbers **F** real numbers

* **28.** The number -2 is a member of which set(s) of numbers?   **A, D, F**
(1, 16)

* **29.** The number $\sqrt{2}$ is a member of which set(s) of numbers?   **E, F**
(1, 16)

* **30.** The number $\frac{1}{2}$ is a member of which set(s) of numbers?   **D, F**
(1, 16)

Early Finishers
Real-World
Application

Uranus is the seventh planet from the Sun and is composed primarily
of rocks and ice. Uranus is turquoise in appearance due to its
atmosphere, which is made up of approximately 82% hydrogen, 15%
helium, and 3% methane. Express each percent as a fraction and as
a decimal.   Hydrogen $= \frac{82}{100} = \frac{41}{50} = 0.82$; Helium $= \frac{15}{100} = \frac{3}{20} = 0.15$; and
Methane $= \frac{3}{100} = 0.03$

Lesson 16   107

▶ See Math Conversations in the sidebar.

3 **Written Practice** (Continued)

Math Conversations

Discussion opportunities are provided below.

Problem 24 (Conclude)

Extend the Problem

*"Explain how you could find elapsed
time if you were given a rate and a
distance."* Divide the distance by the rate.
For example, a distance of 400 miles and an
average rate of 40 miles per hour describe a
time of $400 \div 40$ or 10 hours.

Looking Forward

Working with irrational numbers
prepares students for:

- **Investigation 2,** understanding
  and applying the Pythagorean
  Theorem.

- **Lesson 74,** simplifying square
  roots.

- **Lesson 78,** finding products of
  square roots.

- **Lesson 120,** rationalizing a
  denominator.

•Rounding and Estimating

Objectives

- Round numbers to a given place value.
- Round mixed numbers and decimal numbers to whole numbers.
- Estimate measures.
- Estimate to determine the reasonableness of an answer.

Lesson Preparation

Materials

- **Power Up D** (in *Instructional Masters*)
- **Manipulative Kit: tape measures or yard sticks**
- **Teacher-provided material: calculators, daily newspaper or news magazine, graph paper**

Optional

- **Invetigation Activity 2** (in *Instructional Masters*) or **graph paper**

Power Up D

Math Language

New	English Learners (ESL)
estimate	approximate
reasonable	
round	

Technology Resources

Student eBook Complete student textbook in electronic format.

Resources and Planner CD Assessment, reteaching, and instructional masters, plus a pacing calendar with standards.

Test and Practice Generator CD Create additional practice sheets and custom-made tests.

www.SaxonPublishers.com Visit for more student activities and planning materials.

Inclusion

Adaptations CD Adapted lessons, investigations, practice and assessments.

Meeting Standards

National Council of Teachers of Mathematics (NCTM)

Numbers and Operations

NO.3c Develop and use strategies to estimate the results of rational-number computations and judge the reasonableness of the results

Measurement

ME.2a Use common benchmarks to select appropriate methods for estimating measurements

ME.2b Select and apply techniques and tools to accurately find length, area, volume, and angle measures to appropriate levels of precision

Problem Solving

PS.1b Solve problems that arise in mathematics and in other contexts

Problem-Solving Strategy: Use Logical Reasoning / Make a Table

Daria, Evan, and Fernando went to the cafeteria and each ordered a drink. Daria did not order lemonade. Evan ordered cranberry juice. If their order was for lemonade, cranberry juice, and orange juice, what did each person order?

[Understand] **Understand the problem.**

"What information are we given?"

Three people went to a cafeteria, and each ordered a drink.
   1. Daria did not order lemonade.
   2. Evan ordered cranberry juice.
   3. Somebody ordered orange juice.

"What are we asked to do?"

We are asked to determine which beverage each person ordered.

[Plan] **Make a plan.**

"What problem-solving strategy will we use?"

We will use *logical reasoning* to help us *make a table* to find the solution.

[Solve] **Carry out the plan.**

"How should we begin our table?"

We draw a table with a row for each person and a column for each type of drink. We know that Daria did not order lemonade, so we place an X in the box that corresponds to "Daria orders the lemonade." We know that Evan ordered cranberry juice, so we place a checkmark in the box that corresponds to "Evan orders the cranberry juice."

"How do we fill in the rest of the table?"

Since we know Evan ordered the cranberry juice, we can place X's in the boxes above and below his checkmark. Now we know Daria did not order the cranberry juice or the lemonade, so she must have ordered the orange juice. We place a checkmark in the appropriate box. That means that Fernando must have ordered the lemonade.

	L	C	O
D	X	X	✓
E	X	✓	X
F	✓	X	X

[Check] **Look back.**

"Did we find the answer to the question that was asked?"

Yes. We determined that Daria ordered orange juice, Evan ordered cranberry juice, and Fernando ordered lemonade.

• Rounding and Estimating

1 Power Up

Facts
Distribute **Power Up D** to students. See answers below.

Mental Math
Encourage students to share different ways to mentally compute these exercises. Strategies for exercises **c** and **e** are listed below.

c. Add the Parts
$1\frac{1}{4}$ in. + $1\frac{1}{4}$ in. + $1\frac{1}{4}$ in. =
$(1 + 1 + 1) + (\frac{1}{4} + \frac{1}{4} + \frac{1}{4}) = 3\frac{3}{4}$ in.

Regroup, then Multiply
$3 \times 1\frac{1}{4}$ in. =
$(3 \times 1) + (3 \times \frac{1}{4}) =$
$3 + \frac{3}{4} = 3\frac{3}{4}$ in.

e. Halve and Double
$14 \times 5 = 7 \times 10 = 70$

Regroup, then Multiply
$14 \times 5 = (10 \times 5) + (4 \times 5) =$
$50 + 20 = 70$

Problem Solving
Refer to **Power-Up Discussion,** p. 108B.

2 New Concepts

Instruction
To help students see how much *rounding* and *estimating* are used in reporting news, ask them to look through today's newspaper or a news magazine for rounded numbers or estimated values.

Explain that two reasons for rounding a number are
- to make the number easier to work with when an exact answer is not needed.
- to make it easier to understand the size or value of the number quickly.

Demonstrate the rounding procedures in this lesson's three examples on the board or overhead and have students follow along with you.

(continued)

---

facts   Power Up D

mental math

a. Calculation: Tammy types 20 words per minute. How many words can she type in $2\frac{1}{2}$ minutes?   50

b. Powers/Roots: 25×10^2 2500

c. Fractional Parts: If the folded piece of wire is unfolded, about how long will it be? $3\frac{3}{4}$ in.

d. Algebra: Solve for x: $7x - 1 = 20$.   3

e. Number Sense: 14×5 70

f. Measurement: If Roger walks one kilometer in 8 minutes, how long does it take him to walk 500 meters?   4 min

g. Percent: 25% of 100   25

h. Calculation: $444 \div 2$, $\div 2$, $- 11$, $\div 4$, $\sqrt{}$, $\times 7$, $\times 2$, $+ 20$, $+ 9$, $\div 3$, $\div 3$, $+ 100$ 111

problem solving   Daria, Evan, and Fernando went to the cafeteria and each ordered a drink. Daria did not order lemonade. Evan ordered cranberry juice. If their order was for lemonade, cranberry juice, and orange juice, what did each person order?   Daria: orange juice; Evan: cranberry juice; Fernando: lemonade

New Concept   *Increasing Knowledge*

Parade officials reported that one million people lined the route of the Rose Parade.

Thinking Skill

Connect

What are some everyday activities that require estimation? Sample: When grocery shopping, it is good to have an estimation of the total price of the items in your cart.

The number used in the statement, one million, is a round number and is not exact. The number was obtained not by counting every person along the route but by estimating the size of the crowd. We often use rounding and estimating for situations in which an exact or nearly exact number is not necessary.

We **round** whole numbers by finding a nearby number that ends with one or more zeros. For example, we might round 188 to 190 or to 200 depending on whether we are rounding to the nearest ten or nearest hundred.

```
                                          188
  |---|---|---|---|---|---|---|---|---•|---|
 100 110 120 130 140 150 160 170 180 190 200
```

The mathematical procedure for rounding involves place value. We round a number to a certain place value by inspecting the digit that follows that place and deciding whether to round up or down.

Facts   Simplify each power.

$10^2 = 100$	$20^2 = 400$	$2^2 = 4$	$2^3 = 8$	$5^2 = 25$
$3^2 = 9$	$6^2 = 36$	$9^2 = 81$	$4^2 = 16$	$8^2 = 64$
$7^2 = 49$	$1^2 = 1$	$11^2 = 121$	$30^2 = 900$	$10^3 = 1000$
$12^2 = 144$	$13^2 = 169$	$25^2 = 625$	$15^2 = 225$	$\left(\frac{1}{2}\right)^2 = \frac{1}{4}$

Example 1

Round 1,481,362 to the nearest hundred thousand.

Solution

The number is between the round numbers 1,400,000 and 1,500,000. To help us decide which round number is nearer, we inspect the digit in the ten-thousands place. If the digit is 5 or greater we round up. If the digit is less than 5 we round down.

$$1,4\widehat{8}1,362$$

The digit in the ten-thousands place is 8, so we round up to **1,500,000**.

We round decimal numbers by finding a decimal number with fewer decimal places. The procedure is similar to the one used for whole numbers except that we do not use trailing zeros.

Example 2

Round 3.14159 to two decimal places.

Solution

"Two decimal places" means two places to the right of the decimal point, so we are rounding the number to the nearest hundredth. Thus our choice is between 3.14 and 3.15. We inspect the digit in the thousandths place to decide which number is closer.

$$3.14\widehat{1}59$$

The digit in the thousandths place is 1, which is less than 5, so we round down to **3.14**.

To round a mixed number to the nearest whole number, we decide if the fraction is more than or less than $\frac{1}{2}$. If the numerator is less than half the denominator, then the fraction is less than $\frac{1}{2}$, and we round down. If the numerator is half or greater than half of the denominator, we round up.

Example 3

Round each number to the nearest whole number.

a. $13\frac{5}{12}$ b. 13.512

Solution

a. The mixed number is between 13 and 14. The fraction $\frac{5}{12}$ is less than $\frac{1}{2}$ because 5 is less than half of 12. We round down to **13.**

b. The decimal point separates the whole number from the fraction. Again we choose between 13 and 14. The digit in the first decimal place is 5, so we round up to **14.**

Example 1
Instruction
Stress that once a decision has been made about that place (it stays the same for rounding down or is increased by 1 for rounding up), the remaining digits are dropped and their places filled with zeros.

Example 2
Instruction
The rounding rules work in the same way for decimal places as they do for whole numbers. Be sure that students understand that they do not fill the places that are dropped with zeros.

Example 3
Instruction
For rounding mixed numbers, some students may find it easier to use this approach to think about the fraction part:
• Multiply the numerator by 2.
• If the product is less than the denominator, round down.
• If the product is equal to or greater than the denominator, round up.

This method works well for fractions with denominators that are odd numbers.

(continued)

Math Background

A number of different strategies can be used to make an estimate. One such strategy involves compatible numbers and division. Compatible numbers "get along well" when selected operations are performed with them.

To estimate a quotient, change the dividend, the divisor, or both the dividend and the divisor to nearby compatible numbers. For example, to make an estimate for the quotient 475 ÷ 6.89, change 6.89 to 7 and change 475 to 490. The numbers 7 and 490 are compatible numbers because 7 is a factor of 490.

A reasonable estimate of the quotient 475 ÷ 6.89 is 490 ÷ 7 or 70.

Instruction

After example 3, introduce the concept of estimation. The ability to make good estimates is important for almost any kind of job—for construction workers, cooks, doctors, schedulers, and many others.

Encourage students to practice making estimates for measures and calculations both in school and at home. Suggest that they estimate

- the total before checking out when shopping or the bill at a restaurant.
- the time needed to walk or drive somewhere.
- various lengths and distances.

Have students check their estimates by measuring, if possible.

Following example 4, show how estimation can be used to determine whether an answer is reasonable. Explain that students will probably use this kind of estimate more than others. Point out that estimating is important even when using a calculator as it is easy to press the wrong key when entering many keystrokes. Being good at estimating is also helpful when taking a multiple-choice test as it provides a way to quickly eliminate some of the choices.

Example 5
Instruction

Discuss how rounding one number in an estimate down and another one up can help bring the estimate closer to the actual value when adding or multiplying. In this example, instead of calculating the area of the kitchen floor, 8 ft could have been rounded up to 10 ft and 12 ft could have been rounded down to 10 ft to get an estimated area of 100 square feet. In this case, the answer would be the same, since the actual area was rounded to 100 square feet to estimate the total cost.

(continued)

To **estimate** is to determine an approximate value. We make estimates in our activities throughout the day. In a baseball game, for example, the batter estimates the speed and location of the pitch and swings the bat to arrive at the expected location at just the right time. The awaiting fielder hears the crack of the bat and—in a split second—estimates the ball's trajectory and begins moving to the point where the ball is expected to land. Both players adjust their estimates as they visually gather more information about the path of the baseball.

The estimates we make in athletics are extremely complex, yet with practice we perform them with ease. We can also become proficient at estimating measures and calculations as we practice these skills.

Example 4

Estimate the length of one wall of your classroom in feet.

Solution

There are a variety of ways to estimate a length of several feet. Some people walk a distance using big steps counting three feet (one yard) to a step. Other people will use a reference, such as a door which is about seven feet high, to visually form an estimate. Make a thoughtful estimate, and then use a tape measure or yardstick to find the length of the wall, rounded to the nearest foot.

Sample: For a rectangular classroom, you can estimate the length and width, then double each estimate and add.

Discuss Explain how you might estimate the perimeter of the classroom.

Estimating calculations helps us decide if an answer is **reasonable.** For example, suppose we are calculating the cost of 48 square yards of carpeting priced at $28.95 per square yard. We could round the quantity to 50 square yards and the price to $30 per square yard. Multiplying these numbers mentally we get $1500. If the calculated product is very different, then the results are not reasonable and we will review our calculations.

Example 5

Ivan wants to tile the floor of a kitchen that is 12 feet long and 8 feet wide. The installed tile is $7.89 per square foot. Ivan calculates that the cost to tile the floor is $315.60. Is Ivan's calculation reasonable?

Solution

The cost is based on the number of square feet. The area of the kitchen is 8 feet × 12 feet, or 96 square feet. We can estimate the cost of tiling the floor by multiplying 100 square feet by $8 per square foot. A reasonable estimate of the cost is $800, which is very different from Ivan's calculation. Since Ivan's calculation is **not reasonable,** he should check his calculations.

English Learners

Before example 4, explain the meaning of the word **approximate.** Say:

"To approximate means to get close to something. When you find an approximate value, you get a number which is close to the answer."

Ask students to approximate the following numbers by rounding to the nearest whole number.

3.2   7.9   1.78   3.04 $\frac{4}{3}$

3, 8, 2, 3, 1

Example 6

Richard is paid $11.85 per hour. About how much money does he earn in a year (52 weeks) if he works 40 hours per week?

Solution

We use round numbers and multiply the three values to estimate how much Richard earns in a year.

Total Pay $\approx$ $12 · 40 · 50	Rounded $11.85 and 52
$\approx$ $12 · 2000	Multiplied 50 · 40
$\approx$ $24,000	Multiplied

Richard earns about **$24,000** per year.

g. 40 × $10 = $400; Gus's calculation is

Practice Set

100 times larger than the correct answer. He might have misplaced or not keyed in the decimal point.

h. If we round $11\frac{3}{4}$ to 12 and $10\frac{1}{2}$ to 11, then the area of the room is about 12 · 11 = 132 square feet. Since we rounded up, Grace's calculation seems reasonable.

i. It is reasonable that Eduardo can reach Dallas by 9:00 p.m. because he has nearly three hours to travel 157 miles. At his current rate he can drive about 180 mi in 3 hr.

▶ **a.** In 2000 the population of Dallas was 1,188,580. Round that number to the nearest hundred thousand.   1,200,000

▶ **b.** Round 3.14159 to four decimal places.   3.1416

c. The price of regular unleaded gasoline was 2.19\frac{9}{10}$. Round that price to the nearest cent. $2.20

d. *Estimate* Estimate the height of the ceiling in your classroom in meters and in feet.   Estimates vary. Measure to determine height.

e. Estimate the sum of 3879 and 5276.   9000

f. Estimate the product of $12\frac{3}{8}$ and 9.75 by rounding each number to the nearest whole number before multiplying.   12 × 10 = 120

g. *Evaluate* Gus works 39 hours for $9.85 per hour. He calculates that his weekly paycheck should be $38,415. What is a reasonable estimate of what Gus earns? How do you suppose Gus arrived at his calculation?

h. A rectangular room is $11\frac{3}{4}$ feet long and $10\frac{1}{2}$ feet wide. Grace calculated the area to be about 124 square feet. Explain why her calculation is or is not reasonable.

i. It is 6:05 p.m. and Eduardo is driving to Dallas. If he is 157 miles away and driving at an average speed of 62 miles per hour, is it reasonable that he can reach Dallas by 9:00 p.m.? Explain your answer.

Written Practice   *Strengthening Concepts*

1. In the orchard there were 10 rows with 12 trees in each row. How many
(4) trees were in the orchard?   120

2. At 8 a.m. it was 57°F, and at 1 p.m. it was 72°F. By how many degrees
(3) did the temperature change between 8 a.m. and 1 p.m.?   15°F

3. Write a sequence of numbers with 1 as the first term and a constant
(2) difference of 2 between terms.   {1, 3, 5, 7, …}

▶ See Math Conversations in the sidebar.

Example 6
Instruction

Point out that the estimate could have been done in other ways and ask students to describe a different way. Samples: $11.85 is about $12 an hour, so in 1 week he earns about $480 or about $500, in 1 month he earns about $2000, and in 1 year he earns about $24,000. Earning $11.85 is about $12 an hour, so income for 1 week is about $480 or about $500, income for 2 weeks is about $1000, and income for 52 weeks is 26 times 2 weeks, or about $26,000. Emphasize that estimates can often be done in more than one way and that students should look for different ways to make them.

Practice Set
Problem a [Error Alert]

Make sure students recognize that the hundred-thousands place in a number is the sixth place to the left of the decimal point.

Problem b [Error Alert]

Remind students that rounding a number to four decimal places is the same as rounding that number to the ten-thousandths place.

(continued)

Teacher Tip

Tell students that many people **use personal benchmarks** to help them estimate measures. For example, they might know the length of their pace, arm span from fingertip to fingertip, finger width, or hand span. They know about what a pound or ounce weighs or how much volume a cubic foot takes up.

Suggest that students begin to build their own set of benchmarks. Measuring their hand span and the width of a finger would be a good start. Suggest that they know the measure of their personal benchmarks in both customary and metric measures. For example, if a student's hand span is about 8 inches, it is also about 20 centimeters.

3 Written Practice

Math Conversations

Discussion opportunities are provided below.

Problem 4 Explain

Share with students the generalizations shown below.

- Multiplication is used to change a larger unit to a smaller unit.
- Division is used to change a smaller unit to a larger unit.

Explain that the generalizations can be used to help solve a variety of measurement-related problems.

Problem 5 Generalize

"Should we expect the standard form of 11^2 to be greater than 100 or less than 100? Give a reason to support your answer."
Greater than 100; Sample: Since 10^2 is equal to 100, 11^2 will be greater than 100.

Problem 6 Generalize

Invite a volunteer to describe the relationship shared by problems 5 and 6. Squaring and finding the square root are inverse operations.

Remind students that an inverse operation is an operation that undoes another operation.

Problem 7 Generalize

Challenge volunteers to name the sum and explain how to find the sum using only mental math. Sample: Since $\frac{3}{4}$ equals $\frac{1}{2} + \frac{1}{4}$, the sum of $\frac{1}{2}$ and $\frac{3}{4}$ is $\frac{1}{2} + \frac{1}{2} + \frac{1}{4}$.

Errors and Misconceptions
Problem 20

When finding measures of central tendency (such as mean, median, and mode), students should generalize that more than one of those measures may be the same for a given data set. For example, the same number may represent both the median and the mode.

(continued)

▶ *** 4.** *Explain* Brandon said that 48 yards is equal in length to 4 feet. Explain
(6) why his statement is unreasonable. Forty-eight yards is equal to how many feet?   Yards are greater in length than feet, so the number of feet in 48 yards should be much greater than 48. There are 144 feet in 48 yards.

Generalize Simplify.

▶ *** 5.** 11^2 121
(15)

▶ *** 6.** $\sqrt{121}$ 11
(15)

▶ *** 7.** $\frac{1}{2} + \frac{3}{4}$ $1\frac{1}{4}$
(13)

* 8. $1\frac{2}{3} + \frac{5}{6}$ $2\frac{1}{2}$
(13)

9. Justine will fence a rectangular piece of land that measures 15 yards by
(8) 18 yards, then lay sod within the fencing. Find the length of fencing and the number of square yards of sod that she will need.   66 yd of fencing, 270 yd² of sod

10. *Represent* Express with exponents:
(15)
  a. $5xxy$ $5x^2y$ **b.** $6xyyxy$ $6x^2y^3$

11. Compare:
(15)
  a. $\sqrt{100}$ ⊜ -10 **b.** $\sqrt{25}$ ⊜ $\sqrt{36}$

Solve by inspection.

12. $5x = 45$ $x = 9$
(14)

13. $\frac{x}{12} = 3$ $x = 36$
(14)

14. $x + 7 = 15$ $x = 8$
(14)

15. $18 - x = 10$ $x = 8$
(14)

16. Select an equation from problems **12–15** and write a story for it.
(2, 3) See student work.

17. Evaluate $P = 2(l + w)$ when $l = 7$ in. and $w = 5$ in. $P = 24$ in.
(14)

18. Write the prime factorization of 90. Use exponents for repeated factors.
(9) $2 \cdot 3^2 \cdot 5$

19. Patrice has 18 square tiles that she will lay side-by-side to form a
(9) rectangle. Name the dimensions of three different rectangles she can form.   1 by 18, 2 by 9, 3 by 6

Use the following information to answer problems **20** and **21**.

For two weeks, Destiny recorded the number of red lights at which she had to stop between home and school. These numbers are listed below.

3, 4, 3, 2, 5,

3, 4, 6, 3, 2

20. Find the mean, median, mode, and range of the data.   mean 3.5;
(7) median 3; mode 3; range 4

21. Which measure would you use to report the number of stops that
(7) Destiny most frequently made?   mode, 3

22. Rearrange the numbers to make the calculations easier. What properties
(2) did you use? What is the sum? $17 + 3 + 28 = 48$; Commutative Property of Addition
$17 + 28 + 3$

23. Graph these points on the coordinate plane: $(4, 0)$, $(-2, 3)$, $(0, -\frac{7}{2})$.
(Inv. 1) Which appears to be farthest from the origin?

23.

(-2, 3)

(4, 0)

(0, -7/2)

(4, 0) appears farthest from the origin.

▶ See Math Conversations in the sidebar.

24. Find the area and perimeter of a rectangle with vertices at $(-1, 2)$, $(3, 2)$,
(8, $(3, -5)$, and $(-1, -5)$.   area 28 square units, perimeter 22 units
Inv. 1)

25. Write these numbers from least to greatest:
(10)

$$1.3, 0, 1, \frac{3}{4}, \frac{4}{3}, 1\frac{1}{12} \quad 0, \frac{3}{4}, 1, 1\frac{1}{12}, 1.3, \frac{4}{3}$$

26. Which is a better discount?   **A**
(5, 11)
   A Price of $20 is reduced by 30%.

   B Price of $20 reduced by $\frac{1}{4}$.

   C Price of $20 is reduced by $4.

* 27. *Estimate* Chris budgets $5000 to purchase 6 computers at $789 each.
(17) Is the budget reasonable? Estimate the cost of the computers.
$6 \times \$800 = \$4800$. The budget is reasonable.

▶* 28. Round to the nearest whole number.
(17)
   a. $4\frac{5}{8}$ 5   **b.** 3.199 3

29. Estimate 8.25% sales tax on a $789 computer. $64.00
(12)

* 30. Write 0.24 as a reduced fraction and as a percent. $\frac{6}{25}$; 24%
(12)

▶ See Math Conversations in the sidebar.

Math Conversations
Discussion opportunities are provided below.

Problem 24 *Estimate*
Extend the Problem
"Estimate the location of the point at which the diagonals of the rectangle intersect." A reasonable estimate is $(1, -1\frac{1}{2})$.

Problem 28
When rounding a mixed number or a decimal number to the nearest whole number, students should have an understanding that the whole number portion of the mixed or decimal number will remain the same or increase by 1.

For example, when rounding $4\frac{5}{8}$ to the nearest whole number, the answer will be either 4 or 5. When rounding 3.199 to the nearest whole number, the answer will be either 3 or 4. In each case, no other answers can be correct.

Errors and Misconceptions
Problem 28
Rounding numbers typically involves identifying place values. If students have difficulty identifying place values, encourage them to draw or sketch a place value diagram in their math notebooks or on an index card. The index card can be used as a bookmark, and students can refer to the bookmark or to their notebook as needed.

• Lines and Angles

Objectives

- Classify two-dimensional geometric objects as lines, rays, or segments.
- Understand the concept of planes in geometry.
- Classify pairs of lines as parallel, perpendicular, or skew.
- Name angles using three letters, one letter, or one number.
- Classify angles as acute, right, obtuse, and straight.
- Use a protractor to measure angles.
- Understand there are 360° in one full turn, and 180° in a linear pair.

Lesson Preparation

Materials

- **Power Up D** (in *Instructional Masters*)
- **Manipulative Kit: protractors**
Optional
- **Manipulative Kit: calculators**

Power Up D

Math Language

New		Maintain
acute	line	intersect
angle	parallel	
degrees	perpendicular	
linear pair	plane	
obtuse	ray	
protractor	right	
segment		
skew lines		
straight		

Technology Resources

Student eBook Complete student textbook in electronic format.

Resources and Planner CD Assessment, reteaching, and instructional masters, plus a pacing calendar with standards.

Test and Practice Generator CD Create additional practice sheets and custom-made tests.

www.SaxonPublishers.com Visit for more student activities and planning materials.

Inclusion

Adaptations CD Adapted lessons, investigations, practice and assessments.

Meeting Standards

National Council of Teachers of Mathematics (NCTM)

Geometry

GM.1a Precisely describe, classify, and understand relationships among types of two- and three-dimensional objects using their defining properties

GM.4a Draw geometric objects with specified properties, such as side lengths or angle measures

Measurement

ME.1c Understand, select, and use units of appropriate size and type to measure angles, perimeter, area, surface area, and volume

ME.2b Select and apply techniques and tools to accurately find length, area, volume, and angle measures to appropriate levels of precision

Communication

CM.3d Use the language of mathematics to express mathematical ideas precisely

Problem-Solving Strategy: Find a Pattern/
Make a Table

The Mystery Man gave interesting responses. When Erica said 5, the Mystery Man said 9. When Joseph said 8, the Mystery Man said 15. When Humberto said 12, the Mystery Man said 23. When Wally whispered, the Mystery Man said 19. What did Wally whisper?

(Understand) **Understand the problem.**

"What information are we given?"

We are given several numbers and the Mystery Man's responses.

"What are we asked to do?"

We are asked to determine the number Wally whispered to the Mystery Man.

(Plan) **Make a plan.**

"What problem-solving strategy will we use?"

We will *make a table* to help us *find a pattern.*

(Solve) **Carry out the plan.**

"How do we begin?"

We will record the students' inputs and the Mystery Man's outputs in our table:

Student (s)	Mystery Man (m)
5	9
8	15
12	23

"What rule does the Mystery Man use to find his responses?"

The Mystery Man multiplies the student's number by two, then subtracts one from the product.

"The number 19 is one less than twice what number?"

10

(Check) **Look back.**

"Did we find the answer to the question that was asked?"

Yes. We found that Wally's whispered number was 10.

Facts
Distribute **Power Up D** to students. See answers below.

Mental Math
Encourage students to share different ways to mentally compute these exercises. Strategies for exercises **a, c,** and **f** are listed below.

a. Multiply by Unit Rate
$\frac{1}{4}$ hr $\times$ 20 mi/hr = 5 mi
Use Logical Reasoning
In 1 hour, Dash gallops 20 miles.
In $\frac{1}{4}$ hour, Dash gallops $\frac{1}{4}$ of 20 miles, or 5 miles.

c. Halve and Double
$88 \times 5 = 44 \times 10 = 440$
Regroup, then Multiply
$88 \times 5 = (80 \times 5) + (8 \times 5) =$
$400 + 40 = 440$

f. Multiply by 4, Divide by 4
25% of 40 = 100% of 10 = 10
Find a Fraction
$25\% = \frac{1}{4}$
$\frac{1}{4} \times 40 = 10$

Problem Solving
Refer to **Power-Up Discussion**, p. 114B.

• Lines and Angles

Power Up *Building Power*

facts Power Up D

mental math

a. Calculation: Dash galloped 20 miles per hour for $\frac{1}{4}$ hour. How far did Dash gallop?   5 miles

b. Measurement: How many pints are shown? $1\frac{1}{2}$ cups $+ 2\frac{1}{2}$ cups = 4 cups = 2 pints

c. Number Sense: 88×5 440

d. Proportions: If 3 cans cost \$6, how much would 4 cans cost?   \$8

e. Fractional Parts: $\frac{5}{8}$ of 88   55

f. Percent: 25% of 40   10

g. Power/Roots: $\sqrt{10}$ is between which two consecutive integers?
3 and 4

h. Calculation: $24 \div 6, + 3, \times 9, + 1, \sqrt{}, + 1, \sqrt{}, - 5, + 2, \times 17, + 5 =$ 5

problem solving

The Mystery Man gave interesting responses. When Erica said 5, the Mystery Man said 9. When Joseph said 8, the Mystery Man said 15. When Humberto said 12, the Mystery Man said 23. When Wally whispered, the Mystery Man said 19. What did Wally whisper?   10

New Concept *Increasing Knowledge*

A **line** is a straight path that extends without end in both directions. A **ray** is a part of a line that begins at a point and extends without end in one direction. A **segment** is part of a line with two endpoints.

A — B	A — B	A — B
line AB ($\overleftrightarrow{AB}$)	ray AB ($\overrightarrow{AB}$)	segment AB ($\overline{AB}$)
line BA ($\overleftrightarrow{BA}$)		segment BA ($\overline{BA}$)

Justify Can we change the order of the letters we use to name rays? Why or why not?   No; a ray has only one endpoint and the name of a ray begins with the endpoint.

Facts Simplify each power.

$10^2 = 100$	$20^2 = 400$	$2^2 = 4$	$2^3 = 8$	$5^2 = 25$
$3^2 = 9$	$6^2 = 36$	$9^2 = 81$	$4^2 = 16$	$8^2 = 64$
$7^2 = 49$	$1^2 = 1$	$11^2 = 121$	$30^2 = 900$	$10^3 = 1000$
$12^2 = 144$	$13^2 = 169$	$25^2 = 625$	$15^2 = 225$	$\left(\frac{1}{2}\right)^2 = \frac{1}{4}$

A **plane** is a flat surface that extends without end. Two lines on the same plane either intersect or do not intersect. If the lines do not intersect, then they are **parallel** and remain the same distance apart. Lines that intersect and form square corners are **perpendicular.**

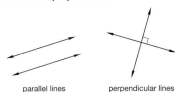

parallel lines   perpendicular lines

Lines that are in different planes that do not intersect are **skew lines.** For example, a wall and the ceiling represent different planes. A line on a wall and a line on the ceiling that do not intersect are skew lines.

Intersecting lines form angles. An **angle** is two rays with the same endpoint. The endpoint is the vertex and the rays are sides of the angle.

Vertex
(plural: vertices)

We can name angles in a variety of ways. If we use three letters, the middle letter is the vertex. We can name an angle by a single letter at the vertex if there is no chance of confusion. Sometimes we use a number to name an angle.

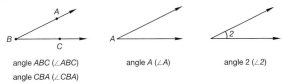

angle *ABC* (∠*ABC*)   angle *A* (∠*A*)   angle 2 (∠2)
angle *CBA* (∠*CBA*)

We can measure angles in **degrees.** A full turn is 360 degrees (360°), so a quarter turn is 90°.

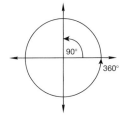

Lesson 18   115

---

2 New Concepts

Instruction
This lesson reviews content students have learned about lines and angles in previous grades. Consider going through the definitions with student books closed and ask volunteers to draw sketches or give examples of the various geometric properties and relationships. Then have students open their books and quickly scan the material just reviewed or move directly to the example.

If some students have difficulty remembering that it is *parallel lines* that do not meet, tell them to notice that the two *l*'s in parallel look like parallel segments.

Note that geometric relationships, such as perpendicular lines and equal angles, will be clearly indicated in the student books.

(continued)

Math Background

There are 360° in a circle. An angle with its vertex at the center of a circle divides the 360° measure of the circle into two parts.

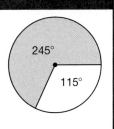

For example, suppose an angle with its vertex at the center of a circle has a measure of 115°. You might think of that as the "inside" measure of the angle. The "outside" measure of the angle (measuring the angle the other way around) is $360° - 115° = 245°$.

An angle whose measure is greater than 180° and less than 360° is a *reflex angle.*

Instruction

If students suggest that two angles that form a straight line are *supplementary* angles, you can agree but explain that two angles do not need to share a side to be supplementary, as long as their angle measures sum to 180°.

Protractors are available in the Manipulative Kit. You may want to let students practice using them before starting the example.

Example

Instruction

Point out that using m to represent the *measure* of an angle is the correct geometric practice, but that students may sometimes see the measure of an angle given without the m.

Be sure that all students are using their protractors correctly. Extend the example by having students measure ∠*QSR* and then check by adding the measures of both angles to see whether they sum to 180°.

(continued)

Angles are commonly described as **acute**, **right**, **obtuse**, or **straight** depending on their measure. Right angles are sometimes indicated by a small square.

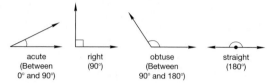

acute · (Between 0° and 90°) right · (90°) obtuse · (Between 90° and 180°) straight · (180°)

If two angles together form a straight angle, the angles are called a **linear pair** and the sum of their measures is 180°. In the figure below, ∠*QSR* and ∠*RST* are a linear pair.

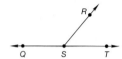

A **protractor** is a tool used to measure angles. To measure an angle we center the protractor on the vertex of the angle and position one of the zero marks on one side of the angle. We find the measure of the angle where the other side of the angle passes through the scale.

Example

Find m∠*RST*.

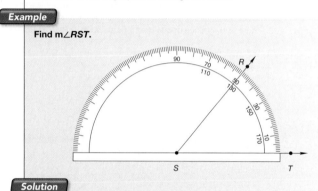

Solution

The abbreviation m∠*RST* means "measure of angle *RST*." Protractors have two scales, one starting from the left side and one starting from the right side. Since side *ST* of this angle is on the right-side zero mark, we read the scale that counts up from zero from the right side. The angle measures **50°**. Another way to decide which scale to use is to determine if we are measuring an acute angle or an obtuse angle. Since this angle is an acute angle, we use the scale with numbers less than 90.

Inclusion

Some students may benefit from a quick physical game that uses the **different types of angles.** After reviewing obtuse, right, acute and straight angles, call out the type of angle and have the students mimic the angle with their arms. Start by calling out the angle types slowly and then increase the pace steadily into rapid rounds.

Practice Set

a. line PQ ($\overleftrightarrow{PQ}$), line QP ($\overleftrightarrow{QP}$)

b. ray PQ ($\overrightarrow{PQ}$)

c. segment PQ ($\overline{PQ}$), segment QP ($\overline{QP}$)

Name each figure in problems **a–c**.

a. $\xleftarrow{\;\;\bullet\overset{P}{}\;\;\bullet\overset{Q}{}\;\;}\rightarrow$

b. $\bullet\overset{P}{}\quad\bullet\overset{Q}{}\rightarrow$

c. $\bullet\overset{P}{}\quad\bullet\overset{Q}{}$

Describe each pair of lines in problems **d** and **e**.

d. $\xleftarrow{\hspace{2cm}}$ parallel
$\xrightarrow{\hspace{2cm}}$

e. perpendicular

▶ **Classify** Describe each angle in problems **f–i** as acute, obtuse, right, or straight.

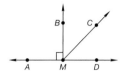

f. ∠CMD   acute

g. ∠CMA   obtuse

h. ∠AMB   right

i. ∠AMD   straight

j. 135°; Angles DMC and CMA form a linear pair, so the sum of their measures is 180°. 180° − 45° = 135°

▶ **j.** If the measure of ∠DMC is 45°, then what is the measure of ∠CMA? Explain how you found your answer.

Written Practice   *Strengthening Concepts*

1. **Estimate** Michaela estimated that there were nine tables in the room
(4)   with about six people seated at each table. About how many people were seated at the tables?   54

▶ **2.** **Analyze** The temperature at 8 a.m. was 65°F. By 11 a.m. the
(3)   temperature had increased 17°. What was the temperature at 11 a.m.?   82°F

3. Of the fifty customers, 35 bought the advertised item. What fraction of
(5, 11) the customers bought the advertised item? What percent? $\frac{7}{10}$; 70%

4. How many cups are in 3 gallons?   48 c
(6)

5. Cleo walked 3 miles in 45 minutes. What was his average rate in
(7)   minutes per mile? In miles per hour?   15 min/mi; 4 mi/hr

▶ See Math Conversations in the sidebar.

Practice Set

Problem b Error Alert
Remind students who name $\overrightarrow{QP}$ as the answer of the proper order of the points when naming rays. Draw and label several different rays on the board or overhead, then ask the students to name each ray by naming the endpoint of each ray first.

Problems f–i Classify
Invite several volunteers to explain how they decide if an angle is acute, right, obtuse, or straight.

Problem j Error Alert
Encourage students to sketch the figure and label the known measures.

3 Written Practice

Math Conversations
Discussion opportunities are provided below.

Problem 2 Analyze
Extend the Problem
"Suppose the rate of increase was constant. What was the temperature at 9:30 a.m.?"
73.5°F

(continued)

Math Conversations

Discussion opportunities are provided below.

Problem 8 Generalize

"Would you expect the difference of these fractions to be greater than 1, about 1, or less than 1? Give a reason to support your answer." less than 1; Sample: Since both fractions are less than 1, the difference of the fractions will be less than 1.

Problem 21 Connect

"What decimal place value is three digits to the right of the decimal point?" thousandths

"What steps are usually followed to change a decimal to a fraction?" Sample: Write the decimal as the fraction named, and then reduce the fraction to lowest terms.

"What steps are usually followed to change a decimal to a percent?" Sample: Multiply the decimal by 100% or move the decimal point two places to the right and write a percent symbol.

Problem 22 Explain

Extend the Problem

Challenge students to explain how to find 15% of $40 using only mental math. Sample: Finding 10% of a number is the same as moving the decimal point in that number one place to the left. So 10% of $40 is $4 and 5% of $40 would be half of that or $2, so 15% of $40 is $4 + $2 or $6.

Problem 24 Analyze

Students should recognize that since $\sqrt{5}$ is closer to $\sqrt{4}$ than to $\sqrt{9}$, the location of $\sqrt{5}$ on a number line is closer to 2 than to 3.

To help decide where to locate $\sqrt{10}$ and $\sqrt{15}$ on a number line, students should compare each to the known square roots of $\sqrt{9}$ and $\sqrt{16}$.

Errors and Misconceptions

Problem 16

You may need to explain that crown molding is installed at the intersection of the walls and the ceiling of a room. Students should assume that Jenna will install the molding after the ceiling has been painted in its entirety.

Problem 18

When working with one-digit prime numbers, a common error is to classify 1 as a prime number. Remind students that 1 is neither prime nor composite, and if necessary, review the definitions of prime and composite numbers with them.

(continued)

Generalize Simplify.

6. 12^2 144
(15)

7. $\sqrt{144}$ 12
(15)

▶ *** 8.** $\frac{5}{8} - \frac{2}{6}$ $\frac{7}{24}$
(13)

* 9. $3\frac{1}{4} + 1\frac{11}{12}$ $5\frac{1}{6}$
(13)

10. Compare:
(15, 16)

   a. $|{-10}| \ominus \sqrt{100}$

   b. $\sqrt{5} \oslash 2$

Solve by inspection.

11. $x - 13 = 20$ $x = 33$
(14)

12. $5 + x = 13$ $x = 8$
(14)

13. $\frac{2x}{5} = 10$ $x = 25$
(14)

14. $8x = 64$ $x = 8$
(14)

15. Write a sequence of four numbers with the first term 5 and a constant difference of 5 between terms.   {5, 10, 15, 20,…}
(2)

▶ **16.** Jenna plans to paint the ceiling of a 15 foot-by-10 foot room, then mount crown molding along the upper edge of the walls. Jenna should buy enough paint to cover what area? What length of crown molding will she need?   150 ft², 50 ft of molding
(8)

▶ **17.** Write the prime factorization of 128. Use exponents for repeated factors. 2^7
(9, 15)

▶ **18.** How many one-digit counting numbers are prime?   four
(9)

19. Write these numbers in order from least to greatest.
(10)

$$0, 1, -1, -\frac{4}{5}, \frac{5}{4} \quad -1, -\frac{4}{5}, 0, 1, \frac{5}{4}$$

20. Compare:
(10, 12)

   a. $\left|-\frac{4}{5}\right| \oslash \left|\frac{5}{4}\right|$

   b. $0.8 \oslash \frac{7}{10}$

▶*** 21.** Connect   Write 0.125 as a fraction and as a percent. $\frac{1}{8}$, 12.5% or $12\frac{1}{2}$%
(12)

▶ ***22.** Compute a 15% tip for a dinner bill of $40. $6
(11)

* 23. Estimate   The sales-tax rate is 8.25%. What is the approximate sales tax for a $104 purchase? $0.08 \times \$100 = \$8$
(12, 17)

▶*** 24.** Analyze   Plot these numbers on a number line.   (See below.)
(8, 16)

$$\sqrt{4}, \sqrt{5}, \sqrt{9}, \sqrt{10}, \sqrt{15}, \sqrt{16}$$

* 25. Estimate   What is the side length of a square with an area of 40 cm²? Measured with a ruler, this side length is between what two consecutive whole centimeters? $\sqrt{40}$ cm; between 6 cm and 7 cm
(8, 16)

24.

▶ See Math Conversations in the sidebar.

Use this diagram to complete problems **26** and **27**.

* 26. **Classify** Describe each angle by type.
  (18)
   a. ∠ABC   **b.** ∠ABD
   c. ∠CBD   **d.** ∠DBE
   a. obtuse, **b.** straight, **c.** acute, **d.** right

* 27. Suppose m∠CBD = 60°. Find the following angle measures.
  (18)
   a. m∠ABC   120°   **b.** m∠ABE   90°

▶ 28. Kiersti drove 58 mph for 1 hour and 52 minutes. Estimate the distance
  (7, 17) she traveled.   60 mph × 2 hr = 120 mi

For problems **29** and **30**, choose from this list *all* correct answers.
   A integers   **B** whole numbers   **C** natural numbers
   D rational numbers   **E** irrational numbers   **F** real numbers

* 29. The number 0 is a member of which set(s) of numbers?   **A, B, D, F**
  (1, 16)

* 30. The number $\sqrt{7}$ is a member of which set(s) of numbers?   **E, F**
  (1, 16)

Early Finishers
Real-World Application

Earth has only one natural satellite, the Moon. The Moon has many effects on Earth. For example, the Moon's gravity affects the tides within the oceans, even though the Moon is 384,403 kilometers away from Earth. If 1 kilometer is 0.62 miles, estimate the distance from Earth to the Moon in miles (round to the nearest thousand).   238,000 miles

▶ See Math Conversations in the sidebar.

Math Conversations
Discussion opportunities are provided below.

Problem 28   Evaluate

Extend the Problem
Challenge students to use a calculator and determine the distance Kiersti drove.
$108.2\overline{6}$ miles

Looking Forward

Working with lines and angles prepares students for:

- **Lesson 19,** working with polygons.
- **Lesson 20,** working with triangles.
- **Lesson 26,** performing transformations.
- **Investigation 5,** graphing transformations.
- **Lesson 54,** understanding and applying angle relationships.
- **Lesson 81,** working with central angles and arcs.
- **Lesson 115,** understanding relative sizes of sides and angles of a triangle.

• Polygons

Objectives

- Understand the three key features of polygons: they are plane figures, they have straight sides, and they are closed.
- Identify regular polygons.
- Name polygons using the number of sides.
- Name polygons using letters at each vertex.
- Identify congruent and similar polygons and understand how dilations relate to similar polygons.

Lesson Preparation

Materials

- **Power Up D** (in *Instructional Masters*)

Optional

- **Teacher-provided material:** pictures of polygons in newspapers, magazines, photographs

Power Up D

Math Language

New	Maintain	English Learners (ESL)
congruent	clockwise	appear
dilation	counterclockwise	
orientation		
polygons		
regular polygon		
similar		
vertex		

Technology Resources

Student eBook Complete student textbook in electronic format.

Resources and Planner CD Assessment, reteaching, and instructional masters, plus a pacing calendar with standards.

Test and Practice Generator CD Create additional practice sheets and custom-made tests.

www.SaxonPublishers.com Visit for more student activities and planning materials.

Inclusion

Adaptations CD Adapted lessons, investigations, practice and assessments.

Meeting Standards

National Council of Teachers of Mathematics (NCTM)

Geometry

GM.1a Precisely describe, classify, and understand relationships among types of two- and three-dimensional objects using their defining properties

GM.1b Understand relationships among the angles, side lengths, perimeters, areas, and volumes of similar objects

GM.1c Create and critique inductive and deductive arguments concerning geometric ideas and relationships, such as congruence, similarity, and the Pythagorean relationship

GM.3a Describe sizes, positions, and orientations of shapes under informal transformations such as flips, turns, slides, and scaling

Problem-Solving Strategy: Make It Simpler/Find a Pattern/Write an Equation

What is the last number in the 20th row?

Row 1	2
Row 2	4　6
Row 3	8　10　12
Row 4	14　16　18　20
Row 5	22　24　26　28　30

Understand We have been given a visual pattern of the even numbers arranged in a triangle, and are asked to find the last number in the 20th row.

Plan We have been asked to find a specific term, so we can *make the problem simpler* by only concerning ourselves with the row numbers and the final numbers in each row. We will *find a pattern,* and *write an equation* to determine the final term in the 20th row.

Solve

Row Number:	1	2	3	4	5
Final Number:	2	6	12	20	30

We notice that the final number in each row equals the row number times the next row number. For example, the final number in the 4th row equals 4 times 5. We can write an equation for this pattern. The equation for finding the final number, F, in a nth row is: $F = n(n + 1)$.

The final number in the 20th row will be $20(21) = 420$.

Check We could have completed the triangle to determine the number, but it would have been time-consuming.

Facts

Distribute **Power Up D** to students. See answers below.

Mental Math

Encourage students to share different ways to mentally compute these exercises. Strategies for exercises **c** and **e** are listed below.

c. Multiply by Numerator First
1 lb = 16 oz
$\frac{3}{4} \times 16 = \frac{48}{4} = 12$ oz

Divide by Denominator First
1 lb = 16 oz
$\frac{3}{4} \times 16 = 3 \times 4 = 12$ oz

e. Use Number Sense
2 tickets = $10
4 tickets = $20

Use a Proportion
$\frac{2}{10} = \frac{4}{c} =$
$2c = 40$
$c = 20$

Problem Solving

Refer to **Power-Up Discussion**, p. 120B.

• Polygons

Power Up *Building Power*

facts | Power Up D

mental math

a. Calculation: Erica rides a snowmobile 20 miles per hour for $2\frac{1}{2}$ hours. How far does Erica ride? 50 miles

b. Powers/Roots: 15×10^2 1500

c. Fractional Parts: Three fourths of a pound is how many ounces? 12 ounces

d. Geometry: What is the measure of ∠ACB? 60°

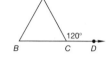

e. Proportions: If 2 tickets cost $10, then how much would four tickets cost? $20

f. Algebra: $3x = 300$ 100

g. Probability: A number cube is rolled once. What is the probability of rolling a number greater than or equal to 4? $\frac{1}{2}$ or 0.5

h. Calculation: $12 \times 2, \div 6, \sqrt{\ }, \times 10, + 5, \sqrt{\ }, \times 4, \times 5, + 1$ 101

problem solving

What is the last number in the 20th row?

Row 1			2		
Row 2			4	6	
Row 3		8	10	12	
Row 4	14	16	18	20	
Row 5	22	24	26	28	30

(Understand) We have been given a visual pattern of the even numbers arranged in a triangle, and are asked to find the last number in the 20th row.

(Plan) We have been asked to find a specific term, so we can *make the problem simpler* by only concerning ourselves with the row numbers and the final numbers in each row. We will *find a pattern* and *write an equation* to determine the final term in the 20th row.

(Solve)

Row Number:	1	2	3	4	5
Final Number:	2	6	12	20	30

We notice that the final number in each row equals the row number times the next row number. For example, the final number in the 4th row equals 4 times 5. We can write an equation for this pattern. The equation for finding the final number, F, in the nth row is $F = n(n + 1)$.

The final number in the 20th row will be 20(21) = **420.**

Facts | Simplify each power.

$10^2 = 100$	$20^2 = 400$	$2^2 = 4$	$2^3 = 8$	$5^2 = 25$
$3^2 = 9$	$6^2 = 36$	$9^2 = 81$	$4^2 = 16$	$8^2 = 64$
$7^2 = 49$	$1^2 = 1$	$11^2 = 121$	$30^2 = 900$	$10^3 = 1000$
$12^2 = 144$	$13^2 = 169$	$25^2 = 625$	$15^2 = 225$	$\left(\frac{1}{2}\right)^2 = \frac{1}{4}$

Check We could have completed the triangle to determine the number, but it would have been time consuming.

New Concept   *Increasing Knowledge*

Polygons are closed plane figures with straight sides. They have the same number of sides as angles.

Example 1

Which of these figures is a polygon?

A   B   C   D

Solution

Figure A is closed but it has a curved side, so it is not a polygon.

Figure B is not closed, so it is not a polygon.

Figure C represents a cube, which is not a plane figure, so it is not a polygon.

Figure D is a plane, closed figure with straight sides, so it is a polygon.

A polygon is **regular** if all its sides are the same length and all its angles are the same size.

Example 2

Which polygon is not regular?

A   B   C   D

Solution

The sides of each figure are equal in length. The angles in figures A, B, and C are of equal size. However, **D** has two acute angles and two obtuse angles, so the figure is not regular.

Instruction

Have students note the three criteria for a *polygon.* closed, flat, straight sides

Example 1
Instruction

Point out that all three criteria must be met in order for a figure to be classified as a polygon.

(continued)

Instruction

Present the chart of names of polygons. Tell students that they need to learn the names of the polygons along with the number of sides each one has.

Ask a volunteer to explain why there can't be a two-sided polygon. *Sample: If there are only two straight sides, they cannot create a closed figure.*

Extend the *Discuss* question by asking why *SVTU* is not a name for the polygon. *Sample: The letters are not in clockwise or counterclockwise order—they are all mixed up.*

Discuss why all congruent polygons are also similar polygons. *Congruent* means "similar and equal." Be sure that students have a good grasp of these vocabulary words: *congruent, similar, orientation,* and *dilation,* and that they understand and know how to use the congruence and similarity symbols.

(continued)

Polygons are named by the number of their sides and angles.

Names of Polygons

Name of Polygon	Number of Sides	Name of Polygon	Number of Sides
Triangle	3	Octagon	8
Quadrilateral	4	Nonagon	9
Pentagon	5	Decagon	10
Hexagon	6	Hendecagon	11
Heptagon	7	Dodecagon	12

A polygon with more than 12 sides may be referred to as an *n*-gon, with *n* being the number of sides. Thus, a polygon with 15 sides is a 15-gon.

The point where two sides of a polygon meet is called a **vertex** (plural: **vertices**). A particular polygon can be identified by naming the letters of its vertices in order. We may name any letter first. The rest of the letters can be named clockwise or counterclockwise.

Math Language
Recall that moving **clockwise** means moving in the same direction as the hands of a clock. Moving **counterclockwise** means moving in the direction opposite to the hands of a clock.

Discuss One name for the polygon below is *USTV*. What are the other seven names? UVTS, STVU, SUVT, TSUV, TVUS, VTSU, VUST

Figures are **congruent** if they are the same shape and size. Figures A and D below are congruent, even though they do not have the same **orientation**. We could slide and turn figure A to perfectly align with figure D.

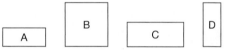

Figures A and C and figures C and D are not congruent, because they are not the same size. They are **similar** because they have the same shape. Figure C appears to be a **dilation** (enlargement) of figures A and D. Using a magnifying glass, we could enlarge the image of figure A or figure D to match figure C. Figure B is not similar to the other figures because its shape is different.

We use the symbol ~ to indicate similarity.

Figure A ~ Figure C

"Figure A is similar to figure C."

Since congruent figures are both similar in shape and equal in measure, we use the symbol ≅ to indicate congruence.

Figure A ≅ Figure D

"Figure A is congruent to figure D."

Teacher Tip

Have students **find pictures of polygons** in newspapers or magazines or take photographs of polygons that they see on their way to school or at home. Make a bulletin board exhibit of "Polygons in Our World" and have students label each polygon with its name and any other information they have about the polygon.

Example 3

a. Which triangles below appear to be similar?

b. Which triangles appear to be congruent?

A   B   C   D

Solution

a. Triangles A, B, and C appear to be similar.

b. Triangles A and C appear to be congruent.

Practice Set ▶

a. Name this polygon. Is it regular or irregular?   hexagon, irregular

b. Which of the following is not a way to name this rectangle?   **C**

  A ☐ *ABCD*   **B** ☐ *ADCB*

  C ☐ *BACD*   **D** ☐ *BADC*

c. What is the name for the shape of a stop sign?   octagon

d. The block H shown is a polygon. Count the sides and name the polygon.   dodecagon

e. *Represent*   Use four letters to correctly name the figure that looks like a square. Start the name with the letter *A*.   ☐ *ABEF* or ☐ *AFEB*

f. In example 3, which triangle appears to be a dilation of triangle **A**? triangle **B**

g. Which figures below appear to be similar and which appear to be congruent?   **A**, **B**, and **D** appear to be similar and **B** and **D** appear to be congruent.

A   B   C   D

Lesson 19   123

▶ See Math Conversations in the sidebar.

Example 3

Instruction

Ask a volunteer to explain why triangles A and C are both similar and congruent. Sample: If two triangles are congruent, then they are also similar.

Students should quickly conclude that triangle D is not similar or congruent to triangles A, B, or C. Encourage students who struggle making the less obvious decisions to trace triangle A and place the tracing on top of triangle B and triangle C. Another tracing can then be used to compare triangle B to triangle C.

Practice Set

Problem b [Error Alert]

Make sure students recognize that rectangles (and other polygons) can be named in a clockwise or counterclockwise direction, but the vertices of the figure must be listed in a consecutive manner. For example, rectangle *ABCD* can be named eight different ways:

    ABCD   *BCDA*   *CDAB*   *DABC*
    ADCB   *DCBA*   *CBAD*   *BADC*

Problem e [Represent]

To provide extra practice naming polygons, you might choose to challenge students to list all of the different ways that the square can be named. There are eight ways altogether: *ABEF*; *BEFA*; *EFAB*; *FABE*; *AFEB*; *FEBA*; *EBAF*; *BAFE*

Math Conversations

Discussion opportunities are provided below.

Problem 8 *Analyze*

"Explain how you can use mental math to name the mixed number that $\frac{7}{2}$ represents." Sample: $6 \div 2 = 3$ and $8 \div 2 = 4$, so $7 \div 2 = 3\frac{1}{2}$.

Problem 9 *Generalize*

"Would you expect the sum of these fractions to be greater than 1, about 1, or less than 1? Give a reason to support your answer." less than 1; Sample: Since both fractions are less than $\frac{1}{2}$, the sum of the fractions will be less than 1.

Problem 21 *Analyze*

Invite several students to write on the board or overhead an expression to represent the given information. Then discuss with students why each expression is correct, or identify the change or changes that must be made to make it correct. Possible expressions include $\frac{30^2}{(5)(6)}$ and $\frac{30 \cdot 30}{5 \cdot 6}$.

Errors and Misconceptions
Problem 4

The following generalizations can be used by students to help make measurement conversions.

- To change from a larger unit to a smaller unit, multiply.
- To change from a smaller unit to a larger unit, divide.

For problem 4, students should change 1 kilometer to meters and then divide 1000 m by 25 m to find the number of laps Kim swam.

(continued)

---

1. One pack of trading cards sells for $1.12. For how much would seven packs sell? $7.84
$^{(4)}$

2. In the 1968 Olympics in Mexico City, Bob Beamon broke Ralph Boston's long jump world record by leaping 890 cm. The former record was 835 cm. How much greater was Beamon's record than Boston's record?   55 cm
$^{(3)}$

3. Kerry had 17 bottles in her collection. Some friends gave her more. Now Kerry has 33 bottles. How many bottles did her friends give her?   16 bottles
$^{(3)}$

▶ **4.** Kim swam one kilometer in 40 minutes. The length of the pool was 25 meters. About how long did it take Kim to swim each length?   1 min
$^{(4)}$

5. What is the mean of the prime numbers between 10 and 20?   15
$^{(7, 9)}$

6. Sketch a number line and plot the approximate location of the following points. $-2, |-3|, \frac{1}{2}, \sqrt{2}$
$^{(10, 15)}$

7. Using prime factorization, reduce $\frac{375}{1000}$. $\frac{3 \cdot 5 \cdot 5 \cdot 5}{2 \cdot 2 \cdot 2 \cdot 5 \cdot 5 \cdot 5} = \frac{3}{8}$
$^{(10)}$

▶ *** 8.** *Analyze* Compare:
$^{(10, 15)}$

    a. $4 \bigcirc \frac{7}{2}$ **b.** $7 \bigcirc \sqrt{49}$

Generalize Simplify.

▶ *** 9.** $\frac{1}{5} + \frac{4}{9}$ $\frac{29}{45}$ *** 10.** $\frac{1}{2} - \frac{1}{10}$ $\frac{2}{5}$
$^{(13)}$ $^{(13)}$

11. Write a fraction and a decimal equivalent to 40%. $\frac{2}{5}$, 0.40
$^{(11, 12)}$

12. Compute 150% of $70. $105
$^{(11)}$

13. Express with exponents:
$^{(15)}$

    a. $y \cdot y \cdot y \cdot y$ y^4 **b.** $3xxyxy$ $3x^3y^2$

* 14. Three coordinates of a rectangle are (0, 4), (2, 4), and (2, −3). Find the fourth coordinate and the area and perimeter of the rectangle.   (0, −3); area: 14 square units; perimeter: 18 units
$^{(8, Inv. 1)}$

Simplify.

15. 2^5 32   **16.** 10^6 1,000,000   **17.** $\sqrt{144}$ 12
$^{(15)}$ $^{(15)}$ $^{(15)}$

* 18. $(12 \text{ in.})^2$ 144 in.^2 *** 19.** 8^3 512   *** 20.** $\sqrt[3]{8}$ 2
$^{(15)}$ $^{(15)}$ $^{(15)}$

▶ *** 21.** *Analyze* What is the quotient when 30^2 is divided by the product of 5 and 6?   30
$^{(1, 15)}$

▶ See Math Conversations in the sidebar.

An area of the playground will be seeded with grass and fenced until the grass grows in. Use this information and the figure to answer problems **22** and **23**.

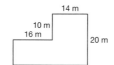

22. The grass seed needs to cover how many square meters?   440 m²
(8)

▶ **23.** How many meters of fencing are needed to surround the area?   100 m
(8)

For problems **24–27,** solve by inspection. Select one equation and write a word problem to match.   See student work.

* **24.** $72 = 36 + m$ $m = 36$ **25.** $w - 11 = 39$ $w = 50$
(14)   (14)

* **26.** $7c = 56$ $c = 8$ **27.** $8 = \frac{72}{x}$ $x = 9$
(14)   (14)

28. Estimate the distance covered by a car traveling at 62 mph for 3 hours and 50 minutes.   60 mph × 4 hr = 240 miles
(7, 17)

* **29.** All rectangles are also parallelograms. The formula for the area of a parallelogram is $A = bh$. Find A when $b = 7$ mm and $h = 9$ mm.
(14) $A = 63$ mm²

30. The number 0 is a member of which sets of numbers?   **A, B, D, F**
(1)
    A integers   **B** whole numbers   **C** counting numbers

    D rational numbers   **E** irrational numbers   **F** real numbers

---

Early Finishers
Real-World Application

Pete, Jim, and John want to change the oil and oil filter in each of their cars. For each oil change, Pete's car needs $4\frac{3}{4}$ quarts of oil, Jim's needs $4\frac{1}{2}$ quarts, and John's needs 5 quarts. Each boy also wants to keep one full quart of oil in his trunk for emergencies. Given that the boys already have one case of oil containing 12 quarts, how many more quarts of oil do they need to buy at the store?   The boys need $5\frac{1}{4}$ quarts of oil, so they should buy 6 quarts at the store.

▶ See Math Conversations in the sidebar.

Math Conversations

Discussion opportunities are provided below.

Problem 23 Evaluate

Extend the Problem

"Suppose the shape of the area to be seeded can be changed, but its perimeter must remain the same. How can the shape be changed to encompass more area? Give an example to support your answer."

Sample: Change the shape to a square with sides of 25 meters. The area of the shape will be $(25 \text{ m})^2$ or 625 m^2.

Looking Forward

Understanding polygons prepares students for:

• **Lesson 20,** working with triangles.

• **Investigation 3,** classifying quadrilaterals.

• **Lesson 35,** working with similar and congruent polygons.

• **Lesson 37,** calculating areas of combined polygons.

• **Lesson 60,** calculating areas of parallelograms.

• **Lesson 65,** performing applications using similar triangles.

• **Lesson 71,** finding percent changes of dimensions.

• **Lesson 75,** calculating areas of trapezoids.

• Triangles

Objectives

- Classify triangles by angle measures (acute, right, obtuse) and by side lengths (equilateral, isosceles, scalene).
- Understand that the total of the angle measures of a triangle is 180°.
- Find an angle measure of a triangle given the other two angle measures.
- Calculate the area of a triangle using the formula $A = \frac{1}{2}bh$.

Lesson Preparation

Materials

- **Power Up D** (in *Instructional Masters*)

Optional

- **Teacher-provided material:** white and colored index cards

Power Up D

Math Language

New	Maintain
acute triangle	congruent
base	perpendicular
equilateral triangle	polygon
height	
isosceles triangle	
obtuse triangle	
right triangle	
scalene triangle	
triangle	

Technology Resources

Student eBook Complete student textbook in electronic format.

Resources and Planner CD Assessment, reteaching, and instructional masters, plus a pacing calendar with standards.

Test and Practice Generator CD Create additional practice sheets and custom-made tests.

www.SaxonPublishers.com Visit for more student activities and planning materials.

Inclusion

Adaptations CD Adapted lessons, investigations, practice and assessments.

Meeting Standards

National Council of Teachers of Mathematics (NCTM)

Geometry

GM.1a Precisely describe, classify, and understand relationships among types of two- and three-dimensional objects using their defining properties

GM.1c Create and critique inductive and deductive arguments concerning geometric ideas and relationships, such as congruence, similarity, and the Pythagorean relationship

GM.4e Recognize and apply geometric ideas and relationships in areas outside the mathematics classroom, such as art, science, and everyday life

Measurement

ME.2c Develop and use formulas to determine the circumference of circles and the area of triangles, parallelograms, trapezoids, and circles and develop strategies to find the area of more-complex shapes

Problem-Solving Strategy: Find a Pattern

Find the next three numbers in this sequence:

$$\frac{1}{16}, \frac{1}{8}, \frac{3}{16}, \frac{1}{4}, \frac{5}{16}, \underline{\quad}, \underline{\quad}, \underline{\quad}$$

(Understand) **Understand the problem.**

"What information are we given?"

The first five terms of a sequence are $\frac{1}{6}, \frac{1}{8}, \frac{3}{16}, \frac{1}{4}$ and $\frac{5}{16}$.

"What are we asked to do?"

We are asked to extend the sequence for three more terms.

(Plan) **Make a plan.**

"What problem-solving strategies could we use?"

We need to *find the pattern* to extend the sequence.

"Do we need to adapt any of the information?"

Because the fractions have different denominators, it is difficult to see right away if the pattern is increasing, decreasing, or fluctuating. It would be easier to evaluate fractions that have the same denominator.

(Solve) **Carry out the plan.**

"How do we begin?"

The lowest common denominator of 16, 8, and 4 is 16. We will convert the fractions to sixteenths:

$$\frac{1}{16} \quad \frac{1}{8} \quad \frac{3}{16} \quad \frac{1}{4} \quad \frac{5}{16}$$
$$\frac{1}{16} \quad \frac{2}{16} \quad \frac{3}{16} \quad \frac{4}{16} \quad \frac{5}{16}$$

"How do we proceed?"

We see that the sequence increases by $\frac{3}{16}$ with each term. We will extend the sequence in sixteenths, and simplify (reduce) the fractions when possible.

$$\frac{1}{16} \quad \frac{1}{8} \quad \frac{3}{16} \quad \frac{1}{4} \quad \frac{5}{16} \quad \mathbf{\frac{3}{8}} \quad \mathbf{\frac{7}{16}} \quad \mathbf{\frac{1}{2}}$$
$$\frac{1}{16} \quad \frac{2}{16} \quad \frac{3}{16} \quad \frac{4}{16} \quad \frac{5}{16} \quad \mathbf{\frac{6}{16}} \quad \mathbf{\frac{7}{16}} \quad \mathbf{\frac{8}{16}}$$

(Check) **Look back.**

"Did we do what we were asked to do?"

Yes, we found the next three terms in the sequence.

• **Triangles**

Facts

Distribute **Power Up D** to students. See answers below.

Mental Math

Encourage students to share different ways to mentally compute these exercises. Strategies for exercises **a** and **d** are listed below.

a. Multiply by Unit Rate
$4\frac{1}{2}$ min $\times$ 20 breaths/min =
$\frac{9}{2} \times 20 = 90$ breaths
Double and Halve
$4\frac{1}{2} \times 20 = 9 \times 10 = 90$ breaths

d. Change to a Fraction and Add
$1.5 = 1\frac{1}{2}$
$1\frac{1}{2} + 1\frac{1}{2} = 3$
Change to a Fraction and Multiply
$1.5 = 1\frac{1}{2}$
$1\frac{1}{2} \times 2 = (1 \times 2) + (\frac{1}{2} \times 2) = 2 + 1 = 3$

Problem Solving

Refer to **Power-Up Discussion**, p. 126B.

Instruction

Have students recall that a *triangle* is a polygon with the least number of sides. Explain that triangles are used in many structures because they provide stability. Suggest that students observe how triangles are used in buildings and bridges.

(continued)

Power Up | Building Power

facts | Power Up D

mental math

a. Calculation: Glenda takes 20 breaths per minute. How many breaths does she take in $4\frac{1}{2}$ minutes?   90 breaths

b. Estimation: $35.8 \div 3.9$ $36 \div 4 = 9$

c. Measurement: If the loop of string is cut and laid out lengthwise, about how long will it be? $1\frac{1}{2}$ in. + $1\frac{1}{2}$ in. = 3 in.

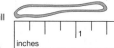

inches

d. Number Sense: 1.5×2 inches   3 inches

e. Geometry: $\angle A$ corresponds to $\angle X$. $\angle B$ corresponds to which angle? $\angle R$

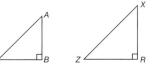

f. Calculation: $7 - 8, + 2, + 10, \times 7, - 2, \div 3, \sqrt{\ }, \times 7, + 7, \div 7, - 7$ -1

problem solving | Find the next three numbers in the sequence:

$$\frac{1}{16}, \frac{1}{8}, \frac{3}{16}, \frac{1}{4}, \frac{5}{16}, \underline{\ \ }, \underline{\ \ }, \underline{\ \ } \quad \frac{3}{8}, \frac{7}{16}, \frac{1}{2}$$

New Concept | Increasing Knowledge

Recall that polygons are closed, plane figures with straight sides. A **triangle** is a polygon with three sides. We classify triangles based on their angle measures and based on the relative lengths of their sides.

Triangles are classified as acute, right, or obtuse based on the measure of their *largest* angle. **The measures of the three angles of a triangle total 180°,** so at least two angles of a triangle are acute.

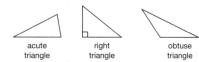

| acute triangle | right triangle | obtuse triangle |

Triangles are also classified by relative side lengths.

- **Equilateral** triangles have three equal-length sides (and three equal angles).
- **Isosceles** triangles have at least two equal-length sides (and at least two equal angles).

126   **Saxon** Math Course 3

Facts | Simplify each power.

$10^2 = 100$	$20^2 = 400$	$2^2 = 4$	$2^3 = 8$	$5^2 = 25$
$3^2 = 9$	$6^2 = 36$	$9^2 = 81$	$4^2 = 16$	$8^2 = 64$
$7^2 = 49$	$1^2 = 1$	$11^2 = 121$	$30^2 = 900$	$10^3 = 1000$
$12^2 = 144$	$13^2 = 169$	$25^2 = 625$	$15^2 = 225$	$\left(\frac{1}{2}\right)^2 = \frac{1}{4}$

• **Scalene** triangles have sides of different lengths (and angles of different measures).

We can use tick marks and arcs to indicate sides and angles that have equal measures.

     equilateral   isosceles   scalene

Any triangle can be classified both by angles and by sides.

Conclude Can an equilateral triangle be an obtuse triangle? Why or why not?

No; equilateral triangles have three equal sides and three equal angles that are acute.

Example 1

Classify triangle *ABC* by angles and by sides.

Solution

The triangle is a **right triangle** and a **scalene triangle**.

Example 2

The roof of the building in the drawing slopes 35°. What is the measure of the angle at the peak of the roof?

Solution

The roof structure forms an isosceles triangle. The measures of the acute base angles total 70°. All three angles total 180°, so the angle at the peak of the roof is **110°.**

$$35° + 35° + 110° = \mathbf{180°}$$

Now we will consider how to find the area of a triangle. Triangle *ABC* is enclosed by a rectangle. What fraction of the area of the rectangle is the area of triangle *ABC*?

Lesson 20   127

2 New Concepts (Continued)

Instruction

Use the *Conclude* question to check students' understanding of classification of triangles. You may need to ask additional questions if you think that the class needs more clarification.

Example 1
Instruction
Emphasize that all triangles can be classified both ways. Sometimes students may see a triangle description that includes both kinds of terms, such as an isosceles right triangle.

Example 2
Instruction
Remind students if needed that the sum of the measures of the three angles in a triangle is 180°.

(continued)

Math Background

It is possible to classify a triangle by its side lengths even if only the angle measures are known. For example:

• If a triangle has a 90° angle, a 60° angle, and a 30° angle, the triangle is a scalene triangle because only scalene triangles have three unequal angles.

• If a triangle has two equal angles, it is an isosceles triangle because the sides opposite the equal angles are equal in length.

• If a triangle has three 60° angles, it is an equilateral triangle.

For each example, the number of congruent sides is known, but the exact length of any side is unknown.

Instruction

To enhance understanding of finding the area of a triangle, model the steps of the explanation from the student page on the board or overhead. Work through the first part of the illustration, helping students see why the triangle represents half of the rectangle.

Continue with the rest of the illustration, emphasizing the meaning of *perpendicular dimensions* as you label the *base* and the *height*. Be sure that students understand why the area of the triangle is half the area of the rectangle.

Example 3

Instruction

Point out that the first step in finding the area of each of these three triangles is determining the perpendicular dimensions, or in simpler words, the base and the height. The term *perpendicular dimensions* is a reminder that the base and height must be perpendicular to each other.

Have students notice that the answers are labeled with square units, as indicated by the exponent 2.

(continued)

Math Language
Recall that *congruent* means "having the same shape and size."

The letters *w*, *x*, *y*, and *z* refer to four regions of the rectangle. Regions *w* and *x* are within the triangle. Regions *y* and *z* are outside the triangle. Notice that regions *w* and *y* are the same size. Also notice that regions *x* and *z* are the same size. These pairs of congruent regions show us that triangle *ABC* occupies half of the rectangle. We will use this fact to help us understand the formula for the area of a triangle.

We start with a rectangle. If we multiply two perpendicular dimensions, the product is the area of a rectangle.

The perpendicular dimensions of a *triangle* are called the **base** and **height**.

Multiplying the base and height of a triangle gives us the area of a rectangle with the same base and height as the triangle. Since the triangle occupies half the area of the rectangle, we can find the area of the triangle by finding half the area of the rectangle.

Area of a Triangle

Area of triangle = $\frac{1}{2}$ base · height

$A = \frac{1}{2}bh$

Example 3

Find the area of each triangle.

a.   b.   c.

Solution

a. One angle is a right angle, so two sides are perpendicular. We multiply the perpendicular sides and find half the product.

$$A = \frac{1}{2}bh$$

$$A = \frac{1}{2}(8 \text{ in.})(6 \text{ in.})$$

$$A = \textbf{24 in.}^2$$

b. We multiply the perpendicular dimensions. As the triangle is oriented the base is 6 cm and the height is 6 cm. We find half the product of the base and height.

$$A = \frac{1}{2}bh$$

Teacher Tip

This game can provide practice with **recognizing and drawing triangles by their classification.**

Write the words *acute*, *right*, and *obtuse* on three white index cards and the words *equilateral*, *isosceles*, and *scalene* on three color index cards. Place the cards face down and mix them up. Have a player choose one color and one white index card. The player should then either draw the triangle described or state that it is impossible to draw.

Other players should verify or deny the player's drawing or conclusion. Players score 2 points for a correct drawing and 3 points for naming an impossible triangle. (Note that there are only two impossible triangles: a right equilateral triangle and an obtuse equilateral triangle.)

$$A = \frac{1}{2} (6 \text{ cm})(6 \text{ cm})$$

$$A = \textbf{18 cm}^2$$

c. The base does not need to be horizontal and the height vertical. The base is 8 m and the height is 7 m. (Turn the book to help you see the relationship.)

$$A = \frac{1}{2}bh$$

$$A = \frac{1}{2} (8 \text{ m})(7 \text{ m})$$

$$A = \textbf{28 m}^2$$

Practice Set ▶ *Classify* Classify each triangle in problems **a–c** by angles and by sides.

a.

5

5

x

right, isosceles

b.

6   6

y

6

acute, equilateral

c.

6

3

4

obtuse, scalene

d. In problems **a** and **b,** the letters x and y represent how many degrees? $x = 45°, y = 60°$

Find the area of each in problems **e–g.**

e.

5 in.

3 in.

4 in.

6 in.²

▶ f.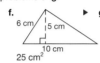

6 cm   5 cm

10 cm

25 cm²

▶ g.

10 ft

6 ft

6 ft

18 ft²

h. right triangle; isosceles triangle; 45°-45°-90°

▶ h. Mr. Torres arranges square floor tiles diagonally in a room. Near each wall he needs to cut the tiles to fit. Sketch the shape of the triangle pieces he needs to cut. Classify the triangle by angle and by sides. Write the measure of each angle.

Written Practice   *Strengthening Concepts*

1. The tram driver collected $50.40 from the 45 passengers. On average, how much did the driver collect per passenger? $1.12
   (4)

2. Mary could carry 12 liters, while Martha could carry 19 liters. How many liters could they carry together?   31 liters
   (3)

3. Practicing quick shots, Roberto made three baskets in ten seconds. At this rate, how many baskets could he make in one minute?
   (4)
   18 baskets

4. Conrad brought home three gallons of milk. How many quarts is that?
   (4)   12 quarts

Lesson 20   **129**

▶ See Math Conversations in the sidebar.

2 New Concepts (Continued)

Practice Set
Problems a–c [Error Alert]
You may need to point out that two names should be used to describe each triangle—one name to describe the sides and one name to describe the angles.

Problems f and g [Error Alert]
Watch for students who do not choose a height perpendicular to the base, and instead choose a side measure to represent the height of one or both triangles.

Problem h [Error Alert]
Some students may benefit from drawing the shape on grid paper. To help recognize that the angles formed by dividing a square along a diagonal measure each measure 45°, encourage students to draw a square that is larger than 1 by 1 to represent a tile (such as 4 by 4), then draw one diagonal of that square and measure using a protractor.

129

3 Written Practice

Math Conversations

Discussion opportunities are provided below.

Problem 7 | Evaluate

"Division is sometimes used to find the median of a set of numbers. Why is division not used to find the median of this set of numbers?" Sample: After arranging the numbers in order from least to greatest or from greatest to least, there is only one middle number.

Lead students to generalize that if a data set contains an odd number of values, division is not used to find the median of those values.

Problem 8 | Evaluate

At the board or overhead, invite volunteers to demonstrate the arithmetic that supports their answers.

Problem 12 | Classify

Make sure students understand that each triangle should be classified two ways: by sides and by angles.

Errors and Misconceptions
Problem 14

Students may not recognize that because two sides of a right triangle are perpendicular, either of the perpendicular sides can be used to represent the height of the triangle.

Use the given triangle to help students recognize that if 3 cm is used to represent the height, 4 cm must be used to represent the base, and if 4 cm is used to represent the height, 3 cm must be used to represent the base.

Either arrangement of bases and heights can be used to name 6 cm² as the area of the triangle.

(continued)

130 *Saxon Math Course 3*

---

5. Write the prime factorization of 60. Use exponents for repeated
(9) factors. $2^2 \cdot 3 \cdot 5$

6.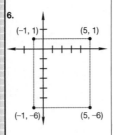

* 6. Plot the following points on a coordinate plane: $(-1, 1)$, $(-1, -6)$,
(4, Inv. 1) $(5, 1)$ and $(5, -6)$. Then draw segments connecting the points to make a rectangle. What is the perimeter of the rectangle?   26 units

Evaluate Use the following information for problems **7** and **8**.

Sergio priced a popular game at several game stores. The prices are recorded below.

$$\$52, \$49, \$48, \$50, \$49, \$50, \$51$$

▶ * 7. **a.** Find the mean, median, mode, and range of the data.   mean $49.86;
(7)   median $50; mode $49, $50; range $4
   b. Which measure would you use to report the spread in the prices?   range $4

▶ 8. If Sergio found the game on sale at a different store for $30, which
(7)   measure of central tendency (mean, median, or mode) would be affected most?   mean

9. Compare: **a.** $\frac{2}{3} \bigcirc \frac{3}{2}$ **b.** $|-7| \bigcirc |7|$
(10)

10. Write a fraction equivalent to $\frac{3}{25}$ that has a denominator of 100. What
(10) decimal is equal to $\frac{3}{25}$? $\frac{12}{100}$; 0.12

* 11. Plot the approximate location of $\sqrt{5}$ on a number line.
(16)

11.

▶* 12. **Classify** Classify each triangle by angles and by sides.
(24)
   a.   **b.**

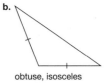

   right, scalene   obtuse, isosceles

* 13. Refer to the figure to answer **a–c.**
(18)
   a. Which angle appears to measure 60°? ∠RMQ or ∠QMR

   b. Which angle appears to measure 120°? ∠PMQ or ∠QMP

   c. Which angle appears to measure 180°? ∠PMR or ∠RMP

▶* 14. Find the area of this triangle: 6 cm²
(20)

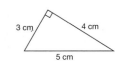
3 cm   4 cm   5 cm

130 *Saxon Math Course 3*

▶ See Math Conversations in the sidebar.

Simplify.

* 15. 9^3 729   **16.** 13^2 169   **17.** $\sqrt{64}$ 8
(15)   (15)   (15)

* 18. $\sqrt[3]{216}$ 6   **19.** $\dfrac{1125}{15}$ 75   **20.** $\dfrac{3}{4} - \dfrac{5}{12}$ $\dfrac{1}{3}$
(15)   (2)   (13)

* 21. Write in exponential form:
(15)
     a. $a \cdot a \cdot a \cdot a \cdot b \cdot b$ a^4b^2 **b.** $2xyxyxyx$ $2x^4y^3$

▶ *** 22.**   Analyze   The coordinates of three vertices of a square are $(-1, -1)$,
(Inv. 1) $(3, -1)$, and $(3, 3)$. What are the coordinates of the fourth vertex? $(-1, 3)$

For problems **23–26,** solve by inspection.

* 23. $m + 90 = 110$ $m = 20$ **24.** $90 - 3x = 60$ $x = 10$
(14)   (14)

* 25. $38 = 2x - 2$ $x = 20$ **26.** $\dfrac{x}{100} = 1$ $x = 100$
(14)   (14)

27. Find $4ac$ when $a = 3$ and $c = 12$.   144
(14)

28. For $A = s^2$, find A when $s = 25$ ft. $A = 625$ ft^2
(14)

* 29. Rearrange the addends to make the calculation easier. Then simplify,
(13)   justifying each step.

$$3\frac{1}{6} + \left(4\frac{1}{6} + 1\frac{2}{3}\right)$$

30. The number -9 is a member of which set(s) of numbers?   **C, E, F**
(10)   **A** whole numbers   **B** counting numbers   **C** integers

     D irrational numbers   **E** rational numbers   **F** real numbers

---

tep:	Justification:
$4\frac{1}{6}) + 1\frac{2}{3}$	Associative Property
$+ 1\frac{2}{3}$	Added $3\frac{1}{6}$ and $4\frac{1}{6}$
9	Added $7\frac{1}{3}$ and $1\frac{2}{3}$

▶ See Math Conversations in the sidebar.

Math Conversations
Discussion opportunities are provided below.

Problem 22   Analyze
Extend the Problem
"The three given vertices form a triangle. Classify the triangle two different ways."
right; isosceles

"The three given vertices, along with a point at $(-1, 3)$, form a square. At what point do the diagonals of the square intersect?" $(1, 1)$

"What is the angle measure of each of the angles formed by the intersection of the diagonals?" $90°$

Looking Forward
Working with triangles prepares students for:

- **Investigation 2,** understanding and applying the Pythagorean Theorem.
- **Lesson 65,** performing applications using similar triangles.
- **Lesson 66,** understanding relationships of sizes and angles of special right triangles.
- **Lesson 112,** writing ratios of side lengths of right triangles.
- **Lesson 115,** ordering relative sizes of sides and angles of a triangle.
- **Lesson 118,** finding sine, cosine, and tangent.
- **Investigation 12,** proving the Pythagorean Theorem.

Assessment *30–40 minutes* *For use after Lesson 20*

Distribute **Cumulative Test 3** to each student. Two versions of the test are available in *Saxon Math Course 3 Course Assessments Book*. Have students complete the **Power-Up Test** first. Allow 10 minutes. Then have students work the 20 numbered items on the **Cumulative Test**. Students may use copies of the answer sheet to record their work. Track individual and class progress with the **Test Analysis** forms.

Power-Up Test 3

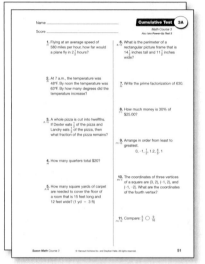

Cumulative Test 3A

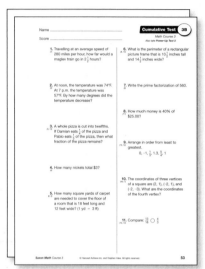

Alternative Cumulative Test 3B

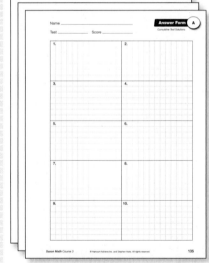

Optional Answer Forms

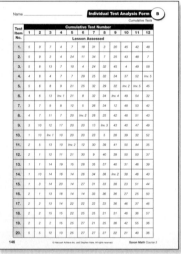

Individual Test Analysis Form

Class Test Analysis Form

Reteaching

Students who score below 80% on the assessment may be in need of reteaching. Look for the causes of student mistakes. If errors are conceptual, refer to the *Reteaching Masters* for reteaching.

Customized Benchmark Assessment

You can develop customized benchmark tests using the Test Generator located on the *Test & Practice Generator CD.*

This chart shows the lesson, the standard, and the test item question that can be found on the *Test & Practice Generator CD.*

LESSON	NEW CONCEPTS	LOCAL STANDARD	TEST ITEM ON CD
11	• Percents		2.11.1
12	• Decimal Numbers		2.12.1
13	• Adding and Subtracting Fractions and Mixed Numbers		2.13.1
14	• Evaluation		2.14.1
	• Solving Equations by Inspection		2.14.2
15	• Powers and Roots		2.15.1
16	• Irrational Numbers		2.16.1
17	• Rounding and Estimating		2.17.1
18	• Lines and Angles		2.18.1
19	• Polygons		2.19.1
20	• Triangles		2.20.1

Using the Test Generator CD

- Develop tests in both English and Spanish.
- Choose from multiple-choice and free-response test items.
- Clone test items to create multiple versions of the same test.
- View and edit test items to make and save your own questions.
- Administer assessments through paper tests or over a school LAN.
- Monitor student progress through a variety of individual and class reports —for both diagnosing and assessing standards mastery.

A Better Cookie Recipe
Assign after Lesson 20 and Test 2

Objectives
- Generate equations from written descriptions.
- Solve and evaluate equations by inspection.
- Perform calculations with whole numbers, fractions, and mixed numbers.
- Select and use appropriate operations to solve a problem.
- Communicate ideas through writing.

Materials
Performance Tasks 3A and **3B**

Preparation
Make copies of **Performance Tasks 3A** and **3B**. (One each per student.)

Time Requirement
25 minutes; Begin in class and complete at home.

Task
Explain to students that they will be modifying a cookie recipe to produce a better recipe that makes 48 cookies. Modifying the recipe will involve performing calculations with whole numbers, fractions, and mixed numbers. Students will be required to generate two equations that modify specific ingredients of the recipe dependent on separate changes to different ingredients. Students must then rewrite the recipe based on their changes and make additions to specified ingredients. Finally students are asked to identify and apply a method for increasing the number of cookies the recipe yields. Point out that all necessary information is provided on **Performance Tasks 3A** and **3B**.

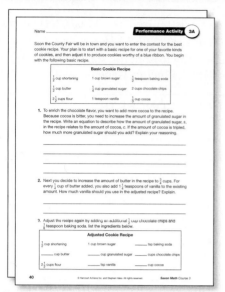

Performance Tasks 3A and 3B

Criteria for Evidence of Learning
- Generates a workable equation that correctly performs the requested function.
- Solves equations correctly by inspection or evaluation.
- Calculates correct values using whole numbers, fractions, and mixed numbers.
- Identifies and applies a working method for correctly adjusting the recipe to yield the specified number of cookies.
- Communicates ideas clearly through writing.

National Council of Teachers of Mathematics (NCTM)

Numbers and Operations

NO.1a Work flexibly with fractions, decimals, and percents to solve problems

NO.1d Understand and use ratios and proportions to represent quantitative relationships

NO.2a Understand the meaning and effects of arithmetic operations with fractions, decimals, and integers

NO.3d Develop, analyze, and explain methods for solving problems involving proportions, such as scaling and finding equivalent ratios

Algebra

AL.2d Recognize and generate equivalent forms for simple algebraic expressions and solve linear equations

AL.3a Model and solve contextualized problems using various representations, such as graphs, tables, and equations

Problem Solving

PS.1b Solve problems that arise in mathematics and in other contexts

Communication

CM.3a Organize and consolidate their mathematical thinking through communication

Connections

CN.4c Recognize and apply mathematics in contexts outside of mathematics

Focus on
• Pythagorean Theorem

Objectives
- Understand and apply the Pythagorean Theorem to find missing side lengths of right triangles.
- Identify Pythagorean triples.
- Use the Pythagorean Theorem to solve word and geometry problems.

Lesson Preparation

Materials
- **Investigation Activity 3**
  Pythagorean Puzzle (in
  Instructional Masters)
- **Teacher-provided material:**
  scissors
- *Optional*
- **Teacher-provided material:**
  envelopes or locking plastic
  bags

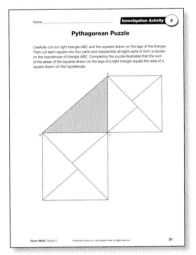

Investigation Activity 3

Math Language

New

hypotenuse

legs

Pythagorean
Theorem

Technology Resources

Student eBook Complete student textbook in electronic format.

Resources and Planner CD Assessment, reteaching, and instructional masters, plus a pacing calendar with standards.

Test and Practice Generator CD Create additional practice sheets and custom-made tests.

www.SaxonPublishers.com Visit for more student activities and planning materials.

Inclusion

Adaptations CD Adapted lessons, investigations, practice and assessments.

Meeting Standards

National Council of Teachers of Mathematics (NCTM)

Geometry

GM.1c Create and critique inductive and deductive arguments concerning geometric ideas and relationships, such as congruence, similarity, and the Pythagorean relationship

GM.4d Use geometric models to represent and explain numerical and algebraic relationships

GM.4e Recognize and apply geometric ideas and relationships in areas outside the mathematics classroom, such as art, science, and everyday life

In this lesson students will learn about the Pythagorean Theorem. Pythagoras who lived almost 3000 years ago, was a Greek mathematician and philosopher who founded a school where both men and women were equal in their study of philosophy, mathematics, and the arts.

Instruction

You may want to allow students to use calculators for this lesson or you may prefer to have the squares of the numbers 11 through 26 posted on the board during this lesson.

$11^2 = 121$	$19^2 = 361$
$12^2 = 144$	$20^2 = 400$
$13^2 = 169$	$21^2 = 441$
$14^2 = 196$	$22^2 = 484$
$15^2 = 225$	$23^2 = 529$
$16^2 = 256$	$24^2 = 576$
$17^2 = 289$	$25^2 = 625$
$18^2 = 324$	$26^2 = 676$

(continued)

Focus on

• Pythagorean Theorem

The longest side of a right triangle is called the **hypotenuse.** The other two sides are called **legs.** Notice that the legs are the sides that form the right angle. The hypotenuse is the side opposite the right angle.

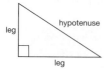

Every right triangle has a property that makes right triangles very important in mathematics. **The area of a square drawn on the hypotenuse of a right triangle equals the sum of the areas of squares drawn on the legs.**

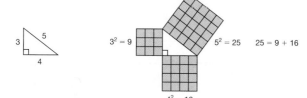

As many as 4000 years ago ancient Egyptians knew of this important and useful relationship between the sides of a right triangle. Today the relationship is named for a Greek mathematician who lived about 550 B.C. The Greek's name was Pythagoras and the relationship is called the Pythagorean Theorem.

The **Pythagorean Theorem** is an equation that relates the sides of a right triangle in this way: the sum of the squares of the legs equals the square of the hypotenuse.

$$\text{leg}^2 + \text{leg}^2 = \text{hypotenuse}^2$$

If we let the letters *a* and *b* represent the lengths of the legs and *c* the length of the hypotenuse, then we can express the Pythagorean Theorem with the following equation.

Pythagorean Theorem
If a triangle is a right triangle, then the sum of the squares of the legs equals the square of the hypotenuse.
$a^2 + b^2 = c^2$

Math Background

Why is it important for students to learn the Pythagorean Theorem?

Throughout elementary school, students study angles, right angles, triangles, square roots, area, and solving equations for an unknown. The Pythagorean Theorem helps students connect all of these mathematical ideas.

It is also a springboard for many ideas in advanced mathematics. This theorem is important in the geometry of Euclid, where it serves as a basis for the definition of distance between two points.

The Pythagorean Theorem is important to the understanding of mathematics, physics, astronomy, and has several real-world applications.

It is helpful to use an area model to solve problems that involve the Pythagorean Theorem. Work through the following examples on your own paper.

Example 1

Copy this triangle. Draw a square on each side. Find the area of each square. Then find *c*.

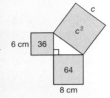

Solution

We copy the triangle and draw a square on each side of the triangle as shown.

We were given the lengths of the legs. The areas of the squares on the legs are 36 cm² and 64 cm². The Pythagorean Theorem says that the sum of the smaller squares equals the area of the largest square.

$$36 \text{ cm}^2 + 64 \text{ cm}^2 = 100 \text{ cm}^2$$

This means that each side of the largest square must be 10 cm long because $(10 \text{ cm})^2$ equals 100 cm². Therefore, $c = $ **10 cm.**

Example 2

Copy this triangle and draw a square on each side. Find the area of each square. Then find *a*.

Solution

We copy the triangle and draw a square on each side. The area of the largest square is 169 in.². The areas of the smaller squares are 144 in.² and a^2. By the Pythagorean Theorem a^2 plus 144 must equal 169.

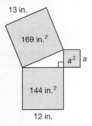

$$a^2 + 144 = 169$$

By inspection we see that

$$a^2 = 25$$

Thus *a* equals **5 in.,** because 5^2 is 25.

Example 1
Instruction
Explain that the hypotenuse always has the largest square because it is the longest length. The longest length of a triangle is always opposite its largest angle, in this case the right angle. Students will learn more about these relationships in Lesson 115.

"If a triangle contains a right angle, why must it be the largest angle?" Sample: The sum of the angle measures of a triangle equals 180°. Since $180° - 90° = 90°$, each of the other angles must be less than 90°.

Example 2
Instruction
Ask a volunteer to write the complete solution on the board.

$$a^2 + 144 = 169$$
$$a^2 = 169 - 144$$
$$a^2 = 25$$
$$a = 5$$

(continued)

Math Conversations

Discussion opportunities are provided below.

Problem 4 *Represent*

Have students rewrite the Pythagorean Theorem to solve for a^2, then for b^2.

$$a^2 = c^2 - b^2$$
$$b^2 = c^2 - a^2$$

Problem 5 *Evaluate*

"How can you identify the base and the height of this triangle?" The base is perpendicular to the height. For this triangle either leg could be the base; the other leg is the height.

Example 3

Instruction

Have students name two more Pythagorean triples and explain their reasoning. Sample: multiply 3-4-5 by 10: 30-40-50; multiply 5-12-13 by 20: 100-240-260

(continued)

---

1. Write the name of the property of right triangles illustrated in examples 1 and 2.   Pythagorean Theorem

2. What is the name for the two sides of a right triangle that form the right angle?   legs

3. What is the name for the side of a right triangle that is opposite the right angle (across the triangle from the right angle)?   hypotenuse

▶ 4. *Represent* Using the letters a and b for the shorter sides of a right triangle and c for the longest side of a right triangle, write the Pythagorean Theorem as an equation. $a^2 + b^2 = c^2$

▶ 5. *Evaluate* Copy the triangle and draw squares on all three sides. Find the area of each square. Then find the length of the longest side of the triangle.

6. Use the Pythagorean Theorem to find a.

5.

256 in.²   144 in.²

400 in.²

20 in.

6.
$$a^2 + b^2 = c^2$$
$$a^2 + 24^2 = 26^2$$
$$a^2 + 576 = 676^2$$
$$a^2 = 100 \text{ cm}^2$$
$$a = 10 \text{ cm}$$

Thinking Skill

Verify

Verify that this multiple of the 5-12-13 triple is a Pythagorean triple: 25-60-65.
$$625 + 3600 = 4225$$

The triangles we have considered so far have sides that are whole numbers. Three whole numbers that can be the side lengths of a right triangle are called a **Pythagorean triple.**

Some Pythagorean Triples

3, 4, 5

5, 12, 13

8, 15, 17

Multiples of Pythagorean triples are also Pythagorean triples. If we multiply 3, 4, and 5 by two, the result is 6, 8, and 10, which is a Pythagorean triple. As we see in this test:

$$a^2 + b^2 = c^2$$
$$6^2 + 8^2 = 10^2$$
$$36 + 64 = 100$$
$$100 = 100$$

Example 3

Are the numbers 2, 3, and 4 a Pythagorean triple?

Solution

If three numbers are a Pythagorean triple, then the sum of the squares of the two lesser numbers equals the square of the greatest number. Since 2^2 plus 3^2 does not equal 4^2, the three numbers **2, 3, and 4 are not a Pythagorean triple.**

a^2	b^2	c^2
2^2	3^2	4^2
4	9	16

▶ See Math Conversations in the sidebar.

The Pythagorean Theorem applies to all right triangles and only to right triangles. If a triangle is a right triangle, then the sides are related by the Pythagorean Theorem. It is also true if the sides of a triangle are related by the Pythagorean Theorem, then the triangle is a right triangle. The latter statement is the **converse** of the Pythagorean Theorem.

Converse of Pythagorean Theorem
If the sum of the squares of two sides of a triangle equals the square of the third side, then the triangle is a right triangle.

We use the converse of the Pythagorean Theorem to determine if a triangle is a right triangle.

Example 4

Cassidy sketched a triangle and carefully measured the sides. Is her triangle a right triangle?

10 in.
7 in.
7 in.

Solution

The triangle might look like a right triangle, but to be a right triangle the side lengths must satisfy the Pythagorean Theorem.

a^2	b^2	c^2
7^2	7^2	10^2
49	49	100

The sum of 49 and 49 is 98, which is nearly 100, but not quite. Therefore, **the triangle is not a right triangle.** (The largest angle of a triangle with these side lengths is about 91°.)

7. Write a multiple of 5, 12, 13, that is a Pythagorean triple.   Answers vary. Possible answers include 10, 24, 26; 15, 36, 39; and 50, 120, 130.

8. Are the numbers 8, 15, and 17 a Pythagorean triple? Explain your answer.   Yes, because $8^2 + 15^2 = 17^2$.

▶ 9. Does a right triangle with the dimensions 8 cm, 9 cm, and 12 cm exist? Explain your answer.   No, although an 8, 9, 12 triangle exists, the triangle is not a right triangle because $8^2 + 9^2$ does not equal 12^2.

Pythagorean triples are used in the building trades to assure that corners being constructed are right angles.

Investigation 2   **135**

▶ See Math Conversations in the sidebar.

Example 4
Instruction
This example asks students to employ the converse of the Pythagorean Theorem to determine if a triangle that appears to be a right triangle actually is a right triangle. A right triangle with legs 7.0 inches long would have a hypotenuse of 9.9 inches.

Math Conversations
Discussion opportunities are provided below.

Problem 9   Analyze
Using a ruler and a protractor, it would be difficult to determine that the triangle is not a right triangle. The largest angle of a triangle with these dimensions is about 89.6°. The hypotenuse of a right triangle with legs of 8 and 9 is about 12.04.

(continued)

Instruction

"Does the Pythagorean Theorem work for every right triangle?" Yes, for every right triangle the sum of the squares of the legs equals the square of the hypotenuse.

"Does every right triangle have side lengths that are whole numbers?" No, when all three of the side lengths of a right triangle are whole numbers, the side lengths are called a Pythagorean triple.

(continued)

Before pouring a concrete foundation for a building, construction workers build wooden forms to hold the concrete. Then a worker or building inspector can use a Pythagorean triple to check that the forms make a right angle. First the perpendicular sides are marked at selected lengths.

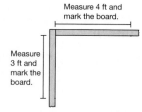
Measure 4 ft and mark the board.
Measure 3 ft and mark the board.

Then the distance between the marks is checked to be sure the three measures are a Pythagorean triple.

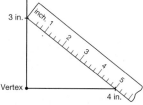
Measure the diagonal. The distance from mark to mark should be 5 ft 0 in.

If the three measures are a Pythagorean triple, the worker can be confident that the corner forms a 90° angle.

You can test your ability to draw a right angle with a pencil and ruler. Draw an angle with sides at least four inches long and mark one side at 3 in. and the other at 4 in. from the vertex.

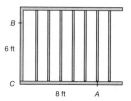
3 in.
Vertex
4 in.

Then measure from mark to mark to see if the distance is 5 inches. If the distance is less than 5 inches, the angle is less than 90°. You can use a protractor to confirm the size of the angle.

10. Britney should push *B* toward *A* to reduce the distance from *A* to *B* to 10 ft 0 inches in order to make a 6-8-10 triple.

10. Britney is framing a wall. She wants the angle at *C* to be a right angle. She marks point *A* 8 feet from *C* and point *B* 6 feet from *C*. She measures from *A* to *B* and finds the distance is 10 ft $1\frac{1}{2}$ in. To make the angle at *C* a right angle, should Britney push *B* toward *A* or pull *B* away from *A*? Why?

B
6 ft
C
8 ft   *A*

As we have seen, some right triangles have three sides with lengths that can be expressed as whole numbers. However, most right triangles have at least one side that cannot be expressed as a whole number.

For example, consider the length of the diagonal of a square. A diagonal of a square is the hypotenuse of two isosceles right triangles. Using the Pythagorean Theorem we find that the length of the hypotenuse is an irrational number.

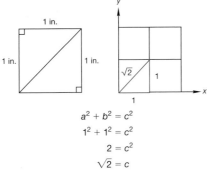

$$a^2 + b^2 = c^2$$
$$1^2 + 1^2 = c^2$$
$$2 = c^2$$
$$\sqrt{2} = c$$

Since the square of the hypotenuse is 2 square inches, the hypotenuse is $\sqrt{2}$ inches. Use an inch ruler to find the length of the diagonal of the square.

From the figure above, we see that on a coordinate plane the diagonal of each square is $\sqrt{2}$ units.

Analyze Find the irrational numbers that represent the lengths of the unmeasured side of each triangle.

▶ **11.** 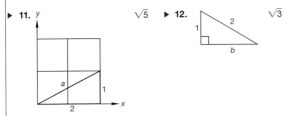 $\sqrt{5}$ ▶ **12.** $\sqrt{3}$

If the side length is an irrational number we can use a calculator to find the approximate length of the side. We will practice doing so in later lessons.

Activity

Pythagorean Puzzle

Materials needed:

• Photocopies of Investigation Activity 3 (1 each per student)

• Scissors

• Envelopes or plastic locking bags (optional)

▶ See Math Conversations in the sidebar.

Rational numbers are any numbers that can be expressed as a ratio of two integers (the denominator of the ratio cannot be zero).

Irrational numbers are numbers that have decimal expansions that are non-ending and nonrepeating. They cannot be expressed as a ratio of two integers.

Math Conversations
Discussion opportunities are provided below.

Problems 11 and 12 Analyze
Have students determine between which two numbers each irrational number lies.
$2^2 = 4$; $3^2 = 9$; so $\sqrt{5}$ is between 2 and 3
$1^2 = 1$; $2^2 = 4$; so $\sqrt{3}$ is between 1 and 2

Extend the Problem
You may wish to ask students to estimate the square root of each number.
Accept any reasonable estimate.
$\sqrt{5}$ is about 2.24
$\sqrt{3}$ is about 1.73

Instruction

You may wish to provide students with a cutout of a square whose sides measure the same as the hypotenuse of the triangle in **Investigation Activity 3.** This square may serve as a template to help students rearrange the pieces of the squares drawn on the legs of the right triangle. Because there can be more than one way to arrange these pieces, ask volunteers to share their solutions.

Cut out and rearrange the pieces of the squares drawn on the legs of the right triangle *ABC* to form a square on the hypotenuse of the triangle.

One solution:

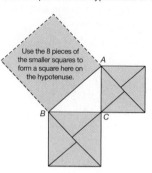

Use the 8 pieces of the smaller squares to form a square here on the hypotenuse.

Looking Forward

Investigating Pythagorean Theorem prepares students for:

• **Investigation 12,** proof of the Pythagorean Theorem.

Lesson Planner

LESSON	NEW CONCEPTS	MATERIALS	RESOURCES
21	• Distributive Property • Order of Operations	none	**Power Up E**
22	• Multiplying and Dividing Fractions	Coins	**Power Up E**
23	• Multiplying and Dividing Mixed Numbers	Recipes	**Power Up E**
24	• Adding and Subtracting Decimal Numbers	Grid paper	**Power Up E**
25	• Multiplying and Dividing Decimal Numbers	none	**Power Up E**
26	• Transformations	Grid paper, construction paper, mirrors, scissors	**Power Up F** **Lesson Activity 4 Transparency** **Investigation Activity 2 Transparency**
27	• Laws of Exponents	Unlined paper, index cards, scissors, grid paper	**Power Up F**
28	• Scientific Notation for Large Numbers	Calculators	**Power Up F**
29	• Ratio	Manipulative Kit: color tiles	**Power Up F**
30	• Repeating Decimals	Calculators	**Power Up F**
Inv. 3	• Classifying Quadrilaterals	Calculators	none

Problem Solving

Strategies

- Act It Out/Make a Model   Lesson 22
- Draw a Diagram   Lessons 23, 26, 28, 29
- Find a Pattern   Lesson 26
- Make a Table   Lessons 21, 24
- Make It Simpler   Lesson 28
- Use Logical Reasoning   Lessons 24, 25, 26
- Use a Graph   Lesson 27
- Work Backwards   Lesson 30

Real-World Applications

pp. 139, 144, 145, 150, 152, 153, 156,
159–161, 163, 164, 166, 167, 174,
175, 178, 180, 183, 187–191, 195

4-Step Process

Student Edition   Lessons 21, 22, 23, 27

Teacher Edition   Lessons 21–30
(Power-Up Discussions)

Communication

Discuss

pp. 148, 173

Explain

pp. 140, 143, 151, 154, 160, 193, 197, 199

Connections

Math and Other Subjects

- Math and Architecture   p. 199
- Math and Art   p. 199
- Math and Geography   p. 183
- Math and History   pp. 156, 167, 174
- Math and Science   pp. 182, 183, 185, 190, 196
- Math and Sports   pp. 150, 161, 167

Math to Math

- Problem Solving and Measurement
  Lessons 21–30, Inv. 3
- Algebra and Problem Solving   Lessons 21, 23,
  26, 29, 30
- Fractions, Percents, Decimals,
  and Problem Solving   Lessons 21–30
- Fractions and Measurement   Lessons 21–25,
  29, 30
- Measurement and Geometry   Lessons 21–30,
  Inv. 3
- Proportional Relationships and
  Geometry   Lessons 26, 29
- Algebra, Measurement, and Geometry
  Lessons 21, 23, 25, 28–30, Inv. 3

Representation

Manipulatives/Hands On

pp. 149, 160, 161, 169, 170–173,
180, 182, 183, 187, 194, 199

Model

pp. 150, 179

Represent

pp. 183, 187, 189

Technology

Student Resources

- eBook, Anytime
- Calculator   Lessons 28, 30, Inv. 3
- Online Resources at
  www.SaxonPublishers.com/ActivitiesC3
  Graphing Calculator Activities   Lessons 23, 28

Teacher Resources

- Resources and Planner CD
- Adaptations CD   Lessons 21–30
- Test & Practice Generator CD
- eGradebook
- Answer Key CD

Students focus on concepts and skills involving rational numbers. The concept of ratio begins here and is extended throughout the year. After discussing the order of operations students learn the laws of exponents. This section closes with experiences involving transformational geometry as well as reflective and rotational symmetry.

Rational Numbers and Operations

Computation with rational numbers is consistently practiced throughout the year.

Review of arithmetic operations with rational numbers is wrapped up in Lessons 22–25 with students multiplying and dividing fractions and mixed numbers, adding and subtracting decimal numbers, and multiplying and dividing decimal numbers. They learn about repeating decimal numbers in Lesson 30.

Algebraic Thinking

The Distributive Property, order of operations, and Laws of Exponents are key algebraic topics.

Students begin simplifying expressions following the order of operations and add the distributive property to the list of properties of operations in Lesson 21. They begin developing a list of Laws of Exponents in Lesson 27. Students apply exponents to express large numbers in scientific notation in Lesson 28.

Proportional Thinking

The concept of ratio is a foundation for many topics in middle school.

Lesson 29 is the first of many lessons on ratio and proportion, which is a major topic of emphasis in this course.

Spatial Thinking

Both language and concepts are emphasized in these geometry lessons.

Students use the language of geometric transformations to describe movement in the plane in Lesson 26. Subsequent lesson will build on the topic. In Investigation 3 students classify quadrilaterals and consider reflective and rotational symmetry.

Assessment

A variety of weekly assessment tools are provided.

After Lesson 25:
- Power-Up Test 4
- Cumulative Test 4
- Performance Activity 4

After Lesson 30:
- Power-Up Test 5
- Cumulative Test 5
- Customized Benchmark Test
- Performance Task 5

LESSON	NEW CONCEPTS	PRACTICED	ASSESSED
21	• Distributive Property	Lessons 21, 22, 25, 26, 28, 29, 31, 32, 33, 34, 35, 36, 37, 38, 40, 41, 42, 44, 47, 55, 56, 59, 60, 63, 64, 65, 66, 67, 69, 70, 72, 74, 76, 81, 82, 87, 90, 91, 94, 96, 97, 102, 109, 110, 111, 112, 113, 117, 118, 119, 120	Tests 5, 10
	• Order of Operations	Lessons 21, 23, 25, 26, 27, 28, 29, 30, 31, 32, 33, 39, 40, 41, 42, 43, 44, 45, 46, 47, 48, 65, 66, 87, 109	Tests 5, 7, 8, 10, 19
22	• Multiplying and Dividing Fractions	Lessons 22, 23, 24, 25, 26, 27, 28, 29, 31, 32, 33, 35, 36, 39, 40, 42, 43, 44, 45, 46, 47, 48, 50, 52, 54, 57, 58, 59, 67, 71, 86, 88, 113, 114	Tests 5–7, 9
23	• Multiplying and Dividing Mixed Numbers	Lessons 23, 24, 25, 26, 27, 29, 30, 31, 32, 33, 34, 35, 38, 39, 40, 41, 47, 49, 50, 56, 63, 81, 82, 84, 87, 88, 89, 90, 91, 102, 104, 105, 106, 107, 108, 111, 112, 116, 120	Tests 7, 8, 10
24	• Adding and Subtracting Decimal Numbers	Lessons 24, 25, 26, 27, 29, 30, 31, 32, 33, 34, 35, 39, 41, 43, 45, 46, 48, 65, 70, 71, 88, 101	Tests 5, 7
25	• Multiplying and Dividing Decimal Numbers	Lessons 25, 26, 27, 28, 29, 30, 31, 32, 33, 34, 35, 36, 38, 39, 40, 41, 43, 44, 46, 48, 49, 59, 60, 63, 65, 70, 71, 76, 77, 78, 81, 83, 84, 85, 86, 87, 88, 89, 90, 91, 92, 97, 98, 99, 100, 101, 103, 104, 105, 106, 107, 108, 109, 110, 111, 112, 113, 114, 117, 119, 120	Tests 5–9, 11, 14, 16, 20
26	• Transformations	Lessons 27, 29, 31, 32, 33, 34, 39, 48, 51, 69, 75	Tests 6, 7
27	• Laws of Exponents	Lessons 27, 28, 29, 30, 31, 32, 33, 34, 35, 36, 38, 39, 40, 41, 43, 44, 46, 47, 48, 50, 53, 54, 55, 56, 57, 60, 61, 62, 64, 65, 66, 67, 68, 69, 70, 71, 72, 73, 74, 75, 77, 78, 79, 80, 82, 83, 84, 98, 99, 100, 102, 103, 105, 106, 108, 111, 112, 113, 114, 115, 116, 117, 118, 119, 120	Tests 6–8, 10, 14, 23,
28	• Scientific Notation for Large Numbers	Lessons 28, 29, 30, 31, 32, 33, 34, 40, 47, 72	Tests 6, 7, 9
29	• Ratio	Lessons 30, 31, 33, 36, 38, 41, 42, 80, 84	Tests 6, 8
30	• Repeating Decimals	Lessons 30, 31, 32, 33, 34, 35, 36, 39, 40, 43, 47, 50, 56, 57	Tests 6, 7
Inv. 3	• Classifying Quadrilaterals	Lessons 34, 39, 40, 41, 44, 49, 52, 74, 76	Test 8

• Distributive Property
• Order of Operations

Objectives

- Use the Distributive Property of Multiplication over Addition to expand and factor expressions.
- Understand the order of operations and use it to simplify arithmetic expressions.

Lesson Preparation

Materials

- **Power Up E** (in *Instructional Masters*)

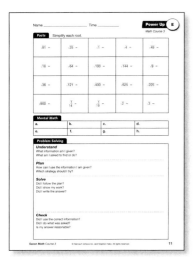

Power Up E

Math Language

New	English Learners (ESL)
distributive property	parentheses
expand	
factor	

Technology Resources

Student eBook Complete student textbook in electronic format.

Resources and Planner CD Assessment, reteaching, and instructional masters, plus a pacing calendar with standards.

Test and Practice Generator CD Create additional practice sheets and custom-made tests.

www.SaxonPublishers.com Visit for more student activities and planning materials.

Inclusion

Adaptations CD Adapted lessons, investigations, practice and assessments.

Meeting Standards

National Council of Teachers of Mathematics (NCTM)

Numbers and Operations

NO.2a Understand the meaning and effects of arithmetic operations with fractions, decimals, and integers

NO.2b Use the associative and commutative properties of addition and multiplication and the distributive property of multiplication over addition to simplify computations with integers, fractions, and decimals

Algebra

AL.2d Recognize and generate equivalent forms for simple algebraic expressions and solve linear equations

Communication

CM.3d Use the language of mathematics to express mathematical ideas precisely

Problem-Solving Strategy: Make a Table

Cameron and Ann are in a chess tournament. The first player to win either two consecutive games, or a total of three games, wins the match and the tournament. How many different ways can their match be played out?

Understand Two players are in a chess tournament, and the winner of the match will be the player who either wins two games in a row, or is the first player to win a total of three games.

Plan We will make a table of the possible outcomes of the match. We will include in our list the number of games it is necessary to play, who won each game, and who the won the match.

Solve

# of Games Played	Who Won Each Game	Match Winner
2 games	CC	Cameron
	AA	Ann
3 games	CAA	Ann
	ACC	Cameron
4 games	CACC	Cameron
	ACAA	Ann
5 games	CACAC	Cameron
	ACACA	Ann
	CACAA	Ann
	ACACC	Cameron

Check Tournaments are a part of almost any competitive activity, and you may be familiar with other formats for determining a winner. Our organized list shows that there are ten different ways the chess match can be played out.

- **Distributive Property**
- **Order of Operations**

facts | Power Up E

mental math

a. **Calculation:** Damian rides his bike 10 miles per hour for $2\frac{1}{2}$ hours. How far does he ride?   25 miles

b. **Estimation:** $3.49 + $1.49 + $6.49 + $3.49 $15

c. **Algebra:** $34 - x = 25$ 9

d. **Power/Roots:** $\sqrt{144}$ 12

e. **Number Sense:** 16×5 80

f. **Fractional Parts:** Three fourths of a dollar is how many cents?   75 cents

g. **Calculation:** $12 \times 3, \sqrt{\ }, \times 7, -2, \div 5, +1, \sqrt{\ }, \div 2$ $1\frac{1}{2}$ or 1.5

problem solving

Cameron and Ann are the two finalists in a chess tournament. The first player to win either two consecutive games, or a total of three games, wins the match and the tournament. How many different ways can their match be played out?

[Understand] Two players are in a chess tournament, and the winner of the match will be the player who either wins two games in a row, or is the first player to win a total of three games.

[Plan] We will make a table of the possible outcomes of the match. We will include in our list the number of games it is necessary to play, who won each game, and who the won the match.

[Solve]

# of Games Played	Who Won Each Game	Match Winner
2 games	CC	Cameron
	AA	Ann
3 games	CAA	Ann
	ACC	Cameron
4 games	CACC	Cameron
	ACAA	Ann
5 games	CACAC	Cameron
	ACACA	Ann
	CACAA	Ann
	ACACC	Cameron

Facts
Distribute **Power Up E** to students. See answers below.

Mental Math
Encourage students to share different ways to mentally compute these exercises. Strategies for exercises **b** and **e** are listed below.

b. Round and Compensate
$3.49 + $1.49 + $6.49 + $3.49 ~
$3 + $1 + $6 + $3 = $13
Add $2 for the four 49¢ parts.
$13 + $2 = $15

Round to Half Dollars
$3.49 + $1.49 + $6.49 + $3.49 ~
$3.50 + $1.50 + $6.50 + $3.50 ~
($3 + $1 + $6 + $3) + ($0.50 × 4) = $15

e. Halve and Double
$16 \times 5 = 8 \times 10 = 80$

Divide by 4, Multiply by 4
$16 \times 5 = (16 \div 4) \times (5 \times 4) = 4 \times 20 = 80$

Problem Solving
Refer to **Power-Up Discussion**, p. 139F.

Facts   Simplify each root.

$\sqrt{81} = 9$	$\sqrt{25} = 5$	$\sqrt{1} = 1$	$\sqrt{4} = 2$	$\sqrt{49} = 7$
$\sqrt{16} = 4$	$\sqrt{64} = 8$	$\sqrt{100} = 10$	$\sqrt{144} = 12$	$\sqrt{9} = 3$
$\sqrt{36} = 6$	$\sqrt{121} = 11$	$\sqrt{400} = 20$	$\sqrt{625} = 25$	$\sqrt{225} = 15$
$\sqrt{900} = 30$	$\sqrt{\frac{1}{4}} = \frac{1}{2}$	$\sqrt{\frac{1}{9}} = \frac{1}{3}$	$\sqrt{2} \approx 1.414$	$\sqrt{3} \approx 1.732$

Instruction

Point out that students may be using the *Distributive Property* intuitively as they do some of the mental math exercises.

Make sure students understand that whether we add before multiplying or multiply before adding, the answer will be the same for the expressions and terms in this lesson. Soon students will learn that the order of operations does matter.

(continued)

Check Tournaments are a part of almost any competitive activity, and you may be familiar with other formats for determining a winner. Our organized list shows that there are ten different ways the chess match can be played out.

New Concepts   *Increasing Knowledge*

distributive property

These two formulas can be used to find the perimeter of a rectangle.

1. $P = 2(l + w)$
2. $P = 2l + 2w$

Using the first formula we add the length and width (12 cm + 8 cm = 20 cm). Then we double this sum (2 × 20 cm = 40 cm).

Using the second formula we double the length (2 × 12 cm = 24 cm) and double the width (2 × 8 cm = 16 cm). Then we add these products (24 cm + 16 cm = 40 cm).

Both formulas produce the same result because the formulas are equivalent.

$$2(l + w) = 2l + 2w$$

These two formulas illustrate the **Distributive Property** (sometimes called the *Distributive Property of Multiplication over Addition*). The Distributive Property gives us a choice when dealing with expressions such as this one.

$$2(12 + 8)$$

One choice is to add before multiplying, 2(20). The other choice is to multiply each addend before adding.

$$2(12 + 8) = 2 \cdot 12 + 2 \cdot 8$$

The second choice distributes the multiplication over the addition. Here we show in symbols the Distributive Property over addition and subtraction.

Distributive Property

$a(b + c) = a \cdot b + a \cdot c$
$a(b + c + d) = a \cdot b + a \cdot c + a \cdot d$
$a(b - c) = a \cdot b - a \cdot c$

The Distributive Property works in two ways. We can **expand** and we can **factor.**

• We expand $2(a + b)$ and get $2a + 2b$.

• We factor $2a + 2b$ and get $2(a + b)$.

Notice that we used the word *factor* as a verb. We factor an expression by writing the expression as a product of two or more numbers or expressions.

Explain How can we factor the expression 15 + 10? Explain and rewrite the expression.   Five is a factor of both 15 and 10. When it is factored out, the expression can be written 5(3 + 2).

Inclusion

Some students need an alternative explanation of the *Distributive Property*. Remind students that multiplication is a version of addition, as in 2 × 3 = 3 + 3. Write the following expressions on the board and ask:

"Knowing that multiplication is addition, how else could you write 2(3 + 4)?" (3 + 4) + (3 + 4)

"Rearrange the 3's and 4's so that they are next to each other." (3 + 3) + (4 + 4)

"Knowing that multiplication is addition, rewrite 3 + 3 and 4 + 4." (2 × 3) + (2 × 4)

"From this exercise of multiplication and addition, what do you know 2(3 + 4) equals?" 2(3 + 4) = (2 × 3) + (2 × 4)

"What property does this exercise demonstrate?" Distributive Property

Example 1

   a. Expand: $3(w + m)$

   b. Factor: $ax + ay$

Solution

   a. To expand, we distribute the multiplication $3(w + m)$.

$$3(w + m) = 3w + 3m$$

   b. To factor, we divide both terms by a.

$$ax + ay = a(x + y)$$

Example 2

   a. Expand: $3(x + 2)$

   b. Factor: $6x + 9$

Solution

   a. We multiply each term within the parentheses by 3.

$$3(x + 2) = 3x + 6$$

   b. We see that 3 is a factor of both terms. We remove by division a factor of 3 from each term.

$$6x + 9 = 3(2x + 3)$$

When factoring, we may prefer to write each term as a product of factors before applying the distributive property.

$6x + 9$	Given expression
$2 \cdot 3 \cdot x + 3 \cdot 3$	Factored each term
$\mathbf{3(2x + 3)}$	Factored 3 from each term

order of operations

If there is more than one operation in an expression, we follow this order.

1. Simplify within **parentheses.**

2. Simplify **exponent** expressions.

3. **Multiply** and **divide** in order from left to right.

4. **Add** and **subtract** in order from left to right.

The first letters of the boldfaced words are also the first letters of the words in the following sentence, which can help us remember this order.

Please **e**xcuse **m**y **d**ear **A**unt **S**ally.

If there are operations within the parentheses we follow the order of operations to simplify within the parentheses.

Example 1

Instruction

Point out that expanding an expression can be done in an automatic way by multiplying each term in the parentheses by the term before the parentheses. Factoring, however, requires that the students look for a common factor that can be removed from all the terms.

Example 2

Instruction

Some people call removing a factor from all the terms *factoring out*. In **b** we factor out a 3.

Instruction

When introducing the order of operations, encourage students to remember the mnemonic.

Point out that multiplication and division are done together as they appear in the problem from left to right—multiplication is not done first from left to right and then division. The same is true for addition and subtraction.

(continued)

English Learners

For example 2 solution, explain the meaning of the word **parentheses.** Write the number 23 with and without parentheses on the board. Point to (23) and say:

"This number is in parentheses."

Point to 23 and say:

"This number is not in parentheses."

Write the following numbers on the board and ask a volunteer to identify the number in parentheses.

   41   36   (53)   68

Math Background

Expressions often contain more than one operation, and there is a need for a consistent way to perform those operations. The order of operations is a *convention* that guides the way an expression is simplified, and ensures that everyone performs the operations in the same order.

A math *convention* is a general agreement about a procedure or principle.

Example 4

Instruction

Be sure that students understand that all grouping symbols should be simplified first. This means that the *Please* in *Please Excuse My Dear Aunt Sally* refers to brackets and braces as well as parentheses, and that these are simplified working from the inside out.

Example 5

Instruction

The parts of this example show how to deal with special grouping situations. These situations are also included in the *Please* part of the mnemonic. Be sure that students understand each of these cases.

(continued)

Example 3

Simplify: $20 - 2 \cdot 3^2 + (7 + 8) \div 5$

Solution

Step:	Justification:
$20 - 2 \cdot 3^2 + 15 \div 5$	Simplified within parentheses
$20 - 2 \cdot 9 + 15 \div 5$	Applied exponent
$20 - 18 + 3$	Multiplied and divided
5	Added and subtracted

Brackets [ ] and braces { } are used as grouping symbols like parentheses. We use brackets to enclose parentheses and braces to enclose brackets.

$$10 - \{8 - [6 - (5 - 3)]\}$$

To simplify expressions with multiple grouping symbols, we begin from the inner most symbols.

Example 4

Simplify: $10 - \{8 - [6 - (5 - 3)]\}$

Solution

We simplify within the parentheses, then the brackets, then the braces.

Step:	Justification:
$10 - \{8 - [6 - (5 - 3)]\}$	Given expression
$10 - \{8 - [6 - 2]\}$	Simplified in parentheses
$10 - \{8 - 4\}$	Simplified in brackets
$10 - 4$	Simplified in braces
6	Subtracted

Absolute value symbols, division bars, and radicals sometimes group multiple terms as well.

Example 5

Simplify:

  a. $|2 - 7|$ b. $\sqrt{9 + 16}$ c. $\dfrac{12 \times 12}{3 + 3}$

Solution

  a. We simplify within the absolute value symbols.
$$|2 - 7| = |-5| = 5$$

  b. We simplify under the radical.
$$\sqrt{9 + 16} = \sqrt{25} = 5$$

c. We simplify above and below the division bar first.

$$\frac{12 \times 12}{3 + 3} = \frac{144}{6} = 24$$

Example 6

Consider this expression: $3 + 3 \times 3 - 3 \div 3$

    a. As written, this expression equals what number?

    b. Copy the expression and place one pair of parentheses so that the expression equals 3. Justify your answer.

Solution

    a. **11**

    b. $3 + 3 \times (3 - 3) \div 3$

$3 + 3 \times 0 \div 3$	Simplified within parentheses
$3 + 0$	Multiplied and divided left to right
3	Added

Practice Set

Perform the indicated multiplication.

▶   **a.** $2(3 + w)$ $6 + 2w$ ▶   **b.** $5(x - 3)$ $5x - 15$

Factor each expression.

▶   **c.** $9x + 6$ $3(3x + 2)$ ▶   **d.** $8w - 10$ $2(4w - 5)$

    e. *Analyze* Which property is illustrated by the following equation?

$$x(y + z) = xy + xz \quad \text{Distributive Property}$$

    f. *Explain* Why might you use the Distributive Property to simplify $3(30 - 2)$? Sample: It is easier to multiply before subtracting: $3(30) - 3(2) = 90 - 6 = 84$.

Simplify.

    g. $2 + 5 \cdot 2 - 1$ **11**   **h.** $(2 + 5) \cdot (2 - 1)$ **7**   **i.** $4 + (11 - 3^2) \cdot 2^3$ **20**

    j. $10 - [8 - (6 - 3)]$ **k.** $\sqrt{36 + 64}$ **10** ▶   **l.** $|8 - 12|$ **4**
    5

    m. The expression $2^2 + 2 \times 2 - 2 \div 2$ equals 7. Copy the expression and insert one pair of parentheses to make the expression equal 11.
    $(2^2 + 2) \times 2 - 2 \div 2$

▶ See Math Conversations in the sidebar.

Example 6
Instruction

Help students understand that they can use parentheses and other grouping symbols to give an expression a particular value. Extend this problem by having students see what other values they can find for the expression by using grouping symbols. Samples: $(3 + 3) \times 3 - (3 \div 3) = 17$ and $(3 + 3) \times [3 - (3 \div 3)] = 12$

Practice Set
Problems a and b ⌊Error Alert⌋

Students should recognize that it is not possible to complete the operation inside the parentheses first because the value of the variable is unknown.

Lead students to generalize that it is only possible to find the sum or difference of like terms, such as $3 + 5$ or $2w - w$.

Problems c and d ⌊Error Alert⌋

An important component of factoring an expression correctly is to identify the greatest common factor, or GCF, of the terms of the expression.

If necessary, review with students how a list can be used to find the common factors, and greatest common factor, of two or more numbers.

Problem l ⌊Error Alert⌋

Watch for the common error of subtracting the absolute value of 12 from the absolute value of 8 $(8 - 12)$ and naming -4 as the simplest form of the expression. Remind students that in some expressions, symbols such as absolute value symbols are used to group more than one term, and those terms must be simplified before the symbols can be applied.

Teacher Tip

Bring writing in math into this lesson by suggesting that students make up their own **order of operations sentences.** This exercise should help reinforce the importance of using the order of operations correctly and help them remember the order. Some students may want to use a word beginning with G for grouping symbols instead of P for parentheses.

Some examples:

• Please explain Mr. Dean's awful song.

• Grace encountered Mike's dog and salamander.

• Pleasant evening, morning dismal, afternoon sunny.

Math Conversations

Discussion opportunities are provided below.

Problem 6 Formulate

Extend the Problem

Ask students to choose mental math or paper and pencil and use that method to solve the following problem.

"What percent of the cost of the room does the tax represent?" 10%

"To solve the problem, did you use paper and pencil, or mental math? Why?"
Sample: Mental math; $7.50 is 10% of $75 because 10% of a number is the same as moving the decimal point in that number one place to the left.

Errors and Misconceptions

Problem 8b

To help factor the expression, students may benefit from first listing all of the factors of each term.

The factors of 9x include 1, 3, 9, and x.
The factors of 12 include 1, 2, 3, 4, 6, and 12.

Students can then list or circle the common factors of the terms, and choose the greatest common factor.

The common factors of the terms are 1 and 3.
The greatest common factor is 3.

(continued)

---

* 1. Bob drove from his home near Los Angeles to his destination in Sacramento in 7 hours. The next time he made his trip, he flew. He drove $\frac{1}{2}$ hour to the airport, spent $1\frac{1}{2}$ hours at the airport, had a 1 hour flight, and arrived at his destination 1 hour after landing. Considering Bob's total travel time, how much time did it save Bob to fly rather than drive?   3 hours
(3)

2. George chopped 8 times in the first 30 seconds. Then he chopped 5 times in the next 20 seconds. Finally he chopped 2 times in the last 10 seconds. How many times did he chop? How long did it take him? When was he chopping the most rapidly?   15 times; 1 minute; the first 30 seconds
(3, 4)

3. John read 66 books in one year. At this rate, how many would he read in four months?   22 books
(7)

* 4. a. How can these numbers be rearranged to make the addition easier?
(2)
$(7 + 13) + 18$
$$7 + (18 + 13)$$

b. What two properties did you use?   Commutative Property of Addition: $7 + (13 + 18)$; Associative Property of Addition: $(7 + 13) + 18$

c. What is the sum?   38

5. Use the Associative and Commutative Properties of Multiplication to find the product of these numbers mentally.
(2)
$$12 \cdot 13 \cdot 5 \cdot 10$$
Write the order in which you multiplied the numbers. What is the product?   For example, $(12 \cdot 5) \cdot 13 \cdot 10 = 7800$

6.
$2(75 + 7.5) = 165$
$2 \cdot 75 + 2 \cdot 7.5 = 165$

▶ *** 6.** Formulate Linda reserved two hotel rooms for $75 each room plus a tax of $7.50 each. Illustrate the Distributive Property by writing two ways to compute the total. What is the total?
(21)

7. Estimate the area of this figure.   24 cm²
(8, 17)

6.3 cm
$4\frac{1}{4}$ cm

* 8. a. Expand: $2(x + 7)$ $2x + 14$
(21)
▶ **b.** Factor: $9x + 12$ $3(3x + 4)$

* 9. Classify this triangle by sides and by angles and state the measure of each angle.   isosceles, right; $m\angle A = 45°$, $m\angle B = 45°$, $m\angle C = 90°$
(20)

▶ See Math Conversations in the sidebar.

10. The numbers of students playing soccer after school Monday through
(7)
Friday were 20, 22, 19, 25, and 24. What was the mean number of
students playing soccer that week?   22

▶ *Generalize* Simplify.

* 11. $1 + 2 + 3 \times 4 + 5$ 20
(21)

* 12. $\dfrac{2 + 5}{1 + 20}$ $\dfrac{1}{3}$
(10, 21)

13. $\dfrac{20}{21} - \dfrac{2}{3}$ $\dfrac{2}{7}$
(13)

14. $1\dfrac{3}{5} + 1\dfrac{1}{10}$ $2\dfrac{7}{10}$
(13)

15. $\dfrac{3660}{12}$ 305
(2)

* 16. $\sqrt{169}$ 13
(15)

* 17. $\sqrt[3]{27}$ 3
(15)

* 18. 3^4 81
(15)

19. Plot the following points, connect the points to make a rectangle, and
(Inv. 1, 8)
find the area and perimeter of the rectangle. $(-5, 7)$, $(3, 7)$, $(3, -2)$,
$(-5, -2)$ $P = 34$ units; $A = 72$ square units

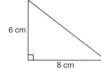

* 20. *Analyze* Compare. $20 - 33$ $\lessgtr$ $|20 - 33|$
(1, 21)

21. Find the two values for r which make this statement true: $|r| = 2$.   2, −2
(1)

* 22. Write in exponential form: $\dfrac{bbrr}{yyyy}$ $\dfrac{b^2 r^2}{y^4}$
(15)

* 23. Find the perimeter and area of this triangle. $P = 24$ cm; $A = 24$ cm²
(20, Inv. 2)

```
     |\
     | \
6 cm |  \
     |   \
     |____\
      8 cm
```

For problems **24–27**, solve by inspection.

24. $27 + w = 35$ $w = 8$
(14)

25. $\dfrac{32}{y} = 2$ $y = 16$
(14)

26. $8n + 2 = 90$ $n = 11$
(14)

27. $2b - 3 = 5$ $b = 4$
(14)

* 28. *Evaluate* Find $b^2 - 4ac$ when $a = 2$, $b = 3$, $c = 1$ 1
(14, 15)

29. How many square yards of carpet are needed to cover the floor of a
(6, 8)
classroom that is 30 ft long and 30 ft wide?   100 yd²

* 30. Name four sets of numbers of which zero is a member.   whole, integers,
(10, 16)
rational, real

▶ See Math Conversations in the sidebar.

Math Conversations

Discussion opportunities are provided below.

Problem 11 *Generalize*

"How many operation symbols appear in this expression?" four

"Which operation is completed first? Explain why." multiplication; The Order of Operations states that multiplication is performed before addition.

Problem 12 *Generalize*

"In this expression, the fraction bar represents division. How does the fraction bar also serve as a grouping symbol?"
Sample: Operations in the numerator and in the denominator must be completed before the quotient can be found.

Problem 20 *Analyze*

Make sure students recognize that the absolute value of $20 - 33$ cannot be determined until the subtraction has been completed.

Problem 28 *Evaluate*

To help students recognize the operations that must be performed, they may find it helpful to make each substitution in parentheses.

$$b^2 - 4ac$$
$$(b)^2 - 4(a)(c)$$
$$(3)^2 - 4(2)(1)$$

The parentheses can help students understand, for example, that the expression $4ac$ represents the product of three factors, not 421.

This technique is especially useful when substitutions involve negative numbers.

Looking Forward

Expanding and factoring expressions using the Distributive Property prepares students for:

• **Lesson 36,** multiplying and dividing terms.

• **Lesson 92,** finding products of binomials.

Learning the order of operations prepares students for:

• **Lesson 50,** solving multi-step equations.

• Multiplying and Dividing Fractions

Objectives

- Use capacity and area models to demonstrate fraction multiplication.
- Find the reciprocal or multiplicative inverse of a given rational number.
- Use a reciprocal to divide fractions.

Lesson Preparation

Materials

- **Power Up E** (in *Instructional Masters*)

Optional

- **Teacher-provided material: coins**

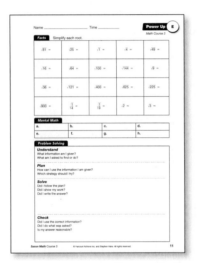

Power Up E

Math Language

New	English Learners (ESL)
multiplicative inverse	approximate
reciprocal	

Technology Resources

Student eBook Complete student textbook in electronic format.

Resources and Planner CD Assessment, reteaching, and instructional masters, plus a pacing calendar with standards.

Test and Practice Generator CD Create additional practice sheets and custom-made tests.

www.SaxonPublishers.com Visit for more student activities and planning materials.

Inclusion

Adaptations CD Adapted lessons, investigations, practice and assessments.

Meeting Standards

National Council of Teachers of Mathematics (NCTM)

Numbers and Operations

NO.1a Work flexibly with fractions, decimals, and percents to solve problems

NO.2a Understand the meaning and effects of arithmetic operations with fractions, decimals, and integers

NO.3a Select appropriate methods and tools for computing with fractions and decimals from among mental computation, estimation, calculators or computers, and paper and pencil, depending on the situation, and apply the selected methods

Geometry

GM.4d Use geometric models to represent and explain numerical and algebraic relationships

Problem-Solving Strategy: Make a Model/Act It Out

These two congruent squares of note paper can be overlapped to form polygons with as few as 4 sides or as many as 16 sides. Are there polygons with other numbers of sides that can be formed by overlapping congruent squares?

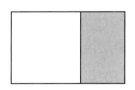   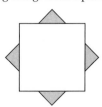

Understand We know that a polygon is a closed shape. The polygons given in the problem are both concave, because it is possible to connect two points located inside the polygon with a segment that goes outside the polygon.

Plan This is a good problem to solve by using a model and acting it out, so we will need to locate or create two congruent squares.

Solve We will leave one of our squares stationary, and rotate and slide the second square:

        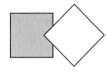

   7 sides   8 sides   9 sides   13 sides

Check We have constructed polygons with 7, 8, 9, and 13 sides by sliding the two squares. We may be able to form different polygons with other numbers of sides. A natural extension of this problem would be to work with a variety of shapes, such as two congruent rectangles, or a square and a rectangle.

•Multiplying and Dividing Fractions

1 Power Up

Facts
Distribute **Power Up E** to students. See answers below.

Mental Math
Encourage students to share different ways to mentally compute these exercises. Strategies for exercises **a** and **g** are listed below.

a. Multiply by Unit Rate
$1\frac{1}{4}$ hr $\times$ 20 pages/hr =
$\frac{5}{4}$ hr $\times$ 20 pages/hr = 25 pages
Regroup, then Multiply
$20 \times 1\frac{1}{4} = 20 \times (1 + \frac{1}{4}) =$
$20 \times 1 + 20 \times \frac{1}{4} = 20 + 5 = 25$ pages

g. Divide by 4, Multiply by 4
25% of 400 = 100% of 100 = 100
Find a Fraction
$25\% = \frac{1}{4}$
$\frac{1}{4} \times 400 = 100$

Problem Solving
Refer to **Power-Up Discussion**, p. 146B.

Power Up   *Building Power*

facts   Power Up E

mental math

a. Calculation: Madrid read 20 pages per hour. How many pages can she read in $1\frac{1}{4}$ hours?   25

b. Geometry: When we write a congruence statement for a polygon, we write the corresponding vertices in the same order for both polygons. Copy and complete this statement: $\triangle ABC \cong \triangle X\_\_$ $\triangle ABC \cong \triangle XWR$

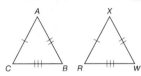

c. Number Sense: $14 \div 4$ $3\frac{1}{2}$

d. Fractional Parts: $\frac{1}{4}$ of 120   30

e. Proportions: If four of the boxes weigh 20 pounds, how much would six of the boxes weigh?   30 pounds

f. Power/Roots: $\sqrt{16} \cdot \sqrt{16}$ 16

g. Percent: 25% of 400   100

h. Calculation: $1000 \div 2, \div 2, \div 2, -25, \div 2, \div 2, -25, \div 2, -25$ -25

problem solving

These two congruent squares of note paper can be overlapped to form polygons with as few as 4 sides or as many as 16 sides. Are there polygons with other numbers of sides that can be formed by overlapping congruent squares?

(**Understand**) We know that a polygon is a closed shape. The polygons given in the problem are both concave, because it is possible to connect two points located inside the polygon with a segment that goes outside the polygon.

(**Plan**) This is a good problem to solve by using a model and acting it out, so we will need to locate or create two congruent squares.

Facts   Simplify each root.

$\sqrt{81} = 9$	$\sqrt{25} = 5$	$\sqrt{1} = 1$	$\sqrt{4} = 2$	$\sqrt{49} = 7$
$\sqrt{16} = 4$	$\sqrt{64} = 8$	$\sqrt{100} = 10$	$\sqrt{144} = 12$	$\sqrt{9} = 3$
$\sqrt{36} = 6$	$\sqrt{121} = 11$	$\sqrt{400} = 20$	$\sqrt{625} = 25$	$\sqrt{225} = 15$
$\sqrt{900} = 30$	$\sqrt{\frac{1}{4}} = \frac{1}{2}$	$\sqrt{\frac{1}{9}} = \frac{1}{3}$	$\sqrt{2} \approx 1.414$	$\sqrt{3} \approx 1.732$

Solve We will leave one of our squares stationary, and rotate and slide the second square:

7 sides   8 sides   9 sides   13 sides

Look Back We have constructed polygons with 7, 8, 9, and 13 sides by sliding the two squares. We may be able to form different polygons with other numbers of sides. A natural extension of this problem would be to work with a variety of shapes, such as two congruent rectangles, or a square and a rectangle.

New Concept   *Increasing Knowledge*

Pictured below are containers for a gallon, a quart, and a pint. We can use these measures to illustrate the multiplication of fractions. A quart is $\frac{1}{4}$ of a gallon, and a pint is $\frac{1}{2}$ of a quart. What fraction of a gallon is a pint?

1 gallon   1 quart   1 pint

A pint is $\frac{1}{2}$ of $\frac{1}{4}$ of a gallon. By multiplying $\frac{1}{2}$ and $\frac{1}{4}$, we find that a pint is $\frac{1}{8}$ of a gallon.

$$\frac{1}{2} \cdot \frac{1}{4} = \frac{1}{8}$$

Notice that the numerator of $\frac{1}{8}$ is the product of the numerators, and the denominator is the product of the denominators. Also notice that $\frac{1}{8}$ is less than both factors.

An area model can also help us visualize the result of multiplying fractions. Here we show a 1 inch-by-1 inch square. Within the square is a small, shaded square that is $\frac{1}{2}$ inch-by-$\frac{1}{2}$ inch. Notice the shaded square is $\frac{1}{4}$ the area of the larger square. This model illustrates the multiplication of $\frac{1}{2}$ and $\frac{1}{2}$.

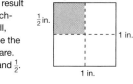

$$\frac{1}{2} \cdot \frac{1}{2} = \frac{1}{4}$$

To multiply fractions we multiply the numerators to find the numerator of the product, and we multiply the denominators to find the denominator of the product.

Example 1

Multiply $\frac{1}{3}$ and $\frac{2}{3}$. Use an area model to illustrate the multiplication.

Lesson 22   **147**

Instruction

Ask students to share any experiences they or their families have had with multiplying and dividing fractions. Possible experiences include:

- Increasing or decreasing the amounts of ingredients in recipes.
- Buying things that come in fractional measures—such as fabric, deli meats and cheeses, wood, and gasoline.
- Sharing pizza, money, or beverages.

Point out that multiplying fractions is simpler than adding or subtracting them. There is no need to think about finding a common denominator.

The area model gives students a visual representation of why the product of two proper fractions (fractions less than 1) is less than either factor.

Example 1

Instruction

Encourage students to sketch a square and divide it as described on the student page. Point out that the square and the divisions do not need to be drawn exactly. What is important is to create a representation of the multiplication of the fractions.

(continued)

2 New Concepts (Continued)

Example 2
Instruction
Use the *Discuss* question to emphasize the advantages of reducing first. Be sure that students understand that the answer will be the same whether they reduce first, reduce partially first, or wait till they multiply to reduce, as long as they simplify the product completely.

Instruction
After going over the information about reciprocals, ask students whether $\frac{b}{a}$ is a reciprocal of $\frac{a}{b}$. **yes** Point out that reciprocals are easy to recognize because the two parts of the fraction have changed places. The reciprocal of a number is the result of dividing 1 by the number, but the same result is more easily accomplished with fractions by interchanging the numerator and denominator.

Example 3
Instruction
After you work through parts **a** and **b**, ask what the difference between a reciprocal and a multiplicative inverse is. Each method produces the same result. Call attention to the relationship between the questions and answers in parts **c** and **d**. The answer is the reciprocal of the fractions. This relationship is the basis for dividing fractions.

(continued)

Solution

Multiply the numerators. Multiply the denominators

$$\frac{1}{3} \cdot \frac{2}{3} = \frac{2}{9}$$

We draw a square and divide two adjacent sides into thirds, extending the divisions across the square. Then we shade an area with sides $\frac{1}{3}$ and $\frac{2}{3}$ long. We see that $\frac{2}{9}$ of the square is shaded.

Example 2

What number is $\frac{3}{4}$ of $\frac{8}{9}$?

Solution

To find $\frac{3}{4}$ of $\frac{8}{9}$ we multiply the fractions. We may reduce before we multiply (cancel).

$$\overset{1}{\cancel{3}} \cdot \overset{2}{\cancel{8}} = \frac{2}{3}$$
$$\underset{1}{\cancel{4}} \cdot \underset{3}{\cancel{9}}$$

Discuss Why might we want to reduce before we multiply? Answers will vary but may include that it is easier and faster to multiply small numbers.

If the product of two fractions is 1, the fractions are **reciprocals**.

$$\underbrace{\frac{2}{3} \cdot \frac{3}{2}}_{\text{reciprocals}} = \frac{6}{6} = 1$$

We can form the reciprocal of a fraction by reversing the numbers of the numerator and denominator of the fraction.

$$\frac{3}{4} \times \frac{4}{3}$$

Some say we *invert* a fraction to form its reciprocal. This expression comes from another name for reciprocal, **multiplicative inverse**.

Example 3

    a. What is the reciprocal of $\frac{5}{6}$?

    b. What is the multiplicative inverse of 3?

    c. How many $\frac{1}{4}$s are in 1?

    d. How many $\frac{2}{3}$s are in 1?

Solution

    a. The reciprocal of $\frac{5}{6}$ is $\frac{6}{5}$.

    b. The multiplicative inverse of 3 (or $\frac{3}{1}$) is $\frac{1}{3}$.

Math Background

A number of different methods involving equivalent division problems can be used when dividing by a fraction. Below we show three different methods to find $8 \div \frac{2}{3}$.

1. Multiply both 8 and $\frac{2}{3}$ by 3 (the denominator). The result is $24 \div 2$, which is 12.

2. Divide both 8 and $\frac{2}{3}$ by 2 (the numerator). The result is $4 \div \frac{1}{3}$. Since there are three $\frac{1}{3}$'s in 1, the number of $\frac{1}{3}$'s in 4 is four times as many, which is 12.

3. Multiply both 8 and $\frac{2}{3}$ by $\frac{3}{2}$ (the reciprocal of $\frac{2}{3}$). The result is $12 \div 1$, which is 12.

The third method, which combines the first and second methods, is the most commonly used method to divide by a fraction. When this method is used, the quotient is immediately obvious once the dividend has been multiplied by the reciprocal of the divisor.

c. The number of $\frac{1}{4}$s in 1 is **4** (or $\frac{4}{1}$), which is the reciprocal of $\frac{1}{4}$.

d. The number of $\frac{2}{3}$s in 1 is the reciprocal of $\frac{2}{3}$, which is $\frac{3}{2}$.

We use reciprocals to help us divide fractions. If we want to know the number of $\frac{3}{4}$s in 2, we divide 2 by $\frac{3}{4}$.

$$2 \div \frac{3}{4}$$

We perform the division in two steps. First we find the number of $\frac{3}{4}$s in 1, which is the reciprocal of $\frac{3}{4}$.

$$1 \div \frac{3}{4} = \frac{4}{3}$$

There are twice as many $\frac{3}{4}$s in 2 as there are in 1, so we multiply $\frac{4}{3}$ by 2.

$$2 \times \frac{4}{3} = \frac{8}{3} = \mathbf{2\frac{2}{3}}$$

We can combine the two steps and multiply by the reciprocal of the divisor.

$$2 \div \frac{3}{4}$$

$$2 \times \frac{4}{3} = \frac{8}{3} = \mathbf{2\frac{2}{3}}$$

Example 4

Thinking Skill

Connect

There are 2 cups in a pint. How many cups are in a gallon? What fraction of a gallon is one cup? How are the two numbers related? 16; $\frac{1}{16}$; They are reciprocals.

A quart is $\frac{1}{4}$ of a gallon. A pint is $\frac{1}{8}$ of a gallon. How many $\frac{1}{8}$s are in $\frac{1}{4}$?

Solution

The question "How many are in...?" is a division question. We divide $\frac{1}{4}$ by $\frac{1}{8}$.

$$\frac{1}{4} \div \frac{1}{8}$$

$$\frac{1}{4} \times \frac{8}{1} = \frac{8}{4} = 2$$

The answer is reasonable. Two $\frac{1}{8}$s equal $\frac{1}{4}$, and two pints equal a quart.

Example 5

Simplify: $\frac{3}{4} \div \frac{1}{3}$

Solution

We show two methods.

First method: Find the number of $\frac{1}{3}$s in 1.

$$1 \div \frac{1}{3} = 3$$

Then find $\frac{3}{4}$ of this number.

$$\frac{3}{4} \cdot 3 = \frac{9}{4} = \mathbf{2\frac{1}{4}}$$

2 New Concepts *(Continued)*

Instruction

When presenting fraction division, emphasize that understanding reciprocals is the key. A division can be changed to a multiplication by using the reciprocal of the divisor. Guide students carefully through this explanation. If necessary, demonstrate each step on the board or overhead.

Example 4

Instruction

Be sure that students understand the steps of the solution. Have volunteers explain in their own words why the answer is reasonable.

Example 5

Instruction

Call attention to the direction line: *Simplify*. Ask students what this means. Sample: The answer must be in simplest form.

Work through the two methods shown for this problem. Let the class discuss which is easier to do. Tell students that they may use whichever one they prefer.

(continued)

Teacher Tip

If some students have difficulty grasping the concept that **the product of two positive fractions less than 1 is less than either fraction,** use coins to represent these situations. Some examples:

Start with a half dollar ($\frac{1}{2}$) and ask what half of that is. a quarter or $\frac{1}{4}$ Guide students to see that a quarter is less than a half dollar and $\frac{1}{4}$ is less than $\frac{1}{2}$.

Start with 6 dimes ($\frac{6}{10}$) and ask what one third of that is. 2 dimes or $\frac{2}{10}$ Guide students to see that 2 dimes are less than 6 dimes and $\frac{2}{10}$ is less than $\frac{1}{3}$.

After working with some coin situations, review the area model and have students draw area models of the coin situations.

2 New Concepts (Continued)

Practice Set

Problem a Model

Students should recognize that the denominators of the fractions represent the divisions of the model. For example, if a rectangle is used to represent $\frac{1}{4} \cdot \frac{1}{2}$, one dimension of the rectangle (such as its length) is divided into 4 equal parts, and the other dimension of the rectangle (its width) is divided into 2 equal parts.

Problem d Generalize

Some students may notice that the numerator 2 and the denominator 6 represent terms of the fractions that can be reduced.

Remind students that reducing the terms of fractions before multiplying often makes the arithmetic easier to complete, and can produce a product that is already in simplest form.

Problems m and n Error Alert

Watch for students who reduce the terms of the fractions before the fractions are rewritten as the product of two factors.

3 Written Practice

Math Conversations

Discussion opportunities are provided below.

Problem 2 Analyze

Students should recognize that only the units are added. Students should simplify their answers.

Errors and Misconceptions

Problem 5

Although students can be expected to recognize the fraction bar as a symbol for division, they may not recognize that the fraction bar also represents a grouping symbol.

Explain that the Order of Operations states that operations in grouping symbols must be completed first. Help students recognize that an application of this concept is that the numerator and the denominator must be simplified before the division can be completed.

Problem 7

Some students may write an equals sign to complete the comparison because the computation on each side of the inequality represents -13. Have these students note the symbol for absolute value on the left side of the inequality, and work with them to understand its meaning.

(continued)

150   *Saxon* Math Course 3

Second method: Rewrite the division problem as a multiplication problem and multiply by the reciprocal of the divisor.

$$\frac{3}{4} \div \frac{1}{3}$$

$$\frac{3}{4} \cdot \frac{3}{1} = \frac{9}{4} = 2\frac{1}{4}$$

Practice Set ▶

a.

a. **Model** Multiply $\frac{1}{4}$ and $\frac{1}{2}$. Use an area model to illustrate the multiplication. $\frac{1}{8}$

b. One half of the students in the class are boys. One third of the boys walk to school. Boys who walk to school are what fraction of the students in the class? $\frac{1}{6}$

Generalize Simplify.

c. $\frac{1}{2} \times \frac{3}{4}$ $\frac{3}{8}$ ▶ d. $\frac{5}{6} \cdot \frac{2}{3}$ $\frac{5}{9}$

e. What number is $\frac{1}{2}$ of $\frac{3}{4}$? $\frac{3}{8}$

f. What number is $\frac{2}{3}$ of $\frac{3}{4}$? $\frac{1}{2}$

For **g** and **h** write the multiplicative inverse (reciprocal) of the number.

g. $\frac{3}{8}$ $\frac{8}{3}$ h. 4 $\frac{1}{4}$

i. How many $\frac{2}{3}$s are in 1? $\frac{3}{2}$ or $1\frac{1}{2}$

j. $1 \div \frac{3}{5}$ $\frac{5}{3}$ or $1\frac{2}{3}$ k. $1 \div \frac{1}{6}$ 6 or $\frac{6}{1}$

l. How many $\frac{1}{2}$s are in $\frac{3}{4}$? $(\frac{3}{4} \div \frac{1}{2})$ $\frac{3}{2}$ or $1\frac{1}{2}$

Simplify.

▶ m. $\frac{2}{3} \div \frac{3}{4}$ $\frac{8}{9}$ ▶ n. $\frac{3}{4} \div \frac{2}{3}$ $\frac{9}{8}$ or $1\frac{1}{8}$

Written Practice   *Strengthening Concepts*

1. Mariya ran 14 miles in one week. At that rate, how many miles would
   (7) she run in 5 days? 10 miles

▶ * 2. *Analyze* The triathlete swam 2 miles in 56 minutes. Then, he rode his
   (3, 7) bicycle 100 miles in 5 hours. Finally, he ran 20 miles in 160 minutes. How many minutes did it take him to complete the course? During which portion of the race did he have the greatest average speed? 516 minutes; bike

* 3. Expand: $3(x + 7)$ $3x + 21$ * 4. Factor: $5x + 35$ $5(x + 7)$
  (21)   (21)

▶ * 5. $\frac{6 + 4}{7 - 2}$ 2   * 6. $6 + 5 \times 4 - 3 + 2 \div 1$ 25
  (21)   (21)

▶ * 7. Compare: $|6 - 19| \bigodot (6 - 19)$
  (1, 21)

* 8. $\frac{3}{4} \cdot \frac{1}{3}$ $\frac{1}{4}$
  (22)

150   *Saxon* Math Course 3

▶ See Math Conversations in the sidebar.

* 9. What number is $\frac{1}{3}$ of $\frac{3}{5}$? $\frac{1}{5}$
(22)

▶* 10. *Generalize* What is the reciprocal of $\frac{1}{7}$?   7
(22)

* 11. What is the multiplicative inverse of $\frac{2}{3}$? $\frac{3}{2}$
(22)

12. Find $x^2 + 2yz$ when $x = 4$, $y = 5$, and $z = 7$.   86
(14)

* 13. $\frac{3}{4} \div \frac{1}{3}$ $\frac{9}{4}$ or $2\frac{1}{4}$
(22)

* 14. *Generalize* Find the perimeter and area of
(8, 20) this triangle. $P = 30$ cm; $A = 30$ cm^2

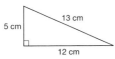
5 cm, 13 cm, 12 cm

▶* 15. *Classify* Classify this triangle by angles and
(20) sides, and state the measure of each angle.
acute, equilateral; $m\angle A = m\angle B = m\angle C = 60°$

16. Find the area of a square with a side length of 17 in.   289 in.^{2}
(8)

17. *Explain* Is this figure a polygon? Explain
(19) why or why not.   No. A polygon cannot have a curved side.

18. Can an obtuse triangle be regular? Explain why or why not.   No. In a
(20) regular triangle, all angles must be equal.

19. Choose the appropriate symbol to complete this statement:
(19) $\triangle EFG \bigcirc \triangle XYZ$ **A**

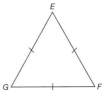
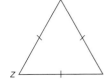

A $\cong$ **B** $\sim$

C $=$ **D** $<$

20. $\angle WYX$ and $\angle XYZ$ form a linear pair. If $m\angle XYZ$ is 60°, find $m\angle WYX$.
(18) 120°

21. Name this figure   **B**
(18)

A $\overrightarrow{EF}$ **B** $\overrightarrow{FE}$ **C** either **A** or **B**

▶ See Math Conversations in the sidebar.

Math Conversations

Discussion opportunities are provided below.

Problem 10   *Generalize*

Extend the Problem

"It is correct to say that $\frac{7}{1}$ is a reciprocal of $\frac{1}{7}$. Is it also correct to say that $\frac{14}{2}$ is a reciprocal of $\frac{1}{7}$? Explain why or why not."

Yes; two numbers whose product is 1 are reciprocals. Because the product of $\frac{1}{7}$ and $\frac{14}{2}$ is $\frac{14}{14}$, and $14 \div 14 = 1$, $\frac{14}{2}$ is a reciprocal of $\frac{1}{7}$.

The value of a reciprocal is unique. However, there are an infinite number of ways to represent that value (or any other value).

Problem 15   *Classify*

To name the measure of each angle, students must recognize that all of the angles are congruent, and recall that the sum of the angle measures of any triangle is 180°.

(continued)

Math Conversations

Discussion opportunities are provided below.

Problem 30 _Generalize_

Ask students to choose mental math or paper and pencil and use that method to solve the problem.

Then ask students to name the method they chose, and explain why that method was chosen. Methods and explanations will vary.

22. A freeway passes under a street. If we think of the freeway and the
(18) street as lines, we would say the lines are: **C**

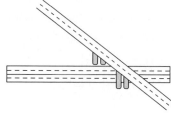

A intersecting   **B** parallel   **C** skew

23. Round $403,500,000 to the nearest million. $404 million
(17)

24. Estimate the product $(17.89)(9\frac{7}{8})$.   180
(17)

25. Name a set of numbers that includes 1, but not zero.
(1) natural (or counting) numbers

26. $\sqrt[3]{64}$ 4   **27.** $1\frac{1}{3} + 1\frac{1}{6}$ $2\frac{1}{2}$
(15)   (13)

28. Write $\frac{7}{8}$ as a decimal number.   0.875
(12)

29. What is $\frac{3}{5}$ of 35?   21
(5)

▶* **30.** _Generalize_   A home in the mountains is going
(20) to be built with a steep roof to keep heavy
snow from accumulating on the roof. If the
roof is at a 70° angle as shown, what is the
angle at the peak?   40°

▶ See Math Conversations in the sidebar.

Looking Forward

Multiplying and dividing fractions prepares students for:

• **Lesson 23,** multiplying and dividing mixed numbers.

• Multiplying and Dividing Mixed Numbers

Objectives

- Multiply and divide mixed numbers by first rewriting them as improper fractions.
- Rewrite mixed numbers and whole numbers as improper fractions.
- Multiply and divide mixed numbers to solve word problems.

Lesson Preparation

Materials

- **Power Up E** (in *Instructional Masters*)

Optional

- **Teacher-provided material:** recipes

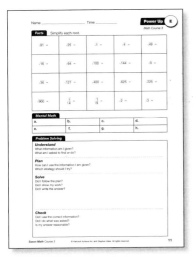

Power Up E

Math Language

Maintain	English Learners (ESL)
improper fractions	eliminate
mixed numbers	

Technology Resources

Student eBook Complete student textbook in electronic format.

Resources and Planner CD Assessment, reteaching, and instructional masters, plus a pacing calendar with standards.

Test and Practice Generator CD Create additional practice sheets and custom-made tests.

www.SaxonPublishers.com Visit for more student activities and planning materials.

Inclusion

Adaptations CD Adapted lessons, investigations, practice and assessments.

Meeting Standards

National Council of Teachers of Mathematics (NCTM)

Numbers and Operations

NO.1a Work flexibly with fractions, decimals, and percents to solve problems

NO.3a Select appropriate methods and tools for computing with fractions and decimals from among mental computation, estimation, calculators or computers, and paper and pencil, depending on the situation, and apply the selected methods

Geometry

GM.4d Use geometric models to represent and explain numerical and algebraic relationships

Problem Solving

PS.1b Solve problems that arise in mathematics and in other contexts

Problem-Solving Strategy: Draw a Diagram

We can use tree diagrams to help us identify possible combinations or possible outcomes of probability experiments.

Problem: The security guard can choose from three different shirts and two different pairs of pants for his uniform. How many different combinations does he have to choose from?

[**Understand**] We are told that the guard has three different shirts and two different pants. We are asked to find the number of different uniform combinations he has to choose from.

[**Plan**] We will make a tree diagram to show the possible combinations. We will use the first set of branches for the three shirts (A, B, C) and the second set of branches for pants (1, 2).

[**Solve**]

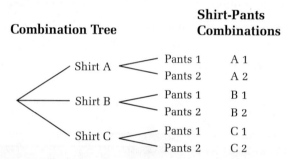

Combination Tree

Shirt-Pants Combinations

Shirt A	Pants 1	A 1
	Pants 2	A 2
Shirt B	Pants 1	B 1
	Pants 2	B 2
Shirt C	Pants 1	C 1
	Pants 2	C 2

We identify 6 different possible combinations.

[**Check**] We look back at the problem with our solution in mind to be sure we have answered the question and that our answer is reasonable. We were asked for the number of combinations of shirts and pants. We answered 6. Our answer is reasonable because for each choice of shirt there are two choices of pants.

• Multiplying and Dividing Mixed Numbers

facts | Power Up E

mental math

  a. Calculation: Robbie ran ten miles per hour. How many minutes would it take Robbie to run 2 miles?   12 minutes

  b. Geometry: Two angles of a triangle are 90° and 35°. What is the measure of the third angle?   55°

  c. Number Sense: $18 ÷ 4 $4.50

  d. Proportions: If 2 pounds cost $5, how much would 3 pounds cost? $7.50

  e. Percent: 25% of 104   26

  f. Algebra: $\frac{54}{x} = 0.54$ 100

  g. Fractional Parts: $\frac{1}{3}$ of 93 $93 ÷ 3 = 31$

  h. Calculation: $7 + 3$, $× 10$, $÷ 2$, $÷ 10$, $+ 2$, $× 9$, $+ 1$, $\sqrt{\ }$, $+ 1$, $\sqrt{\ }$, $+ 1$, $\sqrt{\ }$, $- 1$, $\sqrt{\ }$, $- 1$ 0

problem solving

We can use tree diagrams to help us identify possible combinations or possible outcomes of probability experiments.

Problem: The security guard can choose from three different shirts and two different pairs of pants for his uniform. How many different combinations does he have to choose from?

  Understand We are told that the guard has three different shirts and two different pants. We are asked to find the numbers of different uniform combinations he has to choose from.

  Plan We will make a tree diagram to show the possible combinations. We will use the first set of branches for the three shirts (A, B, C) and the second set of branches for pants (1, 2).

  Solve

Combination Tree	Shirt-Pants Combinations

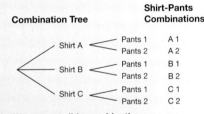

	Pants 1	A 1
Shirt A	Pants 2	A 2
Shirt B	Pants 1	B 1
	Pants 2	B 2
Shirt C	Pants 1	C 1
	Pants 2	C 2

We identify **6 different possible combinations.**

---

1 **Power Up**

Facts
Distribute **Power Up E** to students. See answers below.

Mental Math
Encourage students to share different ways to mentally compute these exercises. Strategies for exercises **b** and **e** are listed below.

  b. Subtract from 180°
    $180° − 90° = 90°$
    $90° − 35° = 55°$
  Sum of the Angles of a Triangle
    $a + 90° + 35° = 180°$
    $a + 135° = 180°$
    $a = 180° − 135° = 55°$
  e. Think Half of Half
    $\frac{1}{2} × 104 = 52$
    $\frac{1}{2} × 52 = 26$
  Multiply by 4, Divide by 4
    25% of 104 = 100% of (104 ÷ 4)
    $(104 ÷ 4) = (100 ÷ 4) + (4 ÷ 4) =$
    $25 + 1 = 26$

Problem Solving
Refer to **Power-Up Discussion,** p. 153B.

Facts   Simplify each root.

$\sqrt{81} = 9$	$\sqrt{25} = 5$	$\sqrt{1} = 1$	$\sqrt{4} = 2$	$\sqrt{49} = 7$
$\sqrt{16} = 4$	$\sqrt{64} = 8$	$\sqrt{100} = 10$	$\sqrt{144} = 12$	$\sqrt{9} = 3$
$\sqrt{36} = 6$	$\sqrt{121} = 11$	$\sqrt{400} = 20$	$\sqrt{625} = 25$	$\sqrt{225} = 15$
$\sqrt{900} = 30$	$\sqrt{\frac{1}{4}} = \frac{1}{2}$	$\sqrt{\frac{1}{9}} = \frac{1}{3}$	$\sqrt{2} \approx 1.414$	$\sqrt{3} \approx 1.732$

2 New Concepts

Instruction

Point out that multiplying and dividing *mixed numbers* may be used even more than multiplying and dividing fractions for cooking, woodworking, home repair, gardening, and sewing projects.

Use the *Explain* question to review how to write a whole number as a fraction.

The method of multiplying the whole number by the denominator and adding the numerator is the one most people use to convert a mixed number to an improper fraction. Be sure that students understand the concept as well as the process. This will help them avoid errors in future lessons.

Example 1

Instruction

Guide students to notice that the multiplication and division of mixed numbers is the same as the process for fractions once the mixed numbers have been converted to improper fractions. Emphasize again the usefulness of reducing or canceling.

Make sure that students notice that the answers are expressed in simplest form.

(continued)

Check We look back at the problem with our solution in mind to be sure we have answered the question and that our answer is reasonable. We were asked for the number of combinations of shirts and pants. We answered 6. Our answer is reasonable because for each choice of shirt there are two choices of pants.

New Concept — *Increasing Knowledge*

Thinking Skill

Explain

How do we write whole numbers as improper fractions? We write the number as the numerator of a fraction with a denominator of 1.

To multiply or divide mixed numbers we first write each mixed number (or whole number) as a fraction. A mixed number can be converted into a fraction as we illustrate.

$$2\frac{1}{4} = \frac{4}{4} + \frac{4}{4} + \frac{1}{4} = \frac{9}{4}$$

Another way to perform the conversion is to multiply the whole number by the denominator and add the numerator to find the numerator of the new fraction.

$$\overset{4 \times 2 + 1 = 9}{2\frac{1}{4} = \frac{9}{4}}$$

If the answer is an improper fraction we might choose to convert the improper fraction to a mixed number. We do so by dividing the numerator by the denominator.

$$\frac{9}{4} = 4\overline{)9} \;\; \begin{array}{r} 2 \\ \underline{-8} \\ 1 \end{array} = 2\frac{1}{4}$$

The remainder becomes the numerator of the fraction part of the mixed number.

Visit www.SaxonPublishers.com/ActivitiesC3 for a graphing calculator activity.

Example 1

Simplify:

a. $2\frac{1}{3} \times 1\frac{1}{2}$ b. $1\frac{2}{3} \div 2\frac{1}{2}$

Solution

a. First we rewrite each mixed number as an improper fraction. Then we multiply.

$$2\frac{1}{3} \times 1\frac{1}{2}$$

$$\frac{7}{3} \times \frac{3}{2} = \frac{21}{6} = 3\frac{3}{6} = 3\frac{1}{2}$$

The product is an improper fraction which we can convert to a mixed number. We reduce the fraction.

Math Background

Fraction terms can be reduced before multiplying because reducing the terms produces the same product as reducing the terms after multiplying.

However, reducing the terms before multiplying makes it easier to simplify the product. For some factors, reducing the terms before multiplying will produce a product that is already in simplest form.

b. We write the mixed numbers as improper fractions. Instead of dividing, we multiply by the reciprocal of the divisor.

$$1\frac{2}{3} \div 2\frac{1}{2}$$

$$\frac{5}{3} \div \frac{5}{2}$$

$$\frac{5}{3} \times \frac{2}{5} = \frac{10}{15} = \frac{2}{3}$$

a and **b** could be reduced before multiplying. We may reduce (or cancel) to eliminate the need to reduce after multiplying.

a. $\dfrac{7}{\overset{1}{\cancel{3}}} \times \dfrac{\overset{1}{\cancel{3}}}{2} = \dfrac{7}{2} = 3\dfrac{1}{2}$

b. $\dfrac{\overset{1}{\cancel{5}}}{3} \times \dfrac{2}{\underset{1}{\cancel{5}}} = \dfrac{2}{3}$

Example 2

A carpenter is nailing horizontal boards to the outside surface of a building. The exposed portion of each board is $6\frac{3}{4}$ in. How many rows of boards are needed to reach to the top of an 8 ft wall?

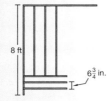

8 ft

$6\frac{3}{4}$ in.

Solution

We begin by converting 8 ft to 96 in. Then we divide 96 in. by $6\frac{3}{4}$ in.

$$96 \div 6\frac{3}{4}$$

$$\frac{96}{1} \div \frac{27}{4}$$

$$\frac{\overset{32}{\cancel{96}}}{1} \cdot \frac{4}{\underset{9}{\cancel{27}}} = \frac{128}{9} = 14\frac{2}{9}$$

Fourteen boards is not enough. To reach to the top of the wall the carpenter will need **15 rows of boards**.

Example 2
Instruction
Work through the problem with students on the board or overhead. It may be helpful to recreate the drawing. Point out that the drawing shows 3 boards that have already been nailed to the outside wall. Note that these boards will be included in the answer.

(continued)

English Learners

For example 1 solution, explain the meaning of the word **eliminate**. Say:

> **"When you eliminate something, you remove it."**

Ask students to eliminate the unneeded zeros from the following numbers:

87.90300   5.8070   107.010
87.903   5.807   107.01

Teacher Tip

To help students see a practical use for the topic of this lesson, ask each student to find and copy a recipe that has at least three **fractions or mixed numbers** in its measurements. Have students exchange recipes and rewrite them twice—once to make two or three times the number of servings and once to make a half or a third of the number of servings.

2 New Concepts (Continued)

Instruction
Take time to review the steps in the table. Be sure that students understand these procedures before starting the practice set and written practice.

Practice Set
Problem a [Error Alert]
When multiplying mixed numbers, it can be difficult for students to know if an exact answer is reasonable.

One way for students to make such a determination when multiplying mixed numbers is to create a range of possible answers by rounding the factors up and rounding the factors down.

Using this method, $2\frac{1}{2} \cdot 1\frac{1}{2}$ rounds to $3 \cdot 2$ and $2 \cdot 1$, creating a range of possible answers from 2 to 6.

3 Written Practice

Math Conversations
Discussion opportunities are provided below.

Problem 1 [Analyze]
You might choose to ask students to write two equations to represent the problem. After solving one equation, students can solve the other equation to check their work. Sample: $n + 109 = 217$; $217 - 109 = n$

Problems 4 and 5
Remind students that an estimate represents a good way to check an exact answer for reasonableness.

"What is a reasonable estimate of the sum of $\frac{5}{6}$ and $\frac{1}{2}$? Explain your answer." Sample: $1\frac{1}{2}$ is a reasonable estimate because $\frac{5}{6}$ is about 1, and the sum of 1 and $\frac{1}{2}$ is $1\frac{1}{2}$.

"What is a reasonable estimate of the difference of $\frac{5}{6}$ and $\frac{1}{2}$? Explain your answer." Sample: $\frac{1}{2}$ is a reasonable estimate because $\frac{5}{6}$ is about 1, and $\frac{1}{2}$ subtracted from 1 is $\frac{1}{2}$.

Ask students to record their estimates and use them to check their exact answers for reasonableness.

(continued)

The following table shows the steps we take to multiply and divide fractions and mixed numbers.

Multiplying and Dividing Fractions and Mixed Numbers

1. Write whole numbers or mixed numbers as fractions.	

2. **Multiplying**	**Dividing**
Multiply numerators. Multiply denominators.	Instead of dividing, multiply by the reciprocal of the divisor.

3. Simplify the answer by reducing if possible. Improper fractions may be expressed as whole or mixed numbers.	

Practice Set ▶

a. What is the area of a rectangle $2\frac{1}{2}$ inches long and $1\frac{1}{2}$ inches wide? $3\frac{3}{4}$ in.^{2}

b. A recipe calls for $1\frac{3}{4}$ cups of milk. How many cups of milk are needed if the recipe is doubled? $3\frac{1}{2}$ cups

c. A tile setter is covering a 5 ft by 5 ft square shower wall. Each tile covers a $4\frac{5}{8}$ in. by $4\frac{5}{8}$ in. square. How many rows of tile are needed to reach 5 feet? How many tiles are needed to cover the 5 ft by 5 ft square? 13 rows, 169 tiles

Write the multiplicative inverse (reciprocal) of each number.

d. $2\frac{2}{3}$ $\frac{3}{8}$ **e.** $\frac{5}{6}$ $\frac{6}{5}$ **f.** 5 $\frac{1}{5}$

Simplify.

g. $1\frac{1}{2} \times 1\frac{2}{3}$ $2\frac{1}{2}$ **h.** $2\frac{1}{2} \cdot 2\frac{1}{2}$ $6\frac{1}{4}$

i. $1\frac{1}{2} \div 2\frac{2}{3}$ $\frac{9}{16}$ **j.** $2\frac{2}{3} \div 1\frac{1}{2}$ $\frac{16}{9}$ or $1\frac{7}{9}$

Written Practice   *Strengthening Concepts*

▶ **1.** *(3)* **[Analyze]** At the wedding the guests sat on either side of the banquet hall. There were 109 guests seated on the left side. If there were 217 guests in all, how many sat on the right side of the aisle? 108 guests

2. *(5)* Visitors to the school's website can follow a link to the school's chorale pictures. If the website had 250 visitors in one week and $\frac{3}{10}$ of them visited the chorale pictures, how many visited the chorale pictures? 75 visitors

3. *(3)* Martin Luther was born in 1483, which was twenty-seven years after the invention of the printing press. In what year was the printing press invented? 1456

▶ ***4.** *(13)* $\frac{5}{6} + \frac{1}{2}$ $1\frac{1}{3}$ ▶ ***5.** *(13)* $\frac{5}{6} - \frac{1}{2}$ $\frac{1}{3}$

*6. *(22)* $\frac{5}{6} \cdot \frac{1}{2}$ $\frac{5}{12}$ ***7.** *(22)* $\frac{5}{6} \div \frac{1}{2}$ $1\frac{2}{3}$ or $\frac{5}{3}$

▶ See Math Conversations in the sidebar.

* 8. $\frac{5}{7} \cdot \frac{7}{10}$ $\frac{1}{2}$
(22)

* 9. $\frac{5}{7} \div \frac{7}{10}$ $1\frac{1}{49}$ or $\frac{50}{49}$
(22)

* 10. $\frac{3}{7} \cdot 2$ $\frac{6}{7}$
(22)

* 11. $\frac{3}{7} \div 2$ $\frac{3}{14}$
(22)

* 12. $2\frac{1}{2} \cdot 1\frac{2}{3}$ $4\frac{1}{6}$ or $\frac{25}{6}$
(23)

* 13. $2\frac{1}{2} \div 1\frac{2}{3}$ $1\frac{1}{2}$ or $\frac{3}{2}$
(23)

Use order of operations to simplify.

▶* 14. $16 - [8 - 4(2 - 1)]$ 12

* 15. $6 + 7 \times (3 - 3)$ 6
(21)

16.
(−1, 2)   (6, 2)
y
x
(−1, −6)   (6, −6)

16. A rectangle has vertices at: (6, 2), (6, −6,), (−1, 2). Write the
(Inv. 1, 8) coordinates of the fourth vertex and find the area and perimeter of the
rectangle.   (−1, −6); A = 56 sq. units; P = 30 units

* 17. _Generalize_ Compare:
(15, 21)

   a. $(5 - 7)$ ⬤ $|5 - 7|$

   ▶ **b.** $\sqrt{64}$ ⬤ $\sqrt[3]{64}$

18. Find the two values that make this statement true: $|x| = 12$
(1) $x = 12, -12$

19. Express with exponents:
(15)

   a. $yyyy$ y^4

   b. $2ababa$ $2a^3b^2$

▶* 20. What is the area of a square with sides $2\frac{1}{2}$ in. long? $6\frac{1}{4}$ in.^{2}
(8, 23)

21. a.
Commutative
Property of
Addition
b. Zero Property
of Multiplication

21. Name the properties illustrated below:
(2)

   a. $a + 5 = 5 + a$

   b. $a \cdot 0 = 0$

* 22. Find the perimeter and area of this triangle. (Dimensions are in meters.)
(8, 20) $P = 60$ m; $A = 150$ m^2

20   12   15
25

For problems **23–28**, solve by inspection.

23. $5 + x = 22$ $x = 17$
(14)

24. $4x + 13 = 25$ $x = 3$
(14)

* 25. $\frac{1}{2} \cdot p = \frac{1}{6}$ $p = \frac{1}{3}$
(14)

26. $\frac{x}{30} = \frac{2}{3}$ $x = 20$
(14)

27. Evaluate $b^2 - 4ac$ when $a = 1$, $b = 6$, and $c = 8$.   4
(14)

* 28. For $A = \frac{1}{2}bh$, find A when b is 6 cm and h is 4 cm. $A = 12$ cm^2
(14)

▶ See Math Conversations in the sidebar.

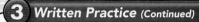

3 _Written Practice (Continued)_

Math Conversations

Discussion opportunities are provided below.

Problem 17b Generalize

Students should generalize that simplifying
- $\sqrt{64}$ involves naming a factor that when used two times, has a product of 64.
- $\sqrt[3]{64}$ involves naming a factor that when used three times, has a product of 64.

Problem 20

"Between which two whole numbers can we expect the exact answer to be? Explain why." 4 and 9; $(2.5)^2$ is greater than 2^2 but less than 3^2.

Errors and Misconceptions
Problem 14

Write the expression on the board or overhead and point out that the grouping symbols are sometimes called nested grouping symbols. Explain that when grouping symbols are nested in an expression, the operations inside the innermost grouping symbols must be completed first.

Demonstrate the steps that are followed to simplify the expression to 12. If students need extra practice working with nested grouping symbols, write the expressions shown below on the board or overhead and ask students to simplify each expression.

$$6 + [2(16 \div 4)] - 5 \quad 9$$

$$3[4 + (6 - 1) - 9] + 1 \quad 1$$

(continued)

Math Conversations

Discussion opportunities are provided below.

Problem 29b *Analyze*

"How is a greatest common factor used to factor an expression?" All of the terms of an expression are divided by the greatest common factor of those terms.

"What is the greatest common factor of 6 and 10?" 2

"Divide each term of this expression by 2." $6x \div 2 = 3x$ and $10y \div 2 = 5y$

Invite a volunteer to write the factored form of the expression on the board or overhead.

---

* 29. *(21)* *Analyze* **a.** Expand: $5(x + 3)$ $5x + 15$

▶ **b.** Factor: $6x - 10y$ $2(3x - 5y)$

* 30. *(Inv. 2)* A steel cable providing tension on a power pole is anchored 16 ft from the pole and reaches 12 feet up the pole. How long is the cable?   20 ft

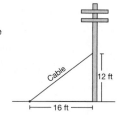

Cable 12 ft 16 ft

Early Finishers
Real-World Application

To complete the bookcase he is building for his mother, Tucker needs 10 pieces of wood each measuring $2\frac{3}{4}$ ft long. Each piece must be whole; he cannot splice together two smaller pieces to create a piece $2\frac{3}{4}$ ft long. One 8-foot length of lumber costs $14.95 and one 10-foot length costs $16.95.

a. If Tucker only purchased 8-foot lengths of wood, how much money would he spend? How much wood would he waste? $74.75; He would waste $12\frac{1}{2}$ ft of wood.

b. If Tucker only purchased 10-foot sections of wood, how much money would he spend? How much wood would he waste? $67.80; He would waste $12\frac{1}{2}$ ft of wood.

c. What is the most economical combination of 8-foot and 10-foot lengths Tucker could buy? What would be the cost and how much wood would be wasted?   two 8-foot lengths and two 10-foot lengths; $63.80; $8\frac{1}{2}$ ft

▶ See Math Conversations in the sidebar.

•Adding and Subtracting Decimal Numbers

Objectives
• Add and subtract decimal numbers by first aligning their decimal points.

Lesson Preparation

Materials
• **Power Up E** (in *Instructional Masters*)

Optional
• **Teacher-provided material: grid paper**

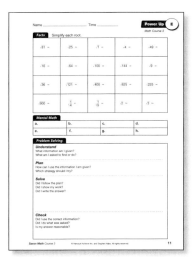

Power Up E

Math Language

Maintain
decimal numbers
place value

Technology Resources

Student eBook Complete student textbook in electronic format.

Resources and Planner CD Assessment, reteaching, and instructional masters, plus a pacing calendar with standards.

Test and Practice Generator CD Create additional practice sheets and custom-made tests.

www.SaxonPublishers.com Visit for more student activities and planning materials.

Inclusion

 Adaptations CD Adapted lessons, investigations, practice and assessments.

Meeting Standards

National Council of Teachers of Mathematics (NCTM)

Numbers and Operations

NO.1a Work flexibly with fractions, decimals, and percents to solve problems

NO.1b Compare and order fractions, decimals, and percents efficiently and find their approximate locations on a number line

NO.3a Select appropriate methods and tools for computing with fractions and decimals from among mental computation, estimation, calculators or computers, and paper and pencil, depending on the situation, and apply the selected methods

NO.3b Develop and analyze algorithms for computing with fractions, decimals, and integers and develop fluency in their use

Problem-Solving Strategy: Use Logical Reasoning/ Make a Table

Franklin, Grover, and Herbert went to a restaurant and each ordered a soup and a salad. Franklin ordered chicken noodle soup and did not order a Caesar salad. Herbert did not order French onion soup but did order a house salad. If their order was for chicken noodle, French onion, and vegetable soups, and their salads were Caesar, house, and fruit, what did each person order?

Understand **Understand the problem.**

"What information are we given?"

Three men went to a restaurant, and each ordered soup and salad.
1. Franklin ordered chicken noodle soup and did not order a Caesar salad.
2. Herbert did not order French onion soup but did order a house salad.
3. Three different soups were ordered: chicken noodle, French onion, and vegetable.
4. Three different salads were ordered: Caesar, house, and fruit.

"What are we asked to do?"

Determine what each man ordered.

Plan **Make a plan.**

"What problem-solving strategy will we use?"

We will *use logical reasoning* and *make a table* to record the facts provided and our deductions and conclusions.

"What size will our table need to be?"

Three rows (for the three men) by six columns (for the three soups + the three salads).

Solve **Carry out the plan.**

	Chicken	Onion	Vegetable	Caesar	House	Fruit
Franklin	Step 1: YES (Fact 1)	Step 2: X (Deduce from fact 1)	Step 2: X (Deduce from fact 1)	Step 1: X (Fact 1)	Step 4: X (Deduce from fact 2)	Step 10: YES (Conclude)
Grover	Step 2: X (Deduce from fact 1)	Step 5: YES (Conclude)	Step 6: X (Conclude)	Step 8: YES (Conclude)	Step 4: X (Deduce from fact 2)	Step 9: X (Conclude)
Herbert	Step 2: X (Deduce from fact 1)	Step 3: X (Fact 2)	Step 7: YES (Conclude)	Step 4: X (Deduce from fact 2)	Step 3: YES (Fact 2)	Step 4: X (Deduce from fact 2)

Check **Look back.**

"Did we find the answer to the question that was asked?"

Yes. We found what each man ordered:
1. Franklin ordered chicken noodle soup and a fruit salad,
2. Grover ordered French onion soup and a Caesar salad, and
3. Herbert ordered vegetable soup and with a house salad.

• Adding and Subtracting Decimal Numbers

Power Up   *Building Power*

facts

Power Up E

mental math

a. Calculation: Maria reads 40 pages per hour. How many pages does she read in 2 hours and 15 minutes?   90

b. Measurement: What is the diameter of the ring?   1.4 cm

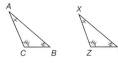

c. Number Sense: $46 \div 4$ 11.5 or $11\frac{1}{2}$

d. Geometry: Which angle in $\triangle XYZ$ corresponds to $\angle B$? $\angle Y$

e. Proportions: If Darrel jogs 2 miles in 16 minutes, how long will it take Darrel to jog 3 miles at that pace?   24 minutes

f. Power/Roots: $\sqrt{400}$ 20

g. Fractions: $\frac{3}{5} = \frac{x}{25}$ 15

h. Calculation: $-5 + 10, +4, \sqrt{}, +1, \sqrt{}, \times 8, \sqrt{}, +1, \times 20, \sqrt{}$ 10

problem solving

Franklin, Grover, and Herbert went to a restaurant and each ordered a soup and a salad. Franklin ordered chicken noodle soup and did not order a Caesar salad. Herbert did not order French onion soup but did order a house salad. If their order was for chicken noodle, French onion, and vegetable soups, and their salads were Caesar, house, and fruit, what did each person order?   Franklin: chicken noodle soup and fruit salad; Grover: French onion soup and Caesar salad; Herbert: vegetable soup and house salad.

New Concept   *Increasing Knowledge*

Performing arithmetic with decimal numbers is similar to arithmetic with whole numbers. We follow a few more rules to keep track of the decimal point. When adding or subtracting decimal numbers, we first align the decimal points. By lining up the decimal points we assure that we are adding or subtracting digits with the same place value.

Lesson 24   159

---

1 Power Up

Facts
Distribute **Power Up E** to students. See answers below.

Mental Math
Encourage students to share different ways to mentally compute these exercises. Strategies for exercises **a** and **g** are listed below.

a. Multiply by Unit Rate
2 hr and 15 min $= 2\frac{1}{4}$ hr $= \frac{9}{4}$ hr
$\frac{9}{4}$ hr $\times$ 40 pages/hr $=$ 90 pages
Use Math Sense
40 pages in 1 hour = 10 pages in $\frac{1}{4}$ hr
$2\frac{1}{4}$ hr $= 9 \times \frac{1}{4}$ hr
9×10 pages $=$ 90 pages

g. Find an Equivalent Fraction
$\frac{3}{5} = \frac{x}{25}$
$5 \times 5 = 25$, so we multiply 3 by 5 to find x.
$x = 15$

Problem Solving
Refer to **Power-Up Discussion**, p. 159B.

2 New Concepts

Instruction
Point out that students have been calculating with money amounts for several years. Adding and subtracting decimal numbers is similar to adding and subtracting money amounts. Explain that this skill is used in almost every business in the country, and that even though most of the computation is done by computer, it is important to know how to carry out the calculations.

(continued)

Facts   Simplify each root.

$\sqrt{81} = 9$	$\sqrt{25} = 5$	$\sqrt{1} = 1$	$\sqrt{4} = 2$	$\sqrt{49} = 7$
$\sqrt{16} = 4$	$\sqrt{64} = 8$	$\sqrt{100} = 10$	$\sqrt{144} = 12$	$\sqrt{9} = 3$
$\sqrt{36} = 6$	$\sqrt{121} = 11$	$\sqrt{400} = 20$	$\sqrt{625} = 25$	$\sqrt{225} = 15$
$\sqrt{900} = 30$	$\sqrt{\frac{1}{4}} = \frac{1}{2}$	$\sqrt{\frac{1}{9}} = \frac{1}{3}$	$\sqrt{2} \approx 1.414$	$\sqrt{3} \approx 1.732$

2 New Concepts (Continued)

Example 1
Instruction
Emphasize the importance of lining up the decimal points. Suggest that students think of an imaginary vertical line that connects all the points.

Use the *Explain* question to discuss why it is possible to fill in empty places with zeros. Be sure students understand that they can do this for both addition and subtraction of decimal numbers.

Example 2
Instruction
You may point out that there is no need to fill in with zeros as both numbers have the same number of decimal places.

Practice Set
Problems c–h [Error Alert]
Write the addend 7.5 from problem **c** on the board or overhead and demonstrate how one zero, or any number of zeros, can be written to the right of the digit 5 in the tenths place. Lead students to conclude that writing any number of zeros to the right of the least place value of a decimal number does not change the value of the number.

Encourage students to write one or more zeros as needed to help maintain correct alignment of the place values.

Problem i [Explain]
Another way to check a sum or difference of decimal numbers is to make an estimate by rounding each decimal number to the nearest whole number. The sum or difference of those whole numbers is then compared to the exact sum or difference.

Example 1

Simplify:

   a. 12.5 + 3.75 + 2   b. 5.2 − 2.88

Solution

Thinking Skill

Explain

Why can we attach zeros to the end of a decimal number? A decimal point "locks" place values, so attaching zeros to the end of a decimal number does not shift the place values of the other digits.

a. We align the decimal points. Since 2 is a whole number we place the decimal point to the right of the 2. We may use zeros to write all the decimal numbers with two decimal places. We add in columns and place the decimal point in the sum aligned with the other decimal points.

$$\begin{array}{r} 12.50 \\ 3.75 \\ +\ 2.00 \\ \hline \mathbf{18.25} \end{array}$$

b. We subtract 2.88 from 5.2. We align the decimal points and fill in with zero so that we can subtract.

$$\begin{array}{r} 5.20 \\ -\ 2.88 \\ \hline \mathbf{2.32} \end{array}$$

Example 2

Gregory's temperature was 100.2°F. The thermometer marked 98.6°F as normal body temperature. How many degrees above normal was Gregory's temperature?

Solution

We are given two temperatures and are asked to find the difference. Therefore we subtract the lower temperature from the higher temperature.

$$100.2 - 98.6 = 1.6$$

Gregory's temperature is **1.6 degrees Fahrenheit** above normal.

Practice Set

a. Arrange these numbers from least to greatest. −1, 0, 0.3, ½, 1.75, 2

   ½, 0, −1, 2, 0.3, 1.75

b. Compare 0.036 ⊘ 0.0354

▶ Simplify:

   c. 7.5 + 12.75   20.25 d. 4.2 + 12   16.2   e. 0.3 + 0.8   1.1

   f. 11.46 − 3.6   7.86   g. 5.2 − 4.87   0.33   h. 3 − 2.94   0.06

i. Answers will vary. Possible answer: Add the difference to the subtrahend; their sum should be the minuend.

▶ i. **Explain** How can you check your answers in problems **f–h**?

j. The weather report stated that the recent storm dropped 1.50 inches of rain raising the seasonal total to 26.42 inches. What was the seasonal total prior to the recent storm? Explain how you found your answer.   24.92 in.; I subtracted 1.50 in. from the current total to find the prior total.

160   **Saxon** *Math Course 3*

▶ See Math Conversations in the sidebar.

Teacher Tip

To help students who are not able to **keep the decimal points aligned,** suggest that they turn their papers a quarter turn and choose a line to use for the decimal points.

$$\begin{array}{r} \overset{1}{9}\,\overset{1}{7}.\overset{1}{3}\,8 \\ 0.4\,6\,5 \\ 7\,8\,8.0\,1 \\ \hline 8\,8\,5.8\,5\,5 \end{array}$$

You may also provide grid paper if it is available.

Math Background

In our number system, it is customary to use a decimal point in a number to separate the place values that are greater than or equal to 1 from the place values that are less than 1.

In some number systems elsewhere in the world, however, decimal points are not used. For example, it is customary in some countries to use a comma instead of a decimal point. In those countries, the number 13,9 means "thirteen and nine tenths."

160   **Saxon** *Math Course 3*

1. Irina ran $\frac{1}{2}$ mile in $3\frac{1}{2}$ minutes. At that rate, how long would it take her to run 2 miles?   14 minutes
(7)

2. There were 180 people watching the football game. If $\frac{7}{10}$ of the people watching the game were sitting on the home team bleachers, how many people were sitting on the home team bleachers?   126
(5)

3. The Pacific team defeated the Atlantic team by a score of 5 runs to 3. What fraction of the runs were scored by the Pacific team? $\frac{5}{8}$
(5)

▶ *** 4.** $1.23 + 12.3 + 123$ 136.53
(24)

* 5. *Analyze*   The average low temperature for November 1 in a certain town is $41.5°F$. The low on November 1 last year was $38.6°F$. How much lower was that temperature than the average? $2.9°$
(24)

Generalize   Solve.

▶ *** 6.** $\frac{4}{5} \cdot 2$ $\frac{8}{5}$ or $1\frac{3}{5}$ *** 7.** $\frac{4}{5} \div 2$ $\frac{2}{5}$
(23)   (23)

▶ *** 8.** $1\frac{1}{3} \cdot \frac{3}{4}$ 1   ▶ *** 9.** $1\frac{1}{3} \div \frac{3}{4}$ $\frac{16}{9}$ or $1\frac{7}{9}$
(23)   (23)

▶ *** 10.** A square has sides $1\frac{2}{3}$ in. long. What is the area of the square? $2\frac{7}{9}$ in.^{2}
(23)

* 11. $\frac{4}{9} \cdot \frac{2}{3}$ $\frac{8}{27}$ *** 12.** $\frac{4}{9} \div \frac{2}{3}$ $\frac{2}{3}$
(22)   (22)

* 13. *Generalize* $4 + 3 \times (5 - 1)$ 16
(21)

* 14. Compare: $|16 - 20| \circledgt (16 - 20)$
(21)

15. Find the perimeter and area of this triangle. $P = 56$ m; $A = 84$ m^2
(8, 20)

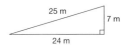

25 m   7 m

24 m

16. Classify this triangle by sides and angles.
(20)   isosceles, right

▶ *** 17.** *Connect*   Terrell built a scale model of his house. The front door of his model is _____ to the front door of his house.   **C**
(19)

    A congruent   **B** equal   **C** similar

18. Which of these is regular?   **A**
(19)

   A   **B**   **C**   **D** all of the above

Lesson 24   161

▶ See Math Conversations in the sidebar.

Math Conversations
Discussion opportunities are provided below.

Problem 6   *Generalize*
Extend the Problem
"To write a whole number such as 2 as an improper fraction, we write 2 as the numerator of a fraction and 1 as the denominator. Why is 1 used as the denominator of the fraction?" Sample: Any number other than 1 will change the value of the whole number; $\frac{2}{1} = 2 \div 1 = 2$.

Problem 8   *Generalize*
After changing $1\frac{1}{3}$ to an improper fraction, encourage students to look for terms of the fractions that can be reduced.

Problem 9   *Generalize*
Remind students that fraction terms can only be reduced during multiplication.

Problem 10
"Between which two whole numbers can we expect the exact answer to be? Explain why." 1 and 4; Sample explanation: $(\frac{5}{3})^2$ is greater than $(\frac{3}{3})^2$ but less than $(\frac{6}{3})^2$.

Problem 17   *Connect*
Extend the Problem
"Why can't the doors be congruent?" Sample: If the doors were congruent, the model would be exactly the same size as the house.

"The door of the scale model and the door of the actual house are similar. Explain what that means." Sample: The corresponding sides of the doors are proportional, and the corresponding angles of the doors are congruent.

Errors and Misconceptions
Problem 4
When adding and subtracting decimal numbers, students sometimes have difficulty maintaining the correct alignment of place values. To help maintain correct alignment, encourage these students to complete the computation on grid paper or on lined paper turned sideways. Students may also draw a vertical segment and align the decimal points on the segment.

(continued)

Math Conversations

Discussion opportunities are provided below.

Problem 19 *Analyze*

"What degree measure represents the sum of the three angles? Explain how you know." 180°; Sample explanation: The sum of the three angle measures is 180° because the three angles form a straight angle, and the measure of a straight angle is 180°.

Errors and Misconceptions
Problem 29

When converting from one measurement unit to another, students may find it helpful to use the following generalizations to make the necessary conversion or to check their work for reasonableness.

- To change from a larger unit to a smaller unit, multiply.
- To change from a smaller unit to a larger unit, divide.

Students should conclude that multiplying by 1000 will change liters to an equivalent number of milliliters, and that multiplying a number by 1000 is the same as moving the decimal point in that number three places to the right.

▶* **19.** *Analyze* Find x. $x = 50°$
(18)

20. Does $\overrightarrow{BA}$ intersect $\overline{CD}$? If so, what is the
(18) point of intersection? Yes, point D

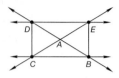

21. Round 6.029 to the nearest tenth. 6.0
(17)

22. Estimate: $\dfrac{24.42}{8\frac{1}{8}}$ 3
(17)

23. Name a set of numbers that includes zero, but not negative one.
(1) whole numbers

24. $\sqrt[3]{125}$ 5
(15)

25. $4^2 + 3^2$ 25
(15)

26. $1\frac{1}{2} + 1\frac{1}{5}$ $2\frac{7}{10}$
(13)

27. $\frac{1}{3} - \frac{1}{4}$ $\frac{1}{12}$
(13)

28. Find the prime factorization of 84. $2^2 \cdot 3 \cdot 7$
(9)

▶ **29.** The capacity of a small glass is 120 mL. How many small glasses can
(6) be completely filled from a 2L pitcher of water? 16

30. There is a 25% discount on bongo drums at the music shop. The
(12) regular price is $56. How much money will be saved? $14

▶ See Math Conversations in the sidebar.

Looking Forward

Adding and subtracting decimal numbers prepares students for:

- **Lesson 25,** multiplying and dividing decimal numbers.
- **Investigation 10,** calculating compound interest.
- **Lesson 102,** calculating growth and decay.
- **Lesson 109,** calculating consumer interest.

• Multiplying and Dividing Decimal Numbers

Objectives

- Multiply decimal numbers by counting the total number of decimal places in the factors.
- Divide whole numbers and decimal numbers by decimal numbers by forming equivalent division problems.
- Multiply and divide decimal numbers to solve word problems.

Lesson Preparation

Materials

- **Power Up E** (in *Instructional Masters*)

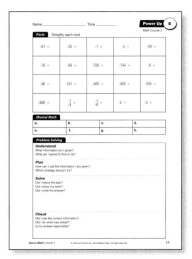

Power Up E

Math Language

Maintain	English Learners (ESL)
dividend	averaged
divisor	
quotient	

Technology Resources

Student eBook Complete student textbook in electronic format.

Resources and Planner CD Assessment, reteaching, and instructional masters, plus a pacing calendar with standards.

Test and Practice Generator CD Create additional practice sheets and custom-made tests.

www.SaxonPublishers.com Visit for more student activities and planning materials.

Inclusion

Adaptations CD Adapted lessons, investigations, practice and assessments.

Meeting Standards

National Council of Teachers of Mathematics (NCTM)

Numbers and Operations

NO.1a Work flexibly with fractions, decimals, and percents to solve problems

NO.2a Understand the meaning and effects of arithmetic operations with fractions, decimals, and integers

NO.3a Select appropriate methods and tools for computing with fractions and decimals from among mental computation, estimation, calculators or computers, and paper and pencil, depending on the situation, and apply the selected methods

NO.3c Develop and use strategies to estimate the results of rational-number computations and judge the reasonableness of the results

Problem-Solving Strategy: Use Logical Reasoning

A trivia game gives 5 points for each correct answer, 0 points for an answer left blank, and −1 points for each incorrect answer. The game has 20 questions. For each of these scores {95, 96, 99, 94}, determine how many answers were correct, how many were left blank, and how many were incorrect. If the score is not possible, say so.

(Understand) **Understand the problem.**

"What information are we given?"

1. A game has 20 questions.
2. A correct answer receives 5 points.
3. An incorrect answer receives −1 points.
4. A blank answer receives 0 points.

"What are we asked to do?"

Determine how many answers were correct and how many were incorrect for scores of 94, 95, 96, and 99.

(Plan) **Make a plan.**

"What problem-solving strategy will we use?"

We will *use logical reasoning.*

(Solve) **Carry out the plan.**

"What can we assume about the number of correct answers if the final scores are greater than 94?"

1. 20 questions correct is already 100 points, with no questions to spare for blank or incorrect answers.
2. 18 questions correct would only produce 90 points, and any incorrect answers would only lower that score.
3. The number of correct answers must be 19 for a final score to be greater than or equal to 94.

"What are the only options for the 20th question's response to be?"

Incorrect, or blank.

"If the 20th question is left blank, what will the final score be?"

$95 + 0 = 95$.

"If the 20th question is incorrect, what will the final score be?"

$95 - 1 = 94$.

"Do we need to check 96 and 99 as possibilities?"

No, they are impossible.

(Check) **Look back.**

"Did we complete the task that was assigned?"

Yes. We determined that only the 94 and the 95 were possible scores. A score of 94 has 19 correct answers, 0 blank answers, and 1 incorrect answer. A score of 95 has 19 correct answers and 1 blank answer.

LESSON 25

Multiplying and Dividing Decimal Numbers

Power Up | *Building Power*

facts | Power Up E

mental math

a. **Calculation:** Luis walked 3 miles per hour on his way home from school, a distance of $1\frac{1}{2}$ miles. How many minutes did it take for Luis to walk home?   30 minutes

b. **Estimation:** $24.97 + $1.97 + $9.99   25 + 2 + 10 = $37

c. **Measurement:**

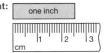

one inch

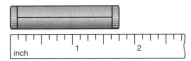

About how many cm are four inches? (Round to the nearest cm.)   10 cm

d. **Number Sense:** $22 divided equally among 4 people $5.50

e. **Measurement:** If four sugarless gum sticks were laid end to end, they would be how long? $1\frac{3}{4} \times 4 = \frac{7}{4} \times 4 = 7$ inches

f. **Geometry:** Rewrite and complete this congruence statement:
$\triangle CBD \cong \triangle G\_\_$ $\triangle CBD \cong \triangle GEF$

g. **Proportions:** If four pencils cost $1.00, how much would eight pencils cost? $2

h. **Fractional Parts:** $\frac{3}{4}$ of $84 $63

i. **Calculation:** $17 + 8$, $\sqrt{\ }$, $+ 1$, square it, $\div 9$, $\sqrt{\ }$, $- 3$, $\times 5$, $+ 10$, $+ 2$ 7

problem solving

A trivia game gives 5 points for each correct answer, 0 points for an answer left blank, and −1 points for each incorrect answer. The game has 20 questions. For each of these scores {95, 96, 99, 94}, determine how many answers were correct, how many were left blank, and how many were incorrect. If the score is not possible, say so.   95–19 correct, 1 left blank, 0 incorrect; 96–not possible, 99–not possible, 94–19 correct, 0 left blank, and 1 incorrect

Lesson 25   163

---

1 Power Up

Facts
Distribute **Power Up E** to students. See answers below.

Mental Math
Encourage students to share different ways to mentally compute these exercises. Strategies for exercises **a** and **d** are listed below.

a. **Make a Unit Rate**
   3 mi in 1 hr $\longrightarrow$ 3 mi in 60 min $\longrightarrow$ 1 mi in 20 min = 20 min/mi
   $1\frac{1}{2}$ mi $= \frac{3}{2}$ mi
   $\frac{3}{2}$ mi $\times$ 20 min/mi = 30 min

d. **Divide by 2 Twice**
   $22 \div 4 = $22 \div 2 \div 2 = $11 \div 2 = $5.50
   Think of Bills and Coins
   $22 = 4 $5 bills and 4 half-dollar coins
   Each person gets 1 of each, or $5.50.

Problem Solving
Refer to **Power-Up Discussion**, p. 163B.

Facts   Simplify each root.

$\sqrt{81} = 9$	$\sqrt{25} = 5$	$\sqrt{1} = 1$	$\sqrt{4} = 2$	$\sqrt{49} = 7$
$\sqrt{16} = 4$	$\sqrt{64} = 8$	$\sqrt{100} = 10$	$\sqrt{144} = 12$	$\sqrt{9} = 3$
$\sqrt{36} = 6$	$\sqrt{121} = 11$	$\sqrt{400} = 20$	$\sqrt{625} = 25$	$\sqrt{225} = 15$
$\sqrt{900} = 30$	$\sqrt{\frac{1}{4}} = \frac{1}{2}$	$\sqrt{\frac{1}{9}} = \frac{1}{3}$	$\sqrt{2} \approx 1.414$	$\sqrt{3} \approx 1.732$

2 New Concepts

Instruction

Remind students that decimals are another way to represent a rational number or a fraction. Be sure that students understand that places to the left of the decimal point (the whole number part) are not included in the decimal places.

Example 1
Instruction

For part a, demonstrate the two ways to multiply three tenths times 12 hundredths on the board or overhead. Guide students to see the answers are the same. Point out that multiplying with the fraction form is a way to check multiplication of decimals.

For part b, reinforce the rule of counting the decimal places and then placing the decimal point that many places from the right.

For part c, call attention to the way the decimal point moves 1 place to the right when a number is multiplied by 10.

Use the *Generalize* question to show students that multiplying any whole or decimal number by a power of 10 simply involves shifting the decimal point to the right the same number of places as the number of zeros in the power of 10.

Example 2
Instruction

After going through the example, ask students to explain why $0.34 and $33.54 are not reasonable answers to the question. Sample: The first one is much less than the price for one pound, and the second one is much more than the price for one pound, and the cost should be close to the price for one pound.

(continued)

New Concept   *Increasing Knowledge*

To multiply decimal numbers with pencil and paper we do not need to align the decimal points. We instead multiply to find the product and then count all the decimal places in the factors to locate the proper position for the decimal point in the product. (Decimal places are places to the right of the decimal point.) In part **a** of the example below, we show the same multiplication in decimal form and in fraction form.

Example 1

Simplify:

   a. 0.3 × 0.12   **b. (1.5)²**   **c. 4.25 × 10**

Solution

a. Three tenths times twelve hundredths equals 36 thousandths.

$$\frac{3}{10} \cdot \frac{12}{100} = \frac{36}{1000}$$

$$\begin{array}{r} 0.12 \\ \times\ 0.3 \end{array} \Big\} \text{ 3 places in factors}$$

$$\underline{}$$

$$.036 \quad \text{3 places in product}$$

We count over three places from the end of the product, filling the empty place with zero. The product, **0.036,** is equivalent to $\frac{36}{1000}$.

b. To simplify $(1.5)^2$ we multiply 1.5 by 1.5.

$$\begin{array}{r} 1.5 \\ \times\ 1.5 \end{array} \Big\} \text{ 2 places}$$

$$\begin{array}{r} 75 \\ 15 \end{array}$$

$$\mathbf{2.25} \quad \text{2 places}$$

Note that the result also means that $\sqrt{2.25}$ is 1.5.

c. We multiply, then count.

$$\begin{array}{r} 4.25 \\ \times\ \ \ 10 \\ \hline \mathbf{42.5} \quad 42.50 \end{array}$$

Multiplying a decimal number by 10 simply shifts the decimal point one place to the right.

Generalize What is 4.25 × 10,000? How many places is the decimal shifted to the right?   42,500; 4 places

Example 2

What is the cost of 0.86 pounds of cheese at $3.90 per pound? Explain why your answer is reasonable.

Math Background

When multiplying decimal numbers, a generalization students can use to check their work is the idea that the total number of decimal places in the factors is equal to the number of decimal places in the product.

The only time this generalization does not *seem* to be true is when a product is expressed in a simpler way. For example, the product 2.4 × 5 can be written as 12.0 or simply as 12. Writing the product as 12 *seems* to invalidate the generalization. But the generalization is still true because 12.0 and 12 are equivalent.

We multiply the quantity in pounds by the price per pound.

$$\$3.90 \times 0.86 = \$3.3540$$

We round the answer to the nearest cent, **$3.35.** The answer is reasonable because 0.86 pounds is a little less than one pound and $3.35 is a little less than $3.90, which is the price per pound.

We distinguish between dividing by a whole number and dividing by a decimal number.

Whole number divisor   Decimal number divisor

$$0.42 \div 6 \qquad\qquad 0.42 \div 0.6$$

When dividing by a whole number the decimal point in the quotient is placed above the decimal point of the dividend. In this example the quotient and dividend have the same number of decimal places. We fill empty places with zero if necessary.

$$\begin{array}{r} 0.07 \\ 6\overline{)0.42} \end{array}$$

Example 3

Simplify:

a. $0.48 \div 8$ b. $4.8 \div 5$ c. $4.8 \div 10^2$

Solution

a. We place the decimal point in the quotient above the decimal point in the dividend. Then we divide like we divide whole numbers. We use zero as a place holder, so **0.06** is the quotient.

$$\begin{array}{r} 0.06 \\ 8\overline{)0.48} \\ \underline{48} \\ 0 \end{array}$$

b. We place the decimal point in the quotient, and then we divide. We do not write remainders with decimal numbers. Instead we affix zero(s) and continue dividing (or we round). We find that **0.96** is the quotient.

$$\begin{array}{r} 0.96 \\ 5\overline{)4.80} \\ \underline{45} \\ 30 \\ \underline{30} \\ 0 \end{array}$$

c. Since 10^2 equals 100, we divide 4.8 by 100. Notice that the quotient has the same digits as the dividend with the decimal points shifted two places.

$$\begin{array}{r} 0.048 \\ 100\overline{)4.800} \end{array}$$

---

2 New Concepts (Continued)

Example 3
Instruction

For part a, emphasize the need to fill any empty places in the quotient with zeros. Ask why the answer would not be correct if the zeros are not included. Sample: The quotient would be greater than what it should be.

For part b, point out that we affix zeros to the dividend and keep dividing. Ask why we can do that. Sample: Those zeros do not change the value of the number.

For part c, call attention to the direction and number of places the decimal point moves. Ask students to compare this result with what happens when a decimal number is multiplied by a power of 10. Sample: The decimal point moves the same number of places as the number of zeros in the power of 10, but in the opposite direction.

(continued)

2 New Concepts (Continued)

Instruction

Introduce dividing by decimal numbers after example 3. To help students understand why there is no change in the quotient when the decimal point in the dividend and the divisor are shifted the same number of places to the right, point out that the process shown on the student page is like finding an equivalent fraction by multiplying both the numerator and denominator by the same number.

Example 4

Instruction

Caution students to be careful when shifting the decimal point. Suggest that they use scallops like those shown on the student page. Sometimes a scallop is used for each place so that the scallops can be counted to be sure that the decimal point has moved the correct number of places.

Example 5

Instruction

Call attention to the need to affix zeros to the dividend to carry on the division. Ask why the result was rounded to 25. Sample: The decimal part of the quotient is greater than one half.

Discuss why 2.5 mi/gal and 246 mi/gal would be unreasonable answers to this problem. Emphasize the importance of checking the answer in the context of the problem situation.

(continued)

When dividing by a decimal number we take an extra step to make an equivalent problem in which the divisor is a whole number. Multiplying the dividend and the divisor by 10 shifts the decimal points one place without changing the quotient. Instead of showing the multiplication we can shift both decimal points the same number of places before we divide.

$$\frac{0.42}{0.6} \cdot \frac{10}{10} = \frac{4.2}{6}$$

$$06.\overline{)04.2}$$

Example 4

Simplify:

    a. 3.6 ÷ 0.6   **b. 3 ÷ 0.06**

Solution

Thinking Skill

Connect

A fraction bar and a division sign both indicate division. What fraction name for 1 do we multiply 3.6 ÷ 0.6 by to make the equivalent division problem 36 ÷ 6? $\frac{10}{10}$

a. We rewrite the problem, shifting both decimal points one place. Then we divide. The quotient, **6,** is a whole number, so the decimal point does not need to be shown.

$$06.\overline{)36.} \quad \begin{array}{r} 6. \\ \underline{36} \\ 0 \end{array}$$

b. The dividend is the whole number 3. To make 0.06 a whole number we shift the decimal point two places. The decimal point to the right of 3 shifts two places, which are filled with zeros. The quotient, **50,** is a whole number and can be written without a decimal point.

$$006.\overline{)300.} \quad 50.$$

Example 5

Chloe drove her car 236.4 miles on 9.6 gallons of gas. Find the number of miles per gallon the car averaged to the nearest mile per gallon.

Solution

To find miles per gallon we divide miles by gallons. Since the divisor is a decimal number we take an extra step to make the divisor a whole number.

$$\frac{mi}{gal} \quad \frac{236.4}{9.6} \cdot \frac{10}{10} = \frac{2364}{96}$$

$$96\overline{)2364.000} \quad 24.625$$

Rounding to the nearest whole number, we find Chloe's car averaged **25 miles per gallon.** The answer is reasonable because 9.6 gallons is nearly 10 gallons and dividing 236 miles by 10 gallons is 23.6 miles per gallon, and this estimate is close to our calculated answer.

English Learners

For example 5, explain the meaning of the word **averaged.** Say:

"An average is a normal or usual amount. For example, I spend an average of $3 on lunch each day."

Make 3 stacks of pennies in the following amounts: 3, 8, and 4. Show students how to average by moving coins to make the stacks equal.

Decimal Arithmetic Reminders

Operation	+ or −	×	÷ by whole (W)	÷ by decimal (D)
	line up	×; then count	up	over, over, up
Memory cue	$\pm\ .\ \_$	$\times\ .\_$ $.\_\_$	$W)\overline{\ .\ }$	$D.)\overline{\ .\ }$

You may need to …
• Place a decimal point to the right of a whole number.
• Fill empty places with zeros.

Practice Set   Simplify.

▶ **a.** 0.4×0.12 0.048   ▶ **b.** $(0.3)^2$ 0.09   **c.** 6.75×10^3 6750

d. $0.144 \div 6$ 0.024   **e.** $1.2 \div 0.06$ 20   **f.** $2.4 \div 0.5$ 4.8

g. Use the answer to **b** to find $\sqrt{0.09}$.   0.3

h. What is the cost of 10.2 gallons of gas at $2.249 per gallon?
$22.94

i. If 1.6 pounds of peaches cost $2.00, then what is the cost per pound? $1.25

Written Practice   *Strengthening Concepts*

* 1. Mr. Villescas typed 16 names in a minute. At that rate, how many names
(7)   could he type in one and a half minutes?   24 names

2. The number of students in four classrooms is 27, 29, 30, and 30. What
(7)   is the average (mean) number of students in the four classrooms?   29

▶ *** 3.** *Analyze*   Al Oerter won the gold medal in the discus in four consecutive
(3, 24)   Olympics, establishing a new Olympic record each time. He won his
first gold medal in 1956 in Melbourne with a throw of 56.36 meters. He
won his fourth gold medal in Mexico City in 1968, throwing 64.78 m. His
1968 winning mark was how much farther than his 1956 mark?   8.42 m

Simplify.

4. $\frac{1}{2} + \frac{2}{3}$ $1\frac{1}{6}$ *** 5.** $\frac{1}{2} \cdot \frac{2}{3}$ $\frac{1}{3}$ *** 6.** $\frac{1}{2} \div \frac{2}{3}$ $\frac{3}{4}$
(13)   (22)   (22)

7. $\frac{2}{3} - \frac{1}{2}$ $\frac{1}{6}$ ▶ *** 8.** $0.9(0.11)$ 0.099   *** 9.** $(3.1)^2$ 9.61
(13)   (25)   (15, 25)

* 10. $4.36 + 0.4$ 4.76   *** 11.** $4.2 - 0.42$ 3.78
(24)   (24)

▶ *** 12.** $\frac{0.144}{4}$ 0.036   *** 13.** $\frac{4.36}{0.4}$ 10.9
(25)   (25)

14. Arrange these numbers in order from least to greatest.
(12)

0.25   0.249   0.251   0.249, 0.25, 0.251

Lesson 25   167

▶ See Math Conversations in the sidebar.

Teacher Tip

It may help students who do not understand why they can shift the decimal point the same number of places in the dividend and the divisor without changing the value of the quotient to **see a problem worked in both fraction and decimal form,** for example: $0.3 \div 0.4$.

Fraction form:

$$\frac{3}{10} \div \frac{4}{10} = \frac{3}{\cancel{10}} \times \frac{\cancel{10}}{4} = \frac{3}{4} \text{ or } 0.75$$

Decimal form:

$$0.4)\overline{0.3} = 4)\overline{3} = 4)\overline{3.00}^{\ 0.75} \text{ or } \frac{3}{4}$$

Point out that the 10's cancelled each other in the fraction form of the division, and that made the numerator and the denominator whole numbers. The same thing happens in the decimal form of the division when the decimal point is shifted in both dividend and divisor.

---

② New Concepts (Continued)

Instruction
Use the table to summarize the lesson. Ask students to compare operations with decimal numbers to operations with whole numbers.

Practice Set
Problems a and b [Error Alert]
Encourage students to check their work by comparing the number of decimal places in the product to the total number of decimal places in the factors.

③ Written Practice

Math Conversations
Discussion opportunities are provided below.

Problem 3 [Analyze]
"Before we find the exact answer, explain how we can make an estimate that can be used to check our exact answer for reasonableness." Sample: Round 64.78 to 65 and round 56.36 to 56, then subtract; an estimate of the distance is 65 − 56 or 9 meters.

Errors and Misconceptions
Problem 8
The need to write a placeholder zero, such as the zero in the tenths place of the product, is sometimes overlooked by students. To check the product of one or more decimals factors, remind students to compare the number of decimal places in the product to the total number of decimal places in the factors; the numbers should be equal unless the product has been written in a simpler way. For example, 0.2 is a simpler way of writing 0.20, the product of 0.5 and 0.4.

Problem 12
When dividing a decimal dividend, students sometimes forget to write a decimal point in the quotient. Point out that it is a good idea to write a decimal point in the quotient before beginning the division of a decimal dividend.

(continued)

Math Conversations
Discussion opportunities are provided below.

Problem 30 Evaluate

Invite a number of volunteers to each describe a step, or demonstrate a step on the board or overhead, that must be completed to simplify the expression.

Step 1: Work inside parentheses; $4ac = 16$

Step 2: Simplify the exponent; $4^2 = 16$

Step 3: Subtract; $16 - 16 = 0$

---

15. **a.** Name a pair of angles in this figure that form a linear pair. $\angle AGB$ and $\angle BGC$, or $\angle AGD$ and $\angle DGC$
(18)
   b. If $\angle AGB$ measures 120°, and if $\angle BGD$ is a right angle, then what is the measure of $\angle BGC$ and $\angle CGD$? $m\angle BGC = 60°$, $m\angle CGD = 30°$

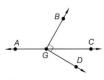

16.
(−7, −1) ... (2, −1)
(−7, −10) ... (2, −10)

16. Find the area and perimeter of a rectangle with vertices at $(-7, -1)$, $(-7, -10)$, $(2, -10)$, and $(2, -1)$. $A = 81$ sq. units; $P = 36$ units
(8, Inv. 1)

17. **a.** Expand: $3(t + 4)$ $3t + 12$
(21)
   b. Factor: $10x - 15$ $5(2x - 3)$

18. Simplify and compare:
(15, 21)
   a. $|11 - 7| \bigcirc |7 - 11|$ $4 = 4$ **b.** $\sqrt{121} \bigcirc \sqrt[3]{1000}$ $11 > 10$

19. Find the two values for z that make this statement true: $|z| = 7$ $z = 7, -7$
(1)

20. Write this expression in exponential form. $\dfrac{k^2 u^3}{r^4 t}$
(15)
$$\frac{k \cdot k \cdot u \cdot u \cdot u}{r \cdot r \cdot r \cdot r \cdot t}$$

21. What is the area of a square window that is $3\frac{1}{2}$ feet on each side? $12\frac{1}{4}$ ft^2
(8, 23)

22. a. Associative Property of Addition,
b. Identity Property of Multiplication

22. Name the properties illustrated.
(2)
   a. $4 + (3 + 1) = (4 + 3) + 1$ **b.** $0.5 \times 1 = 0.5$

* 23. Find the perimeter and area of this triangle: $P = 30$ in.; $A = 30$ in.^{2}
(20, Inv. 2)

12 in. ... 5 in. ... C ... A ... B

* 24. Classify the triangle in problem **23** by angles and sides. If the measure of $\angle A$ is $22\frac{1}{2}°$, what is the measure of $\angle B$?
(20)
right triangle, scalene triangle, $67\frac{1}{2}°$

For problems **25–28**, solve by inspection.

25. $70 = 2r + 10$ $r = 30$
(14)

26. $1 - x = \dfrac{2}{3}$ $x = \dfrac{1}{3}$
(13, 14)

27. $\dfrac{1}{4}p = \dfrac{1}{8}$ $p = \dfrac{1}{2}$
(14, 22)

28. $\dfrac{100}{m} = \dfrac{1}{2}$ $m = 200$
(10, 14)

Evaluate.

29. Find $\frac{1}{2}bh$ when $b = 3$ and $h = 6$. 9
(14)

▶ **30.** Evaluate Find $b^2 - (4ac)$ when $a = 1$, $b = 4$, and $c = 4$. 0
(14)

▶ See Math Conversations in the sidebar.

Looking Forward

Multiplying and dividing decimal numbers prepares students for:

- **Lesson 28,** writing large numbers in scientific notation.
- **Lesson 30,** writing fractions as repeating decimals.
- **Lesson 46,** solving problems using scientific notation.
- **Lesson 50,** solving multi-step equations.
- **Lesson 57,** performing operations with small numbers in scientific notation.

CUMULATIVE ASSESSMENT 4

Assessment 30–40 minutes

For use after Lesson 25

Distribute **Cumulative Test 4** to each student. Two versions of the test are available in *Saxon Math Course 3 Course Assessments Book*. Have students complete the **Power-Up Test** first. Allow 10 minutes. Then have students work the 20 numbered items on the **Cumulative Test.** Students may use copies of the answer sheet to record their work. Track individual and class progress with the **Test Analysis** forms.

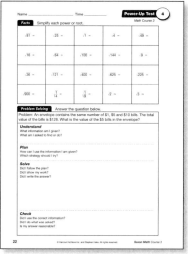

Power-Up Test 4

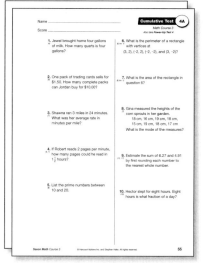

Cumulative Test 4A

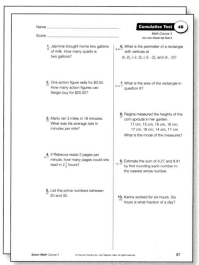

Alternative Cumulative Test 4B

Optional Answer Forms

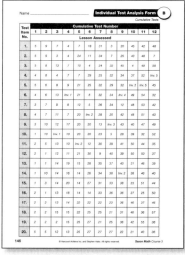

Individual Test Analysis Form

Class Test Analysis Form

Reteaching

Students who score below 80% on the assessment may be in need of reteaching. Look for the causes of student mistakes. If errors are conceptual, refer to the *Reteaching Masters* for reteaching.

Choosing When to Round or Estimate

Assign after Lesson 25

Objectives
- Differentiate between exact and rounded number representations.
- Determine when to use rounded, estimated, or exact values in a given problem situation.
- Construct problems that involve rounding or estimating.
- Communicate ideas through writing.

Materials
Performance Activity 4

Preparation
Make copies of **Performance Activity 4**. (One each per student.)

Time Requirement
15–25 minutes; Begin in class and complete at home.

Performance Activity 4

Activity
Explain to students that they will be investigating the differences between exact, rounded, and estimated values and how each applies to real-world problems. Students will first distinguish between pairs of values and determine which is a less-exact representation. They must then decide whether to round, estimate, or use an exact value for a given real-world situation. Students conclude the task by creating a real-world situation with rounding and one with estimating. Point out that all necessary information is provided on **Performance Activity 4.**

Criteria for Evidence of Learning
- Distinguishes correctly between an exact and a less-exact number representation.
- Determines correctly when to use either exact, rounded, or estimated values in a given real-world problem situation.
- Describes accurately a real-world situation when rounding is appropriate and one when estimating is appropriate.
- Communicates ideas clearly through writing.

National Council of Teachers of Mathematics (NCTM)

Numbers and Operations

NO.1a Work flexibly with fractions, decimals, and percents to solve problems

NO.1b Compare and order fractions, decimals, and percents efficiently and find their approximate locations on a number line

NO.3a Select appropriate methods and tools for computing with fractions and decimals from among mental computation, estimation, calculators or computers, and paper and pencil, depending on the situation, and apply the selected methods

Communication

CM.3b Communicate their mathematical thinking coherently and clearly to peers, teachers, and others

Representation

RE.5a Create and use representations to organize, record, and communicate mathematical ideas

• Transformations

Objectives

- Understand how congruence transformations (reflections, rotations, and translations) affect the orientation of an object.
- Show transformations on a coordinate plane and describe translations with an ordered pair of movements.
- Model transformations with manipulatives.
- Understand how similarity transformations (dilations and contractions) affect an object.

Lesson Preparation

Materials

- **Power Up F** (in *Instructional Masters*)
- **Investigation Activity 2** (in *Instructional Masters*)
- **Lesson Activity 4** (in *Instructional Masters*)
- **Teacher-provided material:** scissors

Optional
- **Teacher-provided material:** mirrors, grid paper

Math Language

New	Maintain
reflection	congruent
rotation	similar
transformations	
translation	

Technology Resources

Student eBook Complete student textbook in electronic format.

Resources and Planner CD Blackline masters, plus a pacing calendar with standards.

Test and Practice Generator CD Create additional practice sheets and custom-made tests.

www.SaxonPublishers.com Visit for more student activities and planning materials.

Inclusion

Adaptations CD Adapted lessons, investigations, practice and assessments.

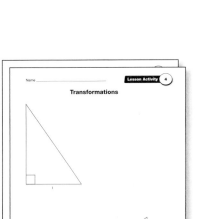

Power Up F

Lesson Activity 4 and Investigation Activity 2

Meeting Standards

National Council of Teachers of Mathematics (NCTM)

Geometry

GM.2a Use coordinate geometry to represent and examine the properties of geometric shapes

GM.3a Describe sizes, positions, and orientations of shapes under informal transformations such as flips, turns, slides, and scaling

GM.3b Examine the congruence, similarity, and line or rotational symmetry of objects using transformations

GM.4e Recognize and apply geometric ideas and relationships in areas outside the mathematics classroom, such as art, science, and everyday life

Measurement

ME.2e Solve problems involving scale factors, using ratio and proportion

Problem-Solving Strategy: Find a Pattern/Use Logical Reasoning/Draw a Diagram

Determine the number of small triangles in the first three figures. Draw the fourth figure, and determine the number of small triangles in it. How are the areas of the four figures related?

(Understand) **Understand the problem.**

"What information are we given?"

We are shown the first three figures in a pattern of squares that are built of small triangles.

"What are we asked to do?"

1. Determine the number of small triangles in the first three figures.
2. Draw the fourth figure.
3. Determine the number of small triangles in the fourth figure.
4. Describe how are the areas of the four figures are related.

(Plan) **Make a plan.**

"What problem-solving strategy will we use?"

We will *use logical reasoning* to help us *draw a diagram* to help us *find a pattern.*

(Solve) **Carry out the plan.**

"How many triangles are in each of the first three figures?"

4, 8, and 16.

"How many triangles might we assume will be in fourth figure?"

The number of triangles seems to double with each new figure, so 16 × 2 = 32 small triangles will make up the fourth figure.

"How could we describe how to draw the fourth figure?"

First we copy the third figure. Each vertex of the third figure will become a mid-point for a side of the fourth square. After drawing the fourth square we extend the pattern into the fourth square.

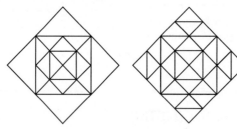

"Is our assumption that the fourth figure would be made up of 32 triangles correct?"

Yes. The fourth figure has twice as many small triangles as the third figure.

"How are the areas of the figures related?"

Just as the number of triangles doubles, the area doubles with each new figure.

(Check) **Look back.**

"Did we find the answers to the questions that were asked?"

Yes.

• Transformations

facts | Power Up F

mental math

a. **Calculation:** The laundromat washes about 90 loads of laundry per day. About how many loads of laundry does it wash per week?   630

b. **Geometry:** Two angles of a triangle are 90° and 10°. What is the third angle? $180° - 100° = 80°$

c. **Number Sense:** $1\frac{1}{2} \times 12$ $12 + 6 = 18$

d. **Power/Roots:** What whole number is closest to $\sqrt{37}$?   6

e. **Proportions:** On the long downhill slope the elevation dropped 100 feet every quarter mile. How much did the elevation drop in one mile?   400 feet

f. **Percent:** 25% of $36 $9

g. **Fractional Parts:** $\frac{2}{3}$ of the 36 students   24

h. **Calculation:** $100 - 50, + 14, \sqrt{}, + 1, \sqrt{}, + 1, \sqrt{}, - 1, \sqrt{}, - 1, \sqrt{}, - 1, \times 9$ -9

problem solving | Determine the number of small triangles in the first three figures. Draw the fourth figure, and determine the number of small triangles in it. How are the areas of the four figures related?   Each figure is twice the area of the preceding figure.

New Concept | *Increasing Knowledge*

Transformations are operations on a geometric figure that alter its position or form. Transformations are used for computer graphics and in animation. In this lesson we will consider four different transformations. Below we illustrate three transformations that move △ABC to its image △A′B′C′ (we read △A′B′C′ as "A prime B prime C prime"). The three transformations are **reflection** (flip), **rotation** (turn), and **translation** (slide). Notice that the size of the figure is not changed in these transformations.

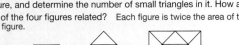

| reflection | rotation | translation |

Lesson 26   **169**

---

1 Power Up

Facts
Distribute **Power Up F** to students. See answers below.

Mental Math
Encourage students to share different ways to mentally compute these exercises. Strategies for exercises **c** and **f** are listed below.

  c. Regroup and Multiply
    $1\frac{1}{2} \times 12 = 1\frac{1}{2} \times 2 \times 6$
    $= 3 \times 6 = 18$
  Use Math Sense
    $1\frac{1}{2} \times 12 = \frac{3}{2} \times 12$
    $= 3 \times 6 = 18$
  f. Think Half of Half
    $\frac{1}{2}$ of $36 = 18$
    $\frac{1}{2}$ of $18 = 9$
  Quadruple and Quarter
    25% of $36 = 100\%$ of $9 = 9$

Problem Solving
Refer to **Power-Up Discussion**, p. 169B.

2 New Concepts

Instruction
Cut out the triangles in **Lesson Activity 4 Transformations** and use one as the original figure and the other as the image on the overhead as you quickly demonstrate the transformations shown on the student page. Use the terms *reflection, rotation,* and *translation* as you move the image triangle. Ask students what other words can be used to describe these transformations. flip, turn, and slide

(continued)

Facts | Express each mixed number as an improper fraction.

$3\frac{1}{3} = \frac{10}{3}$	$1\frac{3}{4} = \frac{7}{4}$	$7\frac{1}{2} = \frac{15}{2}$	$2\frac{2}{3} = \frac{8}{3}$	$2\frac{4}{5} = \frac{14}{5}$
$10\frac{1}{2} = \frac{21}{2}$	$1\frac{7}{8} = \frac{15}{8}$	$33\frac{1}{3} = \frac{100}{3}$	$12\frac{1}{2} = \frac{25}{2}$	$6\frac{2}{3} = \frac{20}{3}$

Express each improper fraction as a mixed number or whole number.

$\frac{8}{4} = 2$	$\frac{11}{5} = 2\frac{1}{5}$	$\frac{7}{2} = 3\frac{1}{2}$	$\frac{14}{3} = 4\frac{2}{3}$	$\frac{11}{4} = 2\frac{3}{4}$
$\frac{16}{5} = 3\frac{1}{5}$	$\frac{24}{6} = 4$	$\frac{23}{10} = 2\frac{3}{10}$	$\frac{19}{6} = 3\frac{1}{6}$	$\frac{16}{7} = 2\frac{2}{7}$

Math Language

Be sure students understand the use of prime and double prime symbols to indicate that the figure is a transformed image of the original figure.

Instruction

Now do each transformation again, using **Investigation Activity 2** Coordinate Plane and the triangles, following the diagrams on the student page and taking time to discuss the points made for each transformation. Emphasize that for all three transformations:

• the triangle does not change shape or size as it is transformed.

• the triangle and its image are congruent figures.

When discussing *reflections,* point out that students may sometimes see or hear the words "reflected in" or "reflected over" as well as "reflected across" in reference to the line of reflection.

As you discuss *rotations,* explain that the point of rotation can be inside, on, or outside the figure.

(continued)

A reflection occurs across a line. Here we show the reflection of △ABC across the y-axis. Each point in the reflection is the same distance from the y-axis as the corresponding point in the original figure. A segment between corresponding points is perpendicular to the line of reflection. Notice that if we were to fold this page along the line of reflection, the figures would coincide exactly.

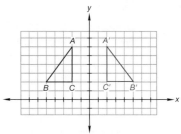

A positive rotation turns a figure counter-clockwise about (around) a point. Here we show a 90° rotation about point B. Point B is the point of rotation —its location is fixed, and the figure spins around it. If we trace the path of any other point during this rotation, we find that it sweeps out an arc of 90°.

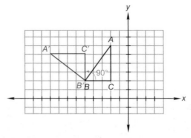

A translation slides a figure a distance and direction without flipping or turning. Here we show a translation of (6, 1), which is 6 units to the right and 1 unit up. For any translation (*a, b*), *a* describes the horizontal shift, and *b* describes the vertical shift for each point of the figure.

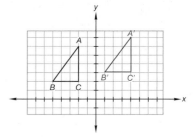

Math Background

This lesson includes a manipulative-based activity. Manipulatives involve students mentally and physically in the learning process, and offer alternative ways to explore a problem. Kinesthetic, visual, and social learners often benefit from activities that allow them to cooperate as they learn concepts by seeing and touching representations of mathematical ideas.

• Manipulatives are especially useful for illustrating elementary concepts, and can also make complex concepts more accessible.

• Manipulatives provide you with alternative ways of exploring a topic, and provide extra practice for students who need reinforcement.

Example 1

Describe the transformations that move △ABC to the location of △A‴B‴C‴.

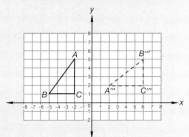

We will use all three transformations. We begin by **reflecting △ABC across line AC.**

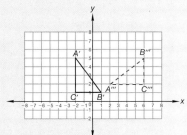

Then we **rotate △A'B'C' 90° about point C.**

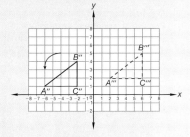

Lesson 26   171

Example 1

Instruction

Continue to use the transparencies of **Investigation Activity 2** Coordinate Plane and the triangles to demonstrate the transformations in this example. When you complete the three moves, point out that the three moves could have been made in any order, and the final image would be the same.

You might explore this idea by having students suggest a different order for the three moves for you or a volunteer to make on the overhead. Note that the reflection must take place across *AC* wherever it is at the time it is to be reflected.

(continued)

Instruction

If you have large sheets of grid paper available, students could work in small groups to carry out this activity. If not, work as a class and have volunteers move the figures on the overhead, using the Coordinate Plane transparency of **Investigation Activity 2.**

2 New Concepts (Continued)

Instruction

Emphasize that the figures after a *dilation* or *contraction* are similar. Photographic enlargements are probably the most familiar dilations for students but some artists use the idea behind dilations when they create pictures with perspective.

(continued)

We finish by **translating △A″B″C″ 8 units to the right and 1 unit up.**

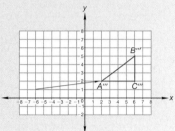

Activity

Describing Transformations

Materials needed:

Copies of Lesson Activity 4. Cut out the two triangles before beginning the activity.

Description of Activity:

The teacher or a student volunteer positions the two figures on the same plane but in different orientations. Then students direct the volunteer to perform the transformations that move one of the figures to the location and orientation of the other figure. Repeat the activity with other volunteers and with other positions of the polygons.

Math Language
The word "isometries" comes from the Greek words "iso" (meaning "equal") and "meter" (meaning "measure").

The three transformations described above do not change the size of the figure. These transformations are called **isometries** or **congruence transformations** because the original figure and its image (result of the transformation) are congruent.

One transformation that does change the size of a figure is a dilation. Recall that a **dilation** is a transformation in which the figure grows larger. (A **contraction** is a transformation in which the figure grows smaller.)

An example of a dilation is a photographic enlargement.

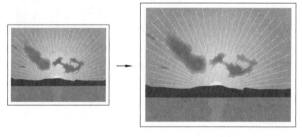

Although a dilation changes the dimensions of a figure, it does not change its shape. The original figure and its image are similar and corresponding lengths are proportional. Thus, dilations and contractions are **similarity transformations**.

Dilations of geometric figures occur away from a fixed point that is the center of the dilation.

Dilation of Rectangle ABCD

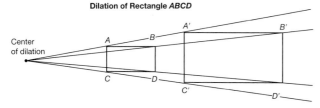

Note that corresponding vertices are on the same rays from the center of dilation and that the corresponding segments of △*ABC* and its image △*A'B'C'* are parallel.

Example 2

Measure the length and width of rectangle *ABCD* above and its dilated image rectangle *A'B'C'D'*.

a. What is the scale factor of the dilation?

b. The perimeter of the image is what multiple of the perimeter of rectangle *ABCD*?

c. The area of the image is what multiple of the area of rectangle *ABCD*?

Solution

The scale factor of the dilation applies to all linear measures, including the perimeter. Since area is a product of two linear measures, area is related by the square of the scale factor (scale factor × scale factor).

Rectangle *ABCD* is 2 cm by 1 cm. Rectangle *A'B'C'D'* is 4 cm by 2 cm.

a. The scale factor is **2**.

b. The perimeter of the image (2 × 2 cm + 2 × 4 cm = 12 cm) is **2 times** the perimeter of rectangle *ABCD* (2 × 1 cm + 2 × 2 cm = 6 cm).

c. The area of the image (2 cm × 4 cm = 8 cm^2) is **4 times** the area of rectangle *ABCD* (1 cm × 2 cm = 2 cm^2).

Discuss How is the scale factor of the dilation related to the relative perimeters and areas?

Practice Set ▶ *Classify* For **a–d** write the meaning of each transformation by selecting a word from this list: turn, flip, enlargement, slide.

a. Translation   slide

b. Rotation   turn

c. Reflection   flip

d. Dilation   enlargement

Lesson 26   173

▶ See Math Conversations in the sidebar.

2 New Concepts (Continued)

Example 2
Instruction

You may want to point out that the *scale factor* is the ratio of the lengths of the sides of the dilated image to the original figure. Note too that a scale factor does not have to be a whole number.

Call attention to the way the answers for parts b and c are similar to the results found in earlier lessons when we looked at the effect of doubling the dimensions of a rectangle—the perimeter doubles, the area quadruples.

As you go over the *Discuss* question, it may be helpful to compare what happens for two different scale factors. We can use 2 and 3 as scale factors.

• In this problem with a scale factor of 2, the perimeter of the image was 2 times the perimeter of the original and the area was 2^2 or 4 times the area of the original.

• For a problem with a scale factor of 3, the perimeter of the image would be 3 times the perimeter of the original and the area of the image would be 3^2 or 9 times the area of the original.

Practice Set
Problems a–d   Classify

For additional practice working with transformations, encourage students to include an informal sketch with each answer. As the sketches are completed, remind students that the size of a figure does not change during a translation (slide), rotation (turn), or reflection (flip).

(continued)

Manipulative Use

You may want to extend the experience with **reflections** described in this lesson. Provide students with reflective devices such as mirrors. Have students draw figures and explore how they change when they are reflected in a mirror. Students may make sketches of what they observe.

Teacher Tip

Make and **keep copies of Investigation Activity 2** Coordinate Plane in a convenient place. The students can use them as they work through this lesson, as well as lessons that follow where transformations may appear in practice exercises.

Problems e–g

Rectangle *PQRS* can be called the preimage of image *P'Q'R'S'*.

The sketches are informal, so it is not necessary to draw the rectangles proportionally.

Math Conversations

Discussion opportunities are provided below.

Problem 7 *Generalize*

After rewriting the expression as $\frac{7}{8} \cdot \frac{6}{1}$, encourage students to look for terms of the fractions that can be reduced.

Problem 8 *Generalize*

"Is 1 a reasonable estimate of the sum of these addends? Explain why or why not." No; Sample explanation: Both addends have a value that is close to 1, so a reasonable estimate of the sum is 1 + 1 or 2.

Problem 9 *Generalize*

"Is 1 a reasonable estimate of the exact difference? Explain why or why not." No; Sample explanation: Both numbers are nearly the same, so the difference of the numbers will be close to 0, not 1.

Errors and Misconceptions
Problem 14

Although students can be expected to connect the radical sign ($\sqrt{}$) with the need to find the root of a number, they may not recognize that the sign also represents a grouping symbol.

Remind students that the Order of Operations must be followed whenever two or more operations are present, and operations in grouping symbols must be completed first. So before finding the root, students must complete the subtraction.

When working with roots of this nature, a common error is to find the root of each term. For example, it is not correct to rewrite $\sqrt{25 - 16}$ as $\sqrt{25} - \sqrt{16}$, which is another name for 1.

(continued)

▶ Rectangle *PQRS* is dilated with a scale factor of 3 forming the rectangle *P'Q'R'S'*. Use this information for **e–g.**

e. Sketch rectangle *P'Q'R'S'* and label its length and width.

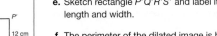

e.

f. The perimeter of the dilated image is how many times the perimeter of rectangle *PQRS*?   3 times

g. The area of the image is how many times the area of rectangle *PQRS*?   9 times

1. Marco Polo, the Italian trader, journeyed from Italy to China with his
(3) father and uncle. They returned to Italy in 1295, which was twenty-four years after they had left Italy. In what year did they leave Italy for China?   1271

2. Of the fifty states in the United States, $\frac{4}{25}$ of them begin with the letter
(5) "M." How many of the fifty states begin with the letter "M"?   8 states

3. On the safari, the average speed traveled by the vehicle was 25 miles
(7) per hour. If the vehicle traveled for 6 hours, how far did it travel?   150 miles

Generalize Simplify.

4. $1\frac{7}{8} + 1\frac{1}{6}$ $3\frac{1}{24}$ (13)   **5.** $\frac{7}{8} - \frac{1}{6}$ $\frac{17}{24}$ (13)

* 6. $\frac{7}{8} \cdot \frac{1}{6}$ $\frac{7}{48}$ (22)   **▶ * 7.** $\frac{7}{8} \div \frac{1}{6}$ $5\frac{1}{4}$ (23)

▶ * 8. $0.9 + 0.85$ 1.75 (24)   **▶ * 9.** $0.9 - 0.85$ 0.05 (24)

* 10. $(0.9)(0.85)$ 0.765 (25)   *** 11.** $\frac{0.828}{0.9}$ 0.92 (25)

12. Write the expressions in exponential from:
(15)
   a. *mmnmn* m^3n^2 **b.** $2xyyxy$ $2x^2y^3$

Use order of operations to simplify.

* 13. $5 \times 4 - [3 \times (2 - 1)]$ 17 (21)   **14.** $|25 - 16| - \sqrt{25 - 16}$ 6 (15, 21)

▶ 15. Find the area and perimeter of a rectangle with vertices at $(-3, -3)$,
(8, Inv. 1) $(-3, 6)$, $(0, -3)$, and $(0, 6)$. $P = 24$ units, $A = 27$ square units

* 16. **a.** Expand: $5(4 - p)$ $20 - 5p$
(21)
   b. Factor: $8y - 12$ $4(2y - 3)$

17. Compare:
(15, 21)
   a. $|1 - 9|$ ⊜ $(9 - 1)$ **b.** $\sqrt{9} + \sqrt{16}$ ⊜ $\sqrt{9 + 16}$

18. Find two values for *x* that make this statement true: $|x| = \frac{1}{2}$ $x = \frac{1}{2}, -\frac{1}{2}$
(1)

▶ See Math Conversations in the sidebar.

Estimate For problems **19** and **20**, estimate each answer.

▶* **19.** $14.3 \div 1.9$ 7   * **20.** 2983×7.02 21,000
(17)   (17)

21. Arrange these numbers in order from least to greatest.
(12)   1.2, 0, 0.12, 1, 2   0, 0.12, 1, 1.2, 2

22. a. Distributive Property,
b. Associative Property of Multiplication

22. Which property is illustrated?
(2, 21)
        a. $3(x - 9) = 3x - 27$ **b.** $3(4 \cdot 2) = (3 \cdot 4)2$

▶* **23.** Analyze Find the perimeter and area of this
(8, 20)   triangle. Dimensions are in mm.
          $P = 60$ mm, $A = 120$ mm^2

24   26
10

Solve by inspection. Choose one equation and write a story
for it.   See student work.

24. $\dfrac{5 + m}{2} = 10$ $m = 15$ **25.** $6m + 2 = 50$ $m = 8$
(14)   (14)

26. $2m = 104$ $m = 52$ **27.** $m + \dfrac{1}{4} = \dfrac{3}{4}$ $m = \dfrac{1}{2}$
(14)   (13, 14)

Evaluate.

28. Find $b^2 - 4ac$ when $a = 2, b = 3,$ and $c = 1$.   1
(14, 15)

29. Write the prime factorization of 200 using exponents. $2^3 \cdot 5^2$
(9, 15)

▶* **30.** Evaluate Banks made a kite with paper
(8,   and string and perpendicular wooden
Inv. 2) cross pieces with the dimensions shown (in
         inches).
         a. What is the distance from A to B?   15 in.
         b. What is the distance from B to C?   20 in.
         c. If there is a loop of string around the kite,
              how long is the loop?   70 in.

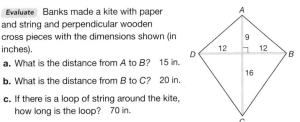
A
9
D   12   12   B
16
C

▶ See Math Conversations in the sidebar.

Math Conversations
Discussion opportunities are provided below.

Problem 19   Estimate
The divisor of this division is a decimal number. Have students recall that a decimal divisor must be changed to a whole number before the division can be completed.

"What number can we multiply 1.9 by to change it to a whole number?" Sample: 10

"If we multiply 1.9 by 10, how many places and in what direction does the decimal point move?" one place to the right

"If we multiply 1.9 by 10, can we begin the division? Explain why or why not." No; if the divisor is multiplied by 10, the dividend must be multiplied by 10 before the division can begin.

Problem 23   Analyze
"To find the area of the triangle, is it easier to use mental math, or paper and pencil? Explain why." Sample: Mental math; One-half of the product of 24 and 10 is the same as the product of 12 and 10, which is 120.

Problem 30   Evaluate
Students must recognize the triangles as right triangles, and conclude that the Pythagorean Theorem is used to find the length of AB and BC.

Looking Forward
Understanding and applying transformations prepares students for:

- **Investigation 5,** graphing transformations.

- **Lesson 91,** investigating the effects of scaling on perimeter, area, and volume.

• Laws of Exponents

Objectives

- Simplify exponential expressions involving factors with the same base using the laws of exponents.
- Explain the laws of exponents using everyday language.

Materials

- **Power Up F** (in *Instructional Masters*)
- **Manipulative Kit: scissors**
- **Teacher-provided material: unlined paper**

Optional

- **Teacher-provided material: index cards, grid paper**

Power Up F

Math Language

New	Maintain
laws of exponents	base
	exponent
	factor

Technology Resources

Student eBook Complete student textbook in electronic format.

Resources and Planner CD Assessment, reteaching, and instructional masters, plus a pacing calendar with standards.

Test and Practice Generator CD Create additional practice sheets and custom-made tests.

www.SaxonPublishers.com Visit for more student activities and planning materials.

Inclusion

Adaptations CD Adapted lessons, investigations, practice and assessments.

Meeting Standards

National Council of Teachers of Mathematics (NCTM)

Numbers and Operations

NO.1e Develop an understanding of large numbers and recognize and appropriately use exponential, scientific, and calculator notation

NO.1f Use factors, multiples, prime factorization, and relatively prime numbers to solve problems

NO.3b Develop and analyze algorithms for computing with fractions, decimals, and integers and develop fluency in their use

Problem-Solving Strategy: Use a Graph

Sharon took Susan to a playground. Use the graph to write a brief story about what Susan was doing on the playground.

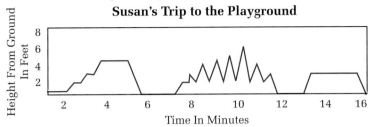

Susan's Trip to the Playground

(Understand) **Understand the problem.**

We have been given a graph that shows how many feet Susan was above the ground over a span of 17 minutes of play on a playground. We are asked to write a brief story of what she was doing while on the playground.

(Plan) **Make a plan.**

The motion graph that we have been provided shows three distinct events in terms of height. The first event shows a gradual rise up, and then a sudden drop down. The second event shows a consistent up-and-down. The third event shows an extended amount of time at approximately 4 feet.

(Solve) **Carry out the plan.**

Susan arrived at the play area and immediately ran to the slide. She waited her turn to climb up the rungs to the top, where she hesitated for a while before finally sliding down. She then walked over to the swings where she began to swing, gradually gaining altitude, and then slowing down so she could get off. Finally, Susan decided to play in the "Tubes and Tunnels." She climbed up the steps, and then spent several minutes crawling through the tunnels before exiting.

(Check) **Look back.**

We were able to write a story because Susan's movement on the playground had been graphed. Other stories may differ from ours.

Facts

Distribute **Power Up F** to students. See answers below.

Mental Math

Encourage students to share different ways to mentally compute these exercises. Strategies for exercises **c** and **f** are listed below.

c. Subtract from 180°

$180° - 80° = 100°$

$100° \div 2 = 50°$

Sum of Angles of Triangle

$x + x + 80° = 180°$

$2x = 180° - 80°$

$2x = 100°$

$x = 50°$

f. Use a Proportion

$\frac{2}{3} = \frac{x}{12}$

$3x = 2 \times 12$

$x = \frac{24}{3} = 8$

Use Math Sense

3 steps = 2 feet

6 steps = 4 feet

12 steps = 8 feet

Problem Solving

Refer to **Power-Up Discussion**, p. 176B.

• Laws of Exponents

Power Up | *Building Power*

facts | Power Up F

mental math

a. Calculation: Roper does 20 pushups per minute. If he can do 50 pushups at this rate, how long will it take? $2\frac{1}{2}$ minutes

b. Number Sense: $2\frac{1}{2} \times 12$ $12 + 12 + 6 = 30$

c. Geometry: Find x.   50°

d. Algebra: $4x - 3 = 25$ 7

e. Fractional Parts: $\frac{2}{5}$ of $55 $22

f. Proportions: Walking up 3 stair steps, Vera rose 2 feet. How many feet did Vera rise walking up 12 stair steps?   8 ft

g. Percent: 25% of 444   111

h. Calculation: $\sqrt{100}$, -1, $\sqrt{}$, $\times 12$, $\sqrt{}$, $\times 4$, $+1$, $\sqrt{}$, $\times 10$, -1, $\sqrt{}$ 7

problem solving

Sharon took Susan to a playground. Use the graph to write a brief story about what Susan was doing on the playground.

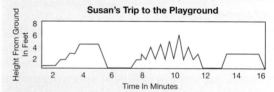

Susan's Trip to the Playground

Understand We have been given a graph that shows how many feet Susan was above the ground over a span of 17 minutes of play on a playground. We are asked to write a brief story of what she was doing while on the playground.

Plan The motion graph that we have been provided shows three distinct events in terms of height. The first event shows a gradual rise up, and then a sudden drop down. The second event shows a consistent up-and-down. The third event shows an extended amount of time at approximately 4 feet.

Solve Susan arrived at the play area and immediately ran to the slide. She waited her turn to climb up the rungs to the top, where she hesitated for a while before finally sliding down. She then walked over to the swings where she began to swing, gradually gaining altitude, and then slowing down so she could get off. Finally, Susan decided to play in the "Tubes and Tunnels." She climbed up the steps, and then spent several minutes crawling through the tunnels before exiting.

Check We were able to write a story because Susan's movement on the playground had been graphed. Other stories may differ from ours.

Facts | Express each mixed number as an improper fraction.

$3\frac{1}{3} = \frac{10}{3}$	$1\frac{3}{4} = \frac{7}{4}$	$7\frac{1}{2} = \frac{15}{2}$	$2\frac{2}{3} = \frac{8}{3}$	$2\frac{4}{5} = \frac{14}{5}$
$10\frac{1}{2} = \frac{21}{2}$	$1\frac{7}{8} = \frac{15}{8}$	$33\frac{1}{3} = \frac{100}{3}$	$12\frac{1}{2} = \frac{25}{2}$	$6\frac{2}{3} = \frac{20}{3}$

Express each improper fraction as a mixed number or whole number.

$\frac{8}{4} = 2$	$\frac{11}{5} = 2\frac{1}{5}$	$\frac{7}{2} = 3\frac{1}{2}$	$\frac{14}{3} = 4\frac{2}{3}$	$\frac{11}{4} = 2\frac{3}{4}$
$\frac{16}{5} = 3\frac{1}{5}$	$\frac{24}{6} = 4$	$\frac{23}{10} = 2\frac{3}{10}$	$\frac{19}{6} = 3\frac{1}{6}$	$\frac{16}{7} = 2\frac{2}{7}$

Increasing Knowledge

Math Language
The **exponent,** or *n*, shows the number of times the **base,** or *x*, is used as a factor.

Recall that a counting-number exponent indicates how many times a base is a factor.

$$x^n = x \cdot x \cdot x \ldots x \qquad \text{(n factors of x)}$$

Applying this knowledge we can begin to develop the **laws of exponents** that describe relationships between exponents for certain operations.

Example 1

Find the missing exponent: $x^5 \cdot x^3 = x^\square$

Solution

We apply the meaning of the exponents.

$$x^5 \cdot x^3 = (x \cdot x \cdot x \cdot x \cdot x)(x \cdot x \cdot x) = x^{\boxed{8}}$$

We see that multiplying x^5 and x^3 means that x is a factor eight times. Notice that the exponent 8 is the sum of the exponents 5 and 3.

Example 2

Find the missing exponent: $\dfrac{3^5}{3^3} = 3^\square$

Solution

We apply the meaning of the exponents and reduce the fraction.

$$\frac{3^5}{3^3} = \frac{3 \cdot \overset{1}{\cancel{3}} \cdot \overset{1}{\cancel{3}} \cdot \overset{1}{\cancel{3}} \cdot 3}{\underset{1}{\cancel{3}} \cdot \underset{1}{\cancel{3}} \cdot \underset{1}{\cancel{3}}} = 3^{\boxed{2}}$$

Notice that the exponent 2 is the difference of the exponents 5 and 3.

Example 3

Find the missing exponent: $(x^3)^2 = x^\square$

Solution

The exponent 2 means that the base x^3 is a factor twice.

$$(x^3)^2 = x^3 \cdot x^3 = xxx \cdot xxx = x^{\boxed{6}}$$

Notice that the exponent 6 is the product of the exponents 2 and 3.

Lesson 27   177

2 New Concepts

Instruction

Explain that this lesson will start with the simplest way to express the meaning of an exponential expression and will build on that to develop the laws for working with exponents.

Use the *Math Language* feature to help students develop the correct vocabulary. As you use these terms in this lesson, encourage students to do so also.

Example 3
Instruction

It may help students differentiate between multiplying exponential expressions and raising them to a power if you point out that parentheses can be used to show that an exponential expression is being raised to a power. Tell them to remember that they multiply the exponents only when they see the parentheses between the two exponents.

(continued)

Math Background

Finding area is one application of the laws of exponents.

For example, the area of a rectangle having a length of 4 cm and a width of 5 cm is 20 cm^2.

$$A = lw$$
$$A = (4 \text{ cm})(5 \text{ cm})$$
$$A = (4 \cdot 5)(\text{cm}^1 \cdot \text{cm}^1)$$
$$A = (20)(\text{cm}^{1+1})$$
$$A = 20 \text{ cm}^2$$

The laws of exponents state that $x^a \cdot x^b = x^{a+b}$, and units of area (such as cm · cm = cm^2) represent one application of those laws.

Instruction

Use the *Connect* question to emphasize that zero cannot be used as a divisor in exponential expressions.

Have students write their responses to the *Summarize* question. Then ask volunteers to read their summaries, and allow others to ask questions or tell what they may not completely understand about the laws. It is important that students understand these fundamental relationships.

Example 4

Instruction

Emphasize that the laws work for letters or numbers as long as the bases are the same.

Practice Set

Problems a–h [Error Alert]

If students have difficulty recalling the laws of exponents, encourage them to record the laws in their math notebooks or on an index card. The index card can be used as a bookmark, and students can refer to the bookmark or to their notebook as needed.

Examples 1, 2, and 3 illustrate the following three laws of exponents.

Thinking Skill

Connect

Why does the table specify that for division, $x \neq 0$? Division by zero is not possible.

Laws of Exponents for Multiplication and Division

$$x^a \cdot x^b = x^{a+b}$$

$$\frac{x^a}{x^b} = x^{a-b}$$

for $x \neq 0$

$$(x^a)^b = x^{a \cdot b}$$

Sample answer: When the bases are the same, and you multiply, you add the exponents; when you divide, you subtract the exponents; when you raise a term with an exponent to a power, you multiply the exponents.

Summarize State the laws of exponents as shown in the table in your own words.

We will expand on these laws in later lessons.

Example 4

Write each expression as a power of ten.

a. $10^8 \cdot 10^6$ b. $\dfrac{10^8}{10^6}$

Solution

The bases are the same, so we can apply the laws of exponents.

a. We add the exponents.

$$10^8 \cdot 10^6 = 10^{14}$$

b. We subtract the exponent of the divisor from the exponent of the dividend.

$$\frac{10^8}{10^6} = 10^2$$

Practice Set ▸ Find the missing exponents.

a. $x^5 \cdot x^2 = x^\square$ 7 b. $\dfrac{x^5}{x^2} = x^\square$ 3 c. $(x^2)^3 = x^\square$ 6

▸ Simplify.

d. $2^3 \cdot 2^2$ 32 e. $\dfrac{2^5}{2^2}$ 8 f. $(2^5)^2$ 1024

▸ Write each expression as a power of 10.

g. $10^6 \cdot 10^3$ 10^9 h. $\dfrac{10^6}{10^2}$ 10^4

Written Practice *Strengthening Concepts*

1. Cynthia planted 12 potted plants in the last 3 weeks. At that rate, how many would she plant in 5 weeks? 20 potted plants
(7)

2. The volleyball team has 5 wins and 7 losses. What fraction of their games will they have won if they win their next 3 games? $\frac{8}{15}$
(5)

3. Of the 2,800 visitors to the fair, only $\frac{3}{70}$ won a prize. How many visitors won prizes? 120 visitors won prizes.
(5)

▸ See Math Conversations in the sidebar.

Teacher Tip

As you review student work for the *Practice Set* and *Written Practice*, **observe whether the papers are neat and organized.** Check that problems are written with each step on a separate line. If papers are disorganized and sloppy, spend some time in the next class discussing good work habits and your expectations for paper work.

Inclusion

Students who have difficulty with the laws of exponents may benefit from another demonstration. Write the following expressions on the board and ask:

"What is the expanded form of $x^3 \cdot x^2$?" $(x \cdot x \cdot x)(x \cdot x)$

"What is the simplified form of $x^3 \cdot x^2$?" x^5

"What is the expanded form of $x^4 \cdot x^2$?" $(x \cdot x \cdot x \cdot x)(x \cdot x)$

"What is the simplified form of $x^4 \cdot x^2$?" x^6

"What is the expanded form of $x^5 \cdot x^2$?" $(x \cdot x \cdot x \cdot x \cdot x)(x \cdot x)$

"What is the simplified form of $x^5 \cdot x^2$?" x^7

"What pattern do you see from the expanded form to simplified form?"
Sample: When multiplying the bases you add the exponents.

Do similar exercises with the other laws and discuss the patterns that the students observe.

* 4. *(Analyze)* Reflect the point (1, 4) across the *y*-axis. What is the image?
(26) (−1, 4)

* 5. *(Classify)* What transformation is shown
(26) at right?   dilation

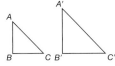

6.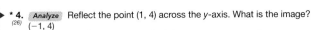

* 6. *(Model)* If this figure is rotated 90° clockwise,
(26) draw the image.

Generalize Simplify.

* 7. $3^2 + 3^1 + 3^0$ 13
(27)

* 8. $2.1 \div 0.7$ 3
(25)

* 9. 6.02×10^6 6,020,000
(25, 27)

10. $4.21 + 42.1 - 0.421$ 45.889
(24)

* 11. $1\frac{1}{2} \cdot \frac{4}{5}$ $\frac{6}{5}$ or $1\frac{1}{5}$
(23)

* 12. $1\frac{1}{2} \div \frac{4}{5}$ $\frac{15}{8}$ or $1\frac{7}{8}$
(23)

13. $\frac{2}{5} \div \frac{4}{5}$ $\frac{1}{2}$
(22)

14. $\frac{4}{5} \div \frac{2}{5}$ 2
(22)

15. $4^2 - 4(2)(2)$ 0
(21)

16. $\sqrt[3]{8} + \sqrt{9}$ 5
(15)

17. $1\frac{1}{10} + \frac{1}{2}$ $1\frac{3}{5}$
(13)

18. Compare: $|16 - 20| \bigcirc (16 - 20)$
(21)

19. Classify this triangle by sides and angles.
(20) isosceles, obtuse

20. Find the perimeter and area of this triangle.
(8, 20) P = 120 m; A = 600 m²

30 m   50 m

40 m

21. A regular triangle has a perimeter of 51 m. How long is each side?   17 m
(19)

22.
not the same size

* 22. *(Verify)* Give a counterexample to disprove the statement "all squares
(19) are congruent."

23. Choose the best word to complete the following sentence. Two lines
(18) that are in different planes and do not intersect are   **B**

  A parallel.

  B skew.

  C perpendicular.

  D diagonal.

24. These lines are perpendicular.
(18) $m \angle 1 + m \angle 3 = \underline{\hspace{1cm}}$.   180°

Lesson 27   179

▶ See Math Conversations in the sidebar.

3 Written Practice

Math Conversations
Discussion opportunities are provided below.

Problem 4 *Analyze*
Encourage students who may have difficulty inferring the answer to use grid paper to complete the reflection.

Problem 5 *Classify*
Students should recognize that image $A'B'C'$ is larger than ABC, and conclude that $A'B'C'$ does not represent a reflection, a rotation, or a translation because those transformations do not change the size of a figure.

Problem 6 *Model*
"When looking at an analog clock, which direction represents clockwise?" to the right

Encourage students to turn their textbooks 90° clockwise to model the transformation.

Problem 9 *Generalize*
"10^6 is another name for one million. How can we complete this problem without multiplying by one million?" When one factor is a power of 10, the exponent indicates the number of places and the direction to move the decimal point in the other factor. The result of moving the decimal point represents the product of the factors.

Problem 12 *Generalize*
"Can the terms of fractions be reduced during division?" no

"During which operation can the terms of fractions be reduced?" multiplication

Errors and Misconceptions
Problem 7
Watch for students who rewrite the expression as 3^{2+1+0} or 3^3.

Another common error is to simplify 3^0 to 0. To remediate this error, write the pattern shown below on the board or overhead to show students that 1 is the result of simplifying 3^0.

3^3	3^2	3^1	3^0
↓	↓	↓	↓
$27 \div 3 =$	$9 \div 3 =$	$3 \div 3 =$	1

(continued)

Math Conversations

Discussion opportunities are provided below.

Problem 28 *Predict*

Extend the Problem

"If Anthony doubles the length of the rectangular pen, and halves the width, will the perimeter of the rectangle remain the same?" Accept all predictions.

Ask students to complete the computation to check their predictions.

"Did doubling the length and halving the width increase or decrease the perimeter? By what amount?" increase; 4.28 m

---

25. Round 7,654,321 to the nearest hundred thousand.   7,700,000
(17)

26. Estimate the difference: $15.81 - 6\frac{1}{4}$ 10
(17)

27. Name a set of numbers that includes −2, but does not include −2.3.
(10) integers

▶ **28.** Anthony is building a rectangular pen 3.54 m long and 2.8 m wide for
(8, 24) his dog. How many meters of fence will Anthony need?   12.68 m

29. Write the prime factorization of 144 using exponents. $2^4 \cdot 3^2$
(9)

30. Solve by inspection.
(14)
    a. $35 - d = 17$ $d = 18$ **b.** $8n = 72$ $n = 9$

Early Finishers
Real-World Application

Each of the 50 states on a US flag are represented by a 5-point star. There is a story that Betsy Ross showed George Washington how to make a 5-point star with one clip of her scissors. To make a 5-point star, fold and cut an $8\frac{1}{2}$ by 10 sheet of unlined paper according to the following directions.

1.

Fold the paper in half to create a left (L) and a right (R) corner.

2.

Crease the folded paper at midlines. Then unfold.

3.

Fold down left corner from vertical midline to horizontal midline.

4.

Fold left corner back to fold shown in step 3.

5.

Fold right corner to left across fold shown in step 4.

6.

Fold right corner back to fold shown in step 5.

7.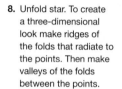

Use scissors to make one cut at about the angle shown.

8. Unfold star. To create a three-dimensional look make ridges of the folds that radiate to the points. Then make valleys of the folds between the points.

▶ See Math Conversations in the sidebar.

Looking Forward

Understanding the Laws of Exponents prepares students for:

- **Lesson 28,** writing large numbers in scientific notation.

- **Lesson 51,** working with negative exponents.

- **Lesson 57,** performing operations with small numbers in scientific notation.

Scientific Notation for Large Numbers

Objectives

- Write numbers in scientific notation, understanding that powers of 10 can be used to indicate place value.
- Write numbers in scientific notation using words.
- Use a calculator to demonstrate scientific notation.

Lesson Preparation

Materials

- **Power Up F** (in *Instructional Masters*)
- **Teacher-provided material:** calculators

Power Up F

Math Language

New	Maintain	English Learners (ESL)
coefficient	power	elevation
scientific notation		

Technology Resources

Student eBook Complete student textbook in electronic format.

Resources and Planner CD Assessment, reteaching, and instructional masters, plus a pacing calendar with standards.

Test and Practice Generator CD Create additional practice sheets and custom-made tests.

www.SaxonPublishers.com Visit for more student activities and planning materials.

Inclusion

Adaptations CD Adapted lessons, investigations, practice and assessments.

Meeting Standards

National Council of Teachers of Mathematics (NCTM)

Numbers and Operations

NO.1e Develop an understanding of large numbers and recognize and appropriately use exponential, scientific, and calculator notation

Communication

CM.3d Use the language of mathematics to express mathematical ideas precisely

Connections

CN.4c Recognize and apply mathematics in contexts outside of mathematics

Problem-Solving Strategy: Draw a Diagram/
Make It Simpler

Aoki, Breann, Chuck, and Dan line up from left to right to take a picture. How many different arrangements are there?

(Understand) **Understand the problem.**

"What information are we given?"

Four people are lining up for a picture.

"What are we asked to do?"

Determine how many different arrangements of four people are possible.

(Plan) **Make a plan.**

"What problem-solving strategy will we use?"

We will *draw a tree diagram* to find the answer. We can *make it simpler* by first looking only for the permutations with Aoki in the left position.

"How will we use the arrangements involving Aoki to find the total number of arrangements?"

The number of arrangements that are possible with Akoi in the first position will be the same number of arrangements possible if Breann, Chuck, or Dan is in the first position.

(Solve) **Carry out the plan.**

"If Aoki stands in the left-most position, how many arrangements of the four students are possible?"

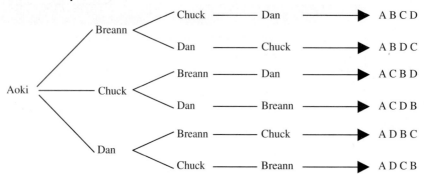

There are six different arrangements of the four students if Akoi stands in the first position.

"What other tree diagrams could we make?"

Three similar tree diagrams exist for placing Breann, Chuck, or Dan in the left-most position.

"How many different arrangements of the four students will be possible?"

Each of the four students has the opportunity to be placed in the first position, with six arrangements of the remaining three students resulting. Therefore, there are $4 \times 6 = 24$ different arrangements of the four students.

(Check) **Look back.**

"Did we do what we were asked to do?"

Yes, we found the number of possible arrangements of the four students.

• Scientific Notation for Large Numbers

facts | Power Up F

mental math

a. **Calculation:** The odometer read 235 miles. Seth drove north until the odometer read 245 miles. Then Seth drove south until the odometer read 254 miles. How far is Seth from where he started?   1 mile

b. **Geometry:** If a spoke is 12 inches long, then the circumference of the wheel is a little more than how many feet?   6 ft

12 in. radius

c. **Number Sense:** $10\frac{1}{2} \times 4$ 42

d. **Proportions:** If 3 gallons cost $7.50, how much would 4 gallons cost? $10.00

e. **Power/Roots:** $\sqrt{900}$ 30

f. **Fractional Parts:** $\frac{5}{6}$ of 48   40

g. **Fractions:** $\frac{1}{7} = \frac{3}{x}$ 21

h. **Calculation:** $180 - 80$, $\div 2$, $\div 2$, $\sqrt{}$, $\times 9$, $+ 4$, $\sqrt{}$, $- 6$, $\times 17$, $- 1$, $\sqrt{}$, $\sqrt{}$ 2

problem solving | Aoki, Breann, Chuck, and Dan line up from left to right to take a picture. How many different arrangements are there?   24 arrangements

New Concept | Increasing Knowledge

Scientific notation is a method of writing a number as a decimal number times a power of 10. Scientific notation is a useful way to express and manipulate very large or very small numbers that take many places to express in standard form. For example, the speed of light is about 300,000,000 meters per second. In scientific notation, we write this number as follows:

$$3.0 \times 10^8$$

"Three point zero times ten to the eighth."

The first number (3.0) is the **coefficient.** The coefficient is written with one non-zero digit to the left of the decimal point. The power of 10 is the multiplier that turns 3.0 into 300,000,000. Notice that the exponent, 8, corresponds to the number of places the decimal point shifts when the number is written in standard form.

Lesson 28   181

Facts | Express each mixed number as an improper fraction.

$3\frac{1}{3} = \frac{10}{3}$	$1\frac{3}{4} = \frac{7}{4}$	$7\frac{1}{2} = \frac{15}{2}$	$2\frac{2}{3} = \frac{8}{3}$	$2\frac{4}{5} = \frac{14}{5}$
$10\frac{1}{2} = \frac{21}{2}$	$1\frac{7}{8} = \frac{15}{8}$	$33\frac{1}{3} = \frac{100}{3}$	$12\frac{1}{2} = \frac{25}{2}$	$6\frac{2}{3} = \frac{20}{3}$

Express each improper fraction as a mixed number or whole number.

$\frac{8}{4} = 2$	$\frac{11}{5} = 2\frac{1}{5}$	$\frac{7}{2} = 3\frac{1}{2}$	$\frac{14}{3} = 4\frac{2}{3}$	$\frac{11}{4} = 2\frac{3}{4}$
$\frac{16}{5} = 3\frac{1}{5}$	$\frac{24}{6} = 4$	$\frac{23}{10} = 2\frac{3}{10}$	$\frac{19}{6} = 3\frac{1}{6}$	$\frac{16}{7} = 2\frac{2}{7}$

1 Power Up

Facts
Distribute **Power Up F** to students. See answers below.

Mental Math
Encourage students to share different ways to mentally compute these exercises. Strategies for exercises **c** and **d** are listed below.

c. Multiply by 2 Twice
$10\frac{1}{2} \times 4 = 10\frac{1}{2} \times 2 \times 2 =$
$21 \times 2 = 42$
Double and Halve
$10\frac{1}{2} \times 4 = 21 \times 2 = 42$

d. Use a Proportion
$\frac{4}{3} = \frac{g}{\$7.50}$
$3g = 4 \times \$7.50$
$3g = \$30$
$g = \$10$
Use Math Sense
3 gal → $7.50
1 gal → $2.50
4 gal → $10.00

Problem Solving
Refer to **Power-Up Discussion**, p. 181B.

2 New Concepts

Instruction
Have students examine the two parts of the number as written in *scientific notation*.

"What is the coefficient?"   3.0

"What is the power of 10?" 10^8

As the class studies the Place Value Table on the next page, be sure that students understand the relationship between the place value name and the power of 10.

(continued)

Example 1

Instruction

Point out that in scientific notation, unlike standard notation, the decimal point in a number is read as "point" and that each digit is read as a single number.

Check that students are using the correct form for scientific notation. Forming good habits now will avoid errors due to carelessness later.

Example 2

Instruction

You may want to discuss when it makes sense to use scientific notation. In this example, expressing 1500 meters in millimeters using scientific notation is not very sensible. Some people have an idea of how long 1500 meters is; almost no one would be able to visualize how long 1.5×10^6 mm is. So the point is that scientific notation should be used for very large (or very small) numbers.

Instruction

If students have scientific calculators, go through this exercise and let students with different calculators compare their displays. As a class do the calculation at the begining of the next page to find the length of a light year in meters.

(continued)

In other words, powers of 10 can be used to indicate place value.

Place Value Table

Trillions			Billions			Millions			Thousands			Units (ones)		
hundreds	tens	ones	hundreds	tens	ones	hundreds	tens	ones	hundreds	tens	ones	hundreds	tens	ones
10^{14}	10^{13}	10^{12}	10^{11}	10^{10}	10^9	10^8	10^7	10^6	10^5	10^4	10^3	10^2	10^1	10^0

Example 1

Earth's average distance from the sun is 93,000,000 miles. Write 93,000,000 in scientific notation.

Solution

The coefficient is written with one digit to the left of the decimal point, so we place the decimal point between 9 and 3. This is seven decimal places from the actual location of the decimal point, so we use the exponent 7. We drop trailing zeros. The answer is read "nine point three times ten to the seventh."

$$9.3 \times 10^7$$

Visit www. SaxonPublishers. com/ActivitiesC3 for a graphing calculator activity.

Example 2

When Brigita finished the 1500 meter run she announced that she had run "one point five times ten to the sixth millimeters." Write that number a in scientific notation and b in standard form.

Solution

a. 1.5×10^6

b. The power of 10 indicates that the actual location of the decimal point is six places to the right.

1500000.

Brigita ran **1,500,000** mm.

Scientific calculators will display the results of an operation in scientific notation if the number would otherwise exceed the display capabilities of the calculator. For example, to multiply one million by one million, we would enter

[1] [0] [0] [0] [0] [0] [0] [×]

[1] [0] [0] [0] [0] [0] [0] [=]

The answer, one trillion, contains more digits than can be displayed by most calculators. Instead of displaying one trillion in standard form, the calculator displays one trillion in some modified form of scientific notation such as

$[\ 1.\ ^{12}\ ]$ or perhaps $[\ 1. \times 10\ ^{12}\ ]$

Teacher Tip

Throughout this lesson, remind students to **use the scallop marks underneath each digit** and to count each place as they shift the decimal point.

Math Background

When finding the product of a counting number and a power of 10 (such as 3.0×10^8), the exponent represents the number of zeros in the standard form of the number.

$10^0 = 1$ (no zeros) $10^5 = 100,000$ (five zeros)

$10^1 = 10$ (one zero) $10^6 = 1,000,000$ (six zeros)

$10^2 = 100$ (two zeros) $10^7 = 10,000,000$ (seven zeros)

$10^3 = 1000$ (three zeros) $10^8 = 100,000,000$ (eight zeros)

$10^4 = 10,000$ (four zeros) $10^9 = 1,000,000,000$ (nine zeros)

The standard form of the product 3.0×10^8 contains eight zeros, and is written 300,000,000.

9.45×10^{16}; We know from the law of exponents that $10 = 10^1$. We also know that $9.45 \times 10^{15} \times 10^1 =$

Practice Set
$9.45 \times 10^{(15+1)} = 9.45 \times 10^{16}$.

Connect On a calculator multiply the speed of light (300,000,000 m/sec), times the approximate number of seconds in a year (31,500,000) to find a light year in meters. 9.45×10^{15} m

Connect Use your calculator to multiply the measure of a light year in meters by 10. Use Laws of Exponents to explain the result.

a. Write "two point five times ten to the sixth" with digits. 2.5×10^6

b. **Represent** Use words to write 1.8×10^8. one point eight times ten to the eighth

▶ Write each number in standard form.

c. 2.0×10^5 200,000

d. 7.5×10^8 750,000,000

e. 1.609×10^3 1609

f. 3.05×10^4 30,500

Write each number in scientific notation.

g. 365,000 3.65×10^5

h. 295,000,000 2.95×10^8

i. 70,500 7.05×10^4

j. 25 million 2.5×10^7

Written Practice   *Strengthening Concepts*

▶ *** 1.** The lowest point on dry land is the shore of the Dead Sea, which is
    (3)   about 1292 feet below sea level. Less than 20 miles from the Dead Sea is the Mount of Olives, which is 2680 feet above sea level. What is the elevation difference between the shore of the Dead Sea and the Mount of Olives? 3972 feet

▶ *** 2.** **Infer** About $\frac{7}{10}$ of Greece's mainland is mountainous. About what
    (11) percent of Greece's mainland is not mountainous? 30%

3. The Great Wall of China is about 1500 miles long. If there are about
 (4) 8 towers distributed along each mile, about how many towers are on the Great Wall of China? about 12,000 towers

4. Classify this triangle by angles and sides and
 (20) find its area. obtuse triangle, scalene triangle, 6 m²

4 m
3 m

5. If the largest angle of the triangle in problem **4** is 104°, then the sum of
 (15) the measures of the two acute angles is how many degrees? 76°

▶ *** 6.** On earth a kilogram mass weighs about 2.2 pounds. A 16-pound
 (6, 25) bowling ball has a mass of about how many kilograms? Express your answer to the nearest whole kilogram. 7 kilograms

Lesson 28   183

▶ See Math Conversations in the sidebar.

Math Conversations

Discussion opportunities are provided below.

Problem 7 Generalize

Prior to simplifying the expressions, invite one or more volunteers to state the Laws of Exponents and write on the board or overhead an example of each law.

Problem 12

If some students have difficulty identifying the measure of $\angle WQY$, explain that $\overline{QY}$ bisects $\angle XQZ$.

Problem 14

If students have difficulty rounding the mixed numbers, encourage them to compare the numerator and the denominator of each fraction, and decide if the numerator represents less than one-half of the denominator, or one-half or more.

(continued)

15.

(−6, 5)   (−1, 5)

(−6, −2)   (−1, −2)

22. a.
Commutative
Property of
Multiplication,
b. Identity
Property of
Multiplication

▶ *Generalize* Simplify using rules of exponents.

* 7. **a.** $m^3 \cdot m^4$ m^7
(27)
b. $\dfrac{m^6}{m^2}$ m^4

Simplify. Remember to follow the order of operations.

* 8. $\dfrac{1}{3} + 1\dfrac{1}{3} \cdot 2\dfrac{1}{4}$ $3\dfrac{1}{3}$
(21, 22)
* 9. $\dfrac{3}{4} - \dfrac{1}{5} \div \dfrac{4}{5}$ $\dfrac{1}{2}$
(21, 22)

* 10. $\dfrac{2 + 1.2}{2 - 1.2}$ 4
(21, 25)
* 11. $(1.5)^2 - 1.5$ 0.75
(21, 25)

▶*** 12.** Find the measure of $\angle WQY$.   135°
(18)

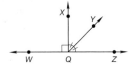

* 13. Evaluate: $x^2 - 2x$ when $x = 5$ 15
(14, 15)

▶*** 14.** Round each number to the nearest whole number.
(17)
a. $3\dfrac{3}{4}$ 4
b. $3\dfrac{3}{10}$ 3
c. 3.10   3

* 15. Plot the following points which are vertices of a rectangle. Locate the
(8, Inv. 1) fourth vertex, and find the area and perimeter of the rectangle. (−1, 5), (−1, −2), (−6, 5)   (−6, −2); A = 35 square units; P = 24 units

16. **a.** Expand: $3(x + r + 5)$
(21) $3x + 3r + 15$
b. Factor: $4x + 6y$
   $2(2x + 3y)$

* 17. **a.** Write 2.97×10^5 in standard notation.   297,000
(28)
b. Write 4,030,000 in scientific notation. 4.03×10^6

* 18. Simplify: $1^3 + 2^3 + 3^1 + 4^0$ 13
(27)

* 19. Estimate: $\dfrac{6870}{6.9}$ 1000
(17)

20. Compare: $\sqrt{25} \ominus \sqrt[3]{27}$
(17)

* 21. What is the multiplicative inverse of $2\dfrac{1}{2}$? $\dfrac{2}{5}$
(23)

22. Which property is illustrated?
(2)
a. $xy = yx$
b. $1 \cdot x = x$

23. If a triangle is equilateral, then each angle measures how many
(20) degrees?   60°

Solve by inspection:

24. $10 \cdot 5 = 10 + h$ $h = 40$
(14)
25. $1 - f = \dfrac{9}{10}$ $f = \dfrac{1}{10}$
(13, 14)

* 26. $\dfrac{10^6}{10^2} = 10^x$ $x = 4$
(27)
27. $\dfrac{18}{x} = \dfrac{9}{10}$ $x = 20$
(10, 14)

28. Simplify.
(21)
a. $2 + 3 \cdot 10 \div 2$ 17
b. $2 \times (3 + 12) + 10$ 40

▶ See Math Conversations in the sidebar.

► **29.** *Analyze* Arrange these numbers in order from least to greatest.
(12)

$$2, 0.2, -2, 0, 0.02$$
$$-2, 0, 0.02, 0.2, 2$$

* 30. What is the length of the hypotenuse of this
(15, isosceles right triangle? $\sqrt{2}$ cm
Inv. 2)

1 cm

1 cm

Early Finishers
Real-World
Application

Flies belong to a group of insects called *Diptera*. The *Diptera* order is one of the four largest groups of living organisms. There are over 120,000 different kinds of flies known in the world today. If a particular species of fly weighs approximately 0.0044 of a pound, how many grams would 12 flies weigh (1 pound = 453.5923 g)? Round your answer to the nearest ten-thousandth.
23.9497 g

► See Math Conversations in the sidebar.

Math Conversations

Discussion opportunities are provided below.

Problem 29 *Analyze*

"Let's try to complete this problem using only mental math. Order the integers from least to greatest." $-2, 0, 2$

"On a number line, the decimal numbers 0.2 and 0.02 would be between which two of those integers?" 0 and 2

"On a number line, which of the decimal numbers would be closer to zero? Explain why." 0.02; Sample explanation: The place value of the tenths place in 0.02 is less than the place value of the tenths place in 0.2.

"What is the order of the numbers from least to greatest?" $-2, 0, 0.02, 0.2, 2$

Looking Forward

Writing large numbers using scientific notation prepares students for:

• **Lesson 46,** solving problems using scientific notation.

• **Lesson 51,** writing small numbers using scientific notation.

• **Lesson 57,** performing operations with small numbers in scientific notation.

• Ratio

Objectives

- Write ratios using the word "to", as fractions, as decimals, and with colons.
- Round ratios when appropriate.
- Find an approximate average rate from a table of data.

Lesson Preparation

Materials

- **Power Up F** (in *Instructional Masters*)

Optional

- **Manipulative Kit: color tiles**

Power Up F

Math Language

New	Maintain
ratio	cancel
	rate

Technology Resources

Student eBook Complete student textbook in electronic format.

Resources and Planner CD Assessment, reteaching, and instructional masters, plus a pacing calendar with standards.

Test and Practice Generator CD Create additional practice sheets and custom-made tests.

www.SaxonPublishers.com Visit for more student activities and planning materials.

Inclusion

Adaptations CD Adapted lessons, investigations, practice and assessments.

Meeting Standards

National Council of Teachers of Mathematics (NCTM)

Numbers and Operations

NO.1d Understand and use ratios and proportions to represent quantitative relationships

NO.3d Develop, analyze, and explain methods for solving problems involving proportions, such as scaling and finding equivalent ratios

Measurement

ME.2f Solve simple problems involving rates and derived measurements for such attributes as velocity and density

Connections

CN.4c Recognize and apply mathematics in contexts outside of mathematics

Problem-Solving Strategy: Draw a Diagram

Mr. Roberts faced west. He walked ten steps forward. Then, without turning, he took five sideways steps to his right. Then, he took seven steps backward. Then, he turned left and walked six steps forward. Then, he turned right and took three steps backward. Which direction is Mr. Roberts facing, and how far is he from where he started?

(Understand) ***Understand the problem.***

"What important *information* are we given?"

Mr. Roberts began a journey facing west. He then:
1. Took 10 steps forward.
2. WITHOUT TURNING, took 5 steps to his right.
3. Took 7 steps BACKWARDS.
4. TURNED LEFT and walked 6 steps forward.
5. TURNED RIGHT and took 3 steps BACKWARDS.

"What are we asked to do?"

Determine (1) the direction Mr. Roberts is facing and (2) how many steps he is from where he began his journey.

(Plan) ***Make a plan.***

"What problem-solving strategy will we use?"

We will *draw a diagram* of Mr. Robert's steps.

"Do we need to adapt any of the information?"

We will also need to mark our diagram with the *direction* Mr. Roberts is always facing.

(Solve) ***Carry out the plan.***

"How do we begin?"

We will sketch Mr. Roberts' path on a grid, being careful to keep track of which direction he is facing at all times (with arrows, for instance).

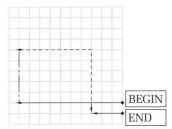

"Which direction is Mr. Roberts facing?"

west

"How far is Mr. Roberts from where he started?"

one step south.

(Check) ***Look back.***

"Did we find the answers to the questions that were asked?"

Yes. Mr. Roberts is facing west, and is only one step from where he began.

1 Power Up

Facts
Distribute **Power Up F** to students. See answers below.

Mental Math
Encourage students to share different ways to mentally compute these exercises. Strategies for exercises **d** and **g** are listed below.

d. Multiply by 2 Twice
$7.5 \times 4 = 7.5 \times 2 \times 2 = 15 \times 2 = 30$
Double and Halve
$7.5 \times 4 = 15 \times 2 = 30$

g. Triple and Third
$33\frac{1}{3}\%$ of $90 = 100\%$ of $30 = \$30$
Find a Fraction
$33\frac{1}{3}\% = \frac{1}{3}$
$\frac{1}{3}$ of $90 = \$30$

Problem Solving
Refer to **Power-Up Discussion**, p. 186B.

2 New Concepts

Instruction
The word *ratio* comes directly to us from the Latin word *ratio,* meaning "calculation." Ratios are used to do many calculations, mostly in proportions, which are equations that show two ratios are equal. Students will encounter proportions in Lesson 34.

Go over the four ways to express a ratio. Ask students to express the ratio of boys to girls in each of the four ways. 4 to 3, $\frac{4}{3}$, $1.\overline{3}$, and 4:3

(continued)

LESSON 29 • Ratio

facts   Power Up F

mental math

a. **Calculation:** Frank flipped 2 hotcakes every 3 seconds. At that rate, how many can he flip in a minute?   40

b. **Estimation:** $449.8 \div 49.7$ $450 \div 50 = 9$

c. **Geometry:** What is the value of *x*?   130°

d. **Number Sense:** 7.5×4 30

e. **Scientific Notation:** Write 7.5×10^6 in standard notation.   7,500,000

f. **Fractional Parts:** $\frac{3}{8}$ of $32 $12

g. **Percent:** $33\frac{1}{3}\%$ of $90 $30

h. **Calculation:** $11, \times 9, + 1, \sqrt{\ }, + 6, \sqrt{\ }, + 5, \sqrt{\ }, + 7 =$ 10

problem solving

Mr. Roberts faced west. He walked ten steps forward. Then, without turning, he took five sideways steps to his right. Then, he took seven steps backward. Then, he turned left and walked six steps forward. Then, he turned right and took three steps backward. Which direction is Mr. Roberts facing, and how far is he from where he started?   He is facing west, one step south of where he started.

New Concept   *Increasing Knowledge*

A **ratio** is a comparison of two numbers by division. For example, if there are 12 girls and 16 boys in a class, then we can express the ratio of girls to boys as a reduced fraction.

$$\frac{girls}{boys} \quad \frac{12}{16} = \frac{3}{4}$$

We read this ratio as "3 to 4." Here we show four ways to write a ratio:

with the word **to**	3 to 4
as a fraction	$\frac{3}{4}$
as a decimal	0.75
with a colon	3:4

Example 1

There are 9 girls and 15 boys in a class. What is the ratio of boys to girls in the class?

Facts   Express each mixed number as an improper fraction.

$3\frac{1}{3} = \frac{10}{3}$	$1\frac{3}{4} = \frac{7}{4}$	$7\frac{1}{2} = \frac{15}{2}$	$2\frac{2}{3} = \frac{8}{3}$	$2\frac{4}{5} = \frac{14}{5}$
$10\frac{1}{2} = \frac{21}{2}$	$1\frac{7}{8} = \frac{15}{8}$	$33\frac{1}{3} = \frac{100}{3}$	$12\frac{1}{2} = \frac{25}{2}$	$6\frac{2}{3} = \frac{20}{3}$

Express each improper fraction as a mixed number or whole number.

$\frac{8}{4} = 2$	$\frac{11}{5} = 2\frac{1}{5}$	$\frac{7}{2} = 3\frac{1}{2}$	$\frac{14}{3} = 4\frac{2}{3}$	$\frac{11}{4} = 2\frac{3}{4}$
$\frac{16}{5} = 3\frac{1}{5}$	$\frac{24}{6} = 4$	$\frac{23}{10} = 2\frac{3}{10}$	$\frac{19}{6} = 3\frac{1}{6}$	$\frac{16}{7} = 2\frac{2}{7}$

Solution

We write the ratio in the order stated—boys to girls.

$$\frac{boys}{girls} \qquad \frac{15}{9} = \frac{5}{3}$$

The ratio of boys to girls is 5 to 3. Notice that we reduce the ratio, but we do not write the ratio as a mixed number.

Example 2

A 30 ft tall tree cast a shadow 18 ft long. What was the ratio of the height of the tree to the length of its shadow?

Solution

We write the ratio in the order specified: height to length.

$$\frac{\text{height of tree}}{\text{length of shadow}} \qquad \frac{30 \text{ ft}}{18 \text{ ft}} = \frac{5}{3}$$

Thinking Skill

Represent

Use words to state the exact ratio of advancers to decliners. seven hundred eighty-nine to five hundred ninety-seven

In some situations we round numbers to express a ratio. For example, in a day of stock-market trading perhaps 789 stocks gained value and 597 lost value. The ratio of advancers to decliners is estimated as

$$\frac{\text{advancers}}{\text{decliners}} \qquad \frac{789 \text{ stocks}}{597 \text{ stocks}} \approx \frac{800}{600}$$

The rounded ratio is reduced, so we might hear a business report stating that advancers led decliners 4 to 3.

Example 3

At the high school football game 1217 fans sat on the home-team side and 896 fans sat on the visiting-team side. What was the approximate ratio of home-team fans to visiting-team fans?

Solution

We arrange the numbers in the stated order, and then we round and reduce the ratio.

$$\frac{\text{home-team fans}}{\text{visiting-team fans}} \qquad \frac{1217 \text{ fans}}{897 \text{ fans}} \approx \frac{1200}{900}$$

The ratio reduces to 12 to 9 which further reduces to $\frac{4}{3}$.

Recall that a rate is a ratio of two measures with different units. The units do not cancel but instead remain part of the rate.

---

2 New Concepts (Continued)

Example 1
Instruction

Caution students that order is important when writing ratios. 3 to 5 is not the ratio of boys to girls, but that of girls to boys. Emphasize that a ratio should be completely reduced but not converted to a mixed number.

Example 2
Instruction

Again note that ratios must be written in the given order. If they are not, then they do not represent the situation. The units must still be present or the numbers have no meaning.

Example 3
Instruction

You may want to mention that there is another number that is implicit in this problem—the total number of fans at the game. That number can also be used to write ratios that can describe the attendance at the game. For example, the ratio of home-team fans to all fans is about 4 to 7.

(continued)

Inclusion

Some students may have difficulty understanding that a reduced ratio is equivalent to its original ratio. For example 1, use the colored tiles from the Manipulative Kit. Have students take 15 tiles of one color to represent the 15 boys in the ratio and use 9 tiles of another color for the 9 girls. Then instruct the students to divide the boy tiles into equal groups. **5 groups of 3 or 3 groups of 5** Instruct the students to divide the girls into equal groups. **3 groups of 3** Ask:

"Which division of the tiles gives an equal number of groups for both boys and girls?" 3 groups of 5 for the boys; 3 groups of 3 for the girls

"What reduced ratio to 15 boys to 9 girls can you see from the groups of tiles?" 5 boys to 3 girls

"What is another equivalent ratio you can find using the groups of tiles?" 10 boys to 6 girls

---

Math Background

A ratio is a comparison of two quantities by division, and can be expressed as a to b, $a:b$, or $\frac{a}{b}$. A ratio is in simplest form when a and b are whole numbers ($b \neq 0$), and the only common factor of a and b is 1.

2 New Concepts (Continued)

Example 4
Instruction
Discuss the data and calculations in the table. Ask students what they notice about Rosa's daily reading rates and her average reading rate. Sample: On 2 days, her daily rate was the same as her average rate.

Practice Set

Problems a–e Error Alert
Before completing the problems, remind students that the order of the terms of a ratio is important, and must be identical to the order of the terms as they are stated in each problem.

Also remind students that whenever possible, a ratio should be expressed in simplest form, and point out that dividing the terms of a ratio by the greatest common factor of the terms is a way to change a ratio that is not in simplest form to a ratio in simplest form.

Problems b, d, and e Error Alert
Watch for students who transpose the terms of a ratio because they assume ratios must have a value that is less than 1.

Example 4

Rosa kept a record of the number of pages and number of minutes she read each night. Find Rosa's approximate reading rate for the book in pages per minute.

Reading Record

Day	Pages	Minutes
M	15	30
T	11	20
W	14	30
Th	20	40
F	27	50

Solution

We are asked for the rate in pages per minute, so the units are pages and minutes. To find Rosa's reading rate we have some choices. We can find the rate for each day to see if the rate is consistent, or we can find the total number of pages and minutes and calculate an average rate. We show both methods in the table. We see that each ratio is equal or very close to 1 page every 2 minutes or about $\frac{1}{2}$ **page per minute.**

Reading Record

Day	Pages	Minutes	p/m
M	15	30	$\frac{1}{2}$
T	11	20	$\frac{11}{20}$
W	14	30	$\frac{7}{15}$
Th	20	40	$\frac{1}{2}$
F	27	50	$\frac{27}{50}$
5 days	87	170	$\frac{87}{170}$

Practice Set

Connect Refer to this information to answer questions **a** and **b**.

In a bag are 14 marbles. Six marbles are red and eight are blue.

▶ **a.** What is the ratio of red marbles to blue marbles? $\frac{3}{4}$

▶ **b.** What is the ratio of blue marbles to red marbles? $\frac{4}{3}$

Refer to this statement to answer questions **c** and **d**.

A 20 ft flagpole casts a shadow 24 feet long.

▶ **c.** What is the ratio of the height of the flagpole to the length of the shadow? $\frac{5}{6}$

▶ **d.** What is the ratio of the length of the shadow to the height of the flagpole? $\frac{6}{5}$

▶ **e.** If 479 stocks advanced in price and 326 declined in price, then what was the approximate ratio of advancers to decliners? 5 to 3

f. Using the table in example 4, find Rosa's approximate reading rate in minutes per page. 2 minutes per page

▶ See Math Conversations in the sidebar.

1. One thousand pounds of grain were packaged in five-pound bags. How
(4) many bags were there?   200

2. The minute hand of a clock changes position by 30° in five minutes.
(10) What fraction of a full 360° turn is this? $\frac{1}{12}$

3. Compute an 18% gratuity on a $3000 banquet fee. $540
(11)

4. If the base and height of a triangle are the lengths of two sides of the
(20) triangle, then the triangle is   **B**

   A acute   **B** right

   C obtuse   **D** cannot be determined

5. Val planted 36 pumpkin seeds in the community garden. In two weeks,
(11) 27 of the seeds had germinated. What percent of the seeds had
germinated?   75%

Simplify.

▶ * 6. $5^2 \cdot 5^1 \cdot 5^0$ 125   ▶ * 7. $10^2 - 10^1 - 10^0$ 89
(27)   (15, 27)

8. $xxwxw$ x^3w^2 9. $(xy)(xy)$ $(xy)^2$ or x^2y^2
(15)   (15)

10. $5\frac{1}{5} \cdot 2\frac{1}{2}$ 13   11. $\frac{1}{2} + \frac{2}{3} \div \frac{3}{4}$ $\frac{25}{18}$ or $1\frac{7}{18}$
(23)   (13, 22)

12. $\frac{1.35 + 0.07}{0.2}$ 7.1   13. $0.01(101 + 10.1)$ 1.111
(24, 25)   (24, 25)

14. Cruz filled his car with 10.2 gallons of gas at $2.89 per gallon. If he
(17) fills his car with about this much gas at about this price once a week,
estimate how much he will have spent on gas after four weeks. $120

▶ * 15. **Analyze** Rectangles *ABCD* and *MNOP* are similar. What scale factor is
(26) used to dilate rectangle *ABCD* to rectangle *MNOP*? Round your answer
to the thousandth.   2.604

16. A triangle has vertices (−2, 1), (3, 1), and (1, 4). What is the area of the
(Inv. 1, triangle? $7\frac{1}{2}$ square units
20)

▶ * 17. **Represent** The product 53(120) is equal to 53(100 + 20). Which of the
(21) following shows how to rewrite 53(100 + 20)?   **C**

   A $53 + 100 \times 53 + 20$ **B** $53 \times 100 + 20$ **C** $53 \times 100 + 53 \times 20$

Lesson 29   189

▶ See Math Conversations in the sidebar.

Teacher Tip

In this and other lessons, students may have difficulty working some of the *Written Practice* problems after class. Suggest that they **work on the more difficult problems** or the ones they don't understand while they are still **in class**. Doing this will allow them to obtain the help they need from you and will make the rest of the assignment easier to complete outside of class.

Math Conversations
Discussion opportunities are provided below.

Problem 15 Analyze
To help students recognize that division is used to identify the scale factor, offer the following simpler problem.

> *"Suppose the measure of side DC was 2 and the measure of side PO was 6. What would the scale factor of the dilation be? Explain why."* The scale factor would be 3 because $6 \div 2 = 3$.

Problem 17 Represent

Point out that students can check their answer by writing the given expression and the expression that was chosen for the answer in standard form. If the standard forms of the expressions are the same, the answer checks.

Errors and Misconceptions
Problem 6
If students rewrite 5^0 as 0, the expression will simplify to 0 because the product of any number of factors and 0 is 0.

To remediate the error of rewriting 5^0 as 0, write the pattern shown below on the board or overhead and explain how it shows that 1 is the result of simplifying 5^0.

$$5^3 \qquad 5^2 \qquad 5^1 \qquad 5^0$$
$$\downarrow \qquad \downarrow \qquad \downarrow \qquad \downarrow$$
$$125 \div 5 = 25 \div 5 = 5 \div 5 = 1$$

Problem 7
Watch for students who simplify the expression by subtracting the exponents. The following example demonstrates this error.

$$10^2 - 10^1 - 10^0 = 10^{2-1-0} = 10^1 = 10$$

Explain to students that one way to recognize an error of this nature is for them to check their work by changing each term of the expression to standard form before subtracting.

$$10^2 - 10^1 - 10^0 = 100 - 10 - 1 = 89$$

(continued)

3 Written Practice (Continued)

Math Conversations

Discussion opportunities are provided below.

Problem 26a Formulate

Remind students that when writing a number in scientific notation, the coefficient must be a number that has one nonzero digit to the left of the decimal point. In other words, the coefficient must be greater than or equal to 1, but less than 10.

Problem 28 Analyze

After solving the problem, ask students to write and solve an equation that is different than $c \times 1.75 = p$, and then compare the solution to the original solution to check their work.

(continued)

18. We know $53(120) = 53 \times 100 + 53 \times 20$. The two products are easy to mentally compute. $53(120) = 5300 + 1060$. We add the products to get the answer: $53(120) = 6360$

18. Explain how the answer to problem **17** can help us calculate $53(120)$.
(21)

19. Arrange in order from least to greatest. $-1, 0, \frac{3}{7}, 0.5, \frac{2}{3}$
(1, 12)
$$\frac{2}{3}, -1, 0.5, 0, \frac{3}{7}$$

20. Chef Paul forgot to put pepper in the gumbo. If each bowl of gumbo needs $1\frac{1}{3}$ teaspoons of pepper, how much pepper will Chef Paul need for 6 bowls of gumbo? 8 teaspoons of pepper
(23)

21. Solve by inspection.
(14)
   a. $22 - n = 10$ $n = 12$ **b.** $\frac{d}{4} = -8$ $d = -32$

22. What is the median for this set of data? 10
(7)

Days	Number of Cars Sold This Week
Monday	13
Tuesday	9
Wednesday	11
Thursday	5
Friday	3
Saturday	16

23. Tedd drove 294 miles in 7 hours. What was his average speed in miles per hour? 42 mph
(7)

Simplify.

24. Expand: $3(2x - y)$ $6x - 3y$
(21)

25. Factor: $18x - 27$ $9(2x - 3)$
(21)

* 26. Formulate The orbit of the moon is elliptical. Its distance from earth ranges from about 226,000 miles to 252,000 miles.
(28)
   ▶ **a.** Write the greater distance in scientific notation. 2.52×10^5 mi.

   b. The greater distance is about what fraction of a million miles? $\frac{1}{4}$ million mi.

27. Classify this triangle by angles and sides. isosceles; right triangle
(20)

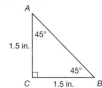

▶* 28. Analyze Marion, a store owner, uses the formula $c \times 1.75 = p$ to price items (c is how much she pays for the item and p is selling price). How much will she charge for music boxes that she purchased for $16 each? $16 \times 1.75 = 28$; $28
(14, 25)

▶ See Math Conversations in the sidebar.

30. No; If the legs of a right triangle are 12 ft and 16 ft, the hypotenuse (longer side) would be 20 12 ft + 16 ft + 20 ft = 48 ft, so a 45-ft roll is not long enough.

▶ **29.** Use this figure to find a and b.
(18, 20) $a = 40°$, $b = 50°$

30. Miles is building a right triangle shaped pen for his chickens. He has a
(Inv. 2)   45 foot roll of chicken wire and plans to make the two shorter sides 12 ft and 16 ft. Will he have enough chicken wire to go all the way around?

Early Finishers
Real-World Application

Computers are able to perform complex and repetitive procedures quickly and reliably by breaking the procedures down into a series of simple instructions. The clock rate of a Central Processing Unit (CPU) measures how many instructions per second a computer can process. Northwood Mid-High is upgrading their office's computer system from a CPU that runs at a clock speed of 1,300,000 cycles/second to a CPU that runs at 2,000,000 cycles/second. What is the difference in clock speed between the two processors? Write your answer in standard form and in scientific notation.   700,000 cycles/second; 7×10^5 cycles per second

Lesson 29   191

▶ See Math Conversations in the sidebar.

Math Conversations
Discussion opportunities are provided below.

Problem 29 `Explain`
Extend the Problem
"Two angles in this figure are not named. These angles are adjacent to ∠a. Explain how to find the measure of each angle."
Sample: The intersection of the extensions of the sides of the triangle creates four angles whose sum is 360°. Since the sum of two of the angles is 80°, the measure of each remaining angle is (360° − 80°) ÷ 2, or 140°.

Looking Forward

Writing and solving problems using ratios prepares students for:

- **Lesson 34,** working with proportions and solving ratio word problems.
- **Lesson 44,** solving proportions using cross products.
- **Lesson 45,** solving ratio problems involving totals.
- **Lesson 69,** working with direct variation.
- **Lesson 70,** solving direct variation problems.
- **Lesson 88,** reviewing proportional and non-proportional relationships.
- **Lesson 112,** writing ratios of side lengths of right triangles.

• Repeating Decimals

Objectives

- Write repeating decimals as a decimal number with a bar over the repetend.
- Compare and order decimal numbers with and without repeating digits.
- Write fractions as decimal numbers with repeating decimals.
- Use a calculator to convert rational numbers from fractions to decimal numbers.

Lesson Preparation

Materials

- **Power Up F** (in *Instructional Masters*)
- **Teacher-provided material:** calculators

Power Up F

Math Language

New	Maintain	English Learners (ESL)
repetend	ellipsis	convenient
	rational number	

Technology Resources

Student eBook Complete student textbook in electronic format.

Resources and Planner CD Assessment, reteaching, and instructional masters, plus a pacing calendar with standards.

Test and Practice Generator CD Create additional practice sheets and custom-made tests.

www.SaxonPublishers.com Visit for more student activities and planning materials.

Inclusion

Adaptations CD Adapted lessons, investigations, practice and assessments.

Meeting Standards

National Council of Teachers of Mathematics (NCTM)

Numbers and Operations

NO.1a Work flexibly with fractions, decimals, and percents to solve problems

NO.1b Compare and order fractions, decimals, and percents efficiently and find their approximate locations on a number line

NO.2a Understand the meaning and effects of arithmetic operations with fractions, decimals, and integers

NO.3b Develop and analyze algorithms for computing with fractions, decimals, and integers and develop fluency in their use

Problem-Solving Strategy: Work Backwards

Copy the problem and fill in the missing digits:

$$8)\overline{} \\ -\underline{} \\ -4\ 8 \\ \overline{0}$$

Understand **Understand the problem.**

"What information are we given?"

A division problem has a divisor of 8, a 3-digit dividend, and a 2-digit quotient with no remainder.

"What are we asked to do?"

Determine the 3-digit dividend and the 2-digit quotient.

Plan **Make a plan.**

"What problem solving strategy will we use?"

We will *work backwards* and use number sense.

Solve **Carry out the plan.**

Step 1:
$$8)\overline{} \\ -\underline{} \\ -4\ 8 \\ \overline{0}$$
quotient _ 6

Step 2:
_ 6, 48, −48, 0

Step 3:
_ 6, __8, 48, −48, 0

Step 4:
1 6, __8, 8, 48, −48, 0

Step 5:
1 6, 8)1 2 8, −8, 48, −48, 0

Check **Look back.**

"Did we complete the task that was assigned?"

Yes. We determined that the missing dividend is 128, and the missing quotient is 16.

"How can we verify the solution is correct?"

We verify the solution by using the inverse operation of multiplication:
$16 \times 8 = 128$

• **Repeating Decimals**

1 Power Up

Facts
Distribute **Power Up F** to students. See answers below.

Mental Math
Encourage students to share different ways to mentally compute these exercises. Strategies for exercises **d** and **f** are listed below.

d. Multiply by 2 Twice
$$4.5 \times 4 = 4.5 \times 2 \times 2 = 9 \times 2 = 18$$
Double and Halve
$$4.5 \times 4 = 9 \times 2 = 18$$

f. Find a Unit Rate
$$\$24 \text{ in } 3 \text{ hr} = \$8/\text{hr}$$
$$5 \text{ hr} \times \$8/\text{hr} = \$40$$
Use a Proportion
$$\frac{3}{24} = \frac{5}{e}$$
$$3e = 5 \times 24$$
$$e = \frac{5 \times 24}{3}$$
$$e = 5 \times 8 = 40$$

Problem Solving
Refer to **Power-Up Discussion,** p. 192B.

2 New Concepts

Instruction
Much of this lesson should be review material for your students. Students were introduced to *repeating decimals* in Lesson 12.

Be sure that students understand that the *repetend* can consist of one or more digits. Suggest that students explore the sevenths to see some interesting repeating decimal patterns.

$\frac{1}{7}$	0.142857142857
$\frac{2}{7}$	0.285714285714
$\frac{3}{7}$	0.428571428571
$\frac{4}{7}$	0.571428571428
$\frac{5}{7}$	0.714285714285
$\frac{6}{7}$	0.857142857142
$\frac{7}{7}$	1.000000000000

(continued)

facts | Power Up F

mental math

a. Calculation: Ronald ran 7 laps of the park in an hour. Enrique ran 4 laps in half an hour. Whose average speed was faster?   Enrique was faster (8 laps per hour)

b. Geometry: Rewrite and complete this congruence statement: $\triangle ABC \cong$
$\triangle ABC \cong \triangle WXY$

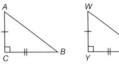

c. Fractional Parts: Jackie rode his bike 20 miles per hour for $1\frac{1}{2}$ hours. How far did he ride?   30 miles

d. Number Sense: 4.5×4 18

e. Scientific Notation: Write 750,000 in scientific notation. 7.5×10^5

f. Proportions: Gina earned $24 in 3 hours. At that rate, how much would she earn in 5 hours? $40

g. Power/Roots: What whole number is closest to $\sqrt{101}$?   10

h. Calculation: $28, \div 4, + 2, \times 7, + 1, \sqrt{}, + 5, \times 2, - 1, \sqrt{}, - 3, \times 50$
100

problem solving

Copy the problem and fill in the missing digits:

$$8\overline{)} \qquad \begin{array}{r} 16 \\ 8\overline{)128} \\ -8 \\ \hline 48 \\ -48 \\ \hline 0 \end{array}$$

$$\begin{array}{r} - \\ \hline -48 \\ \hline 0 \end{array}$$

New Concept | Increasing Knowledge

Recall that to express a ratio as a decimal number, we perform the division indicated. For example, to convert $\frac{3}{4}$ to a decimal number, we divide 3 by 4.

$$4\overline{)3.00}^{\;0.75}$$

Math Language

Recall that the three dots (…) is called an *ellipsis*. It indicates that a sequence continues without end.

Notice that we used a decimal point and zeros to write 3 as 3.00 so that we could perform the division. Some fractions convert to decimal numbers that have repeating digits such as $0.272727\ldots$. The repeating digits are called the **repetend.** We can indicate repeating digits with a bar over the repetend. We write $0.272727\ldots$ as $0.\overline{27}$.

Facts	Express each mixed number as an improper fraction.			
$3\frac{1}{3} = \frac{10}{3}$	$1\frac{3}{4} = \frac{7}{4}$	$7\frac{1}{2} = \frac{15}{2}$	$2\frac{2}{3} = \frac{8}{3}$	$2\frac{4}{5} = \frac{14}{5}$
$10\frac{1}{2} = \frac{21}{2}$	$1\frac{7}{8} = \frac{15}{8}$	$33\frac{1}{3} = \frac{100}{3}$	$12\frac{1}{2} = \frac{25}{2}$	$6\frac{2}{3} = \frac{20}{3}$

Express each improper fraction as a mixed number or whole number.

$\frac{8}{4} = 2$	$\frac{11}{5} = 2\frac{1}{5}$	$\frac{7}{2} = 3\frac{1}{2}$	$\frac{14}{3} = 4\frac{2}{3}$	$\frac{11}{4} = 2\frac{3}{4}$
$\frac{16}{5} = 3\frac{1}{5}$	$\frac{24}{6} = 4$	$\frac{23}{10} = 2\frac{3}{10}$	$\frac{19}{6} = 3\frac{1}{6}$	$\frac{16}{7} = 2\frac{2}{7}$

Example 1

Express each fraction or mixed number as a decimal number.

a. $\dfrac{1}{6}$ b. $2\dfrac{1}{3}$

Solution

a. We divide 1 by 6 and find a repeating pattern. The division does not terminate. Instead the digit 6 repeats in the quotient. The repeating digit or set of digits is called the *repetend*. We place a bar over the first 6 to show that every digit that follows is a 6. Thus, **0.16̄** is the decimal equivalent of $\frac{1}{6}$.

$$
\begin{array}{r}
0.166 \\
6\,\overline{)1.000} \\
\underline{6} \\
40 \\
\underline{36} \\
40 \\
\underline{36} \\
4
\end{array}
$$

b. The mixed number $2\frac{1}{3}$ is a whole number plus a fraction. The whole number, 2, is written to the left of the decimal point. The fraction $\frac{1}{3}$ converts to 0.333…, which we write as $.\overline{3}$.

$$2\dfrac{1}{3} = 2.\overline{3}$$

Recall that converting a rational number to decimal form has three possible outcomes.

1. The rational number is an integer.
2. The rational number is a terminating decimal number.
3. The rational number is a non-terminating decimal with repeating digits.

Non-terminating, non-repeating decimal numbers are *irrational* and do not result from converting a rational number to a decimal.

To perform calculations with repeating decimals we first round the number to a suitable number of decimal places.

Example 2

Find $\dfrac{5}{6}$ of \$12.47.

Solution

Before multiplying, we choose to convert $\frac{5}{6}$ to the decimal $0.8\overline{3}$, rounding to 0.83.

$$0.83 \times 12.47 = 10.3501$$

We round to the nearest cent, **\$10.35.**

Explain   Marsha multiplied $\frac{5}{6}$ and \$12.47 and got \$10.39. Which answer is more accurate? Why is there a difference in the two answers? **\$10.39 is more accurate. Expressing the fraction as a rounded decimal introduces rounding error into the calculation.**

---

2 New Concepts (Continued)

Example 1
Instruction
Make sure that students understand that the bar must go over all digits that repeat and only over those digits. For example, in part **a**, if the bar were placed over the 1 and the 6, it would mean that the decimal was 0.161616…, and not 0.1666….

Instruction
Review the information about outcomes of converting a rational number to decimal form. This was first introduced in Lesson 12.

Example 2
Instruction
Extend the *Explain* question by suggesting that students carry out the fraction computation, especially if anyone says that there cannot be that much difference in the two values. Then suggest that they use calculators to do the following calculations and compare those results to the fraction calculation.

0.83 × 12.47   10.3501

0.833 × 12.47   10.38751

0.8333 × 12.47   10.391251

0.83333 × 12.47   10.3916251

Note that even though the additional decimal place may seem quite trivial, the difference between multiplying by 0.83 and 0.833 is quite noticeable.

(continued)

Math Background

Non-terminating, non-repeating decimal numbers are examples of irrational numbers. Irrational numbers are numbers that cannot be expressed as a ratio of two integers. A number that contains an infinite number of decimal places with non-repeating digits, such as pi (π), is an irrational number. Square roots of whole numbers that are not perfect squares, such as $\sqrt{21}$ and $\sqrt{150}$, are also irrational numbers.

Square roots of decimal numbers may or may not be irrational numbers. For example, $\sqrt{2.25}$ is not an irrational number because it can be expressed as 1.5 (1.5 × 1.5 = 2.25). The square root of 22.5, however, cannot be expressed as a decimal number that terminates or repeats. So, $\sqrt{22.5}$ is an irrational number.

Example 3

Instruction

Discuss how writing the numbers with three decimal places makes it much easier to compare and order them. Explain that it is always wise to use as much information as you can when you are at the *Understand* part of the process of problem solving. Seeing these numbers with three decimal places shows more differences than can be seen in the numbers as they appear in the problem.

Instruction

Have students work on the activity independently, in pairs, or in small groups, depending on the number of calculators that are available. Be sure that all students know how to carry out the three calculations: converting a fraction to a decimal, adding fractions, and finding percents.

If students have different kinds of calculators, check that all the calculators yield the results given here for these exercises. If not, work with students to see what procedure can be used to get the correct answers.

Practice Set

Problems a–d 〔Error Alert〕

Explain that a repetend will be a part of every answer, and students will need to continue each division until each repetend can be identified.

Problems e–h 〔Error Alert〕

Before completing the problem, remind students of the following decimal place value generalizations.

- One digit to the right of a decimal point represents a decimal number in tenths.
- Two digits to the right of a decimal point represents a decimal number in hundredths.
- Three digits to the right of a decimal point represents a decimal number in thousandths.

(continued)

〔**Example 3**〕

Arrange in order from least to greatest.

$$0.3 \quad 0.\overline{3} \quad 0.33$$

〔**Solution**〕

We will write each decimal number with three places to make the comparison easier.

$$0.3 = 0.300$$
$$0.\overline{3} = 0.33\overline{3}$$
$$0.33 = 0.330$$

Now we arrange the given numbers in order.

$$0.3, \quad 0.33, \quad 0.\overline{3}$$

Many calculators do not have functions that enable the user to perform arithmetic with fractions. To convert a fraction to a decimal, we enter the numerator, press the ⊕ key, then key in the denominator and press ⊜. Convert these fractions to decimals.

a. $\frac{10}{11}$ 0.$\overline{90}$ **b.** $\frac{11}{12}$ 0.91$\overline{6}$ **c.** $\frac{17}{80}$ 0.2125

Thinking Skill

Analyze

Write $\frac{1}{6}$ as a decimal rounded to two decimal places. Double the result. Add $\frac{1}{6}$ and $\frac{1}{6}$ as fractions and write the sum as a decimal. Which decimal sum is more accurate? 0.34; 0.$\overline{3}$; The second is more accurate.

To add fractions it is not necessary to enter long repeating decimals and it is not necessary to round the decimal equivalents. For example, to add $\frac{5}{6}$ and $\frac{8}{3}$ on a calculator that has algebraic logic (follows the order of operations), we can use this key stroke sequence:

If your calculator has algebraic logic, the final display should read 3.5, which equals $3\frac{1}{2}$. Try these operations and write the decimal result.

d. $\frac{11}{12} + \frac{11}{6}$ 2.75   **e.** $\frac{17}{24} - \frac{1}{2}$ 0.208$\overline{3}$

Many calculators do not have a percent key. To find a given percent of a number with a calculator, we mentally shift the decimal point two places to the left before we enter the number.

f. Estimate 6.25% of $72.59. Then use a calculator to perform the actual calculation and round the answer to the nearest cent. What decimal number did you enter for 6.25%? About $4.20; rounds to $4.54; enter .0625

Practice Set ▸ Write each fraction in **a–d** as a decimal number.

a. $\frac{3}{11}$ 0.$\overline{27}$ **b.** $\frac{2}{9}$ 0.$\overline{2}$ **c.** $2\frac{2}{3}$ 2.$\overline{6}$ **d.** $\frac{1}{30}$ 0.0$\overline{3}$

▸ Round each decimal number to the nearest thousandth.

e. 0.$\overline{3}$ 0.333   **f.** 0.$\overline{6}$ 0.667   **g.** 0.$\overline{36}$ 0.364   **h.** 1.8$\overline{6}$ 1.867

Arrange in order from least to greatest.

i. 0.6, 0.$\overline{6}$, 0.66 0.6, 0.66, 0.$\overline{6}$ **j.** $\frac{1}{2}$, 0.5, $\frac{1}{3}$, 0.3, 0.0$\overline{6}$ 0.0$\overline{6}$, 0.3, $\frac{1}{3}$, $\frac{1}{2}$, 0.5

▸ See Math Conversations in the sidebar.

Teacher Tip

To vary how you present this or other lessons, **try teaching the lesson with student books closed.** Work the examples on the overhead and have students work along with you. Then go back to the student books, read the examples, and check whether students have any questions about the lesson before beginning the *Practice Set* and *Written Practice*.

1. There are 20 students in the algebra class. One-half of the students
(5)   were boys. One-half of the boys wore T-shirts. How many boys wore
   T-shirts to the algebra class? Boys wearing T-shirts were what fraction
   of the students in the class?   5 boys wore T-shirts; $\frac{1}{4}$

2. The big room measured 19 ft 10 in. by 22 ft 1 in. About how many square
(8, 17)   feet of carpet are needed to re-carpet the big room?   About 440 ft²

▶ *3. **Evaluate** The four pencils in Julio's desk have these lengths: $7\frac{1}{2}$ in., $5\frac{3}{4}$ in.,
(7, 13)   5 in. $2\frac{3}{4}$ in. What is the average (mean) length of the four pencils? $5\frac{1}{4}$ in.

▶ 4. **Analyze** Find the area of the triangle. (Dimensions are in mm.)   10 mm²
(20)

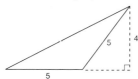

5
4

5

▶ *5. **Classify** Classify the triangle in problem 4 by angles and sides. If each
(20)   acute angle measures $26\frac{1}{2}°$, then what is the measure of the obtuse
   angle?   obtuse triangle, isosceles triangle, 127°

6. The $80.00 DVD player is on sale for 25% off. Find 25% of $80. $20
(12)

*7. What is the ratio of a side length to the perimeter of a square? $\frac{1}{4}$
(29)

Simplify.

8. $\frac{1}{4} + \frac{2}{3} \cdot \frac{1}{2}$ $\frac{7}{12}$
(13, 22)

9. $\frac{7}{8} - \frac{1}{8} \div \frac{1}{4}$ $\frac{3}{8}$
(13, 22)

▶*10. $\dfrac{1.23 + 0.4 + 5}{0.3}$ 22.1
(24, 25)

11. $4^0 + 4 \cdot 5 \cdot 2 - 1^3$ 40
(21, 27)

*12. $0.8 - \{0.6 - [0.4 - (0.2)^2]\}$ 0.56
(21, 24)

*13. **a.** Write $\frac{2}{9}$ as a decimal and a percent. $0.\overline{2}$; $22\frac{2}{9}$%
(30)
   b. Which of the three forms is the most convenient for finding $\frac{2}{9}$ of $27?

*14. Write 70% as a decimal and a fraction.   0.7; $\frac{7}{10}$
(11, 12)

*15. Plot these points and find the area and perimeter of the rectangle with
(8,   these vertices: (5, 11), (5, 1), (−2, 1), (−2, 11).   A = 70 square units;
Inv. 1)   P = 34 units

16. **a.** Expand: $5(x + y + z)$ $5x + 5y + 5z$
(14)
   b. Factor: $wx + wy$ $w(x + y)$

▶*17. Simplify: $\dfrac{x^5 \cdot x^2}{x}$ x^6
(15)

▶ 18. Write 28,000,000 in scientific notation. 2.8×10^7
(28)

Lesson 30   195

▶ See Math Conversations in the sidebar.

13 b. Possible
answer: The most
convenient form
is $\frac{2}{9}$ because I can
find that $\frac{2}{9}$ of $27
is $6 mentally.

5.
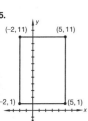
(−2, 11)   (5, 11)

(−2, 1)   (5, 1)

3 Written Practice

Math Conversations
Discussion opportunities are provided below.

Problem 3 Evaluate
*"One way to solve this problem is to add
the whole and mixed numbers, then divide
the sum of the numbers by 4. Another way
is to change each whole and mixed number
to a decimal number, then divide the sum
of the decimal numbers by 4."*

Invite students to choose a method and use
it to solve the problem. To check their work,
ask students to compare their answers to the
answers that were generated by a different
method.

Problem 4 Analyze
*"Which dimension, 4 mm or 5 mm,
represents the height of the triangle?
Explain how you know."* 4 mm; the height
of a triangle is perpendicular to the base of
the triangle.

Problem 5 Classify
Encourage students to give a reason for each
of their answers.

Problem 10
Students should recognize the fraction bar as a
symbol for division and as a grouping symbol.
The grouping symbol should lead students to
infer that the numerator must be simplified
before the division can be completed.

Errors and Misconceptions
Problem 17
Because the variable x appears two times in
the factors x^5 and x^2, watch for the common
error of writing $2x^7$ as the product of the
terms.

Problem 18
You may need to remind students that when
changing the standard form of a number to a
number in scientific notation, the coefficient
must be a number that has one nonzero digit
to the left of the decimal point.

In other words, the coefficient must be greater
than or equal to 1, but less than 10.

(continued)

English Learners
For problem **13b**, explain the
meaning of the word **convenient**.
Say:

*"When something is convenient,
it is easy to do."*

Ask volunteers to describe what
is the most convenient way to get
to school and why. ride the bus,
ride in the car, walk or ride a bike,
according to the location of the
student's home

Math Conversations

Discussion opportunities are provided below.

Problem 30 [Analyze]

Extend the Problem

Using only mental math, challenge students to name the coordinates of each vertex if the triangle was reflected across the y-axis, and name the coordinates of each vertex if the triangle was instead reflected across the x-axis. $A'(-3, 2)$, $B'(-1, 1)$, $C'(-3, 1)$; $A'(3, -2)$, $B'(1, -1)$, $C'(3, -1)$

19. Write the prime factorization of 1,000,000 using exponents. $2^6 \cdot 5^6$
(9, 15)

* 20. Simplify and compare: $\sqrt{169} \bigcirc (3.7)^2$ $13 < 13.69$
(15)

21.
a. Commutative Property of Multiplication,
b. Associative Property of Addition

21. Which property is illustrated below?
(1)

a. $\dfrac{1}{2} \cdot \dfrac{1}{4} = \dfrac{1}{4} \cdot \dfrac{1}{2}$ **b.** $\dfrac{1}{3} + \left(\dfrac{2}{3} + \dfrac{1}{2}\right) = \left(\dfrac{1}{3} + \dfrac{2}{3}\right) + \dfrac{1}{2}$

22. Arrange in order from least to greatest.
(12)

$0.3, \dfrac{2}{5}, 35\%, 0, 1$ $0, 0.3, 35\%, \dfrac{2}{5}, 1$

23. Classify this triangle by side length and angle measure: scalene acute
(20)

Solve by inspection.

* 24. $2.2 = 2m + 0.2$ $m = 1$
(14, 24)

25. $\dfrac{4}{5} = 1 - r$ $r = \dfrac{1}{5}$
(10, 14)

26. $\dfrac{7}{20} = \dfrac{7}{10}h$ $h = \dfrac{1}{2}$
(10, 14)

27. $\dfrac{t + 3}{4} = 5$ $t = 17$
(10, 14)

Evaluate.

28. Find $b^2 - 4ac$ when $a = 4$, $b = 9$, $c = 5$.   1
(14, 20)

29. **Connections** Suspended objects such as apples in a tree or hailstones in a cloud have potential energy equal to their mass (m) times the acceleration of gravity (g) times their height (h). For the equation $E = mgh$, find E when $m = 2$, $g = 9.8$, and $h = 5$. $E = 98$
(14, 25)

▶* 30. **Analyze** In the figure, $\overline{AC}$ is 1 unit and $\overline{BC}$ is 2 units. Use the Pythagorean Theorem to find $\overline{AB}$. $\sqrt{5}$ units
(Inv. 1, Inv. 2)

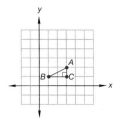

▶ See Math Conversations in the sidebar.

Looking Forward

Converting fractions to repeating decimals prepares students for:

- **Lesson 63,** working with rational numbers, non-terminating decimals, and percents.

- **Lesson 84,** selecting an appropriate rational number.

- **Lesson 110,** converting repeating decimals to fractions.

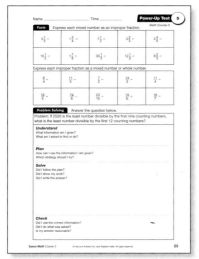

Assessment   30–40 minutes   For use after Lesson 30

Distribute **Cumulative Test 5** to each student. Two versions of the test are available in *Saxon Math Course 3 Course Assessments Book*. Have students complete the **Power-Up Test** first. Allow 10 minutes. Then have students work the 20 numbered items on the **Cumulative Test.** Students may use copies of the answer sheet to record their work. Track individual and class progress with the **Test Analysis** forms.

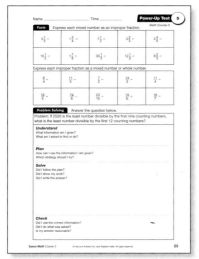

Power-Up Test 5

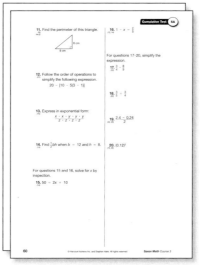

Cumulative Test 5A

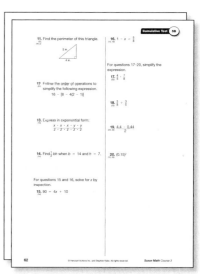

Alternative Cumulative Test 5B

Optional Answer Forms

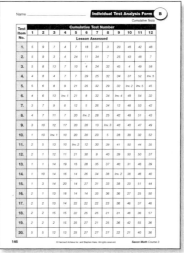

Individual Test Analysis Form

Class Test Analysis Form

Reteaching

Students who score below 80% on the assessment may be in need of reteaching. Look for the causes of student mistakes. If errors are conceptual, refer to the *Reteaching Masters* for reteaching.

Customized Benchmark Assessment

You can develop customized benchmark tests using the Test Generator located on the *Test & Practice Generator CD*.

This chart shows the lesson, the standard, and the test item question that can be found on the *Test & Practice Generator CD*.

LESSON	NEW CONCEPTS	LOCAL STANDARD	TEST ITEM ON CD
21	• Distributive Property		3.21.1
	• Order of Operations		3.21.1
22	• Multiplying and Dividing Fractions		3.22.1
23	• Multiplying and Dividing Mixed Numbers		3.23.1
24	• Adding and Subtracting Decimal Numbers		3.24.1
25	• Multiplying and Dividing Decimal Numbers		3.25.1
26	• Transformations		3.26.1
27	• Laws of Exponents		3.27.1
28	• Scientific Notation for Large Numbers		3.28.1
29	• Ratio		3.28.1
30	• Repeating Decimals		3.30.1

Using the Test Generator CD

• Develop tests in both English and Spanish.

• Choose from multiple-choice and free-response test items.

• Clone test items to create multiple versions of the same test.

• View and edit test items to make and save your own questions.

• Administer assessments through paper tests or over a school LAN.

• Monitor student progress through a variety of individual and class reports —for both diagnosing and assessing standards mastery.

Making Sense of Irrational Lengths
Assign after Lesson 30 and Test 5

Objectives
- Use a calculator to approximate irrational values.
- Use the Pythagorean Theorem to determine an irrational length.
- Draw right triangles with side lengths that are irrational numbers.
- Communicate ideas through writing.

Materials
Performance Tasks 5A and **5B**

Straight edge or ruler
Calculator

Preparation
Make copies of **Performance Tasks 5A** and **5B**. (One each per student.)

Time Requirement
30–45 minutes; Begin in class and complete at home.

Task
Explain to students that for this task they will be examining lengths expressed as irrational numbers by constructing right triangles with irrational lengths for the hypotenuses. To begin, students use their calculators to approximate several irrational numbers. Then students are led through the process of drawing right triangles to produce different irrational lengths for the hypotenuses. Point out that all necessary information is provided on **Performance Tasks 5A** and **5B.**

Criteria for Evidence of Learning
- Uses a calculator to correctly approximate the value of irrational numbers to eight decimal places.
- Generates correct irrational number lengths using the Pythagorean Theorem.
- Draws and constructs right triangles representing given irrational number lengths.
- Communicates ideas clearly through writing.

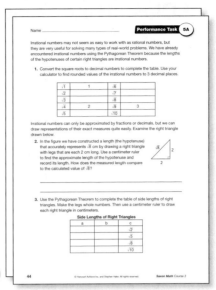

Performance Tasks 5A and 5B

National Council of Teachers of Mathematics (NCTM)

Numbers and Operations

NO.3a Select appropriate methods and tools for computing with fractions and decimals from among mental computation, estimation, calculators or computers, and paper and pencil, depending on the situation, and apply the selected methods

Geometry

GM.1c Create and critique inductive and deductive arguments concerning geometric ideas and relationships, such as congruence, similarity, and the Pythagorean relationship

GM.4a Draw geometric objects with specified properties, such as side lengths or angle measures

GM.4d Use geometric models to represent and explain numerical and algebraic relationships

Problem Solving

PS.1c Apply and adapt a variety of appropriate strategies to solve problems

Connections

CN.4b Understand how mathematical ideas interconnect and build on one another to produce a coherent whole

Focus on
• Classifying Quadrilaterals

Objectives
- Classify quadrilaterals by side lengths and by angle measures.
- Understand how different sets of quadrilaterals relate to one another.
- Use a Venn diagram to show relationships between sets.
- Identify an object's line(s) of symmetry.
- Find the order of rotational symmetry of various shapes.

Lesson Preparation

Materials
- Teacher-provided material: calculators

Math Language

New

parallelogram

reflective symmetry

rhombus

trapezoid

Venn diagram

Technology Resources

Student eBook Complete student textbook in electronic format.

Resources and Planner CD Assessment, reteaching, and instructional masters, plus a pacing calendar with standards.

Test and Practice Generator CD Create additional practice sheets and custom-made tests.

www.SaxonPublishers.com Visit for more student activities and planning materials.

Inclusion

Adaptations CD Adapted lessons, investigations, practice and assessments.

Meeting Standards

National Council of Teachers of Mathematics (NCTM)

Geometry

GM.1a Precisely describe, classify, and understand relationships among types of two- and three-dimensional objects using their defining properties

Communication

CM.3a Organize and consolidate their mathematical thinking through communication

CM.3c Analyze and evaluate the mathematical thinking and strategies of others

CM.3d Use the language of mathematics to express mathematical ideas precisely

Focus on
• Classifying Quadrilaterals

Recall that a four-sided polygon is called a quadrilateral. Refer to the quadrilaterals shown below to answer the problems that follow.

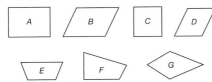

1. Which figures have two pairs of parallel sides?   *A, B, C, D*

2. Which figure has just one pair of parallel sides?   *E*

3. Which figures have no pairs of parallel sides?   *F, G*

One way to classify quadrilaterals is by the number of pairs of parallel sides. A quadrilateral with two pairs of parallel sides is called a **parallelogram.** Here we show four parallelograms. Notice that the sides that are parallel are the same length.

4. Which of the figures *A–G* are parallelograms?   *A, B, C, D*

A quadrilateral with one pair of parallel sides is a **trapezoid.** The figures shown below are trapezoids. Identify each pair of parallel sides. Notice that the parallel sides of a trapezoid are not the same length.

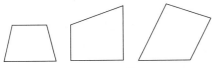

Thinking Skill

Explain

Does the length of the sides affect whether or not the sides are parallel? Explain.   No; no matter how long parallel sides are, they will never intersect.

5. Which of the figures *A–G* is a trapezoid?   *E*

If the non-parallel sides of a trapezoid are equal in length, then the trapezoid is called an **isosceles trapezoid.**

A quadrilateral with no pairs of parallel sides is called a **trapezium.** Below we show two examples. The figure on the right is called a **kite.** A kite has two pairs of adjacent sides of equal length.

Have students define *quadrilateral* using their own words. Then, ask students to find objects in the classroom that are shaped like quadrilaterals. In this lesson students will discuss both quadrilaterals and symmetry.

Instruction

As students identify each shape, have them sketch that shape on their papers. Have a volunteer work at the board.

Point out that on this page they are classifying quadrilaterals by whether they have parallel sides.

You may wish to tell students that sometimes definitions of math terms vary from country to country. For example, in the United States a *trapezium* is a "quadrilateral with no parallel sides." The British definition of a *trapezium* is "a quadrilateral with exactly one pair of parallel sides," which in the United States is called a *trapezoid.*

(continued)

Math Background

How are quadrilaterals classified?

Quadrilaterals are first classified (or sorted) by whether they possess parallel sides.

• Quadrilaterals with two pairs of parallel sides are parallelograms.

• Quadrilaterals with only one pair of parallel sides are trapezoids.

• Quadrilaterals with no parallel sides are trapeziums.

Parallelograms are further classified both by side lengths and angle size.

• If all the side lengths are equal, the parallelogram is a rhombus.

• If all the angles are right angles, the parallelogram is a rectangle.

• If all the side lengths are equal and all the angles are right angles, the parallelogram is a square.

Instruction

Point out that on this page parallelograms are further classified by their sides and angles. Again, have students sketch each shape as they identify it while a volunteer works at the board.

Math Conversations

Discussion opportunities are provided below.

Problem 6

Extend the Problem

"If four sticks are arranged to form a parallelogram, how can a kite be formed by moving only two sticks?" Sample: Reverse the positions of two adjacent sticks.

Instruction

Ask a volunteer to draw the Venn diagram on the board. Then ask students to explain the diagram using their own words.

"How can we show that all the figures are quadrilaterals?" Draw a big circle or oval around all the shapes.

Math Conversations

Discussion opportunities are provided below.

Problem 12 Conclude

"How are the rectangle (A) and the square (C) the same? How are they different?" Sample: both have 4 right angles; the square is also a rhombus because it has all sides the same length

(continued)

▶ **6.** Which of the figures *A–G* are trapeziums? Which is a kite? *F, G; G*

We have sorted figures *A–G* into three categories of quadrilaterals.

Quadrilaterals

Parallelograms (A, B, C, D)	Trapezoids (E)	Trapeziums (F, G)

We can further classify some types of parallelograms.

7. Which of the figures *A–G* have four right angles? *A, C*

A quadrilateral with four right angles is a special kind of parallelogram called a **rectangle.**

8. Which of the figures *A–G* have four sides of equal length? *C, D*

A quadrilateral with four equal-length sides is a specific kind of parallelogram called a **rhombus.**

9. Which figure in *A–G* is both a rectangle and a rhombus? *C*

A figure that is both a rectangle and a rhombus is a **square.** This Venn Diagram illustrates the relationship among parallelograms. A **Venn diagram** is a diagram that uses overlapping circles to represent the relationships among sets.

Thinking Skill

Classify

Nita's polygon had four sides of equal length and no right angles. Sketch a quadrilateral Nita might have drawn. Use the Venn diagram to classify it. Students should sketch a rhombus that is not a square; rhombus

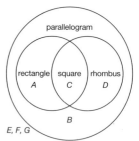

Refer to the Venn diagram and to figures *A–G* to answer questions **10–14.**

10. Which figure is a parallelogram but not a rectangle or a rhombus? *B*

11. Which figure is a parallelogram and a rhombus but not a rectangle? *D*

▶ **12.** *Conclude* Which figure is a parallelogram and a rectangle but not a rhombus? *A*

13. Which figure is a parallelogram, a rectangle, and a rhombus? *C*

▶ See Math Conversations in the sidebar.

Teacher Tip

Point out that baseball is played on what is commonly referred to as a *diamond*, which is a word often used to refer to a *rhombus*. Ask students to think about **baseball diamonds** they have seen and determine whether a baseball diamond is also a rhombus.

Each of these figures is a rhombus.

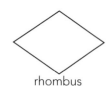

square   square   rhombus

A baseball diamond is a square, so it is also a rhombus.

14. *E, F, G;*
Figures *E, F,* and *G* are not parallelograms because they do not have two pairs of parallel sides.

▶ **14.** *Explain* Which figures on the Venn diagram are not parallelograms? Explain why the figures are not parallelograms.

One special type of rectangle identified by ancient Greeks and found frequently in art and architecture is the "Golden Rectangle." The ratio of the sides of a golden rectangle is not a rational number. If the width is 1, then the length is $1 + \frac{1}{2}(\sqrt{5} - 1)$. Here is an example of a golden rectangle:

If we draw a segment through a golden rectangle to form a square in the rectangle, we also form a smaller golden rectangle.

That is, the original rectangle and the smaller rectangle are similar. Therefore, the process of dividing can continue indefinitely.

All the rectangles that are formed are similar.

15. With a calculator, find the length of the largest golden rectangle shown above to the nearest tenth.   1.6

16. What are some whole number pairs of side lengths that form rectangles that approximate a golden rectangle?   Samples: 10 by 16, 5 by 8

A student made a model of a rectangle out of straws and pipe cleaners (Figure J). Then the student shifted the sides so that two angles became obtuse and two angles became acute (Figure K).

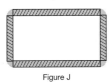
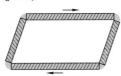

Figure J   Figure K

▶ See Math Conversations in the sidebar.

Manipulative Use

Create a rhombus using four straws of equal length and pipe cleaners to demonstrate the various forms a rhombus may take.

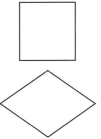

- A rhombus with four right angles is called a square.
- All other rhombuses have two sets of opposite angles that are equal, one set being acute, the other set being obtuse.

Math Conversations
Discussion opportunities are provided below.

Problem 14 *Explain*
Extend the Problem
"Can you draw a trapezoid with a right angle? If so, sketch one." Yes; Sample:

Instruction
Give students an opportunity to make their own model using a pipe cleaner, 2 short straws, and 2 long straws to demonstrate the changes from figure J to figure K.

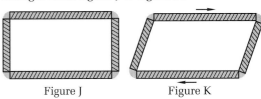

Figure J   Figure K

Ask students how they could support their answers, eliciting ideas such as measuring the sides. Then students can compute the perimeter and area of each figure.

(continued)

Problem 20 `Analyze`

As students manipulate their straw rectangles, ask them why the area is becoming less if the sides are not changing in length. The sides are moving closer together, so the area must be decreasing.

Problem 25 `Model`

Ask students to stand up. Then call out instructions such as,

"Turn 90° clockwise."

Continue until students are able to make turns of varying degrees: 90°, 180°, 270°, 360°.

Problem 27 `Verify`

Point out that the sum of the angle measures of all quadrilaterals is 360°. Ask students to use a protractor to verify the sum of the angle measures of any quadrilateral.

Instruction

The two kinds of symmetry covered in this investigation are *reflective symmetry*, often called line symmetry, and *rotational symmetry*.

Have students work together to devise a way to fold and cut an 8.5 in. × 11 in. sheet of paper into a square.

Fold this corner down.　　Cut this section off.

"What kind of triangle have you formed?"
a right isoceles triangle

"If you unfold the triangle, what shape will you see?" square

Have students fold the square along its other lines of symmetry.

(continued)

Refer to figures J and K from the previous page to answer problems **17–27**.

17. Is figure K a rectangle? Is figure K a parallelogram?　no, yes

18. Did the lengths of the sides change when the angles changed?　no

19. Does the perimeter of figure K equal the perimeter of figure J?　yes

▶ 20. Does the area of figure K equal the area of figure J?　no

21. As the sides of figure K are shifted and the obtuse angles become large and the acute angles smaller, in what way does the area change? The area becomes less as the angles change from 90°.

22. The four angles of figure J total how many degrees? How do you know?

23. What is the sum of the measures of the four angles of figure K?　360°

24. How many degrees is a full turn?　360°

▶ 25. If you trace with your eraser figures J or K, you will find your eraser heading in a direction opposite to the direction it started after tracing two angles. This means your eraser has finished half of a turn. How many degrees is half a turn?　180°

26. In figure K, the measure of an obtuse angle and an acute angle together total how many degrees?　180°

▶ 27. If an obtuse angle of figure K measures 100°, what does an acute angle measure?　80°

28. Figure *ABCD* is a parallelogram. Angle *A* measures 70°. What does ∠*B* measure?　110°

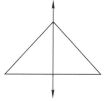

29. In parallelogram *ABCD*, ∠*A* measures 70°, what does ∠*D* measure?　110°

30. Use the information you found in questions 28 and 29 to find the measure of ∠*C*.　70°

A figure has **reflective symmetry** if it can be divided in half by a line so that the halves are mirror images of each other. The triangle in the illustration below has reflective symmetry.

The line that divides the triangle into mirror images is a **line of symmetry.**

22. The four angles total 360°, because right angles measure 90°, and 4 × 90° = 360°

▶ See Math Conversations in the sidebar.

Manipulative Use

Suggest that students **make a parallelogram** by matching one pair of opposite corners of an 8.5 in. by 11 in. sheet of paper together. Then have them crease the paper on the fold and cut off the overlap.

Fold this corner down to meet the opposite corner.

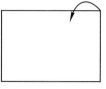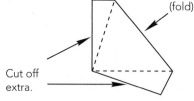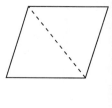

(fold)

Cut off extra.

They can then unfold the paper to find a parallelogram that is not a rectangle.

Some quadrilaterals have one or more lines of symmetry. Trace figures *A, B, C,* and *D,* from the beginning of the lesson and sketch their lines of symmetry.

31. Figure *A* has how many lines of symmetry?   2

32. Figure *B* has how many lines of symmetry?   0

33. Figure *C* has how many lines of symmetry?   4

34. Figure *D* has how many lines of symmetry?   2

35. Does a line of symmetry for figure *A* pass through sides or angles? sides

36. Does a line of symmetry for figure *D* pass through sides or angles? angles

37. Does a line of symmetry for figure *C* pass through sides or angles? Both sides and angles

A figure has **rotational symmetry** if, as the figure turns, its original image reappears in less than a full turn. For example, as we rotate a square, its original image reappears every quarter (90°) turn.

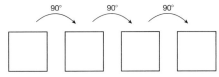

Since the original image appears four times in a full turn we say that a square has rotational symmetry of order four.

▶ **Predict**   Refer to figures *A–G* and state whether the following figures have rotational symmetry. If a figure has rotational symmetry, state its order.

38. Figure *A*
yes, order 2

39. Figure *B*
yes, order 2

40. Figure *D*
yes, order 2

41. Figure *E*
no

42. Figure *F*
no

43. Figure *G*
no

▶ See Math Conversations in the sidebar.

Instruction
Draw a capital S on the overhead. Slowly rotate the sheet and stop at 90°.

"Does the letter look the same as it did in the original position?" no

Continue to rotate it and stop again at 180°. After stopping at 270° and then 360°, summarize the activity.

"The letter S has rotational symmetry of order 2 because the original image appears 2 times in a full turn."

Draw a capital H, and U on the chalkboard.

"Do both letters have reflective symmetry? How many lines?" Yes; H, 2 lines; U, 1 line

"Do both letters have rotational symmetry? What order?" No; H, order 2; U, none

Math Conversations
Discussion opportunities are provided below.

Problems 38–43 *Predict*
"Other than the letter H, can you think of another letter of the alphabet that has both reflective and rotational symmetry?" the letters I, O, X

Looking Forward

Investigating classifying quadrilaterals prepares students for:

• **Lesson 37,** areas of combined polygons.

• **Investigation 4,** drawing geometric solids.

• **Lesson 75,** area of a trapezoid.

Lesson Planner

LESSON	NEW CONCEPTS	MATERIALS	RESOURCES
31	• Adding Integers • Collecting Like Terms	none	Power Up G Lesson Activity 5
32	• Probability	Manipulative Kit: dot cubes	Power Up G
33	• Subtracting Integers	none	Power Up G
34	• Proportions • Ratio Word Problems	none	Power Up G
35	• Similar and Congruent Polygons	none	Power Up G
36	• Multiplying and Dividing Integers • Multiplying and Dividing Terms	Calculators	Power Up H
37	• Areas of Combined Polygons	none	Power Up H
38	• Using Properties of Equality to Solve Equations	none	Power Up H
39	• Circumference of a Circle	Calculators	Power Up H
40	• Area of a Circle	none	Power Up H
Inv. 4	• Drawing Geometric Solids	Manipulative Kit: inch rulers Unlined paper, grid paper	none

Problem Solving

Strategies

- **Find a Pattern**   Lessons 37, 40
- **Guess and Check**   Lesson 35
- **Make a Table**   Lessons 33, 40
- **Make an Organized List**   Lesson 38
- **Make It Simpler**   Lessons 31, 32
- **Use Logical Reasoning**   Lessons 34, 35, 36, 37
- **Draw a Diagram**   Lessons 34, 38, 39
- **Work Backwards**   Lesson 35
- **Write an Equation**   Lessons 31, 32, 38

Real-World Applications

pp. 204, 207–209, 214, 215, 217–222, 224,
226–228, 233, 234, 236–238, 242, 243, 245,
248–250, 253–256, 259–261,
263, 265–267, 269, 270

4-Step Process

Student Edition   Lessons 31, 38
Teacher Edition   Lessons 31–40
   (Power-Up Discussions)

Communication

Discuss

pp. 206, 259, 266

Explain

pp. 227, 258

Connections

Math and Other Subjects

- **Math and Architecture**   p. 233
- **Math and Art**   pp. 208, 221
- **Math and Geography**   p. 228
- **Math and History**   pp. 208, 260
- **Math and Science**   pp. 208, 216, 220, 228, 248, 256, 262
- **Math and Sports**   pp. 214, 249

Math to Math

- **Problem Solving and Measurement**   Lessons 31–40
- **Algebra and Problem Solving**   Lessons 31, 32, 34, 36, 38
- **Fractions, Percents, Decimals, and Problem Solving**   Lessons 31–40
- **Fractions and Measurement**   Lessons 31–35, 38
- **Measurement and Geometry**   Lessons 31–40
- **Proportional Relationships and Geometry**   Lessons 31, 33-35, 37, 38, 40
- **Algebra, Measurement, and Geometry**   Lessons 31–33, 35, 37–40
- **Probability and Statistics**   Lessons 32–35, 37–40

Representation

Manipulatives/Hands On

pp. 214, 240, 246, 247, 259, 260, 269

Model

pp. 207, 219, 228, 256, 268

Represent

pp. 215, 242

Technology

Student Resources

- **eBook**   Anytime
- **Calculator**   Lessons 36, 37, 39
- **Online Resources** at
  www.SaxonPublishers.com/ActivitiesC3
     Graphing Calculator Activities   Lessons 33, 36
     Real-World Investigation 2   after Lesson 34

Teacher Resources

- **Resources and Planner CD**
- **Adaptations CD**   Lessons 31–40
- **Test & Practice Generator CD**
- **eGradebook**
- **Answer Key CD**

These lessons focus on algebraic and proportional thinking. Operations and integers are key topics for these lessons. Proportions are used for solving both ratio problems and geometric problems.

Algebraic Thinking

The operations used in the first 30 lessons now shift from numbers to algebraic terms.

In Lesson 31 students add integers and collect like terms. In Lesson 33 students learn an algebraic method for subtracting integers. And in Lesson 36 students multiply and divide integers and algebraic terms. These skills are used to solve equations in Lesson 38 when students begin employing inverse operations to solve equations. Students will further develop these skills in later lessons.

Problem Solving and Proportional Thinking

A visual organizer helps students translate a ratio problem and set up a proportion.

Ratio and proportion are emphasized in these lessons. Probability is introduced as a ratio in Lesson 32. Students identify and solve proportions in Lesson 34 and use proportions to solve ratio problems. Students work with similar polygons, which have proportional relationships, in Lesson 35. And pi, the ratio of the circumference to the diameter of a circle, is used in Lessons 39 to calculate circumferences and in Lesson 40 to calculate areas.

Geometry and Measurement

Spatial thinking and measurement skills come together in these lessons.

After classifying quadrilaterals in Investigation 3, students develop additional geometric concepts in these lessons including similarity, congruence, scale, and pi. Students calculate circumferences and areas of circles, and in Lesson 36 they divide and find the areas of complex polygons. In Investigation 4 students learn different techniques for drawing geometric solids.

Assessment

A variety of weekly assessment tools are provided.

After Lesson 35:
- Power-Up Test 6
- Cumulative Test 6
- Performance Activity 6

After Lesson 40:
- Power-Up Test 7
- Cumulative Test 7
- Customized Benchmark Test
- Performance Task 7

LESSON	NEW CONCEPTS	PRACTICED	ASSESSED
31	• Adding Integers	Lessons 31, 33, 34, 35, 40, 41, 44, 46, 48, 52, 54, 55, 56, 57, 59, 60, 70, 72, 79, 84, 87, 91	Tests 7, 9, 10, 14, 19
	• Collecting Like Terms	Lessons 31, 34, 35, 38, 41, 43, 46, 48, 49, 52, 53, 55, 56, 57, 58, 59, 61, 120	Tests 10–12, 14, 16, 17, 19
32	• Probability	Lessons 32, 34, 35, 36, 37, 38, 39, 40, 41, 42, 43, 44, 46, 49, 51, 53, 57, 58, 59, 62, 63, 64, 65, 67, 68, 69, 71, 72, 79, 80, 93, 94, 95	Tests 7–9, 11–14, 16, 19
33	• Subtracting Integers	Lessons 33, 34, 35, 40, 41, 42, 44, 48, 51, 54, 56, 58, 64, 66, 70, 90, 97, 104, 110, 111	Tests 7, 8, 17
34	• Proportions	Lessons 36, 37, 42, 43, 45, 54, 55, 78, 97	Tests 7, 8
	• Ratio Word Problems	Lessons 34, 35, 36, 38, 39, 40, 44, 98, 109	Tests 7–9
35	• Similar and Congruent Polygons	Lessons 35, 41, 42, 44, 46, 47, 50, 51, 54, 55, 56, 58, 59, 61, 64, 67, 69, 70, 71, 72, 74, 75, 76, 81, 82, 85, 110, 120	Tests 7, 12
36	• Multiplying and Dividing Integers	Lessons 36, 38, 39, 40, 44, 46, 47, 48, 49, 50, 51, 52, 53, 54, 55, 56, 57, 59, 60, 62, 66, 68, 71, 73, 75, 76, 79, 81, 83, 85, 86, 87, 88, 89, 91, 92, 93, 98, 100, 101, 102, 104, 109, 110, 111, 114, 116, 117, 118, 119, 120	Tests 8, 9, 12, 14, 17, 20, 22, 23
	• Multiplying and Dividing Terms	Lessons 37, 38, 40, 41, 47, 49, 51, 53, 55, 56, 57, 58, 59, 67, 89, 101, 102, 118, 119, 120	Tests 9, 11, 12
37	• Areas of Combined Polygons	Lessons 37, 39, 40, 41, 44, 47, 54, 55, 58, 59, 62, 64, 66, 69, 70, 71, 72, 73, 114	Tests 8, 10–12
38	• Using Properties of Equality to Solve Equations	Lessons 38, 39, 40, 41, 43, 44, 45, 46, 47, 48, 49, 53, 54, 58, 59, 61, 62, 63, 64, 66, 74, 75, 76, 77, 78, 79, 81, 82, 83, 84, 85, 86, 87, 88, 90, 92, 104	Tests 8–10
39	• Circumference of a Circle	Lessons 39, 40, 41, 43, 44, 45, 46, 47, 48, 49, 50, 52, 53, 56, 57, 58, 59, 61, 62, 63, 64, 65, 67, 88, 104, 112	Tests 8–10, 12, 14
40	• Area of a Circle	Lessons 40, 41, 43, 44, 45, 46, 48, 50, 51, 52, 53, 54, 55, 56, 57, 58, 59, 61, 63, 64, 66, 68, 74, 81, 83, 88, 89, 91, 92, 93, 94, 95, 97, 98, 101, 104, 111, 113, 116, 120	Tests 8–12, 14
Inv. 4	• Drawing Geometric Solids	Lessons 42, 43, 45, 49, 51, 52, 54, 55, 57, 62, 64, 65, 74, 78, 86, 89, 92, 94, 96, 101, 103, 106	Test 9

• Adding Integers
• Collecting Like Terms

Objectives
- Adding integers with the same and with opposite signs.
- Apply the addition of integers to problem-solving situations.
- Model the addition of integers on a number line.
- Recognize the additive inverse of a number.

Lesson Preparation

Materials
- **Power Up G** (in *Instructional Masters*)

Optional
- **Lesson Activity 5** (in *Instructional Masters*)

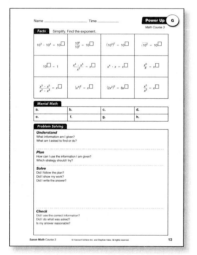

Power Up G

Math Language

New	Maintain
additive inverse	absolute value
	subtrahend

Technology Resources

Student eBook Complete student textbook in electronic format.

Resources and Planner CD Assessment, reteaching, and instructional masters, plus a pacing calendar with standards.

Test and Practice Generator CD Create additional practice sheets and custom-made tests.

www.SaxonPublishers.com Visit for more student activities and planning materials.

Inclusion

Adaptations CD Adapted lessons, investigations, practice and assessments.

Meeting Standards

National Council of Teachers of Mathematics (NCTM)

Numbers and Operations

NO.1g Develop meaning for integers and represent and compare quantities with them

NO.2a Understand the meaning and effects of arithmetic operations with fractions, decimals, and integers

NO.2c Understand and use the inverse relationships of addition and subtraction, multiplication and division, and squaring and finding square roots to simplify computations and solve problems

Algebra

AL.2d Recognize and generate equivalent forms for simple algebraic expressions and solve linear equations

Problem-Solving Strategy: Write an Equation/Make It Simpler

A rectangle has a length of 10 meters and a width of 8 meters. A second rectangle has a length of 6 meters and a width of 4 meters, and overlaps the first rectangle as shown. What is the difference between the areas of the two non-overlapping regions of the two rectangles?

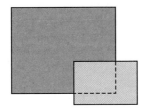

Understand We have been given the dimensions of two rectangles that overlap. We haven't been given the dimensions of the overlapping area, but have been asked to find the difference between the two NON-OVERLAPPING regions of the two rectangles.

Plan We will use the equation for the area of a rectangle ($A = l \times w$). We will need to subtract the overlapping area from each rectangle, and then subtract the remaining areas of each. We will make it simpler by drawing diagrams of the extremes to to see if there is any sort of pattern.

Solve The two extremes of this problem are:
1. None of the smaller rectangle overlaps the larger rectangle.
2. All of the smaller rectangle overlaps the larger rectangle.

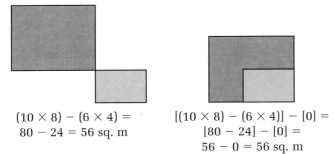

$$(10 \times 8) - (6 \times 4) =$$
$$80 - 24 = 56 \text{ sq. m}$$

$$[(10 \times 8) - (6 \times 4)] - [0] =$$
$$[80 - 24] - [0] =$$
$$56 - 0 = 56 \text{ sq. m}$$

In both cases, the difference of the areas of the non-overlapping regions is 56 sq. m

Check To verify the solution is always going to be 56 sq. m, we can create a simple example of an area of overlap:

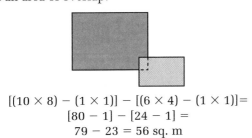

$$[(10 \times 8) - (1 \times 1)] - [(6 \times 4) - (1 \times 1)] =$$
$$[80 - 1] - [24 - 1] =$$
$$79 - 23 = 56 \text{ sq. m}$$

As the smaller rectangle slides into the larger rectangle, the same amount of area is subtracted from both the larger and the smaller rectangles, resulting in no difference of their non-overlapping areas.

Facts

Distribute **Power Up G** to students. See answers below.

Mental Math

Encourage students to share different ways to mentally compute these exercises. Strategies for exercises **c** and **f** are listed below.

c. Use a Fraction

$75\% = \frac{3}{4}$

$\frac{3}{4} \times \$200 = 3 \times 50 = \$150$

Use Math Sense

75% of $100 = $75

75% of $200 = $75 + $75 = $150

f. Use Complementary Angles

$51° + x° = 90°$

$x° = 90° - 51°$

$x° = 39°$

Use Supplementary Angles

$90° + 51° + x° = 180°$

$x° = 180° - (90° + 51°)$

$x° = 180° - 141°$

$x° = 39°$

Problem Solving

Refer to **Power-Up Discussion**, p. 202B.

• **Adding Integers**
• **Collecting Like Terms**

Power Up | *Building Power*

facts | Power Up G

mental math

a. Number Sense: Seventeen people have $200 each. How much money do they have altogether? $3400

b. Fractions: $\frac{5}{4} = \frac{25}{x}$ 20

c. Fractional Parts: 75% of $200 $150

d. Measurement: How long is the paperclip? If 10 paperclips are placed end to end, how far would they reach?   3.1 cm, 31 cm

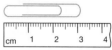

e. Rate: If the space shuttle orbits earth 16 times a day, how many times does it orbit in $2\frac{1}{2}$ days?   40

f. Geometry: Find x

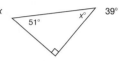

g. Powers/Roots: Estimate $\sqrt{99} - \sqrt{80}$.   10 − 9 = 1

h. Calculation: $45 - 40, \times 2, + 1, \times 6, - 2, \sqrt{\ }, \times 3, + 1, \sqrt{\ }, - 10$ −5

problem solving

A rectangle has a length of 10 meters and a width of 8 meters. A second rectangle has a length of 6 meters and a width of 4 meters, and overlaps the first rectangle as shown. What is the difference between the areas of the two non-overlapping regions of the two rectangles?

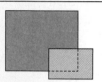

(**Understand**)   We have been given the dimensions of two rectangles that overlap. We have not been given the dimensions of the overlapping area, but have been asked to find the difference between the two **non-overlapping** regions of the two rectangles.

(**Plan**)   We will use the equation for the area of a rectangle ($A = l \times w$). We will need to subtract the overlapping area from the area of each rectangle, and then subtract the remaining areas of each. We will make it simpler by drawing diagrams of the extremes to see if there is any sort of pattern.

Facts | Simplify. Find the exponent.

$10^3 \cdot 10^4 = 10^{\boxed{7}}$	$\frac{10^6}{10^2} = 10^{\boxed{4}}$	$(10^3)^2 = 10^{\boxed{6}}$	$\sqrt{10^2} = 10^{\boxed{1}}$
$10^{\boxed{0}} = 1$	$\frac{x^4 \cdot x^5}{x^3} = x^{\boxed{6}}$	$x^4 \cdot x = x^{\boxed{5}}$	$\frac{x^6}{x} = x^{\boxed{5}}$
$\frac{x^3 \cdot x^5}{x^2 \cdot x^4} = x^{\boxed{2}}$	$(x^4)^2 = x^{\boxed{8}}$	$(2x^2)^3 = 8x^{\boxed{6}}$	$\frac{x^3}{x^2} = x^{\boxed{1}}$

Solve The two extremes of this problem are:

1. None of the smaller rectangle overlaps the larger rectangle.

2. All of the smaller rectangle overlaps the larger rectangle.

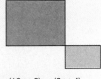

$(10 \times 8) - (6 \times 4) =$ $[(10 \times 8) - (6 \times 4)] - [0] =$
$80 - 24 = 56$ sq. m $[80 - 24] - [0] =$
                              $56 - 0 = 56$ sq. m

In both cases, the difference of the areas of the non-overlapping regions is 56 sq. m.

Check To verify that the solution is always going to be 56 sq. m, we can create a simple example of an area of overlap:

$[(10 \times 8) - (1 \times 1)] - [(6 \times 4) - (1 \times 1)] =$
$[80 - 1] - [24 - 1] =$
$79 - 23 = 56$ sq. m

As the smaller rectangle slides into the larger rectangle, the same amount of area is subtracted from both the larger and the smaller rectangles, resulting in no difference of their non-overlapping areas.

New Concepts   *Increasing Knowledge*

**adding
integers**

Recall that integers include the counting numbers (1, 2, 3, ...), the opposites of the counting numbers (..., −3, −2, −1), and zero. In this lesson we show examples of adding integers.

We see integers on thermometers. On the Celsius scale, 0° marks the freezing temperature of water. Negative numbers indicate temperatures below freezing. Positive numbers indicate temperatures above freezing.

Instruction

Explain that four operations of arithmetic can be done with integers. Addition is studied first because much of what we learn about addition can be applied to the other operations.

Point out that another example of integers in everyday life is the way that score is sometimes kept in golf—the scores are recorded as the number of strokes above or below par, where *par* is the number of strokes considered to be the standard for a hole when played by an expert.

(continued)

2 New Concepts (Continued)

Example 1
Instruction

It may be helpful to draw a vertical number line as a model for a thermometer as you work through this example.

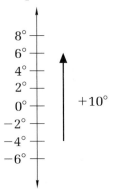

Example 2
Instruction

You might use another vertical number line to show Sam's financial situation.

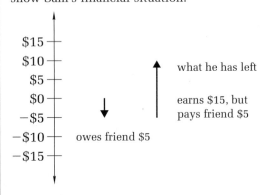

Instruction

Use **Lesson Activity 5** Number Lines to demonstrate the three examples or draw number lines on the board.

If necessary during this discussion, review the meaning of absolute value.

Ask how number sentence C is different from number sentences A and B. Both addends have the same sign. Then discuss how the answers to the bulleted questions for number sentence C are different from those for number sentences A and B.

(continued)

204 **Saxon** *Math Course 3*

Example 1

If the temperature in the morning is −4 degrees but increases 10 degrees by noon, then what is the noontime temperature?

Solution

Counting up 10 degrees from −4, we find that the noontime temperature is **6 degrees above zero.**

$$-4 + 10 = 6$$

Another application of positive and negative numbers is debt and credit. A debt is recorded as a negative number and a credit as a positive number.

Example 2

Sam has no money and owes a friend $5. If Sam earns $15 washing cars, then he can repay his friend and have money left over. Write an equation for this situation and find how much money Sam has after he repays his friend.

Solution

We show Sam's debt as −5 and Sam's earnings as +15.

$$-5 + 15 = 10$$

Sam has **$10** after he pays his friend.

We can show the addition of integers on a number line. We start at zero. Positive integers are indicated by arrows to the right and negative integers by arrows to the left. Here we show three examples.

A. $(-3) + (+5) = (+2)$

B. $(+3) + (-5) = (-2)$

C. $(-5) + (-3) = -8$

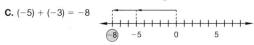

Look at number sentences **A** and **B** above and answer these questions:

- Do the addends have the same sign or opposite signs?   opposite
- How can we determine whether the sign of the sum will be positive or negative?   The answer will take the sign of the addend with the greater absolute value.
- How can we determine the number of the sum?   subtract the addends

Now look at number sentence **C** and answer the same three questions. Then try completing the exercises in example 3 before reading the solution.

Example 3

Find each sum.

a. $(-6) + (+2)$ b. $(+6) + (-2)$

c. $(-6) + (-2)$ d. $(-6) + (+6)$

Solution

Math Language
Recall that the **absolute value** of a number is its distance from 0 on the number line.

a. The signs of the addends are not the same. The number with the greater absolute value is negative, so the sum is negative. The difference of the absolute values is 4, so the sum is **−4.**

b. The signs are different. The number with the greater absolute value is positive. The difference of the absolute values is 4. The sum is positive **4.**

c. The signs are the same and negative, so the sum is **−8.**

d. The numbers are opposites. The sum of opposites is **0.**

Math Language
Recall that the **subtrahend** is the number being subtracted.

Recall that the opposite of a number is also called the **additive inverse.** We can change any subtraction problem into an addition problem by adding the opposite of the subtrahend. For example, instead of subtracting 2 from 6, we can add −2 to 6.

$$6 - 2 = 4 \qquad \text{Subtract 2 from 6.}$$
$$6 + (-2) = 4 \qquad \text{Or add } -2 \text{ to 6.}$$

We use this concept to change subtraction of integers to addition of integers.

Addition with Two Integers

> To find the sum of addends with different signs:
>
> **1.** Subtract the absolute values of the addends.
>
> **2.** Take the sign of the addend with the greater absolute value.
>
> To find the sum of addends with the same sign:
>
> **1.** Add the absolute values of the addends.
>
> **2.** Take the sign of the addends.

collecting like terms

An algebraic **term** is an expression that includes a positive or negative number and may include one or more variables.

Here are some examples of terms:

$$3y, \ x, \ -w^2, \ 3x^2y, \ -2$$

The number part of a term is called its **numerical coefficient** or just coefficient for short. Each of the first four terms has a coefficient that is a positive or negative number.

The coefficient of $3y$ is $+3$.

The numerical coefficient of x is $+1$.

The numerical coefficient of $-w^2$ is -1.

The coefficient of $3x^2y$ is $+3$.

Notice that if the coefficient is 1, it is not written. It is understood to be 1. A term without a variable, such as -2, is called a constant.

Lesson 31   205

Example 3
Instruction

Use the *Math Language* feature to review absolute value if you have not already done so. Ask students to describe the sum when both signs are the same and the numbers are positive. Sample: The numbers are added and the sign is positive.

Instruction

Call attention to the chart. Tell students that these rules must be learned and that rules for the other operations will be added to them in future lessons.

Point out that the negative signs in these terms do not indicate subtraction. They indicate that the numerical coefficient is a negative number.

(continued)

Math Background

Do the rules for adding integers apply to non-integers as well?

"Yes. The rules apply to all real numbers. Consider $(+1.7) + (-4.8)$. The addend -4.8 has the greater absolute value, so the sum is negative. The difference of the absolute values is 3.1, so the sum is -3.1. Now, consider $(-\frac{2}{3}) + (-\frac{1}{4})$. The signs are the same and negative, so the sum is $-\frac{11}{12}$."

Example 4

Instruction

If these three exercises do not provide enough practice for your students, give more by using these terms: $-4x$, $3y^2$, xyz, $-2vt^4$. -4, 3, 1, -2

Instruction

Have students compare the two *like terms*, describing how they are similar and different. Sample: One is negative and the other is positive. They have x and y in them but not the same order. Then explain why they are called like terms. Repeat this procedure for the *unlike terms*.

Use the *Discuss* question to clarify understanding of like and unlike terms. Point out that the numerical coefficients including those that are understood to be 1 tell us how many of each like term we have.

Example 5

Instruction

Use the *Justify* question to help students see why the Commutative Property of Addition can be used to rearrange terms that involve subtraction. It may help students understand how this works if the given expression is rewritten so that it contains only addition signs:

$3x + 2 + (-x) + 3$ Given expression

$3x + (-x) + 2 + 3$ Commutative Property of Addition

(continued)

Example 4

Identify the numerical coefficient of each of these terms.

a. a^2b b. $3y$ c. $-x^2$

Solution

a. $+1$

b. $+3$

c. -1

We can identify like terms by looking at the variables. **Like terms** have identical variable parts, including exponents. The variables may appear in any order.

Like terms: $-5xy$ and yx

Unlike terms: $2xy$ and $-5x^2y$

Discuss Why are $-5xy$ and yx like terms? Why are $2xy$ and $-5x^2y$ unlike terms?

We combine or "collect" like terms by adding their numerical coefficients. The variables do not change.

Step:	Justification:
$-5xy + yx$	Given expression
$-5xy + 1xy$	Express $+yx$ as $+1xy$
$-4xy$	Combined terms ($-5 + 1 = -4$)

xy and yx are like terms because the Commutative Property of Multiplication lets us reorder the terms. xy and x^2y are not like terms because even though the variables are the same, the exponents are different.

Example 5

Simplify this expression by collecting like terms.

$$3x + 2 - x + 3$$

Solution

Thinking Skill

Justify

The Commutative Property of Addition does not apply to subtraction. Why can we use the Commutative Property of Addition to rearrange the terms in this expression that includes subtraction?

Using the commutative property, we rearrange the terms. (The sign moves with the term.)

Step:	Justification:
$3x + 2 - x + 3$	Given expression
$3x - x + 2 + 3$	Commutative Property of Addition

We combine the terms $3x - x$ (which is $3x - 1x$). We also combine the $+2$ and $+3$.

$2x + 5$	Added

$-x$ means the same as $+(-x)$, and the Commutative Property of Addition can be applied to $+(-x)$.

Example 6

What is the perimeter of this rectangle?

Solution

We add the lengths of the four sides.

Step:	Justification:
$P = 2x + 3 + 2x + 3$	Added four sides
$= 2x + 2x + 3 + 3$	Commutative Property of Addition
$= 4x + 6$	Collected like terms

Practice Set

Simplify:

▶ **a.** $(-12) + (-3)$ -15

▶ **b.** $(-12) + (+3)$ -9

▶ **c.** $(+12) + (-3)$ 9

▶ **d.** $(-3) + (+12)$ 9

▶ **e.** (*Model*) Choose any of the problems **a–d.** Show the operation on a number line.   Answers will vary depending on which exercise is chosen.

f. At 6:00 a.m. the temperature was $-12°C$. By noon the temperature increased 8 degrees. Write an equation for this situation and find the temperature at noon. $(-12) + (+8) = -4; -4°C$

g. The hikers started on the desert floor, 182 feet below sea level. After an hour of hiking they had climbed 1,018 ft. Write an equation for the situation and find the hikers' elevation after an hour of hiking.
$-182 + 1018 = 836; 836$ ft above sea level

Collect like terms:

h. $3x + 2xy + xy - x$ $2x + 3xy$

i. $6x^2 - x + 2x + 1$ $6x^2 + x - 1$

j. $2a^3 + 3b - a^3 - 4b$ $a^3 - b$

k. $x + y - 1 - x + y + 1$ $2y$

l. $P = L + W + L + W$ $P = 2L + 2W$

m. $P = s + s + s + s$ $P = 4s$

n. (*Connect*) What is the perimeter of this rectangle? $2x + 6y$ or $6y + 2x$

▶ See Math Conversations in the sidebar.

---

2 New Concepts (Continued)

Example 6
Instruction
You may want to show students that the answer will be the same if you use another formula for the perimeter of a rectangle.

$$P = 2(l + w)$$
$$P = 2(2x + 3)$$
$$P = 4x + 6$$

Have students notice that the answer is the same but that the like terms did not need to be collected.

Practice Set
Problems a–d (Error Alert)
Students who find the sum or difference of the absolute values before naming the sign of the answer may forget to write the sign. Encourage these students to write the sign of the answer before adding or subtracting absolute values.

To help students better understand integer sums, invite volunteers to describe the different steps they followed to complete each computation.

Problem e (Model)
One way for students to check their answers for problems a–d is to use a number line to check all four computations.

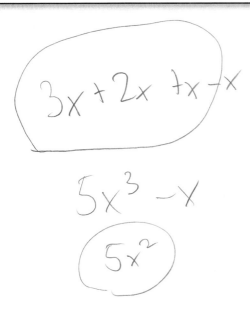

3 Written Practice

Math Conversations

Discussion opportunities are provided below.

Problem 1 Analyze

Remind students that a good way to check an exact answer is to compare that answer to an estimate.

"Explain how we could estimate the amount of money Troy should receive." Sample: 45¢ is a little less than 50¢, or one-half of a dollar, so Troy should receive a little less than $27, which is $\frac{1}{2}$ of $54.

Problem 2 Analyze

"Explain how decimals and improper fractions can each be used to solve this problem." Find the product of 4.25 and 2.5, and reduce the product of $\frac{17}{4}$ and $\frac{5}{2}$ to lowest terms.

Ask students to choose one method and use it to solve the problem, and then use the other method to check their work.

Problem 3 Analyze

After completing the problem, challenge students to explain why the sum of the percents is not 100. Other gases are present in our atmosphere.

Problem 4 Conclude

Extend the Problem

Students should note that when the dimensions of a rectangle are increased by a scale factor of 2 (in other words, doubled), the perimeter of the rectangle doubles, but the area of the rectangle increases by a factor of *four*.

To help recognize this relationship, invite students to compute and then compare the perimeter and the area of each rectangle.

Problem 14 Conclude

Ask several students to give one or two examples to support their answer.

Problem 16 Evaluate

"In the formula W = mg, what operation does mg represent?" the product of two factors

(continued)

Analyze Solve problems **1–3.**

▶ **1.** The Acme Scrap Metal Company pays 45¢ per pound for aluminum
(25)   cans. Troy wants to sell 54.2 lbs of cans. How much money should he
       receive? $24.39

▶ * **2.** A recipe for chili calls for $4\frac{1}{4}$ lbs of beans. Azza wants to make $2\frac{1}{2}$ times
(23)   the recipe. How many pounds of beans will she need? $10\frac{5}{8}$ pounds

▶ * **3.** The atmosphere that we live in is 78.08 percent nitrogen and
(24)   20.95 percent oxygen. What percentage of the atmosphere is made up
        of nitrogen and oxygen?   99.03 percent

▶ * **4.** Marcia developed a roll of film and received 4-inch by 6-inch prints. She
(26)   wants to have one picture enlarged to an 8-inch by 12-inch print. What
        kind of transformation is this? What is the scale factor?   dilation; 2

* **5.** In 1875, an estimated twelve-and-a-half trillion locusts appeared in
(28)   Nebraska. Write the number of locusts in scientific notation. 1.25×10^{13}

6. Patrick has 7 tetras, 4 goldfish, and 22 snails in his fish tank. What is the
(29) ratio of snails to goldfish in Patrick's fish tank? $\frac{11}{2}$

Simplify.

7. $4 + 10 \div 5 \times 2$ 8
(21)

8. $\dfrac{5 + 3 \cdot 10}{5^2 - 10}$ $2\frac{1}{3}$
(15, 21)

9. $\dfrac{3}{4} - \dfrac{1}{6} \div \dfrac{1}{3}$ $\frac{1}{4}$
(13, 22)

10. $\dfrac{2}{3} - \dfrac{1}{12} \cdot \dfrac{1}{2}$ $\frac{5}{8}$
(13, 22)

11. Simplify and compare: $\sqrt{9} + \sqrt{16} \bigcirc \sqrt{9 + 16}$ $3 + 4 > 5$ or $7 > 5$
(15)

12. **a.** Expand: $4(x + 2y + 3)$ $4x + 8y + 12$
(21)

   b. Factor: $6x + 3y$ $3(2x + y)$

13. Rearrange the numbers to make multiplication easier. Then simplify.
(2)   What properties did you use? $(2 \times 5) \times 27 = 10 \times 27 = 270$;
      Associative Property of Multiplication
                                              $2 \times (5 \times 27)$

▶ * **14.** **Conclude**   The addition of the absolute values of two negative integers will
(31)   always be   **B**

   A a negative integer.   **B** a positive integer.

   C zero.   **D** any positive number.

Evaluate:

15. Find $a + b + c$ when $a = 5$, $b = -2$, and $c = -4$. -1
(14, 31)

▶ * **16.** **Evaluate**   The weight of an object on Earth is equal to its mass times
(14, 25)   the acceleration of gravity. For the equation $W = mg$, find W when $m = 5$ and $g = 9.8$.   49

▶ See Math Conversations in the sidebar.

17. *Classify* Classify this triangle by angles
(20) and by sides. Then find the area of the
triangle.   acute; scalene; 9 cm²

3 cm

6 cm

18. Collect like terms: $3x^2 + 2x + 3x - 1$ $3x^2 + 5x - 1$
(31)

Simplify:

19. $47 - 79$ -32
(2)

20. $\dfrac{x^6 \cdot x^2}{x \cdot x^3}$ x^4
(27)

21. $6\dfrac{1}{4} - 3\dfrac{3}{8}$ $2\dfrac{7}{8}$
(13)

22. $6 - 3.67$ 2.33
(24)

▶*** 23.** **a.** $(-3) + (-12)$ -15 **b.** $(-12) + (-3)$ -15
(14)

24. It costs $10 plus $8 per hour to rent a canoe. Brandon and Erin have
(14) $50. Solve the following equation to find how many hours they can rent
a canoe.

$$8h + 10 = 50 \quad h = 5; \text{ 5 hours}$$

* 25. Express $\dfrac{3}{11}$ as a decimal number. $0.\overline{27}$
(30)

26. Use prime factorization to reduce $\dfrac{27}{45}$. $\dfrac{3 \cdot 3 \cdot 3}{3 \cdot 3 \cdot 5} = \dfrac{3}{5}$
(10)

* 27. Julie wrote a 500-word essay. Following the suggestions made by her
(31) English teacher, Julie deleted a 25-word long paragraph and added
a new paragraph 17 words long. How many words long is Julie's final
essay? $500 - 25 + 17 = 492$; 492 words

28.
a. Zero Property
of Multiplication
b. Identity
Property of
Multiplication

28. Name each property illustrated.
(2)
a. $62 \times 0 = 0$ **b.** $27 \times 1 = 27$

* 29. **a.** Find the missing exponent: $x^8 \cdot x^2 \cdot x^{\square} = x^{15}$ 5
(27)
b. Simplify: $2^3 + 2^2 + 2^1 + 2^0$ 15

30. Loose birdseed is priced at $4.29 per pound. Raoul scoops out a small
(25) bag for his birdfeeder. It weighs 1.3 pounds. How much will he pay for
the birdseed (rounded to the nearest cent)? $5.58

▶ See Math Conversations in the sidebar.

Math Conversations

Discussion opportunities are provided below.

Errors and Misconceptions
Problems 23a and 23b

When finding the sum of two integers, some
students may assume that the order of the
addends is important. To remind these
students that addition is a commutative
operation, ask them to reverse the order of the
addends, and then compare the sums of those
addends, in problems **23a** and **23b.**

Looking Forward

Adding integers and collecting like
terms prepares students for:

- **Lesson 33,** subtracting integers.

- **Lesson 38,** using properties of
equality to solve equations.

- **Lesson 50,** solving multi-step
equations.

• Probability

Objectives

- Calculate the probability of an event as a ratio of the number of favorable outcomes to the total number of possible outcomes.
- Convert a probability expressed as a ratio to a chance expressed as a percent.
- Express the odds of a particular event as the ratio of favorable to unfavorable outcomes.
- Find the sample spaces of compound events and use the sample spaces to find the probabilities of specific outcomes.
- Understand how the probabilities of an event and its complement are related.
- Distinguish between experimental and theoretical probability.
- Make and justify predictions using experimental and theoretical probabilities.

Lesson Preparation

Materials

- **Power Up G** (in *Instructional Masters*)

Optional

- **Manipulative Kit: dot cubes**

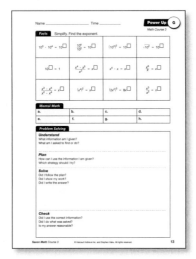

Power Up G

Math Language

New	Maintain	English Learners (ESL)
chance	ratio	random
complement		
experimental probability		
odds		
probability		
sample space		
theoretical probability		

Technology Resources

Student eBook Complete student textbook in electronic format.

Resources and Planner CD Assessment, reteaching, and instructional masters, plus a pacing calendar with standards.

Test and Practice Generator CD Create additional practice sheets and custom-made tests.

www.SaxonPublishers.com Visit for more student activities and planning materials.

Inclusion

Adaptations CD Adapted lessons, investigations, practice and assessments.

Meeting Standards

National Council of Teachers of Mathematics (NCTM)

Data Analysis and Probability

DP.4a Understand and use appropriate terminology to describe complementary and mutually exclusive events

DP.4b Use proportionality and a basic understanding of probability to make and test conjectures about the results of experiments and simulations

DP.4c Compute probabilities for simple compound events, using such methods as organized lists, tree diagrams, and area models

Problem-Solving Strategy: Make It Simpler/ Write an Equation

The diameter of a penny is $\frac{3}{4}$ in. How many pennies placed side by side would it take to make a row of pennies $\frac{3}{4}$ ft long? How many would it take to measure $\frac{3}{4}$ of a yard?

(Understand) **Understand the problem.**

"What information are we given?"

The diameter of a penny is $\frac{3}{4}$ inch.

"What are we asked to do?"

1. Determine how many pennies it will take to make a row that is $\frac{3}{4}$ foot long.
2. Determine how many pennies it will take to measure $\frac{3}{4}$ of a yard.

(Plan) **Make a plan.**

"What problem-solving strategy will we use?"

We will try to *make it simpler*, and then *write equations*.

"Do we need to adapt any of the information?"

$\frac{3}{4}$ foot = 9 inches. $\frac{3}{4}$ of a yard = 27 inches.

"If it seems difficult to visualize more than a few $\frac{3}{4}$ inch pennies, how might we simplify the problem?"

We could add just enough pennies together to achieve a whole number of inches.

(Solve) **Carry out the plan.**

"How many diameters (of pennies) would we have to combine to achieve a whole number of inches?"

$\frac{3}{4} + \frac{3}{4} = 1\frac{1}{2}$, and $1\frac{1}{2} + 1\frac{1}{2} = 3$, so the diameters of four pennies are equal to 3 inches.

"How many 3-inch lengths are in 9 inches?"

There are three 3-inch lengths in 9 inches.

"How many pennies are in a 9-inch ($\frac{3}{4}$ foot) row?"

4 (pennies per 3 inches) × 3 (3-in. lengths in $\frac{3}{4}$ foot) = 12 pennies in $\frac{3}{4}$ foot

"How many 9-inch lengths are in 27 inches?"

three

"How many pennies are in a 27-inch ($\frac{3}{4}$ yard) row?"

12 (pennies per 9 inches) × 3 (9-in. lengths in $\frac{3}{4}$ yard) = 36 pennies in $\frac{3}{4}$ of a yard

(Check) **Look back.**

"Did we answer the questions that were asked?"

Yes. There are 12 pennies in $\frac{3}{4}$ of a foot, and 36 pennies in $\frac{3}{4}$ of a yard.

• Probability

facts | Power Up G

mental math

a. **Number Sense:** 110×200 $22,000

b. **Algebra:** $15 + x = 60$ 45

c. **Measurement:** How long is this rectangle? $3\frac{1}{8}$ in.

d. **Rate:** At a rate of 40 words per minute, how many words can Valerie type in 20 minutes?   800 words

e. **Scientific Notation:** Write 280,000,000 km in scientific notation.
   2.8×10^8 km

f. **Geometry:** In this triangle, x must be between what two numbers?   12 and 32

g. **Powers/Roots:** List the perfect squares from 49 to 100.   49, 64, 81, 100

h. **Calculation:** $25 \times 4, \div 2, -1, \sqrt{}, \times 7, +1, \times 2, -1, \div 11, \sqrt{}, \times 7$
   21

problem solving
The diameter of a penny is $\frac{3}{4}$ in. How many pennies placed side by side would it take to make a row of pennies $\frac{3}{4}$ ft long? How many would it take to measure $\frac{3}{4}$ of a yard?   12, 36

New Concept | *Increasing Knowledge*

Probability is the likelihood that a particular event will occur. To represent the probability of event A we use the notation $P(A)$. We express probability as a number ranging from zero to one.

Range of Probability

```
0                    1/2                    1
|--------------------|--------------------|
Impossible  Unlikely      Likely      Certain
```

Math Language
Recall that a **ratio** is a comparison of two numbers by division.

Probability is a ratio of favorable outcomes to possible outcomes.

$$P(\text{Event}) = \frac{\text{number of favorable outcomes}}{\text{number of possible outcomes}}$$

---

1 Power Up

Facts
Distribute **Power Up G** to students. See answers below.

Mental Math
Encourage students to share different ways to mentally compute these exercises. Strategies for exercises **a, d,** and **f** are listed below.

a. Regroup
$110 \times 200 = $110 \times 2 \times 100 =$
$220 \times 100 = $22,000$

d. Use a Unit Rate
20 min $\times$ 40 words/min = 800 words
Use Math Sense
1 min ➝ 40 words
2 min ➝ 80 words
20 min ➝ 800 words

f. Sides of a Triangle
x has to be less than $22 + 10$
x has to be greater than $22 - 10$
x has to be between 12 and 32

Problem Solving
Refer to **Power-Up Discussion,** p. 210B.

2 New Concepts

Instruction
Tell students that people have been interested in probability for hundreds of years. Blaise Pascal in 1654 began investigating the ideas that we call probability today because he wanted to be able to predict the results of rolling number cubes. Now probability concepts are used to make predictions, such as weather and financial forecasts, and to design research projects, such as tests for new medicines and experiments that involve many variations.

Point out that a probability of 0 means that the event will not occur and a probability of 1 means that the event will definitely occur. Ask students to name events that have probabilities of 0 or 1. Sample: The probability is 0 for the sun setting in the east. The probability is 1 for the sun setting in the west.

(continued)

Facts | Simplify. Find the exponent.

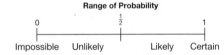

$10^3 \cdot 10^4 = 10^{\boxed{7}}$	$\dfrac{10^6}{10^2} = 10^{\boxed{4}}$	$(10^3)^2 = 10^{\boxed{6}}$	$\sqrt{10^2} = 10^{\boxed{1}}$
$10^{\boxed{0}} = 1$	$\dfrac{x^4 \cdot x^5}{x^3} = x^{\boxed{6}}$	$x^4 \cdot x = x^{\boxed{5}}$	$\dfrac{x^6}{x} = x^{\boxed{5}}$
$\dfrac{x^3 \cdot x^5}{x^2 \cdot x^4} = x^{\boxed{2}}$	$(x^4)^2 = x^{\boxed{8}}$	$(2x^2)^3 = 8x^{\boxed{6}}$	$\dfrac{x^3}{x^2} = x^{\boxed{1}}$

Example 1

The spinner shown at right is spun once. What is the probability the spinner will stop

   a. in sector *A?*

   b. in sector *A* or *B?*

   c. in sector *A, B, C,* or *D?*

Solution

The face of the spinner is divided into fourths. There are four equally likely outcomes.

   a. One outcome, *A*, is favorable.

$$P(A) = \frac{1}{4}$$

   b. To find the probability of *A* or *B* we add the probabilities of each.

$$P(A \text{ or } B) = P(A) + P(B)$$
$$= \frac{1}{4} + \frac{1}{4}$$
$$= \frac{1}{2}$$

   c. The probability of *A, B, C,* or *D* is **1** because every spin results in one of the listed outcomes.

$$P(A, B, C, \text{ or } D) = \frac{4}{4} = 1$$

Probability may be expressed as a fraction, as a decimal, or as a percent. We often use the word **chance** when expressing probability in percent form. In example 1 *P(A)* is 0.25, which means that the spinner has a 25% chance of stopping in sector *A.*

Odds is the ratio of the number of favorable to unfavorable outcomes and is often expressed with a colon. We will calculate the odds of the spinner stopping in sector *A* in example 2.

Example 2

If the spinner in example 1 is spun once, what are the odds the spinner will stop in sector *A?*

Solution

Of the four equally likely outcomes, one is *A* and three are not *A*. So the odds the spinner will stop in sector *A* are **1:3.**

The **sample space** of an experiment is the collection of all possible outcomes. We can record the sample space in a variety of ways, including a list or a table. For example, if a coin is tossed twice, there are four possible outcomes.

Lesson 32   211

Example 1

Instruction

Ask students to name the four equally likely outcomes. stopping in sector A, B, C, or D Have a volunteer explain why they are equally likely. Then ask what an impossible outcome would be. Sample: stopping in sectors B and D at the same time

In each part, call attention to the notation used to represent the different probabilities.

Instruction

Point out to students that they probably hear the word *chance* used more often than any other way to describe probability in their everyday experience because that is what weather forecasters use.

Call attention to the definition of *odds*. Point out that the least value for both odds and probability is zero, but that odds can have values greater than 1. For example, if the probability is $\frac{3}{4}$, then the odds are 3:1.

(continued)

2 New Concepts (Continued)

Instruction

Call attention to the use of braces (also called curly brackets) to contain the *sample space*. Point out that the table is a simple and effective way to be sure that all possible outcomes are included in the *sample space*.

For the *Formulate* question, have a volunteer go to the board and show how she or he found the sample space for spinning the 4-part spinner in example 1 twice. You can extend this question by asking students to use the sample space to name the probability and the odds of spinning the same letter twice. probability: $\frac{1}{4}$; odds: 1:3

Example 3

Instruction

For part a, ask students to explain the reason for the guess in the solution—that we will be more likely to get *A* with two spins than with one. Sample: We have an extra opportunity to spin *A*.

For part b, point out that a two-phase experiment means that the experiment has two steps. In this case, the spinner is spun two times. Call attention to the way that the table shows all the possible outcomes.

For part c, be sure that students notice the notation for the probability of *not A*.

(continued)

In the list and table at right we use H for "heads" and T for "tails."

Sample space = {HH, HT, TH, TT}

Knowing the sample space for an experiment helps us calculate probabilities. Referring to the sample space above, can you find the probability of getting heads at least once in two tosses of a coin? $\frac{3}{4}$

Sample Space

	First Toss	
	H	**T**
Second Toss **H**	HH	TH
T	HT	TT

Formulate If Javier spins the spinner in example 1 twice, what is the sample space for the experiment? {AA, AB, AC, AD, BA, BB, BC, BD, CA, CB, CC, CD, DA, DB, DC, DD}

The **complement** of an event is the set of outcomes in the sample space that are not included in the event. The complement of getting heads at least once in two tosses is not getting heads at least once. The probability of an event and the probability of its complement total one, because it is certain that an event either will occur or will not occur. If we know the probability of an event, we can find the probability of its complement by subtracting the probability from 1.

Example 3

The spinner in example 1 is spun twice.

  a. **Predict: Is the probability of spinning *A* more likely with one spin or with two spins?**

  b. **Find the probability of getting *A* at least once.**

  c. **Find the probability of not getting *A* at least once.**

Solution

  a. We guess that we will be **more likely to get *A* with two spins than with one spin.**

  b. To find the probability of *A* we first determine the sample space. We can make a table or a tree diagram. For a two-part experiment, a table is convenient.

	1st Spin			
	A	**B**	**C**	**D**
2nd Spin **A**	AA	BA	CA	DA
B	AB	BB	CB	DB
C	AC	BC	CC	DC
D	AD	BD	CD	DD

Seven of the 16 outcomes result in *A* at least once, so $P(A) = \frac{7}{16}$. Notice that $\frac{7}{16}$ is greater than $P(A)$ with one spin, which is $\frac{1}{4}$.

  c. The probability of not *A* is the complement of the probability of *A*. One way to find $P(\text{not } A)$ is by subtracting $P(A)$ from 1.

$$P(\text{not } A) = 1 - P(A)$$

Math Background

A bucket contains 2 blue blocks and 2 red blocks. Consider two experiments.

- **Experiment 1:** A block is randomly chosen, returned to the bucket, and then another block is chosen. Consider the events "blue on the first pick" and "blue on the second pick." The probability of getting blue on the second pick is $\frac{1}{2}$, whether or not the first block is blue. For this reason, the events are said to be *independent*.

- **Experiment 2:** A block is randomly chosen, is *not* returned, and then a second block is chosen. If a blue block is chosen on the first pick, then the probability the second block will be blue is $\frac{1}{3}$. If a red block is chosen first, then the probability the second block will be blue is $\frac{2}{3}$. In this case, the probability of getting blue on the second pick depends on whether blue is chosen on the first pick. In this case, the events are *not independent*.

$$P(\text{not } A) = 1 - \frac{7}{16}$$

$$P(\text{not } A) = \frac{9}{16}$$

The answer is reasonable because 9 of the 16 possible outcomes in the table do not include A.

Example 4

Nathan flips a coin three times.

   a. Predict: Which is more likely, that he will get heads at least once or that he will not get heads at least once.

   b. Find the probability of getting heads at least once.

   c. Find the probability of not getting heads at least once.

Solution

a. The probability of getting heads in one toss is $\frac{1}{2}$. Since the opportunity to get heads at least once increases with more tosses, **we predict that getting heads at least once is more likely than not getting heads.**

b. We use a tree diagram to find the sample space. We find eight equally likely possible outcomes.

First Toss	Second Toss	Third Toss	Outcome
		H	HHH
	H	T	HHT
H		H	HTH
	T	T	HTT
		H	THH
	H	T	THT
T		H	TTH
	T	T	TTT

Since 7 of the 8 outcomes have heads at least once, $P(H) = \frac{7}{8}$.

c. The probability of not getting heads is $\frac{1}{8}$.

We distinguish between the **theoretical probability,** which is found by analyzing a situation, and **experimental probability,** which is determined statistically. Experimental probability is the ratio of the number of times an event occurs to the number of trials. For example, if a basketball player makes 80 free throws in 100 attempts, then the experimental probability of the player making a free throw is $\frac{80}{100}$ or $\frac{4}{5}$. The player might be described as an 80% free-throw shooter.

In baseball and softball, a player's batting average is the experimental probability, expressed as a decimal, of the player getting a hit.

Lesson 32   **213**

2 New Concepts *(Continued)*

Example 4

Instruction
Model making the tree diagram on the board or overhead. Have students follow along with you on their papers. Point out that a table works well for experiments with two steps, but that a tree diagram is better for any experiments with more than two steps.

Instruction
Explain that when experimental data is presented in a problem, the experimental probability calculated from the data is often used to answer questions, not the theoretical probability.

(continued)

Inclusion

Some students may need a physical demonstration of theoretical and experimental probabilities. For example 4 have the students flip a coin in triplets and record the results as tally marks in a table similar to the one shown. Instruct them to flip the coin in triplets 24 more times and record the results in their table. Then instruct them to calculate the experimental probability of flipping at least one head in the triplets. You may need to review equivalent fractions for the following. Ask:

   "How does your experimental probability compare to the theoretical probability? Explain." Sample: The probabilities are close but different due to randomness of the experiment.

   "What could be done to bring the experimental probability closer to the theoretical probability?" Sample: more experiments

Outcome	Number
HHH	II
HHT	III
HTH	IIII
HTT	NNI
THH	III
THT	III
TTH	III
TTT	II

Example 5
Instruction

Ask what the probability is that Emily will not get a hit. P(not a hit) = 0.65 Help students see that there are two ways to find this probability:
• It can be calculated by dividing 39 by 60.
• It can be found by subtracting 0.35 from 1.

Practice Set
Problem b Error Alert

Have students who name $\frac{1}{6}$ as the answer note that the word "odds" is present in the problem. Ask these students to explain how odds and probability differ. Odds represent a ratio of favorable outcomes to unfavorable outcomes. Probability represents a ratio of favorable outcomes to the sum of the number of favorable and unfavorable outcomes.

Problem c Justify

Have students note that the answer (80%) is the complement of the given probability.

Problem e Error Alert

Remind students that the sum of the probability of an event and the probability of the complement of that event is 1.

Problem g Error Alert

To help students understand and recall how the terms *theoretical* and *experimental* are different, invite volunteers to define the terms using their own words. Sample: Theoretical represents a prediction of what can be expected to happen. Experimental describes what actually happened.

Example 5

Emily is a softball player who has 21 hits in 60 at-bats. Express the probability that Emily will get a hit in her next at-bat as a decimal number with three decimal places. Emily's coach needs to decide whether to have Emily bat or to use a substitute hitter whose batting average is .300 (batting averages are usually expressed without a 0 in the ones place). How would you advise the coach?

Solution

The ratio of hits to at-bats is 21 to 60. To express the ratio as a decimal we divide 21 by 60.

$$21 \div 60 = 0.35$$

We write the probability (batting average) with three decimal places: **.350**. Since Emily's batting average is greater than the batting average of the substitute hitter, **we advise the coach to have Emily bat.**

Practice Set

a. A number cube is rolled once. What is the probability of rolling an even number? Express the probability as a fraction and as a decimal. $\frac{1}{2}$, 0.5

▶ b. A number cube is rolled once. What are the odds of rolling a 6?   1:5

▶ c. **Justify** If the chance of rain tomorrow is 20%, then is it more likely to rain or not rain? What is the chance it will not rain tomorrow? Explain your reasoning.

c. Sample answer: The chance it will rain and the chance it will not rain total 1, or 100%. Subtracting 20%, the chance it will rain, from 100%, I find the chance it will not rain is 80%. So it is more likely not to rain.

d. A coin is flipped three times. What is the sample space of the experiment?   {HHH, HHT, HTH, HTT, THH, THT, TTH, TTT}

▶ e. Referring to the experiment in **d**, what is the probability of getting heads exactly twice? What is the probability of not getting heads exactly twice? $\frac{3}{8}$, $\frac{5}{8}$

f. Quinn runs a sandwich shop. Since she added turkey melt to the menu, 36 out of 120 customers have ordered the new sandwich. What is the probability that the next customer will order a turkey melt? If Quinn has 50 customers for lunch, about how many are likely to order a turkey melt? $\frac{3}{10}$ or 0.3; $\frac{3}{10} \cdot 50 = 15$

▶ g. State whether the probabilities found in problems **e** and **f** are examples of theoretical probability or experimental probability.   e: theoretical probability, f: experimental probability

Written Practice   *Strengthening Concepts*

1. If postage for an envelope costs 39¢ for the first ounce and 24¢ for each additional ounce, then what is the postage for a 12 ounce envelope? $3.03
(3, 4)

2. An author writes an average of eight pages per day. At this rate, how long would it take to write a 384 page book?   48 days
(4)

▶ See Math Conversations in the sidebar.

Manipulative Use

To give students more hands-on experience with both **theoretical and experimental probability,** suggest that they find the sample space for the sums obtained by rolling two standard number cubes. Then have students work in pairs or small groups to roll two cubes several times and see whether the experimental results come close to the theoretical expectations.

This table shows the sample space.

	1	2	3	4	5	6
1	2	3	4	5	6	7
2	3	4	5	6	7	8
3	4	5	6	7	8	9
4	5	6	7	8	9	10
5	6	7	8	9	10	11
6	7	8	9	10	11	12

Let students decide how to record their data and analyze their results. Suggest that the groups pool their data to see whether more data will more closely match the theoretical results shown by the table.

3. Pete saw that he was 200 yards from shore when he dove out of the
(4) boat. It took him 49 seconds to swim the first 50 yards. At that rate, how
much longer will it take to reach the shore?   147 seconds

▶ * **4.** *Evaluate* Alonzo chose a name from a box, read the name, then
(32) replaced it and mixed the names. He repeated this experiment several
times. Out of the 20 names he chose, 12 were eighth-graders.

   a. What is the experimental probability of choosing the name of an
   eighth-grader based on Alonzo's experiments? $\frac{3}{5}$ or 0.6

   b. If half of the names in the box are eighth-graders, what is the
   theoretical probability of choosing the name of an eighth-grader?
   $\frac{1}{2}$ or 0.5

▶ * **5.** *Analyze* There are 18 marbles in Molly's bag. Two of the marbles are
(32) yellow. If Molly chooses one marble at random, find the theoretical
probability that she will choose a yellow marble. What is the probability
that she will not choose a yellow marble? $\frac{1}{9}$; $\frac{8}{9}$

▶ * **6.** *Connect* Use the figure at right to answer **a**
(8) and **b.**

   a. What is the area of this triangle?
   $A = 24 \text{ m}^2$
   b. What is the perimeter of this triangle?
   $P - 24$ m

10 m

6 m

7. Estimate: $\frac{610 + 195}{398}$ 2
(17)

Simplify.

8. $\frac{1}{5} - \frac{1}{3} \cdot \frac{4}{5}$ $-\frac{1}{15}$ **9.** $\frac{7}{9} - \frac{1}{3} \div \frac{3}{4}$ $\frac{1}{3}$
(13, 23)   (13, 23)

10. $2.05 - (3.1)(0.1)$ 1.74   **11.** $7^2 - 6^1 + 5^0$ 44
(24, 25)   (15, 27)

12 Simplify and compare:
(15, 21)
   a. $\sqrt{3^2 + 4^2} \bigcirc \sqrt{3^2} + \sqrt{4^2}$ 5 < 7

   b. $|-1 + 5| \bigcirc |-1| + |5|$ 4 < 6

▶ **13.** *Represent* Write $\frac{5}{9}$ as a decimal and a percent. $0.\overline{5}$; $55\frac{5}{9}\%$
(30)

* **14.** **a.** Write 60% as a decimal and a reduced fraction.   0.6; $\frac{3}{5}$
(11, 16)
   b. Which form would you find most convenient to use to find 60%
   of $15? Explain.   Using the fraction $\frac{3}{5}$ would be most convenient since
   $15 is easily divided by the denominator, 5.

15.
y
(3, 2)   (7, 2)

x

(3, –5)   (7, –5)

15. These points are vertices of a rectangle: (3, −5), (7, −5), (7, 2). Plot
(8, Inv. 1) these points and locate the fourth vertex. Then find the area and
perimeter of the rectangle.   (3, 2), $A = 28$ units^2; $P = 22$ units

16. **a.** Expand: $3(x + 12)$ $3x + 36$
(21)
   b. Factor: $x^2 + 6x$ $x(x + 6)$

* **17.** Write 6.02×10^{10} in standard notation.   60,200,000,000
(28)

Lesson 32   215

▶ See Math Conversations in the sidebar.

---

3 Written Practice

Math Conversations
Discussion opportunities are provided below.

Problem 4 *Evaluate*
Ask students to also express each probability
as a percent.

Problem 5 *Analyze*
Remind students that one way to check the
probability of an event, and the probability of
the complement of that event, is to compare
the sum of the probabilities to 1.

Problem 6 *Connect*
Students must recognize that finding the
perimeter and the area of the right triangle
involves solving $a^2 + b^2 = c^2$ for a or for b.

Problem 13 *Represent*
Before beginning the arithmetic, invite a
volunteer to explain what a repetend is.

Errors and Misconceptions
Problem 4
When working with probability, a
misconception some students may have is that
in a given scenario, theoretical probability and
experimental probability cannot be described
by the same ratio.

Students should infer from problem 4 that
although Alonzo chose the name of an eighth
grader 12 out of 20 times, it was possible
that he could have chosen the name of an
eighth grader 10 out of 20 times. If that
had happened, the same ratio (10 out of 20
or $\frac{1}{2}$) would represent both the theoretical
probability and experimental probability of
Alonzo randomly choosing an eighth grade
name.

(continued)

English Learners

For problem **5** explain the meaning
of the word **random.** Say:

*"When you choose something
at random, you choose with no
plan. I will choose a random
two-digit number with my
calculator."*

Without looking, press two keys on
a calculator and write the resulting
number on the board. Ask:

"Why is this a random number?"
It was not planned.

Math Conversations

Discussion opportunities are provided below.

Problem 18a | Generalize

Writing the expanded form of the expression can help students understand why m^{12} is the simplest form of $(m^4)^3$, and adding parentheses to the notation can help students see the relationship shared by the exponent 3 and m^4. $(m^4)^3 = m^4 \cdot m^4 \cdot m^4 = (m \cdot m \cdot m \cdot m) \cdot (m \cdot m \cdot m \cdot m) \cdot (m \cdot m \cdot m \cdot m)$

Problem 29 | Evaluate

Write the equation $E = \frac{mv^2}{2}$ on the board or overhead, and explain that it is equivalent to the given equation because dividing a quantity by 2 produces the same result as multiplying that quantity by $\frac{1}{2}$. Students can choose either equation to solve the problem.

(continued)

Generalize Simplify.

* **18.** ▶ **a.** $(m^4)^3$ m^{12}
(27)

b. $\dfrac{r^2 r^5}{r^3}$ r^4

19. **Predict** **a.** On a number line, graph the points 2 and 6. Then graph the
(1, 3)   mean of 2 and 6.

$$-1\ 0\ 1\ 2\ 3\ 4\ 5\ 6\ 7$$

19. b.
$$-6\ -5\ -4\ -3\ -2\ -1\ 0\ 1\ 2$$

b. On a number line, graph the points −5 and 1. Use the number line to predict the mean of −5 and 1. The mean of −5 and 1 is the number halfway between them, which is −2.

20. What numbers are members of both the set of whole numbers and the
(1)   set of integers? the whole numbers {0, 1, 2, 3, ...}

21. Rearrange the addends in this addition problem to make the calculation
(2)   easier. Then simplify. What properties did you use? $(23 + 7) + 18 = 48;$ Associative Property of Addition
$$23 + (7 + 18)$$

22. Find the factors of 2100 using a factor tree. Then write the prime
(9, 15)   factorization of 2100 using exponents. See student work; $2^2 \cdot 3 \cdot 5^2 \cdot 7$

23. The spinner shown is spun twice. What is the
(32)   sample space of the experiment? What is the probability of spinning A at least once? {AA, AB, AC, BA, BB, BC, CA, CB, CC}; $P(A) = \frac{5}{9}$

24. Jon will win more often. The probability of Jon winning is $\frac{5}{9}$, but the probability of Meg winning is only $\frac{3}{9}$.

24. Jon and Meg play a game with the spinner from problem **23**. They take
(32)   turns spinning the spinner twice. Jon earns a point if a player spins at least one A in a turn. Meg earns a point if a player spins "doubles" (AA, BB, or CC). Predict who you think will win more often if they play several times, and justify your prediction.

25. Order these numbers from least to greatest.   −5.4, −3.2, 0, 2.3, 4.5
(12)
$$0, 2.3, -3.2, 4.5, -5.4$$

26. When a page of print is viewed in a mirror the words appear to be
(26)   printed backwards. The image in the mirror is an example of which type of transformation? reflection

27. Solve by inspection: $3x + 20 = 80$ $x = 20$
(14)

Evaluate.

28. Find $\sqrt{b^2 - 4ac}$ when $a = 2$, $b = 5$, $c = 2$.   3
(14, 15)

▶* **29.** **Evaluate** The kinetic energy of an object is given by the equation
(14, 15) $E = \frac{1}{2}mv^2$. Find E when $m = 2$, $v = 3$. $E = 9$

▶ See Math Conversations in the sidebar.

▶* 30. (18, 20) *Analyze* Triangle ∠WXY is isosceles. If m∠W is 40°, then what is the measure of the following angles? **a.** 70°, **b.** 70°, **c.** 110°

a. ∠X

b. ∠WYX

c. ∠WYZ

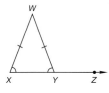

To award door prizes at the winter carnival, the Anderson Intermediate School principal drew the names of five students from a hat. Only seventh and eighth graders go to Anderson Intermediate School.

a. One possible outcome is the principal drawing five seventh-grade students. What are the other possible outcomes? (Order does not matter, so 7-7-7-8-7 is the same as 8-7-7-7-7.)

b. If sixty percent of the names drawn were eighth graders, how many names drawn were seventh graders?
a. five 7th graders, four 7th and one 8th, three 7th and two 8th, two 7th and three 8th, one 7th and four 8th, and five 8th; **b.** 2 students

Lesson 32   217

▶ See Math Conversations in the sidebar.

Looking Forward

Calculating probabilities and identifying sample spaces prepares students for:

• **Lesson 59,** calculating experimental probabilities.

• **Lesson 68,** applying the probability multiplication rule.

• **Investigation 7,** simulating probability experiments.

• **Lesson 83,** calculating probabilities of dependent events.

• **Lesson 101,** calculating geometric probabilities.

• Subtracting Integers

Objectives

• Subtract an integer from another integer by adding its opposite.
• Write and solve equations involving subtracting integers to solve word problems.

Lesson Preparation

Materials

• **Power Up G** (in *Instructional Masters*)

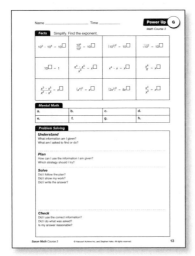

Power Up G

Math Language

Maintain	English Learners (ESL)
subtrahend	descended

Technology Resources

Student eBook Complete student textbook in electronic format.

Resources and Planner CD Assessment, reteaching, and instructional masters, plus a pacing calendar with standards.

Test and Practice Generator CD Create additional practice sheets and custom-made tests.

www.SaxonPublishers.com Visit for more student activities and planning materials.

Inclusion

Adaptations CD Adapted lessons, investigations, practice and assessments.

Meeting Standards

National Council of Teachers of Mathematics (NCTM)

Numbers and Operations

NO.1g Develop meaning for integers and represent and compare quantities with them

NO.2a Understand the meaning and effects of arithmetic operations with fractions, decimals, and integers

NO.2c Understand and use the inverse relationships of addition and subtraction, multiplication and division, and squaring and finding square roots to simplify computations and solve problems

NO.3b Develop and analyze algorithms for computing with fractions, decimals, and integers and develop fluency in their use

Problem-Solving Strategy: Make a Table

Andrew, Amelia, Beth, and Freddy decided to take pictures of two people at a time. How many different pairs of people can be made from these four people?

Understand **Understand the problem.**

"What information are we given?"

Four people wish to be photographed two at a time.

"What are we asked to do?"

Determine how many different pairs of people can be photographed.

Plan **Make a plan.**

"What problem-solving strategy will we use?"

We will *make a table.*

Solve **Carry out the plan.**

"Who should be paired with whom?"

	Andrew	Amelia	Beth	Freddy
Andrew	Not a pair	☺	☺	☺
Amelia	Already paired	Not a pair	☺	☺
Beth	Already paired	Already paired	Not a pair	☺
Freddy	Already paired	Already paired	Already paired	Not a pair

"How many different pairs of people were photographed?"

3 + 2 + 1 = 6 pairs

Check **Look back.**

"Did we find the answer to the question that was asked?"

Yes. We found that there are six different pairs of people that can be photographed from a group of four.

218   *Saxon* Math Course 3

1 Power Up

Facts
Distribute **Power Up G** to students. See answers below.

Mental Math
Encourage students to share different ways to mentally compute these exercises. Strategies for exercises **a** and **b** are listed below.

a. Regroup
$21 \times 400 = 21 \times 4 \times 100 =$
$84 \times 100 = 8400$
Regroup a Different Way
$21 \times 400 = (20 + 1) \times 400 =$
$(20 \times 400) + (1 \times 400) =$
$8000 + 400 = 8400$

b. Triple and Third
$33\frac{1}{3}\%$ of $\$390 = 100\%$ of $\$130 = \$130$
Find A Fraction
$33\frac{1}{3}\% = \frac{1}{3}$
$\frac{1}{3} \times \$390 = \$130$

Problem Solving
Refer to **Power-Up Discussion**, p. 218B.

2 New Concepts

Instruction
Make sure that students have a solid understanding of integer addition before you begin this lesson.

(continued)

•Subtracting Integers

Power Up   *Building Power*

facts | Power Up G

mental math
a. **Number Sense:** 21×400 8400
b. **Fractional Parts:** $33\frac{1}{3}\%$ of \$390   \$130
c. **Measurement:** How long is this strip of paper?   4.7 cm

d. **Rate:** Albert threw only 64 pitches in 7 innings. About how many pitches per inning did Albert throw?   About 9
e. **Scientific Notation:** Write twelve million in scientific notation.
1.2×10^7
f. **Geometry:** Find *x*.   41°

g. **Estimation:** Sam bought 7 at \$2.97 each plus 4 at \$9.97 each. About how much did he spend?   about \$61
h. **Calculation:** $32 \div 4$, $+1$, $\sqrt{\ }$, $+5$, square it, $+1$, $+10$, $\div 3$, $\sqrt{\ }$, $\times 7$ 35

problem solving | Andrew, Amelia, Beth, and Freddy decided to take pictures of two people at a time. How many different pairs of people can be made from these four people?   6

New Concept   *Increasing Knowledge*

Recall that we use a method called algebraic addition to subtract integers. Instead of subtracting a number, we add its opposite. Consider the following examples.

Example 1

Visit www. SaxonPublishers. com/ActivitiesC3 for a graphing calculator activity.

Change each subtraction to addition and find the sum.

a. $(-3) - (+2)$ b. $(-3) - (-2)$

Facts   Simplify. Find the exponent.

$10^3 \cdot 10^4 = 10^{\boxed{7}}$	$\dfrac{10^6}{10^2} = 10^{\boxed{4}}$	$(10^3)^2 = 10^{\boxed{6}}$	$\sqrt{10^2} = 10^{\boxed{1}}$
$10^{\boxed{0}} = 1$	$\dfrac{x^4 \cdot x^5}{x^3} = x^{\boxed{6}}$	$x^4 \cdot x = x^{\boxed{5}}$	$\dfrac{x^6}{x} = x^{\boxed{5}}$
$\dfrac{x^3 \cdot x^5}{x^2 \cdot x^4} = x^{\boxed{2}}$	$(x^4)^2 = x^{\boxed{8}}$	$(2x^2)^3 = 8x^{\boxed{6}}$	$\dfrac{x^3}{x^2} = x^{\boxed{1}}$

Solution

We change the subtraction sign to an addition sign and reverse the sign of the subtrahend (the number being subtracted). Then we add.

Expression a.	Justification	Expression b.
$(-3) - (+2)$	Given	$(-3) - (-2)$
$(-3) + (-2)$	Added opposite	$(-3) + (+2)$
-5	Simplified	-1

Thinking Skill

Verify

Use a number line to prove that $(-3) - (+2)$ and $(-3) + (-2)$ are equal.
See student work.

Example 2

Jocelyn has a checking balance of $1286. In the mail she receives a rebate check for $25 and a utility bill for $128. She deposits the rebate and writes a check for the bill. Write an equation with integers for the situation and find her checking balance after the transactions.

Solution

To find the balance b we add the rebate to and subtract the utility bill from her current balance.

$$b = 1286 + 25 - 128$$

Instead of subtracting 128, we may add negative 128.

$$b = 1286 + 25 + (-128)$$

Both methods result in a balance of **$1183**.

Addition and Subtraction with Two Integers

Operation	Rule
+	To find the sum of addends with different signs: **1.** Subtract the absolute values of the addends. **2.** Take the sign of the addend with the greater absolute value. To find the sum of addends with the same sign: **1.** Add the absolute values of the addends. **2.** Take the sign of the addends.
−	Instead of subtracting a number, add its opposite.

Practice Set Simplify:

▶ **a.** $(-12) - (-3)$ -9

b. $(-12) - (+3)$ -15

c. $(-3) - (-12)$ 9

d. $(-3) - (+12)$ -15

▶ **e.** *Model* Choose any of the problems **a–d**. Show the operation on a number line.   Answers will vary depending on which problem is chosen.

Lesson 33   219

▶ See Math Conversations in the sidebar.

Math Background

Extending subtraction patterns can clarify what it means to subtract a negative number. In the patterns below, each time the subtrahend decreases by 1, the difference increases by 1.

$$3 - 3 = 0 \qquad -1 - 3 = -4$$
$$3 - 2 = 1 \qquad -1 - 2 = -3$$
$$3 - 1 = 2 \qquad -1 - 1 = -2$$
$$3 - 0 = 3 \qquad -1 - 0 = -1$$

These patterns can be extended to differences with negative subtrahends.

$$3 - (-1) = 4 \qquad -1 - (-1) = 0$$
$$3 - (-2) = 5 \qquad -1 - (-2) = 1$$

Example 1
Instruction
Point out that the answers are both 2 units from -3, but in opposite directions. You may want to demonstrate the two examples on a number line.

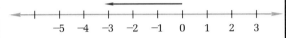

Start at 0. Move left 3 units to show -3.

To add $+2$, we would move right 2 units. To subtract 2, we move left 2 units. The result is -5.

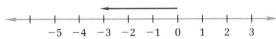

Start at 0. Move left 3 units to show -3.

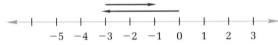

To add -2, we would move left 2 units. To subtract -2, we move right 2 units. The result is -1.

Example 2
Instruction
To check that students understand why they can subtract 128 by adding -128, ask them to explain the procedure.

Instruction
Summarize this lesson by reviewing the chart. Call attention to what has been added to this chart. Students first saw the chart in Lesson 31 where it contained only the information for adding integers. Emphasize again that students must learn this material.

Practice Set
Problem a
To begin each computation, ask students to name the subtrahend and its opposite.

Problem e *Model*
One way for students to check their answers for problems **a–d** is to use a number line to check all four computations.

(continued)

Practice Set
Problem f [Error Alert]
Point out that the equation should involve subtracting a negative integer.

Math Conversations
Discussion opportunities are provided below.

Problem 1 [Analyze]
Ask students to choose mental math or paper and pencil and use that method to solve the problem.

Then ask students to name the method they chose, and explain why that method was chosen. Methods and explanations will vary.

Problem 6 [Evaluate]
Before computing the new depth of the whale, ask students to write an equation that involves subtracting a negative integer to represent the situation.

Problem 7 [Generalize]
To begin each computation, ask students to name the subtrahend and its opposite.

Problem 9 [Analyze]
If students have difficulty recognizing that the difference of $2a^2$ and a^2 is a^2, work with them to help understand that the difference of a simpler problem such as $a^2 - a^2$ is 0.
$1a^2 - 1a^2 = 0a^2 = 0$

Problem 10 [Formulate]
"What is a repetend?" the repeating digits to the right of the decimal point in a decimal quotient

Point out that the division $7 \div 9$ will produce a repetend.

Problem 13 [Generalize]
"This expression contains more than one operation. Describe the operations. Which operation or operations do we complete first?" The fractions $\frac{1}{3}$ and $\frac{1}{4}$ are squared. The squares are multiplied, and then the square root of the product is found. The square root sign is also a grouping symbol. We follow the order of operations within the grouping symbol, so we first square $\frac{1}{3}$ and $\frac{1}{4}$.

(continued)

---

f. Victor owed $386. His creditor forgave (subtracted) $100 of the debt. Write an equation for the situation and find out how much Victor still owes. $-386 - (-100) = -286$; Victor owes $286

▶ *** 1.** [Analyze] At midnight, the temperature was $-5°$F. By 10:00 a.m. the
(31) next morning it had increased by $17°$. What was the temperature at 10:00 a.m.?   **B**

    A $22°$F   **B** $12°$F   **C** $10°$F   **D** $8°$F

* 2. Write the approximate distance from Earth to Venus, 25,000,000 miles,
(28) in scientific notation. 2.5×10^7

3. Enrique bought 6 bags of grass seed to reseed his lawn. Each bag cost
(25) $13.89. How much did Enrique spend on grass seed? $83.34

4. In the city of Austin, Texas, the state sales tax is 6.25%, the city sales
(11) tax is 1%, and the transportation board sales tax is 1%. What percent do the people of Austin pay in sales taxes? Ken, who lives in Austin, purchased a bicycle for $189. How much sales tax did he pay?
8.25%; $15.59

5. What kind of figure is created when these points are connected by line
(19, Inv. 1) segments in the given order?   trapezoid or isosceles trapezoid

$$(-2, 2), (1, 5), (5, 5), (8, 2), (-2, 2)$$

▶ *** 6.** [Evaluate] In a whale ecology study, gray whales were tagged in order
(31) to study their feeding habits. One day, a biologist recorded that a gray whale feeding at a depth of 10 meters (-10 m) suddenly descended 32 meters. What is the new depth of the gray whale? -42 m

[Generalize] Simplify.

▶ *** 7. a.** $8 - (-1)$ 9   **b.** $-1 + (-2)$ 1
(33)

* 8. a. $-6 - 5$ -11 **b.** $-8 + (-12)$ -20
(31)

▶ *** 9.** [Analyze] Collect like terms: $3a + 2a^2 + a - a^2$ $4a + a^2$
(31)

▶ *** 10.** [Formulate] Write $\frac{7}{9}$ as a decimal and a percent. $0.\overline{7}$; $77\frac{7}{9}$%
(30)

11. A spool contains 9 yards of ribbon. How many quarter-yard pieces can
(22) be cut from the spool of ribbon?   36

12. What is the length of side BC?   20 in.
(Inv. 2)

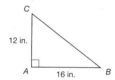

▶ **13.** [Generalize] Simplify: $\sqrt{\left(\frac{1}{3}\right)^2 \cdot \left(\frac{1}{4}\right)^2}$ $\frac{1}{12}$
(22, 15)

▶ See Math Conversations in the sidebar.

For problem **6** explain the meaning of the word **descended**. Say:

"When you descend, you move from a higher to a lower place. When you walked down stairs, you descended."

Ask volunteers to say a short sentence using "descended" and one of the following words:

    staircase   airplane   hikers

John descended the staircase. The airplane descended to land. The hikers descended the mountain.

14. Solve by inspection. $5x - 3 = 27$ $x = 6$
(14)

➤ **15.** **Estimate** Estimate and then calculate. 29×0.3 One estimate: $\frac{1}{10}$ of 30
(25)   is 3 so $\frac{3}{10}$ is about 9; 8.7

16. Add:
(31, 12)
    a. $-17 + (-5)$ **b.** $16 + -4$ **c.** $-12 + 27$ **d.** $-\frac{1}{4} + 0.75$
       -22 12 15 $\frac{1}{2}$ or 0.5

17. **a.** Write 20% as decimal and a reduced fraction. $0.2; \frac{1}{5}$
(11)
    b. Which form would you find most convenient to use to calculate a tip
    of 20% on a meal that cost \$45.00?   Sample: Using $\frac{1}{5}$ would be most
    convenient since \$45 is easily divisible by 5.

Generalize Simplify.

➤ **18.** $9^2 - 7^2 + 6^0$ 33
(15, 27)

19. $1.09 + 0.055 + 3.2$ 4.345
(24)

20. $3.14 - (0.2)(1.5)$ 2.84
(21, 24)

21. $0.5 \div 0.025$ 20
(25)

* **22.** In a shipping carton of juice there are 8 boxes. In each box there are
(15)   8 containers. In each container there are 8 ounces of juice. How many
    ounces of juice are in 8 shipping cartons of juice? Use exponents to find
    the answer. $8^4 = 4096$ fl oz

23. Order these numbers from least to greatest. $-1.8, -\frac{1}{10}, 0.12, \frac{1}{8}, 0.22$
(10, 12)

$$\frac{1}{8}, 0.12, -1.8, 0.22, -\frac{1}{10}$$

24.

* **24.** A triangle has vertices $(-2, 1)$, $(2, 4)$ and $(6, 1)$. Sketch this triangle and
(20,   refer to your sketch to answer questions **a–c.**
Inv. 2)
    a. Classified by sides, what type of triangle is it?   isosceles
    b. What is the area of the triangle?   12 units^2
    c. What is the perimeter of the triangle?   18 units

25. If the triangle in problem **24** is transformed so that the vertices of
(26)   the image are at $(-2, 1)$, $(1, -3)$, and $(-2, -7)$, then what type of
    transformation was performed?   rotation

* **26.** Tanya made a scale drawing of a bookcase she is going to build. The
(29)   height of the bookcase is going to be 60 inches. Her drawing shows the
    height as 4 inches. What is the ratio of the scale drawing height to the
    actual height of the bookcase? $\frac{4}{60} = \frac{1}{15}$

27. Chef Lorelle has a 79.5 ounce block of cheese. She asks her assistant
(25)   to slice the cheese into 0.75 ounce slices. What is the maximum number
    of slices they can get from the block of cheese?   106 slices

➤ See Math Conversations in the sidebar.

---

3 **Written Practice** (Continued)

Math Conversations
Discussion opportunities are provided below.

Problem 15 **Estimate**
Encourage students to share several different
ways to estimate the product. Sample:
Round 29 to 30, round 0.3 to $\frac{1}{3}$, then find $\frac{1}{3}$ of
30; Round 29 to 30, then find the product of
30 and 0.3

Problem 18 **Generalize**
Write the pattern shown below on the board
or overhead if students need to be reminded
that the simplest form of 6^0 is 1.

$$6^3 \qquad 6^2 \qquad 6^1 \qquad 6^0$$

$$216 \;\div 6 = \; 36 \;\div 6 = \; 6 \;\div 6 = \; 1$$

(continued)

Math Conversations

Discussion opportunities are provided below.

Problem 29 *Formulate*

Students should recognize that $\frac{1}{2}$ is a factor which will be used to produce two products.

---

28. Keisha is doing a science experiment. She is measuring the growth
(24) differences that result from using different amounts of water and sunlight on bean seedlings. In one of the pots, a seedling is 6.7 cm tall. In another, the seedling is 5.8 cm tall. How much taller is the first seedling than the second?   0.9 cm

▶* 29. *Formulate* Use the Distributive Property to find $\frac{1}{2}$ of $6\frac{3}{4}$ in the following
(21) expression: $\frac{1}{2}(6 + \frac{3}{4})$. $3\frac{3}{8}$

30. Ryan had an $8\frac{1}{2}$ in.-by-11 in. piece of paper. He cut it into quarters as
(8, 23) shown. What is the length and width of each quarter? What is the area of each quarter?   length $5\frac{1}{2}$ in., width $4\frac{1}{4}$ in.; $23\frac{3}{8}$ in.²

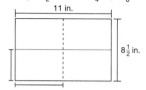

Early Finishers
Real-World Application

"Sea level" refers to the level of the ocean's surface and is used as a benchmark to measure land elevation. Death Valley, California, the lowest point in the United States, is approximately 282 feet below sea level. Denver, the largest city and capital of the state of Colorado, is 5431 feet above sea level. What is the difference in elevation between these two places?
$5431 - (-282) = 5431 + 282 = 5713$ feet

▶ See Math Conversations in the sidebar.

Looking Forward

Subtracting integers prepares students for:

• **Lesson 38,** using properties of equality to solve equations.

• **Lesson 50,** solving multi-step equations.

• Proportions
• Ratio Word Problems

Objectives

- Form proportions from equivalent ratios.
- Determine whether relationships are proportional by testing value pairs for a constant ratio.
- Find missing numbers in a proportion by finding a multiple between the terms of the proportion.
- Use a ratio table to form and solve a proportion from a word problem.

Lesson Preparation

Materials

- **Power Up G** (in *Instructional Masters*)

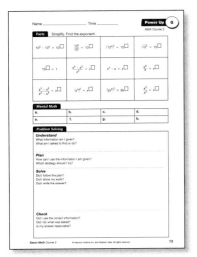

Power Up G

Math Language

New	Maintain	English Learners (ESL)
proportion	ratio	shadow

Technology Resources

Student eBook Complete student textbook in electronic format.

Resources and Planner CD Assessment, reteaching, and instructional masters, plus a pacing calendar with standards.

Test and Practice Generator CD Create additional practice sheets and custom-made tests.

www.SaxonPublishers.com Visit for more student activities and planning materials.

Inclusion

Adaptations CD Adapted lessons, investigations, practice and assessments.

Meeting Standards

National Council of Teachers of Mathematics (NCTM)

Numbers and Operations

NO.1d Understand and use ratios and proportions to represent quantitative relationships

NO.3d Develop, analyze, and explain methods for solving problems involving proportions, such as scaling and finding equivalent ratios

Algebra

AL.2c Use symbolic algebra to represent situations and to solve problems, especially those that involve linear relationships

AL.3a Model and solve contextualized problems using various representations, such as graphs, tables, and equations

Problem Solving

PS.1b Solve problems that arise in mathematics and in other contexts

Problem-Solving Strategy: Draw a Diagram/Use Logical Reasoning

Every block in this cube is labeled with a number and a letter. The block labeled 9A has two blocks behind it (9B and 9C). Which block is not visible from any angle?

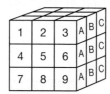

(Understand) **Understand the problem.**

"What information are we given?"

We are given a diagram of a labeled cube, and instructions as to how to name smaller cubes.

"What are we asked to do?"

Determine which block is not visible from any angle.

(Plan) **Make a plan.**

"What problem-solving strategy will we use?"

We will *use the diagram* that has been provided, as well as *logical reasoning*.

(Solve) **Carry out the plan.**

"What prior knowledge do we bring to this problem?"

This larger cube is made up of $3 \times 3 \times 3 = 27$ smaller cubes.

"How many faces of the large cube is it possible to view?"

Six. The diagram shows the front, right, and top views. The faces we cannot see are the back, left, and bottom.

"Of the 27 smaller cubes, which one is not visible from any angle?"

only the one in the very center of the cube

"Which is the label of the block that is not visible from any angle?"

5B

(Check) **Look back.**

"Did we find the answer to the question that was asked?"

Yes. The very center cube is not visible from any angle.

• **Proportions**
• **Ratio Word Problems**

facts | Power Up G

mental math |

a. **Number Sense:** $6.50 × 40 $260

b. **Fractional Parts:** $66\frac{2}{3}\%$ equals $\frac{2}{3}$. Find $66\frac{2}{3}\%$ of $45. $30

c. **Measurement:** Find the temperature indicated on this thermometer.   56°F

d. **Proportions:** Caesar finished 12 problems in 20 minutes. At that rate, how many problems can he do in 60 minutes?   36 problems

e. **Percent:** 20% of 90   18

f. **Geometry:** Find the area of this rectangle.   30.3 m²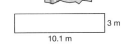
10.1 m | 3 m

g. **Powers/Roots:** List all the perfect squares from 16 to 64, then approximate $\sqrt{26} × 4.9$.   16, 25, 36, 49, 64; 25

h. **Calculation:** $10 - 9, × 8, + 7, ÷ 5, × 6, + 4, - 3, + 2, ÷ 1, ÷ 3, × 2, - 4, × 5, + 6, ÷ 7$ 8

problem solving | Every block in this cube is labeled with a number and a letter. The block labeled 9A has two blocks behind it (9B and 9C). Which block is not visible from any angle?   5B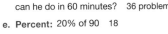

New Concepts | *Increasing Knowledge*

proportions | A proportion is a statement that two ratios are equal. The ratios $\frac{2}{4}$ and $\frac{6}{12}$ are equal and form a proportion.

$$\frac{2}{4} = \frac{6}{12}$$

1 Power Up

Facts
Distribute **Power Up G** to students. See answers below.

Mental Math
Encourage students to share different ways to mentally compute these exercises. Strategies for exercises **b, d,** and **e** are listed below.

b. **Triple and Third**
$66\frac{2}{3}\%$ of $45 = 200\%$ of $15 = 30
Use a Fraction
$\frac{2}{3} × $45 = 2 × 15 = 30

d. **Use Math Sense**
20 min → 12 problems
40 min → 24 problems
60 min → 36 problems

e. **10% Times Two**
10% of 90 = 9
20% of 90 = 18
Find a Fraction
$20\% = \frac{2}{10}$
$\frac{2}{10} × 90 = 2 × 9 = 18$

Problem Solving
Refer to **Power-Up Discussion**, p. 223B.

Facts | Simplify. Find the exponent.

$10^3 \cdot 10^4 = 10^{\boxed{7}}$	$\dfrac{10^6}{10^2} = 10^{\boxed{4}}$	$(10^3)^2 = 10^{\boxed{6}}$	$\sqrt{10^2} = 10^{\boxed{1}}$
$10^{\boxed{0}} = 1$	$\dfrac{x^4 \cdot x^5}{x^3} = x^{\boxed{6}}$	$x^4 \cdot x = x^{\boxed{5}}$	$\dfrac{x^6}{x} = x^{\boxed{5}}$
$\dfrac{x^3 \cdot x^5}{x^2 \cdot x^4} = x^{\boxed{2}}$	$(x^4)^2 = x^{\boxed{8}}$	$(2x^2)^3 = 8x^{\boxed{6}}$	$\dfrac{x^3}{x^2} = x^{\boxed{1}}$

Instruction

Explain that proportions and ratio problems are two of the most important topics in middle school math. Help students understand the idea that a proportion means that the two ratios are equal, and that two equal ratios can be used to form a proportion.

You may want to point out that because the inverse of multiplication is division, there are also division relationships between the numbers in the proportion. For example, in the proportion $\frac{2}{4} = \frac{6}{12}$, you can show that
- in the numerators, $6 \div 2 = 3$.
- in the denominators, $12 \div 4 = 3$.
- within the ratios, going from denominator to numerator, $4 \div 2 = 2$ and $12 \div 6 = 2$.

Use the Thinking Skill *Connect* question to support the reasoning in this part of the instruction. Use the *Justify* question to emphasize further the idea that if the ratios are not equal, a statement is not a proportion.

Example 1

Instruction

Ask students to explain why it makes sense that there is a proportional relationship between Nora's pay and the hours she works. Sample: The hours she works are always multiplied by the same number to get her pay.

(continued)

Equal ratios reduce to the same ratio. Both $\frac{2}{4}$ and $\frac{6}{12}$ reduce to $\frac{1}{2}$. Notice these multiplication relationships between the numbers in the proportion.

$$2 \times 3 = 6$$
$$\frac{2}{4} = \frac{6}{12}$$
$$4 \times 3 = 12$$

$$2 \times 2 = 4 \downarrow \frac{2}{4} = \frac{6}{12} \downarrow \quad 6 \times 2 = 12$$

Thinking Skill

Connect

What mathematical property is illustrated by the equation $\frac{2}{4} \cdot \frac{3}{3} = \frac{6}{12}$? Identity Property of Multiplication

No; The relationship is not proportional because the ratios are not equal. They do not reduce to the same ratio. There is no form of 1 by which one of the ratios can be multiplied to produce the other ratio.

One ratio in a proportion can be expressed as the other ratio by multiplying the terms by a constant factor.

$$\frac{2}{4} \cdot \frac{3}{3} = \frac{6}{12}$$

We can use this method to test whether ratios form a proportion. For example, to park for 2 hours, a lot charges $3. To park for 3 hours, the lot charges $4.

| Time (hr) | 2 | 3 |
| Charge ($) | 3 | 4 |

Justify Is the time parked and the fee charged by the lot a proportional relationship? Why or why not?

Example 1

Nora is paid $12 an hour. Is her pay proportional to the number of hours she works?

Solution

We can make a table of her pay for various hours of work. We see that the ratio of pay to hours worked is constant. The ratio does not change. Any two ratios form a proportion.

$$\frac{\text{Pay (\$)}}{\text{Time (hr)}} \quad \frac{12}{1} = \frac{36}{3}$$

Therefore, Nora's pay **is proportional** to the number of hours she works.

Nora's Pay

Hours	Pay	Pay / Hours
1	12	$\frac{12}{1}$
2	24	$\frac{24}{2} = \frac{12}{1}$
3	36	$\frac{36}{3} = \frac{12}{1}$
4	48	$\frac{48}{4} = \frac{12}{1}$

Example 2

Nelson has a paper route. If he works by himself the job takes 60 minutes. If he splits the route with a friend, it takes 30 minutes. If two friends help, the job takes 20 minutes. Is the amount of time it takes to complete the route proportional to the number of people working?

The table shows the number of workers and the number of minutes needed to complete the job. The ratio of time to workers changes.

$$\frac{60}{1} \neq \frac{15}{1}$$

There is a relationship between the number of workers and the time to complete a job, but the relationship **is not proportional.**

Time for Paper Route

Number Working	Time (min.)	Time / Workers
1	60	$\frac{60}{1}$
2	30	$\frac{30}{2} = \frac{15}{1}$
3	20	$\frac{20}{3}$

We can use proportions to solve problems where one of the numbers in the proportion is missing. A variable represents the missing number in the proportion.

$$\frac{2}{8} = \frac{6}{x}$$

One way to find the missing number in a proportion is to use the multiple between the terms of the ratios. This method is like finding equivalent fractions.

$$2 \times 3 = 6$$
$$\frac{2}{8} = \frac{6}{x}$$
$$8 \times 3 = 24$$

By multiplying $\frac{2}{8}$ by $\frac{3}{3}$, we find that the missing term is 24. Below we show another relationship we can use to find a missing number in a proportion.

$$2 \times 4 = 8 \quad \downarrow \frac{2}{8} = \frac{6}{x} \downarrow \quad 6 \times 4 = 24$$

Again we find that the missing number is 24.

Solve: $\frac{24}{m} = \frac{8}{5}$

We solve the proportion by finding the missing number. We inspect the proportion to find a relationship that is convenient to use in order to calculate the missing number. This time we multiply both terms from right to left.

$$8 \times 3 = 24$$
$$\frac{24}{m} = \frac{8}{5}$$
$$5 \times 3 = 15$$

We find that **m = 15.**

Example 2
Instruction
You can extend this example by asking students to describe the relationship that is constant in this problem. Sample: The number of minutes times the number of people working is always 60.

Instruction
Explain that students can look at proportions with unknown numbers and decide whether they want to multiply across or down or up to find the unknown value. They can use whatever way makes sense or is easier to compute. The unknown value will be the same, as long as the computation was done correctly.

Example 3
Instruction
Ask volunteers to explain how they found the unknown number. You may want to point out that the proportion could have been rewritten as $\frac{8}{5} = \frac{24}{m}$ to make the multiplication relationship easier to see.

(continued)

Instruction

Discuss why it would be important to form the correct proportion when solving a problem. When a proportion is used to solve a problem, it is necessary that the terms in both ratios be in the correct order. The ratio table is an effective way to keep the terms in order.

Example 4
Instruction

Call attention to the way that the proportion can be written directly from the ratio table. Continue to emphasize the importance of entering the numbers in the correct order.

Practice Set
Problem a [Error Alert]

For each pair of ratios, ask students to decide whether the numerators share a constant factor, then decide if the denominators share the same constant factor.

Problem b [Justify]

Students should recognize that multiplying $\frac{3}{6}$ by $\frac{2}{2}$ is the same as multiplying $\frac{3}{6}$ by 1, and recall that multiplying a number by 1 does not change the value of the number.

Problems c–f

Before completing the arithmetic, ask students to name the constant factor that is present in each proportion.

Problems i and j [Analyze]

Remind students that proportions must be written in a consistent way. In problem **i**, for example, if the first ratio that is written represents length divided by width, the second ratio that is written must also represent length divided by width.

---

ratio word problems | Ratio word problems can include several numbers, so we will practice using a table with two columns to sort the numbers. In one column we write the ratio numbers. In the other column we write the actual counts. We can use a ratio table to help us solve a wide variety of problems.

Example 4

The ratio of boys to girls in the class is 3 to 4. If there are 12 girls, how many boys are there?

Solution

We see ratio numbers and one actual count. We record the numbers in a ratio table with two columns and two rows. We let b stand for the actual number of boys. Now we use two rows from the table to write a proportion.

	Ratio	Actual Count
Boys	3	b
Girls	4	12

→ $\frac{3}{4} = \frac{b}{12}$

By multiplying each term of the first ratio by 3, we find that there are **9 boys**.

$$\frac{3}{4} \cdot \frac{3}{3} = \frac{9}{12}$$

Practice Set ▶

a. Which pair of ratios forms a proportion? **B**

A $\frac{3}{6}, \frac{6}{9}$ **B** $\frac{3}{6}, \frac{6}{12}$ **C** $\frac{3}{6}, \frac{6}{3}$

b. Sample: I can multiply $\frac{3}{6}$ by $\frac{2}{2}$ to get $\frac{6}{12}$. There is no form of 1 by which I can multiply $\frac{3}{6}$ to get $\frac{6}{9}$ or $\frac{6}{3}$.

▶ **b.** [Justify] How do you know your choice is correct?

▶ Solve each proportion.

c. $\frac{4}{6} = \frac{c}{18}$ $c = 12$ **d.** $\frac{9}{3} = \frac{18}{d}$ $d = 6$

e. $\frac{e}{9} = \frac{5}{15}$ $e = 3$ **f.** $\frac{4}{f} = \frac{3}{12}$ $f = 16$

g. A wholesaler offers discounts for large purchases. The table shows the price of an item for various quantities. Is the price proportional to the quantity? How do you know? No, the price is not proportional to the quantity because the ratio of price to quantity changes.

Quantity	Price
10	$30
100	$200
1000	$1000

h. Yes, the total price is proportional to the quantity purchased because the ratio of price to quantity does not change.

h. A retailer sells an item for $5. Brenda needs several of the items. Is the total price proportional to the quantity purchased? How do you know?

▶ [Analyze] Solve problems **i** and **j** by creating a ratio table and writing a proportion.

i. The ratio of the length to width of a rectangular room is 5 to 4. If the room is 20 feet long, how wide is the room? $\frac{5}{4} = \frac{20}{w}$, 16 ft

j. The teacher-student ratio in the primary grades is 1 to 20. If there are 100 students in the primary grades, how many teachers are there? $\frac{1}{20} = \frac{t}{100}$, 5 teachers

▶ See Math Conversations in the sidebar.

Teacher Tip

To extend the concept in this lesson, you can explain that **all the terms in a proportion are proportional** in these directions: left and right, and up and down. They are not proportional diagonally. (Students will learn later about the diagonal relationship in a proportion.)

To prove this, show how the terms in a proportion can be rearranged to form three other proportions.

For example, from $\frac{5}{7} = \frac{25}{35}$, we can also write:

- $\frac{5}{25} = \frac{7}{35}$

- $\frac{7}{5} = \frac{35}{25}$

- $\frac{35}{7} = \frac{25}{5}$

▶ *** 1.** ₍₂₃₎ [Analyze] Marc's cell phone company charges users $33\frac{1}{3}$ cents for every minute they go over their plan. If Marc goes 27 minutes over his plan, how much money will his cell phone company charge him? $9.00

2. ₍₂₄₎ Juan ran the 100-meter dash in 11.91 seconds. Steve finished behind Juan with a time of 12.43 seconds. How many seconds slower than Juan was Steve?   0.52 seconds

▶ *** 3.** ₍₃₄₎ The ratio of the base of a certain triangle to its height is 3 to 2. If the base of the triangle is 24 inches, what is the height of the triangle?
$\frac{3}{2} = \frac{24}{h}$, $h = 16$ inches

* 4. ₍₂₆₎ A sculpture in the center of the bank lobby casts a triangular shadow on the west floor when sunlight shines through the east window in the morning. In the afternoon, the sun shines through the west window casting the sculpture's shadow on the east floor. The change in the position of the shadow from morning to afternoon corresponds to what kind of geometric transformation?   reflection

* 5. _(31, 33) Simplify: $(-3) + (-4) - (-5) - (+6)$ -8

* 6. _(Inv. 3) [Explain] True or false: Some rectangles are rhombuses. Explain.

6. True; Sample explanation: A rhombus has four congruent sides, so any square is a rectangle and also a rhombus.

Simplify.

▶ **7.** ₍₂₇₎ $\frac{7^7 \cdot 7^0}{7^5 \cdot 7^2}$ 1

8. _(24, 25) $\frac{3 + 2.7}{3 - 2.7}$ 19

9. _(15, 21) $3^3 + 4[21 - (7 + 2 \cdot 3)]$ 59

10. _(13, 23) $\frac{9}{5} \cdot \frac{1}{3} - \frac{1}{10}$ $\frac{1}{2}$

11. _(15, 21) $\sqrt{1^3 + 2^3 + 3^3}$ 6

* 12. ₍₃₃₎ $-2 - (-13 + 20)$ -9

▶ *** 13.** ₍₃₂₎ [Evaluate] The spinner at right is spun once. What is the probability that the spinner will stop

a. in sector A? $\frac{1}{2}$

b. in sector B? $\frac{1}{4}$

c. in sector A or C? $\frac{3}{4}$

* 14. ₍₃₁₎ Collect like terms to simplify.
a. $7xy - 3y + 4y - 18yx$ **b.** $13b^2 + 8ac - ac + 4$
$\quad - 11xy + y$ $13b^2 + 7ac + 4$

15. _(3, 24) On one shipping pallet of water there are 30 boxes. In each box are 10 cases. In each case are 24 bottles. In each bottle are 20 fluid ounces of water. How many ounces are in 2 shipping pallets?   288,000 fluid ounces

Lesson 34   227

▶ See Math Conversations in the sidebar.

3 Written Practice

Math Conversations
Discussion opportunities are provided below.

Problem 1 [Analyze]
Ask students to choose mental math or paper and pencil and use that method to solve the problem. Then ask students to name the method they chose, and explain why that method was chosen. Sample: Mental math; since $33\frac{1}{3}$ cents is $\frac{1}{3}$ of a dollar, divide 27 by 3 to find the number of dollars. Marc's cost is $9.

Problem 13 [Evaluate]
"What fraction of the whole spinner does each outcome represent?" $A: \frac{1}{2}$; $B: \frac{1}{4}$; $C: \frac{1}{4}$

"Suppose the spinner is used for 1000 spins. Predict the number of times you would expect an outcome of C, and explain your prediction." 250; find $\frac{1}{4}$ of 1000

Errors and Misconceptions
Problem 3
Some students may assume that there is only one correct way to write a proportion. Use problem 3 to demonstrate that there are a number of ways, as long as the ratios in each proportion are written in a consistent way. For example:
- If the first ratio is established as base to height, the proportion shown below can be used to solve the problem.
$$\frac{3}{2} = \frac{24}{h}$$
- If the first ratio is established as height to base, the proportion shown below can be used.
$$\frac{2}{3} = \frac{h}{24}$$

Both proportions can be used to solve the problem. In each proportion, students should note that the same constant factor (8) is present.

Problem 7
Watch for students who attempt to simplify the expression by first writing the standard form of each term. Review the laws of exponents with these students, and then help them apply the laws to simplify the expression.

(continued)

Math Conversations

Discussion opportunities are provided below.

Problem 16b Analyze

Have students note that enough information is given to solve the problem by proportion.

Problem 25 Connect

Some students may infer that the transformation also includes a rotation because the puck is likely to spin to some degree as it slides.

Problem 28 Evaluate

Make sure students write an equation that represents subtracting a negative integer.

---

* **16.** (19, Inv. 3) **Analyze** Parallelograms *ABCD* and *WXYZ* are similar.

   a. What is the measure of ∠*Y*? 100°

▶   **b.** What is the length of side *WX*? 6 in.

For problems **17–20**, find all values of *b* that make the equation true.

17. (14) $3|b| = 21$ $b = 7, b = -7$ **18.** (14, 31) $b + 2b = 15$ $b = 5$

19. (14) $\frac{81}{b} = 9$ $b = 9$ **20.** (14) $|b| + |b| = 12$ $b = 6, b = -6$

* **21.** (11, 30) Write $\frac{1}{3}$ as a decimal and a percent. $0.\overline{3}, 33\frac{1}{3}\%$

22. (28) Alfred was studying the mass of several planets. He found that Pluto's mass is 4.960×10^{27} kg, Neptune's is 1.028×10^{27} kg, Jupiter's is 1.894×10^{30} kg, and Earth's is 5.976×10^{27} kg. Order the planets from greatest to least mass. Jupiter, Earth, Pluto, Neptune

23.

-5   0   5

23. (1) **Model** On a number line, graph −3 and two numbers that are 4 units away.

24. (32) Brittanie's gasoline credit card bill was $70.92 in September, $38.15 in October, and $52.83 in November. Altogether, what were her gasoline charges for these months? **C**

    A $109.07   **B** $150.90   **C** $161.90   **D** $207.70

▶ **25.** (26) **Connect** The hockey puck slid across the ice from point A to point B. This movement corresponds to what geometric transformation? translation

Solve for *y*.

* **26.** (34) $\frac{10}{y} = \frac{2}{7}$ 35   * **27.** (34) $\frac{4}{5} = \frac{16}{y}$ 20

28. $134 - (-129)$ $= t; t = 134 +$ $129; t = 263$ The difference between coldest and hottest temperatures recorded is 263°.

▶* **28.** (33) **Evaluate** Vostok, Antarctica holds the world's record for the coldest temperature, which is −129°F. Death Valley, California holds the record for the hottest recorded temperature, which is 134°F. Write an equation with integers for finding the difference between these two temperatures and then solve it.

29. (14) Evaluate $a^2 + b^2 - 2ab$ for $a = 4$ and $b = 2$. 4

30. (Inv. 1) In which quadrant is the point $(2, -3)$? fourth quadrant

▶ See Math Conversations in the sidebar.

Looking Forward

Working with proportions and solving ratio word problems prepares students for:

- **Lesson 44,** solving proportions using cross products.
- **Lesson 45,** solving ratio problems involving totals.
- **Lesson 49,** solving rate problems with proportions and equations.
- **Lesson 88,** reviewing proportional and non-proportional relationships.

Math Background

If two variables, *x* and *y*, are proportional, then pairs of (*x*, *y*) values will fall on a line that passes through the origin. This is because the ratio of *y* to *x* is a constant *k*. In symbols, $\frac{y}{x} = k$. This can be written as $y = kx$, which represents a line with *y*-intercept 0. This graph shows some (*hours, pay*) pairs for a person who earns $12 per hour. The points fall on the line $y = 12x$.

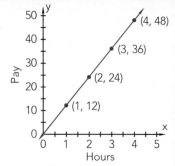

• Similar and Congruent Polygons

Objectives

- Identify corresponding parts of similar and congruent polygons and understand the relationships between them.
- Determine that triangles are similar when their corresponding sides are proportional in length.
- Determine that triangles are similar when their angles are congruent.
- Use the relationships between sides and angles of similar and congruent polygons to find missing side and angle measures.

Lesson Preparation

Materials

- **Power Up G** (in *Instructional Masters*)

Optional

- **Investigation Activity 2** (in *Instructional Masters*) **or graph paper**

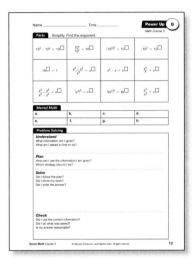

Power Up G

Math Language

Maintain	English Learners (ESL)
congruent	tick mark
corresponding parts	
similar	

Technology Resources

Student eBook Complete student textbook in electronic format.

Resources and Planner CD Assessment, reteaching, and instructional masters, plus a pacing calendar with standards.

Test and Practice Generator CD Create additional practice sheets and custom-made tests.

www.SaxonPublishers.com Visit for more student activities and planning materials.

Inclusion

Adaptations CD Adapted lessons, investigations, practice and assessments.

Meeting Standards

National Council of Teachers of Mathematics (NCTM)

Geometry

GM.1a Precisely describe, classify, and understand relationships among types of two- and three-dimensional objects using their defining properties

GM.1b Understand relationships among the angles, side lengths, perimeters, areas, and volumes of similar objects

GM.1c Create and critique inductive and deductive arguments concerning geometric ideas and relationships, such as congruence, similarity, and the Pythagorean relationship

Connections

CN.4a Recognize and use connections among mathematical ideas

Problem-Solving Strategy: Use Logical Reasoning/ Guess and Check/Work Backwards

Find each missing digit. (Hint: If the remainder is 8, then the divisor must be greater than 8.)

$$
\begin{array}{r}
\_\ \_\ \text{r }8 \\
\_\ )\overline{1\ \_\ \_} \\
=\ = \\
\_\ \_ \\
\underline{=\ =} \\
\_
\end{array}
$$

Understand   **Understand the problem.**

"What information are we given?"

A division problem has a remainder of 8, but the divisor, the quotient, and two of the digits of the dividend are missing.

"What are we asked to do?"

We are asked to find the missing digits.

Plan   **Make a plan.**

"What problem-solving strategy will we use?"

We will *use logical reasoning* and number sense to *guess and check* as to the missing digits. Because we do have the remainder, we will also *work backwards.*

"If the remainder is 8, what are the possible divisors?"

only 9

Solve   **Carry out the plan.**

$$
\begin{array}{r}
\_\ \_\ \text{R }8 \\
9)\overline{1\ \_\ \_} \\
-\ == \\
\_\ \_ \\
-\ \underline{=}\\
8
\end{array}
\qquad
\begin{array}{r}
2\ \_\ \text{R }8 \\
9)\overline{1\ \_\ \_} \\
-\ \underline{1\ 8} \\
\_\ \_ \\
-\ \underline{=}\\
8
\end{array}
\qquad
\begin{array}{r}
2\ \_\ \text{R }8 \\
9)\overline{1\ 9\ \_} \\
-\ \underline{1\ 8} \\
1\ \_ \\
-\ \underline{=}\\
8
\end{array}
\qquad
\begin{array}{r}
2\ 1\ \text{R }8 \\
9)\overline{1\ 9\ \_} \\
-\ \underline{1\ 8} \\
1\ \_ \\
-\ \underline{9}\\
8
\end{array}
\qquad
\begin{array}{r}
2\ 1\ \text{R }8 \\
9)\overline{1\ 9\ 7} \\
-\ \underline{1\ 8} \\
1\ 7 \\
-\ \underline{9}\\
8
\end{array}
$$

Check   **Look back.**

"How can we verify the solution is correct?"

We can use the inverse operation of division, which is multiplication: $(21 \times 9) + 8 = 189 + 8 = 197$.

• Similar and Congruent Polygons

facts | Power Up G

mental math

  a. Number Sense: $22 ÷ 4 $5.50

  b. Algebra: $x - 12 = 48$ 60

  c. Measurement: Find the temperature indicated on this thermometer.   24°C

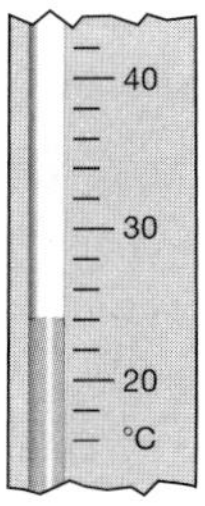

  d. Rate: Mei Ling walked 100 yards in 1 minute. How many feet per minute is that?   300 ft/min

  e. Scientific Notation: Write five billion in scientific notation. $5 × 10^9$

  f. Geometry: Two sides of a triangle are 7 and 9. The third side must be between what two numbers?   2 and 16

  g. Estimation: 3 at $19.98 plus 2 at $3.48 $67

  h. Calculation: $25 × 3, + 6, \sqrt{}, \sqrt{}, × 9, - 2, \sqrt{}, × 9, + 4, \sqrt{}$ 7

problem solving | Find each missing digit. (Hint: If the remainder is 8, then the divisor must be greater than 8.)

```
        _ _ r 8          21 r 8
    _)1 _ _         9)197
        _ _            18
        _ _            17
        _ _             9
        _               8
```

Recall that two figures are **similar** if they have the same shape even though they may vary in size. In the illustration below, triangles *A*, *B* and *C* are similar. To see this, we can imagine dilating △*B* as though we were looking through a magnifying glass. By enlarging △*B*, we could make it the same size as △*A* or △*C*. Likewise, we could reduce △*C* to the same size as △*A* or △*B*.

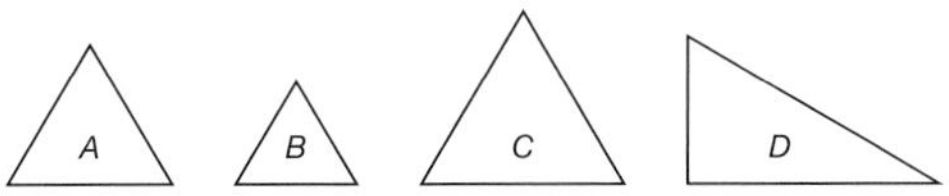

△*D* is not similar to the other three triangles, because its shape is different. Reducing or enlarging △*D* will change its size, but not its shape.

---

1 **Power Up**

Facts
Distribute **Power Up G** to students. See answers below.

Mental Math
Encourage students to share different ways to mentally compute these exercises. Strategies for exercises **a, d,** and **f** are listed below.

  a. Divide by 2 Twice
    $22 ÷ 4 = 22 ÷ 2 ÷ 2 =$
    $11 ÷ 2 = 5.50

  d. Use a Unit Rate
    100 yd × 3 ft/yd = 300 ft

  f. Sides of a Triangle
    The third side must be less than the sum of the other two sides and greater than the difference of the other two sides. It must be less than 16 and greater than 2.

Problem Solving
Refer to **Power-Up Discussion,** p. 229B.

Facts   Simplify. Find the exponent.

$10^3 \cdot 10^4 = 10^{\boxed{7}}$	$\dfrac{10^6}{10^2} = 10^{\boxed{4}}$	$(10^3)^2 = 10^{\boxed{6}}$	$\sqrt{10^2} = 10^{\boxed{1}}$
$10^{\boxed{0}} = 1$	$\dfrac{x^4 \cdot x^5}{x^3} = x^{\boxed{6}}$	$x^4 \cdot x = x^{\boxed{5}}$	$\dfrac{x^6}{x} = x^{\boxed{5}}$
$\dfrac{x^3 \cdot x^5}{x^2 \cdot x^4} = x^{\boxed{2}}$	$(x^4)^2 = x^{\boxed{8}}$	$(2x^2)^3 = 8x^{\boxed{6}}$	$\dfrac{x^3}{x^2} = x^{\boxed{1}}$

2 New Concepts

Instruction

Remind students about the terms *dilation* and *contraction* that they learned in Lesson 26. Ask them to define the words.

Point out that dilated or contracted figures are similar to the original figure and ask a volunteer to explain why. Sample: They are the same shape but a different size.

Discuss what makes figures congruent and why the transformations of reflection, rotation, and translation produce congruent images.

On the board or overhead demonstrate how single, double, and triple tick marks and arcs are used to identify congruent *corresponding* sides and angles.

Review the similarity and congruence symbols. Point out the congruence symbol consists of the equals sign and the similarity symbol.

Call attention to the definitions of similar polygons and congruent polygons. Tell students that they must learn these definitions.

(continued)

Also recall that figures that are the same shape and size are not only similar, they are also **congruent**. All three of the triangles below are similar, but only triangles △ABC and △DEF are congruent. Figures may be reflected (flipped) or rotated (turned) without affecting their similarity or congruence.

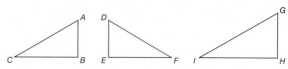

When inspecting polygons to determine whether they are similar or congruent, we compare their **corresponding parts**. Referring back to the illustration of △ABC and △DEF, we identify the following corresponding parts:

Corresponding Angles	Corresponding Sides
∠A corresponds to ∠D	$\overline{AB}$ corresponds to $\overline{DE}$
∠B corresponds to ∠E	$\overline{BC}$ corresponds to $\overline{EF}$
∠C corresponds to ∠F	$\overline{CA}$ corresponds to $\overline{FD}$

We use tick marks on corresponding side lengths that have equal length and arcs on corresponding angles that have the same measure.

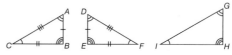

The symbol ~ represents similarity. Since △ABC is similar to △GHI, we can write △ABC ~ △GHI.

The symbol ≅ represents congruence. Since △ABC and △DEF are congruent, we can write △ABC ≅ △DEF.

Notice that when we write a statement about the similarity or congruence of two polygons, we name the letters of the corresponding vertices in the same order. Below we define similar and congruent polygons in a way that enables us to draw conclusions about their side lengths and angle measures.

Similar Polygons

> Similar polygons have corresponding angles which are the same measure and corresponding sides which are proportional in length.

Congruent Polygons

> Congruent polygons have corresponding angles which are the same measure and corresponding sides which are the same length.

English Learners

For problem **4** demonstrate the meaning of the word **tick mark.** Draw a 0 to 6 number line with tick marks for 0 and each whole number. Point to a tick mark and say:

"This is a tick mark. The tick marks on this number line show the position of 0, 1, 2, 3, 4, 5, and 6. Who would like to add a tick mark to show the position of $2\frac{1}{2}$?"

Ask for volunteers to add tick marks for other numbers.

Example 1

Which two quadrilaterals are similar?

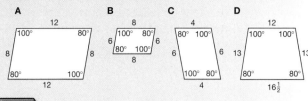

Polygons are similar if:

1. The corresponding angles are congruent.
2. The corresponding sides are proportional.

All four quadrilaterals have two 100° angles and two 80° angles. Figures A and B have the same orientations so it is clear that their corresponding angles are congruent. We could rotate (turn) figure C so that it has the same orientation as figures A and B and see that its corresponding angles are also congruent. The sequence of angles in figure D does not match the corresponding angles of the other figures, so we remove figure D from consideration for similarity.

Now we consider the side lengths to see if corresponding sides have proportional lengths.

	A	B	C
shorter sides	8	6	4
longer sides	12	8	6

We see that $\frac{8}{12}$ and $\frac{4}{6}$ are equal ratios, as both reduce to $\frac{2}{3}$. Thus the side lengths of figures A and C are proportional, and **figures A and C are similar**.

The ratio of side lengths of figure B does not reduce to $\frac{2}{3}$, so it is not similar to figures A and C.

The relationship between the sides and angles of a triangle is such that the lengths of the sides determine the size and position of the angles. For example, with three straws of different lengths, we can form one and only one shape of triangle. Three other straws of twice the length would form a similar triangle with angles of the same measure. Knowing that two triangles have proportional corresponding side lengths is enough to determine that they are similar.

Side-Side-Side Triangle Similarity

> If two triangles have proportional corresponding side lengths, then the triangles are similar.

Lesson 35　231

Example 1
Instruction

Remind students that it is not necessary for figures to have the same orientation to be similar or congruent. It is easier to see and decide which parts are corresponding when figures have the same orientation, so sometimes we redraw figures to help determine corresponding parts.

You can connect this lesson to earlier lessons on finding equivalent fractions by pointing out that knowing how to find equivalent fractions is necessary in determining proportionality.

(continued)

Math Background

Can any three segments form a triangle?

"No. To form a triangle, the sum of the lengths of the two shorter segments must be greater than the length of the longest segment."

Suppose you have segments of length 2 cm, 4 cm, and 8 cm. Imagine joining the 2 cm and 4 cm segments first. You could not form an angle with these segments so that the unconnected ends would reach the ends of the 8 cm segment.

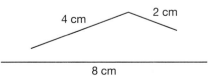

Instruction

You may want to demonstrate this relationship. Give all students sets of three straws or strips of paper that are different lengths (but the same three lengths for all students). Have them work in pairs to try to form two different triangles. They will not be able to do this.

Explain that triangles have some special side and angle relationships that are not the same as for other polygons, which make it easier to determine whether two triangles are similar. To help students understand this, have them compare this problem with the quadrilaterals in example 1 that had congruent sides or congruent angles but were not similar.

Example 2
Instruction

Guide students to understand that the reason we can say that the ratios form a proportion is because we know that the corresponding sides of similar triangles are proportional.

Point out that *scale factor* was introduced in the lesson on transformations. We use it for similar triangles just as we did for other figures.

Call attention to the ways that perimeter and area change when a side length is changed. The perimeter varies directly with the scale factor in length; the area varies as the square of the scale factor.

(continued)

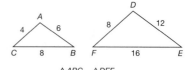

△ABC ~ △DEF

Consider the three triangles below. They have corresponding angles with equal measures.

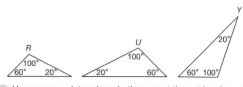

Measure the side lengths and check whether corresponding sides are proportional.

Analyze How can you determine whether or not these triangles are similar?

We might make the conjecture that these triangles are similar and that any triangle with the same angle measures would be similar to these. We will accept this basic assumption about similar triangles: all triangles with the same set of angle measures are similar. Thus, knowing that two triangles have congruent corresponding angles is sufficient information to conclude that the triangles are similar.

Angle-Angle-Angle Similarity

> If the angles of one triangle are congruent to the angles of another triangle, then the triangles are similar and their corresponding side lengths are proportional.

Example 2

Thinking Skill
Analyze

Is the perimeter of the triangle on the right three times the perimeter of the triangle on the left? Is the area three times as great? The perimeter of the larger triangle is three times the perimeter of the smaller triangle, but the area of the larger triangle is 9 times the area of the smaller triangle.

The triangles are similar. Find x.

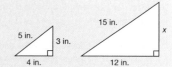

Solution

We pick two sides from the right triangle to write a ratio and include x. We pick the two corresponding sides from the left triangle to write a ratio.

Left Triangle	Right Triangle
4	12
3	x

Inclusion

Students will benefit from a discussion on how *scale factors* are used in the real world. Ask:

"Where have you seen scales used?" Samples: maps, models, paintings

"Why is it important to use a constant ratio (scale) in these real-world applications?" Sample: If you do not use a common ratio for each part of your model, the two objects related by the scale will not be similar.

Since the triangles are similar, the ratios form a proportion. We solve the proportion for x.

$$4 \times 3 = 12$$
$$\frac{4}{3} = \frac{12}{x}$$
$$3 \times 3 = 9$$

The constant factor that relates the ratios of similar polygons is called the **scale factor**. In this case the scale factor is 3. Since 3×3 is 9, we find that the side of the triangle is **9 inches.**

Example 3

An architect makes a scale drawing of a building.

  a. If one inch on the drawing represents 4 feet, then what is the scale factor from the drawing to the actual building?

  b. What is the length and width of a room that is 5 in. by 4 in. on the drawing?

Solution

A scale drawing is similar to the view of the object it represents.

  a. If 1 inch represents 4 feet, then 1 inch represents 48 inches. Therefore, the scale is 1:48 and the scale factor is **48.**

  b. Each inch represents 4 ft, so 5 in. represents $5 \times 4 = 20$ ft, and 4 in. represents $4 \times 4 = 16$ ft. The room is **20 ft long and 16 ft wide.**

Practice Set

Refer to the following figures for problems **a–e**.

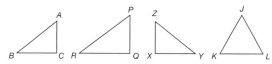

  ▶ **a.** Which triangle is congruent to $\triangle ABC$? $\triangle ZYX$ (only answer)

  b. Which triangle is similar but not congruent to $\triangle XYZ$? $\triangle QRP$ (only answer)

  c. Which triangle is not similar to $\triangle PQR$? $\triangle JKL$ (any letter arrangement)

  ▶ **d.** Which angle in $\triangle ZYX$ corresponds to $\angle A$ in $\triangle ABC$? $\angle Z$

  ▶ **e.** Which side of $\triangle PRQ$ corresponds to side XY in $\triangle ZYX$? Side QR (only answer)

f. No; The triangles are not similar because the lengths of the corresponding sides are not proportional.

  ▶ **f.** _Justify_ Are these two triangles similar? How do you know?

▶ See Math Conversations in the sidebar.

Example 3
Instruction
Ask students to explain why the scale factor is not used to answer the question in part b. Sample: it is easier to use the scale and work with feet, rather than use the scale factor and work with inches.

Practice Set
Problem a [Error Alert]
Remind students who need assistance that a tracing can be used to help decide if two figures are congruent.

Problems d and e [Error Alert]
If the different orientations of the triangles make it difficult for students to identify corresponding angles and sides, ask them to trace and label the given triangle, then orient the tracing to be the same as the similar triangle.

Problem f [Justify]
Ask students to use arithmetic to prove that the triangles are not proportional. Any ratio describing two sides of one triangle is not equivalent to the ratio that describes the corresponding sides of the other triangle. Sample: $\frac{5}{3} \neq \frac{12}{6}$.

Teacher Tip

To help students **connect** the topics in this lesson **to everyday experiences,** consider asking an architect or a designer to speak to the class about how he or she uses geometric ideas, such as similarity and scale factor, in his or her work.

Math Conversations

Discussion opportunities are provided below.

Problem 2 Analyze

"How many factors does every prime number have?" two

"Is 1 a prime number, or a composite number, or neither? Explain your answer."
Neither; Sample explanation: A composite number has more than two factors. A prime number has exactly two factors. The number 1 has only one factor—itself.

Problem 4a Evaluate

The fractions $\frac{8}{25}$ and $\frac{17}{20}$ represent the probabilities expressed as a fraction in lowest terms.

(continued)

---

g. These quadrilaterals are similar. Find the missing side length. What is the scale factor from the smaller figure to the larger? (Units are inches.)
12 in.; 3

For **h–j**, draw two rectangles, one 2 cm-by-1 cm and the other 4 cm-by-2 cm. Then answer the following questions.   See student work.

h. What is the scale factor from the smaller to larger rectangle?   2

i. The perimeter of the larger rectangle is how many times the perimeter of the smaller rectangle?   2 times

j. The area of the larger rectangle is how many times the area of the smaller rectangle?   4 times

k. On a scale drawing of a house, one inch represents 8 feet. How wide is the garage if it is $2\frac{1}{2}$ inches wide on the drawing?   20 ft

Written Practice Strengthening Concepts

1. Yes, the distance Mr. Connors drives commuting is proportional to the number of days he works because the ratio of miles driven and days worked is constant.

* **1.** Mr. Connors drives his car 11 miles each day to and from work. Is the
(34) distance Mr. Connors drives commuting to work proportional to the number of days he works? How do you know?

▶ * **2.** Analyze If a number cube is rolled, what is the probability of rolling a
(9, 32) prime number? $\frac{1}{2}$

3. Adam worked 8 hours per week before his workload was increased.
(3, 4) After the increase, he worked 4 hours per day for six days each week. How many more hours per week did he work after the increase than he worked before the increase?   16 hours

* **4.** One hundred residents of the city were randomly selected for a survey
(32) regarding the new gymnasium design. Thirty-two residents approved of Design A and 85 residents approved of Design B.

▶ a. Evaluate Use these experimental results to calculate the probability that any city resident selected at random would approve of Design A. Then calculate the probability for Design B.   0.32, 0.85

b. Based on the results of the survey, which design would you recommend?   Design B

* **5.** Expand then collect like terms: $3(x + 2) + x + 2$ $4x + 8$
(21, 31)

6. Plot these points on a coordinate plane, then draw segments from
(20, Inv. 2) point to point to form a triangle: (0, 0), (4, 0), (0, 3). Use the Pythagorean Theorem to find the length of the hypotenuse. What is **a** the perimeter and **b** the area of the triangle?   a. 12 units, b. 6 square units

▶ See Math Conversations in the sidebar.

7. Find the
(Inv. 2)
    a. area and   24 cm²
    b. perimeter of the triangle.   24 cm

8 cm

6 cm

Generalize Simplify.

* 8. a. $(-3) + (-15)$ -18 ▶ **b.** $(-3) - (-15)$ 12
(31, 33)

9. a. $(-15) + (-3)$ -18 **b.** $(-15) - (-3)$ -12
(31, 33)

▶*** 10.** $1\frac{2}{3} + 2\frac{3}{4}$ $4\frac{5}{12}$ **11.** $\frac{1}{8} + \frac{7}{8} \div \frac{7}{8}$ $1\frac{1}{8}$
(13)   (13, 22)

12. $\frac{9}{10} - \frac{2}{3} \cdot \frac{3}{5}$ $\frac{1}{2}$ **13.** $\frac{(2.54) + 1.21}{0.03}$ 125
(13, 22)   (24, 25)

* 14. $7^2 - 4(7 + 3) + 1^{20} - \sqrt{64}$ ▶ **15.** $(0.3^2 - 0.2^2) - (0.3 - 0.2)^2$
(15, 21) 2   (24, 25) 0.04

16. Find each missing exponent.
(27)
    a. $10^5 \cdot 10^6 = 10^{\square}$ 11   **b.** $\frac{10^5}{10^2} = 10^{\square}$ 3

17. Triangles *ABE* and *ACD* are similar.
(35)
    a. Which side of △*ABE* corresponds to
    side *CD*? side *BE*

    b. Compare: m∠*AEB* ⊜ m∠*D*

For problems **18** and **19** refer to this spinner. It is
divided into five congruent sectors.

18. a. What is the ratio of even numbers to odd
(32)   numbers on the spinner? $\frac{2}{3}$

    b. What is the probability of spinning an
    even number? $\frac{2}{5}$

    c. What is the probability of not spinning an even number? $\frac{3}{5}$

19. a. Sample Space =
$\begin{Bmatrix} H1, H2, H3, H4, H5 \\ T1, T2, T3, T4, T5 \end{Bmatrix}$

19. a. If a coin is tossed once and the spinner is spun once, what is the
(32)   sample space of the experiment?

    b. What is the probability of getting heads and an even number? $\frac{1}{5}$

20. b. Example: I
would choose the
fraction because
it is easy to
mentally compute
$\frac{1}{8} \cdot 4 = \frac{1}{2}$ and
parts of inches
are often reported
as fractions.

* 20. a. *Formulate* Write $\frac{1}{8}$ as a decimal and a percent. 0.125, 12.5% or $12\frac{1}{2}$%
(12)

    b. Which of the three forms would be most convenient to use to find a
    part of 4 inches?

Lesson 35   **235**

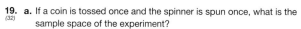
▶ See Math Conversations in the sidebar.

Math Conversations
Discussion opportunities are provided below.

Problem 8b Generalize
*"This expression can be rewritten to make
the arithmetic easier to complete. Explain
how you would rewrite the expression."*
Subtracting -15 is the same as adding $+15$;
rewrite the expression as $(-3) + (+15)$
or $-3 + 15$.

Problem 10 Generalize
To find the sum, students may add $\frac{2}{3}$ and $\frac{3}{4}$.
Remind these students that one way to check
their answer is to change each mixed number
to an improper fraction, then find the sum of
the improper fractions.

Errors and Misconceptions
Problem 15
Students who name 0 as the answer
incorrectly simplified $(0.3^2 - 0.2^2)$ to $(0.1)^2$.
To remediate this error, write the simpler
problem $3^2 - 2^2$ on the board or overhead.
Demonstrate that squaring each number
($3^2 = 9$ and $2^2 = 4$) produces the correct
answer ($9 - 5 = 4$), and subtracting before
squaring ($3^2 - 2^2 = 1^2$) does not ($1^2 = 1$). So
$(0.3^2 - 0.2^2) \neq (0.1)^2$.

(continued)

Math Conversations

Discussion opportunities are provided below.

Problem 30 `Analyze`

"Sides PQ and PR each display a tick mark. What do the tick marks represent?" congruency (The sides have exactly the same measure.)

"Because two sides of the triangle are congruent, two angles of the triangle are also congruent. Explain how you can identify which two of the three angles of the triangle are congruent." Sample: The angles opposite the congruent sides are congruent.

Errors and Misconceptions
Problem 24

Students may have difficulty finding the value of x because the constant factor of the proportion is not obvious.

Remind students that fractions in lowest terms are often easier to work with than fractions that are not in lowest terms. Ask students to reduce $\frac{7}{28}$ to lowest terms and then name the constant factor of the proportion. $\frac{1}{4}$; 9

For additional practice with this skill, invite students to solve $\frac{x}{24} = \frac{15}{40}$ for x. $x = 9$

For problems **21–24,** use inspection to find all values of x which make the equations true.

21. $|x| = 4$ $x = 4, -4$
(1, 14)

* 22. $2x + 5 = 29$ $x = 12$
(14)

* 23. $\frac{3}{x} = \frac{12}{20}$ $x = 5$
(14, 34)

▶ *** 24.** $\frac{7}{28} = \frac{9}{x}$ $x = 36$
(14, 34)

25. Use prime factorization to reduce $\frac{144}{360}$. $\frac{2}{5}$
(9)

26. On a number line, graph the negative integers.
(1)

26.
```
-+-•+•+•+•+•+|-+-|-+-|-+-|-+
     -5      0       5
```

27. Estimate: $\dfrac{(39)(1.9) + 1.1}{8.89}$ 9
(17)

28. `Evaluate` The floor of Memorial Arena measures 100 ft wide by 200 ft long. The facility is used for arena football games, which are played on similar rectangular field that is 150 ft long.
(35)

   a. What is the width of the football field?   75 ft

   b. What is the perimeter of the football field?   450 ft

29. One sheet of paper in a notebook is $8\frac{1}{2}$ in. × 11 in. A smaller notebook has a similar shape, and its pages are $5\frac{1}{2}$ in. long. What is the width of the paper in the smaller notebook? $4\frac{1}{4}$ in.
(35)

30. `Analyze` Triangle PQR is isosceles and $\angle PRS$ measures 130°. Find:
(20)

   a. $m\angle PRQ$ 50°

   b. $m\angle Q$ 50°

   c. $m\angle P$ 80°

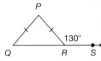

▶ See Math Conversations in the sidebar.

Looking Forword

Understanding the relationships between similar and congruent polygons prepares students for:

- **Investigation 5,** graphing transformations.
- **Lesson 65,** performing applications using similar triangles.
- **Lesson 71,** finding percent change of dimensions.
- **Lesson 87,** solving scale drawing word problems.
- **Lesson 91,** investigating the effects of scaling on perimeter, area, and volume.
- **Lesson 101,** calculating geometric probabilities.
- **Lesson 108,** working with similar solids.

Distribute **Cumulative Test 6** to each student. Two versions of the test are available in *Saxon Math Course 3 Course Assessments Book*. Have students complete the **Power-Up Test** first. Allow 10 minutes. Then have students work the 20 numbered items on the **Cumulative Test.** Students may use copies of the answer sheet to record their work. Track individual and class progress with the **Test Analysis** forms.

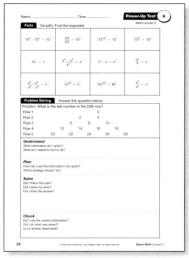

Power-Up Test 6

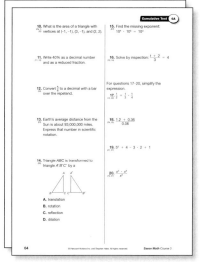

Cumulative Test 6A

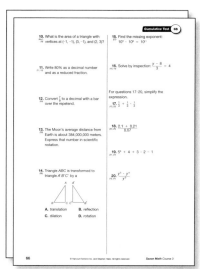

Alternative Cumulative Test 6B

Optional Answer Forms

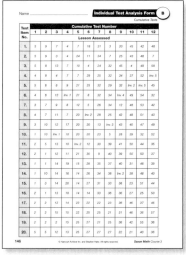

Individual Test Analysis Form

Class Test Analysis Form

Reteaching

Students who score below 80% on the assessment may be in need of reteaching. Look for the causes of student mistakes. If errors are conceptual, refer to the *Reteaching Masters* for reteaching.

The Vastness of Space

Assign after Lesson 35

Objectives

- Calculate distance given time or rate.
- Use appropriate operations with scientific notation to solve application problems.
- Round answers to the appropriate level of accuracy.
- Communicate ideas through writing.

Materials

Performance Activity 6

Calculator

Preparation

Make copies of **Performance Activity 6.** (One per student.)

Time Requirement

15–30 minutes; Begin in class and complete at home.

Activity

Tell students they will be calculating large numbers using scientific notation that describe our solar system. Students will first use the speed of light in miles per second and the time it takes light to reach each planet in seconds to determine the distance from the Sun to each planet in miles. Their answers should be expressed in scientific notation. Students then compare the distances between objects in space. Point out that all necessary information is provided on **Performance Activity 6.**

Criteria for Evidence of Learning

- Correctly calculates the distance between the Sun and each planet of the solar system using values of time and rate.
- Demonstrates knowledge of operations with scientific notation by accurately comparing relative distances in space.
- Communicates ideas clearly through writing.

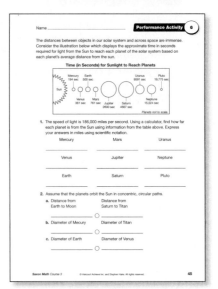

Performance Activity 6

Meeting Standards

National Council of Teachers of Mathematics (NCTM)

Numbers and Operations

NO.1e Develop an understanding of large numbers and recognize and appropriately use exponential, scientific, and calculator notation

NO.2a Understand the meaning and effects of arithmetic operations with fractions, decimals, and integers

NO.3a Select appropriate methods and tools for computing with fractions and decimals from among mental computation, estimation, calculators or computers, and paper and pencil, depending on the situation, and apply the selected methods

Measurement

ME.2f Solve simple problems involving rates and derived measurements for such attributes as velocity and density

Problem Solving

PS.1b Solve problems that arise in mathematics and in other contexts

Communication

CM.3d Use the language of mathematics to express mathematical ideas precisely

• Multiplying and Dividing Integers
• Multiplying and Dividing Terms

Objectives

- Multiply and divide integers and assign the appropriate sign to the product.
- Multiply and divide integers to solve word problems.
- Distinguish between the square roots of a number and its principal square root.

Lesson Preparation

Materials

- **Power Up H** (in *Instructional Masters*)
- **Teacher-provided material:** calculators

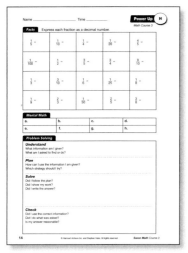

Power Up H

Math Language

Maintain	English Learners (ESL)
square root	deducted

Technology Resources

Student eBook Complete student textbook in electronic format.

Resources and Planner CD Assessment, reteaching, and instructional masters, plus a pacing calendar with standards.

Test and Practice Generator CD Create additional practice sheets and custom-made tests.

www.SaxonPublishers.com Visit for more student activities and planning materials.

Inclusion

Adaptations CD Adapted lessons, investigations, practice and assessments.

Meeting Standards

National Council of Teachers of Mathematics (NCTM)

Numbers and Operations

NO.1g Develop meaning for integers and represent and compare quantities with them

NO.2a Understand the meaning and effects of arithmetic operations with fractions, decimals, and integers

NO.2c Understand and use the inverse relationships of addition and subtraction, multiplication and division, and squaring and finding square roots to simplify computations and solve problems

Power-Up Discussion

For use with Power Up, p. 237

Problem-Solving Strategy: Use Logical Reasoning

The item cost \$4.59. Abraham paid with a \$5 bill. The clerk gave Abraham 4 coins. What were they?

Understand **Understand the problem.**

"What information are we given?"

Abraham used a \$5 bill to pay for a \$4.59 item. The clerk gave him 4 coins in change.

"What are we asked to do?"

Determine what the four coins are.

Plan **Make a plan.**

"What problem-solving strategy will we use?"

We will *use logical reasoning* to count by pennies, nickels, dimes, and/or quarters from \$4.59.

Solve **Carry out the plan.**

"Which coin will we begin with?"

\$4.59 + one penny = \$4.60.

"How do we proceed?"

\$4.60 + one nickel = \$4.65 + one dime = \$4.75 + one quarter = \$5.00

Check **Look back.**

"Did we find the answer to the question that was asked?"

Yes. The four coins Abraham received in change were a penny, a nickel, a dime, and a quarter.

- • Multiplying and Dividing Integers
- • Multiplying and Dividing Terms

Power Up | *Building Power*

facts

Power Up H

mental math

a. **Number Sense:** $280 ÷ 40 $7

b. **Fractional Parts:** $66\frac{2}{3}$% of $66 $44

c. **Measurement:** Approximate the measure of this angle.   Answers may vary between 50° and 55°.

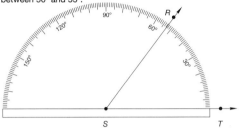

d. **Rate:** Kerry wrote 12 pages in 2 hours. What was her rate in pages per hour?   6 pages per hour

e. **Proportions:** The ratio of sheep to goats in a petting zoo is 3 to 1. There are 12 sheep. How many goats are there?   4

f. **Geometry:** Two angles of a triangle measure 30° and 60°. Find the measure of the third angle.   90°

g. **Powers/Roots:** List all the perfect squares from 1 to 100. Then, approximate $\sqrt{101} - \sqrt{38}$.   1, 4, 9, 16, 25, 36, 49, 64, 81, 100; 4

h. **Calculation:** $8 + 8, \sqrt{\ }, \sqrt{\ }, × 10, + 1, ÷ 3, × 7, \sqrt{\ }, - 8$ -1

problem solving

The item cost $4.59. Abraham paid with a $5 bill. The clerk gave Abraham 4 coins. What were they?   quarter, dime, nickel, penny

New Concepts | *Increasing Knowledge*

multiplying and dividing integers

On this number line we illustrate multiplication and division of integers. The arrows show that 3 times -2 is -6.

$$3(-2) = -6$$

Lesson 36   **237**

Power Up

Facts
Distribute **Power Up H** to students. See answers below.

Mental Math
Encourage students to share different ways to mentally compute these exercises. Strategies for exercises **a, d,** and **e** are listed below.

a. **Divide by 10, Then by 4**
   $280 ÷ 40 = 280 ÷ 10 ÷ 4 =$
   $28 ÷ 4 = 7$
   Divide by 4, Then by 10
   $280 ÷ 40 = 280 ÷ 4 ÷ 10 =$
   $70 ÷ 10 = 7$

d. **Use Math Sense**
   12 pages in 2 hours
   $\frac{12}{2}$ pages in $\frac{2}{2}$ hours
   6 pages per hour

e. **Look for a Multiplier**
   $1 × 3 = 3$
   $? × 3 = 12$
   $? = 4$

Problem Solving
Refer to **Power-Up Discussion,** p. 237B.

Facts | Express each fraction as a decimal number.

$\frac{1}{5}$ = 0.2	$\frac{1}{10}$ = 0.1	$\frac{1}{4}$ = 0.25	$\frac{1}{20}$ = 0.05	$\frac{4}{5}$ = 0.8
$\frac{1}{100}$ = 0.01	$\frac{1}{2}$ = 0.5	$\frac{3}{5}$ = 0.6	$\frac{3}{4}$ = 0.75	$\frac{9}{10}$ = 0.9
$\frac{1}{3}$ = 0.$\overline{3}$	$\frac{3}{10}$ = 0.3	$\frac{1}{6}$ = 0.1$\overline{6}$	$\frac{1}{25}$ = 0.04	$\frac{1}{8}$ = 0.125
$\frac{1}{9}$ = 0.$\overline{1}$	$\frac{2}{3}$ = 0.$\overline{6}$	$\frac{1}{50}$ = 0.02	$\frac{2}{5}$ = 0.4	$\frac{3}{8}$ = 0.375

2 New Concepts

Instruction

Ask students to explain how and why the example on the number line shows each of the three relationships. Sample: It shows us that $3(-2) = -6$ because we can show -2 by moving 2 units to the left, so moving 2 units to the left 3 times is 3 times -2, and that is either $-2 + -2 + -2$ or $3 \times (-2)$.

Students may not accept that these relationships between the signs of the factors (or dividend and divisor) and the sign of the product (or quotient) will be true for all integers. Explain that it is and that they will learn more about this in a later lesson. Suggest that they observe the patterns and use them as a way to remember the relationships.

Example 1

Instruction

Discuss each problem, and help students apply the rules to decide the sign of the answer. For part c, you can show students a different way to find the answer that may help them understand why the rules work.

$$\frac{-10}{-5} = \frac{(\cancel{-}1)(10)}{(\cancel{-}1)(5)} = \frac{10}{5} = 2$$

Example 2

Instruction

Ask students to write an addition expression for Newton's internet service charges. $(-25) + (-25) + (-25) + (-25) + (-25) + (-25)$

Help students see that $(-25) + (-25) + (-25) + (-25) + (-25) + (-25)$ is the same as $6(-25)$.

(continued)

The illustration also shows that if we divide -6 into 3 parts, each part is -2.

$$\frac{-6}{3} = -2$$

Likewise, the illustration shows that the number of -2s in -6 is 3.

$$\frac{-6}{-2} = 3$$

From these illustrations notice these relationships:

$$3(-2) = -6$$

different signs → negative product

$$\frac{-6}{3} = -2$$

different signs → negative quotient

$$\frac{-6}{-2} = 3$$

same signs → positive quotient

When we multiply two negative numbers like $(-3)(-2)$, we can think about the multiplication as "the opposite of 3 times -2." Since $3(-2)$ is -6, the opposite of $3(-2)$ is the opposite of -6, which is positive 6.

$$(-3)(-2) = 6$$

same signs → positive product

Visit www. SaxonPublishers. com/ActivitiesC3 *for a graphing calculator activity.*

Example 1

Simplify:

a. $(-10)(-5)$ b. $(+10)(-5)$

c. $\dfrac{-10}{-5}$ d. $\dfrac{10}{-5}$

Solution

We multiply or divide as indicated. If the two numbers have the same sign, the answer is positive. If the two numbers have different signs, the answer is negative.

a. $(-10)(-5) = 50$ b. $(10)(-5) = -50$

c. $\dfrac{-10}{-5} = 2$ d. $\dfrac{10}{-5} = -2$

Example 2

Every month $25 is automatically deducted from Newton's checking account to pay for Internet service. Write an expression using integers that shows the effect on Newton's account of six months of charges.

English Learners

For problem **4** explain the meaning of the word **deducted**. Say:

> *"To deduct means to take away or subtract. If you used a $5 coupon when you paid for groceries, the clerk deducted $5 from the total cost."*

Write the following equations on the board and ask volunteers what was deducted in each case.

$120 – $12 = $108 $12 deducted

$45 – 25% = $33.75 25% deducted

Each month's charge subtracts $25 from Newton's checking account. We can represent each change as -25. Therefore, six months of charges is **6(-25), or -150.** Six months of charges would deduct $150 from Newton's account.

Since the product of two negative numbers is a positive number, squaring a negative number results in a positive number.

$$(-5)^2 = (-5)(-5) = 25$$

However, cubing a negative number results in a negative number.

$$(-2)^3 = (-2)(-2)(-2)$$

The product of -2 and -2 is 4.

$$[(-2)(-2)](-2) = (4)(-2)$$

The product of 4 and -2 is -8.

$$(4)(-2) = (-8)$$

Example 3

Simplify.

  a. $(-1)^5$ b. $(-1)^6$

Solution

Every pair of negative factors has a positive product, so an even number of negative factors is positive and an odd number is negative.

  a. $(-1)^5 = -1$ b. $(-1)^6 = 1$

Example 4

  a. For $y = x^2$, find y if x is -2.

  b. If $x^2 = 9$, then x can be which two numbers?

Solution

  a. We are asked to find the value of x^2 when x is -2. Since x^2 means $x \cdot x$, we multiply $(-2)(-2)$. The product is **4.**

  b. Both **3** and **-3** make the equation true.

$$3^2 = 9 \qquad (-3)^2 = 9$$

We could have solved example **4b** by finding the square root of x^2 and 9.

Thinking Skill

Connect

Use digits and symbols to show both square roots of 41. $\sqrt{41}$; $-\sqrt{41}$

We distinguish between the words "square root" and the ($\sqrt{}$). The radical indicates the **principal square root,** which is the positive square root of a positive real number.

- The square roots of 9 are 3 and -3.
- $\sqrt{9} = 3$

---

2 New Concepts *(Continued)*

Instruction

Understanding the difference between squaring and cubing negative integers will be needed when students learn to find square and cube roots.

Example 3

Instruction

Have students demonstrate understanding of these relationships by asking them to restate the explanation in the solution in their own words.

Example 4

Instruction

Remind students that an exponent tells how many times the base is used as a factor.

Instruction

You might ask students why they think the positive square root is the *principal square root.* Sample: We use positive numbers more than negative numbers.

(continued)

Math Background

Extending multiplication patterns can illustrate why the product of two negative numbers is positive. In this pattern, the second factor is always -5. Each time the first factor decreases by 1, the product increases by 5.

$$(+3)(-5) = -15$$
$$(+2)(-5) = -10$$
$$(+1)(-5) = -5$$
$$(0)(-5) = 0$$

We can extend the pattern to see what happens when the second factor becomes negative.

$$(-1)(-5) = 5$$
$$(-2)(-5) = 10$$
$$(-5)(-2) = 10$$

Calculator Activity

Have students check to see where the *reverse sign* key is on their calculators. Explain that this key is used to enter a negative number. Let everyone follow these instructions. Give assistance to those whose calculators may not work as described.

2 New Concepts (Continued)

Instruction

The summary of the rules for "Arithmetic with Two Integers" completes the table begun in earlier lessons. Stress the importance of learning these rules. Call attention to the way the sign of the result depends on the signs of the integers.

Example 5
Instruction

Ask volunteers to describe what happens in each step. Note in part **a** that the answer is given with the numerical coefficient first, followed by the variables. The variables may be listed in any order.

For part **b**, the fraction is written in simplest form. You can show students why the negative sign can move from the denominator to the numerator and to the fraction itself this way:

$$\frac{3x}{-z} = \frac{-1}{-1} \times \frac{3x}{(-1)z} = \frac{(-1)3x}{(-1)(-1)(z)} = \frac{-3x}{z}$$

$$= (-1)\left(\frac{3x}{z}\right) = -\frac{3x}{z}$$

(continued)

Below we summarize the rules for arithmetic with two integers.

Arithmetic with Two Integers

Operation	Rule
+	To find the sum of addends with different signs: **1.** Subtract the absolute values of the addends. **2.** Take the sign of the addend with the greater absolute value. To find the sum of addends with the same sign: **1.** Add the absolute values of the addends. **2.** Take the sign of the addends.
−	Instead of subtracting a number, add its opposite.
× ÷	**1.** Multiply or divide as indicated. **2.** If the two numbers have the same sign, the answer is positive. If the two numbers have different signs, the answer is negative.

Activity

Reversing Signs on a Calculator

Most calculators have a [+/−] key that reverses the sign of the displayed number. To key in a negative number, such as −5, we first key in its absolute value, in this case 5, and then press the [+/−] key to make the entry negative. Here is the keystroke sequence for adding −5 and −3 on most calculators:

The display should be −8. Try the following exercises:

a. $(-5) + (-3)$ −8   b. $(-15) - (-3)$ −12

c. $(-12)(-8)$ 96   d. $\frac{144}{-8}$ −18

---

multiplying and dividing terms

In Lesson 31 we added and subtracted terms. In this lesson we will multiply and divide terms.

Example 5

Simplify.

a. $(6x^2y)(-2xyz)$ b. $\frac{6x^2y}{-2xyz}$

Solution

a. We can use the commutative and associative properties of multiplication to rearrange and regroup the factors.

Teacher Tip

To help students avoid errors when working with problems involving **many negative signs,** suggest that they write terms with negative signs in parentheses. This will help them see the signs more easily when doing the computation. They can also strike completely through the parentheses when they reduce and avoid inadvertently changing a negative sign to a positive sign.

Step:	Justification:
$(6x^2y)(-2xyz)$	Given expression
$(6)(-2)x^2 \cdot x \cdot y \cdot y \cdot z$	Commutative and associative properties
$-12x^3y^2z$	Multiplied and grouped with exponents

b. We can factor the dividend and divisor and then reduce. The quotient assumes that no variables are zero.

Step:	Justification:
$\dfrac{6x^2y}{-2xyz}$	Given expression
$\dfrac{2 \cdot 3 \cdot x \cdot x \cdot y}{-2 \cdot x \cdot y \cdot z}$	Factors
$\dfrac{\overset{1}{2} \cdot 3 \cdot \overset{1}{\cancel{x}} \cdot x \cdot \overset{1}{\cancel{y}}}{-\underset{1}{\cancel{2}} \cdot \underset{1}{\cancel{x}} \cdot \underset{1}{\cancel{y}} \cdot z}$	Reduced
$-\dfrac{3x}{z}$	Simplified

Notice that in example 5, part **b,** we expressed the quotient as a negative fraction. The following three forms are equivalent; however, we avoid expressing a denominator as a negative number.

$$\frac{3x}{-z} = \underbrace{\frac{-3x}{z}}_{\text{Preferred}} = -\frac{3x}{z}$$

Example 6

Expand.

a. $3x(2x - 4)$ **b.** $-3x(2x - 4)$

Solution

a. We apply the distributive property and multiply the terms within the parenthesis by $3x$.

$$3x(2x - 4) = 6x^2 - 12x$$

b. We multiply by $-3x$. Notice that $-3x$ times -4 is $+12x$.

$$-3x(2x - 4) = -6x^2 + 12x$$

Practice Set ▶ Simplify:

a. $(-12)(-3)$ 36   **b.** $(-12)(+3)$ -36

c. $\dfrac{-12}{-3}$ 4   **d.** $\dfrac{-12}{+3}$ -4

e. $(-6)^2$ 36   **f.** $(-1)^2$ 1

g. $(-3)^3$ -27 **h.** $(-2)^4$ 16

▶ **i.** Solve: $x^2 = 100$ (Write two possible solutions.) $10, -10$

Lesson 36   241

▶ See Math Conversations in the sidebar.

New Concepts (Continued)

Example 6
Instruction
Point out that in both parts a and b, the expression in the parentheses contains two terms. This is the reason that the expanded forms have two terms.

Practice Set
Problems a–h
Before completing the arithmetic, ask students to name the sign of each product or quotient, and explain why that sign was named.

Problem i (Error Alert)
If students struggle identifying -10 as a solution, point out that 100 is a positive integer, and remind them that the product of two negative integers is a positive integer.

(continued)

Lesson 36   **241**

2 New Concepts (Continued)

Practice Set

Problem k Represent

A pattern can be used to help students write the expression. Point out that the ends of the drill rods are at depths of −8 m, −16 m, −24 m, −32 m, and so on, and explain that the depths are negative because each depth represents a distance *below* the surface of the water.

3 Written Practice

Math Conversations

Discussion opportunities are provided below.

Problem 4 Analyze

"What should we remember when we use a proportion to solve a problem?" Sample: Set two ratios equal to each other and write the terms of the ratios in an orderly way.

Problems 5 and 6 Justify

Invite one or more volunteers to explain how to identify the constant factor that is present in each proportion.

Problem 7 Evaluate

Students must recognize that finding the perimeter of the right triangle involves solving $a^2 + b^2 = c^2$ for c.

Problem 8 Generalize

Extend the Problem

"What is the sum of the angle measures of quadrilateral ABCD?" 360°

"What is the sum of the angle measures of quadrilateral PQRS?" 360°

"Rectangles and squares are other examples of quadrilaterals. What is the sum of the angle measures of a rectangle or a square? Explain how you know." 360°; Each figure has four 90° angles, and 4 × 90° = 360°.

"What generalization can you make about the sum of the angle measures of any quadrilateral?" The sum of the angle measures of any quadrilateral is 360°.

(continued)

242 **Saxon** *Math Course 3*

---

j. What are the square roots of 100? What is $\sqrt{100}$?   10, −10; 10

▶ k. Represent Drilling for core samples in the sea floor, the driller used 12 drill rods 8 meters long to reach from the surface of the ocean to the lowest core sample. Write an equation using integers that shows the depth of the core sample with respect to sea level.   12(−8) = −96

Simplify:

l. $(-12xy^2z)(3xy)$ $-36x^2y^3z$

m. $\dfrac{-12xy^2z}{3xy}$ $-4yz$

Expand:

n. $2x(2x - 5)$ $4x^2 - 10x$

o. $-2x(2x - 5)$ $-4x^2 + 10x$

Written Practice   *Strengthening Concepts*

1. A water company charges customers $1.081 for each CCF (hundred cubic feet) of water used. If one customer uses 70 CCF of water, how much will the water company charge the customer? $75.67
   (4, 25)

2. Each box of cards contains forty-five packs. Each pack contains eight cards. How many cards are in two boxes?   720 cards
   (4)

3. Doug read three books that averaged 156 pages each. He also read 12 short stories that were each six pages long. How many pages did Doug read altogether?   540 pages
   (3, 4)

▶ * 4. Analyze A bank prefers to have a customer-to-teller ratio of 3 to 1. If there are 9 customers in the bank, how many tellers should be available?   3 tellers
   (29)

Justify Solve for x. Check your solution.

▶ * 5. $\dfrac{x}{12} = \dfrac{2}{3}$ $x = 8$; See student work.   ▶ * 6. $\dfrac{1}{5} = \dfrac{4}{x}$ $x = 20$; See student work.
   (34)   (34)

▶ * 7. Evaluate Find the **a** area and **b** perimeter of the triangle with vertices (2, 3), (5, 3), and (5, −1).   **a.** 6 square units **b.** 12 units
   (Inv. 1, 20)

▶ * 8. Quadrilaterals *ABCD* and *PQRS* are similar.
   (19)

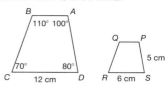

   a. What is the measure of ∠S?   80°

   b. What is the length of side *AD*?   10 cm

9. **a.** Expand: $-2(3x - 4)$ $-6x + 8$ **b.** Factor: $7x - 21$ $7(x - 3)$
   (21, 36)

242   **Saxon** *Math Course 3*

▶ See Math Conversations in the sidebar.

▶* 10. *Analyze* What is the probability of rolling an odd number on a number
(17) cube? How does that compare to the probability of rolling an even
number? $\frac{1}{2}$, same probability

Simplify problems **11–18.**

▶* 11. $(-4)\left(\frac{1}{2}\right)(-3)$ 6
(22, 36)

* 12. $\dfrac{-72xy}{6}$ $-12xy$
(36)

13. $\dfrac{2}{3} + \dfrac{3}{4} \div \dfrac{1}{2}$ $2\frac{1}{6}$
(21, 22)

14. $\dfrac{1}{2} - \dfrac{2}{3} \cdot \dfrac{3}{4}$ 0
(21, 22)

15. $(-2)^2 \cdot (-2)^3$ -32
(36)

16. $\dfrac{10^3 \cdot 10^2}{10^4}$ 10
(27)

17. $1\frac{2}{3} + 3\frac{3}{4} \div 1\frac{1}{2}$ $4\frac{1}{6}$
(21, 23)

18. $\dfrac{64}{0.16}$ 400
(25)

* 19. **a.** Write $\frac{1}{25}$ as a decimal and as a percent. 0.04; 4%
(12, 25)

b. Instead of dividing a number by 25, we can multiply by any form
of $\frac{1}{25}$. Show how to use multiplication and one of the forms of the
reciprocal of 25 to find $80 \div 25$. $80 \times 0.04 = 3.2$

20. Arrange these numbers in order from least to greatest. 12.5%, 0.15, $\frac{1}{6}$
(12, 30)

$$12.5\%, \frac{1}{6}, 0.15$$

21. Sample:

* 21. Draw quadrilateral WXYZ so that sides WX and YZ are parallel and sides
(18, 19) XY and YZ are perpendicular. Make side YZ longer than side WX.
See student work.

For problems **22–25,** find all values of x which make the equation true.

22. $-3|x| = -6$ $x = 2, -2$
(1, 14)

23. $x + x = 26$ $x = 13$
(14)

* 24. $2x - 1 = 19$ $x = 10$
(14)

* 25. $x^2 - 1 = 24$ $x = 5, -5$
(14, 36)

26.
(1)

26. *Model* On a number line, graph the whole numbers less than 5.

27. Fritz recorded the daily high temperature in degrees Fahrenheit for a
(7) week.

S	M	T	W	T	F	S
81°	78°	79°	74°	70°	77°	80°

Find the mean high temperature for the week. 77°F

Evaluate.

* 28. Find $\sqrt{b^2 - 4ac}$ when $a = 2, b = -5, c = -3$. 7
(21, 36)

▶ See Math Conversations in the sidebar.

---

③ Written Practice

Math Conversations
Discussion opportunities are provided below.

Problem 10 *Analyze*
Remind students that whenever they choose
to use a fraction to represent probability, the
fraction should be written in lowest terms.

Errors and Misconceptions
Problem 11
Students must recall that the product and
quotient rules (shown below) represent
arithmetic with *two* integers, and infer that
because problem 11 represents the product of
three factors, the rules must be applied twice
to learn the sign of the product of those factors.

• different signs: negative product or quotient
• same signs: positive product or quotient

Point out that the rules are first applied to
name the sign of the product of (-4) and $(\frac{1}{2})$,
and applied a second time to name the sign of
the product of (-2) and (-3).

(continued)

Math Conversations

Discussion opportunities are provided below.

Problem 29 Evaluate

"What is the probability of each outcome?"
$P(vowel) = \frac{1}{2}$ and $P(odd) = \frac{2}{3}$

"What operation is used to find the probability of both outcomes?"
multiplication

"Suppose each spinner is spun once. Is it likely that the spinners will stop on a vowel and an odd number? Give a reason to support your answer." No; Sample: Any probability greater than $\frac{1}{2}$ represents a likely event. $P(vowel)$ and $P(odd)$ is $\frac{1}{2} \cdot \frac{2}{3}$, or $\frac{1}{3}$, which is less than $\frac{1}{2}$.

▶* **29.** **Evaluate** Both spinners are spun once.
(32)

a. What is the sample space of the experiment? Sample space = {A1, A2, A3, B1, B2, B3}
b. What is the probability that the spinners stop on a vowel and an odd number? $\frac{1}{3}$

30. **Classify** In the figure, right triangle *ABC* is
(20) divided into two smaller triangles by segment *CD*. Classify the three triangles by sides.

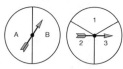

a. △*ABC*   scalene

b. △*BCD*   isosceles

c. △*ADC*   equilateral

Early Finishers
Real-World Application

To make a small fruit smoothie, Prianka used juice, ice, 5 strawberries and 15 blueberries. She is planning a party this weekend and would like to make small smoothies for all her guests.

a. If Prianka used 270 blueberries to make all the smoothies for the party, how many strawberries did she use?   90 strawberries

b. How many guests attended Prianka's pool party?   18 guests

▶ See Math Conversations in the sidebar.

Looking Forward

Multiplying and dividing integers prepares students for:

• **Lesson 38,** using properties of equality to solve equations.

• **Lesson 44,** solving proportions using cross products.

• **Lesson 50,** solving multi-step equations.

• **Lesson 77,** working with inequalities with negative coefficients.

Multiplying and dividing terms prepares students for:

• **Lesson 92,** finding products of binomials.

•Areas of Combined Polygons

Objectives
- Find the areas of complex polygons by dividing them into less complex shapes.
- Estimate the areas of complex polygons.

Materials
- **Power Up H** (in *Instructional Masters*)

Power Up H

Math Language

Maintain

polygon

Pythagorean Theorem

Technology Resources

Student eBook Complete student textbook in electronic format.

Resources and Planner CD Assessment, reteaching, and instructional masters, plus a pacing calendar with standards.

Test and Practice Generator CD Create additional practice sheets and custom-made tests.

www.SaxonPublishers.com Visit for more student activities and planning materials.

Inclusion

Adaptations CD Adapted lessons, investigations, practice and assessments.

Meeting Standards

National Council of Teachers of Mathematics (NCTM)

Geometry

GM.1b Understand relationships among the angles, side lengths, perimeters, areas, and volumes of similar objects

Measurement

ME.2a Use common benchmarks to select appropriate methods for estimating measurements

ME.2b Select and apply techniques and tools to accurately find length, area, volume, and angle measures to appropriate levels of precision

ME.2c Develop and use formulas to determine the circumference of circles and the area of triangles, parallelograms, trapezoids, and circles and develop strategies to find the area of more-complex shapes

Problem-Solving Strategy: Find a Pattern/
Use Logical Reasoning

A newspaper is made of folded sheets of paper. The outside sheet contains pages 1, 2, 35, and 36. The next sheet has pages 3, 4, 33, and 34. The inside sheet contains what pages?

(Understand) Understand the problem.

"What information are we given?"

The outside sheet of paper pulled from a newspaper contains pages 1, 2, 35, and 36. The next sheet has pages 3, 4, 33, and 34.

"What are we asked to do?"

Determine which pages the inner-most sheet has.

"Can we presume that the inside sheet contains 4 pages (as opposed to 2-pages on a half-sheet of paper)?"

Yes, because 36 pages ÷ 4 pages per sheet of paper = 9 *full* sheets of paper.

(Plan) Make a plan.

"What problem-solving strategy will we use?"

We will try to *find a pattern* and *use logical reasoning*.

(Solve) Carry out the plan.

"Is there a pattern to the sums of the pages?"

"Opposite" pages sum to 37 (1 + 36, 2 + 35, 3 + 34, 4 + 33).

"Which page will you have finished when you are exactly half-way through the newspaper?"

$\frac{1}{2}$ of 36 pages = page 18

"Which page is next to page 18 (and sums to 37 when added to 18)?"

page 19

"Which pages are "behind" pages 18 and 19 (and sum to 37)?"

pages 17 and 20

(Check) Look back.

"Did we find the answer to the question that was asked?"

Yes. We found that the inside sheet contains pages 17, 18, 19, and 20.

• **Areas of Combined Polygons**

facts | Power Up H

mental math

a. **Number Sense:** $180 ÷ 40$ $4.50

b. **Measurement:** Find the temperature indicated on this thermometer.   32°F

c. **Proportions:** $\frac{4}{16} = \frac{2}{x}$ 8

d. **Rate:** The walkers maintained a pace of 4 miles per hour for $3\frac{1}{2}$ hours. To complete the 15-mile course, how much farther do they need to walk?   1 mile

e. **Scientific Notation:** Write 125,000 in scientific notation. 1.25×10^5

f. **Geometry:** Two angles of a triangle measure 30° and 50°. Find the measure of the third angle.   100°

g. **Estimation:** 7 at $4.97 each plus 2 at $34.97 each $105

h. **Calculation:** $77 ÷ 7, -2, \times 11, +1, \sqrt{\ }, -1, \sqrt{\ }, -10$ −7

problem solving | A newspaper is made of folded sheets of paper. The outside sheet contains pages 1, 2, 35, and 36. The next sheet has pages 3, 4, 33, and 34. The inside sheet contains what pages?   17, 18, 19, 20

New Concept   *Increasing Knowledge*

The area of some polygons can be found by dividing the polygon into smaller parts and finding the area of each part.

Example 1

Find the area of this figure.

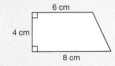
6 cm
4 cm
8 cm

Facts
Distribute **Power Up H** to students. See answers below.

Mental Math
Encourage students to share different ways to mentally compute these exercises. Strategies for exercises **c**, **d**, and **f** are listed below.

c. Multiply Down
$4 \times \mathbf{4} = 16$
$2 \times \mathbf{4} = 8$
Divide Across
$4 ÷ 2 = 2$
$16 ÷ 2 = 8$

d. Two Steps: Find Distance/Subtract
$3\frac{1}{2}$ hr $\times$ 4 mi/hr $= \frac{7}{2}$ hr $\times$ 4 mi/hr $=$
$7 \times 2 = 14$ mi traveled
15 mi − 14 mi = 1 mi to go

f. Sum of Angles of Triangle
$t + 30° + 50° = 180°$
$t = 180° − (30° + 50°)$
$t = 180° − 80° = 100°$

Problem Solving
Refer to **Power-Up Discussion**, p. 245B.

Instruction
Some students may remember a formula for the area of a trapezoid. Tell them not to use it to solve this lesson's problems because this lesson is about decomposing figures into simpler shapes.

(continued)

Facts	Express each fraction as a decimal number.			
$\frac{1}{5} = 0.2$	$\frac{1}{10} = 0.1$	$\frac{1}{4} = 0.25$	$\frac{1}{20} = 0.05$	$\frac{4}{5} = 0.8$
$\frac{1}{100} = 0.01$	$\frac{1}{2} = 0.5$	$\frac{3}{5} = 0.6$	$\frac{3}{4} = 0.75$	$\frac{9}{10} = 0.9$
$\frac{1}{3} = 0.\overline{3}$	$\frac{3}{10} = 0.3$	$\frac{1}{6} = 0.1\overline{6}$	$\frac{1}{25} = 0.04$	$\frac{1}{8} = 0.125$
$\frac{1}{9} = 0.\overline{1}$	$\frac{2}{3} = 0.\overline{6}$	$\frac{1}{50} = 0.02$	$\frac{2}{5} = 0.4$	$\frac{3}{8} = 0.375$

New Concepts (Continued)

Example 1

Instruction

When you finish going through the example, use the *Evaluate* question to promote the idea that most complex figures can be subdivided in many ways. Point out the polygon can be divided into two triangles two ways using the diagonals: either diagonal will produce two triangles.

Example 2

Instruction

If needed, review the Pythagorean Theorem: for any right triangle, the sum of the squares of the measures of the legs is equal to the square of the measure of the hypotenuse. Remind students of the formula:

$$c^2 = a^2 + b^2$$

where c is the measure of the hypotenuse and a and b are the measures of the legs.

You may want to point out that the polygon can also be divided into two triangles using either diagonal. Students may be interested in knowing that the areas of the two larger triangles are equal as are the areas of the two smaller triangles, regardless of which diagonal is used.

If you have time, demonstrate how to find the area both ways and compare the answers to the answer found by dividing the polygon into a rectangle and a triangle. The larger triangles will have areas of 5300 ft² and the smaller triangles will have areas of 3000 ft² for total areas of 8300 ft².

(continued)

You can divide the polygon into two triangles: one with a base of 6 cm and a height of 4 cm and the other with a base of 8 cm and a height of 4 cm. The areas of the triangles are 12 cm² and 16 cm². So the area of the whole polygon is 28 cm². This is the same area as was found in the example above.

Solution

One way to find the area of this figure is to divide the polygon into a rectangle and a triangle. Then we find the area of each part and add the areas.

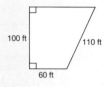

Area of rectangle =   6 cm · 4 cm = 24 cm²
+ Area of triangle = $\frac{1}{2}$ · 4 cm · 2 cm =   4 cm²
Area of polygon   = **28 cm²**

Evaluate There is another way to find the area of the polygon by dividing it into parts. Describe this way and use it to find the area of the polygon. Compare the result to the answer above.

Example 2

Use a calculator to estimate the area of this lot.

Solution

We divide the figure into a rectangle and a triangle. We use the Pythagorean Theorem to find the unknown dimension of the right triangle.

$$x^2 + 100^2 = 110^2$$
$$x^2 + 10,000 = 12,100$$
$$x^2 = 2100$$
$$x \approx 46$$

The base and height of the triangle are 100 ft and about 46 ft. We add the area of the triangle and the area of the rectangle.

Area of triangle $\approx \frac{1}{2}$(100 ft)(46 ft) $\approx$ 2300 ft²
+ Area of rectangle =   (100 ft)(60 ft) = 6000 ft²
Area of lot   ≈ **8300 ft²**

Example 3

In the figure, *AD* is 40 cm and *DC* is 30 cm. Point *B* is the midpoint of $\overline{AC}$ and Point *E* is the midpoint of $\overline{AD}$. Find the perimeter and area of quadrilateral *BCDE*.

Inclusion

Some students may need to study an actual polygon to understand why the areas must be combined. Find an area, like the classroom or hallway, that is not a rectangle. Explain that their job is to find out how much carpet or tile is needed for the area. Ask:

"Can we calculate the area simply using the room's length and width? Explain." Sample: No, because the area is not a rectangle.

"If the floor is not a rectangle, how can we calculate its area?" Sample: Break up the floor into polygons whose areas we can calculate and add those areas to find the total area.

Have the students discuss where the polygons lie in the chosen area. Then have them measure the dimensions of those polygons, calculate the areas, and add the areas to find the total area.

Since triangle *ACD* is a right triangle we can find that *AC* is 50 cm. A midpoint of a segment divides a segment in half. We sketch the figure again recording the dimensions (in cm) we are given and have calculated.

To find the length of segment *EB* we can use the Pythagorean Theorem or we can solve a proportion since the smaller and larger triangles are similar.

	△*ACD*	△*ABE*	
Longer Leg	40	20	$\frac{40}{30} = \frac{20}{x}$
Shorter Leg	30	*x*	

Since the dimensions of the smaller triangle are half the dimensions of the larger triangle, segment *EB* is 15 cm long.

We find the perimeter of *BCDE* by adding the lengths of the four sides.

Perimeter of *BCDE* = 25 cm + 30 cm + 20 cm + 15 cm

= **90 cm**

We can find the area of figure *BCDE* by subtracting the area of the smaller triangle from the area of the larger triangle. The dimensions of the larger triangle are 2 times the dimensions of the smaller triangle, so the area is 2^2 times the area of the smaller triangle.

Area of △*ACD* $(\frac{1}{2})(40\text{ cm})(30\text{ cm}) = 600\text{ cm}^2$

− Area of △*ABE* $(\frac{1}{2})(20\text{ cm})(15\text{ cm}) = 150\text{ cm}^2$

Area of figure *BCDE* = **450 cm²**

Practice Set

Find the area of each polygon by dividing the polygons into rectangles or triangles. (Angles that look like right angles are right angles).

▶ **a.**

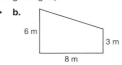

80 ft²

▶ **b.**

6 m
3 m
8 m

36 m²

▶ **c.** Find the area of the shaded region by subtracting the area of the smaller triangle from the area of the larger triangle. Dimensions are in cm.   1200 cm²

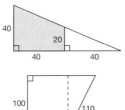

d. Use a calculator to help estimate the area of a lot with the given dimensions. Dimensions are in feet.   9300 ft²

100
110
70

▶ See Math Conversations in the sidebar.

Example 3
Instruction

You may want to work through this example on the board or overhead. Because there are several steps involved, point out the importance of keeping the work organized, using labels to show what is known, and writing each step on a new line.

After you show how to find the area of *BCDE*, ask whether anyone can describe a different way to find that area. Samples: It will be 3 times the area of triangle *ABE*. It could be divided into 2 triangles two different ways.

Ask students which transformations of △*ABE* will position three congruent triangles in ___ quadrilateral *BCDE*. Reflect △*ABE* across $\overline{BE}$. Translate △*ABE* so that side *AB* is positioned on side *BC*. Reflect △*ABE* to occupy the remaining area of quadrilateral *BCDE*.

Practice Set
Problems a–c

Sketch each figure on the board or overhead, and ask students to sketch each figure on paper. For each figure, use input from the students to:

• divide the figure into two or more parts (if necessary).
• name the missing measures.
• find the area of each part.
• complete the arithmetic.

As you work with each figure, ask students to duplicate your actions on their sketches.

Math Conversations

Discussion opportunities are provided below.

Problem 2 `Analyze`

Make sure students infer that the number of striped cats can be found by writing and solving a proportion. Then ask students to choose mental math or paper and pencil and use that method to solve the problem.

Invite volunteers to name the method they chose, and explain why that method was chosen. Sample: Mental math; The answer is the product of 5 and 6 because 6 is the constant factor of 2 and 12.

Problem 3

When writing a proportion, remind students that the order of the terms of the ratios is very important.

Problem 5 `Generalize`

Before completing the problem, sketch a square on the board or overhead and label one side of the square with an arbitrary measure (such as 10, for example). Ask students to name the perimeter of the square and make a generalization about how the perimeter of a square compares to the length of one of its sides. The perimeter of a square is four times the length of one side.

Problem 6b `Connect`

Remind students of the following conversion generalizations.
• Multiplication is used to change a larger unit to a smaller unit.
• Division is used to change a smaller unit to a larger unit.

(continued)

---

1. Of the 1800 people at the zoo, three-fifths were children. How many
(4) children were at the zoo? 1080 children

▶ *** 2.** `Analyze` At the zoo, the ratio of spotted cats to striped cats was 2 to 5.
(34) If there were 12 spotted cats, how many striped cats were there? 30

▶ *** 3.** In the reptile section, the ratio of lizards to snakes was 2 to 9. If there
(34) were 36 snakes, how many lizards were there? 8

* 4. If the space shuttle travels completely around the world in 90 minutes,
(4) how many times will it circle the globe in a full week? 112

5. See student work. For each pair of numbers the perimeter should be four times the side length.

▶ *** 5.** `Generalize` The perimeter of a square is four
(8) times the length of one of its sides. In this table we show the perimeter of a square with a side length of 3 units. Copy this table on your paper. Imagine two more squares with different side lengths. Record the side lengths and perimeters of those squares in your table.

$P = 4s$

Side Length	Perimeter
3	12

6. `Connect` A stop sign is the shape of a regular octagon. Many stop signs
(6, 8) have sides 12 inches long.

    a. What is the perimeter of a regular octagon with sides 12 inches long? 96 inches

▶   **b.** Convert your answer in part **a** to feet. 8 feet

* 7. Triangles *ABD* and *ECD* are similar.
(18, 20)

    a. If $m\angle A = 60°$, then what is the measure of $\angle CED$? 60°

    b. What is the measure of $\angle D$? 30°

    c. Which side of $\triangle ECD$ corresponds to side *AD* of $\triangle ABD$? Side *ED*

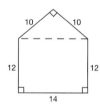

8. Solve $\frac{6}{10} = \frac{x}{15}$ 9
(34)

9. Solve $\frac{x}{5} = \frac{4}{20}$ 1
(34)

10. Find the **a** area and **b** perimeter of the triangle with the vertices (0, 0),
(8, Inv. 1) (−5, 0) and (0, −12). A = 30 square units; P = 30 units

11. Find the **a** area and **b** perimeter of this
(8, 37) pentagon. Dimensions are in ft. **a.** 218 ft² **b.** 58 ft

▶ See Math Conversations in the sidebar.

▶* 12. *Analyze* **a.** Expand: $-3(x - y + 5)$ **b.** Factor: $4x - 2$
(21, 36) $-3x + 3y - 15$ $2(2x - 1)$

13. Write each of the following as a reduced fraction and as a decimal:
(12)
    a. 99% $\frac{99}{100}$, 0.99   ▶ **b.** $\frac{180}{360}$ $\frac{1}{2}$, 0.5

Generalize Simplify.

▶* 14. $\frac{35x}{-7}$ $-5x$ **15.** $\frac{x^3}{x^4 x}$ $\frac{1}{x^2}$
(36)   (27)

16. $10 + 10(10^2 - 10 \cdot 3^2)$ 110   *** 17.** $(-2)^3 + (-3)^2$ 1
(15, 21)   (31, 36)

18. $\frac{9}{10} - \frac{3}{4} \cdot \frac{2}{5}$ $\frac{3}{5}$ **19.** $\frac{6}{7} \div \frac{2}{7} + \frac{1}{2}$ $3\frac{1}{2}$
(13, 22)   (13, 22)

Collect like terms.

20. $x^2 + x + 1 + 3x + x^2 + 2$ $2x^2 + 4x + 3$
(36)

21. $5x - x + 2y - y$ $4x + y$
(36)

Find all values for x which make the equation true.

22. $x^2 = 1$ $x = 1, -1$ **23.** $|x| + 1 = 3$ $x = 2, -2$
(7, 8)   (1, 7)

24. Simplify: $(-2) + (-3) - (-4) + (-5)(-2)$ 9
(31, 36)

25. Chandra bowled five games. Her scores were 89, 97, 112, 104, and 113.
(7)   What is her mean score for the five games?   103

26. The number $-\frac{1}{2}$ is a member of which sets of numbers?   **A and C**
(10)
     A real numbers   **B** integers

     C rational numbers   **D** irrational numbers

27. Write the prime factorization of 77,000 using exponents. $2^3 \cdot 5^3 \cdot 7 \cdot 11$
(9, 15)

28. Find $n(n - 1)$ when n is 10.   90
(14)

▶ 29. *Evaluate* The teacher asked for two volunteers. Andy, Benito, Chen,
(32)   and Devina raised their hands. If the teacher picks two of the four
     volunteers,

     a. what is the sample space?   Sample space = {AB, AC, AD, BC, BD,
     CD} (Letters may be reversed.)
     b. what is the probability Benito will be picked? $\frac{1}{2}$ or 0.5

30. The measure of $\angle ABD$ is 145°. Find
(18, 20)   the measure of

     a. $\angle CBD$ 35°

     b. $\angle CDB$ 55°

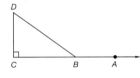

▶ See Math Conversations in the sidebar.

Math Background

You can derive the area formula for a trapezoid with height h and base lengths a and b by dividing the trapezoid into two triangles.

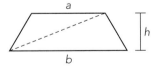

The area of the trapezoid is the sum of the areas of the triangles.

Area of trapezoid $= \frac{1}{2}ah + \frac{1}{2}bh$
$= \frac{1}{2}h(a + b)$

Looking Forward

Calculating the areas of combined polygons prepares students for:

- **Lesson 43,** calculating surface areas.

- **Lesson 60,** calculating areas of parallelograms.

- **Lesson 75,** calculating areas of trapezoids.

- **Lesson 101,** calculating geometric probabilities.

---

③ Written Practice (Continued)

Math Conversations

Discussion opportunities are provided below.

Problem 12a   *Analyze*

"To expand this expression, how many products must you write? Explain your answer." Three; Sample explanation: each of the three terms inside the parentheses is multiplied by -3, the factor outside the parentheses.

Problem 14   *Generalize*

Ask students to name the sign of the quotient, and explain why they chose that sign. Negative; Sample: the rules for arithmetic with two integers state that a quotient is negative if the sign of the dividend is different than the sign of the divisor.

Problem 29   *Evaluate*

Tell students that they should use the first letter of each volunteer's name to represent an outcome. For example, use A for Andy and use B for Benito.

Errors and Misconceptions

Problem 13b

When reducing $\frac{180}{360}$ to lowest terms, some students may cancel the zero in the numerator and the zero in the denominator, but not understand why the zeros can be canceled.

Ask these students to divide 180 by 10 and compare the location of the decimal point in the dividend to the location of the decimal point in the quotient. Use the comparison to help students generalize that dividing a number by 10 is the same as moving the decimal point in that number one place to the left, and conclude that canceling the zeros in $\frac{180}{360}$ is the same as dividing both the numerator and the denominator by 10.

Problem 29

Explain to students who name 12 possible outcomes in the sample space that outcomes such as AB and BA represent only one outcome because in the problem, the order in which the volunteers are chosen is not important.

•Using Properties of Equality to Solve Equations

Objectives
- Demonstrate how inverse operations "undo" each other.
- Manipulate and solve equations using the properties of equality.

Lesson Preparation

Materials
- **Power Up H** (in *Instructional Masters*)

Power Up H

Math Language

Maintain	English Learners (ESL)
inverse operations	isolate

Technology Resources

Student eBook Complete student textbook in electronic format.

Resources and Planner CD Assessment, reteaching, and instructional masters, plus a pacing calendar with standards.

Test and Practice Generator CD Create additional practice sheets and custom-made tests.

www.SaxonPublishers.com Visit for more student activities and planning materials.

Inclusion

 Adaptations CD Adapted lessons, investigations, practice and assessments.

Meeting Standards

National Council of Teachers of Mathematics (NCTM)

Numbers and Operations

NO.2c Understand and use the inverse relationships of addition and subtraction, multiplication and division, and squaring and finding square roots to simplify computations and solve problems

Problem Solving

PS.1a Build new mathematical knowledge through problem solving

PS.1b Solve problems that arise in mathematics and in other contexts

PS.1c Apply and adapt a variety of appropriate strategies to solve problems

PS.1d Monitor and reflect on the process of mathematical problem solving

Problem-Solving Strategy: Draw a Diagram/ Write an Equation/Make an Organized List

Problem solving usually requires us to use multiple strategies.

Problem: Sergio used 20 yards of fence to enclose a rectangular garden on the side of his house. He used the wall of his house for one side of the garden. He wanted the rectangle to have the greatest possible area. Find the dimensions and the area of Sergio's garden.

(**Understand**) Twenty yards of fencing material is used to enclose three sides of a garden. We are asked to determine the dimensions that will result in the greatest possible area for the garden.

(**Plan**) We will begin by drawing a diagram of the house and fenced garden. We will then write an equation for the perimeter of the three fenced sides of the garden, and use the formula for the area of a rectangle when we make an organized list of possible garden sizes.

(**Solve**) Our diagram of the yard shows a garden that is adjacent to the house and that is fenced on only three sides.

The formula for the perimeter of a rectangle is $2l + 2w = P$. Since one side of the garden is enclosed by the wall, we will use the formula $l + 2w = 20$.

The possible dimensions and the resulting area for the garden are:

Length	Width	Resulting Area
18 yards	1 yard	18 sq. yards
16 yards	2 yards	32 sq. yards
14 yards	3 yards	42 sq. yards
12 yards	4 yards	48 sq. yards
10 yards	5 yards	50 sq. yards
8 yards	6 yards	48 sq. yards
6 yards	7 yards	42 sq. yards
4 yards	8 yards	32 sq. yards
2 yards	9 yards	18 sq. yards

(**Check**) We found the dimensions for the garden that result in the maximum garden area. A garden that is 10 yd × 5 yd will use 20 yards of fencing $(10 + 2(5) = 20)$, and will have 50 sq. yards of area in which to plant.

1 Power Up

Facts

Distribute **Power Up H** to students. See answers below.

Mental Math

Encourage students to share different ways to mentally compute these exercises. Strategies for exercises **a** and **d** are listed below.

a. Double and Halve
$$\$55 \times 4 = 110 \times 2 = \$220$$
Regroup
$$\$55 \times 4 = (50 \times 4) + (5 \times 4) =$$
$$200 + 20 = \$220$$
d. Find a Fraction
$$30\% = \frac{3}{10}$$
$$\frac{3}{10} \times \$60 = 3 \times \$6 = \$18$$
Use Math Sense
10% of $60 = $6
20% of $60 = $12
30% of $60 = $18

Problem Solving

Refer to **Power-Up Discussion**, p. 250B.

• Using Properties of Equality to Solve Equations

Power Up
Building Power

facts   Power Up H

mental math

  a. Number Sense: $55 × 4 $220

  b. Fractional Parts: $\frac{7}{8}$ of $72 $63

  c. Measurement: Find the diameter of the quarter in millimeters.   25 mm

  d. Percent: 30% of $60 $18

  e. Proportion: Daniel finished 4 problems in two minutes. At that rate, how many problems can he finish in 20 minutes?   40 problems

  f. Geometry: Two sides of a triangle measure 7 inches and 12 inches. The length of the third side must be between what two lengths?   between 5 inches and 19 inches

  g. Powers/Roots: Approximate $\sqrt{26} + \sqrt{80} - \sqrt{5}$. $5 + 9 - 2 = 12$

  h. Calculation: $\sqrt{1} + \sqrt{4} + \sqrt{9} + \sqrt{16} + \sqrt{25} + \sqrt{36} + \sqrt{49} - \sqrt{64} - \sqrt{81} - \sqrt{100}$ 1

problem solving

Problem solving usually requires us to use multiple strategies.

Problem: Sergio used 20 yards of fence to enclose a rectangular garden on the side of his house. He used the wall of his house for one side of the garden. He wanted the rectangle to have the greatest possible area. Find the dimensions and the area of Sergio's garden.

(**Understand**) Twenty yards of fencing material is used to enclose three sides of a garden. We are asked to determine the dimensions that will result in the greatest possible area for the garden.

(**Plan**) We will begin by drawing a diagram of the house and fenced garden. We will then write an equation for the perimeter of the three fenced sides of the garden, and use the formula for the area of a rectangle when we make an organized list of possible garden sizes.

Facts	Express each fraction as a decimal number.			
$\frac{1}{5} = 0.2$	$\frac{1}{10} = 0.1$	$\frac{1}{4} = 0.25$	$\frac{1}{20} = 0.05$	$\frac{4}{5} = 0.8$
$\frac{1}{100} = 0.01$	$\frac{1}{2} = 0.5$	$\frac{3}{5} = 0.6$	$\frac{3}{4} = 0.75$	$\frac{9}{10} = 0.9$
$\frac{1}{3} = 0.\overline{3}$	$\frac{3}{10} = 0.3$	$\frac{1}{6} = 0.1\overline{6}$	$\frac{1}{25} = 0.04$	$\frac{1}{8} = 0.125$
$\frac{1}{9} = 0.\overline{1}$	$\frac{2}{3} = 0.\overline{6}$	$\frac{1}{50} = 0.02$	$\frac{2}{5} = 0.4$	$\frac{3}{8} = 0.375$

Solve Our diagram of the yard shows a garden that is adjacent to the house and that is fenced on only three sides.

The formula for the perimeter of a rectangle is $2l + 2w = P$. Since one side of the garden is enclosed by the wall, we will use the formula $l + 2w = 20$.

The possible dimensions and the resulting area for the garden are:

Length	Width	Resulting Area
18 yards	1 yard	18 sq. yards
16 yards	2 yards	32 sq. yards
14 yards	3 yards	42 sq. yards
12 yards	4 yards	48 sq. yards
10 yards	5 yards	50 sq. yards
8 yards	6 yards	48 sq. yards
6 yards	7 yards	42 sq. yards
4 yards	8 yards	32 sq. yards
2 yards	9 yards	18 sq. yards

A garden measuring 10 yd by 5 yd will enclose the maximum area using 20 yd of fencing.

Check We found the dimensions for the garden that result in the maximum garden area. A garden that is 10 yd × 5 yd will use 20 yards of fencing $(10 + 2(5) = 20)$, and will have 50 sq. yards of area in which to plant.

New Concept *Increasing Knowledge*

We have practiced solving equations by inspection using logical reasoning. In this lesson we will use inverse operations to solve equations. Inverse operations "undo" each other.

- Addition and subtraction are inverse operations. $(n + 5 - 5 = n)$
- Multiplication and division are inverse operations. $(n \times 5 \div 5 = n)$

Any number may be used for n in the equations above to perform the operations. The result in every case is n.

We use inverse operations to isolate the variable in an equation. We can illustrate the process with a balance-scale model:

Lesson 38   251

2 New Concepts

Instruction

Students may be using inverse operations informally or intuitively when they solve equations by inspection. For example, to solve $x + 8 = 13$, a student may think $13 - 8 = x$, and $x = 5$.

The balance scale model helps give a structure for the idea of an equation. Students can think of the equals sign as the balancing point of the equation.

(continued)

English Learners

Explain the meaning of the word **isolate.** Say:

"To isolate means to place something alone. When you isolate a variable, you take steps to get it alone. Watch while I isolate the variable in this equation."

$$2a = 6 \qquad a = \frac{6}{2}$$

"I isolated the variable a. Who can isolate the variable in this equation?"

Write $b + 2 = 6$ on the board.

As you discuss the Operation Properties of Equality and the *Formulate* question, discuss with students how to decide what operation will isolate a variable. Sample: I choose an operation that will undo the expression. If the expression is $3x = 15$, I undo 3 times x by dividing by 3.

Example 1
Instruction

As you discuss the example, point out the importance of writing each part of each step. As students progress through the program, they may be able to shorten this process, but for now, writing each part of each step will help strengthen their understanding of the process.

(continued)

The balanced scale shows that the weight on the left side equals the weight on the right side. We can represent the relationship with this equation:

$$x + 5 = 12$$

To isolate x we need to remove the 5. Since 5 is added to x, we remove the 5 by subtracting (which is the inverse operation of addition). However, if we subtract 5 from the left side, we must also subtract 5 from the right side to keep the scale balanced.

$$x + 5 - 5 = 12 - 5$$
$$x = 7$$

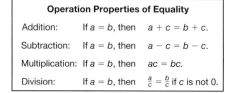

We find that x equals 7.

Isolating a variable means that the variable, like x, is "alone" on one side of the equals sign.

Notice these two aspects of isolating a variable.

1. We choose the operation that isolates the variable.
2. We perform the operation on both sides of the equals sign to keep the equation balanced.

Performing the same operation on both sides of an equation preserves the equality of the equation. Below are four **properties of equality** we can use to manipulate equations.

Operation Properties of Equality		
Addition:	If $a = b$, then	$a + c = b + c$.
Subtraction:	If $a = b$, then	$a - c = b - c$.
Multiplication:	If $a = b$, then	$ac = bc$.
Division:	If $a = b$, then	$\frac{a}{c} = \frac{b}{c}$ if c is not 0.

Formulate Use numbers to give an example of each property. See student work.

Example 1

After spending $2.30, Robert had $5.70. How much money did he have before he spent $2.30? Solve this equation to find the answer.

$$x - 2.30 = 5.70$$

Solution

We see that 2.30 is subtracted from x. To isolate x we add 2.30 to the left side to undo the subtraction, and we add 2.30 to the right side to keep the equation balanced. The result is a simpler equivalent equation.

Math Background

Does taking the square root of a number "undo" squaring?

"Yes, but you need to be careful. Remember that a positive number has two square roots. For example, consider the equation $(x + 1)^2 = 16$. When you take the square root of both sides, there are two possibilities, which lead to two possible solutions."

Step:	Justification:
$(x + 1)^2 = 16$	Given
$x + 1 = 4$ or $x + 1 = -4$	Took the square root of both sides
$x = 3$ or $x = -5$	Solved each equation separately

Step:	Justification:
$x - 2.30 = 5.70$	Given equation
$x - 2.30 + 2.30 = 5.70 + 2.30$	Added 2.30 to both sides
$x = 8.00$	Simplified

We find that Robert had **$8.00.**

Example 2

If a 12-month subscription to a magazine costs $8.40, what is the average cost per month? Solve this equation to find the answer.

$$12m = 8.40$$

Solution

The variable is multiplied by 12. To isolate the variable we divide the left side by 12. To keep the equation balanced we divide the right side by 12.

Step:	Justification:
$12m = 8.40$	Given equation
$\dfrac{12m}{12} = \dfrac{8.4}{12}$	Divided both sides by 12
$1m = 0.70$	Simplified
$m = 0.70$	Simplified

Explain In the context of the problem, what does $m = 0.70$ mean?   The average cost per month for the subscription is $0.70.

Example 3

Solve: $\dfrac{2}{3}w = \dfrac{3}{4}$

Solution

Thinking Skill

Connect

When the variable is multiplied by a fraction, why do we multiply by the reciprocal to help us isolate the variable?   The product of a number and its reciprocal is always 1, so we multiply by the reciprocal to get $1x$, or x.

The variable is multiplied by $\frac{2}{3}$. Instead of dividing by $\frac{2}{3}$, we multiply both sides by the multiplicative inverse (reciprocal) of $\frac{2}{3}$.

Step:	Justification:
$\dfrac{2}{3}w = \dfrac{3}{4}$	Given equation
$\dfrac{3}{2} \cdot \dfrac{2}{3}w = \dfrac{3}{2} \cdot \dfrac{3}{4}$	Multiplied both sides by $\frac{3}{2}$
$1w = \dfrac{9}{8}$	Simplified
$w = \dfrac{9}{8}$	Simplified

2 New Concepts *(Continued)*

Example 2
Instruction
Use the *Explain* question to stress the importance of going back to the context of the problem to check whether the answer makes sense and is reasonable.

Example 3
Instruction
Use the Thinking Skill *Connect* question to point out that multiplying both sides of the equation by the reciprocal of the coefficient of w is an efficient way to isolate the variable because it changes the coefficient of the variable to 1. Ask whether there are other ways to isolate the variable in this equation. Samples: Dividing both sides by $\frac{2}{3}$. Multiplying both sides by 3 and then dividing both sides by 2, or vice versa.

(continued)

Instruction

Help students remember this property by suggesting that they relate reversing an equation to a geometric reflection. Ask what the equals sign would represent. the line of symmetry

Example 4
Instruction

Ask students how the steps would be different if the Symmetric Property were applied at the first step.

Step:	Justification:
$1.5 = x - 2.3$	Given equation
$x - 2.3 = 1.5$	Symmetric Property
$x - 2.3 + 2.3 = 1.5 + 2.3$	Added 2.3 to both sides
$x = 3.8$	Simplified

Point out that the answer does not change.

Practice Set
Problems d–g Justify

Before completing any paper and pencil arithmetic, ask students to describe the inverse operation for each problem that can be used to isolate x.

Problem d: subtract $\frac{1}{2}$ from each side
Problem e: add 1.3 to each side
Problem f: multiply each side by 4
Problem g: multiply each side by $\frac{5}{3}$

Problem i Error Alert

Encourage students to use a number line or count back 5 from $+2$ to check their work.

3 Written Practice

Math Conversations

Discussion opportunities are provided below.

Errors and Misconceptions
Problem 2

To help write the ratios of a proportion in a consistent way, encourage students to write a label for each term of a ratio.

For example, a proportion with labels to represent problem **2** is shown below.

$$\frac{3 \text{ whole milk bottles}}{7 \text{ skim milk bottles}} = \frac{n \text{ whole milk bottle}}{210 \text{ skim milk bottles}}$$

It is important for students to generalize that the ratios of a proportion must be written in a consistent way.

(continued)

It is customary to express a solution with the variable on the left side of the equal sign. Since the quantities on either side of an equal sign are equal, we can reverse everything on one side of an equation with everything on the other side of the equation. This property of equality is called the **symmetric property.**

Symmetric Property of Equality

If $a = b$, then $b = a$.

Example 4

Solve: $1.5 = x - 2.3$

Solution

We may apply the Symmetric Property at any step.

Step:	Justification:
$1.5 = x - 2.3$	Given equation
$1.5 + 2.3 = x - 2.3 + 2.3$	Added 2.3 to both sides
$3.8 = x$	Simplified
$x = 3.8$	Symmetric Property

Practice Set

a. What does "isolate the variable" mean? Manipulate the equation so that the variable is alone on one side of the equation.

b. Which operation is the inverse of subtraction? addition

c. Which operation is the inverse of multiplication? division

See solutions manual for steps and justification.

▶ Justify Solve each equation. Justify the steps.

d. $x + \frac{1}{2} = \frac{3}{4}$ $x = \frac{1}{4}$
e. $x - 1.3 = 4.2$ $x = 5.5$

f. $1.2 = \frac{x}{4}$ $x = 4.8$
g. $\frac{3}{5}x = \frac{1}{4}$ $x = \frac{5}{12}$

h. Peggy bought 5 pounds of oranges for $4.50. Solve the equation $5x = \$4.50$ to find the price per pound. $0.90 per pound

▶ **i.** From 8 a.m. to noon, the temperature rose 5 degrees to 2°C. Solve the equation $t + 5 = 2$ to find the temperature at 8 a.m. -3°C

Written Practice   *Strengthening Concepts*

1. It is 4:35 p.m. and dinner is at 5:00 p.m. If each task takes five minutes to complete, how many tasks can be completed before dinner?   5
(3, 4)

▶ *** 2.** The ratio of whole milk bottles to skim milk bottles at the dairy was 3 to 7. If there were 210 bottles of skim milk, how many bottles of whole milk were there?   90 bottles
(34)

▶ See Math Conversations in the sidebar.

* 3. (6, 25) ▸ **Justify** Printed on the label of the one-gallon milk bottle was 3.78 L.

    a. How many milliliters is 3.78 liters? 3780 mL

    b. Which is more, a liter of milk or a quart of milk? How do you know? A liter is a little more than a quart, because it takes four quarts to equal a gallon but only 3.78 liters.

▸ **4.** (7) **Analyze** Bob drives 28 miles every half hour. If he drives for $2\frac{1}{2}$ hours, how far does he drive? 140 miles

▸ **Analyze** Solve problems **5–8** using inverse operations.

    * 5. (38) $x - 2.9 = 4.21$ $x = 7.11$ *** 6.** (38) $\frac{2}{3} + x = \frac{5}{6}$ $x = \frac{1}{6}$

    * 7. (38) $\frac{3}{5}x = \frac{6}{7}$ $x = \frac{10}{7}$ *** 8.** (38) $\frac{x}{2.2} = 11$ $x = 24.2$

▸ *** 9.** (34) Solve $\frac{7}{x} = \frac{21}{30}$ $x = 10$

10. (Inv. 1, 20) Find the **a** area and **b** perimeter of the triangle with vertices $(-4, 1)$, $(2, 1)$, and $(2, -7)$. **a.** 24 square units; **b.** 24 units

▸*** 11.** (8, 20) **Evaluate** Find the **a** area and **b** perimeter of the figure below. (Dimensions are in ft.) **a.** 150 ft²; **b.** 50 ft

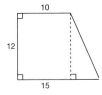

12. (21, 36) **a.** Expand: $-4x(2x - 9)$ $-8x^2 + 36x$

    b. Factor: $3x + 3$ $3(x + 1)$

13. (11, 12) Write 32% as a decimal and as a reduced fraction. $0.32; \frac{8}{25}$

Simplify.

14. (8, 11) $26 + 3(8^2 - 4 \cdot 4^2)$ 26   **15.** (15, 25) $21 - 20(0.5)^2$ 16

16. (36) $\frac{-48mx}{-8x}$ $6m$ **17.** (13, 23) $\frac{2}{5} - \frac{4}{7} \div 1\frac{5}{7}$ $\frac{1}{15}$

18. (13, 22) $\frac{1}{9} + \frac{4}{6} \cdot \frac{4}{12}$ $\frac{1}{3}$ **19.** (27) $\frac{x^5}{x^2x} \cdot \frac{y^4}{y}$ x^2y^3

Generalize Combine like terms to simplify.

▸*** 20.** (31) $xyz + yxz - zyx - x^2yz$ $xyz - x^2yz$

▸*** 21.** (31) $gh - 4gh + 7g - 8h + h$ $-3gh + 7g - 7h$

▸ See Math Conversations in the sidebar.

---

3 Written Practice *(Continued)*

Math Conversations
Discussion opportunities are provided below.

Problem 3a Justify
"What part of 1 liter is 1 milliliter?" $\frac{1}{1000}$

"One liter is equivalent to what number of milliliters?" 1000

Problem 4 Analyze
Extend the Problem
"Suppose that Bob's $2\frac{1}{2}$ hour elapsed time includes a rest stop of 10 minutes. What was Bob's average speed in miles per hour during the driving portion of his trip?" 60 miles per hour

Problems 5–8 Analyze
Before completing any paper and pencil arithmetic, ask students to describe the inverse operation for each problem that can be used to isolate *x*.
Problem 5: add 2.9 to each side
Problem 6: subtract $\frac{2}{3}$ from each side
Problem 7: multiply each side by $\frac{5}{3}$
Problem 8: multiply each side by 2.2

Problem 9
Challenge volunteers to name the constant factor, then solve the proportion, using only mental math.

Problem 11 Evaluate
"One leg of the triangle has a measure of 12 feet. Explain how to find the measure of the other leg of the triangle." Subtract 10 feet from 15 feet.

"To find the measure of the hypotenuse of the right triangle, we must solve $a^2 + b^2 = c^2$ for which variable?" *c*

Problems 20 and 21 Generalize
Ask students to identify the like terms that are present before collecting any terms.

(continued)

Math Conversations

Discussion opportunities are provided below.

Problem 26 Evaluate

Students can use a pattern of numbers, like the pattern shown below, to help recognize the equation or to check their answer.

Number of Minutes	0	1	2	3	4	5
Number of Bacteria	1	2	4	8	16	32

22. The triangles are similar. Find x and y. $x = 24, y = 22$
(19, 20)

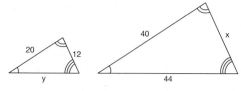

For problems **23** and **24,** find all values of x which make the equations true.

23. $x^2 = 100$ $10, -10$
(14, 15)

24. $3 + |x| = 9$ $6, -6$
(1, 14)

25. There are twelve sheep in the field. Eduardo notices that there are
(29)   more goats in the field than there are sheep. Which of the following is a possible ratio of sheep to goats?   **D**

   A $\frac{12}{5}$ **B** $\frac{12}{12}$ **C** $\frac{17}{12}$ **D** $\frac{12}{17}$

▶* **26.** Evaluate A strain of bacteria doubles every minute. Beginning with one
(15)   bacteria, how many would there be after 12 minutes? Write an equation using exponents and powers of 2. You may use a calculator to find the number. $n = 2^{12}; n = 4096$

27. Model On a number line, graph the integers that are greater than -3
(1)   and less than 3.

27.

28. Dharma has a bag that contains six pens; three are black, two are blue
(32)   and one is red. If Dharma takes one pen out of the bag without looking,

   a. what is the probability of selecting a blue pen? $\frac{1}{3}$

   b. what is the complement of selecting a blue pen? $\frac{2}{3}$

29. Use 3.14 for π to find $2\pi r$ when $r = 5$.   31.4
(14, 25)

30. Refer to this figure to answer the following
(18)   questions.

   a. Which angle is acute? $\angle BOC$ (or $\angle COB$)

   b. Which angle is obtuse? $\angle AOB$ (or $\angle BOA$)

   c. Which angle is straight? $\angle AOC$ (or $\angle COA$)

   d. Which two angles form a linear pair? $\angle AOB$ (or $\angle BOA$) and $\angle BOC$ (or $\angle COB$)

▶ See Math Conversations in the sidebar.

Looking Forward

Using properties of equality to solve equations prepares students for:

• **Lesson 50,** solving multi-step equations.

• **Lesson 62,** graphing solutions to inequalities on a number line.

• **Lesson 77,** working with inequalities with negative coefficients.

• **Lesson 79,** transforming formulas.

• **Lesson 93,** solving equations with exponents.

• Circumference of a Circle

Objectives

- Identify the radius, diameter, and circumference of a circle and understand how they are related.
- Use approximations for pi when appropriate.
- Use the formula for circumference to solve word problems involving circles.

Lesson Preparation

Materials

- **Power Up H** (in *Instructional Masters*)
- **Teacher-provided material:** calculators

Optional

- **Teacher-provided material:** string and rulers

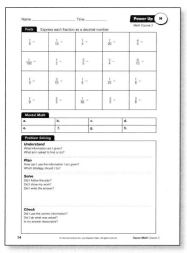

Power Up H

Math Language

New	Maintain	English Learners (ESL)
circumference	perimeter	pivot
diameter		
pi		
radius		

Technology Resources

Student eBook Complete student textbook in electronic format.

Resources and Planner CD Assessment, reteaching, and instructional masters, plus a pacing calendar with standards.

Test and Practice Generator CD Create additional practice sheets and custom-made tests.

www.SaxonPublishers.com Visit for more student activities and planning materials.

Inclusion

Adaptations CD Adapted lessons, investigations, practice and assessments.

Meeting Standards

National Council of Teachers of Mathematics (NCTM)

Algebra

AL.1a Represent, analyze, and generalize a variety of patterns with tables, graphs, words, and, when possible, symbolic rules

Geometry

GM.1b Understand relationships among the angles, side lengths, perimeters, areas, and volumes of similar objects

Measurement

ME.1c Understand, select, and use units of appropriate size and type to measure angles, perimeter, area, surface area, and volume

ME.2c Develop and use formulas to determine the circumference of circles and the area of triangles, parallelograms, trapezoids, and circles and develop strategies to find the area of more-complex shapes

Problem-Solving Strategy: Draw a Diagram

A robot is programmed to follow this sequence of commands: forward 3, rotate 90° clockwise, backward 1, rotate 90° counterclockwise, forward 2. If the robot begins at space 7 D facing the top of the page, where does it end, and which direction is it facing?

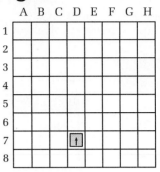

[**Understand**] **Understand the problem.**

"What information are we given?"

A robot begins at space 7 D and follows this sequence of commands:

1. Forward 3.
2. Rotate 90° clockwise.
3. Backward 1.
4. Rotate 90° counterclockwise.
5. Forward 2.

"What are we asked to do?"

Determine in which space the robot ends, and in which direction it is facing.

[**Plan**] **Make a plan.**

"What problem-solving strategy will we use?"

We will *draw a diagram* of the robot's path.

[**Solve**] **Carry out the plan.**

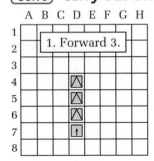
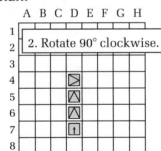
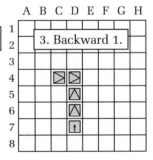

[**Check**] **Look back.**

"Did we complete the task that was assigned?"

Yes. We determined that the robot will end his journey in space 2 C facing the top of the page.

• Circumference of a Circle

Power Up   *Building Power*

facts | Power Up H

mental math

a. **Number Sense:** $4\frac{1}{2}$ inches $+ 13\frac{1}{2}$ inches   18 in.

b. **Algebra:** $\frac{1}{x} = \frac{1}{2}$ 2

c. **Measurement:** Find the length of this object in inches. $2\frac{5}{8}$ in.

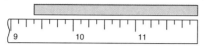

d. **Rate:** Peter picked 6 peppers per minute. What was his rate in peppers per hour?   360 peppers per hour

e. **Proportions:** There are 10 computers to every 30 students in the school. What is the ratio of computers to students? If there are 600 students in the school, how many computers does the school own? 1 to 3; 200

f. **Scientific Notation:** Write 2×10^6 in standard notation.   2,000,000

g. **Geometry:** Approximate the area of this rectangle.   100 cm²

4.9 cm
20.2 cm

h. **Calculation:** $48 \div 4, -3, \sqrt{\ }, -4, \times 2, +3, \times 9, \times 4, \sqrt{\ }, -6$ 0

problem solving

A robot is programmed to follow this sequence of commands: forward 3, rotate 90° clockwise, backward 1, rotate 90° counterclockwise, forward 2. If the robot begins at space 7 D facing the top of the page, where does it end, and which direction is it facing?   2 C, top of the page

1 Power Up

Facts
Distribute **Power Up H** to students. See answers below.

Mental Math
Encourage students to share different ways to mentally compute these exercises. Strategies for exercises **b, d,** and **g** are listed below.

b. By Inspection
   $x = 2$, because the numerators are equal, so the denominators have to be equal.

d. Use Math Sense
   1 min → 6 peppers
   10 min → 60 peppers
   60 min → 360 peppers
   Use a Unit Rate
   6 peppers/min × 60 min/hour =
   360 peppers/hour

g. Round to Estimate
   4.9 cm ≈ 5 cm
   20.2 cm ≈ 20 cm
   5 cm × 20 cm = 100 cm²

Problem Solving
Refer to **Power-Up Discussion**, p. 257B.

Facts   Express each fraction as a decimal number.

$\frac{1}{5} = 0.2$	$\frac{1}{10} = 0.1$	$\frac{1}{4} = 0.25$	$\frac{1}{20} = 0.05$	$\frac{4}{5} = 0.8$
$\frac{1}{100} = 0.01$	$\frac{1}{2} = 0.5$	$\frac{3}{5} = 0.6$	$\frac{3}{4} = 0.75$	$\frac{9}{10} = 0.9$
$\frac{1}{3} = 0.\overline{3}$	$\frac{3}{10} = 0.3$	$\frac{1}{6} = 0.1\overline{6}$	$\frac{1}{25} = 0.04$	$\frac{1}{8} = 0.125$
$\frac{1}{9} = 0.\overline{1}$	$\frac{2}{3} = 0.\overline{6}$	$\frac{1}{50} = 0.02$	$\frac{2}{5} = 0.4$	$\frac{3}{8} = 0.375$

2 New Concepts

Instruction

Use the Thinking Skill *Generalize* question to check understanding of the relationship of a radius and a diameter of a circle.

To help students understand the constant nature of the relationship between the circumference and diameter of a circle, you may want to have students use string and rulers or meter/yard sticks to measure the circumference and diameter of several circular objects and then calculate the ratio of the circumference to the diameter. Explain that this ratio is always constant and is equal to π.

Doing this activity will also give students extra support for understanding the two formulas that are given for finding the circumference of a circle.

Use the *Reading Math* feature to note that because π is irrational, we have to use approximations to calculate with π, and we indicate that the answers are also approximations by using the symbol $\approx$ for "approximately equals" instead of an equals sign.

(continued)

New Concept Increasing Knowledge

To draw a circle we can use a compass, a tool with a pivot point and a drawing point. As we swing the compass around its pivot point the drawing point traces a circle. Every point on the circle is the same distance from the center. The distance from the center to a point on the circumference of the circle is its **radius** (plural: **radii**).

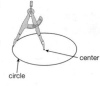

The distance across a circle measured through its center is its **diameter**.

Thinking Skill

Generalize

How does the diameter of a circle relate to its radius? How does the radius of a circle relate to its diameter? The diameter of a circle is twice its radius. The radius of a circle is half its diameter.

The distance around a circle is its **circumference**. Circumference is the specific name for the perimeter of a circle. The distance around a circle is related to the distance across the circle. If we take lengths equal to the diameter and wrap them around a circle, we would find that it takes a little more than three diameter lengths to complete the circumference.

The circumference of a circle is about 3.14 or $3\frac{1}{7}$ diameters, but these numbers are approximations of a special constant. A circumference is exactly π **(pi)** diameters. Thus the ratio of the circumference to the diameter of a circle is π.

$$\frac{\text{circumference}}{\text{diameter}} = \pi$$

These are two commonly used formulas for the circumference of a circle.

Circumference of a Circle

$$c = \pi d \qquad c = 2\pi r$$

To find a circle's circumference using the formula on the left, we multiply its diameter by π.

Explain How would you use the formula on the right to find circumference? Double its radius and multiply by π.

Multiplying by π involves approximation, because π is an irrational number. There is no decimal or fraction that exactly equals π. This book will use two commonly used approximations for π.

$$\pi \approx 3.14 \qquad \pi \approx \frac{22}{7}$$

Reading Math

Recall that when numbers are approximate, we use $\approx$ in place of $=$.

Applications that require greater precision may use closer approximations for π, such as 3.14159. For rough mental estimations or to check the reasonableness of a calculation we may use 3 for π.

English Learners

Explain the meaning of the word **pivot** in the term pivot point. Say:

"To pivot means to turn on a point. Watch while I pivot."

Turn in place and then say:

"When you draw a circle with a compass, you put the pivot point in the center. Then, you turn the pencil around the pivot point."

Use a compass to draw several circles. Have students identify the pivot point of each circle.

Some calculators have a key or keystroke sequence for π.

   a. If your calculator displays π, write its value to the number of places shown.   3.14159265358979323...

   b. Arrange these numbers in order from least to greatest.   3.14, π, $\frac{22}{7}$

$$3.14, \frac{22}{7}, \pi$$

Example 1

The diameter of the truck wheel is 35 inches. About how far does the wheel roll in one turn? (Use $\frac{22}{7}$ for π.)

Solution

The distance the wheel rolls in one turn equals the circumference of the wheel. To find the circumference we multiply the diameter by the given approximation for π.

$$c = \pi d$$
$$c \approx \frac{22}{7} \cdot 35 \text{ inches}$$
$$c \approx 110 \text{ inches}$$

We calculate that the wheel rolls about **110 inches** in one turn. The answer seems reasonable because π is a little more than 3, and 3×35 in. is 105 in.

> The calculation is easier using $\frac{22}{7}$ when the diameter is a multiple of 7.

Discuss   Why might you choose to use $\frac{22}{7}$ for π instead of 3.14?

Example 2

The fan belt on Fernando's car wraps around two circular pulleys. One pulley has a diameter of 8 cm. The other has a diameter of 12 cm. What is the ratio of the pulleys' circumferences?

Solution

The circumferences are 8π and 12π, so the ratio of the circumferences is

$$\frac{8\pi}{12\pi} = \frac{8}{12} = \frac{2}{3}$$

All circles are similar, so the radii, diameters, and circumferences of any two circles are proportional. The scale factor from the large to small pulley is $\frac{2}{3}$. From the smaller to the larger pulley, the scale factor is $\frac{3}{2}$.

Example 3

What effect does doubling the diameter of a circle have on the circumference?

Lesson 39   259

2 New Concepts (Continued)

Calculator Activity

Call attention to the order of the numbers in the answer to part b. Ask what this order tells us about calculations that might be performed using these numbers. Calculations with 3.14 will be less than the exact value, calculations with π will be the exact value, and calculations with $\frac{22}{7}$ will be greater than the exact value.

Example 1
Instruction

Extend the *Discuss* question by pointing out that 3.14 is usually used when working with decimal numbers, but that either approximation or the approximation obtained with a calculator key may be used for any problem that does not specify which value of π to use.

Example 2
Instruction

Ask a volunteer to explain why all circles are similar. They are all the same shape. Point out that the ratio of the circumferences of two circles is the same as the ratio of their diameters and as the ratio of their radii.

Example 3
Instruction

Point out that the same relationship is true for doubling the side lengths of any polygon.

(continued)

Teacher Tip

You may want to give students **more information about π.** In addition to 3.14 and $\frac{22}{7}$, other approximations for π have been derived, but most are very complex. A simple approximation that is accurate to 7 significant digits is $\frac{355}{113}$.

An unusual fact is that in the late 1800's a bill attempting to define π was introduced in the Indiana legislature but it failed to pass into law, partly because it contained three different values for π, one of which was 3. Pi can be an interesting and challenging topic for a research project.

2 New Concepts (Continued)

Example 4
Instruction

Compare the two answers to the order of the digits obtained in the calculator activity. Ask how the answer that could be found using $\frac{22}{7}$ to approximate π would compare to these two values. It would be greater.

Practice Set
Problem e Error Alert

Explain that one formula should describe how to find circumference given a radius (r), and the other formula should describe how to find circumference given a diameter (d).

Problem h Connect
Extend the Problem

Invite students to describe a situation in which each approximation might be used. Sample: Use 3.14 if a situation involves decimal numbers, and use $\frac{22}{7}$ if a situation involves whole numbers, fractions, or mixed numbers.

Problem k Estimate

Write $C = \pi d$ on the board or overhead and invite a volunteer to demonstrate how the formula is used to solve the problem.

Then invite a volunteer to demonstrate how $C = 2\pi r$ can be used to solve the problem.

Solution

The circumference is a length. Applying a scale factor to a figure applies the scale factor to all lengths. Therefore, **doubling the diameter doubles the circumference.** For example, if the diameter of a 6 inch circle is doubled to 12 inches, the circumference doubles from 6π inches to 12π inches.

Example 4

George Ferris designed a Ferris Wheel for the 1893 World Columbian Exposition in Chicago. The wheel was 75 meters in diameter. Calculate the circumference of the wheel to the nearest meter. (Use a calculator if available.)

Solution

Using a calculator we can multiply 75 m by 3.14 or by using the π function. Here we show sample displays.

$$\text{Using } 3.14 = 235.5$$
$$\text{Using } \pi \text{ key} = 235.619449$$

Rounding to the nearest meter we find the circumference of the wheel was about **236 m.**

Practice Set

a. The diameter of a circle on the playground is 12 ft. What is the radius of the circle?   6 ft

b. A spoke on the bike wheel is about 12 inches long. The diameter of the wheel is about how many inches?   24 in.

c. What is the name for the perimeter of a circle?   circumference

d. How many diameters equal a circumference? π

▶ e. Write two formulas for the circumference of a circle. $c = \pi d$, $c = 2\pi r$

f. Which of these terms does not apply to π?   **A**

   A rational number   **B** irrational number   **C** real number

g. π does not exactly equal any fraction, so it is an irrational number. Real numbers are all the rational and irrational numbers.

g. Justify Explain your choice for problem **f.**

▶ h. Write a decimal number and a fraction commonly used as approximations for π.   3.14, $\frac{22}{7}$

i. What is incorrect about the following equation?
$$\pi = 3.14$$

i. The equal sign should not be used because 3.14 is an approximation of π.

j. To roughly estimate calculations involving π or to check if a calculation is reasonable, we can use what number for π?   3

▶ k. Estimate A bicycle tire with a diameter of 30 inches rolls about how many inches in one turn?   about 94 inches

▶ See Math Conversations in the sidebar.

Math Background

An *arc* of a circle is a continuous path on the circumference of a circle between two points. You can find the length of an arc using the measure of the central angle whose sides intersect the two points. Just find the ratio of the central angle to 360° (the number of degrees in a full rotation) and multiply the ratio by the circumference of the circle.

$$\text{Length of arc } CD = \frac{60}{360} \cdot 2\pi r$$
$$= \frac{60}{360} \cdot 2\pi(4\text{in.})$$
$$= \frac{1}{6} \cdot 8\pi \text{ in.}$$
$$\approx \left(\frac{1}{6}\right)(8)(3.14) \text{ in.}$$
$$\approx 4.19 \text{ in.}$$

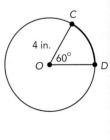

l. *Justify* The diameter of a circle painted on the playground is 7 yards. The distance around the circle is about how many yards? What number did you use for π and why did you use that number? 22 yds; Sample: I used $\frac{22}{7}$ because the diameter can be divided by 7, so the calculation is easier than multiplying by 3.14.

m. The diameter of the earth at the equator is about 7927 miles. About how many miles is the circumference of the earth at the equator? Use a calculator with a π function if available. Round to the nearest hundred miles. 24,900 mi

Written Practice *Strengthening Concepts*

1. The dump truck traveled north 20 miles to pick up a load of rocks. Then
(3) it traveled south 7 miles to dump the load. How far is the truck from where it started? (It might be helpful to draw a picture.) 13 miles

2. A puzzle has 330 pieces. How long will it take to complete the puzzle if
(4) 60 pieces are put together each hour? $5\frac{1}{2}$ hours

3. Sarah laughed once the first hour, twice the second hour, three times
(3) the third hour, etc. If this pattern continued nine hours, how many times did Sarah laugh in all? 45 times

▶ * **4.** Leah will win the board game on her next turn if she rolls a number
(30, 32) greater than 2 with one number cube. Find her chances of winning on her next turn. Express your answer as a ratio in simplest form and as a percent rounded to the nearest whole percent. $\frac{2}{3}$, 67%

▶ * **5.** *Analyze* In a coin collection, the ratio of buffalo nickels to non-buffalo
(34) nickels is 2 to 8. If there are 96 non-buffalo nickels, how many buffalo nickels are in the collection? $\frac{2}{8} = \frac{b}{96}$, $b = 24$; there are 24 buffalo nickels in the collection.

Simplify.

* **6.** $(-3)(-5)(-2)$ $\quad -30$
(36)

* **7.** $\dfrac{(-5)(-12)}{-10}$ $\quad -6$
(36)

* **8.** $\dfrac{-6}{-3} + \dfrac{-10}{5}$ $\quad 0$
(36)

* **9.** $\dfrac{-12x}{-2}$ $\quad 6x$
(36)

* **10.** $1\frac{1}{4} + 2\frac{1}{2} \div 1\frac{1}{3}$ $\quad 3\frac{1}{8}$
(13, 23)

11. $\dfrac{1}{5} - \dfrac{1}{5} \cdot \dfrac{1}{2}$ $\quad \frac{1}{10}$
(21, 22)

12. $\dfrac{4.28 - 1}{(2)(0.2)}$ $\quad 8.2$
(24, 25)

13. $\sqrt{5^2 + 12^2}$ $\quad 13$
(15, 21)

* **14.** $\dfrac{x^0 \cdot x^5}{x^2}$ $\quad x^3$
(27)

▶ ***15.** $2^6 \cdot 3 \cdot 5^6$ (*Hint:* pair 2's and 5's) 3,000,000
(15, 27)

16. One side of a rectangle has vertices $(-2, -5)$ and $(-9, -5)$. What is the
(8, Inv. 1) length of an adjacent side if the area of the rectangle is 21 square units? Find two possible locations for the other pair of vertices. 3; $(-9, -2)$, $(-2, -2)$ or $(-9, -8)$, $(-2, -8)$.

Lesson 39 **261**

▶ See Math Conversations in the sidebar.

3 Written Practice

Math Conversations
Discussion opportunities are provided below.

Problem 4 *Justify*
Extend the Problem
Write the terms *more likely* and *less likely* on the board or overhead. Ask students to decide if Leah is more likely or less likely to win the game on her next toss of the cube, and give a reason to support their answer. More likely; Sample: The probability of an event ranges from 0 to 1, and $\frac{1}{2}$ represents equally likely outcomes. Since Leah's probability of winning is $\frac{2}{3}$, and $\frac{2}{3}$ is greater than $\frac{1}{2}$, her probability of winning is more likely than not winning.

Problem 5 *Analyze*
Challenge students to write two different proportions on the board or overhead that can be used to solve the problem. Sample: $\frac{2}{8} = \frac{x}{96}$ and $\frac{96}{x} = \frac{8}{2}$

For each correct proportion that is written, have students note how the ratios are written in an orderly way.

Errors and Misconceptions
Problem 15
One way for students to check if they paired the 2's and 5's correctly is to solve a simpler problem that does not involve lengthy arithmetic. For example, ask students to simplify $2^2 \cdot 3^2$ and $(2 \cdot 3)^2$, then compare the standard form of each expression.

$$2^2 \cdot 3^2 = 4 \cdot 9 = 36$$
$$(2 \cdot 3)^2 = (6)^2 = 36$$

Because the standard form of each expression is the same, students should generalize that the expression $2^2 \cdot 3^2$ can be rewritten as $(2 \cdot 3)^2$, and for problem 15, infer that $2^6 \cdot 3 \cdot 5^6$ can be rewritten as $3 \cdot (2 \cdot 5)^6$ or $3 \cdot 10^6$.

(continued)

3 Written Practice (Continued)

Math Conversations

Discussion opportunities are provided below.

Problem 18 `Justify`

Invite students to name, or list on the board or overhead, a variety of other frequently-used fraction and decimal equivalents.

Sample: $\frac{1}{2} = 50\%$; $\frac{1}{3} = 33\frac{1}{3}\%$; $\frac{3}{4} = 75\%$; $\frac{1}{5} = 20\%$; $\frac{2}{5} = 40\%$; $\frac{3}{5} = 60\%$; $\frac{4}{5} = 80\%$; $\frac{1}{10} = 10\%$; $\frac{3}{10} = 30\%$; $\frac{7}{10} = 70\%$; $\frac{9}{10} = 90\%$

Problem 19 `Analyze`

Encourage students to trace the letters and move the tracings to help decide if either type of symmetry is present.

Problem 23

"What is the sign of the product of two negative integers?" positive

Problems 24 and 25 `Analyze`

Before completing any paper and pencil arithmetic, ask students to describe the inverse operation for each problem that can be used to isolate x.

Problem 24: subtract 0.9 from each side
Problem 25: divide each side by 0.9

18. b. See student work. Using $\frac{1}{4}$ is probably more convenient because finding $\frac{1}{4}$ of $24 seems easier than multiplying $24 by 0.25.

17. A corner was cut from a 5-inch square. Find the **a** area of the square, **b** the area of the triangle that was cut from the original square, and **c** the area of the remaining shape. (Hint: subtract) **a.** 25 in.²; **b.** 6 in.²; **c.** 19 in.²

18. `Justify` **a.** Write 25% as a reduced fraction and a decimal. $\frac{1}{4}$, 0.25
(12)
    b. Which form would you find most convenient to compute 25% of $24? Explain.

19. `Analyze` Consider these upper-case letters:
(26, Inv. 3)
                X Y Z
    a. Which letter does not have reflective symmetry? Z
    b. Which letter does not have rotational symmetry? Y

20. Estimate by rounding first: $\frac{2.8^2 + 1.1^2}{1.9}$ 5
(17)

21. A coin is tossed and a number cube is rolled. What is the sample space for the experiment? What is the probability of tossing heads and rolling 1? Sample space = {H1, H2, H3, H4, H5, H6, T1, T2, T3, T4, T5, T6}; $\frac{1}{12}$

22. How would you rearrange these numbers so they are easier to multiply?
(1, 22) Name the properties you use.
$$3\left(2 \cdot \frac{1}{3}\right)$$
Sample: $(3 \cdot \frac{1}{3}) \cdot 2 = 2$; Commutative and Associative Properties of Multiplication
Solve by inspection.

23. Find two values of x that make this equation true.
(15, 36)
$$x^2 = 16 \quad x = 4, -4$$

`Analyze` Solve using inverse operations.

24. $0.9 + x = 2.7$ x = 1.8   **25.** $0.9x = 2.7$ x = 3
(38)   (38)

26. The moon is about a quarter of a million miles from earth.
(5, 28)
    a. The moon is about how many miles from earth? 250,000 mi
    b. Express your answer to part **a** in scientific notation. 2.5×10^5 mi

27. Refer to the diagram.
(18)
    a. Find m∠ a. 30°
    b. Find m∠ b. 60°

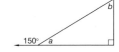

Evaluate.

28. Sketch a circle with a diameter of 2 inches. What is the circumference of a circle with a diameter of 2 inches? (Use 3.14 for π.) 6.28 in.
(39)

▶ See Math Conversations in the sidebar.

▶* 29. Rafters are lengths of wood, often 2 by 6s or
(Inv. 2) 2 by 8s, that support the roof. Find the length
of the rafters for the building shown.   **13 feet**

* 30. A smaller square is cut from a larger square.
(37) What is the area of the remaining figure?
16 in.²

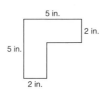

Early Finishers
*Real-World
Application*

Luz wants to place a fence around the edge of her garden and fertilize the
soil inside. A scale drawing of her garden is shown below. She plans to put
support posts 4 feet apart around the edge of the garden and to string wire
fencing between the posts. Each post costs $5.00 and the wire fencing costs
$1.50 per foot. One box of fertilizer costs $4.00 and covers 500 sq. ft. How
much will it cost Luz to fence and fertilize her garden?   **$268**

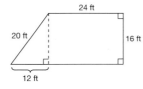

Lesson 39   263

▶ See Math Conversations in the sidebar.

Math Conversations

Discussion opportunities are provided below.

Problem 29   Evaluate

Extend the Problem

To check their work, challenge students
to divide the figure into three parts, then
compare the sum of the areas of those parts to
their original answer. Sample: $(2 \times 2) +
2(3 \times 2) = 16$

Looking Forword

Calculating the circumferences of circles prepares students for:

• **Lesson 40,** calculating areas of circles.

• **Lesson 43,** calculating surface areas.

• **Lesson 81,** working with central angles and arcs.

• **Lesson 85,** calculating surface areas of cylinders and prisms.

• **Lesson 91,** investigating the effects of scaling on perimeter, area, and
volume.

• **Lesson 100,** calculating surface areas of right pyramids and cones.

• **Lesson 111,** calculating volumes and surface areas of spheres.

• Area of a Circle

Objectives

- Use the formula $A = \pi r^2$ to calculate the areas of circles and to solve problems involving the areas of circles.
- Identify central angles and arcs of a circle and classify arcs as major or minor.
- Calculate the area of a sector of a circle.
- Understand the effect doubling the radius of a circle has on its area.

Lesson Preparation

Materials

- **Power Up H** (in *Instructional Masters*)

Optional

- **Teacher-provided material: grid paper**

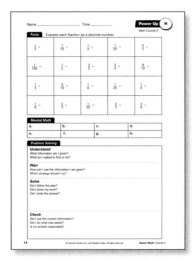

Power Up H

Math Language

New	Maintain	English Learners (ESL)
arc	circumference	occupies
central angle	diameter	
sector	radius	

Technology Resources

Student eBook Complete student textbook in electronic format.

Resources and Planner CD Assessment, reteaching, and instructional masters, plus a pacing calendar with standards.

Test and Practice Generator CD Create additional practice sheets and custom-made tests.

www.SaxonPublishers.com Visit for more student activities and planning materials.

Inclusion

Adaptations CD Adapted lessons, investigations, practice and assessments.

Meeting Standards

National Council of Teachers of Mathematics (NCTM)

Measurement

ME.1c Understand, select, and use units of appropriate size and type to measure angles, perimeter, area, surface area, and volume

ME.2b Select and apply techniques and tools to accurately find length, area, volume, and angle measures to appropriate levels of precision

ME.2c Develop and use formulas to determine the circumference of circles and the area of triangles, parallelograms, trapezoids, and circles and develop strategies to find the area of more-complex shapes

Problem-Solving Strategy: Find a Pattern/
Make a Table

The mystery man listened and replied. When Bobby said 7, the mystery man said 16. When Jack said 11, the mystery man said 24. When Bao said 99, the mystery man said 200. Wally whispered. The mystery man said 40. What did Wally whisper?

(Understand) **Understand the problem.**

"What important information are we given?"

A 7 results in a 16; 11 becomes 24; 99 becomes 200; and a whispered number becomes 40.

"What are we asked to do?"

Determine the number Wally whispered.

(Plan) **Make a plan.**

"What problem-solving strategy will we use?"

We will *make a table* to help us *find the pattern*.

(Solve) **Carry out the plan.**

"How do we begin?"

We will record the students' inputs and the mystery man's outputs.

Student	Possible rule(s)	Mystery Man
7	$n + 9$; $(n \times 2) + 2$	$= 16$
11	$(n \times 2) + 2$	$= 24$
99	$(n \times 2) + 2$	$= 200$
19	$(n \times 2) + 2$	$= 40$

"How did we algebraically solve for Wally's whispered number?"

$(40 - 2) \div 2 = 19$

(Check) **Look back.**

"Did we find the answer to the question that was asked?"

Yes. We found that Wally's whispered number was 19.

264   **Saxon** Math Course 3

1 Power Up

Facts
Distribute **Power Up H** to students. See answers below.

Mental Math
Encourage students to share different ways to mentally compute these exercises. Strategies for exercises **a, b,** and **c** are listed below.

  a. Regroup
$$2 \times 128 = 2 \times (100 + 20 + 8)$$
$$= 200 + 40 + 16 = 256$$

  b. Use Math Sense
    There is only one 6, so the probability is the same: $\frac{1}{6}$.

  c. Multiply
    $\frac{3}{8} \times \$48 = 3 \times 6 = \$18$

  Use a Unit Fraction
    $\frac{1}{8}$ of \$48 = \$6
    $\frac{3}{8}$ of \$48 = \$18

Problem Solving
Refer to **Power-Up Discussion,** p. 264B.

2 New Concepts

Instruction
Explain that although π is the ratio of the circumference of a circle to its diameter (or the number of diameters that make up the circumference of a circle), students will also find it used in many other calculations, such as finding the area of a circle. Point out that the value of π is always the same, regardless of how it is used.

(continued)

LESSON
40   • **Area of a Circle**

Power Up   *Building Power*

facts | Power Up H

mental math

  a. Number Sense: 2×128 256

  b. Probability: The probability of rolling a 3 on a number cube is $\frac{1}{6}$, because there is only one "3" out of six possible outcomes. What is the probability of rolling a 6? $\frac{1}{6}$

  c. Fractional Parts: $\frac{3}{8}$ of \$48   \$18

  d. Measurement: The odometer read 0.8 miles when she left. When she returned, it read 2.2 miles. How many miles did she travel?   1.4 mi

  e. Rate: Danielle drinks 8 cups of fluids a day. How long will it take her to drink 56 cups of fluids?   7 days

  f. Geometry: Find the area of the rectangle, and then find the area of the shaded triangle.   36 cm², 18 cm²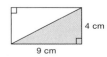

  g. Estimation: $6 \times \$2.98 + 2 \times \$7.48 + \$39.98$ \$73

  h. Calculation: $200 - 50, \div 3, -1, \sqrt{\ }, +2, \sqrt{\ }, \times 20, +4, \sqrt{\ }, +4, \div 4$, square it   9

problem solving | The mystery man listened and replied. When Bobby said 7, the mystery man said 16. When Jack said 11, the mystery man said 24. When Bao said 99, the mystery man said 200. Wally whispered. The mystery man said 40. What did Wally whisper?   19

New Concept   *Increasing Knowledge*

The area of a circle is related to the area of a square on the radius. The area of a circle is π times the area of a square on the radius. A formula for the area of a circle is

$$A = \pi r^2$$

The area of a circle is related to the area of a square on its radius. The area is greater than the area of three of these squares but less than the area of four such squares. The area of the circle is π times the area of the square of the radius as we see in the formula above.

area of circle $> 3r^2$ area of circle $< 4r^2$

264   *Saxon Math Course 3*

Facts   Express each fraction as a decimal number.

$\frac{1}{5} = 0.2$	$\frac{1}{10} = 0.1$	$\frac{1}{4} = 0.25$	$\frac{1}{20} = 0.05$	$\frac{4}{5} = 0.8$
$\frac{1}{100} = 0.01$	$\frac{1}{2} = 0.5$	$\frac{3}{5} = 0.6$	$\frac{3}{4} = 0.75$	$\frac{9}{10} = 0.9$
$\frac{1}{3} = 0.\overline{3}$	$\frac{3}{10} = 0.3$	$\frac{1}{6} = 0.1\overline{6}$	$\frac{1}{25} = 0.04$	$\frac{1}{8} = 0.125$
$\frac{1}{9} = 0.\overline{1}$	$\frac{2}{3} = 0.\overline{6}$	$\frac{1}{50} = 0.02$	$\frac{2}{5} = 0.4$	$\frac{3}{8} = 0.375$

Example 1

A circular table in the library has a diameter of 6 feet. If four students sit around the table, then each student has about how many square feet of work area?

Solution

First we find the area of the tabletop. The diameter is 6 feet, so the radius is 3 feet, and the radius squared is 9 square feet. We multiply 9 square feet by π, using 3.14.

$$A = \pi r^2$$
$$A \approx 3.14 \, (9 \text{ ft}^2)$$
$$A \approx 28.26 \text{ ft}^2$$

The area of the tabletop is about 28 square feet. If four students equally share the area, then each student has about **7 square feet** of work area.

Example 2

Express the answers to a and b in terms of π.

a. What is the circumference of this circle?

b. What is the area of this circle?

6 in.

Solution

Instead of multiplying by an approximation for π, we leave π in the answer as a factor. The parts of the answer are written in this order: rational number, irrational number, units.

a. The circumference is π times the diameter. The diameter is 12 inches. Thus the circumference is **12π in.**

b. The area of a circle is π times the radius squared. The square of the radius is 36 in.^{2}. Thus the area of the circle is **36π in.^{2}**.

A **sector** of a circle is a portion of the interior of a circle enclosed by two radii and an **arc** which is part of the circle.

The angle formed by the radii, called a **central angle**, determines the fraction of the area of the circle the sector occupies.

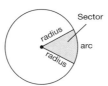

Sector

radius

arc

radius

---

2 New Concepts (Continued)

Example 1
Instruction
Call attention to the use of the approximation symbol and to the way the calculation is done. Ask why the result of the calculation is not the answer, and discuss ways to check the answer. Sample: First check that the area of the tabletop is correct by using 3 as an approximation of π and then decide if that number is close to 4×7.

Example 2
Instruction
Have students note that if we had written the steps to these calculations instead of doing them mentally, we could have used the equals sign, as the answers 12π in. and 36π in.^{2} are exact.

(continued)

English Learners

After example 2 explain the meaning of the word **occupies.** Say:

"To occupy means to fill in a space. When you occupy a seat, you fill the space in that seat."

Point to some object in the room and say what it occupies. For example, the wastebasket occupies this corner. Ask students what occupies other spaces in the classroom. Ex.: The blackboard occupies the entire wall.

2 New Concepts (Continued)

Example 3

Instruction

Students may find it helpful to make a sketch of the problem before beginning the calculation.

You might ask why the approximation $\frac{22}{7}$ was used instead of 3.14, and then discuss why using an approximation is more practical than using π. Sample: It is not easy to know how large an area described by π really is; even though an approximation is not exact, it is close enough to have a sense of how large the area is.

Example 4

Instruction

Ask students to describe another situation in which doubling a length of a figure quadrupled its area. Sample: If you double the length of the side of a square, its area is four times as great.

Example 5

Instruction

Discuss the definitions of *sector* and *central angle*.

For part **a**, you might point out that the fraction circles used earlier in the instruction on fractions are actually sectors. To find the area of a sector, find the fraction of the area of the circle that the sector occupies and then multiply the area of the circle by that fraction.

For part **b**, remind students that *semi-* is a prefix that means "half." So for a semicircle, we don't have to find the fraction of the circle that the sector is, because we know that it is $\frac{1}{2}$.

(continued)

Example 3

A lawn sprinkler waters a circular portion of a yard. The radius of the circular portion is 7 ft. Calculate the area of the yard watered by the sprinkler to the nearest square foot.

Solution

Thinking Skill

Discuss

Why might we choose to use $\frac{22}{7}$ for π in this instance? Since the radius is divisible by 7, it is convenient to use $\frac{22}{7}$ instead of 3.14 because we can cancel.

We choose to use $\frac{22}{7}$ for π.

$$A = \pi r^2$$
$$\approx \frac{22}{7}(7 \text{ ft})^2$$
$$\approx \frac{22}{7}(\overset{7}{\cancel{49}} \text{ ft}^2)$$
$$\approx 154 \text{ ft}^2$$

The sprinkler system waters about **154 ft²**.

Example 4

What effect does doubling the diameter of a circle have on the area of the circle?

Solution

Doubling the diameter doubles the radius. The radius is squared to calculate the area, so doubling the radius results in a circle with an area **four times** (2^2) as large. For example, if the diameter is doubled from 6 in. to 12 in. the area of the circle increases fourfold from 9π in.² to 36π in.².

Example 5

Find the area of each sector. Express in terms of π.

a.   b.

Solution

a. Sector *RMS* is bounded by angle *RMS* and arc *RS*. The 45° central angle indicates that the sector occupies $\frac{1}{8}$ of the area of the circle.

$$\frac{45°}{360°} = \frac{1}{8}$$

The area of a circle with a radius of 4 cm is 16π cm².

Step:	Justification:
$A = \pi r^2$	Area formula
$= \pi(4 \text{ cm})^2$	Substituted 4 cm for r
$= 16\pi \text{ cm}^2$	Simplified

Math Background

To see why the area formula for a circle makes sense, imagine cutting a circular region into equal wedges and arranging the wedges like this.

 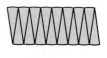

This shape resembles a parallelogram. The more wedges you cut the circle into, the smoother the bases will be and the more vertical the sides will be. In other words, the parallelogram will look more like a rectangle. The height of the rectangle will be the radius of the circle r. The base will be half of the circumference, or πr. So, the area will be $r \cdot \pi r$, or πr^2.

The area of the sector is $\frac{1}{8}$ of the area of the circle.

$$\text{Area of sector} = \frac{1}{8} \cdot 16\pi \text{ cm}^2$$

$$= 2\pi \text{ cm}^2$$

b. A sector that is half a circle is called a **semicircle**. We first find the area of the whole circle. The diameter is 16 cm, so the radius is 8 cm.

Step:	Justification:
$A = \pi r^2$	Area formula
$= \pi (8 \text{ cm})^2$	Substituted 8 cm for r
$= 64\pi \text{ cm}^2$	Simplified

The area of the semicircle is half of the area of the circle.

$$\text{Area of sector} = \frac{1}{2}(64\pi \text{ cm}^2)$$

$$= 32\pi \text{ cm}^2$$

Practice Set ▸ For **a** and **b**, find the area of each circle.

a.   78.5 cm²

5 cm

(Use π = 3.14)

b.   225π m²

15 m

(Express in terms of π)

▸ **c.** What is the scale factor from the circle in **a** to the circle in **b?** The area of the circle in **b** is how many times the area of the circle in **a?** scale factor is 3; area is 9 times as great

▸ **d.** A 140 ft diameter helicopter landing pad covers an area of about how many square feet? What value did you use for π and why did you choose it?   about 15,400 ft²; I used $\frac{22}{7}$ because the radius is divisible by 7, so the calculation is easier.

▸ **e.** A semicircular window with a radius of 36 inches allows light through an area of how many square feet? You may use a calculator if one is available. Round your answer to the nearest square foot.   14 ft²

r = 36 in.

▸ In the figure, segment AC is a diameter of circle O and measures 12 cm. Central angle BOC measures 60°. Find the area of the sectors named in **f–h** below. Express each area in terms of π.

f. Sector BOC 6π cm²

g. Sector BOA 12π cm²

h. Sector AOC 18π cm²

▸ See Math Conversations in the sidebar.

Practice Set
Problems a–h (Error Alert)
Remind students that units of area are square units, and point out that typical units of area include square centimeters (cm^2), square meters (m^2), and square feet (ft^2).

Problem e (Error Alert)
Since the radius of the window is given in inches and students are asked to find a number of square feet, they should recognize that changing 36 inches to 3 feet before finding the area will reduce the amount of arithmetic that needs to be completed.

Problems f–h (Error Alert)
Before expressing each area in terms of pi, students must determine the fraction of the circle each sector represents.

Sector BOC represents $60° \div 360°$, or $\frac{1}{6}$.
Sector BOA represents $(180° - 60°) \div 360°$, or $\frac{1}{3}$.
Sector AOC represents $180° \div 360°$, or $\frac{1}{2}$.

Math Conversations

Discussion opportunities are provided below.

Problem 6 | Model

"How can we use the rule to produce ordered pairs that we can plot?" Substitute values for x and solve for y.

"What values can we substitute for x?" Any numbers can be substituted for x.

Work with students to generalize that it is helpful to substitute even numbers for x so that the product of those numbers and $\frac{1}{2}$ is an integer.

Problems 9 and 10 | Analyze

Before completing any paper and pencil arithmetic, ask students to describe the inverse operation for each problem that can be used to isolate x.

Problem 9: multiply each side by 4 or $\frac{4}{1}$
Problem 10: subtract 2.9 from each side

Problem 11 | Evaluate

Ask students to sketch and label the figure, then divide it into two parts—a rectangle and a triangle.

"The hypotenuse of the triangle is 5 feet and we can use subtraction to find the measure of one of the legs of the triangle. Explain how to find that measure."
6 ft − 2 ft = 4 ft

"To find the measure of the other leg of the right triangle, we must solve $a^2 + b^2 = c^2$ for which variable?" a or b

Errors and Misconceptions
Problem 4

Watch for students who do not recognize that the length of the diameter must be halved when using the formula $A = \pi r^2$ to find the area of the circle.

Problem 5

Watch for students who do not recognize that the length of the radius must be doubled when using the formula $C = \pi d$ to find the circumference of the circle.

Problem 6

Make sure students understand that it is difficult to recognize a substitution or plotting error if only two points are graphed.

(continued)

---

1. How many hours and minutes is it from 3:45 p.m. on Tuesday to
(3) 6:30 a.m. on Wednesday?   14 hours and 45 minutes

2. The ratio of heroes to evil characters in the trilogy is 7 to 8. How many
(34) evil characters were there if there were 84 heroes?   96 evil characters

3. The four books Sergio read during the summer contained 186 pages,
(7) 210 pages, 246 pages, and 206 pages. What was the mean number of pages in the four books?   212 pages

▶ *** 4.** Find the area and circumference of the circle with diameter 6 m. Express
(40) answers in terms of π. $9\pi\,\text{m}^2, 6\pi\,\text{m}$

▶ *** 5.** Find the **a** area and **b** circumference of the circle with radius 10 m. Use
(40) 3.14 for π.   **a.** 314 m²; **b.** 62.8 m

▶ *** 6.** The rule for this table is $y = \frac{1}{2}x$. Graph the
(Inv. 1) (x, y) pairs on a coordinate plane.

x	y
−4	−2
−2	−1
0	0
2	1
4	2

6.

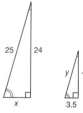

* 7. The triangles are similar.
(19, 20) **a.** Find x.   7
  b. Find y.   12.5
  c. What is the scale factor from the smaller to larger triangle?   2

* 8. Arrange the numbers in order from least to greatest: **A, D, C, B**
(30) **A** $\frac{2}{5}$ **B** $0.8\overline{8}$ **C** 0.8   **D** $0.4\overline{4}$

▶ **Analyze** Solve.

* 9. $\frac{1}{4}x = 5$ $x = 20$
(38)

* 10. $2.9 + x = 3.83$ $x = 0.93$
(24, 38)

▶ *** 11.** **Evaluate** Find the **a** area and **b** perimeter
(Inv. 2, 37) of the figure. (Dimensions are in ft.)   **a.** 30 ft²; **b.** 24 ft

▶ See Math Conversations in the sidebar.

* 12. Find the **a** area and **b** perimeter of a triangle with vertices located at
(Inv. 1, 20) (2, 1), (2, −5), (−6, −5).   **a.** 24 square units **b.** 24 units

13. Expand and collect like terms: $x(2x − 3) − x^2 − x$ $x^2 − 4x$
(21, 36)

Simplify.

14. $\dfrac{27x^2y^2}{3xy}$ $9xy$
(27)

15. $(7^2 − 2^2) − (4^2 − 1^2)$ 30
(15, 21)

16. $\left(\dfrac{1}{2}\right)^2 − \left(\dfrac{1}{2}\right)^3$ $\dfrac{1}{8}$
(15, 22)

17. $5 + 5(10)^2$ 505
(15, 21)

18. $\dfrac{1}{2} − \dfrac{3}{4} \cdot 1\dfrac{1}{2}$ $−\dfrac{5}{8}$
(13, 23)

19. $\dfrac{2}{7} + \dfrac{5}{14} \div \dfrac{1}{2}$ 1
(13, 22)

20. $(−2) − (−6) + (−4)$ 0
(31, 33)

21. $\dfrac{(−2)(−6)}{(−4)}$ −3
(36)

For problems **22** and **23** find all values of x which make the equations true.

22. $x^2 + 1 = 26$ 5, −5
(14, 15)

23. $|x| − 16 = 2$ 18, −18
(1, 14)

* 24. **Classify** Which terms below describe
(Inv. 3) this figure? Choose all terms that
apply.   **A, B, D**

A rectangle

B parallelogram

C trapezoid

D quadrilateral

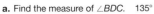

▶* 25. **Analyze** Which quadrilateral named below does not have rotational
(Inv. 3) symmetry?   **D**

A rectangle   **B** rhombus   **C** parallelogram **D** trapezoid

26. Write 4.93×10^8 in standard form.   493,000,000
(28)

* 27. Segment *AC* is a diameter of circle *D* and
(18, 40) measures 8 cm. Central angle $\angle ADB$
measures 45°.

a. Find the measure of $\angle BDC$.   135°

b. Find the area of sector *ADB* expressed in
terms of π. 2π cm²

28. In baseball, the pitcher's mound has a diameter of 18 feet. Which is the
(39) best estimate of the circumference of the pitcher's mound?   **D**

A 48 ft   **B** 50 ft   **C** 52 ft   **D** 54 ft

29. Evaluate: Find *Fd* when *F* = 2.2. and *d* = 10.   22
(14, 25)

▶ See Math Conversations in the sidebar.

Math Conversations

Discussion opportunities are provided below.

Problem 25 **Analyze**

Encourage students to draw an example of
each figure on grid paper, then rotate the
paper to help decide.

(continued)

3 Written Practice (Continued)

Math Conversations
Discussion opportunities are provided below.

Problem 30b [Justify]

Extend the Problem

"Is the probability of getting tails and an odd number likely or unlikely? Explain why." Unlikely: Sample: Probability ranges from 0 to 1, and $\frac{1}{2}$ represents equally likely outcomes. Since $\frac{1}{4}$ is less than $\frac{1}{2}$, $\frac{1}{4}$ represents an unlikely probability.

---

30. [Evaluate] A coin is flipped and the spinner
(32) is spun.

    a. Write the sample space for the experiment. Sample space = {H1, H2, H3, H4, T1, T2, T3, T4}

▶   **b.** What is the probability of getting tails and an odd number? P(T and Odd) = $\frac{1}{4}$

Early Finishers
Real-World Application

The Reliant Astrodome is located in Houston, Texas. It was the first sports stadium in the nation to install Astroturf, a type of artificial grass that requires minimal maintenance. Suppose that to improve the Astrodome's outward appearance, the management wants to install new lights at 10-foot intervals around the structure of the stadium where the dome meets the vertical walls. The diameter of the Astrodome is 710 feet. How many lights would the management need to buy to implement their plan? Use 3.14 for π and round your answer to the nearest whole number. 223 lights

▶ See Math Conversations in the sidebar.

Looking Forward

Calculating the areas of circles prepares students for:

- **Lesson 43,** calculating surface areas.
- **Lesson 76,** calculating volumes of prisms and cylinders.
- **Lesson 81,** working with central angles and arcs.
- **Lesson 85,** calculating surface areas of cylinders and prisms.
- **Lesson 86,** calculating volumes of pyramids and cones.
- **Lesson 100,** calculating surface areas of right pyramids and cones.
- **Lesson 101,** calculating geometric probabilities.
- **Lesson 111,** calculating volumes and surface areas of spheres.

Assessment
30–40 minutes
For use after Lesson 40

Distribute **Cumulative Test 7** to each student. Two versions of the test are available in *Saxon Math Course 3 Course Assessments Book*. Have students complete the **Power-Up Test** first. Allow 10 minutes. Then have students work the 20 numbered items on the **Cumulative Test.** Students may use copies of the answer sheet to record their work. Track individual and class progress with the **Test Analysis** forms.

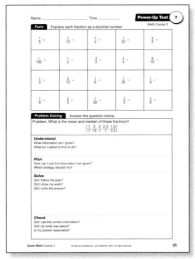
Power-Up Test 7

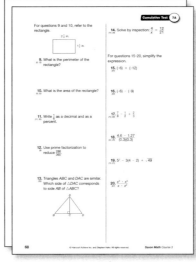
Cumulative Test 7A

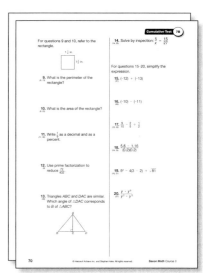
Alternative Cumulative Test 7B

Optional Answer Forms

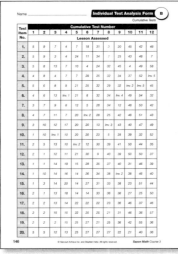
Individual Test Analysis Form

Class Test Analysis Form

Reteaching

Students who score below 80% on the assessment may be in need of reteaching. Look for the causes of student mistakes. If errors are conceptual, refer to the *Reteaching Masters* for reteaching.

Customized Benchmark Assessment

You can develop customized benchmark tests using the Test Generator located on the *Test & Practice Generator CD.*

This chart shows the lesson, the standard, and the test item question that can be found on the *Test & Practice Generator CD.*

LESSON	NEW CONCEPTS	LOCAL STANDARD	TEST ITEM ON CD
31	• Adding Integers		4.31.1
32	• Probability		4.32.1
33	• Subtracting Integers		4.33.1
34	• Proportions		4.34.1
	• Ratio Word Problems		4.34.2
35	• Similar and Congruent Polygons		4.35.1
36	• Multiplying and Dividing Integers		4.36.1
	• Multiplying and Dividing Terms		4.36.2
37	• Areas of Combined Polygons		4.37.1
38	• Using Properties of Equality to Solve Equations		4.38.1
39	• Circumference of a Circle		4.39.1
40	• Area of a Circle		4.40.1

Using the Test Generator CD

- Develop tests in both English and Spanish.
- Choose from multiple-choice and free-response test items.
- Clone test items to create multiple versions of the same test.
- View and edit test items to make and save your own questions.
- Administer assessments through paper tests or over a school LAN.
- Monitor student progress through a variety of individual and class reports —for both diagnosing and assessing standards mastery.

Design a Floor Plan

Assign after Lesson 40 and Test 7

Objectives

- Interpret and follow complex directions.
- Design a reasonable floor plan for a home.
- Calculate the area of a complex shape consisting of squares, rectangles, triangles, and semicircles.
- Determine a method for estimating the area of a floor plan.
- Communicate ideas through writing.

Materials

Performance Tasks 7A and **7B**

Preparation

Make copies of **Performance Tasks 7A** and **7B**. (One each per student.)

Time Requirement

25 minutes; Begin in class and complete at home.

Task

Explain to students that they will be designing their own floor plans for a 3-bedroom, 2-bath home and that it should be different from the example floor plan provided. Stress to the students that the design requirements must be followed but the instructions do allow for individual creativity in the design. After the floor plan is complete, each student will need to calculate the area of each room and the total area of the design using 3.14 for π. Students must then describe a method for estimating the overall area of their floor plans. Point out that all necessary information is provided on **Performance Tasks 7A** and **7B**.

Criteria for Evidence of Learning

- Designs a reasonable floor plan for a home that correctly meets all design criteria.
- Calculates correctly the area of each room and the area of the entire floor plan.
- Determines a viable method for estimating the overall area of the design.
- Communicates ideas clearly through writing.

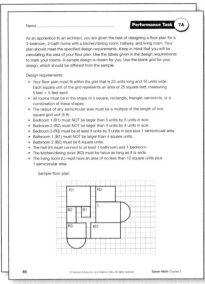

Performance Tasks 7A and 7B

Meeting Standards

National Council of Teachers of Mathematics (NCTM)

Numbers and Operations

NO.3c Develop and use strategies to estimate the results of rational-number computations and judge the reasonableness of the results

Algebra

AL.3a Model and solve contextualized problems using various representations, such as graphs, tables, and equations

Geometry

GM.4d Use geometric models to represent and explain numerical and algebraic relationships

GM.4e Recognize and apply geometric ideas and relationships in areas outside the mathematics classroom, such as art, science, and everyday life

Measurement

ME.2b Select and apply techniques and tools to accurately find length, area, volume, and angle measures to appropriate levels of precision

ME.2c Develop and use formulas to determine the circumference of circles and the area of triangles, parallelograms, trapezoids, and circles and develop strategies to find the area of more-complex shapes

Communication

CM.3a Organize and consolidate their mathematical thinking through communication

Focus on
• Drawing Geometric Solids

Objectives
- Identify a geometric solid's faces, edges, and vertices.
- Classify geometric solids, including prisms, pyramids, cylinders, cones, and spheres.
- Sketch prisms and cylinders using parallel projection.
- Sketch cones and pyramids from different viewpoints.
- Draw a multi-view projection of a three-dimensional object.
- Sketch prisms and cylinders using one-point projection.

Lesson Preparation

Materials
- Teacher-provided material: unlined paper
- Manipulative Kit: inch rulers

Optional
- Teacher-provided material: grid paper

Math Language

New

apex	geometric solid
edge	vertex
face	

Technology Resources

Student eBook Complete student textbook in electronic format.

Resources and Planner CD Assessment, reteaching, and instructional masters, plus a pacing calendar with standards.

Test and Practice Generator CD Create additional practice sheets and custom-made tests.

www.SaxonPublishers.com Visit for more student activities and planning materials.

Inclusion

Adaptations CD Adapted lessons, investigations, practice and assessments.

Meeting Standards

National Council of Teachers of Mathematics (NCTM)

Geometry

GM.4a Draw geometric objects with specified properties, such as side lengths or angle measures

Communication

CM.3b Communicate their mathematical thinking coherently and clearly to peers, teachers, and others

Focus on
• Drawing Geometric Solids

Closed figures that we draw on paper, like polygons and circles, are two-dimensional. They have length and width, but they are flat, lacking depth. Physical objects in the world around us are three-dimensional; they have length and width and depth.

Two-dimensional figures are called plane figures because they are contained in a plane. Three-dimensional figures are sometimes called space figures, because they occupy space and cannot be contained in a plane. Space figures are also called **geometric solids.**

The terms **face**, **edge**, and **vertex** (pl. vertices) refer to specific features of solids. The face of a polyhedron is a polygon. Two faces meet at an edge and edges intersect at a vertex.

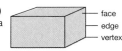

face
edge
vertex

In the table below we name, illustrate, and describe some geometric solids.

Geometric Solids

Polyhedron (pl. polyhedra)		A general term that identifies a solid with faces that are polygons. A polyhedron has no curved surfaces or edges.
Prism		A type of polyhedron with parallel congruent bases.
Pyramid		A type of polyhedron with lateral surfaces that narrow to a point (apex).
Cylinder		In this book we will use the term **cylinder** to refer to a right circular cylinder as illustrated.
Cone		In this book we will use the term **cone** to refer to a right circular cone as illustrated.
Sphere		A smooth curved solid every point of which is the same distance from its center.

Investigation 4 **271**

Math Background

A polyhedron is a 3-dimensional solid with faces that are polygons. It is important that students understand and be able to recognize the attributes of polyhedra and other solids. Students will build on this knowledge in later lessons when they measure volume and surface area. The key properties of some common polyhedra are in the chart below.

Polyhedron	Faces	Vertices	Edges
Cube/Rectangular Prism	6 square or rectangular	8	12
Triangular Prism	2 triangular and 3 rectangular	6	9
Square/Rectangular Pyramid	4 triangular and 1 square/rectangular	5	8
Triangular Pyramid	4 triangular	4	6

In this lesson students will draw three-dimensional figures. Invite students to look around the room and describe some of the geometric solids they see. Some examples might include the following:
• Book (rectangular prism)
• Pen or pencil (cylinder)
• Globe (sphere)

Instruction
Draw these shapes on the board.

Ask students to visualize a three-dimensional solid for which each polygon could be a face or base. Sample: square: cube, rectangular prism, square pyramid; triangle: triangular prism or pyramid; circle: cylinder or cone

(continued)

Instruction

Discuss the faces of a prism.

> **"How many bases does a prism always have?"** two

> **"How many sides can the base of a prism have?"** any number of sides

Point out to students that the faces of a prism that are not the bases are always rectangles.

Example

Instruction

Discuss the faces of a pyramid.

> **"How many bases does a pyramid always have?"** one

> **"How many sides can the base of a pyramid have?"** any number of sides

> **"The faces of a pyramid that are not the base are always what shape?"** triangle

Ask a volunteer to represent the relationship of faces and bases in a table. The student should work at the board or overhead.

Pyramid

Number of Sides of the Base (s)	3	4	5	6
Number of Faces (f)	4	5	6	7

Lead students to see that we can use the letters s and f to write an equation representing their relationship: $f = s + 1$. Have another volunteer do the same for a prism. Students will learn more about functions in Lesson 41.

(continued)

Prisms can be further classified by the shapes of their bases.

Triangular Prism   Rectangular Prism   Hexagonal Prism

One type of prism is a **rectangular prism** in which all faces are rectangles. One type of rectangular prism is a **cube** in which all faces are congruent squares.

Example

The pyramids of Egypt have square bases. A pyramid with a square base has how many faces, edges, and vertices?

Solution

A pyramid with a square base has **5 faces** (one square and four triangles), **8 edges**, and **5 vertices**.

Conclude How do the number of faces of a pyramid relate to the shape of its base? How do the number of faces of a prism relate to the shape of its base? The number of faces of a pyramid is 1 + the number of sides of the base; the number of faces of a prism is 2 + the number of sides of the base.

1. A triangular prism has how many faces, edges, and vertices? 5 faces, 9 edges, 6 vertices

2. **A** prism or rectangular prism; **B** pyramid; **C** cone; **D** prism or triangular prism; **C** A cone is not a polyhedron because it is curved.

2. Name each figure. Which is not a polyhedron? Explain your choice.

A   B

C   D

Geometric solids are three-dimensional figures. They have length, width, and depth (or height); they take up space. Flat surfaces like pages in a book, billboards, and artists' canvases are two-dimensional and lack depth. Thus, to represent a three-dimensional figure on a two-dimensional surface we need to create the illusion of depth. In this investigation we will practice ways to draw and represent three-dimensional figures in two dimensions.

Teacher Tip

Simple geometric solids are often found in architecture. Encourage students to observe buildings in their area or to research famous buildings online or in the library. Ask them to find an example of each solid they learned about in this lesson. They should record the names of the solids and the building on which it was found. If possible, they should sketch pictures of the solids and share their research with the class.

Samples: Tacoma Museum of Glass (Tacoma, WA) cone-like
Capitol Records (Los Angeles, CA) cylinder-like
Trans America Building (San Francisco, CA) pyramid-like
Spaceship Earth (Orlando, FL) sphere-like

Parallel projection is one way to sketch prisms and cylinders. Recall that prisms and cylinders have two congruent bases, one at each end of the figure. Using parallel projection, we draw the base twice, one offset from the other. We draw each base the same size.

Then we draw parallel segments between the corresponding vertices (or the corresponding opposite sides of the circles).

The resulting figures show all the edges as though the prisms were made with wire. If we were drawing a picture of a box or tube, the hidden edges would be erased.

In geometric sketches we often show hidden edges with dashes.

Activity 1

Sketching Prisms and Cylinders Using Parallel Projection

Materials needed:

- unlined paper
- pencil

Description of activity:

Sketch a rectangular prism, a triangular prism, and a cylinder using parallel projection. Make the bases of each figure congruent. Show hidden edges with dashes. To sketch the figures from different viewpoints, shift the position of the more distant base.

To draw pyramids and cones we can begin by sketching the base. To represent a square base of a pyramid we can draw a parallelogram. To represent the circular base of a cone we can draw an **ellipse,** which looks like a stretched or tilted circle.

Read through each step of the drawing instructions before students attempt to sketch any figures.

Some students may need to practice sketching polygons before they sketch three-dimensional figures.

(continued)

Activity 1

Students should draw on unlined paper. However, some students may feel more comfortable using grid paper.

Ask a volunteer to work at the board as other students work at their desks.

Instruction

Again, some students may need practice sketching the bases before they sketch pyramids and cones.

(continued)

Activity 2

A pyramid with a triangular base is called a tetrahedron. This word comes from the Greek words *tetra* meaning four-faced and *hedron* meaning a three-dimensional solid. A regular tetrahedron has four equilateral triangles as faces.

Ask a volunteer to work at the board as other students work at their desks.

Instruction

To provide students practice with visualizing multiview projection displays, pick up a classroom object and hold it so students have a front view. Have a volunteer sketch the view on the board. Then turn the object so students can see a different view. Ask questions about the object as you display the different views.

"Do you think the back view is different from the front view? Why or why not?"

"Do you think the side view is different from the back view? Why or why not?"

"Predict what the bottom view will look like."

Ask a volunteer to draw each view on the board as you turn the object. Choose another classroom object and encourage students to sketch all its views without turning it. When the sketches are complete, turn the object so students can see the different views and determine if their predictions were correct.

Math Language
A pyramid's **apex** is also one of its vertices.

Sample: 1. Draw a triangular base. 2. Draw a dot above the triangle. 3. Draw segments from the dot to the vertices of the base. 4. Erase the hidden edges or change them to dashes.

Centered above the base we draw a dot for the **apex,** or peak, of the pyramid or cone. Then we draw segments to the vertices of the base of the pyramid (or opposite points of the circular base of the cone).

We erase hidden edges or represent them with dashes.

Activity 2

Sketching Pyramids and Cones

Sketch a few pyramids and cones from different viewpoints.

Model Sketch a pyramid that has a triangular base.   See student work.

Discuss What steps will you follow to draw a pyramid with a triangular base?

Multiview projection displays three-dimensional objects from three perpendicular viewpoints, **top, front,** and **side** (usually the right side). An **isometric** view is often included, which is an angled view of the object, as shown in the projection below.

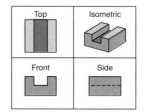

Notice that hidden edges do not appear in the isometric drawing but do appear in the other views as dashes. Notice that the width of the figure is the same in the top and front views. The height is the same in the front and side views, and the length is the same in the top and side views.

Activity 3

Create a Multiview Drawing

Materials needed:

- unlined paper
- pencil
- ruler

Description of activity:

Divide your paper into four equal sections. In the isometric section copy the sketch below. Then draw the top, front, and side views.

extensions

1. Build a figure from unit cubes and create a multiview projection for the figure.

2. Create a multiview projection for a building on your school's campus or in your school's neighborhood.

Parallel projection and isometric drawings do not provide the same perspective of depth our eyes perceive in the three-dimensional world. Objects appear to diminish in size the farther they are from us. For example, if we look down a straight road it may appear to nearly vanish at the horizon.

Using a **vanishing point** can provide a **perspective** to a figure as its more distant edges are shorter than corresponding nearer edges. Below we show a triangular prism drawn toward a vanishing point.

To create a one-point perspective drawing of a prism, draw a polygon in the foreground and pick a location for the vanishing point.

Then lightly draw segments from the vertices of the polygon to the vanishing point.

Investigation 4 **275**

Activity 3

Ask four volunteers to work at the board as they sketch the different views. Lead a class discussion on whether they agree or disagree with the students' drawings.

Instruction

In art, we use perspective when we want objects to appear to go into the distance. The vanishing point is the point from which all lines radiate. The closer the object is to the vanishing point, the smaller it is drawn.

If you have students who are particularly good at drawing, you might have them bring to class any drawing that has a vanishing point. The students should identify the vanishing point and discuss how the objects in the drawing relate to the vanishing point.

After students have drawn prisms using a vanishing point, have volunteers share their drawings.

Determine the depth you want to portray and draw corresponding segments *parallel* to the sides of the polygon in the foreground. Darken the edges between the two bases. Use dashes to show hidden edges.

Activity 4

One-Point Perspective Drawing

Materials needed:

- unlined paper
- pencil
- ruler

Description of activity:

Create one-point perspective drawings of some prisms. Place the vanishing point in different locations to change the point of view. Try different polygons for the bases of the prisms.

Looking Forward

Investigating drawing geometric solids prepares students for:

- **Lesson 42,** volume.
- **Lesson 43,** surface area.
- **Lesson 55,** nets of prisms, cylinders, pyramids, and cones.
- **Lesson 76,** volumes of prisms and cylinders.
- **Lesson 85,** surface areas of cylinders and prisms.
- **Lesson 86,** volumes of pyramids and cones.
- **Lesson 100,** surface areas of right pyramids and cones.
- **Lesson 107,** volume and surface area of compound solids.
- **Lesson 108,** similar solids.

Lesson Planner

LESSON	NEW CONCEPTS	MATERIALS	RESOURCES
41	• Functions	none	Power Up I
42	• Volume	Manipulative Kit: inch rulers Rectangular box, calculators, plastic liter bottles	Power Up I
43	• Surface Area	Manipulative Kit: inch rulers Rectangular box	Power Up I
44	• Solving Proportions Using Cross Products • Slope of a Line	none	Power Up I Lesson Activity 6
45	• Ratio Problems Involving Totals	none	Power Up I
46	• Solving Problems Using Scientific Notation	Calculators	Power Up J
47	• Graphing Functions	Calculators	Power Up J Lesson Activity 7
48	• Percent of a Whole	none	Power Up J
49	• Solving Rate Problems with Proportions and Equations	none	Power Up J
50	• Solving Multi-Step Equations	none	Power Up J
Inv. 5	• Graphing Transformations	Tracing paper, overhead marker	Investigation Activity 1 Transparency Investigation Activity 2

Problem Solving
Strategies
- **Find a Pattern**   Lessons 42, 44, 48
- **Make a Table, Make a Chart or Draw a Graph**   Lessons 45, 48
- **Make It Simpler**   Lessons 41, 43, 46, 47
- **Use Logical Reasoning**   Lessons 43, 45, 49, 50
- **Write an Equation**   Lesson 44
- **Guess and Check**   Lessons 49, 50

Real-World Applications
pp. 279, 281, 284–291, 295, 297–299, 303, 305–312, 315–320, 322–325, 327–329, 332–334, 336, 338, 340, 341

4-Step Process
Teacher Edition   Lessons 41–50 (Power-Up Discussions)

Communication
Discuss
pp. 281, 283

Explain
pp. 303, 319

Formulate a Problem
pp. 283, 292

Connections
Math and Other Subjects
- **Math and Architecture**   pp. 288, 289
- **Math and Art**   pp. 286, 288, 305, 312
- **Math and Science**   pp. 312, 315, 316, 329, 335
- **Math and Sports**   pp. 306, 332

Math to Math
- **Problem Solving and Measurement** Lessons 41–50
- **Algebra and Problem Solving**   Lessons 41, 43–50
- **Fractions, Percents, Decimals, and Problem Solving**   Lessons 42–50
- **Fractions and Measurement**   Lessons 42, 44, 46
- **Measurement and Geometry**   Lessons 41–50
- **Proportional Relationships and Geometry**   Lessons 44, 46, 47, 50, Inv. 5
- **Algebra, Measurement, and Geometry** Lessons 41, 43, 44, 46–48, Inv. 5
- **Probability and Statistics**   Lessons 41–44, 46, 49

Representation
Manipulatives/Hands On
pp. 289, 291, 296, 297, 322

Model
pp. 284, 285, 299, 310, 316

Represent
pp. 304, 323, 341

Formulate an Equation
pp. 292, 293, 298, 309, 311, 318, 329

Technology

Student Resources
- **eBook**   Anytime
- **Calculator**   Lessons 42, 47
- **Online Resources** at wwwSaxonPublisher.com/ActivitiesC3
  - **Graphing Calculator Activities**   Lesson 47 and Inv. 5
  - **Real-World Investigation 3**   after Lesson 47

Teacher Resources
- **Resources and Planner CD**
- **Adaptations CD**   Lessons 41–50
- **Test & Practice Generator CD**
- **eGradebook**
- **Answer Key CD**

Algebraic and proportional thinking are emphasized as students solve problems by writing both equations and proportions. Students use the coordinate plane to graph both functions and transformations.

Algebraic Thinking

The emphasis on algebra continues with both functions and equations.

Students identify functions in Lesson 41 and graph functions in Lesson 47. Students extend their equation-solving skills in Lesson 50 as they solve multi-step equations using inverse operations and justify each step of simplification. A practical skill for science, students begin solving problems by multiplying and dividing large numbers in scientific notation in Lesson 46.

Problem Solving and Proportional Thinking

Students use a ratio box to solve a wide variety of ratio problems.

Students learn additional skills as they work with proportional relationships. In Lesson 44 students solve proportions using cross products. In Lesson 45 they learn helpful techniques for solving ratio problems that involve totals. Students solve percent problems with proportions in Lesson 48 and rate problems with proportions in Lesson 49.

Geometry and Measurement

Volume and surface area are presented in these lessons.

Following the introduction to geometric solids in Investigation 4, students calculate volumes of rectangular solids in Lesson 42 and the surface areas and lateral surface area of these solids in Lesson 43. Students merge geometric and algebraic concepts in Investigation 5 as they graph geometric transformations on the coordinate plane.

Assessment

A variety of weekly assessment tools are provided.

After Lesson 45:
- Power-Up Test 8
- Cumulative Test 8
- Performance Activity 8

After Lesson 50:
- Power-Up Test 9
- Cumulative Test 9
- Customized Benchmark Test
- Performance Task 9

LESSON	NEW CONCEPTS	PRACTICED	ASSESSED
41	• Functions	Lessons 41, 42, 43, 44, 45, 46, 47, 48, 49, 50, 53, 54, 55, 56, 60, 61, 62, 63, 64, 65, 66, 67, 68, 69, 73, 75, 77, 79, 87, 88, 89, 90, 91, 97, 98, 103, 105, 112, 115, 118	Test 9
42	• Volume	Lessons 43, 44, 45, 46, 47, 48, 49, 50, 51, 52, 53, 55, 57, 59, 62, 64, 76, 83, 86, 92, 98, 102	Tests 9–13
43	• Surface Area	Lessons 43, 44, 45, 46, 47, 48, 50, 52, 53, 57, 59, 60, 61, 64, 65, 75, 79, 89, 93, 102	Tests 9, 10, 12, 14
44	• Solving Proportions Using Cross Products	Lessons 44, 47, 57, 58, 69, 70, 72, 73, 74, 75, 76, 77, 78, 83, 84, 85, 86, 88, 89, 90, 91, 97, 98, 99, 101, 103, 104, 105, 106, 107, 108, 109, 110, 111, 112, 113, 114, 117, 119	Tests 11, 12, 15,18, 22
44	• Slope of a Line	Lessons 45, 46, 47, 48, 52, 53, 54, 56, 60, 64	Test & Practice Generator
45	• Ratio Problems Involving Totals	Lessons 45, 47, 48, 49, 50, 51, 52, 53, 54, 56, 57, 58, 59, 60, 62, 65, 66, 67, 68, 69, 70, 71, 72, 74, 75, 76, 77, 84, 85, 88, 89, 93, 105	Tests 9, 10, 12, 15
46	• Solving Problems Using Scientific Notation	Lessons 46, 47, 48, 49, 50, 51, 53, 54, 60, 61, 89, 90, 97, 101, 103, 105, 117	Tests 10–12, 18
47	• Graphing Functions	Lessons 51, 55, 56, 57, 82, 83, 87, 107	Test 11
48	• Percent of a Whole	Lessons 48, 49, 50, 58, 59, 60, 62, 63, 64, 65, 67, 68, 69, 70, 71, 73, 75, 76, 78, 79, 80, 82, 84, 96, 97, 100, 102, 103, 104, 106, 108, 114, 115, 117, 118, 119	Tests 10–12
49	• Solving Rate Problems with Proportions and Equations	Lessons 49, 51, 52, 53, 54, 55, 57, 60, 83, 87, 107	Tests 10–12
50	• Solving Multi-Step Equations	Lessons 50, 52, 53, 54, 55, 56, 57, 58, 60, 61, 62, 63, 64, 65, 66, 67, 68, 70, 71, 72, 74, 75, 76, 77, 79, 80, 85, 87, 88, 89, 90, 92, 93, 94, 96, 97, 98, 99, 100, 101, 102, 103, 104, 105, 107, 108, 110, 111, 112, 113, 114, 116, 118, 119, 120	Tests 10–15, 17–21, 23
Inv. 5	• Graphing Transformations	Lessons 51, 52, 56, 58, 59, 60, 68, 71, 76, 79, 81, 83, 85, 93, 96, 98, 108, 111, 114, 115, 118, 119	Tests 5, 11, 12, 18

• Functions

Objectives

- Determine whether a relationship between two sets of numbers is a function.
- Express functions in words and with equations, tables, and graphs.
- Graph equations by first creating function tables of value pairs.
- Determine whether functions are proportional or not proportional.

Lesson Preparation

Materials

- **Power Up I** (in *Instructional Masters*)

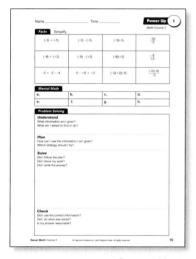

Power Up I

Math Language

New	Maintain
function	formula
linear function	quadrant

Technology Resources

Student eBook Complete student textbook in electronic format.

Resources and Planner CD Assessment, reteaching, and instructional masters, plus a pacing calendar with standards.

Test and Practice Generator CD Create additional practice sheets and custom-made tests.

www.SaxonPublishers.com Visit for more student activities and planning materials.

Inclusion

Adaptations CD Adapted lessons, investigations, practice and assessments.

Meeting Standards

National Council of Teachers of Mathematics (NCTM)

Algebra

AL.1c Identify functions as linear or nonlinear and contrast their properties from tables, graphs, or equations

AL.2c Use symbolic algebra to represent situations and to solve problems, especially those that involve linear relationships

AL.3a Model and solve contextualized problems using various representations, such as graphs, tables, and equations

Problem-Solving Strategy: Make It Simpler

Find the sum of the whole numbers from 1 to 15.

(Understand) **Understand the problem.**

"What information are we given?"

We will be working with the whole numbers from 1 to 15.

"What are we asked to do?"

Find the sum of the whole numbers from 1 to 15.

(Plan) **Make a plan.**

"What problem solving strategy will we use?"

We will *make it simpler* by using the pairing technique.

(Solve) **Carry out the plan.**

"What is the sum of the pair of addends that are at either end of the list?"

$1 + 15 = 16$.

"Where are there other pairs of addends that sum to 16?"

By working inward from both ends of the list we find other pairs (2 and 14, 3 and 13, 4 and 12, ...) that each have a sum of 16.

"How many pairs of 16 exist?"

15 numbers ÷ 2 per pair = 7 pairs, and one "spare" number.

"Which number is un-paired?"

The middle number of the sequence of whole numbers from 1 to 15: 1, 2, 3, 4, 5, 6, 7, **8**, 9, 10, 11, 12, 13, 14, 15.

"How will we now find the sum?"

$(16 \times 7) + 8 = 120$.

(Check) **Look back.**

"Did we find the answer to the question that was asked?"

Yes. We found that the sum of the whole numbers from 1 to 15 is 120.

• Functions

facts Power Up I

mental math

a. **Number Sense:** 19×20 380

b. **Probability:** The probability of rolling a number less than 3 on a number cube is $\frac{2}{6}$, because there are 2 numbers less than 3 (1 and 2) out of 6 possible outcomes. Find the probability of rolling a number less than 6. $\frac{5}{6}$

c. **Fractional Parts:** 75% of $36 $27

d. **Measurement:** Find the length of this piece of cable. $2\frac{3}{8}$ in.

e. **Scientific Notation:** Write 4.06×10^6 in standard notation. 4,060,000

f. **Rate:** The town's garbage trucks dump 7.7 tons of garbage per week. On average, how many tons per day is that? 1.1 tons per day

g. **Geometry:** To find volume of a rectangular prism, we multiply $l \times w \times h$. Approximate the volume of this rectangular prism. 18 m³

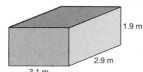

h. **Calculation:** $41 + 14$, $\div 11$, $\times 7$, $+ 1$, $\sqrt{}$, $+ 3$, square it, $+ 19$, $\sqrt{}$, $+ 3$ 13

problem solving Find the sum of the whole numbers from 1 to 15. 120

The formula for the perimeter of a square, $P = 4s$, identifies the relationship between two variables, the length of a side of a square (s) and its perimeter (P). This formula is an example of a function.

1 Power Up

Facts
Distribute **Power Up I** to students. See answers below.

Mental Math
Encourage students to share different ways to mentally compute these exercises. Strategies for exercises **a, c,** and **f** are listed below.

a. **Regroup, then Multiply**
   $19 \times 20 = 19 \times 2 \times 10 =$
   $38 \times 10 = 380$

c. **Find a Fraction**
   $75\% = \frac{3}{4}$
   $\frac{3}{4} \times \$36 = 3 \times 9 = \$27$
   Multiply by 4, Divide by 4
   75% of $36 = 300\%$ of $9 = \$27$

f. **Use a Rate**
   7.7 tons/week $\times$ 1 week/7days $=$
   $\frac{7.7}{7}$ tons/day $= 1.1$ tons/day

Problem Solving
Refer to **Power-Up Discussion,** p. 277B.

Facts Simplify.

$(-3) + (-5)$	$(-3) - (-5)$	$(-3)(-5)$	$\dfrac{-30}{-5}$
-8	2	15	6
$(-8) + (+2)$	$(-8) - (+2)$	$(-8)(+2)$	$\dfrac{-8}{+2}$
-6	-10	-16	-4
$-3 + -2 - -4$	$-5 - +6 + +2$	$(-3)(+2)(-6)$	$\dfrac{(-2)(-6)}{-3}$
-1	-9	36	-4

Instruction

Explain that along with ratio and proportion, functions are key mathematical ideas for the middle grades. As noted, the formula for the perimeter of a square is a function. A formula such as $P = 4s$ is a function because it shows the relationship between two sets of numbers.

Stress the importance of each input number having one and only one output number. This is the key difference between a function and an equation. Students sometimes think that all equations represent functions, but that is not true. For some equations there can be more than one value for the dependent variable for each value of the independent variable.

Point out that a function need not be expressed as an equation. Words, tables, and graphs are also ways to represent functions.

Example 1

Instruction

For part **a**, you can point out that if the formula $P = s + s + s$ was used instead of $P = 3s$, the rest of the example would still be the same, because the value of P is the same for any s using either formula. If necessary, draw an equilateral triangle on the board or overhead.

As students complete part **b**, tell them that using small whole-number values for the side lengths will make their work easier.

Provide graph paper for part **c**. Students will be making graphs throughout this lesson. As they move through the program, you can encourage them to make simple sketches of coordinate planes on plain paper instead of using prepared coordinate planes or graph paper.

Extend part **c** by suggesting that students select a point that is aligned with the other points and test whether its coordinates satisfy the function.

(continued)

A **function** is a mathematical rule that identifies a relationship between two sets of numbers. A function's rule is applied to an input number to generate an output number. **For each input number there is one and only one output number.** In the formula $P = 4s$, the input is the side length and the output is the perimeter.

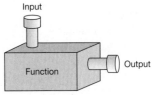

A function may be described with words or expressed with an equation, as in the formula for the perimeter of a square. We may illustrate functional relationships in tables or in graphs.

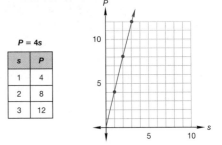

$P = 4s$

s	P
1	4
2	8
3	12

Here is a table that shows the perimeter of a square for some given side lengths, and a graph that shows other pairs of numbers that represent side lengths and perimeters of squares.

In this lesson we will consider function tables and graph some functions.

Example 1

The perimeter of an equilateral triangle is three times the length of one of its sides.

a. Write an equation that expresses this relationship. Use *P* for perimeter and *s* for side length.

b. Choose four different side lengths. Make a function table that shows the side lengths and the perimeters of the equilateral triangles.

c. Graph the pairs of numbers from the table on a coordinate plane. Let the horizontal axis represent side length (*s*) and the vertical axis represent perimeter (*P*).

2 **New Concepts** *(Continued)*

Example 2
Instruction
In example 1, students were given the function. Now they are asked to find the rule given input and output values that satisfy the rule.

Emphasize that the way to test the rule is to substitute the value of the *x*-coordinate of a point in the equation and see if the *y*-value calculated is the same as the *y*-coordinate for that point. Note that when using the rule, once the *x*-value is chosen, the *y*-value is decided by the rule.

(continued)

Solution

a. To find the perimeter (P) of an equilateral triangle we multiply the length of a side (s) by 3.

$$P = 3s$$

b. We can use the equation to help us fill in the table. The input number is on the left; the output number is on the right. We choose four side lengths such as 1, 2, 3, and 4. We apply the rule (multiply the side length by 3) to find each perimeter.

$P = 3s$

s	P
1	3
2	6
3	9
4	12

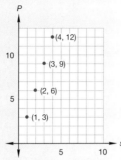

c. We graph the (s, P) pairs just as we graph (x, y) pairs. Since lengths are only positive, all possible pairs are in the first quadrant. Notice that the points are aligned.

Example 2

Xavier and Yolanda are playing a game. When Xavier says a number, Yolanda performs an operation with Xavier's number and says the result. The table shows four numbers Xavier said and Yolanda's replies. Describe the rule Yolanda uses, and write the rule as an equation. Then graph the (x, y) pairs from the table and all other pairs of numbers Xavier and Yolanda could say.

x	y
2	4
3	5
4	6
5	7

Solution

Yolanda adds 2 to the number Xavier says. The equation is

$$y = x + 2.$$

We graph the x, y pairs from the table and see that the points are aligned. We suspect other points along this line also meet the conditions of the problem. We draw a line through and beyond the graphed points and test some x, y pairs on the line to see if they fit the equation $y = x + 2$. Any point we choose on the line satisfies the equation. We conclude that the graph of all possible pairs of numbers Xavier and Yolanda could say using the rule are represented by points on the graphed line.

Lesson 41   279

2 New Concepts (Continued)

Instruction

Extend the Thinking Skill *Verify* questions by exploring similar questions for example 1.

As students examine ratios of output to input for the two *linear* equations following example 2, ask them to note how the two equations differ. Sample: In example 1, the operation is multiplication, and in example 2, the operation is addition.

Point out that the two listed characteristics will be present in all graphs of proportional functions, even for those functions in which the coefficient of *x* is a fraction.

(continued)

280   *Saxon Math Course 3*

Thinking Skill

Verify

Select and name coordinates of points on the graphed line that are not in the table. What do the two numbers for each selected point represent? Do the number pairs fit the rule of the game Xavier and Yolanda are playing? Various points could be selected. The coordinates of each point represent Xavier's number and Yolanda's reply. Each pair of numbers should fit the rule with Yolanda's number being two more than Xavier's number, even if both numbers are fractions or mixed numbers.

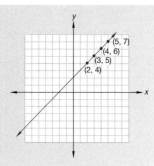

Examples 1 and 2 illustrate special classes of functions. We noted that the points plotted in both examples are aligned. If all the input-output pairs of a function fall on a line, then the function is **linear**. The functions in examples 1 and 2 are linear functions.

However, there is an important difference between the functions in example 1 and example 2. Notice that the ratio of output to input in example 2 is not constant.

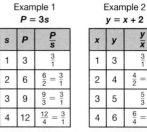

	Example 1 $P = 3s$	
s	**P**	$\frac{P}{s}$
1	3	$\frac{3}{1}$
2	6	$\frac{6}{2} = \frac{3}{1}$
3	9	$\frac{9}{3} = \frac{3}{1}$
4	12	$\frac{12}{4} = \frac{3}{1}$

Proportional

	Example 2 $y = x + 2$	
x	**y**	$\frac{y}{x}$
1	3	$\frac{3}{1}$
2	4	$\frac{4}{2} = \frac{2}{1}$
3	5	$\frac{5}{3}$
4	6	$\frac{6}{4} = \frac{3}{2}$

Not Proportional

This means the relationship of perimeter to side length is **proportional,** but the relationship of Yolanda's number to Xavier's number is **not proportional.** Graphs of proportional functions have these two characteristics.

1. The function is linear.

2. The points are aligned with the origin (0, 0).

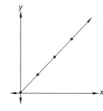

280   *Saxon Math Course 3*

Example 3

The area of a square is a function of its side length. The graph of an area function is different from the graph of a perimeter function. For the function $A = s^2$, describe the rule with words and make a table that shows at least four pairs of numbers that satisfy the function. Then graph the (s, A) pairs and predict the graph of other points for the function.

Solution

The rule is, **"To find A, square s."** We may choose any four numbers for s to put into the function. To keep our calculations simple we choose 0, 1, 2, and 3. Then we find A for each value of s.

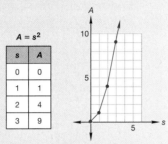

$A = s^2$

s	A
0	0
1	1
2	4
3	9

We graph the pairs of numbers from the table with s on the horizontal axis and A on the vertical axis. We see that the points are not aligned. Instead, the points seem to be on a curve that becomes steeper and steeper as the side length increases.

Discuss Is the function of side length to area linear? Is the function proportional? The function is not linear; the graph is a curve. If the function is not linear it cannot be proportional.

Example 4

Yanos is playing a numbers game. When Xena says a number, Yanos says a number that is twice Xena's number.

a. Write an equation for the game using x for the number Xena says and y for the number Yanos says.

b. Make a table that shows some pairs of numbers for the game.

c. Graph all the possible pairs of numbers for the game.

2 **New Concepts** *(Continued)*

Example 3
Instruction
As you work through this example, you may want to suggest that using small whole-number values for s will make the work easier. Point out that choosing 0 as a value for s is allowed.

After students have made their graphs, ask why the line gets steeper as you move to the right. Sample: There is a greater difference between the A values than between the corresponding s values.

Use the *Discuss* questions to apply the two characteristics of a functional proportion listed on the previous page as a check for proportionality.

Example 4
Instruction
After students complete their work on this example, take time to discuss the work. For part **a**, have volunteers explain how they wrote the equation. For part **b**, ask students to tell what numbers they selected and explain why they chose those numbers. For part **c**, ask other students to tell whether the function is a proportional function and to explain their answers.

(continued)

Math Background

The formula for the area of a square, $A = s^2$, is an example of a *quadratic function*. A quadratic function has an equation of the form $y = ax^2 + bx + c$, where a, b, and c are constants and $a \neq 0$. Quadratic functions have U-shaped graphs called *parabolas*. If $a > 0$, the parabola opens up. If $a < 0$, the parabola opens down.

In the case of a square, only positive values of s apply, because lengths are not negative. When applying quadratic functions in the real world, we are careful to consider which values are possible.

Example 5
Instruction

You may want to model graphing this function on the board or overhead as students work on their papers. When the graph is completed, ask whether the function is proportional and have students explain their answers. Sample: The function is not proportional because it does not pass through the origin.

(continued)

Solution

a. $y = 2x$

b. We write some numbers Xena could say in the *x*-column. Then we find each number Yanos would say for each of Xena's numbers and write them in the *y*-column.

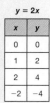

$y = 2x$	
x	**y**
0	0
1	2
2	4
−2	−4

c. The numbers in the function table form ordered pairs of numbers we can graph on a coordinate plane. We graph the ordered pairs and draw a line through the graphed points. Every point on the line represents an (x, y) pair of numbers that meets the conditions of the game.

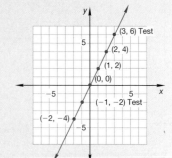

To check our work we can test some (x, y) pairs on the line to see if the pairs meet the conditions of the problem. We choose (3, 6) and (−1, −2). If Xena says 3, Yanos doubles the number and says 6. If Xena says −1, Yanos doubles the number and says −2. These pairs of numbers satisfy the problem, which verifies our work.

Example 5

Graph the function $y = \frac{1}{2}x - 2$.

Solution

In this lesson we will graph functions by first making a function table of (x, y) pairs that satisfy the equation. We choose values for *x* and calculate each corresponding value for *y*. Since *x* is multiplied by $\frac{1}{2}$, we choose even numbers for *x* so that *y* is a whole number. Then we plot the (x, y) ordered pairs and draw a line through them to complete graphing the equation.

Teacher Tip

To provide extra practice with **the concept of functions,** play *What's The Rule?* as a class activity. Start by telling students that the rule is the same until you announce that you are using a new rule. Explain that you will tell them the input and output and they will try to find the rule. Tell the students that each rule will have only one step (for example, "add 20" rather than "multiply by 5, then add 20").

Say:

"If the input is 10 and the output is 20, what's the rule?" Add 10 or multiply by 2.

Elicit both answers. Then continue with an input of 5 and output of 10 and ask whether they can tell which rule it is. **Yes, multiply by 2.**

Continue with other pairs of inputs and outputs depending on the needs of your class.

Some possible answers are:
- Words are easy to understand but do not show values and are not visual.
- Equations make it easy to generate values but do not show values.
- Tables show values, but only a few. The relationship might not be obvious in a table.
- A graph visually represents all values or a pattern of values but the relationship might not be as clearly understood as a description.

Practice Set

a. $n = 12i$

i	n
1	12
2	24
3	36
4	48

Yes, the relationship is both linear and proportional.

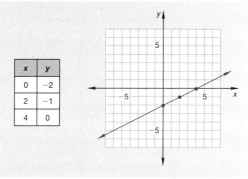

x	y
0	-2
2	-1
4	0

In this lesson, we have described functions with words and expressed functions with equations. We have listed pairs of numbers in tables that satisfy selected functions and represented these functions in graphs.

Discuss Describe some of the benefits and limitations of each of these four ways of expressing a function.

▶ **a.** *Connect* The relationship between feet and inches is a function. Write an equation that shows how to find the number of inches (n, output) if you know the number feet (i, input). Then make a function table that shows the number of inches in 1, 2, 3, and 4 feet. Is the relationship linear? Is the relationship proportional?

▶ **b.** Yolanda played a new number game with Xavier. She used this equation to generate her response to each number Xavier said:

$$y = x - 2$$

Describe with words the rule Yolanda uses. Then make a function table that shows the numbers Yolanda says for four numbers Xavier might say. Use 0 for one of Xavier's numbers and three more numbers of your choosing. Is the function linear? Is it proportional? (See below.)

▶ **c.** *Formulate* This table shows the capacity in ounces of a given number of pint containers. Describe with words the rule of the function and write an equation that relates pints (p) to ounces (z). Then find the number of ounces in 5 pints. To find the number of ounces, multiply the number of pints by 16. Equation: $z = 16p$. Five pints is 5(16) = 80 ounces

Pints	Ounces
1	16
2	32
3	48
4	64

b. Yolanda subtracts 2 from every number Xavier says. Table values vary. Some possible values are shown. The function is linear; the input-output pairs are aligned. The relationship is not proportional; (0, 0) is not a solution pair.

x	y
0	-2
1	-1
2	0
3	1

Lesson 41   283

▶ See Math Conversations in the sidebar.

Instruction

Use the *Discuss* feature to summarize the lesson and to check understanding of these important ideas about functions.

Practice Set
Problem a [Error Alert]

Because feet are being changed to inches, students should recognize that feet (f) represent the input, and inches (i) represent the output. Explain that the relationship 1 foot = 12 inches will be used to write the equation.

Problem b [Error Alert]

To help decide if the relationship is linear and proportional, students should plot the points from the function table. Explain that one condition must be present for the relationship to be linear: the points must fall on a line, and if the relationship is proportional, three conditions must be present: the points must fall on a line, the points must be aligned with the origin, and the line must rise to the right.

Problem c [Formulate]

Remind students to use the relationship 1 pint = 16 ounces to write the equation. Since the equation relates pints (p) to ounces (z), students should conclude that p represents the input of the equation and z represents the output.

(continued)

Problem g Model

Help students understand that it is sensible to substitute even numbers for x because the product of an even number and $\frac{1}{2}$ is an integer.

③ **Written Practice**

Math Conversations

Discussion opportunities are provided below.

Problem 2 Analyze

Extend the Problem

"How many different combinations of one serving of vegetables and one serving of fruit are possible from six vegetable choices and eight fruit choices?"

6×8 or 48

Problem 4 Verify

"How will we know if the given values satisfy the function?" Sample: Substitute 2 for x. If the right side of the equation simplifies to 4, the values $x = 2$ and $y = 4$ satisfy the equation.

(continued)

---

d. State why the relationship between the numbers in this table is not a function. A function has only one output for each input. Since the input (1) has two outputs (1 and −1), the relationship is not a function.

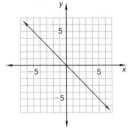

x	y
0	0
1	1
1	−1
2	2

e. Answers vary. Sample table:

x	y
0	0
1	−1
2	−2
3	−3

Rule: Xena says a number and Yanos says its opposite. Equation: $y = -x$

e. Yanos and Xena played a numbers game. This graph shows all the possible pairs of numbers they could say following the rule of the game. Make a function table that lists four pairs of numbers they could say. Then describe the rule Yanos followed and write an equation for the rule.

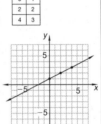

f. Formulate Make up a numbers game Yanos and Xena could play. Describe the rule and write an equation for the rule. Make a function table that has four pairs of numbers they could say. Graph all possible pairs of numbers for the game you create. Answers vary. Check students' work.

▶ g. Model For the function $y = \frac{1}{2}x + 1$, make a function table and use it to graph the equation.

Written Practice *Strengthening Concepts*

g.

x	y
0	1
2	2
4	3

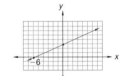

1. Cathy makes $18 teaching a half-hour piano lesson. She makes $32 an
(3, 4) hour as a chef at a restaurant. How much does she make in a week if she works as a chef for 2 hours every Friday and teaches piano lessons for one hour on Mondays and 2 hours on Tuesdays? $172

▶ *2. Analyze The cafeteria offered six choices of vegetables and eight
(29) choices of fruits. What was the ratio of fruit to vegetable choices? $\frac{4}{3}$

3. Socks are sold four pairs per pack. Bobby put three complete packages
(3, 4) of socks in the laundry. He later noticed that he had 21 socks. How many socks were misplaced in the laundry? 3 socks

▶ *4. Verify Shown is a graph of the function
(41) $y = \frac{1}{2}x + 3$. Does $x = 2$ and $y = 4$ satisfy the function? Demonstrate your answer by substituting the values and simplifying. Yes. $4 = (\frac{1}{2})2 + 3, 4 = 4$

▶ See Math Conversations in the sidebar.

5.

▶ *** 5.** (Inv. 3) **Model** Sketch a rectangle and draw its lines of symmetry.

▶ *** 6.** (35) **Conclude** Which pair of words correctly completes the following sentence? "Similar polygons have corresponding angles that are _____ and corresponding sides lengths that are _____." **B**

    A similar, congruent   **B** congruent, proportional

    C acute, straight   **D** vertexes, lines

▶ *** 7.** (39, 40) **Generalize** Use $\frac{22}{7}$ for π to find the **a** area and **b** circumference of a circle with a diameter of 14 meters.   **a.** 154 m², **b.** 44 m

▶ *** 8.** (39, 40) Find the **a** area and **b** circumference of the circle with radius 1 cm. Express answers in terms of π.   **a.** π cm², **b.** 2π cm

  9. (33) At 7 p.m. the wind-chill temperature was 4°F. By 10 p.m., it had fallen 11 degrees. Write an equation to show the wind-chill temperature at 10 p.m., then solve the equation. $(4) - (+11) = t$, $t = -7$.

Solve.

▶*** 10.** (25, 38) $-3m = 4.2$ $m = -1.4$ ▶*** 11.** (24, 38) $30.7 - x = 20$ $x = 10.7$

  Analyze For problems **12** and **13,** refer to the figure at right. (Dimensions are in meters.)

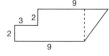

▶ **12.** (37) Find the area of the figure.   36 m²

▶ **13.** (8, Inv. 2) Find the perimeter of the figure.   30 m

  14. (11, 18) **a.** Expand: $-4(2m - 7x + 9)$ $-8m + 28x - 36$

    b. Factor: $3x^2 + 3x + 3$ $3(x^2 + x + 1)$

Simplify.

  15. (27) $\frac{32xmz}{-4mz}$ $-8x$ **16.** (13, 23) $\frac{2}{5} + 4\frac{2}{7} \div 1\frac{11}{49}$ $3\frac{9}{10}$

  17. (23) $\frac{2}{3} \cdot 2\frac{1}{4} \cdot 1\frac{4}{5}$ $2\frac{7}{10}$ **18.** (21) $36 \div [2(1 + 2)^2]$ 2

  19. (31, 36) $\frac{(-3) + (-5)}{-4}$ 2   **20.** (6, 12) $\left(\frac{1}{3}\right)^2 - \left(\frac{1}{3}\right)^3$ $\frac{2}{27}$

  21. (27, 36) $(-3)^2 + (-3)^1 + (-3)^0$ 7   **22.** (27, 36) $(2x^2y)^3$ $8x^6y^3$

  23. (12) Write $\frac{11}{20}$ as a **a** decimal and **b** percent.   **a.** 0.55 **b.** 55%

  24. (32) Three alphabet tiles are face down. The letters on the tiles are S, A, and M. Danielle picks one tile, keeps it, and picks up another.

    a. What is the sample space of the experiment? Sample Space = {SA, SM, AS, AM, MS, MA}

    b. What is the probability that one of the tiles she picks up will be an A? $\frac{2}{3}$

▶ See Math Conversations in the sidebar.

Math Conversations

Discussion opportunities are provided below.

Problem 5 Model

Point out that the rectangle should be longer in one dimension than the other.

After completing the problem, ask:

"Is it possible for a rectangle to have more than two lines of symmetry? Explain your answer." Yes; a square is a rectangle and a square has four lines of symmetry.

Problem 6 Conclude

To help decide which responses are correct, you might choose to ask students to draw two similar rectangles that are not congruent on grid paper. Students can then count unit squares to help recognize that the corresponding side lengths of two similar figures are proportional.

Problem 7 Generalize

"Name the formula that is used to find the area of a circle." $A = \pi r^2$

"What is the radius of the given circle?" 7 m

Problem 10

Before completing any paper and pencil arithmetic, ask students to describe an inverse operation that can be used to isolate x. divide each side by -3

Problem 12 Analyze

Encourage students to check their work by dividing the figure into four parts, and compare the sum of the areas of those parts to their original answer. Sample: $(2 \times 3) + 2(2 \times 6) + \frac{(3 \cdot 4)}{2} = 36$

Errors and Misconceptions

Problem 8

When a radius of 1 cm is substituted into the formula $A = \pi r^2$, students should recognize that the square of 1 is 1, and the product of any number and 1 is that number.

Students should also recognize that because the radius of the given circle is 1 cm, the value of d that is substituted into the equation $C = \pi d$ is 2 cm.

Problem 11

Some students may infer that two inverse operations are needed to simplify the equation. For example, subtract 30.7 from both sides of the equation to isolate $-x$, then multiply each term of the equation by -1 to change $-x$ to x.

(continued)

Math Conversations

Discussion opportunities are provided below.

Problems 30b and 30c Evaluate

Before writing the equation, explain that x should represent the numbers Xena said and y should represent the numbers Yanos said.

Students should conclude that the graph represents a linear function because the points fall on a line.

Combine like terms to simplify.

25. $2xy - xy - y + 7y - xy$ $6y$
(31)

26. $9x^2 - 4x + 7x - 6x^2 + 3$ $3x^2 + 3x + 3$
(31)

Evaluate.

27. For $E = \frac{1}{2}mv^2$, find E when $m = 5$ and $v = 4$. $E = 40$
(14, 15)

28. The radius of the sector shown is 3 ft. State the area of the sector in terms of π. 3π ft^2
(11)

29. Florence bought 50 cm of thin leather cord to make jewelry. She used 16 cm of it for a bracelet and 34 cm for a necklace. How many centimeters of leather cord were left? $50 - 16 - 34 = 0$ cm
(31)

* 30. *Evaluate*   Xena and Yanos played a number game. In the table are four numbers Xena said and the numbers Yanos said in reply.
(41)

a. Use words to describe the rule Yanos followed.   Yanos subtracts three from Xena's number.

▸ **b.** Write an equation that shows the rule. $y = x - 3$

▸ **c.** Sketch a graph that shows all the pairs of numbers that fit the rule. Then draw a line through the points to show other x, y pairs of numbers that fit the rule.

X	Y
3	0
0	−3
2	−1
5	2

30. c.

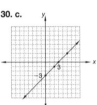

▸ See Math Conversations in the sidebar.

Looking Forward

Describing functions with words, equations, and graphs prepares students for:

- **Lesson 47,** graphing functions.
- **Lesson 56,** writing the slope-intercept equation of a line.
- **Lesson 73,** writing formulas for sequences.
- **Lesson 79,** transforming formulas.
- **Lesson 89,** solving problems with two unknowns by graphing.
- **Lesson 97,** writing recursive rules for sequences.
- **Lesson 98,** determining whether relationships between two variables are functions.
- **Investigation 11,** working with non-linear functions.

• Volume

Objectives

- Use the formulas $V = Bh$ and $V = lwh$ to calculate the volumes of prisms and rectangular prisms.
- Apply the formulas for the volume of a prism to solve word problems.
- Calculate the volumes of complex geometric solids by dividing them into smaller rectangular prisms.

Lesson Preparation

Materials

- **Power Up I** (in *Instructional Masters*)
- **Manipulative Kit: inch rulers**
- **Teacher-provided material: rectangular box, calculators**

Optional

- **Teacher-provided material: plastic liter bottles**

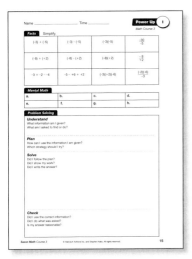

Power Up I

Math Language

New	Maintain
volume	prism

Technology Resources

Student eBook Complete student textbook in electronic format.

Resources and Planner CD Assessment, reteaching, and instructional masters, plus a pacing calendar with standards.

Test and Practice Generator CD Create additional practice sheets and custom-made tests.

www.SaxonPublishers.com Visit for more student activities and planning materials.

Inclusion

Adaptations CD Adapted lessons, investigations, practice and assessments.

Meeting Standards

National Council of Teachers of Mathematics (NCTM)

Geometry

GM.4b Use two-dimensional representations of three-dimensional objects to visualize and solve problems such as those involving surface area and volume

GM.4e Recognize and apply geometric ideas and relationships in areas outside the mathematics classroom, such as art, science, and everyday life

Measurement

ME.1c Understand, select, and use units of appropriate size and type to measure angles, perimeter, area, surface area, and volume

ME.2b Select and apply techniques and tools to accurately find length, area, volume, and angle measures to appropriate levels of precision

Problem Solving

PS.1b Solve problems that arise in mathematics and in other contexts

Problem-Solving Strategy: Find a Pattern

In each bowling lane, 10 pins are arranged in four rows forming a triangle as shown:

If the pins from 12 lanes are combined to make one big triangle of pins, how many rows will it have?

(Understand) **Understand the problem.**

"What information are we given?"

Bowling lanes each have 10 pins arranged in four rows that form a triangle.

"What are we asked to do?"

Determine how many rows will be in one big triangle made from the pins of 12 lanes.

(Plan) **Make a plan.**

"What problem solving strategy will we use?"

We will *find a pattern* of the number of pins and the number of rows.

"How many pins will we be using in our one large triangle?"

12 lanes × 10 pins per lane = 120 pins.

(Solve) **Carry out the plan.**

"What would the pattern of triangles made of less than 10, or greater than 10, pins look like?"

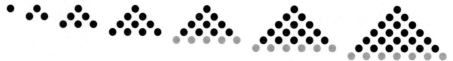

"How can the terms in this sequence be written as numbers?"

1, 3, 6, 10, 15, 21, 28, ...

"How can the terms in this sequence be written as sums?"

1, 1 + 2, 1 + 2 + 3, 1 + 2 + 3 + 4, 1 + 2 + 3 + 4 + 5, 1 + 2 + 3 + 4 + 5 + 6, 1 + 2 + 3 + 4 + 5 + 6 + 7, etc.

"What is the rule of the pattern?"

The first term has 1 row, the second term has 2 rows, the third row has 3 terms, etc. Add to the previous term the same number of pins as the number of rows the new term will have.

"How far do we need to extend the pattern?"

Until we can account for at least 120 pins.

	+5	+6	+7	+8	+9	+10	+11	+12	+13	+14	+15
10	15	21	28	36	45	55	66	78	91	105	120

"How many rows of pins will there be in a triangle made up of 120 pins?"

15

(Check) **Look back.**

"Did we find the answer to the question that was asked?"

Yes. We found that the triangle formed by 120 pins has 15 rows.

• Volume

facts   Power Up I

mental math

  a. Number Sense: 2×256 512

  b. Algebra: $\frac{x}{4} = 6$ 24

  c. Measurement: Find the length of the piece of cable. $4\frac{1}{8}$ in.

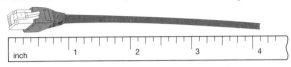

  d. Percent: 75% of 40 $\frac{3}{4} \times 40 = 3 \times 10 = 30$

  e. Scientific Notation: Write 6.05×10^5 in standard notation.   605,000

  f. Rate: Robert biked 12 miles in an hour. On average, how many minutes did it take him to ride each mile?   5 minutes

  g. Geometry: Approximate the volume: 100 cm^3

2.1 cm
5.2 cm   9.8 cm

  h. Calculation: $\sqrt{100}$, $\times 6$, $+ 4$, $\sqrt{\ }$, $\times 6$, $+ 1$, $\sqrt{\ }$, $\times 9$, $+ 1$, $\sqrt{\ }$, $+ 1$, $\sqrt{\ }$ 3

problem solving

In each bowling lane, 10 pins are arranged in four rows forming a triangle as shown:

If the pins from 12 lanes are combined to make one big triangle of pins, how many rows will it have?   15 rows

In this lesson we will find the volumes of rectangular prisms. In later lessons we will find the volumes and surface areas of other geometric solids.

The **volume** of a solid is the total amount of space occupied or enclosed by the solid. Volume is measured in cubic units such as cubic centimeters (cm^3), cubic inches (in.^3), and cubic feet (ft^3). The following diagram illustrates volume.

Lesson 42   **287**

---

1 **Power Up**

Facts
Distribute **Power Up I** to students. See answers below.

Mental Math
Encourage students to share different ways to mentally compute these exercises. Strategies for exercises **a**, **f**, and **g** are listed below.

  a. Regroup, then Multiply
$$2 \times 256 = 2 \times 250 + 2 \times 6 =$$
$$500 + 12 = 512$$

  f. Use a Unit Rate
$$1 \text{ hr}/12 \text{ mi} \times 60 \text{ min}/1 \text{ hr} =$$
$$60 \text{ min}/12 \text{ mi} = 5 \text{ min}/\text{mi}$$

  Use Math Sense
12 mi in 1 hr $\longrightarrow$
12 mi in 60 min $\longrightarrow$
1 mi in 5 min

  g. Round and Multiply
5.2 cm $\approx$ 5 cm
9.8 cm $\approx$ 10 cm
2.1 cm $\approx$ 2 cm
$V = 5 \text{ cm} \times 10 \text{ cm} \times 2 \text{ cm} = 100 \text{ cm}^3$

Problem Solving
Refer to **Power-Up Discussion**, p. 287B.

Facts   Simplify.

$(-3) + (-5)$	$(-3) - (-5)$	$(-3)(-5)$	$\frac{-30}{-5}$
-8	2	15	6
$(-8) + (+2)$	$(-8) - (+2)$	$(-8)(+2)$	$\frac{-8}{+2}$
-6	-10	-16	-4
$-3 + -2 - -4$	$-5 - +6 + +2$	$(-3)(+2)(-6)$	$\frac{(-2)(-6)}{-3}$
-1	-9	36	-4

2 New Concepts

Instruction

After introducing the term *volume,* ask students to name other cubic units they may have used when they worked with volume in earlier grades. Samples: cubic yards (yd³), cubic meters (m³), cubic millimeters (mm³)

After using the cubes to develop the formulas for volume of a prism and a rectangular prism, ask whether the same number of cubes could be used to form a prism that is 3 cubes wide, 4 cubes long, and 5 cubes high. **yes** Ask if the cubes could form a prism that is 5 cubes wide, 6 cubes long, and 2 cubes high. **yes** Then ask whether these prisms would have the same volume as the given prism and have students explain their answers. Samples: They both have the same number of cubes as the given prism. Using the formula, all three cubes have the same volume.

Example 1
Instruction

This example gives students an everyday use of measurement. Ask students to name the percent difference in the volume if the room were 9 feet high instead of 10 feet high. **10%**

Ask students to predict how the heating and cooling costs of a room having a 9-foot ceiling might compare to the same room with a 10-foot ceiling. Sample: It would be cheaper to heat and cool the room with the 9-foot ceiling, because you would have to heat and cool a smaller volume.

Example 2
Instruction

Use this example to clarify the difference between a 2-foot cube and 2 cubic feet. A 2-foot cube is 2 ft × 2 ft × 2 ft, or 8 cubic feet. That is 4 times the volume of 2 cubic feet.

(continued)

Thinking Skill

Analyze

Why are the formulas $V = Bh$ and $V = lwh$ equivalent formulas for the volume of a rectangular prism? The base of a rectangular prism is a rectangle with an area of lw. Since $B = lw$, $V = Bh$ becomes $V = lwh$.

The bottom layer of this solid has 4 rows of cubes with 5 cubes in each row. Therefore, there are 20 cubes on the bottom layer. There are three layers of cubes, so there are 3×20, or 60 cubes in all.

Notice that we found the volume (*V*) by multiplying the area of the base (*B*) by the height (*h*). We can use this formula for any prism.

Volume of a Prism

$$V = Bh$$

The area of the base of a rectangular prism equals the length (*l*) times the width (*w*). Thus, the specific formula for a rectangular prism is:

Volume of a Rectangular Prism

$$V = lwh$$

Example 1

To calculate the heating and cooling requirement for a room, one factor architects consider is the room's volume. A classroom that is 30 feet long, 30 feet wide, and 10 feet high contains how many cubic feet?

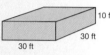

Solution

We can find the volume by multiplying the room's length, width, and height.

$$V = lwh$$
$$V = (30 \text{ ft})(30 \text{ ft})(10 \text{ ft})$$
$$\mathbf{V = 9000 \text{ ft}^3}$$

Example 2

A sculptor carved a 2-foot cube of ice into a swan. At 57 pounds per cubic foot, what did the 2-foot cube weigh before it was carved?

Solution

A 2-foot cube is a cube with edges 2 feet long. The specific formula for the volume of a cube is $V = s^3$, where *s* is the edge length. We will use this formula to find the volume of the cube.

Step:	Justification:
$V = s^3$	Volume of a cube
$V = (2 \text{ ft})^3$	Substituted
$V = 8 \text{ ft}^3$	Simplified

The volume of the ice before it was carved was 8 ft³. At 57 pounds per ft³, the weight of the 2-ft cube was 8×57, or **456 pounds.**

Math Background

How many cubic inches are in a cubic foot?

A cubic foot can be represented by a cube with edges of length 1 foot. Because 1 foot equals 12 inches, each edge has length 12 inches. This means the volume is (12 in.)³, or 1728 in.³ Therefore, there are 1728 cubic inches in a cubic foot.

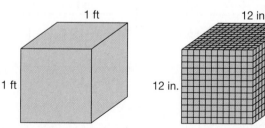

Analyze Why are the formulas $V = Bh$ and $V = s^3$ equivalent formulas for the volume of a cube?   The base of a cube is a square, so its area is s^2. The height of a cube is also s, and $s^2 \cdot s$ equals s^3.

Activity

Volume of a Box

Find a box in the classroom such as a tissue box. Measure the length, width, and height of the box and estimate its volume after rounding the dimensions to the nearest inch.

Example 3

Many buildings (and other objects) are shaped like combinations of geometric solids. Find the volume of a building with this shape. All angles are right angles.

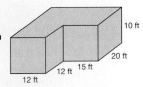

Solution

First we find the area of the building's base. We sketch the base and divide it into two rectangles. We add the area of the two rectangles to find the area of the base (684 ft²). Now we find the volume.

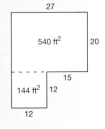

$$V = Bh$$
$$= (684 \text{ ft}^2)(10 \text{ ft})$$
$$= \mathbf{6840 \text{ ft}^3}$$

Example 4

Find the volume of this cube.

② New Concepts (Continued)

Instruction

Students will use these connections among the metric measures of volume, capacity, and weight for 1000 cm³ of water at standard conditions in problems throughout the rest of the book and in their science classes.

Practice Set

Problem a [Error Alert]

To help students to remember to label measures of volume in cubic units, write the solution to problem **a** (shown below) on the board or overhead.

4 in. × 5 in. × 9 in. = (4 × 5 × 9)(in. × in. × in.)

$$180 \qquad in.^3$$

Problem d [Error Alert]

To identify each relationship, students should divide the greater measure by the lesser measure. $6 \div 2 = 3$; $216 \div 8 = 27$

Problem e [Error Alert]

Students may divide the block into parts, then find the sum of the volumes of the parts.

Problem f [Estimate]

Give students an opportunity to share their findings with their classmates.

---

③ Written Practice

Math Conversations

Discussion opportunities are provided below.

Problem 1 [Evaluate]

Invite a small group of volunteers to demonstrate how to organize the information and solve the problem on the board or overhead. Sample:

Monday: 2 × $15 = $30
Wednesday: 2 × $15 = $30
Friday: 4 × $15 = $60
Weekend: 4 × $25 = $100
$30 + $30 + $60 + $100 = $220

(continued)

We can choose from three formulas to calculate the volume of a cube. A cube is a prism, so we may use the formula $V = Bh$. A cube is a rectangular prism, so we may use the formula $V = lwh$. Also, since every edge (s) of a cube is the same length, we may use the formula $V = s^3$.

$$V = s^3$$
$$V = (10 \text{ cm})^3$$
$$\mathbf{V = 1000 \text{ cm}^3}$$

The cube in example 4 is a special cube. The metric system relates volume to capacity. The capacity of this cube (1000 cm³) is equal to one liter. That means a container of this size and shape will hold one liter of liquid. Furthermore, if the liter of liquid is water, then in standard conditions its mass would be one kilogram.

Predict How would the volume of a cube change if you doubled its dimensions?   It would be eight times greater

Practice Set ▸

a. What is the volume of a tissue box with the dimensions shown?   180 in³

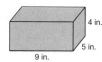

b. What is the volume of a cube with edges 2 inches long?   8 in.³

c. Find the volume of a cube with edges 6 inches long.   216 in.³

▸ **d.** How many times greater are the dimensions of the cube in problem **c** than the cube in problem **b?** How many times greater is the volume?   dimensions: 3 times; volume: 27 times.

▸ **e.** What is the volume of this block T? (All angles are right angles).   64 cm³

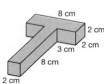

▸ **f.** [Estimate] Find a box at home that is the shape of a rectangular prism (such as a cereal box) and measure its dimensions. Then sketch the box on your paper and record its length, width, and height. Estimate the capacity of the box in cubic inches by rounding the measurements to the nearest inch before using the volume formula.   see student work.

Written Practice   *Strengthening Concepts*

▸ **1.** [Evaluate] Jason has two part-time jobs. He earns $15 an hour working at the help desk at a local library. He also mows lawns earning $25 per lawn. How much does he earn in a week if he works at the help desk for 2 hours each on Monday and Wednesday and for 4 hours on Friday and he mows 4 lawns on the weekend? $220
(3, 4)

▸ See Math Conversations in the sidebar.

Manipulative Use

To give students hands-on experience with the **metric relationships** described at the end of the lesson, find some plastic liter bottles and fill them with water. Pass them around so that students can see what volume 1000 cm³ of water takes up, get a mental picture of the capacity of a liter, and feel about how heavy a kilogram is.

2. There were 35 plastic cups and 15 one-liter bottles of water on a table. What was the ratio of plastic cups to bottles of water? $\frac{7}{3}$
(29)

▸ **3.** The dimensions of a rectangular Olympic-sized swimming pool are 2 meters deep, 25 meters wide, and 50 meters long. What is the volume of the pool? If 1 m^3 is equivalent to about 264 gallons, how many gallons of water does the pool hold?   2500 m^3; The pool holds about 660,000 gallons of water.
(42)

▸ **4.** **Justify** Shown is a graph of the function $y = \frac{1}{4}x + 1$. Does $x = 8$ and $y = 3$ satisfy the function? Demonstrate your answer by substituting the values and simplifying.   yes; $3 = (\frac{1}{4})8 + 1$, $3 = 2 + 1$, $3 = 3$
(41)

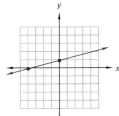

5. a.

5. a. Using the figure and vanishing point shown below, draw a polyhedron.
(Inv. 4)

    b. What is the name of the polyhedron you drew?   triangular prism

vanishing point
•

▸ **6.** Lars stitched three right triangular sails for sailboats as shown. Which statement about the sails is true?   **D**
(35)

    A △A and △B are congruent.

    B △A and △C are congruent.

    C △C and △B are similar, but not congruent.

    D △B and △C are congruent and both are similar to △A

7. Use a calculator to find the **a** area and **b** circumference of a circle with a diameter of 28 feet. Use $\frac{22}{7}$ for π.   **a.** 616 ft^2, **b.** 88 ft
(4)

▸ **8.** **Evaluate** On Saturday, Margo bought six packages of rawhide treats for her dog. Each package contained 8 treats. By the following Saturday there were 44 treats left. If Margo continues to give her dog treats at this rate, how many weeks will the treats she bought last?   12 weeks
(3, 4)

Lesson 42   291

▸ See Math Conversations in the sidebar.

Math Conversations

Discussion opportunities are provided below.

Problem 3   Estimate

Extend the Problem

Tell students the weight of water (shown below), or ask them to research its weight, then estimate the weight in pounds of the water in the pool.

One gallon of water weighs approximately $8\frac{1}{3}$ pounds. Accept reasonable estimates; the water in the pool weighs approximately 5,500,000 pounds

Problem 4   Justify

"How will we know if the given values satisfy the function?" Sample: Substitute 8 for x. If the right side of the equation simplifies to 3, the values $x = 8$ and $y = 3$ satisfy the equation.

Problem 8   Evaluate

"One way to solve this problem is to use a proportion. What ratios could we use to write the proportion?" Sample: 4 treats in 1 week is the same as 48 treats in what number of weeks?

Write the proportion $\frac{4}{1} = \frac{48}{n}$ on the board or overhead. Ask students to choose mental math or paper and pencil and use that method to solve the proportion for n.

Then ask students to name the method they chose, and explain why that method was chosen. Sample: Mental math; the constant factor of the proportion is $48 \div 4$ or 12, and the product of 1 and 12 is 12.

Errors and Misconceptions
Problem 6

One way for students to prove that triangles B and C are similar to triangle A is to compare the ratios of the corresponding sides. One such comparison is shown below.

$$\frac{18}{12} = \frac{3}{2} \text{ and } \frac{12}{8} = \frac{3}{2}$$

Explain that if the ratios are equal, the corresponding sides are proportional, and if the corresponding sides are proportional, the triangles are similar.

(continued)

Math Conversations

Discussion opportunities are provided below.

Errors and Misconceptions
Problem 9b

After writing the equation, encourage students to substitute the given ordered pairs into the equation to check if the equation is correct for all of the ordered pairs. Point out that substituting more than one ordered pair will help increase the likelihood of discovering an error if one exists.

(continued)

9. c.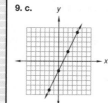

9. Use this table to answer **a–c**.
(18, 41)

x	y
−2	−6
0	−2
2	2
4	6

a. Use words to describe the rule shown in the table.   Multiply x times 2, then subtract 2.

▶ b. Write an equation that shows the rule.
$y = 2x − 2$

c. Sketch a graph that shows the pairs of numbers in the table. Then draw a line through the points to show other (x, y) pairs of numbers that fit the rule.

Simplify.

10. $3 \times 2(6 − 4)^3$ 48
(15, 21)

11. $\frac{5}{8} + 3\frac{2}{3} \div 1\frac{1}{21}$ $4\frac{1}{8}$
(13, 22)

12. $\frac{4}{9} \cdot \frac{10}{9} \cdot \frac{3}{8}$ $\frac{5}{27}$
(13, 22)

13. $48 \div [3(4 − 2)^2]$ 4
(15, 21)

14. $\left(\frac{1}{2}\right)^3 − \left(\frac{1}{2}\right)^4$ $\frac{1}{16}$
(13, 22)

15. $\frac{105xyz}{−5yz}$ $−21x$
(15, 27)

Solve.

16. $−5s = 21.5$ $s = −4.3$
(13, 22)

17. $45.6 − m = 25$ $m = 20.6$
(13, 22)

18. If the thickness of an average sheet of 8.5-inch by 11-inch copy paper is 0.004 inches (or about 0.1 mm) then what is the volume of the sheet of paper in cubic inches?   0.374 in.³
(42)

19. a. Expand: $−3(4n − 6w + 5)$ $−12n + 18w − 15$
(18, 21)

b. Factor: $8y^2 + 8y + 8$ $8(y^2 + y + 1)$

20. The spinner is spun once. What is the probability the spinner will stop
(32)

a. in sector A? $\frac{1}{5}$

b. in sector A, B or C? $\frac{3}{5}$

21. Find the a circumference and b area of a circle with a diameter of 8 meters. Express the answers in terms of π.   a. 8π m, b. 16π m²
(40)

22. In a parking lot, the ratio of cars to trucks is 5 to 1. If there are 20 trucks in the parking lot, how many cars are there? Write a proportion and use it to solve the problem. $\frac{5}{1} = \frac{c}{20}$, $c = 100$
(34)

For problems **23–26**, find all values of x, if any, that make the equations true.

23. $x^2 + 3 = 7$ 2, −2
(14, 15)

24. $−5|x| = 25$ no solution
(14)

25. $3x^2 = 27$ 3, −3
(14, 15)

26. $|x| − 4 = 12$ 16, −16
(14)

▶ See Math Conversations in the sidebar.

▶ **27.** *Formulate* A submarine was at a depth of 255 meters below sea
(33)   level. The submarine rose 65 m. Then it dove 25 m. Write an equation
with integers to express the situation. Then find the new depth of the
submarine. Sample: $-255 + 65 - 25 = d$; $d = -215$; The new depth is
215 m.

Combine like terms to simplify.

28. $3xy - xy - 2y + 5y$
(21) $2xy + 3y$

29. $5x^2 - 3x + 5x - 4x^2 + 6$
(21) $x^2 + 2x + 6$

* **30.** Recall that the graph of a proportional relationship has these
(41)   characteristics:

    1. The graph is a line or aligned points.

    2. The graph is aligned with the origin.

Which graph below indicates a proportional relationship? Explain why
the other graphs do not show a proportional relationship.

30. C; In A and B
the graph does
not align with the
origin; in D the
graph is not a line.

A.

B.

C.

D.

▶ See Math Conversations in the sidebar.

Math Conversations
Discussion opportunities are provided below.

Problem 27 *Formulate*
Before students write the equation, ask them
to decide if the final depth of the submarine
will be greater than or less than the its initial
depth. less than

Looking Forward

Understanding and calculating
volume prepares students for:

- **Lesson 76,** calculating volumes of
  prisms and cylinders.

- **Lesson 91,** investigating the
  effects of scaling on perimeter,
  area, and volume.

- **Lesson 106,** reviewing the effects
  of scaling on volume.

- **Lesson 107,** calculating volumes
  and surface areas of compound
  solids.

- **Lesson 111,** calculating volumes
  and surface areas of spheres.

• Surface Area

Objectives

- Distinguish between surface area and lateral surface area.
- Calculate surface areas of rectangular and other types of prisms by adding the areas of the faces.
- Calculate the lateral surface area of a prism by finding the perimeter of its base, then multiplying by its height.
- Use nets to strengthen understanding of surface area.

Lesson Preparation

Materials

- **Power Up I** (in *Instructional Masters*)
- **Manipulative Kit: inch rulers**
- **Teacher-provided material: rectangular box**

Power Up I

Math Language

New

lateral surface area

surface area

Technology Resources

Student eBook Complete student textbook in electronic format.

Resources and Planner CD Assessment, reteaching, and instructional masters, plus a pacing calendar with standards.

Test and Practice Generator CD Create additional practice sheets and custom-made tests.

www.SaxonPublishers.com Visit for more student activities and planning materials.

Inclusion

Adaptations CD Adapted lessons, investigations, practice and assessments.

Meeting Standards

National Council of Teachers of Mathematics (NCTM)

Geometry

GM.4b Use two-dimensional representations of three-dimensional objects to visualize and solve problems such as those involving surface area and volume

Measurement

ME.1c Understand, select, and use units of appropriate size and type to measure angles, perimeter, area, surface area, and volume

ME.2d Develop strategies to determine the surface area and volume of selected prisms, pyramids, and cylinders

Problem-Solving Strategy: Use Logical Reasoning/ Make It Simpler

Rolling a number cube has 6 different possible outcomes (from 1 to 6). Rolling two number cubes has 11 different possible outcomes (from 2 to 12). How many different possible outcomes does rolling 5 number cubes have?

(Understand) **Understand the problem.**

"What information are we given?"

We are reminded that rolling a single number cube can give 6 different results, and rolling two number cubes can give us 11 different results.

"What are we asked to do?"

Determine how many different totals can result from rolling 5 number cubes.

(Plan) **Make a plan.**

"What problem-solving strategy will we use?"

We will *use logical reasoning* to *make it simpler.*

(Solve) **Carry out the plan.**

"What is the greatest possible total for a roll of five number cubes?"

thirty (by rolling five 6's)

"What is the least possible total for a roll of five number cubes?"

five (by rolling five 1's)

"What are the only counting numbers that are not possible to roll?"

1, 2, 3, and 4

"How many different totals can be achieved?"

30 − 4 "unobtainable" numbers = 26 different totals

(Check) **Look back.**

"Did we find the answer to the question that was asked?"

Yes. We found there are 26 different totals possible when rolling 5 number cubes.

• **Surface Area**

Power Up

Facts
Distribute **Power Up I** to students. See answers below.

Mental Math
Encourage students to share different ways to mentally compute these exercises. Strategies for exercises **a**, **b**, and **d** are listed below.

a. Divide by 100, Then by 2
$700 \div 200 = 700 \div 100 \div 2 =$
$7 \div 2 = 3.5$
Cancel Zeros
$700 \div 200 = 7 \div 2 = 3\frac{1}{2}$

b. Multiply by 3, Divide by 3
$33\frac{1}{3}\%$ of $\$243 = 100\%$ of $\$81 = \$81$
Find a Fraction
$33\frac{1}{3}\% = \frac{1}{3}$
$\frac{1}{3} \times \$243 = \$81$

d. Use Equal Ratios
Half an hour is 30 min.
$\frac{6}{10} = \frac{x}{30}$
$10 \times 3 = 30$
$6 \times 3 = 18$
$x = 18$ pages
Use Unit Rate
$\frac{6 \text{ pages}}{10 \text{ minutes}} = 0.6$ pages/min
0.6 pages/min $\times 30$ min $= 18$ pages

Problem Solving
Refer to **Power-Up Discussion**, p. 294B.

facts | Power Up I

mental math

a. **Number Sense:** $700 \div 200$ 3.5 or $3\frac{1}{2}$

b. **Fractional Parts:** $\frac{1}{3}$ of $\$243$ $\$81$

c. **Scientific Notation:** Write 38,100 in scientific notation. 3.81×10^4

d. **Proportions:** If Darla can read 6 pages in 10 minutes, how many pages can she read in half an hour?   18 pages

e. **Geometry:** Find the area of the rectangle. Then find the area of the shaded triangle. 18 m^2; 9 m^2

3 m
6 m

f. **Proportions:** $\frac{7}{3} = \frac{x}{9}$ 21

g. **Powers/Roots:** Estimate $\sqrt{120} - \sqrt{99} + \sqrt{80}$ 10

h. **Calculation:** $77 - 7, \div 7, - 7, \times 7, + 7, \div 7 + 7, \times 7$ 77

problem solving | Rolling a number cube has 6 different possible outcomes (from 1 to 6). Rolling two number cubes has 11 different possible outcomes (from 2 to 12). How many different possible outcomes does rolling 5 number cubes have?
26

New Concept | *Increasing Knowledge*

The surface area of a solid is the combined area of the surfaces of the solid. We distinguish between total surface area and lateral surface area, which is the combined area of surfaces on the sides of a solid and does not include the area(s) of the base(s). We can find the lateral surface area of prisms and cylinders by multiplying the perimeter or circumference of the base by the height.

Example 1

The figure represents a cube with edges 10 cm long.

 a. Find the total surface area of the cube.

 b. Find the lateral surface area of the cube.

10 cm

New Concepts

Instruction
Use a rectangular box or a rectangular prism that is not a cube to help students see an important difference between *surface area* and *lateral surface area*. Hold up the box or prism and ask what sides (or faces) are included in the surface area. all of the faces Then ask which sides (or faces) are included in the lateral surface area. the four that are not bases Turn the box or prism and assign two different sides to be bases. Ask if the total surface area has changed. no Ask if the lateral surface area has changed. Sample: Yes, because two of the four faces have changed.

(continued)

Facts | Simplify.

$(-3) + (-5)$	$(-3) - (-5)$	$(-3)(-5)$	$\frac{-30}{-5}$
-8	2	15	6
$(-8) + (+2)$	$(-8) - (+2)$	$(-8)(+2)$	$\frac{-8}{+2}$
-6	-10	-16	-4
$-3 + -2 - -4$	$-5 - +6 + +2$	$(-3)(+2)(-6)$	$\frac{(-2)(-6)}{-3}$
-1	-9	36	-4

Solution

a. All edges of a cube are the same length. So the length, width, and height of the cube are each 10 cm. Thus, the shape of each face is a square with an area of 100 cm^2. Since the cube has six congruent faces, the total surface area is

$$6 \times 100 \text{ cm}^2 = \mathbf{600 \text{ cm}^2}$$

b. The lateral surface area of the cube is the combined area of the four side faces, not including the area of the top or bottom of the cube. One way to find the lateral surface area of a cube is to multiply the area of one face of the cube by 4.

$$\text{Lateral surface area of the cube} = 4 \times 100 \text{ cm}^2$$
$$= \mathbf{400 \text{ cm}^2}$$

Another way to find the lateral surface area is to multiply the perimeter of the base by the height of the cube.

$$\text{Lateral surface area} = \text{perimeter of base} \cdot \text{height}$$
$$= 40 \text{ cm} \cdot 10 \text{ cm}$$
$$= \mathbf{400 \text{ cm}^2}$$

Example 2

Before buying paint for the sides of this building, Malia calculated its lateral surface area. Find its lateral surface area.

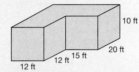

Solution

We can find the lateral surface area by multiplying the perimeter of the base by the height of the building.

$$\text{Lateral surface area} = \text{perimeter of base} \cdot \text{height}$$
$$= 118 \text{ ft} \cdot 10 \text{ ft}$$
$$= \mathbf{1180 \text{ ft}^2}$$

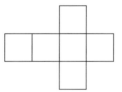

A net is a two-dimensional image of the surfaces of a solid. A net can help us visualize a solid's surfaces. Here is a net of a cube. We see the six square faces of the cube.

Example 1
Instruction

For part **a**, point out that a cube is a special type of rectangular prism. Since all its faces are the same, the surface area can be found simply by multiplying the area of one face by 6.

As you work on part **b**, you might note that a cube has the same lateral surface area regardless of which face is serving as the base. Point out that the two methods for calculating the lateral surface area give the same result. Ask whether anyone can think of a formula for the lateral surface area of a cube. Samples: $4s \cdot s$, $4s^2$

Example 2
Instruction

Ask if there is another way to find the lateral surface area of the building. Sample: Find the area of each outside wall and then add the areas. Point out that finding the perimeter and multiplying it by the height is usually the easiest way to find the lateral surface area.

(continued)

Activity

You may do the activity as a whole class or let students work in pairs or small groups, depending on how many boxes are available. When step 4 is completed, have students check to see whether the cut-apart box matches the net that they drew.

2 New Concepts (Continued)

Example 3

Instruction

After you complete the example and the discussion of the Thinking Skill *Connect* question, ask whether anyone can think of a way to use the fact that the box consists of three pairs of congruent faces to compute the surface area. Sample: You could multiply 96 in.² by 2, multiply 24 in.² by 2, and multiply 36 in.² by 2, and add the products.

Point out that any of these methods may be used, and students can select the method they like or the one that would be easiest for a particular problem.

(continued)

Activity

Surface Area of a Box

Find a box in the classroom that has six complete faces.

1. Identify the faces with terms such as front, back, top, bottom, left side, right side.

2. Which faces are congruent? Sample answer: front and back, top and bottom, left side and right side.

3. Sketch a net of the box predicting its appearance if some edges were cut and the box were unfolded.

4. Unfold the box, cutting and taping as necessary, to reveal a net of six rectangles. Find the surface area by adding the areas of the six rectangles.

3. example

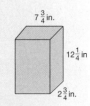

Example 3

Thinking Skill
Connect

How could we use the lateral surface area of the box to find the total surface area? We could find the lateral surface area of the box (by multiplying the perimeter of the base by the height), and then we could add the area of the top and bottom of the box to the lateral surface area.

The figure shows the dimensions of a cereal box. Estimate the surface area of the box.

$7\frac{3}{4}$ in.

$12\frac{1}{4}$ in

$2\frac{3}{4}$ in.

Solution

We round to the nearest whole number before performing the calculations.

To estimate the surface area we estimate the area of the six surfaces.

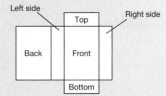

Area of front	8 in. × 12 in. = 96 in.²
Area of back	8 in. × 12 in. = 96 in.²
Area of top	8 in. × 3 in. = 24 in.²
Area of bottom	8 in. × 3 in. = 24 in.²
Area of left side	12 in. × 3 in. = 36 in.²
Area of right side	12 in. × 3 in. = 36 in.²
Total Surface Area	= 312 in.²

The surface area of the box is **about 312 in.²**

Math Background

How do you find the surface area of a right triangular prism?

The same method you used to find the surface area of a box works for any right prism. For example, the perimeter of the base of the triangular prism at right is 12 cm, and the height is 4 cm. So, the lateral surface area is (4 cm)(12 cm) = 48 cm². To find the total surface area, add the areas of the two bases. The area of each base is $(\frac{1}{2})$(3 cm)(4 cm), or 6 cm², so the total surface area is 48 cm² + 12 cm² = 60 cm².

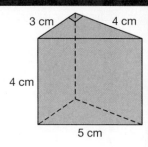

3 cm   4 cm

4 cm

5 cm

Practice Set ▶

a. What is the lateral surface area of a tissue box with the dimensions shown? 112 in.²

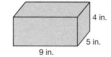
4 in.
5 in.
9 in.

b. What is the total surface area of a cube with edges 2 inches long? 24 in²

▶ c. Estimate the surface area of a cube with edges 4.9 cm long. 150 cm²

▶ d. *Analyze* Kwan is painting a garage. Find the lateral surface area of the building. 640 ft²

20 ft
8 ft
20 ft

e. Find a box at home (such as a cereal box) and measure its dimensions. Sketch the box on your paper and record its length, width, and height. Then estimate the number of square inches of cardboard used to construct the box. see student work

Written Practice   *Strengthening Concepts*

▶ **1.** Desiree drove north for 30 minutes at 50 miles per hour. Then, she drove
(7) south for 60 minutes at 20 miles per hour. How far and in what direction is Desiree from where she started? 5 miles north

2. In the forest, the ratio of deciduous trees to evergreens is 2 to 7. If there
(34) are 400 deciduous trees in the forest, how many trees are in the forest? 1800 trees

3. Reginald left his house and rode his horse east for 3 hours at 9 miles
(7) per hour. How fast and in which direction must he ride to get back to his house in an hour? 27 miles per hour west

▶ *** 4.** *Analyze* What is the volume of a shipping box with dimensions
(42) $1\frac{1}{2}$ inches × 11 inches × 12 inches? 198 in.³

5. How many square inches is the surface area of the shipping box
(43) described in problem **4**? 333 in.²

* 6. How many edges, faces, and vertices does a
(Inv. 4) triangular pyramid have? 6 edges, 4 faces, 4 vertices

7.
$y = -2x + 3$
(0, 3)
(4, −5)
(4, −11)

▶ *** 7.** Graph $y = -2x + 3$. Is (4, −11) on the line? no
(41)

* 8. Find **a** the area and **b** circumference of the circle with a radius of 6 in.
(39, 40) Express your answer in terms of π. **a.** 36π in.² **b.** 12π in.

Lesson 43   297

▶ See Math Conversations in the sidebar.

---

2 New Concepts (Continued)

Practice Set
Problem a [Error Alert]

The lateral surface area of the tissue box does not include the area of its top or its bottom. Students who include those areas in their computation are likely to name 202 cm² as the lateral surface area.

Problem c [Error Alert]

Point out that an exact answer is not required, and encourage students to make an estimate using only mental math. Sample: 5 × 5 = 25, and 25 + 25 + 25 + 25 + 25 + 25 = 150

Problem d [Analyze]

Challenge students to write an expression that uses exactly three factors to represent the lateral surface area of the garage. Sample: 4(8 ft × 20 ft)

3 Written Practice

Math Conversations

Discussion opportunities are provided below.

Problem 4 [Analyze]

To solve the problem, students may change $1\frac{1}{2}$ to a decimal or to an improper fraction, and check their work using the other form.

Errors and Misconceptions
Problem 1

To determine the distance Desiree drove in each direction, students must recognize that the rate is given in hours and the elapsed times are given in minutes. Students should change minutes to hours.

Problem 7

To graph the equation, remind students that they should first use it to produce more than two ordered pairs. Any two points form a line, but plotting more than two points provides a check.

Also explain that one way for students to check their yes or no answer is to substitute 4 for x and −11 for y in the equation $y = -2x + 3$. If the equation remains true after the substitutions, the point will be on the line.

(continued)

Math Conversations

Discussion opportunities are provided below.

Problem 9 [Formulate]

Remind students that substitution is a good way for them to check their equations. For example, if the substitution of *x* and *y* from each ordered pair in the table always produces a true statement, students can assume that the equation they wrote is correct.

Problem 12 [Evaluate]

Students should assume that each measure of the figure represents yards.

Problem 14 [Justify]

Extend the Problem

"How many products will be formed when this expression is expanded? Explain your answer." Three; Sample explanation: each of the three terms in parentheses represents one factor of a product that has −5 as its other factor.

(continued)

▶ *** 9.** [Formulate] A hotel shuttles 50 people per
(41)   bus to an amusement park. The table at the right charts the number of busses *x* and the corresponding number of people *y* shuttled to the park. Write an equation that shows the relationship in this table. $y = 50x$

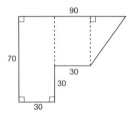

x	y
1	50
2	100
3	150
4	200

For problems **10** and **11**, solve using inverse operations:

10. $\dfrac{x}{1.1} = 11$ 12.1
(25, 38)

11. $x + 3.2 = 5.14$ 1.94
(24, 38)

At right is a diagram of a grassy schoolyard. Refer to this diagram to answer problems **12** and **13**. Dimensions are in yards.

▶ *** 12.** [Evaluate] How many square yards are there to mow?   3900 yd²
(37)

13. The athletes do cardiovascular conditioning by running laps around the
(8,
Inv. 2) perimeter of the entire schoolyard. How far do they run in one lap?
300 yards

▶ *** 14.** **a.** Expand: $-5(x^2 - x + 4)$ $-5x^2 + 5x - 20$
(21, 36)

   b. Factor: $7x + 7$ $7(x + 1)$

Simplify.

15. $\dfrac{20\,wx^2}{5\,x^2}$ 4w
(27)

16. $\left(\dfrac{1}{4}\right)^2 - \left(\dfrac{1}{2}\right)^4$ 0
(13, 27)

17. $\dfrac{7}{8} - \dfrac{12}{13} \div \dfrac{16}{13}$ $\dfrac{1}{8}$
(13, 22)

18. $\dfrac{1}{2} \cdot \dfrac{2}{3} \cdot \dfrac{3}{4}$ $\dfrac{1}{4}$
(22)

19. $\dfrac{1 + 3^2}{(1 + 3)^2}$ $\dfrac{5}{8}$
(15, 21)

20. $\dfrac{(-3)(-4)}{(-3) - (-4)}$ 12
(33, 36)

For problems **21–22**, find all values of *x* which make the equations true.

21. $\dfrac{x^2}{2} = 18$ $x = 6, -6$
(14, 15)

22. $\dfrac{|x|}{5} = 10$ $x = 50, -50$
(1, 14)

23. Write 0.005 **a** as a percent and **b** as a reduced fraction.
(11, 12)   **a.** 0.5% or $\frac{1}{2}$%, **b.** $\frac{1}{200}$

24. Express $\frac{5}{6}$ **a** as a decimal number, and **b** as a percent.   **a.** $0.8\overline{3}$, **b.** $83\frac{1}{3}$%
(30)

25. Write the prime factorization of 9000 with exponents. $2^3 \cdot 3^2 \cdot 5^3$
(9)

▶ See Math Conversations in the sidebar.

26. Todd wondered if students were likely to favor certain numbers when choosing a number between 1 and 10, so he conducted a survey. He asked 60 students to pick a number from 1 to 10 and tallied the choices.

1	2	3	4	5	6	7	8	9	10
III	IIII	IIII I	III	IIII IIII I	IIII	IIII IIII IIII	IIII	III	IIII

Before the survey, Todd guessed that all numbers were equally likely to be chosen. Based on his hypothesis,

  a. What is the theoretical probability that a student would choose the number 7? $\frac{1}{10}$ or 0.1.

  b. Based on Todd's survey, what is the experimental probability that a student will choose the number 7? $\frac{1}{4}$ or 0.25.

  c. Was Todd's hypothesis confirmed in the survey? No, the numbers were picked with different frequencies.

27. Combine like terms to simplify: $x^2 + 4x + 4 + 2x^2 - 3x - 4$ $3x^2 + x$
(31)

28. Find mgh when $m = 3$, $g = 9.8$, and $h = 10$. 294
(14)

29. Segment PR is a diameter of circle M and measures 20 in. Central angle QMR measures $60°$.
(18, 40)

  a. Find m $\angle QMP$. $120°$

  b. Find the area of the semicircle RMP (Use $\pi \approx 3.14$). 157 in.^{2}

▶* 30. **Model** For **a–c,** refer to this figure constructed of 1-cm cubes.
(Inv. 4, 42, 43)

  a. On grid paper draw the front view, top view, and right-side view of this figure.

  b. What is the total surface area of this figure? 46 cm^2

  c. What is the volume of this figure? 14 cm^3

a.

ront view Top view Right-side view

▶ See Math Conversations in the sidebar.

Math Conversations

Discussion opportunities are provided below.

Problem 30 Model

Encourage students who struggle drawing one or more of the views to use blocks and build a model of the figure.

Looking Forward

Understanding and calculating surface area prepares students for:

- **Lesson 55,** sketching and constructing nets of prisms, cylinders, pyramids, and cones.

- **Lesson 85,** calculating surface areas of cylinders and prisms.

- **Lesson 91,** investigating the effects of scaling on perimeter, area, and volume.

- **Lesson 100,** calculating surface areas of right pyramids and cones.

- **Lesson 107,** calculating volumes and surface areas of compound solids.

- **Lesson 111,** calculating volumes and surface areas of spheres.

• Solving Proportions Using Cross Products
• Slope of a Line

Objectives

- Use cross products to solve proportions.
- Find the slope of a line by finding the ratio of rise to run.
- Visually determine whether a line's slope is positive, negative, zero, or undefined.
- Use slope to help solve rate problems.

Lesson Preparation

Materials

- **Power Up I** (in *Instructional Masters*)

Optional

- **Lesson Activity 6** (in *Instructional Masters*)

Power Up I

Math Language

New	Maintain
cross product	proportion
rise	
run	
slope	

Technology Resources

Student eBook Complete student textbook in electronic format.

Resources and Planner CD Assessment, reteaching, and instructional masters, plus a pacing calendar with standards.

Test and Practice Generator CD Create additional practice sheets and custom-made tests.

www.SaxonPublishers.com Visit for more student activities and planning materials.

Inclusion

Adaptations CD Adapted lessons, investigations, practice and assessments.

Meeting Standards

National Council of Teachers of Mathematics (NCTM)

Numbers and Operations

NO.1d Understand and use ratios and proportions to represent quantitative relationships

NO.3d Develop, analyze, and explain methods for solving problems involving proportions, such as scaling and finding equivalent ratios

Algebra

AL.2b Explore relationships between symbolic expressions and graphs of lines, paying particular attention to the meaning of intercept and slope

Problem Solving

PS.1b Solve problems that arise in mathematics and in other contexts

Problem-Solving Strategy: Find a Pattern/
Write an Equation

   a. Find the square root of the sum of the first 2 positive odd numbers.

   b. Find the square root of the sum of the first 3 positive odd numbers.

   c. Find the square root of the sum of the first 4 positive odd numbers.

   d. Describe the pattern.

   e. Using the pattern you noticed, what do you think is the square root of the sum of the first 17 positive odd numbers?

(Understand) **Understand the problem.**

"What information are we given?"

We are given five steps that will lead us to finding a pattern about the square roots of sums of odd numbers.

"What are we asked to do?"

Complete each of the five steps.

(Plan) **Make a plan.**

"What problem solving strategy will we use?"

We will *write the equations* that have been recommended to help us *find a pattern* to use.

(Solve) **Carry out the plan.**

"What is the square root of the sum of the first 2 odd numbers?"

$\sqrt{(1 + 3)} = \sqrt{4} = 2$

"What is the square root of the sum of the first 3 odd numbers?"

$\sqrt{(1 + 3 + 5)} = \sqrt{9} = 3$

"What is the square root of the sum of the first 4 odd numbers?"

$\sqrt{(1 + 3 + 5 + 7)} = \sqrt{16} = 4$

"How can we describe the pattern?"

The number of consecutive odd numbers we are to add is equal to the square root of the sum.

"According to the pattern, what will be the square root of the sum of the first 17 odd numbers?"

17

(Check) **Look back.**

"Did we find the answer to the question that was asked?"

Yes. We found the square roots to three sets of sums of odd numbers, described the pattern we noticed, and then applied the pattern to determine that the square root of the sum of the first 17 odd numbers is 17.

• **Solving Proportions Using Cross Products**
• **Slope of a Line**

facts | Power Up I

mental math | a. **Number Sense:** $6\frac{1}{2} \times 20$ 130

b. **Fractional Parts:** David tipped $\frac{1}{5}$ of the $35 meal bill. What was his tip? $7

c. **Measurement:** Find the temperature indicated on this thermometer.   32° F

d. **Rate:** Charlene drove 55 miles per hour for 4 hours. Ralph drove 50 miles per hour for 5 hours. How far did each drive?   Charlene: 220 miles; Ralph: 250 miles

e. **Geometry:** Two sides of a triangle are 16 m and 20 m. The third side is between what two lengths?   between 4 m and 36 m

f. **Scientific Notation:** Write 2.38×10^7 in standard notation.   23,800,000

g. **Estimation:** Approximate the total for this shopping bill: 3 items at $1.99 each, 4 items at $2.49 each, and 2 items at $6.99 each. $30

h. **Calculation:** $5 + 2, \times 6, \div 7, \times 8, + 1, \div 7, \div 7, \times 12, \div 3, \times 5, + 1, \div 7$ 3

problem solving | a. Find the square root of the sum of the first 2 positive odd numbers.
$\sqrt{4} = 2$
b. Find the square root of the sum of the first 3 positive odd numbers.
$\sqrt{9} = 3$
c. Find the square root of the sum of the first 4 positive odd numbers.
$\sqrt{16} = 4$
d. Describe the pattern.   number of odd numbers = square root of sum
e. Using the pattern you noticed, what do you think is the square root of the sum of the first 17 positive odd numbers?   17

New Concepts   *Increasing Knowledge*

solving proportions using cross products | We have solved proportions by finding equivalent ratios just as we found equivalent fractions. To solve some proportions it is helpful to use another method. In this lesson we will practice using cross products to solve proportions.

Power Up

Facts
Distribute **Power Up I** to students. See answers below.

Mental Math
Encourage students to share different ways to mentally compute these exercises. Strategies for exercises **b** and **g** are listed below.

b. **Use a Fraction**
$\frac{1}{5} \times \$35 = \$7$
Divide by 5
$\$35 \div 5 = \$7$

g. **Round and Compensate**
$\$1.99 \approx \$2, \$2.49 \approx \$2, \$6.99 \approx \$7$
$3 \times \$2 + 4 \times \$2 + 2 \times \$7 =$
$6 + 8 + 14 = \$28$
Add $2 because 49¢ is close to 50¢ and $4 \times 50¢ = \$2$.
$\$28 + \$2 = \$30$
Round to Half Dollars
$\$1.99 \ \$2, \$2.49 \ \$2.50, \$6.99 \ \$7$
$3 \times \$2 + 4 \times \$2.50 + 2 \times \$7 = \$30$

Problem Solving
Refer to **Power-Up Discussion**, p. 300B.

Facts   Simplify.

$(-3) + (-5)$	$(-3) - (-5)$	$(-3)(-5)$	$\frac{-30}{-5}$
-8	2	15	6
$(-8) + (+2)$	$(-8) - (+2)$	$(-8)(+2)$	$\frac{-8}{+2}$
-6	-10	-16	-4
$-3 + -2 - -4$	$-5 - +6 + +2$	$(-3)(+2)(-6)$	$\frac{(-2)(-6)}{-3}$
-1	-9	36	-4

A **cross product** is the result of multiplying the denominator of one fraction and the numerator of another fraction. A characteristic of equal ratios is that their cross products are equal.

$$8 \cdot 3 = 24 \qquad 4 \cdot 6 = 24$$

If we know that two ratios are equal, we can use cross products to help us find an unknown term in one of the ratios.

$$4n \qquad 6 \cdot 6$$

We do not know n, but we know that the cross product $4n$ equals the cross product $6 \cdot 6$.

$$4n = 6 \cdot 6$$

We can solve this equation to find n.

Step:	Justification:
$4n = 6 \cdot 6$	Equal ratios have equal cross products
$\dfrac{4n}{4} = \dfrac{6 \cdot 6}{4}$	Divide both sides by 4.
$n = 9$	Simplified

Example 1

Solve using cross products: $\dfrac{m}{10} = \dfrac{15}{25}$

Solution

The ratios are equal. We find the cross products and solve for m.

Step:	Justification:
$\dfrac{m}{10} = \dfrac{15}{25}$	Given proportion
$25m = 10 \cdot 15$	Equal ratios have equal cross products.
$\dfrac{25m}{25} = \dfrac{10 \cdot 15}{25}$	Divide both sides by 25.
$m = 6$	Simplified

Justify Explain how we can check the solution. We replace the m in the original proportion with 6 then we simply both ratios. If the ratios reduce to the same ratio, then they are equal. Both $\frac{6}{10}$ and $\frac{15}{25}$ reduce to $\frac{3}{5}$, so our solution is correct.

Lesson 44   301

2 New Concepts

Instruction

You may want to review quickly the equivalent ratios method for solving proportions. This should refresh understanding of proportions.

Some students may not be willing to accept the idea that the cross products of equal ratios are equal without some proof. The following proof is fairly easy to follow and is based on multiplying both sides of the equation by the reciprocal of one of the ratios.

Step:	Justification:
$\dfrac{a}{b} = \dfrac{c}{d}$	A general proportion where no variable is equal to zero.
$\dfrac{a}{b} \cdot \dfrac{b}{a} = \dfrac{c}{d} \cdot \dfrac{b}{a}$	Multiply both sides of the equation by $\frac{b}{a}$, the reciprocal of $\frac{a}{b}$.
$1 = \dfrac{cb}{da}$	Simplified
$da = cb$	Multiply both sides of the equation by da.
$d \cdot a = c \cdot b$	The cross products of the proportion are equal.

Point out that this proof shows that the relationship is true for any equal ratios.

Example 1
Instruction

Suggest that students use the equivalent ratios method to solve this proportion after they solve it using cross products. They will discover that because $25 \times \frac{2}{5} = 10$, they need to find $\frac{2}{5}$ of 15 to find m. Note that the answer, $m = 6$, is the same. Then ask students to compare the two methods. Sample: For this problem, using cross products is better because I could reduce to make the computation easier.

(continued)

2 New Concepts (Continued)

Instruction

Go over the information on slope carefully. Some students may be familiar with slope from last year's work in mathematics. The first part of the instruction helps students decide by inspection whether the slope is positive or negative. Guide students to understand that when we say that the slope is "uphill" or "downhill", we are referring to its direction from left to right.

You might use **Lesson Activity 6** Slope to demonstrate how to use the *rise* and *run* to determine the slope of a line. Emphasize that it is helpful to avoid fractional values for the rise and run. To do this, students can use any two points on the line that are at the intersections of the lines on the grid.

The rise or run can be calculated using any two points on the graph, not necessarily points that are nearest to each other. To avoid a negative run students should select a first point that is to the left of the second point.

(continued)

---

slope of a line

In Lesson 41 we graphed lines to illustrate the relationship between two variables. Lines on a coordinate plane may be horizontal, vertical, or slanted one way or the other. We use a number called the *slope* to indicate the steepness of the line and whether the line is slanted "uphill" (positive) or "downhill" (negative).

Slope

> The **slope** of a line is the ratio of the **rise** to the **run** between any two points on the line.
>
> $$\text{slope} = \frac{\text{rise}}{\text{run}}$$

These two graphs illustrate the rise and run of two lines.

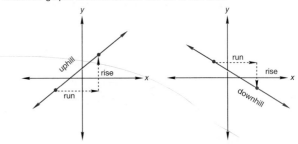

The *run* starts from a point on the line and moves over to the right.

The *rise* starts at the end of the run and moves up or down to meet the line.

Train your eyes to read lines on graphs from left to right like you read words.

"Uphill" lines have a positive slope.

"Downhill" lines have a negative slope.

The graph on the left has a positive slope. The graph on the right has a negative slope.

Infer Which of the graphs above has a positive slope? Which has a negative slope?

Here are four examples of calculating slope.

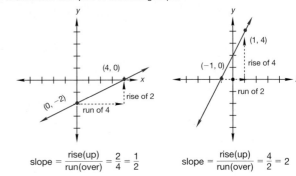

$$\text{slope} = \frac{\text{rise(up)}}{\text{run(over)}} = \frac{2}{4} = \frac{1}{2} \qquad \text{slope} = \frac{\text{rise(up)}}{\text{run(over)}} = \frac{4}{2} = 2$$

The graph on the right. Sample: The graph on the right looks steeper and a slope of 2 is greater than a slope of $\frac{1}{2}$.

Infer Which of the two graphs on the previous page has the steeper slope? Support your answer.

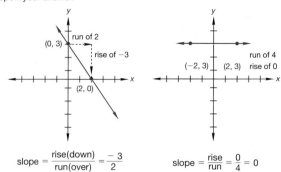

$$\text{slope} = \frac{\text{rise(down)}}{\text{run(over)}} = \frac{-3}{2}$$

$$\text{slope} = \frac{\text{rise}}{\text{run}} = \frac{0}{4} = 0$$

Thinking Skill

Explain

Can we use the words *uphill* and *downhill* to describe a line with a slope of zero? Explain. No; if the slope of a line is 0, it is horizontal and does not have an uphill or downhill slant.

Note that **the slope of a horizontal line is zero.** We do not assign a slope to a vertical line. Instead, we say that **the slope of a vertical line is undefined.**

Discuss Why is the slope of a vertical line undefined? (Hint: Think about the run of a vertical line.) Sample: The run of a vertical line is 0. Since we cannot divide by 0, the slope of a vertical line is undefined.

Two points on a graph represent an interval. The slope between the two points is the average **rate of change** of one variable relative to the other in that interval.

Example 2

Derek drives the highway at a steady rate, noting the time and distance he has traveled. This graph describes the distance Derek travels when driving at a constant rate of 50 mph. Find the average rate of change in miles per hour Derek drives over these three intervals: zero and 1 hour, 1 hour and 3 hours, and 3 hours and 4 hours.

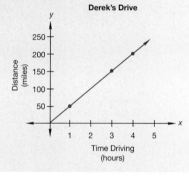

Derek's Drive

Lesson 44   303

Instruction

Emphasize that a negative coordinate in one of the points on the line does not make the rise, the run, or the slope negative. It is only the distance and direction between two points that determine the sign of the slope.

Emphasize the phrase "rise over run" to students. Students may create their own mnemonic device, but they should know that the rise is the numerator of the ratio and the run is the denominator.

(continued)

Math Background

The slope of the line that passes through points (x_1, y_1) and (x_2, y_2) can be calculated by dividing the difference in y-coordinates by the difference in x-coordinates.

$$\text{slope} = \frac{y_2 - y_1}{x_2 - x_1}$$

It does not matter which point is considered (x_1, y_1) as long as both subtractions begin from the same point. For example, both calculations below give the slope of the line through (1, 6) and (4, 2).

$$\text{slope} = \frac{2 - 6}{4 - 1} = \frac{-4}{3} \qquad \text{slope} = \frac{6 - 2}{1 - 4} = \frac{4}{-3}$$

Example 2

Instruction

In this example, point out that because the function is linear, the slope between any two points is the same. So whether the slope is determined from 0 to 4 hours or between any two points on the line, it will represent an average rate of 50 miles per hour. Have students notice that the average distance traveled each hour is the same: 50 miles.

Practice Set

Problems a–d Analyze

Have students note that the constant factor of each proportion is not obvious, and then point out that the use of cross products represents a useful way to solve such proportions.

Problems e–g Error Alert

Remind students to use the rules described below each time they write the slope of a line in simplest form.

- If the signs of two integers are the same, the product or quotient of those integers is positive.
- If the signs of two integers are different, the product or quotient of those integers is negative.

Problem i Represent

You might choose to challenge volunteers to explore how the x- and y-coordinates of the ordered pairs (2, −4) and (0, 0) can be arranged to represent the slope of the line.

$$\frac{-4 - 0}{2 - 0} \text{ or } \frac{0 - (-4)}{0 - 2}$$

Solution

We find that the average rate of change is **50 miles per hour** for each of the three intervals.

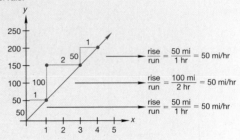

$$\frac{\text{rise}}{\text{run}} = \frac{50 \text{ mi}}{1 \text{ hr}} = 50 \text{ mi/hr}$$

$$\frac{\text{rise}}{\text{run}} = \frac{100 \text{ mi}}{2 \text{ hr}} = 50 \text{ mi/hr}$$

$$\frac{\text{rise}}{\text{run}} = \frac{50 \text{ mi}}{1 \text{ hr}} = 50 \text{ mi/hr}$$

Notice that if a function is linear (the points are aligned as on the graph above), then the slope between any two points is constant.

Practice Set   *Analyze* Use cross products to solve the proportions in **a–d**.

▸ **a.** $\frac{8}{12} = \frac{12}{w}$ $w = 18$ ▸ **b.** $\frac{3}{12} = \frac{x}{1.6}$ $x = 0.4$

▸ **c.** $\frac{y}{18} = \frac{16}{24}$ $y = 12$ ▸ **d.** $\frac{0.8}{z} = \frac{5}{1.5}$ $z = 0.24$

▸ Find the slope of lines **e–g.** **e.** $\frac{1}{2}$, **f.** 1, **g.** 2

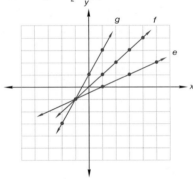

h. *Generalize* Which statement best describes the relationship between the slope and the steepness of the line? **B**

A The greater the uphill steepness, the less the slope.

B The greater the uphill steepness, the greater the slope.

C The less the uphill steepness, the greater the slope.

▸ **i.** *Represent* Graph the line that passes through the origin and (2, −4). Then find the slope of the line.

i.

slope = −2

j. What is the slope of a line passing through (1, 1) and (5, −1)? $-\frac{1}{2}$

▸ See Math Conversations in the sidebar.

1.

	Case 1	Case 2
Undersized lobsters	3	u
Total number	5	260

$\frac{3}{5} = \frac{u}{260}$; Since $5 \times 52 = 260$ then $3 \times 52 = u$; $u = 156$

1. A marine biologist reported the results of a survey that found 3 out of
(34) 5 lobsters are undersized and if caught, must be put back in the water. If a lobsterman traps 260 lobsters, about how many should he expect to toss back? Write a proportion and solve.

2. During their third season, a baseball team played 36 games and won $\frac{5}{9}$
(22) of them. How many games did they win?   **A**

    A 20   **B** 25   **C** 30   **D** 45

▶ *** 3.** **Connect** Tomás plans to build a circular pen for his dog. The radius of
(39) the pen will be 17.5 feet. Approximately, how many feet of fencing will Tomás use for the pen?   about 110 ft

▶ *** 4.** **Analyze** The dimensions of a pasta box are 14 in. by 1.5 in. by 3 in.
(43) What is the surface area of the box?   135 in.^{2}

* 5. Geri wants to fill a rectangular planter box with soil. If the dimensions
(42) of the box are $2\frac{1}{2}$ ft by $1\frac{3}{4}$ ft by 4 ft long. How many cubic feet of soil will Geri need?   17.5 ft^3

6. $y = 4x$; The function is linear and it is proportional.

Number of Coin Purses	Amount Collected in Dollars
1	4
2	8
3	12
4	16

* 6. Anna makes leather coin purses and donates them to the local
(41) children's hospital fundraiser fair. The coin purses sell for $4 each. Make a function table that relates the number of coin purses sold to the amount of money collected. Write an equation for the rule. Is the function linear? Is it proportional?

* 7. An artist makes rugs by painting intricate designs on canvas. He has
(40) been commissioned by a local store to create a 12-foot diameter circular rug. He prices his rugs by their area. About what is the area of this 12-foot rug?   About 113 ft^2

* 8. **Justify** Consider the function $y = \frac{2}{3}x - 1$.
(41)
▶   **a.** Does $(9, -5)$ satisfy this function? Why or why not?   No, when x is 9, y is 5.

▶   **b.** If the value of x is 15, what is y? Write your answer as an ordered pair. $(15, 9)$

Simplify.

9. $6\frac{3}{4} - \frac{3}{5} \div \frac{1}{5}$ $3\frac{3}{4}$
(13, 22)

10. $(2.5)^2 - \left(\frac{3}{2}\right)^2$ 4
(15, 25)

11. $(-10) - (-4)$ -6
(33)

12. $\frac{(-4)(-8) \div (-2)}{-2}$ 8
(36)

* 13. $(3x^2y)(-2xy)^3$ $-24x^5y^4$
(27, 36)

▶***14.** $5(40) \div [-5(1-3)^3]$ 5
(21, 36)

15. $\left[\frac{3}{5} - \left(-\frac{1}{2}\right)^2 + \frac{9}{10}\right]^0$ 1
(13, 27)

16. $\frac{10^8}{10^3}$ 10^5
(27)

▶ See Math Conversations in the sidebar.

Math Conversations
Discussion opportunities are provided below.

Problem 3 **Connect**
"What measure of the circle are we being asked to find?" its circumference, or distance around

"What formula is used to find circumference?" $C = \pi d$

"In the problem, the radius is given. In the formula for circumference, d represents diameter. How can we change the radius to a diameter?" Sample: double its length

Problem 4 **Analyze**
"The pasta box is shaped like a rectangular prism. How many pairs of congruent faces does a rectangular prism have?" three pairs

After completing the problem, challenge students by asking:

"Is the surface area of the box greater than one square foot? Explain why or why not." No; one square foot is 12 inches by 12 inches, or 144 square inches, and 135 is less than 144.

Problem 8a **Justify**
"How will we know if the given values satisfy the function?" Sample: Substitute 9 for x. If the right side of the equation simplifies to -5, the values $x = 9$ and $y = -5$ satisfy the equation.

Errors and Misconceptions
Problem 4
Watch for students who do not read the problem carefully and compute the volume of the box instead of its surface area.

Problem 8b
You may need to remind students that when writing ordered pairs, the x-value is written first because all ordered pairs are of the form (x, y).

Problem 14
Watch for students who simplify $(-2)^3$ as if it was $-(2)^3$.

Make sure students understand that $-(2)^3$ represents $-(2 \cdot 2 \cdot 2)$ and $(-2)^3$ represents $(-2) \cdot (-2) \cdot (-2)$. This concept is especially important when the exponent is an even number.

(continued)

Math Conversations

Discussion opportunities are provided below.

Problem 20 [Justify]

Extend the Problem

Challenge students to describe two different ways mental math can be used to estimate the number of turn-of-the-century farmers that were needed to feed 130 people. Sample: Round 130 to 125, then divide 125 by 25 to conclude that about five times as many farmers were needed then as now; round 2600 to 2500, then divide by 25 to learn that about 100 farmers were needed.

Problem 25 [Verify]

Extend the Problem

Invite a volunteer to demonstrate on the board or overhead how two inverse operations can be used to check the solution. Sample: Subtract 3 from each side of the equation, then divide each side of the equation by 5.

(continued)

---

17. For Francisco: $P(F) = \frac{31}{75} = 0.413$; for Rafael: $P(R) = \frac{40}{83} = 0.482$. Rafael is more likely to get a hit in his next at-bat.

17. Francisco and Rafael are baseball players. Francisco has had 31 hits in
(32) 75 at-bats, while Rafael has had 40 hits in 83 at-bats. Between the two, who is more likely to get a hit in his next at-bat? Explain your answer.

18. A 1-inch garden hose had a small leak. Ali patched the leak by wrapping
(39) plastic tape around the hose 6 times. About how many inches of tape did Ali use? **C**

   A 6 in.   **B** 12 in.   **C** 18 in.   **D** 21 in.

19. There was very little rain in Austin one summer. In June, the depth
(31) of Lake Travis fell 3 inches from its usual level. In July, it went down another 5 inches. In August it finally rained, adding 2 inches to the lake's depth. How many inches below the usual level was the lake at that point? $-3 + (-5) + 2 = -6$; 6 inches below normal.

▶ **20.** It is estimated that at the turn of the 20th century, one farmer in the U.S.
(34) could feed 25 people, whereas today, that ratio is about 1 to 130. How many farmers would it take today to feed 2600 people? 20 farmers

21. Pedro collects baseball caps. Three-fourths of the caps are red, and he
(38) has 12 red caps. How many caps does Pedro have? Write an equation and solve. $\frac{3}{4}c = 12$; $c = 16$; Pedro has 16 caps

22. The larger triangle is a dilation of the smaller
(35) triangle. What is the scale factor? 2

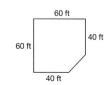

23. Sergio's front yard has the shape shown. He
(37) is going to sod his lawn. Before he buys the sod, Sergio needs to know the area. What is the area of the front yard? 3400 ft²

24. a. Write 4% as a reduced fraction and as a decimal. $\frac{1}{25}$; 0.04
(11)

    b. Which form would you find most convenient to answer the following question? "If 4% of a class of 25 students were absent, how many were absent?" $\frac{1}{25}$ since it is easy to divide 25 by 25

▶ **25.** Solve by inspection. $5x + 3 = 28$ $x = 5$
(14)

26. Find the mean time of Bert's last five downhill skiing runs: 98 sec,
(7) 90 sec, 102 sec, 97 sec, and 113 sec. 100 sec.

27. Find the area and perimeter of the quadrilateral with vertices $(-4, -1)$,
(8, Inv. 3) $(-4, 7)$, $(4, 7)$ and $(4, -1)$. What kind of quadrilateral is it? $A = 64$ units²; $P = 32$ units; square

▶ See Math Conversations in the sidebar.

29. Slope = 2.

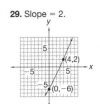

28. The science club charges $1.00 to join and 50¢ dues per week so that
(14) they can go on a field trip at the end of the year. The equation for dues
(*d*) collected and the number of weeks (*w*) is $d = 0.50w + 1$. Katja has
been a member for 18 weeks. How much has she paid? $10

29. A line passes through points (4, 2) and (0, −6). Sketch the line and find
(44) its slope.

▶* **30.** *Evaluate*   At Hilbert's hat store, Hilbert has a strategy for pricing hats.
(41) The rates are shown on the graph below.

Explain Hilbert's pricing strategy. Is the relation proportional? Why or why
not? If it is a proportional relationship, write an equation that describes
the graph and state the constant of proportionality.   (See below.)

Early Finishers
Real-World Application

A local rental company rents cars for $45.50 per day plus $0.10 per mile.
Azam rented a car for one day to take a drive along the coast. Write a
function that represents the cost of his trip (use *c* to represent cost and *m* to
represent distance in miles) and create a function table showing the cost of a
50-mile trip, a 125-mile trip, and a 160-mile trip. $c = \$45.50 + (\$0.10)m$;

m	*c*
50	$50.50
125	$58.00
160	$61.50

30. Hilbert charges $10 for the first hat purchased and $5 for each additional
hat. The relationship is NOT proportional, therefore there is no constant of
proportionality.

Lesson 44   307

▶ See Math Conversations in the sidebar.

Math Conversations
Discussion opportunities are provided below.

Problem 30   Evaluate
The points on the graph meet only one of
the two conditions that must be present for
a relationship to be proportional—they fall on
a line. However, the second condition—the
points are aligned with the origin—is absent,
so the relationship is not proportional.

Looking Forward

Solving proportions using cross products prepares students for:

• **Lesson 49,** solving rate problems with proportions and equations.

• **Lesson 88,** reviewing proportional and non-proportional relationships.

Calculating the slopes of lines prepares students for:

• **Lesson 56,** writing the slope-intercept equation of a line.

• **Lesson 69,** working with direct variation.

• **Lesson 70,** solving direct variation problems.

Ratio Problems Involving Totals

Objectives

- Use a three-row ratio table to solve ratio problems involving totals.

Lesson Preparation

Materials

- **Power Up I** (in *Instructional Masters*)

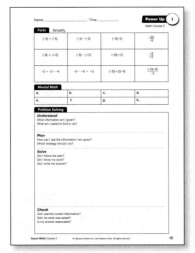

Power Up I

Math Language

Maintain	English Learners (ESL)
cross product	minimum
proportion	
ratio	

Technology Resources

Student eBook Complete student textbook in electronic format.

Resources and Planner CD Assessment, reteaching, and instructional masters, plus a pacing calendar with standards.

Test and Practice Generator CD Create additional practice sheets and custom-made tests.

www.SaxonPublishers.com Visit for more student activities and planning materials.

Inclusion

Adaptations CD Adapted lessons, investigations, practice and assessments.

Meeting Standards

National Council of Teachers of Mathematics (NCTM)

Numbers and Operations

NO.1d Understand and use ratios and proportions to represent quantitative relationships

NO.3d Develop, analyze, and explain methods for solving problems involving proportions, such as scaling and finding equivalent ratios

Algebra

AL.3a Model and solve contextualized problems using various representations, such as graphs, tables, and equations

Problem Solving

PS.1b Solve problems that arise in mathematics and in other contexts

Problem-Solving Strategy: Use Logical Reasoning/ Make a Table

Three friends ordered 3 different sandwiches and 3 different drinks. Annie ordered tuna, but didn't order water. Bernice ordered lemonade. Calvin did not order grilled cheese. Who ordered the cranberry juice? Who ordered the chicken sandwich?

Understand **Understand the problem.**

"What information are we given?"

Three friends each ordered a sandwich and a drink.

1. Annie ordered tuna and did not order water.
2. Bernice ordered lemonade.
3. Calvin did not order grilled cheese.
4. Someone ordered cranberry juice.
5. Someone ordered a chicken sandwich.

"What are we asked to do?"

Determine who ordered the cranberry juice and who ordered the chicken sandwich.

Plan **Make a plan.**

"What problem solving strategy will we use?"

We will *use logical reasoning* and *make a table* to record the facts provided and our deductions and conclusions.

"What size will our table need to be?"

Three rows (for the three friends) by six columns (for the three sandwiches + the three drinks).

Solve **Carry out the plan.**

	Tuna	Cheese	Chicken	Water	Lemonade	Cranberry
Annie	Step 1: YES (Fact 1)	Step 2: X (Deduce from fact 1)	Step 2: X (Deduce from fact 1)	Step 1: X (Fact 1)	Step 4: X (Deduce from fact 2)	Step 10: YES (Conclude)
Bernice	Step 2: X (Deduce from fact 1)	Step 6: YES (Conclude)	Step 7: X (Conclude)	Step 4: X (Deduce from fact 2)	Step 3: YES (Fact 2)	Step 4: X (Deduce from fact 2)
Calvin	Step 2: X (Deduce from fact 1)	Step 5: X (Fact 3)	Step 8: YES (Conclude)	Step 9: YES (Conclude)	Step 4: X (Deduce from fact 2)	Step 11: X (Conclude)

Check **Look back.**

"Did we find the answer to the questions that were asked?"

Yes. We found that Annie ordered the cranberry juice, and Calvin ordered the chicken sandwich.

• Ratio Problems Involving Totals

facts   Power Up I

mental math

a. **Number Sense:** $8\frac{1}{2} \times 4$ 34

b. **Probability:** What is the probability of rolling a number less than 1 on a number cube? $\frac{0}{6}$ or 0

c. **Algebra:** $12x = 6$ 0.5 or $\frac{1}{2}$

d. **Measurement:** Find the length of the object in inches: $1\frac{7}{8}$ in.

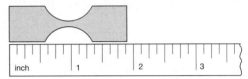

e. **Scientific Notation:** Write 40,800 in scientific notation. 4.08×10^4

f. **Rate:** Nathaniel drives north at a rate of 60 miles per hour. Sally drives south at a rate of 60 miles per hour. If they started at the same place and time, how far apart are they after one hour?   120 miles

g. **Geometry:** Approximate the volume of this box: 135 cm³

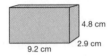

   4.8 cm   9.2 cm   2.9 cm

h. **Calculation:** 10×10, $+ 44$, $\sqrt{\ }$, $- 3$, $\sqrt{\ }$, $- 3$, $\sqrt{\ }$ 0

problem solving

Three friends ordered 3 different sandwiches and 3 different drinks. Annie ordered tuna, but didn't order water. Bernice ordered lemonade. Calvin did not order grilled cheese. Who ordered the cranberry juice? Who ordered the chicken sandwich?   Annie; Calvin

New Concept   *Increasing Knowledge*

Some ratio problems require us to consider the total to solve the problem. For these problems we add a third row for the total to our ratio table.

Example 1

Acrobats and clowns converged on the center ring in the ratio of 3 to 5. If a total of 24 acrobats and clowns performed in the center ring, how many were clowns?

Teacher Edition (left page)

Facts
Distribute **Power Up I** to students. See answers below.

Mental Math
Encourage students to share different ways to mentally compute these exercises. Strategies for exercises **a** and **f** are listed below.

a. Regroup, then Multiply
$8\frac{1}{2} \times 4 = 8\frac{1}{2} \times 2 \times 2 = 17 \times 2 = 34$
Multiply Whole Numbers, then Fractions
$8\frac{1}{2} \times 4 = 8 \times 4 + \frac{1}{2} \times 4 =$
$32 + 2 = 34$

f. Use the Rates
Nathaniel: 1 hr × 60 mi/hr = 60 mi
Sally: 1 hr × 60 mi/hr = 60 mi
60 mi north + 60 mi south = 120 mi apart
Use Math Sense
Nathaniel: 1 hr ⟶ 60 mi north from start
Sally: 1 hr ⟶ 60 mi south from start
60 mi north + 60 mi south = 120 mi apart

Problem Solving
Refer to **Power-Up Discussion**, p. 308B.

Instruction
Briefly review what has been taught about ratios and problem solving. Remind students how to use ratio tables.

(continued)

Facts   Simplify.

$(-3) + (-5)$	$(-3) - (-5)$	$(-3)(-5)$	$\frac{-30}{-5}$
-8	2	15	6
$(-8) + (+2)$	$(-8) - (+2)$	$(-8)(+2)$	$\frac{-8}{+2}$
-6	-10	-16	-4
$-3 + -2 - -4$	$-5 - +6 + +2$	$(-3)(+2)(-6)$	$\frac{(-2)(-6)}{-3}$
-1	-9	36	-4

Solution

We are given the ratio of acrobats to clowns. We can add the ratio numbers to find a ratio number for the total. We are given the actual total.

	Ratio	Actual Count
Acrobats	3	a
Clowns	5	c
Total	8	24

There are three rows in the table. We can use the numbers in two rows to write a proportion. We use the row for the number we want to find (clowns), and we use the row in which we know both numbers (total).

	Ratio	Actual Count
Acrobats	3	a
Clowns	5	c
Total	8	24

$$\rightarrow \quad \frac{5}{8} = \frac{c}{24}$$
$$c = 15$$

We solve the proportion and find that there were **15 clowns.**

Connect What is the relationship between the ratios and the actual counts in example 1? How could you use this information to solve the proportion a different way?

Thinking Skill

Formulate

Write and solve a proportion to find the total number of acrobats.
$\frac{3}{8} = \frac{a}{24}$; $a = 9$

The actual counts are three times the numbers in the ratios; I can multiply the ratio number for clowns by 3 to find the actual count of clowns:
$3 \times 5 = 15$.

Example 2

A bus company has small and large buses in the ratio of 2 to 7. If the company has 84 large buses, how many buses does it have?

Solution

The question involves the total number of buses, so we use a three-row table. To write the proportion, we use numbers from the row with two known numbers and from the row with the unknown we want to find.

	Ratio	Actual Count
Small Buses	2	s
Large Buses	7	84
Total	9	t

$$\rightarrow \quad \frac{7}{9} = \frac{84}{t}$$
$$7t = 9 \cdot 84$$
$$t = 108$$

The answer is reasonable because the ratio of 2 to 7 means that there are fewer small buses than large buses. Therefore, the total number of buses is just a little more than the number of large buses.

2 New Concepts (Continued)

Example 1
Instruction
Explain that the value for the third row in the ratio column can be found by adding the numbers of the ratio. Stress the importance of putting the numbers in the correct boxes, especially with an extra row in the table.

Use the Thinking Skill *Formulate* question in the sidebar to extend the example. As you discuss the *Connect* question, you may want to point out that the proportion could also have been solved using cross products.

Example 2
Instruction
After you complete this example, ask students to describe a different way to solve this problem. Sample: The relationship between the ratios and the actual counts is that the actual counts are 12 times the ratios.

Urge students to look for the simplest way to solve ratio problems. This will save them time and help them avoid errors.

(continued)

Teacher Tip

If some students spend a lot of time making the ratio tables, remind them that the purpose of the table is simply **to organize information.** Students should be able to sketch a table in a few seconds using abbreviations.

	R	AC
A	3	a
C	5	c
T	8	24

Practice Set
Problems a–c [Error Alert]

Remind students that the order of the terms of the ratios in a proportion is very important.

Have students write a ratio table to represent each problem, and write a proportion from each ratio table to make sure that the order of the terms in the proportion is correct.

3 Written Practice

Math Conversations
Discussion opportunities are provided below.

Problem 1 [Analyze]

To use a proportion to solve the problem, students must recognize that the ratio of 7 house finches to 3 goldfinches implies that for every 10 birds, 3 of the birds are goldfinches. So the proportion $\frac{3}{10} = \frac{g}{80}$ is used to represent the problem.

	Ratio	Actual Count
house finches	7	h
goldfinches	3	g
total	10	80

To solve for the unknown in a proportion, remind students to use an inverse operation to isolate the unknown.

Problem 6 [Explain]
Extend the Problem

Challenge students to explain how to find the volume of the cabinet in cubic feet. Then use a calculator to name that volume to the nearest tenth of a cubic foot. Sample: A cubic foot measures 12 inches by 12 inches by 12 inches, so divide the volume of the cabinet in cubic inches by the cube of 12 inches; $(704 \text{ in.}^3) \div (12 \text{ in.})^3 \approx 0.4 \text{ ft}^3$.

Problem 7 [Model]

After plotting the points and drawing the line, invite a volunteer to explain the arithmetic that is used to determine the slope of the line.

Remind students to always express the slope of a line in simplest form.

Errors and Misconceptions
Problem 7

Students should recognize that if a negative integer is substituted for x in the equation $y = -x$, the value of y will be a positive integer. Have students recall that this is because the opposite of a negative is a positive.

(continued)

Practice Set

a. 80 girls; If 80 of the 180 students are girls, then there are 100 boys, and the ratio of boys to girls is $\frac{100}{80}$ which reduces to $\frac{5}{4}$.

▶ **a.** The ratio of boys to girls at the assembly was 5 to 4. If there were 180 students at the assembly, how many girls were there? Explain why your answer is reasonable.

▶ **b.** The coin jar was filled with pennies and nickels in the ratio of 7 to 2. If there were 28 nickels in the jar, how many coins were there?   126 coins

▶ **c.** The ratio of football players to soccer players at the park was 5 to 7. If the total number of players was 48, how many were football players?   20 football players

Written Practice   *Strengthening Concepts*

▶ *** 1.** [Analyze] The ratio of house finches to goldfinches is 7 to 3. If there are 80 in all, how many goldfinches are there?   24 goldfinches
(45)

2. If it was 113.5 degrees in Amarillo and 95.7 degrees in Phoenix, how much hotter was it in Amarillo than it was in Phoenix?   17.8 degrees
(24)

* 3. The ratio of hours that the power is on to the hours that the power is off is 5 to 7. If there are 720 hours in the month, how many hours is the power on?   300 hours
(45)

* 4. Two guests out of every 25 guests at an amusement park bought popcorn. If there were 5175 guests at the amusement park, how many bought popcorn?   414 guests
(45)

5. a. A pentagonal prism has how many faces, edges, and vertices?   7 faces, 15 edges, 10 vertices
(Inv. 4)
   b. Sketch a net of the prism.

5. b.

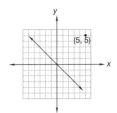

▶ *** 6.** Find the volume of a speaker cabinet with dimensions 8 in. by 8 in. by 11 in.   704 in.³
(42)

▶ *** 7.** [Model] Graph the equation $y = -x$. Is (5, 5) on the line? What is the slope of the line?   no; slope = −1
(41, 44)

▶ See Math Conversations in the sidebar.

Math Background

If you know that two quantities are proportional, how can you conclude that either quantity is proportional to the total?

If two quantities x and y are proportional, then $\frac{y}{x} = k$, where k is a constant. This can be rewritten as $y = kx$. The ratio of x to the total is $\frac{x}{x + y}$. We can show that this ratio is also constant.

$$\frac{x}{x + y} = \frac{x}{x + kx}$$ Because $y = kx$, substituted kx for y

$$= \frac{x}{x(1 + k)}$$ Factored x from the denominator

$$= \frac{1}{1 + k}$$ Simplified

Because k is a constant, $\frac{1}{1 + k}$ is too. So, x and $x + y$ are proportional.

* 8. *(40)* **Evaluate** Radius *DB* measures 6, $m\angle ADB = 120°$.

▶ **a.** Find the area of the circle. (Leave in terms of π.) 36π units²

▶ **b.** What fraction of the area of the circle does sector *ADB* cover? $\frac{1}{3}$

c. Find the area of sector *ADB*. (Leave in terms of π.) 12π units²

▶ *** 9.** *(41)* Write an equation for the function shown in the table: $y = x + 1.5$

x	y
−1	.5
0	1.5
1	2.5
2	3.5

▶ **10.** *(20)* **Classify** **a.** Classify this triangle by sides. isosceles

b. What is its area? 60 m²

c. What is its perimeter? 36 m

Solve for *x*.

11. *(13, 22)* $\frac{2}{3}x = 10$ $x = 15$ **12.** *(13)* $x - \frac{2}{3} = \frac{1}{9}$ $x = \frac{7}{9}$

For problems **13–14**, find all values of *x* which make the equations true.

13. *(38)* $x^2 + 1 = 145$ $x = 12, -12$ **14.** *(38)* $7 - |x| = 1$ $x = 6, -6$

Simplify.

15. *(15)* $\frac{mn}{2m^2}$ $\frac{n}{2m}$ **16.** *(13, 22)* $\frac{4}{5} - \frac{1}{5} \div \frac{1}{4}$ 0

17. *(13, 22)* $\frac{2}{7} \cdot \frac{3}{4} + \frac{11}{14}$ 1 **18.** *(13, 15)* $\left(\frac{3}{5}\right)^2 + \frac{3}{5}$ $\frac{24}{25}$

19. *(21, 31)* Simplify and compare: $\frac{-5 + \sqrt{25-16}}{2} \bigcirc \frac{-5 - \sqrt{25-16}}{2}$ $-1 > -4$

* 20. *(11, 25)* Simplify and compare: 0.5% of 1000 $\bigcirc$ 101% of 5 $5 < 5.05$

21. *(11)* **a.** Write 45% as a decimal and as a reduced fraction. $0.45, \frac{9}{20}$

b. Which of the three forms would be convenient for computing a 45% discount of a $40 shirt?   For example, the fraction can be used to find the product mentally: $\frac{9}{20} \cdot 40 = 18$; The shirt is discounted $18.

22. *(89, 40)* A chalk artist draws the earth as a circle with a diameter of 14 m. Find the **a** area and **b** circumference of the circle. Express the measures in terms of π.   **a.** 49π m²; **b.** 14π m

▶ See Math Conversations in the sidebar.

---

3 **Written Practice** *(Continued)*

Math Conversations
Discussion opportunities are provided below.

Problem 8a Evaluate
"When we use the formula A = πr^2 to find the area of a circle, we must square the radius of the circle. Why doesn't 12 represent the square of the radius of this circle?" $6^2 = 36$

Problem 8b Evaluate
"To find the fraction of the circle sector ADB represents, what two measures do we need to know?" the degree measure of the sector, and the degree measure of a circle

"How can we use the degree measure of the sector and of a circle to find solve the problem?" reduce $\frac{120°}{360°}$ to lowest terms

Problem 10 Classify
Make sure students realize that all of the measures that will be used to name the perimeter and the area of the triangle are given.

Errors and Misconceptions
Problem 9
Make sure students check their work by substituting the values of each ordered pair into the equation. If the substitutions always produce a true statement, students should assume that the equation is correct.

(continued)

Math Conversations

Discussion opportunities are provided below.

Problem 27 [Analyze]

Explain that all six faces of the cushion will be covered by the material Maria purchases, and students should assume no overlap of that material.

23. Consider the drawing from problem **22.**
(39, 40)
   a. The number of square meters of a drawing gives the artist an indication of how much chalk is needed. Estimate the number of square meters the drawing will cover.   about 150 m²

   b. The artist will rope off the drawing to protect the work in progress. Estimate the length of rope needed to rope off the art.   about 45 m

24. For $E = \frac{1}{2}mv^2$, find E when $m = 6$ and $v = 2$.   12
(14)

25. Which shows how to rewrite $7 \cdot 3 + 7 \cdot 5$?   **C**
(21)
   A $7 + 3 \times 7 + 5$ **B** $7 \times 7 + 3 \times 5$

   C $7(3 + 5)$ **D** $8(7 + 7)$

26. Frank earned $80.00 this week working at a supermarket. He owed his
(31) father $12.00 for a book and $6.00 for drawing paper that he bought for school last week. How much money does Frank still have from his weekly pay? $-12 - 6 + 80 = 62$; Frank still has $62.

▶*** 27.** [Analyze]   Maria wants to make a cover
(43) for the cushion on her chair. She needs to know the total surface area before she buys material. Find the total surface area of the cushion.   1224 in.²

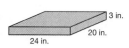
3 in.
20 in.
24 in.

* 28. Venus and Earth are often called twin planets because they are
(39) almost the same size. Earth has a circumference of 40,070 km. Venus has a diameter of 12,100 km. Which planet is larger? Hint: find the circumference of Venus. $3.14 \times 12,100 = 37,994$ km; Earth is larger.

* 29. Lisa stood next to a Ponderosa pine tree that is 5 times her height. If
(38) the tree is 6.85 meters high, how tall is Lisa? Write an equation and solve. $5h = 6.85$, $h = 1.37$, Lisa is 1.37 meters tall.

* 30. Leora's lasagna recipe required 3
(34) cups of spaghetti sauce to make 4 servings. Leora is serving lasagna to a large group of people. Leora makes a table that shows the number of cups of sauce she needs for multiples of four servings. Copy and complete the table. What is the constant of proportionality? Use the information in the table to find the minimum number of cups of sauce she will need to serve 18 people.   constant of proportionality is $\frac{3}{4}$; Leora will need at least 13.5 cups of sauce.

Number (n) of Servings	Number of Cups of Sauce (s)	Ratio $\frac{s}{n}$
4	3	$\frac{3}{4}$
8	6	$\frac{3}{4}$
12	9	$\frac{3}{4}$
16	12	$\frac{3}{4}$
20	15	$\frac{3}{4}$

▶ See Math Conversations in the sidebar.

Looking Forward

Solving ratio problems involving totals prepares students for:

• **Lesson 67,** finding percents of change.

English Learners

For problem **30** explain the meaning of the word **minimum.** Say:

   "The minimum is the smallest part needed."

Write the following on the board and ask students to identify the minimum in each case.

five or more examples

at least 10 students

4 to 6 cups of flour

The minimum is five. The minimum is 10. The minimum is 4.

Assessment   *30–40 minutes*   *For use after Lesson 45*

Distribute **Cumulative Test 8** to each student. Two versions of the test are available in *Saxon Math Course 3 Course Assessments Book*. Have students complete the **Power-Up Test** first. Allow 10 minutes. Then have students work the 20 numbered items on the **Cumulative Test.** Students may use copies of the answer sheet to record their work. Track individual and class progress with the **Test Analysis** forms.

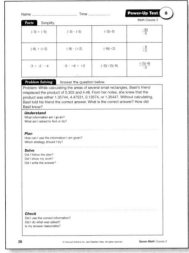

Power-Up Test 8

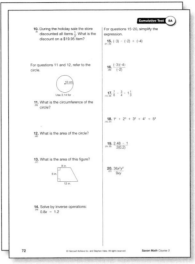

Cumulative Test 8A

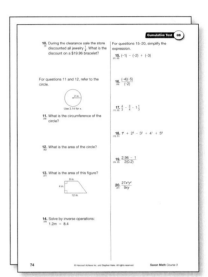

Alternative Cumulative Test 8B

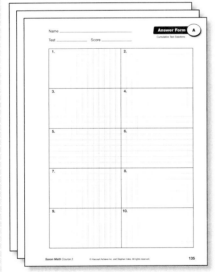

Optional Answer Forms

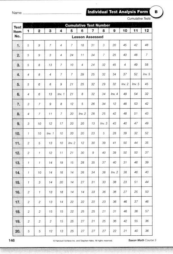

Individual Test Analysis Form

Class Test Analysis Form

Reteaching

Students who score below 80% on the assessment may be in need of reteaching. Look for the causes of student mistakes. If errors are conceptual, refer to the *Reteaching Masters* for reteaching.

Building Blocks
Assign after Lesson 45

Objectives
- Construct two cubes from drawn nets.
- Draw the net for a rectangular prism of specified size.
- Calculate the volume of a rectangular prism from its net.
- Communicate ideas through writing.

Materials
Performance Activities 8A, 8B, and **8C**

Scissors

Tape

Straight edge

Preparation
Make copies of **Performance Activities 8A, 8B,** and **8C.**
(One each per student.)

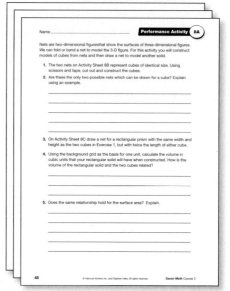

Performance Activity 8A, 8B, and 8C

Time Requirement
15–30 minutes; Begin in class and complete at home.

Activity
Tell students that for this activity they will be building blocks from paper cut-outs of drawn nets. Students will first cut out and construct two cubes from two different nets. Students then draw their own nets for a rectangular prism of given dimensions and calculate the volumes of the prisms from their nets. Students should be allowed time to cut out and construct their nets if they so choose. Students finish by investigating the relationships between the volumes and surface areas of their prism with those of the two cubes. Point out that all necessary information is provided on **Performance Activities 8A, 8B,** and **8C.**

Criteria for Evidence of Learning
- Constructs two cubes from their respective nets correctly.
- Recognizes that other nets are possible for a cube and gives a correct example.
- Draws an accurate net for a rectangular prism of a given size.
- Determines the correct volume of the rectangular prism from its net.
- Communicates ideas clearly through writing.

National Council of Teachers of Mathematics (NCTM)

Geometry

GM.4a Draw geometric objects with specified properties, such as side lengths or angle measures

GM.4b Use two-dimensional representations of three-dimensional objects to visualize and solve problems such as those involving surface area and volume

GM.4c Use visual tools such as networks to represent and solve problems

GM.4d Use geometric models to represent and explain numerical and algebraic relationships

Measurement

ME.2d Develop strategies to determine the surface area and volume of selected prisms, pyramids, and cylinders

Communication

CM.3a Organize and consolidate their mathematical thinking through communication

•Solving Problems Using Scientific Notation

Objectives

- Multiply and divide numbers written in scientific notation.
- Write equations using numbers in scientific notation to solve word problems.

Lesson Preparation

Materials

- **Power Up J** (in *Instructional Masters*)
- **Teacher-provided material:** calculators

Power Up J

Math Language

Maintain	English Learners (ESL)
scientific notation	modifications

Technology Resources

Student eBook Complete student textbook in electronic format.

Resources and Planner CD Assessment, reteaching, and instructional masters, plus a pacing calendar with standards.

Test and Practice Generator CD Create additional practice sheets and custom-made tests.

www.SaxonPublishers.com Visit for more student activities and planning materials.

Inclusion

Adaptations CD Adapted lessons, investigations, practice and assessments.

Meeting Standards

National Council of Teachers of Mathematics (NCTM)

Numbers and Operations

NO.1e Develop an understanding of large numbers and recognize and appropriately use exponential, scientific, and calculator notation

NO.1g Develop meaning for integers and represent and compare quantities with them

NO.2a Understand the meaning and effects of arithmetic operations with fractions, decimals, and integers

NO.2b Use the associative and commutative properties of addition and multiplication and the distributive property of multiplication over addition to simplify computations with integers, fractions, and decimals

Communication

CM.3b Communicate their mathematical thinking coherently and clearly to peers, teachers, and others

Problem-Solving Strategy: Make It Simpler

Find the sum of all the multiples of 3 from 30 to 81. (30 + 33 + 36 + ... + 75 + 78 + 81).

(Understand) **Understand the problem.**

"What important information are we given?"

We will be working with the multiples of 3 from 30 to 81.

"What are we asked to do?"

Find the sum of the multiples of 3 from 30 to 81.

(Plan) **Make a plan.**

"What problem-solving strategy will we use?"

We will *make it simpler* by using the pairing technique.

(Solve) **Carry out the plan.**

"What is the sum of the pair of addends that are at either end of the list?"

30 + 81 = 111

"Which multiple of 3 is 30, and which multiple of 3 is 81?"

Since 30 = 3 × 10, it is the 10th multiple of 3. Since 81 = 3 × 27, it is the 27th multiple of 3.

"How many numbers are in the sequence of multiples of 3 from 30 to 81?"

The first nine multiples of 3 are not in the list, so we subtract 9 from 27. There are 18 multiples.

"How many pairs of 111 exist?"

18 multiples ÷ 2 per pair = 9 pairs

"What is the sum?"

9 × 111 = 999

(Check) **Look back.**

"Did we find the answer to the question that was asked?"

Yes. We found that the sum of the multiples of 3 from 30 to 81 is 999.

• Solving Problems Using Scientific Notation

facts | Power Up J

mental math

a. **Number Sense:** $10\frac{1}{2} \times 16$ 168

b. **Probability:** What is the probability of rolling an odd number with one roll of a number cube? $\frac{3}{6} = \frac{1}{2}$

c. **Fractional Parts:** $\frac{2}{5}$ of the 30 students were girls. How many girls were there?   12

d. **Ratio:** The ratio of the length to width of a rectangular field is 4 to 2. If the field is 100 yards long, how wide is the field?   50 yards

e. **Measurement:** Find the length of this object: 4.1 cm

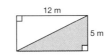

f. **Geometry:** Find the area of the rectangle. Then find the area of the shaded triangle.   Rectangle: 60 m², Triangle: 30 m²

12 m
5 m

g. **Powers/Roots:** $\sqrt{10 \cdot 10}$ 10

h. **Calculation:** $7 \times 6, + 3, \div 5, \sqrt{\ }, \times 8, + 1, \sqrt{\ }, \times 10, - 1, \sqrt{\ }$ 7

problem solving | Find the sum of all the multiples of 3 from 30 to 81. (30 + 33 + 36 + ... + 75 + 78 + 81).   There are 9 pairs of numbers (30 + 81, 33 + 78, ...) that total 111. Thus, the sum is 111 × 9 = 999

To multiply numbers written in scientific notation, we multiply the coefficients to find the coefficient of the product. Then we multiply the powers of 10 by adding the exponents.

Steps:	**Justification:**
$(1.2 \times 10^6)(4 \times 10^8)$	Given
$(1.2 \times 4)(10^6 \times 10^8)$	Assoc. and Comm. Properties
4.8×10^{14}	Simplified

If the product is not in the proper form of scientific notation, we revise the product so that there is one digit to the left of the decimal point.

Lesson 46   313

---

1 Power Up

Facts
Distribute **Power Up J** to students. See answers below.

Mental Math
Encourage students to share different ways to mentally compute these exercises. Strategies for exercises **a** and **c** are listed below.

a. **Double and Halve**
$10\frac{1}{2} \times 16 = 21 \times 8 =$
$42 \times 4 = 84 \times 2 = 168$

Regroup
$10\frac{1}{2} \times 16 = (10 \times 16) + (\frac{1}{2} \times 16) =$
$160 + 8 = 168$

c. **Multiply by Numerator First**
$\frac{2}{5} \times 30 = \frac{60}{5} = 12$

Divide by Denominator First
$\frac{2}{5} \times 30 = 2 \times 6 = 12$

Problem Solving
Refer to **Power-Up Discussion**, p. 313B.

2 New Concepts

Instruction
Have a volunteer tell what the proper form for scientific notation is. Sample: Scientific notation has two parts: a coefficient that must have one digit to the left of the decimal point (the digit must not be zero) and a power of 10.

(continued)

---

1. The distance around a circle is its _____ circumference _____.

2. Every point on a circle is the same distance from the _____ center _____.

3. The distance across a circle through its center is its _____ diameter _____.

4. The distance from a circle to its center is its _____ radius _____.

5. Two or more circles with the same center are _____ concentric _____ circles.

6. A segment between two points on a circle is a _____ chord _____.

7. Part of a circumference is an _____ arc _____.

8. A portion of a circle and its interior, bound by an arc and two radii, is a _____ sector _____.

9. Half of a circle is a _____ semicircle _____.

10. An angle whose vertex is the center of a circle is a _____ central _____ angle.

Instruction

After you go through this multiplication exercise and the *Generalize* question, extend this concept by discussing whether the coefficient of a product when multiplying numbers written in scientific notation is likely to be less than 1. Sample: No, because both coefficients being multiplied are equal to or greater than one. Point out that for multiplication with scientific notation sometimes the product of the coefficients will be greater than 10. In that case, students will need to move the decimal point of the coefficient one place to the left and add 1 to the exponent of the power of 10.

Example 1
Instruction

For part **a,** ask why there is no need to change the coefficient. Sample: It is in proper form.

For part **b,** after discussing how to change the coefficient so that it is in proper form, ask what must be done to the exponent of the power of 10. It must be increased by 1.

Instruction

Introduce division of numbers written in scientific notation. Discuss why division can result in a coefficient being less than 1. Sample: If the dividend is less than the divisor, the quotient will be less than 1. Note that moving the decimal point in the coefficient to the right means that the exponent of the power of 10 must be reduced by 1.

Use the *Conclude* question to summarize what has been taught about dividing with numbers written in scientific notation and to solidify understanding of proper scientific notation form.

(continued)

Steps:	Justification:
$(7.5 \times 10^4)(2 \times 10^3)$	Given
$(7.5 \times 2)(10^4 \times 10^3)$	Assoc. and Comm. Properties
15.0×10^7	Simplified (but incorrect form)
$1.5 \times 10^1 \times 10^7$	$15.0 = 1.5 \times 10^1$
1.5×10^8	Proper form ($10^1 \times 10^7 = 10^8$)

Look carefully at the last three steps. The coefficient 15.0 is not the correct form. We write 15.0 in scientific notation (1.5×10^1) and simplify again.

Generalize Write a rule that explains how moving the decimal point of the coefficient changes the exponent.

Moving the decimal point one place to the right decreases the exponent by 1. Moving the decimal point one place to the left increases the exponent by 1.

Example 1

Find each product

a. $(1.2 \times 10^5)(3.0 \times 10^5)$ b. $(4.0 \times 10^4)(5.0 \times 10^5)$

Solution

a. We multiply the coefficients and add the exponents.

$$(1.2 \times 10^5)(3.0 \times 10^5) = 3.6 \times 10^{10}$$

b. We multiply the coefficients and add the exponents.

$$(4.0 \times 10^4)(5.0 \times 10^5) = 20.0 \times 10^9$$

The answer is not in proper form because the coefficient has two digits left of the decimal point. We reposition the decimal point.

$$20.0 \times 10^9 = \mathbf{2.0 \times 10^{10}}$$

To divide numbers in scientific notation we divide the coefficients, and we divide the powers of 10 by subtracting the exponents.

$$\frac{4.8 \times 10^6}{4.0 \times 10^3} = \frac{4.8}{4.0} \times \frac{10^6}{10^3} = 1.2 \times 10^3$$

If the quotient is not in the proper form, we reposition the decimal point and change the exponent.

$$\frac{1.0 \times 10^8}{4.0 \times 10^3} = 0.25 \times 10^5 = 2.5 \times 10^4$$

When changing the exponent of a number written in scientific notation, first decide whether the shifting decimal point makes the coefficient larger or smaller, then compensate by changing the exponent.

$$0.25 \times 10^5 \longrightarrow 2.5 \times 10^4$$

The coefficient becomes 10 times larger, so we remove one power of ten.

Conclude Can the coefficient for a number written in scientific notation ever be greater than or equal to 10? Explain your answer.   No; If the coefficient is 10, we move the decimal point one place to the left and increase the exponent by 1.

Thinking Skill

Justify

Write 1.2×10^3 in standard form. Explain how you found your answer.   1,200; I moved the decimal point in the coefficient three places to the right since the coefficient is multiplied by 10 to the third power.

Math Background

Can you add and subtract numbers written in scientific notation?

"Yes, but you must be sure both numbers have the same exponent."

For example: $4.252 \times 10^6 + 2.443 \times 10^8$;

• Rewrite the problem so that both numbers have the same exponent:

$4.252 \times 10^6 + 244.3 \times 10^6$;

• Apply the distributive property: $(4.252 + 244.3) \times 10^6$;

• Simplify inside the parentheses: 248.552×10^6;

• Write the number in scientific notation: 2.48552×10^8.

Example 2

Light travels at a speed of about 300,000 kilometers per second. An hour is 3600 seconds. Write both numbers in scientific notation. Then estimate the distance light travels in an hour using scientific notation.

Solution

The rate 300,000 km/sec is equal to 3.0×10^5 **km/sec.**

The measure 3600 sec is equal to 3.6×10^3 **sec.**

The product of 3.0×10^5 km/sec and 3.6×10^3 sec is 10.8×10^8 km. The product is not in proper form for scientific notation, so we adjust the answer. The distance light travels in one hour is about 1.08×10^9 **km,** which is more than 1 billion kilometers.

Example 3

Find each quotient

a. $\dfrac{1.44 \times 10^{12}}{1.2 \times 10^8}$ b. $\dfrac{3.0 \times 10^8}{4.0 \times 10^4}$ c. $\dfrac{7.5 \times 10^6}{2.5 \times 10^6}$

Solution

We divide the coefficients and subtract the exponents.

a. $\dfrac{1.44 \times 10^{12}}{1.2 \times 10^8} = 1.2 \times 10^4$

b. $\dfrac{3.0 \times 10^8}{4.0 \times 10^4} = 0.75 \times 10^4$

  The quotient is not in proper form. We move the decimal point one place to the right and subtract 1 from the exponent.

$$0.75 \times 10^4 = 7.5 \times 10^3$$

c. $\dfrac{7.5 \times 10^6}{2.5 \times 10^6} = 3 \times 10^0$

  Recall that 10^0 equals 1. Thus the quotient is simply **3.**

Example 4

Earth's average distance from the sun is about 150 million kilometers. Light travels about 300 thousand kilometers per second. Express both numbers in scientific notation and estimate how long it takes the sun's light to reach Earth.

Solution

We rewrite 150 million km as 1.5×10^8 **km.**

We rewrite 300 thousand km/sec as 3.0×10^5 **km/sec.**

Dividing 1.5×10^8 km by 3.0×10^5 km/sec equals 0.5×10^3 sec. We rewrite the answer in proper form. To reach Earth, light from the sun travels about 5×10^2 **seconds,** which is **500 seconds.**

Lesson 46   315

Example 2
Instruction

If some students are confused by the concept "light hour," explain that they should think of it as the distance that light would travel in one hour. Connect it to *light year,* the distance that light travels in one year.

Example 3
Instruction

For part **a,** discuss why the answer did not need further work to put it in proper scientific notation form.

In part **b,** if some students are still having difficulty with rewriting the quotient in proper scientific notation form, you might tell them to think of the process as multiplying the coefficient by 10 and dividing the power of 10 by 10.

As you work through part **c,** note that there is a pair of common factors in the numerator and the denominator that can be cancelled to reduce the fraction.

Example 4
Instruction

Discuss how using scientific notation makes computation simpler, especially if scientific calculators are not available. Students can do the computation with the coefficients without a calculator and adjust the exponent of the power of 10 mentally.

(continued)

Teacher Tip

If your students are using their own calculators, have students with **different calculators** do the computation in this lesson and see whether everyone gets the same results. If not, compare the way that the calculators display answers. If some calculators do not have a display for scientific notation, help students to develop procedures for multiplying and dividing with numbers written in scientific notation.

Practice Set

Problems a–d [Error Alert]

Before completing any arithmetic for each problem, ask students to name the factors that will be used to find the coefficient of the product, and name the exponent of the product of the powers of 10.

Problem a: 2.4×2; 11
Problem b: 1.25×2; 10
Problem c: 4×4; 10
Problem d: 2.5×5; 13

Problem e [Error Alert]

To estimate the distance in kilometers that the sun's light travels in one day, students should multiply the number of seconds in one day (8.64×10^4) by the number of kilometers the sun's light travels in one second (3.0×10^5), and express the product (25.92×10^9) in scientific notation (2.592×10^{10}).

Problem h [Error Alert]

Watch for students who do not recognize 10^0 as another name for 1.

Write the pattern shown below on the board or overhead if students need to be reminded that $10^0 = 1$.

10^3 10^2 10^1 10^0

↓   ↓   ↓   ↓

$1000 \div 10 =$ $100 \div 10 =$ $10 \div 10 =$ 1

---

3 Written Practice

Math Conversations

Discussion opportunities are provided below.

Problem 6 [Model]

Challenge students to explain why it is helpful to select even numbers for x. In simplest form, the product of $\frac{3}{2}$ and an even number is an integer.

Problem 8 [Analyze]

Point out that a CD is shaped like a rectangular prism, and then ask students to name the formula that is used to find the volume of a rectangular prism. $V = lwh$

Errors and Misconceptions

Problem 8

After substituting for l, w, and h in the formula $V = lwh$, students should recall that that the Commutative and Associative Properties of Multiplication enable them to multiply the factors in any order.

(continued)

Practice Set | Find each product in **a–d**.

▶ **a.** $(2.4 \times 10^6)(2.0 \times 10^5)$ 4.8×10^{11}

▶ **b.** $(1.25 \times 10^4)(2 \times 10^6)$ 2.5×10^{10}

▶ **c.** $(4.0 \times 10^5)(4.0 \times 10^5)$ 1.6×10^{11}

▶ **d.** $(2.5 \times 10^6)(5 \times 10^7)$ 1.25×10^{14}

▶ **e.** One day is 86,400 seconds. Express this number in scientific notation and estimate how far the sun's light travels in a day. 8.64×10^4 sec; 2.592×10^{10} km

f. [Analyze] What operation did you use for the exponents in problems **a–e**? addition

Find each quotient in **g–j**.

g. $\dfrac{3.6 \times 10^{10}}{3.0 \times 10^6}$ 1.2×10^4

▶ **h.** $\dfrac{6.0 \times 10^8}{4.0 \times 10^8}$ $1.5 \times 10^0 = 1.5$

i. $\dfrac{1.2 \times 10^7}{3.0 \times 10^3}$ 4.0×10^3

j. $\dfrac{3 \times 10^9}{8 \times 10^4}$ 3.75×10^4

k. If Mars is 225 million kilometers from the sun, how long does it take light from the sun to reach Mars? 7.5×10^2 sec or 750 seconds

l. [Analyze] What operation did you apply to the exponents in problems **g–k**? subtraction

Written Practice   *Strengthening Concepts*

* **1.** The ratio of the cat's weight to the rabbit's weight is 7 to 4. Together, they weigh 22 pounds. How much does the rabbit weigh? 8 pounds
(45)

* **2.** The ratio of the weight of the Guinea pig to the weight of the Goliath beetle is 8 to 1. Together, they weigh 27 ounces. How much does the Goliath beetle weigh? 3 oz.
(45)

3. The mass of a flea is about 0.005 grams. How many fleas does it take to make 1 gram? 200 fleas
(6, 25)

* **4.** Simplify: $\dfrac{3.36 \times 10^7}{2.1 \times 10^4}$ 1.6×10^3
(46)

* **5.** Simplify: $(9.0 \times 10^2)(1.1 \times 10^7)$ 9.9×10^9
(46)

▶ * **6.** [Model] Graph the equation $y = \frac{3}{2}x - 2$. (Hint: For the table select even numbers for x.) What is the slope of the line? slope $= \frac{3}{2}$
(41, 44)

6.

7. Find the **a** area and **b** the circumference of a circle that has a diameter of 100. (Use a decimal approximation for π.) **a.** 7,850 square units **b.** 314 units
(39, 40)

▶ * **8.** [Analyze] Find the volume of a plastic CD case with dimensions 12.0 cm by 12.5 cm by 0.3 cm. 45 cm³
(42)

9. It will cost a manufacturer $45 to make machinery modifications in order to produce a new product. Each item will cost $10 to manufacture. To the right is a chart of the number of items (x) that are manufactured and the total cost (y). Write an equation that shows the relationship in the table. $y = 10x + 45$
(41)

x	y
0	45
1	55
2	65
3	75

▶ See Math Conversations in the sidebar.

English Learners

For problem **9** explain the meaning of the word **modifications**. Say:

"When you make a modification, you change a part of something."

Draw a figure composed of three 2-D figures. Then say you are going to make modifications to your figure. Change it in two or three ways. Ask:

"What modifications or changes did I make to the figure?"

Invite volunteers to make another modification to the figure.

10. Find the **a** area and **b** perimeter of this
(8, 37) figure. **a.** 78 ft² **b.** 46 ft

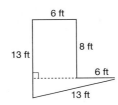

Solve for *x*.

11. $\frac{1}{2}x = \frac{3}{7}$ $x = \frac{6}{7}$
(22, 38)

12. $x + \frac{1}{12} = \frac{1}{2}$ $x = \frac{5}{12}$
(13, 38)

13. $x - 1.2 = 1.95$ $x = 3.15$
(24, 38)

14. $\frac{x}{16} = \frac{30}{20}$ $x = 24$
(36)

15. **a.** Expand: $-6(x^2 - 18x + 81)$ **b.** Factor: $9x - 3$
(21, 36) $-6x^2 + 108x - 486$ $3(3x - 1)$

16. **a.** Write $\frac{11}{20}$ as a decimal and percent.   0.55, 55%
(12)

    b. Which of the three forms is most appropriate for a store owner
to describe a discount of $11 from a $20 item?   Sample: 55%;
discounts are customarily reported as percents.

Simplify:

17. $\frac{mr}{3mr}$ $\frac{1}{3}$
(27)

18. $\frac{(-12) - (-2)(3)}{(-2)(-3)}$ -1
(33, 36)

19. $\frac{1}{2} \div \frac{3}{4} - \frac{1}{3}$ $\frac{1}{3}$
(13, 22)

20. $(0.15)^2$ 0.0225
(25)

Combine like terms to simplify:

21. $x^3 + 2x^2y - 3xy^2 - x^2y$ $x^3 + x^2y - 3xy^2$
(31)

▸ **22.** **Connect** Simplify $5(x - 3) + 2(3 - x)$ (Hint: expand first using the
(31, 36) Distributive Property.) $3x - 9$

23. Find all values of *x* which make the equation true: $x^2 - 9 = 0$ 3, −3
(14, 36)

24. Claire flips a coin twice.
(32)

    a. Use the sample space to find the
probability of Claire getting tails at least
once. $\frac{3}{4}$

    b. Find the probability of Claire getting
heads twice. $\frac{1}{4}$

25. Consider the similar triangles.
(35)

    a. What is the scale factor from the smaller
to the larger triangle? $\frac{3}{2}$ or 1.5

    b. Find *x*. $7\frac{1}{2}$ or 7.5

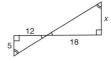

Lesson 46   317

▸ See Math Conversations in the sidebar.

---

3 **Written Practice** *(Continued)*

Math Conversations

Discussion opportunities are provided below.

Problem 22 **Connect**

*"How many products will be formed when
this expression is expanded? Explain your
answer."* Four; Sample explanation: each
of the four terms in parentheses represents
one factor of a product that has 5 or 2 as its
other factor.

*"What is the next step to be completed
after finding those products?"* collect like
terms

After the problem has been completed and
students understand why $3x - 9$ is the correct
answer, challenge volunteers to factor $3x - 9$.
$3(x - 3)$

(continued)

Math Conversations
Discussion opportunities are provided below.

Problem 26a [Evaluate]
Invite a number of volunteers to each write a proportion on the board or overhead that can be used to solve the problem. Discuss the proportions with students and identify those which correctly represent the problem. Then ask students to choose a proportion and use it to solve the problem. Sample: $\frac{6}{30} = \frac{1}{n}$

Problem 26b [Evaluate]
"Explain how division can be used to find the floor plan dimensions of the kitchen."
Since the actual kitchen is 10 feet by 20 feet and we know that 1 inch in the drawing represents 5 feet, divide 10 feet by 5 and divide 20 feet by 5 to find the number of inches.

Problem 27 [Analyze]
Point out that a trapezoid has two bases and the terms b_1 and b_2 represent those bases.

Errors and Misconceptions
Problem 27
Watch for students who assume that the subscripts 1 and 2 in the formula $A = \frac{b_1 + b_2}{2}$ represent exponents.

Explain that the subscripts are simply used to distinguish one base of the trapezoid from the other base. In the formula, students should note that because the addition of two addends is commutative, the bases are interchangeable.

▶* **26.** [Evaluate] Richard drew the floor plan of his dream house. On his scale drawing of a kitchen, he drew a 6 in. segment to represent a distance of 30 ft.
(35)
   a. Each inch in the drawing represents what distance in the house? 5 ft
   b. If Rick's kitchen is to measure 10 ft by 20 ft, what are the dimensions of the floor plan of the kitchen? 2 in. by 4 in.

▶* **27.** [Analyze] We can use this formula to find the area of a trapezoid.
(21)
$$A = \frac{b_1 + b_2}{2} \cdot h$$
   Solve for A if $b_1 = 5$, $b_2 = 7$, and $h = 3$. (Units are in centimeters.) 18 cm²

28. What is the length of the hypotenuse? **A**
(Inv. 2)
   A $\sqrt{80}$ **B** $\sqrt{81}$
   C 9.1   **D** 9.3

* **29.** Miguel is going to build a storage cube for his sports equipment. How many square feet of wood will he need to make a three-foot cube? 54 ft²
(43)

* **30.** A bakery produces 144 loaves (*l*) of bread per hour (*h*) every day. Which graph represents the relationship of time and the number of loaves baked? Is this a proportional relationship? How do we know? Write an equation that describes the relationship. What is the constant of proportionality?
(41)

Graph **B**; The relationship is proportional because the graph is a line that intersects the origin. *l* = 144*h* (*l* is number of loaves baked, *h* is the number of hours); 144 is the constant of proportionality.

▶ See Math Conversations in the sidebar.

Looking Forward
Solving problems using scientific notation prepares students for:
- **Lesson 51,** writing small numbers in scientific notation.
- **Lesson 57,** performing operations with small numbers in scientific notation.

• Graphing Functions

Objectives

- Identify a function's domain and range.
- Graph step functions and continuous functions on a coordinate plane.
- Use a function's graph to determine whether it is continuous and whether it is a direct proportion.

Materials

- **Power Up J** (in *Instructional Masters*)
- **Teacher-provided material: calculators**

Optional

- **Lesson Activity 7** (in *Instructional Masters*)

Power Up J

Math Language

New	Maintain
continuous function	function
direct proportion	
domain	
range	
step function	

Technology Resources

Student eBook Complete student textbook in electronic format.

Resources and Planner CD Assessment, reteaching, and instructional masters, plus a pacing calendar with standards.

Test and Practice Generator CD Create additional practice sheets and custom-made tests.

www.SaxonPublishers.com Visit for more student activities and planning materials.

Inclusion

Adaptations CD Adapted lessons, investigations, practice and assessments.

Meeting Standards

National Council of Teachers of Mathematics (NCTM)

Algebra

AL.1a Represent, analyze, and generalize a variety of patterns with tables, graphs, words, and, when possible, symbolic rules

AL.1b Relate and compare different forms of representation for a relationship

AL.1c Identify functions as linear or nonlinear and contrast their properties from tables, graphs, or equations

AL.4a Use graphs to analyze the nature of changes in quantities in linear relationships

Problem-Solving Strategy: Make It Simpler

Three painters paint a house in 3 days. How many houses could 6 painters paint in 6 days working at the same rate?

(Understand) **Understand the problem.**

"What information are we given?"

In 3 days, 3 men can paint 1 house.

"What makes this ratio problem unique?"

There are *three* values in proportion: men, houses, and days.

"What are we asked to do?"

Determine how many houses 6 men can paint in 6 days.

(Plan) **Make a plan.**

"What problem-solving strategy will we use?"

A ratio is a relationship between two values. We will work with this proportional reasoning problem that involves more than two ratios (such as the men to houses to days) by *making it simpler.*

"How will we efficiently deal with the three different values?"

We will compare two values at a time:
1. how an increase in the number of days affects the number of houses, and then
2. how the increase in men affects the number of houses.

(Solve) **Carry out the plan.**

"If 3 men paint 1 house every 3 days, how many houses can the 3 men paint in 6 days?"

The same number of men will be able to paint twice as many houses in twice as many days. The three men will be able to paint 2 houses in 6 days.

"If 3 men working together can paint 2 houses in 6 days, how many houses can 6 men paint in 6 days?"

Twice as many men in the same amount of time (6 days) will be able to paint twice as many houses. Six men will be able to paint 4 houses in 6 days.

(Check) **Look back.**

"Did we find the answer to the question that was asked?"

Yes. We found that 4 houses will be painted by 6 men in 6 days.

• Graphing Functions

facts | Power Up J

mental math

a. **Number Sense:** $8\frac{1}{2} \times 10$ $80 + 5 = 85$

b. **Statistics:** Find the mean of 5, 6, and 10. 7

c. **Fractional Parts:** Calculate a 20% tip on a bill of $30. $6

d. **Measurement:** The odometer read 5306.5 miles at the end of her trip. When she started, the odometer read 5103.5. How long was her trip? 203 miles

e. **Proportions:** If Zollie can write 40 multiplication facts in 2 minutes, how many can she write in 5 minutes? 100

f. **Geometry:** Two angles of a triangle measure 80° and 20°. Is the triangle a right triangle, an acute triangle, or an obtuse triangle? Explain. acute triangle (The third angle is 80°, so all 3 angles are acute.)

g. **Estimation:** Approximate the total: $2.47 plus $3.47 plus 5 at $6.99 $41

h. **Calculation:** Square 10, × 5, ÷ 10, × 2, $\sqrt{\ }$, × 4, − 4, $\sqrt{\ }$ 6

problem solving

Three painters paint a house in 3 days. How many houses could 6 painters paint in 6 days working at the same rate? 4 houses

Recall that a **function** is a rule that pairs one output number with each input number. The following picture of a function machine and two buckets illustrates the relationship between the **domain** (set of inputs) and **range** (set of outputs) of a function.

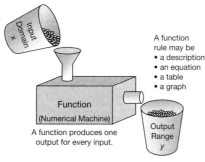

Input Domain x

A function rule may be
• a description
• an equation
• a table
• a graph

Function
(Numerical Machine)

A function produces one output for every input.

Output Range y

A function machine takes each element (member) from the domain "bucket" (set) and produces one element for the range "bucket."

Facts   Write the word that completes each sentence.

1. The distance around a circle is its _____ circumference _____.

2. Every point on a circle is the same distance from the _____ center _____.

3. The distance across a circle through its center is its _____ diameter _____.

4. The distance from a circle to its center is its _____ radius _____.

5. Two or more circles with the same center are _____ concentric _____ circles.

6. A segment between two points on a circle is a _____ chord _____.

7. Part of a circumference is an _____ arc _____.

8. A portion of a circle and its interior, bound by an arc and two radii, is a _____ sector _____.

9. Half of a circle is a _____ semicircle _____.

10. An angle whose vertex is the center of a circle is a _____ central _____ angle.

---

1 Power Up

Facts
Distribute **Power Up J** to students. See answers below.

Mental Math
Encourage students to share different ways to mentally compute these exercises. Strategies for exercises **a**, **c**, and **e** are listed below.

a. **Think of a Decimal**
$8\frac{1}{2} = 8.5$
$8.5 \times 10 = 85$
Multiply Whole Numbers, then Fractions
$8\frac{1}{2} \times 10 = 8 \times 10 + \frac{1}{2} \times 10 =$
$80 + 5 = 85$

c. **Use Math Sense**
10% of $30 = $3
20% of $30 = $6
Find a Fraction
$20\% = \frac{1}{5}$
$\frac{1}{5} \times \$30 = \$6$

e. **Write a Unit Rate**
40 facts in 2 min → 20 facts in 1 min
5 min × 20 facts/min = 100 facts
Use Math Sense
2 min → 40 facts
1 min → 20 facts
5 min → 100 facts

Problem Solving
Refer to **Power-Up Discussion**, p. 319B.

2 New Concepts

Math Language
In this lesson, students build additional vocabulary for working with functions: the terms *domain* and *range*. You may provide this aid for remembering which word refers to inputs: domain ends with *in*, and input begins with *in*.

(continued)

2 New Concepts (Continued)

Instruction

Provide students with copies of **Lesson Activity 7** Four Coordinate Planes or with graph paper. Continue to encourage sketching of the graphs on plain paper.

Example 1
Instruction

As you discuss part **a,** you might explain that zero hours would mean that a driver had not entered the lot. Point out that the inputs for the domain are the number of hours that a car is parked in the lot, not the number of hours that have passed since the lot opened.

For part **b,** ask why it is not possible for the parking charge to be an even number of dollars. Sample: After the first hour when the charge was $1, the charge is $2 more for every hour until $15 is reached. An odd number plus an even number is always an odd number.

After you finish part **c,** extend the example by asking students to use the information on the sign and the graph to decide when the cost per hour of parking is the least, the greatest, and the same. Cost per hour is least (94¢ an hour) if the driver parks for 16 hours; it is greatest ($1.875 an hour) for eight hours of parking; and it is the same ($1 an hour) for parking 1 hour or 15 hours.

(continued)

A checkout scanner at a store is a real-world example of a function machine. The input is the product code the scanner reads and the domain is the set of codes programmed for the scanner. The output is the price the register records for that product code and the range is the set of prices of the coded items. The function pairs a code with a price.

For each coded item there is only one price. Different coded items may have the same price, but each coded item has only one price.

Functions may be expressed with descriptions, equations, tables, or graphs. The sign in example 1 is an example of a description for a function that pairs the number of hours parked and the number of dollars charged for parking.

Example 1

The sign at right describes a function—a rule that relates hours parked to dollars charged.

a. What is the domain of the function?

b. What is the range of the function?

c. Graph the function.

> *Parking*
>
> **$1.00 for first hour**
> **$2.00 for each additional**
> **hour or part thereof**
> **$15.00 maximum**
> **Lot open 6 a.m. to 10 p.m.**
> **No overnight parking**

Solution

a. The domain of the function is the number of hours a car can be parked in the lot. Since the lot is open from 6:00 a.m. to 10:00 p.m., the domain is from a few moments in the lot up to a maximum of 16 hours, so the domain is the set of real numbers from **0–16.**

b. The range is the number of dollars charged for parking. For up to one hour the charge is $1.00. Any time during the second hour the charge is $3.00 ($1.00 + $2.00). During the third hour the charge is $5.00. The pattern of odd dollar charges continues to $15.00: **$1, $3, $5, ... $13, $15.**

c. We use the horizontal axis for the domain and the vertical axis for the range.

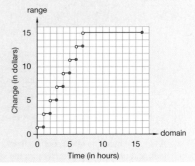

320   *Saxon* Math Course 3

Inclusion

Students may find graphing a step function difficult. Ask:

"Is a person who uses the parking garage only parking on the hour or is time continuous?" No, time is continuous.

"Is the cost continuous? That is, if a person parked for an hour and half, would he/she be charged less than $2? Explain." Sample: No, the charge jumps from $1 in the first hour then to $2 for the entire second hour.

Explain that the reason why the graph in example 1 covers each hour with a segment is because time is continuous. However, the reason why the graph uses steps for the cost is because the charge jumps at each hour up to hour 8.

The parking charge during an hour is flat, but as the hour passes the charge increases by two dollars until the maximum charge is reached. Because of the stair step pattern, this type of function is sometimes called a **step function**. The small filled and empty circles on each step of the graph mean that at the exact hour the charge is the lower amount, not the higher amount. The next minute the charge jumps to the next level.

A formula can be an example of a function expressed as an equation. Consider the formula that computes the perimeter of a square given a side length.

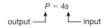

$$P = 4s$$

output ──── input

Example 2

Consider the function $P = 4s$.

a. What is the domain?

b. What is the range?

c. Create a table for some function pairs.

d. Graph the function.

Solution

a. The domain is any number that can represent a side length. Lengths are positive, so any positive number on the number line can represent a length. Thus the domain is **all positive real numbers.**

b. The range is any number that can represent the perimeter. A perimeter is a length, so any positive number on the number line can represent the perimeter of a square. The range is **all positive real numbers.**

c. To create a table we choose input numbers (side length) and use the function rule to find the output (perimeter). Although we may choose any positive real number for s, we decide to select numbers that are easy to compute and graph.

$P = 4s$

s	P
1	4
2	8
3	12

d. Since lengths are positive, the graph of the function is in the first quadrant only. We graph the pairs from the table and notice that the points are aligned. We could have chosen and graphed (4, 16), (0.5, 2), (1.5, 6), (0.1, 0.4), or countless other pairs. All such pairs would be aligned with these points. By drawing a line from the origin through the points from the table, the line becomes a representation of all possible side-length and perimeter pairs for the function.

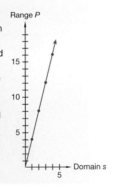

Range P

Domain s

Lesson 47   321

2 New Concepts *(Continued)*

Example 2
Instruction

For parts **a** and **b**, you may want to point out that zero is not part of the domain or the range because it is not a positive real number.

For part **c**, you may explain that the graph seems to begin at the origin. This is because the point (0, 0) would satisfy the equation, but that point is actually not included in the graph because zero is not positive and cannot represent a length.

Ask a volunteer to explain what a point on the line represents. Sample: The x-coordinate represents the side length of a square, and the y-coordinate represents the perimeter of that square.

(continued)

Math Background

The *floor function*, also called the *greatest integer function*, is a well-known step function. The floor function, denoted $y = \lfloor x \rfloor$, gives the greatest integer less than x. For example, $\lfloor 5.8 \rfloor = 5$ and $\lfloor -1.3 \rfloor = -2$. The domain of the floor function is all real numbers, and the range is the set of integers.

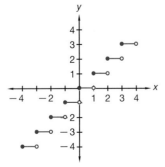

Instruction

After example 2, discuss the features that make this function a continuous function. Ask whether the graph is proportional and have students explain their answers. Sample: Yes, because the line is aligned with the origin and rises to the right.

As you discuss the *Verify* question, you may want to check that students remember how to use cross products to check that two ratios form a proportion.

Example 3

Instruction

For part **a**, remind students to choose values for p that are easy to work with.

As students work on part **b**, circulate and check that all students are graphing the function correctly.

Discuss answers to part **c**. Ask students how the equation for this function is different from the equation for example 2.

(continued)

One way to verify is to reduce both ratios. Since both ratios reduce to $\frac{1}{4}$, the ratios are equal and form a proportion. Another way to verify is to cross multiply to see if the cross products are equal. Since $8 \cdot 3 = 2 \cdot 12$, the ratios are equal and form a proportion.

Visit www.SaxonPublishers.com/ActivitiesC3 for a graphing calculator activity.

Notice how the graph in example 2 is different from the graph in example 1. The graph in example 2 is not interrupted with gaps. This means that the function $P = 4s$ is a **continuous function**.

Notice two more important features of the graph in example 2.

  1. The graph begins at the origin.

  2. All points in the graph are aligned.

Together, these two features indicate that the function is a **direct proportion**. We will be studying direct proportions in many lessons in this book. Any two pairs from a direct proportion form a proportion. Take (2, 8) and (3, 12) for example.

$$\frac{2}{8} = \frac{3}{12}$$

Verify How can we verify that these two ratios form a proportion?

Example 3

An online auction service charges a 30¢ listing fee plus 6% of the selling price for items up to $25. The total service charge (*c*) is a function of the selling price (*p*) of an item.

$$c = 0.30 + 0.06p$$

  a. Use a calculator to generate a table of pairs of values for the selling price and service charge.

  b. Graph the function on axes like the ones below.

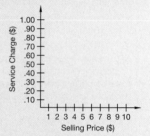

  c. Is the relationship a proportion? How do you know?

Solution

  a. We choose input values (selling prices) that are easy to calculate.

p	c
1	0.36
2	0.42
3	0.48
4	0.54
5	0.60

Teacher Tip

Make plenty of **extra copies of Lesson Activity 7** Four Coordinate Planes. Students who need the structure of a premade coordinate plane should have access to them for use during class or for homework.

Encourage students to try sketching a coordinate plane and their graphs on plain paper.

b. We graph the points from our table on the given axes and draw a line connecting the points.

c. The relationship is not proportional. The graph does not intercept zero and the price/charge ratio is not constant.

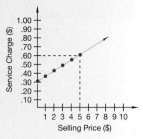

Service Charge ($) / Selling Price ($)

Practice Set

a. *Represent* The directions on the can of paint described a function: One gallon covers 400 sq. ft of a sealed, non-textured surface. On graph paper draw and extend axes like the ones illustrated. Then create a function table relating quantity of paint in gallons (*g*) to area (*A*) covered in square feet. Use numbers from the table to graph the function on your paper.

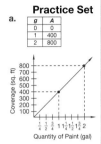

g	A
0	0
1	400
2	800

Coverage (sq. ft) / Quantity of Paint (gal)

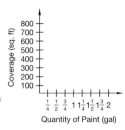

Coverage (sq. ft) / Quantity of Paint (gal)

b. Referring to problem **a,** which equation below describes the relationship between the number of gallons (*g*) of paint and the area (*A*) covered in square feet? **B**

A $A = 400 + g$ **B** $A = 400g$ **C** $A = \frac{400}{g}$ **D** $A = \frac{g}{400}$

c. Referring to problem **a,** painting 700 square feet of wall would require about how many *quarts* of paint?   7 quarts

d. Janine works in a high-rise building. When she wants to go to upper floors she enters an elevator and pushes a button (input), and the elevator takes her a distance above street level (output). Assuming that the building has 12 floors and that floors are 10 feet apart, graph the relationship between the floor Janine is on and her distance (elevation) above street level. Let the tick marks on the vertical axis (output) increase by tens.

e. In problem **d,** what is the domain of the function?   The domain is the counting numbers through 12 (or 1, 2, 3, 4, 5, 6, 7, 8, 9, 10, 11, 12).

f. Is the relationship described in problem **d** proportional? Why or why not?   The relationship is not proportional. Although the points are aligned, they are not aligned with the origin because there is no zero floor. The first floor is at street level. Therefore, the elevation/floor number ratios are not constant. (For example, $\frac{20}{3} \neq \frac{40}{5}$.)

Practice Set
Problem a Represent

Draw the following function table on the board or overhead. Explain that *g* represents the number of gallons of paint, and *A* represents the coverage area in square feet. Ask students to substitute values for *g* and use the relationship 1 gallon = 400 ft² to complete the table.

g	A

Make sure students understand that although countless numbers can be substituted for *g*, substituting whole numbers makes the arithmetic easier to complete.

Problem b Error Alert

If students did not use substitution to choose an equation, ask them to use substitution to check their answer.

Problem c Error Alert

Since the vertical axis interval is by tens, students should infer that the vertical axis represents distance above street level, and the horizontal axis is to be labeled from 1 to 12 by ones because it represents the various floors in the building.

Problem f Error Alert

Students should recall that in order for the relationship to be proportional, the points must fall on a straight line and must be aligned with the origin.

Math Conversations

Discussion opportunities are provided below.

Problem 1 *Analyze*

Before students complete any arithmetic, encourage them to discuss the problem, and describe one or more ways to make an estimate that gives a general idea of what to expect for an exact answer. Sample: The ratio of 2 buses to 11 cars tells us that most of the vehicles that entered the lot were cars. So we should expect most of the 650 vehicles in the lot to be cars.

After solving the problem, ask students to decide the reasonableness of the exact answer by comparing it to the estimate.

Problem 4 *Generalize*

"What factors will we use to find the coefficient of the product?" 4×3

"What exponent will be in the product of the powers of 10?" 7

"Ten to the seventh power is not a part of the correct answer. What does this fact tell you about the coefficient of the product of the factors?" Sample: The coefficient is greater than or equal to 10, or it is less than 1.

Problem 5 *Model*

Remind students that plotting only two points makes it difficult to recognize if the graph of the equation is incorrect because any two points form a line.

Also remind students that one way to check their yes or no answer is to substitute 3 for x and 1 for y in the equation $y = x - 1$. If the equation remains true after the substitutions, the point will be on the line.

(continued)

▶ *** 1.** *(45)* *Analyze* The ratio of buses to cars entering the lot was 2 to 11. If 650 vehicles entered the lot all together, how many were cars? 550 cars

2. *(45)* A pack of 8 collectable cards contains 1 rare card, 3 uncommon cards, and 4 common cards. If Javier has 45 packs of cards, how many more uncommon cards does he have than rare cards? 90 more

3. *(3, 4)* Kimberly used coupons worth $1.00 off and $1.25 off and two coupons for $1.50 off. If the discount of each of these coupons were doubled, how much would Kimberly save? $10.50

▶ *** 4.** *(28, 46)* *Generalize* Simplify: $(4.0 \times 10^3)(3.0 \times 10^4)$ 1.2×10^8

▶ *** 5.** *(41)* *Model* Graph the equation $y = x - 1$. Is the point $(3, 1)$ on the line? no

6. *(40)* Find the **a** area and **b** circumference of a circle with a radius of 5 in. Express the measures in terms of π. **a.** $25\,\pi$ in.^{2} **b.** $10\,\pi$ in.

7. *(42)* Find the volume of an aquarium with dimensions 1 ft $\times$ 2 ft $\times$ 1.5 ft. 3 ft^3

8. *(39)* Polly's pie shop is famous for its 12-inch blueberry pies. Is the circumference of Polly's pie greater or less than 1 yard? $3.14 \times 12 = 37.68$; 37.68 in. > 36 in.; the pie has a circumference greater than 1 yard.

For problems **9** and **10**, refer to the following information. Salvador has a yard of this shape. (Dimensions are in meters.) He would like to lay sod and fence his yard.

9. *(37)* How many square meters of sod will he need? 76 m^2

10. *(8, Inv. 2)* What length of fencing will he need if he fences all but one 10-meter edge of his yard? 26 m

Solve.

11. *(22, 38)* $\frac{4}{3}x = 12$ $x = 9$

12. *(13, 38)* $x - \frac{2}{5} = 12$ $x = 12\frac{2}{5}$

13. *(36, 38)* $4x^2 = 64$ $x = 4, -4$

14. *(44)* $\frac{24}{x} = \frac{15}{20}$ $x = 32$

15. *(21, 36)* **a.** Expand: $-5(4r - 2d - 1)$ $-20r + 10d + 5$ **b.** Factor: $4x - 28$ $4(x - 7)$

* 16. *(12)* **a.** Write 0.005 as a percent and as a reduced fraction. $\frac{1}{2}\%$ or 0.5%, $\frac{1}{200}$

b. Which of the three forms would be most convenient for finding 0.5% of $1000? See student work. Sample: The decimal form can be quickly multiplied: 0.005 ($1000) = $5

Simplify.

17. *(27, 36)* $\frac{24wx^2y}{-12xy}$ $-2wx$

18. *(13, 22)* $\frac{3}{8} - \frac{1}{2} \cdot \frac{2}{3} \cdot \frac{3}{4}$ $\frac{1}{8}$

5. [graph showing line with point (3, 1)]

19. $1\frac{2}{3} \div 3\frac{1}{3} + 1\frac{5}{6}$ $2\frac{1}{3}$
(13, 23)

20. $\dfrac{(-12)-(-2)(-3)}{-(-2)(-3)}$ 3
(33, 36)

21. $\dfrac{1.2-0.12}{0.012}$ 90
(24, 25)

22. $(-1)^2 + (-1)^3$ 0
(36)

23. Combine like terms: $2(x + 1) + 3(x + 2)$ (Hint: Expand first using the
(31, 36)   distributive property.) $5x + 8$

▶ **24.**   *Analyze*   Find the slope of the line that passes through points (0, 0) and
(44) $(2, -4)$. -2

* 25. The radius of this circle is 10 ft.
(40)
   a. Using 3.14 for π, what is the area of the
   circle? $314\ \text{ft}^2$

   b. What fraction of the circle is shaded?

   c. What is the combined area of the shaded
   regions? (Round to the nearest square
   foot.) $70\ \text{ft}^2$

25. b. $\frac{80}{360} = \frac{2}{9}$

* 26. For **a–c**, refer to these triangles.
(35)
   a. Redraw △*ABE* and △*ACD* as two
   separate triangles.

   b. Explain how you know that
   △*ABE* ~ △*ACD*.

   c. What is the scale factor from △*ABE* to
   △*ACD*? $\frac{5}{3}$

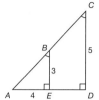

26. a.

26. b. Since the
measure of ∠*A*
equals itself, and
given the other
corresponding
angle measures
are equal, we see
that the triangles
satisfy the angle-
angle-angle
similarity criteria.

27. For the equation $E = mc^2$, find E when $m = 0.001$ and $c = 3.0 \times 10^8$.
(28) 9.0×10^{13}

28. Express $\frac{1}{12}$ **a** as a decimal number and **b** as a percent.   **a.** $0.08\overline{3}$ **b.** $8\frac{1}{3}\%$
(30)

▶* **29.** Amelia is making a scratching post for her cat. She has a rectangular
(43)   prism post that is 4 inches wide by 4 inches deep by 18 inches tall. How
   much carpet does Amelia need to go around the post without covering
   the top or bottom of the post? $288\ \text{in.}^2$

30. Two business partners split their profits
(41)   evenly. The table shows possible *x*- and
   y-values with *x* representing their profit and
   y representing the amount they each receive.

   a. Write an equation for the function shown in
   the table. $y = \frac{1}{2}x$ or $y = \frac{x}{2}$

   b. Graph the function.

   c. Is the relationship proportional? Explain
   your answer.

x	y
0	0
2	1
4	2
6	3
8	4

30. b.

Possible explanations:
   1. The table includes 0, 0, and all other pairs form a constant $\frac{y}{x}$ ratio of $\frac{1}{2}$.
   2. The equation $y = \frac{1}{2}x$ matches the $y = kx$ equation for a proportional
   relationship.
   3. The graph of the function is a line intersecting the origin.

Lesson 47   **325**

▶ See Math Conversations in the sidebar.

Math Conversations
Discussion opportunities are provided below.

Problem 24   *Analyze*
Before students write the slope in simplest
form, have them recall the rules for
determining the sign of the product or
quotient of two integers.

• If the signs of two integers are the same,
  the product or quotient of those integers
  is positive.
• If the signs of two integers are different,
  the product or quotient of those integers
  is negative.

Errors and Misconceptions
Problem 29
To find the area of the four faces, some
students may assume that the sum of
four addends represents the area. Because
multiplication is, generally speaking, easier to
complete than a number of repeated additions,
help students infer that the four faces to be
carpeted are congruent, and the product of 4
and the area of one face represents the amount
of carpeting Amelia will need.

Looking Forward
Graphing functions prepares students for:

• **Lesson 56,** writing the slope-intercept equation of a line.

• **Investigation 8,** working with scatterplots.

• **Lesson 82,** graphing equations using intercepts.

• **Lesson 89,** solving problems with two unknowns by graphing.

• **Lesson 98,** determining whether relationships between two variables are
  functions.

• **Investigation 11,** working with non-linear functions.

• Percent of a Whole

Objectives

• Use a three-row ratio table to solve word problems involving percent of a whole.

Lesson Preparation

Materials

• **Power Up J** (in *Instructional Masters*)

Power Up J

Math Language

Maintain	English Learners (ESL)
percent	successive
proportion	
ratio	

Technology Resources

Student eBook Complete student textbook in electronic format.

Resources and Planner CD Assessment, reteaching, and instructional masters, plus a pacing calendar with standards.

Test and Practice Generator CD Create additional practice sheets and custom-made tests.

www.SaxonPublishers.com Visit for more student activities and planning materials.

Inclusion

 Adaptations CD Adapted lessons, investigations, practice and assessments.

Meeting Standards

National Council of Teachers of Mathematics (NCTM)

Numbers and Operations

NO.1a Work flexibly with fractions, decimals, and percents to solve problems

NO.1d Understand and use ratios and proportions to represent quantitative relationships

NO.3d Develop, analyze, and explain methods for solving problems involving proportions, such as scaling and finding equivalent ratios

Algebra

AL.1a Represent, analyze, and generalize a variety of patterns with tables, graphs, words, and, when possible, symbolic rules

AL.3a Model and solve contextualized problems using various representations, such as graphs, tables, and equations

Problem-Solving Strategy: Make a Table/Find a Pattern

The mystery man listened and replied. Juan said 1, the mystery man said 13. Samantha said 11, the mystery man said 113. Francisco said 5, the mystery man said 53. Wally whispered. The mystery man said 5283. What did Wally whisper?

(Understand) **Understand the problem.**

"What important *information are we given?*"

A 1 results in a 13; 11 becomes 113; 5 becomes 53; and a whispered number becomes 5283.

"What are we asked to do?"

Determine the number Wally whispered.

(Plan) **Make a plan.**

"What problem-solving strategy will we use?"

We will *make a table* to help us *find the pattern.*

(Solve) **Carry out the plan.**

"How do we begin?"

We will record the students' input and the mystery man's output.

"What are possible rules?"

Have students list several possible rules for the input of 1 resulting in an output of 13 to give them a substantial list to eliminate from when they consider the other input-output pairs.

Student	Possible rule(s)	Mystery Man
1	$n + 12$; $n \times 13$	$= 13$
11	$(n \times 11) - 8$; $(n \times 10) + 3$	$= 113$
5	$(n \times 10) + 3$	$= 53$
528	$(n \times 10) + 3$	$= 5283$

"How did we algebraically solve for Wally's whispered number?"

$(5283 - 3) \div 10 = 528$

(Check) **Look back.**

"Did we find the answer to the question that was asked?"

Yes. We found that Wally's whispered number was 528.

"Someone said the mystery man is just adding a 3 to the end of the number a person says. How is that rule similar to or different from the rule we found?"

"Adding a 3" is the same in both rules. However, "adding a 3 to the end of a number" means every other digit of the number shifts to the left one place. That shift happens by multiplying by ten. To write the mathematical rule as a formula, we need to show the operations that produce the output from the input.

• Percent of a Whole

1 Power Up

Facts
Distribute **Power Up J** to students. See answers below.

Mental Math
Encourage students to share different ways to mentally compute these exercises. Strategies for exercises **a** and **c** are listed below.

a. Regroup, then Multiply
$\$3.25 \times 4 = \$3 \times 4 + 25¢ \times 4$
$= \$12 + \$1 = \$13$

Double and Halve
$\$3.25 \times 4 = \$6.50 \times 2 = \$13.00$

c. Use a Decimal
75% of $\$1000 = 0.75 \times \$1000 = \$750$

Find a Fraction
$75\% = \frac{3}{4}$
$\frac{3}{4} \times \$1000 = \$750$

Problem Solving
Refer to **Power-Up Discussion,** p. 326B.

2 New Concepts

Instruction
Ask students to tell what everyday experiences they have had with percents. Possible responses include:
• Buying jeans on sale
• Calculating a tip at a restaurant
• Sales tax
• Chance for rain in the weather forecast

Remind students that they used a three-row ratio table when they solved ratio problems involving totals.

(continued)

Power Up   *Building Power*

facts   Power Up J

mental math

a. Number Sense: $\$3.25 \times 4$ $\$13$

b. Measurement: How many degrees below "freezing" is the temperature shown on the thermometer? (Water freezes at 32°F.)   6°

c. Percent: How much is 75% of $1,000? $750

d. Scientific Notation: Write 63,400,000 in scientific notation. 6.34×10^7

e. Rate: Maria walks 4 miles per hour south, while Reginald strolls 3 miles per hour north. If they start at the same place and same time, how long will it take them to be 14 miles apart?   2 hours

f. Algebra: $x + 3 = 5.8$ 2.8

g. Geometry: Approximate the volume of this prism.   210 m³

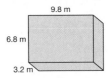

9.8 m
6.8 m
3.2 m

h. Calculation: $12 \div 4, \times 3, \times 4, \sqrt{}, \times 8, + 1, \sqrt{}, \times 9, + 1, \sqrt{}$ 8

problem solving
The mystery man listened and replied. Juan said 1, the mystery man said 13. Samantha said 11, the mystery man said 113. Francisco said 5, the mystery man said 53. Wally whispered. The mystery man said 5283. What did Wally whisper?   528

New Concept   *Increasing Knowledge*

Percents are commonly used to describe part of a whole.

• Shanna answered 92% of the questions correctly.
• A basketball player has made 80% of her free throws.
• The governor was elected with 56% of the vote.

In this lesson we will use a three-row ratio table to help us solve percent problems about parts of a whole. A percent is a ratio, with the given percent representing the part and 100% representing the total.

Facts   Write the word that completes each sentence.

1. The distance around a circle is its _____ circumference.
2. Every point on a circle is the same distance from the _____ center.
3. The distance across a circle through its center is its _____ diameter.
4. The distance from a circle to its center is its _____ radius.
5. Two or more circles with the same center are _____ concentric _____ circles.
6. A segment between two points on a circle is a _____ chord.
7. Part of a circumference is an _____ arc.
8. A portion of a circle and its interior, bound by an arc and two radii, is a _____ sector.
9. Half of a circle is a _____ semicircle.
10. An angle whose vertex is the center of a circle is a _____ central _____ angle.

Example 1

Thirty percent of the students ride the bus. If 210 do not ride the bus, how many students are there in all?

Solution

We draw a three-row ratio table and fill it in as completely as possible.

If 30% ride the bus, then 70% do not. To write a proportion we use the row with two known numbers and the row with the number we want to find.

	Percent	Count
Bus	30	a
Not Bus	(70)	210
Total	100	t

$$\frac{70}{100} = \frac{210}{t}$$

$$70t = 21{,}000$$

$$t = 300$$

There were **300 students** in all.

Example 2

Thinking Skill

Analyze

How could we use the answer to find what percent of the questions Shanna answered incorrectly?
Subtract:
100% − 85% = 15%. Shanna answered 15% of the questions incorrectly.

Shanna correctly answered 17 of the 20 questions on the game show. What percent of the questions did she answer correctly?

Solution

In an earlier lesson we found the fraction of correct answers and then found the equivalent percent. Here we use a proportion to find the percent Shanna answered correctly. We draw a three-row ratio table and fill it in as completely as possible. We want to find the percent for the number correct, so we use the numbers in the first and third rows to write the proportion.

	Percent	Count
Correct	c	17
Incorrect	n	3
Total	100	20

$$\frac{c}{100} = \frac{17}{20}$$

$$20c = 17 \cdot 100$$

$$\frac{20c}{20} = \frac{17 \cdot 100}{20}$$

$$c = 85$$

We find that **85%** of Shanna's answers were correct.

Practice Set ▶ *Formulate* Solve each of these problems using a proportion. Begin by making a ratio table.

  a. Mariah has read 135 of the 180 pages in the book. What percent of the book has she read?   75%

▶ See Math Conversations in the sidebar.

Example 1
Instruction

Ask why we can write 70 in the row labeled "Not Bus." Sample: We know that Bus plus Not Bus will total 100%, so since Bus is 30%, we subtract 30% from 100% to get 70%.

Point out that the proportion could also have been solved by noticing that the relationship between the Counts and the Percents shows that a Count is 3 times a Percent.

Example 2
Instruction

Emphasize the importance of filling in the table accurately. If the numbers are not entered correctly, the proportion will not represent the situation and the answer will be wrong.

Extend the Thinking Skill *Analyze* question by asking how the ratio table could be used to find the percent of questions Shanna answered incorrectly. Sample: Use the Incorrect row and the Total row to form this proportion: $\frac{n}{100} = \frac{3}{20}$.

Practice Set
Problems a–d (Error Alert)

Remind students that one way to check an exact answer for reasonableness is to make an estimate before solving a problem, and then compare the exact answer to the estimate after the problem has been solved.

Before solving problems **a–d**, ask students to make and record an estimate of each exact answer, or ask them to discuss the problems as a class and make the estimates collectively.

After the problems have been solved, have students check for reasonableness by comparing the exact answers to the estimates.

Math Background

Does it ever make sense to talk about more than 100% of a whole?

Yes. For example, airlines often sell more than 100% of the seats on a flight. Suppose an airplane has seats for 160 passengers, but the airline sells 175 tickets for the flight. What percent of the total number of seats did they sell? You can answer this question by solving a proportion.

Step:	Justification:
$\frac{175}{160} = \frac{x}{100}$	Wrote a proportion
$17{,}500 = 160x$	Cross multiplied
$\frac{17{,}500}{160} = x$	Divided both sides by 160
$x \approx 109\%$	Simplified

3 Written Practice

Math Conversations

Discussion opportunities are provided below.

Problem 1 **Analyze**

Have students describe one or more ways to make an estimate that gives a general idea of what to expect for an exact answer. Sample: The ratio of 5 people watching whales to 7 people fishing tells us that a few more people were fishing than were watching whales. So we should expect that a few more than one-half of the 72 people were fishing.

After solving the problem, ask students to decide the reasonableness of the exact answer by comparing it to the estimate.

Problem 5 **Evaluate**

"In what quadrant is the point (−2, 2) located?" second

"On which axis is the point (2, 0) located?" the x-axis

"When we use a number to describe the slope of the line that passes through these points, do you expect that number to be positive, or negative? Explain why." Negative; Sample explanation: because the leftmost point (−2, 2) is above the x-axis and the rightmost point (2, 0) is on the x-axis, the line slopes downward from left to right and a downward slope is negative.

Problem 15

Explain that the notation following each whole number represents inches.

Errors and Misconceptions

Problem 1

If students write ratio tables to represent the problem and then compare those tables, they may find different arrangements of the terms. However, each table can be used to solve the problem if it correctly represents the relationship of the terms in the problem. For example, two different ratio tables to represent problem 1 are shown below.

Whale Watching	5	w
Fishing	7	f
Total	12	72

Fishing	7	f
Whale Watching	5	w
Total	12	72

Although the arrangement of the terms in each table is different, and the proportions derived from those terms are different, the values of f (f = 42) and w (w = 30) are the same.

(continued)

---

b. McGregor is growing alfalfa on 180 acres, which is 30% of his farmland. McGregor has how many acres of farmland? 600 acres

c. The frequency of the letter *e* in written English is about 13%. On a page of a novel that has about 2000 letters per page, about how many occurrences of the letter *e* can we expect to find? 260

d. The Springfield Sluggers won 64% of their games and lost 9 games. How many games did the Sluggers win? 16 games

Written Practice   *Strengthening Concepts*

▶ *** 1.** **Analyze** The ratio of people watching whales to people fishing was 5 to 7. If there were 72 in all, how many people were fishing? 42
(45)

2. Sergio purchased 4 items for $1.50 each. Sales tax was 8.25%. What was the total price? $6.50
(4, 11)

3. At back-to-school night, $\frac{1}{2}$ of the algebra students came, and $\frac{1}{3}$ of the pre-algebra students came. If there are 62 algebra students and 66 pre-algebra students, how many of the students came to back-to-school night? 53 students
(5)

4. Betsy correctly answered 19 of the 25 trivia questions. What percent of the questions did she answer correctly? 76%
(48)

▶ *** 5.** **Evaluate** Find the slope of the line passing through points (−2, 2) and (2, 0). $-\frac{1}{2}$
(44)

Simplify.

6. $\frac{a^2b^2c}{12a^2c^2}$ $\frac{b^2}{12c}$
(27)

7. $\frac{4}{9} \div \frac{2}{3} - \frac{1}{2}$ $\frac{1}{6}$
(13, 22)

8. $3^3 \div 3 + 3 - 3(3)$ 3
(15, 21)

9. $\left(\frac{2}{5}\right)^2 - \left(\frac{1}{5}\right)^2$ $\frac{3}{25}$
(13, 15)

* 10. $\frac{5.2 \times 10^7}{1.3 \times 10^4}$ 4×10^3
(46)

* 11. $(5.0 \times 10^7)(3.0 \times 10^4)$ 1.5×10^{12}
(46)

12. $(12.4 + 2)(1 - 0.998)$ 0.0288
(24, 25)

* 13. Graph $y = x - 3$. Is the point (3, 0) on the line? yes
(41)

* 14. Find the **a** area and **b** the circumference of a circle that has a diameter of 40 cm. Use 3.14 for π.   **a.** 1256 cm²; **b.** 125.6 cm
(39, 40)

▶ *** 15.** Find the volume of a drawer with dimensions 10" × 15" × 4".   600 in.³
(42)

16. For **a–c**, refer to this triangle.
(20, Inv. 2)
  a. Classify the triangle by angles. right
  b. Find the area of the triangle. 120 cm²
  c. Find the perimeter of the triangle. 60 cm

Solve.

17. $x - 3\frac{1}{3} = 2\frac{1}{2}$ $x = 5\frac{5}{6}$
(13, 38)

18. $x - \frac{2}{3} = \frac{5}{6}$ $x = 1\frac{1}{2}$
(13, 38)

13.
(3, 0)

▶ See Math Conversations in the sidebar.

21. b. Possible answer: Using the percent, I may compute 200% (double) then add 50% (half): $320,000 + $80,000 = $400,000

19. $4x^2 = 400$ $x = 10, -10$
(36, 38)

* 20. $\frac{1.2}{3} = \frac{x}{2}$ $x = 0.8$
(44)

21. **a.** Write 250% as a decimal and reduced fraction. $2.5, \frac{5}{2}$ or $2\frac{1}{2}$
(11, 12)

b. Which of the three forms would you choose to find the price of a home that is now worth 250% of its original price of $160,000?

Combine like terms to simplify.

22. $abc - cab + bac - 2b^2$ **23.** $5x^2y - 4yx^2 + 2x - x$ $x^2y + x$
(31) $abc - 2b^2$ (31)

* 24. At a high-rise hotel, the ground floor is 3 feet
(41) above street level. Each successive floor is
10 feet above the one below it. At the right is
a chart of the number of floors (x) a person
is above the ground floor and how high they
are in feet (y) above street level. Write an
equation for the function shown in the table.
Is the function a proportional relationship?
How do you know? $y = 10x + 3$; The relationship is not proportional
because the ratio $\frac{y}{x}$ is not constant.

x	y
1	13
2	23
3	33
4	43

* 25. A circle with a radius of 4 in. is divided into congruent sectors, each with
(40) a central angle of 30°.

a. How many sectors cover the circle?   12

b. What is the area of one sector? (Round to the nearest square inch.)
4 in.²

26. 13.1 mi/hr

▶ **26.** A rate formula is $r = \frac{d}{t}$. Find r when $d = 26.2$ miles and $t = 2$ hours.
(14, 25)

27. An entomologist recorded the lengths of two newly discovered species
(24) of beetles. The first beetle was 2.76 cm and the second was 3.14 cm
long. What is the difference in their lengths?   0.38 cm

28. When Jon began eating lunch the clock read 12:30. Fifteen minutes
(26) later the clock read 12:45. Describe the transformation of the minute
hand on the clock between 12:30 and 12:45.   90° rotation

▶*** 29.** _Evaluate_ Rivera is creating a package for a new product. The package
(43) is a box that is 5 in. by 9 in. by 14 in. He needs to let the manufacturer
know the amount of surface area for each box. What is the surface
area?   482 in.²

* 30. The graph shows the relationship between
(41) the number of servings of soup (s) and
the number of teaspoons (t) of salt in the
soup. Is the relationship proportional? If the
relationship is proportional, write an equation
for the relationship and state the constant
of proportionality, k.   The relationship is
proportional. The equation is $s = \frac{5}{3}t$ or $t = \frac{3}{5}s$
(s is the number of servings and t is the number
of teaspoons of salt); $k = \frac{5}{3}$

Number of People Soup Can Serve

Teaspoons of Salt

▶ See Math Conversations in the sidebar.

Math Conversations
Discussion opportunities are provided below.

Problem 26 Connect
Extend the Problem
Challenge students to use inverse operations
to solve $r = \frac{d}{t}$ for d, and then solve it for t.
$d = rt$ and $t = \frac{d}{r}$

Problem 29 Evaluate
Ask students to write an equation that can be
used to find the surface area of the box and
represents the fact that the opposite faces of
the box are congruent. Sample:
$A = 2(5$ in. $\times 9$ in.$) + 2(5$ in. $\times 14$ in.$) +$
$2(9$ in. $\times 14$ in.$)$

English Learners
For problem **24** explain the
meaning of the word **successive.**
Say:

_"Successive means to follow an
order without a break."_

Write the following lists of numbers
on the board and ask which one
shows successive numbers. Ask why
the numbers are successive.

2, 3, 4, 5, 6, 7, 8

5, 6, 9, 12, 13, 14

The first list is successive because
there is no break in the numbers.

Looking Forward
Calculating percents of wholes
prepares students for:

• **Lesson 58,** solving percent
problems with equations.

• **Lesson 67,** finding percents of
change.

• **Lesson 71,** finding percent
changes of dimensions.

• Solving Rate Problems with Proportions and Equations

Objectives
- Solve rate problems by writing and solving proportions.
- Solve rate problems by writing an equation using the unit rate.

Lesson Preparation

Materials
- **Power Up J** (in *Instructional Masters*)

Power Up J

Math Language

Maintain
rate
unit rate

Technology Resources

Student eBook Complete student textbook in electronic format.

Resources and Planner CD Assessment, reteaching, and instructional masters, plus a pacing calendar with standards.

Test and Practice Generator CD Create additional practice sheets and custom-made tests.

www.SaxonPublishers.com Visit for more student activities and planning materials.

Inclusion

Adaptations CD Adapted lessons, investigations, practice and assessments.

Meeting Standards

National Council of Teachers of Mathematics (NCTM)

Numbers and Operations

NO.1d Understand and use ratios and proportions to represent quantitative relationships

NO.3d Develop, analyze, and explain methods for solving problems involving proportions, such as scaling and finding equivalent ratios

Algebra

AL.2c Use symbolic algebra to represent situations and to solve problems, especially those that involve linear relationships

AL.3a Model and solve contextualized problems using various representations, such as graphs, tables, and equations

Measurement

ME.2f Solve simple problems involving rates and derived measurements for such attributes as velocity and density

Problem-Solving Strategy: Use Logical Reasoning/ Guess and Check

Problem: Five coins totaled $1. What are the coins?

(Understand) **Understand the problem.**

"What important *information are we given?*"

Five coins total $1.00.

"What are we asked to do?"

Determine what the five coins are.

(Plan) **Make a plan.**

"What problem-solving strategy will we use?"

We will *use logical reasoning* to intelligently *guess and check.*

(Solve) **Carry out the plan.**

"Which coin can we eliminate entirely from our options?"

The penny. We would need to use pennies in groups of five to to have a result that is a multiple of 5 or 10 (which $1.00 is), but we can only have five coins total for this problem, so the use of pennies is not an option.

"Can five coins total a dollar without using a half dollar?"

No. Four quarters total a dollar with four coins. Three quarters total 75¢, but no two coins total 25¢. Two quarters total 50¢, but three coins less than a quarter cannot total 50¢.

"What combinations of coins that include a half dollar total $1.00?"

HD	Q	D	N	TOTAL
2				2 coins
1	2			3 coins
1	1	2	1	5 coins
1	1	1	3	6 coins

(Check) **Look back.**

"Did we find the answer to the question that was asked?"

Yes. We found that the five coins that total $1.00 are a half dollar, a quarter, two dimes, and a nickel.

"What problem-solving strategy could we use to verify that the solution is correct?"

We can *write a number sentence:* $1(.50) + 1(.25) + 2(.10) + 1(.05) = \$1.00$.

Facts
Distribute **Power Up J** to students. See answers below.

Mental Math
Encourage students to share different ways to mentally compute these exercises. Strategies for exercises **a**, **f**, and **g** are listed below.

a. Multiply by 2 Twice
$10.5 \times 4 = 10.5 \times 2 \times 2 =$
$21 \times 2 = 42$
Regroup, then Multiply
$10.5 \times 4 = (10 \times 4) + (0.5 \times 4) =$
$40 + 2 = 42$

f. Cross Products
$\frac{6}{x} = \frac{12}{2}$
$12x = 12$
$x = 1$
Use Math Sense
$12 \times \frac{1}{2} = 6$, so we multiply 2 by $\frac{1}{2}$ to find x.
$2 \times \frac{1}{2} = 1$

g. Use Math Sense
$\sqrt{x \cdot x} = x$
$\sqrt{3 \cdot 3} = 3$ and $\sqrt{2 \cdot 2} = 2$
$3 + 2 = 5$

Problem Solving
Refer to **Power-Up Discussion**, p. 330B.

2 New Concepts

Instruction
Use the *Math Language* feature in the sidebar to review rates. Explain that this lesson shows how to use two methods (proportions and equations) to solve rate problems. It is important for students to know how to use both of these methods, but they should feel free to use whichever method they prefer or is easier for a particular problem.

Point out that sometimes the directions in the student book will tell which method to use, and that in those cases, the prescribed method should be used.

(continued)

LESSON 49

• Solving Rate Problems with Proportions and Equations

facts   Power Up J

mental math

a. **Number Sense:** 10.5×4 42

b. **Statistics:** Find the mean of 13, 3, and 2.   6

c. **Fractional Parts:** Because of the sale, Liz only had to pay 75% of the original price of $28. How much did she pay? What was the percent of discount? $21, 25%

d. **Measurement:** Find the length of this section of cable. $2\frac{3}{8}$ in.

e. **Geometry:** Two angles of a triangle measure 50° and 30°. Is the triangle acute, obtuse, or right?   obtuse

f. **Proportions:** $\frac{6}{x} = \frac{12}{2}$ 1

g. **Powers/Roots:** $\sqrt{3 \cdot 3} + \sqrt{2 \cdot 2}$ 5

h. **Calculation:** Start with a dozen, $\times 4$, $+ 1$, $\sqrt{\ }$, $\times 5$, $+ 1$, $\sqrt{\ }$, $- 2$, $\sqrt{\ }$, $- 2$, $\sqrt{\ }$ 0

problem solving   Five coins total $1. What are the coins?   half dollar, quarter, dime, dime, nickel

New Concept   Increasing Knowledge

Math Language
Recall that a **rate** is a ratio that compares two different units. A **unit rate** is a rate with a denominator of 1 unit.

Recall that a rate is a ratio of two measures. For example, speed is a rate that is a ratio of distance to time. If an object's speed is constant, then the ratio of its distance traveled to time of travel is constant. A car traveling at an average speed of 50 miles per hour travels the following distances in the given time periods.

$\frac{50 \text{ miles}}{1 \text{ hour}}$	$\frac{100 \text{ miles}}{2 \text{ hours}}$	$\frac{150 \text{ miles}}{3 \text{ hours}}$	$\frac{200 \text{ miles}}{4 \text{ hours}}$

These ratios are equivalent, and each reduces to 50 miles/1 hour, which is the unit rate. Therefore, the relationship is proportional, and any two of these ratios form a proportion. Thus we may solve rate problems two ways: with proportions or by multiplying by the unit rate.

Facts   Write the word that completes each sentence.

1. The distance around a circle is its _____.   circumference

2. Every point on a circle is the same distance from the _____.   center

3. The distance across a circle through its center is its _____.   diameter

4. The distance from a circle to its center is its _____.   radius

5. Two or more circles with the same center are _____ circles.   concentric

6. A segment between two points on a circle is a _____.   chord

7. Part of a circumference is an _____.   arc

8. A portion of a circle and its interior, bound by an arc and two radii, is a _____.   sector

9. Half of a circle is a _____.   semicircle

10. An angle whose vertex is the center of a circle is a _____ angle.   central

These two methods are based on two forms of the rate equation.

1. The ratio is constant: $\frac{y}{x} = k$
2. The unit rate is constant: $y = kx$

All proportional relationships can be expressed with these two equations. Examples 1 and 2 show how we can use a proportion or multiplying by the unit rate to solve the same problem.

Example 1

If 6 books weigh 15 pounds, how much would 20 books weigh?

Solution

We do not need to find the weight per book. Instead we can use the given information to write a proportion. We are given the ratio of books to weight in one case and we are asked to complete the ratio in another case. We record the information in a table with the headings Case 1 and Case 2.

Thinking Skill

Connect

What method did we use to find the weight of 20 books? Why is the relationship proportional? We wrote and solved a proportion. Because the weight per book is constant.

	Case 1	Case 2
Books	6	20
Weight (lbs)	15	p

$$\rightarrow \frac{6}{15} = \frac{20}{p}$$

$$6p = 15 \cdot 20$$

$$p = \frac{15 \cdot 20}{6}$$

$$p = 50$$

We find that 20 books would weigh **50 pounds.**

Example 2

If 6 books weigh 15 pounds, what is the unit rate? What is the weight of 20 books? Write an equation that shows how to find the weight (w) of books knowing the number (n) of books and the unit rate.

Solution

To find the unit rate (weight of one book), we divide:

$$\frac{\text{weight } (w)}{\text{number } (n)} = \frac{15 \text{ pounds}}{6 \text{ books}} = 2.5 \text{ pounds per book}$$

To find the weight of a number of books, we multiply the number by the unit rate:

$$w = 2.5n$$

To find the weight of 20 books, we multiply the unit rate by 20:

$$w = 2.5 \cdot 20 = 50 \text{ lbs}$$

2 New Concepts (Continued)

Example 1

Instruction

Explain that estimating first is a good habit to develop. After solving the problem, we can quickly compare our answer to our estimate to determine whether our answer is reasonable.

We can begin by estimating so that we have an expectation for a reasonable answer. We are told the weight of 6 books and asked for the weight of 20 books. Since 20 is a little more than 3 times 6, we expect 20 books to weigh a little more than 3 times 15 pounds, that is, a little more than 45 pounds.

If necessary, use the Thinking Skill *Connect* question to review how to use cross products to solve a proportion. You might ask why a three-row ratio table is not used for this problem. Sample: There are no totals and it is not a percent problem.

Example 2

Instruction

Help students understand that they first need to find the unit rate (weight of one book) before they can write an equation to solve the problem. Explain that in some problems, the rate may be given, and in those cases, an equation using the rate can be written first.

Point out that the problems in examples 1 and 2 are the same. They were solved using two different methods, but the answer is the same. Take some time to compare the two methods and ask students to discuss which method they prefer to use. Sample: I prefer to use the ratio table to form a proportion because I do not need to know the unit rate to solve the problem.

(continued)

Lesson 49   331

Example 3
Instruction

As you discuss the *Predict* question, note that this is a way to estimate the answer before starting to solve the problem.

Once the ratio table is filled in, ask students to predict whether the value for *m* will be greater than or less than 50 and to explain their predictions. Sample: 27 is greater than 15, so *m* has to be greater than 50.

Example 4
Instruction

Extend this example by showing students how $d = \frac{5}{9}t$ can be written so that the variable for time, *t*, is isolated on the left side of the equation: $t = \frac{9}{5}d$ for the whole race. Ask students to compare solving the equation with solving the equation $m = \frac{50 \cdot 27}{15}$ in example 3. Sample: The computation is easier when you find the rate first.

(continued)

Example 3

Julio is riding in a 50 km bike race. He passed the 15 km mark in 27 minutes. If Julio continues to ride at the same rate, what will be his time for the whole race?

Solution

At the 15 km mark, Julio was less than one-third of the way through the race and he had been riding for nearly half an hour.

Predict Will it take Julio more or less than one hour to complete the whole race?   more than 1 hour

To solve the problem we can write a proportion. We use the given distance/time ratio for one point in the race and the incomplete ratio for the end of the race.

	One Point in the Race	End of the Race
Distance (km)	15	50
Time (min)	27	m

$$\frac{15}{27} = \frac{50}{m}$$

$$15m = 50 \cdot 27$$

$$m = \frac{50 \cdot 27}{15}$$

$$m = 90$$

If Julio continues riding at the same rate, his time for the whole race will be **90 minutes,** which is $1\frac{1}{2}$ hours.

Example 4

In example 3, what is Julio's rate in km/min? Write an equation that relates Julio's distance to time riding.

Solution

The ratio of distance to time is:

$$\frac{d}{t} = \frac{15 \text{ km}}{27 \text{ min}}$$

$$\frac{d}{t} = \frac{5 \text{ km}}{9 \text{ min}}$$

This can also be expressed:

$$d = \frac{5}{9}t$$

Math Background

In the graph of a rate equation, $y = kx$, the rate *k* is equal to the slope of the line. For example, if a car travels at a constant rate of 50 mph, then the distance traveled *d* in *h* hours is given by the equation $d = 50h$. In the graph of this equation, the slope is 50.

Notice that the slope is determined by the values of variables, not by the appearance of the graph. The slope appears slight because different scales are applied to the axes.

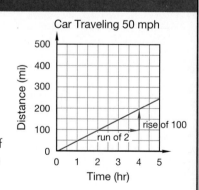

Example 5

Three tickets cost $20.25. How much would 7 tickets cost? What is the unit cost?

Solution

Since 7 is more than double 3, we expect 7 tickets to cost more than twice as much as 3 tickets, that is, more than $40.

We record the information in a ratio table. Then we write and solve a proportion.

	Actual	Estimate
Tickets	3	7
Price ($)	20.25	p

$$\frac{3}{20.25} = \frac{7}{p}$$

$$3p = 7 \cdot 20.5$$

$$p = \frac{7 \cdot 20.25}{3}$$

$$p = 47.25$$

Seven tickets would cost **$47.25,** which agrees with our original estimate. We find the unit cost by dividing $20.25 by 3. The unit cost is **$6.75.**

Practice Set

For problems **a–c** below record the information in a ratio table. Estimate an answer and then solve the problem by writing and solving a proportion.

▶ **a.** If 5 pounds of seedless grapes cost $3.80, how much would 9 pounds cost? $6.84

▶ **b.** If 8 cows eat 200 pounds of hay a day, how many pounds of hay would 20 cows eat in a day? 500 lbs

▶ **c.** Darcie can type 135 words in 3 minutes. At that rate, how many minutes would it take her to type 450 words? 10 min

▶ **d.** **Analyze** Find the price per pound of grapes in **a**, the pounds of hay per cow in **b**, and the words per minute in **c**. $0.76/pound, 25 pounds/cow, 45 words/min

e. Solve problems **a** and **b** again using a rate equation instead of a proportion. See student work and answers to **a** and **b**.

Written Practice *Strengthening Concepts*

Evaluate For problems **1–2**, record the information in a ratio table. Estimate and then solve by writing and solving a proportion.

▶ * **1.** Marcus can run 3 miles in 18 minutes. At that rate, how long will it take
 (49) him to run 7 miles? 42 minutes

* **2.** Felicia's pets eat thirty pounds of food in two weeks. How many pounds
 (49) of food would they eat in five weeks? 75 pounds

Lesson 49   333

▶ See Math Conversations in the sidebar.

---

2 New Concepts (Continued)

Example 5
Instruction
Discuss whether a better approach to solving the problem would be to find the unit cost first and write an equation given that the problem asked for the unit cost. Samples: Finding the unit cost first makes more sense, and the math might be easier.

Practice Set
Problems a–c Error Alert
Remind students to compare their exact answers to their estimates to help decide if the exact answers are reasonable.

Problem d Analyze
Point out that the answers represent the unit rate in problems **a, b,** and **c**. Choose one of the unit rates and use it to demonstrate how it can be used to solve the problem.

Point out that because proportions and unit rates can both be used to solve rate problems, students can use one method to solve the problem and the other method to check their work.

3 Written Practice

Math Conversations
Discussion opportunities are provided below.

Problem 1 Evaluate
"Name a proportion that can be used to solve the problem." Sample: $\frac{3}{18} = \frac{7}{t}$

"What is the unit rate in this problem?"
$\frac{6 \text{ minutes}}{1 \text{ mile}}$

Ask students to use the unit rate to solve the problem, then compare the answer to the answer found by using a proportion. The comparison should lead them to generalize that either method can be used to solve a rate problem.

(continued)

③ Written Practice *(Continued)*

Math Conversations

Discussion opportunities are provided below.

Problem 3 `Analyze`

Remind students who choose to express the probabilities as fractions to make sure the fractions are reduced to lowest terms.

Have students recall that *P*(not green) is the complement of *P*(green), and the sum of the probabilities is 1.

Problem 4 `Evaluate`

"If we use the given information to write and solve a proportion, what will we find?" The number of stripes for 10,000 stars.

"What other operation must we complete in order to solve the problem? Explain your answer." Subtraction; to compare stars to stripes, subtract the number of stripes from the number of stars.

Problem 11 `Analyze`

A three-row ratio table can help students identify the unstated information in the problem. Draw the table shown below on the board or overhead and ask students to copy the table on their papers.

	Percent	Count
Remembered	70	
Forgot		21
Total		

Help students infer that 100% represents the total membership and 100% − 70%, or 30% of the members forgot the password.

After 100% and 30% have been written in the percent column of the table, ask students to write a proportion that can be used to solve the problem. $\frac{30}{100} = \frac{21}{t}$

(continued)

► *** 3.** `Analyze` In a bag of 60 marbles, 18 are green. If one marble is drawn
$^{(32)}$ from the bag, what is the probability the marble is

   a. green? $\frac{3}{10}$ **b.** not green? $\frac{7}{10}$

► *** 4.** `Evaluate` At the flag shop, for every 13 stripes there are 50 stars.
$^{(45)}$ If there are 10,000 stars, then how many more stars are there than stripes?
7,400 more stars than stripes.

5. The shipping charges for the store include a $3.50 base fee plus
$^{(3, 4)}$ $0.65 per pound. How much would it cost to ship a 10 pound order? $10

Solve.

6. $1.4x = 84$ $x = 60$ **7.** $x + 2.6 = 4$ $x = 1.4$
$^{(25, 38)}$ $^{(24, 38)}$

8. $\frac{x}{3} = 1.2$ $x = 3.6$ *** 9.** $x - 7 = -2$ $x = 5$
$^{(25, 38)}$ $^{(31, 38)}$

* 10. Austin has answered 21 of the 25 questions. What percent of the
$^{(48)}$ questions has he answered? 84%

► *** 11.** `Analyze` If 70% of the members remembered the password but 21
$^{(48)}$ members forgot, then how many members were there in all? 70

* 12. Refer to the graph of lines *a* and *b* to
$^{(Inv. 1, 44)}$ answer the following questions.

   a. What is the slope of line *a*? 4

   b. Which line is perpendicular to the x-axis? line *b*

   c. Which line intersects the y-axis at positive 4? line *a*

   d. In which quadrant do lines *a* and *b* intersect? 1st

13. Yes

* 13. Graph $y = 3$. Is the point (6, 3) on the line?
$^{(41)}$

14. At the park is a circular wading pool 20 feet in diameter. If parents
$^{(39)}$ are seated on the edge of the pool about every three feet, how many parents are sitting on the edge of the pool? 21

15. Find the volume of an oven with inside dimensions 3 ft by 1.5 ft
$^{(42)}$ by 3 ft. 13.5 ft³

16. How many edges, vertices, and faces does a number cube have?
$^{(Inv. 4)}$ 12 edges, 8 vertices, 6 faces

17. Which of the following is not a parallelogram? **C**
$^{(Inv. 3)}$

   A square   **B** rectangle   **C** trapezoid   **D** rhombus

18. Find *x* and *y*. $x = 48°, y = 42°$
$^{(18, 20)}$

► See Math Conversations in the sidebar.

19. About twenty-one percent of the earth's atmosphere is oxygen. Write
(11, 12) 21% as a decimal and a fraction. $0.21, \frac{21}{100}$

20. Find $\frac{1}{2}mv^2$ when $m = 8$ and $v = 2$.   16
(14, 15)

* 21. Sketch a triangular prism that has an equilateral base.
(Inv. 4)

21.
Sample:

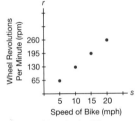

22. Yanos and Xena play a numbers game. The table shows some numbers
(41) Xena says and the numbers Yanos says in response.

X	6	2	1	−2
Y	3	1	$\frac{1}{2}$	−1

a. Describe the rule Yanos uses.   The number Yanos says is $\frac{1}{2}$ of Xena's number.
b. Write the rule as an equation beginning with $y =$. $y = \frac{1}{2}x$

c. Sketch a graph that shows all the pairs of numbers Xena and Yanos could say using the rule.

22. c.

graph

Combine like terms to simplify.

23. $5(x + 3) - 2(x + 4)$ $3x + 7$
(31, 36)

24. $-7x + 2(x^2 + 4x - 1)$ $2x^2 + x - 2$
(31, 36)

Simplify.

* 25. $\dfrac{-(-3)}{-6}$ $-\frac{1}{2}$
(36)

* 26. $-(-4) - 3$ 1
(31, 33)

▶* 27. $\left(1\frac{1}{2}\right)^2 - 1\frac{1}{2}$ $\frac{3}{4}$
(23, 13)

* 28. $\dfrac{(5.2 \times 10^9)}{(4 \times 10^7)}$ 1.3×10^2
(46)

29. Find all values of x: $3|x| = 6$ $x = 2, -2$
(1, 14)

▶ 30. *Evaluate* What relationship does
(41) the graph show? Is the relationship proportional? How do you know? Using the information given, calculate the number of revolutions per minute at one mile per hour. Then write an equation for the relationship. If it is proportional, state the constant of proportionality, k.   The graph shows the relationship between the speed of a bicycle and the RPMs (revolutions per minute) of its wheels. It is proportional. We know because the points are aligned with the origin. $r = 13s$ (r is number of RPMs and s is the speed of bike.); $k = 13$

graph: Wheel Revolutions Per Minute (rpm) vs Speed of Bike (mph); y-axis values 65, 130, 195, 260; x-axis values 5, 10, 15, 20

Lesson 49   335

▶ See Math Conversations in the sidebar.

3 **Written Practice** (Continued)

Math Conversations
Discussion opportunities are provided below.

Problem 30   Evaluate
"The points on the graph show a relationship. How can we tell from those points if the relationship is proportional?" The points will form a straight line that is aligned with the origin, and the line will have a positive slope.

Errors and Misconceptions
Problem 27
A common error when raising an improper fraction to a power is to raise only the numerator of the fraction to that power. For example:

$$\left(1\frac{1}{2}\right)^2 = \left(\frac{3}{2}\right)^2 = \frac{3^2}{2} = \frac{9}{2} = 4\frac{1}{2}$$

Students who make this error simplifying problem **27** are likely to name 3 as the answer. Emphasize that students must also square the denominator for their calculations to be correct.

Looking Forward

Solving rate problems with proportions and equations prepares students for:

• **Lesson 69,** working with direct variation.

• **Lesson 70,** solving direct variation problems.

• **Lesson 105,** solving compound rate and average problems.

Lesson 49   335

• Solving Multi-Step Equations

Objectives

- Use the properties of equality to solve multi-step equations.
- Write and solve multi-step equations to help solve word problems.

Lesson Preparation

Materials

- **Power Up J** (in *Instructional Masters*)

Power Up J

Math Language

Maintain	English Learners (ESL)
equation	holds

Technology Resources

Student eBook Complete student textbook in electronic format.

Resources and Planner CD Assessment, reteaching, and instructional masters, plus a pacing calendar with standards.

Test and Practice Generator CD Create additional practice sheets and custom-made tests.

www.SaxonPublishers.com Visit for more student activities and planning materials.

Inclusion

Adaptations CD Adapted lessons, investigations, practice and assessments.

Meeting Standards

National Council of Teachers of Mathematics (NCTM)

Algebra

AL.2d Recognize and generate equivalent forms for simple algebraic expressions and solve linear equations

Problem Solving

PS.1b Solve problems that arise in mathematics and in other contexts

PS.1c Apply and adapt a variety of appropriate strategies to solve problems

Connections

CN.4a Recognize and use connections among mathematical ideas

Problem-Solving Strategy: Use Logical Reasoning/
Guess and Check

$\sqrt{900} = 30$; $\sqrt{1600} = 40$; $\sqrt{2500} = 50$; Find $\sqrt{2025}$

Understand **Understand the problem.**

"What information are we given?"

$\sqrt{900} = 30$, $\sqrt{1600} = 40$, and $\sqrt{2500} = 50$

"What are we asked to do?"

Find $\sqrt{2025}$

Plan **Make a plan.**

"What problem-solving strategy will we use?"

We will *use logical reasoning* to intelligently *guess and check* to find the square root of 2025.

"What do we anticipate our answer to be in the range of?"

Because $\sqrt{2025}$ is between $\sqrt{1600}$ and $\sqrt{2500}$ we know that the answer will be between 40 and 50.

Solve **Carry out the plan.**

"What factor can produce a product that has a 5 in the ones position when squared?"

Only $5 \times 5 = 25$.

"What would be an intelligent guess to check for $\sqrt{2025}$?"

45, and 45×45 does $= 2025$.

Check **Look back.**

"Did we find the answer to the question that was asked?"

Yes. We found that $\sqrt{2025} = 45$.

• **Solving Multi-Step Equations**

1 Power Up

Facts
Distribute **Power Up J** to students. See answers below.

Mental Math
Encourage students to share different ways to mentally compute these exercises. Strategies for exercises **a, c,** and **e** are listed below.

a. **Multiply by 2 Twice**
   $6.4 \times 4 = 6.4 \times 2 \times 2 = 12.8 \times 2 = 25.6$

c. **Use a Unit Fraction**
   $\frac{1}{8} \times 32 = 4$
   $3 \times 4 = 12$

e. **Use Math Sense**
   1 hr → R − S = 8 − 7 = 1 mi
   2 hr → double 1 mi to get 2 mi

Problem Solving
Refer to **Power-Up Discussion,** p. 336B.

2 New Concepts

Instruction
Ask students to describe the equations that they have solved in this book so far. Lead them to see that these equations all required only one step to solve.

Use the Thinking Skill *Connect* question to help students see that reversing the order of operations is a good strategy for deciding how to undo the operations in a multi-step equation.

(continued)

---

mental math

a. **Number Sense:** 6.4×4 25.6

b. **Statistics:** Find the mean of 5, 6, and 1. 4

c. **Fractional Parts:** Three-eighths of the class wore jackets. There were 32 students in the class. How many wore jackets? 12 students

d. **Scientific Notation:** Write 4.05×10^5 in standard notation. 405,000

e. **Rate:** Robert rode 8 miles per hour north. Stephen rode 7 miles per hour north. If they start at the same place and time, how far apart are they after 1 hour? After 2 hours? 1 mile, 2 miles

f. **Geometry:** Find the area of the rectangle, then the area of the shaded triangle. 28 cm², 14 cm²

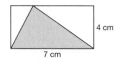

g. **Estimation:** Approximate the total for this shopping trip: $3.47 + 2 \times$ $5.99 + $39.97 + $1.47 $57

h. **Calculation:** $8 + 7, \div 5, \times 9, - 2, \sqrt{\ }, \times 11, + 1, \div 7, + 1, \sqrt{\ }, \times 1000$ 3000

problem solving | $\sqrt{900} = 30; \sqrt{1600} = 40; \sqrt{2500} = 50;$ Find $\sqrt{2025}$ 45

New Concept | *Increasing Knowledge*

We have used inverse operations to isolate a variable in an equation. The equations we will solve in this lesson require two or more steps to isolate the variable. Recall that isolating a variable, such as x, actually means that $1x + 0$ is on one side of the equal sign.

Example 1

Thinking Skill

Connect

How are the steps to solving and checking an equation related to the order of operations?

Suppose a taxi charges $1.20 to start a ride plus $3 per mile. If a ride costs $5.40, how far was the ride? Let x represent the distance traveled in miles. Solve this equation to find the length of the ride.

$$3x + 1.20 = 5.40$$

When checking an equation we follow the order of operations as we simplify the expression. When solving an equation we reverse the order of operations to isolate the variable.

Facts | Write the word that completes each sentence.

1. The distance around a circle is its _____ circumference.

2. Every point on a circle is the same distance from the _____ center.

3. The distance across a circle through its center is its _____ diameter.

4. The distance from a circle to its center is its _____ radius.

5. Two or more circles with the same center are _____ concentric circles.

6. A segment between two points on a circle is a _____ chord.

7. Part of a circumference is an _____ arc.

8. A portion of a circle and its interior, bound by an arc and two radii, is a _____ sector.

9. Half of a circle is a _____ semicircle.

10. An angle whose vertex is the center of a circle is a _____ central angle.

We see that x is multiplied by 3 and that 1.20 is added to that product. We undo these operations in reverse order. First we subtract 1.20 from both sides of the equation, which leaves $3x$ on the left side. Then we divide both sides by 3 to isolate x. We find that x equals 1.4.

Step:	Justification:
$3x + 1.20 = 5.40$	Given
$3x + 1.20 - 1.20 = 5.40 - 1.20$	Subtracted 1.2 from both sides
$3x = 4.20$	Simplified
$\dfrac{3x}{3} = \dfrac{4.20}{3}$	Divided both sides by 3
$x = 1.4$	Simplified

The solution means that the taxi ride was **1.4 miles.**

We check the solution by substituting 1.4 for x in the original equation. Then we simplify.

$3(1.4) + 1.20 = 5.40$	Substituted
$4.20 + 1.20 = 5.40$	Simplified $3(1.4)$
$5.40 = 5.40$	Simplified

Solve: $-2x - 5 = 9$

We see that x is multiplied by -2 and 5 is subtracted from that product. First we add 5 to both sides of the equation. Then we divide both sides by -2.

Step:	Justification:
$-2x - 5 = 9$	Given
$-2x - 5 - 5 = 9 + 5$	Added 5 to both sides
$-2x = 14$	Simplified
$\dfrac{-2x}{-2} = \dfrac{14}{-2}$	Divided both sides by -2
$x = -7$	Simplified

We check the solution in the original equation.

$-2(-7) - 5 = 9$	Substituted -7 for x
$14 - 5 = 9$	Simplified $-2(-7)$
$9 = 9$	Simplified $14 - 5$

Every step in solving an equation forms a new equation with the same solution. Step by step we form simpler equations until the final equation states the value(s) of the variable.

2 New Concepts (Continued)

Example 1
Instruction

Call attention to the two terms on the left side of this equation. Explain that this lesson is about solving equations like this one for which multiple steps are required to find the value of the variable.

Ask whether anyone can explain why the operations are undone in reverse order. Lead students to see that if the multiplication were undone first, all the terms would have to be divided by 3 and the computation would be more complicated.

Example 2
Instruction

Guide students through solving the equation. Call attention to the way each step is written on a separate line, making it easy to follow the process and check the work. Point out that no shortcuts are taken. Explain that this is a model students should use as they solve multi-step equations.

Tell students that checking the answer is an important part of solving an equation. You may want to explain how you would like them to check their work on the Practice Set and Written Practice.

(continued)

Inclusion

Students may have difficulty understanding the algorithm for solving a multi-step equation. An alternative method where parts of the equation are solved separately may help. For example 2, instead of first subtracting 5 and then dividing by -2, have the students do the following steps.

$-2x + 5 = 9$	write down the equation
$? + 5 = 9$	replace the $-2x$ with a ?
$? = 4$	subtract 5 from both sides

Now have the students replace the ? with $-2x$ and do the final steps.

$-2x = 4$	write down the equation
$-2? = 4$	replace the x with a ?
$? = -2$	divide both sides by -2

Connect the separated steps with the algorithm used for example 2.

Example 3

Instruction

Use this example to summarize the process for solving multi-step equations. You might ask students to describe how they would explain the way to solve this equation for a student who was absent today.

Practice Set

Problems a–h Justify

For each problem, ask students to name the inverse operations, and the order those operations will be used, to solve for the variable.

Problems a–i Error Alert

Encourage students to check their work by substituting the solution into the given equation and simplifying the expression on the left side of the equals sign. If the result is a true statement (such as $50 = 50$ for problem a), the solution checks.

Problems g and h Error Alert

Students must recognize the need for collecting like terms before using inverse operations.

---

3 Written Practice

Math Conversations

Discussion opportunities are provided below.

Problem 1 Analyze

Point out that a ratio table with a third row labeled "Total" should be used to represent the problem.

Problem 2 Explain

Extend the Problem

Challenge students to explain how to find the cost of the food using only mental math. Sample: Break apart $15 to $10 and $5, multiply $10 and $5 by 50, and add the products; $50 \times \$10 + 50 \times \$5 = \$500 + \$250$ or $750.

(continued)

Example 3

Solve: $3x + 4 - x = 28$

Solution

We write a sequence of simpler but equivalent equations until the variable is isolated.

In this equation the variable appears twice. We collect like terms and then proceed to isolate the variable.

Step:	Justification:
$3x + 4 - x = 28$	Given equation
$(3x - x) + 4 = 28$	Commutative and Associative Properties
$2x + 4 = 28$	Added $3x$ and $-x$
$2x = 24$	Subtracted 4 from both sides
$x = 12$	Divided both sides by 12

We check the solution by replacing each occurrence of x with 12 in the original equation.

Step:	Justification:
$3x + 4 - x = 28$	Given equation
$3(12) + 4 - (12) = 28$	Substituted 12 for x
$36 + 4 - 12 = 28$	Simplified
$28 = 28 ✓$	Simplified

Practice Set ▶ **Justify** Solve. Check your work.

a. $3x + 5 = 50$ $x = 15$ **b.** $4x - 12 = 60$ $x = 18$

c. $30n + 22 = 292$ $n = 9$ **d.** $\frac{x}{5} + 4 = 13$ $x = 45$

e. $-2x + 17 = 3$ $x = 7$ **f.** $3m - 1.5 = 4.2$ $m = 1.9$

g. $4x + 10 + x = 100$ $x = 18$ **h.** $7x - 12 - x = 24$ $x = 6$

i. A computer repair shop charges $40 per hour plus the cost of parts. If a repair bill of $125 includes $35 in parts, then how long did the repair shop work on the computer? Solve this equation to find the answer. (Express your answer in both decimal form and in hours and minutes.)

$40x + 35 = 125$ 2.25 hr; 2 hr 15 min

Written Practice   *Strengthening Concepts*

▶ *** 1.** **Analyze** The ratio of in-state to out-of-state visitors at the zoo is
  (45)   approximately 7 to 3. If 2000 people visited the zoo, about how many people were from out of state?   about 600

▶ **2.** Arnold is planning a party for his friends. Renting the facilities will cost
  (3, 4) $500. Feeding each friend will cost $15. What will the total cost of the party be if Arnold invites 50 friends? $1250

▶ See Math Conversations in the sidebar.

▶ * 3. *(35)* **Generalize** Consider the quadrilaterals below.

Choose the correct word to complete the conjecture: Quadrilaterals with corresponding sides of equal length are _____ (sometimes/always/never) congruent." **sometimes**

▶ Analyze Solve.

* 4. *(50)* $5x + 25 = 100$ $x = 15$ *** 5.** *(50)* $\frac{x}{2} + 8 = 16$ $x = 16$

* 6. *(50)* $2x - 1.2 = 3$ $x = 2.1$ *** 7.** *(50)* $-4m + 5.5 = 9.5$ $x = -1$

* 8. *(50)* $-2w + 22 = 30$ $x = -4$ *** 9.** *(50)* $\frac{1}{2}x - \frac{1}{3} = \frac{2}{3}$ $x = 2$

Generalize Simplify.

▶* 10. *(36)* $-3^2 + (-3)^2$ 0 **11.** *(13, 22)* $\frac{1}{3} + \frac{5}{6} \cdot \frac{4}{5}$ 1

▶ 12. *(27)* $\frac{mc^2xc}{mx^2}$ $\frac{c^3}{x}$ **13.** *(13, 23)* $1\frac{1}{2} \cdot 2\frac{2}{3} - 3\frac{3}{4}$ $\frac{1}{4}$

▶* 14. *(28, 46)* $\frac{2.7 \times 10^8}{9 \times 10^3}$ 3×10^4 **15.** *(24, 25)* $\frac{0.24 - 0.024}{0.02}$ 10.8

16. *(39, 40)* Find the **a** area and **b** circumference of the circle with radius 1 meter. Express the measures in terms of π.   **a.** $\pi \, m^2$ **b.** $2\pi \, m$

17. *(42)* Estimate the volume in cubic feet of a cabinet with height 4 feet 2 inches, depth 13 inches, and width 2 feet 11 inches. $12 \, ft^3$

18. *(8)* Find the **a** area and **b** perimeter of this figure.   **a.** $64 \, m^2$ **b.** $40 \, m$

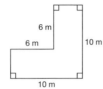

19. a. Sample:

x	y
0	0
1	40
2	80

19. *(41)* The company will charge $40 for each item it sells.

   a. Make a function table of possible x- and y-values with x representing the number of items sold and y representing the revenue from the sales.

   b. Write an equation for the function table: $y = 40x$

Lesson 50   339

▶ See Math Conversations in the sidebar.

Math Conversations

Discussion opportunities are provided below.

Problem 3 **Generalize**

Make sure students can recognize the sides of the quadrilaterals that are corresponding sides.

Problems 4–9 **Analyze**

"When two inverse operations are used to solve an equation, which operation is used first?" The inverse operations are used in reverse order of the order of operations.

Before students solve each problem, ask them to name the inverse operation that will be used first, and used second, to solve for the variable.

Problem 14 **Generalize**

Students should recall that dividing numbers in scientific notation involves dividing the coefficients, and dividing the powers of 10 by subtracting the exponents.

"What numbers represent the coefficients of the numerator and the denominator?" 2.7 and 9

"What operation does a fraction bar represent?" division

"What is the quotient of the coefficients?" 0.3

"What is the quotient of the powers of 10? Explain your answer." 10^5; to divide like bases such as powers of 10, subtract the exponents.

Errors and Misconceptions

Problem 10

A common error is to assume -3^2 simplifies to 9. Students who make this assumption are likely to name 18 as the answer to problem 10.

Remind students that an exponent represents the number of times a base is used as a factor. Point out that the base of -3^2 is 3, and then demonstrate the arithmetic that is used to write it in simplest form. $-3^2 = -(3 \cdot 3) = -(9) = -9$

Problem 12

When simplifying an algebraic fraction, one way for students to check their work is to rewrite the fraction without exponents, then simplify.

$$\frac{mc^2xc}{mx^2} = \frac{mccxc}{mxx} = \frac{\not{m}cc\not{x}c}{\not{m}\not{x}x} = \frac{ccc}{x} = \frac{c^3}{x}$$

(continued)

Math Conversations

Discussion opportunities are provided below.

Problem 24 [Analyze]

Show students how the Distributive Property applies to this problem. Students have the choice of multiplying the length (l) of each wall by the height (h) and then adding $hl_1 + hl_2 + hl_3 + hl_4$, or multiplying the perimeter of the room by the height: $h(l_1 + l_2 + l_3 + l_4)$. Each method produces the lateral surface area.

Problem 27 [Evaluate]

Students may want to solve this problem without writing and solving an equation. In doing so they would subtract $3.50 from $20, leaving $16.50 to spend on games, and then find the number of $5.50 games Rita could play for $16.50. Point out that these are the very steps they would take to solve the equation $3.50 + 5.50y = 20$.

---

20. Write 7.5% **a** as a decimal and **b** as a reduced fraction.   **a.** 0.075, **b.** $\frac{3}{40}$
(11, 12)

21. a. All corresponding angle pairs have the same measure.

* 21. Consider the triangles.
(35)
   a. Explain how you know that the triangles are similar.

   b. What is the scale factor from $\triangle ABC$ to $\triangle QRS$? $\frac{4}{10}$ or $\frac{2}{5}$ or 0.4

   c. Find x.   6

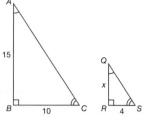

22. Find $\frac{r^2 - 4r}{t}$ when $r = 3$ and $t = -1$.   3
(14, 15)

23.

Number sold x	Money collected y
2	6
4	12
6	18
8	24

23. Carlos was making necklaces to sell at the school carnival. He sold
(41) each necklace for $3. Make a function table that relates the number of necklaces sold to the amount of money collected. Write an equation for the rule. Is the function linear? Is it proportional? $y = 3x$; The function is linear and it is proportional.

▶* 24. [Analyze]   Geraldo is going to paint the interior walls of the lobby of the
(43) local history museum. The room is 40 ft by 60 ft. Its height is 16 ft. In order to purchase the right amount of paint, Geraldo must calculate the lateral surface area of the room. What is the lateral surface area?   3200 ft²

* 25. There are approximately 2.25×10^{12} grains of sand on a stretch of
(46) beach. If a bucket holds 1.25×10^9 grains of sand, how many buckets would it take to remove all of the sand from the beach? 1.8×10^3 buckets

26.

	Percent	Count
Days Missed	m	2
Days Not Missed	n	18
Total	100	20

* 26. Last month, Andrea missed two days of school because she had a
(48) cold. What percent of school days did Andrea miss? Hint: Assume that there are 20 school days in a month. $\frac{2}{20} = \frac{m}{100}$; $20m = 2 \cdot 100$; $m = 10$. Andrea missed 10% of school days.

▶* 27. [Evaluate]   If the bowling alley charges $3.50 for a pair of shoes and
(50) $5.50 per game, how many games will Rita be able to play with a $20 dollar bill? Write and solve an equation and check the solution.   3 games; (See below.)

28. Write the mixed number $1\frac{1}{9}$ as a decimal. $1.\overline{1}$
(30)

27.
$$3.50 + 5.50g = 20$$
$$5.50g + 3.50 - 3.50 = 20 - 3.50$$
$$5.50g = 16.50$$
$$\frac{5.50g}{5.50} = \frac{16.50}{5.50}$$
$$g = 3$$

Check:
$$3.50 + 5.50(3) = 20$$
$$3.50 + 16.50 = 20$$
$$20 = 20$$

▶ See Math Conversations in the sidebar.

English Learners

For problem **26** explain the meaning of the word **holds**. Say:

"When you have something in your hands, you are holding it. A box or a cup can hold something."

Draw a picture of a cereal-type box and a cup on the board. Ask:

"What could the box hold? What could the cup hold?"

Have students use the word *hold* in their answers. For example, the cup holds hot tea.

29.

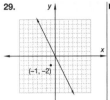

(−1, −2)

30. A; The relation is not proportional. Although the points are aligned, they are not aligned with the origin.

▶* **29.** Represent Graph $y = -2x$. Is the point $(-1, -2)$ on the line? What is the slope of the line?   No; Slope = −2
(41, 44)

30. For a promotion, the clothes shop is giving every customer 2 free T-shirts. If the customers want more T-shirts, they must buy them for $5 each. Which graph represents the relationship between the number of shirts a customer receives and the amount of money the customer pays for the shirts? Is the relationship proportional? Why or why not?
(41)

A

B

C

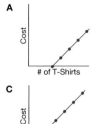

D

Early Finishers
Real-World Application

Ferdinand is planting four rose bushes in the city park. He is planning to place the bushes into four rectangular planters that are 3 feet long, 1 foot wide and 1.5 feet deep. How many bags containing 1.25 feet of cubic soil will he need to fill all four planters two-thirds full?   Volume of Planter = *lwh*; V = (3)(1)(1.5) = 4.5 cubic feet; Two-thirds full = ($\frac{2}{3}$)(4.5) = 3 cubic feet; Four Planters = (4)(3) =12 cubic feet; 12 ÷ 1.25 = 9.6 bags of soil. Ferdinand would need 10 bags of soil.

Lesson 50   341

▶ See Math Conversations in the sidebar.

Math Conversations

Discussion opportunities are provided below.

Problem 29 Represent

Before computing the slope, remind students that they can learn the sign of the slope simply by looking at the line. If the line falls from left to right, the sign of the slope is negative. If the line rises from left to right, the sign of the slope is positive.

Looking Forward

Solving multi-step equations prepares students for:

- **Lesson 62,** graphing solutions to inequalities on a number line.

- **Lesson 73,** writing formulas for sequences.

- **Lesson 77,** working with inequalities with negative coefficients.

- **Lesson 79,** transforming formulas.

- **Lesson 89,** solving problems with two unknowns by graphing.

Assessment   30–40 minutes   For use after Lesson 50

Distribute **Cumulative Test 9** to each student. Two versions of the test are
available in *Saxon Math Course 3 Course Assessments Book*. Have students
complete the **Power-Up Test** first. Allow 10 minutes. Then have students work
the 20 numbered items on the **Cumulative Test.** Students may use copies of the
answer sheet to record their work. Track individual and class progress with the
Test Analysis forms.

Power-Up Test 9

Cumulative Test 9A

Alternative Cumulative Test 9B

Optional Answer Forms

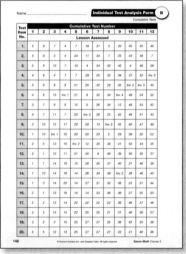

Individual Test Analysis Form

Class Test Analysis Form

Reteaching

Students who score below 80% on the assessment may be in need of reteaching.
Look for the causes of student mistakes. If errors are conceptual, refer to the
Reteaching Masters for reteaching.

You can develop customized benchmark tests using the Test Generator located on the *Test & Practice Generator CD*.

This chart shows the lesson, the standard, and the test item question that can be found on the *Test & Practice Generator CD*.

LESSON	NEW CONCEPTS	LOCAL STANDARD	TEST ITEM ON CD
41	• Functions		5.41.1
42	• Volume		5.42.1
43	• Surface Area		5.43.1
44	• Solving Proportions Using Cross Products		5.44.1
	• Slope of a Line		5.44.2
45	• Ratio Problems Involving Totals		5.45.1
46	• Solving Problems Using Scientific Notation		5.46.1
47	• Graphing Functions		5.47.1
48	• Percent of a Whole		5.48.1
49	• Solving Rate Problems with Proportions and Equations		5.49.1
50	• Solving Multi-Step Equations		5.50.1

Using the Test Generator CD

• Develop tests in both English and Spanish.

• Choose from multiple-choice and free-response test items.

• Clone test items to create multiple versions of the same test.

• View and edit test items to make and save your own questions.

• Administer assessments through paper tests or over a school LAN.

• Monitor student progress through a variety of individual and class reports —for both diagnosing and assessing standards mastery.

Transformations in Art

Assign after Lesson 50 and Test 9

Objectives
- Perform transformations on two dimensional figures.
- Create a dilated image using a scale factor of 2.
- Communicate ideas through writing.

Materials
Copy a $\frac{1}{4}$-inch grid on transparency film for each student, large enough to cover a small photograph.

Activity Masters 9A, 9B, and **9C**

Preparation
Make copies of **Performance Tasks 9A, 9B,** and **9C.** (One each per student.)

Time Requirement
25 minutes; Begin in class and complete at home.

Task
Explain to students that they will be using a dilation technique used by artists to create enlargements of pictures. Students will use grids provided—a transparency with quarter-inch squares, and drawing paper with half-inch squares—to perform a 200% dilation of a complex photographed object. Note that drawing from a gridded photograph to squares with doubled dimensions is a dilation of scale factor 2. Point out that all necessary information is provided on **Performance Tasks 9A, 9B,** and **9C.**

Criteria for Evidence of Learning
- Performs dilations correctly on a two-dimensional shape.
- Performs rotations correctly of two-dimensional figures around the origin (Extension).
- Performs reflections across the *y*-axis correctly (Extension).
- Communicates ideas clearly through writing.

Performance Tasks 9A, 9B, and 9C

National Council of Teachers of Mathematics (NCTM)

Geometry

GM.3a Describe sizes, positions, and orientations of shapes under informal transformations such as flips, turns, slides, and scaling

GM.4e Recognize and apply geometric ideas and relationships in areas outside the mathematics classroom, such as art, science, and everyday life

Measurement

ME.2e Solve problems involving scale factors, using ratio and proportion

Problem Solving

PS.1c Apply and adapt a variety of appropriate strategies to solve problems

Focus on
• Graphing Transformations

Objectives

• Graph reflections, rotations, translations, and dilations on a coordinate plane.

Lesson Preparation

Materials

• **Investigation Activity 2** (in *Instructional Masters*)
• **Investigation Activity 1 Transparency** (in *Instructional Masters*)
• **Teacher-provided material:** tracing paper, overhead marker

Math Language

Maintain	
dilation	transformations
reflection	translation
rotation	

Technology Resources

Student eBook Complete student textbook in electronic format.

Resources and Planner CD Assessment, reteaching, and instructional masters, plus a pacing calendar with standards.

Test and Practice Generator CD Create additional practice sheets and custom-made tests.

www.SaxonPublishers.com Visit for more student activities and planning materials.

Inclusion

Adaptations CD Adapted lessons, investigations, practice and assessments.

Meeting Standards

National Council of Teachers of Mathematics (NCTM)

Geometry

GM.3a Describe sizes, positions, and orientations of shapes under informal transformations such as flips, turns, slides, and scaling

GM.3b Examine the congruence, similarity, and line or rotational symmetry of objects using transformations

GM.4d Use geometric models to represent and explain numerical and algebraic relationships

INVESTIGATION 5

In this investigation, students will explore a variety of transformations. In some transformations (such as reflections, rotations, and translations), the image and the given figure will be congruent. In other transformations (such as dilations and contractions), the image will be larger or smaller than the given figure, but similar to it.

Instruction

Have students note from the examples that:
- the reflection and the rotation changed the orientation of the given figures.
- the reflection, the rotation, and the translation produced an image that is congruent to the given figures.
- a dilation does not preserve congruency, but it does preserve similarity.

Provide students with more practice working with reflections by writing the coordinates of the given figure and its reflection (shown below) on the board or overhead. Then ask students to explain how a reflection across the *y*-axis affects the (*x*- and *y*-coordinates) of the corresponding vertices. Sample: The *x*-coordinates are opposite; the *y*-coordinates do not change.

Point	Given Figure	Image
A	(−2, 6)	(2, 6)
B	(−5, 2)	(5, 2)
C	(−2, 2)	(2, 2)

Make sure students also infer that a reflection of points across the *x*-axis changes the *y*-coordinates to the opposites of their corresponding points.

Math Conversations

Discussion opportunities are provided below.

Problem 3

Students should recognize that the equation *x* = 1 describes a vertical line because the *x*-value of every point on the line is 1.

After completing the reflection, ask

"How does the size and shape of triangle A″B″C″ compare to triangle A′B′C′?" Sample: The triangles are the same size and the same shape.

"What mathematical term describes two figures that are the same size and the same shape?" congruent

(continued)

INVESTIGATION 5

Focus on
• Graphing Transformations

Recall that **transformations** are operations on a geometric figure that alter its position or size. In this investigation we will graph different transformations on the coordinate plane.

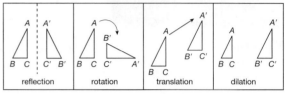

| reflection | rotation | translation | dilation |

A **reflection** occurs across a line. Below we show the reflection of △*ABC* across the *y*-axis. If we positioned a vertical mirror on the line, the reflection of △*ABC* would appear to be on the other side of the *y*-axis and the same distance from the *y*-axis as △*A′B′C′* (read "A prime, B prime, C prime"). A segment between corresponding points of a figure and its reflection is perpendicular to the line of reflection. If we were to fold a graph along the line of reflection, the figures would align exactly.

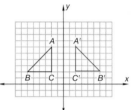

1.

2. The *x*-coordinates of the reflection match the *x*-coordinates of the figure but the *y*-coordinates of the reflection are the opposite of the *y*-coordinates of the figure.

3.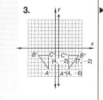

▶ **1.** On a coordinate plane draw triangle *ABC* with *A* at (−2, 6), *B* at (−5, 2), and *C* at (−2, 2). Then draw the reflection of △*ABC* across the *x*-axis. Label the coordinates of the vertices. *A′* (−2, −6), *B′* (−5, −2), *C′* (−2, −2)

2. Describe how the coordinates of the reflection across the *x*-axis compare with the coordinates of the original triangle.

▶ **3.** On the same coordinate plane as problem 1, draw a vertical line through the *x*-axis at *x* = 1. (The line should be parallel to the *y*-axis.) Then graph the reflection of △*A′B′C′* across the line *x* = 1. Name the reflection △*A″B″C″* (read "A double prime, B double prime, C double prime") and label the coordinates of the vertices. *A″* (4, −6), *B″* (7, −2), *C″* (4, −2)

▶ See Math Conversations in the sidebar.

Math Language

Recall that **counterclockwise** means "in the opposite direction as the movement of the hands of a clock," or "to the left."

A positive **rotation** turns a figure counterclockwise about (around) a point. Here we show a 90° rotation about point B. Point B is the point of rotation; its location is fixed, and the figure spins around it. If we trace the path of any other point during this rotation, we find that it sweeps out an arc of 90°.

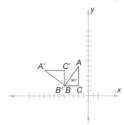

To graph a rotation it is helpful to have a piece of transparency film and a transparency marker. Otherwise use a piece of paper thin enough to use for tracing.

▶ **4.** On a coordinate plane graph △ABC as illustrated above. We will rotate △ABC 90° about the origin. Place a piece of transparency film or tracing paper on the coordinate plane so that it covers △ABC and the origin. Trace △ABC and mark an inch or so of the x and y-axes through the origin as illustrated below.

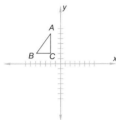

Press a pencil point on the tracing sheet at the origin and rotate the tracing sheet counterclockwise 90° so that the x-axis on the tracing paper aligns with the y-axis on the original coordinate plane below, and the y-axis on the tracing paper aligns with the x-axis below.

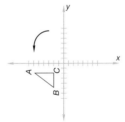

Investigation 5 **343**

▶ See Math Conversations in the sidebar.

Instruction

Make sure students can differentiate counterclockwise rotations from clockwise rotations. If an analog clock is not present in your classroom, invite volunteers to share different ways to remember the direction of each rotation.

To help students visualize the rotation, you might choose to cut out and label two congruent right triangles, and then model the rotation on an overhead grid transparency.

Explain that a point of rotation can be on a figure, inside a figure, or outside a figure.

Math Conversations

Discussion opportunities are provided below.

Problem 4

Make sure students have sufficient materials to complete the transformations, and use the points $A(-2, 6)$, $B(-5, 2)$, and $C(-2, 2)$ as the vertices of the given triangle.

"What fraction of a whole turn is a 90° turn? Explain how you know." Sample: A 90° turn is the same as a $\frac{1}{4}$ or quarter turn because there are 360° in a circle and $\frac{90°}{360°} = \frac{1}{4}$.

(continued)

Math Conversations

Discussion opportunities are provided below.

Problem 5

After completing the rotations for problems **4** and **5,** ask students to use the Pythagorean Theorem to compare the lengths of the corresponding hypotenuses and state a conclusion. Sample: The distances of the corresponding hypotenuses are the same, which means that the rotation preserved length.

Instruction

Have students note that because the integers of the ordered pair (6, 1) are both positive, they represent a horizontal movement of 6 units to the right, followed by a vertical movement of 1 unit up.

Problem 6

Make sure students understand that a translation of 7 units to the right is the same as adding 7 to the x-coordinates of the given vertices, and a translation of 8 units down is the same as subtracting 8 from the y-coordinates of the given vertices. The vertices of the image will be:

$$A' \ (-2 + 7, 6 - 8) \text{ or } A' \ (5, -2)$$
$$B' \ (-5 + 7, 2 - 8) \text{ or } B' \ (2, -6)$$
$$C' \ (-2 + 7, 2 - 8) \text{ or } C' \ (5, -6)$$

Problem 7

"What ordered pair describes the location of point A?" (−2, 6)

"By moving point A from (−2, 6) to the origin, how will the x-coordinate and y-coordinate of the point change?" The x-coordinate will increase by 2 and the y-coordinate will decrease by 6.

Students should conclude that the x-coordinates of points B and C will also increase by 2 and the y-coordinates will also decrease by 6.

Instruction

Ask students to explain how similarity transformations are different from congruence transformations. Sample: In a congruence transformation, the image is the same size and the same shape as the given figure. In a similarity transformation, the image is the same shape, but not the same size, as the given figure.

Explain that drawing rays through corresponding vertices is a way to check if an image produced by a dilation is correct. If the rays are drawn through corresponding vertices of the given figure and its image converge at one point, students can assume that the dilation is correct.

4.

5.

6.

Visit www.SaxonPublishers.com/ActivitiesC3 *for a graphing calculator activity.*

Use the position of the traced image to help you draw the rotated image on the coordinate plane. Name the rotated image △*A'B'C'* and label the coordinates of the vertices.   *A'* (−6, −2), *B'* (−2, −5), *C'* (−2, −2)

▶ **5.** On the same coordinate plane rotate △*ABC* 180°. Name the image △*A"B"C"* and label the coordinates of the vertices.   *A"* (2,−6), *B"* (5, −2), *C"* (2, −2)

A **translation** slides a figure a distance and direction without flipping or turning. Here we show a translation of (6, 1). For any translation (*a, b*), *a* describes the horizontal shift and *b* describes the vertical shift for each point of the figure.

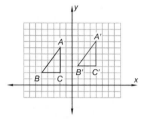

▶ **6.** Draw triangle *ABC* as illustrated on a coordinate plane. Then draw its image △*A'B'C'* translated 7 units to the right and 8 units down, or (7, −8). Label the coordinates of △*A'B'C'*.   *A'* (5, −2), *B'* (2, −6), *C'* (5, −6)

▶ **7.** If △*ABC* is translated so that the image of point *A* at *A"* is located at the origin, then what would be the coordinates of points *B"* and *C"*? Describe the translation.   *B"* (−3, −4), *C"* (0, −4); The translation is 2 units to the right and down 6, or (2, −6).

Recall that reflections, rotations, and translations are called **isometries** (meaning "same measures"), or **congruence transformations,** because the original figure and its image are congruent. A **dilation** is a transformation in which the figure grows larger, while a **contraction** is a transformation in which the figure grows smaller. Dilations and contractions are **similarity transformations,** because the original figure and its image are similar and corresponding lengths are proportional.

Dilations of geometric figures occur away from a fixed point called the center of the dilation. On a coordinate plane the center of a dilation may be any point. In this book the center of dilation will be the origin.

Dilation of Triangle ABC

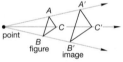

Note that corresponding vertices are on the same rays from the center of the dilation and that the corresponding segments of △*ABC* and its image △*A'B'C'* are parallel.

▶ See Math Conversations in the sidebar.

Math Background

Rotations, translations, and reflections are examples of isometries. An isometry is a transformation in which the size and the shape of a figure do not change. Isometries are sometimes called *rigid* transformations because they preserve distance, such as the distance between two points, while not preserving placement and/or orientation.

An additional example of an isometry or rigid transformation is a *glide reflection*. A glide reflection is a combination of a reflection and a translation.

Recall that to graph a dilation on a coordinate plane we prescribe a scale factor, such as 2. If the center of dilation is the origin, we may multiply the coordinates of the vertices of the figure by the scale factor. For example, using a scale factor of 3, a vertex at (1, 3) in the original figure would have a corresponding vertex at (3, 9) in its image after dilation.

8.

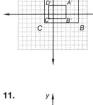

▶ **8.** On a coordinate plane draw rectangle *ABCD* with *A* at (6, 4), *B* at (6, −2), *C* at (−2, −2), and *D* at (−2, 4). Then draw its image □*A'B'C'D'* using scale factor $\frac{1}{2}$, with the center of the contraction at the origin. What are the coordinates of the vertices of □*A'B'C'D'*?   *A'* (3, 2), *B'* (3, −1), *C'* (−1, −1), *D'* (−1, 2)

▶ **9.** What fraction of the dimensions of □*ABCD* are the dimensions of □*A'B'C'D'*? What fraction of the perimeter of □*ABCD* is the perimeter of □*A'B'C'D'*? $\frac{1}{2}, \frac{1}{2}$

▶ **10.** What fraction of the area of □*ABCD* is the area of □*A'B'C'D'*? $\frac{1}{4}$

11.

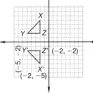

In the following table we summarize the transformations graphed in this investigation.

Transformations

Preserving Congruence	Preserving Similarity
Translation (slide)	Dilation (scale increased)
Rotation (turn)	Contraction (scale reduced)
Reflection (flip)	

▶ For review, graph the following transformations on a coordinate plane.

12.

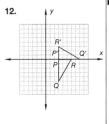

11. Draw △*XYZ* with *X* at (−2, 5), *Y* at (−5, 2), and *Z* at (−2, 2). Then draw its reflection across the *x*-axis. Correctly label the corresponding vertices of △*X'Y'Z'*.

12. Draw △*PQR* with *P* at (3, 0), *Q* at (3, −5), and *R* at (6, 0). Then draw its image △*P'Q'R'* after a 90° counterclockwise rotation about point *P*.

13. Draw △*DEF* with *D* at (−2, −2), *E* at (2, −2), and *F* at (0, 2). Then draw its image △*D'E'F'* after a translation of (5, 3).

13.

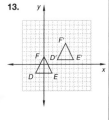

14. Draw △*JKL* with *J* at (1, 2), *K* at (−1, −2), and *L* at (1, −2). Then draw its image △*J'K'L'* after a dilation of scale factor 2.

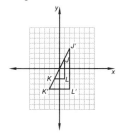

▶ See Math Conversations in the sidebar.

Looking Forward

Investigating transformations prepares students for:

• **Lesson 65,** working with similar triangles and their applications.

Math Conversations

Discussion opportunities are provided below.

Problem 8

Remind students that $\frac{1}{2}$ is a unit fraction, and multiplying the *x*- and *y*-coordinates by $\frac{1}{2}$ is the same as dividing the coordinates by 2.

Problem 9

Extend the Problem

Ask students to state a generalization about the problem and its answer. Sample: If a rectangle is contracted by a given factor, its perimeter decreases by the same factor.

Challenge students to use examples to prove, or nonexamples to disprove, that the same generalization applies to other polygons.

Problem 10

Ask students to state a generalization about the problem and its answer. Sample: If a rectangle is contracted by a given factor, its area decreases by the square of the same factor.

Challenge students to use examples to prove, or nonexamples to disprove, that the same generalization applies to other polygons.

Problem 11

Make sure students recognize that a reflection across the *x*-axis changes only the *y*-coordinates of the given vertices.

Problem 12

Point out that the rotation should be counterclockwise, and remind students that *P*—the point of rotation—does not move. The same ordered pair describes the location of *P* and *P'*.

Problem 13

Students should recognize that a translation of (5, 3) represents adding 5 to the *x*-coordinates of the given vertices and adding 3 to the *y*-coordinates.

Problem 14

Make sure students understand that a dilation of scale factor 2 will produce an image that is larger than the given figure. Recognize that the *x*- and *y*-coordinates of the figure's vertices will be multiplied by 2.

Lesson Planner

LESSON	NEW CONCEPTS	MATERIALS	RESOURCES
51	• Negative Exponents • Scientific Notation for Small Numbers	Calculators	Power Up K
52	• Using Unit Multipliers to Convert Measures • Converting Mixed-Unit to Single-Unit Measures	Measuring tools: rulers, yardsticks	Power Up K
53	• Solving Problems Using Measures of Central Tendency	none	Power Up K
54	• Angle Relationships	Isometric dot paper, protractors	Power Up K
55	• Nets of Prisms, Cylinders, Pyramids, and Cones	Unlined paper, compasses, scissors, glue or tape, grid paper	Power Up K
56	• The Slope-Intercept Equation of a Line	none	Power Up L Lesson Activity 7 or graph paper
57	• Operations with Small Numbers in Scientific Notation	none	Power Up L
58	• Solving Percent Problems with Equations	none	Power Up L Fraction-Decimal-Percent Equivalents poster
59	• Experimental Probability	none	Power Up L
60	• Area of a Parallelogram	Manipulative Kit: inch rulers Scissors, graph paper	Power Up L
Inv. 6	• Collect, Display, and Interpret Data	none	none

Problem Solving

Strategies

- **Draw a Diagram**   Lesson 59
- **Find a Pattern**   Lesson 51
- **Guess and Check**   Lesson 53, 55
- **Make It Simpler**   Lesson 58
- **Use Logical Reasoning**   Lessons 53, 54, 59
- **Work Backwards**   Lesson 60
- **Write an Equation**   Lessons 51, 52, 56, 57

Real-World Applications

pp. 350, 351, 354–358, 362–367,
370–373, 378–382, 386–389, 391, 392,
394–398, 401–404, 406, 409–411

4-Step Process

Teacher Edition   Lessons 51–60
(Power-Up Discussions)

Connections

Math and Other Subjects

- **Math and Architecture**   p. 392
- **Math and Art**   pp. 373, 409
- **Math and Geography**   p. 405
- **Math and Science**   pp. 350, 380, 381, 391, 397, 399, 403, 405, 409
- **Math and Sports**   pp. 356, 364, 382, 392, 401, 403
- **Math and Social Studies**   p. 362

Math to Math

- **Problem Solving and Measurement**   Lessons 51–60, Inv. 6
- **Algebra and Problem Solving**   Lessons 51, 55, 56, 58, 60
- **Fractions, Decimals, Percents, and Problem Solving**   Lessons 51, 53–60, Inv. 6
- **Fractions and Measurement**   Lessons 52–60
- **Measurement and Geometry**   Lessons 51–60
- **Proportional Relationships and Geometry**   Lessons 51, 52, 54–56, 58–60
- **Algebra, Measurement, and Geometry**   Lessons 51–60
- **Probability and Statistics**   Lessons 51–53, 55, 57–59

Communication

Explain

pp. 372, 390, 402, 403, 405, 406

Formulate a Problem

p. 379

Representation

Manipulatives/Hands On

pp. 347, 377, 407

Model

pp. 374, 378, 408

Represent

pp. 357, 386, 388, 392

Technology

Student Resources

- **eBook**   Anytime
- **Calculator**   Lesson 51
- **Online Resourses** at
  www.SaxonPublishers.com/ActivitiesC3
    Graphing Calculator Activities   Lesson 51
  and Inv. 6

Teacher Resources

- **Resources and Planner CD**
- **Adaptations CD**   Lessons 51–60
- **Test & Practice Generator CD**
- **eGradebook**
- **Answer Key CD**

For geometry and measurement, students work with nets and calculate area. In statistics students represent data in a variety of displays and solve problems involving measures of central tendency.

Algebraic and Proportional Thinking

Students write equations to solve percent problems and write the equations of lines.

Students consolidate their gains in algebra in mixed practice and add the skill of solving percent problems using equations in Lesson 58. They explore the important algebraic topic of slope, the ratio of the rise to the run of a line, in Lesson 56. Students are introduced to negative exponents and their application in scientific notation for small numbers in Lesson 51, and they multiply and divide small numbers expressed in scientific notation in Lesson 57.

Geometry and Measurement

Students make nets and relate surface area formulas to the nets.

Furthering their geometric studies, students explore angle relationships in Lesson 54, work with nets of prisms, cylinders, pyramids, and cones in Lesson 55, and actively calculate the areas of parallelograms in Lesson 60. Students learn to convert linear measures using unit multipliers in Lesson 52 and will later use the skills learned to convert between units of area and volume.

Probability and Statistics

Students make predictions using experimental probability and discuss surveys and sampling.

In Lesson 59, students distinguish between theoretical and experimental probability and use data to calculate probabilities. Students solve problems involving measures of central tendency in Lesson 53 and collect, display, and interpret data in Investigation 6.

Assessment

A variety of weekly assessment tools are provided.

After Lesson 55:	**After Lesson 60:**
• Power-Up Test 10	• Power-Up Test 11
• Cumulative Test 10	• Cumulative Test 11
• Performance Activity 10	• Customized Benchmark Test
	• Performance Task 11

LESSON	NEW CONCEPTS	PRACTICED	ASSESSED
51	• Negative Exponents	Lessons 52, 54, 56, 60, 63, 66, 69, 70, 72, 73, 74, 76, 77, 78, 79, 80, 81, 82, 83, 85, 87, 90, 99, 100, 101, 102, 104, 105, 106, 107, 108, 111, 112, 113, 114, 115, 116, 117, 118, 120	Tests 11, 13–18, 20, 23
	• Scientific Notation for Small Numbers	Lessons 51, 53 58	Test 11
52	• Using Multipliers to Convert Measures	Lessons 52, 53, 54, 55, 56, 57, 58, 59, 60, 61, 67, 73, 90, 96, 97, 98, 99, 101, 108	Tests 11, 12, 22
	• Converting Mixed-Unit to Single-Unit Measures	Lessons 52, 53, 59, 60	Test & Practice Generator
53	• Solving Problems Using Measures of Central Tendency	Lessons 53, 54, 55, 56, 57, 58, 59, 60, 63, 64, 66, 77, 90, 96, 97, 98, 99, 101, 105	Tests 11, 13
54	• Angle Relationships	Lessons 54, 55, 56, 58, 59, 60, 61, 62, 63, 64, 65, 66, 67, 68, 69, 70, 72, 95, 101, 105	Tests 11, 13
55	• Nets of Prisms, Cylinders, Pyramids, and Cones	Lessons 56, 57, 60, 87, 92, 94, 97, 103, 109	Tests 11, 15
56	• The Slope-Intercept Equation of a Line	Lessons 56, 57, 58, 59, 61, 62, 66, 67, 68, 69, 70, 71, 72, 73, 74, 76, 77, 78, 83, 84, 85, 86, 88, 96, 104, 111, 112, 113, 114, 118, 119, 120	Tests 13, 14, 16, 22, 23
57	• Operations with Small Numbers in Scientific Notation	Lessons 59, 79, 118	Tests 12–14
58	• Solving Percent Problems with Equations	Lessons 58, 59, 60, 65, 66, 67, 68, 71, 72, 77, 86, 95, 96	Tests 12, 13
59	• Experimental Probability	Lessons 59, 71, 75, 85	Test 15
60	• Area of a Parallelogram	Lessons 60, 66, 73, 75, 76, 77, 79, 80, 96, 104, 109, 112, 114	Tests 13, 15, 18
Inv. 6	• Collect, Display, and Interpret Data	Lessons 61, 64, 71, 72, 77, 80, 81, 90, 99, 108	Test & Practice Generator

• Negative Exponents
• Scientific Notation for Small Numbers

Objectives

- Understand the Law of Exponents for Negative Exponents ($x^{-n} = \frac{1}{x^n}$).
- Simplify expressions involving negative exponents.
- Use negative exponents to write very small numbers in scientific notation.

Lesson Preparation

Materials

- **Power Up K** (in *Instructional Masters*)
- **Teacher-provided material: calculators**

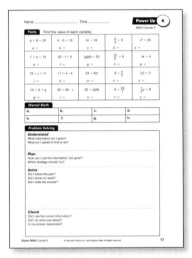

Power Up K

Math Language

Maintain	English Learners (ESL)
reciprocal	mixes
scientific notation	

Technology Resources

Student eBook Complete student textbook in electronic format.

Resources and Planner CD Assessment, reteaching, and instructional masters, plus a pacing calendar with standards.

Test and Practice Generator CD Create additional practice sheets and custom-made tests.

www.SaxonPublishers.com Visit for more student activities and planning materials.

Inclusion

Adaptations CD Adapted lessons, investigations, practice and assessments.

Meeting Standards

National Council of Teachers of Mathematics (NCTM)

Numbers and Operations

NO.1e Develop an understanding of large numbers and recognize and appropriately use exponential, scientific, and calculator notation

Algebra

AL.2d Recognize and generate equivalent forms for simple algebraic expressions and solve linear equations

Connections

CN.4b Understand how mathematical ideas interconnect and build on one another to produce a coherent whole

Problem-Solving Strategy: Find a Pattern/Write an Equation

The first four numbers Hexa said were 16, 32, 48, and 64. If she keeps counting this way, what is the 99th number Hexa will say?

(Understand) **Understand the problem.**

"What information are we given?"

The first four terms of a sequence are 16, 32, 48, and 64.

"What are we asked to do?"

Determine the 99th term of the sequence.

(Plan) **Make a plan.**

"What problem-solving strategy will we use?"

We will *find the pattern,* and *write an equation* for determining a specific term of the sequence.

"What do we anticipate our answer might be in the range of?"

Encourage several students to guess.

(Solve) **Carry out the plan.**

POSITION:	1st	2nd	3rd	4th
TERM:	16	32	48	64
PROCESS:	1×16	2×16	3×16	4×16

"What is the formula (rule) for determining the value of a term?"

$V_t = 16t$

"What is the 99th number Hexa will say?"

$99 \times 16 = \mathbf{1584}$.

(Check) **Look back.**

"Did we find the answer to the question that was asked?"

Yes. We determined that 1584 is the 99th number Hexa will say.

"How could we find the answer using mental math?"

The 100th number Hexa would say is 1600, because $100 \times 16 = 1600$. The 99th number would be 16 less than 1600, which is 1584.

- **Negative Exponents**
- **Scientific Notation for Small Numbers**

1 Power Up

Facts
Distribute **Power Up K** to students. See answers below.

Mental Math
Encourage students to share different ways to mentally compute these exercises. Strategies for exercises **a, c,** and **h** are listed below.

a. Multiply by 2 Twice
$$3.3 \times 4 = 3.3 \times 2 \times 2 = 6.6 \times 2 = 13.2$$

Regroup, then Multiply
$$3.3 \times 4 = 3 \times 4 + 0.3 \times 4 =$$
$$12 + 1.2 = 13.2$$

c. Isolate the Variable
$$25x = 250$$
$$x = \frac{250}{25} = 10$$

Solve By Inspection
$$25x = 250$$
$$x = 10$$

h. Square Roots of Perfect Squares
$$3 + 4 - 5 = 2$$

Problem Solving
Refer to **Power-Up Discussion,** p. 346F.

2 New Concepts

Instruction
To prepare students for this lesson, go over this review of dividing exponential expressions with the same base. Explain that this lesson will add to what students know about dividing exponential expressions.

(continued)

---

facts Power Up K

mental math

a. **Number Sense:** 3.3×4 13.2

b. **Measurement:** What temperature is indicated on this thermometer? $-24°C$

c. **Algebra:** $25x = 250$ 10

d. **Proportions:** There are 2 oranges to every 3 apples in a fruit basket. If there are 8 oranges, how many apples are in the basket? 12

e. **Percent:** How much is a 10% down payment on a $20,000 car? $2000

f. **Scientific Notation:** Write 250 in scientific notation. 2.5×10^2

g. **Geometry:** Approximate the volume of this object. $\approx 60 \text{ mm}^3$

2.9 mm

5.2 mm   4.1 mm

h. **Calculation:** $\sqrt{9} + \sqrt{16} - \sqrt{25}$ 2

problem solving The first four numbers Hexa said were 16, 32, 48, and 64. If she keeps counting this way, what is the 99th number Hexa will say? $99 \times 16 = 1584$

New Concepts
Increasing Knowledge

negative exponents

Recall from Lesson 27 that we subtract the exponents when dividing exponential expressions that have the same base.

$$x^5 \div x^3 = x^2$$

We can understand this law by applying what we know about exponents and division.

$$\frac{x^5}{x^3} = \frac{\overset{1}{\cancel{x}} \cdot \overset{1}{\cancel{x}} \cdot \overset{1}{\cancel{x}} \cdot x \cdot x}{\underset{1}{\cancel{x}} \cdot \underset{1}{\cancel{x}} \cdot \underset{1}{\cancel{x}}} = x^2$$

Now consider the result when we reverse the numbers in the division. Following the Laws of Exponents, the exponent of the quotient is negative.

$$x^3 \div x^5 = x^{-2} \text{ (because } 3 - 5 = -2)$$

Facts   Find the value of each variable.

$a + 8 = 20$	$b - 6 = 18$	$3c = 24$	$\frac{d}{4} = 8$	$x^2 = 25$
$a = 12$	$b = 24$	$c = 8$	$d = 32$	$x = 5 \text{ (and } -5)$
$7 + e = 15$	$20 - f = 5$	$(g)(4) = 20$	$\frac{12}{h} = 6$	$\sqrt{w} = 4$
$e = 8$	$f = 15$	$g = 5$	$h = 2$	$w = 16$
$18 = j + 11$	$17 = k - 4$	$24 = 6m$	$6 = \frac{n}{3}$	$\|z\| = 3$
$j = 7$	$k = 21$	$m = 4$	$n = 18$	$z = 3, -3$
$14 = 5 + q$	$30 = 40 - r$	$32 = (s)(4)$	$8 = \frac{24}{t}$	$\frac{1}{2}y = 8$
$q = 9$	$r = 10$	$s = 8$	$t = 3$	$y = 16$

We will apply what we know about exponents and division to understand the meaning of x^{-2}.

$$\frac{x^3}{x^5} = \frac{\overset{1}{\cancel{x}} \cdot \overset{1}{\cancel{x}} \cdot \overset{1}{\cancel{x}}}{\underset{1}{\cancel{x}} \cdot \underset{1}{\cancel{x}} \cdot \underset{1}{\cancel{x}} \cdot x \cdot x} = \frac{1}{x^2}$$

Math Language
Recall that the product of a number and its **reciprocal** is 1.

By performing the division we find that x^{-2} means $\frac{1}{x^2}$. We see that x^{-2} is the reciprocal of x^2. This fact is another law of exponents.

**Law of Exponents for
Negative Exponents**

$$x^{-n} = \frac{1}{x^n}$$

Applying this law to powers of 10, we see the following pattern. Note that $10^0 = 1$.

$$10^2 = 100$$
$$10^1 = 10$$
$$10^0 = 1$$
$$10^{-1} = \frac{1}{10} \text{ or } 0.1$$
$$10^{-2} = \frac{1}{100} \text{ or } 0.01$$

Evaluate Use the Laws of Exponents to find the product of 10^2 and 10^{-2}.
$10^2 \cdot 10^{-2} = 10^{2-2} = 10^0 = 1$
Very small numbers may exceed the display capabilities of a calculator. One millionth of one millionth is more than zero, but it is a very small number. On a calculator we enter

The product, one trillionth, contains more digits than can be displayed by many calculators. Instead of displaying one trillionth in standard form, the calculator displays the number in a modified form of scientific notation:

$$\boxed{\text{\textit{l.} }^{-12}} \text{ or perhaps } \boxed{\text{\textit{l.} } \times 1\text{\textit{0}}^{-12}}$$

Example 1

Which of the following does not equal 10^{-3}?

A $\frac{1}{10^3}$ B $\frac{1}{1000}$ C 0.001   D −1000

Solution

An exponential expression with a negative exponent is the reciprocal of the expression with the opposite exponent, as shown in A. Since 10^3 equals 1000, B is just an alternate form of A. Choice C is the decimal equivalent of B. The only number that does not equal 10^{-3} is choice **D, −1000**. A negative exponent does not imply a negative number. Actually, 10^{-3} is a positive number.

Lesson 51   347

---

2 New Concepts (Continued)

Instruction
Use the *Math Language* feature to check on students' understanding of reciprocals. Ask students to explain why the product of a number and its reciprocal is 1. Sample: When you multiply a number and its reciprocal, you are forming a fraction equal to 1.

Guide students through the division starting with the use of the Division Law of Exponents and ending with the new Law of Exponents for Negative Exponents: $x^{-n} = \frac{1}{x^n}$. Note that we used our understanding of the exponent laws and reciprocals to develop this new relationship.

Have volunteers describe and explain the pattern in the list of powers of 10 and their standard forms. For the *Apply* question, have students recall that any number raised to the zero power is 1.

Example 1
Instruction
Work through the elimination process to find the answer. Then call attention to the different ways of expressing one thousandth.

(continued)

New Concepts (Continued)

Example 2
Instruction

Explain that the Laws of Exponents apply to negative exponents as well as positive exponents. To find the answers to **a** and **b**, students must remember how to add and subtract negative numbers.

Use the *Verify* feature to provide proof that the laws work for negative numbers. Ask whether using the laws or simplifying the expressions is a better way to solve parts **a** and **b** of this example.

Example 3
Instruction

Extend this example by comparing the two expressions and their simplified values. Note that the exponent laws make the manipulation of the numbers and symbols very different even though the problems look very similar.

(continued)

348 **Saxon** *Math Course 3*

Example 2

Find each missing exponent.

a. $10^{-2} \cdot 10^{-4} = 10^{\square}$

b. $\dfrac{10^{-2}}{10^{-4}} = 10^{\square}$

Solution

a. $\frac{1}{100} \cdot \frac{1}{10,000} =$
$\frac{1}{1,000,000} = \frac{1}{10^6}$
$= 10^{-6}$

b. $\frac{1}{100} \div \frac{1}{10,000} =$
$\frac{1}{100} \cdot \frac{10,000}{1} =$
$100 = 10^2$

a. To multiply exponential expressions with the same base we can add the exponents. We add -2 and -4.
$$(-2) + (-4) = -6$$
The missing exponent is **−6.**

b. To divide exponential expressions with the same base we can subtract the exponents. In this case we subtract -4 from -2. Instead of subtracting a negative, we add its opposite.
$$(-2) - (-4)$$
$$(-2) + (+4) = 2$$
The missing exponent is **2.**

Verify Find the answers to **a** and **b** by simplifying each exponential expression and performing the multiplication and division.

Example 3

Simplify:

a. 2^{-3} 　　　　　　　 b. $(-2)^3$

Solution

We distinguish between negative powers and powers of negative numbers.

a. To simplify 2^{-3} we rewrite the expression with a positive exponent.
$$2^{-3} = \frac{1}{2^3}$$
Then we apply the positive exponent to the base.
$$\frac{1}{2^3} = \frac{1}{2 \cdot 2 \cdot 2} = \frac{1}{8}$$

b. The expression $(-2)^3$ is written with a positive exponent. Three negative factors produce a negative product.
$$(-2)^3 = (-2)(-2)(-2) = -8$$

348 **Saxon** *Math Course 3*

Example 4

Simplify: $3^2 \cdot 3^{-2}$

Solution

To simplify $3^2 \cdot 3^{-2}$ we add the exponents. Adding the exponents 2 and -2 results in the exponent zero.

$$3^2 \cdot 3^{-2} = 3^0$$

Recall that $x^0 = 1$ if x is not zero. Therefore $3^0 = 1$. We can confirm this by applying what we have learned about negative exponents. We will rewrite the multiplication by expressing 3^{-2} with a positive exponent.

Step:	Justification:
$3^2 \cdot 3^{-2}$	Given expression
$3^2 \cdot \dfrac{1}{3^2}$	Wrote 3^{-2} with positive exponent
$9 \cdot \dfrac{1}{9}$	Applied exponents
1	Simplified

We confirm that the expression 3^0 equals **1**.

Example 5

Express with positive exponents and simplify: $2x^{-1}yx^2y^{-2}z$

Solution

A negative exponent indicates a reciprocal, so x^{-1} is $\frac{1}{x}$ and y^{-2} is $\frac{1}{y^2}$. A quick way to change the sign of the exponent is to draw a division bar and shift the exponential expression to the opposite side of the division bar.

$$\frac{2x^{-1}yx^2y^{-2}z}{1} = \frac{2yx^2z}{xy^2}$$

All exponents are positive. Now we reduce.

$$\frac{2yx^2z}{xy^2} = \frac{2\cancel{y}\cancel{x}xz}{\cancel{x}\cancel{y}y} = \frac{\mathbf{2xz}}{\mathbf{y}}$$

> We can add the exponents of the x and y factors: $2x^{-1}x^2y^1y^{-2}z = 2xy^{-1}z$

Connect How can we apply the Multiplication Law of Exponents to simplify the original expression?

> *scientific notation for small numbers*

We use negative powers of 10 to write small numbers in scientific notation. By small numbers we mean numbers between 0 and 1.

Positive numbers named with negative powers of 10.

Lesson 51   349

Example 4
Instruction
Explain that proof is an important part of mathematical thinking. For simple exercises and problems, checking the answers is a kind of proof. In many mathematical situations, it is necessary to go further—to show why each step is valid, and to show how each step connects to the next step.

The informal proof given here has more structure than simply checking the answer. Exposure to such explanations prepares students for writing formal proofs in their future work with mathematics.

Example 5
Instruction
Point out that once the expression is rewritten with positive exponents, the simplification process is the same as in earlier work with expressions. Use the *Connect* question to show how using the Multiplication Law of Exponents relates to the simplest form of the expression.

Instruction
Introduce scientific notation for small numbers. Explain that this definition of small numbers is only for writing numbers between 0 and 1 in scientific notation.

(continued)

Math Background

Can an exponent be a fraction?

Yes. If x is a positive real number, p is a positive integer, and q is an integer, then $x^{\frac{p}{q}} = \sqrt[q]{x^p} = (\sqrt[q]{x})^p$.

Here are some examples.

$$25^{\frac{1}{2}} = \sqrt[2]{25^1} = \sqrt[2]{25} = 5 \qquad 8^{\frac{2}{3}} = (\sqrt[3]{8})^2 = 2^2 = 4$$

$$16^{\frac{5}{4}} = (\sqrt[4]{16})^5 = 2^5 = 32 \qquad 27^{\frac{2}{3}} = (\sqrt[3]{27})^2 = 3^2 = 9$$

2 New Concepts (Continued)

Example 6
Instruction

Ask students to explain why this number is in proper scientific notation form. Sample: The coefficient has one and only one digit to the left of the decimal point, and the digit is not zero.

Example 7
Instruction

Tell students that they can make scallops under each digit as they move the decimal point to help them keep track of the number of places the point moves.

$$0.000007$$

Example 8
Instruction

Emphasize that no matter how small a positive number is, it will always be greater than 0 or any negative number.

Instruction

Work with students to see how their calculators display this number. If students have different calculators, be sure that all students know how their calculators display small numbers in scientific notation.

Practice Set
Problems a and b [Error Alert]

Students should generalize that a negative exponent indicates a reciprocal.

Explain to students who name $\frac{1}{3^2}$ and $\frac{1}{2^3}$ as answers that the denominators 3^2 and 2^3 each represent an operation that has not been completed.

Problem d [Error Alert]

Watch for students who multiply the bases and rewrite 4^0 as 1.

Problem e [Analyze]

Remind students that a negative exponent indicates a reciprocal, then challenge them to write or name the order using only mental math.

Problems f and g [Error Alert]

Make sure students recognize that the expressions represent the product or quotient of like bases.

(continued)

Visit www.SaxonPublishers.com/ActivitiesC3 for a graphing calculator activity.

Example 6

Write this number in standard form.

$$1.5 \times 10^{-3}$$

Solution

The power 10^{-3} equals 0.001. If we perform the multiplication we find the product is 0.0015.

$$1.5 \times 10^{-3}$$
$$1.5 \times 0.001 = \mathbf{0.0015}$$

Notice that we can find the product simply by shifting the decimal point in the coefficient three places to the left. Thus the power of ten indicates both the direction and the number of places the decimal shifts.

Visit www.SaxonPublishers.com/ActivitiesC3 for a graphing calculator activity.

Example 7

The diameter of a red blood cell is about 0.000007 meters. Write that number in scientific notation.

Solution

The coefficient is 7. In standard form the decimal point is six places to the left, so the power of 10 is −6.

$$0.000007 = \mathbf{7 \times 10^{-6}}$$

Example 8

Compare: $1 \times 10^{-6} \bigcirc -10$

Solution

The expression 1×10^{-6} is a positive number, though a small one (0.000001). Any positive number is greater than a negative number.

$$1 \times 10^{-6} > -10$$

Practice Set   Simplify:

▶ **a.** 3^{-2} $\frac{1}{9}$ ▶ **b.** 2^{-3} $\frac{1}{8}$ **c.** 5^0 1   ▶ **d.** $2^{-3} \cdot 2^3$ 1

▶ **e.** [Analyze] Arrange in order from least to greatest:

$\frac{1}{2}, 0, 1, 2^{-2}, -1, 0.1$ $-1, 0, 0.1, 2^{-2}, \frac{1}{2}, 1$

[Evaluate] Find the missing exponent in problems **f–g**. Check your answers by substituting the exponent answer into each equation and solving.

▶ **f.** $10^{-3} \cdot 10^{-4} = 10^{\square}$ −7   ▶ **g.** $\frac{1}{1} = 10^{\square}$ −3

▶ See Math Conversations in the sidebar.

Teacher Tip

If your students do not have scientific calculators, explain that they can use **ordinary calculators to help** them **calculate** with **scientific notation.**

- They multiply or divide the coefficients with their calculators first to find the coefficient of the answer.

- Next they do the computation with the powers of 10 mentally to get the power of 10 for the answer.

- Then they combine the coefficient and the power of 10 and check whether they need to rewrite the expression in proper scientific notation form.

Simplify:

h. $x^{-3}y^2xy^{-1}$ $\frac{y}{x^2}$ **i.** $\frac{6x^{-2}y^3z^{-1}}{2xy}$ $\frac{3y^2}{x^3z}$

j. Write 10^{-4} as a decimal number.   0.0001

k. Write 5×10^{-5} in standard form.   0.00005

l. Write 2.5×10^{-2} in standard form.   0.025

▶ **m.** Write 0.008 in scientific notation. 8×10^{-3}

▶ **n.** Write 0.000125 in scientific notation. 1.25×10^{-4}

o. If lightning strikes a mile away the sound reaches us in about 5 seconds, but its light reaches us in about 5 millionths of a second. Write 5 millionths in scientific notation. 5×10^{-6}

p. A nanometer is 10^{-9} meters. Write that number in standard form.   0.000000001

Written Practice   *Strengthening Concepts*

Evaluate For problems **1–2,** record the information in a ratio table. Estimate an answer and then solve by writing and solving a proportion.

▶ *** 1.** Ruben wrote 2 pages in 3 hours. At that rate, how long will it take him to write 9 pages? $13\frac{1}{2}$ hours
   (49)

▶ *** 2.** If 9 gallons of gas cost $20.25, how much would it cost to fill a 25 gallon tank? $56.25
   (49)

▶ *** 3.** On a piano, the ratio of black keys to white keys is 9 to 13. If there are 88 keys on a piano, how many are black?   36 black keys
   (45)

▶ *** 4.** Kerry mixes apple slices and raisins at a 3 to 1 ratio to make her fruit salad. If she wants 16 cups of fruit salad, how many cups of apple slices will she need?   12 cups
   (45)

5. The shipping charges totaled $9.26. Included in the charge was a $3.50 flat fee. The rest of the cost was for weight, at $0.64 per pound. How much did the package weigh?   9 pounds
   (3, 4)

Solve:

▶ *** 6.** $12x - 3 = 69$ $x = 6$ ▶ *** 7.** $\frac{x}{4} + 1 = 12$ $x = 44$
   (50)   (50)

▶ *** 8.** $\frac{x}{3} - 4 = 5$ $x = 27$ ▶ *** 9.** $-x + 1 = 6$ $x = -5$
   (50)   (50)

▶ *** 10.** $1 - m = -1$ $m = 2$ ▶ *** 11.** $3x + 2x - 1 = 99$ $x = 20$
   (50)   (50)

Lesson 51   351

▶ See Math Conversations in the sidebar.

English Learners

For problem **4,** explain the meaning of the word **mixes.** Say:

> *"When you mix two or more things, you put them together. You can mix marbles by putting them all together in a bag."*

Ask students which ingredients they need to mix to make pancakes. Mention that there are some things that after you mix them, you cannot separate them anymore—unlike the marbles, which can be easily separated.   milk, eggs, flour, baking powder, sugar

---

New Concepts *(Continued)*

Practice Set
Problems m and n   Error Alert

You may need to remind students that the coefficient must have only one nonzero digit to the left of its decimal point.

Written Practice

Math Conversations

Discussion opportunities are provided below.

Problem 1   Evaluate

Explain that the problem can be solved by proportion or by unit rate. Ask students to choose one method and use it to solve the problem, then use the other method to check their work.

Problem 2   Evaluate

Before completing the arithmetic, encourage students to make and record an estimate of the cost. After completing the problem, students should decide the reasonableness of the exact answer by comparing it to the estimate.

Problem 3   Analyze

Students who use a ratio table to represent the problem should infer that because 88 keys represent the total number of keys, a third row titled "total" should be included in the table.

Problem 4   Analyze

Make sure students understand that because the 3 to 1 ratio describes the relationship of apple slices to raisins in the whole fruit salad, the ratio also describes any portion of that whole, such as one cup.

Problems 6–11   Analyze

Before completing the arithmetic for each problem, ask students to identify the inverse operation(s), and the order of the inverse operations, that will be used to isolate the variable.

For problem **11,** students should recognize the need to collect like terms before applying inverse operations.

Errors and Misconceptions
Problems 6–11

When inverse operations are used to solve for a variable, watch for students who use those operations in the *same* order as the order of operations. When solving for a variable, remind students to use inverse operations in *reverse* order of the order of operations.

(continued)

Lesson 51   **351**

Math Conversations

Discussion opportunities are provided below.

Problem 14 Evaluate

You may need to point out that the measures of the diameters must be halved because r in the formula $A = \pi r^2$ represents the length of a radius.

Encourage students to sketch the circles and label the radii.

(continued)

---

* 12. Refer to the graph of lines *a* and *b* to
(Inv. 1) answer the following questions.

    a. Which line intersects the *y*-axis at −4? line *a*

    b. Which line is perpendicular to the *y*-axis? line *b*

    c. What is the slope of line *a*? $-\frac{4}{3}$

    d. In which quadrant do lines *a* and *b* intersect? 2nd

13.

* 13. Graph $y = 4x + 1$. Is (3, 13) on the line? Yes
(47)

▶*** 14.** The figure shows three concentric (meaning
(40) "same center") circles. The diameters of the three circles are 4 cm, 8 cm, and 12 cm. Find the area of the shaded region. Use 3.14 for π and round the answer to the nearest square centimeter. 38 cm²

* 15. Sketch a model of a book that measures 2 in. by 10 in. by 8 in. What is
(Inv. 4, 42) the volume of the book? 160 in.³

* 16. Write 3.4×10^{-5} in decimal notation. 0.000034
(51)

Combine like terms to simplify:

17. $9(x - 3) + 5(x + 5)$
(31, 36) $14x - 2$

18. $3x^2 - 3x + x - 1$
(31) $3x^2 - 2x - 1$

Simplify:

* 19. $\dfrac{(2xy)(3x^2y)}{6xy^2}$ x^2
(36)

* 20. $-6 - (-5)$ -1
(33)

21. $2\frac{1}{2} \cdot 1\frac{3}{5} - 2\frac{3}{8}$ $1\frac{5}{8}$
(13, 23)

* 22. $(2.3 \times 10^4)(1.5 \times 10^3)$ 3.45×10^7
(46)

23. Compare $0.62 \;\bigcirc\!\!< \; \frac{5}{8}$
(12)

24. Write $\frac{7}{10}$ **a** as a decimal and **b** as a percent. **a.** 0.7; **b.** 70%
(12)

25. a.

$a = 70°$
$b = 70°$

25. **a.** Redraw the triangles separately and find *a*
(35) and *b*.

    b. Explain how you know that the two triangles are similar. Angle-Angle-Angle similarity criteria

    c. Find the scale factor from the smaller to the larger triangle, then find *x*. scale factor: 1.5, *x* = 5.4

▶ See Math Conversations in the sidebar.

26. Find $\sqrt{b^2 - 4ac}$ when $a = 6$, $b = 5$, and $c = -1$.   7
(14, 36)

* 27. James is building a 10-inch by 12-inch rectangular picture frame. To
(Inv. 2) assure the frame has right angles, James measures the two diagonals
to see if they are equal. When the diagonals are equal, how long
is each diagonal? (Express your answer to the nearest tenth of an
inch.)   15.6 in.

28. Arnold flipped a coin twice and it landed heads up both times. If he flips
(32) the coin again, what is the probability the coin will land heads up? $\frac{1}{2}$

29. Find all possible values of x for the equation $x^2 - 16 = 0$.   4, −4
(14, 36)

▶ **30.** **a.** Which figure—A, B, or C—is a translation of figure *MNOPQR*?
(Inv. 5)   Figure C
       b. For the figure you chose, give the coordinates that locate M', N', O',
       P', Q', and R'. M' (2, −2), N' (4, −2), O' (4, −4), P' (7, −4), Q' (7, −6),
       and R' (2, −6).

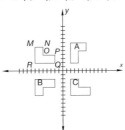

Early Finishers

Real-World
Application

In a vacuum, the speed of light is constant at approximately 300,000,000
meters/second. If the distance from the Earth to the Sun is about
149,000,000,000 meters, about how many seconds does it take light to reach
the Earth? Express your answer in scientific notation.

$\frac{1.49 \times 10^{11}}{3.0 \times 10^8} = \frac{1.49}{3.0} \times \frac{10^{11}}{10^8} = 0.49\overline{66} \times 10^3 = 4.97 \times 10^2$ seconds

▶ See Math Conversations in the sidebar.

Math Conversations

Discussion opportunities are provided below.

Errors and Misconceptions
Problem 30

If students have difficulty understanding how
translations, reflections, and rotations are
different, remind them that other words can
be used to describe the transformations.

translation: slide
reflection: flip
rotation: turn

Work with these students to sketch a figure,
then sketch a translation, a reflection, and a
rotation of that figure.

Looking Forward

Working with negative exponents
and scientific notation for small
numbers prepares students for:

- **Lesson 57,** performing operations
  with small numbers in scientific
  notation.

- **Lesson 63,** simplifying fractions
  with negative exponents.

• Using Unit Multipliers to Convert Measures
• Converting Mixed-Unit to Single-Unit Measures

Objectives

- Use unit multipliers to convert between units of measure.
- Solve word problems that require unit multipliers.
- Convert between mixed-unit measures and single-unit measures with and without using unit multipliers.

Lesson Preparation

Materials

- **Power Up K** (in *Instructional Masters*)

Optional

- Teacher-provided material: measuring tools (rulers, yardsticks)

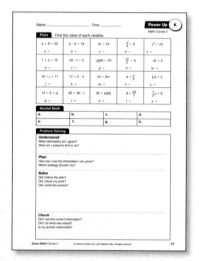

Power Up K

Math Language

New

unit multiplier

Technology Resources

Student eBook Complete student textbook in electronic format.

Resources and Planner CD Assessment, reteaching, and instructional masters, plus a pacing calendar with standards.

Test and Practice Generator CD Create additional practice sheets and custom-made tests.

www.SaxonPublishers.com Visit for more student activities and planning materials.

Inclusion

Adaptations CD Adapted lessons, investigations, practice and assessments.

Meeting Standards

National Council of Teachers of Mathematics (NCTM)

ME.1a Understand both metric and customary systems of measurement

ME.1b Understand relationships among units and convert from one unit to another within the same system

Connections

CN.4a Recognize and use connections among mathematical ideas

Problem-Solving Strategy: Write an Equation

A number is divided by 2 and then added to 11. The result is 19. What is the number? Explain your thinking.

(Understand) **Understand the problem.**

"What information are we given?"

A number is first divided by two, and the resulting quotient is then added to 11.

"What are we asked to do?"

Determine the number and explain how we determined the number.

(Plan) **Make a plan.**

"What problem-solving strategy will we use?"

We will *write an equation.*

"How can we know how many steps this problem will require to be solved?"

Both division and addition are mentioned, so it will require at least two steps.

(Solve) **Carry out the plan.**

"How will we indicate the unknown number in the equation?"

with a letter like n

"What is the first operation performed on the unknown number and how do we show that?"

The number is divided by 2, which we show as $\frac{n}{2}$.

"Then what operation is performed to make the result 19?"

The quotient is added to 11. $\frac{n}{2} + 11 = 19$

"What must the quantity $\frac{n}{2}$ equal?"

8, because $8 + 11 = 19$

"If $\frac{n}{2}$ equals 8, what does n equal?"

16, because $16 \div 2 = 8$

"How can we use the equation to verify that our solution is correct?"

We can verify 16 is the correct solution by substituting it back into that original equation: $\frac{16}{2} + 11 = 8 + 11 = 19$.

(Check) **Look back.**

"Did we complete the task that was assigned?"

Yes. We explained how we were able to determine that 16 was the number that when divided by two and added to eleven produces 19.

• Using Unit Multipliers to Convert Measures
• Converting Mixed-Unit to Single-Unit Measures

1 Power Up

Facts

Distribute **Power Up K** to students. See answers below.

Mental Math

Encourage students to share different ways to mentally compute these exercises. Strategies for exercises **a, e,** and **f** are listed below.

a. Multiply by 10, Then by 2

$7.5 \times 20 = 7.5 \times 10 \times 2 = 75 \times 2 = 150$

Regroup, then Multiply

$7.5 \times 20 = 7 \times 20 + 0.5 \times 20 = 140 + 10 = 150$

e. Use Each Rate, then Subtract

J: $\frac{1}{2}$ hr $\times$ 50 problems per hr = 25 problems

R: $\frac{1}{2}$ hr $\times$ 40 problems per hr = 20 problems

J − R = 25 − 20 = 5 problems

f. Sum of Angles of Triangle

$m + 60° + 60° = 180°$

$m = 180° - (60° + 60°)$

$m = 180° - 120°$

$m = 60°$

All 3 angles are equal, so the triangle is equilateral.

Problem Solving

Refer to **Power-Up Discussion,** p. 354B.

2 New Concepts

Instruction

Point out that the two unit multipliers are reciprocals, and that this is true for all unit multipliers. Explain that either form can be used to convert from one unit to another, and that the form we choose to use depends on the unit that is needed for the answer. The unit that is needed for the answer should be above the division bar of the unit multiplier.

(continued)

Power Up   *Building Power*

facts   Power Up K

mental math

a. **Number Sense:** 7.5×20 150

b. **Statistics:** The mean of two numbers is the number halfway between. What is the mean of 10 and 20?   15

c. **Fractional Parts:** How much do you save if a $90 item is 10% off? $9

d. **Scientific Notation:** Write 0.0051 in scientific notation. 5.1×10^{-3}

e. **Rate:** Jackie finishes 50 problems per hour. Ray finishes 40 problems per hour. How many more problems will Jackie finish than Ray if they work for 30 minutes?   5

f. **Geometry:** Two angles of a triangle are 60° and 60°. Find the measure of the third angle. What type of triangle is the triangle?   60°; equilateral

g. **Powers/Roots:** List the perfect squares from 1 to 169.   1, 4, 9, 16, 25, 36, 49, 64, 81, 100, 121, 144, 169

h. **Calculation:** $22, + 2, \times 2, + 2, \times 2, \sqrt{}$ 10

problem solving

A number is divided by 2 and then added to 11. The result is 19. What is the number? Explain your thinking.   Before it was added to 11, the result was 8. Before 8 was divided by 2, it was 16. Original number = 16

New Concepts   *Increasing Knowledge*

using unit multipliers to convert measures

A unit multiplier is a ratio in which the numerator and denominator are equivalent measures but different units. Since 12 inches equal one foot, we can write these two unit multipliers for that relationship.

$$\frac{12 \text{ in.}}{1 \text{ ft}} \qquad \frac{1 \text{ ft}}{12 \text{ in.}}$$

Each of these ratios equals 1 because the measures above and below the division bar are equivalent. Since multiplying by 1 (or a form of 1) does not change a quantity, we can multiply by a unit multiplier to convert a measure from one unit to another unit.

Example 1

The sapling apple tree is 64 inches tall. Convert 64 inches to feet by multiplying 64 inches by $\frac{1 \text{ ft}}{12 \text{ in.}}$.

354   *Saxon Math Course 3*

Facts   Find the value of each variable.

$a + 8 = 20$	$b - 6 = 18$	$3c = 24$	$\frac{d}{4} = 8$	$x^2 = 25$
$a = 12$	$b = 24$	$c = 8$	$d = 32$	$x = 5$ (and −5)
$7 + e = 15$	$20 - f = 5$	$(g)(4) = 20$	$\frac{12}{h} = 6$	$\sqrt{w} = 4$
$e = 8$	$f = 15$	$g = 5$	$h = 2$	$w = 16$
$18 = j + 11$	$17 = k - 4$	$24 = 6m$	$6 = \frac{n}{3}$	$|z| = 3$
$j = 7$	$k = 21$	$m = 4$	$n = 18$	$z = 3, -3$
$14 = 5 + q$	$30 = 40 - r$	$32 = (s)(4)$	$8 = \frac{24}{t}$	$\frac{1}{2}y = 8$
$q = 9$	$r = 10$	$s = 8$	$t = 3$	$y = 16$

Thinking Skill

Explain

Is canceling
units of measure
like canceling
numbers?
Explain.   Yes; We
cancel numbers
by pairing a
numerator and
denominator that
have a
common
factor. We cancel
units by pairing
a numerator and
denominator that
have a common
unit.

Solution

The unit multiplier cancels inches and leaves feet as the unit.

$$64 \text{ in.} \times \frac{1 \text{ ft}}{12 \text{ in.}} = \frac{64}{12}\text{ft} = 5\frac{1}{3} \text{ ft}$$

Example 2

A certain double feature at a theater is 270 minutes long. Use a unit multiplier to convert 270 minutes to hours.

Solution

Since 60 minutes equal one hour, we have a choice of two unit multipliers.

$$\frac{60 \text{ min}}{1 \text{ hr}} \qquad \frac{1 \text{ hr}}{60 \text{ min}}$$

To cancel minutes we choose the unit multiplier with minutes below the division bar.

$$270 \text{ min} \times \frac{1 \text{ hr}}{60 \text{ min}} = \frac{270}{60} \text{ hr} = 4\frac{1}{2} \text{ hr}$$

Connect   In addition to canceling units in examples 1 and 2, could we also cancel numbers? Explain.

We can use unit multipliers to convert measures to desired or appropriate units. Appropriate units are correct and meaningful to the intended reader.

Example 3

Daniel is buying refreshments for a meeting. He wonders if four quarts of juice is enough for 30 students. Is four quarts a reasonable amount of juice for the meeting? If not, suggest a more reasonable quantity.

Solution

If each student has the same amount of juice, then one serving is 4 quarts divided by 30.

$$\frac{4 \text{ quarts}}{30 \text{ students}} = \frac{4}{30} \text{ quarts per student}$$

The answer is not very meaningful. A more appropriate unit is ounces. We convert 4 quarts to ounces and then we divide by 30.

$$4 \text{ qt} \cdot \frac{32 \text{ oz}}{1 \text{ qt}} = 128 \text{ oz}$$

$$\frac{128 \text{ oz}}{30 \text{ students}} = 4 \text{ ounces per student}$$

Since four ounces is half a cup, **four quarts is probably not enough juice.** If Daniel buys **eight quarts,** then each student could have a full cup (8 ounces) of juice.

Example 1
Instruction
Explain that the unit multiplier $\frac{1 \text{ ft}}{12 \text{ in.}}$ was used because the desired unit for the answer is feet. Because the unit multiplier has feet above the division bar, feet will be the unit of the answer. Ask whether the answer could be expressed in a different way or with different units. Samples: 5 ft 4 in.; 5.$\overline{3}$ ft

Example 2
Instruction
Ask a volunteer to explain why we want to cancel minutes. Sample: We want the answer to be in hours. Use the Thinking Skill *Explain* question to stress that canceling units is needed to be sure that the computation will display the correct unit.

As you discuss the *Connect* question, explain that students should always look for opportunities to cancel when converting measures. Because canceling makes the computation simpler, there are likely to be fewer errors.

Example 3
Instruction
Extend this problem by asking students if Daniel could have used a different approach to deciding how much juice to buy for 30 students. Sample: I would have started by thinking about how much juice each student might drink and then multiply that amount by 30.

(continued)

Math Background

Some conversions involve multiplying by more than one unit multiplier. For example, these steps convert 352 ounces to gallons.

$$352 \text{ oz} \cdot \frac{1 \text{ c}}{8 \text{ oz}} \cdot \frac{1 \text{ pt}}{2 \text{ c}} \cdot \frac{1 \text{ qt}}{2 \text{ pt}} \cdot \frac{1 \text{ gal}}{4 \text{ qt}} = 2.75 \text{ gal}$$

These steps convert 1 year to minutes.

$$1 \text{ yr} \cdot \frac{365 \text{ day}}{1 \text{ yr}} \cdot \frac{24 \text{ hr}}{1 \text{ day}} \cdot \frac{60 \text{ min}}{1 \text{ hr}} = 525,600 \text{ min}$$

Students will learn about these types of conversions in Lesson 72.

Instruction

Discuss how Mr. Seymour's height could have been converted to inches. Sample: Convert 6 feet to inches using a unit multiplier and then add 3 inches.

Example 4

Instruction

Ask a volunteer to explain how to find Samantha's driving time in minutes. Sample: Convert 1 hour to minutes and add 45 minutes. You might extend this problem by asking students to calculate Samantha's average driving rate in miles per hour. About 57 miles per hour

Example 5

Instruction

Have a student explain why it would not make sense to find Noel's running time in seconds. Sample: The number would be too big and it would be hard to compare with other running times. We generally express measures using the most appropriate unit.

Example 6

Instruction

Point out that 13 ft 6 in. is converted first to a single-unit measure because a single unit can more easily be used in the computation for conversion to yards.

Connect this problem to everyday experiences by explaining that because carpeting is sold by the yard, someone who is going to buy carpeting would want to know the dimensions of the room in yards.

(continued)

---

converting mixed-unit to single-unit measures

Some units like feet and inches are used together to express a measure.

Mr. Seymour is 6 ft 3 in. tall.

To express Mr. Seymour's height with a single unit we could give his height in inches (75 in.) or in feet. Below we show his height in feet. Three inches is $\frac{3}{12}$ of a foot, which equals $\frac{1}{4}$ ft or 0.25 ft. We can combine 6 ft with $\frac{1}{4}$ ft or 0.25 ft.

$$6 \text{ ft } 3 \text{ in.} = 6\frac{1}{4} \text{ ft} = 6.25 \text{ ft}$$

Example 4

Samantha drove 100 miles in an hour and 45 minutes. How many hours did it take for Samantha to drive 100 miles?

Solution

We express 45 minutes as $\frac{45}{60}$ of an hour.

$$45 \text{ min} = \frac{45}{60} \text{ hr} = \frac{3}{4} \text{ hr} = 0.75 \text{ hr}$$

Samantha drove for 1 hr 45 min, which is **$1\frac{3}{4}$ hr or 1.75 hr.**

Example 5

Noel ran one mile in 7 minutes and 30 seconds. Find Noel's time in minutes. Express the result as a mixed number and as a decimal number.

Solution

We convert 30 sec to $\frac{30}{60}$ minutes which is $\frac{1}{2}$ or 0.5 min.

$$7 \text{ min } 30 \text{ sec} = 7\frac{1}{2} \text{ min} = 7.5 \text{ min}$$

Example 6

To measure a room for carpeting, Juan converts the length and width of the room from feet and inches to yards. A room that is 13 ft 6 in. long is how many yards long?

Solution

First we convert 13 ft 6 in. to feet.

$$13 \text{ ft } 6 \text{ in.} = 13\frac{6}{12} \text{ ft} = 13.5 \text{ ft}$$

Then we convert feet to yards.

$$13.5 \text{ ft} \cdot \frac{1 \text{ yd}}{3 \text{ ft}} = \frac{13.5 \text{ yd}}{3} = 4.5 \text{ yd}$$

The room is **4.5 yd** long.

Manipulative Use

To give students **hands-on experience with converting measures,** provide measuring tools so each student can measure the length of five objects in the classroom. After students make their measurements, have them convert the measures to a different unit. Ask students to express any mixed-unit measures in two ways: with mixed units and with a single unit.

You may also want to display a poster of common equivalents for measures or develop a class list of equivalent measures the students are likely to need for problems.

Practice Set

Problems a and b [Error Alert]

Make sure students understand that a unit multiplier is a ratio that is equal to 1 and consists of two equivalent measures.

Problem c [Error Alert]

Review capacity relationships with those students who do not know that 1 pint and 16 ounces are equivalent measures.

Problem d [Error Alert]

Watch for opportunities to remind students that units can be canceled if the same unit is in a numerator and in a denominator of the factors.

Also point out that numbers can be canceled in the same way, and have students recall that if the numbers are different, they should divide by a common factor, or by the greatest common factor, of the numbers.

Problems g and j [Error Alert]

To convert the measures, students will need to use two different unit multipliers.

Problem h [Error Alert]

Remind students that unit multipliers such as $\frac{1 \text{ min}}{60 \text{ sec}}$ and $\frac{60 \text{ sec}}{1 \text{ min}}$ represent the same unit multiplier, and either can be used to solve the problem. Have students note that both unit multipliers are ratios equal to 1, and made up of two equivalent measures.

Practice Set ▶

a. $\frac{1 \text{ day}}{24 \text{ hr}}, \frac{24 \text{ hr}}{1 \text{ day}}, \frac{24 \text{ hr}}{1 \text{ day}},$ I would choose the multiplier with days as the denominator because I want to cancel days.

d. $\frac{50 \text{ in}}{1} \cdot \frac{2.54 \text{ cm}}{1 \text{ in.}}$ = 127 cm

▶ **a.** *Justify* One day is 24 hours. Write two unit multipliers that have days and hours as the units. Identify the unit multiplier you would use to convert days to hours. Explain your choice.

▶ **b.** *Represent* Write two unit multipliers for this equivalence: $\frac{1 \text{ pt}}{16 \text{ oz}}, \frac{16 \text{ oz}}{1 \text{ pt}}$

  16 oz = 1 pt

▶ **c.** A gallon is 128 oz. Convert 128 oz. to pints using a unit multiplier.   8 pt

▶ **d.** An inch is 2.54 cm. A bookcase that is 50 inches high is how many centimeters high? Use a unit multiplier to perform the conversion.

  e. Convert 24 quarts to gallons using a unit multiplier. (1 gal = 4 qt)   6 gal

  f. Carter claims he can run 10,000 centimeters in 14 seconds. Express his claim in more appropriate terms.   100 meters in 14 seconds

▶ **g.** The newborn child was 21 inches long and weighed 8 pounds 4 ounces. Convert these measures to feet and to pounds respectively, expressed as mixed numbers and as decimal numbers. $1\frac{3}{4}$ ft, 1.75 ft, $8\frac{1}{4}$ lb, 8.25 lb

▶ **h.** Marsha swam 400 meters in 6 minutes and 12 seconds. Convert that time to minutes.   6.2 min

  i. A room is 11 ft 6 in. long and 11 ft 3 in. wide. Find the perimeter of the room in feet.   45.5 ft

▶ **j.** Convert 11 ft 3 in. to feet. Then use a unit multiplier to convert that measure to yards.   3.75 yd

Written Practice   *Strengthening Concepts*

1. The hen to rooster ratio in the barnyard is 11 to 2. If there are 26 hens and roosters in all, how many are roosters?   4
  (45)

2. Sally sells popcorn for $1 and beverages for $2. What will be her total sales if 19 people each buy one bag of popcorn and one beverage? $57
  (3, 4)

3. For a collect call, a phone company charges a $1 connection fee, then 4 cents per minute for the duration of a call. How much will it cost for an 11 minute call? $1.44
  (3, 4)

For problems **4–6,** record the information in a ratio table. Estimate an answer and then solve by writing and solving a proportion.

* 4. Cynthia sews four dresses in 3 hours. How many dresses could she sew in 9 hours?   12 dresses
  (49)

* 5. Sergio estimates that his trip will take 3 hours and 30 minutes. Express Sergio's estimate as a mixed number of hours and as a decimal number of hours. $3\frac{1}{2}$ hours; 3.5 hours
  (52)

▶ See Math Conversations in the sidebar.

3 Written Practice

Math Conversations

Discussion opportunities are provided below.

Problems 7 and 8 | Analyze

"When two inverse operations are used to isolate a variable, which operation is used first?" The inverse operations are used in reverse order of the order of operations.

Before students solve each problem, ask them to name the inverse operation that will be used first, and second, to solve for the variable.

Problem 9 | Analyze

"To isolate x, what step should we complete before we use an inverse operation?" collect the like terms; $x + x = 2x$

Problem 12a | Analyze

"Is the point at 5 on the y-axis above or below the origin?" above

"What ordered pair describes the location of that point?" $(0, 5)$

Problem 12b | Analyze

After computing the slope, remind students that they can check if the sign of the slope is correct simply by looking at the line. If the line falls from left to right, the sign of the slope should be negative. If the line rises from left to right, the sign of the slope should be positive.

Problem 19 | Generalize

"Explain how to simplify 5^{-2} using only mental math." Sample: The negative exponent indicates the reciprocal of 5^2. Since 5^2 is 25 and $25 = \frac{25}{1}$, $5^{-2} = \frac{1}{25}$.

Problem 20 | Generalize

"Complete this sentence: Subtracting a negative is the same as adding … ." Sample: its opposite

Errors and Misconceptions
Problem 19

The generalization that a negative exponent represents a negative number is a common misconception some students have when working with negative exponents.

Have students note that 5^{-2} simplifies to a positive number.

(continued)

---

* 6. A light is left on for 40 days. Convert 40 days to hours using a unit multiplier. If the light bulb has an estimated life of 1400 hours, is the light likely to still be on after 40 days?   960 hours, yes
(52)

Analyze Solve.

▶ *** 7.** $20x + 50 = 250$ $x = 10$ ▶ *** 8.** $\frac{x}{3} + 5 = 7$ $x = 6$
(50)   (50)

▶ *** 9.** $x + 5 + x = 25$ $x = 10$ *** 10.** $14 - m = 24$ $m = -10$
(50)   (50)

11. Victoria is playing a board game with two number cubes. She rolls both
(32)   cubes once.

    a. List the possible totals (sample space).

    b. Predict: Which totals do you predict are least likely and which totals are most likely. Justify your prediction.

11. a. The possible totals are 2, 3, 4, 5, 6, 7, 8, 9, 10, 11, 12;
b. The least likely totals are 2 and 12 because there is only way to make each total. The most likely is 7 because there are more combinations that total 7 than any other number.

* 12. *Analyze* Refer to the graph of lines
(Inv. 1, 44) a and b to answer the following questions.

    ▶ **a.** Which line intersects the y-axis at 5?   line a

    ▶ **b.** What is the slope of line b? -1

    c. In which quadrant do lines a and b intersect?   2nd

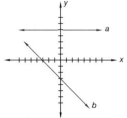

13. Triangle ABC with vertices at (2, 1), (1, 4), and (2, 2) is reflected in the
(Inv. 5) x-axis. What are the coordinates of the vertices of $\triangle A'B'C'$? $(2, -1)$, $(1, -4)$, $(2, -2)$

14. A 14-inch diameter circular porthole (window) is framed in a brass ring
(39, 40) and mounted in the side of a ship.

    a. Find the area of the glass. Round your answer to the nearest square inch.   154 in.²

    b. What is the inner circumference of the brass mounting ring? (Use $\frac{22}{7}$ for π.)   44 in.

15. Find the volume of a box with dimensions 5 in. by 5 in. by 8 in. Sketch
(42) the box resting on a square face and indicate its dimensions.   200 in.³

15.

8 in.

5 in.

5 in.

16. Find the surface area of the box in exercise **15**.   210 in.²
(43)

Generalize Simplify:

17. $4(x - 4) - 2(x - 6)$ **18.** $b + h + b + h$
(31, 36) $(2x - 4)$ (31) $2b + 2h$

▶*** 19.** 5^{-2} $\frac{1}{25}$ ▶*** 20.** $(-3) - (-7)$ 4
(51)   (33)

21. $\dfrac{(4.2 \times 10^7)}{(1.4 \times 10^2)}$ 3×10^5 **22.** $\left(\dfrac{2}{3}\right)^2 + \dfrac{2}{3}$ $1\frac{1}{9}$
(46)   (13, 22)

▶ See Math Conversations in the sidebar.

▶* **23.** *Connect* **a.** Write $\frac{19}{20}$ as a decimal and as a percent. 0.95; 95%
  (12)

   b. How would you report your score on a test for which you answered 19 out of 20 questions correctly? 95%

24. The pentagons are similar.
  (35)
   a. Find a. 80°

   b. What is the scale factor from the smaller to the larger pentagon? $\frac{5}{3}$

   c. Find x. $\frac{10}{3}$ or $3\frac{1}{3}$

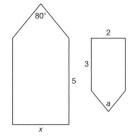

▶ **25.** Simplify and express with positive exponents. $\frac{y}{x^2}$
  (51)

$$\frac{x^{-1}y^2}{xy}$$

* **26.** Chester needs a length of 2-by-4 to make a diagonal brace for a wooden gate that has the dimensions shown. The 2-by-4 must be at least how many inches long? 45 in.
  (Inv. 2)

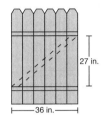

27 in.

36 in.

* **27.** An ant weighs about 10^{-5} kg. Write this as a decimal number. 0.00001 kg
  (51)

28. Sample:

trapezoid

28. Sketch a quadrilateral with just one pair of parallel sides. What type of quadrilateral did you sketch?
  (Inv. 3)

Find all values of x.

29. a. $7x^2 = 7$ 1, −1   **b.** $|x| - 15 = 5$ 20, −20
  (14, 36)

30.

Front

Right   Top

30. Sketch the front, right side, and top views of this figure.
  (Inv. 4)

Top

Right

Front

Lesson 52   359

▶ See Math Conversations in the sidebar.

3 **Written Practice** *(Continued)*

Math Conversations

Discussion opportunities are provided below.

Problem 23 *Connect*

Ask students to choose mental math or paper and pencil and use that method to solve the problem.

Then ask students to name the method they chose, and explain why that method was chosen. Methods and explanations will vary.

Errors and Misconceptions
Problem 25

Watch for students who cancel the x's.

Looking Forward

Using unit multipliers to convert measures and converting mixed-unit to single-unit measures prepares students for:

• **Lesson 64,** using a unit multiplier to convert a rate.

• **Lesson 72,** using multiple unit multipliers.

• **Lesson 80,** adding and subtracting mixed measures.

• Solving Problems Using Measures of Central Tendency

Objectives

- Interpret and create line plots and histograms to display data.
- Calculate the mean, median, mode, and range of a data set and choose the most appropriate measure of central tendency to convey an idea about the data.
- Discuss how certain measures of central tendency might be misleading in some situations.

Lesson Preparation

Materials

- **Power Up K** (in *Instructional Masters*)

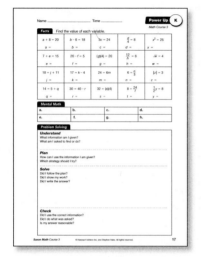

Power Up K

Math Language

New	Maintain	English Learners (ESL)
histogram	mean	compute
line plot	median	
	mode	
	range	

Technology Resources

Student eBook Complete student textbook in electronic format.

Resources and Planner CD Assessment, reteaching, and instructional masters, plus a pacing calendar with standards.

Test and Practice Generator CD Create additional practice sheets and custom-made tests.

www.SaxonPublishers.com Visit for more student activities and planning materials.

Inclusion

Adaptations CD Adapted lessons, investigations, practice and assessments.

Meeting Standards

National Council of Teachers of Mathematics (NCTM)

Data Analysis and Probability

DP.1b Select, create, and use appropriate graphical representations of data, including histograms, box plots, and scatterplots

DP.2a Find, use, and interpret measures of center and spread, including mean and interquartile range

DP.2b Discuss and understand the correspondence between data sets and their graphical representations, especially histograms, stem-and-leaf plots, box plots, and scatterplots

Problem Solving

PS.1b Solve problems that arise in mathematics and in other contexts

Representation

RE.5a Create and use representations to organize, record, and communicate mathematical ideas

RE.5b Select, apply, and translate among mathematical representations to solve problems

Problem-Solving Strategy: Use Logical Reasoning/ Guess and Check

About how many sheets of paper the thickness of this page would make a stack 1 cm high? About how many centimeters thick is this page? What should be the product of your two answers?

(Understand) **Understand the problem.**

"What information are we given?"

We will be working with sheets of paper the thickness of this page.

"What are we asked to do?"

1. Estimate how many sheets of paper with the same thickness as this page would make a stack 1 cm high.
2. Estimate how many centimeters thick is this page.
3. Determine the product of the two answers.

(Plan) **Make a plan.**

"What problem-solving strategy will we use?"

We will *use logical reasoning* to effectively estimate and intelligently *guess and check.*

(Solve) **Carry out the plan.**

"How might we estimate how many sheets of paper with the same thickness as this page would make a stack 1 cm high?"

If students "pinch" approximately 1 centimeter of pages of this book between two fingers, they should have approximately 250 pages, which would be 125 sheets.

"How might we estimate how thick this page is in centimeters?"

Students may recognize that 100 sheets in 1 cm would make each sheet 0.01. Because our paper is actually thinner than that, we could estimate it to be 0.008 cm.

"What should be the product of our two answers?"

The number of sheets of paper multiplied by the thickness of each sheet should equal 1 centimeter. (125 sheets of paper $\times$ 0.008 cm thick each = a 1 centimeter stack.)

"What do we call two numbers whose product is 1?"

reciprocals

(Check) **Look back.**

"Did we find the answers to the questions that were asked?"

Yes.

1 Power Up

Facts
Distribute **Power Up K** to students. See answers below.

Mental Math
Encourage students to share different ways to mentally compute these exercises. Strategies for exercises **b** and **d** are listed below.

b. Cross Products
$$25x = 4 \cdot 100$$
$$x = \frac{400}{25}$$
$$x = 16$$
Multiply Down
$$25 \times 4 = 100$$
$$4 \times 4 = 16$$

d. Count Up
$$2901 \rightarrow 3001 = 100$$
$$3001 \rightarrow 3247 = 246$$
$$246 + 100 = 346 \text{ mi}$$
Count Down
$$3247 \rightarrow 2947 = 300$$
$$2947 \rightarrow 2901 = 46$$
$$300 + 46 = 346 \text{ mi}$$

Problem Solving
Refer to **Power-Up Discussion**, p. 360B.

• Solving Problems Using Measures of Central Tendency

Power Up   *Building Power*

facts | Power Up K

mental math
- **a. Number Sense:** 7.5×20 150
- **b. Proportions:** $\frac{25}{100} = \frac{4}{x}$ 16
- **c. Probability:** A spinner has 8 equal sections numbered 1–8. What is the probability that the spinner will stop on a number greater than 5? $\frac{3}{8}$
- **d. Measurement:** The odometer read 2901 mi at the beginning of the trip. At the end of the trip, it read 3247 mi. How long was the trip?   346 mi
- **e. Scientific Notation:** Write 2.08×10^7 in standard notation.   20,800,000
- **f. Geometry:** Find the area of the rectangle, then find the area of the shaded triangle.   6 in.², 3 in.²

3 in.

2 in.

- **g. Estimation:** Estimate the total cost of items priced at: $2.45 plus $7.45 plus 3 items at $9.95. $40
- **h. Calculation:** $\sqrt{121}$, $\times 9$, $+ 1$, $\sqrt{\ }$, $- 1$, $\times 7$, $+ 1$, $\sqrt{\ }$, $\times 6$, $+ 1$, $\sqrt{\ }$ 7

problem solving
About how many sheets of paper the thickness of this page would make a stack 1 cm high? About how many centimeters thick is this page? What should be the product of your two answers?   Answers vary: about 125 sheets; about 0.008 cm; if precisely measured the product should be 1 cm.

New Concept   *Increasing Knowledge*

To summarize data, we often report an average of some kind, like the **mean**, **median**, or **mode**.

Facts   Find the value of each variable.

$a + 8 = 20$	$b - 6 = 18$	$3c = 24$	$\frac{d}{4} = 8$	$x^2 = 25$
$a = 12$	$b = 24$	$c = 8$	$d = 32$	$x = 5$ (and -5)
$7 + e = 15$	$20 - f = 5$	$(g)(4) = 20$	$\frac{12}{h} = 6$	$\sqrt{w} = 4$
$e = 8$	$f = 15$	$g = 5$	$h = 2$	$w = 16$
$18 = j + 11$	$17 = k - 4$	$24 = 6m$	$6 = \frac{n}{3}$	$|z| = 3$
$j = 7$	$k = 21$	$m = 4$	$n = 18$	$z = 3, -3$
$14 = 5 + q$	$30 = 40 - r$	$32 = (s)(4)$	$8 = \frac{24}{t}$	$\frac{1}{2}y = 8$
$q = 9$	$r = 10$	$s = 8$	$t = 3$	$y = 16$

Suppose a popular television show received these ratings over its season:

16.0	15.2	15.3	15.5
15.7	15.1	14.8	15.6
15.0	14.6	14.4	15.8
15.3	14.7	14.2	15.7
14.9	15.4	14.9	16.1

```
                 x    x    x
            x  x xxxxxxxxxxxxx  xx
        ←───+─────────+─────────+─────────+───→
           14        15        16        17
```

The data above are displayed on a **line plot.** Each data point is represented with an X above its value on a number line.

The **mean** TV rating is:

$$\text{mean} = \frac{16.0 + 15.7 + \ldots + 16.1}{20}$$

$$\text{mean} = 15.21$$

Recall that the **median** of an ordered list of numbers is the middle number or the mean of the two central numbers. There are an even number of data, so the numbers 15.2 and 15.3 share the central location. We compute the mean of these two numbers to find the median.

$$\text{median} = \frac{15.2 + 15.3}{2} = 15.25$$

The **mode** is the most frequently occurring number in a set. In this example, there are three modes: 14.9, 15.3, and 15.7.

The **range** of this data is the difference between the highest and lowest ratings.

$$\text{range} = 16.1 - 14.2$$

$$\text{range} = 1.9$$

We may also consider separating the data into intervals such as: 14.0–14.4, 14.5–14.9, 15.0–15.4, 15.5–15.9, 16.0–16.4. Data organized in this way can be displayed in a **histogram,** as shown below.

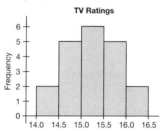

TV Ratings

Data which fall within specified ranges are counted, and the tallies are represented with a bar. For example, the tallest bar tells us that 6 data points fall within the range 15.0–15.4.

The highest peak of a histogram will always indicate the mode of the data ranges.

Lesson 53   361

Example 1

Instruction

Tell students that graph paper is not needed to make a line plot.

For **a,** ask students what they notice about the data. Samples: Two data points are greatly separated from the rest of the data. There is no mode.

As you discuss **b,** ask why the range suggests that the mean may not accurately represent the age of the average customer. Sample: The range is so great that if the data is not evenly spread across the range, the mean can't show a true average. Point out that only two customers were older than the mean age.

(continued)

At the end of a season, Neilsen Ratings reports the mean season rating as a measure of a show's success. For various types of data, the mean is a frequently reported statistic. It is commonly referred to as the "average," even though the median and mode are other averages.

Example 1

The owner of a cafe was interested in the age of her customers in order to plan marketing. One day she collected these data on customers' ages.

28	33	31	41	42
27	75	73	38	35

a. Make a line plot of the data, then find the mean, median, mode, and range.

b. Which measure (mean, median, mode, or range) best represents the typical age of the customers?

Solution

a.

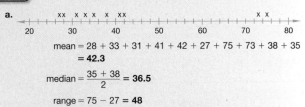

$$\text{mean} = 28 + 33 + 31 + 41 + 42 + 27 + 75 + 73 + 38 + 35$$
$$= \textbf{42.3}$$

$$\text{median} = \frac{35 + 38}{2} = \textbf{36.5}$$

$$\text{range} = 75 - 27 = \textbf{48}$$

There is no number that occurs more frequently than the others, so the mode is **not reported.**

b. The **median** gives the best description of the typical age of the customers. Half of the customers surveyed were younger than 36.5, and half were older. The mean, on the other hand, is much higher than the median because of a few customers that were older than the rest.

It is common to see medians used to report median age of residents by state, or median home prices by state.

Example 2

Suppose the median age of residents of a certain state was 30. Twenty years later it was 37. What changes in the population may have occurred in the twenty years?

Solution

When the median age was 30, half of the residents were younger than 30 and half were older. Twenty years later the median age had raised to 37. **This might happen if fewer children are born, if older people live longer, or if people younger than 37 move out of state or people older than 37 move into the state.** Any of these factors would contribute to an "older" population.

Inclusion

Some students will confuse the types of data that can be summarized with mean, median, and mode. A quick activity grouping students by quantitative and categorical data may help. Instruct the students to line up in order by the number of people in their households. Then ask:

"Can we find the mean or median from our grouping of household size? Explain." Sample: Yes we can find the median because we are in order from least to greatest number.

Instruct the students to sort themselves by hair color. Then ask:

"Can we find the mean or median from our grouping of hair color? Explain." Sample: No because there is no order to hair color.

Discuss the difference in the types of data and what measures of central tendency can be calculated. Sample: You can find the mean, median and mode for numbered data but only the mode for non-numbered data.

Example 3

Thinking Skill

Analyze

Which measure of central tendency would most accurately convey the salary a prospective employee could expect from the company? Why? median; The median tells us the middle salary. Half the employees make more and half make less.

Consider the salaries of the employees of a small business. In an interview, a prospective employee was told that the average salary of employees is $50,000. How might this information be misleading?

Yearly Salary (in thousands $)

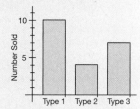

32	43
34	45
32	67
30	85
37	95

mean: 50

median: 40

mode: 32

range: 65

Solution

The interviewer reported the mean salary, which is much higher than the median because of a few salaries which are greater than most of the others. A prospective employee who heard that the average salary is $50,000 would be disappointed if his or her starting salary is near $30,000.

Example 4

Josiah sells three different hats to test their popularity. His sales are reported in a bar graph below. The height of each bar corresponds to the number of hats of that type Josiah sold.

Find the mode of the data. Why are we not interested in the mean or median?

Solution

The mode of the types of hats is Type 1, the most popular choice. **In this case, the data Josiah collected was qualitative data (hat type), not quantitative data (numbers),** so mean and median are not important.

2 New Concepts (Continued)

Example 3
Instruction

Ask volunteers to tell which measure of central tendency best describes this data and to explain their thinking. Sample: None of them really do. The median comes closest, because half are above and half are below it, but the difference between the lowest value and the median is $10,000 and the difference between the median and the greatest value is $55,000, almost six times more. Then have others explain why each measure does not accurately reflect the data.

Example 4
Instruction

Ask students to describe the impression they get of the data by looking at the bar graph. Sample: Type 2 is not very popular. Point out that the visual nature of a bar graph can give a strong impression of a data set.

(continued)

Teacher Tip

To help students see **how often data displays are used to convey information** or to present a particular viewpoint, have students look for data displays in newspapers or magazines. Ask each student to choose one display and write a few sentences describing the data and the impression that the data display leaves with the reader.

Alternatively, you might gather data displays before class and take some class time to review them.

2 New Concepts (Continued)

Practice Set

Problem a [Error Alert]
When making a line plot, students must identify the greatest and least values in the data set to ensure that all the values in the set can be plotted.

Problem b [Analyze]
Encourage students to name as many of the measures as possible using only mental math.

Problem c [Error Alert]
Students should recognize that the word "difference" implies a comparison, and subtraction.

Problem f [Error Alert]
The month of February can have 28 or 29 days. Since students are to represent $\frac{1}{2}$ of those days with a temperature colder than 30°F, they should choose 28 days for February because in the context of the problem, $\frac{1}{2}$ of 29 or 14.5 is not a sensible number of days.

3 Written Practice

Math Conversations
Discussion opportunities are provided below.

Problem 2 [Evaluate]
If students have difficulty writing a proportion, encourage them to make a ratio table and use the given information to complete the table.

Problem 4 [Conclude]
"What is the sum of the angle measures of an equilateral triangle?" 180°

"Is 180° the sum of the angle measures of any triangle, or only an equilateral triangle?" any triangle

Problem 5 [Connect]
Have students recall that a unit multiplier is a ratio that is equal to 1, and consists of two equivalent measures.

"One meter is equivalent to what number of centimeters?" 100

(continued)

Practice Set The amount of electricity (in kWh) used by one household each month of a year is listed below.

420 450 480 440 420 490 580 590 510 450 430 480

▶ a. Make a line plot of the data.

▶ b. [Analyze] Find the mean, median, mode, and range of the data.   mean: 478; median: 465; mode: 420, 450, 480; range: 170

▶ c. Which measure would you report to describe the difference between the most electricity used in a month and the least?   range, 170 KWh

d. Which measure would you report to someone who wanted to compute the total amount of electricity used in the year? Explain your answer.   mean, the total is 12 times this value

e. If the greatest data point (590) were changed to 500, which measure of central tendency (mean, median, or mode) would change the most?   mean; the median and mode would not be affected

▶ f. [Evaluate] Make a list of data values that fits the statement "Half of the days of February were colder than 30° F." Find the mean, median, mode and range of the data.   See student work.

Written Practice   Strengthening Concepts

1. The ratio of adults to children attending the concert was 2 to 3. If there
   (45) were 54 children, how many adults were there?   36

▶ * 2. [Evaluate] Each team in the league has five starters and two alternates.
   (49) If there are 30 starters in all, how many alternates are there?   12 alternates

3. It takes Robert one minute to gather his materials to begin his
   (3)   homework, then an additional minute for each problem on his assignment. If it takes him 20 minutes to complete the assignment, how many problems were on his assignment?   19 problems

▶ * 4. [Conclude] Each angle of an equilateral triangle measures how many
   (20) degrees?   60°

▶ * 5. [Connect] The pole vaulter cleared the bar at 490 cm. Convert 490 cm
   (52) to meters using a unit multiplier. $\frac{490 \text{ cm}}{1} \cdot \frac{1 \text{ m}}{100 \text{ cm}} = 4.9 \text{ m}$

▶ See Math Conversations in the sidebar.

* 6. *(53)* **Analyze** Find the mean, median, and mode of the five temperature readings at each hour from 10 a.m. to 2 p.m. According to the graph, for half the time between 10 a.m. and 2 p.m., it was warmer than what temperature?   mean 35.6°, median 36°, mode 38°; Half the time it was warmer than 36°.

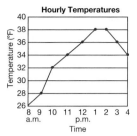

Hourly Temperatures

Analyze Solve.

* 7. *(50)* $-2x = -16$ $x = 8$

8. *(38)* $\frac{w}{2} = 1.5$ $w = 3$

* 9. *(50)* $-z + 3 = 7$ $z = -4$

* 10. *(50)* $23 - p = 73$ $p = -50$

11. *(52)* A meter is about 3.3 ft, so 4.9 m is about   **C**
   A 2 ft   **B** 8 ft   **C** 16 ft   **D** 20 ft

12. *(Inv. 1, 44)* Refer to the graphed lines to answer the following questions.

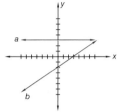

   a. What is the slope of line b? $\frac{2}{3}$

   b. Line b intersects the y-axis at what point? $(0, -2)$

   c. In which quadrant do lines a and b intersect?   1st

13. *(41)* Graph $y = -x$ and the point $(4, -5)$. Is the point on the line?   No

14. *(39, 40)* Find the **a** area and **b** circumference of a circle with a diameter of 18 inches. Express your answer in terms of π.   **a.** 81π in.²; **b.** 18π in.

15. *(42)* Find the volume of a crate with dimensions 4 ft by 3 ft by 2 ft.   24 ft³

16. *(51)* A type of spider weighs about 1×10^{-4} lb. Write this as a decimal number.   0.0001 lb

Simplify.

17. *(31, 36)* $3(x - y) - 2(x + y)$ $x - 5y$

* 18. *(31)* $5x^2 - 3x - 2x^2 + 4x$ $3x^2 + x$

* 19. *(27)* $\frac{2^3 \cdot 2^0}{2^1 \cdot 2^2}$ 1

20. *(27)* $\frac{x^3 y^3 z}{xy^2 z^3}$ $\frac{x^2}{z^2}$

* 21. *(31)* $-5 - (-7)$ 2

22. *(46)* $(1.5 \times 10^3)(1.5 \times 10^{-2})$ 2.25×10

23. *(12)* **a.** Write 98% as a decimal and reduced fraction. 0.98; $\frac{49}{50}$

   b. For a $50,000 fundraising campaign, 98% of the funds have been raised. Which of the three forms would you choose to mentally calculate this amount?   Answers may vary. Sample: The fraction: $\frac{49}{50}(\$50,000) = \$49,000$

Lesson 53   365

▶ See Math Conversations in the sidebar.

13.
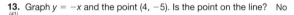

Math Conversations

Discussion opportunities are provided below.

Problem 6   Analyze

"The graph shows eight temperatures. How many of those temperatures will we use to solve the problem?" five

Problems 7–10   Analyze

For problems **7–10**, ask:

"To isolate the variable, how many times will we need to use an inverse operation?"

"Name the operation."

Make sure students understand that if the inverse operations used to isolate a variable are used in the *reverse* order of the order of operations, the arithmetic is often easier to complete.

Problem 16   Connect

Extend the Problem

"How many spiders of the type described in the problem would weigh 1 pound?" 10,000

Errors and Misconceptions

Problem 6

It is a misconception to assume that two or more measures of central tendency can never be the same. To remediate this misconception in a simple way, write the data set {2, 3, 3, 4} on the board or overhead. Using mental math, ask students to name the mean, median, and mode of the set.   mean = 3; median = 3; mode = 3

(continued)

Math Conversations

Discussion opportunities are provided below.

Problem 24

When substituting for the variable in terms such as $2m$, a common error is to not recognize that the term represents the product of 2 and the variable. To help students substitute correctly, encourage them to include parentheses with each substitution For example, to substitute $-\frac{1}{2}$ for m in the term $2m$, students should write $2(-\frac{1}{2})$.

26. Yes, Sergio's claim means he can lift 10 kilograms over his head. $10{,}000 \text{ g} \cdot \frac{1 \text{ kg}}{1000 \text{ g}} = 10 \text{ kg}$; Ten kilograms is about 22 pounds, which is a reasonable weight to lift overhead. $10 \text{ kg} \cdot \frac{2.2 \text{ lbs}}{1 \text{ kg}} \approx 22 \text{ pounds}$

27. Sample space **B** is more useful because each outcome is equally likely, so it is easier to calculate probabilities. The $P(\text{H and 1}) = \frac{1}{4}$.

▶ **24.** Find $\frac{x}{2m}$ when $x = 5$ and $m = -5$. $-\frac{1}{2}$
  (14, 36)

* **25.** Express with all positive exponents: $6x^{-1}yyz^{-2}$ $\frac{6y^2}{xz^2}$
  (51)

* **26.** Sergio claims he can lift 10,000 grams over his head. Is his claim
  (52) reasonable? Justify your answer.

* **27.** A coin is flipped and the spinner is spun.
  (32) Which sample space is most useful? Why?

  A Sample Space {H1, H2, H3, T1, T2, T3}

  B Sample Space {H1, H1, H1, H2, H2, H3, T1, T1, T1, T2, T2, T3}
  Find $P(\text{H and 1})$.

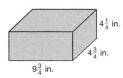

28. Kellie high jumped 5 ft 3 in. Express that height as a mixed number of
  (52) feet and as a decimal number of feet. $5\frac{1}{4}$ ft, 5.25 ft

29. Find all values of x which are solutions.
  (14, 36) **a.** $x^2 + 2 = 27$ $x = 5, -5$ **b.** $-5|x| = -15$ $x = 3, -3$

30. Estimate the **a** volume and **b** surface area
  (42, 43) of this tissue box.   **a.** 200 in.³; **b.** 220 in.²

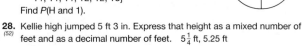

$4\frac{1}{4}$ in.
$4\frac{3}{4}$ in.
$9\frac{3}{4}$ in.

Early Finishers | While traveling on vacation, Mr. and Mrs. Rodriguez decide to spend an
Real-World Application | afternoon biking. There are two bike-rental companies nearby to choose from. Buck's Bikes charges $10 per hour per bike. Cycles Galore charges $4 per hour per bike plus an initial fixed fee of $15 per bike. Let x represent the time (in hours) that the bikes are rented and y represent the total cost.

  a. Write an equation to represent the total amount it would cost Mr. and
  Mrs. Rodriguez to rent two bikes from Buck's Bikes.   Buck's Bikes: $y = 20x$

  b. Write an equation to represent the total amount it would cost Mr. and
  Mrs. Rodriguez to rent two bikes from Cycles Galore.   Cycles Galore: $y = 8x + 30$

  c. Graph both equations on the same coordinate plane.   See student work.

  d. Use your graph to determine which company would be cheaper if Mr.
  and Mrs. Rodriguez want to ride for three hours.   Cycles Galore

▶ See Math Conversations in the sidebar.

Looking Forward

Solving problems using measures of central tendency prepares students for:

• **Lesson 103,** working with line plots and box-and-whisker plots.

• Angle Relationships

Objectives

- Understand the relationships between angles formed by two intersecting lines and apply the knowledge to solve geometry problems.
- Understand the relationships between angles formed by parallel lines intersected by a transversal and apply the knowledge to solve geometry problems.

Lesson Preparation

Materials

- **Power Up K** (in *Instructional Masters*)

Optional
- Teacher-provided material: isometric dot paper
- Manipulative Kit: protractors

Power Up K

Math Language

New	Maintain	English Learners (ESL)
adjacent angles	acute angle	alternate
alternate exterior angles	obtuse angle	
	parallel	
alternate interior angles	right angle	
	straight angle	
complementary angles		
corresponding angles		
opposite angles		
supplementary angles		
transversal		
vertical angles		

Technology Resources

Student eBook Complete student textbook in electronic format.

Resources and Planner CD Assessment, reteaching, and instructional masters, plus a pacing calendar with standards.

Test and Practice Generator CD Create additional practice sheets and custom-made tests.

www.SaxonPublishers.com Visit for more student activities and planning materials.

Inclusion

Adaptations CD Adapted lessons, investigations, practice and assessments.

Meeting Standards

National Council of Teachers of Mathematics (NCTM)

Geometry

GM.1a Precisely describe, classify, and understand relationships among types of two- and three-dimensional objects using their defining properties

Measurement

ME.2b Select and apply techniques and tools to accurately find length, area, volume, and angle measures to appropriate levels of precision

Problem Solving

PS.1c Apply and adapt a variety of appropriate strategies to solve problems

Problem-Solving Strategy: Use Logical Reasoning

At first, one-third of the class were boys. Then another boy joined the class. Now $\frac{3}{8}$ of the class are boys. How many students are in the class now? (Hint: There are fewer than 40 students in the class.)

(Understand) **Understand the problem.**

"What information are we given?"

$\frac{1}{3}$ of a class are boys until a new boy is added to the class, and then the fraction of boys in the class is $\frac{3}{8}$.

"What are we asked to do?"

Determine how many students are now in the class.

(Plan) **Make a plan.**

"What problem-solving strategy will we use?"

We will *use logical reasoning* and our number sense about what equivalent fractions represent.

(Solve) **Carry out the plan.**

"What are the fractions equivalent to $\frac{1}{3}$ that do not exceed a denominator of 40?"

$$\frac{1}{3} \quad \frac{2}{6} \quad \frac{3}{9} \quad \frac{4}{12} \quad \frac{5}{15} \quad \frac{6}{18} \quad \frac{7}{21} \quad \frac{8}{24} \quad \frac{9}{27} \quad \frac{10}{30} \quad \frac{11}{33} \quad \frac{12}{36} \quad \frac{13}{39}$$

"What are the fractions equivalent to $\frac{3}{8}$ that do not exceed a denominator of 40?"

$$\frac{3}{8} \quad \frac{6}{16} \quad \frac{9}{24} \quad \frac{12}{32} \quad \frac{15}{40}$$

"How will we compare the two sets of equivalent fractions to determine the number of students in the class?"

When one boy was added to the class, both the number of boys increased by one *and* the class size as a whole increased by one. We need to look for a fraction equivalent to $\frac{3}{8}$ that has both a numerator *and* a denominator that is greater by 1 than the numerator and denominator of a fraction equivalent to $\frac{1}{3}$.

"In comparing the two sets of equivalent fractions, which fractions have numerators that differ by 1 and denominators that differ by 1?"

$\frac{5}{15}$ and $\frac{6}{16}$

$$\frac{1}{3} \quad \frac{2}{6} \quad \frac{3}{9} \quad \frac{4}{12} \quad \mathbf{\frac{5}{15}} \quad \frac{6}{18} \quad \frac{7}{21} \quad \frac{8}{24} \quad \frac{9}{27} \quad \frac{10}{30} \quad \frac{11}{33} \quad \frac{12}{36} \quad \frac{13}{39}$$

$$\frac{3}{8} \quad \mathbf{\frac{6}{16}} \quad \frac{9}{24} \quad \frac{12}{32} \quad \frac{15}{40}$$

"How many students total are now in the class?"

16

(Check) **Look back.**

"Did we find the answer to the question that was asked?"

Yes. Originally 5 of the 15 students were boys, which is $\frac{1}{3}$ of the class. Then one more boy joined the class, so 6 of 16 students were boys, which is $\frac{3}{8}$.

• Angle Relationships

facts | Power Up K

mental math

a. **Number Sense:** 3.5×8 28

b. **Fractional Parts:** 20% is $\frac{1}{5}$. How much is a 20% tip on a bill of $45? $9

c. **Algebra:** $x^2 = 81$ 9 and −9

d. **Scientific Notation:** Write 5 trillion in scientific notation.
$5,000,000,000,000 = 5 \times 10^{12}$

e. **Rate:** Vu and Tim began running at the same time and from the same place. Vu ran west at 8 miles per hour. Tim ran east at 9 miles per hour. After 30 minutes, how far had each run and how far were they from each other? $4 + 4\frac{1}{2} = 8\frac{1}{2}$ miles

f. **Geometry:** Estimate the volume of this box. Sample: 3 cm^3

2.9 cm
0.9 cm
1.1 cm

g. **Proportions:** A survey of 50 students at a college found that 30 could name the Vice President. If the survey was representative of all 5000 students, then about how many of all the students could name the Vice President?   3000

h. **Calculation:** $\sqrt{49}$, $\times 5$, $+ 1$, $\sqrt{}$, $\times 4$, $+ 1$, $\sqrt{}$, $\times 3$, $+ 1$, $\sqrt{}$, $\times 2$, $+ 1$, $\sqrt{}$ 3

problem solving | At first, one-third of the class were boys. Then another boy joined the class. Now $\frac{3}{8}$ of the class are boys. How many students are in the class now? (Hint: There are fewer than 40 students in the class.)   16 students

New Concept | Increasing Knowledge

Intersecting lines form pairs of adjacent angles and pairs of opposite angles.

Adjacent angles:
∠1 and ∠3
∠3 and ∠4
∠4 and ∠2
∠2 and ∠1

Opposite angles:
∠1 and ∠4
∠2 and ∠3

Adjacent angles share a common vertex and a common side but do not overlap.

Opposite angles are formed by two intersecting lines and share the same vertex but do not share a side. Opposite angles are also called **vertical angles.** Vertical angles are congruent.

Lesson 54   367

Facts
Distribute **Power Up K** to students. See answers below.

Mental Math
Encourage students to share different ways to mentally compute these exercises. Strategies for exercises **a**, **b**, and **g** are listed below.

a. **Double and Halve**
$3.5 \times 8 = 7 \times 4 = 28$
Multiply by 2 Three Times
$3.5 \times 8 = 3.5 \times 2 \times 2 \times 2 =$
$7 \times 2 \times 2 = 14 \times 2 = 28$

b. **Find a Fraction**
$20\% = \frac{1}{5}$
$\frac{1}{5} \times \$45 = \$9$
Multiply by 5, Divide by 5
20% of $45 = 100% of $9 = $9

g. **Use Math Sense**
$5000 \div 50 = 100$
$30 \times 100 = 3000$

Problem Solving
Refer to **Power-Up Discussion**, p. 367B.

2 New Concepts

Instruction
Discuss what it means for angles to be *congruent*. Samples: They are the same size. They have the same angle measure.

(continued)

Facts   Find the value of each variable.

$a + 8 = 20$	$b - 6 = 18$	$3c = 24$	$\frac{d}{4} = 8$	$x^2 = 25$
$a = 12$	$b = 24$	$c = 8$	$d = 32$	$x = 5$ (and −5)
$7 + e = 15$	$20 - f = 5$	$(g)(4) = 20$	$\frac{12}{h} = 6$	$\sqrt{w} = 4$
$e = 8$	$f = 15$	$g = 5$	$h = 2$	$w = 16$
$18 = j + 11$	$17 = k - 4$	$24 = 6m$	$6 = \frac{n}{3}$	$|z| = 3$
$j = 7$	$k = 21$	$m = 4$	$n = 18$	$z = 3, -3$
$14 = 5 + q$	$30 = 40 - r$	$32 = (s)(4)$	$8 = \frac{24}{t}$	$\frac{1}{2}y = 8$
$q = 9$	$r = 10$	$s = 8$	$t = 3$	$y = 16$

Instruction

Demonstrate the angle relationships that exist between the angles formed by two intersecting lines. Discuss why knowing the measure of one of the four angles formed by the intersecting lines means that we can find the measure of the other three angles. Sample: Connecting what we know about the angle relationships and the measure of a straight angle to the measure of one angle gives us everything we need to find the measures of the other angles.

Be sure that students understand that two angles are *supplementary angles* because the sum of their angle measures is 180° and not because the two angles form a straight angle.

Many words used to describe angle relationships can help students remember the relationship.

• Intersecting lines are lines that cross each other like an intersection of two streets.
• Adjacent angles are next to each other because they share a vertex and a side; adjacent means "adjoining" or "next to."
• Opposite or vertical angles are across from each other, sharing only a vertex.
• A straight angle looks like a straight line, and has an angle measure of 180°.

Example 1
Instruction

Call attention to the logical and systematic way that the measures of the angles can be determined.

Extend the *Analyze* question by asking students if they can find a shorter way to determine the measure of one of the acute angles of a right triangle when the measure of the other acute angle is known. Guide students to see the sum of the two acute angles will always be 90°, so the known measure of one of the acute angles can be subtracted from 90° to obtain the measure of the other acute angle.

(continued)

Angles formed by two intersecting lines are related. If we know the measure of one of the angles, then we can find the measure of the other angles.

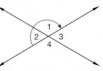

Reading Math

We can use symbols to abbreviate an angle's measure. We read the expression "$m\angle 1 = 120°$" as "the measure of angle 1 is 120 degrees."

Together ∠1 and ∠2 form a straight angle measuring 180°. If ∠1 measures 120°, then ∠2 measures 60°. Likewise, ∠1 and ∠3 form a straight angle, so ∠3 also measures 60° and vertical angles 2 and 3 both measure 60°.

Since ∠3 and ∠4 together form a straight angle (as do ∠2 and ∠4), we find that $m\angle 4 = 120°$. Thus, vertical angles 1 and 4 both measure 120°.

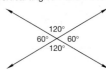

Two angles whose measures total 180° are called **supplementary angles**. We say that ∠2 is the supplement of ∠1 and that ∠1 is the supplement of ∠2. Supplementary angles may be adjacent angles, like ∠1 and ∠2, but it is not necessary that they be adjacent angles.

Angle Pairs Formed by Two Intersecting Lines

Adjacent angles are supplementary.
Opposite angles (vertical angles) are congruent.

Example 1

Refer to this figure to find the measures of angles 1, 2, 3, and 4.

Solution

• Angle 1 is the supplement of a 40° angle, so $m\angle 1 = 140°$.
• Angle 2 is the supplement of ∠1. Since ∠1 measures 140°, $m\angle 2 = 40°$.
• Angle 3 and ∠2 are the acute angles of a right triangle. The sum of the angle measures of a triangle is 180°, so $m\angle 3 = 50°$.
• Angle 4 is the supplement of ∠3, so $m\angle 4 = 130°$.

The sum of the two acute angles of a right triangle is 90°. Subtract the measure of one acute angle from 90° to find the measure of the other.

Analyze When you know the measure of one of the acute angles of a right triangle, how do you find the measure of the other acute angle?

368   *Saxon Math Course 3*

Notice that the measures of angles 2 and 3 in example 1 total 90°. Two angles whose measures total 90° are **complementary angles,** so ∠3 is the complement of ∠2, and ∠2 is the complement of ∠3.

Angles Paired by Combined Measures

Supplementary: Two angles totaling 180°
Complementary: Two angles totaling 90°

In the following figures we name several pairs of angles formed by parallel lines cut by a third line called a **transversal.** If the transversal were perpendicular to the parallel lines, then all angles formed would be right angles. The transversal below is not perpendicular, so there are four obtuse angles that are the same measure, and four acute angles that are the same measure. We will provide justification for these conclusions in a later lesson.

Corresponding angles are on the same side of the transversal and on the same side of each of the parallel lines. Corresponding angles of parallel lines are congruent. One pair of corresponding angles is ∠1 and ∠5. Name three more pairs of corresponding angles.   ∠3 and ∠7, ∠2 and ∠6, ∠4 and ∠8

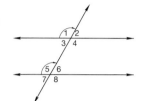

Alternate interior angles are on opposite sides of the transversal and between the parallel lines. Alternate interior angles of parallel lines are congruent. One pair of alternate interior angles is ∠3 and ∠6. Name another pair of alternate interior angles.   ∠4 and ∠5

Alternate Sides of Transversal

Alternate exterior angles are on opposite sides of the transversal and outside the parallel lines. Alternate exterior angles of parallel lines are congruent. One pair of alternate exterior angles is ∠1 and ∠8. Name another pair of alternate exterior angles.   ∠2 and ∠7

Congruent Angle Pairs Formed by a Transversal Cutting Two Parallel Lines

Corresponding angles: Same side of transversal, same side of lines
Alternate interior angles: Opposite sides of transversal, between lines
Alternate exterior angles: Opposite sides of transversal, outside of lines

In summary, if parallel lines are cut by a non-perpendicular transversal, the following relationships exist.

- All the obtuse angles that are formed are congruent.
- All the acute angles that are formed are congruent.
- Any acute angle formed is supplementary to any obtuse angle formed.

Lesson 54   369

2 New Concepts (Continued)

Instruction

Introduce the term *complementary angles.* Be sure that students understand that two angles are complementary because the sum of their angle measures is 90° and not necessarily because they are the acute angles in a right triangle.

Make a drawing on the board or overhead to demonstrate the relationships among the angles formed when parallel lines are cut by a transversal. Students will have to accept for now that the four obtuse angles are congruent and that the four acute angles also are congruent.

Remind students that they identified corresponding angles and sides when they studied similar and congruent polygons.

Help students understand how the names *alternate interior angles* and *alternate exterior angles* tell us what position these angles occupy in the figure. Use your drawing to show which angles are congruent. You may want to use single and double arcs to identify the corresponding congruent angles.

(continued)

English Learners

While discussing vocabulary words, explain the meaning of the word **alternate.** Say:

"When you alternate you go back and forth between two choices. The colors on the U.S. flag alternate because they start with a red stripe, followed by a white one, then red again, and so on."

Ask students to stand up and alternate standing on their right foot and then their left foot.

Example 2
Instruction
As you work through this example, point out that only one angle measure is given by the relationship of angle pairs formed by a transversal cutting parallel lines. All the others are derived from the relationships of supplementary angles and of vertical angles.

Example 3
Instruction
Discuss why knowing the measure of one acute angle in the truss is enough to find the measure of any other angle. Sample: I also know that the measure of each right angle is 90° and I can use that with the one measure we know to work out all the other angles.

(continued)

Example 2

In the figure parallel lines *p* and *q* are cut by transversal *t*. The measure of ∠8 is 55°. What are the measures of angles 1 through 7?

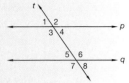

Solution

We are told that *p* and *q* are parallel. Angle 1 and ∠8 are alternate exterior angles and are congruent.

Statement:	Justification:
m∠1 = 55°	Alternate exterior angle to ∠8
m∠2 = 125°	∠2 and ∠1 are supplementary
m∠3 = 125°	∠3 and ∠1 are supplementary
m∠4 = 55°	∠4 and ∠1 are vertical and congruent
m∠5 = 55°	∠5 and ∠8 are vertical and congruent
m∠6 = 125°	∠6 and ∠8 are supplementary
m∠7 = 125°	∠7 and ∠8 are supplementary

Example 3

Structural engineers design triangles into buildings, bridges, and towers because triangles are rigid. The sides of triangles do not shift when force is applied like the sides of quadrilaterals do.

A railroad bridge built with a steel truss is strengthened by triangles that keep the bridge straight under the weight of a train.

Knowing one acute angle in this truss is sufficient to find the measures of all the angles. Find the measures of angles *ABF, FBC,* and *FGB.* Segments that look parallel are parallel, and segments that look perpendicular are perpendicular.

Solution

Angle *ABF* and the 40° angle are alternate interior angles between parallel lines. So **m∠ABF = 40°**. Together angles *ABF* and *FBC* form a straight angle (180°), so **m∠FBC = 140°**. Angle *FGB* is a right angle, so **m∠FGB = 90°**.

Teacher Tip

Some students may need to explore these concepts in a more concrete way. Suggest that they draw intersecting angles or parallel lines cut by a transversal and use a protractor to measure all the angles that are formed. Then have them **examine whether the measures of the angles support the relationships** described in the lesson.

Math Background

Why are triangles rigid figures?

The shape of a triangle is completely determined by the length of its sides. In other words, if two triangles have the same side lengths, then they must be congruent. Therefore, it is impossible to change the shape of a triangle by pressing on its sides or vertices. This is not true of other polygons. For example, the quadrilaterals below all have the same side lengths, but their shapes are very different.

Practice Set

Conclude Refer to Figure 1 for exercises **a–c**.

▶ **a.** Name two pairs of vertical angles. $\angle a$ and $\angle c$, $\angle b$ and $\angle d$

▶ **b.** Name four pairs of supplementary angles. $\angle a$ and $\angle b$, $\angle b$ and $\angle c$, $\angle c$ and $\angle d$, $\angle d$ and $\angle a$

▶ **c.** If $m\angle a$ is 110°, then what are the measures of angles, b, c, and d? $m\angle b$ = 70°, $m\angle c$ = 110°, and $m\angle d$ = 70°

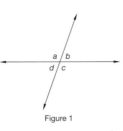

Figure 1

Refer to Figure 2 for exercises **d–f**.

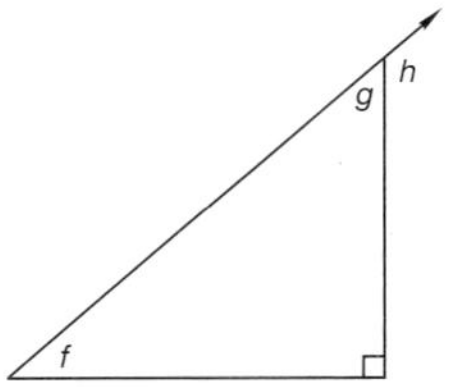

▶ **d.** Which angle is the complement of $\angle g$? $\angle f$

e. Which angle is the supplement of $\angle g$? $\angle h$

f. If $m\angle h$ is 130°, then what are the measures of $\angle g$ and $\angle f$? $m\angle g$ = 50°, $m\angle f$ = 40°

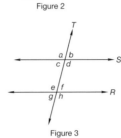

Figure 2

In Figure 3 parallel lines R and S are cut by transversal T. Refer to this figure for exercises **g–j**.

g. Which angle corresponds to $\angle f$? $\angle b$

h. Name two pairs of alternate interior angles. $\angle c$ and $\angle f$, $\angle d$ and $\angle e$

i. Name two pairs of alternate exterior angles. $\angle a$ and $\angle h$, $\angle b$ and $\angle g$

j. If $m\angle a$ is 105°, what is the measure of $\angle f$? $m\angle f$ = 75°

Figure 3

Written Practice   *Strengthening Concepts*

1. The ratio of stars to stripes is 50 to 13. If there were 400 stars in the parade, how many stripes were there?   104 stripes
(45)

▶ *** 2.** **Connect** From the front to the back of the property Wally stepped off 40 paces. He estimated that each pace was a yard. Convert 40 yards to feet using a unit multiplier to estimate the depth of the property in feet. $\frac{40 \text{ yds}}{1} \cdot \frac{3 \text{ ft}}{1 \text{ yd}}$ = 120 ft
(52)

Lesson 54   371

▶ See Math Conversations in the sidebar.

② New Concepts (Continued)

Practice Set
Problem a [Conclude]
Remind students that vertical angles occur in pairs, and both angles of any pair have the same measure.

Problem b [Error Alert]
Have students recall that adjacent angles share a common vertex and a common side, and then ask them to decide if all of the supplementary angles in the figure are also adjacent angles. yes

It is important for students to note, however, that supplementary angles are not always adjacent angles.

To demonstrate this concept, draw two perpendicular lines on the board or overhead. Label the right angles formed at the intersection from 1 to 4 (clockwise or counterclockwise). Then have students note that although angles 1 and 3 and angles 2 and 4 are supplementary because the sum of their measures is 180°, the angles are not adjacent angles.

Problem c [Conclude]
After completing the problem, ask students to name the sum of the four angle measures. 360°

Point out that the four angles form a circle, and the degree measure of any circle is 360.

Problem d [Error Alert]
Make sure students understand that $\angle f$ and $\angle g$ are complementary because the sum of the angle measures of any triangle is 180°, and since one angle measure of the triangle is 90°, the sum of the measures of the other two angles must be 180° − 90° or 90°.

③ Written Practice

Math Conversations
Discussion opportunities are provided below.

Problem 2 [Connect]
Have students recall that a unit multiplier is a ratio that is equal to 1, and consists of two equivalent measures.

(continued)

Lesson 54   **371**

Math Conversations

Discussion opportunities are provided below.

Problem 4b [Evaluate]

"Explain how you can decide the mode of the data simply by looking at the line plot." The mode is the tallest column, or tallest columns if two or more columns are the same height.

Remind students that the data in a set may have one mode, more than one mode, or no mode.

Problems 7–10 [Analyze]

"How can we check our work whenever we solve an equation for a variable?" check by substitution

For problem **8**, students should recognize the opportunity to collect like terms before applying inverse operations.

Errors and Misconceptions
Problem 11

Students should infer that the term x^0 is another name for 1, and because it is one of several factors in the expression, it can simply be canceled because multiplying a number by 1 does not change the value of the number.

(continued)

---

4. a.

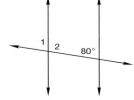

5. 80° because the lines are parallel and ∡1 corresponds to the 80° angle.

13.

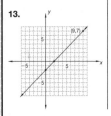

---

3. Solve by writing and solving a proportion: The recipe calls for 2 cups of flour and 7 cranberries. Cathy is multiplying the recipe so that it feeds more people. If the new recipe calls for 49 cranberries, how many cups of flour are needed?   14 cups of flour
(49)

* **4.** [Evaluate] For 5 minutes every day at 10 a.m., James counted the number of birds that came to the bird feeder outside his window. Over 10 days, he collected this data: 3, 5, 4, 5, 5, 4, 6, 5, 6, 6.
(53)

   a. Display the data with a line plot.

▶ **b.** Find the range and the mean, median, and mode of the data.   range: 3, mean: 4.9, median: 5, mode: 5

   c. James said, "Most often, there were 5 birds that came to the bird feeder." Which measure of central tendency did he use?   mode

For problems **5** and **6,** use the figure of the parallel lines cut by a transversal.

* **5.** Find $m\angle 1$. Justify your answer.
(54)

* **6.** Find $m\angle 2$. Justify your answer.   100° because $\angle 2$ and $\angle 1$ are supplementary, so the sum of their measures is 180°.
(54)

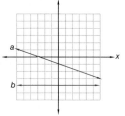

[Analyze] Solve. Then select one equation and write a story for it.   See student work.

▶ * **7.** $3 = 2x + 3$ $x = 0$
   (50)

▶ * **8.** $3x + 7 - x = 21$ $x = 7$
   (50)

▶ * **9.** $20 - x = 1$ $x = 19$
   (50)

▶ * **10.** $-2w = -3$ $x = \frac{3}{2}$
   (36)

▶ **11.** Simplify and express with all positive exponents. $\frac{1}{y}$
   (51)
$$xyx^0y^{-2}x^{-1}$$

  12. Refer to the graphed lines to answer the following questions.
(Inv. 1, 44)

   a. Which line intersects the y-axis at -1?   line a

   b. What is the slope of line b?   0

   c. Which line is horizontal?   line b

   d. In which quadrant do the lines intersect?   4th

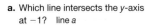

  13. Graph $y = x - 2$. Is the point (9, 7) on the line?   yes
(41)

▶ See Math Conversations in the sidebar.

► * **14.** **Generalize** Naomi cuts circles from squares with sides 20 cm long.
(40)
   a. What is the diameter of the largest circle she can cut from the square?   20 cm

   b. What is the area of the largest circle? (Use 3.14 for π.)   314 cm²

   c. What is the area of the waste to the nearest sq. cm?   86 cm²

15. Find the **a** area and **b** perimeter of the figure
(37, Inv. 2) to the right. (Units are inches.) **a.** 24 in.²
    b. 30 in.

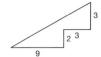

Simplify:

 16. $-(x - y) - (x + y)$ $-2x$ **17.** $2x^2 - 3x - x^2 + 5$ $x^2 - 3x + 5$
(31, 36)   (31)

 18. $\dfrac{2.9 \times 10^{12}}{2.9 \times 10^3}$ 10^9 **19.** $-2 - (-2)$ 0
(46)   (33)

 20. $\dfrac{x^9 y}{x^8 y}$ x **21.** $\left(\dfrac{-1}{2}\right)^3 + \dfrac{7}{8}$ $\dfrac{3}{4}$
(27)   (22, 36)

22. The desktop measured 76.2 cm wide. Convert this measure to meters
(51) and write in scientific notation. 7.62×10^{-1} m

23. Write 100% **a** as a decimal and **b** as a reduced fraction.   **a.** 1 **b.** 1
(12)

► * **24.** **Analyze** Raul planned a painting of his mountain cabin. The cabin
(35) stands 20 ft tall and the trees around it are 30 ft tall. The height of the cabin in his painting will be 6 inches.

   a. What is the scale from the actual cabin to the painting?   10 ft: 3 in. or 40:1

   b. How tall should Raul paint the trees?   9 in.

* **25.** Kyla constructed a simple tent with stakes,
(Inv. 2) ropes, and a length of plastic sheeting. She used the plastic sheeting for the roof and floor of the tent, leaving the ends open. The tent stands 1 m tall and 2 m wide at the base. What is the minimum length of plastic used? (Round up to the next whole meter.)   5 m

Find all solutions.

 26. $\dfrac{x}{12} = \dfrac{12}{9}$ 16   **27.** $\dfrac{x^2}{2} = 18$ 6, −6
(34)   (14, 36)

 28. $-3|x| = -3$ 1, −1   **29.** $\dfrac{m}{5} = 0.2$ 1
(1, 14)   (38)

Lesson 54   373

► See Math Conversations in the sidebar.

Math Conversations

Discussion opportunities are provided below.

Problem 14   Generalize

Have students use 3.14 for pi.

When problems are not accompanied by a drawing, remind students that they can always draw a sketch to help understand the relationship of the information in the problem.

Problem 24   Analyze

"A scale is a ratio. The order of the terms in a ratio is very important. In what order should we write the ratio in this problem?" the height of the actual cabin to the height of the cabin in the painting

(continued)

Math Conversations

Discussion opportunities are provided below.

Problem 30 Model

You may wish to provide students with isometric dot paper for this and similar drawings.

30.

▶ **30.** Use the views shown to draw a three-dimensional view of the figure.
(Inv. 4)

Top View,
Bottom View

Left-side
View

Front View,
Back View

Right-side
View

Early Finishers
Real-World
Application

Mike can swim the 100-yard freestyle in two minutes. If he swims at the same rate, how many seconds will it take him to swim 50 meters (1 meter ≈ 1.09 yard)? $\frac{100 \text{ yds}}{1} \cdot \frac{1 \text{ m}}{1.09 \text{ yard}} = 91.74$ meters; $\frac{91.74 \text{ meters}}{120 \text{ seconds}} \cdot \frac{50 \text{ meters}}{x} = 91.74x = 6000$ seconds; $x = 65.40$ seconds

▶ See Math Conversations in the sidebar.

Looking Forward

Understanding and applying angle relationships prepares students for:

- **Lesson 65,** performing applications using similar triangles.

- **Lesson 81,** working with central angles and arcs.

Nets of Prisms, Cylinders, Pyramids, and Cones

Objectives

- Sketch a geometric solid when given its net.
- Understand how nets are related to formulas for surface area.
- Sketch a net for a given geometric solid.

Lesson Preparation

Materials

- Power Up K (in *Instructional Masters*)
- Teacher-provided material: unlined paper, compass, scissors, glue or tape

Optional

- Teacher-provided material: grid paper

Power Up K

Math Language

Maintain	English Learners (ESL)
cone	particular
cylinder	
net	
prism	
pyramid	

Technology Resources

Student eBook Complete student textbook in electronic format.

Resources and Planner CD Assessment, reteaching, and instructional masters, plus a pacing calendar with standards.

Test and Practice Generator CD Create additional practice sheets and custom-made tests.

www.SaxonPublishers.com Visit for more student activities and planning materials.

Inclusion

Adaptations CD Adapted lessons, investigations, practice and assessments.

Meeting Standards

National Council of Teachers of Mathematics (NCTM)

Geometry

GM.4b Use two-dimensional representations of three-dimensional objects to visualize and solve problems such as those involving surface area and volume

Measurement

ME.2d Develop strategies to determine the surface area and volume of selected prisms, pyramids, and cylinders

Representation

RE.5c Use representations to model and interpret physical, social, and mathematical phenomena

Problem-Solving Strategy: Guess and Check

Two brothers are 5 years apart, and the sum of their ages is 41. What are the ages of the brothers?

(Understand) **Understand the problem.**

"What information are we given?"

Two brothers are 5 years apart, and the sum of their ages is 41.

"What are we asked to do?"

Determine the ages of the two brothers.

(Plan) **Make a plan.**

"What problem-solving strategy will we use?"

We will *guess and check.*

"What do we anticipate the ages to be in the range of?"

If the brothers were twins, they would be $41 \div 2 = 20\frac{1}{2}$ years old, so one is a little younger and one is a little older than 20 years.

(Solve) **Carry out the plan.**

"If the brothers were one year apart how old would they be?"

20 and 21 years old.

"Making the younger brother a year younger and the older brother a year older, makes the brothers how old and how many years apart?"

They would be 19 and 22, which is 3 years apart.

"If we repeat this method one more time, how old are the brothers?"

They are 18 and 23 years old.

(Check) **Look back.**

"Did we find the answer to the question that was asked?"

Yes. We found the ages of two brothers whose combined age is 41 years, and who are 5 years apart.

• **Nets of Prisms, Cylinders, Pyramids, and Cones**

facts | Power Up K

mental math |

a. **Number Sense:** 1.5×8 12

b. **Statistics:** Find the mean of 16 and 20. 18

c. **Fractional Parts:** $66\frac{2}{3}\%$ of $81 $54

d. **Probability:** What is the probability of rolling a number less than 3 on a number cube? $\frac{2}{6}$ or $\frac{1}{3}$

e. **Geometry:** Two angles of a parallelogram measure 80° and 100°. Find the measure of the other two angles. 80° and 100°

f. **Measurement:** The odometer read 2388 mi at the end of the trip. At the beginning, it had read 1208 mi. How long was the trip? 1180 miles

g. **Rate:** Ronnie ran $\frac{1}{4}$ mile in 1 minute. At that rate, how long would it take him to run a mile? 4 minutes

h. **Calculation:** $200 \div 2, \sqrt{\ }, \times 5, -1, \sqrt{\ }, \times 2, +2, \sqrt{\ }, \times 2, +1, \sqrt{\ }$ 3

problem solving | Two brothers are 5 years apart, and the sum of their ages is 41. What are the ages of the brothers? 18 and 23

New Concept Increasing Knowledge

If we think of the surface of a solid as a hollow cardboard shell, then cutting open and spreading out the cardboard creates a net of the solid. For example, here we show a net for a pyramid with a square base.

Example 1

This net represents the surfaces of what geometric solid? Sketch the solid and describe how this surface area formula relates to each part of the net:

$$s = 2\pi rh + 2\pi r^2$$

 Power Up

Facts
Distribute **Power Up K** to students. See answers below.

Mental Math
Encourage students to share different ways to mentally compute these exercises. Strategies for exercises **a** and **c** are listed below.

a. **Multiply by 2 Three Times**
$1.5 \times 8 = 1.5 \times 2 \times 2 \times 2 = 3 \times 2 \times 2 = 6 \times 2 = 12$
Double and Halve
$1.5 \times 8 = 3 \times 4 = 12$

c. **Multiply by 3, Divide by 3**
$66\frac{2}{3}\%$ of $81 = 200\%$ of $27 = 54
Find a Fraction
$66\frac{2}{3}\% = \frac{2}{3}$
$\frac{2}{3} \times $81 = 2 \times 27 = 54

Problem Solving
Refer to **Power-Up Discussion**, p. 375B.

---

2 New Concepts

Instruction
Explain that for some figures, such as cubes, the shape of the net can vary depending on how the figure is taken apart.

Example 1
Instruction
Ask a volunteer to explain how this net would go together to form a cylinder. Sample: Roll the rectangle so it looks like a can and tape it. Then fold the circles down to cover the holes and tape them in place.

(continued)

Facts Find the value of each variable.

$a + 8 = 20$	$b - 6 = 18$	$3c = 24$	$\frac{d}{4} = 8$	$x^2 = 25$
$a = 12$	$b = 24$	$c = 8$	$d = 32$	$x = 5$ (and −5)
$7 + e = 15$	$20 - f = 5$	$(g)(4) = 20$	$\frac{12}{h} = 6$	$\sqrt{w} = 4$
$e = 8$	$f = 15$	$g = 5$	$h = 2$	$w = 16$
$18 = j + 11$	$17 = k - 4$	$24 = 6m$	$6 = \frac{n}{3}$	$|z| = 3$
$j = 7$	$k = 21$	$m = 4$	$n = 18$	$z = 3, -3$
$14 = 5 + q$	$30 = 40 - r$	$32 = (s)(4)$	$8 = \frac{24}{t}$	$\frac{1}{2}y = 8$
$q = 9$	$r = 10$	$s = 8$	$t = 3$	$y = 16$

2 New Concepts (Continued)

Example 2

Instruction

Ask if anyone can describe a different net for this prism. Sample: The triangles could be at the ends of the first or last rectangle rather than the middle rectangle.

Example 3

Instruction

There are several ways to construct a net for this figure; however, all the nets will include six rectangles, two each of the rectangles for the front, top, and side of the figure.

(continued)

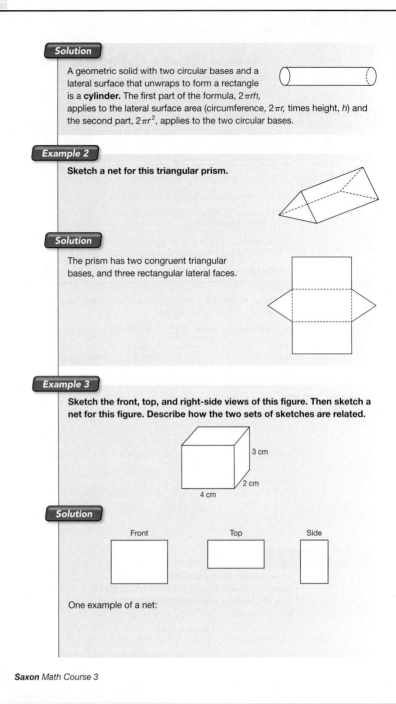

Solution

A geometric solid with two circular bases and a lateral surface that unwraps to form a rectangle is a **cylinder.** The first part of the formula, $2\pi rh$, applies to the lateral surface area (circumference, $2\pi r$, times height, h) and the second part, $2\pi r^2$, applies to the two circular bases.

Example 2

Sketch a net for this triangular prism.

Solution

The prism has two congruent triangular bases, and three rectangular lateral faces.

Example 3

Sketch the front, top, and right-side views of this figure. Then sketch a net for this figure. Describe how the two sets of sketches are related.

3 cm
2 cm
4 cm

Solution

Front   Top   Side

One example of a net:

Teacher Tip

Suggest students **make nets for various prisms and pyramids.** Provide grid paper to make drawing the nets easier. When they complete drawing the nets, have them fold and tape them to see whether the net produces the desired solid figure.

The front, top and right-side views are the three different rectangles that appear in the net. Each rectangle appears twice, because the front and back faces are congruent, as are the top and bottom faces and the left and right faces.

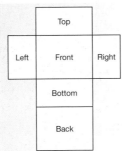

Activity

Instruction

Have students work in pairs to make and disassemble the cones.

The Thinking Skill *Connect* and *Extend* features provide more information and hands-on experience with cones and the surface area and lateral surface area of cones.

Activity

Net of a Cone

Materials needed: unlined paper, compass, scissors, glue or tape, ruler.

Using a compass, draw a circle with a radius of at least two inches. Cut out the circle and make one cut from the edge to the center of the circle. Form the lateral surface of a cone by overlapping the two sides of the cut. The greater the overlap, the narrower the cone. Glue or tape the overlapped paper so that the cone holds its shape.

To make the circular base of the cone, measure the diameter of the open end of the cone and use a compass to draw a circle with the same diameter. (Remember, the radius is half the diameter.) Cut out the circle and tape it in place using two pieces of tape.

Now disassemble the cone to form a net. Cut open the cone by cutting the circular base free on one side. Unroll the lateral surface by making a straight cut to the point (apex) of the cone. The net of a cone has two parts, its circular base and a sector of a circle that forms the lateral surface of the cone.

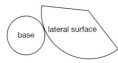

base   lateral surface

Thinking Skill

Connect

The formula for the surface area of a cone is $s = \pi r l + \pi r^2$. Which parts of the formula apply to which parts of the net? $\pi r l$ applies to the lateral surface and πr^2 applies to the circular base.

Extend An alternate method for calculating the area of the lateral surface of a cone is to calculate the area of the portion of a circle represented by the net of the lateral surface. Use a protractor to measure the central angle of the lateral surface of the cone you created. The measure of that angle is the fraction of a 360° circle represented by the lateral surface. Use a ruler to measure the radius. Find the area of a whole circle with that radius. Then find the area of the sector by multiplying the area of the whole circle by the fraction $\frac{\text{central angle}}{360}$. Answers will vary.

central angle

radius

Lesson 55   377

Math Background

How many different nets are there for a cube?

There are exactly 11 different nets that form a cube.

Practice Set
Problem b [Error Alert]
Some students may find it helpful to sketch on grid paper.

Invite students to compare sketches to learn that a variety of nets are possible.

If students have any uncertainty about the nets that were drawn, ask them to cut and fold the nets to check their work.

Problem c [Error Alert]
Students who have difficulty drawing the net may benefit from working with a completed tetrahedron and cutting it apart using scissors.

Problem d [Error Alert]
Drawing the views and the net on grid paper will make it easier for students to model the proportions of the prism.

Math Conversations
Discussion opportunities are provided below.

Problem 3 [Justify]
Accept all answers that are supported by sensible reasoning.

Have students recall that measures of central tendency include mean, median, and mode. Then extend the problem by asking:

"Suppose Yueling read a sixth book that was 200 pages long. Using only mental math, explain how that number of pages would affect the mean, median, and mode of the five books he previously read." The mean and median would increase, and the mode would be unchanged.

"Which measure would show a greater increase, the mean or the range? Give a reason to support your answer." Range; Sample explanation: The range would increase more because it is a measure of the minimum and maximum data values; its increase is more than tenfold, from 9 (105 − 96) to more than 100 (200 − 96).

Problem 6 [Conclude]
Sketch the figure on the board or overhead and challenge volunteers to use the sketch and demonstrate more than one way to find the measure of ∠x.

(continued)

Practice Set
a. Cone

c. one example:

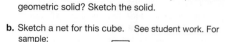

d.
Back   Top   Right side

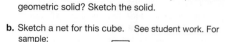

one example:

3 cm
3 cm
4 cm / 5 cm
5 cm
6 cm

▶ **a.** The net created in this lesson's activity represents the surfaces of what geometric solid? Sketch the solid.

▶ **b.** Sketch a net for this cube.   See student work. For sample:

▶ **c.** This pyramid is called a tetrahedron. All of its faces are congruent equilateral triangles. Draw a net of this pyramid.

▶ **d.** Sketch the back, top, and right side views of this triangular prism. Then sketch a net for the figure and label the dimensions.

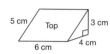

5 cm / Top / 3 cm
6 cm   4 cm

e. [Model] Build a model of the figure in exercise **c** by cutting, folding, and taping the net.   See student work.

Written Practice   *Strengthening Concepts*

1. A manufacturing company has a debt to equity ratio of 3 to 2. If the
(34) company has a debt of $12 million, how much does it have in equity? $8 million

2. It takes Jack 5 minutes to drive from home to the nearest ATM machine.
(3, 4) Then it takes 2 minutes in line at the ATM for each customer ahead of him. How long will it be before Jack can use the ATM if he leaves from home and then waits behind 3 customers?   11 minutes

3. Sample: "Yueling read 5 books that averaged 100 pages each." I selected the mean because 5 times the mean gives the total number of pages he read.

▶ * **3.** [Justify] Yueling read 5 books of these lengths: 105, 97, 96, 99, 103.
(53) Write a statement using a measure of central tendency to communicate how many pages Yueling read. Explain your choice.

4. $(-2)^2 + (-2)^3$ −4
(31, 36)

5. $\frac{4}{3} = \frac{x}{1.5}$ $x = 2$
(44)

▶ * **6.** [Conclude] A transversal cuts parallel lines.
(54) Find x.   75°

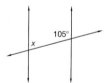

105°
x

▶ See Math Conversations in the sidebar.

Solve. Then select one of the equations and write a word problem for it. see student work

7. $4 = -m + 11$ $m = 7$
(50)

8. $9x + 9 = 90$ $x = 9$
(50)

9. $-5 - x = -9$ $x = 4$
(50)

10. $3y - y - 1 = 9$ $y = 5$
(36)

11. Describe each of the following views of this figure as top, right, or front.
(Inv. 4)

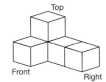

Top

Front   Right

a.    front

b. right

c. top

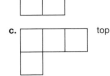

12. Sample:
Both Roger
and Simon are
correct. Roger's
sample space
is more helpful
because each
outcome listed
is equally likely,
so probabilities
can be calculated
from the sample
space.

12. If the spinner is spun once, Roger says the sample space is {A, A, A, B, B, C}. Simon says the sample space is {A, B, C}. Who is correct? Explain your answer.
(32)

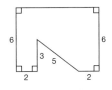

14.

y

(5, 2)

x

13. Garrett does an Internet search for the nearest location of a particular store. He requests a search of a location within a 60 mi radius of his home. About how many square miles does the search cover? about 11,304 mi²
(40)

14. Graph $y = \frac{4}{5}x - 2$. Is the point (5, 2) a solution?   yes
(47)

15. Find the perimeter and area of this figure. (Units are in ft.) $P = 32$ ft, $A = 42$ ft²
(37)

6   6
3
5
2   2

* 16. *Analyze* Moving at a uniform rate the train traveled 200 miles in five hours.
(49)

▶ **a.** Express the average speed of the train as a unit rate.   40 mi/hr

b. How long did it take the train to travel 100 miles?   2.5 hr

Lesson 55   379

▶ See Math Conversations in the sidebar.

Math Conversations

Discussion opportunities are provided below.

Problem 17 | Analyze

"What unit multiplier should we use to make the conversion? Explain why you chose that unit multiplier." $\frac{1\text{ yd}}{3\text{ ft}}$; one yard and three feet are equivalent measures

Problem 19 | Generalize

Make sure students recognize that all of the terms of the expression are factors, a negative exponent indicates a reciprocal, and the factor y^0 is another name for 1.

"Why can we simply cancel y^0?" It is a factor and another name for 1, and multiplying a number by 1 does not change that number.

(continued)

17.
$440 \text{ ft} \cdot \frac{1\text{ yd}}{3\text{ ft}} = 146\frac{2}{3} \text{ yd}$

▶* **17.** (52) **Analyze** Convert 440 ft to yards. Use a unit multiplier.

18. (42) The dimensions of an air mattress are 80 inches by 33 inches by 5 inches. What is the volume of the air mattress? If the average set of human lungs can hold about 244 in.^{3}, about how many breaths will it take to inflate the mattress? 13,200 in.^{3}, about 54 breaths

Generalize Simplify.

▶* **19.** (27, 51) $9^{-2}x^{-1}y^0x$ $\frac{1}{81}$

20. (27) $\frac{x^5m^2}{mx}$ x^4m

21. (22) $\left(\frac{1}{3}\right)^2 \div \frac{2}{3}$ $\frac{1}{6}$

22. (25) $1.2 \div 0.05$ 24

23. (12) **a.** Write $\frac{1}{100}$ as a decimal and percent. 0.01, 1%

b. How does $\frac{1}{100}$ compare to 0.009? $\frac{1}{100}$ is greater

24. (21) Factor:

a. $6x - 15$ $3(2x - 5)$ **b.** $x^2 - x$ $x(x - 1)$

25. (35) The triangles are similar.

a. What is the scale factor from the small to large triangle? 3

b. Find x. 18

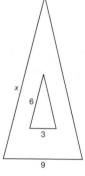

26. (52) Brooke finished the facts practice test in 1 minute and 18 seconds. Express her time as a mixed number of minutes and as a decimal number of minutes. $1\frac{3}{10}$ min, 1.3 min

27. (36) Rahm is playing his favorite video game. Every time his player grabs a wrong object, Rahm loses 5 points. If Rahm accidentally grabs a wrong object 23 times, what is the effect on his score? Rahm loses 115 points.

28. (51) A human hair measures 50 millionths (50×10^{-6}) of a meter. Which is thicker, 100 human hairs or a nickel that is $\frac{2}{10^3}$ meter thick? 100 human hairs are $2\frac{1}{2}$ times as thick as the nickel.

▶ See Math Conversations in the sidebar.

⚐ **29.** Combine like terms to simplify.
  (31, 36)
  a. $2(x + b) - (-x - b)$ $3x + 3b$ **b.** $2x + 1 - 3x + 4$ $-x + 5$

30. As humans get older, their maximum heart rate decreases. Which of
  (41) the following graphs illustrates this relationship? Is it a proportional
        relationship?

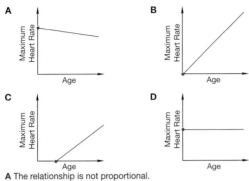

A The relationship is not proportional.

Early Finishers

Real-World
Application

A manager at the local movie theater wants to increase popcorn profits.
The cost of a bucket of popcorn is $0.05 for popcorn kernels, $0.02 for
butter, and $0.25 for the bucket. If the manager wants to sell 115 buckets
of popcorn a night and make a profit of $365.00, how much should the
manager charge for each bucket of popcorn? Note: The profit is the amount
of money made after subtracting the cost.   Cost of Popcorn Bucket = $0.32;
Profit = Amount Collected − Cost; $365.00 = x − 115($0.32); x = $401.80.
Cost of Popcorn Bucket = Amount Collected ÷ Buckets of Popcorn;   Cost of
Popcorn Bucket = $401.80 ÷ 115 = $3.49 per bucket.

3 **Written Practice** *(Continued)*

Math Conversations

Discussion opportunities are provided below.

Problem 29

*"Instead of subtracting a number we may
add its opposite. What is the opposite of
(−x − b)?"* $x + b$

Errors and Misconceptions
Problems 29a and 29b

Make sure students recognize that collecting
like terms involves addition and subtraction
(such as in problem **29b**), but other operations
may be present (such as in problem **29a**).
When other operations are present, students
must recall that the order of operations
governs the order in which those operations
are to be completed. So students should
conclude that in problem **29a**, combining like
terms using addition and subtraction is not
the first step to be completed.

Looking Forward

Sketching and constructing nets of prisms, cylinders, pyramids, and cones
prepares students for:

- **Lesson 85,** calculating surface areas of cylinders and prisms.

- **Lesson 91,** investigating the effects of scaling on perimeter, area, and
  volume.

- **Lesson 100,** calculating surface areas of right pyramids and cones.

- **Lesson 107,** calculating volumes and surface areas of compound solids.

Assessment   30–40 minutes   For use after Lesson 55

Distribute **Cumulative Test 10** to each student. Two versions of the test are available in *Saxon Math Course 3 Course Assessments Book*. Have students complete the **Power-Up Test** first. Allow 10 minutes. Then have students work the 20 numbered items on the **Cumulative Test**. Students may use copies of the answer sheet to record their work. Track individual and class progress with the **Test Analysis** forms.

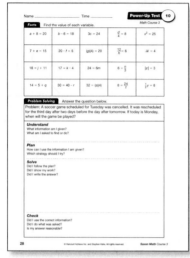
Power-Up Test 10

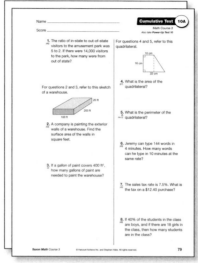
Cumulative Test 10A

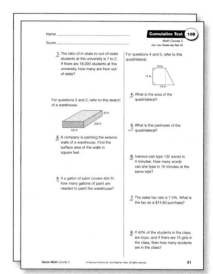
Alternative Cumulative Test 10B

Optional Answer Forms

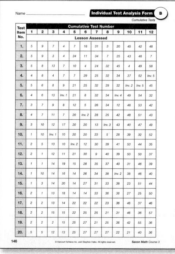
Individual Test Analysis Form

Class Test Analysis Form

Reteaching

Students who score below 80% on the assessment may be in need of reteaching. Look for the causes of student mistakes. If errors are conceptual, refer to the *Reteaching Masters* for reteaching.

Harvest

Assign after Lesson 55

Objectives
- Solve ratio problems involving totals.
- Solve for an unknown using equivalent ratios.
- Communicate ideas through writing.

Materials
Copies of **Performance Activity 10A** and **10B**

Time Requirement
15–30 minutes; Begin in class and complete at home.

Activity
Explain to students that in this activity they will use ratios to draw conclusions about the quality of a harvest and make predictions about the revenue it will bring. First, students will find ratios to complete a table. Then students will use these results and ratios to predict revenue. They will adjust their predictions when new information is given to them. Point out that all necessary information is provided on **Performance Activity 10A** and **10B**.

Criteria for Evidence of Learning
- Uses ratios to draw reasonable conclusions about a total.
- Finds a ratio correctly, given information about a total.
- Uses rates to reasonably predict revenue.
- Adjusts conclusions using percents.
- Communicates ideas clearly through writing.

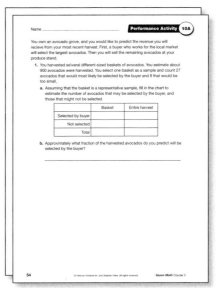

Performance Activity 10A and 10B

Meeting Standards

National Council of Teachers of Mathematics (NCTM)

Numbers and Operations

NO.1d Understand and use ratios and proportions to represent quantitative relationships

NO.3d Develop, analyze, and explain methods for solving problems involving proportions, such as scaling and finding equivalent ratios

Problem Solving

PS.1b Solve problems that arise in mathematics and in other contexts

PS.1c Apply and adapt a variety of appropriate strategies to solve problems

Reasoning and Proof

RP.2b Make and investigate mathematical conjectures

Communication

CM.3a Organize and consolidate their mathematical thinking through communication

Connections

CN.4c Recognize and apply mathematics in contexts outside of mathematics

• The Slope-Intercept Equation of a Line

Objectives

- Describe the graph of a linear function given its equation in slope-intercept form.
- Write an equation for a linear function in slope-intercept form given its graph.
- Graph linear equations given in slope-intercept form.

Lesson Preparation

Materials

- **Power Up L** (in *Instructional Masters*)
- **Lesson Activity 7** (in *Instructional Masters*) **or graph paper**

Power Up L

Math Language

Maintain
slope
y-intercept

Technology Resources

Student eBook Complete student textbook in electronic format.

Resources and Planner CD Assessment, reteaching, and instructional masters, plus a pacing calendar with standards.

Test and Practice Generator CD Create additional practice sheets and custom-made tests.

www.SaxonPublishers.com Visit for more student activities and planning materials.

Inclusion

Adaptations CD Adapted lessons, investigations, practice and assessments.

Meeting Standards

National Council of Teachers of Mathematics (NCTM)

Algebra

AL.2b Explore relationships between symbolic expressions and graphs of lines, paying particular attention to the meaning of intercept and slope

Connections

CN.4a Recognize and use connections among mathematical ideas

Problem-Solving Strategy: Write an Equation

A hiker estimates his hiking time by using the following rule: $\frac{1}{2}$ hour for every 1 mile, plus $\frac{1}{2}$ hour for each 1000-foot rise in elevation. A pair of hikers is planning a 12-mile hike to the summit of a mountain with a 5000-ft rise in elevation. They want to reach the summit by 3:00 p.m. At what time should they begin hiking?

(Understand) *Understand the problem.*

"What information are we given?"

1. A rule for estimating hiking time is: $\frac{1}{2}$ hour per 1 mile, plus $\frac{1}{2}$ hour per 1000 feet in elevation.
2. A planned hike will cover 12 miles and rise to 5000 feet in elevation.
3. The hikers would like to reach the summit by 3:00pm.

"What are we asked to do?"

Determine what time the hikers should begin their hike.

(Plan) *Make a plan.*

"What problem-solving strategy will we use?"

We will *write equations* to solve for total time and the time the hike should begin.

(Solve) *Carry out the plan.*

"How many hours are required to hike 12 miles?"

12 miles at $\frac{1}{2}$ hour per mile requires $12 \times \frac{1}{2} = 6$ hours to hike

"How many additional hours are required for the 5000-foot climb?"

A 5000-ft rise in elevation adds $\frac{1}{2}$ hour per 1000 feet, so $\frac{1}{2}(5000 \div 1000) = \frac{1}{2}(5) = 2\frac{1}{2}$ hours.

"How long could the hike to the summit take?"

6 hours $+ 2\frac{1}{2}$ hours $= 8\frac{1}{2}$ hours

"By what time should the hikers begin their hike?"

3:00 p.m. $- 8\frac{1}{2}$ hours $= 6:30$ a.m.

(Check) *Look back.*

"Did we find the answer to the question that was asked?"

Yes. We determined that the hikers should leave by 6:30 a.m. to reach the summit by 3:00 p.m.

382   Saxon Math Course 3

The Slope-Intercept Equation of a Line

1 Power Up

Facts
Distribute **Power Up L** to students. See answers below.

Mental Math
Encourage students to share different ways to mentally compute these exercises. Strategies for exercises **a** and **d** are listed below.

a. Regroup, then Multiply
$6 \times 3.1 = (6 \times 3) + (6 \times 0.1) =$
$18 + 0.6 = 18.6$

d. Find a Fraction
$75\% = \frac{3}{4}$
$\frac{3}{4} \times 84 = 3 \times 21 = 63$
Multiply by 4, Divide by 4
75% of $84 = 300\%$ of $21 = 63$

Problem Solving
Refer to **Power-Up Discussion**, p. 382B.

---

facts   Power Up L

mental math

a. **Number Sense:** 6×3.1 18.6

b. **Powers/Roots:** $\sqrt{2 \cdot 2} \cdot \sqrt{3 \cdot 3}$ 6

c. **Scientific Notation:** Write 4.013×10^{-4} in standard form.   0.0004013

d. **Percent:** 75% of 84   63

e. **Geometry:** Can the sides of a triangle measure 7 ft, 3 ft, and 3 ft?   no

f. **Fractional Parts:** The gas tank holds 20 gallons when full. About how much gas is in the tank now?   10 gallons

g. **Rate:** Tommy rode his bike 20 miles per hour north. Christina rode 15 miles per hour south. If they started at the same place and time, how far apart are they after 1 hour? After 2 hours?   35 miles; 70 miles

h. **Calculation:** 6×7, -2, $\div 4$, square it, -1, $\div 9$, $+5$, $\div 2$, $\div 2$, $\div 2$ 2

problem solving   A hiker estimates his hiking time by using the following rule: $\frac{1}{2}$ hour for every 1 mile, plus $\frac{1}{2}$ hour for each 1000 foot rise in elevation. A pair of hikers is planning a 12-mile hike to the summit of a mountain with a 5000 ft rise in elevation. They want to reach the summit by 3:00 p.m. At what time should they begin hiking?   6:30 a.m.

New Concept   Increasing Knowledge

If the equation of a line is written in slope-intercept form, we can read the slope and y-intercept directly from the equation.

$$y = (slope)x + (y\text{-intercept})$$

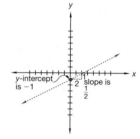

Facts   Write each number in scientific notation.

$186,000 = 1.86 \times 10^5$	$0.0002 = 2 \times 10^{-4}$
$2,050,000 = 2.05 \times 10^6$	$\frac{1}{1,000,000} = 1 \times 10^{-6}$
15 million $= 1.5 \times 10^7$	12 thousandths $= 1.2 \times 10^{-2}$

Write each number in standard form.

$3 \times 10^5 = 300,000$	$1 \times 10^{-3} = 0.001$
$3.75 \times 10^4 = 37,500$	$3.5 \times 10^{-5} = 0.000035$
$4.05 \times 10^3 = 4050$	$2.04 \times 10^{-2} = 0.0204$

The slope-intercept equation of the line graphed on the previous page is $y = \frac{1}{2}x - 1$.

$$y = \frac{1}{2}x - 1$$

The slope is $\frac{1}{2}$. ↑   ↑ The y-intercept is −1.

Many books show the slope-intercept form this way:

Slope-intercept equation

$$y = mx + b$$

The number for **m** is the slope.

The number for **b** is the y-intercept.

Consider the following equations and their graphs.

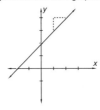

- Slope is 1
- y-intercept is zero

  y = x

- Slope is 1
- y-intercept is +2

  y = x + 2

- Slope is 2
- y-intercept is zero

  y = 2x

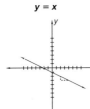

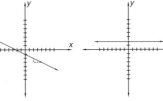

- Slope is $-\frac{1}{2}$
- y-intercept is −1

  $y = -\frac{1}{2}x - 1$

- Slope is zero
- Intersects y-axis at +2

  y = 2

- Slope is undefined
- Every point has
  x-coordinate −3

  x = −3

Notice that a horizontal line has zero slope and can be expressed with slope-intercept form, $y = 0x + 2$, which simplifies to $y = 2$. A vertical line cannot be expressed in slope-intercept form.

Generalize Can the slope of a vertical line be determined? Why or why not?

Thinking Skill

Analyze

What is the value of b in the following equation: $y = 3x$.

0

No; The slope of a vertical line cannot be determined because every point on the line has the same x-coordinate. This means the run is zero. A number divided by zero is undefined.

Example 1

Refer to this equation to answer the questions that follow.

$$y = \frac{2}{3}x - 4$$

Lesson 56   383

Instruction

If this topic is new to your students, be sure to spend enough time developing understanding so that they will be able to work independently on the Practice Set and Written Practice problems.

As you begin discussion of the slope-intercept equation, explain that when the graph for an equation is drawn, the y-intercept is the point where the line passes through the y-axis. Use the Thinking Skill *Analyze* question to help students see that the y-intercept may be 0, and when it is, it is not included in the line's slope-intercept equation.

Discuss the equations and their graphs. Guide students to relate the steepness and direction of the line to the coefficient of x. Point out that when there is a nonzero second term on the right side of an equation, it represents the y-intercept of the graph.

Call attention to the equation for the last graph ($x = -3$). Ask how it is different from the others. It does not include a y term. Then use the *Generalize* question to explore the reasons why a vertical line has an undetermined (or undefined) slope. Sample: There is no run.

(continued)

Example 1

Instruction

Be sure that students do not try to graph the equation to find the answers for **a** and **b.** Tell them that they need only to look at the equation to get the information they need.

For **b,** tell students that we "read" graphs the way we read sentences: from left to right. We always decide whether a line is rising or falling by seeing how it moves from left to right.

Example 2

Instruction

Explain that we can also write an equation of a line in slope-intercept form by inspecting the graph of the equation. We determine the slope by calculating rise over run, and locate the point where the line crosses the *y*-axis.

Point out that we can see the point of intersection of the two lines on the graph. Use the *Justify* feature to introduce the idea that we can tell whether two lines intersect by checking to see if they share a common point.

(continued)

---

a. Where does the graph of the equation cross the *y*-axis?

b. Does the line rise to the right or fall to the right?

> **Solution**

> **a.** The graph of the equation crosses (intercepts) the *y*-axis at **−4,** which is 4 units down from the origin.

> **b.** The line **rises to the right** because the slope is $\frac{2}{3}$ which is positive.

> **Example 2**

Write the equations of lines *a* and *b* in slope-intercept form. At what point do lines *a* and *b* intersect?

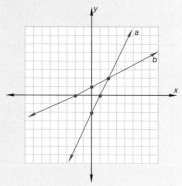

> **Solution**

Line *a* has a slope of 2 and intercepts the *y*-axis at −2.

$$y = 2x - 2$$

Line *b* has a slope of $\frac{1}{2}$ and intercepts the *y*-axis at +1.

$$y = \tfrac{1}{2}x + 1$$

Lines *a* and *b* intersect at **(2, 2).**

Justify Prove that these lines intersect at (2, 2) by substituting for *x* in both equations and solving for *y*. For both equations, students should find that $y = 2$ when $x = 2$.

> **Example 3**

Graph each equation using the given slope and *y*-intercept.

    a. $y = 2x - 3$ b. $y = -\dfrac{1}{2}x + 2$

> **Teacher Tip**

> Be sure to **keep extra copies of Lesson Activity 7 Four Coordinate Planes or graph paper available** for students to use for the problems in this lesson and in the Written Practice in following lessons. Continue to encourage students to try sketching coordinate planes and their graphs on plain paper.

a. We study the equation to understand what the numbers mean.

$$y = 2x - 3$$

This number means ↑   ↑ This means the line
the slope is positive 2   intersects the y-axis
(over 1, up 2).   at −3.

We start by graphing the point of the y-intercept. From there we graph additional points by going over 1 and up 2. The direction of "over" is to the right. Then we draw a line through the points.

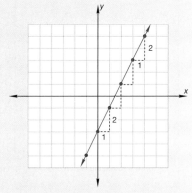

b. If the slope is a fraction, the denominator represents the "over" number and the numerator represents the "up or down" number.

$$y = -\frac{1}{2}x + 2$$

The slope is $-\frac{1}{2}$ ↑   ↑ y -intercept is
(over 2, down 1).   at +2.

We start at +2 on the y-axis and count over 2, then down 1.

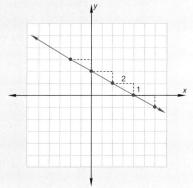

---

2 New Concepts (Continued)

Example 3
Instruction

You might demonstrate how to use only the slope and the y-intercept to graph these equations. Provide copies of **Lesson Activity 7** Four Coordinate Planes or graph paper for students. Point out that from each equation we can learn the slope and the y-intercept.

For **b**, give extra help to students who may not understand how to graph additional points using a slope that is a fraction.

(continued)

Math Background

What does the equation of a vertical line look like?

The equation of a vertical line that crosses the x-axis at the point (c, 0) is x = c. For example, the equation of the line below is x = 3.

Note that this graph and equation do not represent a function. The only input value, 3, corresponds to an infinite number of output values.

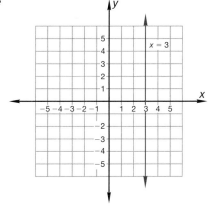

Practice Set

Problem a [Analyze]

Write the general form of the slope-intercept equation ($y = mx + b$) on the board or overhead and ask students to compare the given equations to it.

Problem b [Error Alert]

Make sure students recognize that when an equation of a line is in slope-intercept form, m describes the slope of the line and b describes the y-intercept, or point at which the line passes through the y-axis. The equations and arrows shown below can be copied on the board or overhead.

$$y = mx + b$$
$$\downarrow \qquad \downarrow$$
$$y = -\frac{1}{3}x + 2$$
$$m = \text{slope} \qquad b = y\text{-intercept}$$

Problem g [Error Alert]

Make sure students understand that in order to graph an equation using the slope and y-intercept given by that equation, the equation must be in the form $y = mx + b$.

Before plotting points, ask students to decide if each equation is in slope-intercept form (yes), and then ask them to identify the slope and the y-intercept of the line.

---

3 Written Practice

Math Conversations

Discussion opportunities are provided below.

Problem 1 [Analyze]

Students should recognize the need for a row labeled "total" if they use a ratio table to represent the problem.

Problem 3 [Represent]

"What range of numbers should appear on the horizontal axis of the plot? Explain your answer." The minimum range is from 4 to 8 because 4 cm and 8 cm represent the least and the greatest data values in the set.

Problem 4 [Conclude]

Before completing the problem, invite volunteers to describe or sketch examples of complementary, supplementary, alternate interior, and alternate exterior angles.

(continued)

Practice Set ▶ **a.** [Analyze] Which of the following equations is written in slope intercept form?   **C**

   A $x = 2y + 3$ **B** $y + 2x = 3$ **C** $y = 2x + 3$

▶ **b.** What is the slope and y-intercept of the graph of this equation?

$$y = -\frac{1}{3}x + 2 \quad \text{slope: } -\frac{1}{3}; y\text{-intercept: } +2$$

[Represent] Write equations for lines **c–f** in slope-intercept form.

c. $y = x + 5$

d. $y = 3$

e. $y = -\frac{1}{2}x + 1$

f. $y = -\frac{3}{2}x - 3$

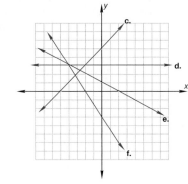

g.

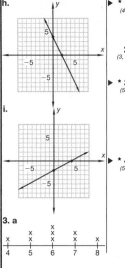

Graph the following equations using the given slope and y-intercept.

▶ **g.** $y = x - 2$ **h.** $y = -2x + 4$ **i.** $y = \frac{1}{2}x - 2$

h.

i.

Written Practice   *Strengthening Concepts*

▶ *** 1.** [Analyze] The ratio of arable land (land that can be used for growing crops) to non-arable land in a certain county is 3 to 7. If the county has an area of 21,000 sq km, what area of the land is arable?   6300 sq km
(45)

2. A lamp costs \$10 and a package of 4 light bulbs costs \$3. How much would it cost to buy 8 lamps and one light bulb for each lamp?   \$86.00
(3, 4)

▶ *** 3.** [Represent] Mary measures the heights of the young plants in her garden to the nearest cm and collects this data: 4 cm, 5 cm, 6 cm, 6 cm, 7 cm, 8 cm, 6 cm, 7 cm, 5 cm
(53)

   a. Display the data with a line plot.

   b. Find the range and the mean, median, and mode of the data.   range: 4 cm; mean: 6 cm; median: 6 cm; mode: 6 cm

▶ *** 4.** [Conclude] Two of the lines are parallel.
(54) Find x.   120°

3. a

X
X X X
X X X X X
4   5   6   7   8

▶ See Math Conversations in the sidebar.

5.

5. Use the slope-intercept method to graph the equation $y = 2x - 4$. Is
(56) (3, 2) a solution?   Yes

6. Find the **a** area and **b** circumference of the circle with radius 1. Use
(39, 40) 3.14159 for π.   **a.** 3.14159, **b.** 6.28318

* 7. The Mid-Atlantic Ridge spreads along the ocean floor an average of
(52) about 10 cm every 4 years.

    a. Express this rate as a unit rate.   2.5 cm/yr

    b. **Connect** This rate is equal to what distance of spread every one
    million years? (Express in km.)   25 km

* 8. Convert 1600 m to km. Use a unit multiplier. $1600\text{m} \cdot \frac{1\text{ km}}{1000\text{ m}} = 1.6$ km
(52)

Solve.

9. $\frac{0.6}{x} = \frac{0.12}{5}$ $x = 25$ *** 10.** $2x - x = 1.5$ $x = 1.5$
(44)   (50)

* 11. $0.6x + 1.2 = 3$ $x = 3$ *** 12.** $7m - 9m = -12$ $m = 6$
(50)   (50)

* 13. a. Write $\frac{2}{5}$ as a decimal and as a percent.   0.4, 40%
(12)

    b. Select any one of these three forms to represent the fact that
    10 students out of 25 had visited the national park.   Sample: 40% of
    the students had visited the national park.

* 14. Factor:
(21)
    a. $2x^2 + 14x$ $2x(x + 7)$ **b.** $15x - 20$ $5(3x - 4)$

* 15. A square with vertices at (2, 2), (−2, 2), (−2, −2), and (2, −2) is dilated
(Inv. 5) by a scale factor of 2. The area of the original square is what fraction of
    its dilated image? $\frac{1}{4}$

16.

cylinder

* 16. The figure is a net for a geometric solid.
(55) Sketch and name the solid.

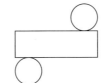

Generalize Simplify:

17. $-5(x + 2) - 2x + 9$ ▶*** 18.** $(-4)^2 - (-4)^3$ 80
(31, 36) $-7x - 1$ (33, 36)

* 19. $\frac{(-15)(-12)}{(-15) - (-12)}$ -60 ▶ **20.** $\frac{wr^2d}{r^3d}$ $\frac{w}{r}$
(33, 36)   (27)

21. $2 \cdot 1\frac{1}{2} - \left(1\frac{1}{2}\right)^2$ $\frac{3}{4}$ **22.** $\frac{6}{8} = \frac{9}{x}$ $x = 12$
(13, 23)   (44)

23. $\frac{4.8 \times 10^7}{1.6 \times 10^4}$ 3×10^3 **24.** $\sqrt{10^2 - 8^2}$ 6
(46)   (15, 21)

25. Simplify and express using only positive exponents. $\frac{a}{c}$
(27, 51)
        $a^0b^1ab^{-1}c^{-1}$

Lesson 56   387

▶ See Math Conversations in the sidebar.

Math Conversations
Discussion opportunities are provided below.

Problem 18 *Generalize*
Ask students to name the sign of the products $(-4)^2$ and $(-4)^3$ before completing the arithmetic.   +; −

Errors and Misconceptions
Problem 20
Remind students who include negative exponents in their answer (such as wr^{-1}) that an expression is not in simplest form if it contains one or more negative exponents. Point out that the reciprocal of the base is used to clear a negative exponent such as r^{-1} from an expression.

(continued)

Math Conversations

Discussion opportunities are provided below.

Problem 27 ~Represent~

Remind students that since the quadrilaterals are to be similar, the corresponding sides of those quadrilaterals must be proportional.

26. Arrange in order from least to greatest: 3%, 0.3, 0.33, $\frac{1}{3}$
(12, 30)

$$0.3, \frac{1}{3}, 0.33, 3\%$$

27.
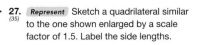

▶ **27.** ~Represent~ Sketch a quadrilateral similar to the one shown enlarged by a scale factor of 1.5. Label the side lengths.
(35)

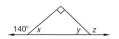

28. Find the measures of angles x, y, and z.
(18, 20) $m\angle x = 40°$, $m\angle y = 50°$; $m\angle z = 130°$

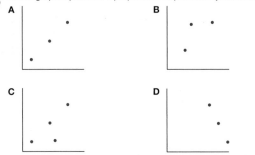

29. Find the slope of the line passing through the points (3, 4) and
(44) $(-4, -3)$.   1

30. Which graph represents a proportion? Explain how you know.
(41)

A

B

C

D

A; It is a proportion because all the points are in a line, and the line appears to intersect with the origin.

▶ See Math Conversations in the sidebar.

Looking Forward

Writing the slope-intercept equation of a line prepares students for:

• **Lesson 69,** working with direct variation.

• **Lesson 70,** solving direct variation problems.

• **Investigation 8,** working with scatterplots.

• **Lesson 82,** graphing equations using intercepts.

• **Lesson 89,** solving problems with two unknowns by graphing.

• **Investigation 11,** working with non-linear functions.

• **Lesson 113,** using scatterplots to make predictions.

• Operations with Small Numbers in Scientific Notation

Objectives
- Multiply and divide numbers written in scientific notation with both positive and negative exponents.
- Multiply and divide numbers written in scientific notation to solve word problems.

Lesson Preparation

Materials
- **Power Up L** (in *Instructional Masters*)

Power Up L

Math Language

Maintain	English Learners (ESL)
scientific notation	certain

Technology Resources

Student eBook Complete student textbook in electronic format.

Resources and Planner CD Assessment, reteaching, and instructional masters, plus a pacing calendar with standards.

Test and Practice Generator CD Create additional practice sheets and custom-made tests.

www.SaxonPublishers.com Visit for more student activities and planning materials.

Inclusion

Adaptations CD Adapted lessons, investigations, practice and assessments.

Meeting Standards

National Council of Teachers of Mathematics (NCTM)

Numbers and Operations

NO.1e Develop an understanding of large numbers and recognize and appropriately use exponential, scientific, and calculator notation

NO.2a Understand the meaning and effects of arithmetic operations with fractions, decimals, and integers

Connections

CN.4b Understand how mathematical ideas interconnect and build on one another to produce a coherent whole

Problem-Solving Strategy: Write an Equation

A plane leaves Minneapolis, Minnesota, at 1 p.m. and flies non-stop to Honolulu in 8 hours. If Hawaii is four time zones earlier than Minnesota, what time does the plane arrive? If the return flight also takes 8 hours, what time does the plane arrive back in Minneapolis if it leaves Honolulu at 8 p.m.?

(Understand) *Understand the problem.*

"What information are we given?"

1. A plane leaves Minneapolis at 1 p.m. and flies non-stop to Honolulu in 8 hours.

2. Hawaii is four times zones earlier than Minnesota.

3. The return flight leaves Honolulu at 8 p.m and also takes 8 hours.

"What is the time equivalent of one time zone?"

One hour.

"In which direction are we traveling?"

West then East.

"What are we asked to do?"

1. Determine what time the plane arrived in Honolulu.

2. Determine what time the plane will return to Minneapolis.

(Plan) *Make a plan.*

"What problem-solving strategy will we use?"

We will *write an equation* for each of the trips.

(Solve) *Carry out the plan.*

"A plane that leaves Minneapolis at 1 p.m. will arrive in Honolulu at what time?"

1 p.m. departure + 8 hours in the air = 9 p.m.
9 p.m. − 4 time zones = 5 p.m. arrival in Honolulu.

"A plane that leaves Honolulu at 8 p.m. will arrive in Minneapolis at what time?"

8 p.m. departure + 8 hours in the air = 4 a.m.
4 a.m. + 4 time zones = 8 a.m. arrival in Minneapolis.

"How many hours will an actual 8 hour trip appear to take when 4 time zones are traversed?"

4 hours if traveling west, or 12 hours if traveling east.

(Check) *Look back.*

"Did we find the answers to the questions that were asked?"

Yes. We will arrive in Honolulu at 5 p.m. and in Minneapolis at 8 a.m.

● **Operations with Small Numbers in Scientific Notation**

facts | Power Up L

mental math |

a. **Number Sense:** 25×36 900

b. **Statistics:** Find the mean of 30 and 40.   35

c. **Fractional Parts:** $66\frac{2}{3}\%$ of $300 $200

d. **Probability:** What is the probability of rolling a number greater than 1 with one roll of a number cube? $\frac{5}{6}$

e. **Proportions:** $\frac{x}{24} = \frac{3}{8}$ 9

f. **Geometry:** Two angles of a parallelogram measure 80° and 80°. What are the measures of the other two angles?   100° and 100°

g. **Measurement:** Find the length of this nail.   5.4 cm

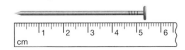

h. **Calculation:** 10×8, $+ 1$, $\sqrt{}$, $\sqrt{}$, $\times 10$, $+ 6$, $\sqrt{}$, $- 7$, square it.   1

problem solving | A plane leaves Minneapolis, Minnesota, at 1 p.m. and flies non-stop to Honolulu in 8 hours. If Hawaii is four time zones earlier than Minnesota, what time does the plane arrive? If the return flight also takes 8 hours, what time does the plane arrive back in Minneapolis if it leaves Honolulu at 8 p.m.?   5 p.m., 8 a.m. the next day

New Concept | Increasing Knowledge

In Lesson 51 we practiced writing small numbers between 0 and 1 in scientific notation. In this lesson we will multiply and divide those numbers.

Recall that to multiply powers of 10 we add the exponents and to divide we subtract.

$$10^5 \cdot 10^3 = 10^8 \qquad \frac{10^5}{10^3} = 10^2$$

Lesson 57   389

Facts
Distribute **Power Up L** to students. See answers below.

Mental Math
Encourage students to share different ways to mentally compute these exercises. Strategies for exercises **a, c,** and **e** are listed below.

a. **Multiply by 4, Divide by 4**
$25 \times 36 = 100 \times 9 = 900$

c. **Multiply by 3, Divide by 3**
$66\frac{2}{3}\%$ of $300 = 200\%$ of $100 = $200
Find a Fraction
$66\frac{2}{3}\% = \frac{2}{3}$
$\frac{2}{3} \times $300 = 200

e. **Cross Products**
$8x = 3 \cdot 24$
$x = \frac{3 \cdot 24}{8}$
$x = 3 \cdot 3 = 9$
Multiply Across
$8 \times 3 = 24$
$3 \times 3 = 9$

Problem Solving
Refer to **Power-Up Discussion,** p. 389B.

2 New Concepts

Instruction
Explain that the only difference in this lesson when compared to the first lesson on multiplying and dividing numbers in scientific notation is that we will be operating on small numbers between 0 and 1.

(continued)

Facts | Write each number in scientific notation.

$186{,}000 = 1.86 \times 10^5$	$0.0002 = 2 \times 10^{-4}$
$2{,}050{,}000 = 2.05 \times 10^6$	$\dfrac{1}{1{,}000{,}000} = 1 \times 10^{-6}$
15 million $= 1.5 \times 10^7$	12 thousandths $= 1.2 \times 10^{-2}$

Write each number in standard form.

$3 \times 10^5 = 300{,}000$	$1 \times 10^{-3} = 0.001$
$3.75 \times 10^4 = 37{,}500$	$3.5 \times 10^{-5} = 0.000035$
$4.05 \times 10^3 = 4050$	$2.04 \times 10^{-2} = 0.0204$

Example 1

Instruction

Ask a volunteer to explain why the answer is in proper scientific notation form. Sample: The coefficient has one and only one non-zero digit to the left of the decimal point and it is multiplied by a power of 10 written in exponential form. Point out that the standard form of the number may make more sense as an answer, but that the calculation is less complicated using scientific notation.

Example 2

Instruction

For **c** and **d**, discuss why the results of the calculations with scientific notation needed to be adjusted and how the adjustments were made.

Use the Thinking Skill *Explain* feature to summarize how the calculations with the powers of 10 were done. If necessary, review the laws of exponents for multiplication and division.

Practice Set

Problems a–h [Error Alert]

Before completing any arithmetic, ask students to name the operation that is to be performed with the coefficients (multiplication or division), and then name the operation that is to be performed with the exponents of the powers of 10 (addition or subtraction).

Students may find it helpful to review how to find the sums and differences of integers.

Problems e, g, and h [Error Alert]

You may need to remind students that subtracting a negative is the same as adding its opposite.

(continued)

The Laws of Exponents implied on the previous page apply to negative exponents as well. We exercise care adding and subtracting the exponents. Here we show some examples.

$$10^{-5} \cdot 10^{-3} = 10^{-8} \qquad 10^5 \cdot 10^{-3} = 10^2$$

$$\frac{10^{-5}}{10^{-3}} = 10^{-2} \qquad \frac{10^5}{10^{-3}} = 10^8$$

Example 1

If a sheet of notebook paper is 0.01 cm thick, how tall is a stack of 2500 sheets of notebook paper? Express each number in scientific notation and perform the calculation in scientific notation.

Solution

We multiply 1×10^{-2} and 2.5×10^3.

$$(1 \times 10^{-2})(2.5 \times 10^3) = 2.5 \times 10^1$$

The stack of paper is 2.5×10^1 cm which is **25 cm.**

Example 2

Perform each indicated calculation and express the result in scientific notation.

a. $(2.4 \times 10^{-6})(2 \times 10^{-2})$ b. $\dfrac{2.4 \times 10^{-8}}{2 \times 10^{-2}}$

c. $(4 \times 10^{-6})(5 \times 10^{-4})$ d. $\dfrac{4 \times 10^{-8}}{5 \times 10^{-2}}$

Solution

Thinking Skill

Explain

Describe how the power of 10 for each product or quotient in **a–d** is found. Add the exponents when multiplying and subtract the exponents when dividing.

a. $(2.4 \times 10^{-6})(2 \times 10^{-2}) = \mathbf{4.8 \times 10^{-8}}$ $(-6) + (-2) = -8$

b. $\dfrac{2.4 \times 10^{-8}}{2 \times 10^{-2}} = \mathbf{1.2 \times 10^{-6}}$ $(-8) - (-2) = -6$

c. $(4 \times 10^{-6})(5 \times 10^{-4}) = 20 \times 10^{-10}$ (improper form) $(-6) + (-4) = -10$

Adjustment: $20 \times 10^{-10} = 2 \times 10^1 \times 10^{-10} = \mathbf{2 \times 10^{-9}}$

d. $\dfrac{4 \times 10^{-8}}{5 \times 10^{-2}}$ (improper form) $(-8) - (-2) = -6$

Adjustment: $0.8 \times 10^{-6} = 8 \times 10^{-1} \times 10^{-6} = \mathbf{8 \times 10^{-7}}$

Practice Set

▶ Find each product or quotient.

a. $(4 \times 10^{10})(2 \times 10^{-6})$ 8×10^4 b. $(1.2 \times 10^{-6})(3 \times 10^3)$ 3.6×10^{-3}

c. $(1.5 \times 10^{-5})(3 \times 10^{-2})$ 4.5×10^{-7} d. $(7.5 \times 10^{-3})(2 \times 10^{-4})$ 1.5×10^{-6}

e. $\dfrac{7.5 \times 10^5}{3 \times 10^{-2}}$ 2.5×10^7 f. $\dfrac{4.8 \times 10^{-3}}{3 \times 10^2}$ 1.6×10^{-5}

g. $\dfrac{8.1 \times 10^{-4}}{3 \times 10^{-7}}$ 2.7×10^3 h. $\dfrac{1.2 \times 10^{-8}}{3 \times 10^{-4}}$ 4×10^{-5}

▶ See Math Conversations in the sidebar.

$$(7 \times 10^8)(3 \times 10^{-3})$$

$$21 \times 10^5$$

▶ **i.** A dollar bill weighs about 0.001 kg. What is the weight of 1,000,000 dollar bills? Express each number in scientific notation and perform the calculation in scientific notation. $1 \times 10^{-3} \cdot 1 \times 10^{6} = 1 \times 10^{3}$ kg, which is a metric ton, about 2200 pounds.

1. In a certain state, the ratio of weddings held in spring or summer to
(45) weddings held in autumn or winter is about 3 to 2. If there were 46,000 weddings in a year, how many were in spring or summer?   27,600

* 2. Sixty percent of the days in the desert were hot and dry. Out of the
(48) 365 days, how many were hot and dry?   219 days

▶ *** 3.** [Analyze] Martin completed 60% of his math assignment during class.
(48) If his math assignment consists of 30 problems, how many problems does he have left to do?   12 problems

* 4. Allison collected these donations for a charity:
(53)
$50, $75, $100, $50,

$60, $75, $80, $50, $75

a. Display the data with a line plot.

b. Find the range and the mean, median, and mode.   range $50; mean ≈ $68; median $75; mode $50 and $75

c. Write a description of the data using the mode.   The most common amounts that people donated were $50 and $75.

5. $\frac{6}{7} = \frac{x}{10.5}$ $x = 9$
(44)

* 6. Two of the lines are parallel. Find x.   30°
(54)

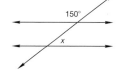

150°

x

7. The spinner is spun twice.
(32)
a. Write the sample space of 16 equally-likely outcomes.   {AA, AA, AA, AA, AB, AB, AC, AC, BA, BA, BB, BC, CA, CA, CB, CC}

b. What is the probability the spinner will stop on A at least once in two spins? $\frac{12}{16} = \frac{3}{4}$

B | A
A | C

▶ **8.** Use the slope-intercept method to graph $y = x - 1$. Then graph the
(56) point $(-2, -3)$. Is $x = -2$, $y = -3$ a solution?   yes

Solve.

9. $0.3m - 0.3 = 0.3$ $m = 2$
(50)

10. $4x + 7x = 99$ $x = 9$
(50)

11. $\frac{2}{3}x + \frac{1}{2} = \frac{2}{3}$ $x = \frac{1}{4}$
(50)

12. $7 = -2p - 5p$ $p = -1$
(50)

4. a.

x x x x x x x
50 60 70 80 90 100

8.

y

x

(−2, −3)

Lesson 57   391

▶ See Math Conversations in the sidebar.

Practice Set
Problem i [Error Alert]
Prior to completing the problem, have students recall that the coefficient of a number in scientific notation must have only one nonzero digit to the left of its decimal point.

Math Conversations
Discussion opportunities are provided below.

Problem 3 [Analyze]
"One way to solve the problem involves finding 60% of 30. Another way involves finding 40% of 30. Explain how each percent can be used to solve the problem." Subtract 60% of 30 from 30 or find 40% of 30.

Invite students to choose one method and use it to solve the problem, and use the other method to check the exact answer for reasonableness.

Errors and Misconceptions
Problem 8
Make sure students recognize that the equation is in slope-intercept form, and x represents a slope of 1 because the product of 1 and any number such as x is x.

Also remind students that the point $(-2, -3)$ can be checked by substitution.

(continued)

English Learners

For problem **1,** explain the meaning of the word **certain.** Say:

"When you talk about a certain person, you may not tell the name, but you are talking about a particular person. For example, a certain person told me you like apples."

Pick a student in the room and give clues to his/her identity for students to guess.

"A certain person in the room has …(finish with clues to the student's identity)."

Math Conversations

Discussion opportunities are provided below.

Problem 17 [Represent]

Ask students to explain how the distance Maggie drove in 5 hours can be found by proportion and by using a unit rate. $\frac{3}{195} = \frac{5}{n}$; 65 mph · 5 h

Problem 20 [Evaluate]

"What units should we use to label our answers?" in.^{3} or cubic inches (volume); in.^{2} or square inches (surface area)

Problem 21 [Generalize]

Make sure students who simply cancel $\frac{b^3}{b^3}$ understand that the terms can be canceled because the fraction is equivalent to 1; the quotient of any number divided by itself is 1.

Problem 24 [Classify]

Extend the Problem

Invite volunteers to graph the relationship to check their answer.

(continued)

Refer to the following information to solve problems **13** and **14**.

A circular tetherball court 6 meters in diameter is painted on the playground. A stripe divides the court into two equal parts.

13. What is the circumference of the tetherball court to the nearest meter? 19 m
(39)

14. What is the area of each semicircle to the nearest square meter? 14 m^2
(40)

15. Collect like terms: $x(x + 2) + 2(x + 2)$ $x^2 + 4x + 4$
(31, 36)

* 16. Simplify and compare: $\left(\frac{1}{2}\right)^2 \bigcirc \left(-\frac{1}{2}\right)^2$ $\frac{1}{4} = \frac{1}{4}$
(22)

▶*** 17.** [Represent] Maggie drove 195 miles in 3 hours.
(49)
   a. At that rate, how many miles will she drive in 5 hours? 325 mi

   b. Express 195 miles in 3 hours as a unit rate. 65 mi/hr

* 18. A mile is 5280 ft. Use a unit multiplier to convert 5280 ft to yards. 1760 yd
(52)

[Evaluate] For **19** and **20** refer to this description.

Diego is building an architectural rendering of a house. For a portion of the roof Diego cuts and folds a net (pattern) for a triangular prism. The base of the prism is an isosceles triangle. The triangle has a base of 24 in. and a height of 5 in. The distance between the triangular bases is 20 in.

19. a.

20 in. ⟋ 5 in.
24 in.

b.

20 in.
24 in.
5 in.

* 19. **a.** Make an isometric sketch of the folded prism.
(Inv. 4, 55)
   b. Make a sketch of the net of the prism.

▶*** 20.** **a.** Find the volume of the prism. 1200 in.^{3}
(42, 43)
   b. Find the surface area of the prism. 1120 in.^{2}

▶ **21.** [Generalize] Simplify: $\frac{b^3 r^4}{mb^3 r^2}$ $\frac{r^2}{m}$
(27)

22. Simplify, then compare: $\sqrt{\frac{4}{9}} \bigcirc \frac{\sqrt{4}}{\sqrt{9}}$ $\frac{2}{3} = \frac{2}{3}$
(15)

23. Write $\frac{11}{12}$ **a** as a percent and **b** as a decimal. **a.** $91\frac{2}{3}\%$; **b.** $0.91\overline{6}$
(30)

▶*** 24.** [Classify] The fare charged for a taxi ride was $1.50 plus 40¢ for each $\frac{1}{5}$ of a mile. What term best describes the relationship between the distance traveled and the fare charged? **B**
(47)
   A continuous function   **B** step function   **C** direct proportion

25. The spinner is spun twice.
(32)
   a. What is the sample space of the experiment? Sample space = {AA, AB, AC, BA, BB, BC, CA, CB, CC}

   b. What is the probability the spinner stops on A at least once? $\frac{5}{9}$

   c. What is the probability the spinner does not stop on A in two spins? $\frac{4}{9}$

▶ See Math Conversations in the sidebar.

26. Evaluate the expression $-b + \sqrt{b^2 - 4ac}$ when $a = 3$, $b = 4$, and
(14, 15) $c = 1$. -2

27. Using the slope-intercept form,
(56) write the equation of each line at the
right. $a: y = x + 2$; $b: y = x - 2$

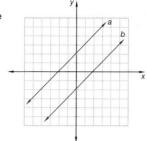

▶ **28.** If a line has a slope of $\frac{1}{2}$ and if it intersects the y-axis at -1, then what is
(56) the equation of the line in slope-intercept form? $y = \frac{1}{2}x - 1$

29. Find all solutions: $9x^2 = 36$ $x = 2, -2$
(14, 15)

30. Use this figure to answer the following
(Inv. 4) questions.

Back

Front   Right Side

a. Which of the following is the front view
of this figure? **A**

A   B

C 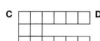 D

b. Which of these is the right-side view? **B**

A   B

C   D

Lesson 57   393

▶ See Math Conversations in the sidebar.

3 Written Practice (Continued)

Math Conversations
Discussion opportunities are provided below.

Errors and Misconceptions
Problem 28
Students must recognize that $y = mx + b$ represents the slope-intercept form of a line, and m and b have a special significance in the equation. Invite volunteers to describe different ways to remember that m represents slope and b represents the y-intercept.

•Solving Percent Problems with Equations

Objectives

• Write equations to solve percent word problems.

Materials

• Power Up L (in *Instructional Masters*)

Optional

• Fraction-Decimal-Percent Equivalents poster

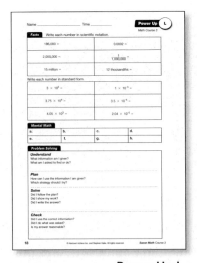

Power Up L

Math Language

Maintain

percent

Technology Resources

Student eBook Complete student textbook in electronic format.

Resources and Planner CD Assessment, reteaching, and instructional masters, plus a pacing calendar with standards.

Test and Practice Generator CD Create additional practice sheets and custom-made tests.

www.SaxonPublishers.com Visit for more student activities and planning materials.

Inclusion

Adaptations CD Adapted lessons, investigations, practice and assessments.

Meeting Standards

National Council of Teachers of Mathematics (NCTM)

Numbers and Operations

NO.1a Work flexibly with fractions, decimals, and percents to solve problems

Algebra

AL.2a Develop an initial conceptual understanding of different uses of variables

AL.2c Use symbolic algebra to represent situations and to solve problems, especially those that involve linear relationships

Problem Solving

PS.1c Apply and adapt a variety of appropriate strategies to solve problems

Problem-Solving Strategy: Make it Simpler

A store sells three sizes of the same candle—a "regular" size with radius r and height h. Candle B is twice as tall as Candle A but has the same radius. Candle C is just the reverse, with twice the radius of Candle A but the same height. If both large Candles B and C are made of the same material, which of them is heavier? Why?

(Understand) **Understand the problem.**

"What information are we given?"

1. Candle B is twice as tall as Candle A but has the same radius.
2. Candle C has twice the radius as Candle A but the same height.
3. Candles B and C are both made of the same material.

"What prior knowledge do we bring to this problem?"

The formula for finding the volume of a cylinder is $V = \pi r^2 h$.

"What can we infer?"

Candle A is the candle that is the "regular" size, with radius r and height h.

"What are we asked to do?"

Determine if Candle B or Candle C is the heaviest.

(Plan) **Make a plan.**

"What problem solving strategy will we use?"

We can *make it simpler* by assigning values for the radius and the height that will be easy to compute.

"What do we anticipate our answer to be?"

Students may assume that doubling the radius or doubling the height will affect the volume in the same way.

(Solve) **Carry out the plan.**

"What is the volume of Candle B?"

$V = \pi(1)^2 (2) = 2\pi$

"What is the volume of Candle C?"

$V = \pi(2)^2 (1) = 4\pi$

"What is the relationship between the volumes of Candle B and Candle C?"

Candle C has twice the volume of Candle B.

(Check) **Look back.**

"Did we find the answer to the question that was asked?"

Yes. Candle C is heavier than Candle B.

"Will the answer change if we change the assumed measures of Candle A?"

Students may assume other measures for Candle A, but the results will be the same.

Facts

Distribute **Power Up L** to students. See answers below.

Mental Math

Encourage students to share different ways to mentally compute these exercises. Strategies for exercises **a, c, d,** and **e** are listed below.

a. Use Math Sense
The least possible number would be 100, using 10×10, so the answer is no.

c. Sum of Angles of a Quadrilateral
$f = 360° - (50 + 90 + 100)°$
$f = 360° - (240)°$
$f = 120°$

d. Use Math Sense
$100\% - 40\% = 60\%$

e. Isolate the Variable
$12x + 1 = 145$
$12x = 144$
$x = 12$

Problem Solving

Refer to **Power-Up Discussion,** p. 394B.

2 **New Concepts**

Instruction

Explain that choosing the fraction or decimal form of the percent depends on factors such as the numbers involved, what kind of calculation a person prefers, and whether a calculator is available for the computation.

(continued)

LESSON

58

• **Solving Percent Problems with Equations**

Power Up | *Building Power*

facts | Power Up L

mental math

a. Number Sense: Can we produce a 2-digit whole number by multiplying two 2-digit whole numbers?   no

b. Scientific Notation: Write 0.0019 in scientific notation. 1.9×10^{-3}

c. Geometry: Three angles of a trapezoid measure 50°, 90° and 100°. Find the measure of the fourth angle.   120°

d. Fractional Parts: If coats are on sale for 40% **off** the regular price, then the sale price is what percent **of** the regular price?   60%

e. Algebra: $12x + 1 = 145$ 12

f. Measurement: The bicycle odometer read 24.2 miles when she left. It read 29.5 miles when she returned. How far did she ride?   5.3 miles

g. Rate: Kenneth read 35 pages per hour. Shana read 40 pages per hour. After 2 hours, how many more pages has Shana read than Kenneth?   10

h. Calculation: $\sqrt{9}, \times 8, \times 2, + 1, \sqrt{\ }, \times 8, - 1, \div 5, \times 3, - 1, \div 4$ 8

problem solving | A store sells three sizes of the same candle—a "regular" size with radius r and height h. Candle B is twice as tall as Candle A but has the same radius. Candle C is just the reverse, with twice the radius of Candle A but the same height. If both large Candles B and C are made of the same material, which of them is heavier? Why?   Candle C is heavier because the volume is twice the volume of Candle B.

New Concept | *Increasing Knowledge*

We may solve percent problems using proportions (as we did in Lesson 48) or by solving a percent equation.

A **percent** of a **whole** is a **part.**

$$\% \times W = P$$

The factors and product in the equation above are the percent, the whole, and the part. If two of the three numbers are known, we can write and solve an equation to find the unknown number. If we are given the percent, we convert the percent to a fraction or decimal before performing the calculation.

For any percent problem we may choose to express the percent as a decimal or as a fraction. We might make the choice based on which form seems easier to calculate. For some problems the calculations are tedious, so we might choose to express the percent as a decimal and use a calculator. For other problems, expressing the percent as a fraction is the best choice.

Facts   Write each number in scientific notation.

$186,000 = 1.86 \times 10^5$	$0.0002 = 2 \times 10^{-4}$
$2,050,000 = 2.05 \times 10^6$	$\dfrac{1}{1,000,000} = 1 \times 10^{-6}$
15 million $= 1.5 \times 10^7$	12 thousandths $= 1.2 \times 10^{-2}$

Write each number in standard form.

$3 \times 10^5 = 300,000$	$1 \times 10^{-3} = 0.001$
$3.75 \times 10^4 = 37,500$	$3.5 \times 10^{-5} = 0.000035$
$4.05 \times 10^3 = 4050$	$2.04 \times 10^{-2} = 0.0204$

Example 1

Thirty-two ounces is 25% of a gallon. How many ounces is a gallon?

Solution

We are given the percent and the part. We are asked for the whole. We write the percent as a decimal or as a fraction and solve for the unknown.

As a decimal:	**As a fraction:**
32 oz is 25% of a gallon	32 oz is 25% of a gallon
$32 = 0.25g$	$32 = \frac{1}{4}g$
$\frac{32}{0.25} = g$	$\frac{4}{1} \cdot 32 = \frac{4}{1} \cdot \frac{1}{4}g$
$g = 128$	$g = 128$

A gallon is **128 ounces.**

Example 2

Mr. Villescas bought a used car for $8,500. The sales-tax rate was 7%. How much did Mr. Villescas pay in tax?

Solution

The sales tax will be added to the price, but the amount of tax is based on the price. In this case the tax is 7% of the price. We translate the sentence to an equation using = for "is" and × for "of." We substitute the known numbers and solve for the unknown. We may write the percent as a decimal or a fraction before performing the calculation.

As a decimal:	**As a fraction:**
Tax is 7% of the price	Tax is 7% of the price
$t = 0.07 \times \$8500$	$t = \frac{7}{\underset{1}{100}} \times \overset{\$85}{\$8500}$
$t = \$595$	$t = \$595$

The sales tax on the car was **$595.** Notice that the amount of tax on large-dollar purchases might seem high. However, it is correct. Seven percent of the price is less than 10% but more than 5%. Since 10% of $8500 is $850, and 5% is half of that ($425), our answer of $595 is reasonable.

Example 3

For the following percent problems, decide whether it is better to express the percent as a decimal or as a fraction.

    a. The sales-tax rate is 8.25%. What is the sales tax on a $18.97 purchase?

    b. Shirts are on sale for $33\frac{1}{3}$% off the regular price. How much is saved on a $24 shirt?

Lesson 58   **395**

Example 1

Instruction

Ask volunteers to explain how they would check whether the answer is reasonable. Sample: Round 32 oz to 30 oz. Because 25% is equal to $\frac{1}{4}$, multiply 30 by 4 to get 120 oz. The answer should be a little more than 120 oz, and it is, so the answer is reasonable.

Example 2

Instruction

Call attention to the way that estimates are used to check the reasonableness of the answer.

(continued)

Math Background

Suppose an item costs $70 and the sales tax is 6%. Here are two ways to find the total cost.

Method 1:

Calculate the amount of the tax.

$$\text{Tax} = 6\% \text{ of } \$70 = 0.06 \times \$70 = \$4.20$$

Add the tax to the price.

$$\text{Total cost} = \$70 + \$4.20 = \$74.20$$

Method 2:

Use the fact that 100% of the price + 6% of the price = 106% of the price.

$$\text{Total cost} = 106\% \text{ of } \$70 = 1.06 \times \$70 = \$74.20$$

Example 3
Instruction
Ask whether anyone had a different answer or a different reason for his or her answer. If so, ask the student or students to share their thinking with the class and discuss whether anyone else would change their answer based on the explanations.

Use the *Connect* questions to explore different ways to work with $33\frac{1}{3}\%$. Because this number is such a common percent, several ways to calculate with it gives students the ability to be flexible in their computations and can help them recognize when they can use mental math to solve an equation.

Example 4
Instruction
Point out that students have now used the equation given at the beginning of the lesson to solve for all three parts of a percent problem—part, whole, and percent.

Practice Set
Problem a [Justify]
Invite students to discuss, or encourage them to share, different ways to estimate 6% of $4500.

Problem b [Error Alert]
Watch for students who do not use a multiplication sign to represent "of" and an equals sign to represent "is" when translating the words to an equation.

Problem d [Error Alert]
You may need to help students recognize that expressing the percent as a fraction (rather than a decimal) will make the computation less tedious.

Problem e [Error Alert]
Solving the percent equation leaves the answer as a decimal or fraction. Students may need to be reminded to convert to a percent to answer the question.

Thinking skill
[Connect]

What is the decimal form of $33\frac{1}{3}\%$? Why would we need to round the decimal to perform the calculation? 0.3; The decimal form is a non-terminating decimal number. We cannot enter an infinite number of 3s after the decimal point, so we would need to round to 0.3 or 0.33 before calculating.

Solution

a. Whether we change the percent to a fraction or decimal, we must multiply a 4-digit number by a 3-digit number. Converting the percent to a fraction further complicates the arithmetic. To calculate an exact answer we would **convert the percent to a decimal** and use a calculator if one was readily available.

b. To write the percent as a decimal we would need to round. Expressing the percent as the fraction $\frac{1}{3}$ is more accurate, and we can perform the calculation mentally. We would **express the percent as a fraction.**

Example 4

Blanca correctly answered 23 of the 25 questions. What percent of the questions did she answer correctly?

Solution

We are given the whole and the part. We are asked for the percent. After solving the equation, we convert the fraction or decimal solution to a percent.

$$\text{What percent of 25 is 23?}$$
$$P \cdot 25 = 23$$
$$\frac{P \cdot 25}{25} = \frac{23}{25}$$
$$P = \frac{23}{25} \text{ or } 0.92$$

We convert 0.92 to **92%**.

Practice Set

Solve by writing and solving equations. In **a–d** choose whether to express the percent as a fraction or as a decimal.

▶ a. [Justify] Six percent of $4500 is how much money? Explain why your answer is reasonable. $270; one answer: Six percent is a little more than 5%. Since 10% of the price is $450, 5% is $225, and $270 is a little more than $225.

▶ b. Twenty percent of what number is 40?   200

c. How much is a 15% tip on a $13.25 meal? Round your answer to the nearest dime. $2.00

▶ d. How much money is $16\frac{2}{3}\%$ of $1200? $200

▶ e. What percent of 50 is 32?   64%

f. Dixon made a $2,000 down payment on an $8,000 car. The down payment was what percent of the price?   25%

g. Kimo paid $24 for the shirt which was 75% of the regular price. What was the regular price? $32

▶ See Math Conversations in the sidebar.

Teacher Tip

Explain to students that they will have an easier time solving percent problems if they know the fraction and decimal equivalents for commonly used percents. Students may use the *Student Reference Guide* for a list of equivalents that they can study.

Display the **Fraction-Decimal-Percent Equivalents** concept poster so that students can refer to it while working on percent problems in this lesson and in upcoming lessons.

▶ *** 1.** *(45)* **Analyze** In water, the ratio of hydrogen atoms to oxygen atoms is 2 to 1. If there are 3×10^{23} atoms in a sample of water, how many are hydrogen atoms? 2×10^{23}

* 2. *(48, 58)* Sixty percent of the voters favored the initiative, and 12,000 did not favor it. How many voters favored the initiative?   18,000

3. *(3, 4)* A bank charges customers $10 per month for a checking account, plus 10 cents for each check that is written. If Jessie uses 13 checks in a month, what will this bank charge for the month? $11.30

▶ *** 4.** *(53)* **Evaluate** The sales revenue of a retail store for one week was (in thousands of dollars):

$$2.9, 1.6, 1.4, 1.3, 1.5, 2.5, 2.8$$

a. Display the data in a line plot.

b. Find the mean, median, mode, and range of the data.   mean = 2.0; median = 1.6; mode = none; range = 1.6

c. Which measure would you choose to report the sales most favorably?   mean

5. *(32)* Brad is trying to remember the combination to a lock. He knows the three numbers are 15, 27, and 18, but he cannot remember the order.

a. What are the possible orders of the numbers?   {15-27-18, 15-18-27, 27-15-18, 27-18-15, 18-15-27, 18-27-15}

b. What is the probability that Brad finds the correct order on his first try? $\frac{1}{6}$

Solve for x.

6. *(44)* Solve for x. $\frac{x}{5} = \frac{14}{20}$ $x = 3.5$

▶ *** 7.** *(54)* These two lines are parallel. Find x.   110°

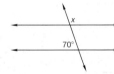

x

70°

8. *(56)* Use the slope-intercept method to graph $y = \frac{1}{2}x - 2$.

9. *(39)* The circumference of the earth at the equator is about 25,000 miles. Estimate the diameter of the earth to the nearest thousand miles. Explain how you found your answer.

Analyze Solve.

▶ *** 10.** *(50)* $3m - 6 + 2m = 4$ $m = 2$ ▶ *** 11.** *(50)* $x - 3x = 18$ $x = -9$

4. a.

xxxx   x xx

1.0   2.0   3.0

8.

y

5

x

-5

9. 8,000 mi; Example answer: The circumference is roughly three times the diameter, so I divided 25,000 by 3 and rounded the quotient down to 8,000.

▶ See Math Conversations in the sidebar.

Math Conversations

Discussion opportunities are provided below.

Problem 1   Analyze

To solve the problem by writing a ratio box, students must recognize that because 3×10^{23} represents the total number of atoms, the ratio box should contain a row titled "total."

To solve the problem using fractions, work with students to help them find the fraction of atoms that are hydrogen. The ratio of hydrogen atoms to the total number of atoms is $\frac{2}{3}$; so $\frac{2}{3}$ of the atoms are hydrogen atoms. (See Errors and Misconceptions note below.)

Problem 4   Evaluate

If students plot the decimals numbers as given, remind them that those numbers will have no meaning unless they include a label in their plot such as "in thousands of dollars."

You might choose to invite a group of volunteers to draw the plot on the board or overhead, and ask the remainder of the students to check their work.

Problem 7

Sketch the figure on the board or overhead. Ask volunteers to label the measures (and explain how to find those measures) of the angles that must be known to find the measure of $\angle x$.

Problems 10 and 11   Analyze

"To begin to simplify the equation, which like terms can we combine?" Problem 10: $3m + 2m = 5m$; Problem 11: $x - 3x = -2x$

After combining like terms, ask students to name the inverse operations that can be used to isolate the variable in each equation.

Errors and Misconceptions

Problem 1

To find $\frac{2}{3}$ of 3×10^{23}, students might try finding $\frac{2}{3}$ of the power of ten as well. Students should find $\frac{2}{3}$ of the coefficient, 3, and not change the power of ten.

(continued)

Math Conversations

Discussion opportunities are provided below.

Errors and Misconceptions
Problem 12

If students have difficulty finding $1x$ from $\frac{2}{3}x$, write $\frac{1}{4} \cdot \frac{4}{1}$ on the board or overhead and ask students to name the product in simplest form (1). Point out that the product of any number and its reciprocal is 1.

Then write $\frac{2}{3}x$ and ask students to name the fraction, name its reciprocal, and name the product of the term and its reciprocal.

$\frac{2}{3}, \frac{3}{2}; \frac{3}{2} \cdot \frac{2}{3}x = \frac{6}{6}x = 1x = x$

(continued)

---

12. $\frac{2}{3}x + \frac{1}{2} = \frac{5}{6}$ $x = \frac{1}{2}$
(50)

13. $\frac{y}{8} = 0.375$ $y = 3$
(38)

14. Isabel wonders whether a beach ball with a 50 inch circumference will pass through a basketball hoop with an 18 inch diameter. What do you predict? Justify your answer.
(39)

14. See student work. Sample answer: I predict the beach ball will pass through the hoop because the circumference of the hoop is more than 54 inches (3×18).

15. One corner is cut from a small rectangle of note paper. Find the **a** area and **b** perimeter of the resulting piece of paper.
(37)
a. 42 cm², **b.** 26 cm

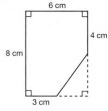

16. Sarah just got her hair cut. If Sarah's hair grows $1\frac{1}{4}$ inches every month, how much longer will it be in $4\frac{1}{2}$ months if she does not cut it? $5\frac{5}{8}$
(23)

17. Use a unit multiplier to convert 2.5 ft to inches. $2.5 \text{ ft} \times \frac{12 \text{ in.}}{1 \text{ ft}} = 30 \text{ in.}$
(52)

Simplify.

18. $\left(\frac{2}{5}\right)^2$ $\frac{4}{25}$
(22)

19. $\frac{ssr^5}{s^2r^4}$ r
(27)

20. $\frac{2}{15} + \frac{2}{5} \cdot \frac{1}{6}$ $\frac{1}{5}$
(13, 22)

21. $x^2 + 2x + x + 2$ $x^2 + 3x + 2$
(31)

22. **a.** Write 55% as a decimal and reduced fraction. $0.55, \frac{11}{20}$
(12, 48)
    b. Choose one form and use it to find 55% of $1200. $660

23. Express $\frac{1}{7}$ as a decimal rounded to three decimal places.   0.143
(30)

24. Find $\frac{n + m}{m}$ when $n = 100$ and $m = -10$. -9
(31, 36)

25. **a.** Explain why the triangles are similar.
(35)
    b. Find x.   24
    c. Find y.   26

25a AAA Triangle Similarity

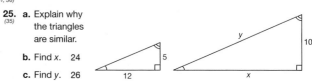

26. An ant weighs as little as 0.00001 kilograms. Write the minimum weight of an ant using an exponent. 10^{-5} kg
(51)

27. Last month, Andrea missed two days of school because she had a cold. What percent of school days did Andrea miss that month? (Hint: Assume that there are 20 school days in a month.)   10%
(48)

28. The Giant Water Lily of the Amazon River is the world's largest lily. Its pads are almost perfectly round. One lily pad usually measures about 6 feet in diameter. What is the approximate surface area of one lily pad?   about 28.26 ft²
(40)

▶ See Math Conversations in the sidebar.

30.

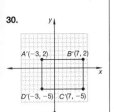

$A'(-3, 2)$ $B'(7, 2)$

$D'(-3, -5)$ $C'(7, -5)$

▶ **29.** On the equator, the earth rotates about its axis about 25,000 miles in
(7)   24 hours. Express this rate in miles per hour. (Round to the nearest
hundred.)   **1000 mph**

30. What set of coordinates represents the
(Inv. 5)   translation of rectangle *ABCD* 3 units to
the right and 2 units down? Sketch the
rectangle on graph paper to illustrate
the transformation. $A'(-3, 2), B'(7, 2),$
$C'(7, -5), D'(-3, -5)$

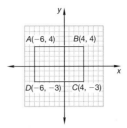

$A(-6, 4)$ $B(4, 4)$

$D(-6, -3)$ $C(4, -3)$

Early Finishers
*Real-World
Application*

Below are the weight in grams (g) of a neutron, a proton and an electron.
First write each particle's weight in standard form. Then list the particles in
order from lightest to heaviest.

neutron 1.6750×10^{-24} neutron: 0.0000000000000000000000016750 g;

proton 1.6726×10^{-24} proton: 0.0000000000000000000000016726 g;

electron 9.1083×10^{-28} electron: 0.00000000000000000000000000091083 g;
electron, proton, neutron

Lesson 58   399

▶ See Math Conversations in the sidebar.

---

3 **Written Practice** (Continued)

Math Conversations

Discussion opportunities are provided below.

Problem 29 Estimate

Extend the Problem

Challenge students to estimate the distance
in miles that a location on the equator rotates
in one year, and express that estimate in
scientific notation. Sample: 9×10^6 miles

Looking Forward

Solving percent problems with
equations prepares students for:

- **Lesson 63,** working with rational
  numbers, non-terminating
  decimals, and percents.

- **Lesson 67,** finding percents of
  change.

- **Lesson 71,** finding percent
  changes of dimensions.

•Experimental Probability

Objectives

- Calculate experimental probabilities.
- Compare the experimental probability of an event with its theoretical probability and offer explanations for any differences.
- Use a model to simulate an event to calculate an experimental probability.

Materials

- **Power Up L** (in *Instructional Masters*)

Power Up L

Math Language

New	Maintain
experimental probability	outcome
theoretical probability	probability

Technology Resources

Student eBook Complete student textbook in electronic format.

Resources and Planner CD Assessment, reteaching, and instructional masters, plus a pacing calendar with standards.

Test and Practice Generator CD Create additional practice sheets and custom-made tests.

www.SaxonPublishers.com Visit for more student activities and planning materials.

Inclusion

Adaptations CD Adapted lessons, investigations, practice and assessments.

National Council of Teachers of Mathematics (NCTM)

Data Analysis and Probability

DP.4a Understand and use appropriate terminology to describe complementary and mutually exclusive events

DP.4b Use proportionality and a basic understanding of probability to make and test conjectures about the results of experiments and simulations

Representation

RE.5c Use representations to model and interpret physical, social, and mathematical phenomena

Problem-Solving Strategy: Draw a Diagram/ Use Logical Reasoning

A square is divided as shown. Regions B and C combine to equal what fraction of the area of the square?

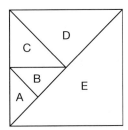

(Understand) **Understand the problem.**

"What information are we given?"

We are shown a square divided into several labeled regions.

"What are we asked to do?"

We are asked to determine what fraction of the square's area is covered by regions B and C.

(Plan) **Make a plan.**

"What problem-solving strategy will we use?"

We will *use the diagram* provided and *logical reasoning* to find the answer.

(Solve) **Carry out the plan.**

"What do we notice about the area of region E relative to the area of the square?"

Region E is one half of the original square.

"What is the relationship between the areas of regions D and E?"

The area of region D is one half the area of region E.

"Does this pattern continue?"

Yes, the area of region C is half the area of region D, and regions A and B are each half the area of region C.

"What fraction of the area of the original square is region C?"

$$\frac{1}{2} \times \frac{1}{2} \times \frac{1}{2} = \frac{1}{8}$$

"What fraction of the area of the original square is region B?"

$$\frac{1}{2} \times \frac{1}{2} \times \frac{1}{2} \times \frac{1}{2} = \frac{1}{16}$$

"Altogether, what fraction of the area of the original square is covered by the two regions?"

$$\frac{1}{8} + \frac{1}{16} = \frac{3}{16}$$

(Check) **Look back.**

"Did we find the answer to the question that was asked?"

Yes, we found the fraction of the area of the square covered by regions B and C.

Facts

Distribute **Power Up L** to students. See answers below.

Mental Math

Encourage students to share different ways to mentally compute these exercises. Strategies for exercises **a** and **f** are listed below.

a. Guess and Check
Use multiples of 10. Try 90 × 90.
90 × 90 = 8100. The answer is yes.

f. Use Math Sense
The third side must be between 8 inches and 18 inches.
12 inches → yes
7 inches → no
19 inches → no

Problem Solving

Refer to **Power-Up Discussion**, p. 400B.

• Experimental Probability

Power Up | *Building Power*

facts | Power Up L

mental math

a. Number Sense: Can we produce a 4-digit number by multiplying two 2-digit numbers?   Yes

b. Statistics: The mean of equally spaced numbers equals the median of the numbers. Find the mean of 30, 40, and 50.   40

c. Fractional Parts: A tip of 15% to 20% is customary. Sam tipped $\frac{1}{6}$ of the bill on a bill of $24. What was the tip? $4

d. Ratio: There are 16 pens in a drawer. Six of the pens are blue and the other 10 are black. What is the ratio of black pens to blue pens? $\frac{5}{3}$

e. Probability: What is the probability of rolling an even number with one roll of a number cube? $\frac{3}{6}$ or $\frac{1}{2}$

f. Geometry: Two sides of a triangle are 5 inches and 13 inches. Can the third side be 12 inches long? 7 inches? 19 inches?   yes, no, no

g. Measurement: What temperature is indicated on this thermometer?   −8°C

h. Calculation: Start with a dollar, add 50%, give away half, subtract 25¢, add a dime, give away half. How much is left?   30¢

problem solving   A square is divided as shown. Regions B and C combine to equal what fraction of the area of the square? $\frac{3}{16}$

Facts   Write each number in scientific notation.

186,000 = 1.86 × 10^5	0.0002 = 2 × 10^{-4}
2,050,000 = 2.05 × 10^6	$\frac{1}{1,000,000}$ = 1 × 10^{-6}
15 million = 1.5 × 10^7	12 thousandths = 1.2 × 10^{-2}

Write each number in standard form.

3 × 10^5 = 300,000	1 × 10^{-3} = 0.001
3.75 × 10^4 = 37,500	3.5 × 10^{-5} = 0.000035
4.05 × 10^3 = 4050	2.04 × 10^{-2} = 0.0204

Increasing Knowledge

When discussing probability, we distinguish between the **theoretical probability**, which is found by analyzing a situation, and the **experimental probability**, which is determined statistically. Experimental probability is the ratio of the number of times an event occurs to the number of trials.

$$\text{experimental probability} = \frac{\text{number of times an event occurs}}{\text{number of trials}}$$

If we want to experimentally determine the probability that a flipped coin will land heads up, we would flip the coin a number of times, counting the number of trials and the number of heads.

Trial	1st	2nd	3rd	4th	5th	6th	7th	8th	9th	10th
Outcome	H	H	T	H	T	H	T	T	T	H
Probability $H \div t$	1.00	1.00	0.67	0.75	0.60	0.67	0.57	0.50	0.44	0.50

As the number of trials grows, the experimental probability tends to approach the theoretical probability of an experiment. Therefore, we want a large number of trials when conducting probability experiments.

Experimental probability is used widely in sports. If a basketball player makes 80 free throws in 100 attempts, then the probability of the player making a free throw is $\frac{80}{100}$ or $\frac{4}{5}$. The player might be described as an 80% free throw shooter. In baseball and softball, a player's batting average is the probability, expressed as a decimal, of the player getting a hit.

Example 1

A softball player has 21 hits in 60 at-bats. Express the probability the player will get a hit in her next at-bat as a decimal number with three decimal places.

Solution

The ratio of hits to at-bats is 21 to 60. To express the ratio as a decimal we divide 21 by 60.

$$21 \div 60 = 0.35$$

It is customary to write the probability (batting average) with three decimal places and without a zero in the ones place: **.350**

Thinking Skill

Analyze

Marcia has a batting average of .330. In one game she has 2 hits in 5 at bats. Will this raise or lower her batting average?

Experimental probabilities are used not only in sports but in many fields such as business, weather forecasting, insurance, and banking. Theoretical probability is commonly applied to designing games of chance.

raise; her batting average for this game is higher than .330, which raises her seasonal batting average.

Instruction

The concept of *experimental probability* was introduced briefly in Lesson 32. The applications to sports will likely have the most appeal for some students. Be sure that students understand the difference between experimental and theoretical probability.

Example 1

Instruction

Some students may want to discuss the idea that whenever a person is at bat, the probability that the person will get a hit is $\frac{1}{2}$. This view oversimplifies a complex situation. Point out that whenever actual data is available, experimental probability is often used instead of theoretical probability because actual experimental results include the effects of variables that theoretical calculations might miss.

Use the Thinking Skill *Analyze* question to show how experimental probability in the form of a batting average is continually updated throughout the playing season.

(continued)

Example 2
Instruction

As you discuss the *Predict* question, ask students whether it is likely that exactly 250 of the next 400 shoppers will accept the free samples. Sample: It is unlikely because actual results often vary and cluster. Although the experimental probability might remain about $\frac{5}{8}$, for any given count the ratio may vary above and below that number.

Example 3
Instruction

Explain that *simulations* are used in many research projects for predicting what factors most affect the outcome of an experiment. Such simulations help researchers make decisions about how to design actual research projects.

Carefully go through the experiment described in this example to help students prepare for carrying out a simulation of their own. Use the *Explain* question to generate ideas for ways to carry out the simulation.

Have students follow the directions given in the *Represent* feature to carry out their own simulation. Students may work independently or in pairs to collect their data. Encourage students to tell what experimental probability they found. Then put together the data from all the students to see whether the experimental probability will change with more data.

(continued)

Example 2

A salesperson distributed free samples at the mall. Fifty shoppers accepted the samples and thirty did not. What is the probability that a shopper at the mall will accept the salesperson's samples?

Solution

Fifty out of eighty shoppers accepted the sample, so the probability is $\frac{5}{8}$.

Predict If the salesperson from example 2 expects to see 400 customers at the mall during the next shift, how many samples should the salesperson have ready? Explain your reasoning.

The salesperson might expect $\frac{5}{8}$ of the 400 customers to accept the samples. The salesperson may need at least 250 samples.

Sometimes experiments are impractical to conduct, so to find an experimental probability, we **simulate** the event using models such as spinners, number cubes, coins, or marbles.

Example 3

The commuter plane flight arrives on schedule $\frac{2}{3}$ of the time on any given weekday. Heather wonders what the probability is that it will arrive on schedule on a Tuesday, Wednesday, and Thursday in the same week.

   a. How could the experimental probability be found? Why is this impractical?

   b. How could the spinner at right be used to simulate the experiment?

Solution

For example, rolling 1, 2, 3, or 4 on a number cube can represent "on time" arrival, and rolling 5 or 6 "late arrival." Using three marbles, 2 blue and 1 red, selecting a red marble can represent "on time" arrival, and selecting a blue marble "late arrival."

   a. **Heather could check the flight arrival time on Tuesdays, Wednesdays, and Thursdays for several weeks.** The experimental probability is the number of times the flight arrives on schedule all 3 days in a row divided by the total number of selected 3-day periods. **This experiment would take a very long time to conduct.**

   b. Each spin can represent one flight. The probability of an on-time arrival is $\frac{2}{3}$. **Heather can spin the spinner three times in a row and repeat this for many trials to find the experimental probability.**

Explain How might a number cube or marbles be used to simulate this experiment?

Represent Select one of the models described in the lesson and use it to simulate Heather's experiment. Conduct 12 trials, which is 36 spins, rolls, or draws. What experimental probability do you find? See student work.

Math Background

How do meteorologists determine the probability of rain?

The National Weather Service uses weather balloons and satellites to collect data about weather conditions, including wind speed and direction, temperature, barometric pressure, and humidity. Meteorologists then compare the current conditions to historical data to determine how often rain occurred on days with the same weather conditions. For example, if meteorologists find that it rained on 40 out of the last 100 days on which the conditions were the same as they are now, they would predict a 40% chance of rain.

Practice Set ▶

a. The probability of him making each free throw is $\frac{6}{20}$ or 30%, which is half the probability of him making a two-point shot. This means that making one of the two free throws (1 point) is as likely as making a two-point shot. The opposing team should choose to foul him.

Explain When a member of the opposing team fouls a basketball player who is shooting, the player shoots two free throws. Near the end of a close game a player has made 6 out of 20 free throws, and he has made 60% of his 2-point shots. When the player has the ball in 2-point range, should the opposing team foul him or risk the shot? Explain your answer in terms of probability.

▶ **b** Quinn runs a sandwich shop. Since she added a turkey melt to the menu, 36 out of 120 customers have ordered the new sandwich. What is the probability that the next customer will order a turkey melt? $\frac{3}{10}$, or 0.3

▶ **c** *Predict* Quinn ordinarily has 200 customers on a busy afternoon, about how many turkey melts should she expect to sell? 60

▶ **d** To prepare premium rates (the amounts customers pay) for an insurance plan, an insurance company conducts an extensive risk study to determine the probability that a member of a certain group may require a pay-off. Based on these probabilities, the expected amount of payoff is charged to the customer as part of the premium. Explain why car insurance companies charge a higher premium for teenage drivers with a clean driving record than for adult drivers with a clean driving record. Sample: Insurance companies charge higher rates for teenage drivers because teens have a higher incidence of accidents.

e. Sample: Flip a coin and specify

e Meghan is a 50% free throw shooter. Select a model to simulate a game in which Meghan shoots 10 free throws.

Written Practice — *Strengthening Concepts*

either heads or tails as making a free throw. Flip the coin in trials of 10 flips and record the results.

▶ ***1** *Analyze* In carbon dioxide, the ratio of carbon atoms to oxygen atoms
   (45) is 1 to 2. If there are 12×10^{23} oxygen atoms in a sample of carbon dioxide, how many atoms are there in all? 18×10^{23}

*2. In the triple-jump competition, Lee jumped 28 ft, 32 ft, 29 ft, 30 ft, and
   (53) 33 ft.
   a Find the mean, median, mode, and range of Lee's marks.
      mean: 30.4; median: 30; mode: none; range: 5
   b Which measure gives the difference between her shortest and longest jumps? range

▶ ***3.** *Formulate* Twelve of the 30 students in the class brought their lunches
   (48, 58) from home. What percent of the students brought their lunches from home? 40%

*4 If a student from the class in problem **3** were selected at random, what
   (59) is the probability that the student would be one who brought his or her lunch from home? $\frac{2}{5}$

▶ **5.** These triangles are similar. Find the scale
   (35) factor from the larger triangle to the smaller triangle and solve for x. $\frac{1}{2}$; $x = 2$

Lesson 59 **403**

▶ See Math Conversations in the sidebar.

---

2 **New Concepts** *(Continued)*

Practice Set
Problem a [Explain]
Point out that a free throw scores one point and a shot from the paint scores 2 points.

Problem b [Error Alert]
Make sure students recognize that the probability is $\frac{36}{120}$ reduced to lowest terms, or to its decimal equivalent.

Problem c [Predict]
You might choose to point out that $\frac{3}{10}$ or 0.3 is a little less than $\frac{1}{3}$, then encourage students to make an estimate of the solution by estimating $\frac{1}{3}$ of 200. Estimating enables students to decide the reasonableness of the solution by comparing it to the estimate.

Problem d [Discuss]
The question and sample answer is likely to provoke some discussion. Point out that premiums for insurance coverage of all types is based on probabilities.

3 **Written Practice**

Math Conversations
Discussion opportunities are provided below.

Problem 1 [Analyze]
Work with students to draw a ratio box on the board or overhead that can be used to solve the problem. The ratio of all the atoms to oxygen atoms is $\frac{3}{2}$ or 1.5.

Problem 3 [Formulate]
"Describe two different methods that can be used to solve this problem."

Invite a volunteer to demonstrate the arithmetic for each method on the board or overhead. Sample methods: Change $\frac{12}{30}$ to a decimal, then change the decimal to a percent by moving the decimal point two places to the right; solve $\frac{12}{30} = \frac{n\%}{100\%}$ for n.

Errors and Misconceptions
Problem 5
When naming a scale factor, students must recognize the corresponding sides of the figure and choose a pair of corresponding sides whose measures are known. Division of the known measures is then used to identify the scale factor.

Explain that the order of the terms of the scale factor in problem **5** is described, and watch for students who complete the computation $3 \div 1.5$ and name the scale factor as $\frac{2}{1}$, 2:1, or 2.

(continued)

Math Conversations

Discussion opportunities are provided below.

Problems 8 and 9 [Analyze]

Remind students to use substitution to check their solutions whenever they solve equations.

Problems 13a and 13b [Evaluate]

Ask students to use their reasoning skills, and not paper and pencil arithmetic, to answer the questions.

After answering the questions, challenge students to complete the paper and pencil arithmetic that is necessary to name the perimeter and the area of the figure.
$P = 28$ m; $A = 26$ m^2

Problem 22 [Evaluate]

"Which word—likely or unlikely—best describes the probability that Van will select the can of yellow paint? Explain your answer." Likely; the probability of any event ranges from 0 to 1, and a probability of $\frac{1}{2}$ represents equally likely events. Since $\frac{2}{3} > \frac{1}{2}$, Van is more likely than less likely to select the can of yellow paint.

(continued)

---

* **6.** Two of the lines are parallel. Solve for x.
(54) $x = 135°$

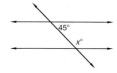

7.

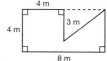

(0, −2)

7. Use slope-intercept to graph $y = -2x + 4$. Is the point (0, −2) a
(56) solution?   No.

[Analyze] Solve.

► * **8.** $3(x - 4) = 15$ $x = 9$
(14, 21)

► * **9.** $2x - x - 2 = 12$ $x = 14$
(14, 31)

10. $\frac{x}{3} = 0.7$ $x = 2.1$
(25, 38)

11. $\frac{1}{2}x = \frac{1}{3}$ $x = \frac{2}{3}$
(22, 38)

12. Find **a** the area and **b** the circumference of a circle that has a radius
(39, 40) of 13 units. Express your answer in terms of π.   **a.** 169π units^2,
b. 26π units

* **13.** [Evaluate] Compare the figure to a 4 m by
(37) 8 m rectangle.

► **a.** Is the area of the figure greater than or less than the area of the rectangle?   The area is less than the area of the rectangle.

► **b.** Is the perimeter of the figure greater than or less than the perimeter of the rectangle?   The perimeter is greater than the perimeter of the rectangle.

14. Express as a unit rate: 2400 miles in 48 hours.   50 mi/hr
(7)

* **15.** Use a unit multiplier to convert 3.5 minutes to seconds.
(52) $3.5 \text{ min} \cdot \frac{60 \text{ sec}}{1 \text{ min}} = 210$ sec

16. The door is 6 ft 9 in. high. Express the height of the door as a mixed
(52) number of feet and as a decimal number of feet. $6\frac{3}{4}$ ft, 6.75 ft

Simplify.

17. $3^{-2} \cdot 2^{-2}$ $\frac{1}{36}$
(51)

18. $\frac{h^3 p^2}{ph}$ $h^2 p$
(27)

19. $\frac{5}{18} - \frac{5}{18} \cdot \frac{1}{5}$ $\frac{4}{18}$ or $\frac{2}{9}$
(13, 22)

20. $0.3 - 0.2(0.1)$ 0.28
(24, 25)

21. a. Write 0.95 as a percent and reduced fraction.   95%, $\frac{19}{20}$
(12)

   b. Order 0.95, $\frac{39}{40}$, and $\frac{9}{10}$ from least to greatest. $\frac{9}{10}$, 0.95, $\frac{39}{40}$.

►* **22.** [Evaluate] Van selected two unmarked paint cans from a shelf with
(32) three unmarked cans. Inside two cans is white paint and inside one can is yellow paint. Van will open the cans as he looks for the yellow paint.

   a. In a list, record the sample space for the experiment. (Hint: Use the abbreviations W_1, W_2, Y.)   Sample space: $\{W_1W_2, W_1Y, W_2Y\}$

   b. What is the probability that one of the two cans Van selected contains yellow paint? $\frac{2}{3}$

► See Math Conversations in the sidebar.

23. The Wilsons traveled the 2400 miles of Route 66 from Chicago, IL to
(7)   Santa Monica, CA. If their total driving time was 50 hours, what was
their average rate?   48 mph

24. What is the amount of sales tax for $315.90 if the tax rate is 7%?
(58)   (Round to the nearest cent.) $22.11

* **25.** If Dori answers 23 of 25 questions correctly, what percent of the
(58)   questions did she answer correctly?   92%

26. Combine like terms: $x(x + 1) - 1(x + 1)$ $x^2 - 1$
(31, 36)

27. Estimate the volume and surface area of a
(42, 43)   cereal box that has these dimensions.
264 in.^{3}, 290 in.^{2}

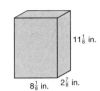

$11\frac{1}{8}$ in.

$8\frac{1}{8}$ in. $2\frac{7}{8}$ in.

28. Some lichens grow at a rate of 0.0000000000625 miles per hour. What
(51)   is the same number expressed in scientific notation? 6.25×10^{-11}

29. If the ink in the period at the end of this sentence weighs 1.3×10^{-8} lb,
(57)   and if there are 30,000 periods printed in this book, then how much does
this ink weigh altogether? Express each number in scientific notation
and perform the calculation in scientific notation.
$(1.3 \times 10^{-8})(3.0 \times 10^4) = 3.9 \times 10^{-4} = 0.00039$ lb

30. The coordinates of the vertices of
(Inv. 5) $\triangle ABC$ are $A(1, 3)$, $B(3, 6)$ and $C(4, 3)$. A
translation of $\triangle ABC$ is used to produce
$\triangle A'B'C'$. Vertex B' is located at $(5, 7)$.
Choose the coordinates of the vertices
A' and C'.   **D**

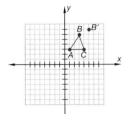

  A $A'(3, 5)$ and $C'(6, 5)$

  B $A'(2, 4)$ and $C'(4, 7)$

  C $A'(5, 3)$ and $C'(4, 7)$

  D $A'(3, 4)$ and $C'(6, 4)$

Lesson 59   **405**

 See Math Conversations in the sidebar.

3 **Written Practice** *(Continued)*

Math Conversations
Discussion opportunities are provided below.

Problem 24 Explain

Extend the Problem
*"Explain how to use the idea of 1% of a
number to estimate the amount of sales
tax."* Sample: Finding 1% of a number is
the same as moving the decimal point in
that number two places to the left. Since 1%
of $315.90 is $3.1590, or a little more than
$3, the sales tax will be a little more than
$3 × 7 or $21.

Looking Forward

Finding experimental probabilities
prepares students for:

• **Lesson 68,** using the probability
multiplication rule.

• **Investigation 7,** simulating
probability experiments.

• **Lesson 83,** calculating
probabilities of dependent
events.

•Area of a Parallelogram

Objectives

- Use the formula $A = bh$ to calculate the area of parallelograms.
- Verify the formula for the area of a parallelogram by using a model.
- Compare the perimeters and areas of similar parallelograms.

Lesson Preparation

Materials

- **Power Up L** (in *Instructional Masters*)
- **Manipulative Kit:** inch rulers
- **Teacher-provided material:** graph paper, scissors

Power Up L

Math Language

Maintain	English Learners (ESL)
parallelogram	tripled
rhombus	

Technology Resources

Student eBook Complete student textbook in electronic format.

Resources and Planner CD Assessment, reteaching, and instructional masters, plus a pacing calendar with standards.

Test and Practice Generator CD Create additional practice sheets and custom-made tests.

www.SaxonPublishers.com Visit for more student activities and planning materials.

Inclusion

Adaptations CD Adapted lessons, investigations, practice and assessments.

Meeting Standards

National Council of Teachers of Mathematics (NCTM)

Geometry

GM.2a Use coordinate geometry to represent and examine the properties of geometric shapes

GM.2b Use coordinate geometry to examine special geometric shapes, such as regular polygons or those with pairs of parallel or perpendicular sides

GM.3a Describe sizes, positions, and orientations of shapes under informal transformations such as flips, turns, slides, and scaling

GM.4d Use geometric models to represent and explain numerical and algebraic relationships

Measurement

ME.2c Develop and use formulas to determine the circumference of circles and the area of triangles, parallelograms, trapezoids, and circles and develop strategies to find the area of more-complex shapes

Problem-Solving Strategy: Work Backwards

Victor makes three different purchases at three different stores one afternoon. Each time, he spends $\frac{1}{3}$ of the money he is carrying. If he ends the day with $16, how much money did he have at the start of the day?

(Understand) **Understand the problem.**

"What information are we given?"

Victor makes three different purchases at three different stores, and each time he spends $\frac{1}{3}$ of the money he is carrying. He ends the day with $16.

"What are we asked to do?"

Determine how much money he had at the start of the day.

(Plan) **Make a plan.**

"What problem-solving strategy will we use?"

We will *work backwards* from the $16 Victor has left.

(Solve) **Carry out the plan.**

"If Victor spent $\frac{1}{3}$ of what he had when he entered the third store, what fraction represents the $16 he has remaining?"

$\frac{2}{3}$

"If $16 is $\frac{2}{3}$ of Victor's money, what is $\frac{1}{3}$?"

$8

"How much did Victor enter the third store with, and how much did he spend?"

He entered with $24, and spent $\frac{1}{3}$ of it, or $8 (and left with $\frac{2}{3}$ of it, the $16 he ended the day with).

"If Victor spent $\frac{1}{3}$ of what he had when he entered the second store, what fraction represents the $24 he had when he left the second store and headed to the third?"

$\frac{2}{3}$

"If $24 is $\frac{2}{3}$ of Victor's money, what is $\frac{1}{3}$?"

$12

"How much did Victor enter the second store with, and how much did he spend?"

He entered with $36, and spent $\frac{1}{3}$ of it, or $12 (and left with $24 to take to the third store).

"If Victor spent $\frac{1}{3}$ of what he had when he entered the first store, what fraction represents the $36 he had when he left the first store and headed to the second?"

$\frac{2}{3}$

"If $36 is $\frac{2}{3}$ of Victor's money, what is $\frac{1}{3}$?"

$18

"How much did Victor enter the first store with, and how much did he spend?"

He entered with $54, and spent $\frac{1}{3}$ of it, or $18 (and left with $36 to take to the second store).

(Check) **Look back.**

"Did we find the answer to the question that was asked?"

Yes. We determined that Victor had $54 at the start of his day of shopping.

Facts

Distribute **Power Up L** to students. See answers below.

Mental Math

Encourage students to share different ways to mentally compute these exercises. Strategies for exercises **a, c,** and **g** are listed below.

a. Use Math Sense

No, because the least 5-digit number is 10,000 and that is the product of 100 times 100. No two 2-digit numbers can have a product equal to or greater than 10,000.

Guess and Check

We try multiplying the largest two-digit numbers: $99 \times 99 = 9801$. It is impossible for two two-digit numbers to have a five-digit product.

c. Sides of a Triangle

The third side must be greater than 5 in. and less than 29 in.

4 in. ➔ no

19 in. ➔ yes

29 in. ➔ no

g. Cross Products

$18x = 12 \times 6$

$x = \frac{12 \times 6}{18}$

$x = \frac{12}{3} = 4$

Multiply Up

$6 \times 3 = 18$

$x \times 3 = 12$

$x = 4$

Problem Solving

Refer to **Power-Up Discussion,** p. 406B.

Instruction

After reviewing the formula for the area of a rectangle, use the *Explain* question to review why the formula for the area of a triangle is half that of a rectangle with the same perpendicular dimensions.

(continued)

Power Up   *Building Power*

facts   Power Up L

mental math

a. Number Sense: Can we produce a 5-digit whole number by multiplying two 2-digit whole numbers?   No

b. Algebra: If $x^3 = 8$, then x equals what number or numbers?   2

c. Geometry: Two sides of a triangle measure 17 inches and 12 inches. Can the third side measure 4 inches? 19 inches? 29 inches?   no; yes; no

d. Fractional Parts: $\frac{5}{9}$ of the 72 athletes were on the home team. How many were on the home team?   40 athletes

e. Scientific Notation: Write 0.000507 in scientific notation. 5.07×10^{-4}

f. Rate: Brad ran north up the trail at 8 miles per hour. Skip walked the trail at 4 miles per hour north. After 30 minutes, how far apart are they if they started at the same place and time?   2 miles

g. Proportions: $\frac{18}{6} = \frac{12}{x}$ 4

h. Calculation: $6 \times 7, -2, \div 2, +1, \div 3, +2, \sqrt{\ }, \times 12, \sqrt{\ }, -\frac{1}{2}$ $5\frac{1}{2}$

problem solving   Victor makes three different purchases at three different stores one afternoon. Each time, he spends $\frac{1}{3}$ of the money he is carrying. If he ends the day with $16, how much money did he have at the start of the day? $54

New Concept   *Increasing Knowledge*

Recall that to find the area of a rectangle we multiply the length and width, which are the perpendicular dimensions of a rectangle.

Thinking Skill

Explain

Why does the formula $A = \frac{1}{2}bh$ work for finding the area of a triangle? The area of a triangle is $\frac{1}{2}$ the area of the rectangle with the same perpendicular dimensions as the triangle.

Also recall that to find the area of a triangle, we multiply the perpendicular base and height as the first step to calculating the area. Then we find half of that product.

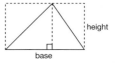

Facts   Write each number in scientific notation.

$186,000 = 1.86 \times 10^5$	$0.0002 = 2 \times 10^{-4}$
$2,050,000 = 2.05 \times 10^6$	$\frac{1}{1,000,000} = 1 \times 10^{-6}$
15 million $= 1.5 \times 10^7$	12 thousandths $= 1.2 \times 10^{-2}$

Write each number in standard form.

$3 \times 10^5 = 300,000$	$1 \times 10^{-3} = 0.001$
$3.75 \times 10^4 = 37,500$	$3.5 \times 10^{-5} = 0.000035$
$4.05 \times 10^3 = 4050$	$2.04 \times 10^{-2} = 0.0204$

Likewise, to find the area of a parallelogram we multiply the perpendicular base and height. Again, the product is the area of a rectangle, but the area of the rectangle is equal to the area of the parallelogram. In the figure below, notice that the part of the parallelogram outside the rectangle matches the missing portion of the rectangle.

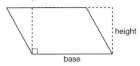

The formula for the area of a parallelogram is

$$A = bh$$

in which A represents area, b represents the length of the base, and h represents the height. Two parallel sides are the bases of a parallelogram. The perpendicular distance between the bases is the height.

Activity

Area of a Parallelogram

Materials needed: $\frac{1}{2}$ sheet of graph paper per student, scissors, ruler, pencil

On graph paper, draw a parallelogram that is not a rectangle. Trace over lines on the background grid to make one pair of parallel sides. Make sure that the vertices of the parallelogram are at intersections of the background grid and then cut out your parallelogram.

Next, on a grid line (such as the dashed line in the example), cut the parallelogram into two parts. Then, rearrange the two pieces to form a rectangle and find the area of the rectangle. Does the area of the rectangle equal the product of the base and height of the parallelogram?   yes

Connect Repeat this activity by drawing a parallelogram and one of its diagonals. How does this area of each triangle you formed compare to the area of the parallelogram? How does the formula for the area of a triangle compare to the formula for the area of a parallelogram?   The area of each triangle is $\frac{1}{2}$ the area of the parallelogram because the triangles are congruent. The formula for the area of a triangle is $A = \frac{1}{2}bh$, while the formula for the area of a parallelogram is $A = bh$.

---

2 New Concepts (Continued)

Instruction

If necessary, use this alternative explanation of why the formula for the area of a parallelogram is the same as that for the area of a rectangle. Note that students will do this in the following activity.

- A parallelogram can be divided into two pieces that will fit exactly over a rectangle with the same perpendicular dimensions (base and height).
- This means that both figures have the same area, so the same formula can be used.

(continued)

Activity

Instruction

Provide students with graph paper and scissors. Have students follow the directions. When everyone has finished, discuss the results. Point out that all the parallelograms made by members of the class are not the same nor were they cut apart in the same way, but all the results are the same, so the formula is likely to apply to all parallelograms.

Use the *Connect* question to strengthen understanding of how the formula for the area of a triangle is related to the formula for the area of a rectangle or parallelogram.

Math Background

How can you prove that four points are the vertices of a parallelogram?

A quadrilateral is a parallelogram if both pairs of opposite sides are parallel. You can use the coordinates of the vertices of a quadrilateral to calculate the slopes of its sides. If opposite sides have the same slope, then they are parallel. For example, consider the quadrilateral with vertices $A(2, 1)$, $B(1, -1)$, $C(-2, -1)$ and $D(-1, 1)$.

Slope of $\overline{AB} = \dfrac{-1 - 1}{1 - 2} = 2$ Slope of $\overline{CD} = \dfrac{1 - (-1)}{-1 - (-2)} = 2$

Slope of $\overline{BC} = \dfrac{-1 - (-1)}{-2 - 1} = 0$ Slope of $\overline{AD} = \dfrac{1 - 1}{-1 - (2)} = 0$

$\overline{AB}$ and $\overline{CD}$ are parallel and $\overline{BC}$ and $\overline{AD}$ are parallel. Therefore, $ABCD$ is a parallelogram.

Example 1

Instruction

Ask whether anyone can describe another way to find the perimeter of this parallelogram. Sample: Find 6 × 2 and 8 × 2 and add the products.

As students work on the *Model* task, ask why they are able to draw so many different parallelograms with an area of 24 in.² Sample: 24 has many factor pairs that can be used for the base and height.

Ask students how many different rectangles there are that have an area of 24 in.² with sides that are whole numbers, 4; with sides that can be any positive real number, an infinite number

Example 2

Instruction

For parts **a** and **b**, provide graph paper if necessary. Suggest that students try sketching the coordinate plane and the two figures on plain paper.

For part **c**, ask whether anyone can describe similar relationships for the areas of circles and squares. Sample: When we used a scale factor to change the length of a radius or a side, the area changed by the square of the scale factor.

(continued)

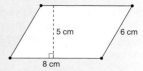

Example 1

Find the perimeter and area of this parallelogram.

Solution

We find the perimeter of the parallelogram by adding the lengths of the four sides.

$$8 \text{ cm} + 6 \text{ cm} + 8 \text{ cm} + 6 \text{ cm} = 28 \text{ cm}$$

We find the area of the parallelogram by multiplying the perpendicular dimensions of the base and the height.

Step:	Justification:
$A = bh$	Formula
$A = 8 \text{ cm} \cdot 5 \text{ cm}$	Substituted
$A = 40 \text{ cm}^2$	Simplified

Check student's drawing. Accept any parallelogram for which the product of the base and height is 24 in.², such as a parallelogram with a base of 8 in. and a height of 3 in.

Model Draw a parallelogram with an area of 24 in.² Label its dimensions.

Example 2

a. On a coordinate plane sketch and find the area of parallelogram *ABCD* with vertices *A* (2, 1), *B* (1, −1), *C* (−2, −1) and *D* (−1, 1).

b. Graph the dilation of parallelogram *ABCD* with scale factor 3. What is the area of the image?

c. The area of the image is how many times the area of parallelogram *ABCD*? Why?

Solution

a. The area of parallelogram *ABCD* is **6 sq. units**.

b. The area of the dilated image is **54 sq. units**.

c. The area of the image is **9 times** the area of parallelogram *ABCD* because the scale factor tripled the base and tripled the height. Therefore, when we multiply the base and height, the product (the area) is 9 times as great.

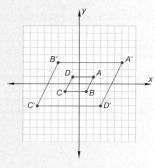

English Learners

For example **2c** solution, explain the meaning of the word **tripled**. Say:

"To triple means to make three times as large. If you triple the number of coins you have, you will have 3 times that amount. If you triple one quarter, you will have 3 quarters or 75¢."

Ask students to triple the following amounts: 3 dollar bills, 2 erasers, 5 pencils, a pair of shoes, 4 dimes. $3 × 3 = $9, 2 × 3 = 6, 5 × 3 = 15, 1 pair × 3 = 3 pairs, 4 × 10¢ × 3 = $1.20

Practice Set ▸ **a.** The base and the height of a parallelogram are always   **A**

         A perpendicular   **B** parallel

         C sides   **D** congruent

b. What is the area of this parallelogram? 56 in.^2

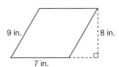

9 in.   8 in.   7 in.

Math Language

Recall that a **rhombus** is a parallelogram with four sides of equal length.

▸ **c.** The sides of a square and another rhombus are 3 cm long. Find the perimeter and area of each parallelogram.   square: $P = 12$ cm, $A = 9 \text{ cm}^2$; rhombus: $P = 12$ cm, $A = 6 \text{ cm}^2$

3 cm

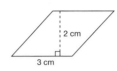
2 cm   3 cm

▸ **d.** Find the area of a parallelogram with vertices at $(4, 2)$, $(2, -2)$, $(-2, -2)$ and $(0, 2)$. What would be the area of a dilation of this parallelogram with a scale factor of 3?   16 sq. units, 144 sq. units

Possible answer: Each of the three congruent parallelograms has a base of 4 ft and a height of 6 ft. The area of the front surface of each is 4 ft × 6 ft, or 24 ft^2. The total area of the front surface of the N is 3 × 24 ft², or 72 ft^2.

▸ **e.** *Evaluate* A brass sculpture of the letter N is formed from one long metal parallelogram folded into three congruent parallelograms. What is the area of one of the smaller parallelograms? What is the total area of the long metal parallelogram? 24 ft^2; 72 ft^2

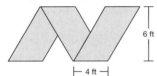
6 ft   4 ft

f. *Justify* How do you know your answer to problem **e** is correct?

Written Practice   *Strengthening Concepts*

▸ *** 1.** Gina has a coupon for 15% off at the video store. If she purchases a
  (58) video marked $16.80, how much will she pay using the coupon?
     $14.28

▸ *** 2.** Scientists know that the diameter of a normal cell is 0.000025 cm. How
  (51) is that number written in scientific notation? 2.5×10^{-5} cm

▸ **3.** A triangle has vertices at $(0, 5)$, $(-10, 1)$, and $(10, 1)$. What is the area of
  (Inv. 1, the triangle?   40 sq. units
  20)

▸ See Math Conversations in the sidebar.

Practice Set

Problem a [Error Alert]

Asking students to draw and label a sketch can help reinforce the concept that the height of a parallelogram must be perpendicular to its base.

Problem c

Remind students that a rhombus is a parallelogram with four congruent sides.

Problem d [Error Alert]

Watch for students who do not recognize that the vertices of the image are found by multiplying the coordinates of the preimage vertices by 3.

Students should conclude that $(12, 6)$, $(6, -6)$, $(-6, -6)$, and $(0, 6)$ represent the image vertices.

Problem e [Evaluate]

An alternative way for students to justify their answer is to sketch and label a net of the sculpture.

---

3 Written Practice

Math Conversations

Discussion opportunities are provided below.

Problem 1 [Explain]

Extend the Problem

"Explain how 10% of a number can be used to estimate the savings." Sample: 10% of a number is the same as moving the decimal point in that number one place to the left. Since 10% of $16.80 is $1.68, Gina's savings are about $1.68 plus one-half of $1.68.

Problem 3 [Verify]

Extend the Problem

"Is the triangle isosceles? Give a reason to support your answer." Yes; Sample: The triangle can be divided into two congruent right triangles. The hypotenuses of the two right triangles are congruent, so the original triangle is isosceles.

Errors and Misconceptions

Problem 2

Watch for students who do not write a coefficient that is greater than or equal to 1 and less than 10.

(continued)

3 Written Practice (Continued)

Math Conversations
Discussion opportunities are provided below.

Problem 6 Analyze
"Finding 25% of an amount is the same as finding what fraction of that amount?" $\frac{1}{4}$

Problem 11 Generalize
Demonstrate on the board or overhead how the expression simplifies to 125. Then ask students to simplify $\frac{(2^2)^3}{2^2}$. 16

Problem 18 Evaluate
"The dilation will produce an image. Explain how to find the vertices of that image." Multiply the coordinates of the preimage vertices by 2.

"Using only mental math, name the vertices of the image." $(-4, 0)$; $(12, 0)$; $(2, 6)$; $(18, 6)$

Problem 21 Analyze
After identifying choice C as the correct choice, invite volunteers to explain why the other nets represent cubes.

(continued)

20.
$25m + 75 - 75$
$= 125 - 75$
$25m = 50$
$\frac{25m}{25} = \frac{50}{25}$
$m = 2$
Jodi will be able to go to the gym for 2 months.
Check :
$25(2) + 75 = 125$
$50 + 75 = 125$
$125 = 125$

---

* 4. The bill for a family of four at a restaurant was $62. Simon paid $72 for the meal and tip. How much was the tip? What percent was the tip? $10; about 16%
(58)

5. Marshall knows that 0.01 is equal to 10^{-2}. How would he represent this using factors? **B**
(51)
  A 8   **B** $\frac{1}{10} \times \frac{1}{10}$ **C** -20 **D** $10 \times (-2)$

* 6. Analyze Some stores have a layaway plan for customers. This means that the customer will pay for the item in installments and will be able to take the item home when it is fully paid for. One store requires that the person make a minimum down payment of 25%. Kayla wants to put a $60 item on layaway at that store. What is the minimum down payment she must make? $15.00
(58)

Generalize Simplify.

7. $-13 + (-4)(-2)$ -5 *** 8.** $256 \div [2(6 - (-2))^2]$ 2
(31, 36)   (21)

9. $(1.6 \times 10^4)(2.0 \times 10^5)$ 3.2×10^9 *** 10.** $(1.5)^2(-2)^4$ 36
(46)   (25, 36)

* 11. $\frac{(5^3)^2}{5^3}$ $5^3 = 125$
(27)

Solve.

12. $\frac{1}{3}x - 1 = 4$ $x = 15$ **13.** $-5k - 11 = 14$ $k = -5$
(50)   (50)

14. $\frac{x}{7} = -2$ $x = -14$ **15.** $5(2t + 4) = 140$ $t = 12$
(50)   (50)

16. $-4m + 1.8 = -4.2$ $m = 1.5$ **17.** $27 = 8b - 5$ $b = 4$
(50)   (50)

* 18. Evaluate Find the area of a parallelogram with vertices at $(-2, 0)$, $(6, 0)$, $(1, 3)$, and $(9, 3)$. What is the area of a dilation of this parallelogram with a scale factor of 2? $A = 24$ units²; The area of the dilation is 96 units².
(Inv. 5, 60)

* 19. The Great Wall of China extends approximately 4163 miles long. A mile is approximately 1.61 kilometers. Find the length of the Great Wall to the nearest kilometer. 4163 mi $\cdot \frac{1.61 \text{ km}}{1 \text{ mi}} \approx 6{,}702$ km
(25, 52)

20. Jodi is joining a fitness center. The application fee is $75 and the monthly rate is $25. She wants to pay $125 now. Solve this equation to find out how many months (m) she will she be able to go to the fitness center for this amount of money.
(50)
$$25m + 75 = 125$$

* 21. Analyze Which of these nets is not a net of a cube? **C**
(55)

410   *Saxon* Math Course 3

▶ See Math Conversations in the sidebar.

22. In parallelogram *ABCD*, *m∠B* is 128°.
(54) What is the measure of ∠*C*?
∠*C* = 52°

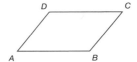

23. What is the median of this data?
(53) 29 inches; 26 + 32 = 58; 58 ÷ 2 = 29

24. The pet store sells guppies for 8 for
(49) $1.50. How much would 36 guppies
cost? Write a proportion and solve.
$\frac{8}{1.5} = \frac{36}{g}$, *g* = 6.75; $6.75

25. At Washington Middle School, 64% of
(48) the students play a sport. If 192 play
a sport, how many students attend
Washington Middle School?   300

26. Will a $25\frac{1}{2}$-inch umbrella fit into a gift
(Inv. 2) box that is 10 inches wide by
24 inches long? (Hint: Will it fit if it
is placed diagonally? Use the
Pythagorean Theorem.)   Yes, The diagonal measurement is 26 inches.

**Average Annual Precipitation
for Selected Texas Cities**

City	Inches
Brownsville	26
Dallas-Fort Worth	32
El Paso	9
Houston	47
Midland-Odessa	14
Port Arthur	55

27. A bakery sells two kinds of bread, whole wheat and white, in a ratio of
(45) 3 whole wheat to 2 white. If the bakery made 60 loaves of bread, how
many were whole wheat?   36

28. Lou makes pancakes at a pancake house. He makes 12 pancakes
(44) in 4 minutes. At that rate, how long would it take him to make
54 pancakes?   18 minutes

29. Wallpaper comes in rolls that cover 80 square feet. Vicki wants to
(43) wallpaper the walls and ceiling of her living room. The room is 15 feet
wide by 18 feet long by 9 feet high. How many rolls of wallpaper will she
need?   The surface area is 864 square feet so she will need 11 rolls.

* 30. *Conclude* Tran earns $7.50 per hour at
(41) his part-time job. Copy and complete the
function table for 1, 2, 3, and 4 hours of
work. Then write an equation for
the function. Start the equation with
P =. Is the relationship between the
number of hours worked and amount
of pay proportional?   *P* = 7.5*h*; Yes, the
relationship is proportional.

Number of Hours (*h*)	Amount of Pay (*P*)
1	7.50
2	15
3	22.50
4	30

▶ See Math Conversations in the sidebar.

Math Conversations

Discussion opportunities are provided below.

Problem 30 Conclude

Work with students to make a reasonable
inference about the proportionality of the
relationship without graphing the equation.
Explain that if each pair of numbers in the
table was simplified, each would simplify to
the same number. And to decide if the line
passes through (0, 0), students can substitute 0
for *P* and 0 for *h* into the equation to find that
0 = 0 and the substitution makes the equation
true. So students can reasonably infer that the
relationship is proportional.

Errors and Misconceptions
Problem 22

You may need to remind students to check
their work using the fact that the sum of the
angle measures of a quadrilateral is 360°.

Looking Forward

Calculating areas of parallelograms
prepares students for:

• **Lesson 75,** calculating areas of
trapezoids.

• **Lesson 76,** calculating volumes of
prisms and cylinders.

• **Lesson 85,** calculating surface
areas of cylinders and prisms.

Assessment   30–40 minutes   For use after Lesson 60

Distribute **Cumulative Test 11** to each student. Two versions of the test are available in *Saxon Math Course 3 Course Assessments Book.* Have students complete the **Power-Up Test** first. Allow 10 minutes. Then have students work the 20 numbered items on the **Cumulative Test.** Students may use copies of the answer sheet to record their work. Track individual and class progress with the **Test Analysis** forms.

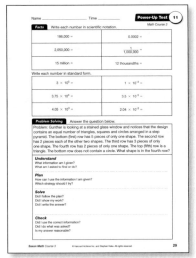

Power-Up Test 11

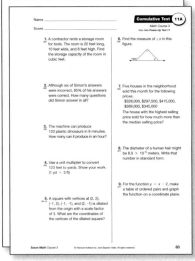

Cumulative Test 11A

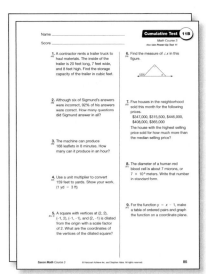

Alternative Cumulative Test 11B

Optional Answer Forms

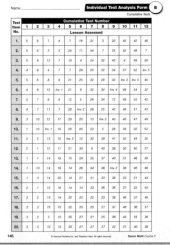

Individual Test Analysis Form

Class Test Analysis Form

Reteaching

Students who score below 80% on the assessment may be in need of reteaching. Look for the causes of student mistakes. If errors are conceptual, refer to the *Reteaching Masters* for reteaching.

Customized Benchmark Assessment

You can develop customized benchmark tests using the Test Generator located on the *Test & Practice Generator CD.*

This chart shows the lesson, the standard, and the test item question that can be found on the *Test & Practice Generator CD.*

LESSON	NEW CONCEPTS	LOCAL STANDARD	TEST ITEM ON CD
51	• Negative Exponents		6.1.1
	• Scientific Notation for Small Numbers		6.1.2
52	• Using Unit Multipliers to Convert Measures		6.2.1
	• Converting Mixed-Unit to Single-Unit Measures		6.2.2
53	• Solving Problems Using Measures of Central Tendency		6.3.1
54	• Angle Relationships		6.4.1
55	• Nets of Prisms, Cylinders, Pyramids and Cones		6.5.1
56	• The Slope-Intercept Equation of a Line		6.6.1
57	• Operations with Small Numbers in Scientific Notation		6.7.1
58	• Solving Percent Problems with Equations		6.8.1
59	• Experimental Probability		6.9.1
60	• Area of a Parallelogram		6.10.1

Using the Test Generator CD
- Develop tests in both English and Spanish.
- Choose from multiple-choice and free-response test items.
- Clone test items to create multiple versions of the same test.
- View and edit test items to make and save your own questions.
- Administer assessments through paper tests or over a school LAN.
- Monitor student progress through a variety of individual and class reports
  —for both diagnosing and assessing standards mastery.

Exploring Carbon Nanotubes

Assign after Lesson 60 and Test 11

Objectives

- Convert between standard form and scientific notation for large and small numbers.
- Perform basic operations on large and small numbers in scientific notation.
- Use rates to solve problems involving proportional relationships.
- Communicate ideas through writing.

Materials

Performance Task 11A and **11B**

Calculator

Preparation

Make copies of **Performance Task 11A** and **11B**. (One each per student.)

Time Requirement

25 minutes; Begin in class and complete at home.

Task

Tell students they will be investigating the size and structure of a single-walled carbon nanotube, a hexagonal cylinder of carbon with unique properties. Students begin by examining the measurements of several small structures and writing the size of each in standard form. Students will then calculate the number of nanotubes it takes to equal the diameter of a human hair. They are asked to explain their calculations in terms of how they manipulate the exponents. Students next determine the number of carbon atom diameters that are equivalent to the diameter of a carbon nanotube. Students finish by using the ratio of a nanotube's length to its diameter to calculate the length of a nanotube in scientific notation and in standard form. Point out that all necessary information is provided on **Performance Task 11A** and **11B**.

Criteria for Evidence of Learning

- Correctly converts very small numbers in scientific notation to standard form.
- Uses scientific notation to correctly represent very small numbers.
- Calculates the equivalence between the diameters of a carbon nanotube and a carbon atom.
- Calculates the correct length in scientific notation and standard form of a carbon nanotube.
- Communicates ideas clearly through writing.

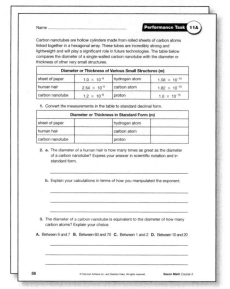

Performance Task 11A and 11B

National Council of Teachers of Mathematics (NCTM)

Numbers and Operations

NO.1d Understand and use ratios and proportions to represent quantitative relationships

NO.1e Develop an understanding of large numbers and recognize and appropriately use exponential, scientific, and calculator notation

NO.2a Understand the meaning and effects of arithmetic operations with fractions, decimals, and integers

Geometry

GM.4e Recognize and apply geometric ideas and relationships in areas outside the mathematics classroom, such as art, science, and everyday life

Communication

CM.3b Communicate their mathematical thinking coherently and clearly to peers, teachers, and others

Connections

CN.4c Recognize and apply mathematics in contexts outside of mathematics

Focus on

• Collect, Display, and Interpret Data

Objectives

- Understand why it is usually necessary to conduct a survey over only a sample of a population.
- Conduct surveys and display the results in an appropriate manner.
- Distinguish between qualitative and quantitative data.
- Create bar graphs, circle graphs, and histograms from given and collected data.

Lesson Preparation

Materials

None

Math Language

New

bias	qualitative data
circle graph	quantitative data
histogram	sample
opinion survey	statistics
population	

Technology Resources

Student eBook Complete student textbook in electronic format.

Resources and Planner CD Assessment, reteaching, and instructional masters, plus a pacing calendar with standards.

Test and Practice Generator CD Create additional practice sheets and custom-made tests.

www.SaxonPublishers.com Visit for more student activities and planning materials.

Inclusion

 Adaptations CD Adapted lessons, investigations, practice and assessments.

Meeting Standards

National Council of Teachers of Mathematics (NCTM)

Data Analysis and Probability

DP.1a Formulate questions, design studies, and collect data about a characteristic shared by two populations or different characteristics within one population

DP.1b Select, create, and use appropriate graphical representations of data, including histograms, box plots, and scatterplots

DP.2b Discuss and understand the correspondence between data sets and their graphical representations, especially histograms, stem-and-leaf plots, box plots, and scatterplots

In this investigation students will collect and interpret quantitative and qualitative data. They will also learn how data can be organized and displayed in a variety of visual ways, including circle graphs, bar graphs, and histograms.

Instruction

Encourage students to share any familiarities they may have with surveys or polls. Some students may explain that surveys are often used to predict the winner of a presidential election before all of the votes have been officially counted. Others may describe a door-to-door survey or a survey that a family member participated in while shopping at a mall.

Use the scenarios described by students to help them generalize that a sample is a way to survey the preferences of a relatively small number of people, which are used to predict the preferences of a larger number of people.

Give students an opportunity to compare the frequency table to the bar graph. Students should conclude that both are simply different ways of displaying the same data.

Ask students to choose the table or graph and describe a benefit of how it displays data. Sample: The data in a bar graph can be quickly compared.

Focus on
• Collect, Display, and Interpret Data

Statistics is the science of collecting data and interpreting the data in order to draw conclusions and make predictions.

Suppose the managers of a theme park plan to build a new restaurant on its grounds, and the managers want to know the preference of the park attendees. The managers can collect this information by conducting a survey.

The group of people that researchers want to study is called the **population** of the study. In the case of the theme park, the population would be all park visitors. Often it is not practical to survey an entire population, so researchers select a smaller **sample** of the population to survey. Researchers use sampling methods to ensure that the sample is representative of the larger population and to avoid **bias** or slant toward a particular point of view. For example, the managers of the theme park might ask every 100th person who walks through the gates to participate in the survey.

1. Discuss various difficulties as a class, including costs, time, and space required to survey everyone, the fact that different people attend the park every day, and that some attendees would decline to participate.

1. Consider the survey that the theme park managers wish to conduct. Discuss the difficulties of surveying the entire population, that is, all park visitors.

2. If the survey were conducted only among people in one of the other restaurants at the park, would the sample be representative of the entire population?

2. Sampling in park restaurants might not be representative. People at one restaurant may share similar food preferences that may differ from other visitors. This may bias the data.

3. Conduct a **closed-option** survey (multiple choice, not free response) among your classmates. As a class, choose three restaurant options for the theme park. Ask each student to write their preference on a piece of paper, then collect and tally the results. Display the data in a **bar graph.** (See below.)

4. **Evaluate** Which type of restaurant is most popular among your classmates? Do you think the survey results would differ if it were conducted among a sample of park attendees?

4. In the sample results, the pizza parlor is most popular, indicated by the tallest bar. Teenagers and adults often have different food preferences, so a survey conducted at a theme park with many adults may have different results.

In the survey, we collected **qualitative data** (data that falls into categories), in this case, types of restaurants. Data that is numerical is called **quantitative data.**

3. Sample: A frequency table and bar graph are shown below.

Type of Restaurant	Tally	Frequency
Sandwich shop	ⅢⅠ ⅢⅠ	10
Fish and chips	ⅢⅠ ⅠⅠ	7
Pizza parlor	ⅢⅠ ⅢⅠ ⅠⅠⅠ	13

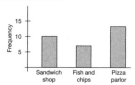

Math Background

Collecting and displaying data often involves the use of tally marks. A tally mark is a way to record frequency. In the United States, our customary system of tallying involves the use of vertical line segments to represent ones and a diagonal line segment to represent a group of five.

$$| \quad || \quad ||| \quad |||| \quad ||||$$

Our system of tallying, however, is not universal. Elsewhere in the world, other cultures use different representations to tally by ones and fives. Two such representations are shown below.

Suppose we want to know about how much time the students in your grade spend doing homework each day. We may select a sample of students, then ask them to record how much time they spent doing homework that day. Sample data for nine responses are shown below.

Time Spent on Homework

1 hr, 10 min	2 hr, 5 min	20 min
55 min	30 min	1 hr, 40 min
1 hr, 30 min	1 hr, 45 min	2 hr

We could then display this data in a **histogram**. A histogram displays quantitative data in adjacent intervals, represented by bars that touch. We show an example for the homework sample data. We sort the data into 30 minute intervals.

Time	Tally	Frequency
:00–:29	I	1
:30–:59	II	2
1:00–1:29	I	1
1:30–1:59	III	3
2:00–2:29	II	2

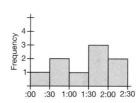

▶ See Math Conversations in the sidebar.

Thinking Skill

Discuss

Why would a bar graph *not* represent the data well? In this case there would be 9 different categories (one for each amount of time) and each bar would be the same height. The graph would do little to help us interpret the data, as compared to a histogram which displays intervals rather than categories. Bar graphs are better used for displaying qualitative data.

▶ **5.** A movie theater collected data on the ages of customers attending a new movie. The ages are listed below. Create a frequency table for the data by setting intervals and tallying the numbers for each interval. Then create a histogram to display the data.   See student work.

```
 7   8   8   9   9   9   10  10  11  12
12  12  13  14  15  16  16  17  18  20
23  28  32  33  34  34  35  37  40  41
48  51  53  57  58  62  68  70  72  75
```

Discuss How does changing the interval affect the display?
See student work.

Another kind of survey that is often conducted is an **opinion survey**. Sample results of an opinion survey are shown below.

"Do You Favor or Oppose Ballot Measure A?"

Response	Number	%
Favor	546	42
Oppose	520	40
Undecided	234	18

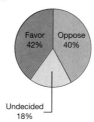

Investigation 6   **413**

Instruction

Ask students to give reasons why the data represent quantitative data and not qualitative data.

Help students recognize that the frequency table and the data bars of the histogram represent a range of times. Students should also recognize that it is not possible to know the exact length of time each student studied.

Math Conversations ·

Discussion opportunities are provided below.

Problem 5
Extend the Problem
"Explain how we can check our work."
Sample: Compare the sum of the tallies in the frequency table to the total number of values in the given data set. Then compare those sums to the data displayed by the histogram. All of the comparisons should be the same.

Instruction

Discuss how to find the number of degrees that each sector of the circle graph represents. Find 42% of 360° (151°), 40% of 360° (144°) and 18% of 360° (65°), rounded to nearest whole number.

(continued)

Problem 6

Before completing the activity, encourage students to share ideas about opinions that could be surveyed and questions that could be asked to elicit those opinions.

Arrange for students to complete the activity in pairs or in small groups.

Problem 7
Extend the Problem

Ask a volunteer who completed a bar graph to duplicate the graph on the board or overhead.

Challenge students to explain how increasing or decreasing an axis interval of the graph will affect the heights of the bars. Sample: Increasing the interval will make the height differences of the bars less obvious. Decreasing the interval will make the height differences of the bars more obvious.

The data are summarized and displayed in a **circle graph.** A circle graph is often used to display qualitative data and is particularly useful to illustrate the relative sizes of parts of a whole. The central angle of a sector is computed by multiplying the fraction or percent of responders by 360°.

▶ **6.** Conduct a closed-option opinion survey in your class, tally the results, and display the data in a circle graph.   See student work.

▶ **7.** One hundred eighth graders were surveyed and asked what extra-curricular activities they planned to be involved with in high school. The students were given several choices and could select as many as they wanted. The results are shown below.

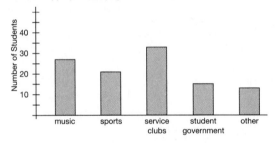

music	𝗍𝖧𝖫 𝗍𝖧𝖫 𝗍𝖧𝖫 𝗍𝖧𝖫 𝗍𝖧𝖫 II
sports	𝗍𝖧𝖫 𝗍𝖧𝖫 𝗍𝖧𝖫 𝗍𝖧𝖫 I
service clubs	𝗍𝖧𝖫 𝗍𝖧𝖫 𝗍𝖧𝖫 𝗍𝖧𝖫 𝗍𝖧𝖫 𝗍𝖧𝖫 𝗍𝖧𝖫 III
student government	𝗍𝖧𝖫 𝗍𝖧𝖫 𝗍𝖧𝖫
other	𝗍𝖧𝖫 𝗍𝖧𝖫 III

Visit www. SaxonPublishers. com/ActivitiesC3 for a graphing calculator activity.

Choose a type of graph (bar graph, histogram, or circle graph) for representing these data, and explain your choice. Then graph the data. Bar graph; Bar graphs and circle graphs are appropriate for qualitative (or categorical) data. However, sectors of circle graphs represent fractions of the whole. In this case, the fractions of students add to more than 1 because students were allowed to select multiple categories. Therefore a circle graph would not be an appropriate display.

▶ See Math Conversations in the sidebar.

Looking Forward ○

Investigating data prepares students for:

• **Investigation 8,** working with scatterplots.

A

absolute value
valor absoluto
(1)

The distance from the graph of a number to the origin on a number line. The symbol for absolute value is a vertical bar on each side of a numeral or variable, e.g., $|-x|$.

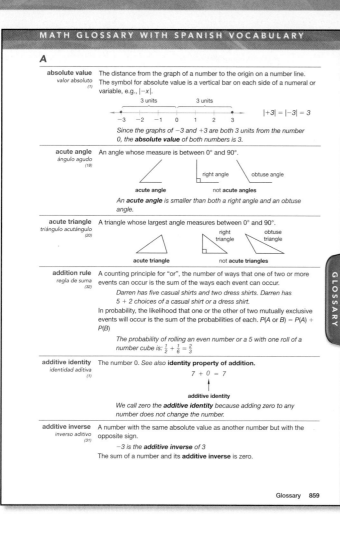

$|+3| = |-3| = 3$

Since the graphs of -3 and $+3$ are both 3 units from the number 0, the **absolute value** of both numbers is 3.

acute angle
ángulo agudo
(18)

An angle whose measure is between 0° and 90°.

right angle   obtuse angle

acute angle   not **acute** angles

An **acute angle** is smaller than both a right angle and an obtuse angle.

acute triangle
triángulo acutángulo
(20)

A triangle whose largest angle measures between 0° and 90°.

right triangle   obtuse triangle

acute triangle   not **acute triangles**

addition rule
regla de suma
(32)

A counting principle for "or", the number of ways that one of two or more events can occur is the sum of the ways each event can occur.

Darren has five casual shirts and two dress shirts. Darren has $5 + 2$ choices of a casual shirt or a dress shirt.

In probability, the likelihood that one or the other of two mutually exclusive events will occur is the sum of the probabilities of each. $P(A \text{ or } B) = P(A) + P(B)$

The probability of rolling an even number or a 5 with one roll of a number cube is: $\frac{1}{2} + \frac{1}{6} = \frac{2}{3}$

additive identity
identidad aditiva
(1)

The number 0. See also **identity property of addition**.

$7 + 0 = 7$

additive identity

We call zero the **additive identity** because adding zero to any number does not change the number.

additive inverse
inverso aditivo
(31)

A number with the same absolute value as another number but with the opposite sign.

-3 is the **additive inverse** of 3

The sum of a number and its **additive inverse** is zero.

---

adjacent angles
ángulos adyacentes
(54)

Two angles that have a common side and a common vertex but do not overlap. The angles lie on opposite sides of their common side.

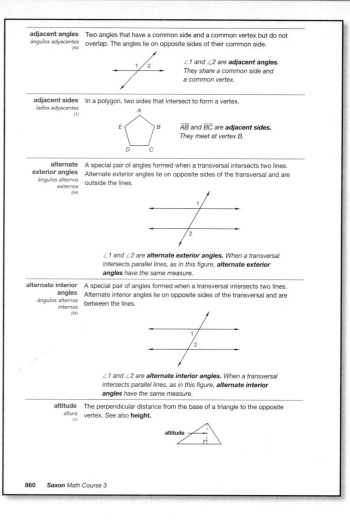

$\angle 1$ and $\angle 2$ are **adjacent angles**. They share a common side and a common vertex.

adjacent sides
lados adyacentes
(1)

In a polygon, two sides that intersect to form a vertex.

$\overline{AB}$ and $\overline{BC}$ are **adjacent sides**. They meet at vertex B.

alternate exterior angles
ángulos alternos externos
(54)

A special pair of angles formed when a transversal intersects two lines. Alternate exterior angles lie on opposite sides of the transversal and are outside the lines.

$\angle 1$ and $\angle 2$ are **alternate exterior angles**. When a transversal intersects parallel lines, as in this figure, **alternate exterior angles** have the same measure.

alternate interior angles
ángulos alternos internos
(54)

A special pair of angles formed when a transversal intersects two lines. Alternate interior angles lie on opposite sides of the transversal and are between the lines.

$\angle 1$ and $\angle 2$ are **alternate interior angles**. When a transversal intersects parallel lines, as in this figure, **alternate interior angles** have the same measure.

altitude
altura
(1)

The perpendicular distance from the base of a triangle to the opposite vertex. See also **height**.

altitude

---

angle
ángulo
(18)

Two rays with the same endpoint. The endpoint of the rays is the vertex of the angle.

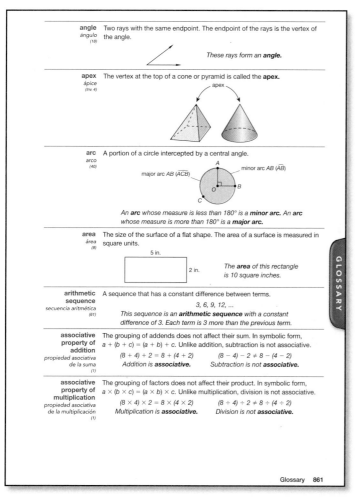

These rays form an **angle**.

apex
ápice
(Inv. 4)

The vertex at the top of a cone or pyramid is called the **apex**.

apex

arc
arco
(40)

A portion of a circle intercepted by a central angle.

major arc AB ($\overset{\frown}{ACB}$)   minor arc AB ($\overset{\frown}{AB}$)

An **arc** whose measure is less than 180° is a **minor arc**. An **arc** whose measure is more than 180° is a **major arc**.

area
área
(8)

The size of the surface of a flat shape. The area of a surface is measured in square units.

5 in.

2 in.

The **area** of this rectangle is 10 square inches.

arithmetic sequence
secuencia aritmética
(61)

A sequence that has a constant difference between terms.

3, 6, 9, 12, ...

This sequence is an **arithmetic sequence** with a constant difference of 3. Each term is 3 more than the previous term.

associative property of addition
propiedad asociativa de la suma
(1)

The grouping of addends does not affect their sum. In symbolic form, $a + (b + c) = (a + b) + c$. Unlike addition, subtraction is not associative.

$(8 + 4) + 2 = 8 + (4 + 2)$ $(8 - 4) - 2 \neq 8 - (4 - 2)$
Addition is **associative**.   Subtraction is not **associative**.

associative property of multiplication
propiedad asociativa de la multiplicación
(1)

The grouping of factors does not affect their product. In symbolic form, $a \times (b \times c) = (a \times b) \times c$. Unlike multiplication, division is not associative.

$(8 \times 4) \times 2 = 8 \times (4 \times 2)$ $(8 \div 4) \div 2 \neq 8 \div (4 \div 2)$
Multiplication is **associative**.   Division is not **associative**.

---

average
promedio
(7)

The number found by dividing the sum of the elements of a set by the number of elements; one of several measures of central tendency, also called *mean*.

To find the **average** of the numbers 5, 6, and 10, add.
$5 + 6 + 10 = 21$
There were three addends, so divide the sum by 3.
$21 \div 3 = 7$
The **average** of 5, 6, and 10 is 7.

B

base
base
(20)

1. A designated side (or face) of a geometric figure.

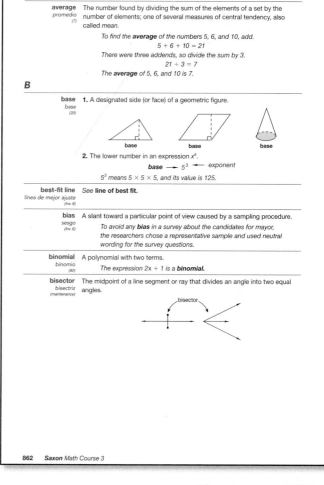

base   base   base

2. The lower number in an expression x^a.

base $\longrightarrow 5^3 \longleftarrow$ exponent

5^3 means $5 \times 5 \times 5$, and its value is 125.

best-fit line
línea de mejor ajuste
(Inv. 8)

See **line of best fit**.

bias
sesgo
(Inv. 6)

A slant toward a particular point of view caused by a sampling procedure.

To avoid any **bias** in a survey about the candidates for mayor, the researchers chose a representative sample and used neutral wording for the survey questions.

binomial
binomio
(80)

A polynomial with two terms.

The expression $2x + 1$ is a **binomial**.

bisector
bisectriz
(maintenance)

The midpoint of a line segment or ray that divides an angle into two equal angles.

bisector

box-and-whisker plot *gráfica de frecuencias acumuladas* (103)	A graph that displays the median, quartiles, and extremes of a set of data. The quantities are the three numbers that divide the set of data into quarters.

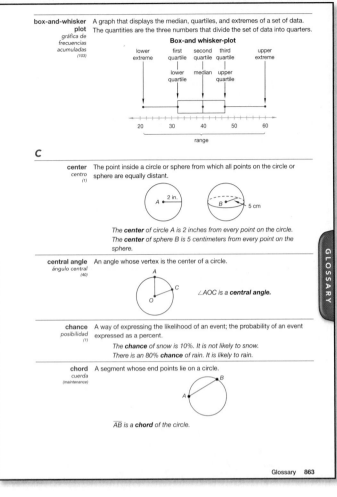

C

center *centro* (1)	The point inside a circle or sphere from which all points on the circle or sphere are equally distant.

The **center** of circle A is 2 inches from every point on the circle. The **center** of sphere B is 5 centimeters from every point on the sphere.

central angle *ángulo central* (40)	An angle whose vertex is the center of a circle.

∠AOC is a **central angle**.

chance *posibilidad* (1)	A way of expressing the likelihood of an event; the probability of an event expressed as a percent.

The **chance** of snow is 10%. It is not likely to snow.
There is an 80% **chance** of rain. It is likely to rain.

chord *cuerda* (maintenance)	A segment whose end points lie on a circle.

$\overline{AB}$ is a **chord** of the circle.

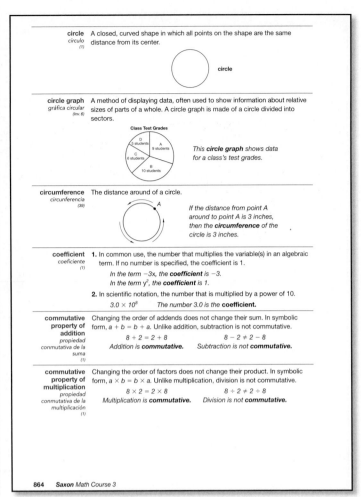

circle *círculo* (1)	A closed, curved shape in which all points on the shape are the same distance from its center.

circle

circle graph *gráfica circular* (Inv. 6)	A method of displaying data, often used to show information about relative sizes of parts of a whole. A circle graph is made of a circle divided into sectors.

Class Test Grades
D 5 students
A 9 students
C 6 students
B 10 students

This **circle graph** shows data for a class's test grades.

circumference *circunferencia* (39)	The distance around a circle.

If the distance from point A around to point A is 3 inches, then the **circumference** of the circle is 3 inches.

coefficient *coeficiente* (1)	1. In common use, the number that multiplies the variable(s) in an algebraic term. If no number is specified, the coefficient is 1. In the term $-3x$, the **coefficient** is -3. In the term y^2, the **coefficient** is 1. 2. In scientific notation, the number that is multiplied by a power of 10. 3.0×10^8 The number 3.0 is the **coefficient**.

commutative property of addition *propiedad conmutativa de la suma* (1)	Changing the order of addends does not change their sum. In symbolic form, $a + b = b + a$. Unlike addition, subtraction is not commutative. $8 + 2 = 2 + 8$ $8 - 2 \neq 2 - 8$ Addition is **commutative**. Subtraction is not **commutative**.

commutative property of multiplication *propiedad conmutativa de la multiplicación* (1)	Changing the order of factors does not change their product. In symbolic form, $a \times b = b \times a$. Unlike multiplication, division is not commutative. $8 \times 2 = 2 \times 8$ $8 \div 2 \neq 2 \div 8$ Multiplication is **commutative**. Division is not **commutative**.

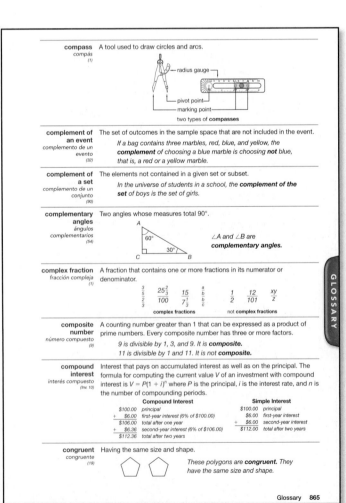

compass *compás* (1)	A tool used to draw circles and arcs.

radius gauge
pivot point
marking point
two types of **compasses**

complement of an event *complemento de un evento* (32)	The set of outcomes in the sample space that are not included in the event. If a bag contains three marbles, red, blue, and yellow, the **complement** of choosing a blue marble is choosing **not** blue, that is, a red or a yellow marble.

complement of a set *complemento de un conjunto* (90)	The elements not contained in a given set or subset. In the universe of students in a school, the **complement of the set** of boys is the set of girls.

complementary angles *ángulos complementarios* (54)	Two angles whose measures total 90°.

∠A and ∠B are **complementary angles**.

complex fraction *fracción compleja* (1)	A fraction that contains one or more fractions in its numerator or denominator. $\dfrac{\frac{3}{5}}{\frac{2}{3}}$ $\dfrac{25\frac{2}{3}}{100}$ $\dfrac{15}{7\frac{1}{3}}$ $\dfrac{\frac{a}{b}}{\frac{b}{c}}$ $\dfrac{1}{2}$ $\dfrac{12}{101}$ $\dfrac{xy}{z}$ **complex fractions** not complex fractions

composite number *número compuesto* (9)	A counting number greater than 1 that can be expressed as a product of prime numbers. Every composite number has three or more factors. 9 is divisible by 1, 3, and 9. It is **composite**. 11 is divisible by 1 and 11. It is not **composite**.

compound interest *interés compuesto* (Inv. 10)	Interest that pays on accumulated interest as well as on the principal. The formula for computing the current value V of an investment with compound interest is $V = P(1 + i)^n$ where P is the principal, i is the interest rate, and n is the number of compounding periods.

Compound Interest		Simple Interest	
$100.00	principal	$100.00	principal
+ $6.00	first-year interest (6% of $100.00)	$6.00	first-year interest
$106.00	total after one year	+ $6.00	second-year interest
+ $6.36	second-year interest (6% of $106.00)	$112.00	total after two years
$112.36	total after two years		

congruent *congruente* (19)	Having the same size and shape.

These polygons are **congruent**. They have the same size and shape.

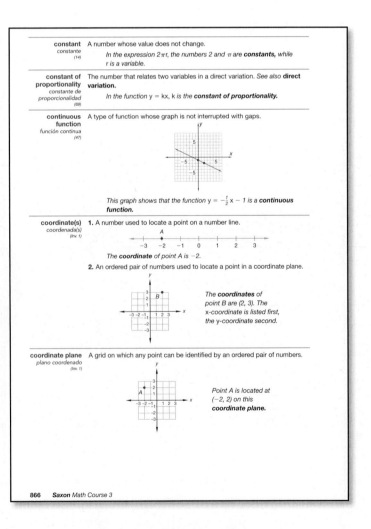

constant *constante* (14)	A number whose value does not change. In the expression $2\pi r$, the numbers 2 and π are **constants**, while r is a variable.

constant of proportionality *constante de proporcionalidad* (69)	The number that relates two variables in a direct variation. *See also* **direct variation.** In the function $y = kx$, k is the **constant of proportionality**.

continuous function *función continua* (47)	A type of function whose graph is not interrupted with gaps.

This graph shows that the function $y = -\frac{1}{2}x - 1$ is a **continuous function**.

coordinate(s) *coordenada(s)* (Inv. 1)	1. A number used to locate a point on a number line.

The **coordinate** of point A is -2.

2. An ordered pair of numbers used to locate a point in a coordinate plane.

The **coordinates** of point B are (2, 3). The x-coordinate is listed first, the y-coordinate second.

coordinate plane *plano coordenado* (Inv. 1)	A grid on which any point can be identified by an ordered pair of numbers.

Point A is located at $(-2, 2)$ on this **coordinate plane**.

Term	Definition

correlation
correlación
(Inv. 8)

A measure of the degree of relationship between two variables.

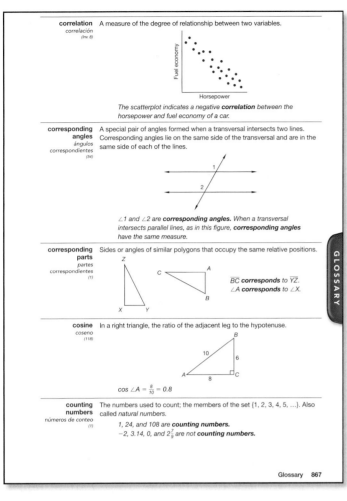

*The scatterplot indicates a negative **correlation** between the horsepower and fuel economy of a car.*

corresponding angles
ángulos correspondientes
(54)

A special pair of angles formed when a transversal intersects two lines. Corresponding angles lie on the same side of the transversal and are in the same side of each of the lines.

∠1 and ∠2 are **corresponding angles**. When a transversal intersects parallel lines, as in this figure, **corresponding angles** have the same measure.

corresponding parts
partes correspondientes
(1)

Sides or angles of similar polygons that occupy the same relative positions.

$\overline{BC}$ corresponds to $\overline{YZ}$.
∠A corresponds to ∠X.

cosine
coseno
(118)

In a right triangle, the ratio of the adjacent leg to the hypotenuse.

$\cos \angle A = \frac{8}{10} = 0.8$

counting numbers
números de conteo
(1)

The numbers used to count; the members of the set {1, 2, 3, 4, 5, …}. Also called *natural numbers*.

1, 24, and 108 are **counting numbers.**
−2, 3.14, 0, and $2\frac{2}{9}$ are not **counting numbers.**

---

cross products
productos cruzados
(44)

The product of the numerator of one fraction and the denominator of another.

$5 \times 16 = 80$ $20 \times 4 = 80$

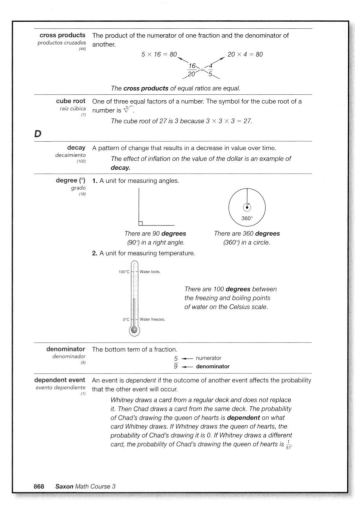

*The **cross products** of equal ratios are equal.*

cube root
raíz cúbica
(1)

One of three equal factors of a number. The symbol for the cube root of a number is $\sqrt[3]{}$.

The cube root of 27 is 3 because $3 \times 3 \times 3 = 27$.

D

decay
decaimiento
(102)

A pattern of change that results in a decrease in value over time.

*The effect of inflation on the value of the dollar is an example of **decay**.*

degree (°)
grado
(18)

1. A unit for measuring angles.

*There are 90 **degrees** (90°) in a right angle.*   *There are 360 **degrees** (360°) in a circle.*

2. A unit for measuring temperature.

*There are 100 **degrees** between the freezing and boiling points of water on the Celsius scale.*

denominator
denominador
(5)

The bottom term of a fraction.

$\frac{5}{9}$ ← numerator
      ← **denominator**

dependent event
evento dependiente
(1)

An event is *dependent* if the outcome of another event affects the probability that that other event will occur.

*Whitney draws a card from a regular deck and does not replace it. Then Chad draws a card from the same deck. The probability of Chad's drawing the queen of hearts is **dependent** on what card Whitney draws. If Whitney draws the queen of hearts, the probability of Chad's drawing it is 0. If Whitney draws a different card, the probability of Chad's drawing the queen of hearts is $\frac{1}{51}$.*

---

dependent variable
variable dependiente
(69)

The variable in an equation whose value is determined by the value chosen for one or more other variables. *See also **independent variable.***

*In $y = 2x + 1$, the **dependent variable** is y.*

diagonal
diagonal
(1)

A line segment, other than a side, that connects two vertices of a polygon.

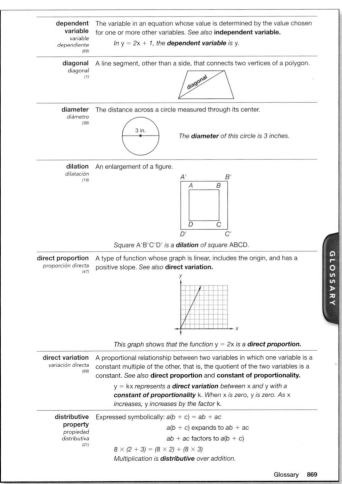

diameter
diámetro
(39)

The distance across a circle measured through its center.

*The **diameter** of this circle is 3 inches.*

dilation
dilatación
(19)

An enlargement of a figure.

*Square A′B′C′D′ is a **dilation** of square ABCD.*

direct proportion
proporción directa
(47)

A type of function whose graph is linear, includes the origin, and has a positive slope. *See also **direct variation.***

*This graph shows that the function $y = 2x$ is a **direct proportion**.*

direct variation
variación directa
(69)

A proportional relationship between two variables in which one variable is a constant multiple of the other, that is, the quotient of the two variables is a constant. *See also **direct proportion** and **constant of proportionality.***

*$y = kx$ represents a **direct variation** between x and y with a **constant of proportionality** k. When x is zero, y is zero. As x increases, y increases by the factor k.*

distributive property
propiedad distributiva
(21)

Expressed symbolically: $a(b + c) = ab + ac$

$a(b + c)$ expands to $ab + ac$
$ab + ac$ factors to $a(b + c)$
$8 \times (2 + 3) = (8 \times 2) + (8 \times 3)$
*Multiplication is **distributive** over addition.*

---

divisible
divisible
(9)

Able to be divided by a counting number without a remainder.

$4\overline{)20}$ gives 5 — *The number 20 is **divisible** by 4, since $20 \div 4$ has no remainder.*

$3\overline{)20}$ gives 6 R 2 — *The number 20 is not **divisible** by 3, since $20 \div 3$ has a remainder.*

domain
dominio
(47)

The set of inputs of a function.

*In the function $y = 3x$, the values of x are the **domain**.*

E

edge
arista
(Inv. 4)

A line segment formed where two faces of a polyhedron intersect.

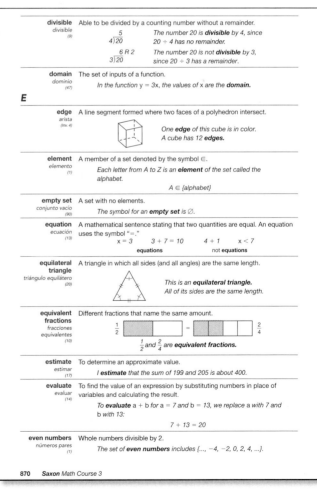

*One **edge** of this cube is in color. A cube has 12 **edges**.*

element
elemento
(1)

A member of a set denoted by the symbol ∈.

*Each letter from A to Z is an **element** of the set called the alphabet.*

$A \in \{alphabet\}$

empty set
conjunto vacío
(90)

A set with no elements.

*The symbol for an **empty set** is ∅.*

equation
ecuación
(13)

A mathematical sentence stating that two quantities are equal. An equation uses the symbol "=."

$x = 3$ $3 + 7 = 10$ $4 + 1$ $x < 7$
equations   not **equations**

equilateral triangle
triángulo equilátero
(20)

A triangle in which all sides (and all angles) are the same length.

*This is an **equilateral triangle**. All of its sides are the same length.*

equivalent fractions
fracciones equivalentes
(10)

Different fractions that name the same amount.

$\frac{1}{2}$ = $\frac{2}{4}$

$\frac{1}{2}$ and $\frac{2}{4}$ are **equivalent fractions.**

estimate
estimar
(17)

To determine an approximate value.

*I **estimate** that the sum of 199 and 205 is about 400.*

evaluate
evaluar
(14)

To find the value of an expression by substituting numbers in place of variables and calculating the result.

*To **evaluate** $a + b$ for $a = 7$ and $b = 13$, we replace a with 7 and b with 13:*

$7 + 13 = 20$

even numbers
números pares
(1)

Whole numbers divisible by 2.

*The set of **even numbers** includes {…, −4, −2, 0, 2, 4, …}.*

experimental probability *probabilidad experimental* (32)	Probability of an outcome that is determined statistically. Experimental probability is the ratio of the number of times an event occurs to the number of trials. *If you toss heads 7 times out of 10 tosses, the **experimental probability** of tossing heads again is $\frac{7}{10}$.*
exponent *exponente* (1)	The upper number in an expression x^a. If the exponent is a counting number, it indicates how many times the base is to be used as a factor. base → 5^3 ←**exponent** 5^3 *means* $5 \times 5 \times 5$, *and its value is 125.*
exterior angle *ángulo externo* (maintenance)	In a polygon, the supplementary angle of an interior angle. 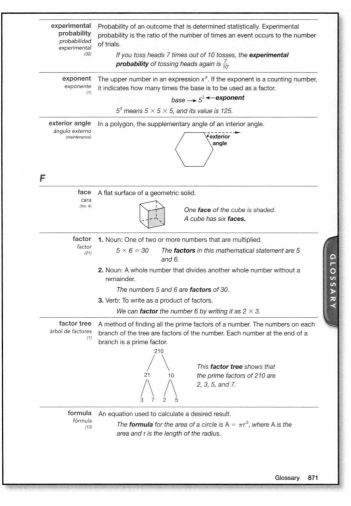

F

face *cara* (Inv. 4)	A flat surface of a geometric solid. *One **face** of the cube is shaded.* *A cube has six **faces**.*
factor *factor* (21)	**1.** Noun: One of two or more numbers that are multiplied. $5 \times 6 = 30$ *The **factors** in this mathematical statement are 5 and 6.* **2.** Noun: A whole number that divides another whole number without a remainder. *The numbers 5 and 6 are **factors** of 30.* **3.** Verb: To write as a product of factors. *We can **factor** the number 6 by writing it as* 2×3.
factor tree *árbol de factores* (1)	A method of finding all the prime factors of a number. The numbers on each branch of the tree are factors of the number. Each number at the end of a branch is a prime factor. *This **factor tree** shows that the prime factors of 210 are 2, 3, 5, and 7.*
formula *fórmula* (13)	An equation used to calculate a desired result. *The **formula** for the area of a circle is* $A = \pi r^2$, *where A is the area and r is the length of the radius.*

Glossary   871

---

fraction *fracción* (1)	A number that names part of a whole. 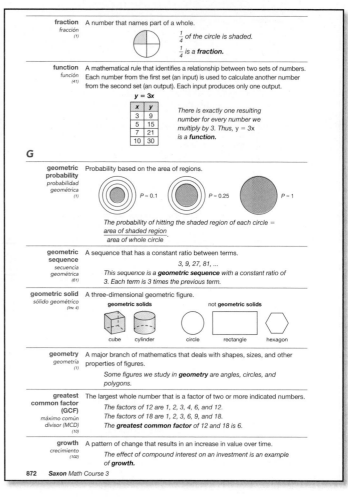 $\frac{1}{4}$ *of the circle is shaded.* $\frac{1}{4}$ *is a **fraction**.*
function *función* (41)	A mathematical rule that identifies a relationship between two sets of numbers. Each number from the first set (an input) is used to calculate another number from the second set (an output). Each input produces only one output. 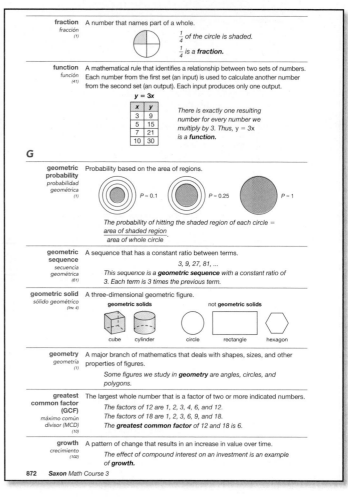

G

geometric probability *probabilidad geométrica* (1)	Probability based on the area of regions. 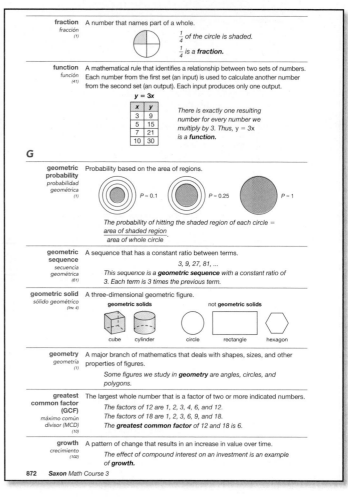 *The probability of hitting the shaded region of each circle =* $\dfrac{\text{area of shaded region}}{\text{area of whole circle}}$
geometric sequence *secuencia geométrica* (61)	A sequence that has a constant ratio between terms. 3, 9, 27, 81, ... *This sequence is a **geometric sequence** with a constant ratio of 3. Each term is 3 times the previous term.*
geometric solid *sólido geométrico* (Inv. 4)	A three-dimensional geometric figure. 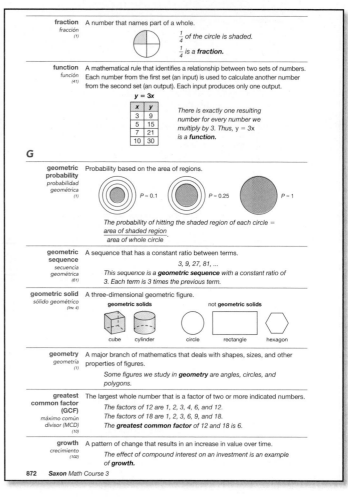
geometry *geometría* (1)	A major branch of mathematics that deals with shapes, sizes, and other properties of figures. *Some figures we study in **geometry** are angles, circles, and polygons.*
greatest common factor (GCF) *máximo común divisor (MCD)* (10)	The largest whole number that is a factor of two or more indicated numbers. *The factors of 12 are 1, 2, 3, 4, 6, and 12.* *The factors of 18 are 1, 2, 3, 6, 9, and 18.* *The **greatest common factor** of 12 and 18 is 6.*
growth *crecimiento* (102)	A pattern of change that results in an increase in value over time. *The effect of compound interest on an investment is an example of **growth**.*

872   *Saxon Math Course 3*

H

height *altura* (20)	The perpendicular distance from the base to the opposite side of a parallelogram or trapezoid; from the base to the opposite face of a prism or cylinder; or from the base to the opposite vertex of a triangle, pyramid, or cone. *See also **altitude**.* 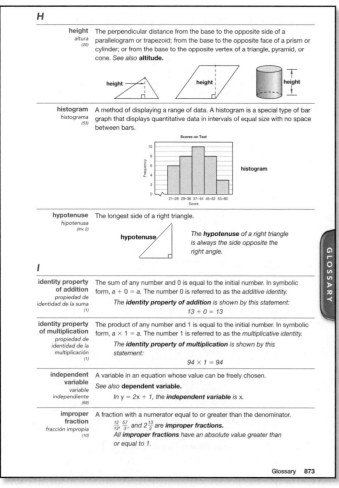
histogram *histograma* (53)	A method of displaying a range of data. A histogram is a special type of bar graph that displays quantitative data in intervals of equal size with no space between bars. 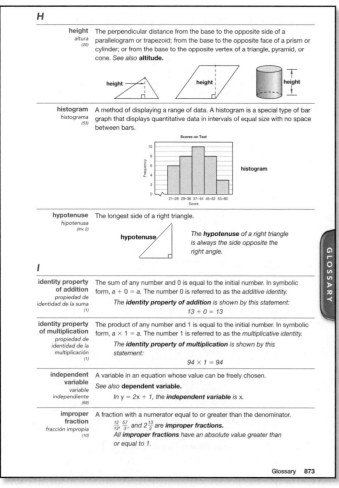
hypotenuse *hipotenusa* (Inv. 2)	The longest side of a right triangle. 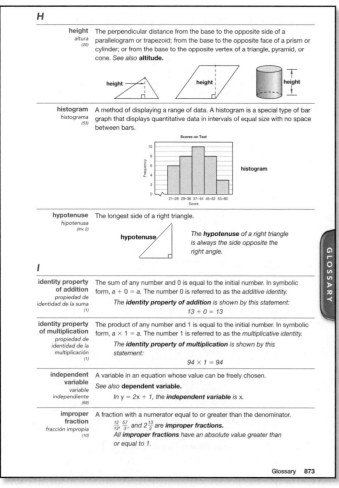 *The **hypotenuse** of a right triangle is always the side opposite the right angle.*

I

identity property of addition *propiedad de identidad de la suma* (1)	The sum of any number and 0 is equal to the initial number. In symbolic form, $a + 0 = a$. The number 0 is referred to as the *additive identity*. *The **identity property of addition** is shown by this statement:* $13 + 0 = 13$
identity property of multiplication *propiedad de identidad de la multiplicación* (1)	The product of any number and 1 is equal to the initial number. In symbolic form, $a \times 1 = a$. The number 1 is referred to as the *multiplicative identity*. *The **identity property of multiplication** is shown by this statement:* $94 \times 1 = 94$
independent variable *variable independiente* (69)	A variable in an equation whose value can be freely chosen. *See also **dependent variable**.* *In* $y = 2x + 1$, *the **independent variable** is x.*
improper fraction *fracción impropia* (10)	A fraction with a numerator equal to or greater than the denominator. $\frac{12}{12}, \frac{57}{3}$, *and* $2\frac{13}{2}$ *are **improper fractions**.* *All **improper fractions** have an absolute value greater than or equal to 1.*

Glossary   873

---

independent events *eventos independientes* (1)	Two events are *independent* if the outcome of one event does not affect the probability that the other event will occur. *If a number cube is rolled twice, the outcome of the first roll does not affect the probability of any outcome on the second roll. The first and second rolls are **independent events**.*
index *índice* (1)	A number associated with a radical sign that indicates a root of a number. *The small 5 in* $\sqrt[5]{32}$ *is the **index** of the root.* $\sqrt[5]{32}$ *means the fifth root of 32, which equals 2.*
indirect measure *medida indirecta* (65)	A measurement technique that uses a proportional relationship between given measures to calculate an unknown measure. ***Indirect measurement** is used when an object or distance cannot be measured with a measurement tool such as a ruler. For example, we can use an **indirect measure** to find the height of a flag pole or the distance across a lake.*
inequalities *desigualdades* (62)	A mathematical statement that has $<$, $>$, $\le$, or $\ge$ as a symbol of comparison. $x \le 4$ $2 < 7$ $x = 2$ $9 + 10$ **inequalities** not **inequalities**
inscribed *inscrito* (maintenance)	In geometry, one figure drawn within another figure; an angle with its vertex on a circle and with sides that are chords. 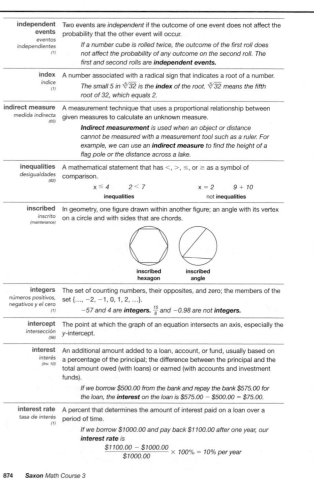 inscribed hexagon inscribed angle
integers *números positivos, negativos y el cero* (1)	The set of counting numbers, their opposites, and zero; the members of the set $\{..., -2, -1, 0, 1, 2, ...\}$. -57 *and 4 are **integers**.* $\frac{15}{8}$ *and* -0.98 *are not **integers**.*
intercept *intersección* (56)	The point at which the graph of an equation intersects an axis, especially the y-intercept.
interest *interés* (Inv. 10)	An additional amount added to a loan, account, or fund, usually based on a percentage of the principal; the difference between the principal and the total amount owed (with loans) or earned (with accounts and investment funds). *If we borrow $500.00 from the bank and repay the bank $575.00 for the loan, the **interest** on the loan is* $\$575.00 - \$500.00 = \$75.00$.
interest rate *tasa de interés* (1)	A percent that determines the amount of interest paid on a loan over a period of time. *If we borrow $1000.00 and pay back $1100.00 after one year, our **interest rate** is* $\dfrac{\$1100.00 - \$1000.00}{\$1000.00} \times 100\% = 10\%$ *per year*

874   *Saxon Math Course 3*

interior angle *ángulo interno* *(maintenance)*	An angle that opens to the inside of a polygon.

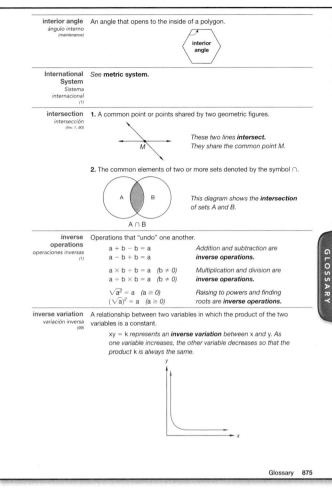

International System *Sistema internacional* *(1)*	See **metric system.**
intersection *intersección* *(Inv. 1, 90)*	1. A common point or points shared by two geometric figures.

These two lines **intersect.**
They share the common point M.

2. The common elements of two or more sets denoted by the symbol ∩.

This diagram shows the **intersection**
of sets A and B.

A ∩ B

inverse operations *operaciones inversas* *(1)*	Operations that "undo" one another.

$a + b - b = a$ Addition and subtraction are
$a - b + b = a$ **inverse operations.**

$a \times b \div b = a$ $(b \neq 0)$ Multiplication and division are
$a \div b \times b = a$ $(b \neq 0)$ **inverse operations.**

$\sqrt{a^2} = a$ $(a \geq 0)$ Raising to powers and finding
$(\sqrt{a})^2 = a$ $(a \geq 0)$ roots are **inverse operations.**

inverse variation *variación inversa* *(99)*	A relationship between two variables in which the product of the two variables is a constant.

$xy = k$ represents an **inverse variation** between x and y. As one variable increases, the other variable decreases so that the product k is always the same.

irrational numbers *números irracionales* *(16)*	Numbers that cannot be expressed as a ratio of two integers. Their decimal expansions are nonending and nonrepeating. π and $\sqrt{3}$ are **irrational numbers.**
isosceles triangle *triángulo isósceles* *(20)*	A triangle with at least two sides of equal length. At least two angles of an isosceles triangle are also equal.

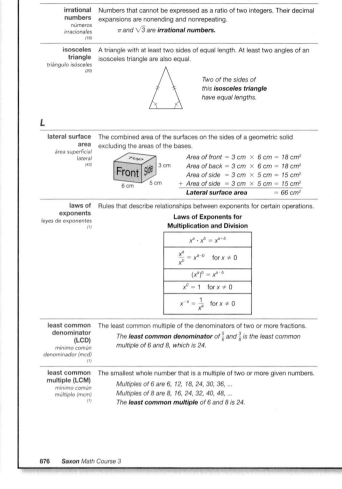

Two of the sides of
this **isosceles triangle**
have equal lengths.

lateral surface area *área superficial lateral* *(43)*	The combined area of the surfaces on the sides of a geometric solid excluding the areas of the bases.

Area of front = 3 cm × 6 cm = 18 cm²
Area of back = 3 cm × 6 cm = 18 cm²
Area of side = 3 cm × 5 cm = 15 cm²
+ Area of side = 3 cm × 5 cm = 15 cm²
Lateral surface area   = 66 cm²

laws of exponents *leyes de exponentes* *(1)*	Rules that describe relationships between exponents for certain operations.

Laws of Exponents for Multiplication and Division

$x^a \cdot x^b = x^{a+b}$
$\dfrac{x^a}{x^b} = x^{a-b}$ for $x \neq 0$
$(x^a)^b = x^{a \cdot b}$
$x^0 = 1$ for $x \neq 0$
$x^{-a} = \dfrac{1}{x^a}$ for $x \neq 0$

least common denominator (LCD) *mínimo común denominador (mcd)* *(1)*	The least common multiple of the denominators of two or more fractions. The **least common denominator** of $\frac{5}{6}$ and $\frac{3}{8}$ is the least common multiple of 6 and 8, which is 24.
least common multiple (LCM) *mínimo común múltiplo (mcm)* *(1)*	The smallest whole number that is a multiple of two or more given numbers. Multiples of 6 are 6, 12, 18, 24, 30, 36, ... Multiples of 8 are 8, 16, 24, 32, 40, 48, ... The **least common multiple** of 6 and 8 is 24.

legs *catetos* *(Inv. 2)*	The two shorter sides of a right triangle that form a 90° angle at their intersection.

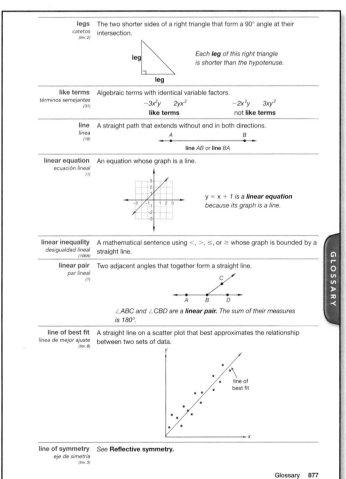

Each **leg** of this right triangle
is shorter than the hypotenuse.

like terms *términos semejantes* *(31)*	Algebraic terms with identical variable factors.

$-3x^2y$ $2yx^2$ $-2x^2y$ $3xy^2$
like terms   not **like terms**

line *línea* *(18)*	A straight path that extends without end in both directions.

A   B
line AB or **line BA**

linear equation *ecuación lineal* *(1)*	An equation whose graph is a line.

$y = x + 1$ is a **linear equation**
because its graph is a line.

linear inequality *desigualdad lineal* *(106A)*	A mathematical sentence using <, >, ≤, or ≥ whose graph is bounded by a straight line.
linear pair *par lineal* *(1)*	Two adjacent angles that together form a straight line.

∠ABC and ∠CBD are a **linear pair.** The sum of their measures
is 180°.

line of best fit *línea de mejor ajuste* *(Inv. 8)*	A straight line on a scatter plot that best approximates the relationship between two sets of data.

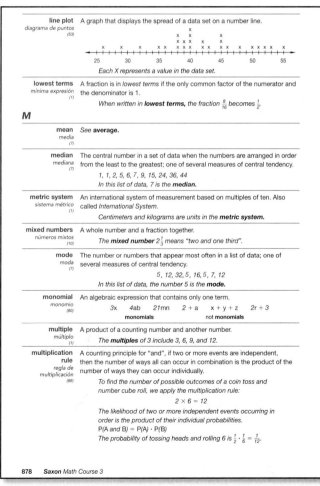

line of
best fit

line of symmetry *eje de simetría* *(Inv. 3)*	See **Reflective symmetry.**

line plot *diagrama de puntos* *(53)*	A graph that displays the spread of a data set on a number line.

Each X represents a value in the data set.

lowest terms *mínima expresión* *(1)*	A fraction is in *lowest terms* if the only common factor of the numerator and the denominator is 1. When written in **lowest terms**, the fraction $\frac{8}{16}$ becomes $\frac{1}{2}$.
mean *media* *(7)*	See **average.**
median *mediana* *(7)*	The central number in a set of data when the numbers are arranged in order from the least to the greatest; one of several measures of central tendency. 1, 1, 2, 5, 6, 7, 9, 15, 24, 36, 44 In this list of data, 7 is the **median.**
metric system *sistema métrico* *(1)*	An international system of measurement based on multiples of ten. Also called *International System.* Centimeters and kilograms are units in the **metric system.**
mixed numbers *números mixtos* *(10)*	A whole number and a fraction together. The **mixed number** $2\frac{1}{3}$ means "two and one third".
mode *moda* *(7)*	The number or numbers that appear most often in a list of data; one of several measures of central tendency. 5, 12, 32, 5, 16, 5, 7, 12 In this list of data, the number 5 is the **mode.**
monomial *monomio* *(80)*	An algebraic expression that contains only one term. $3x$ $4ab$ $21mn$ $2 + a$ $x + y + z$ $2r + 3$ **monomials** not **monomials**
multiple *múltiplo* *(1)*	A product of a counting number and another number. The **multiples** of 3 include 3, 6, 9, and 12.
multiplication rule *regla de multiplicación* *(68)*	A counting principle for "and"; if two or more events are independent, then the number of ways all can occur in combination is the product of the number of ways they can occur individually.

To find the number of possible outcomes of a coin toss and number cube roll, we apply the multiplication rule:

$2 \times 6 = 12$

The likelihood of two or more independent events occurring in order is the product of their individual probabilities.
P(A and B) = P(A) · P(B)
The probability of tossing heads and rolling 6 is $\frac{1}{2} \cdot \frac{1}{6} = \frac{1}{12}$.

multiplicative identity *identidad multiplicativa* (1)	The number 1. *See also* **identity property of multiplication.** $$-2 \times 1 = -2$$ multiplicative identity The number 1 is called the **multiplicative identity** because multiplying any number by 1 does not change the number.
multiplicative inverse *inverso multiplicativo* (22)	*See* **reciprocal.**

N

natural numbers *números naturales* (1)	*See* **counting numbers.**
net *malla* (1)	A two-dimensional image of the surfaces of a solid. 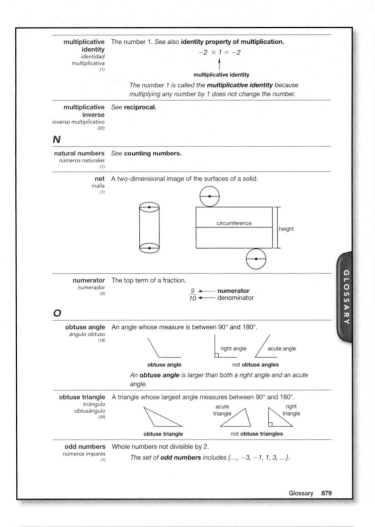
numerator *numerador* (5)	The top term of a fraction. $\dfrac{9}{10}$ ← **numerator** ← **denominator**

O

obtuse angle *ángulo obtuso* (18)	An angle whose measure is between 90° and 180°. right angle acute angle obtuse angle not **obtuse angles** An **obtuse angle** is larger than both a right angle and an acute angle.
obtuse triangle *triángulo obtusángulo* (20)	A triangle whose largest angle measures between 90° and 180°. acute triangle right triangle obtuse triangle not **obtuse triangles**
odd numbers *números impares* (1)	Whole numbers not divisible by 2. The set of **odd numbers** includes {..., −3, −1, 1, 3, ...}.

Glossary   879

odds *posibilidad* (32)	A way of describing the likelihood of an event; the ratio of favorable outcomes to unfavorable outcomes. If you roll a number cube, the **odds** of getting a 3 are 1 to 5, or 1:5.
opinion survey *operaciones aritméticas* (Inv. 6)	A survey in a free-response format without predetermined choices. An **opinion survey** about food preferences might ask, "What is your favorite food?"
opposite angles *ángulos opuestos* (54)	*See* **vertical angles.**
opposites *opuestos* (1)	Two numbers whose sum is zero; a positive number and a negative number whose absolute values are equal. $$(-3) + (+3) = 0$$ The numbers +3 and −3 are **opposites.**
origin *origen* (1)	1. The location of the number 0 on a number line. 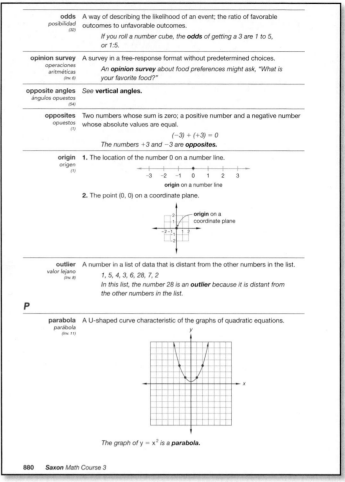 **origin** on a number line 2. The point (0, 0) on a coordinate plane. **origin** on a coordinate plane
outlier *valor lejano* (Inv. 8)	A number in a list of data that is distant from the other numbers in the list. 1, 5, 4, 3, 6, 28, 7, 2 In this list, the number 28 is an **outlier** because it is distant from the other numbers in the list.

P

parabola *parábola* (Inv. 11)	A U-shaped curve characteristic of the graphs of quadratic equations. The graph of y = x² is a **parabola.**

880   *Saxon* Math Course 3

parallel lines *líneas paralelas* (18)	Lines in the same plane that do not intersect. Parallel lines remain the same distance apart. **parallel lines**
parallelogram *paralelogramo* (Inv. 3)	A quadrilateral that has two pairs of parallel sides. **parallelograms** not a **parallelogram**
percent *por ciento* (1)	A fraction whose denominator of 100 is expressed as a percent sign (%). $\dfrac{99}{100} = 99\% = 99$ **percent**
perfect square *cuadrado perfecto* (15)	Commonly used for a number that is a square of a counting number. The number 9 is a **perfect square** because 9 = 3².
perimeter *perímetro* (8)	The distance around a closed, flat shape. 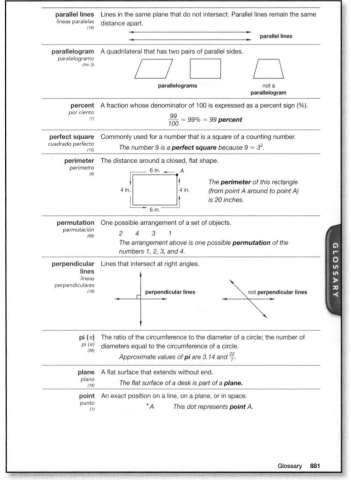 The **perimeter** of this rectangle (from point A around to point A) is 20 inches.
permutation *permutación* (68)	One possible arrangement of a set of objects. 2 4 3 1 The arrangement above is one possible **permutation** of the numbers 1, 2, 3, and 4.
perpendicular lines *líneas perpendiculares* (18)	Lines that intersect at right angles. **perpendicular lines** not **perpendicular lines**
pi (π) *pi (π)* (39)	The ratio of the circumference to the diameter of a circle; the number of diameters equal to the circumference of a circle. Approximate values of **pi** are 3.14 and $\frac{22}{7}$.
plane *plano* (18)	A flat surface that extends without end. The flat surface of a desk is part of a **plane.**
point *punto* (1)	An exact position on a line, on a plane, or in space. •A This dot represents **point** A.

Glossary   881

polygon *polígono* (19)	A closed, plane figure with straight sides. 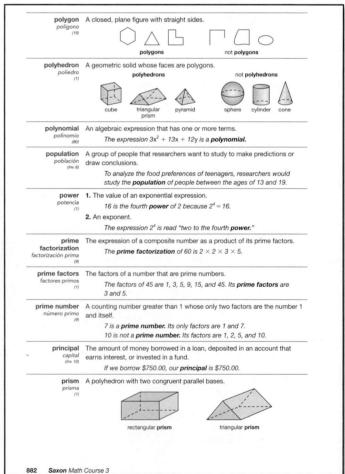 **polygons** not **polygons**
polyhedron *poliedro* (1)	A geometric solid whose faces are polygons. **polyhedrons** cube triangular prism pyramid not **polyhedrons** sphere cylinder cone
polynomial *polinomio* (80)	An algebraic expression that has one or more terms. The expression 3x² + 13x + 12y is a **polynomial.**
population *población* (Inv. 6)	A group of people that researchers want to study to make predictions or draw conclusions. To analyze the food preferences of teenagers, researchers would study the **population** of people between the ages of 13 and 19.
power *potencia* (1)	1. The value of an exponential expression. 16 is the fourth **power** of 2 because 2⁴ = 16. 2. An exponent. The expression 2⁴ is read "two to the fourth **power.**"
prime factorization *factorización prima* (9)	The expression of a composite number as a product of its prime factors. The **prime factorization** of 60 is 2 × 2 × 3 × 5.
prime factors *factores primos* (1)	The factors of a number that are prime numbers. The factors of 45 are 1, 3, 5, 9, 15, and 45. Its **prime factors** are 3 and 5.
prime number *número primo* (9)	A counting number greater than 1 whose only two factors are the number 1 and itself. 7 is a **prime number.** Its only factors are 1 and 7. 10 is not a **prime number.** Its factors are 1, 2, 5, and 10.
principal *capital* (Inv. 10)	The amount of money borrowed in a loan, deposited in an account that earns interest, or invested in a fund. If we borrow $750.00, our **principal** is $750.00.
prism *prisma* (1)	A polyhedron with two congruent parallel bases. rectangular **prism** triangular **prism**

882   *Saxon* Math Course 3

T864   *Saxon* Math Course 3

probability probabilidad (32)	The likelihood that a particular event will occur. *See also* **theoretical probability** and **experimental probability.** *The **probability** of rolling a 3 with a standard number cube is $\frac{1}{6}$.*
proof prueba (Inv. 12)	A method that uses logical steps to describe how certain given information can lead to a certain conclusion. *For an example of a **proof**, please see the **proof** of the Pythagorean theorem in Investigation 12.*
proportion proporción (34)	A statement that two ratios are equal. $$\frac{6}{10} = \frac{9}{15}$$ *These two ratios are equal, so this is a **proportion.***
protractor transportador (1)	A tool that is used to measure and draw angles. 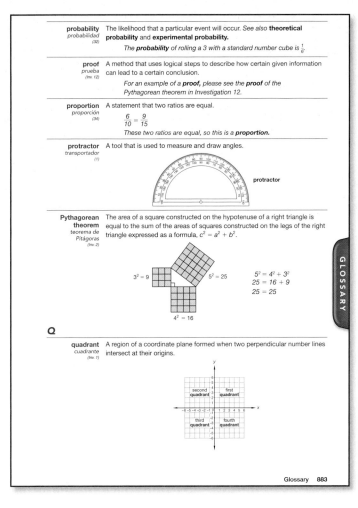 protractor
Pythagorean theorem teorema de Pitágoras (Inv. 2)	The area of a square constructed on the hypotenuse of a right triangle is equal to the sum of the areas of squares constructed on the legs of the right triangle expressed as a formula, $c^2 = a^2 + b^2$. $3^2 = 9$ $5^2 = 25$ $5^2 = 4^2 + 3^2$ $25 = 16 + 9$ $25 = 25$ $4^2 = 16$

Q

quadrant cuadrante (Inv. 1)	A region of a coordinate plane formed when two perpendicular number lines intersect at their origins. second quadrant first quadrant third quadrant fourth quadrant

quadratic equation ecuación cuadrática (93)	An equation containing a variable with an exponent of 2 (but no greater exponents). $2x^2 + 7x = 45$ and $x^2 = 25$ *are **quadratic equations.***
qualitative data datos cualitativos (Inv. 6)	Data that falls into categories. *People's preferences for types of restaurants, books, or movies are examples of **qualitative data.***
quantitative data datos cuantivatos (Inv. 6)	Data that is numerical. *The number of people who see a movie each night of the week is an example of **quantitative data.***
quartile cuartil (103)	*See* **box-and-whisker plot.**

R

radicand radical (15)	The number under a radical sign. *See also* **radical expression.**
radical expression expresión radical (1)	An expression that indicates the root of a number. A radical expression contains a radical sign, $\sqrt{}$. $\sqrt{15^2}$ $\sqrt{9}$ $2 + 4$ 16 $\sqrt{x}$ $2 + \sqrt{13}$ xy 4133 **radical expressions** not **radical expressions**
radius radio (39)	(Plural: *radii*) The distance from the center of a circle or sphere to a point on the circle or sphere. 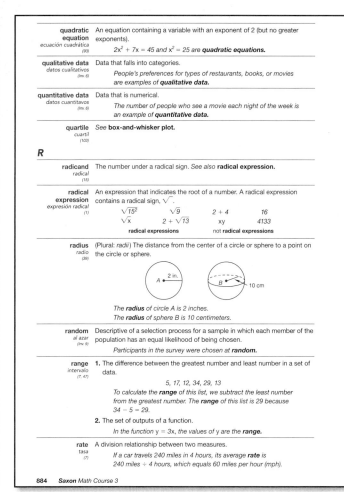 *The **radius** of circle A is 2 inches.* *The **radius** of sphere B is 10 centimeters.*
random al azar (Inv. 9)	Descriptive of a selection process for a sample in which each member of the population has an equal likelihood of being chosen. *Participants in the survey were chosen at **random.***
range intervalo (7, 47)	1. The difference between the greatest number and least number in a set of data. *5, 17, 12, 34, 29, 13* *To calculate the **range** of this list, we subtract the least number from the greatest number. The **range** of this list is 29 because $34 - 5 = 29$.* 2. The set of outputs of a function. *In the function $y = 3x$, the values of y are the **range.***
rate tasa (7)	A division relationship between two measures. *If a car travels 240 miles in 4 hours, its average **rate** is 240 miles ÷ 4 hours, which equals 60 miles per hour (mph).*

rate of change tasa de cambio (44)	How quickly one variable changes as a related variable changes; the slope. *The inflation rate is the **rate of change** of the cost of living per year.*
ratio razón (29)	A comparison of two numbers by division. △△△ ☆☆☆☆☆☆ *There are 3 triangles and 6 stars. The **ratio** of triangles to stars is 3:6 (or 1:2), which is read as "3 to 6" (or "1 to 2").*
rational numbers números racionales (10)	All numbers that can be written as a ratio of two integers. $\frac{15}{16}$ *and 37 are **rational numbers.*** $\sqrt{2}$ *and π are not **rational numbers.***
ray rayo (18)	A part of a line that begins at a point and extends without end in one direction. A •————————→ B **ray AB**
real numbers números reales (16)	All the numbers that can be represented by points on a number line. *The set of **real numbers** is composed of all rational and irrational numbers.*
reciprocal recíproco (22)	The result of inverting a number; also called **multiplicative inverse.** *The **reciprocal** of $\frac{3}{4}$ is $\frac{4}{3}$.* *The product of a number and its **reciprocal** is 1.* $\frac{3}{4} \times \frac{4}{3} = \frac{12}{12} = 1$
rectangle rectángulo (1)	A quadrilateral that has four right angles. 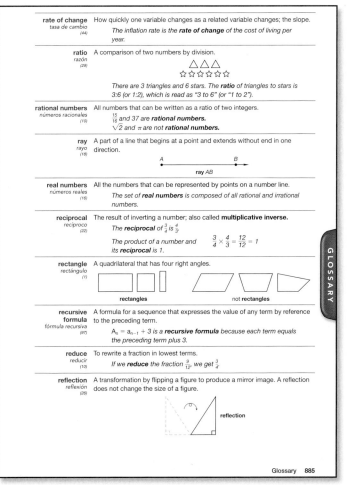 **rectangles** not **rectangles**
recursive formula fórmula recursiva (97)	A formula for a sequence that expresses the value of any term by reference to the preceding term. $A_n = a_{n-1} + 3$ *is a **recursive formula** because each term equals the preceding term plus 3.*
reduce reducir (10)	To rewrite a fraction in lowest terms. *If we **reduce** the fraction $\frac{9}{12}$, we get $\frac{3}{4}$.*
reflection reflexión (26)	A transformation by flipping a figure to produce a mirror image. A reflection does not change the size of a figure. reflection

reflective symmetry simetría de reflexión (Inv. 3)	A characteristic of a figure that can be divided into mirror images by a line or plane; also known as line symmetry. 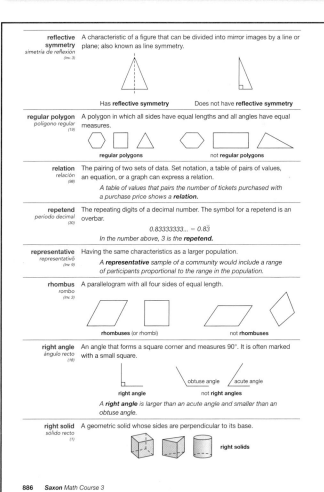 Has **reflective symmetry** Does not have **reflective symmetry**
regular polygon polígono regular (19)	A polygon in which all sides have equal lengths and all angles have equal measures. **regular polygons** not **regular polygons**
relation relación (98)	The pairing of two sets of data. Set notation, a table of pairs of values, an equation, or a graph can express a relation. *A table of values that pairs the number of tickets purchased with a purchase price shows a **relation.***
repetend período decimal (30)	The repeating digits of a decimal number. The symbol for a repetend is an overbar. $0.83333333... = 0.8\bar{3}$ *In the number above, 3 is the **repetend.***
representative representativõ (Inv. 9)	Having the same characteristics as a larger population. *A **representative** sample of a community would include a range of participants proportional to the range in the population.*
rhombus rombo (Inv. 3)	A parallelogram with all four sides of equal length. **rhombuses (or rhombi)** not **rhombuses**
right angle ángulo recto (18)	An angle that forms a square corner and measures 90°. It is often marked with a small square. **right angle** obtuse angle acute angle not **right angles** *A **right angle** is larger than an acute angle and smaller than an obtuse angle.*
right solid sólido recto (1)	A geometric solid whose sides are perpendicular to its base. **right solids**

GLOSSARY

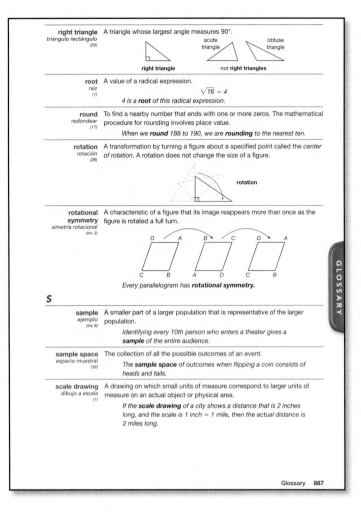

right triangle *triángulo rectángulo* ₍₂₀₎	A triangle whose largest angle measures 90°.

right triangle   not right triangles

root *raíz* ₍₁₎	A value of a radical expression. $\sqrt{16} = 4$ *4 is a **root** of this radical expression.*
round *redondear* ₍₁₇₎	To find a nearby number that ends with one or more zeros. The mathematical procedure for rounding involves place value. *When we **round** 188 to 190, we are **rounding** to the nearest ten.*
rotation *rotación* ₍₂₆₎	A transformation by turning a figure about a specified point called the *center of rotation.* A rotation does not change the size of a figure.

rotation

rotational symmetry *simetría rotacional* _(Inv. 3)	A characteristic of a figure that its image reappears more than once as the figure is rotated a full turn.

*Every parallelogram has **rotational symmetry.***

S

sample *ejemplo* _(Inv. 6)	A smaller part of a larger population that is representative of the larger population. *Identifying every 10th person who enters a theater gives a **sample** of the entire audience.*
sample space *espacio muestral* ₍₃₂₎	The collection of all the possible outcomes of an event. *The **sample space** of outcomes when flipping a coin consists of heads and tails.*
scale drawing *dibujo a escala* ₍₁₎	A drawing on which small units of measure correspond to larger units of measure on an actual object or physical area. *If the **scale drawing** of a city shows a distance that is 2 inches long, and the scale is 1 inch = 1 mile, then the actual distance is 2 miles long.*

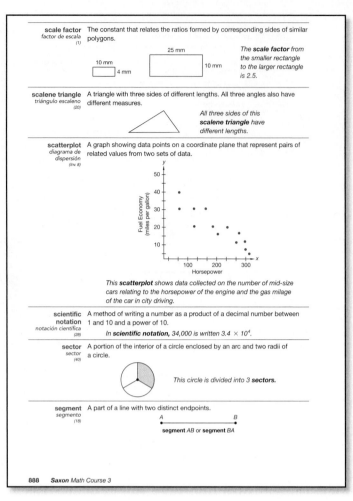

scale factor *factor de escala* ₍₁₎	The constant that relates the ratios formed by corresponding sides of similar polygons.

10 mm   4 mm   25 mm   10 mm

*The **scale factor** from the smaller rectangle to the larger rectangle is 2.5.*

scalene triangle *triángulo escaleno* ₍₂₀₎	A triangle with three sides of different lengths. All three angles also have different measures.

*All three sides of this **scalene triangle** have different lengths.*

scatterplot *diagrama de dispersión* _(Inv. 8)	A graph showing data points on a coordinate plane that represent pairs of related values from two sets of data.

Fuel Economy (miles per gallon)
Horsepower

*This **scatterplot** shows data collected on the number of mid-size cars relating to the horsepower of the engine and the gas milage of the car in city driving.*

scientific notation *notación científica* ₍₂₈₎	A method of writing a number as a product of a decimal number between 1 and 10 and a power of 10. *In **scientific notation**, 34,000 is written 3.4×10^4.*
sector *sector* ₍₄₀₎	A portion of the interior of a circle enclosed by an arc and two radii of a circle.

*This circle is divided into 3 **sectors**.*

segment *segmento* ₍₁₈₎	A part of a line with two distinct endpoints.

A ———— B

segment AB or **segment** BA

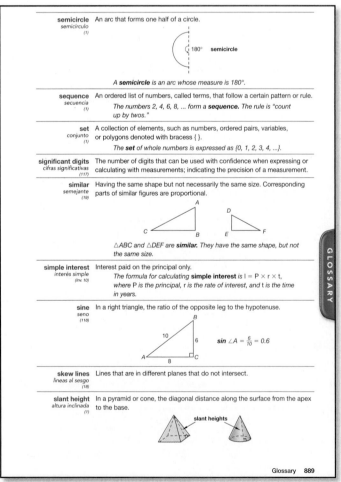

semicircle *semicírculo* ₍₁₎	An arc that forms one half of a circle.

180°   semicircle

*A **semicircle** is an arc whose measure is 180°.*

sequence *secuencia* ₍₁₎	An ordered list of numbers, called terms, that follow a certain pattern or rule. *The numbers 2, 4, 6, 8, ... form a **sequence**. The rule is "count up by twos."*
set *conjunto* ₍₁₎	A collection of elements, such as numbers, ordered pairs, variables, or polygons denoted with bracess { }. *The **set** of whole numbers is expressed as {0, 1, 2, 3, 4, ...}.*
significant digits *cifras significativas* ₍₁₁₇₎	The number of digits that can be used with confidence when expressing or calculating with measurements; indicating the precision of a measurement.
similar *semejante* ₍₁₉₎	Having the same shape but not necessarily the same size. Corresponding parts of similar figures are proportional.

*△ABC and △DEF are **similar**. They have the same shape, but not the same size.*

simple interest *interés simple* _(Inv. 10)	Interest paid on the principal only. *The formula for calculating **simple interest** is I = P × r × t, where P is the principal, r is the rate of interest, and t is the time in years.*
sine *seno* ₍₁₁₈₎	In a right triangle, the ratio of the opposite leg to the hypotenuse.

sin $\angle A = \frac{6}{10} = 0.6$

skew lines *líneas al sesgo* ₍₁₈₎	Lines that are in different planes that do not intersect.
slant height *altura inclinada* ₍₁₎	In a pyramid or cone, the diagonal distance along the surface from the apex to the base.

slant heights

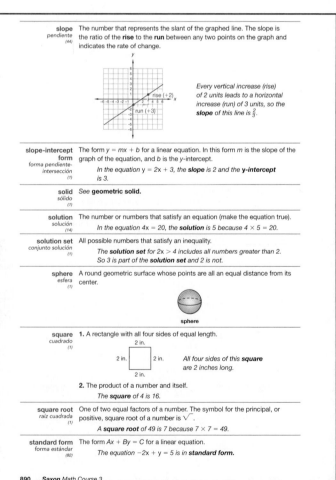

slope *pendiente* ₍₄₄₎	The number that represents the slant of the graphed line. The slope is the ratio of the **rise** to the **run** between any two points on the graph and indicates the rate of change.

rise (+2)   run (+3)

*Every vertical increase (rise) of 2 units leads to a horizontal increase (run) of 3 units, so the **slope** of this line is $\frac{2}{3}$.*

slope-intercept form *forma pendiente-intersección* ₍₁₎	The form y = mx + b for a linear equation. In this form m is the slope of the graph of the equation, and b is the y-intercept. *In the equation y = 2x + 3, the **slope** is 2 and the **y-intercept** is 3.*
solid *sólido* ₍₁₎	See **geometric solid**.
solution *solución* ₍₁₄₎	The number or numbers that satisfy an equation (make the equation true). *In the equation 4x = 20, the **solution** is 5 because 4 × 5 = 20.*
solution set *conjunto solución* ₍₁₎	All possible numbers that satisfy an inequality. *The **solution set** for 2x > 4 includes all numbers greater than 2. So 3 is part of the **solution set** and 2 is not.*
sphere *esfera* ₍₁₎	A round geometric surface whose points are all an equal distance from its center.

sphere

square *cuadrado* ₍₁₎	1. A rectangle with all four sides of equal length.

2 in.   2 in.   2 in.   2 in.

*All four sides of this **square** are 2 inches long.*

2. The product of a number and itself.

*The **square** of 4 is 16.*

square root *raíz cuadrada* ₍₁₎	One of two equal factors of a number. The symbol for the principal, or positive, square root of a number is $\sqrt{\ }$. *A **square root** of 49 is 7 because 7 × 7 = 49.*
standard form *forma estándar* ₍₈₂₎	The form Ax + By = C for a linear equation. *The equation −2x + y = 5 is in **standard form**.*

statistics *estadística* (Inv. 6)	The science of collecting data and interpreting the data in order to draw conclusions or make predictions.
stem-and-leaf plot *diagrama de tallo y hojas* (maintenance)	A method of graphing a collection of numbers by placing the "stem digits" (or initial digits) in one column and the "leaf" digits (or remaining digits) out to the right.

```
Stem | Leaf
  2  | 1 3 5 6 6 8
  3  | 0 0 2 2 4 5 6 6 8 9
  4  | 0 0 1 1 1 2 3 3 5 7 7 8
  5  | 0 1 1 2 3 5 8
```

*In this **stem-and-leaf plot**, 3|2 represents 32.*

step function *función escalón* (47)	A type of function whose graph has a stair step pattern.

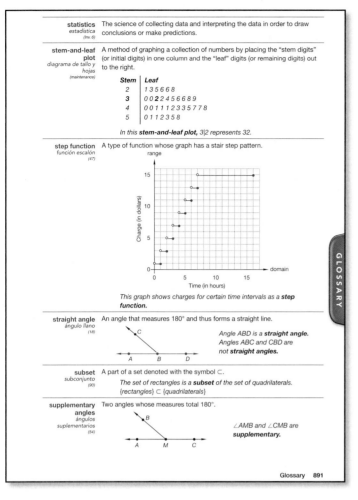

*This graph shows charges for certain time intervals as a **step function**.*

straight angle *ángulo llano* (18)	An angle that measures 180° and thus forms a straight line.

*Angle ABD is a **straight angle**.*
*Angles ABC and CBD are not **straight angles**.*

subset *subconjunto* (90)	A part of a set denoted with the symbol ⊂.

*The set of rectangles is a **subset** of the set of quadrilaterals.*
{rectangles} ⊂ {quadrilaterals}

supplementary angles *ángulos suplementarios* (54)	Two angles whose measures total 180°.

*∠AMB and ∠CMB are **supplementary**.*

---

surface area *área superficial* (43)	The combined area of the surfaces of a geometric solid.

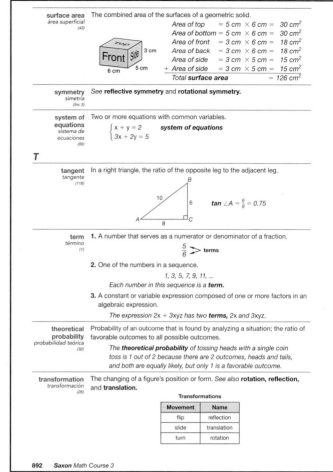

Area of top	= 5 cm × 6 cm =	30 cm²
Area of bottom	= 5 cm × 6 cm =	30 cm²
Area of front	= 3 cm × 6 cm =	18 cm²
Area of back	= 3 cm × 6 cm =	18 cm²
Area of side	= 3 cm × 5 cm =	15 cm²
+ Area of side	= 3 cm × 5 cm =	15 cm²
Total surface area		= 126 cm²

symmetry *simetría* (Inv. 3)	See **reflective symmetry** and **rotational symmetry**.
system of equations *sistema de ecuaciones* (89)	Two or more equations with common variables.

$$\begin{cases} x + y = 2 \\ 3x + 2y = 5 \end{cases} \quad \textbf{system of equations}$$

T

tangent *tangente* (118)	In a right triangle, the ratio of the opposite leg to the adjacent leg.

$\tan \angle A = \frac{6}{8} = 0.75$

term *término* (1)	**1.** A number that serves as a numerator or denominator of a fraction.

$\frac{5}{6}$ terms

2. One of the numbers in a sequence.

1, 3, 5, 7, 9, 11, ...

*Each number in this sequence is a **term**.*

3. A constant or variable expression composed of one or more factors in an algebraic expression.

*The expression 2x + 3xyz has two **terms**, 2x and 3xyz.*

theoretical probability *probabilidad teórica* (32)	Probability of an outcome that is found by analyzing a situation; the ratio of favorable outcomes to all possible outcomes.

*The **theoretical probability** of tossing heads with a single coin toss is 1 out of 2 because there are 2 outcomes, heads and tails, and both are equally likely, but only 1 is a favorable outcome.*

transformation *transformación* (26)	The changing of a figure's position or form. See also **rotation**, **reflection**, and **translation**.

Transformations

Movement	Name
flip	reflection
slide	translation
turn	rotation

---

translation *traslación* (26)	A transformation by sliding a figure from one position to another without turning or flipping the figure. A translation does not change the size of a figure.

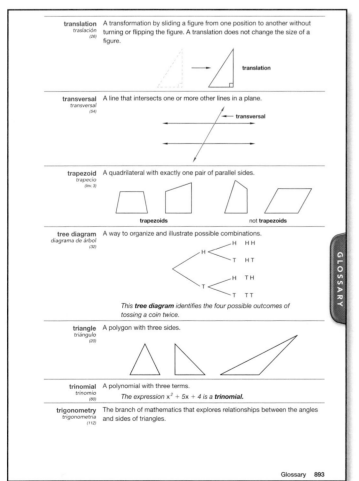

transversal *transversal* (54)	A line that intersects one or more other lines in a plane.

trapezoid *trapecio* (Inv. 3)	A quadrilateral with exactly one pair of parallel sides.

trapezoids   **not trapezoids**

tree diagram *diagrama de árbol* (32)	A way to organize and illustrate possible combinations.

*This **tree diagram** identifies the four possible outcomes of tossing a coin twice.*

triangle *triángulo* (20)	A polygon with three sides.

trinomial *trinomio* (80)	A polynomial with three terms.

*The expression $x^2 + 5x + 4$ is a **trinomial**.*

trigonometry *trigonometría* (112)	The branch of mathematics that explores relationships between the angles and sides of triangles.

U

union *unión* (90)	The combining of two sets, denoted by the symbol ∪.

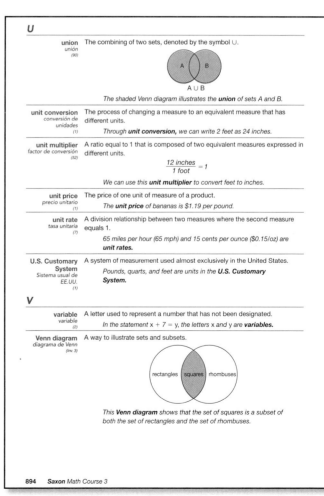

A ∪ B

*The shaded Venn diagram illustrates the **union** of sets A and B.*

unit conversion *conversión de unidades* (1)	The process of changing a measure to an equivalent measure that has different units.

*Through **unit conversion**, we can write 2 feet as 24 inches.*

unit multiplier *factor de conversión* (52)	A ratio equal to 1 that is composed of two equivalent measures expressed in different units.

$\frac{12 \text{ inches}}{1 \text{ foot}} = 1$

*We can use this **unit multiplier** to convert feet to inches.*

unit price *precio unitario* (1)	The price of one unit of measure of a product.

*The **unit price** of bananas is $1.19 per pound.*

unit rate *tasa unitaria* (7)	A division relationship between two measures where the second measure equals 1.

*65 miles per hour (65 mph) and 15 cents per ounce ($0.15/oz) are **unit rates**.*

U.S. Customary System *Sistema usual de EE.UU.* (1)	A system of measurement used almost exclusively in the United States.

*Pounds, quarts, and feet are units in the **U.S. Customary System**.*

V

variable *variable* (2)	A letter used to represent a number that has not been designated.

*In the statement x + 7 = y, the letters x and y are **variables**.*

Venn diagram *diagrama de Venn* (Inv. 3)	A way to illustrate sets and subsets.

rectangles   squares   rhombuses

*This **Venn diagram** shows that the set of squares is a subset of both the set of rectangles and the set of rhombuses.*

vertex *vértice* *(19)*	(Plural: *vertices*) A point of an angle, polygon, or polyhedron where two or more lines, rays, or segments meet.

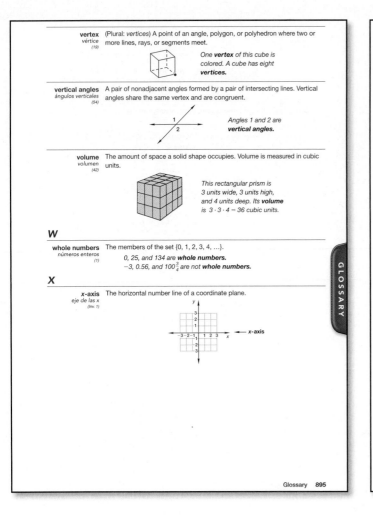

One **vertex** of this cube is colored. A cube has eight **vertices.**

vertical angles *ángulos verticales* *(54)*	A pair of nonadjacent angles formed by a pair of intersecting lines. Vertical angles share the same vertex and are congruent.

Angles 1 and 2 are **vertical angles.**

volume *volumen* *(42)*	The amount of space a solid shape occupies. Volume is measured in cubic units.

This rectangular prism is 3 units wide, 3 units high, and 4 units deep. Its **volume** is $3 \cdot 3 \cdot 4 = 36$ cubic units.

W

whole numbers *números enteros* *(1)*	The members of the set {0, 1, 2, 3, 4, …}.

0, 25, and 134 are **whole numbers.**
−3, 0.56, and $100\frac{3}{4}$ are not **whole numbers.**

X

x-axis *eje de las x* *(Inv. 1)*	The horizontal number line of a coordinate plane.

Y

y-axis *eje de las y* *(Inv. 1)*	The vertical number line of a coordinate plane.

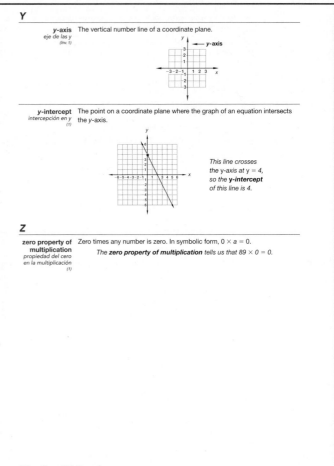

y-intercept *intercepción en y* *(1)*	The point on a coordinate plane where the graph of an equation intersects the *y*-axis.

This line crosses the y-axis at y = 4, so the **y-intercept** of this line is 4.

Z

zero property of multiplication *propiedad del cero en la multiplicación* *(1)*	Zero times any number is zero. In symbolic form, $0 \times a = 0$.

The **zero property of multiplication** tells us that $89 \times 0 = 0$.

A

Abbreviations. *See also* Symbols and
 signs
 Celsius (C), 203–204
 centimeters (cm), 36
 cubic centimeters (cm³), 287
 cubic feet (ft³), 287
 feet (ft), 36
 grams (g), 36
 inch (in.), 36
 kilograms (kg), 36
 kilometers (km), 36
 liters (L), 36
 meters (m), 36
 miles (mi), 36
 milliliters (mL), 36
 millimeters (mm), 36
 square feet (ft²), 51, 99
 square inch (in.²), 99
 "trig", 769
 yard (yd), 36
Absolute value
 on number lines, 8
 signed numbers and, 205
 symbol for, 8
Act it out or make a model. *See* Problem-
 solving strategies
Activities
 area of parallelograms, 406–409
 best-fit line, 543–544
 calculating interest and growth, 672–673
 cones
  nets of, 374
  sketching, 270
 coordinate plane, 70–71
 cylinders, sketching, 269–270
 geometric solids
  multiview drawing, 270–271
  one-point perspective drawing, 272
 parallelograms, area of, 404
 prisms, sketching, 269–270
 probability simulation, 476–477
 pyramids, sketching, 270
 Pythagorean puzzle, 137–138
 random number generators, 607–608
 scatterplots, 543–544
  used to make predictions, 744–745
 sketching
  cones and pyramids, 269–270
  cylinders and prisms, 269–270
 surface area of a box, 292
 transformations, 172
 using the graph of a quadratic function,
  729–730
Acute angles, 116–117, 546
 measuring, with protractors, 116
Addends, 13
 missing, 20
Addition, 12–13
 addends, 13, 20
 associative property of, 14
 collecting like terms, 205, 534, 640,
  801, 805
 commutative property of, 14
 of decimal numbers, 159–160

distributive property of multiplication
 over division, 140–141
 of fractions, 85–90
 identity property of, 14
 of integers, 203–205, 217, 238
 as inverse of subtraction, 247
 missing numbers in, 20
 of mixed measures, 532–533
 of mixed numbers, 85–89
 and order of operations, 141
 of polynomials, 801–803
 in problems about combining, 19–20
 properties of, 14, 15, 140–141
 of radicals, 640, 805–807
 of signed numbers, 204–205, 238
 significant digits in, 765
 simplifying, with multiplication, 27
 word problems, 19–25
Additive inverse, 205
Adjacent angles, 367–368
Algebra. *See also* Addition; Division:
 Multiplication: Subtraction
 algebraic addition, 218–219
 equations, modeling, 617–618, 819
 evaluating expressions, 93, 837, 840
 factoring expressions, 140–141, 822–823,
  829–830, 837–839
 fractions vs. decimals for computation,
  427, 563
 graphing in the coordinate plane, 69–71,
  538–541, 791–795, 797–801, 831–837,
  840–844, 851–855
  with integers. See Integers
 prefixes for number of terms, 533
 solving equations. See Solving
  equations
 terms
  adding and subtracting, 205–207,
   801–802, 818–821
  multiplying and dividing, 328, 619–620,
   803–804
 variables and expressions, 249–250
 writing algebraic expressions, 420,
  814–815
Algebraic addition, 218–219
Algebraic expressions
 evaluating, 93
 factoring, 140–141
 prefixes for number of terms, 533
 variables and, 251–252
 writing, 420
Algebraic terms, dividing and multiplying,
 237–238
Alternate exterior angles, 369
Alternate interior angles, 369
"and" in inequalities, 629–630
Angles, 115–117
 acute, 116–117, 546
 adjacent, 367
 alternate, 369
 central, 265, 545–549
 in circles, 545
 complementary, 369
 corresponding, 230, 369
  in similar figures, 441
 degrees of, 115

exterior, 369
 formed by transversals, 369–370
 interior, 369
 linear pairs, 116
 measuring, with protractors, 116
 obtuse, 116, 546
 opposite, 367
 parallel lines and, 369–370
 relationships between, 369–370
 right, 116
 straight, 116, 546
 supplementary, 368
 of triangles. *See* Triangles, angles
  of vertical, 367
Apex, 274, 635–636
Approximately equal to symbol (≈), 37,
 122, 509
Approximations, 258
 values of square roots, 448, 498
Arcs, 265
 measuring, 546–547
 minor and major, 546
 symbol for, 547
Area, 48–51
 activities
  parallelograms, 406
  surface area of a box, 296
 of bases, 294–296
 calculating as a sweep, 748–751
 of circles, 264–267
 of combined polygons, 245–247
 converting with unit multipliers, 486–488
 cross-sectional of spheres, 733–734
 effect of scalings on, 479–482, 611,
  612, 703
 of parallelograms, 406–409, 501
 percent change calculations, 479–482
 probability based on, 676–677
 of rectangles, 49, 234, 502
  with variable dimensions, 617–620
 of sectors, 264–267
 of semicircles, 267
 of squares, 99, 264
 surface. *See* Surface area
 of trapezoids, 502–504
 of triangles, 69, 127–128, 246–247, 406
  equilateral, 448
 units of, 99
Arithmetic. *See also* Addition; Division;
 Multiplication; Subtraction
 with decimal numbers, 159–160
 with integers. *See* Integers
 operations of, 12–18, 141–143
Arithmetic sequence, 416–417
Assessment. *See* Cumulative assessment;
 Customized benchmark assessment;
 Power-Up tests
Associative property, 14
Average, 41–43, 360–363. *See also*
 Central tendency; Mean
 compound, 697–698
Average speed, 42
Axis (Axes)
 on coordinate planes, 68–69
 intercepts on, 382, 551

B

Bar graphs, 412
Base 10 number system, 78
Bases, numeric
  of exponential expressions, 98, 177
  with negative exponents, 431–432
Bases of geometric figures
  area, 294–296
  of prisms and cylinders, 507–509,
    568–570
  of trapezoids, 502
  of triangles, 128
  and volume, 287, 507–509
Best-fit line, 539–544, 654
Bias, in surveys, 412, 609
Binomials, 533
  adding, 534
  factoring quadratic equations to, 822–824,
    837–839
  products of, 619–621
Box-and-whisker plots, 686–688

C

Calculators. *See also* Graphing calculator
  compound interest, 672–673
  converting fractions to decimals, 194
  division by zero, 758
  exponent key, 672–673
  finding terms of a sequence, 492–493
  graphing, 542
  graphing sequences, 799
  irrational numbers, 103–104
  negative exponents, 347
  percents, 194
  pi, 259
  reversing signs, 240
  scientific notation, 182–183, 347
  sine, cosine, tangent, 770
  square roots, 103–104
Capacity
  equivalent measures, 37
  metric system, 37, 691–694
  U.S. Customary system, 37
Celsius (C), 203–204
Centimeters (cm), 36
  cubic (cm³), 287–288
Central angle, 265, 545–549
Central tendency, 43–44
  See also Average; Mean; Median, Mode
Chance, 211
Circle graphs, 412
Circles
  arcs on, 546–547
  area of, 264–267
    calculated as a sweep, 749–750
  as bases of cylinders, 509–511, 568–
    570
  central angle measures in, 265, 545–
    546
  circumference of, 257–260
  diameter of, 258
  drawing, with compass, 258
  great circle of a sphere, 734
  radius of, 258
  sectors of, 265–266
  semicircles, 267
Circumference, 257–260
Clockwise/counterclockwise, 122, 343
Closed-option surveys, 414

Coefficients, 181
  mathematical operation performed by,
    789
  negative, 514–516
Combining, word problems about, 19–20
Common denominators, 63–64, 788–790
  adding and subtracting, 86–89
    in fractions, 86–87
    in mixed numbers, 87–89
  least common denominator, 87
Communication
  Discuss, 78, 87, 94, 110, 122, 148, 173,
    206, 259, 266, 274, 281, 283, 442,
    454, 502, 509, 564, 626, 631
  Formulate a problem, 22, 29, 34, 46, 52,
    66, 283, 293, 379, 494, 609
  Writing about mathematics, 16, 58, 61,
    67, 70, 93, 98, 104, 105, 112, 140,
    143, 151, 154, 160, 193, 197, 199,
    227, 258, 303, 310, 338, 372, 390,
    402, 403, 405, 406, 419, 424, 441,
    497, 500, 503, 512, 522, 527, 546,
    547, 560, 562, 565, 572, 575, 581,
    589, 599, 604, 612, 630, 636, 641,
    644, 660, 679, 682, 700, 751, 756,
    761, 765, 780
Commutative property, 14
Comparing
  fractions, 32, 63–64
  fractions-decimals-percents, 430–431
  integers, 6–8
  word problems about, 21–22
Comparison symbols
  greater than (>), 8
  less than (<), 8
  reasons for reversing, 514–516
Compass, 258
Complementary angles, 369
Complements, 212
Composite numbers, 55
Compound average and rate problems,
  697–699
Compound interest, 670–674
Compound solids, surface area and
  volume, 707–709
Conditional probability, 558
Cones, 271
  area, 377
  drawing, 274
  nets of, 375–378
  right, 664–666
  slant height, 664–666
  surface area, 635, 664–666
    lateral, 666, 750–751
  volume, 574–577
Congruence
  in geometric figures, 122–123, 128
  in polygons, 229–233
  in triangles, 441–442
  symbol for, 122, 230
Congruence transformations, 172, 344
Constant of proportionality (*k*), 463, 471–
  472, 585–586
Constants, 93, 533
Content highlights. *See* Section overviews
Content trace. *See* Section overviews
Contractions, 172, 344
Converse of Pythagorean Theorem, 135

Conversion
  of decimals
    fraction equivalents, 79–80, 192,
      429–430, 722–724
    percent equivalents, 81–82, 396,
      429–430
    rational numbers to, 81
    repeating, to fractions, 723
    to whole numbers, 787
  of fractions
    decimal equivalents, 79–80, 192, 396
    decimal equivalents, non-terminating,
      429–430, 722–724
    percent equivalents, 73–76, 82
  of percents
    decimal equivalents, 81–82, 429–430
    fraction equivalents, 429–430
  of units
    of measure, 36–40
    between metric and U.S. Customary
      system, 53
    multiple unit multipliers, 486–488
    single unit multipliers, 435–437
    within metric system, 37–38
    within U.S. Customary system,
      37–38
Coordinate plane. *See also* Graphing, the
  coordinate plane
  activities, 70–71
  coordinates on, 68–69
  graphing numbers on, 69–71, 538–541,
    790–800, 817, 831–837, 840–845
  graphing linear inequalities, 831–833,
    835–836
  quadrants of, 68
  graphing systems of inequalities on,
    840–841
Coordinates, 68–69
Correlation of data, 539–544, 654, 743
Corresponding angles, 369
Corresponding parts, 230
Cosine, 768–772
Counterclockwise/clockwise, 122, 343
Counting numbers, 100
  on number line, 7
  set of (ℕ), 601
Cross products, 300–301, 304, 472, 587,
  625–626, 803–804
Cube roots, 99
Cubes, 271
  volume of, 288–290
Cubic centimeters (cm³), 287–288
Cumulative assessment, 67A, 102A, 131A,
  168A, 196A, 236A, 270A, 312A, 341A,
  381A, 411A, 445A, 475A, 506A, 537A,
  573A, 605A, 639A, 669A, 701A, 726A,
  757A, 781A
Curves
  graphs of, 281
  parabolic, 727
Customized benchmark assessment, 67B,
  131B, 196B, 270B, 341B, 411B, 475B,
  537B, 605B, 669B, 726B, 781B
Customary system of measure. *See* U.S.
  Customary system
Cylinders, 271
  drawing, 273
  nets of, 375–377
  similar, 712
  surface area, 568–573
    lateral, 569, 750
  volume, 507–511 , 574, 731–733

D

Data
  collecting, 412–414
  correlated, 539–544, 654, 743
  displaying, 412–414
    bar, 412
    box-and-whisker plots, 687–688
    circle, 413–414
    histograms, 413
    line plots, 686–688
    scatterplots, 654, 742–747
  on graphs
    correlated, 539–544, 654, 743
    outliers, 539
  interpreting, 413–414, 654
  paired, 538–542, 651, 742–743
  predictions using scatterplots, 742–747
  qualitative, 412
  quantitative, 412
  quartiles in, 687
  range of, 44
  in relations, 654
  sampling error, 608
  sampling methods, 606–609
  trends in, 654
Decay and growth, 681–685
Decimal numbers, 78–83
  adding, 159–160
  converting
    fraction equivalents, 79–80, 192, 430–431, 722–726
    percent equivalents, 81, 393, 430–431
    rational numbers to, 81
  dividing, 163–67
  fractions versus, for computations, 429, 563–564
  multiplying, 163–67
  repeating, 192–194, 429–434, 563, 722–726
  rounding, 109
  scientific notation and, 346–350
  solving equations with, 787–788
  subtracting, 159–160
  terminating, 429
Degree of a polynomial, 533–534
Degrees
  90° measurement, 115
  180° measurement, 116, 368
  360° measurement, 115
  of angles. See Angles
Denominators, 31, 62
  common, 63–64, 86–89, 788–789
  least common, 87
  percents and, 73
  rationalizing, 778–781
Dependent events, probability of, 557–562
Diagrams
  factor tree, 498
  for finding area, 246–247
  for fraction problems, 54–55
  for probability experiments, 153–154
  tree, 153–154, 457–458, 558
  Venn, 198–199
Diameter, 258
Difference, 13
Digits
  rounding, 108–109
  significant, 763–767
  symbol for repeating, 429, 723

Dilations, 122, 172–173, 344–345
  percent change, 479
Dimensions, percent change of, 479–482
Direct proportions, 322
Direct variation
  characteristics of, 464, 674
  dependent vs. independent variables, 465–466
  formula for, 463–464
  graphs of, 465–467, 586
  solving problems
    with equations, 471–473
    by graphing, 465–466
    using tables, 464–466, 471
    writing proportions, 472
Distributive property, 140–141, 789
Dividends, 13
Divisibility tests, 56–57
Division, 13–14
  of decimal numbers, 163–167
  of exponential expressions, 178
  of fractions, 148–150, 156
  of integers, 61, 237–240
  as inverse of multiplication, 251, 759–760
  of measurements, 765
  of mixed numbers, 153–156
  order of operations in and, 15, 141
  of numbers in scientific notation, 314–315
  of signed numbers, 238–239
  significant digits in, 765
  simplifying complex fractions using, 774–775
  of small numbers, 389–390
  symbols for, 14
  of terms, 240–241
  word problems, 26–28
  by zero, 61, 178, 758–760
Divisors, 13
Domain, 319–321, 652
Draw a picture or diagram. See Problem-solving strategies

E

Early finishers. See Enrichment
Edges, 271
Elapsed time, 22
Elements of sets ($\in$), 599–600
Elimination, solving systems of equations using, 827–829
Ellipsis (...), 7, 193, 415, 429, 599
Empty set ($\emptyset$), 602
English learners
English learner vocabulary is specified on applicable lesson opener and investigation opener pages.
  10, 15, 22, 28, 33, 44, 49, 63, 74, 81, 88, 99, 110, 123, 141, 151, 155, 166, 179, 183, 195, 215, 220, 227, 230, 238, 251, 258, 265, 278, 295, 312, 316, 329, 340, 351, 364, 371, 379, 391, 408, 416, 423, 430, 441, 461, 464, 473, 484, 487, 494, 503, 512, 523, 528, 546, 553, 565, 578, 583, 586, 596, 618, 636, 642, 648, 660, 683, 714, 739, 743, 760
English system. See U.S. Customary system

Enrichment
  Early Finishers
    Real-world applications 11, 25, 40, 53, 107, 119, 125, 158, 180, 185, 191, 217, 222, 244, 263, 270, 307, 341, 353, 366, 374, 381, 399, 439, 462, 475, 485, 530, 567, 573, 584, 592, 598, 605, 623, 645, 657, 669, 690, 736, 741, 747
    Extend the problem, 23, 24, 30, 33, 45, 58, 70, 71, 83, 91, 107, 125, 131, 137, 144, 151, 180, 191, 196, 199, 208, 242, 255, 270, 284, 306, 310, 329, 365, 399, 405, 409, 413, 414
Equal groups, in word problems, 27–29
Equality
  properties of, using to solve equations, 250–254
  symmetric property of, 254
Equal sign (=), 8
Equations. See also Representation
  arithmetic operations in, 12–18
  distributive property, 789
  with exponents, 624–626
  formulas. See Formulas
  graphing. See Graphing equations
  linear, 382–386, 551, 790–797, 851–853
  for percent problems, 394–396
  quadratic, 624–626, 822–824, 829–831
  simplifying, 141–143, 787–790
  simultaneous, 594
  slope-intercept form of linear, 382–386, 551, 790–792, 795–797, 851–857
  solving. See Solving equations
  standard form of linear, 550–553
  system of, 594
  for terms of a sequence, 491–492
  multi-step, 336–338
  with two variables, 593–596, 658
    solving using substitution, 807–808
    writing, 814–815
  in word problems, 19–20
  writing
    for lines on graphs, 790–791, 852–853
    with two variables, 814–815
Equilateral triangles, 126–127, 278–279, 446–449
Equivalent fractions, 62–64
Errors and Misconceptions, 10, 18, 24, 29, 35, 40, 45, 52, 57, 58, 66, 76, 77, 83, 84, 91, 101, 106, 113, 118, 124, 130, 144, 150, 157, 161, 162, 167, 174, 179, 183, 189, 195, 209, 215, 227, 235, 236, 243, 249, 254, 261, 268, 285, 291, 292, 297, 305, 310, 311, 316, 318, 325, 328, 335, 339, 351, 353, 358, 359, 365, 372, 373, 381, 387, 391, 393, 397, 398, 409, 411, 419, 428, 433, 438, 439, 444, 450, 456, 474, 483, 490, 495, 500, 501, 505, 513, 517, 522, 523, 528, 535, 536, 548, 554, 561, 565, 571, 579, 583, 590, 597, 616, 623, 627, 628, 632, 638, 644, 645, 649, 655, 656, 661, 662, 669, 678, 680, 684, 690, 695, 696, 700, 705, 714, 720, 726, 735, 736, 739, 746, 753, 757, 762, 767, 772, 776, 777, 780
Estimation, 110–112
Evaluation of expressions, 93
Even numbers, 8

Events
    dependent, calculating probabilities,
        557–560
    independent, calculating probabilities,
        459–460, 557, 559
Expanded expressions, 140–141
Experimental probability, 211, 400–403,
    475
Experiments in more than one part, 459–
    460
Exponential vs. linear growth, 674
Exponents, 98
    dividing, 178, 389–390
    equations with, 624–629
    fractions with negative, 431–432
    laws of, 176–178, 346–347, 390
    multiplying, 178, 348–349, 389–390
    negative, 346–349, 431–432
    order of operations and, 141
    polynomials and, 533
    scientific notation, 181–183
Expressions
    distributive property and, 140–141
    evaluation of, 93
    expanding, 140–141
    factoring, 140–141
    order of operations in, 141–143
    simplifying, 14–15, 141–143
    value of the nth term (a_n), 417
Exterior angles, 369

F

Faces, geometric, 271
Factoring
    expressions, 140–141
    of quadratic equations, 822–824
    solving quadratic equations using,
        829–831, 837–839
Factorization, prime. See Prime
    factorization
Factors, 13, 177
    greatest common factor, 62–63
    of algebraic expressions, 140–141
    of perfect squares, 498–499
    prime, 498
    scale. See Scale factor
    simplifying square roots using,
        498–499, 519
Facts Practice (Power Up)
    Each lesson Power Up presents a facts
        practice that builds fluency in basic
        math facts.
Feet (ft), 36
    cubic (ft³), 287–288
    square (ft²), 99
Figures. See Geometric figures; Similar
    figures
Find a pattern. See Problem-solving
    strategies
FOIL algorithm, 620
Formulas, 93
    area
        of circles, 264
        of parallelograms, 502
        of rectangles, 49, 502
        of squares, 99
        of trapezoids, 503
        of triangles, 128, 406, 448, 665
    circumference, 258
    for combining word problems, 19
    generating terms of a sequence, 646–648

lateral surface area
    of cones, 751
    of cylinders, 750
    of prisms, 569
perimeter
    of circles. See Circumference
    of rectangles, 49, 93, 140
    of squares, 93, 277
proportional relationships, 463–464, 588
quadratic, 846–850
recursive, 647–648
sequences, 415, 491–494
slope, 302–304
standard, for a linear equation, 525
surface area, 294–296
    of cones, 377, 666
    of cylinders, 569–570
    of prisms, 569–570
    of pyramids, 665
    of spheres, 734
transforming, 525–530
of variation, direct and inverse, 463–464,
    658
volume
    of cones, 575
    of cubes, 288, 508
    of cylinders, 574, 732–733
    of prisms, 288, 574
    of pyramids, 576
    of rectangular prisms, 508
    of spheres, 733
    of triangular prisms, 508–509
Four-step problem-solving process, 6, 12,
    26, 47, 54, 72, 92, 97, 120, 139, 146, 153,
    176, 202, 250
45°-45°-90° triangles, 447–449
Fractions, 31–35, See also Mixed numbers
    adding, 85–90
    comparing, 32, 63–64
    complex, 773–777
    converting
        decimal equivalents, 79–80, 192, 395
        decimal equivalents, non-terminating,
            429–430, 722–726
        percent equivalents, 75–76, 82
    decimals versus, for computations, 429,
        563–564
    dividing, 146–150, 156
    equal to one, 486, 774
    equivalent, 62–64
    improper, 64–65, 86
    least common denominator, 87
    multiplying, 146–150, 156
    with negative exponents, 431–432
    rates as, 435
    rationalizing denominators, 778–781
    reciprocals of, 148–149, 432
    regrouping, 88
    rewriting mixed numbers as, 154
    simplest form of, 62
    simplifying, 62–63, 148
    solving equations containing, 788–790
    subtracting, 85–90
Function notation, 816–817
Functions
    characteristics of, 652
    defined, 280
    graphing, 280–283, 319–323, 817
    illustrating, 280
    linear, 279–283
    non-linear, 727–730
    proportional, 280–281

quadratic, 728–729
relations and, 651–655
step, 321

G

Geometric figures. See also Height of
    geometric figures
    apex of, 634–636, 664
    bases of. See Bases of geometric
        figures
    height of
        defined, 634
        prisms and cylinders, 507–508
        slant, 634–639
    transformations of, 169–174
Geometric measures with radicals, 640–645
Geometric probability, 675–680
Geometric sequence, 416–417, 681
Geometric solids. See also specific solids
    drawing, 271–276
    nets of, 375–378
    similar, 712–716
    surface area of, 294–297, 707–711
    volume of, 287–290, 707–711
Golden Rectangle, 199
Grams (g), 36
Graphing. See also Calculators; Graphing
    calculator
    calculators for, 542
    the coordinate plane, 69–71, 538–541,
        831–836
    equations
        slope-intercept form, 381–386, 551,
            790–792, 795–797, 851–853
        standard form of linear equations,
            550–553
        with two unknowns, 593–598
        union of solutions, 631
        using intercepts, 550–553
    functions, 278–284, 319–323, 817
    on number lines, 8–9
        inequalities, 422–426, 514
        inequality pairs, 629–633
    sequences, 415, 798–800
    systems of inequalities, 840–841
    transformations, 342–345
Graphing calculator. See also Calculators.
    Graphing Calculator Activities,
        references to, 44, 69, 89, 100, 154,
        182, 218, 238, 322, 344, 350, 414,
        464, 478, 492, 542, 551, 594, 660,
        687, 718, 764, 770
Graphs
    arrowheads on lines in, 423, 466
    bar, 412
    best-fit line, 539–544, 654
    box-and-whisker plots, 686–688
    circle, 414
    of direct-variation relationships, 465–
        466, 586
    histograms, 361, 413
    of inverse-variation relationships, 660
    linear, 465, 586
    line plot, 361, 686–688
    lines on. See Lines
    of non-linear functions, 727–730
    points on. See Points on a graph
    of proportional relationships, 465–466,
        586
    quadratic functions, 728–730
    scatterplots, 538–544, 654, 742–747

of sequences, 417
slope. *See* Slope
vertical line test, 652
x- and *y*- intercepts on, 383, 551,
790–791
Great circles of spheres, 734
Greater than symbol (>), 8
Greatest common factor, 63
Growth and decay, 681–685
Guess and check. *See* Problem-solving
strategies

H

Half circles. *See* Semicircles
Height of geometric figures
defined, 635
of parallelograms, 407
prisms and cylinders, 508–509
slant, 634–639
of trapezoids, 503–504
of triangles, 128
and volume, 288
Heptagons, 122
Hexagons, 122
Histograms, 413
Horizontal lines, 303, 320, 383
Hypotenuse, 132

I

Identity property
of addition, 14
of multiplication, 14, 63, 86, 224, 774
Improper fractions, 64–65, 86, 154
Inch (in.), 36
cubic (in.^{3}), 287–288
Inclusion, 8, 13, 56, 62, 104, 116, 140, 178,
187, 213, 232, 246, 320, 337, 362, 425,
459, 482, 498, 508, 515, 564, 576, 612,
630, 652, 660, 703
Indexes of roots, 100
Indirect measurement, 441–442, 770
Inequalities
graphing, 422–426, 515, 629–634
on the coordinate plane, 831–836
systems of, 840–844
properties of, 515
solving
as equations, 423, 514
with negative coefficients, 514–519
writing, 422
Infinity symbol (∞), 759
Input number, 278
Inspection, solving equations by, 93–94
Integers, 61. *See also* Signed numbers
adding, 203–205, 219, 240
comparing, 6–11
dividing, 237–240
multiplying, 237–240
ordering, 6–11
rational numbers and, 61
ratios using, 429
set of (ℤ), 599, 601
subtracting, 218–219, 240
symbols for, 601
Intercepts
graphing equations using, 382–386,
550–556
x- and *y*-, 383, 551, 790–792
Interest
compound, 670–674
consumer, 717–721

defined, 670
Rule of 72, 673
simple, 670
Interior angles, 369
Intersect, 68, 115
Intersecting lines, 367–370, 595
Intersection of sets (∩), 601, 602
Inverse operations
defined, 625
multiplication and division, 759–760
using, to solve equations, 251–254, 336
Inverse proportion, 659
Inverse variation, 658–663
Investigations
classifying quadrilaterals, 197–201
collect, display, and interpret data,
412–414
compound interest, 670–674
coordinate plane, 68–71
drawing geometric solids, 271–276
graphing transformations, 342–345
non-linear functions, 727–730
probability simulation, 476–478
Pythagorean Theorem, 132–138
Pythagorean Theorem proof, 782–784
sampling methods, 606–609
scatterplots, 538–544
Irrational numbers, 103–105, 193
Isometries, 172, 344
Isosceles trapezoids, 197
Isosceles triangles, 126–127, 447, 635

K

k, constant of proportionality, 463, 471,
586
Kilograms (kg), 36
Kilometers (km), 36
Kites, 197, 198

L

Lateral surface area, 294–297
of prisms, 569
of right cones, 666
of right pyramids, 665
Laws of exponents, 176–178, 346, 347, 389
Least common denominator, 87
Legs of a right triangle, 132
Length
equivalent measures, 37
estimating, 110
of rectangles, 49
scaling's effect on, 612, 703
units of
metric system, 37
U.S. Customary system, 37
Less than symbol (<), 8
Lesson highlights. *See* Section overviews
Lesson planner. *See* Section overviews
Like terms, collecting, 205–206, 534, 640
Linear equations
slope-intercept form, 382–386, 551,
790–792, 795–797, 851–853
standard form of, 550–557
Linear functions, 281–284
Linear growth, 674
Linear pairs, 116
Line plots, 361, 686–688
Lines, 114–117. *See also* Lines on graphs;
Number lines
best-fit, 539–544, 654
graphing, 302–304, 382–385

intersecting, 367–370, 595
intersecting the origin, 465, 586
linear vs. exponential, 674
parallel, 115, 368–370, 851–853
perpendicular, 115, 854–857
skew, 115
slope of, 302–304, 315
defined, 302, 790
finding using two points, 793–795
writing equations using, 790–792
of symmetry, 200–201
writing equations
given slope and one point, 790–792
given two points, 795–797
parallel to a given line through a
given point, 851–853
perpendicular to a given line through
a given point, 854–857
in slope-intercept form, 379–383, 551,
790–792, 795–797, 851–853
Liters (L), 36
Logical reasoning. *See* Problem-solving
strategies
Looking Forward, 11, 18, 25, 30, 35, 40,
46, 53, 67, 71, 77, 84, 91, 102, 107, 119,
125, 131, 138, 145, 152, 162, 168, 175,
180, 185, 191, 196, 201, 209, 217, 222,
228, 236, 244, 249, 256, 263, 270, 276,
286, 293, 299, 307, 312, 325, 329, 335,
341, 345, 353, 359, 366, 374, 381, 388,
405, 411, 414, 421, 428, 434, 451, 456,
462, 469, 475, 478, 485, 490, 495, 501,
506, 513, 518, 524, 530, 537, 544, 549,
556, 573, 579, 584, 592, 616, 623, 639,
657, 669, 674, 685, 706, 730, 741

M

Make an organized list. *See* Problem-
solving strategies
Make it simpler. *See* Problem-solving
strategies
Make or use a table, chart, or graph. *See*
Problem-solving strategies
Manipulative Use, 32, 38, 50, 64, 88, 173,
199, 200, 214, 290, 356, 460, 559, 577,
693
Mass
in the metric system, 691–696
weight and, 37
Math Background, 7, 13, 20, 27, 32, 37, 42,
48, 55, 61, 68, 73, 79, 86, 93, 98, 104,
109, 115, 127, 132, 141, 148, 154, 160,
164, 170, 177, 182, 187, 193, 197, 205,
212, 219, 228, 231, 239, 249, 252, 260,
266, 271, 281, 288, 296, 303, 310, 314,
321, 327, 332, 344, 349, 355, 361, 370,
377, 385, 395, 402, 407, 412, 418, 424,
431, 437, 442, 448, 453, 458, 465, 471,
476, 481, 488, 493, 497, 504, 510, 516,
522, 527, 534, 538, 547, 551, 558, 564,
569, 576, 582, 588, 595, 602, 607, 611,
619, 625, 631, 635, 641, 647, 653, 659,
666, 673, 676, 682, 688, 692, 698, 704,
708, 713, 719, 723, 729, 732, 738, 743,
749, 755, 759, 764, 769, 775, 779
Math language, 21, 61, 68, 86, 93, 115,
122, 128, 172, 192, 205, 210, 274, 301,
330, 343, 347, 407, 409, 435, 441, 459,
463, 486, 497, 519, 533, 551, 606, 625,
723, 728, 769, 789, 790, 805

Math to math
Algebra, Measurement, and Geometry, 6B, 72B, 139B, 202B, 277B, 346B, 415B, 479B, 545B, 610B, 675B, 731B
Algebra and Problem Solving, 6B, 72B, 139B, 202B, 277B, 346B, 415B, 479B, 545B, 610B, 675B, 731B
Fractions and Measurement, 6B, 72B, 139B, 202B, 277B, 346B, 415B, 479B, 545B, 610B, 675B
Fractions, Percents, Decimals, and Problem Solving, 6B, 72B, 139B, 202B, 277B, 346B, 415B, 479B, 545B, 610B, 675B, 731B
Measurement and Geometry, 6B, 72B, 139B, 202B, 277B, 346B, 415B, 479B, 545B, 610B, 675B, 731B
Probability and Statistics, 202B, 277B, 346B, 415B, 479B, 545B, 610B, 675B, 731B
Problem Solving and Measurement, 6B, 72B, 139B, 202B, 277B, 346B, 415B, 479B, 545B, 610B, 675B, 731B
Proportional relationships and geometry, 139B, 202B, 277B, 346B, 415B, 479B, 545B, 610B, 675B, 731B
Math and other subjects
architecture, 199, 233, 288, 289, 392, 581, 636, 644, 684, 695, 704, 713
art, 199, 208, 221, 286, 288, 305, 312, 373, 409, 611, 626, 657, 663, 689, 713, 753
geography, 39, 111, 183, 228, 405, 562
history, 22, 45, 95, 106, 156, 167, 174, 208, 260, 631, 671
science, 107, 119, 182, 183, 185, 190, 196, 208, 216, 220, 228, 248, 256, 262, 312, 315, 316, 329, 335, 350, 380, 381, 391, 397, 399, 403, 405, 409, 463, 490, 517, 529, 603, 643, 663, 669, 679, 682, 683, 697, 743, 753, 765
social studies, 362
sports, 20, 29, 38, 45, 53, 106, 124, 150, 161, 167, 214, 249, 306, 332, 356, 364, 382, 392, 401, 403, 427, 488, 506, 532, 561, 570, 584, 698, 699
Mean, 42–44, 360–363
Measures
of angles, 115–116
of area. See Area
of central tendency, 43–44, 360–364
converting
mixed-unit to single-unit, 356–357
units of, 36–40, 53
using unit multipliers, 354–356
counts vs. measures, 763
equivalent measures, 37
exactness in, 763–764
indirect, 441–442, 770
of length. See Length.
of liquids, 147
multiplying and dividing, 765
rate problems, 330–333
rates and average of, 41–43
significant digits in, 764
similar figures for indirect, 441–442, 770
of volume. See Volume
Measures of central tendency. See Central tendency
Median, 43–44, 360–362

Mental math. *A variety of mental math skills and strategies are developed in the lesson Power Ups.*
Meters (m), 36
Metric system, 37–38
volume, capacity and mass in, 691–696
Miles (mi), 36
Milliliters (mL), 36
Millimeters (mm), 36
Minuends, 13, 21
Missing numbers
in addition problems, 20
in division problems, 15, 28
in equal groups problems, 27–29
equations with two unknowns, 593–598
in multiplication problems, 27, 28
in proportion problems, 225
solving problems with, 12–13
in subtraction problems, 21
Mixed measures, 356
adding and subtracting, 531–537
Mixed numbers, 64–65. *See also* Fractions
adding and subtracting, 85–90
converting
decimal equivalents, 79–80, 192–193
to improper fractions, 154
multiplying and dividing, 153–156
rounding, 109
Mode, 43–44, 360–361
Models, 458, 713
See also Act it out or make a model
Money
compound interest, 670–674
consumer interest, 717–721
simple interest, 670
Monomials, 533
Multiplication, 13–14
of algebraic terms, 401
associative property of, 14
of binomials, 619–623
commutative property of, 14
of decimal numbers, 163–167
distributive property of, 140–141
of expressions with exponents, 178, 348–349
of fractions, 146–149, 156
by fractions vs. decimals, 563–567
identity property of, 14, 63, 86, 224, 774
of inequalities, by negative numbers, 514
of integers, 237–240
as inverse of division, 251, 759–760
of measurements, 765
of mixed numbers, 153–156
and order of operations, 141
properties of, 14, 15, 140–141
repeated, with exponents, 98
rule for dependent events, 558
of numbers in scientific notation, 313–316
of signed numbers, 238–239, 620
significant digits in, 765
of small numbers, 389–391
of square roots, 497–498, 519–524
symbols for, 14
of two variables, 658–661
of variables, by coefficients, 789
word problems, 26–30
zero in, 811–813
zero property of, 14
Multiplication Counting Principle, 458
Multiplication Rule for Probability, 457–460
multiplicative inverse, 148–149
Multiview projection, 274–275

N

Negative coordinates, 68
Negative exponents, 346–349, 431–432
Negative numbers. *See also* Signed numbers
adding, 204–205, 240
dividing, 238–239
multiplying, 238–239
on number line, 7
subtracting, 240
Nets, 291, 375–378
Non-linear functions, 727–730
Non-proportional relationships, 585–592
*n*th root, 100
Number lines. *See also* Graphs; Lines
absolute value and, 8
graphing inequalities on, 422–426, 515
graphing inequality pairs on, 629–633
graphs on, 8–9
integers on, 8–9, 237
line plot graphs on, 686–688
rational numbers on, 61
real numbers on, 104
zero on, 758–759
Number pairs
inequalities, 629–633
relations, 651
Number sentences, 4
Numerators, 31, 62

O

Obtuse angles, 116, 546
Odd numbers, 9, 41
Odds, 211
Operations
of arithmetic, 12–18
order of, 141–143
Opinion surveys, 413
Opposite angles, 367–368
Opposite solutions symbol (±), 624
Order of operations, 141–143
Origin, 7, 68
Outcomes, counting. *See* Probability
Outliers, 539
Output number, 278

P

Parabolic curve, 727
Parallel lines, 115
angle relationships and, 368–370
Parallelograms, 197, 198
area of, 406–409, 502
Parallel projection, 273–274
Patterns. *See also* Sequence; Problem-solving strategies
counting, 60
Pentagons, 122
Percent change
dilation, 479
of dimensions, 479–483
fractions vs. decimals for determining, 563–564
ratio tables in calculating, 452–456
reduction (contraction), 479
scale factor in calculating, 479–482
Percents
converting to
decimal equivalents, 81–82, 395, 430
fraction equivalents, 73–76, 82, 395, 430

INDEX

Q

Quadrants, 68
Quadratic equations, 624–626
  factoring, 822–824
  quadratic function, 728
  solving
    by factoring, 829–831, 837–839
    using the quadratic formula, 846–851
Quadrilaterals, 122
  classification of, 197–201
Qualitative data, 412
Quantitative data, 412
Quotients, 13, 601

R

Radicals. *See also* Roots
  adding, 640, 805–806
  in fractions, 778–781
  geometric measures with, 640–645
Radical sign ($\sqrt{}$), 99, 239, 519, 625
Radicand, 99, 519, 805
Radius (radii), 258
Random number generators, 607–608
Random sample, 606–608
Range, 44, 319–321, 361
Rate, 41–43
  of change, 303
  converting with unit multipliers, 435–437
  as ratios, 435
  unit, 41
Rate problems, 330–333, 698
Rational numbers, 60–62, 429–432
  converting to decimals, 81, 193
  and equivalent fractions, 62–64
  as ratios, 429
  selecting appropriate, 563–567
  square roots of, 103–104
  symbol for, 601
Ratios, 186–188, 210
  of areas, 611, 612
  constant, 416, 681
  of dimensions. *See* Scale factor
  of direct-variation variables, 463, 471
  equivalent, 787–788
  horizontal/vertical in graphs, 790
  of lengths, 611, 612
  of percents, 326–328
  of perimeters, 611
  proportions, 223–225, 318
  in rate problems, 330–333
  rates as, 435
  rational numbers as, 429
  ratio tables, 452–454, 580–581
  reducing equal, 224
  scale factors as. *See* Scale factor
  of side lengths, 231–232
  side lengths of right triangles, 737–741, 768–772
  in similar figures. *See* Similar figures
  slope, 302, 790–793
  in trigonometry, 768
  unit multipliers, 354–356
  word problems, 226
    involving totals, 308–310
Rays, 114
Reading math, 7, 37, 99, 258, 368, 415, 420, 427, 508, 759
Reading mathematical expressions
  "and" in inequalities, 631
  angle measures, 368
  approximately equal to, 37, 258, 508

"between" in inequalities, 422–423
  ellipsis, 7, 415, 429
  inequalities, 422–423, 629, 631
  infinity, 759
  opposite solutions, 624
  "or" in inequalities, 631
  square inch, 99
  term in a sequence, 416–417
Real numbers, 104, 601
Real-world application problems, 11, 19–23, 25, 27–29, 32–34, 37–40, 42–45, 51–53, 57, 58, 66, 75, 76, 82–84, 89–92, 94–97, 100, 101, 105–108, 110–113, 117, 118, 124, 125, 127, 129–130, 138, 139, 144, 145, 150, 152, 153, 156, 159–161, 163, 164, 166, 167, 174, 175, 178, 180, 183, 187–191, 195, 204, 207–209, 214, 215, 217–222, 224, 226–228, 233, 234, 236-238, 242, 243, 245, 248–250, 253–256, 259–261, 263, 265–267, 269, 270, 279, 281, 284–291, 295, 297–299, 303, 305–312, 315–320, 322–325, 327–329, 332–334, 336, 338, 340, 341, 350, 351, 354–358, 362–367, 370–373, 378–382, 386–389, 391, 392, 394–398, 401–404, 406, 409–411, 419–421, 424, 426–428, 431–433, 436, 437, 440–445, 448–456, 460–462, 466–468, 471–475, 479, 481, 483–491, 494, 495, 499–501, 503–506, 511, 516, 517, 522, 528, 532, 533, 535–537, 546–549, 553–555, 558, 560–562, 564–567, 569–572, 574, 575, 577, 578, 581, 582, 585, 588–592, 596, 597, 603, 604, 610, 611, 613–616, 618, 621, 622, 624, 626–628, 633, 637, 638, 642–645, 650, 654–662, 667, 675, 676, 678–684, 688, 689, 692–695, 697–700, 703–705, 707, 710, 712–714, 718–722, 724, 725, 734, 735, 737, 739, 742, 743, 745, 748, 752, 756, 761, 764–766, 771, 776, 780
Reasonable answers, 110
Reciprocals, 148–149, 347
  of fractions, 432
  negative exponents and, 431–432
Rectangles, 198
  area of, 49, 231, 502
    with variable dimensions, 617–623
  Golden Rectangle, 199
  perimeter of, 49, 93, 140
Rectangular prisms, 272
Reduction. *See* Contractions
Reflections, 169–170, 342
Reflective symmetry, 200–201
Regrouping, 88
  for subtracting mixed measures, 532
Regular polygons, 121
Relationships
  correlation of data, 539–544, 654, 743
  and functions, 651–657
  linear, 465, 586
  proportional. *See* Proportional relationships
  between variables in scatterplots, 742–743
Repeating decimals. *See* Repetends
Repetends, 192–194, 429, 723
  symbol (¯), 429, 723
Representation
  Formulate an equation, 292, 293, 298, 309, 311, 318, 329, 425, 451, 467, 494, 517, 624, 638, 650, 655, 675, 684, 703, 767, 781

Manipulatives/Hands On, 80, 84, 88, 103, 104, 149, 160, 161, 169, 170–173, 180, 182, 183, 187, 194, 199, 214, 240, 246, 247, 259, 260, 269, 289, 291, 296, 297, 322, 347, 377, 407, 420, 443, 449, 460, 482, 490, 492, 493, 499, 513, 546, 559, 576, 577, 581-584, 612, 634, 654, 679, 687, 693, 703, 732, 744, 758, 770, 771
  Model, 9, 39, 57, 65, 66, 150, 179, 207, 219, 228, 256, 268, 284, 285, 299, 310, 316, 324, 374, 378, 408, 439, 445, 451, 461, 484, 504, 517, 521, 535, 537, 548, 554, 561, 582, 583, 597, 604, 615, 621, 627, 632, 656, 662, 677, 695, 699, 709, 710, 714, 720, 735, 746, 757
  Represent, 14, 15, 29, 34, 57, 65, 66, 84, 91, 106, 112, 123, 183, 187, 189, 215, 242, 304, 323, 341, 357, 386, 388, 392, 420, 438, 455, 458, 466, 581, 631, 649, 772
Representative samples, 606
Rhombus, 198, 409
Right angles, 116
Right cones, 664–669
Right pyramids, surface area, 664–669
Right triangles
  characteristics of, 737–738
  hypotenuse of, 132, 497, 738
  legs of, 132
  naming angles and sides of, 737–738
  Pythagorean Theorem of, 132–138, 497, 782–784
  ratio of side lengths, 737–741, 768–772
  as slant height of cones and pyramids, 635
Rise and run, 302
Roots, 99–101
Rotational symmetry, 201
Rotations, 169–170, 343–344
Rounding, 108–109, 187
Rule of 72, 673
Rules
  for probability, 457–460
  multiplication of dependent events, 558
  recursive, 646–650
  for sequences, 415, 417, 491–492, 646–650
Run. *See* Rise and run

S

Sample, 412
  random sample, 606
  sampling error, 608
  sampling methods, 606–609
Sample space, 211–212, 458–460
Scale factor, 233, 259
  conversion using, 580–581
  of dilations, 173
  drawing with, 580–584
  model building using a, 713
  in percent change, 479–482
  relationship to area and volume, 479–482, 611–612, 702–706, 713
  relationship to length, 479–482, 611, 612, 703
Scalene triangles, 127
Scatterplots, 538–544, 654, 742–747
Scientific calculators. *See* Calculators
Scientific notation
  for large numbers, 181–183

NUMBERS AND OPERATIONS	COURSE 1	COURSE 2	COURSE 3
Numeration			
digits	●		
read and write whole numbers and decimals	●	●	▲
place value to trillions	●	●	▲
place value to hundred trillions		●	▲
number line (integers, fractions)	●	●	▲
number line (rational and irrational numbers)		●	●
expanded notation	●	●	
comparison symbols (=, <, >)	●	●	▲
comparison symbols (=, <, >, ≤, ≥)		●	▲
compare and order rational numbers	●	●	▲
compare and order real numbers		●	●
scientific notation		●	●
Basic operations			
add, subtract, multiply, and divide integers	●	●	▲
add, subtract, multiply, and divide decimal numbers	●	●	▲
add, subtract, multiply, and divide fractions and mixed numbers	●	●	▲
add, subtract, multiply, and divide algebraic terms		●	●
add and subtract polynomials			●
add, subtract, multiply, and divide radical expressions			●
multiply binomials			●
mental math strategies	●	●	●
regrouping in addition, subtraction, and multiplication	●	●	▲
multiplication notations: $a \times b$, $a \cdot b$, $a(b)$	●	●	▲
division notations: division box, division sign, and division bar	●	●	▲
division with remainders	●	●	▲
Properties of numbers and operations			
even and odd integers	●	●	▲
factors, multiples, and divisibility	●	●	▲
prime and composite numbers	●	●	▲
greatest common factor (GCF)	●	●	▲
least common multiple (LCM)	●	●	▲
divisibility tests (2, 3, 5, 9, 10)	●	▲	▲
divisibility tests (4, 6, 8)		●	▲
prime factorization of whole numbers	●	▲	▲
positive exponents of whole numbers, decimals, fractions	●	●	▲
positive exponents of integers		●	▲
negative exponents of whole numbers		●	▲
negative exponents of rational numbers			●
square roots	●	●	●
cube roots		●	●
order of operations	●	●	▲
inverse operations	●	●	●

● Introduce and Develop
▲ Maintain and Apply

SCOPE AND SEQUENCE

	COURSE 1	COURSE 2	COURSE 3
Estimation			
round whole numbers, decimals, mixed numbers	●	●	▲
estimate sums, differences, products, quotients	●	●	▲
estimate squares and square roots	●	●	●
determine reasonableness of solution	●	●	●
approximate irrational numbers		●	●
ALGEBRA			
Ratio and proportional reasoning			
fractional part of a whole, group, set, or number	●	●	▲
equivalent fractions	●	●	▲
convert between fractions, terminating decimals, and percents	●	●	▲
convert between fractions, repeating decimals, and percents		●	▲
reciprocals of numbers	●	●	▲
complex fractions involving one term in numerator/denominator		●	●
complex fractions involving two terms in numerator/denominator			●
identify/find percent of a whole, group, set, or number	●	●	▲
percents greater than 100%	●	●	▲
percent of change		●	●
solve proportions with unknown in one term	●	●	▲
find unit rates and ratios in proportional relationships	●	●	●
apply proportional relationships such as similarity, scaling, and rates	●	●	●
estimate and solve applications problems involving percent	●	●	●
estimate and solve applications problems involving proportional relationships such as similarity and rate		●	●
compare and contrast proportional and non-proportional linear relationships (direct and inverse variation)			●
Patterns, relations, and functions			
generate a different representation of data given another representation of data		●	●
use, describe, extend arithmetic sequence (with a constant rate of change)	●	●	●
input-output tables	●	●	●
analyze a pattern to verbalize a rule	●	●	▲
analyze a pattern to write an algebraic expression			●
evaluate an algebraic expression to extend a pattern		●	●
compare and contrast linear and nonlinear functions		●	●
Variables, expressions, equations, and inequalities			
solve equations using concrete and pictorial models	●	●	▲
formulate a problem situation for a given equation with one unknown variable		●	●
formulate an equation with one unknown variable given a problem situation	●	●	●
formulate an inequality with one unknown variable given a problem situation			●
solve one-step equations with whole numbers	●	▲	▲
solve one-step equations with fractions and decimals		●	▲
solve two-step equations with whole numbers	●	●	▲
solve two-step equations with fractions and decimals		●	●
solve equations with exponents			●

● Introduce and Develop
▲ Maintain and Apply

	COURSE 1	COURSE 2	COURSE 3
solve systems of equations with two unknowns by graphing			●
graph an inequality on a number line		●	●
graph pairs of inequalities on a number line			●
solve inequalities with one unknown		●	●
validate an equation solution using mathematical properties		●	●
GEOMETRY			
Describe basic terms			
point	●	●	▲
segment	●	●	▲
ray	●	●	▲
line	●	●	▲
angle	●	●	▲
plane	●	●	▲
Describe properties and relationships of lines			
parallel, perpendicular, and intersecting	●	●	●
horizontal, vertical, and oblique	●	●	●
slope		●	●
Describe properties and relationships of angles			
acute, obtuse, right	●	●	●
straight		●	●
complementary and supplementary	●	●	●
angles formed by transversals	●	●	●
angle bisector	●	●	
vertical angles		●	●
adjacent angles		●	●
calculate to find unknown angle measures	●	●	●
Describe properties and relationships of polygons			
regular	●	●	●
interior and exterior angles	●	●	
sum of angle measures	●	●	●
diagonals		●	●
effects of scaling on area		●	●
effects of scaling on volume		●	●
similarity and congruence	●	●	●
classify triangles		●	●
classify quadrilaterals	●	●	●
Use Pythagorean theorem to solve problems			
Pythagorean theorem involving whole numbers		●	●
Pythagorean theorem involving radicals			●
trigonometric ratios			●
3-Dimensional figures			
represent in 2-dimensional world using nets	●	●	●
draw 3-dimensional figures	●	●	●
Coordinate geometry			
name and graph ordered pairs	●	●	●
intercepts of a line		●	●
determine slope from the graph of line		●	●
formulate the equation of a line		●	●

● Introduce and Develop
▲ Maintain and Apply

SCOPE AND SEQUENCE

	COURSE 1	COURSE 2	COURSE 3
identify reflections, translations, rotations, and symmetry	●	●	●
graph reflections across the horizontal or vertical axes	●	●	●
graph translations		●	●
graph rotations			●
graph dilations			●
graph linear equations		●	●

MEASUREMENT

Measuring physical attributes

	COURSE 1	COURSE 2	COURSE 3
use customary units of length, area, volume, weight, capacity	●	●	●
use metric units of length, area, volume, weight, capacity	●	●	●
use temperature scales: Fahrenheit, Celsius	●	●	●
use units of time	●	●	●

Systems of measurement

	COURSE 1	COURSE 2	COURSE 3
convert units of measure	●	●	●
convert between systems	●	●	●
unit multipliers	●	●	●

Solving measurement problems

	COURSE 1	COURSE 2	COURSE 3
perimeter of polygons, circles, complex figures	●	●	●
area of triangles, rectangles, and parallelograms	●	●	●
area of trapezoids		●	●
area of circles	●	●	●
area of semicircles and sectors		●	●
area of complex figures	●	●	●
surface area of right prisms and cylinders	●	●	●
surface area of spheres		●	●
surface area of cones and pyramids			●
estimate area	●	●	●
volume of right prisms, cylinders, pyramids, and cones	●	●	●
volume of spheres		●	●
estimate volume	●	●	●

Solving problems of similarity

	COURSE 1	COURSE 2	COURSE 3
scale factor	●	●	●
similar triangles		●	●
indirect measurement		●	●
scale drawings: two-dimensional	●	●	●
scale drawings: three-dimensional			●

Use appropriate measurement instruments

	COURSE 1	COURSE 2	COURSE 3
ruler (U.S. customary and metric)	●	●	▲
compass	●	●	●
protractor	●	●	●
thermometer	●	●	▲

DATA ANALYSIS AND PROBABILITY

Data collection and representation

	COURSE 1	COURSE 2	COURSE 3
collect and display data	●	●	●
tables and charts	●	●	▲

● Introduce and Develop
▲ Maintain and Apply

	COURSE 1	COURSE 2	COURSE 3
frequency tables	●	●	●
pictographs	●	●	
line graphs	●	●	▲
histograms	●	●	▲
bar graphs	●	●	▲
circle graphs	●	●	▲
Venn diagrams		●	●
scatter plots			●
line plots	●	●	▲
stem-and-leaf plots	●	●	▲
box-and-whisker plots		●	●
choose an appropriate graph	●	●	●
identify bias in data collection		●	▲
analyze bias in data collection			●
draw and compare different representations	●	●	●
Data set characteristics			
mean, median, mode, and range	●	●	▲
select the best measure of central tendency for a given situation		●	●
determine trends from data		●	●
predict from graphs		●	●
recognize misuses of graphical or numerical information		●	●
evaluate predictions and conclusions based on data analysis		●	●
Probability			
experimental probability	●	●	●
make predictions based on experiments	●	●	●
accuracy of predictions in experiments	●	●	●
theoretical probability	●	●	●
sample spaces	●	●	▲
simple probability	●	●	▲
probability of compound events	●	●	●
probability of the complement of an event	●	●	●
probability of independent events	●	●	●
probability of dependent events		●	●
select and use different models to simulate an event			●
PROBLEM SOLVING			
Connections			
identify and apply mathematics to everyday experiences	●	●	●
identify and apply mathematics to activities in and outside of school	●	●	●
identify and apply mathematics in other disciplines	●	●	●
identify and apply mathematics to other mathematical topics	●	●	●
Problem-solving skills and tools			
use a problem-solving plan	●	●	▲
evaluate for reasonableness	●	●	▲
use a proportion	●	●	▲
use a calculator	●	●	▲
use estimation	●	●	▲
use manipulatives	●	●	▲

● Introduce and Develop
▲ Maintain and Apply

SCOPE AND SEQUENCE

	COURSE 1	COURSE 2	COURSE 3
use mental math	●	●	▲
use number sense	●	●	▲
use formulas	●	●	▲
Problem-solving strategies			
choose a strategy	●	●	▲
draw a picture or diagram	●	●	▲
find a pattern	●	●	▲
guess and check	●	●	▲
act it out	●	●	▲
make a table, chart, or graph	●	●	▲
work a simpler problem	●	●	▲
work backwards	●	●	▲
use logical reasoning	●	●	▲
write a number sentence or equation	●	●	▲
Communication			
relate mathematical language to everyday language	●	●	●
communicate mathematical ideas using efficient tools	●	●	●
communicate mathematical ideas with appropriate units	●	●	●
communicate mathematical ideas using graphical, numerical, physical, or algebraic mathematical models	●	●	●
evaluate the effectiveness of different representations to communicate ideas	●	●	●
Reasoning and proof			
justify answers	●	●	●
make generalizations	●	●	●
make conjectures from patterns	●	●	●
make conjectures from sets of examples and nonexamples	●	●	●
validate conclusions using mathematical properties and relationships	●	●	●
ALGEBRA TOPICS APPENDIX			
graph sequences			●
formulate the equation of a line with given characteristics			●
formulate the equation of a line parallel/perpendicular to a given line			●
solve proportions with an unknown in two terms			●
graph linear inequalities			●
factor quadratics			●
solve quadratic equations			●
solve systems of linear equations using substitution			●
solve systems of linear equations using elimination			●
formulate an equation with two unknown variables given a problem situation			●
solve systems of linear inequalities with two unknowns			●
graph systems of linear inequalities			●

● Introduce and Develop
▲ Maintain and Apply